ROAD ATL

FRANCE

C000265356

Contents

Driving in France	inside front cover
Key to map pages	II–III
Route planner 1:1,250,000 scale	IV–XV
Map legend	XVI
Road maps 1:250,000 scale	1–207
Central Paris with the Périphérique	208–209
Environs maps 1:100,000 scale	210–220

Bordeaux	220	Nantes	218
Lille	217	Paris	210–213
Lyon	214–215	Rennes	218
Marseille	216	Strasbourg	219
Montpellier	219	Toulouse	220

Town plans	221–249

Aix-en-Provence	221	la Rochelle	231	Perpignan	241
Angers	222	Lille	232	Poitiers	242
Avignon	223	Lyon	233	Reims	243
Bordeaux	224	Marseille	234	Rennes	244
Brest	225	Metz	235	Rouen	245
Caen	226	Montpellier	236	Strasbourg	246
Cannes	227	Nancy	237	Toulon	247
Clermont-Ferrand	228	Nantes	238	Toulouse	248
Dijon	229	Nice	239	Tours	249
Grenoble	230	Nîmes	240		

Département map	250
Index to place names	251–304
Distances and journey times	inside back cover

21st edition June 2018

© AA Media Limited 2018

Original edition printed 1999

Copyright: © IGN-FRANCE 2017
The IGN data or maps in this atlas are from the latest IGN edition, the years of which may be different. www.ign.fr.
Licence number 40000556.

Distances and journey times data © OpenStreetMap contributors.

All rights reserved. No part of this publication may be reproduced, stored in a retrieval system, or transmitted in any form or by any means - electronic, mechanical, photocopying, recording or otherwise - unless the permission of the publisher has been obtained beforehand (A05579).

Published by AA Publishing (a trading name of AA Media Limited, whose registered office is Fanum House, Basing View, Basingstoke, Hampshire RG21 4EA, UK.
Registered number 06112600).

ISBN: 978 0 7495 7965 4

A CIP catalogue record for this book is available from The British Library.

Printed by 1010 Printing International Ltd.

The contents of this atlas are believed to be correct at the time of printing. However, the publishers cannot be held responsible for loss occasioned to any person acting or refraining from action as a result of any material in this atlas, nor for any errors, omissions or changes in such material. This does not affect your statutory rights.

Scale 1:250,000
or 3.95 miles to 1 inch
(2.5km to 1cm)

II

MAJOR TOWN INDEX

Agen (47) 151
Ajaccio (2A) 204
Albi (81) 170
Alençon (61) 60
Amiens (80) 7
Angers (49) 76-77
Angoulême (16) 122
Annecy (74) 132
Arras (62) 8
Auch (32) 167
Aurillac (15) 140
Auxerre (89) 83
Avignon (84) 174-175
Bar-le-Duc (55) 47
Bastia (2B) 203
Beauvais (60) 20
Belfort (90) 88
Besançon (25) 103
Blois (41) 79-80
Bobigny (93) 42
Bordeaux (33) 135
Bourg-en-Bresse (01) 116-117
Bourges (18) 97
Caen (14) 14
Cahors (46) 152
Carcassonne (11) 187
Châlons-en-Champagne (51) 45
Chambéry (73) 131
Charleville-Mézières (08) 24
Chartres (28) 62
Châteauroux (36) 96
Chaumont (52) 67
Clermont-Ferrand (63) 127
Colmar (68) 71
Créteil (94) 42
Digne-les-Bains (04) 160
Dijon (21) 85
Épinal (88) 69
Évreux (27) 40
Évry (91) 42
Foix (09) 185
Gap (05) 160
Grenoble (38) 145
Guéret (23) 111
Laon (02) 22
Laval (53) 58
Lille (59) 3
Limoges (87) 124
Lons-le-Saunier (39) 102
Lyon (69) 130
Mâcon (71) 116
le Mans (72) 60
Marseille (13) 192
Melun (77) 64
Mende (48) 156
Metz (57) 26
Mont-de-Marsan (40) 166
Montauban (82) 169
Montpellier (34) 173
Moulins (03) 113
Nancy (54) 48
Nanterre (92) 42
Nantes (44) 74
Nevers (58) 98
Nice (06) 195
Nîmes (30) 174
Niort (79) 107
Orléans (45) 80
Paris (75) 42
Pau (64) 182
Périgueux (24) 137
Perpignan (66) 201
Poitiers (86) 109
Pontoise (95) 42
Privas (07) 143
le Puy-en-Velay (43) 142
Quimper (29) 53
Rennes (35) 57
la Roche-sur-Yon (85) 91
la Rochelle (17) 106
Rodez (12) 154
Rouen (76) 18
Saint-Brieuc (22) 33
Saint-Étienne (42) 129
Saint-Lô (50) 37
Strasbourg (67) 51
Tarbes (65) 183
Toulon (83) 193
Toulouse (31) 169
Tours (37) 78
Troyes (10) 66
Tulle (19) 139
Valence (26) 144
Vannes (56) 55
Versailles (78) 42
Vesoul (70) 87

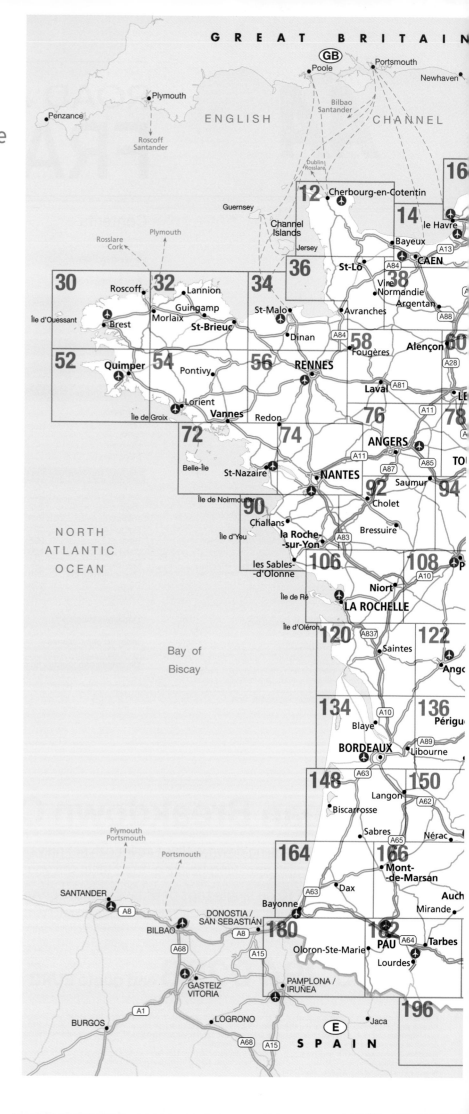

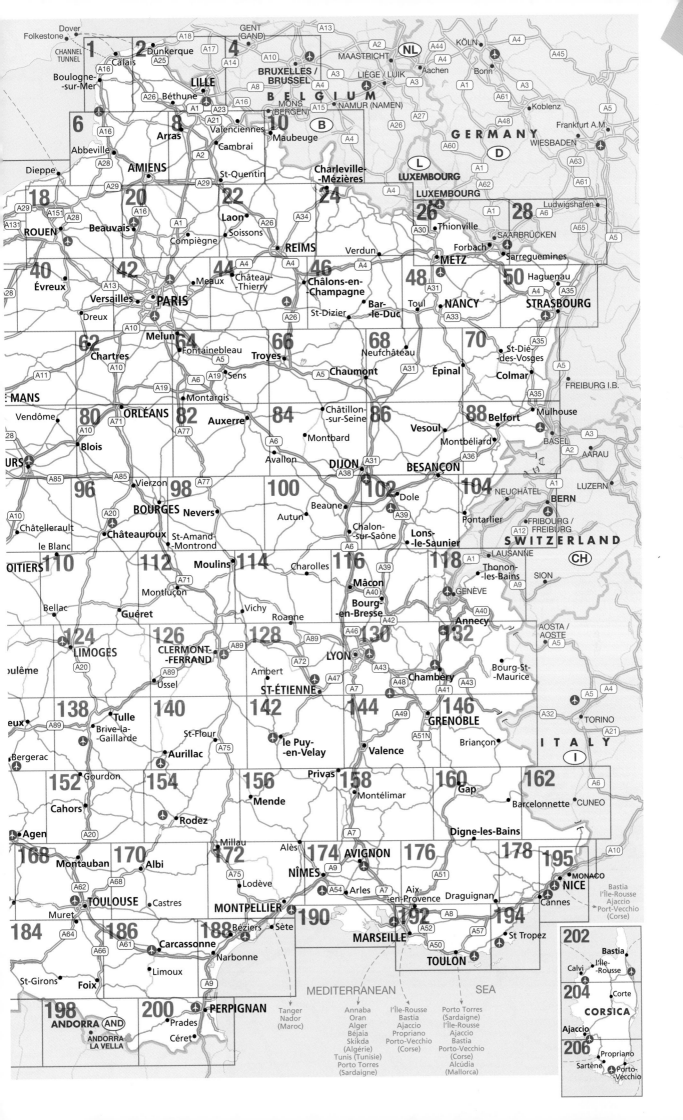

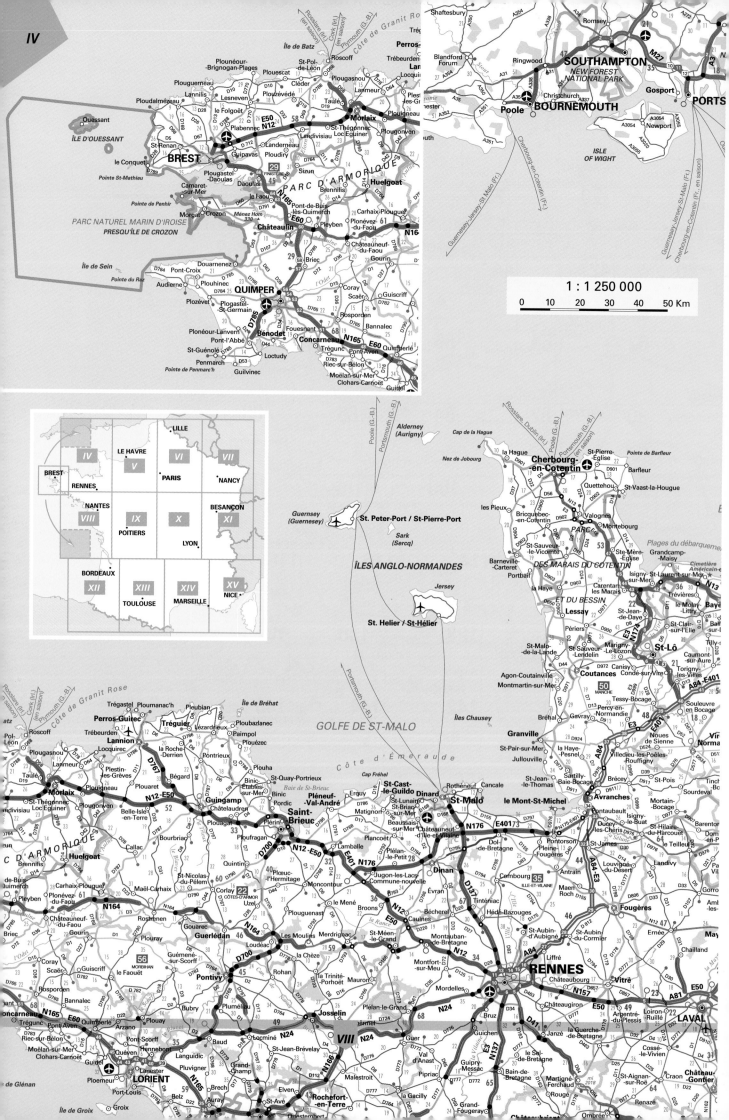

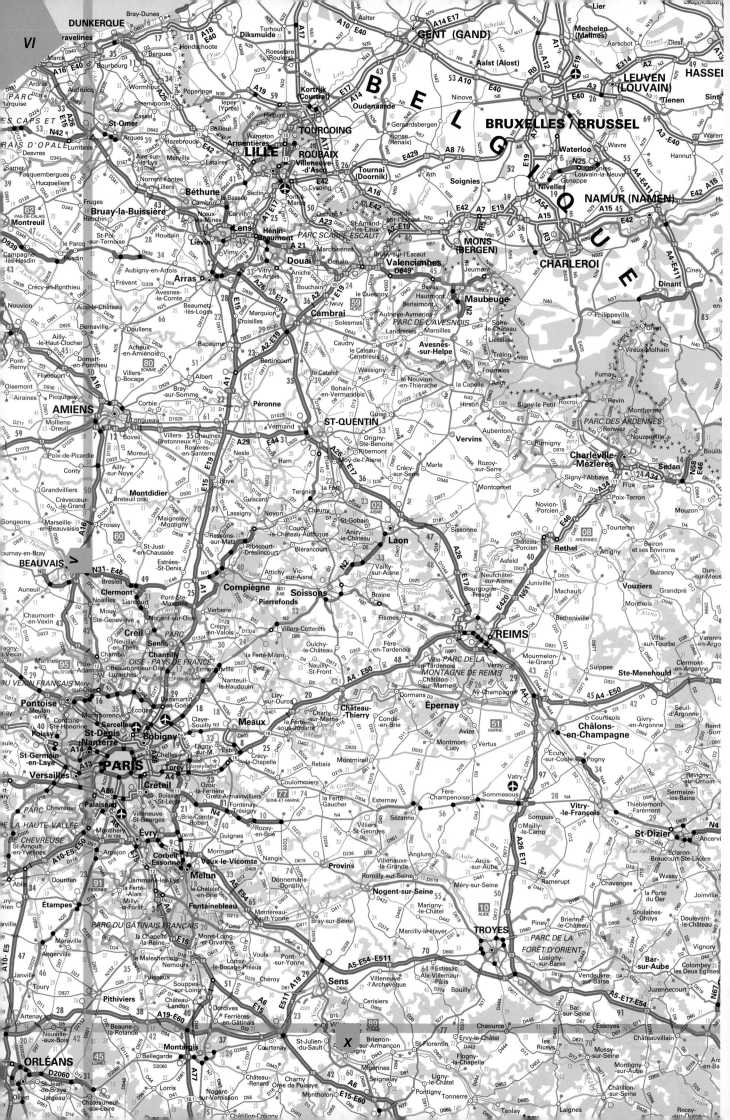

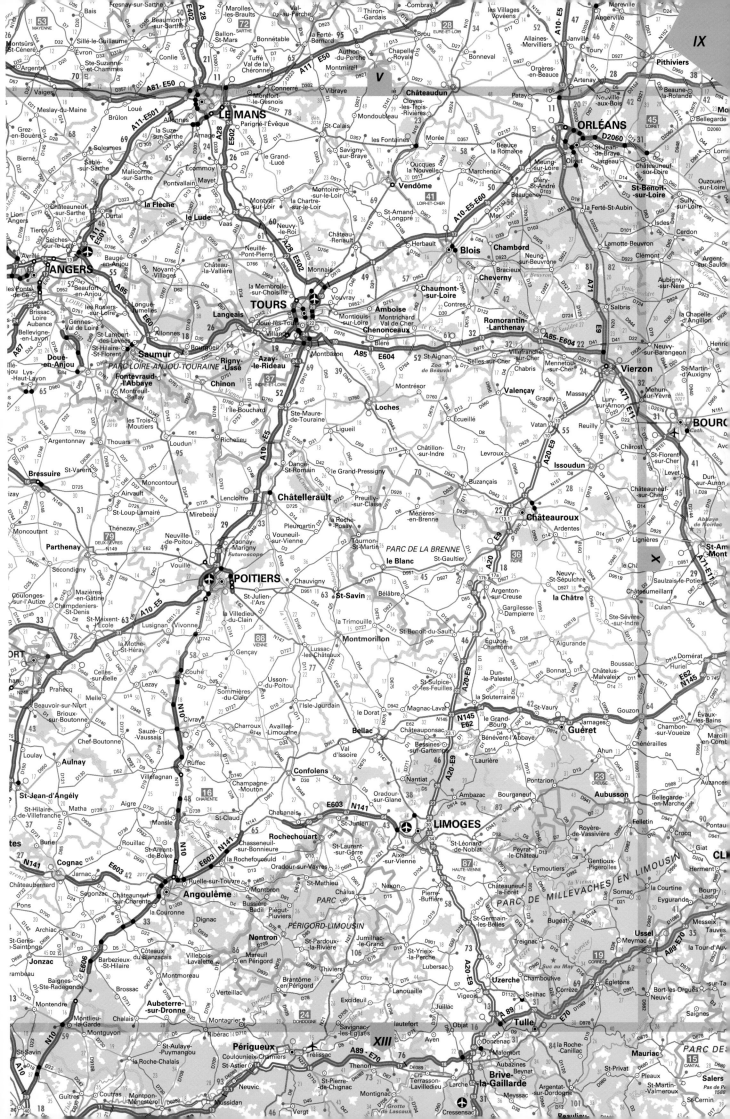

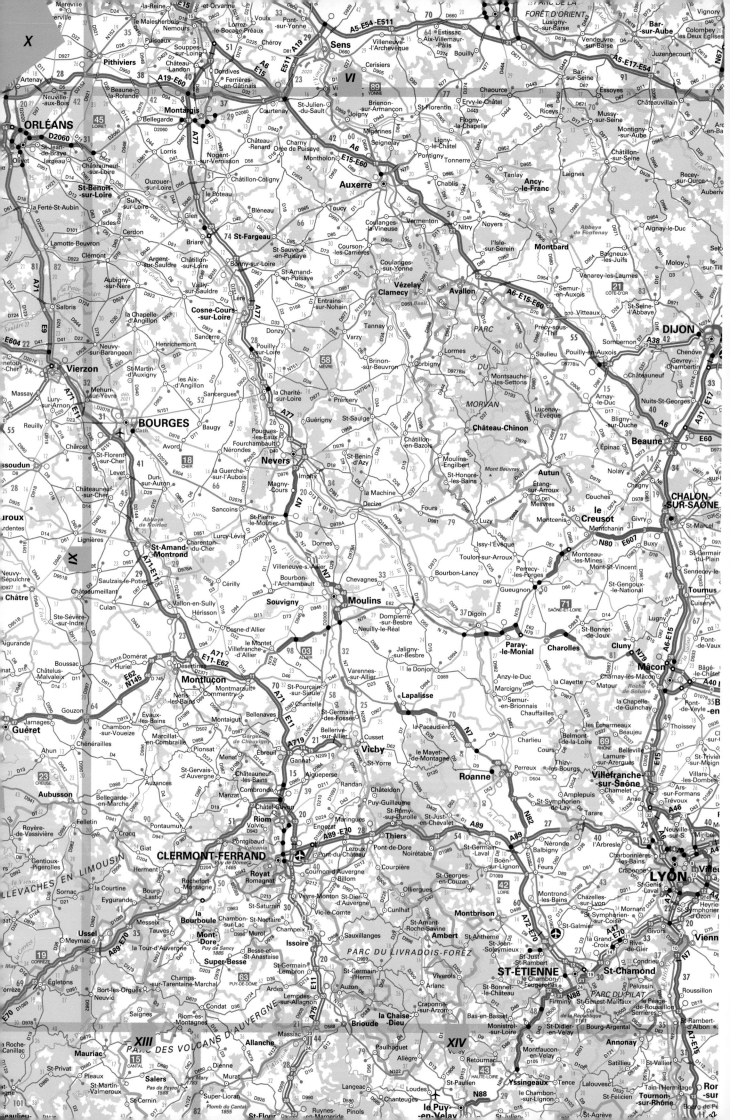

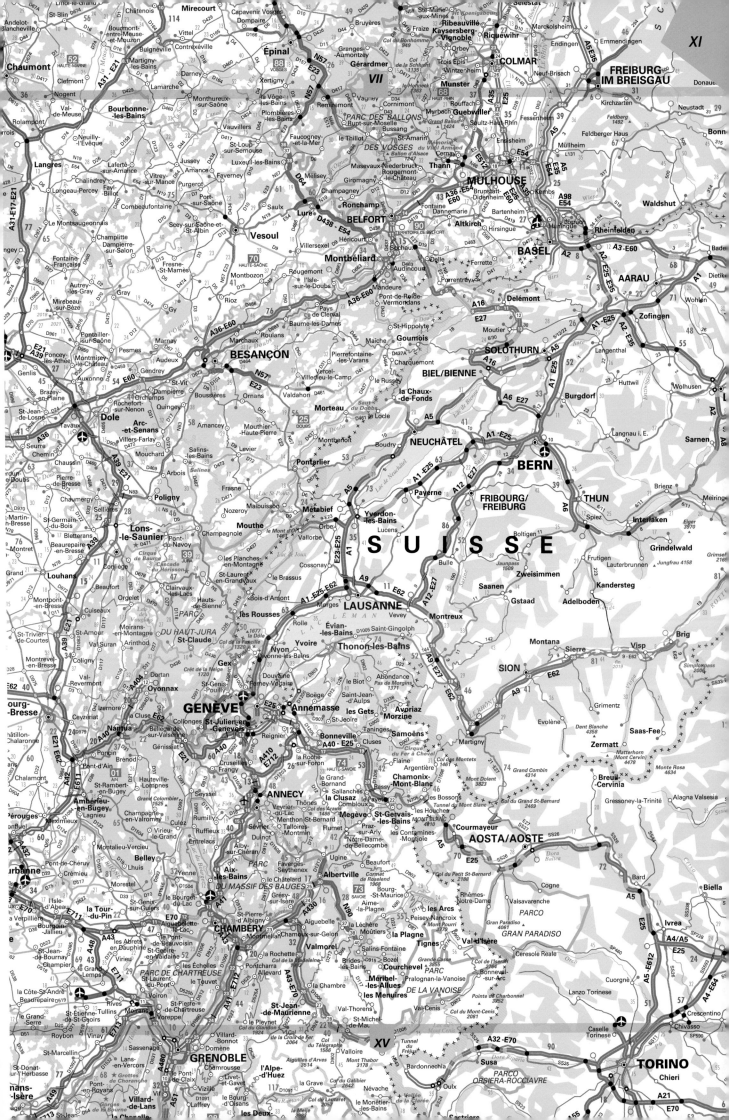

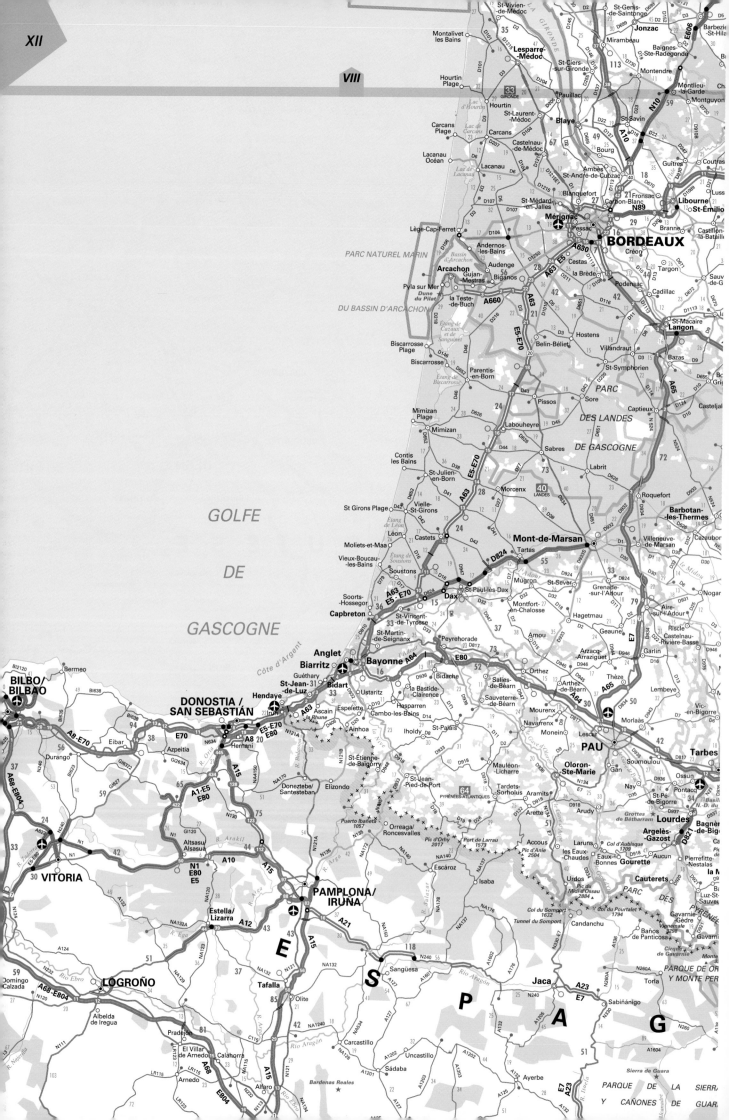

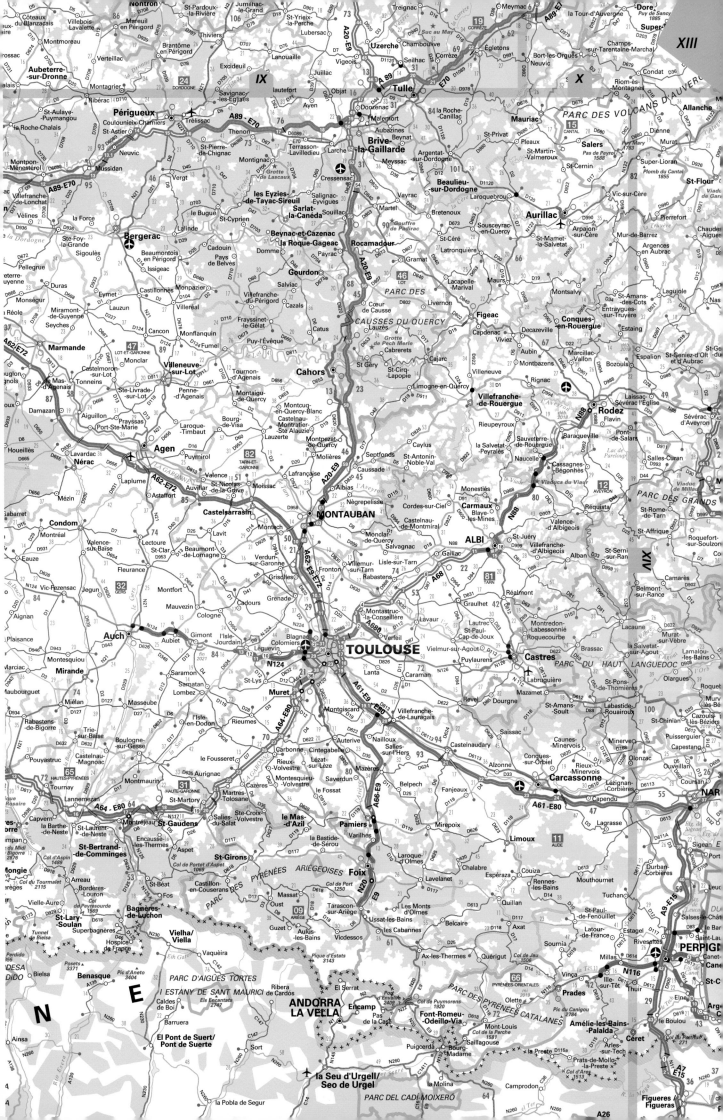

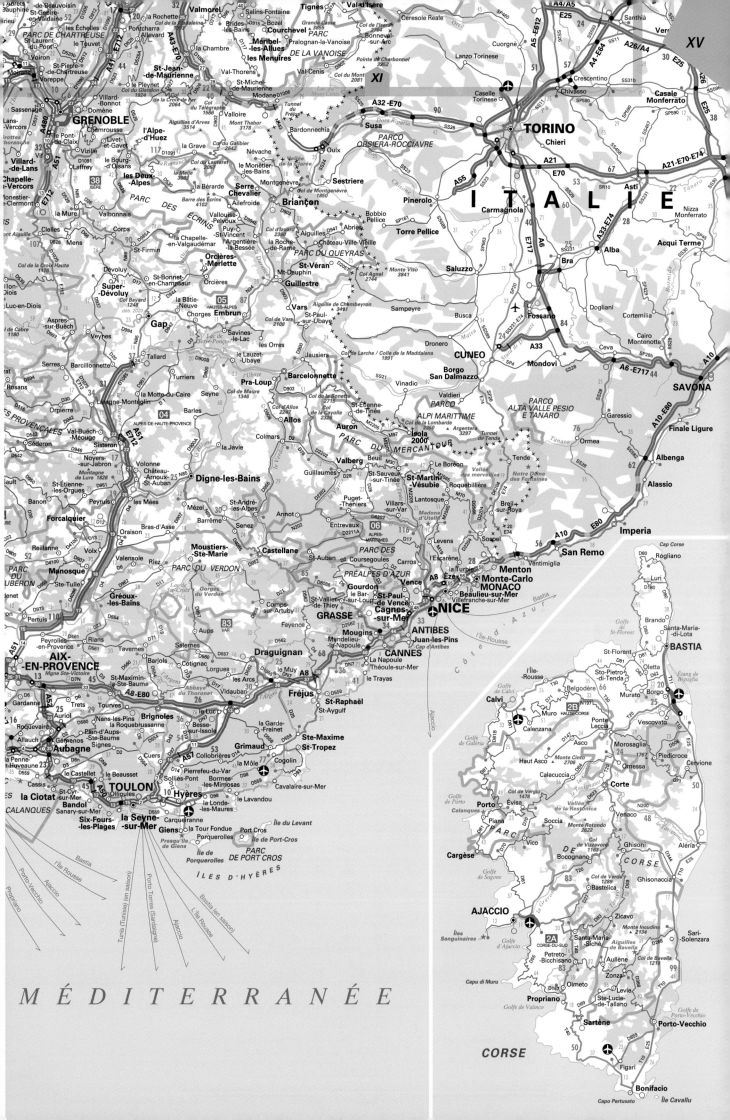

 GB Legend   F Légende

Motorway, toll section (1), Motorway, toll-free section (2), Dual carriageway with motorway characteristics (3)		Autoroute, section à péage (1), Autoroute, section libre (2), Voie à caractère autoroutier (3)
Tollgate (1), Service area (2), Rest area (3)	Péage Loire Neulise	Barrière de péage (1), Aire de service (2), Aire de repos (3)
Junction: complete (1), restricted (2), number	6 73	Échangeur: complet (1), partiel (2), numéro
Motorway under construction		Autoroute en construction
Connecting road between main towns (green road sign)(1), Dual carriageway (2)		Route appartenant au réseau vert (1), Route à quatre voies (2)
Main road (1), Regional connecting road (2), Other road (3)		Route de liaison principale (1), Route de liaison régionale (2), Autre route (3)
Road under construction		Route en construction
Not regularly maintained road (1), Footpath (2)		Route irrégulièrement entretenue (1), Chemin (2)
Tunnel (1), Prohibited road (2)		Tunnel (1), Route interdite (2)
Distances in kilometres (km) on motorway, Road numbering: Motorway	E11 5 A75	Distances kilométriques (km), Numérotation: Autoroute, type autoroutier
Distances in kilometres on road, Road numbering: Other road	3 2 5 D197	Distances kilométriques sur route, Numérotation: Autre route
Railway, station, halt, tunnel		Chemin de fer, gare, arrêt, tunnel
Airport (1), Airfield (2), Ferry route (3)	Bastia	Aéroport (1), Aérodrome (2), Liaison maritime (3)
Built-up area (1), Industrial park (2), Woodland (3)		Zone bâtie (1), Zone industrielle (2), Bois (3)
Département (1), International boundary (2)	+ + + + + + +	Limite de département (1), Limite d'État (2)
Military camp boundary (1), Park boundary (2)		Limite de camp militaire (1), Limite de Parc (2)
Marsh (1), Salt pan (2), Glacier (3)		Marais (1), Marais salants (2), Glacier (3)
Dry sand (1), Wet sand (2)		Région sableuse (1), Sable humide (2)
Cathedral (1), Abbey (2), Church (3), Chapel (4)		Cathédrale (1), Abbaye (2), Église (3), Chapelle (4)
Castle (1), Castle open to the public (2), Museum (3)	M	Château (1), Château ouvert au public (2), Musée (3)
Town or place of tourist interest	**LA ROCHELLE**	Localité d'intérêt touristique
Settlement (1), Municipality with isolated town hall (2)		Commune (1), Commune avec mairie isolée (2)
Lighthouse (1), Mill (2), Place of interest (3), Military cemetery (4)	★ ★	Phare (1), Moulin (2), Curiosité (3), Cimetière militaire (4)
Cave (1), Megalith (2), Antiquities (3), Ruins (4)		Grotte (1), Mégalithe (2), Vestiges antiques (3), Ruines (4)
Viewpoint (1), Panorama (2), Waterfall or spring (3), Gorge (4)	★ ★	Point de vue (1), Panorama (2), Cascade ou source (3), Gorge (4)
Spa resort (1), Winter sports resort (2), Refuge hut (3), Leisure activities (4)		Station thermale (1), Sports d'hiver (2), Refuge (3), Activités de loisirs (4)
Park visitor centre (1), Nature reserve (2), Park or garden (3)		Maison du Parc (1), Réserve naturelle (2), Parc ou jardin (3)
Tourist railway (1), Aerial cableway (2)		Chemin de fer touristique (1), Téléphérique (2)
Height in metres (1), Mountain pass (2)	614 • 963	Taille en mètres (1), Col (2)

1: 250,000

0	5	km	15	20	25

0	5	miles	10	15

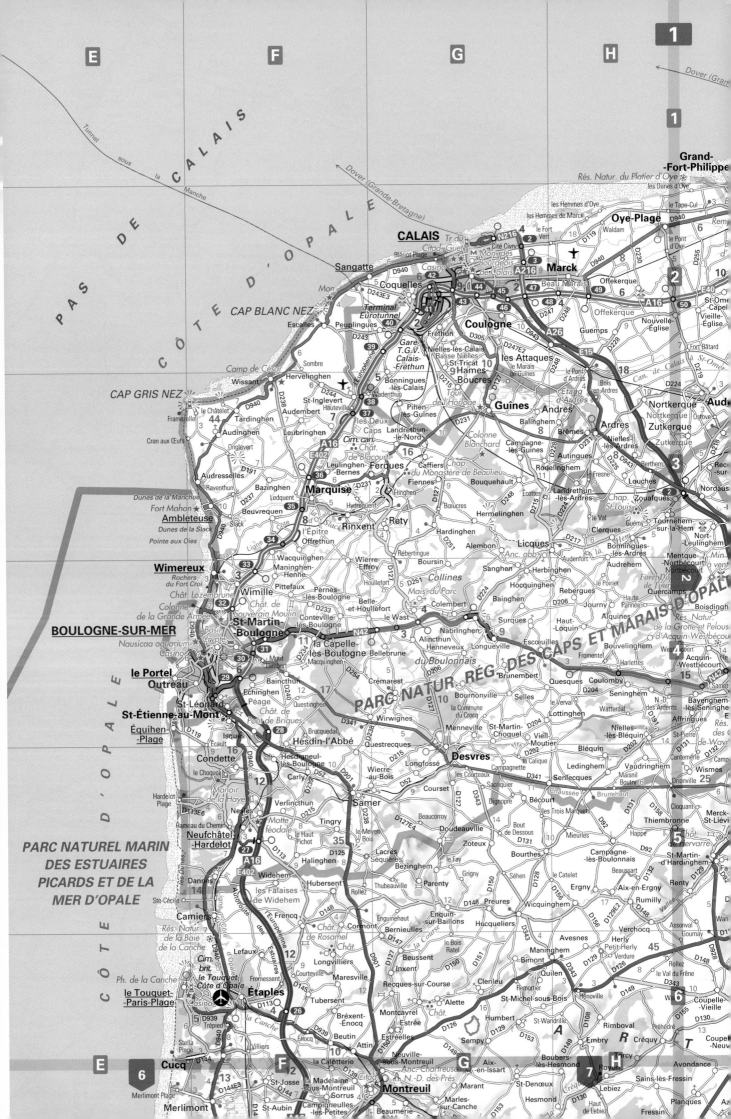

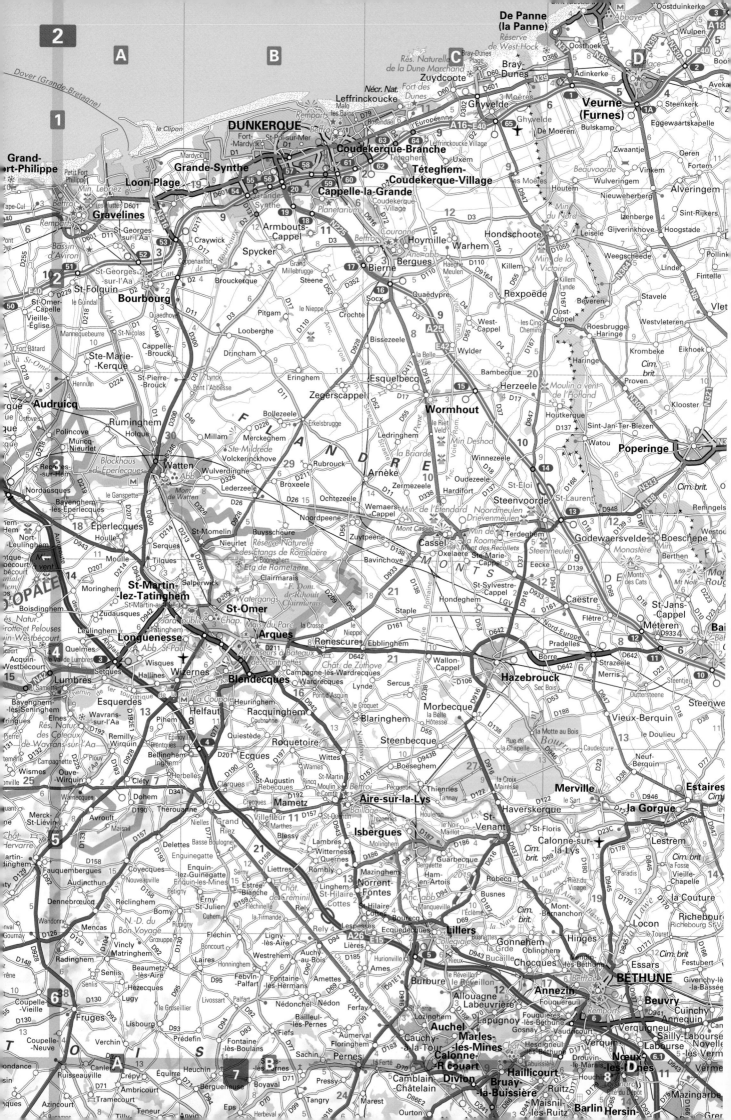

Lille environs map p.217

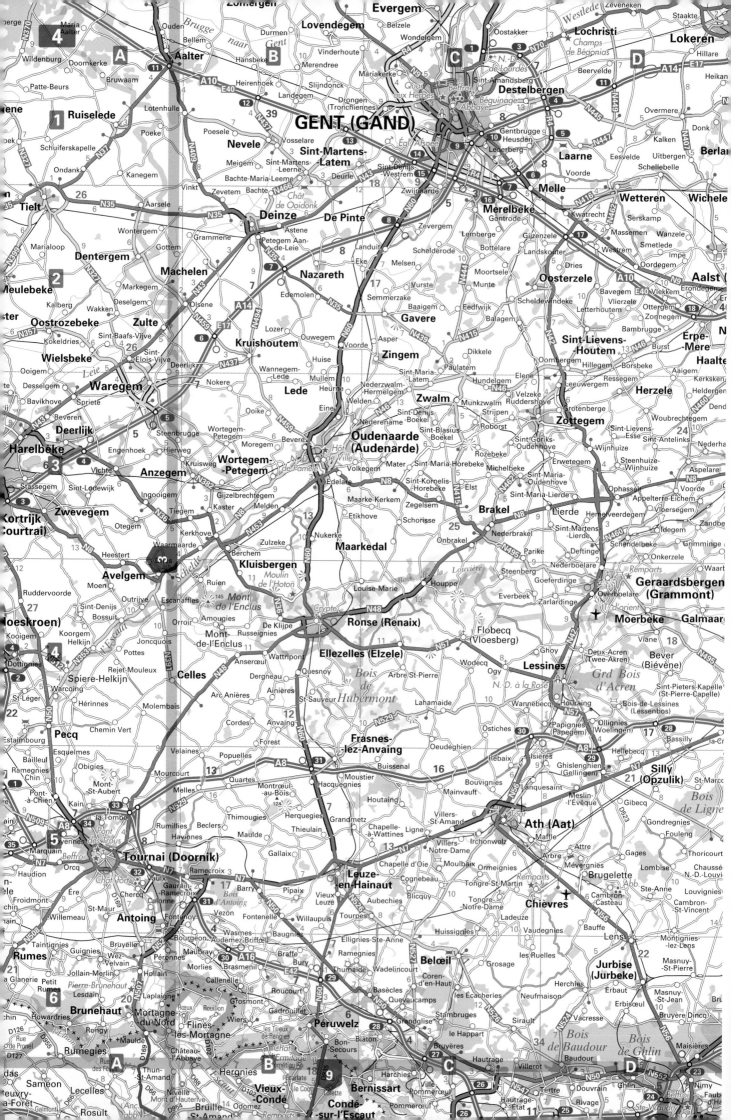

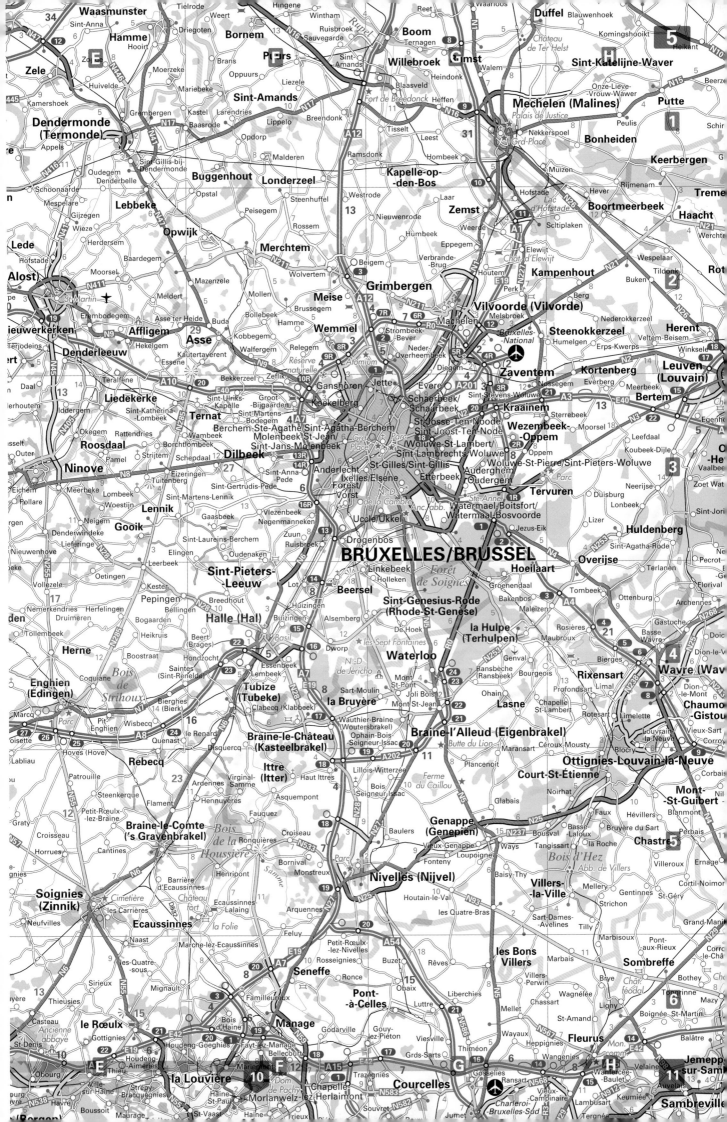

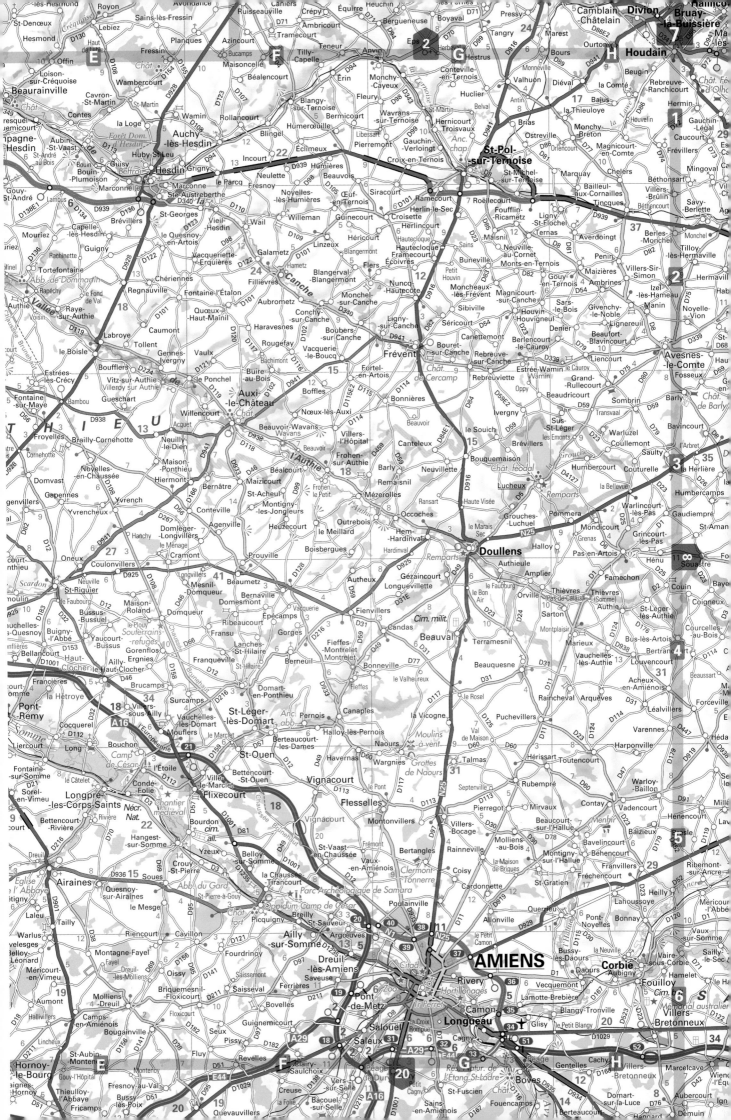

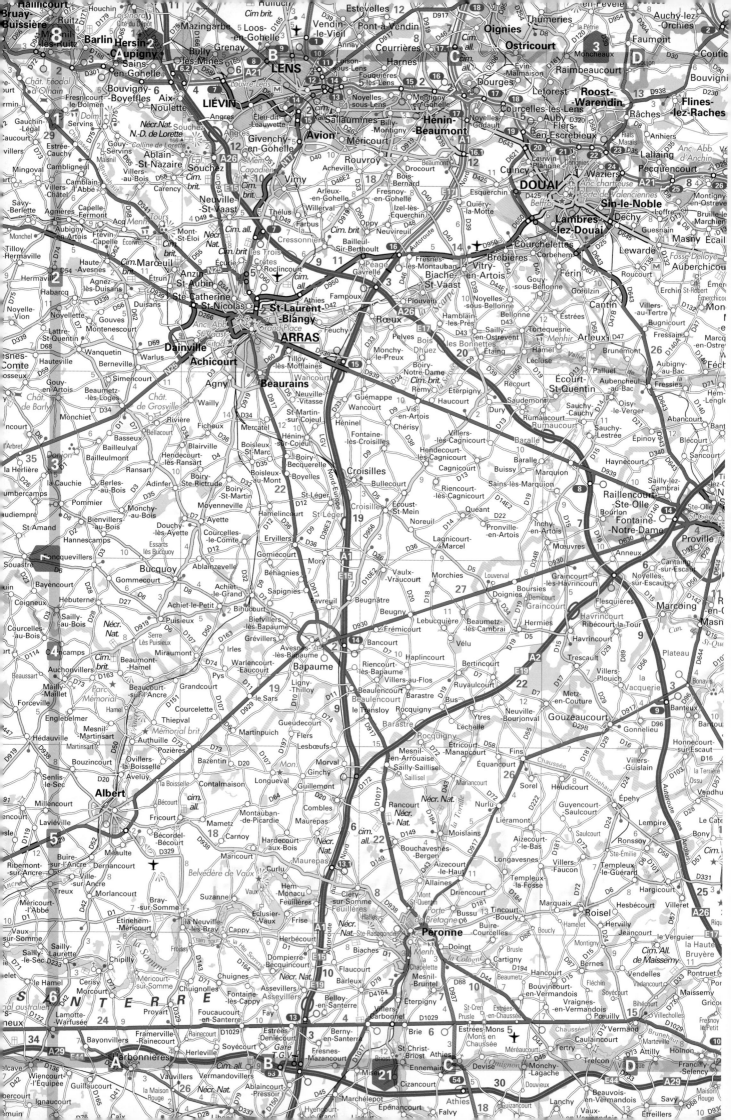

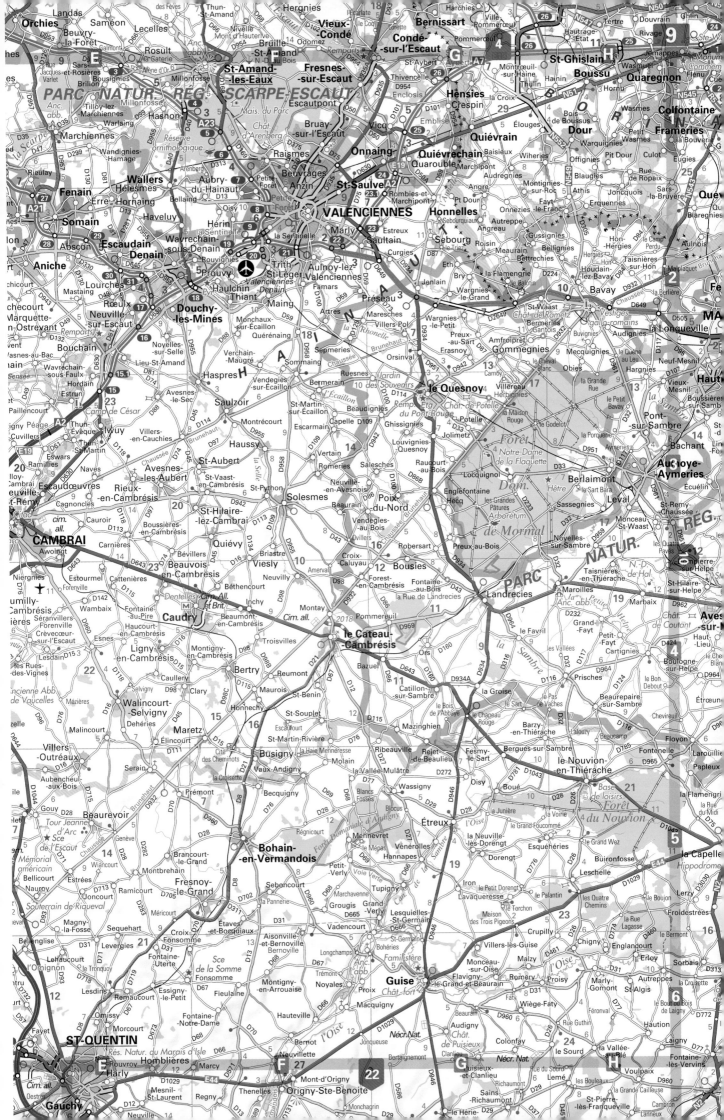

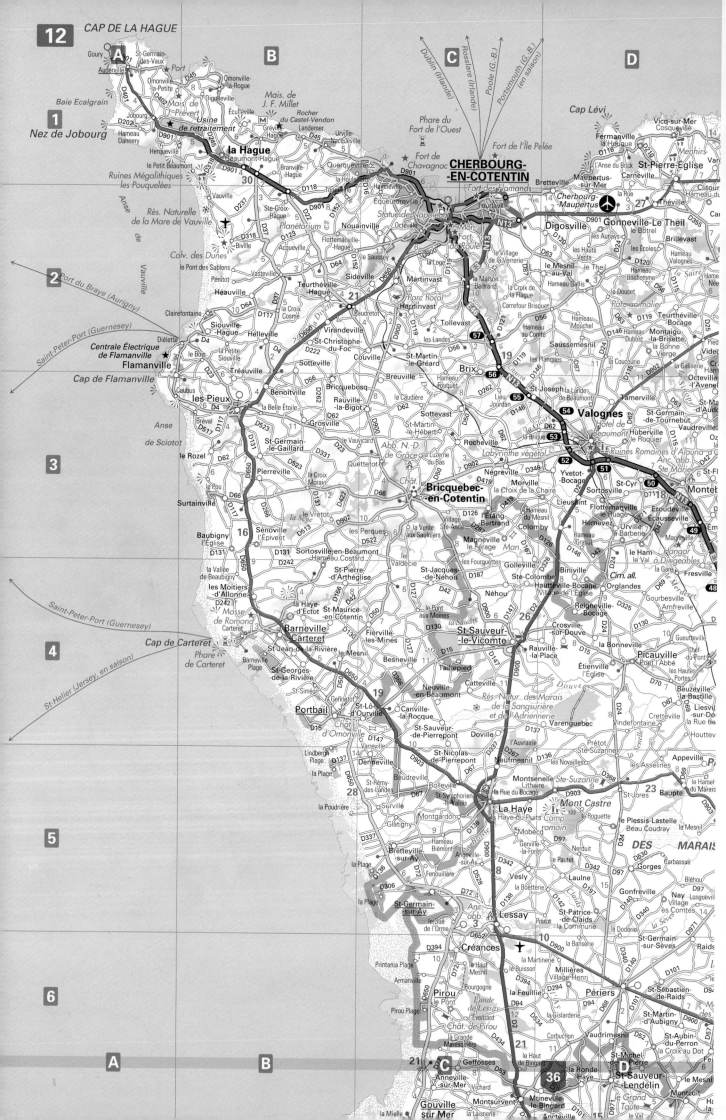

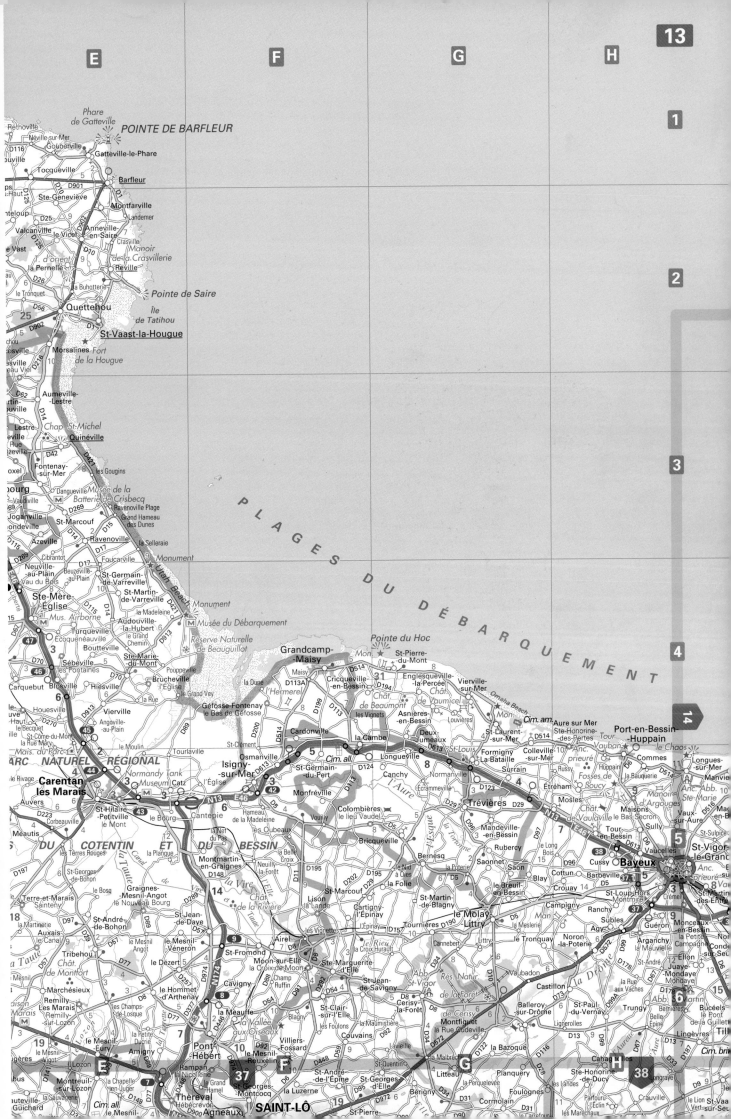

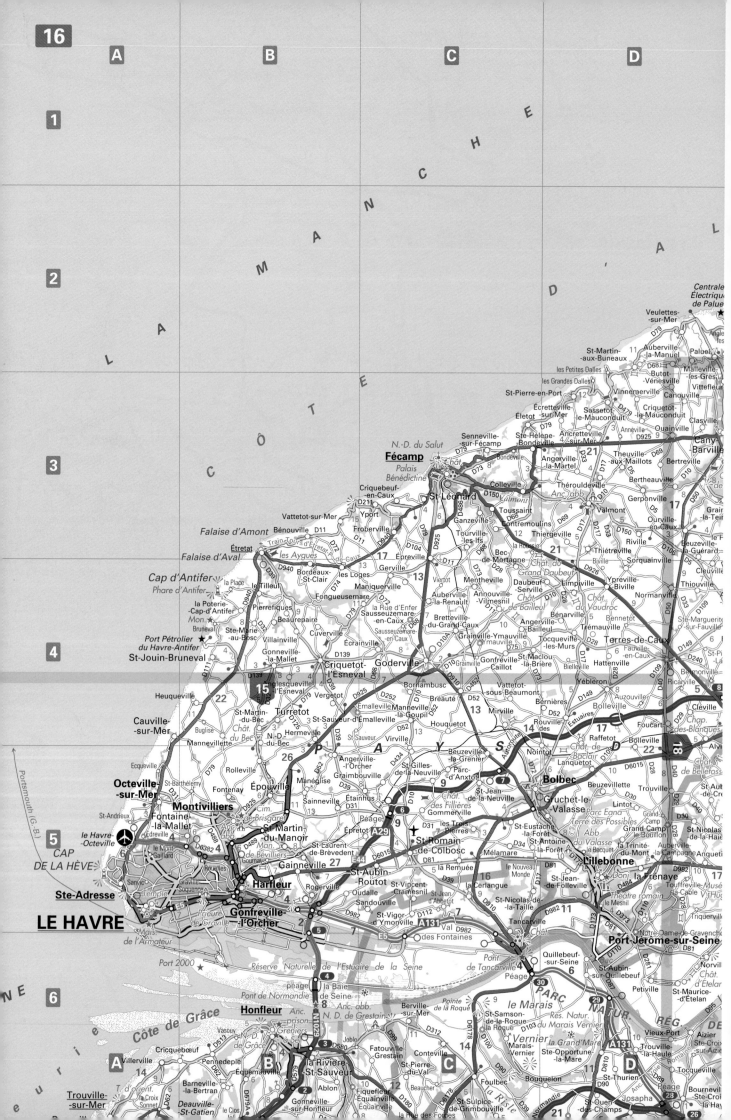

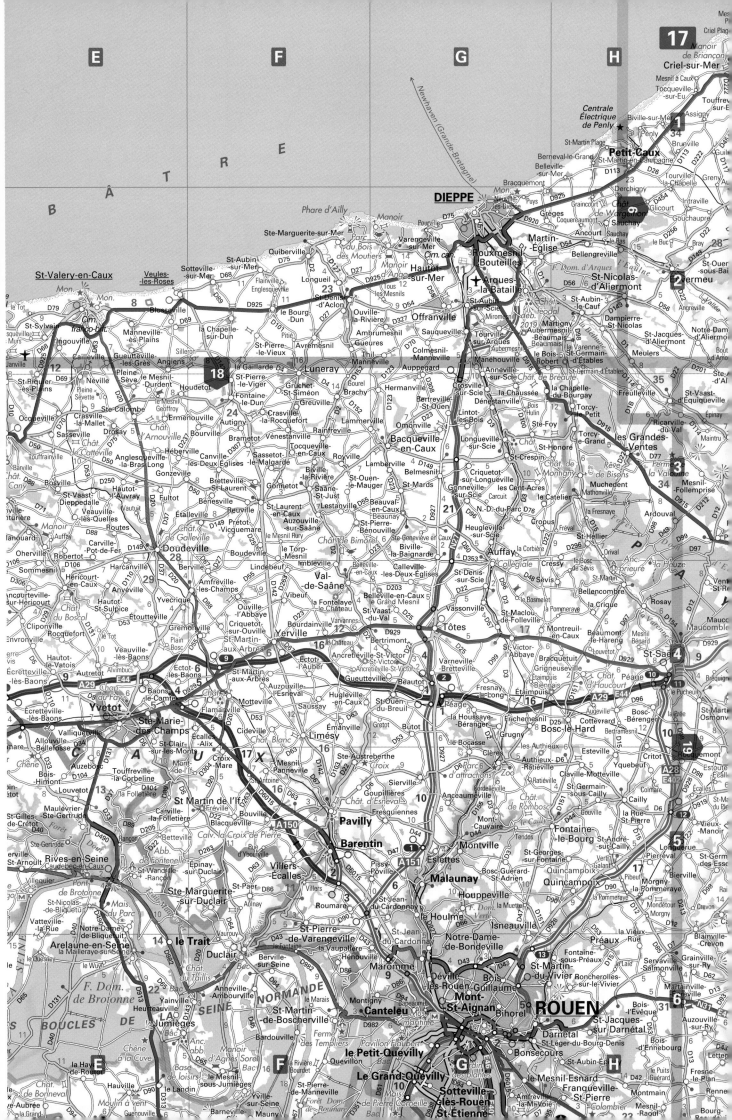

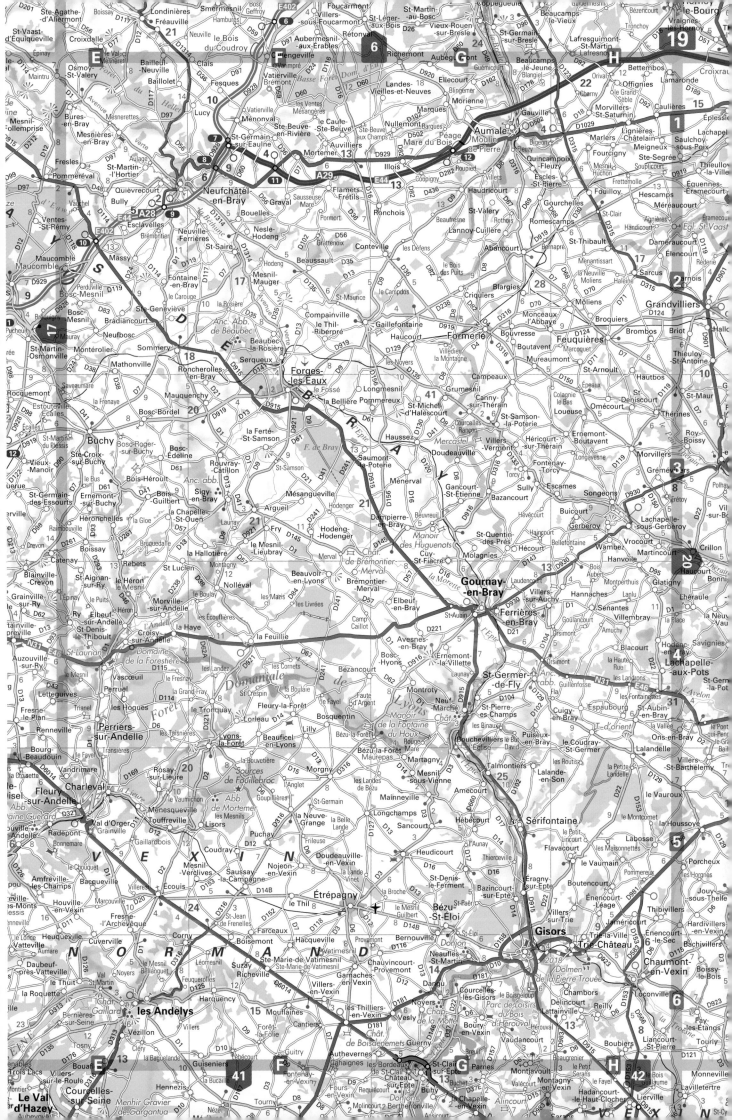

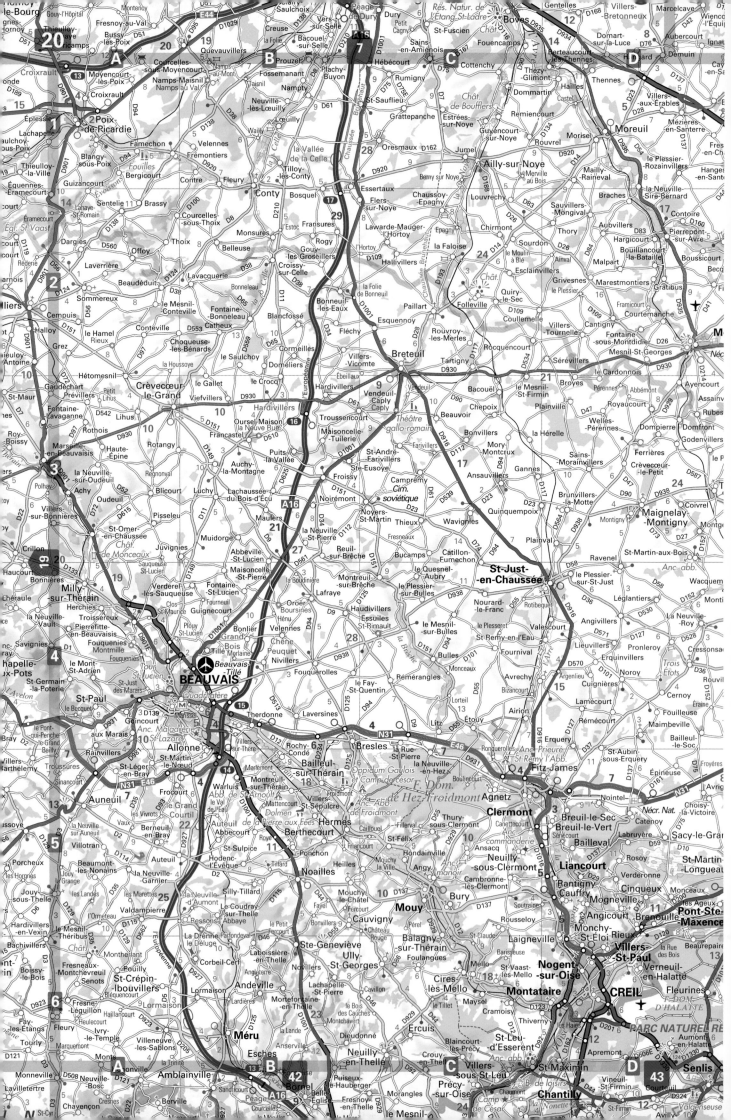

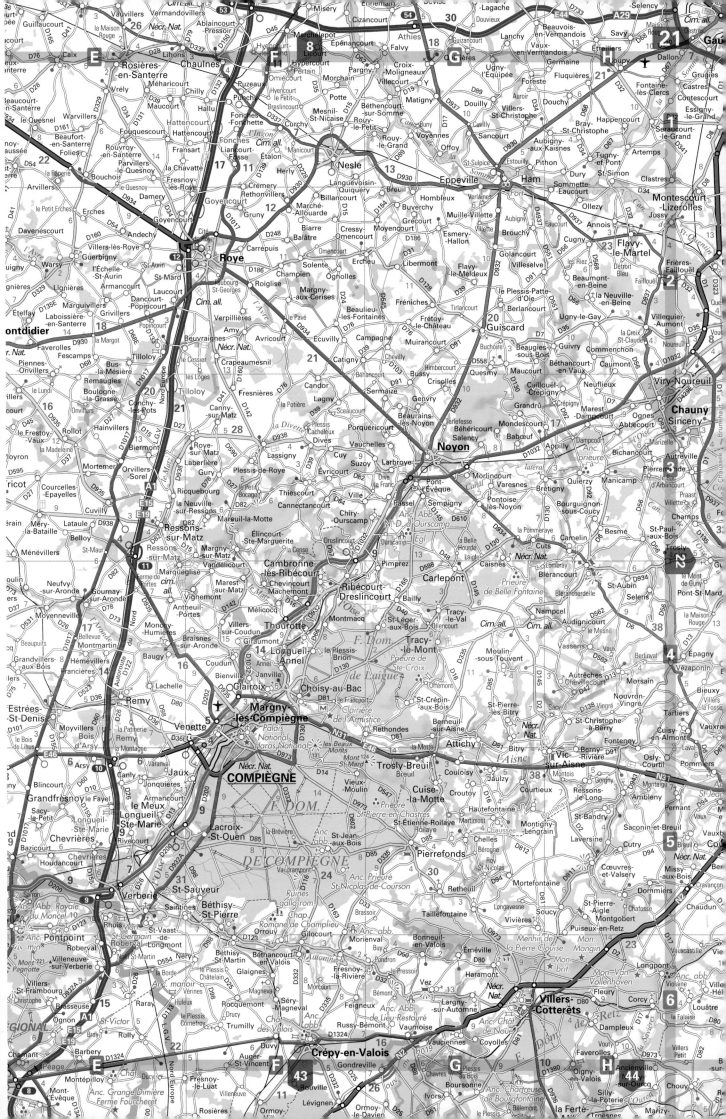

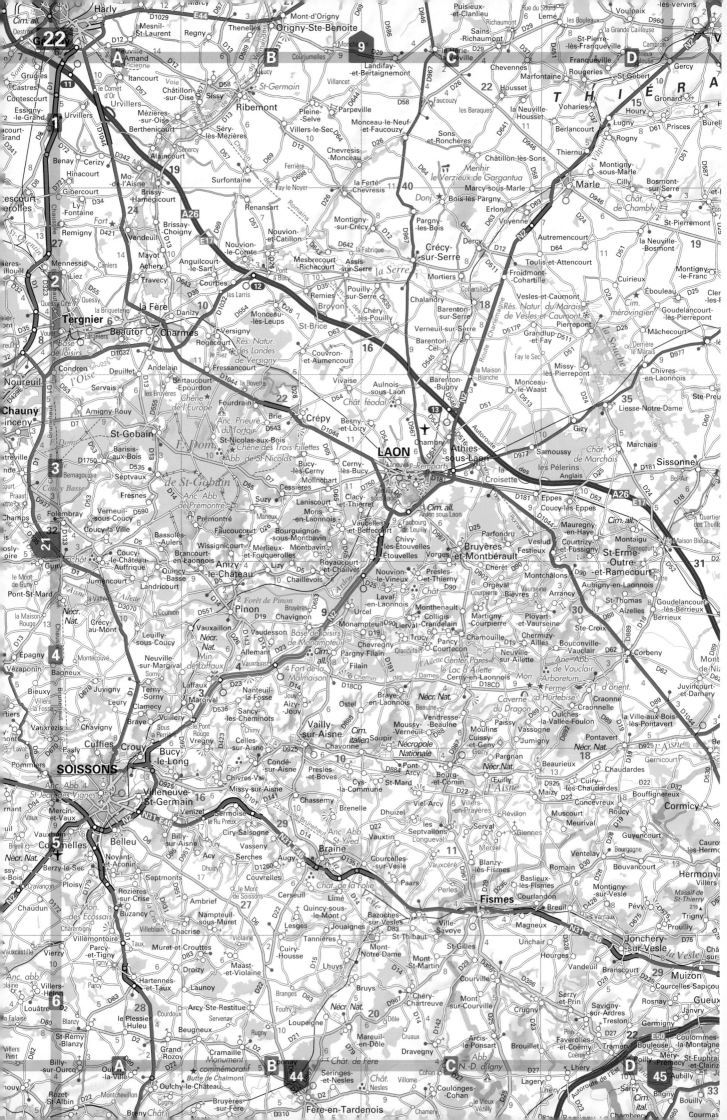

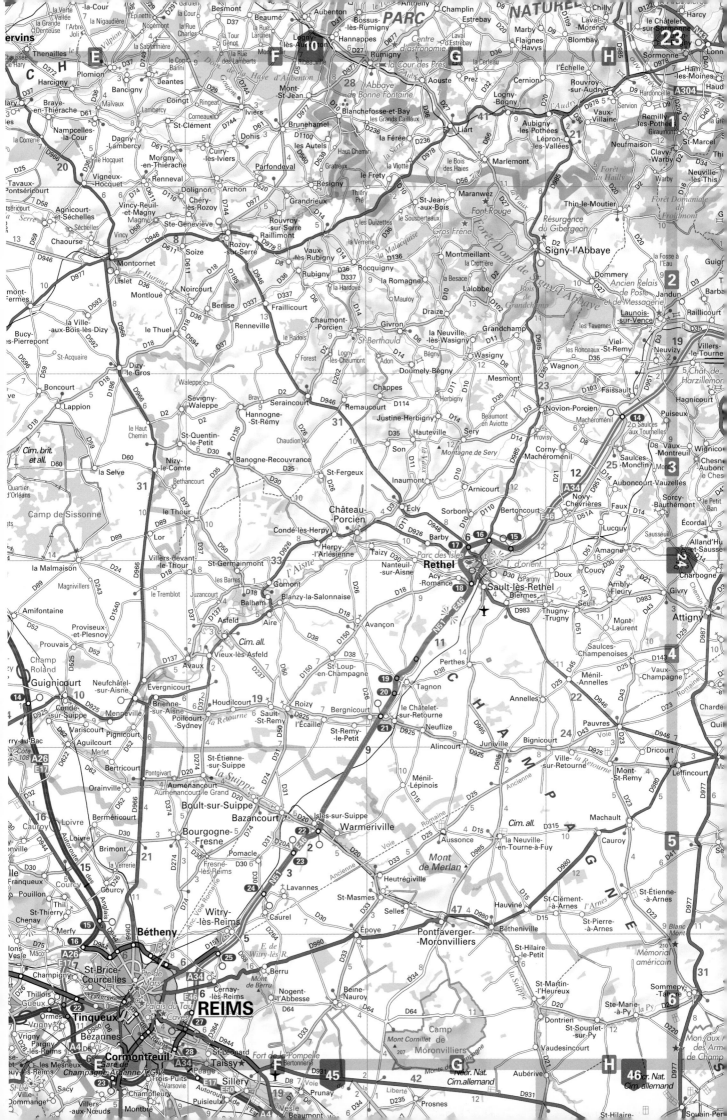

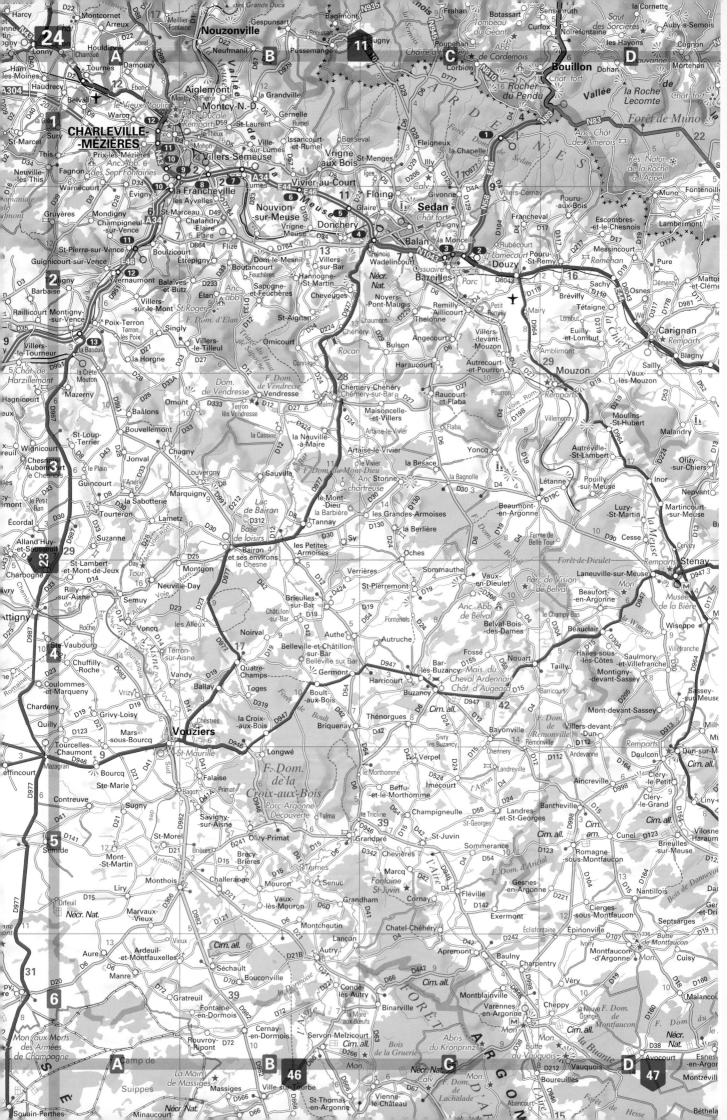

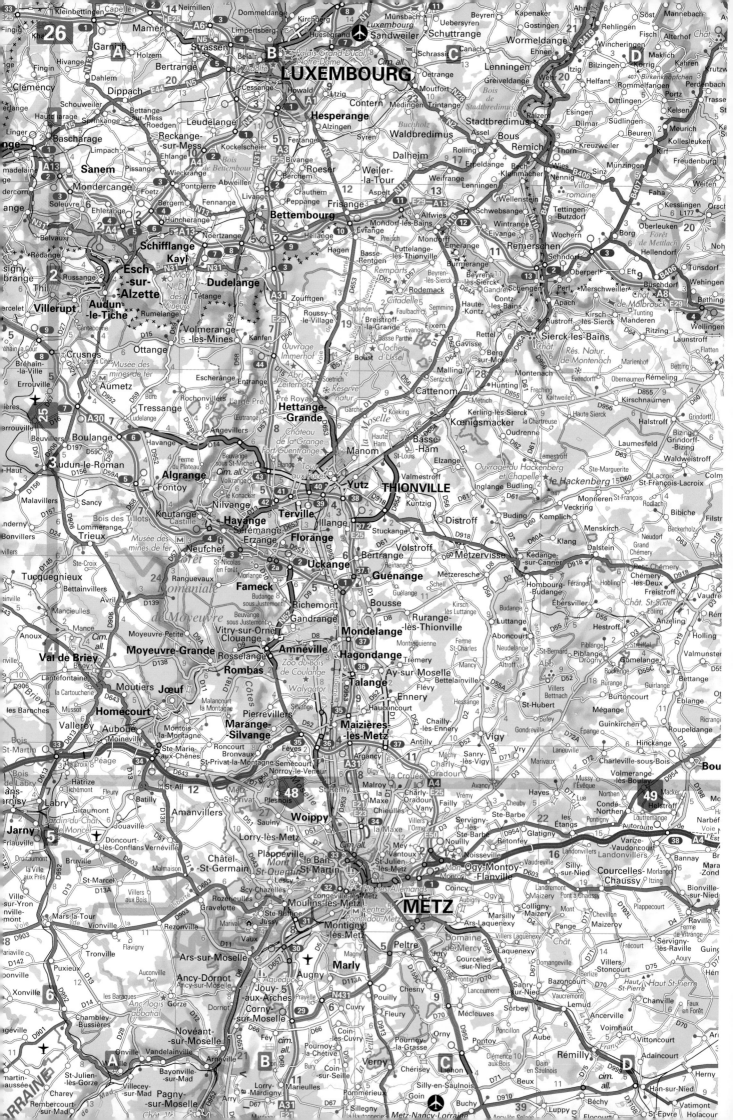

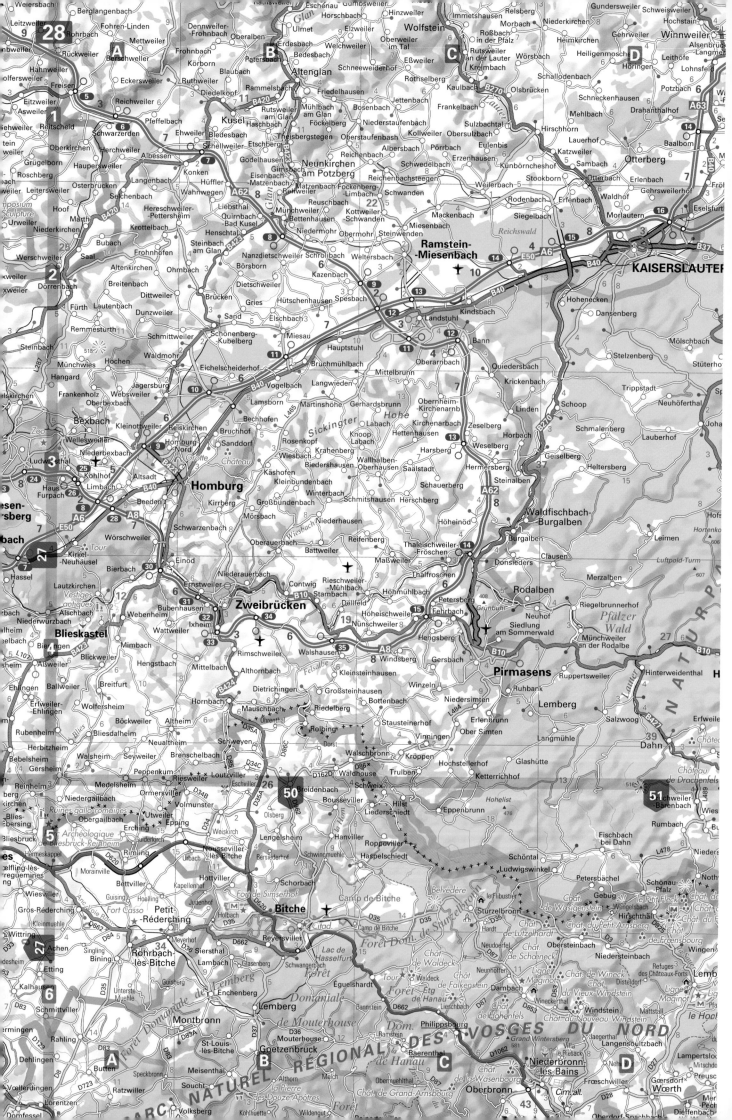

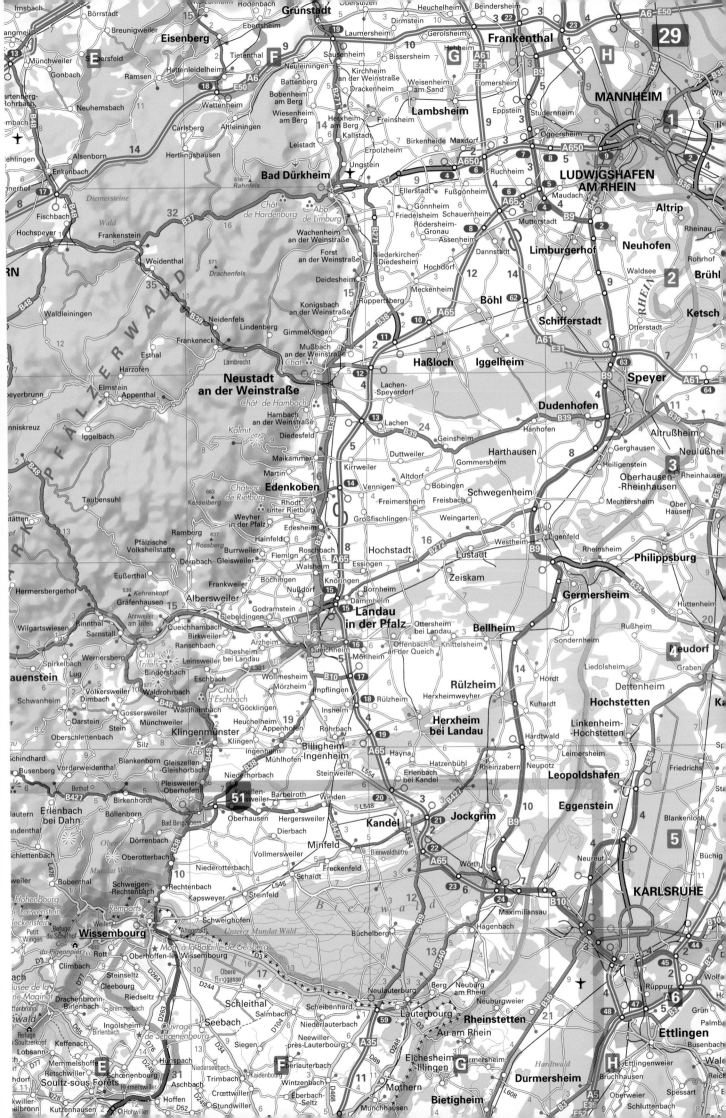

A   B   C   D

1

2

3

CÔTE   DES   LÉG

les   Abers

Île Vierge ⚲ Phare de l'Île V

Kélerdut

St-Cava

Plouguerneau

Presqu'île
Ste-Marguerite

l'Aber Wrac'h

Landéda

Aber Benoît

D1

D128

D13

Côum

3 Morgan

Lannilis

12

Trémazan
Portsall

Chât.

Lampaul-
-Ploudalmézeau

St-Pabu

Tréglonou

D26

D28

Tariec

D3

Pointe de Landunvez

9

Kersaint

D168

Ploudalmézeau

Plouguin

D26

Coat-Méal

Landunvez

5   D21

D28

Menhir
de Kervignen

Tréouergat

Bourg-
Blanc

Radénoc

Argenton

15

Milizac-
Guipronvel

14

Île d'Ouessant

Porspoder

Kersant

Plourin

D68

17

Guipronvel

les Trois
Curés

Phare du Stiff

D21

Ménhirs

Brélès

Lanner

Milizac

la-Récré
des Trois Curés

Phare de
Créac'h

Niou
Huella

Frugullou

Manoir
de
Bel-air

Château
de Kergroadez

Lanvéoc

Lanrivoaré

Kerviniou

Gou

Notre-Dame
de Bon Voyage

Lampaul-
Ouessant

Melon

Perros

Lanildut

D28

l'Aber Ildut

12   D27

6

Gui

Faunteun Vélen

Lampaul-
-Plouarzel

Erragounan

14

St-Renan

Guilers

10

Phare de la
Jument

4

Passage du Fromveur

Phare
de Trézien

Keresca

Plouarzel

4   D5

Menhir
de Kerloas

Lamber

D105

Bohars

Ruscumunoc

Kerhornou

5

D5

Rest

Pointe de Corsen

Kerlazou

Trégorff

le Bouguen
Arsenal

Île-Molène

Kerhornou

Ploumoguer

16   D67

Plouzané

D205

Île
Molène

Illien

D28

4

Locmaria-
Plouzané

Plouzané

Castel-Névez

Réserve Naturelle
d'Iroise

Trébabu

3

Keramzaze

St-Pierre
Quilibignon

B

Île de Béniguet

le Conquet

D789

Porsmilin

23

la Trinité

D789

Lochrist

Ste-Anne
du Portzic

le Trez Hir

Trégana

D8

St-Mathieu

Plougonvelin

M   D85

Pointe du
Petit Minou

Goulet de Brest

RADE   DE

Abbaye

POINTE DE ST-MATHIEU

5

D355

Roscanvel

PARC   NATUREL   MARIN   D'IROISE

Lanvernazal

Fort ★

Quélern

Taladerc'h

N.-D. de Roc

Amadour

St-Fiacre

Lanvéo

Camaret-
-sur-Mer

Tour Vauban

D55

P R E S Q U ' Î L E   L

Alignements de Lagatjar

D355

D55

Monument

POINTE DE PEN-HIR

3

9

Croz

les Tas de Pois

Gaoulac'h

6

Pointe de Dinan

D308

Morgan

Pointe
des Grot

la Palue

Grottes

St-Ha

M   Maison
des minéraux

Cap de
la Chèvre

Rostudel

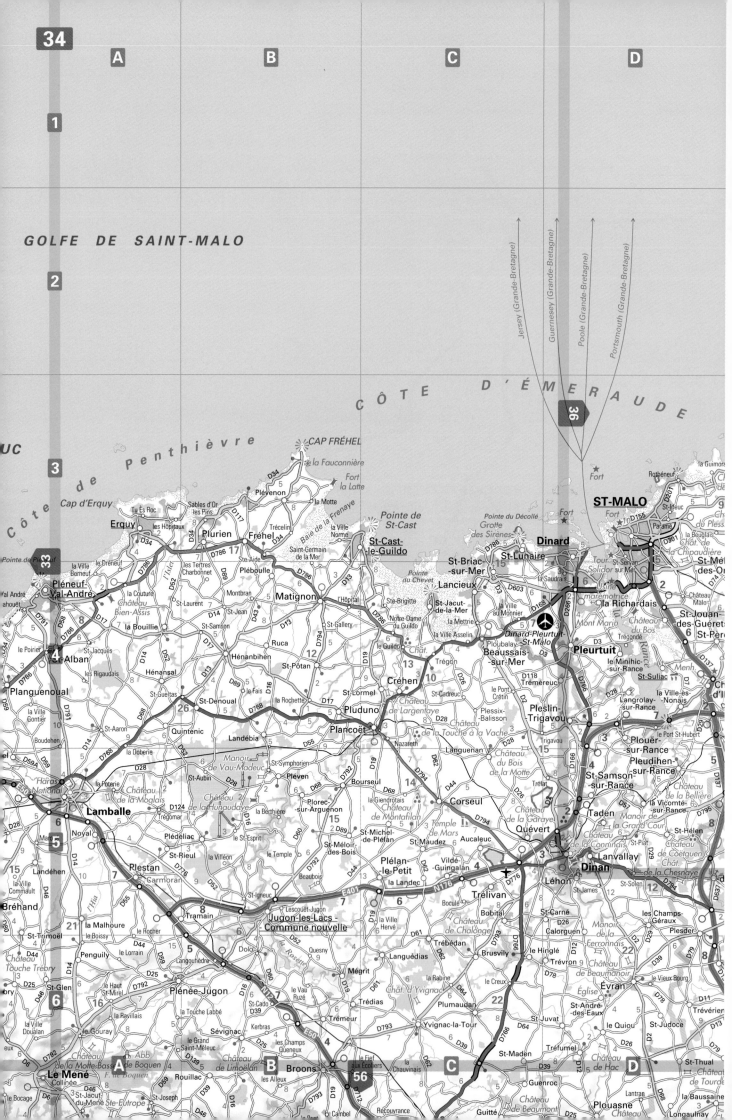

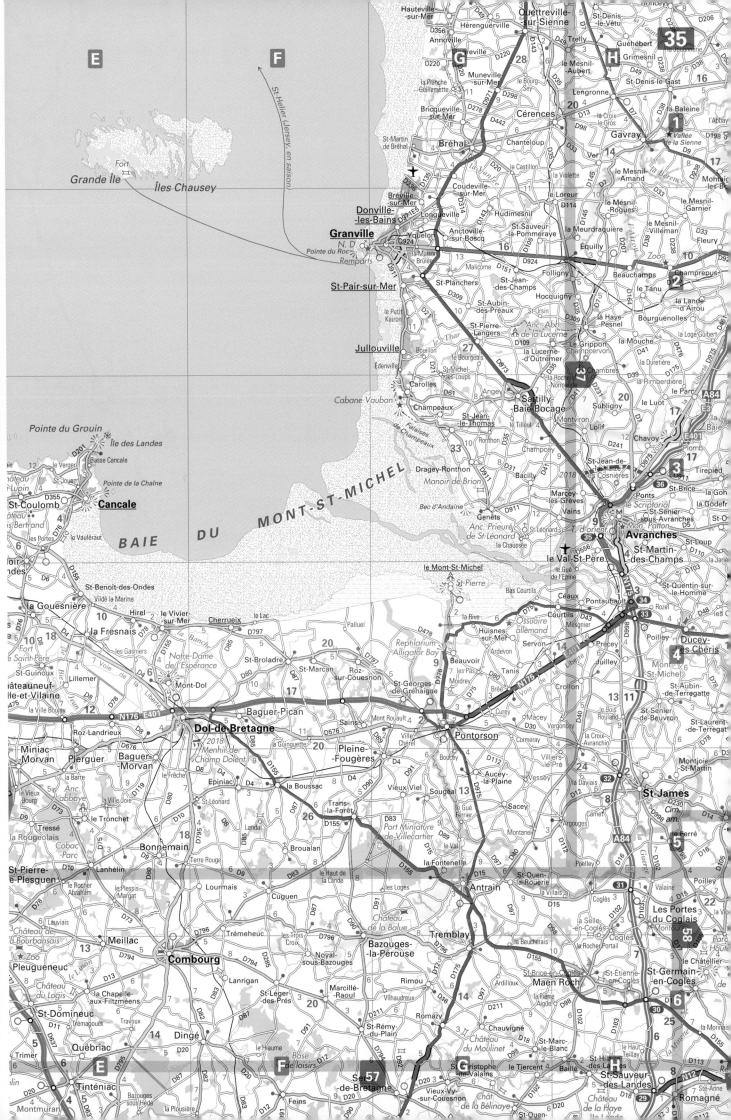

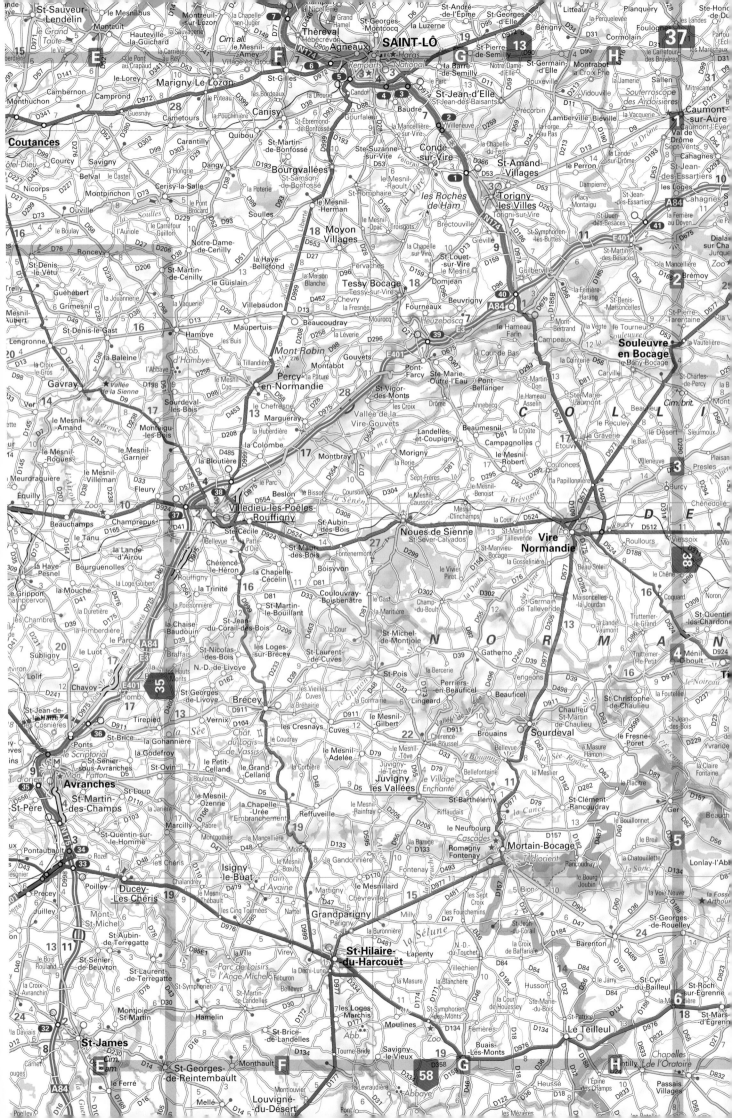

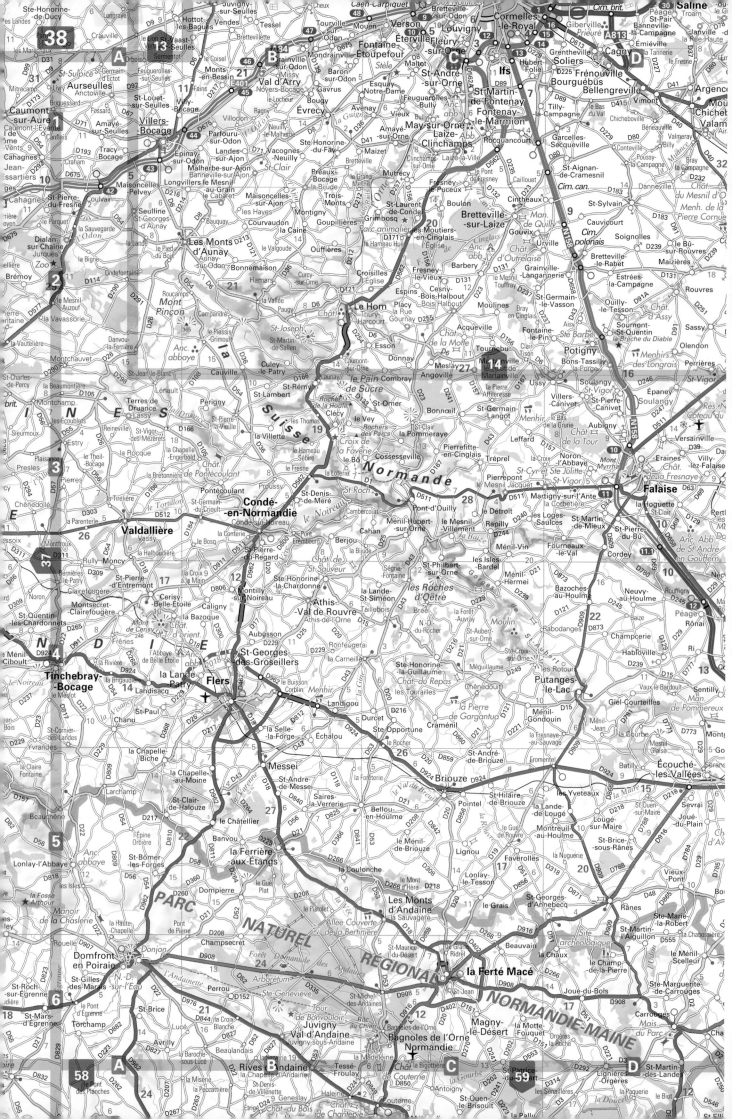

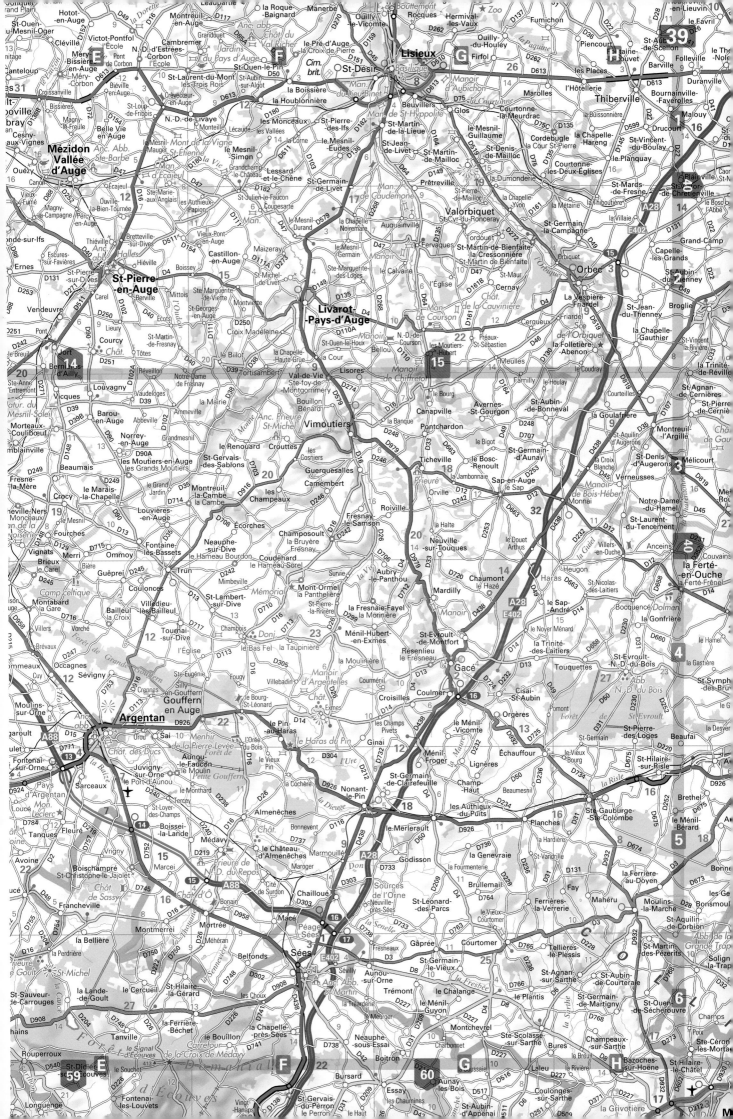

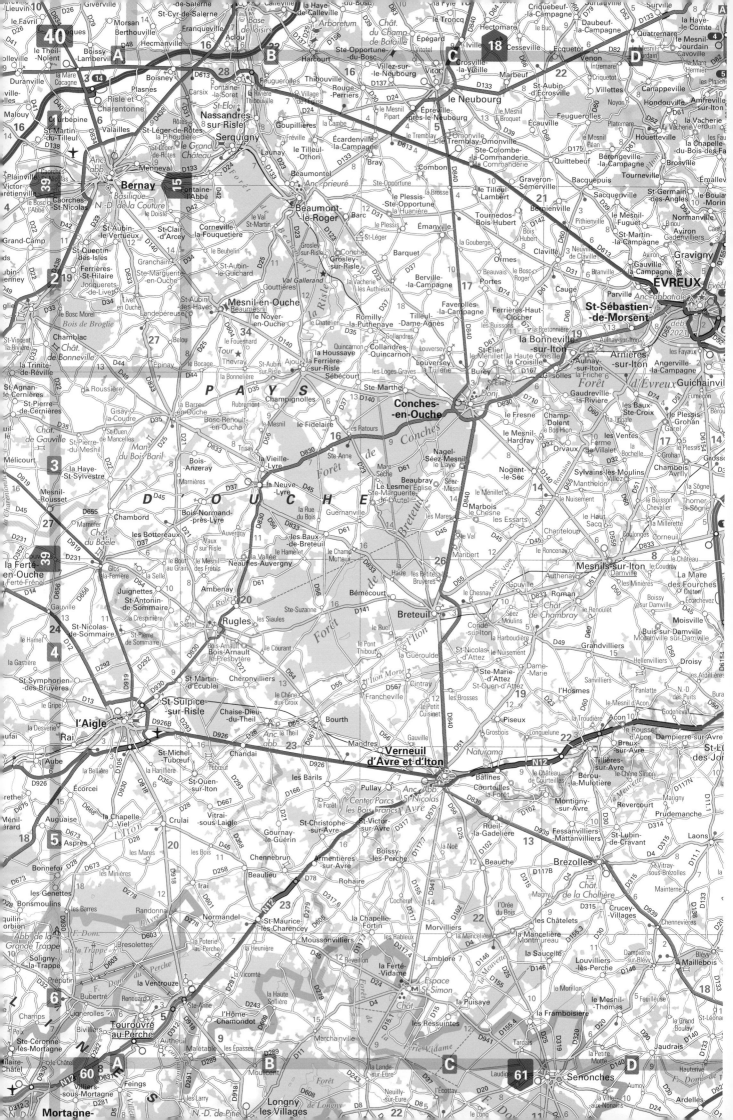

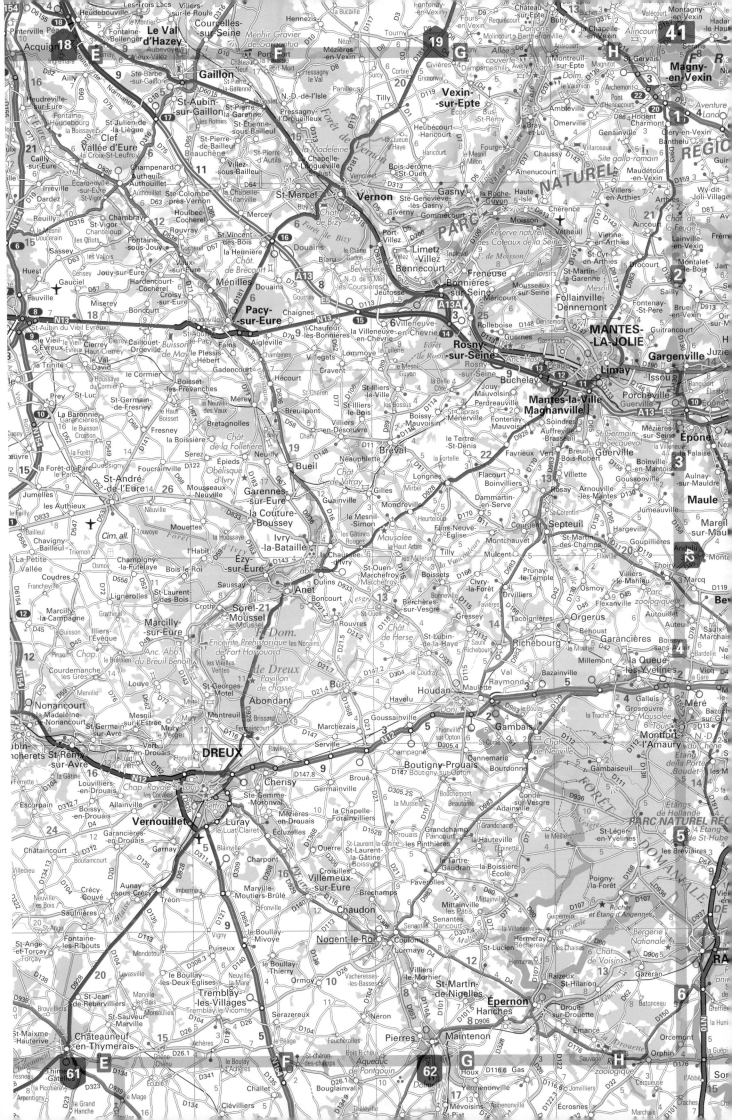

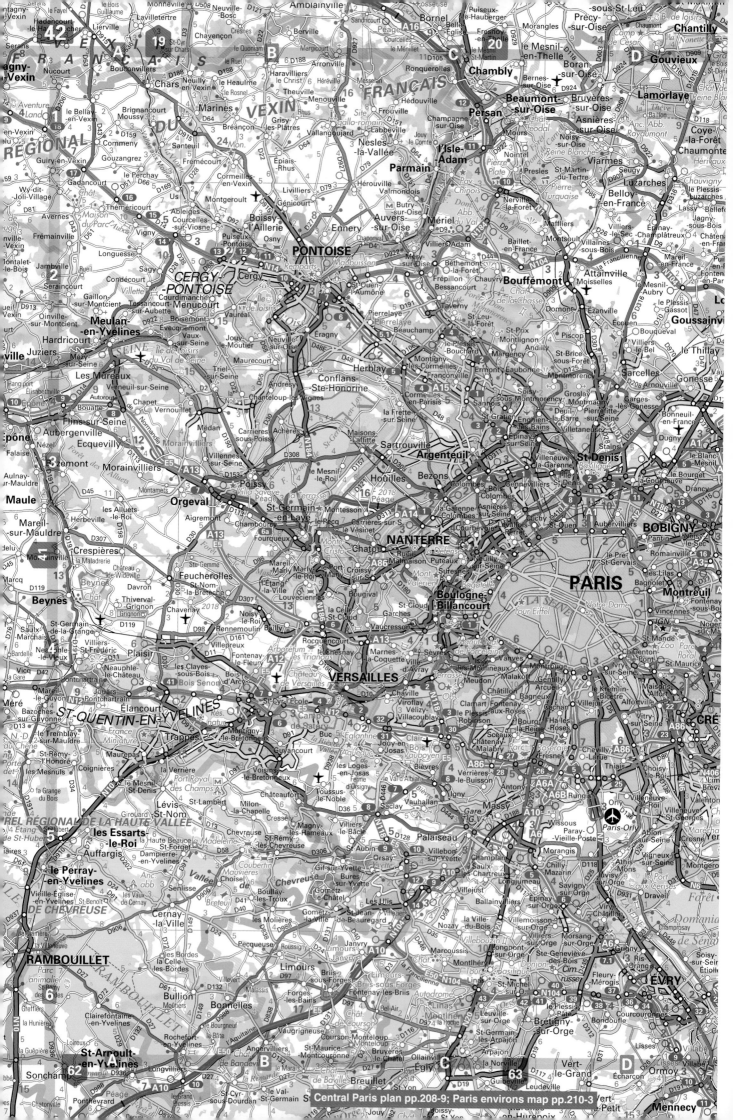

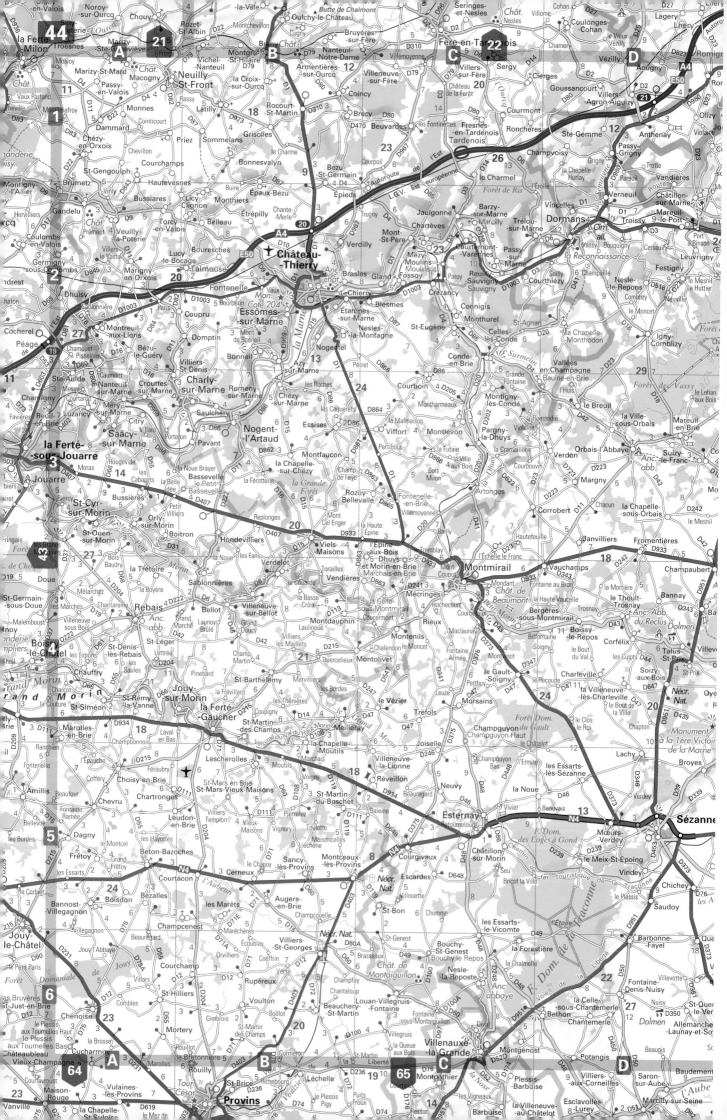

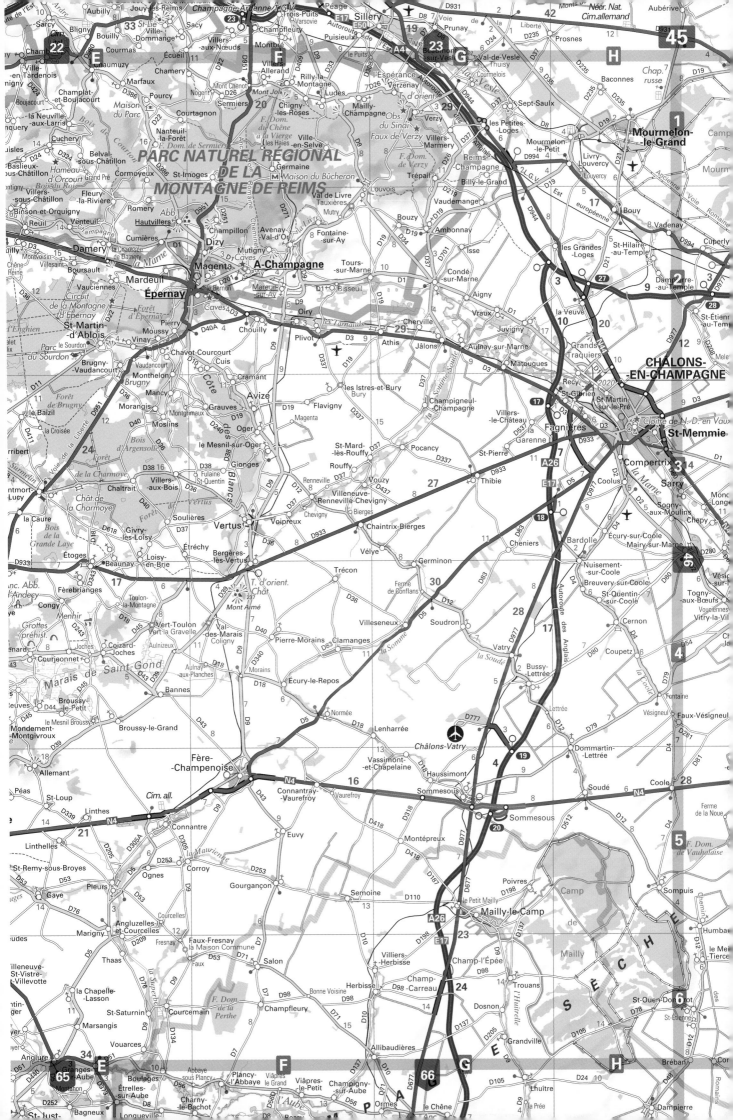

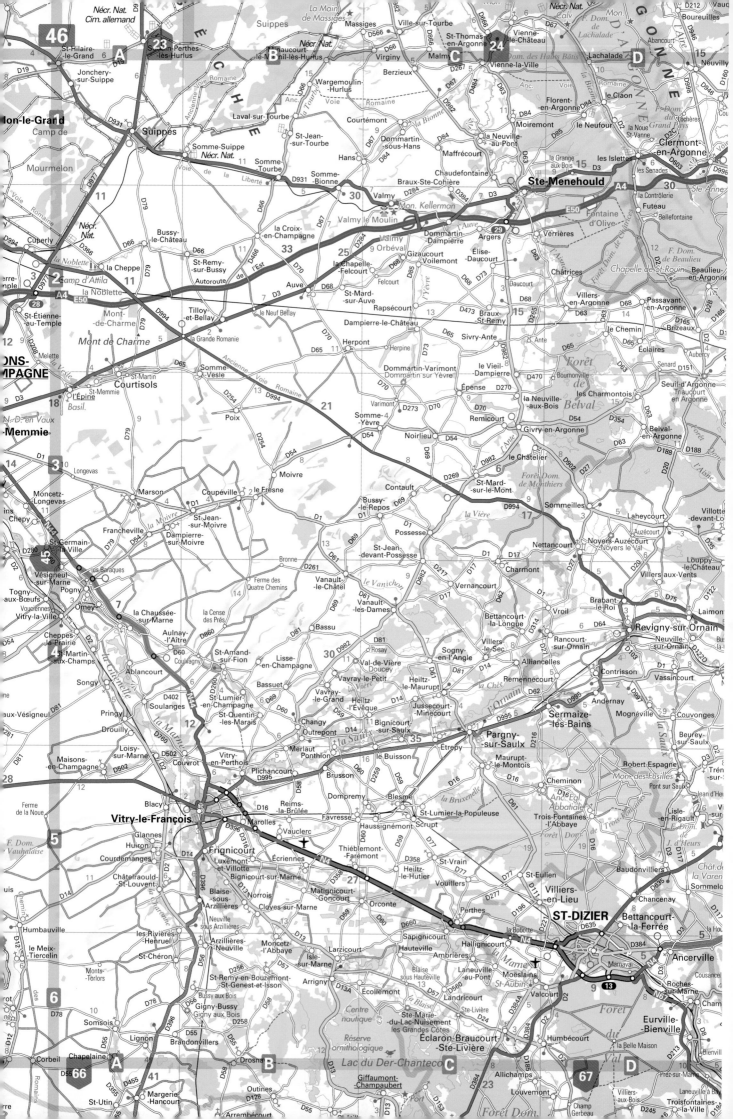

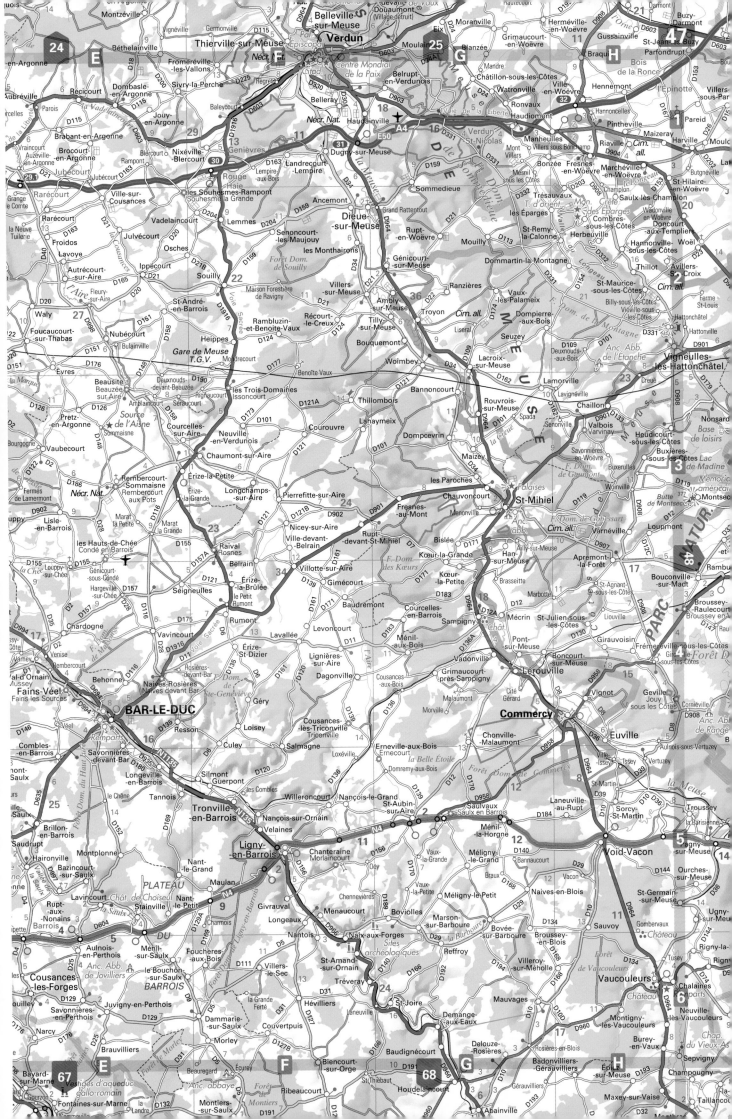

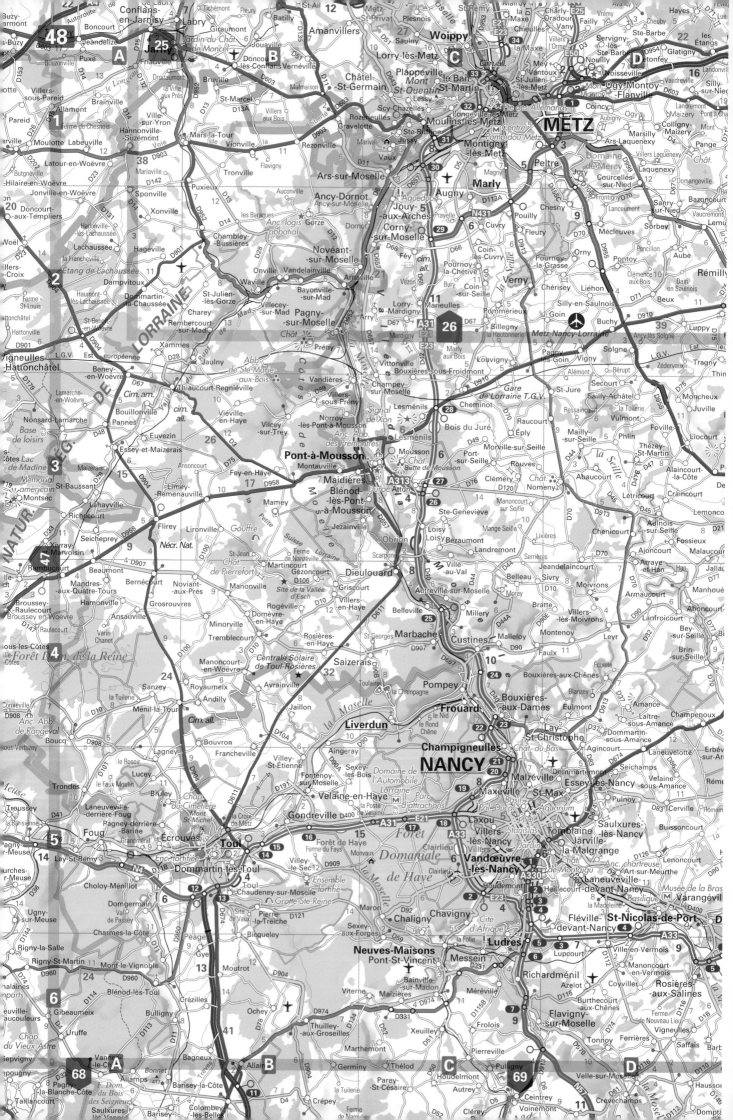

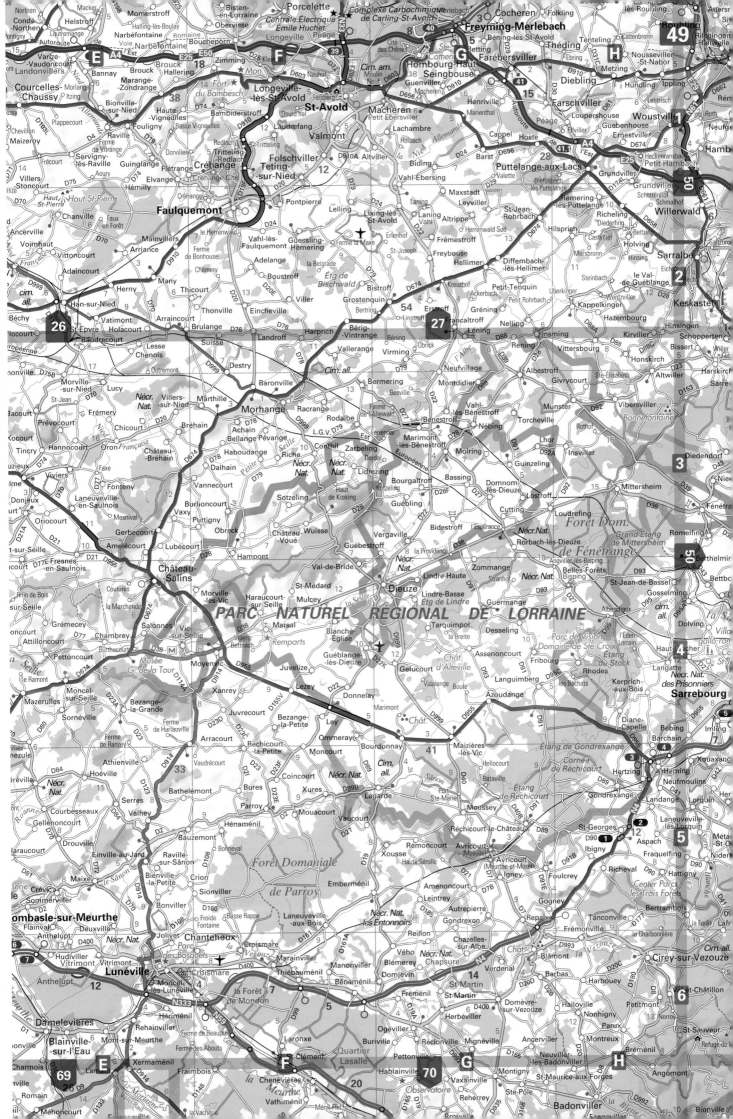

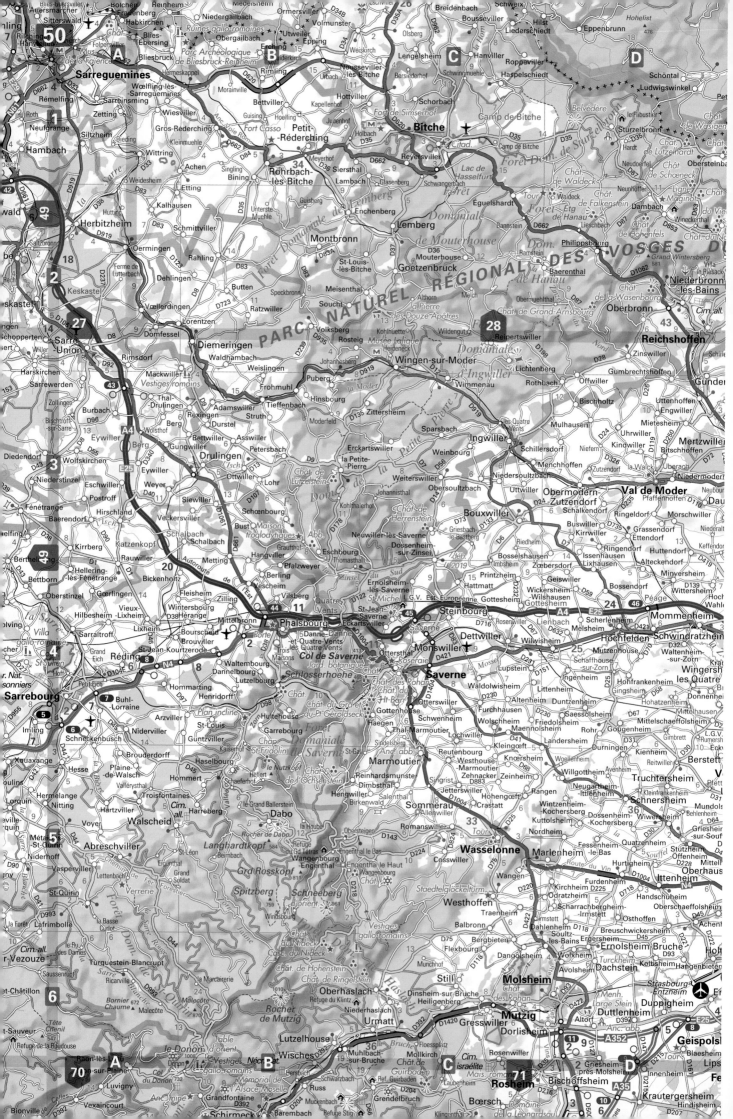

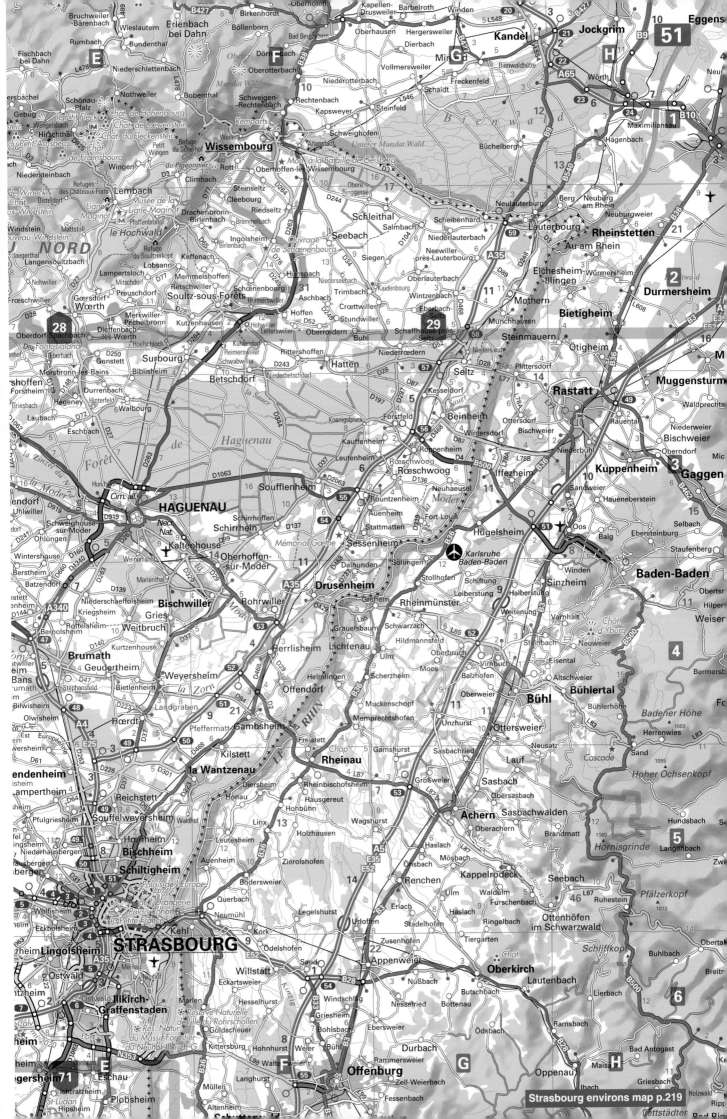

Strasbourg environs map p.219

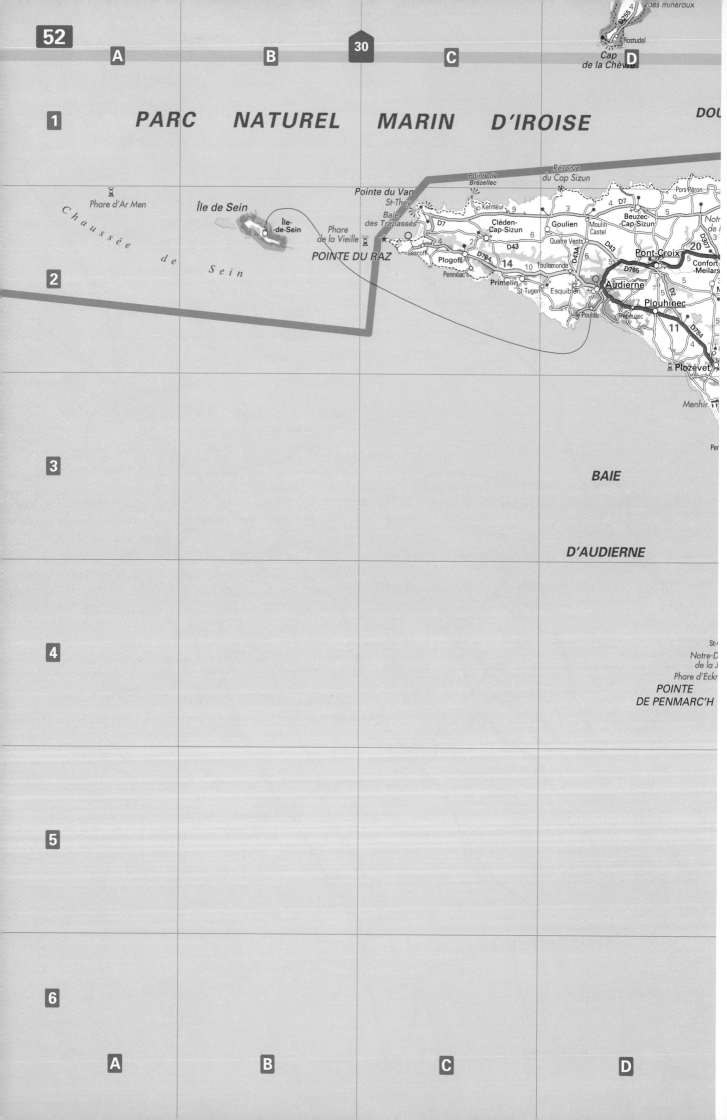

1

PARC NATUREL MARIN D'IROISE

DOU

Cap
de la Chèvre

des minéraux

D255

Rostudel

Phare d'Ar Men

Île de Sein

Île
-de-Sein

Chaussée de

Sein

Phare
de la Vieille

POINTE DU RAZ

Pointe de
Brézellec

*Réserve
du Cap Sizun*

Pointe du Van
St-They

Baie
des Trépassés

Pointe de

Pors-Péron

Kermeur   9

Cléden-
Cap-Sizun

D7

Goulien

3

Moulin
Castel

Beuzec-
Cap-Sizun

4   D7

5

Notr
de l

D7

D43

Quatre Vents

D43A

D43

Pont-Croix

D307

20

2

Lescoff

4

Plogoff

2

D784

14

Toulemonde

10

6

5

Confort-
Meilars

Pennéac'h

Primelin

Esquibien

Audierne

D765

D2

St-Tugen

Le Pouldu

Trébeuzec

Plouhinec

7

11

D784

4

Plozévet

Menhir

Per

3

BAIE

D'AUDIERNE

4

St-
Notre-D
de la J

Phare d'Eckr

*POINTE
DE PENMARC'H*

5

6

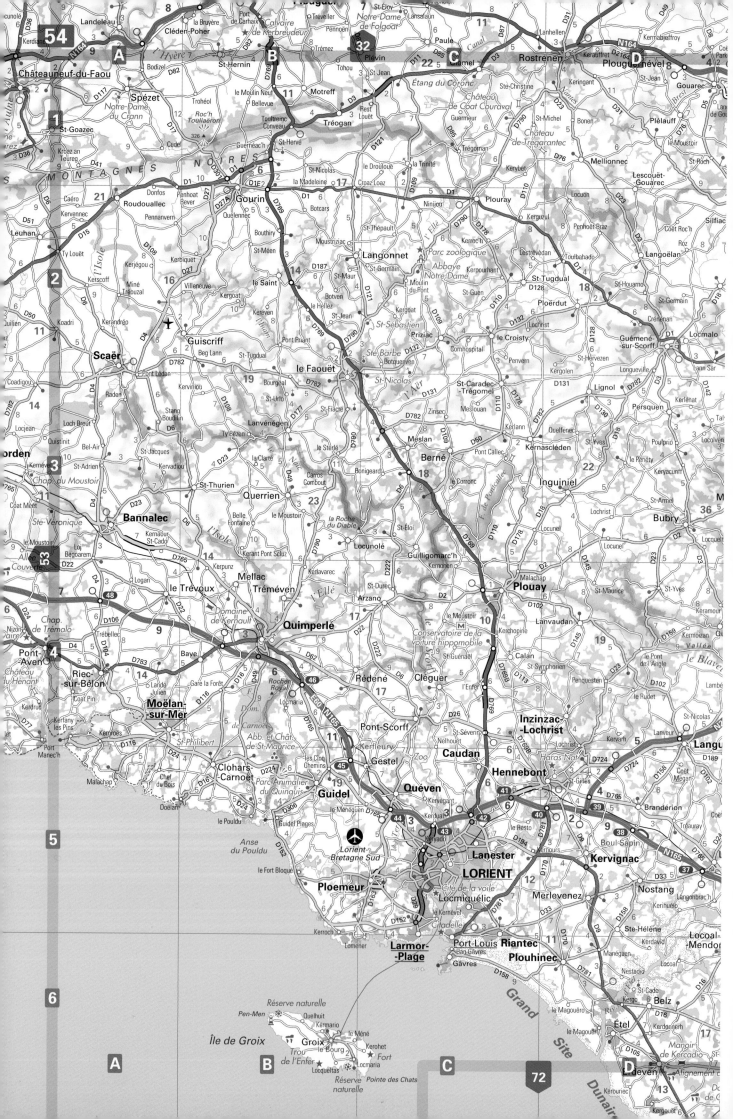

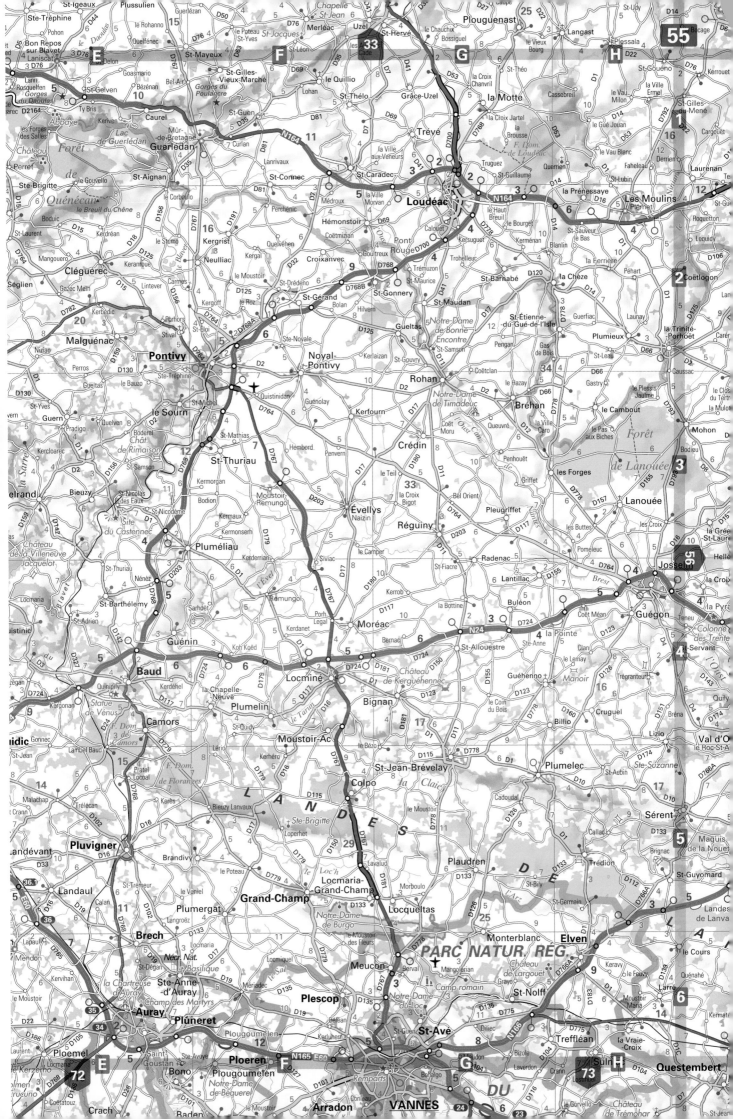

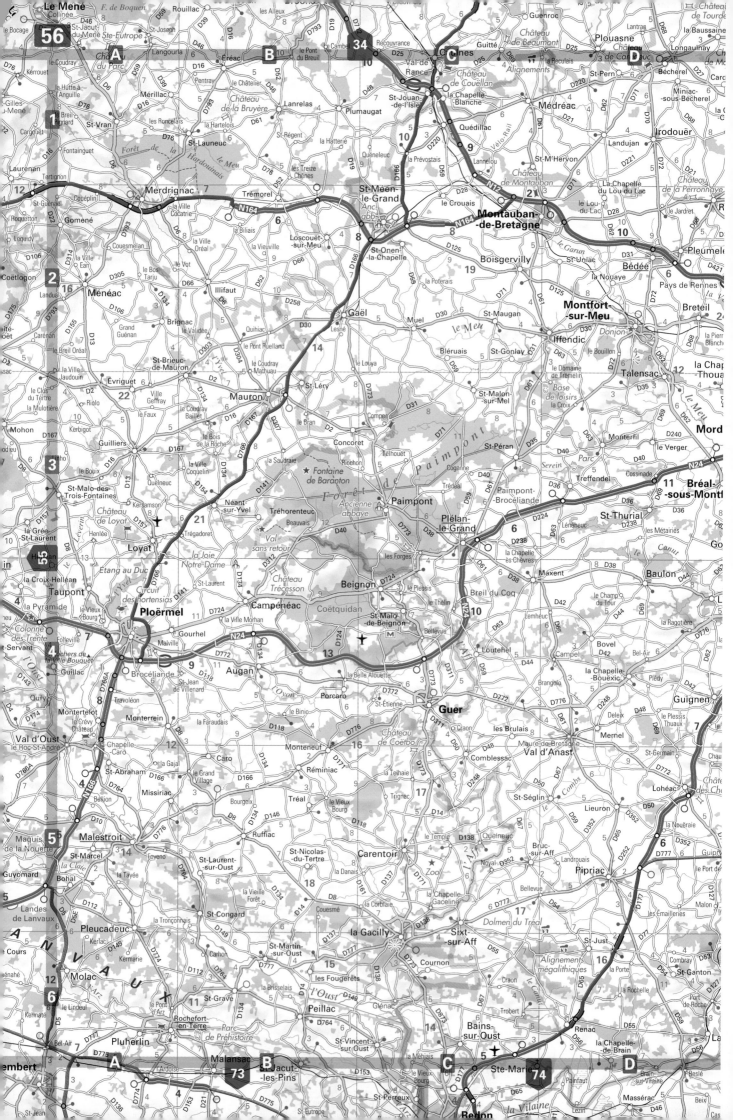

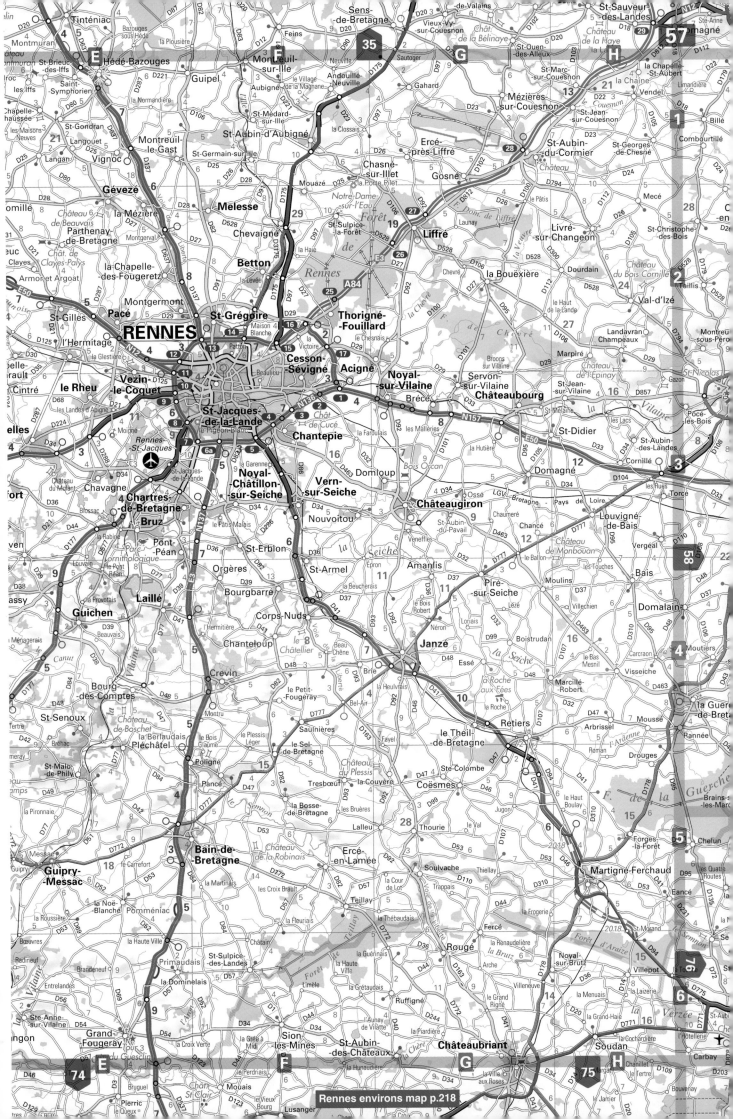

Rennes environs map p.218

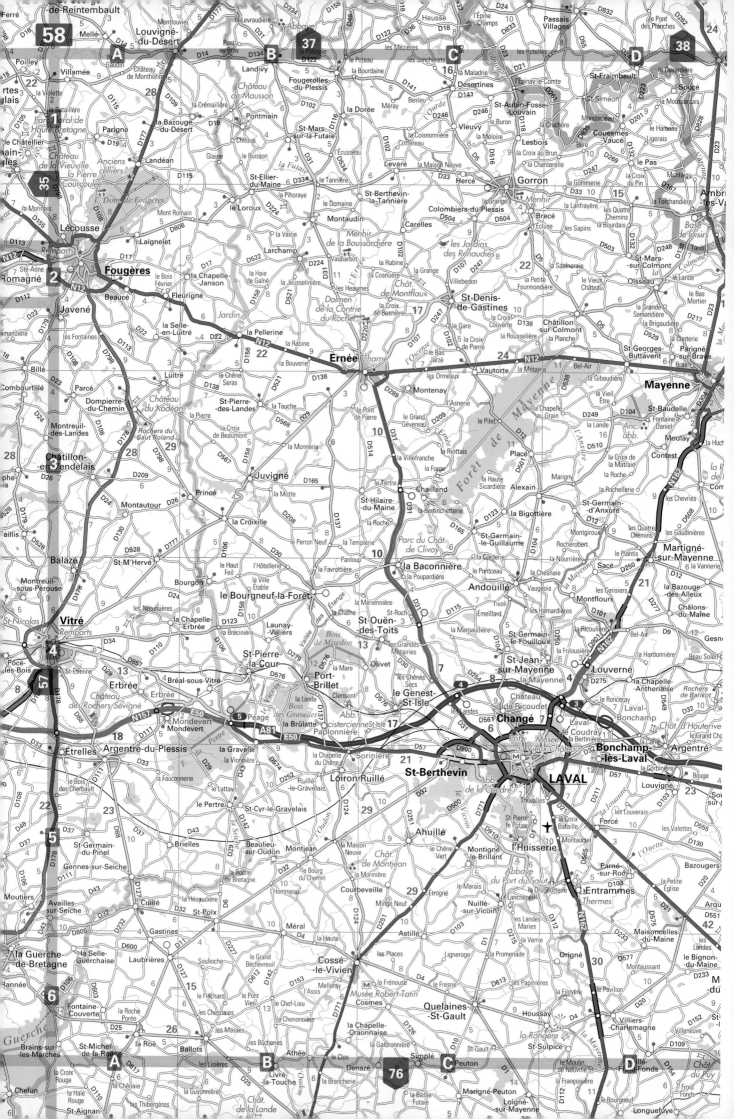

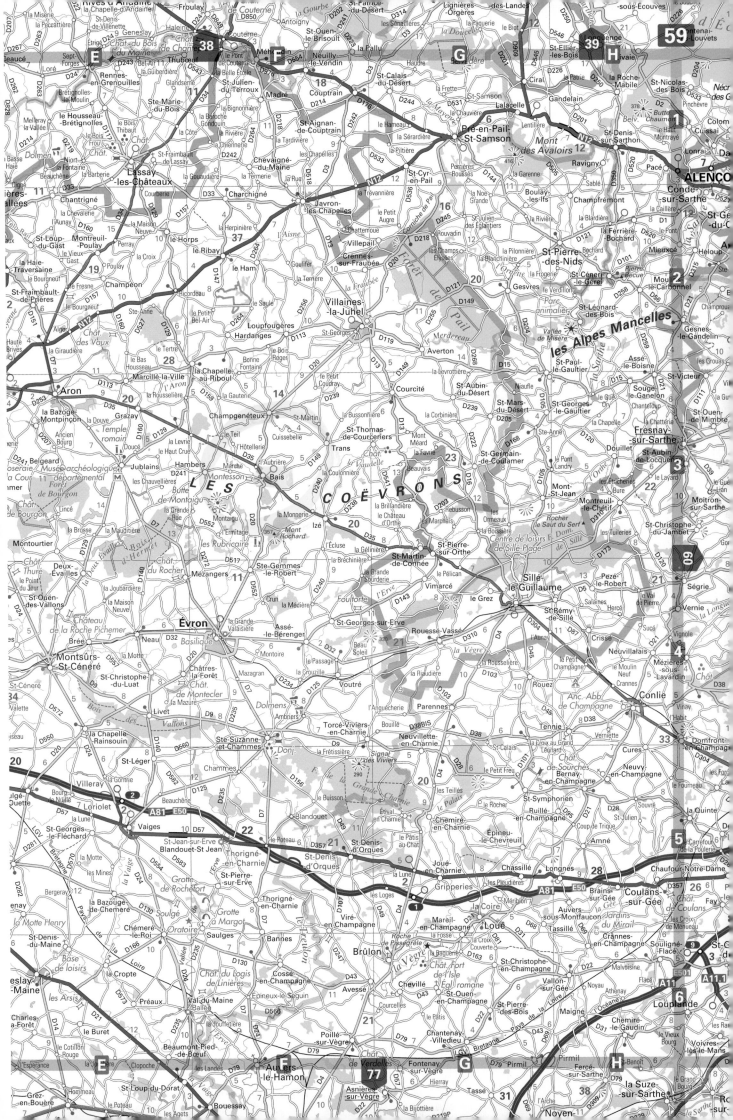

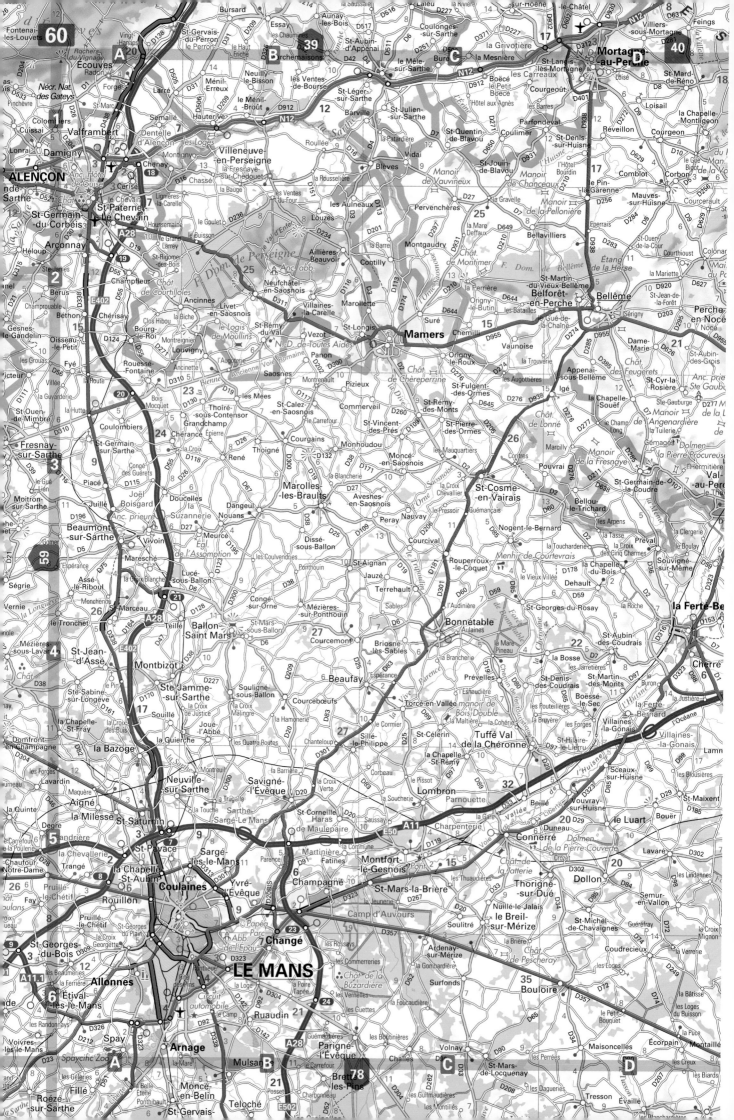

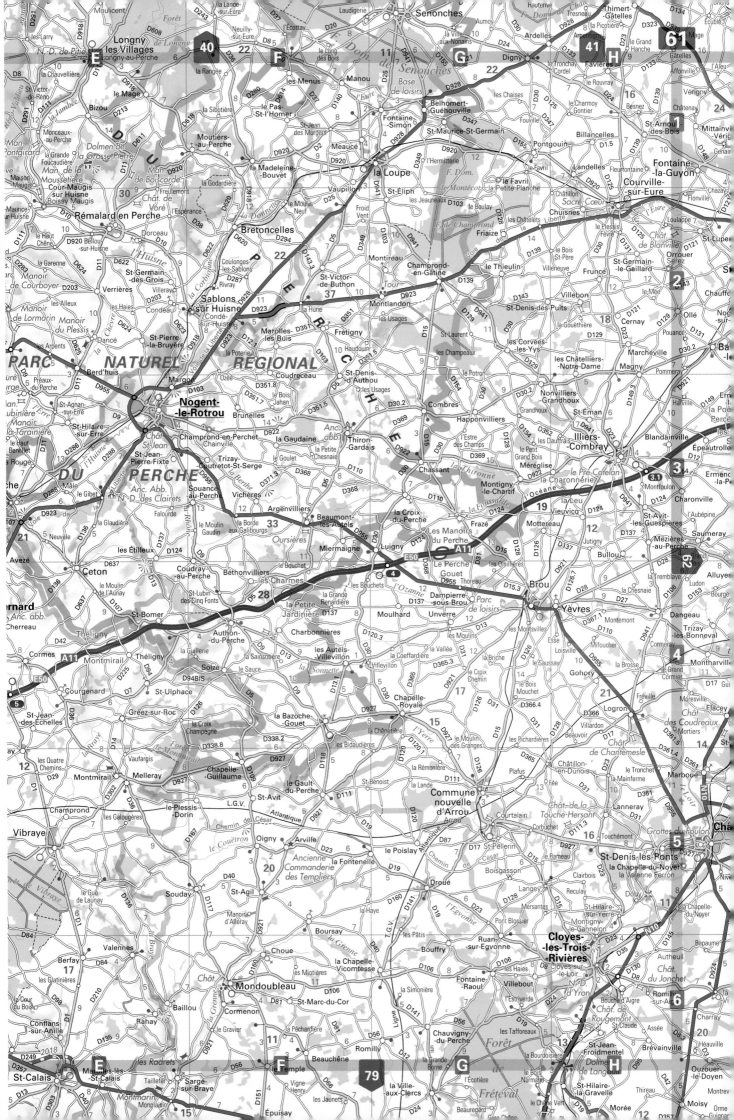

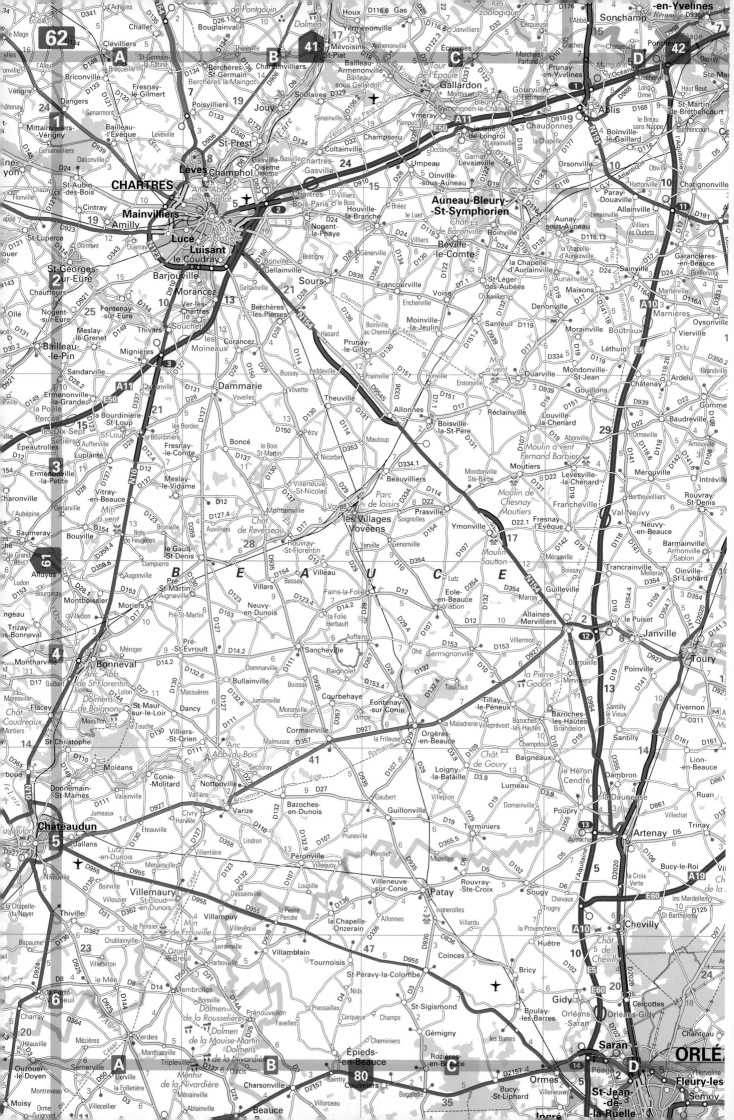

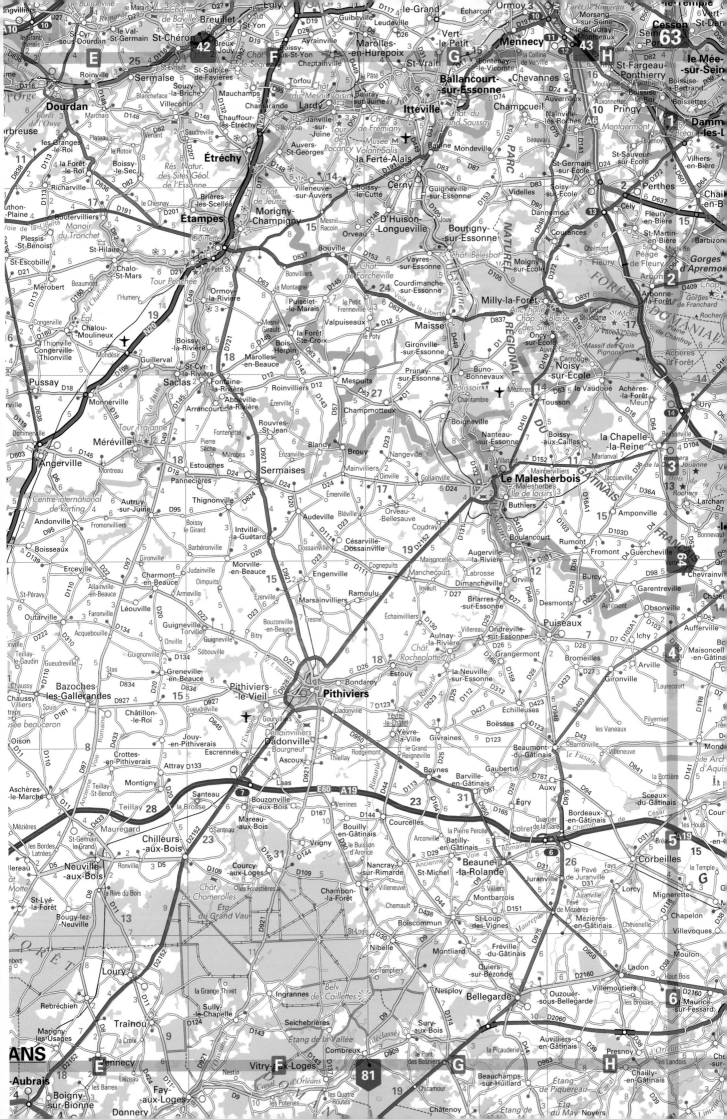

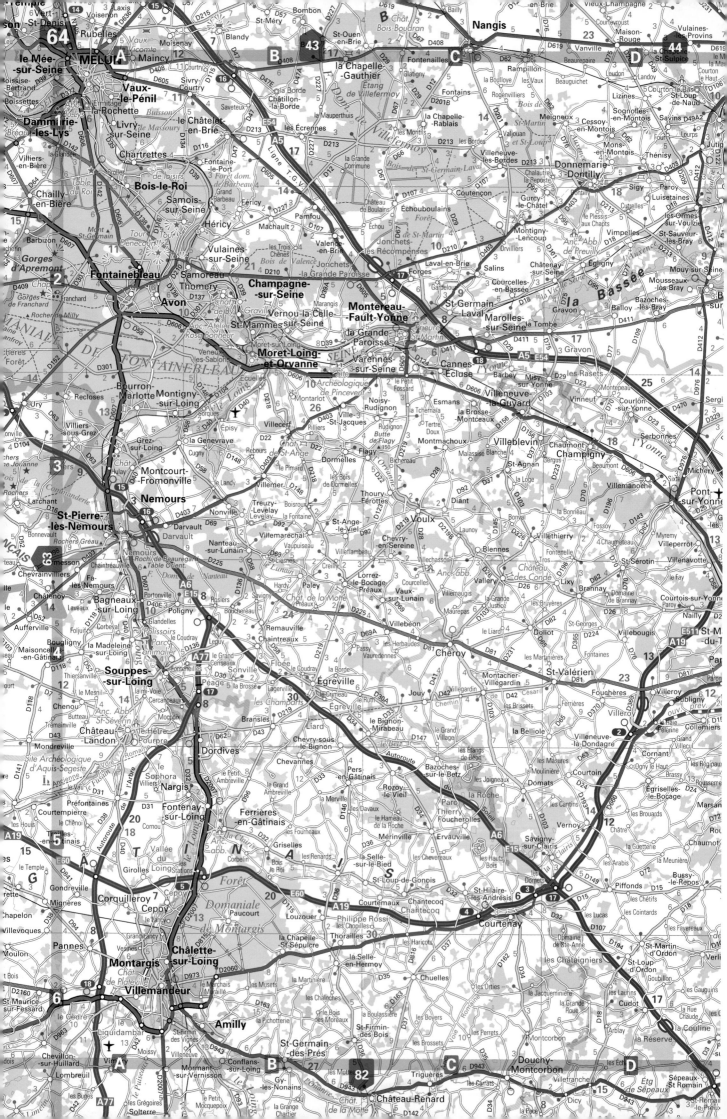

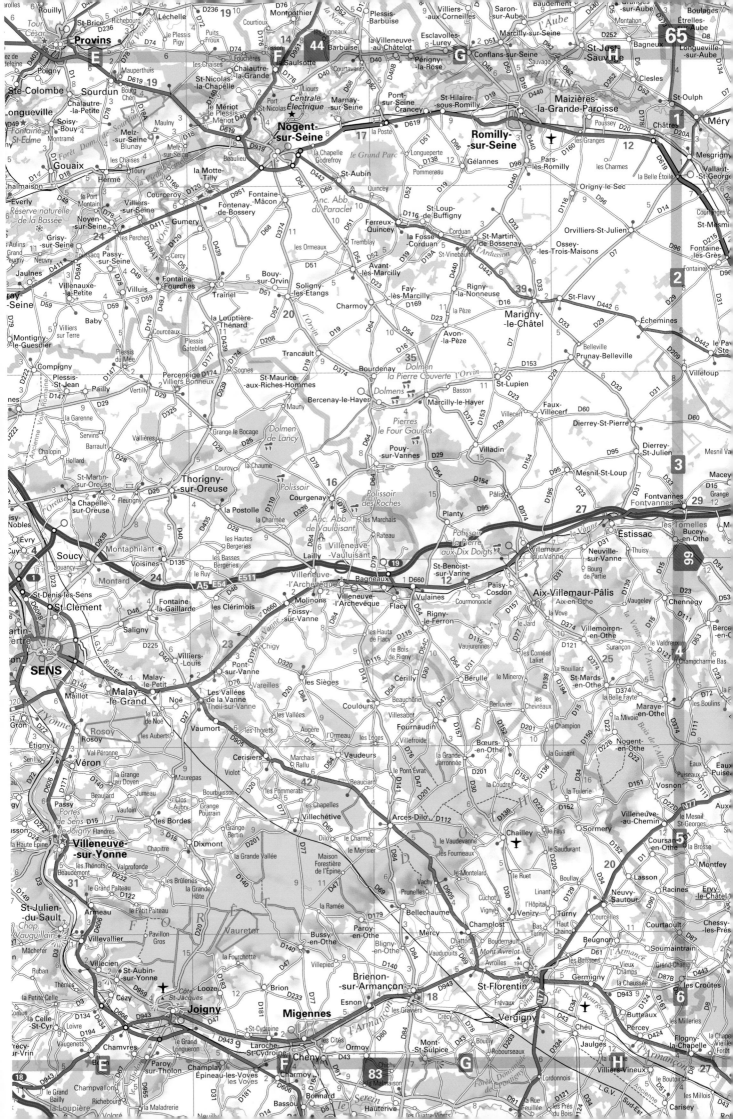

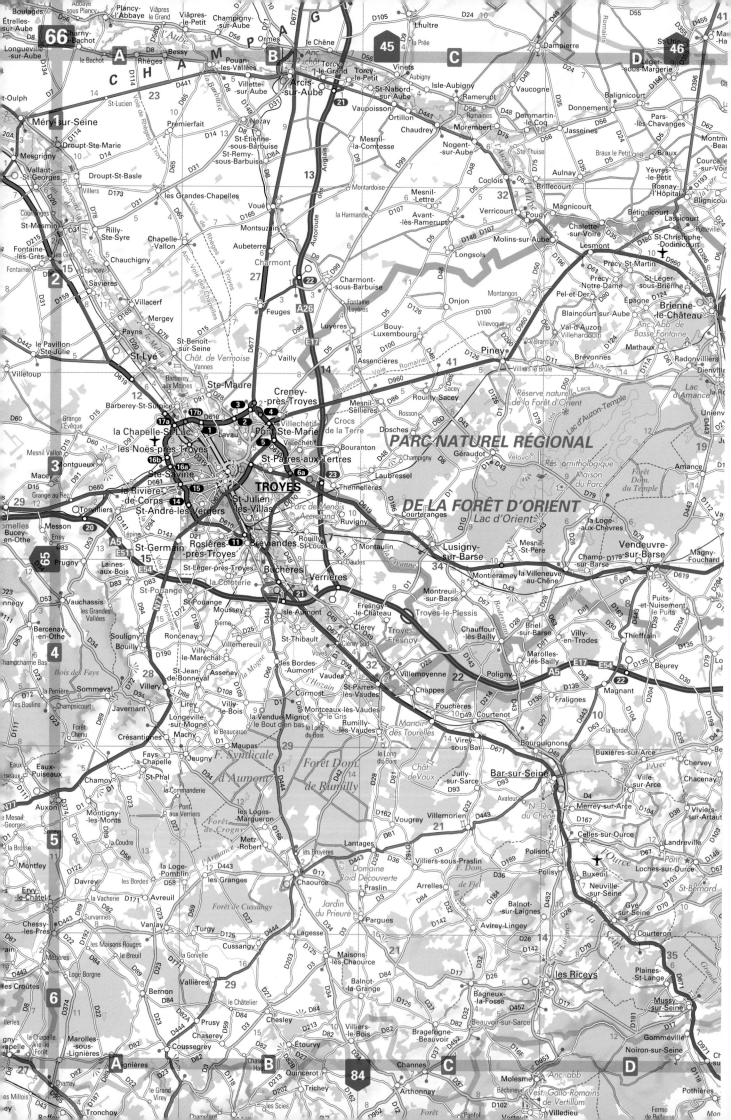

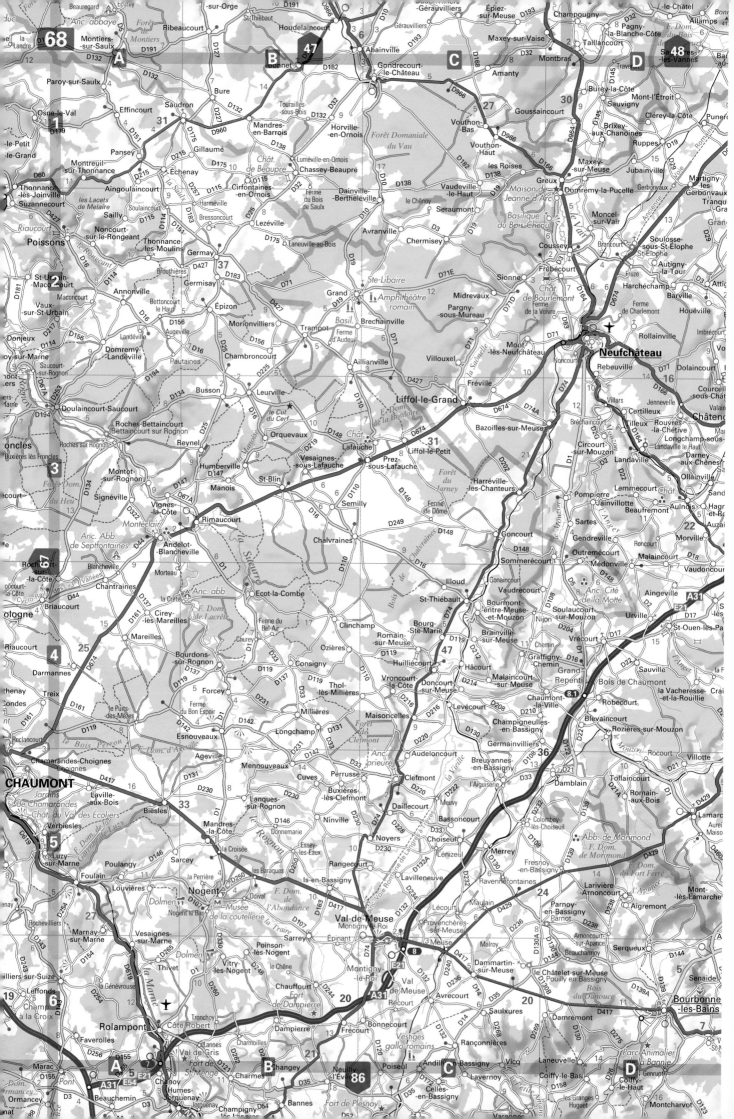

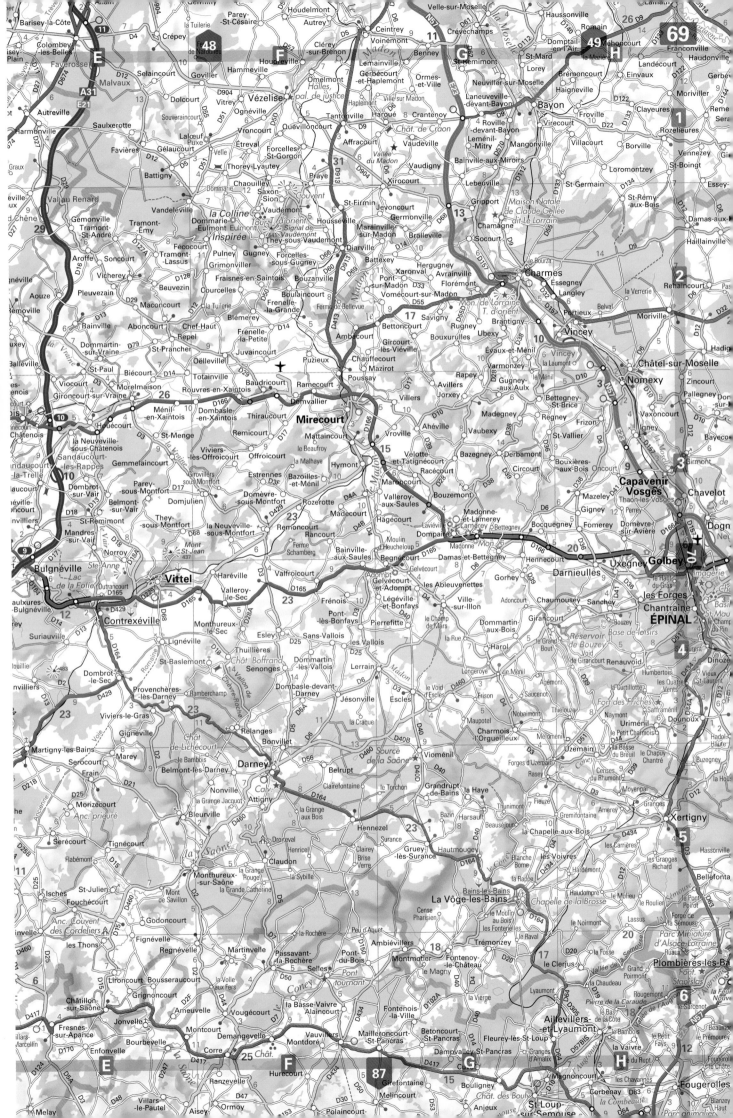

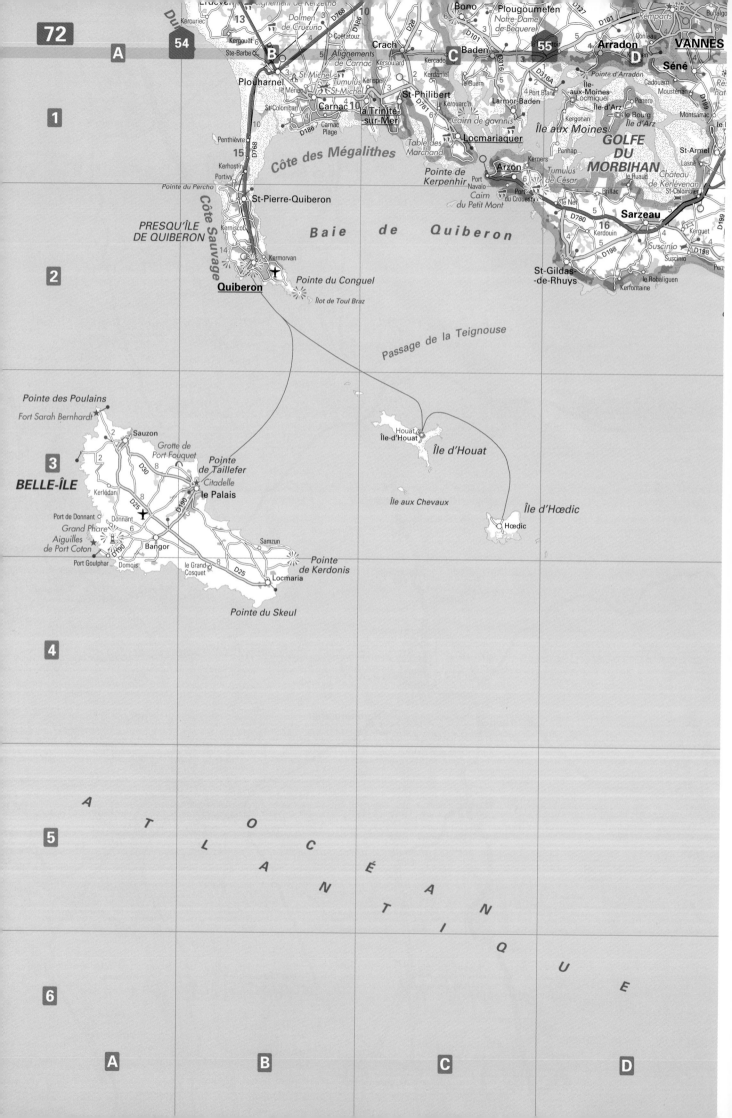

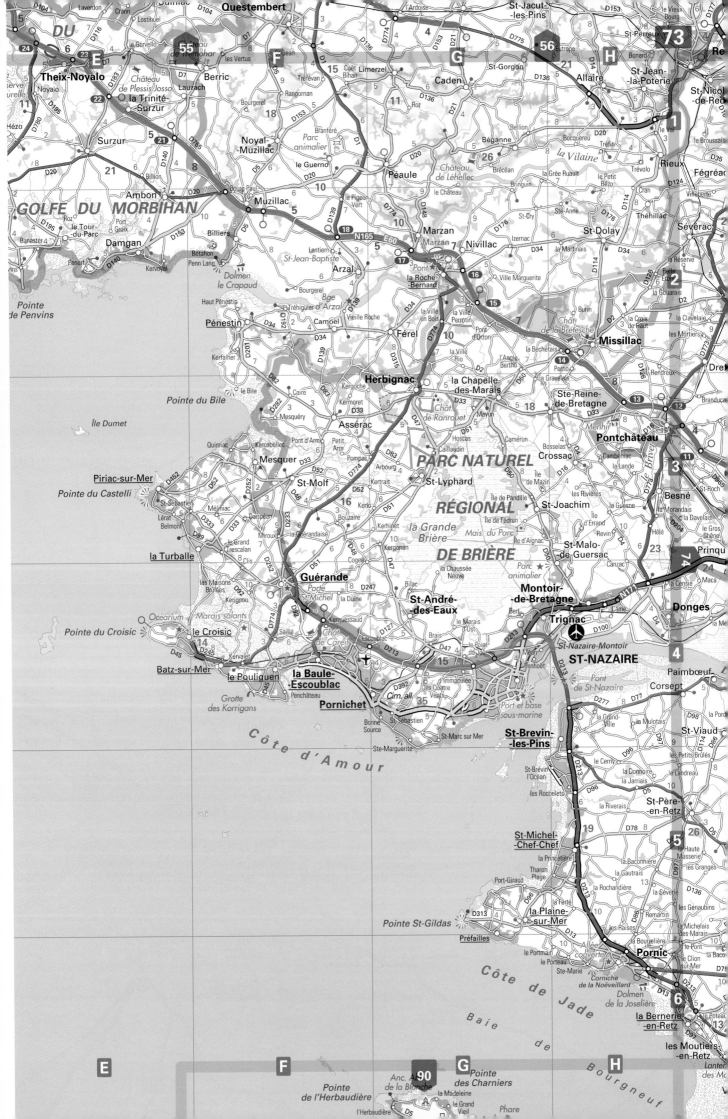

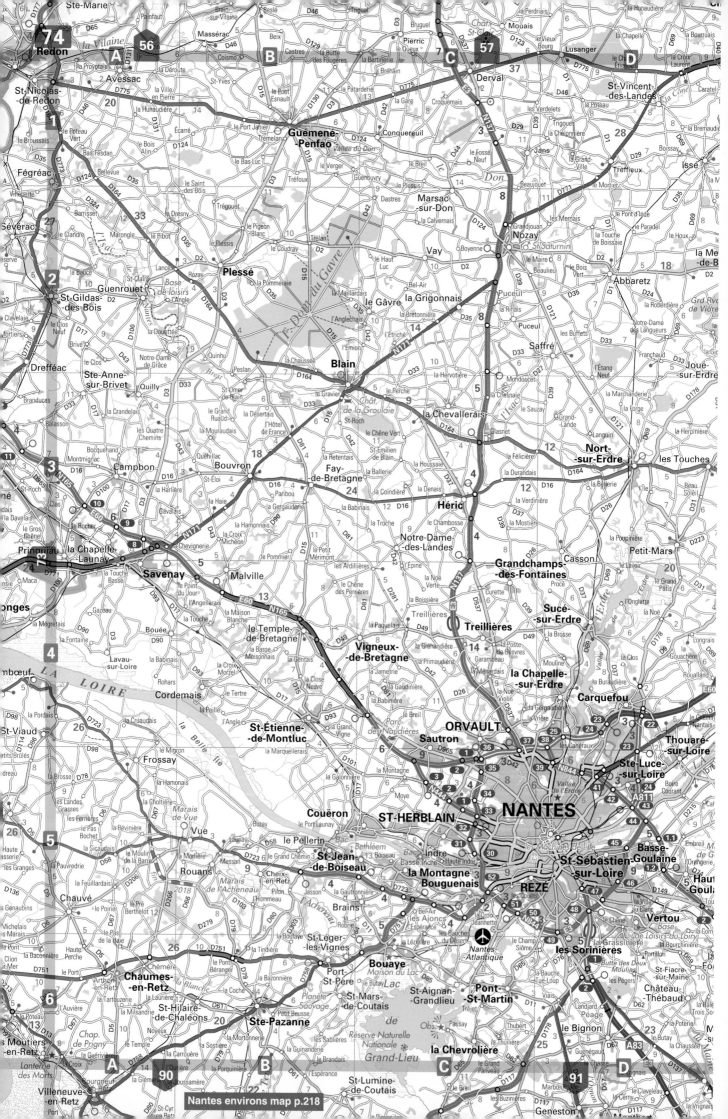

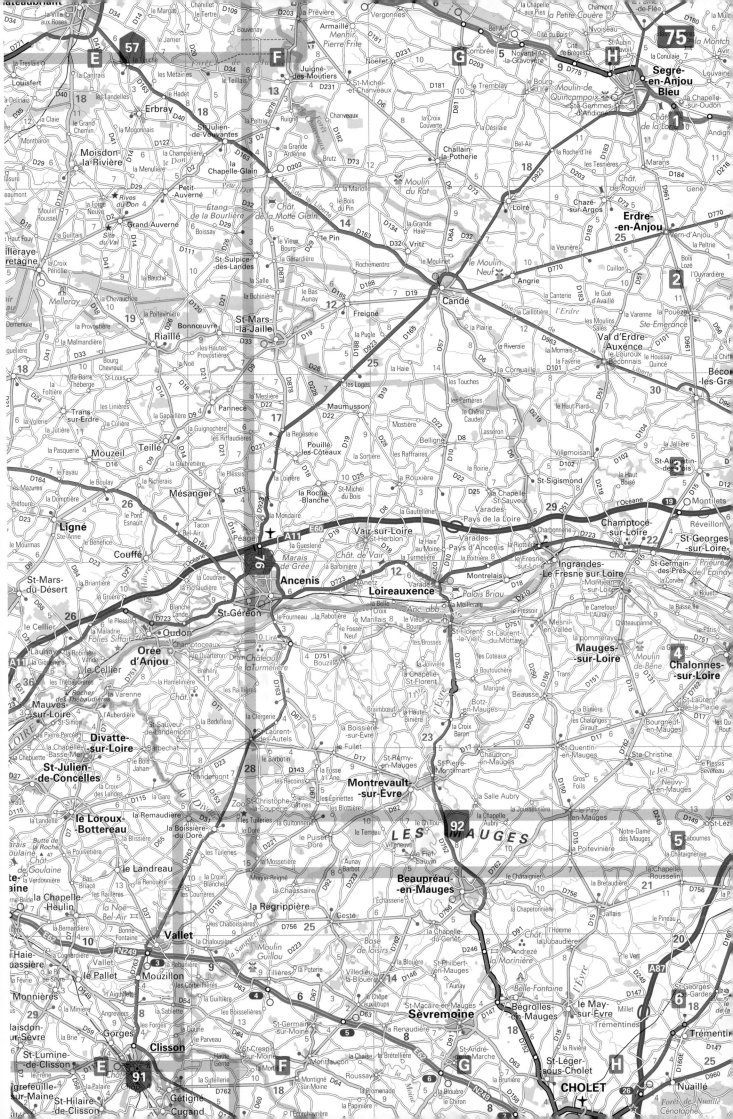

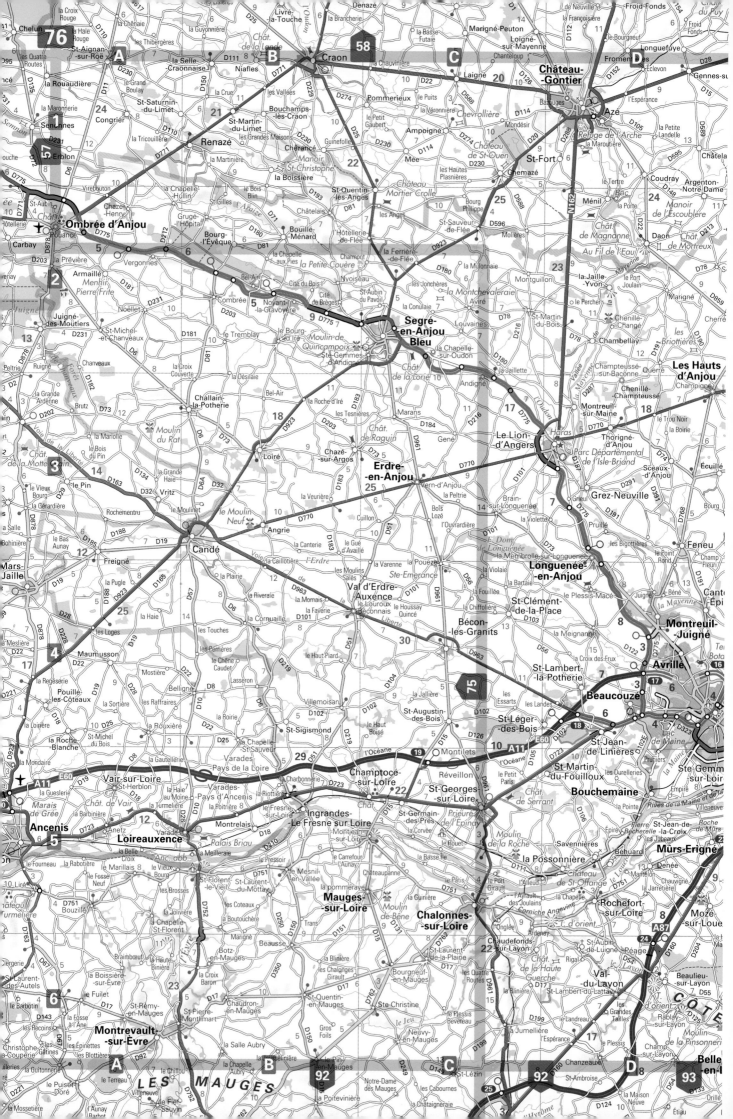

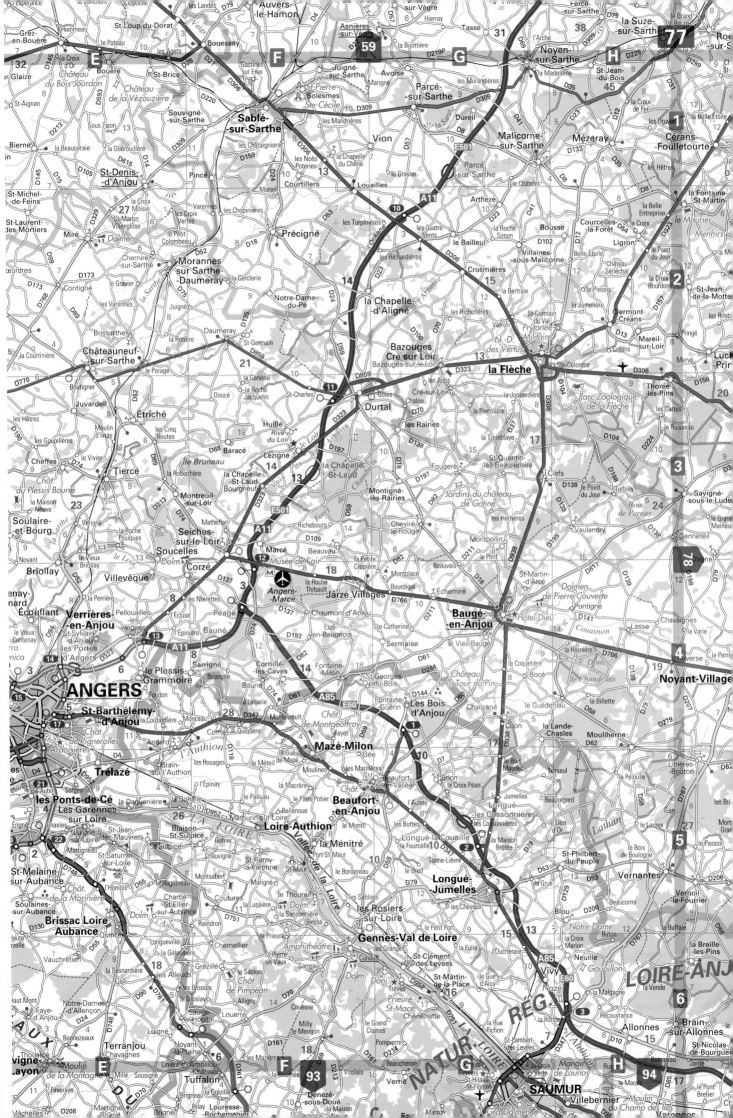

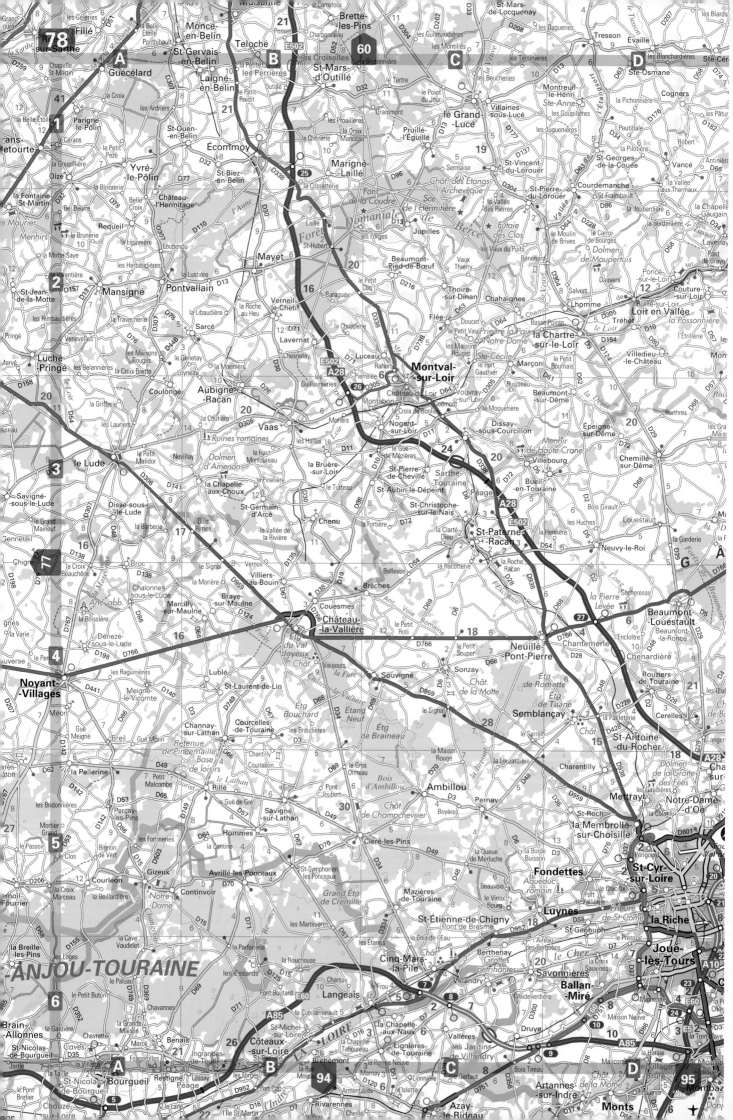

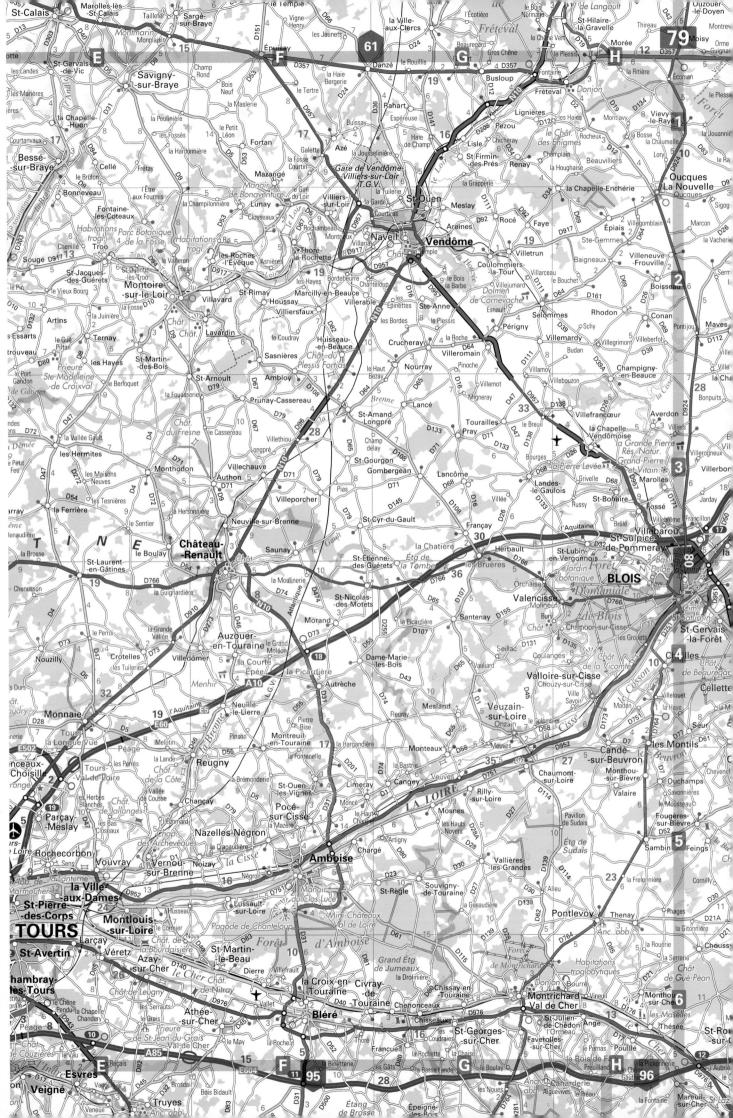

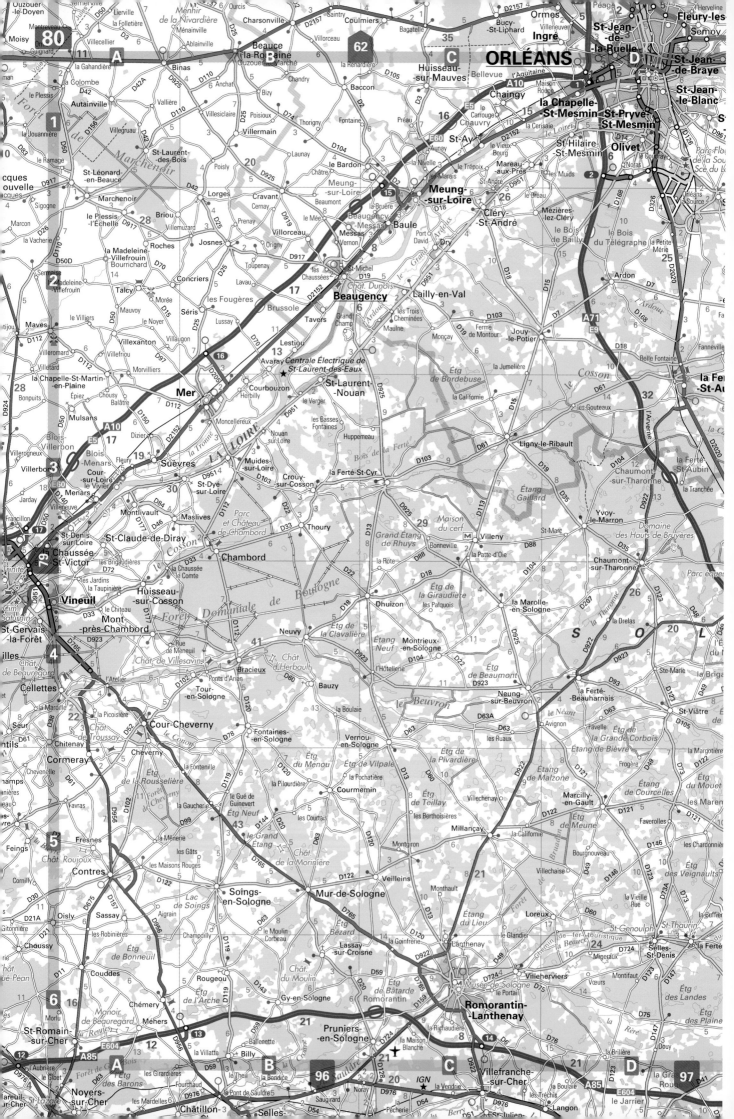

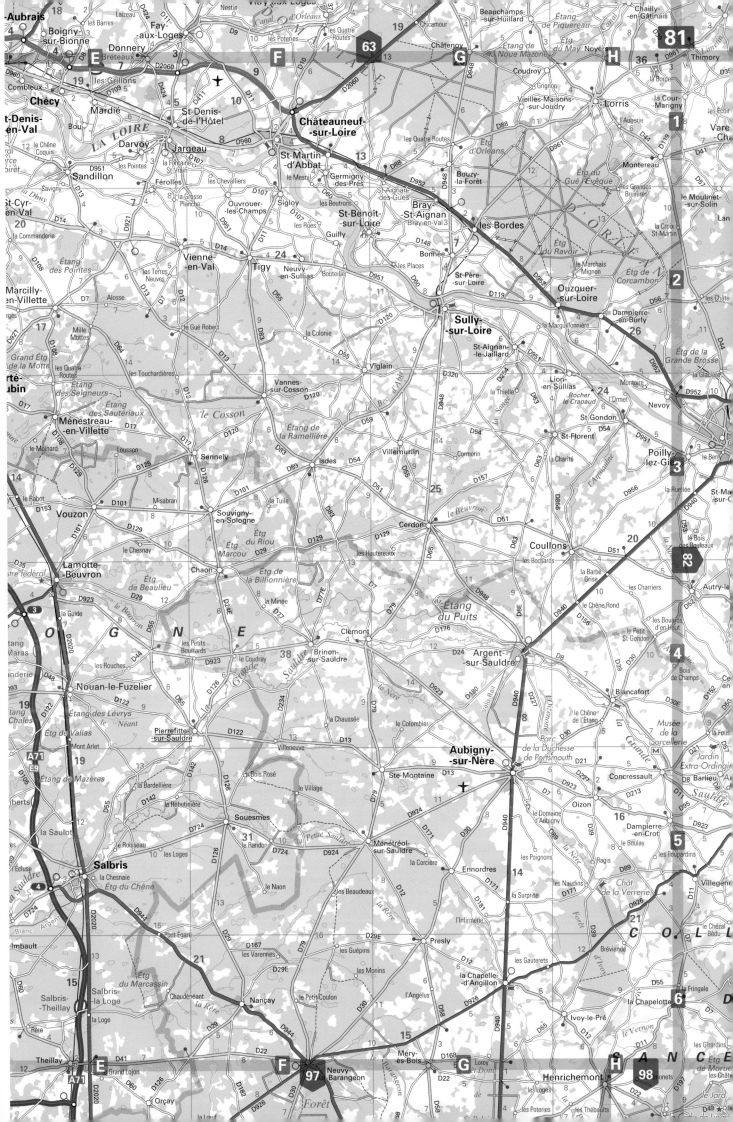

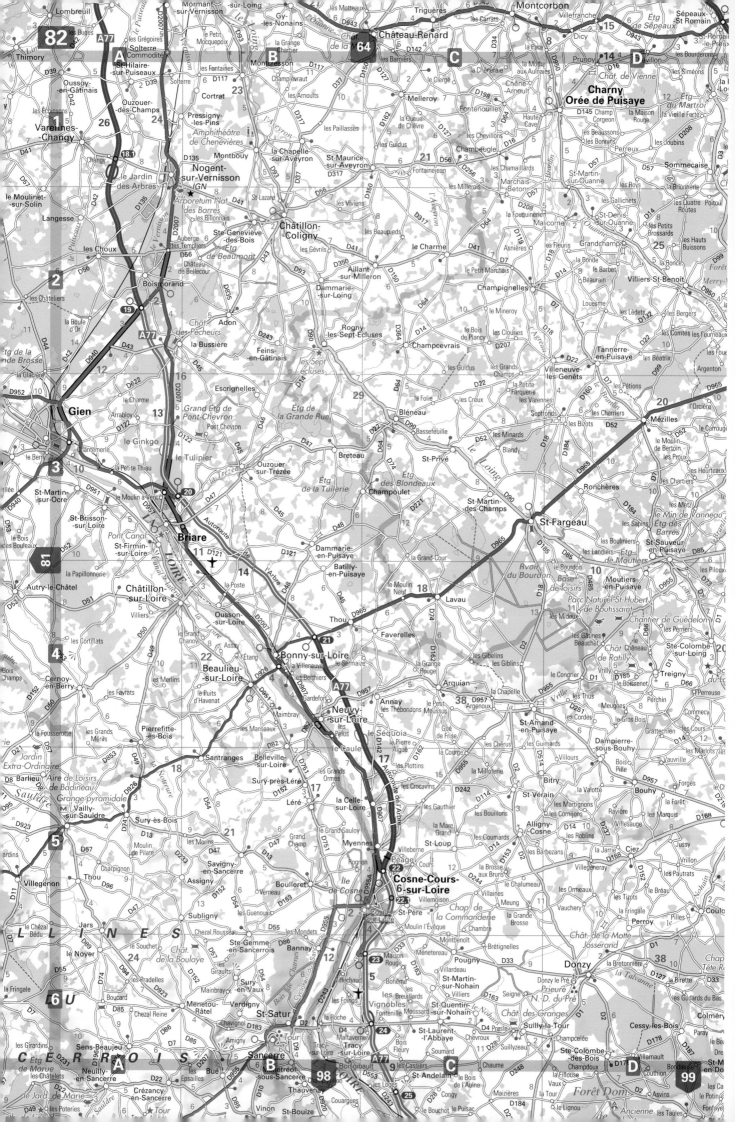

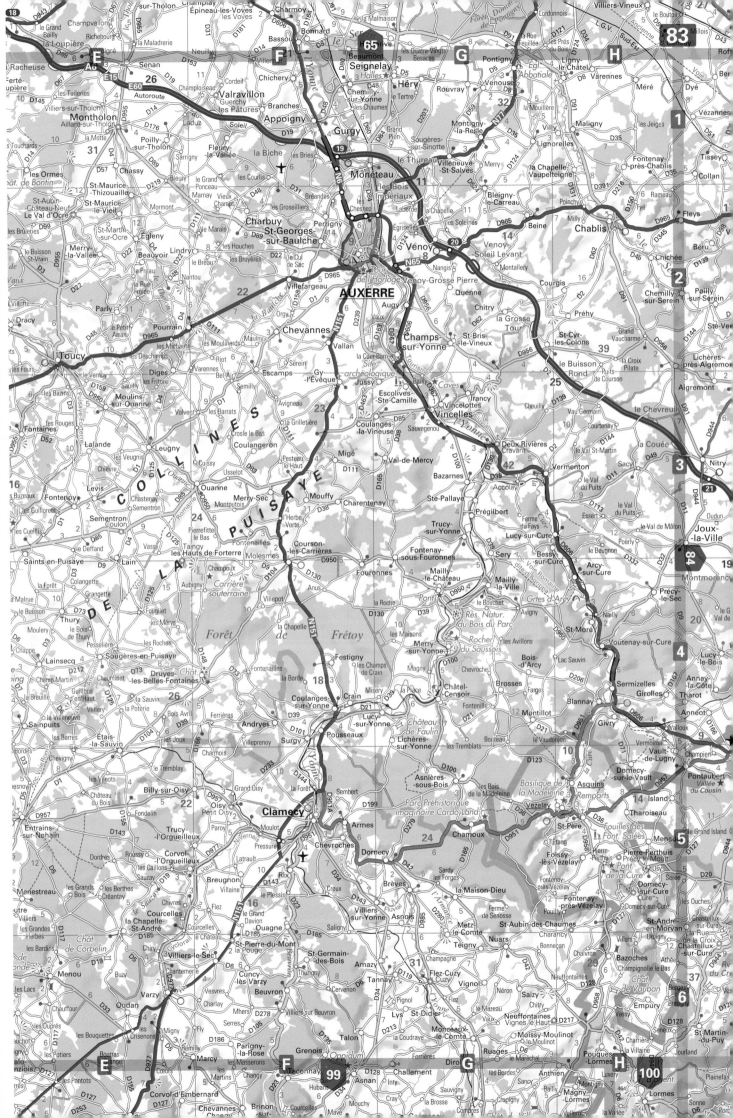

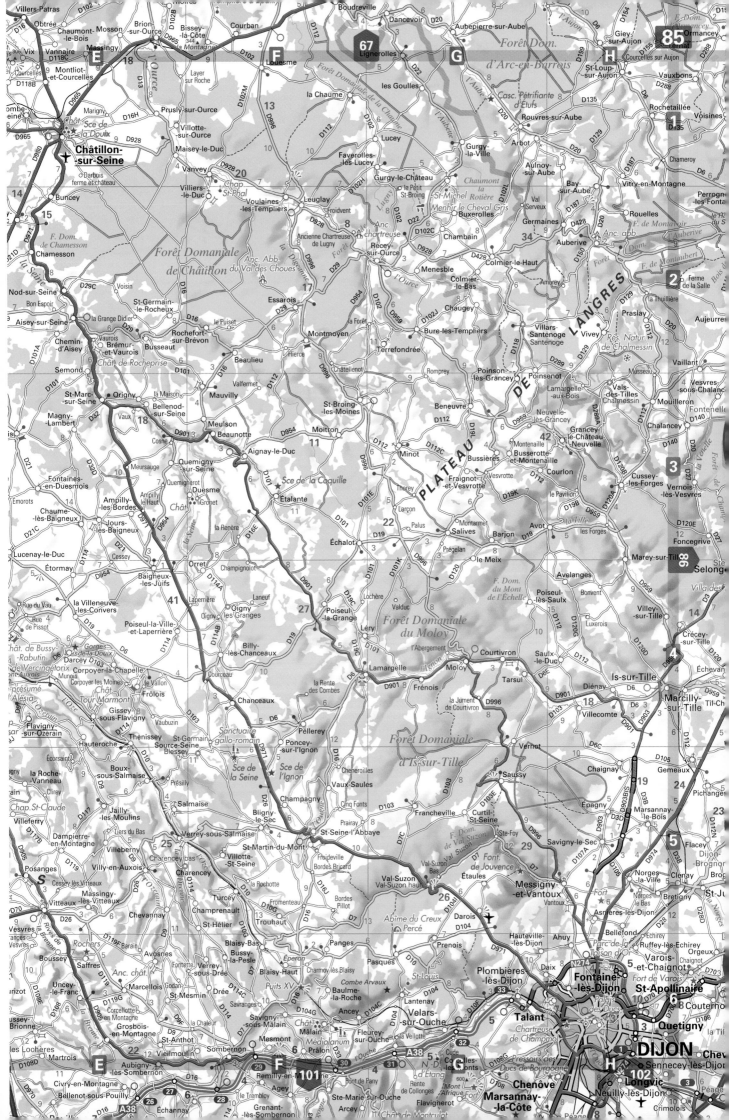

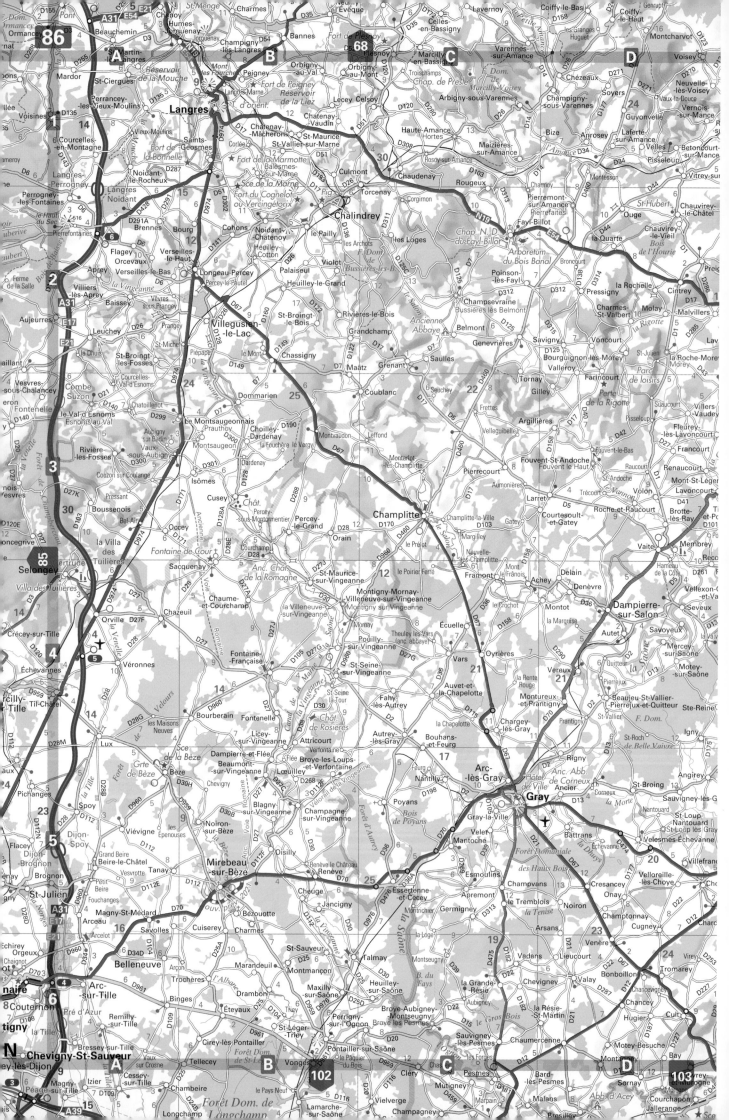

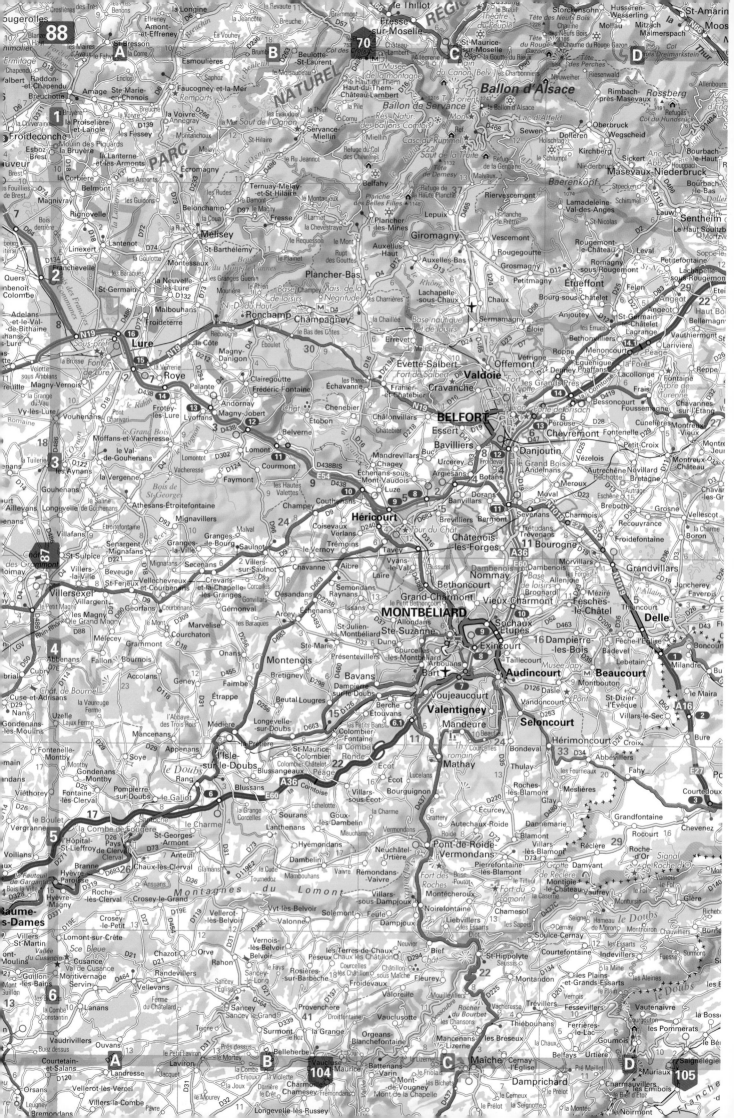

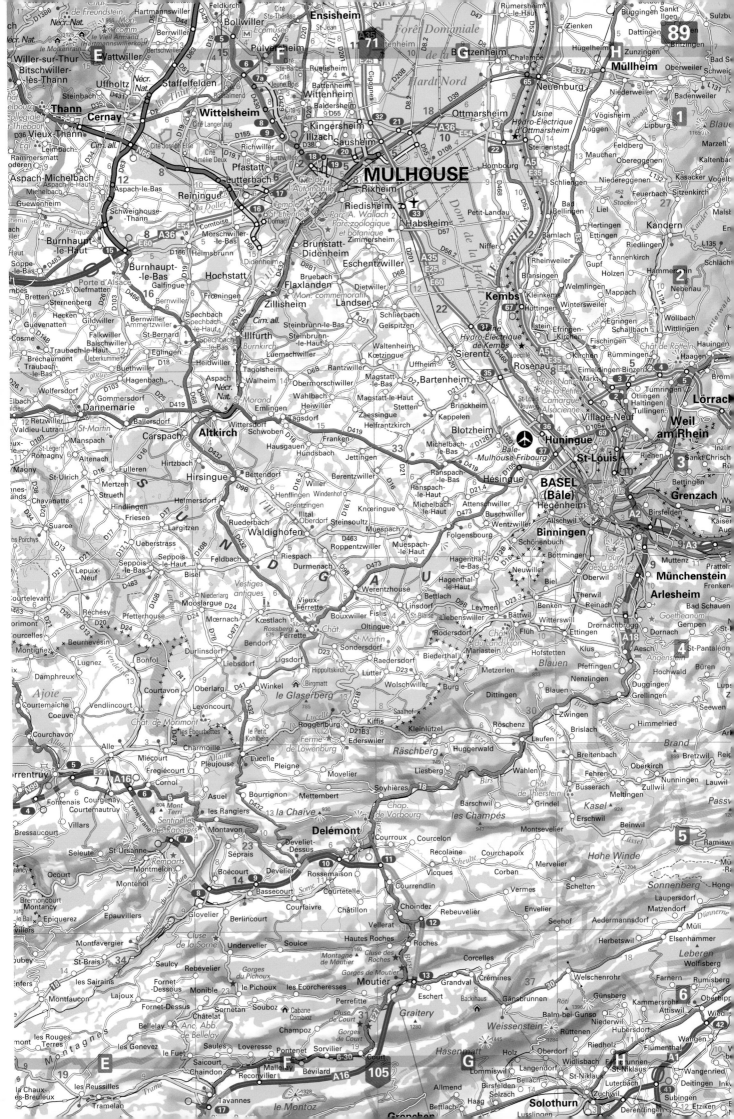

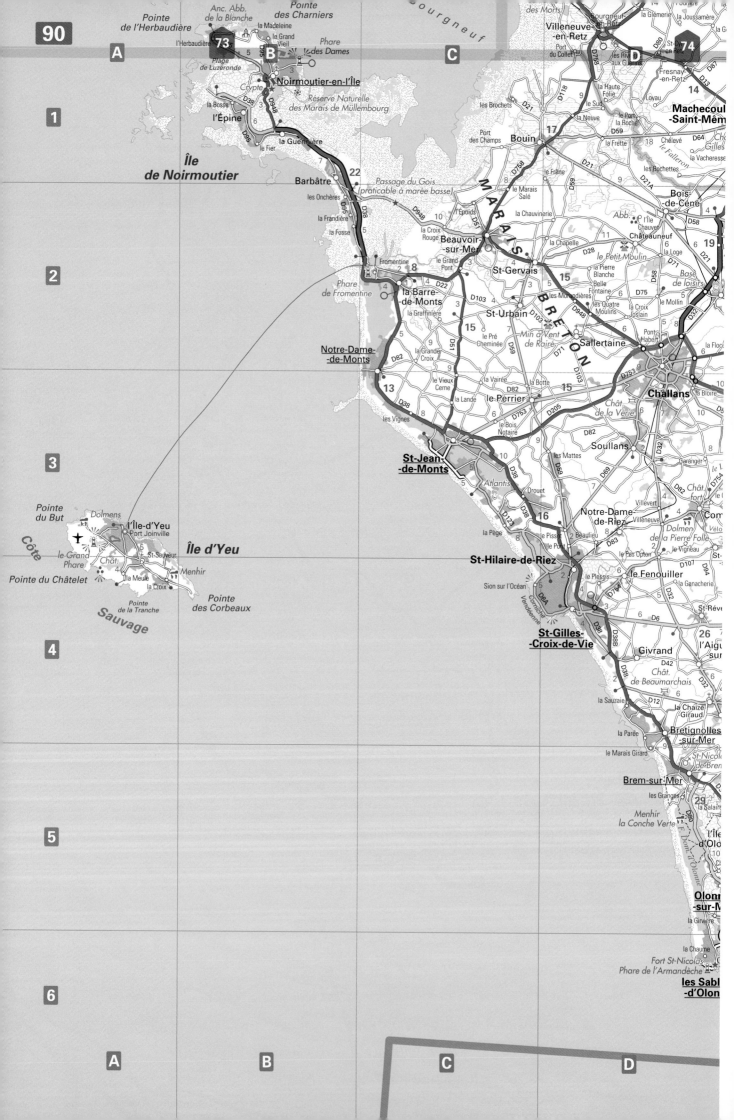

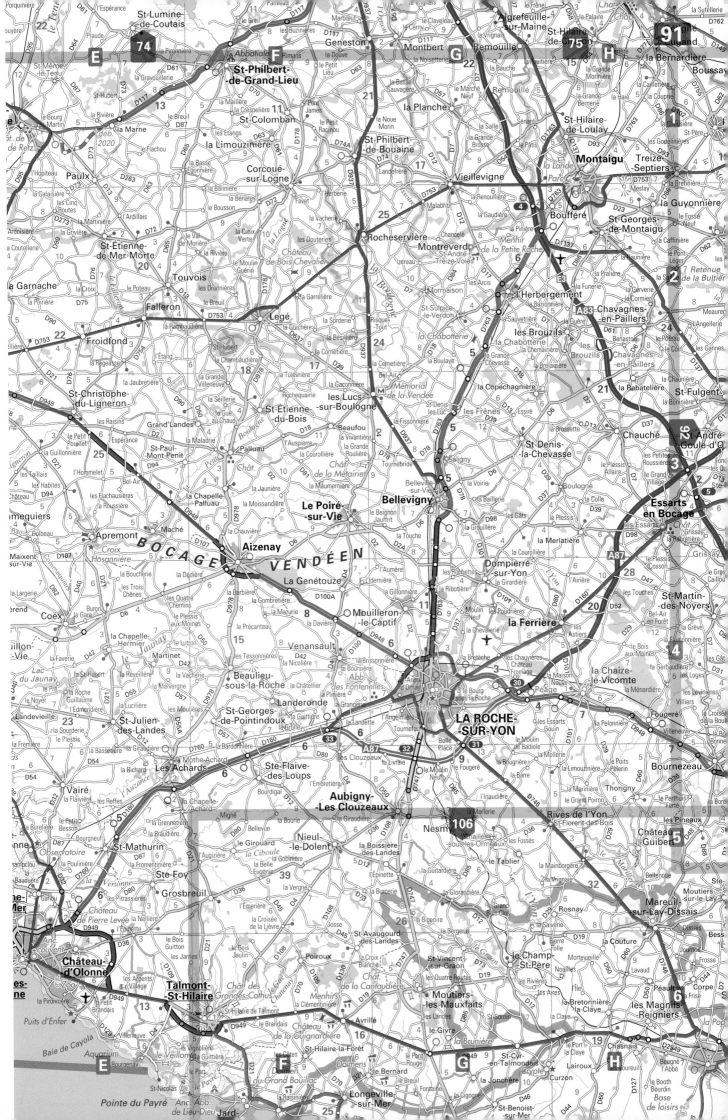

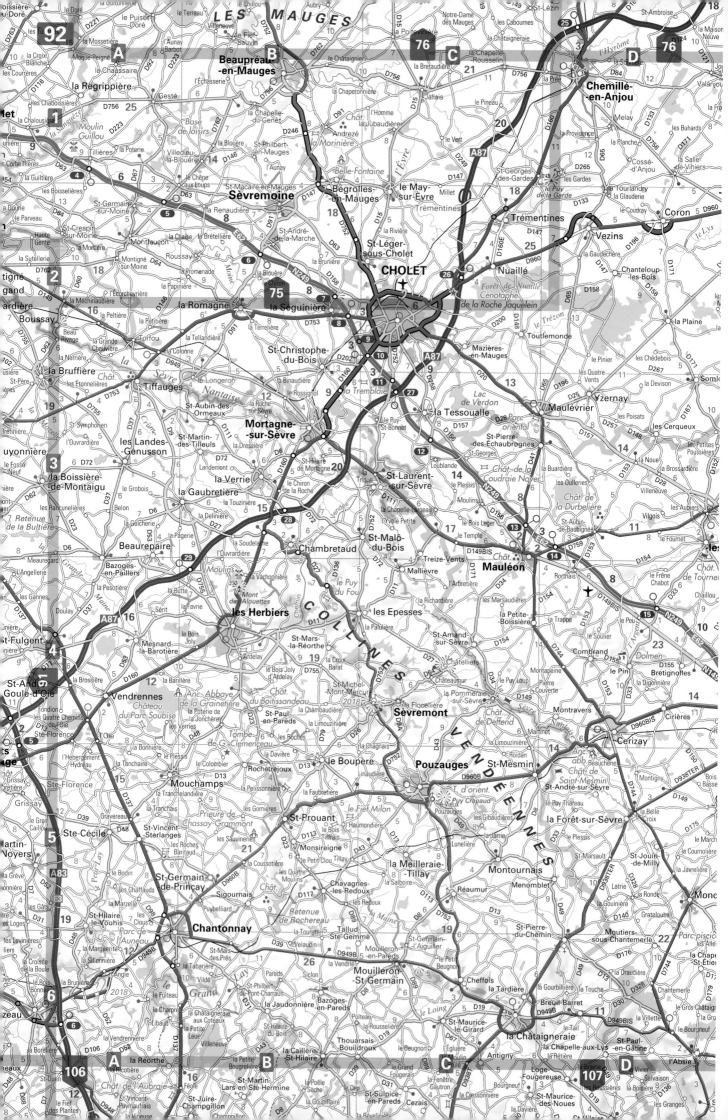

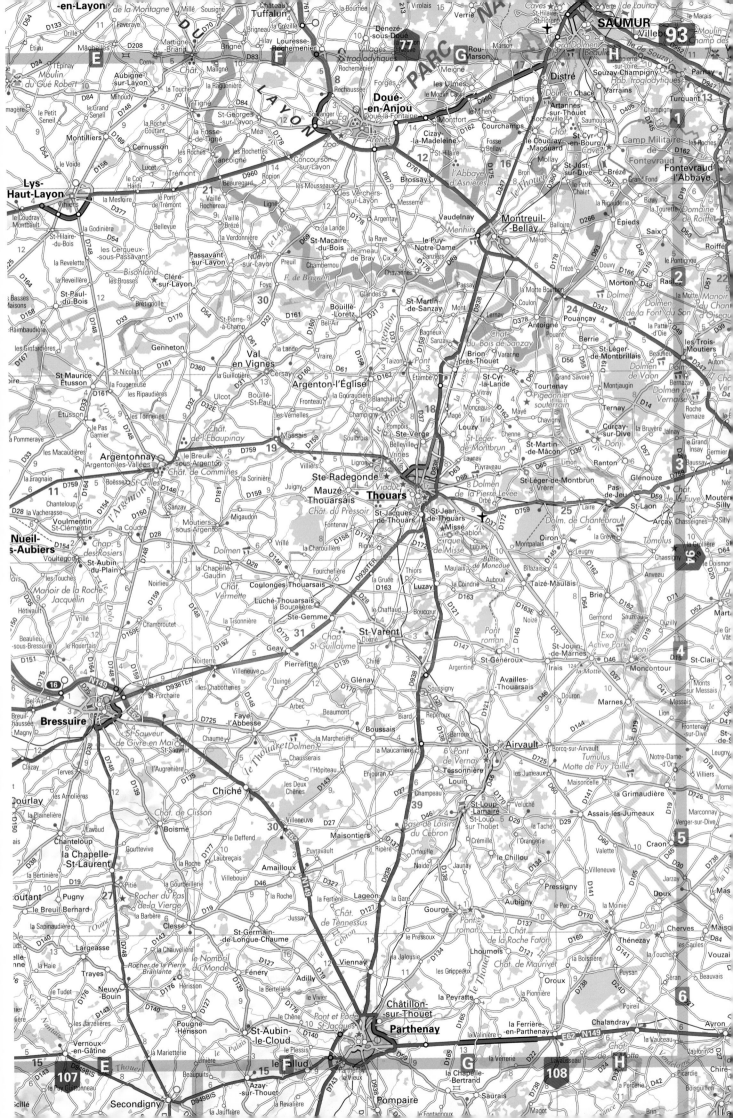

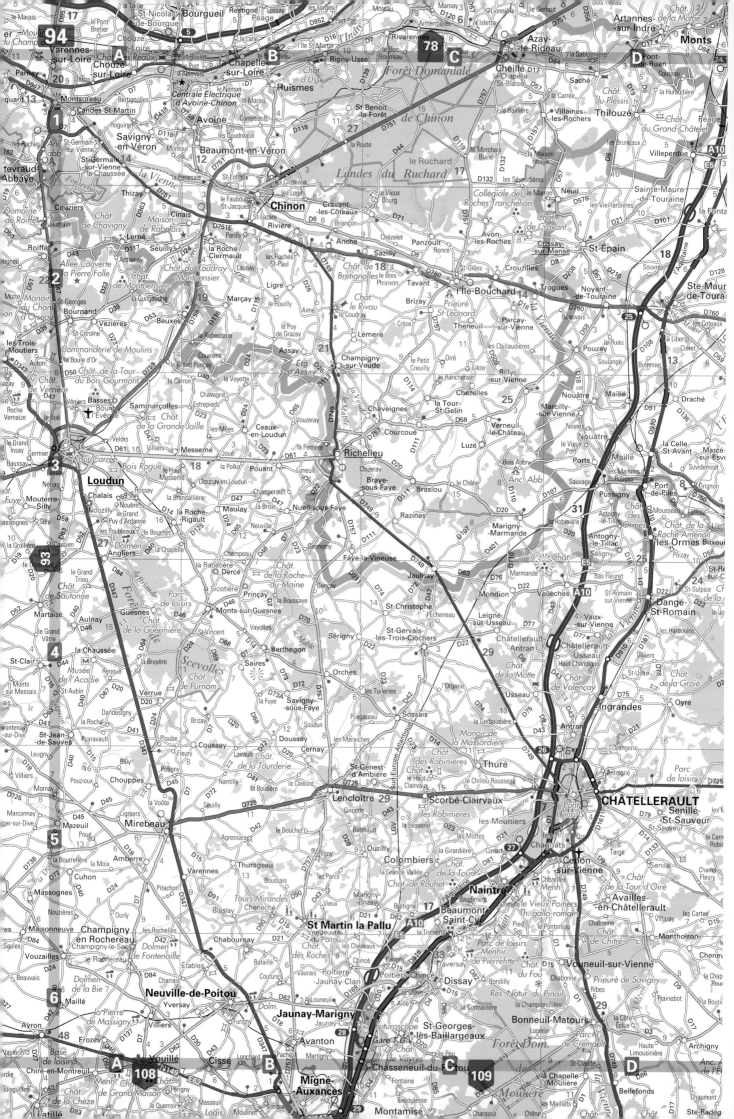

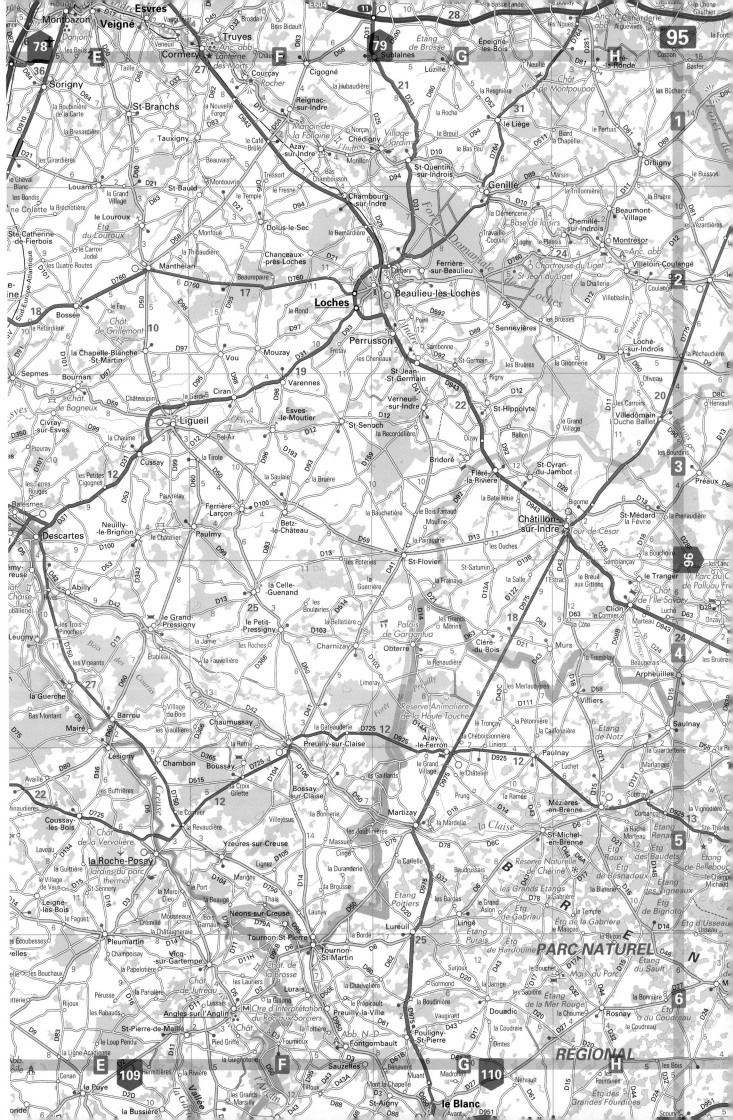

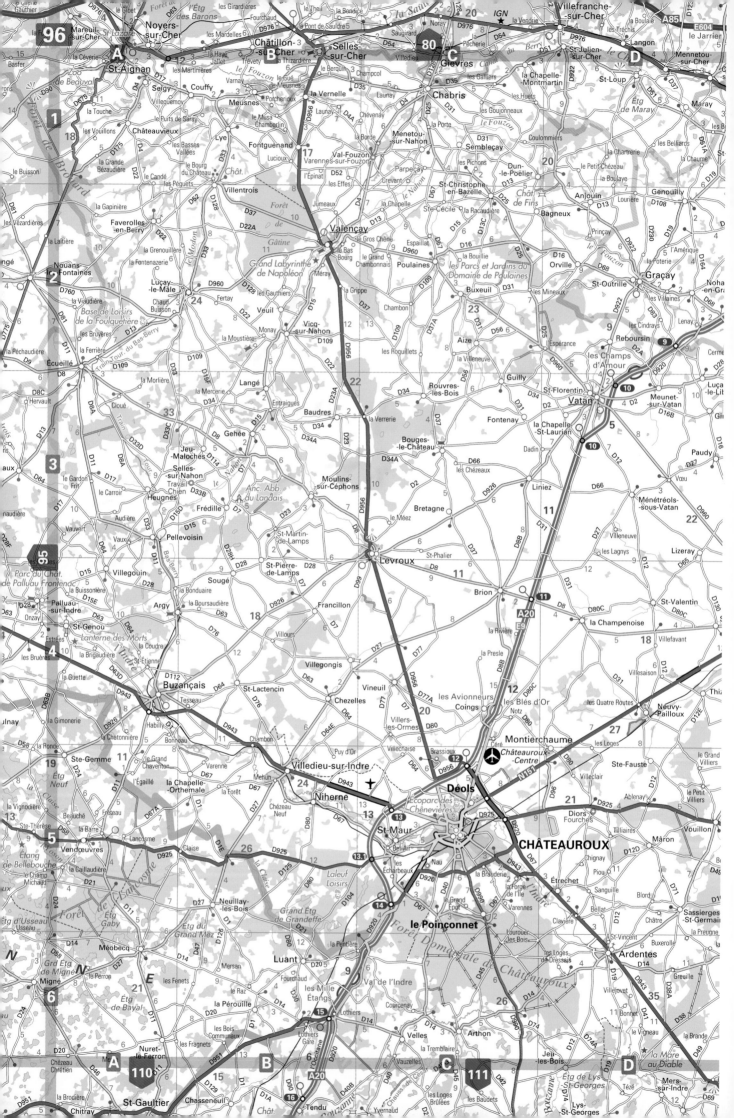

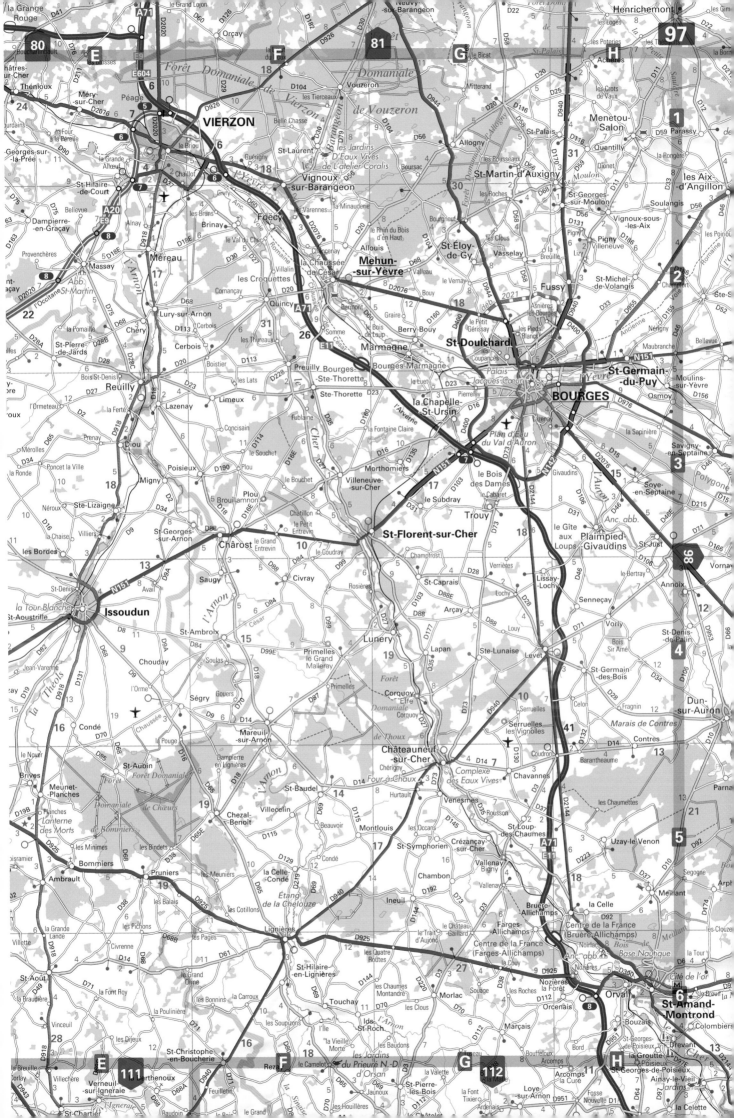

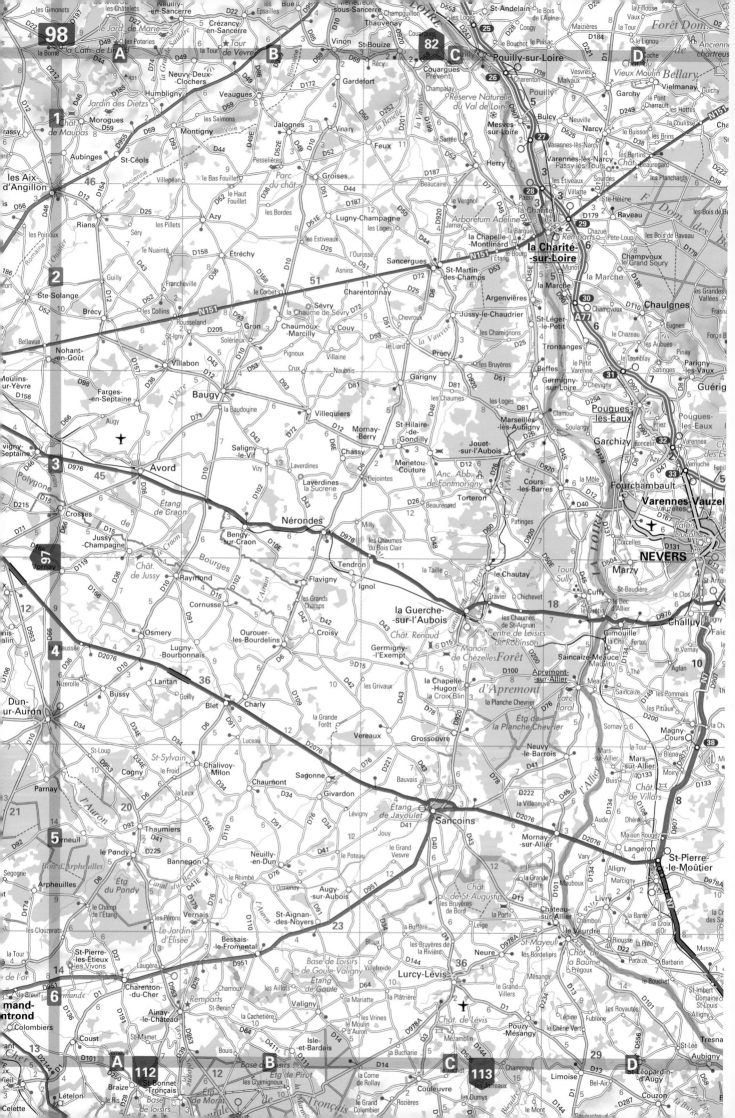

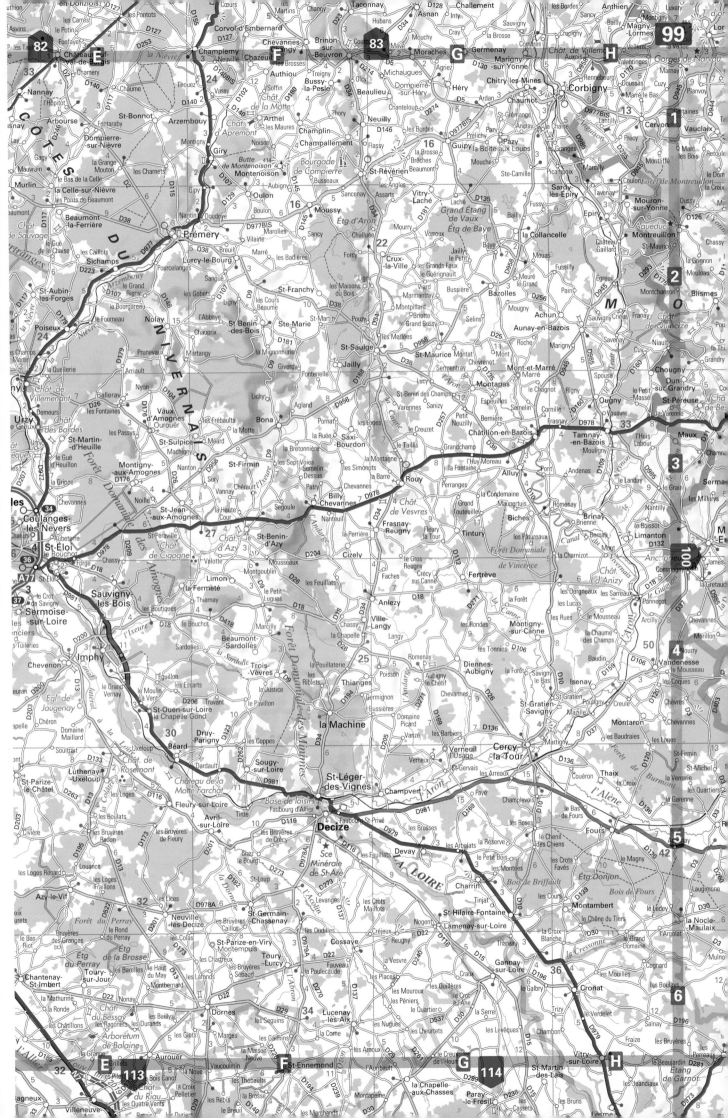

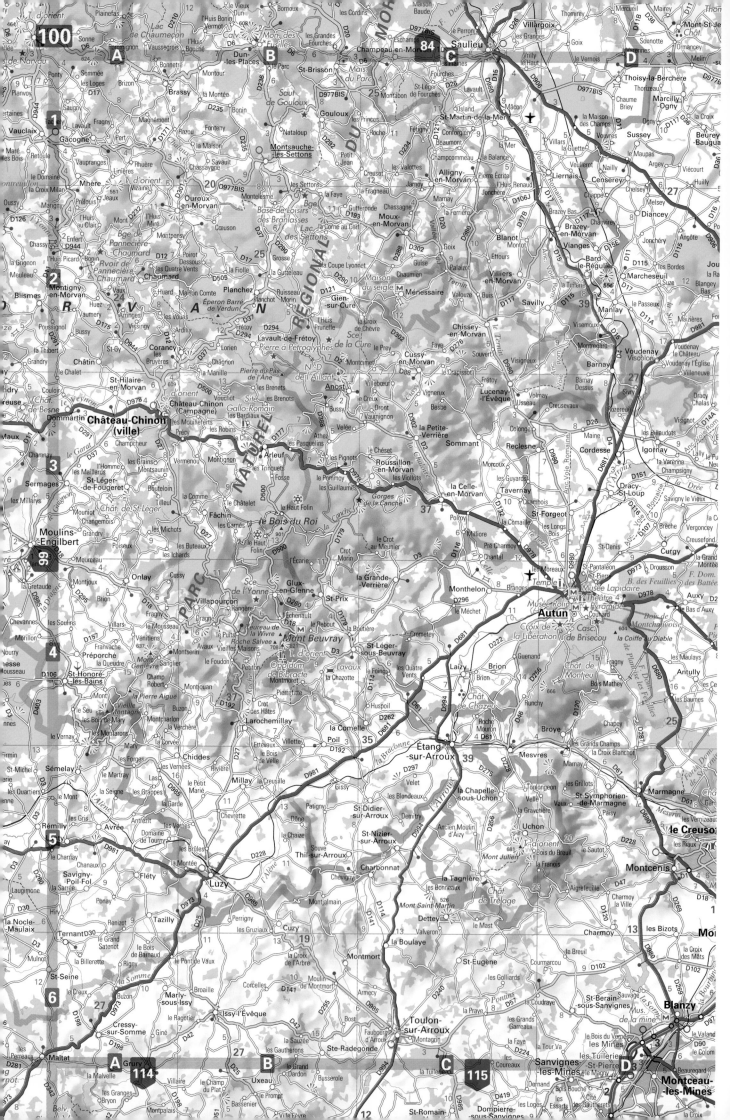

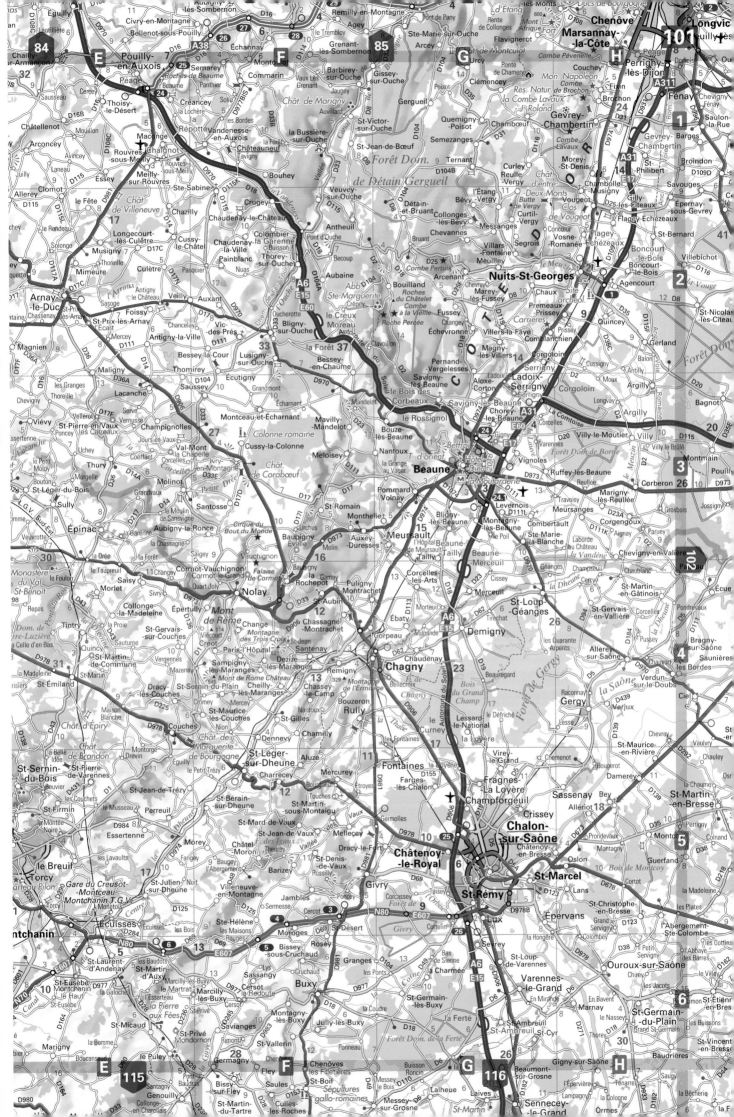

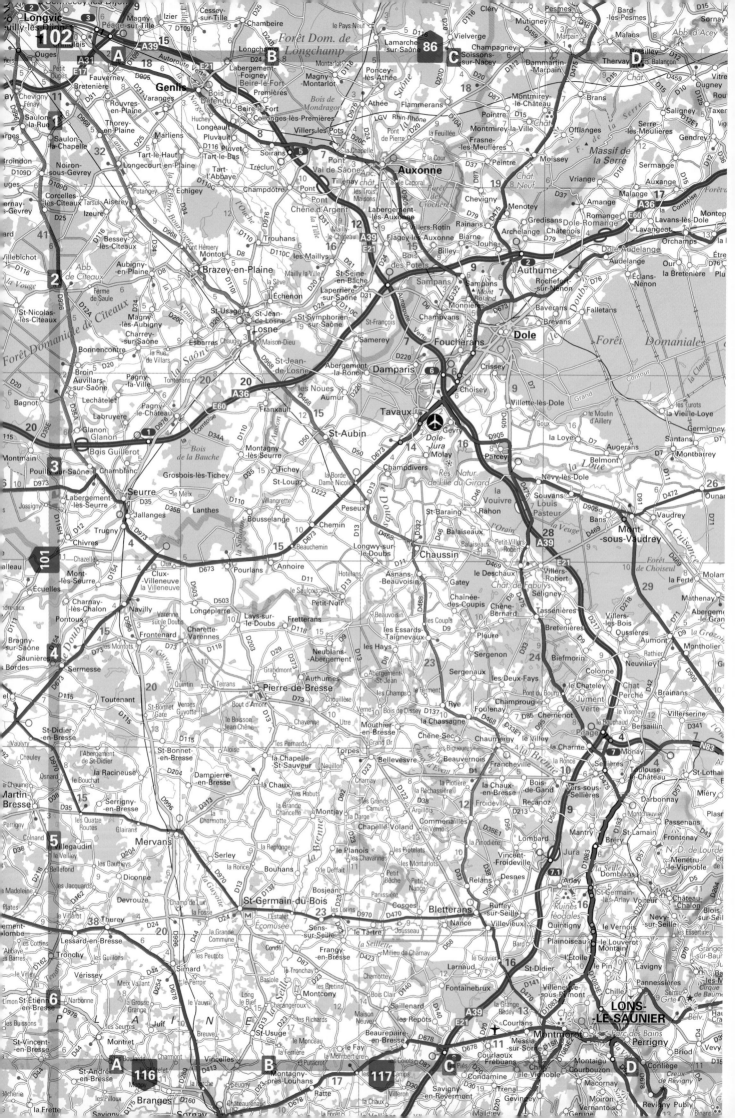

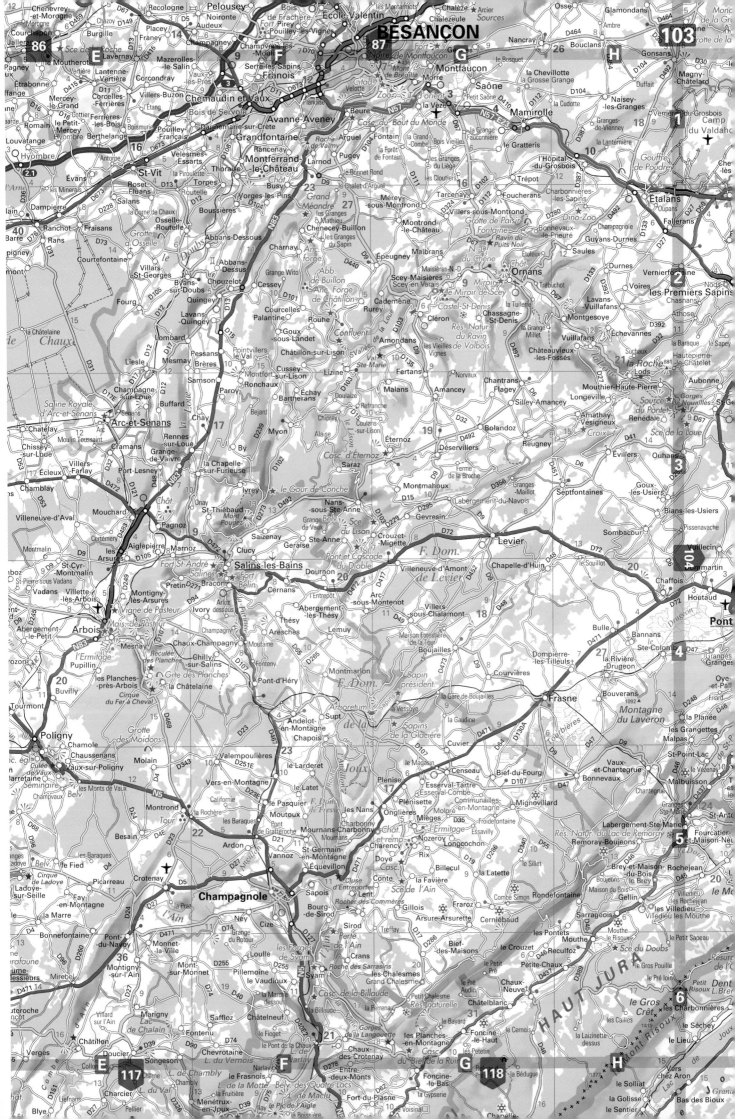

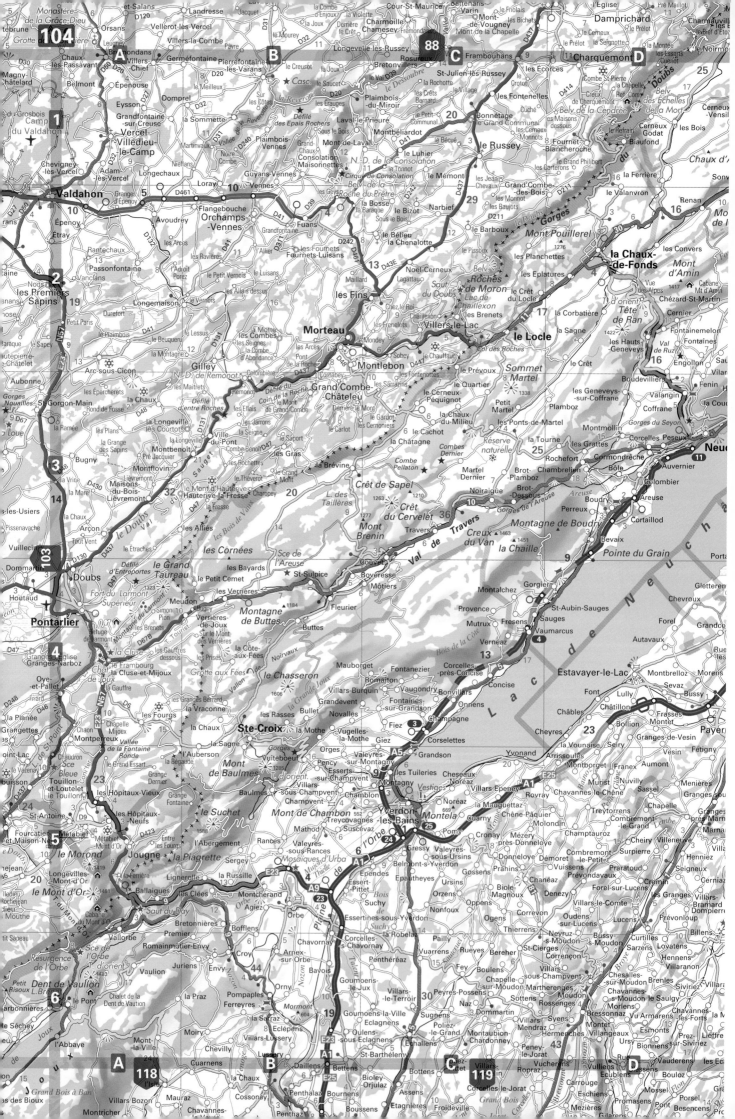

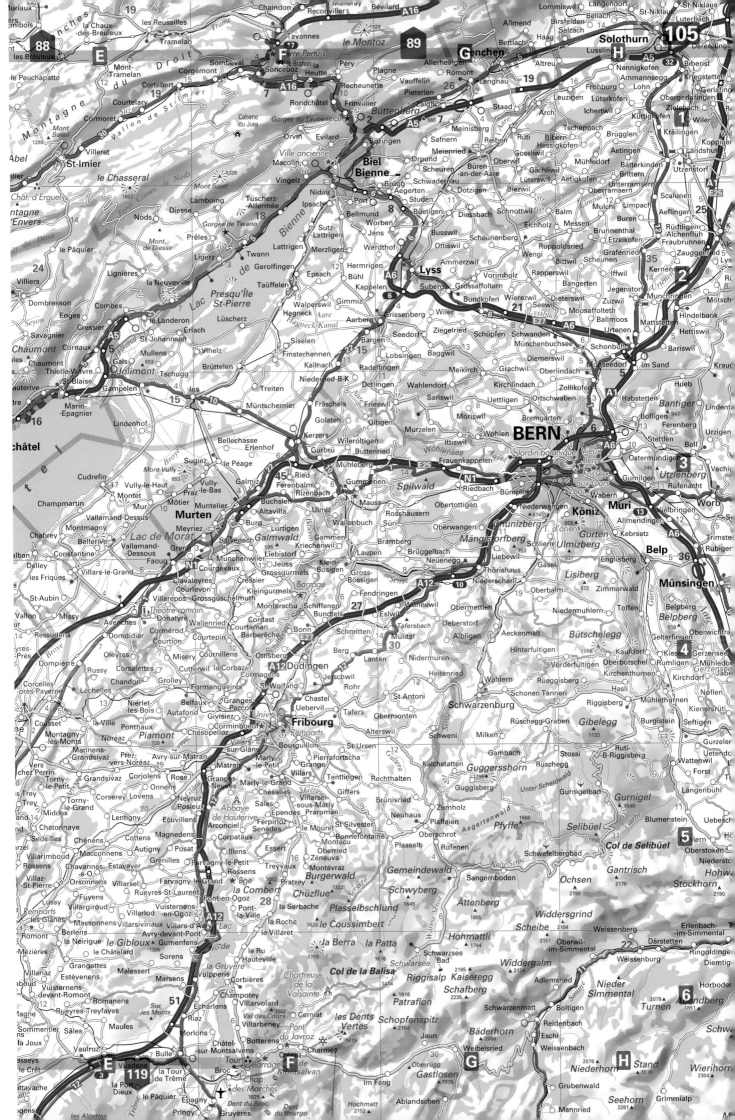

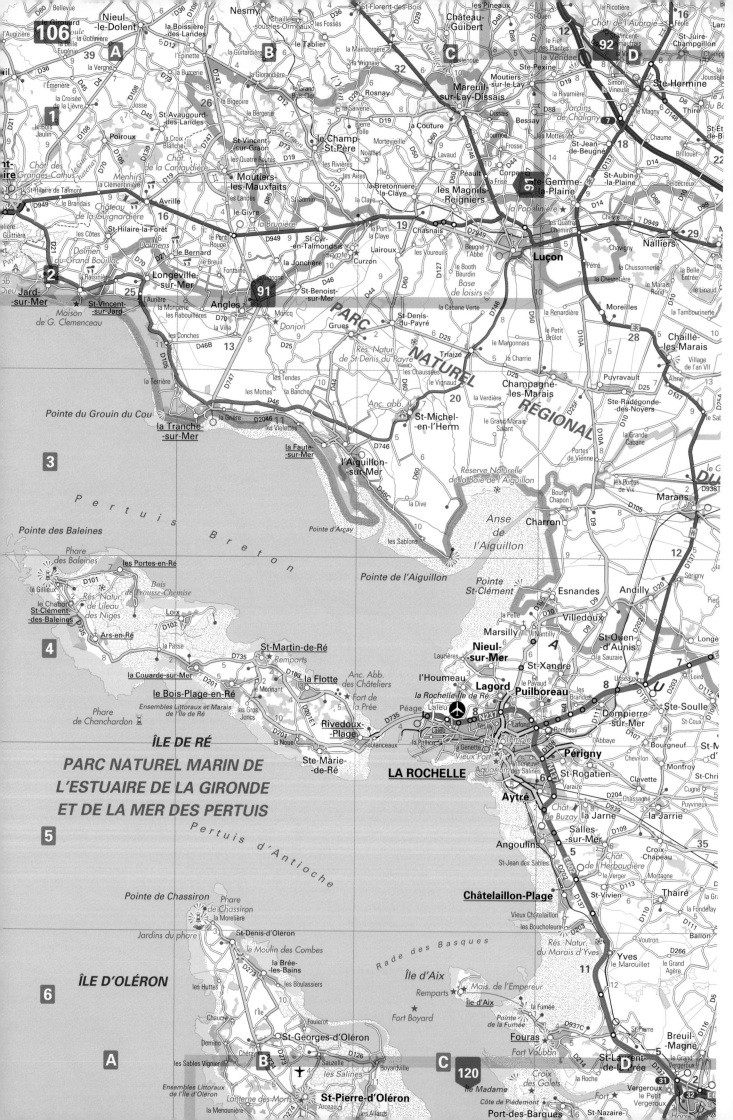

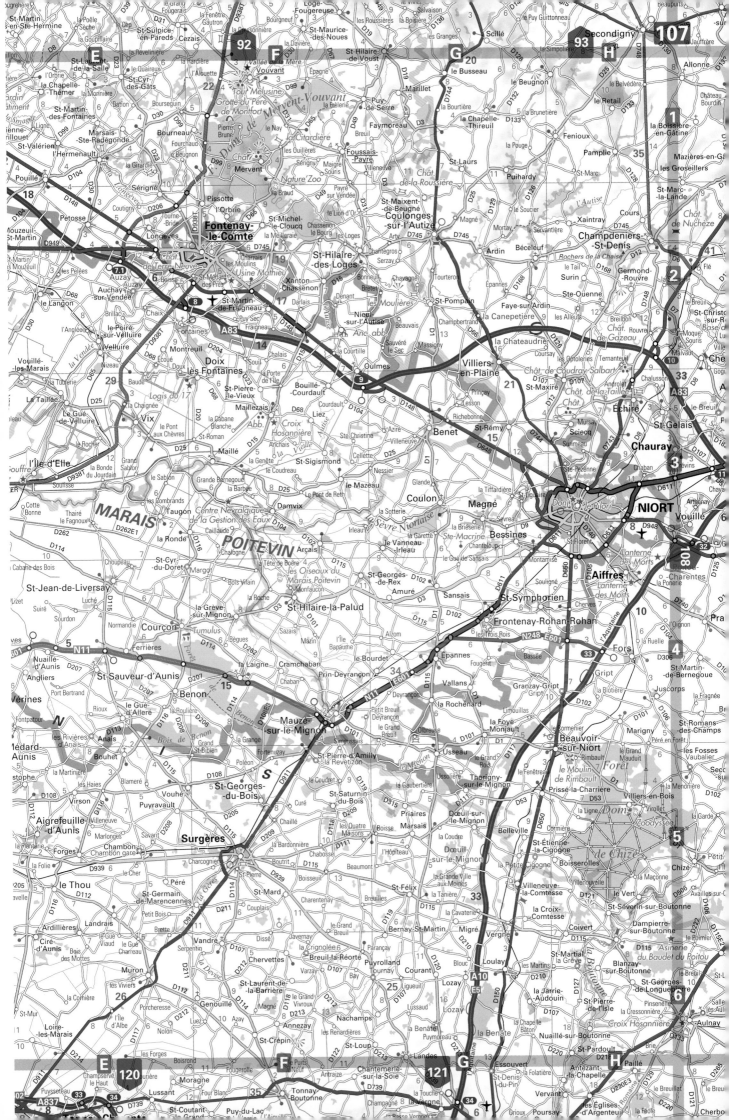

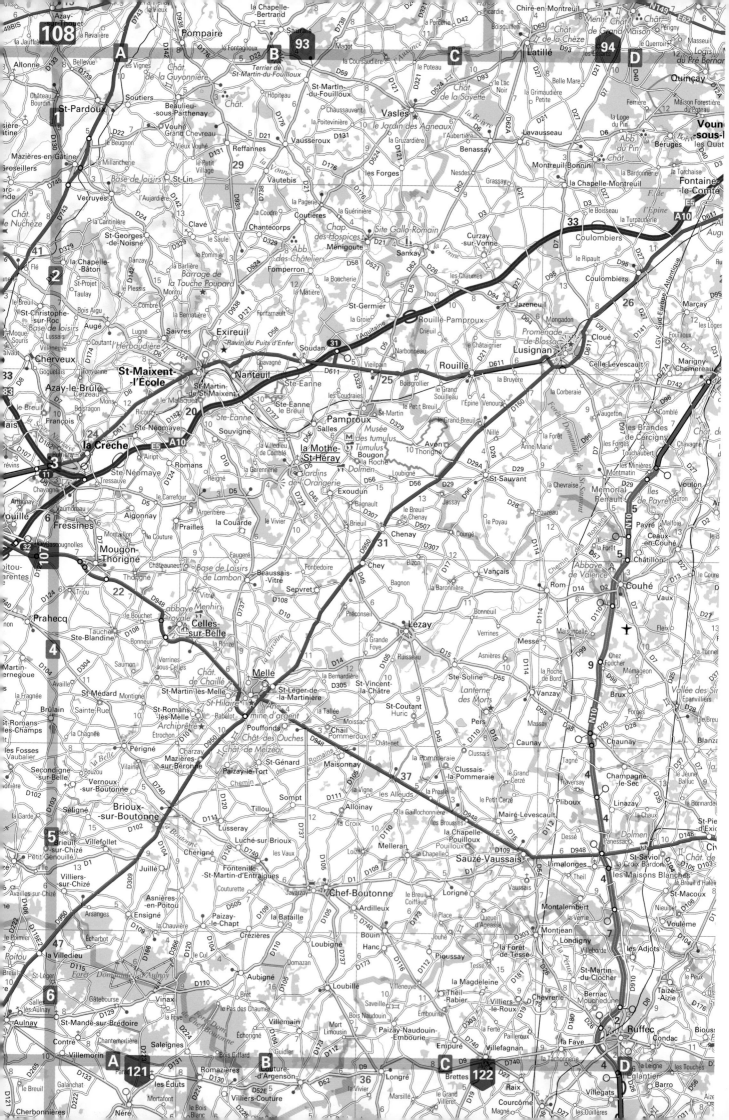

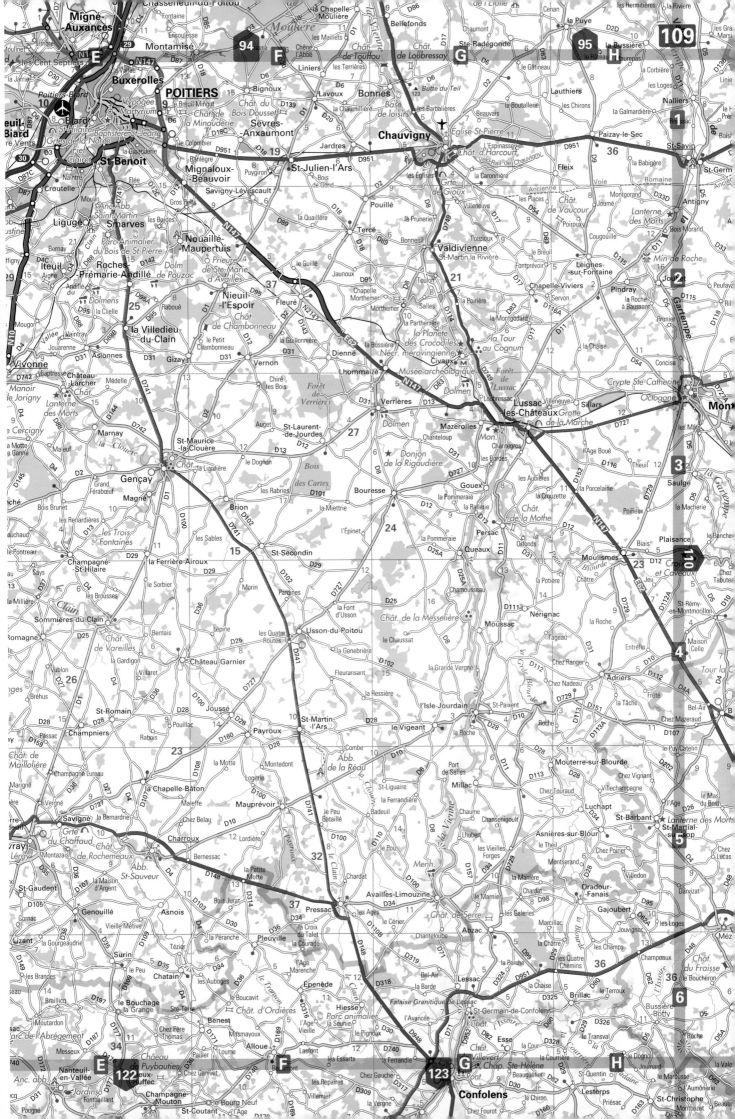

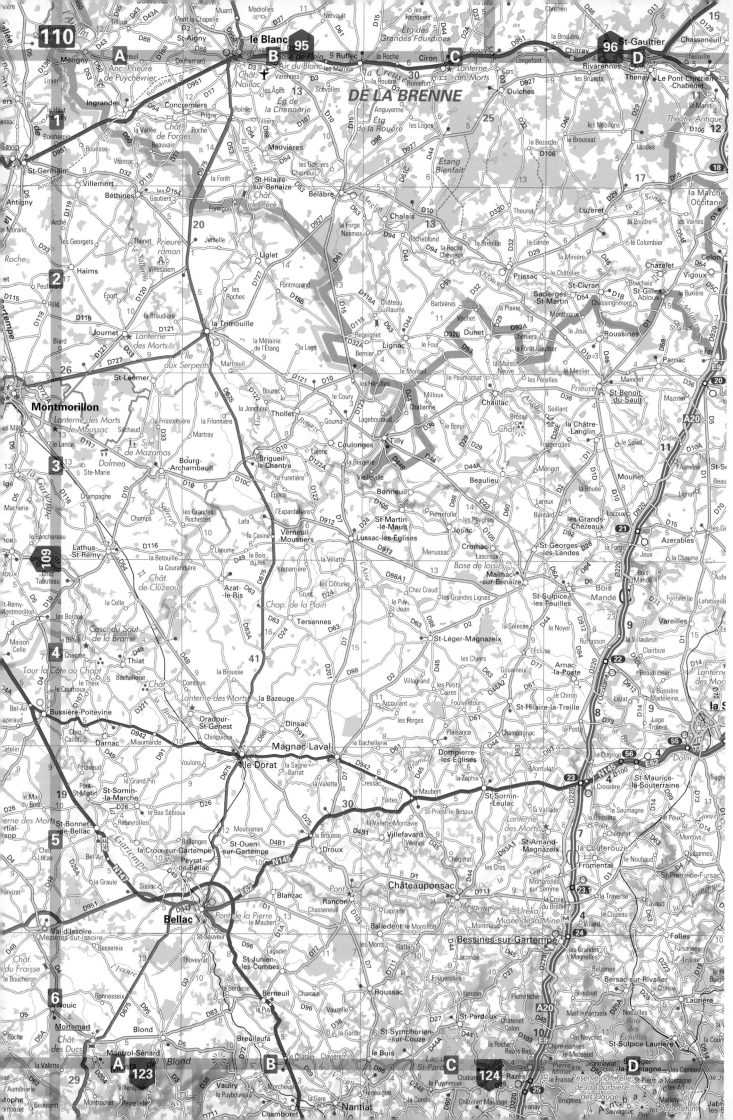

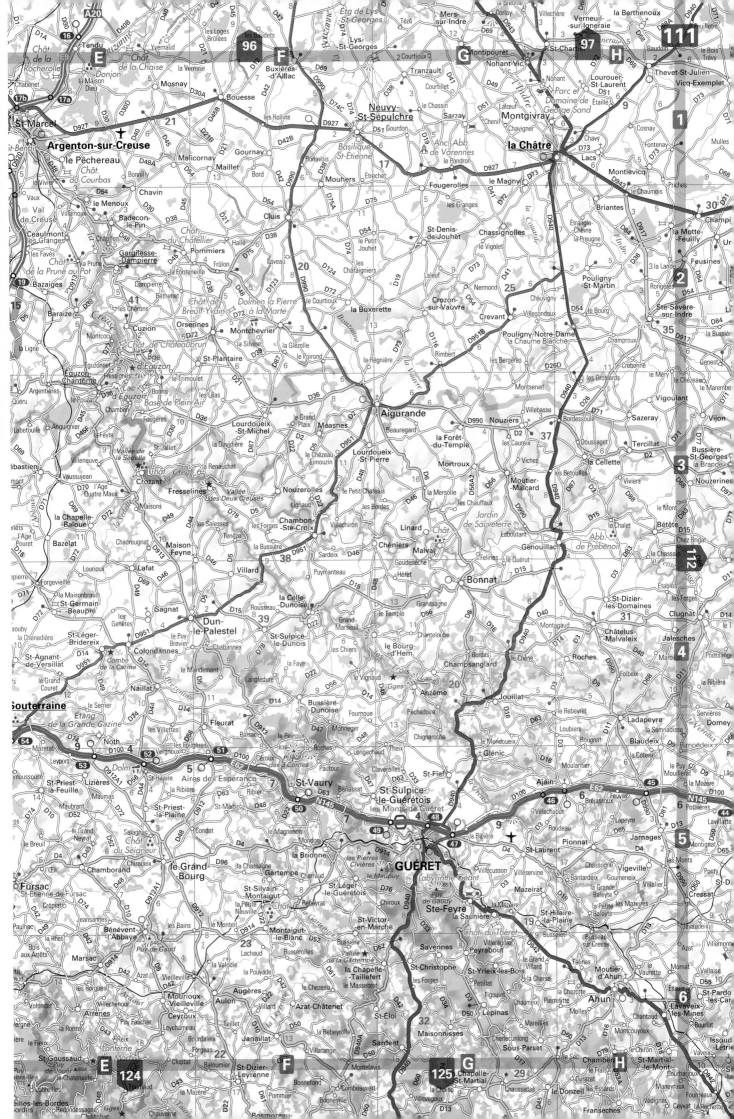

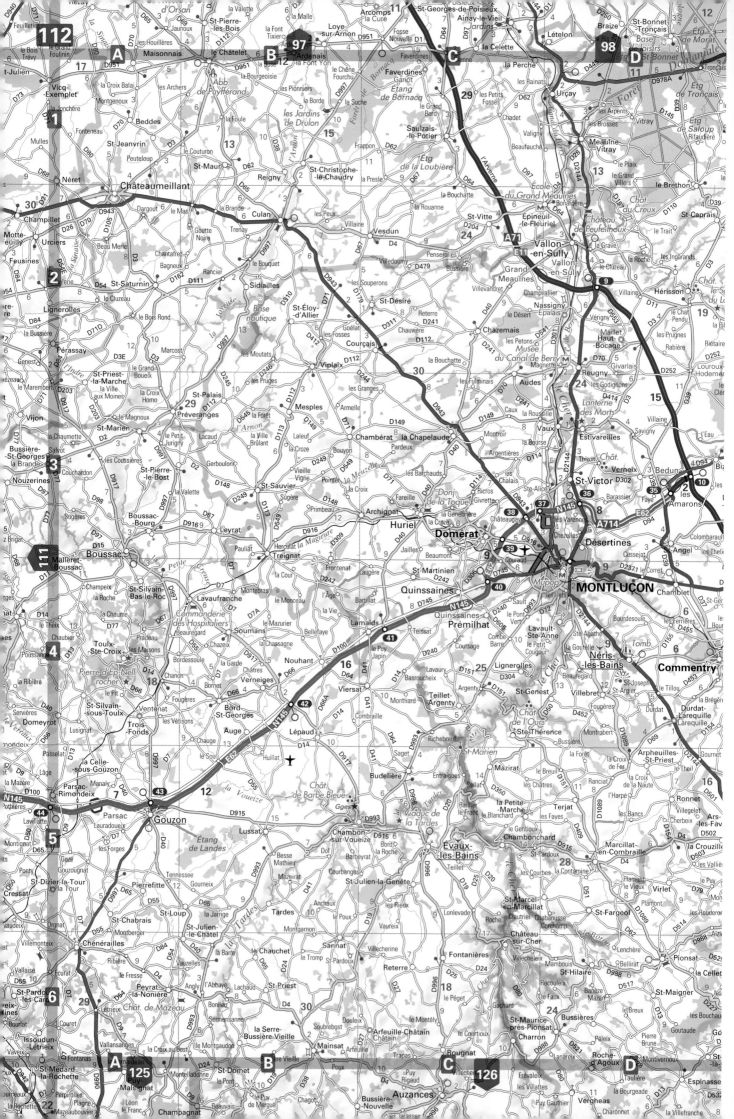

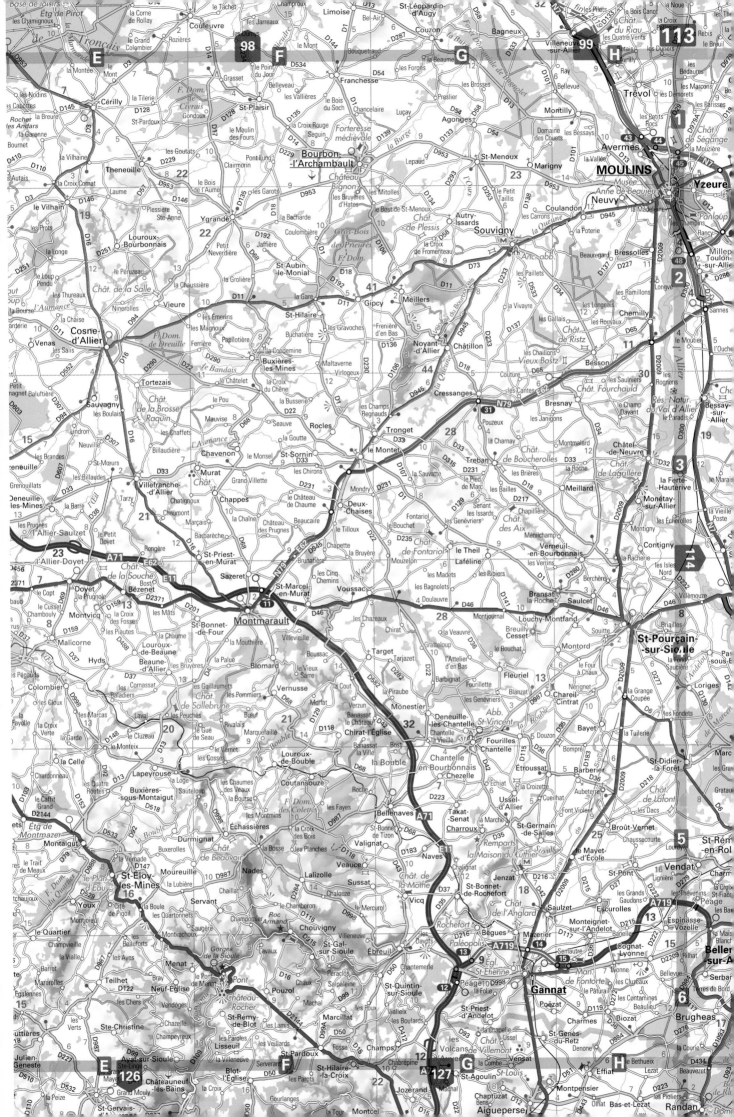

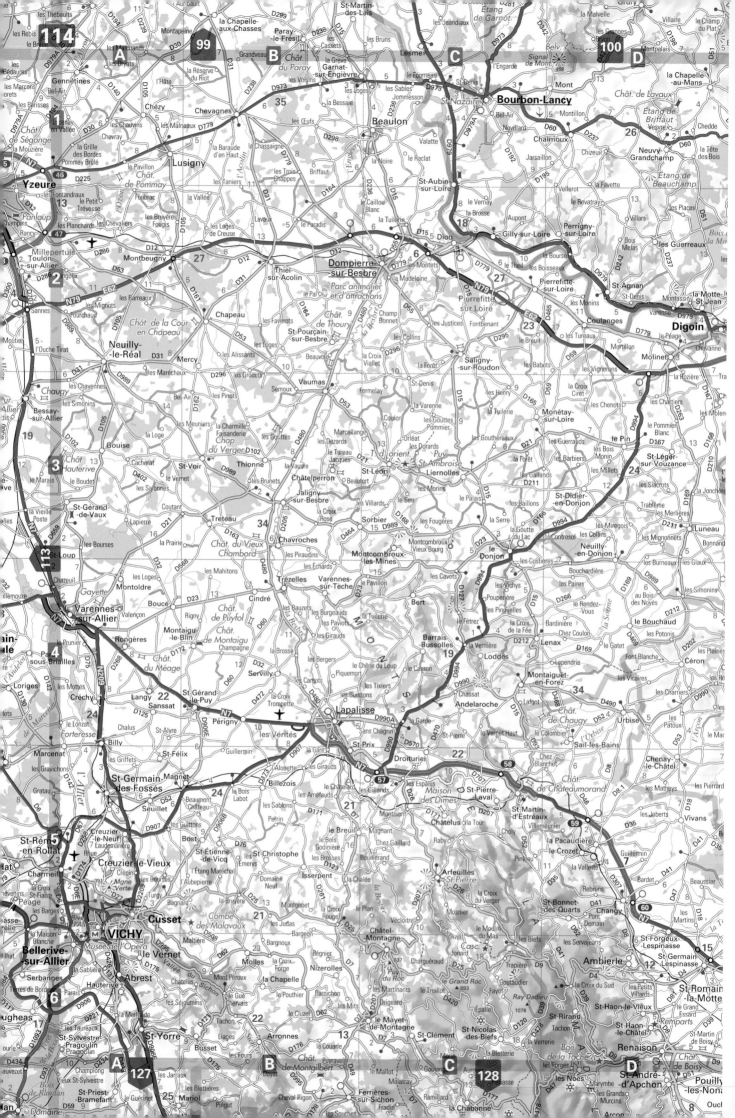

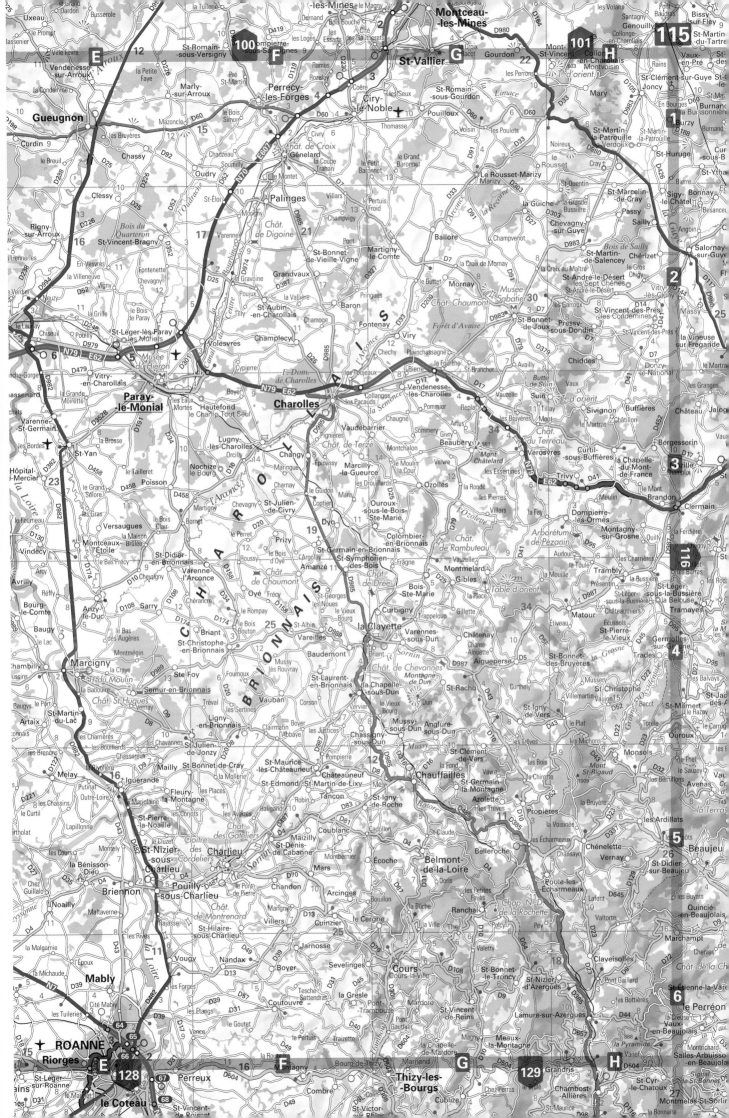

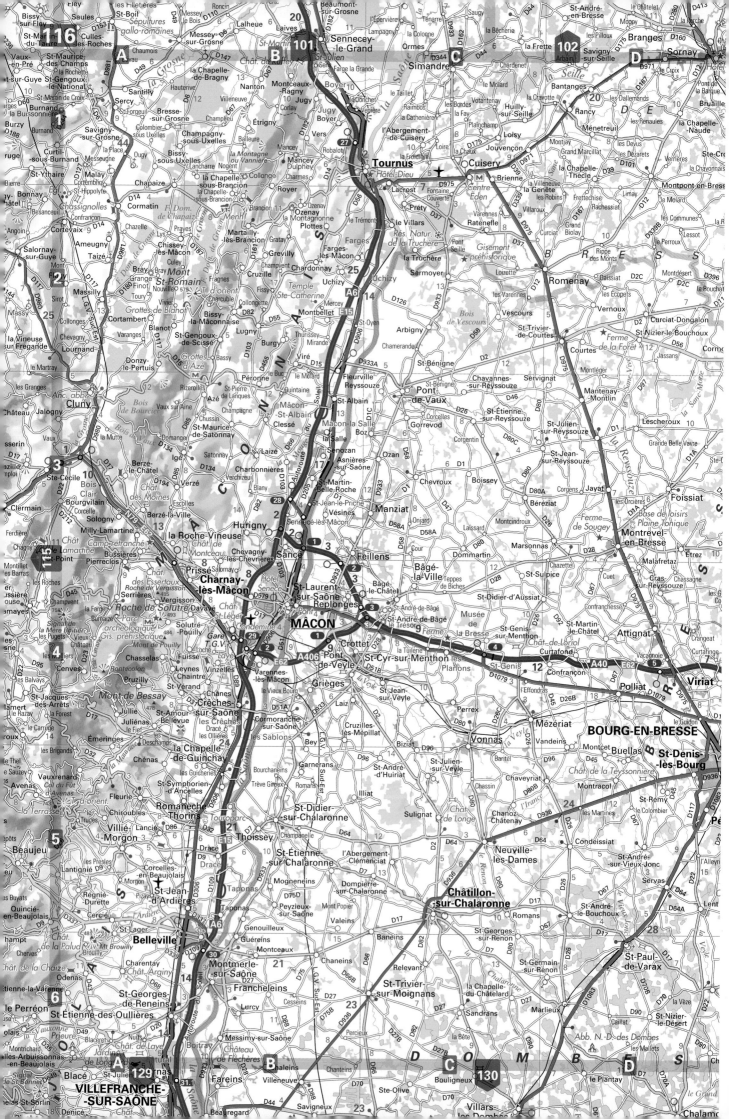

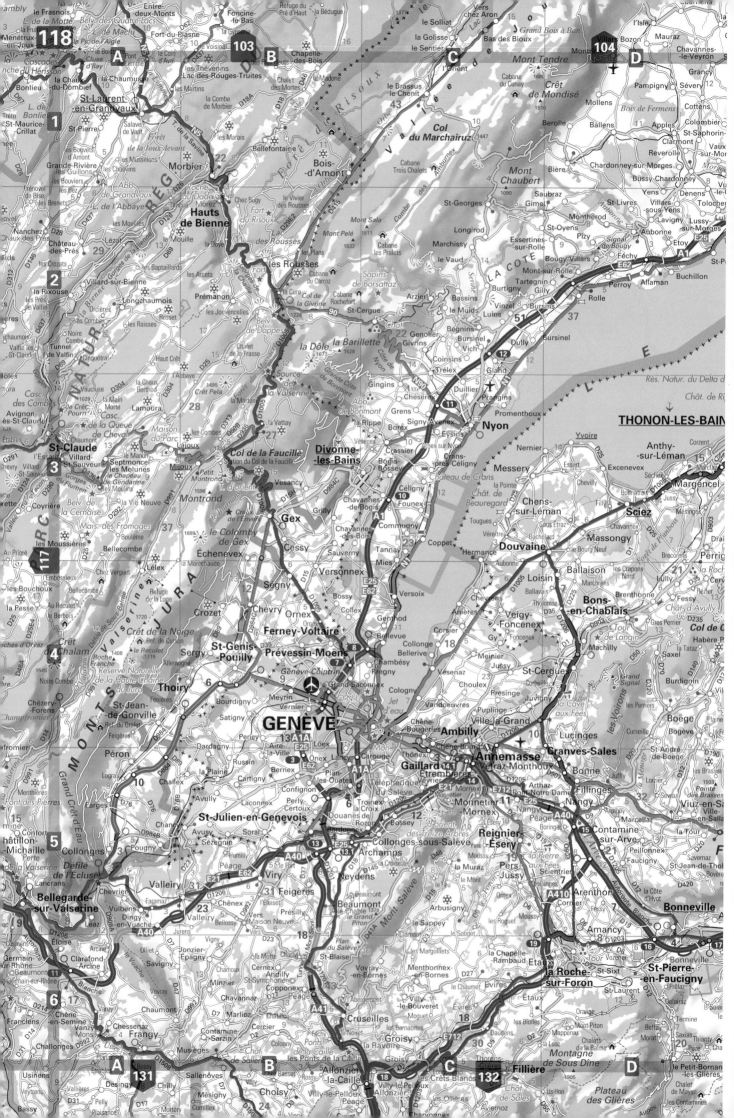

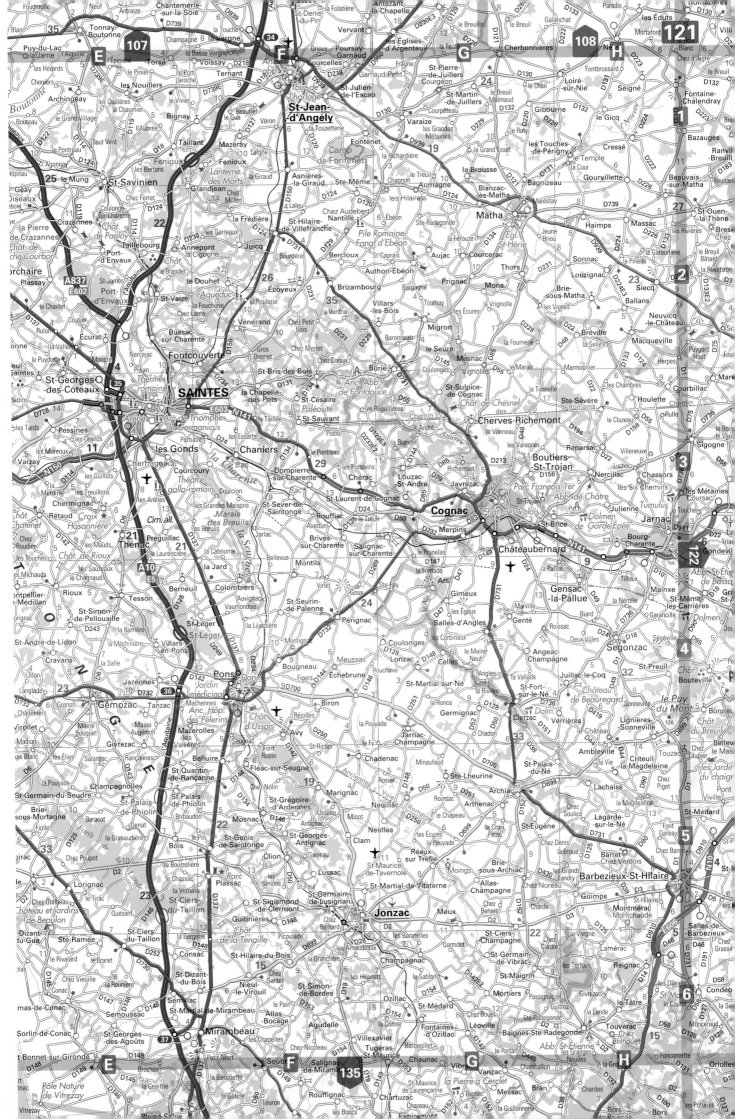

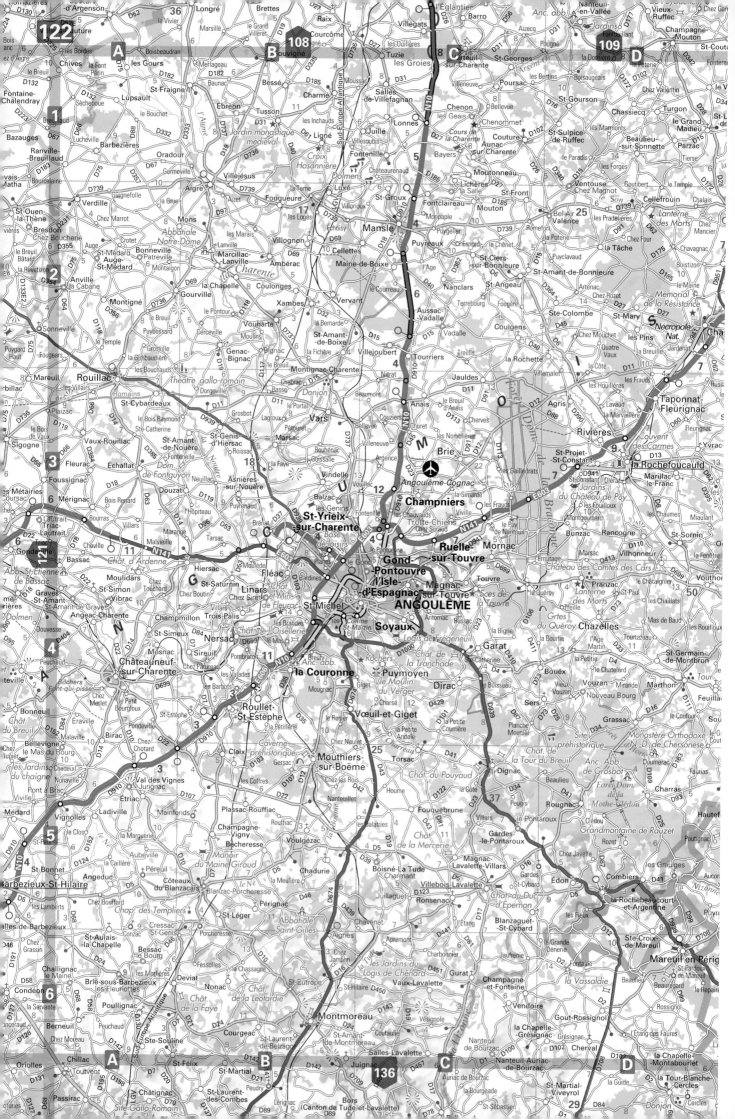

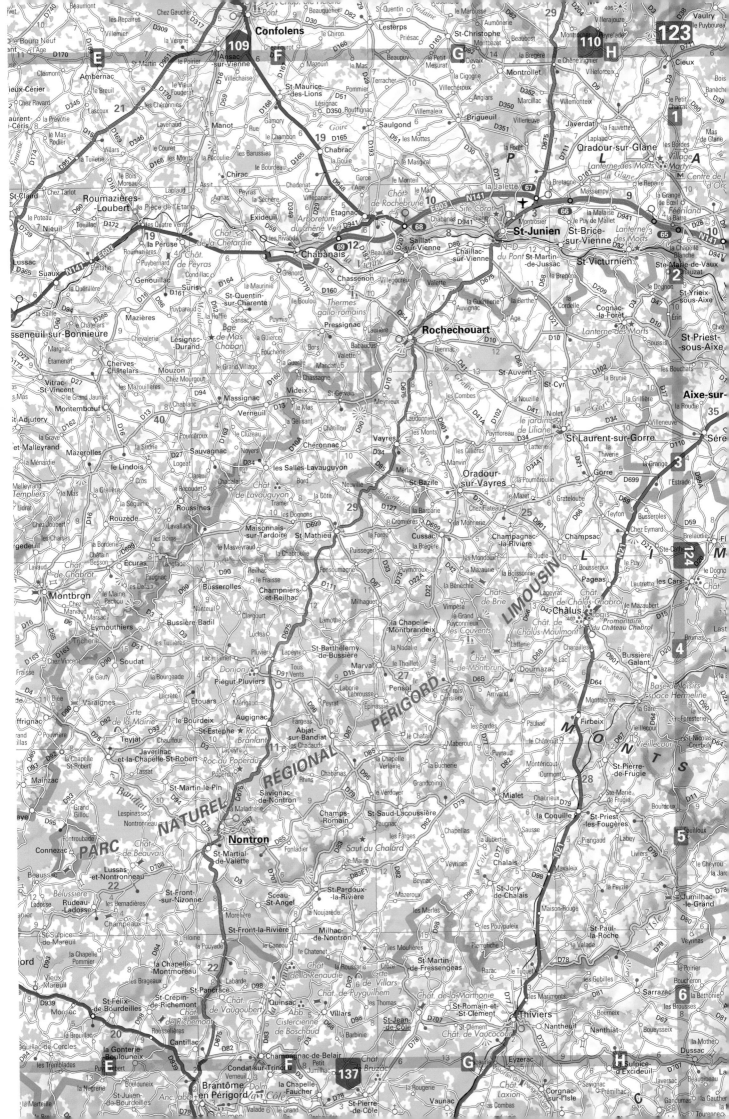

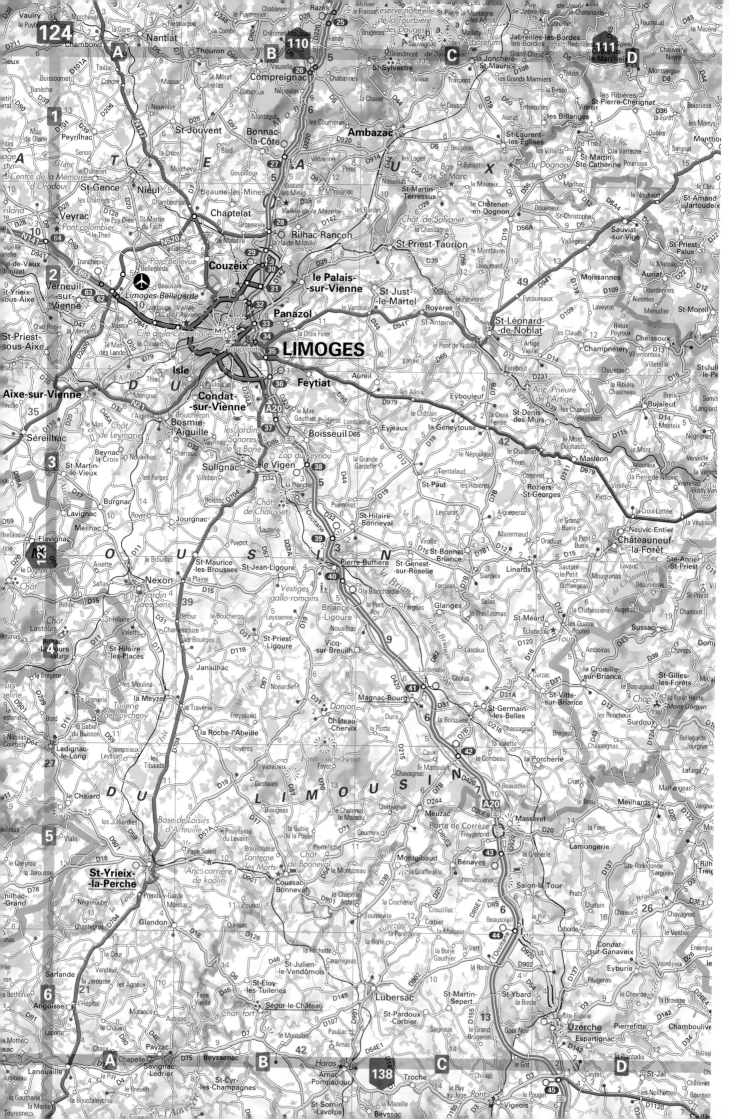

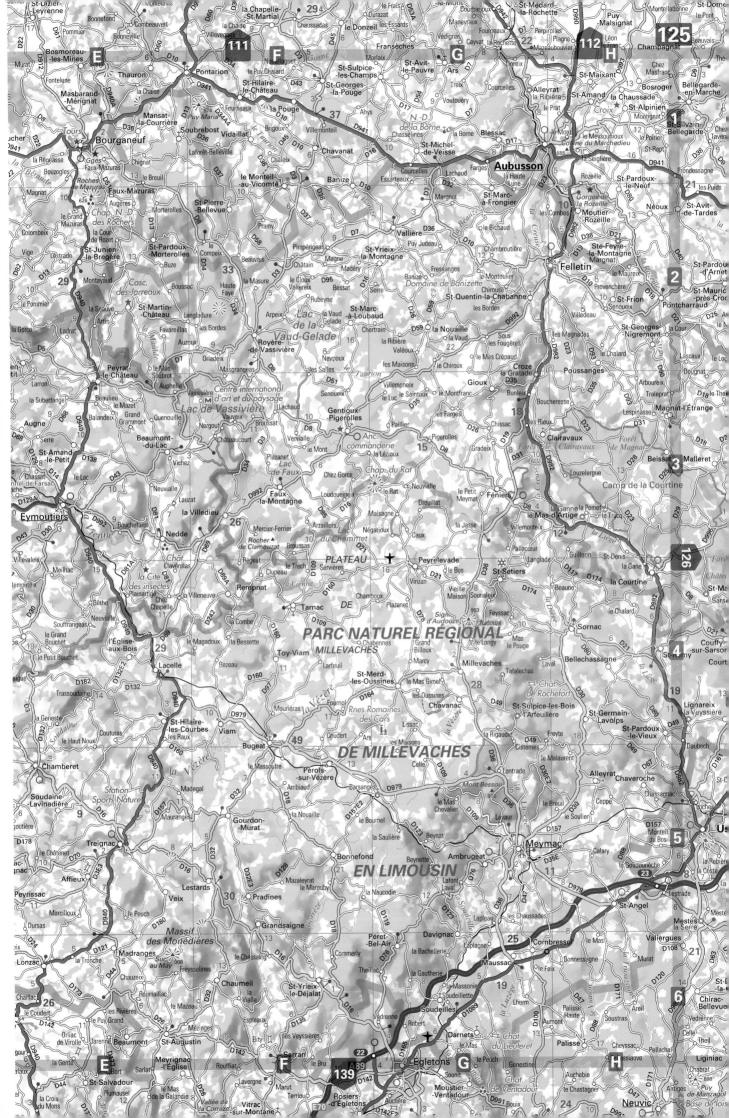

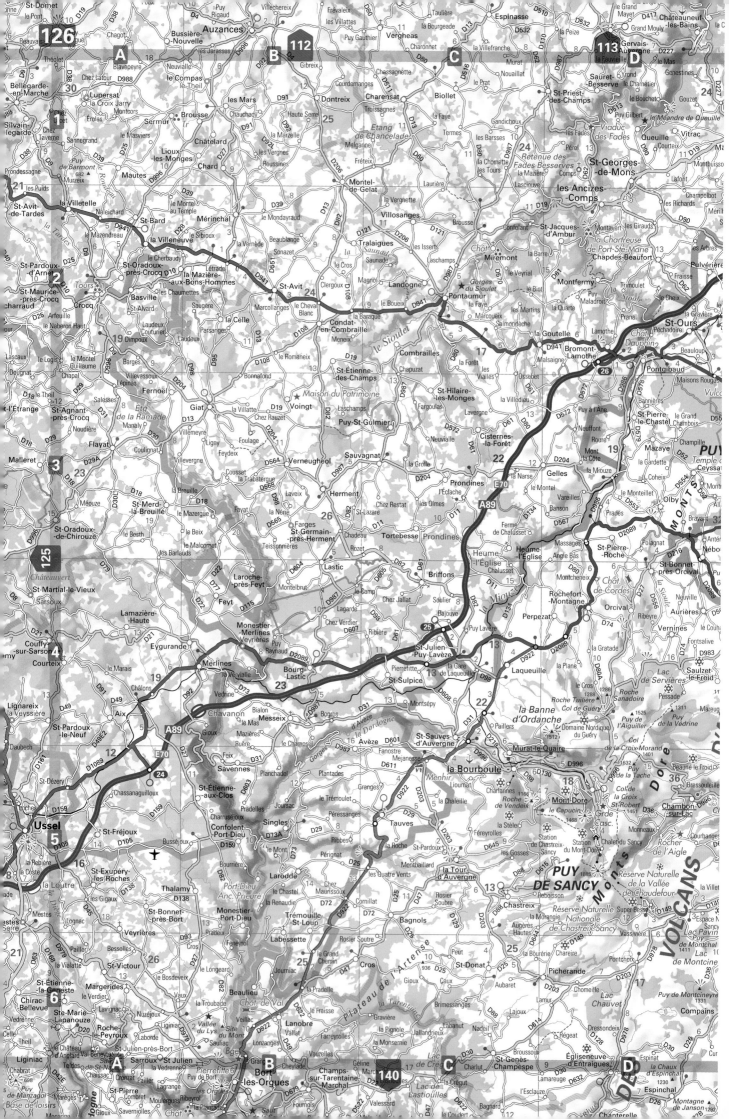

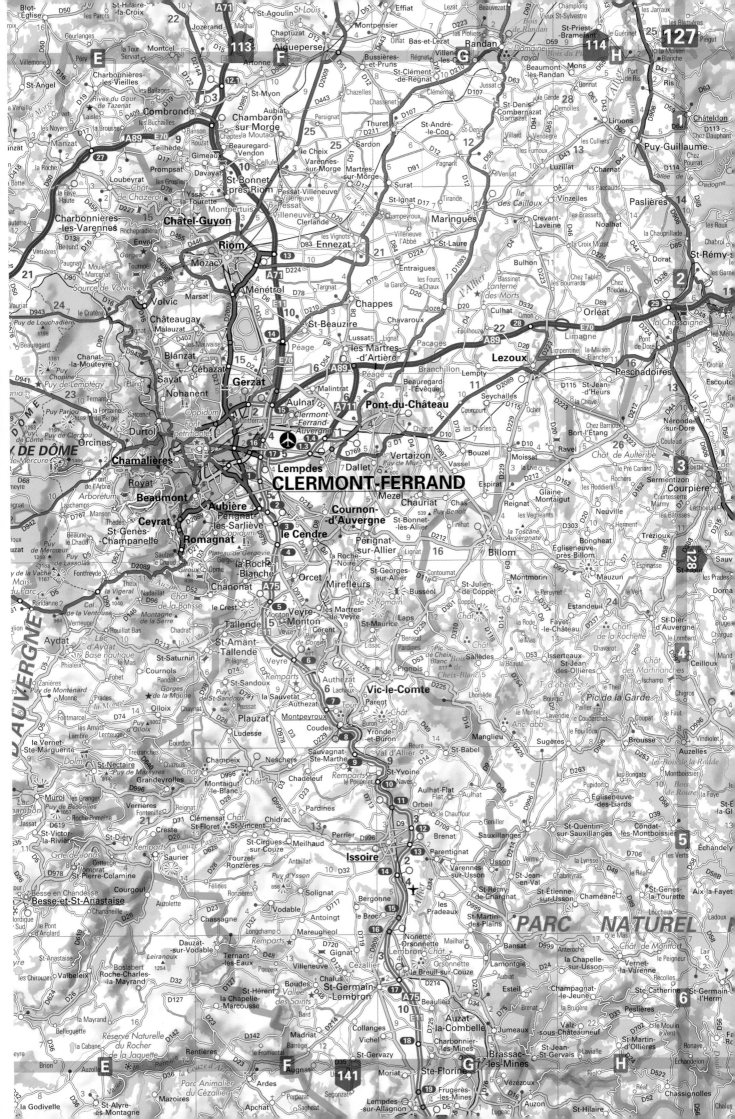

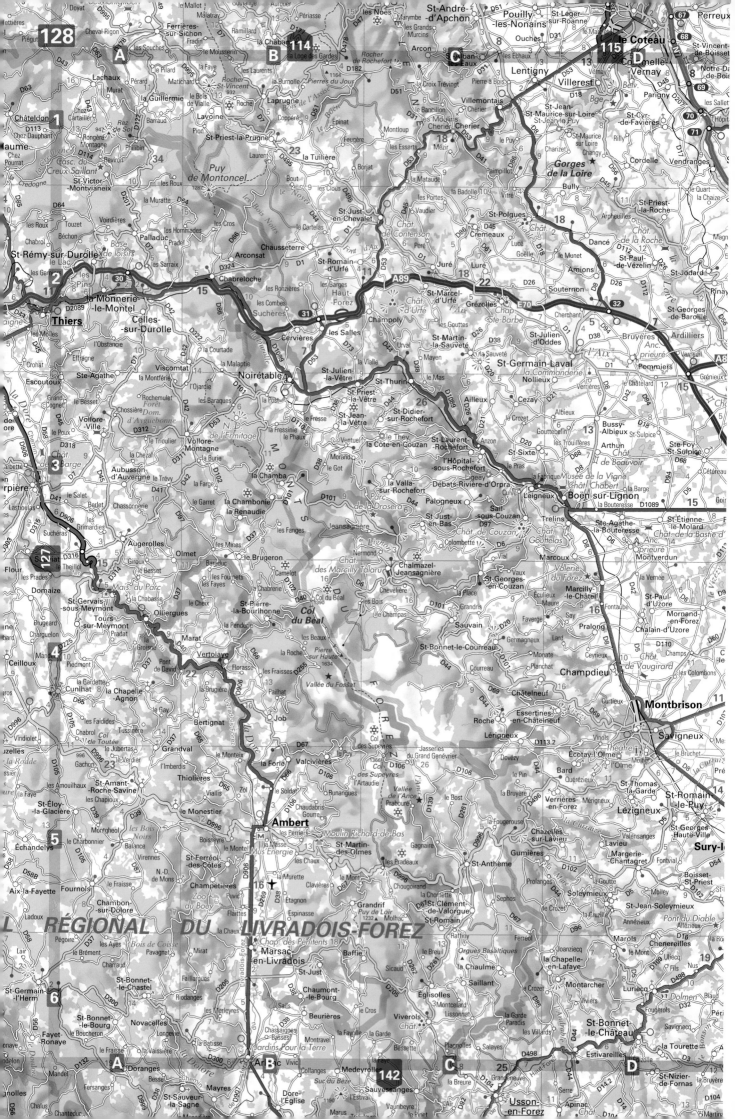

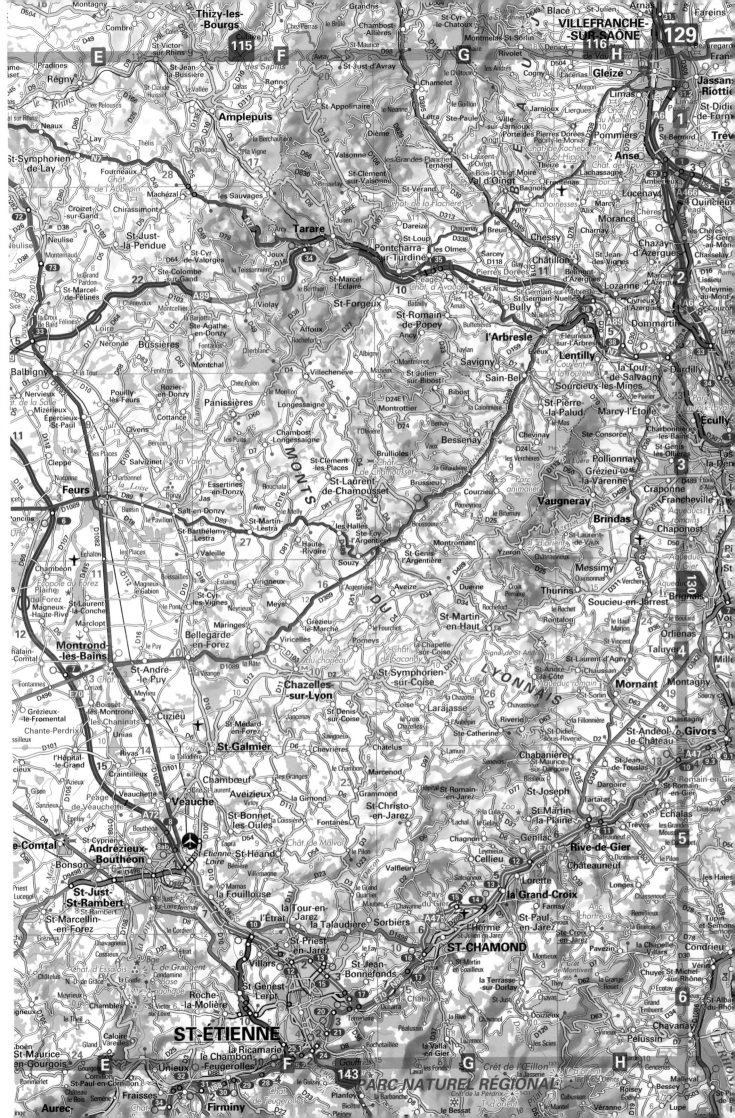

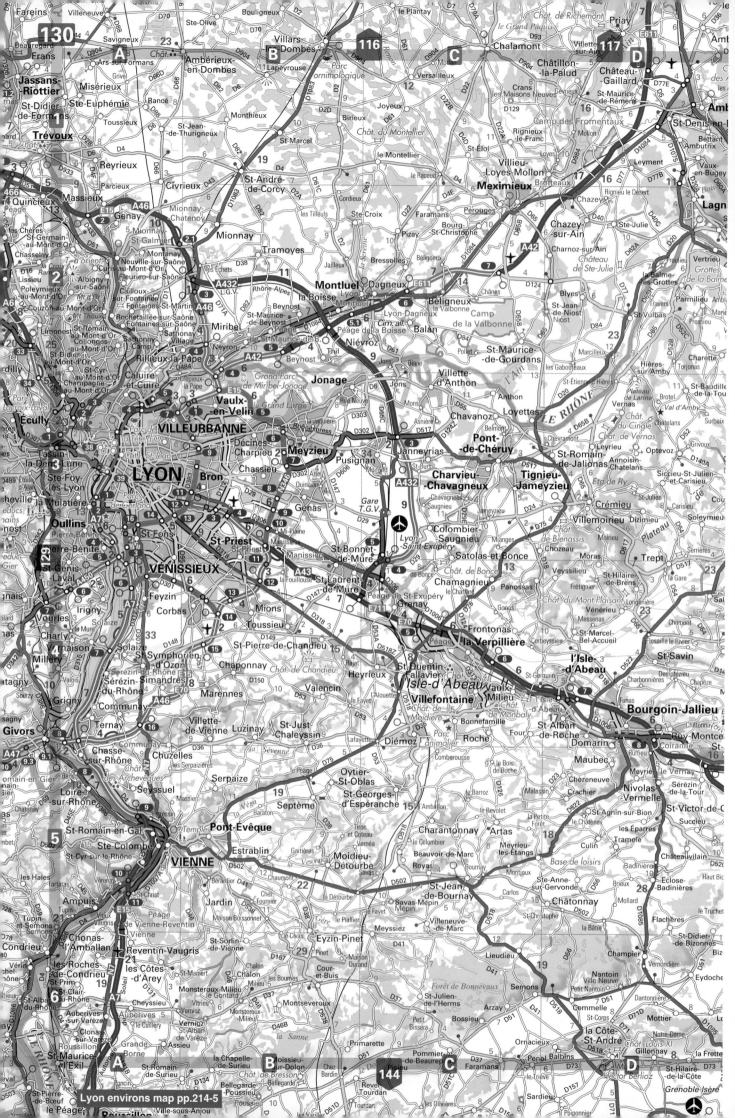

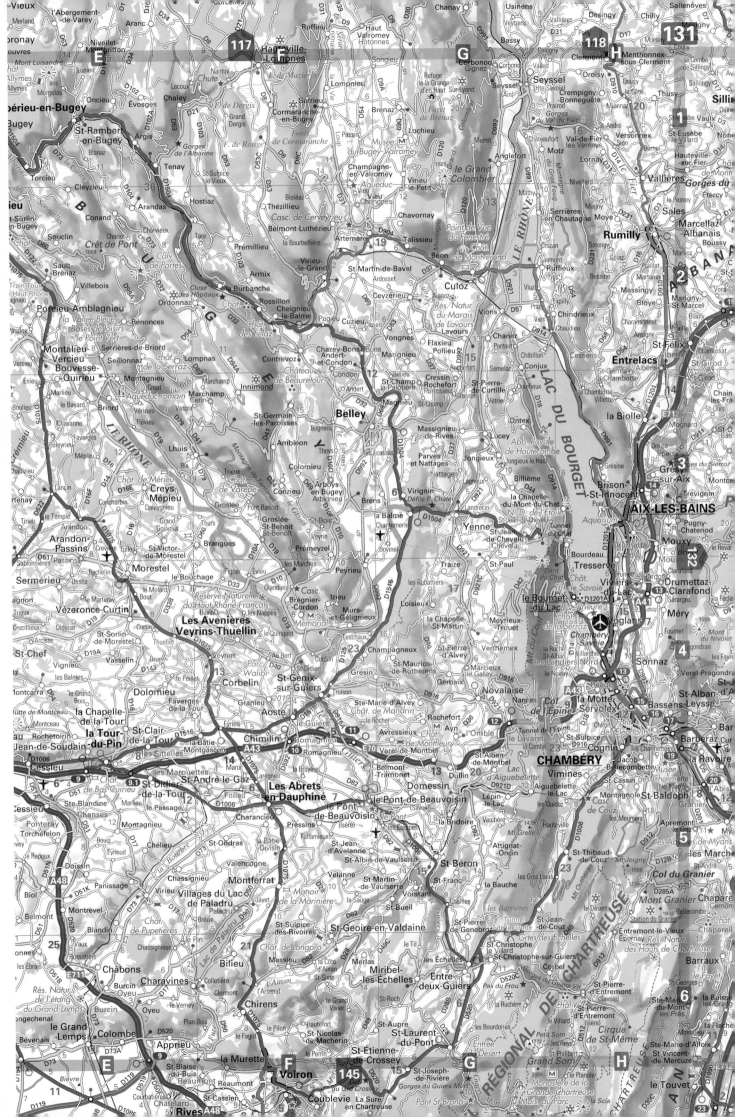

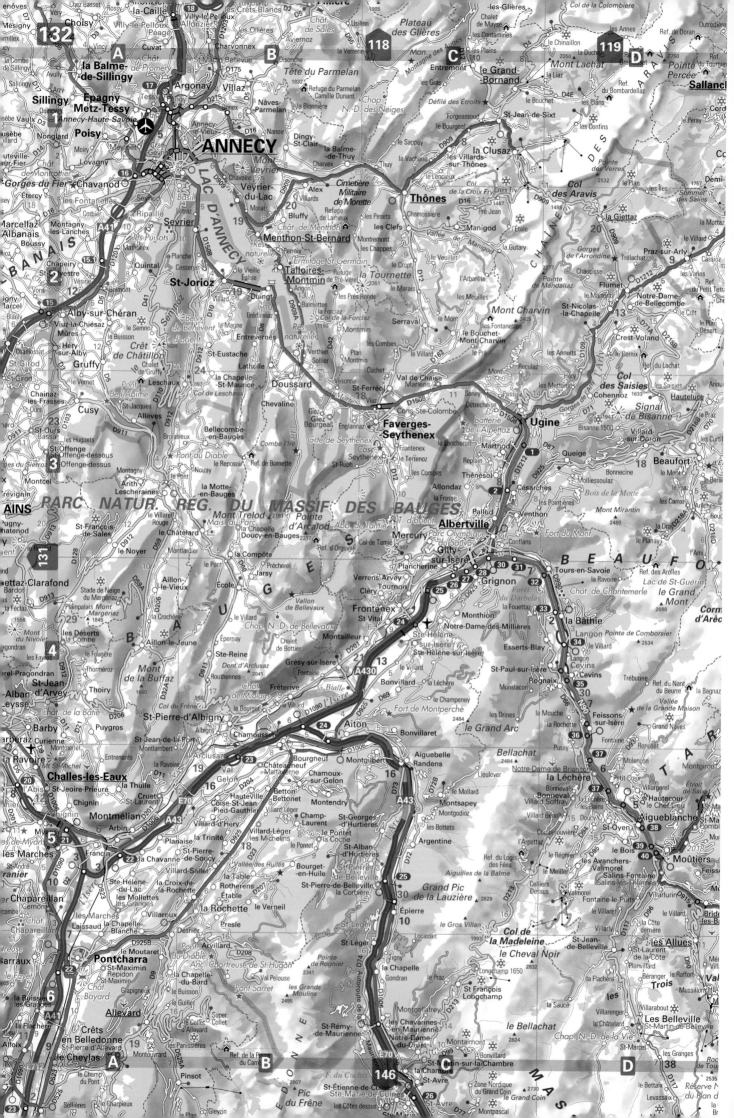

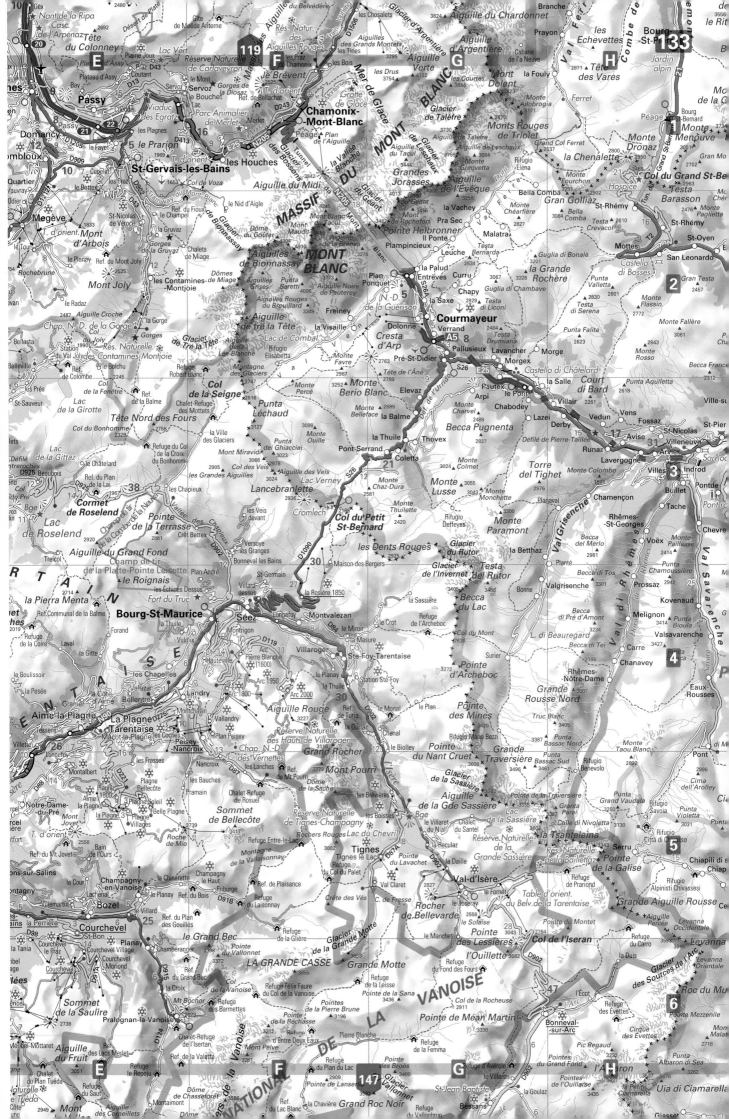

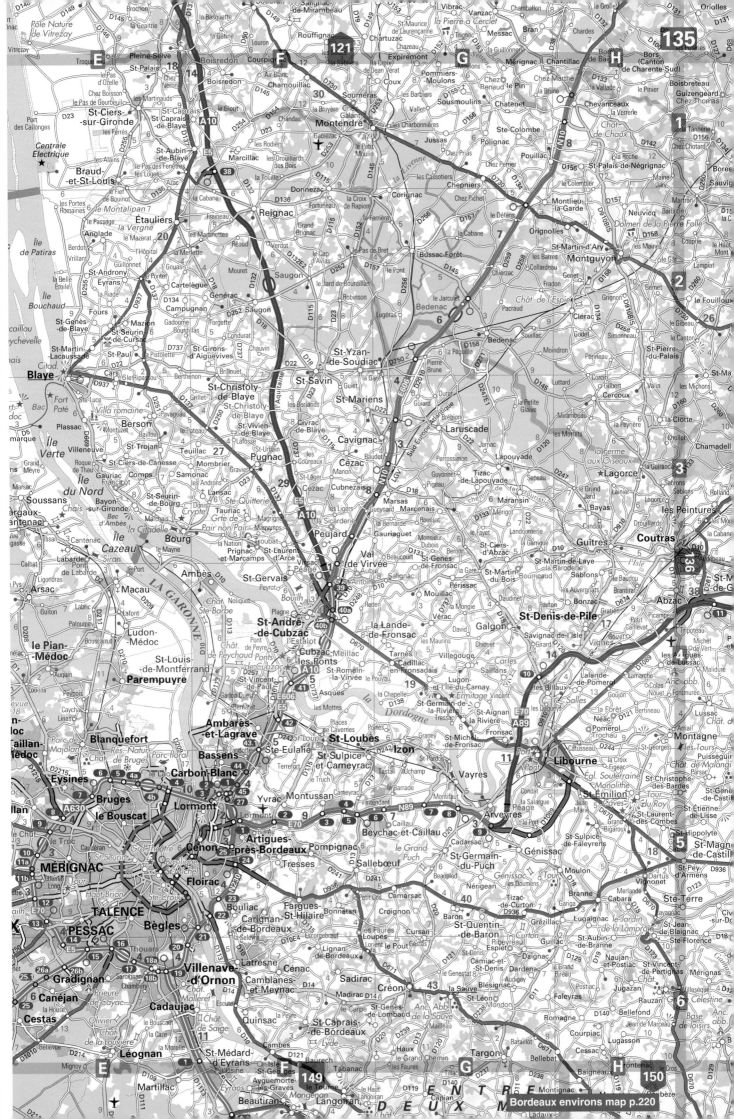

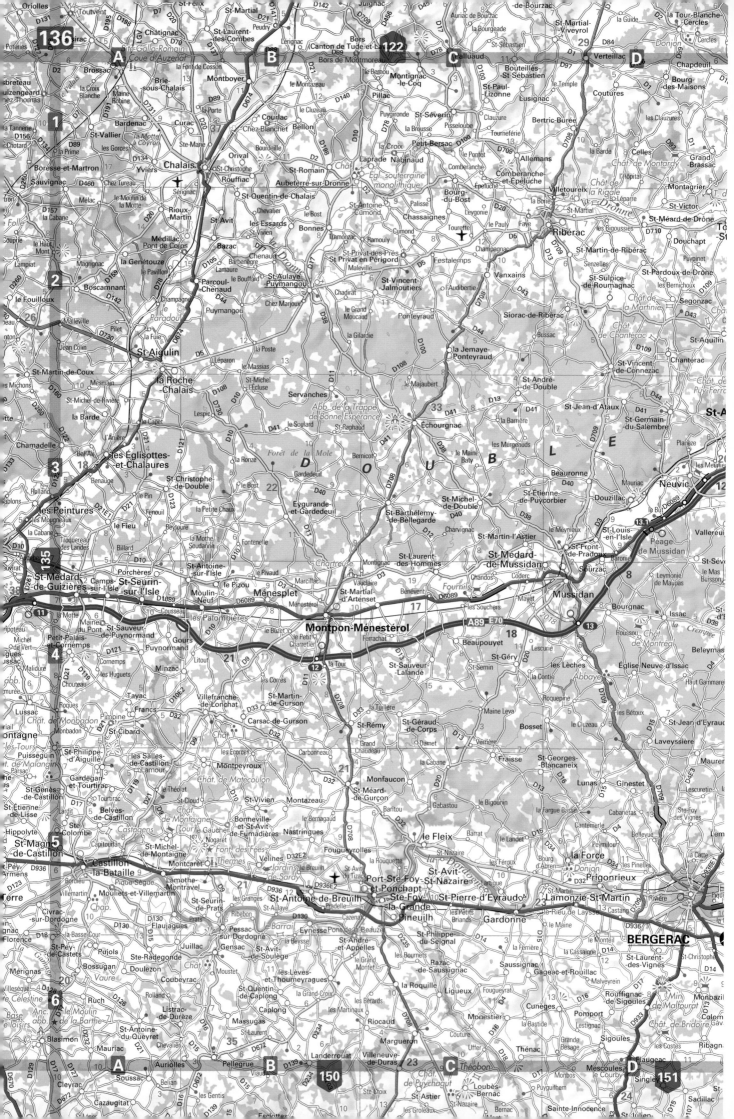

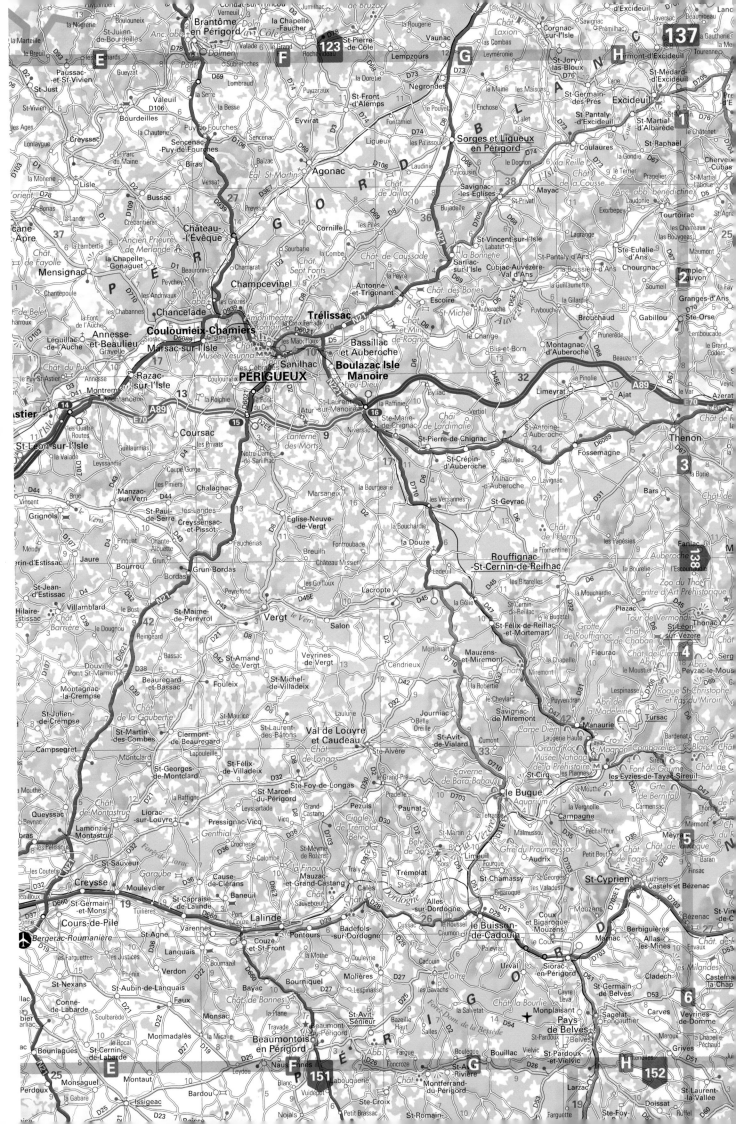

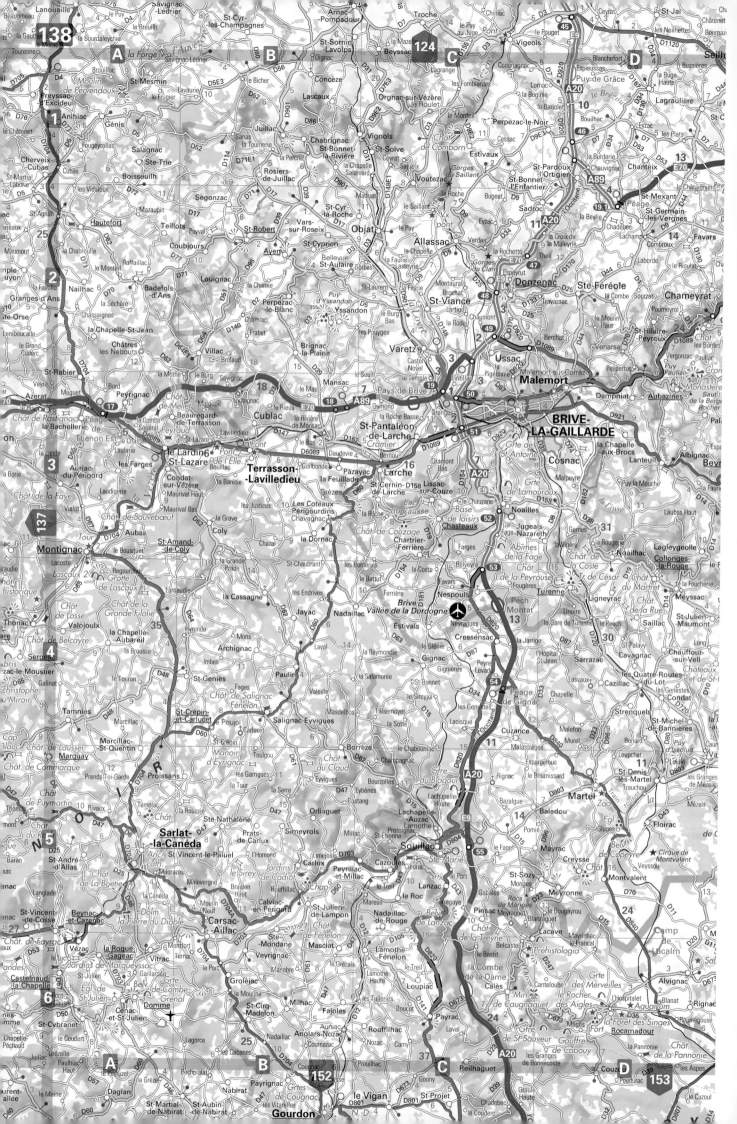

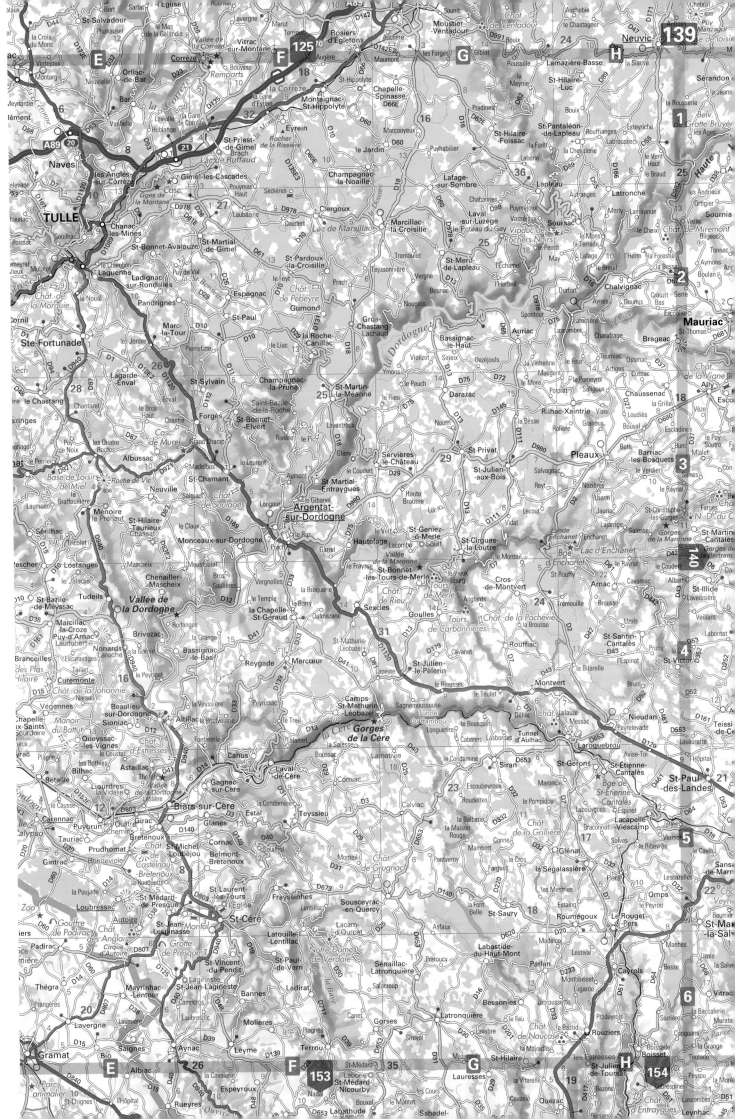

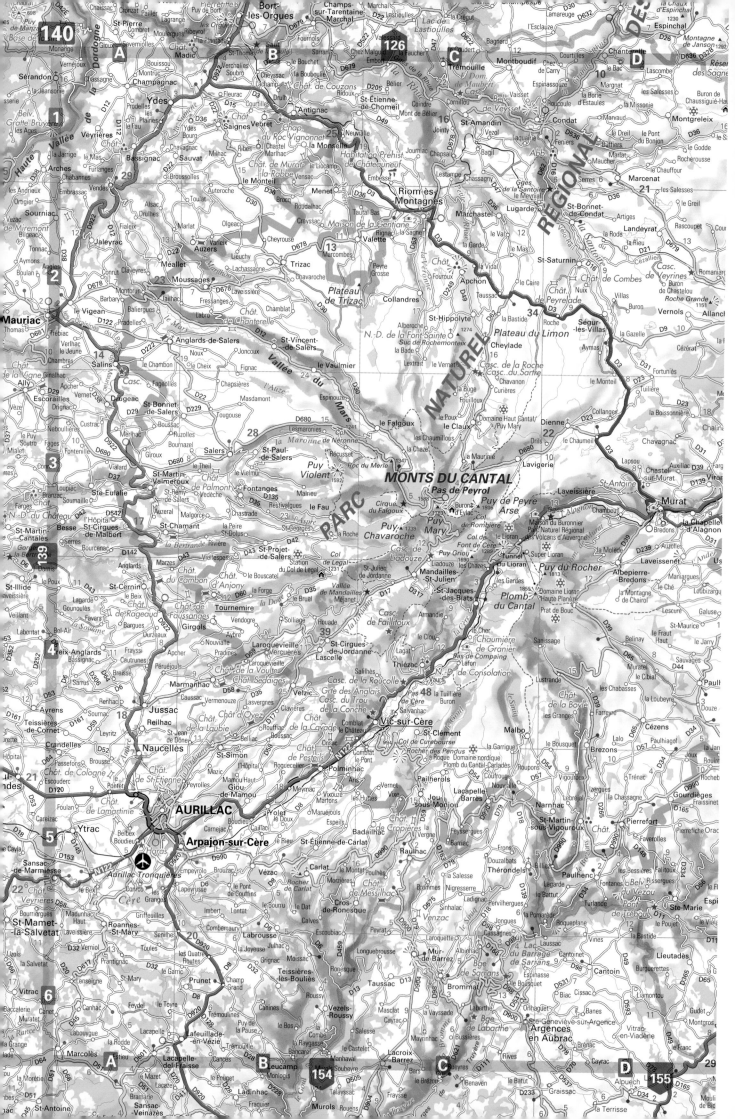

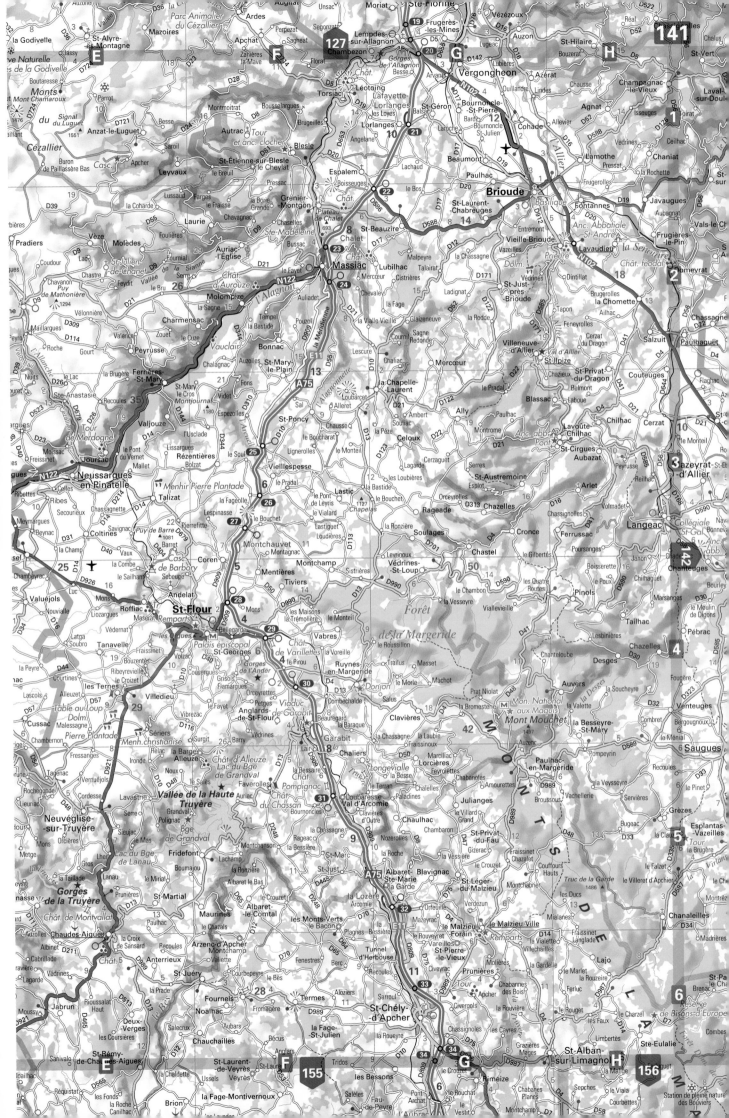

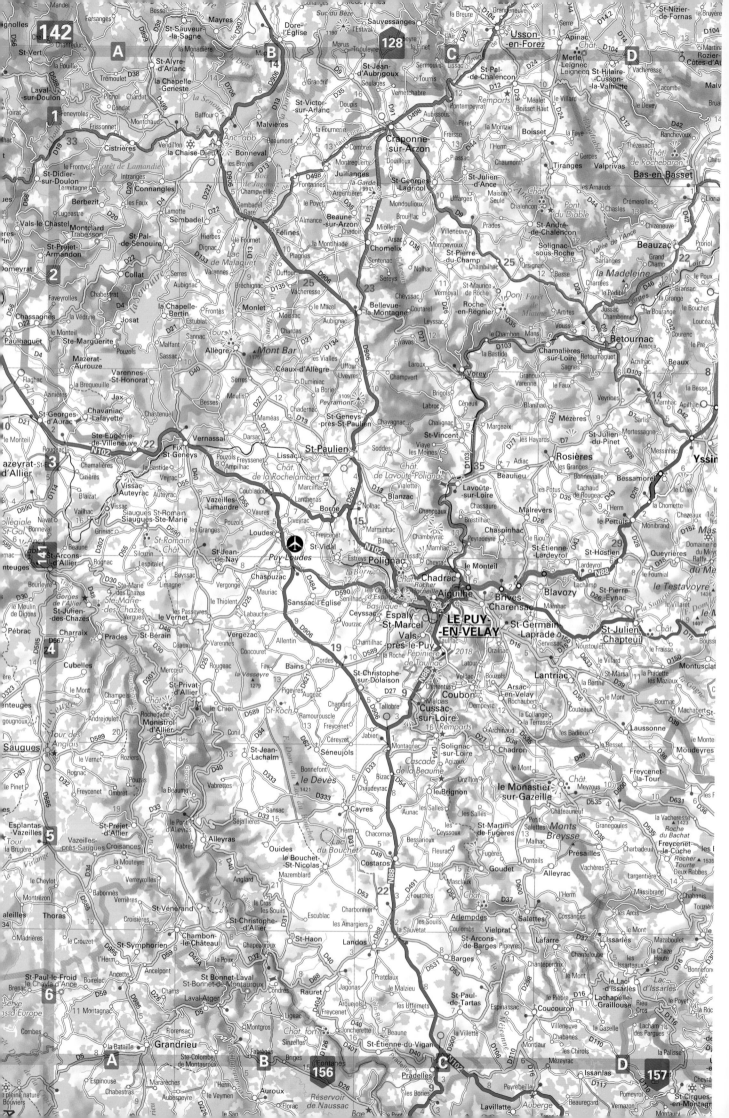

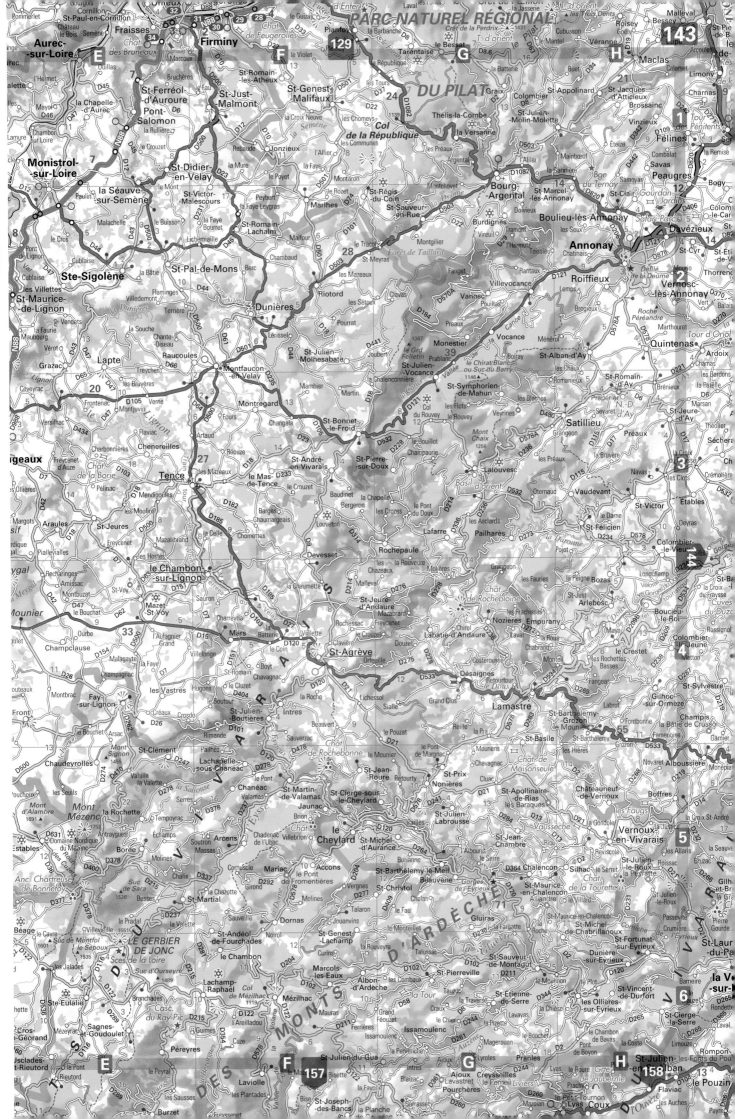

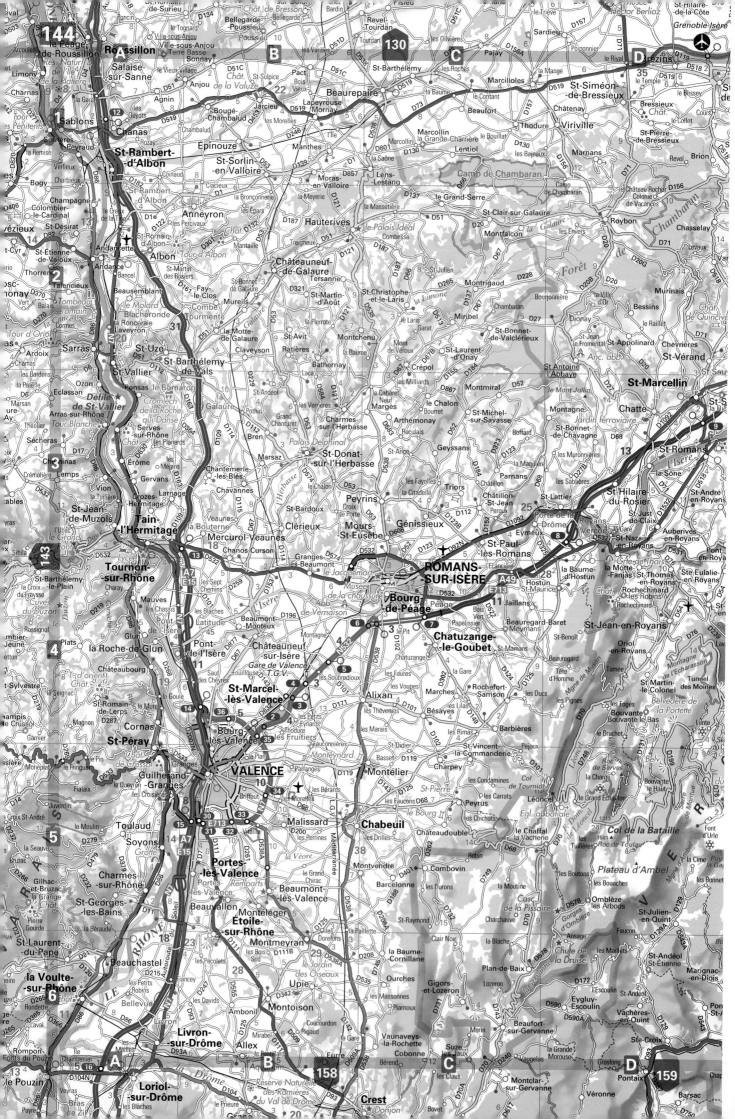

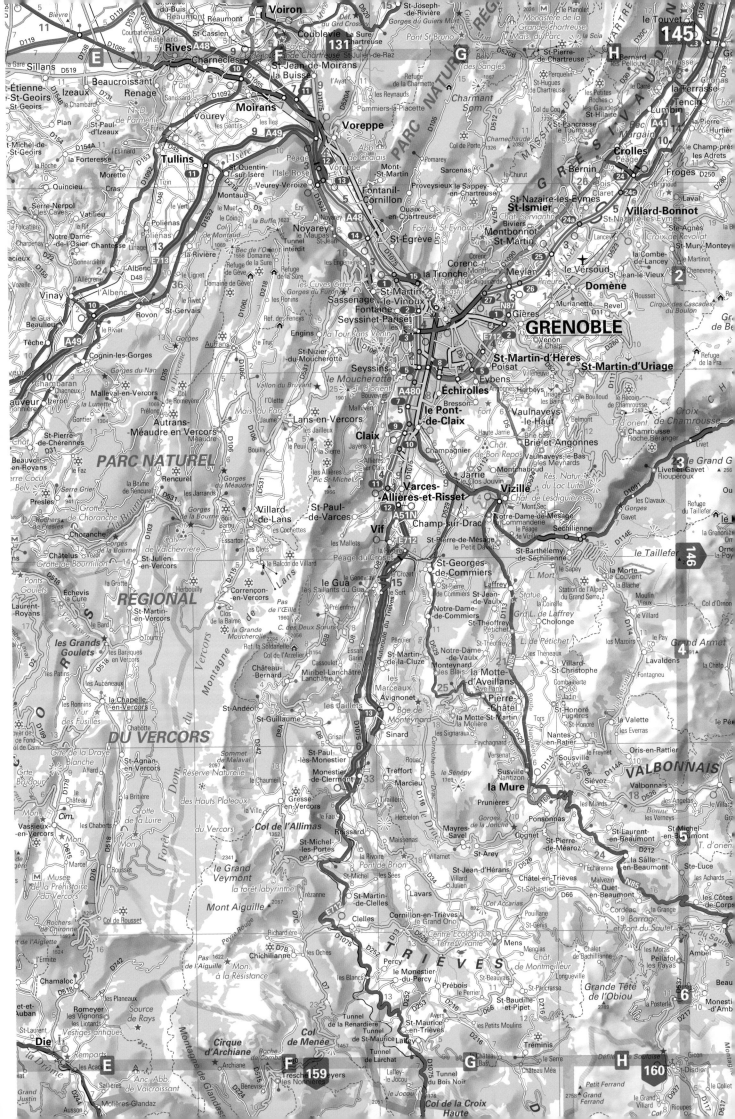

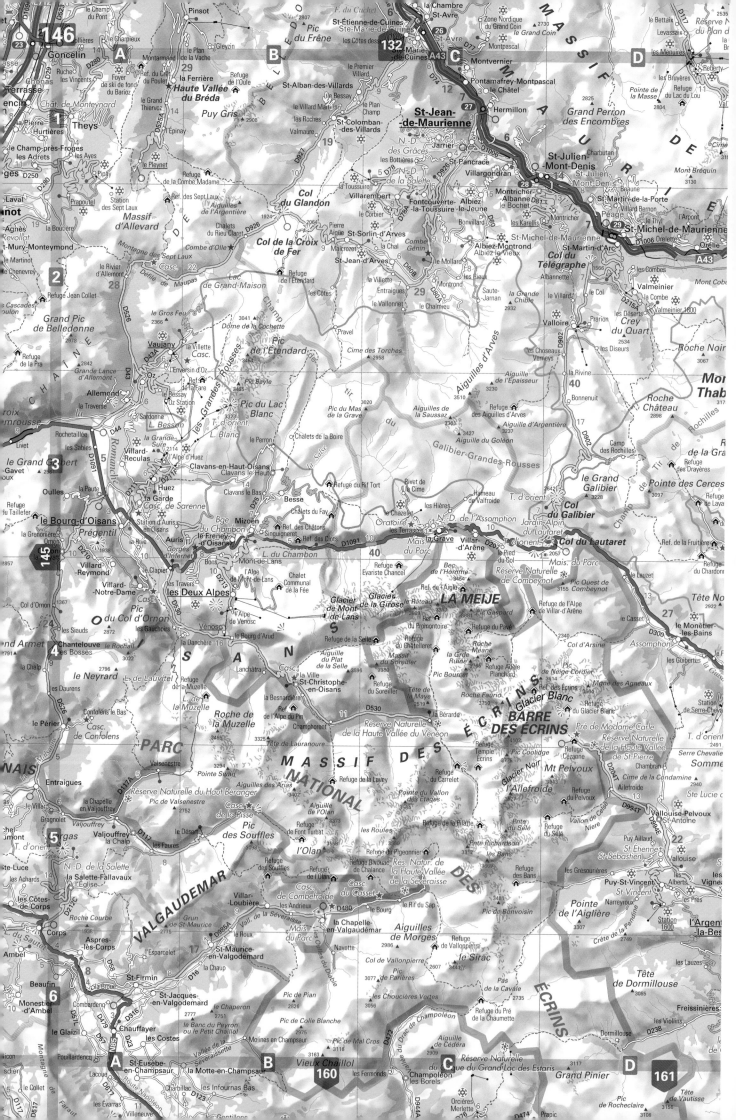

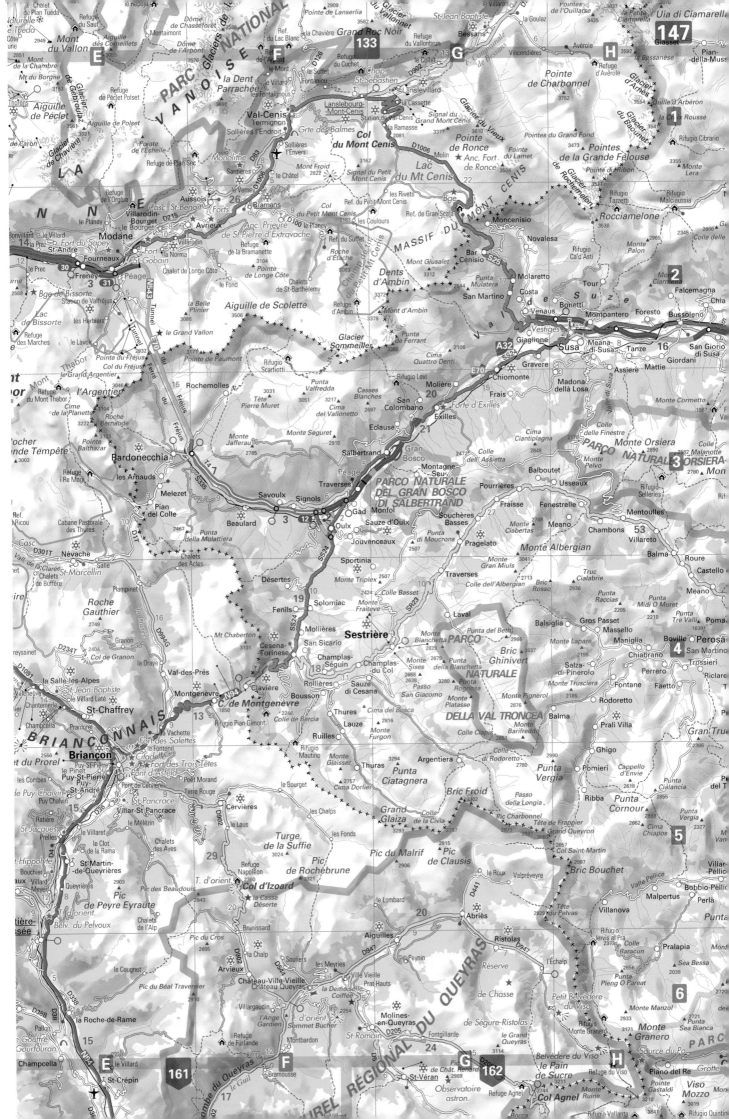

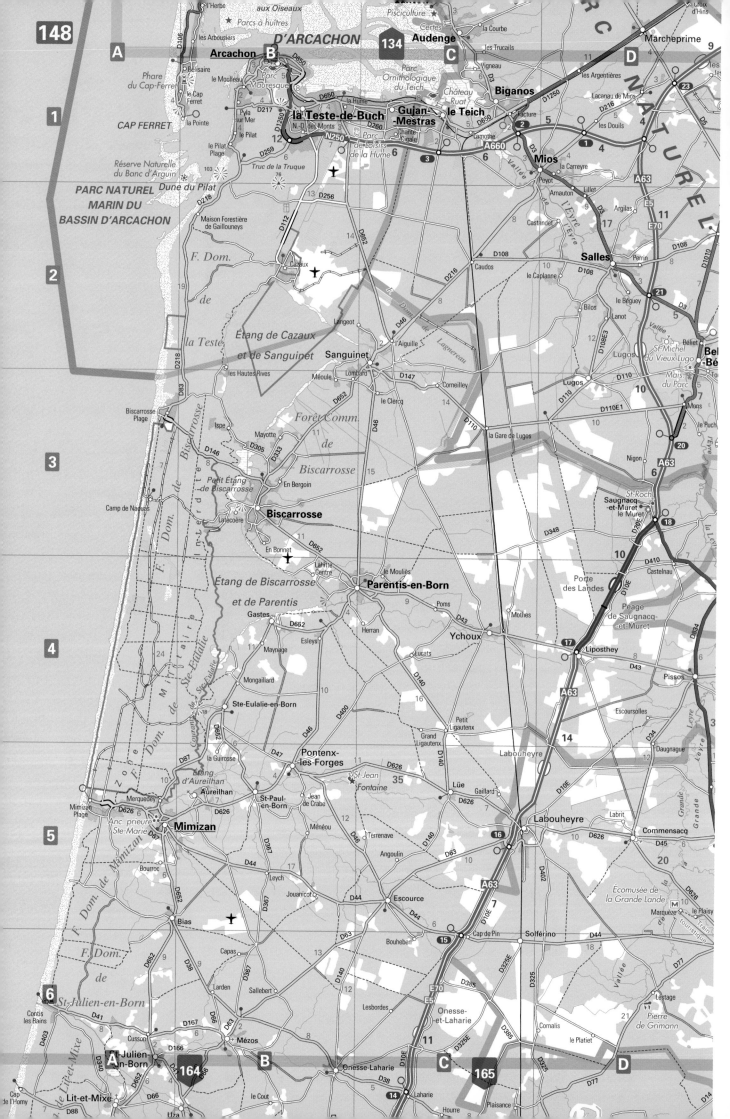

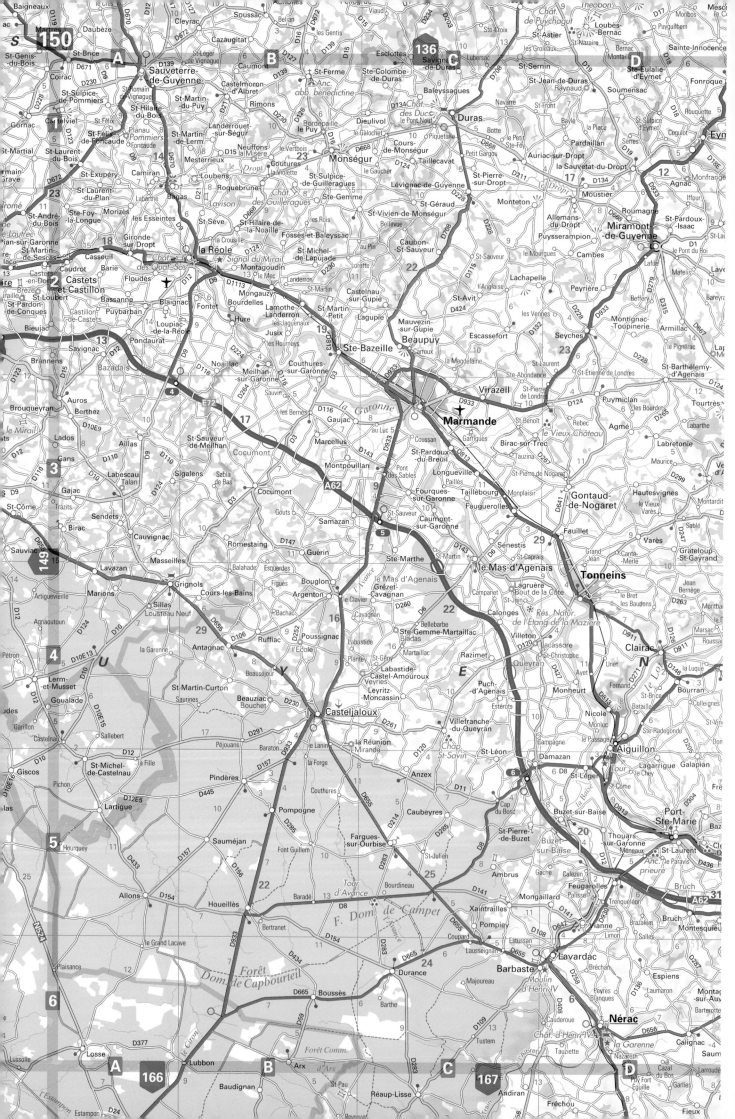

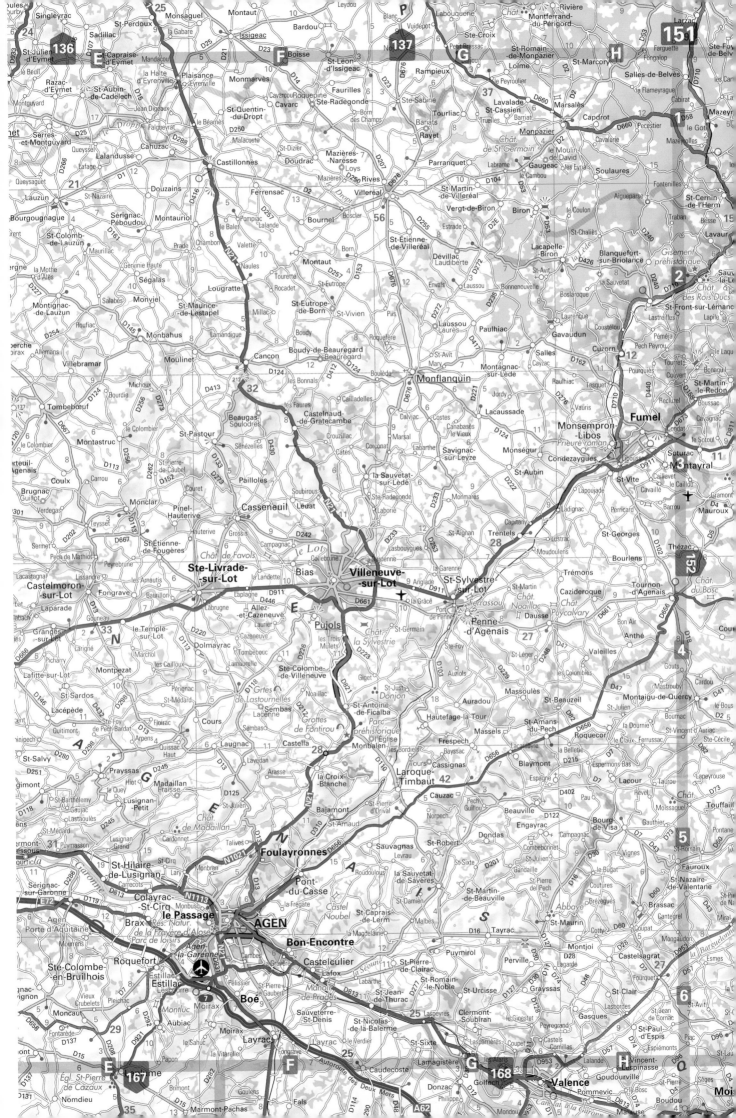

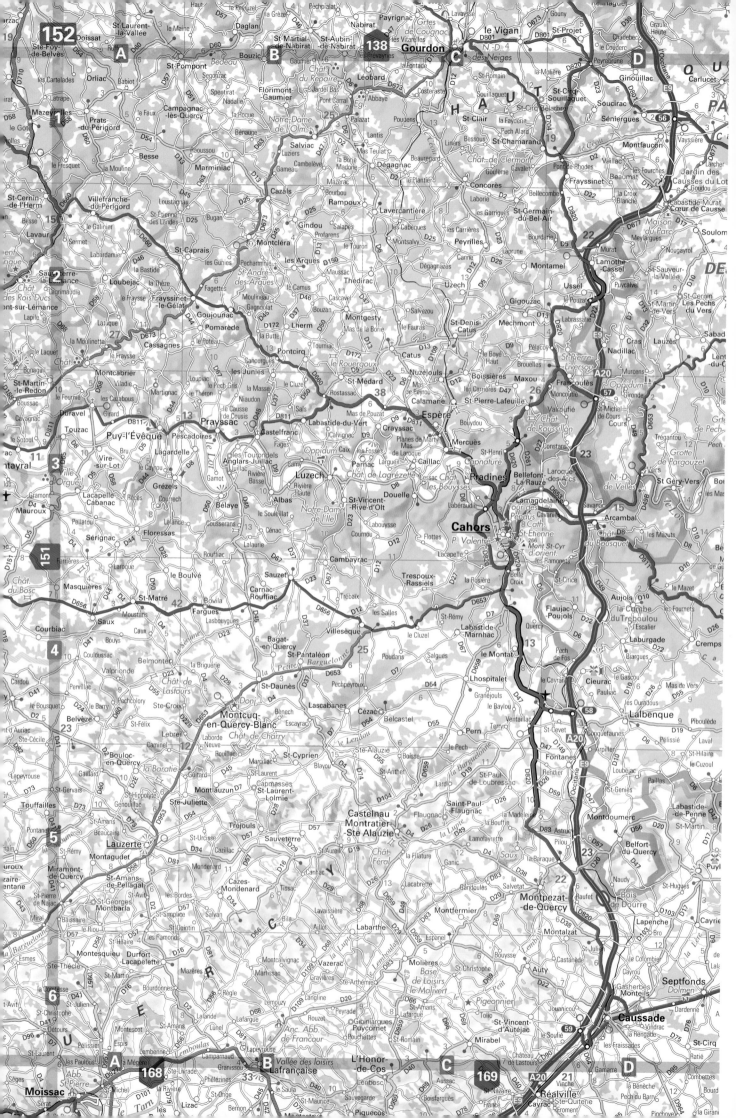

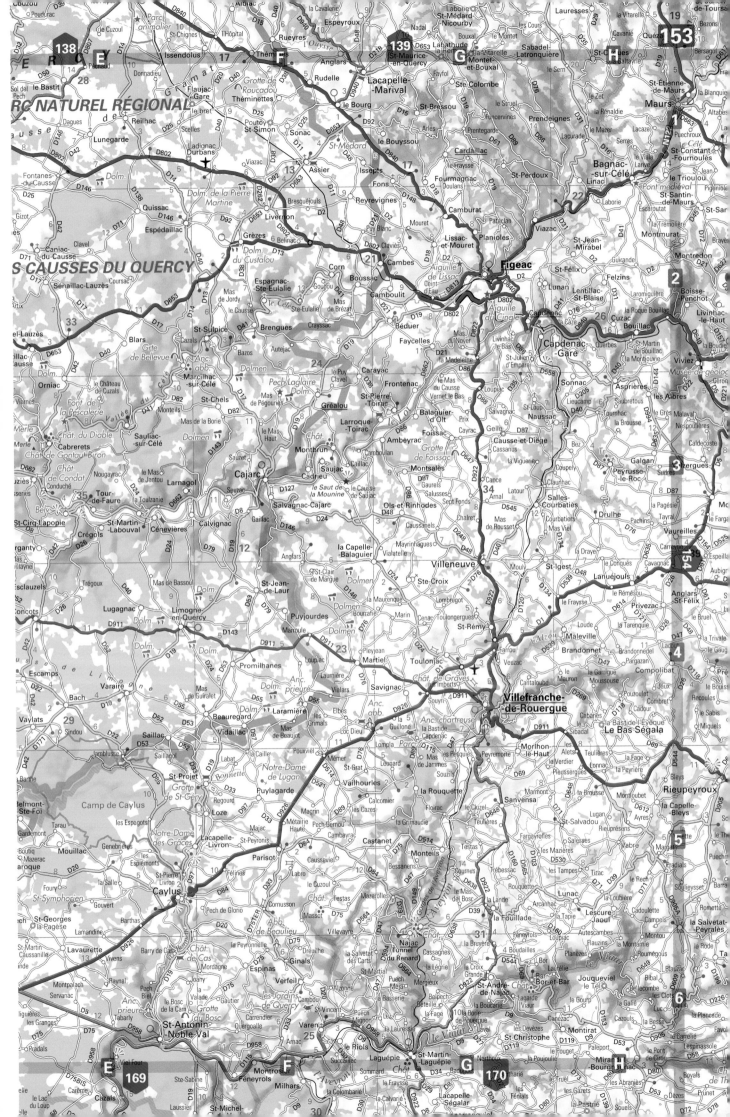

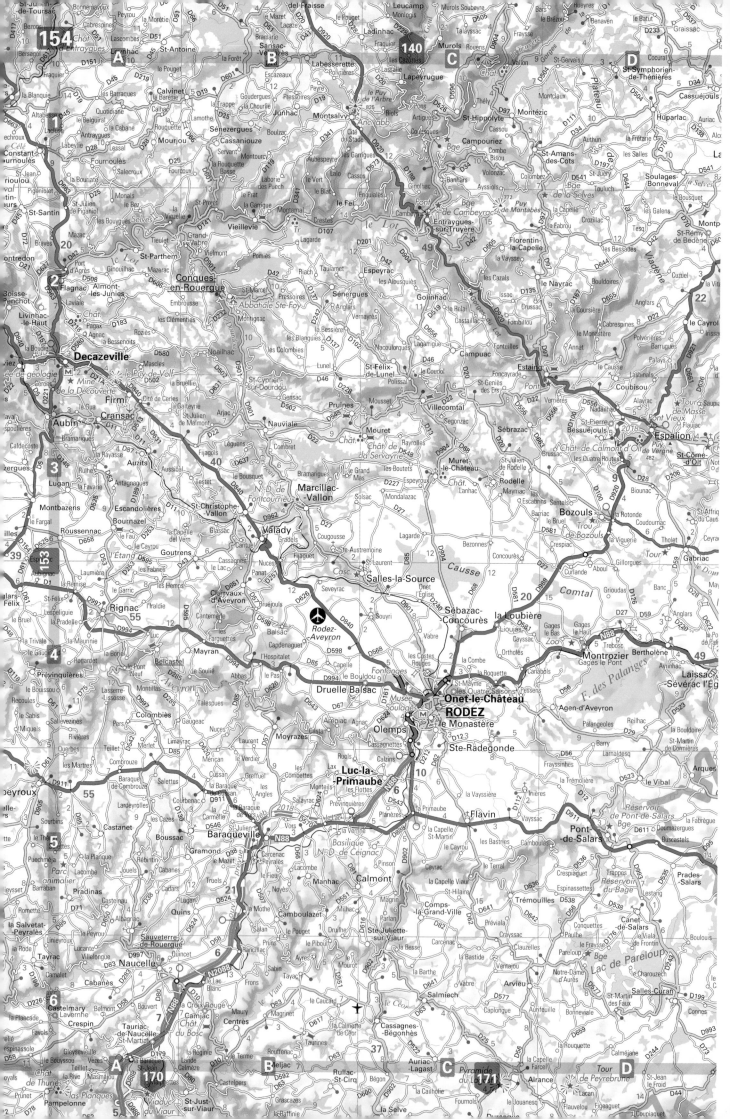

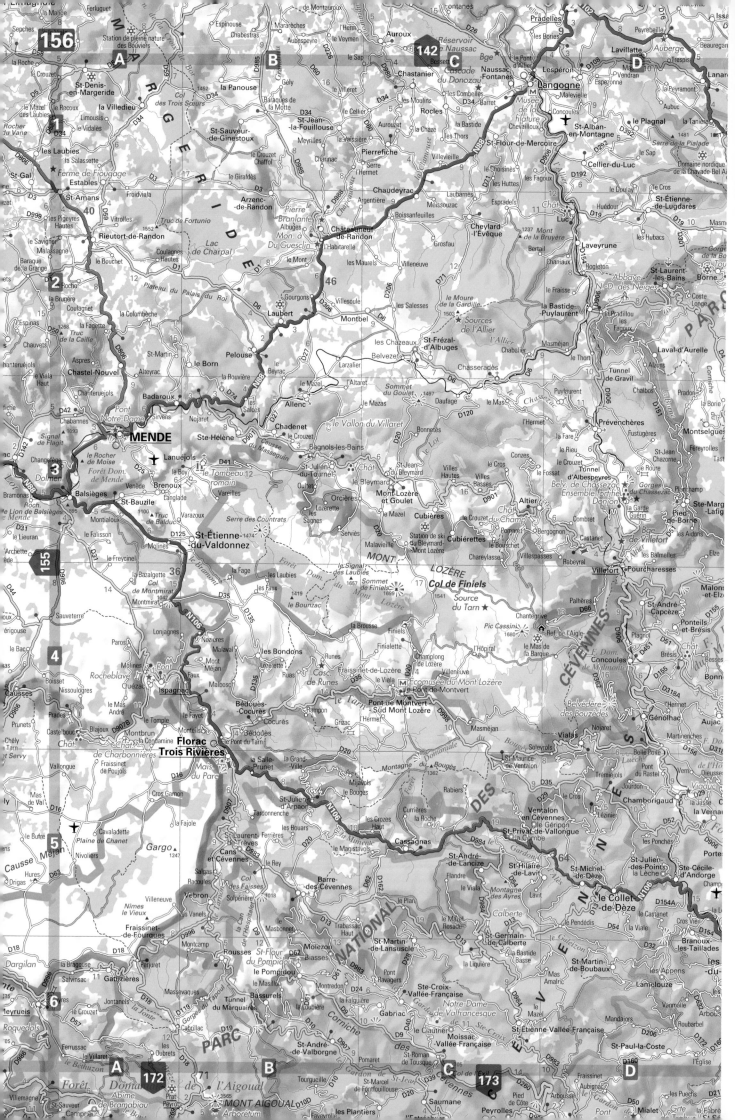

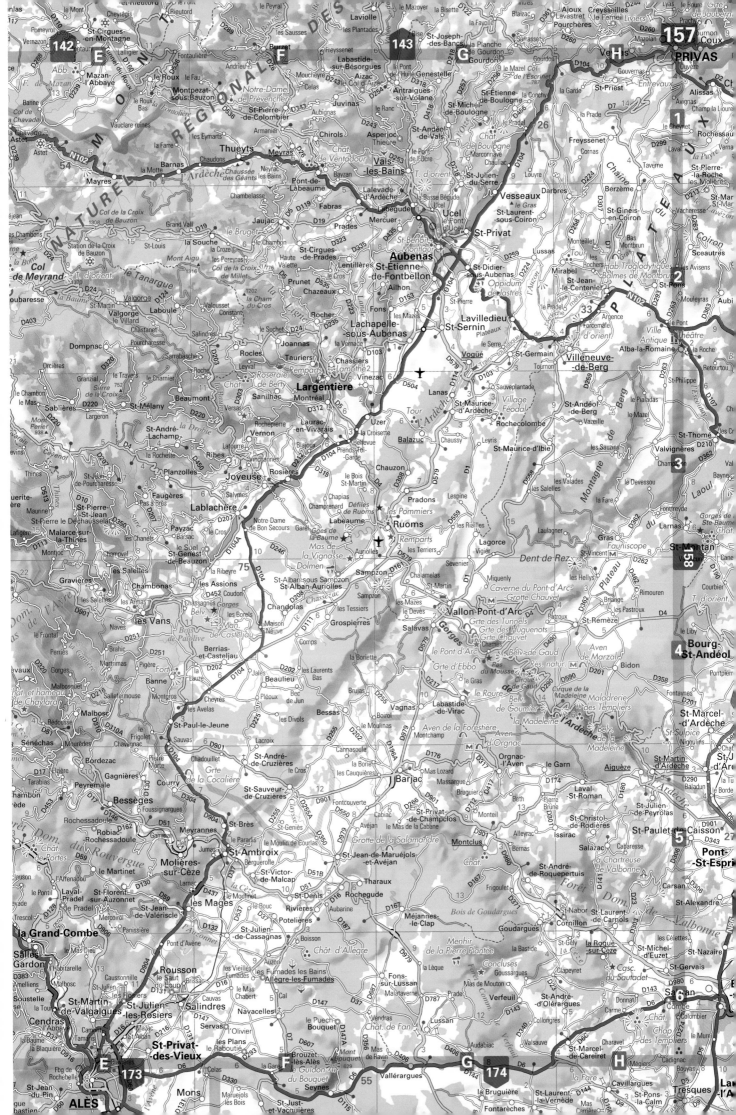

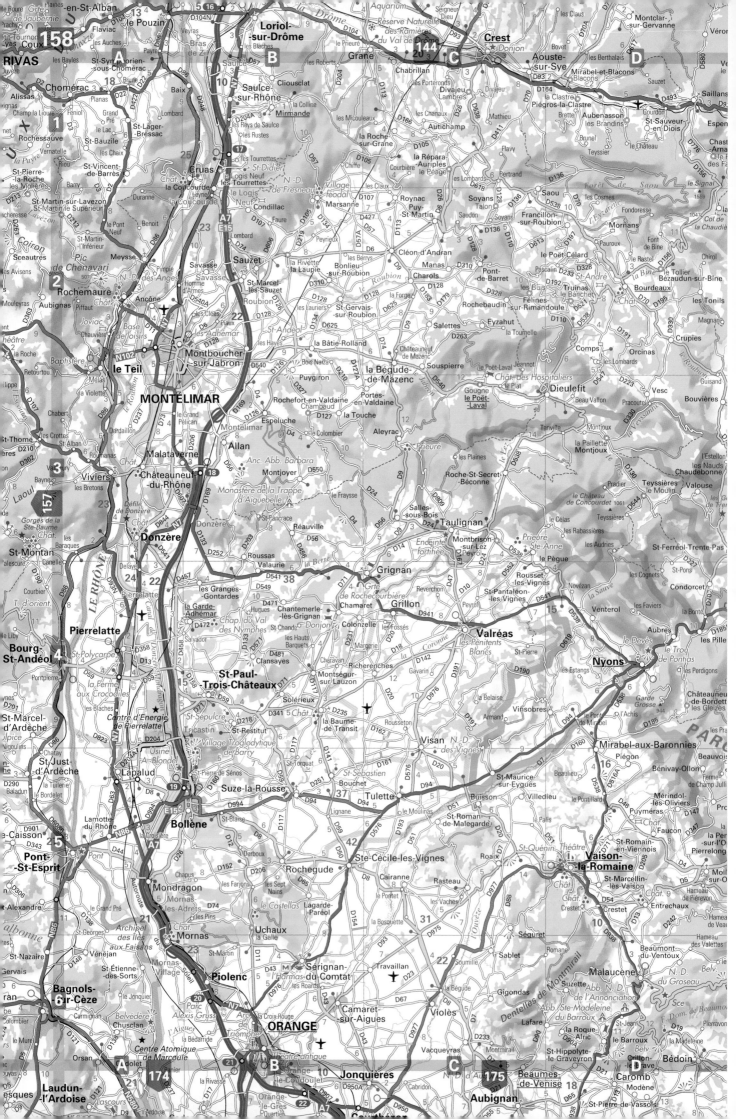

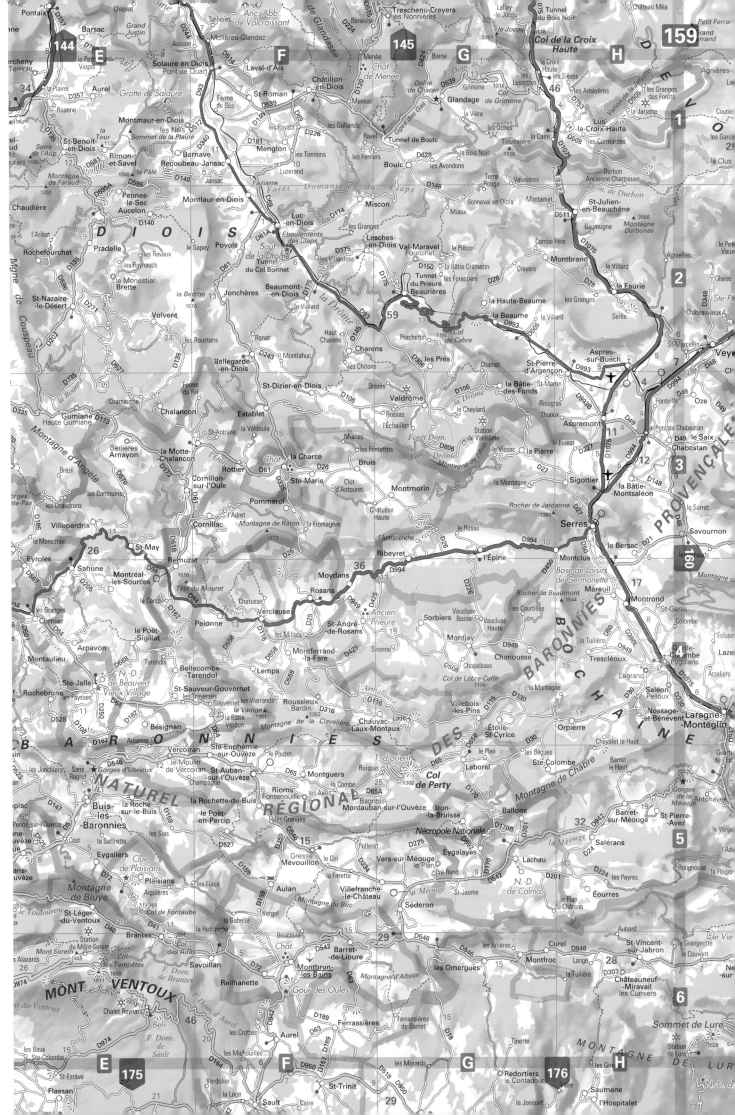

GAP

CHAMPSAUR

la Bâtie-Neuve

Chorges

Sisteron

Château-Arnoux-St-Auban

DIGNE-LES-BAINS

Laragne-Montéglin

Veynes

la Roche-des-Arnauds

Montmaur

Tallard

la Saulce

Monêtier-Allemont

Ventavon

Upaix

le Poët

Mison

Peipin

Volonne

Seyne

St-Martin-lès-Seyne

Selonnet

Montclar

le Grand Puy

la Motte-du-Caire

le Caire

Bayons

Clamensane

Valavoire

Châteaufort

St-Geniez

Authon

Thoard

Barles

Verdaches

Beaujeu

la Javie

le Brusquet

Marcoux

Orcières

Prapic

Réallon

St-Apollinaire

Pontis

le Sauze-du-Lac

Ubaye
Serre-Ponçon

St-Vincent-les-Forts

Gigors

Bréziers

Bellaffaire

Turriers

Faucon-du-Caire

St-Bonnet-en-Champsaur

la Motte-en-Champsaur

Champoléon

St-Michel-de-Chaillol

St-Jean-St-Nicolas

St-Léger-les-Mélèzes

Ancelle

la Fare-en-Champsaur

Poligny

le Noyer

St-Julien-en-Champsaur

Buissard

Forest-St-Julien

Rambaud

Montgardin

Avançon

St-Étienne-le-Laus

Valserres

Remollon

Théus
Espinasses
Rousset

Châteauvieux

Jarjayes

Neffes

Pelleautier

la Freissinouse

Manteyer

St-André

Sigoyer

Esparron

Barcillonnette

Lardier-et-Valença

Vitrolles

Curbans

Venterol

Piégut

Rochebrune

Lettret

Châteauneuf-d'Oze

Oze

St-Auban-d'Oze

Furmeyer

Laye

Station de Laye

Chaudun

Pic de Bure

Observatoire du Plateau de Bure

Superdévoluy

Col du Festre

St-Étienne-en-Dévoluy

Dévoluy

Agnières-en-Dévoluy

Lachaup

Mison
les Armands

Val Buëch-Méouge
Ribiers

Ventavon

Claret

Sigoyer

Thèze

Vaumeilh

Nibles

Valernes

Salignac

Sourribes

Entrepierres

Vilhosc

St-Symphorien

le Castellard-Mélan

Hautes-Duyes
St-Estève

la Robine-sur-Galabre

Champtercier

Bevons

Noyers-sur-Jabron

Valbelle
les Richaud

Aubignosc

Châteauneuf-Val-St-Donat

l'Escale

Barras

Sommet du Ruth

Montagne de Lure

Pierre Écrite

Défilé de la Pierre Écrite

Citadelle

N.-D. des Pommiers

les Monges

Montagne de Jouère

Clues de Verdaches

Clues de Barles

Site de l'Ichtyosaure

Centre Géologique de St-Benoît

A51

Route Napoléon

Durance

D900

D994

D942

D1085

D4

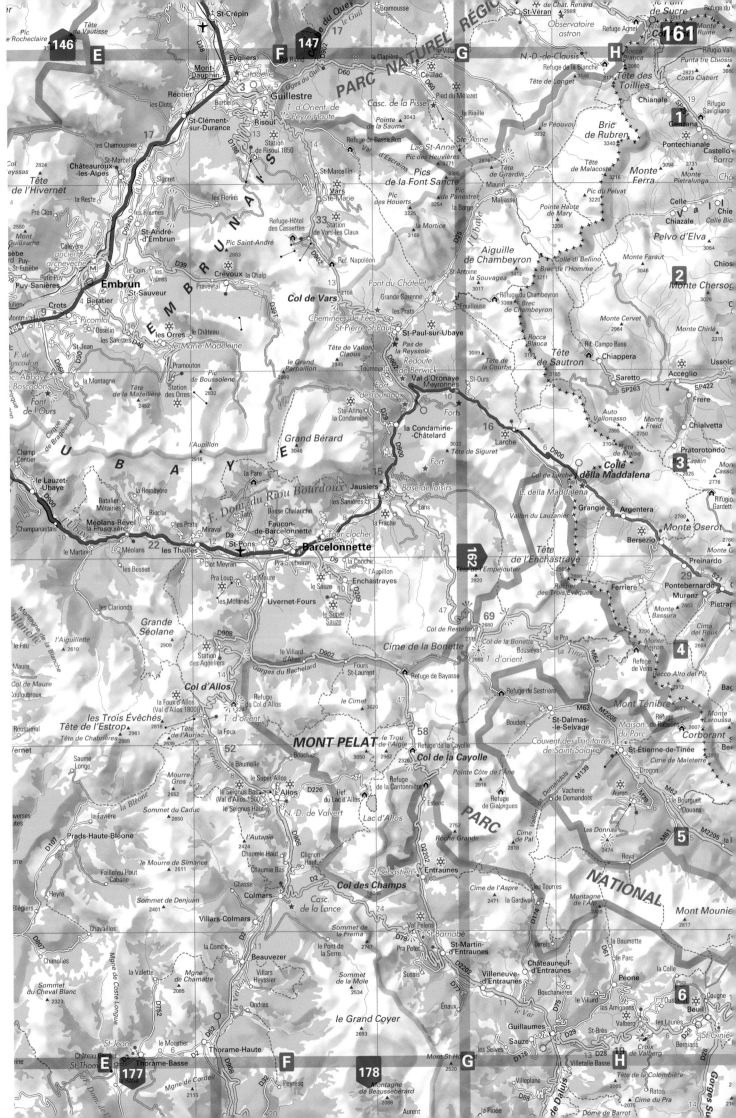

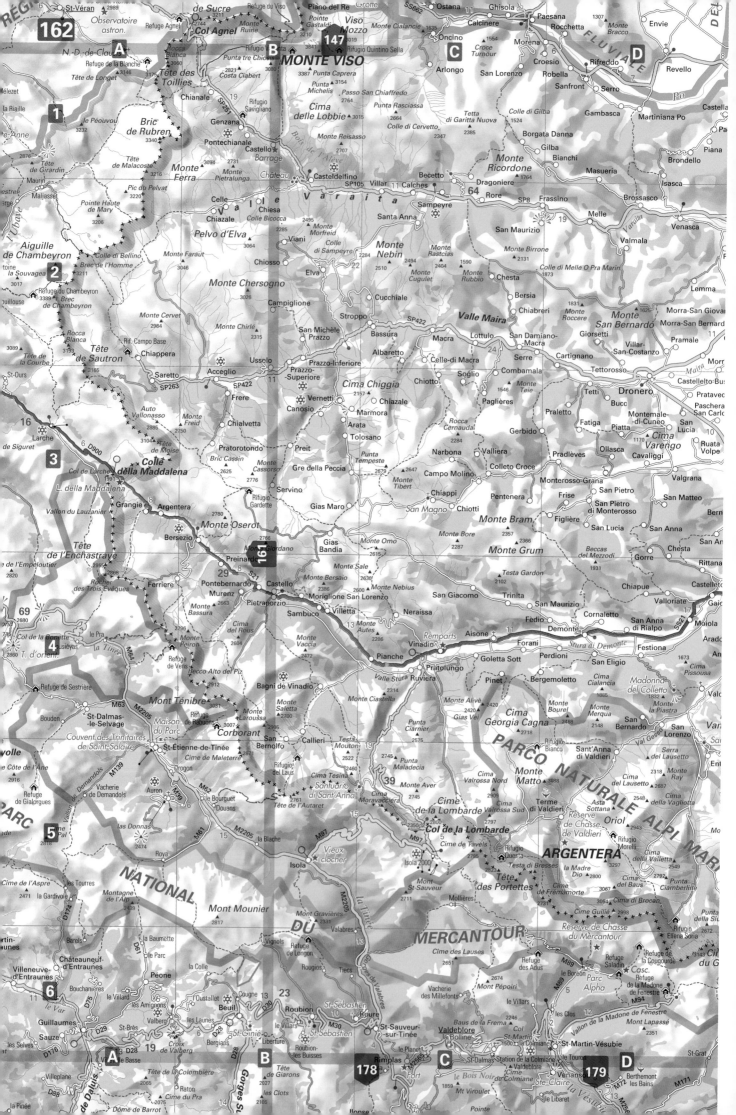

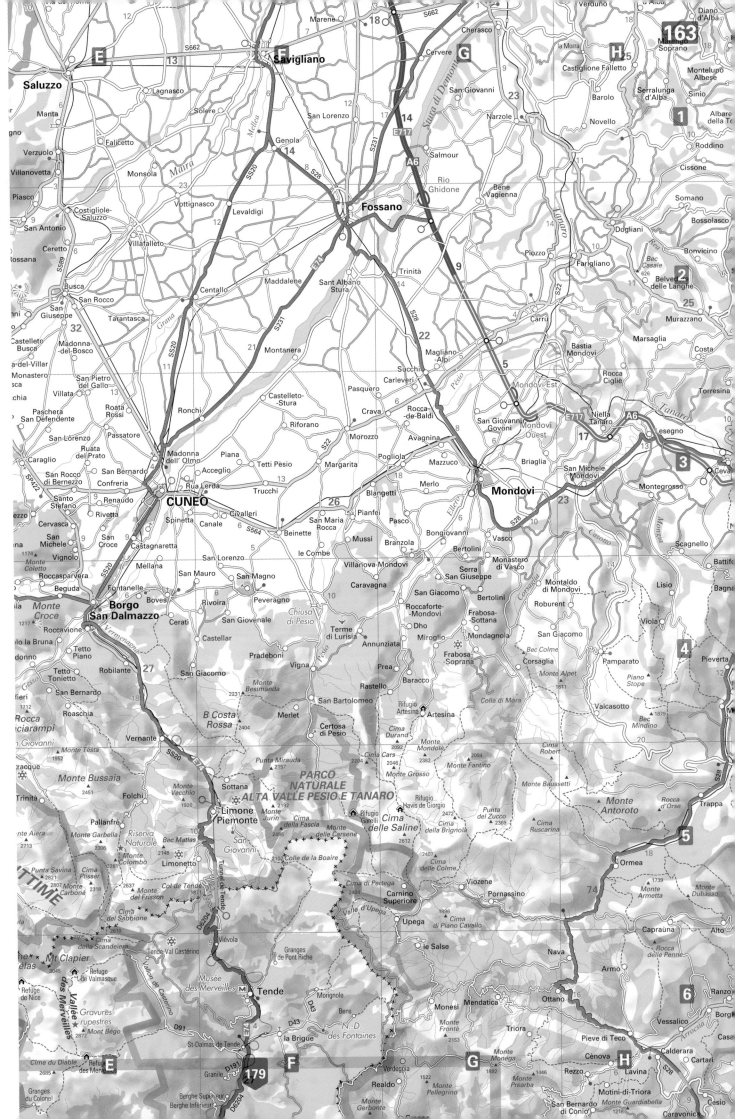

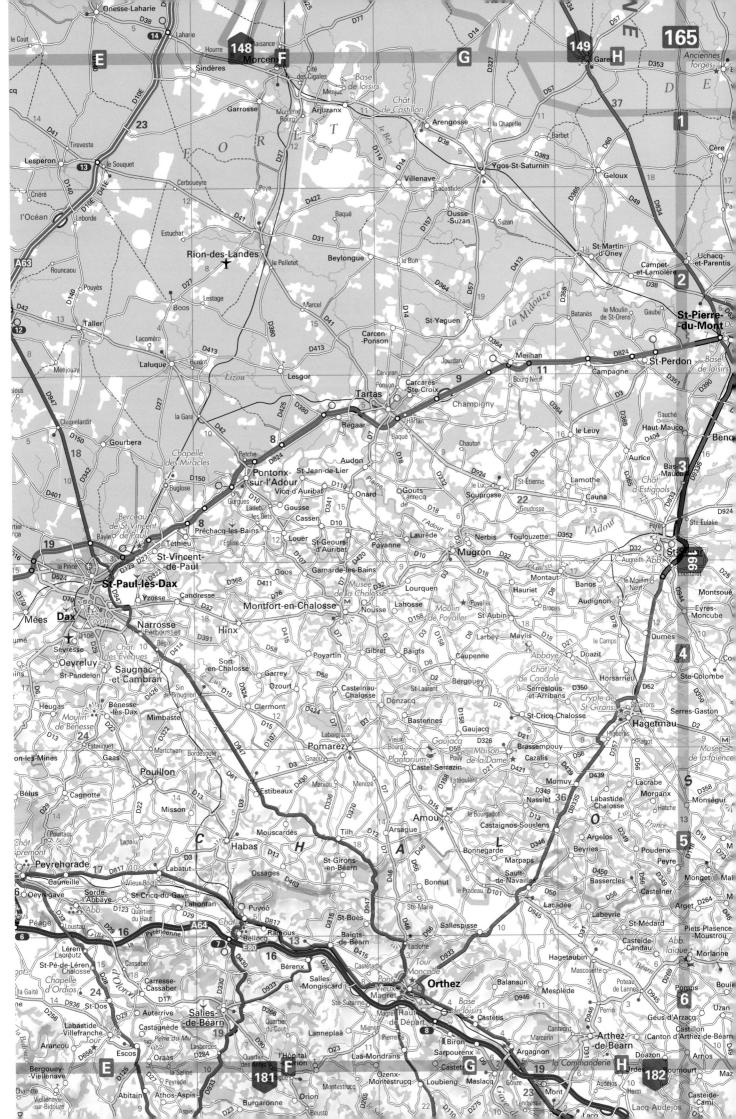

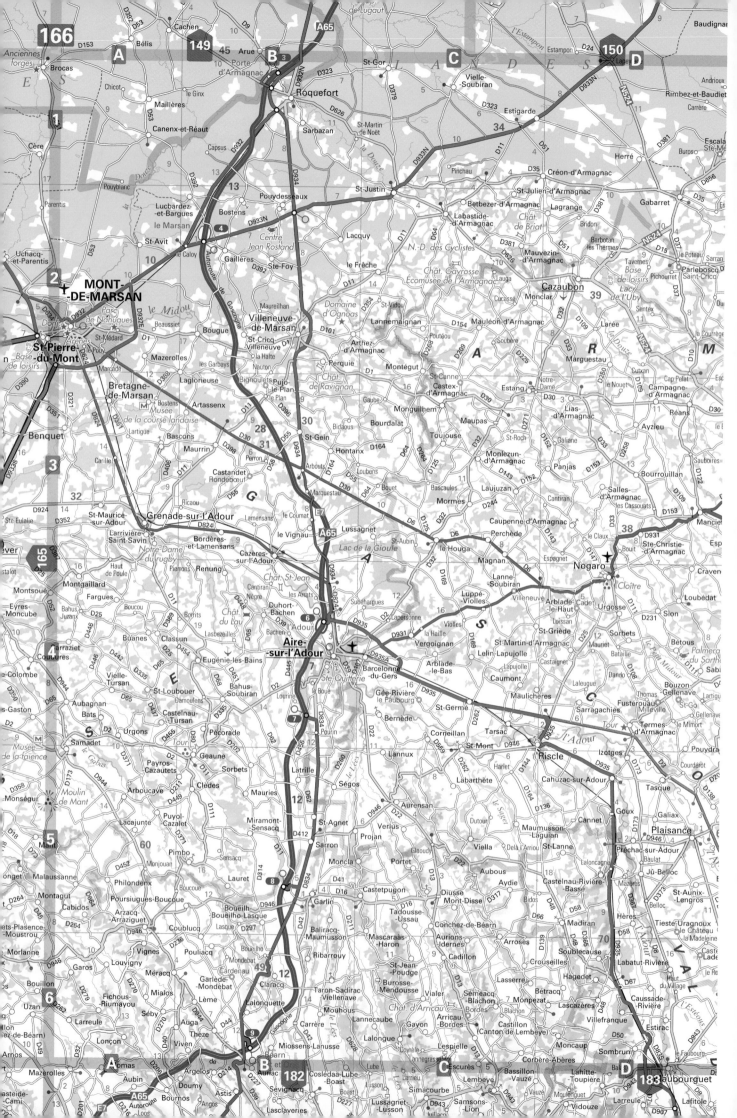

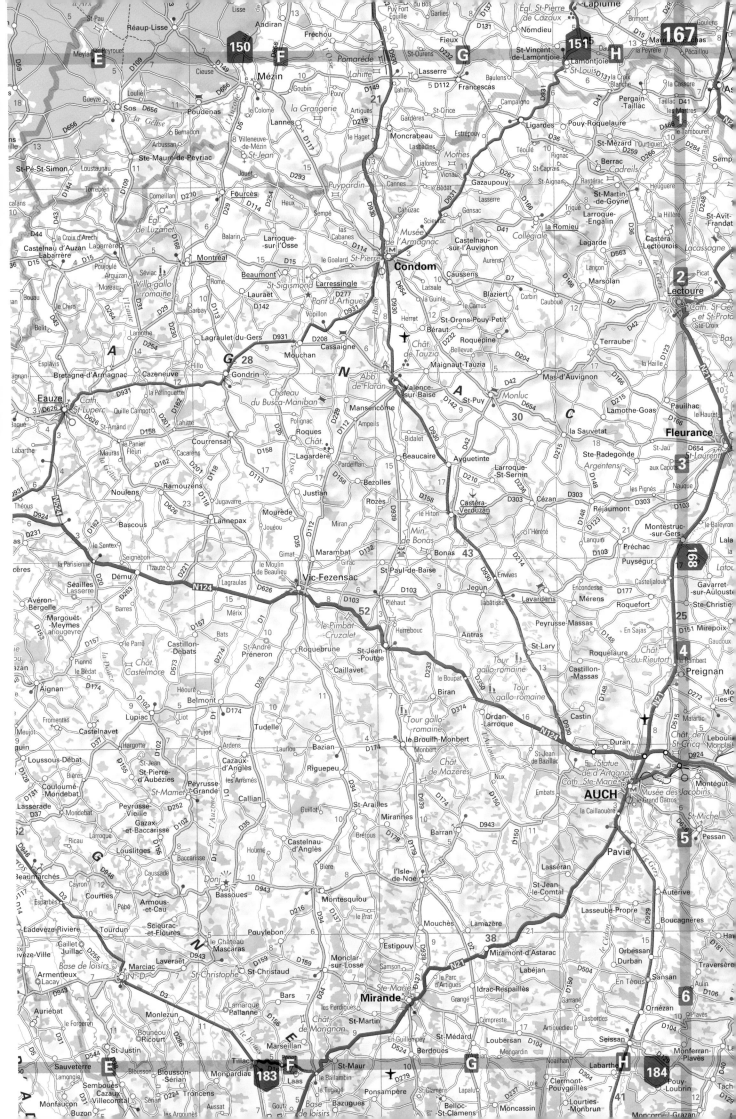

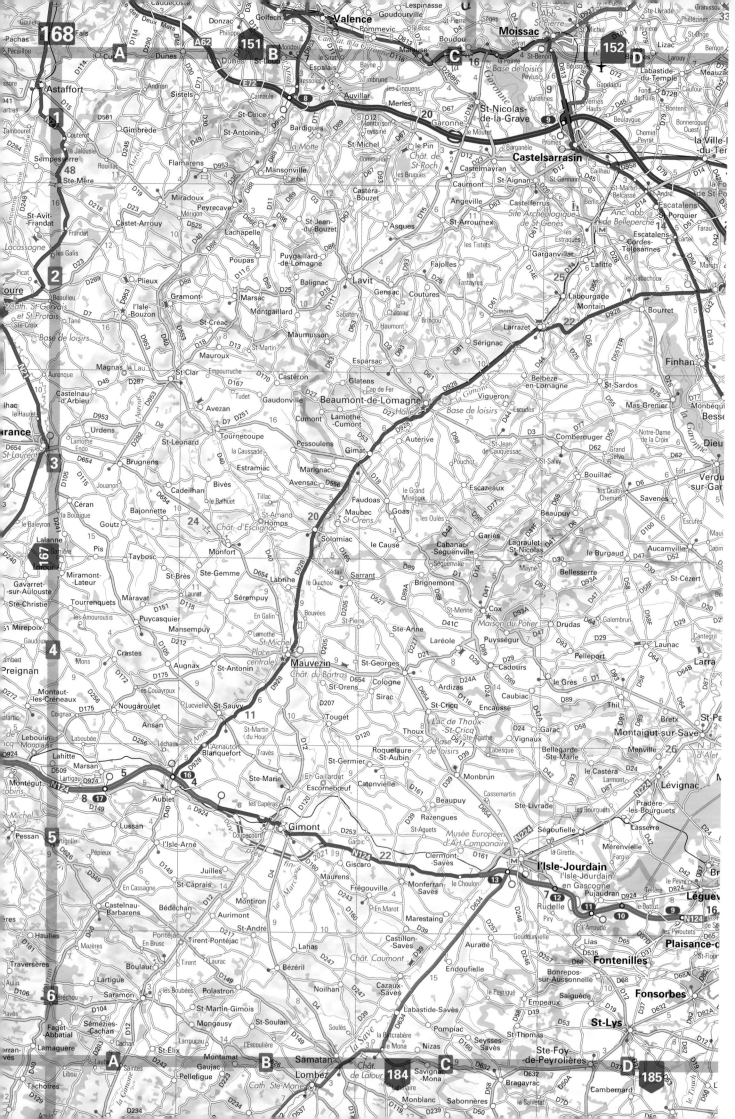

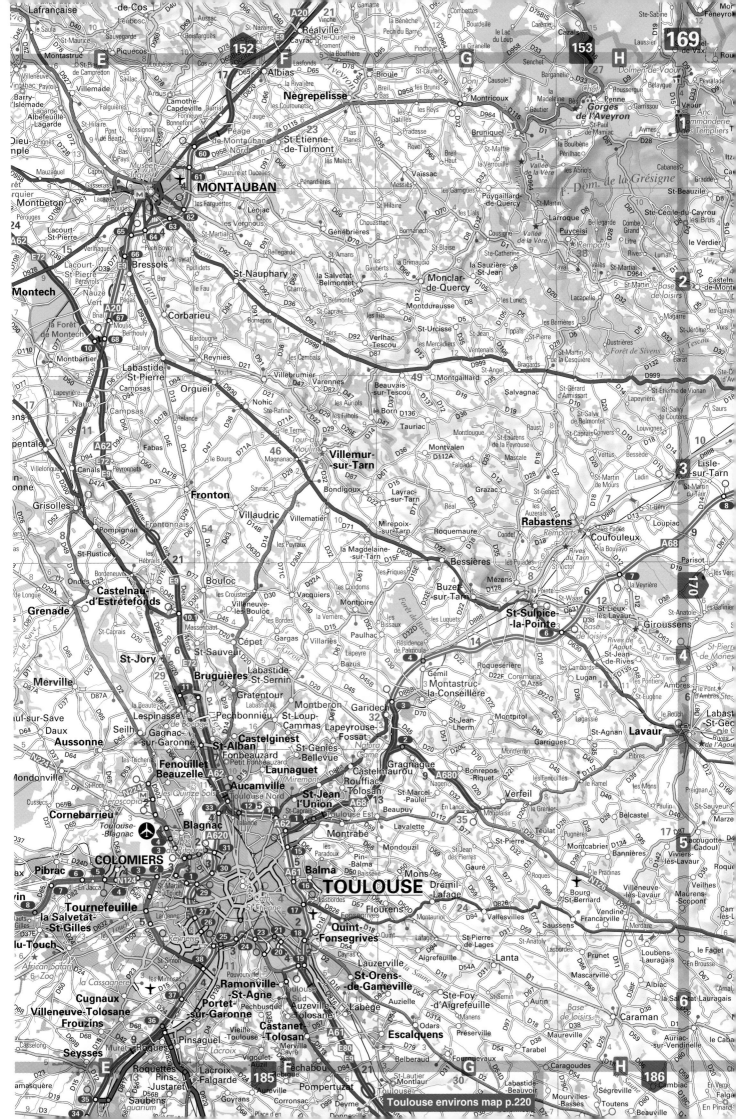

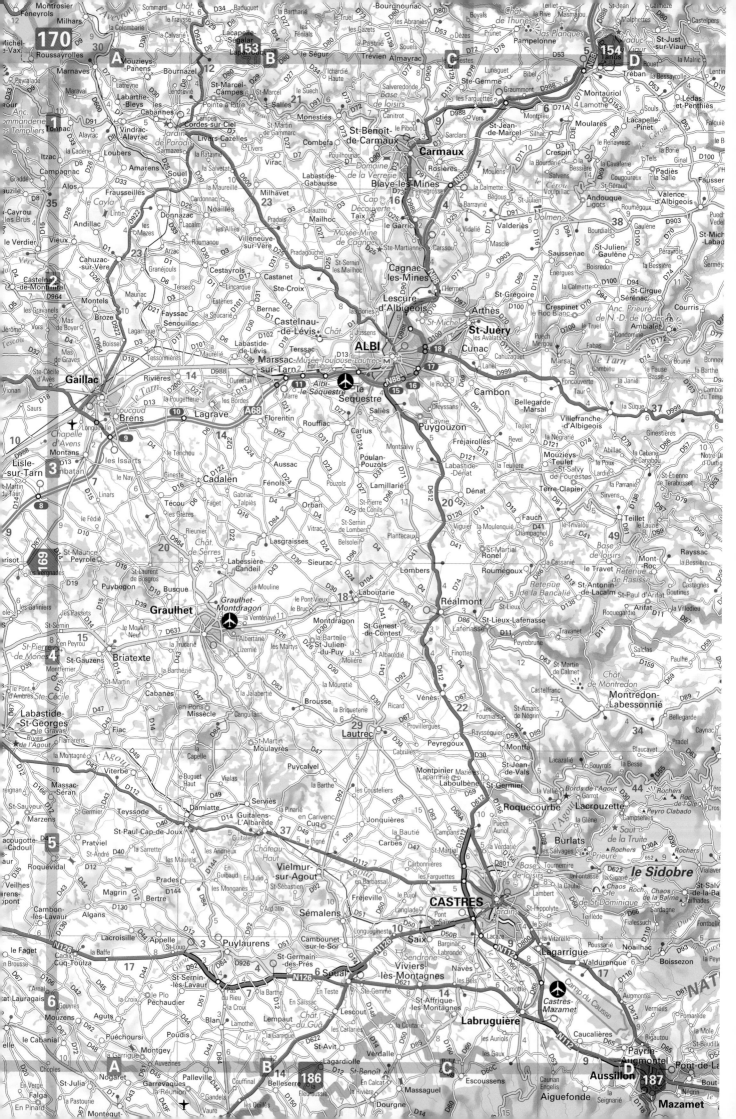

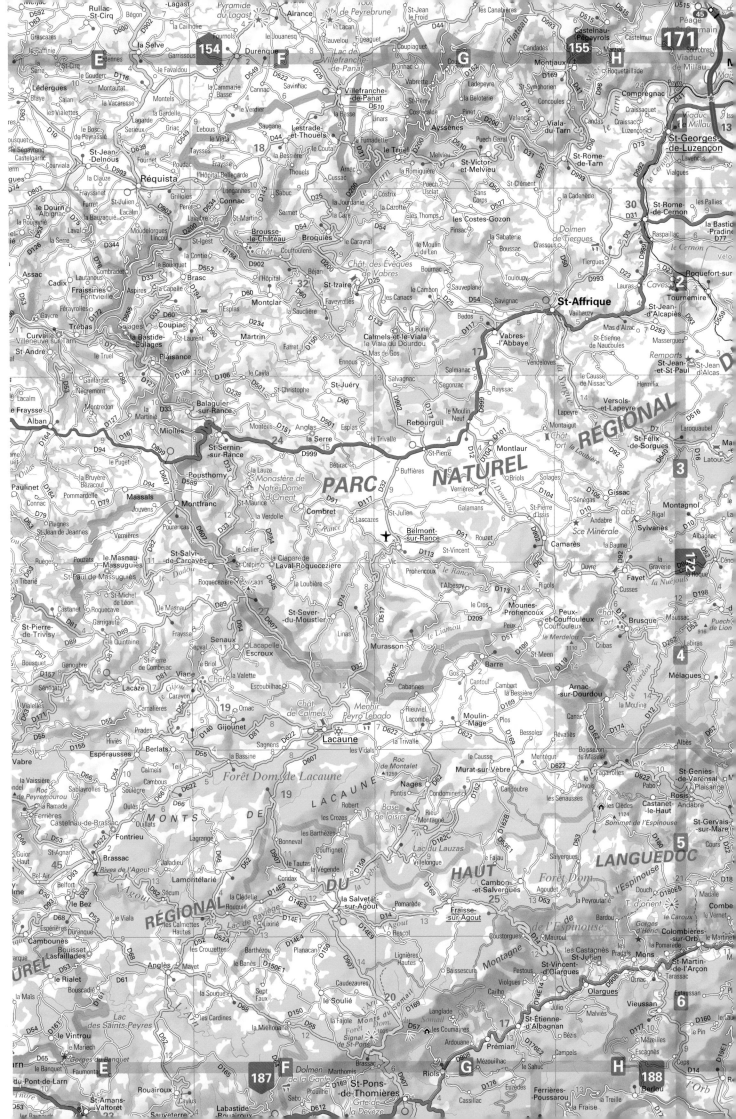

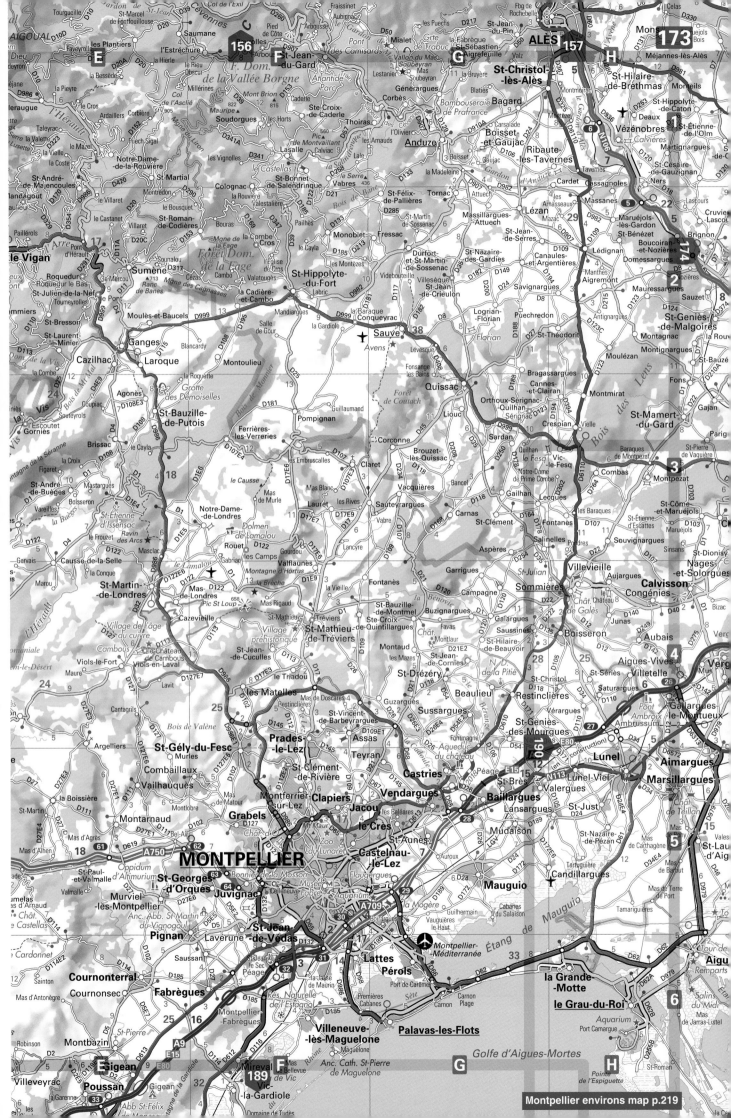

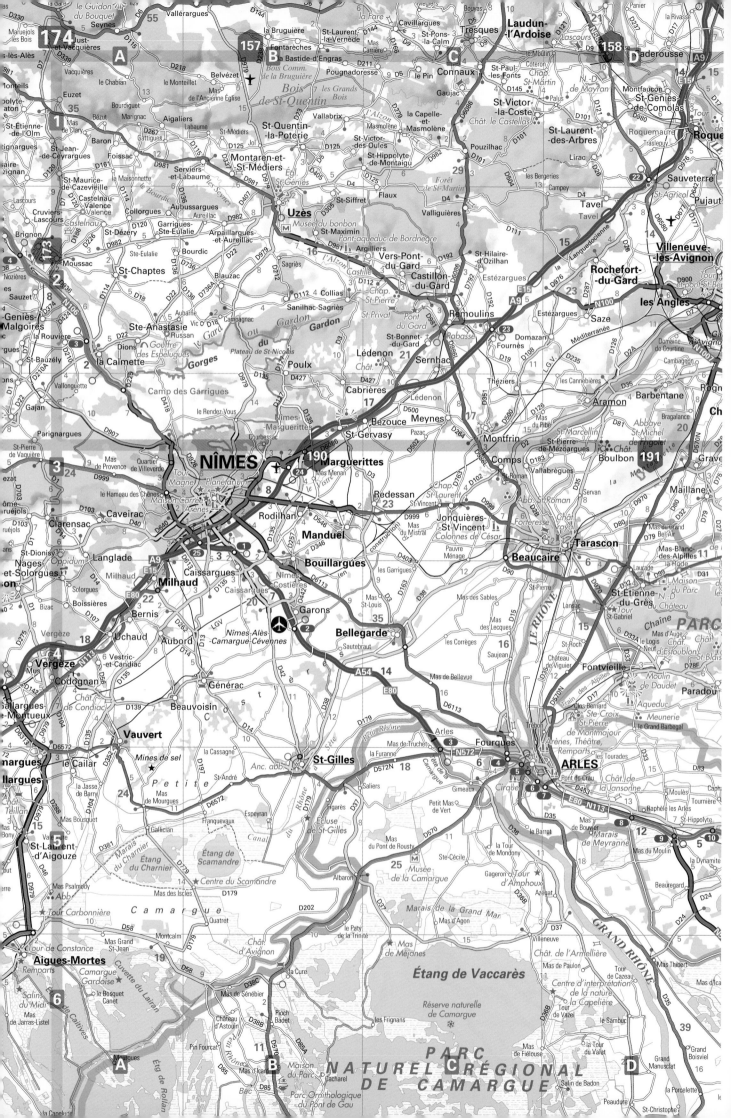

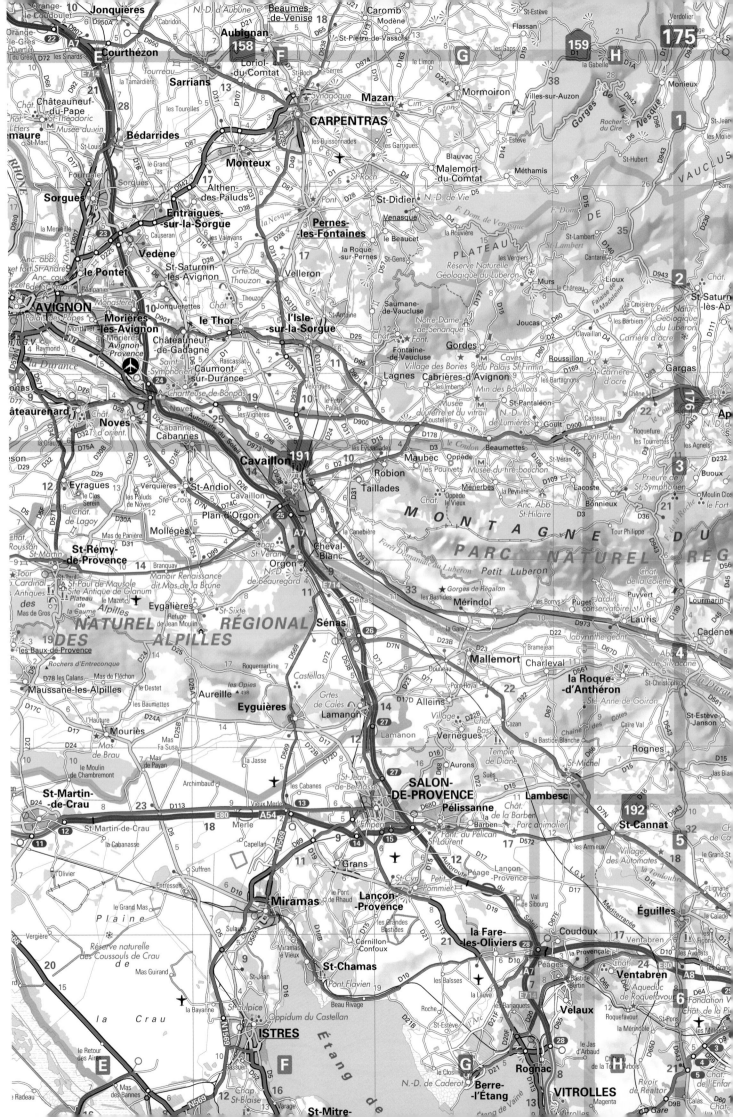

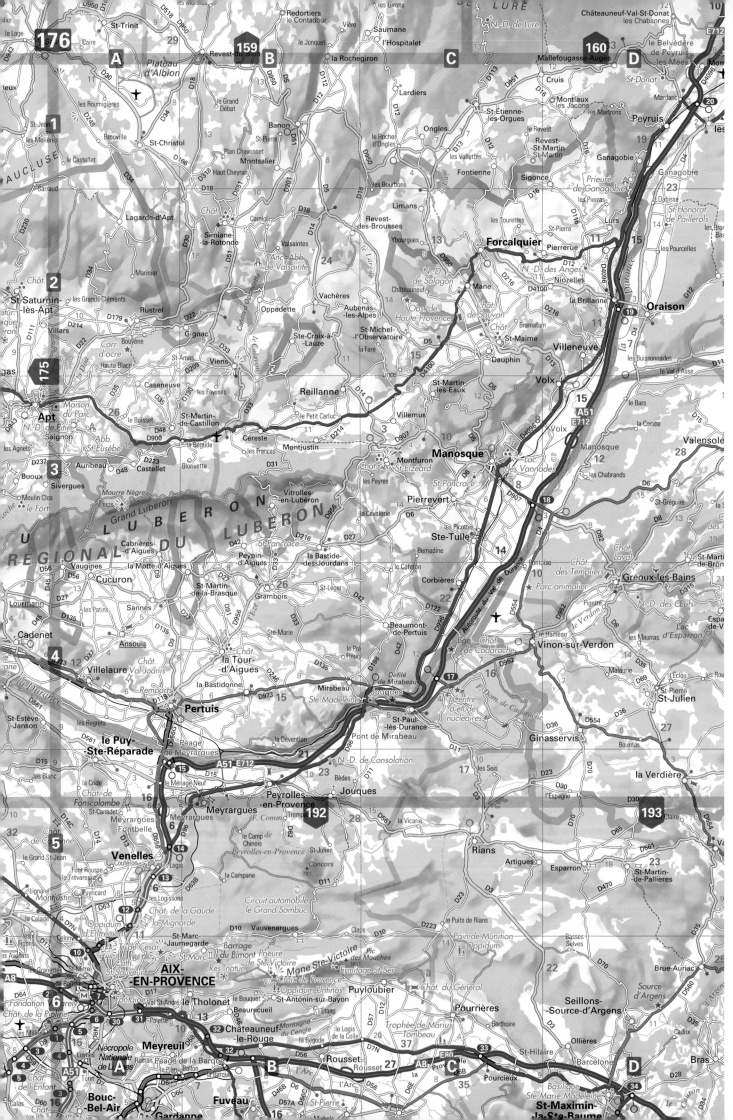

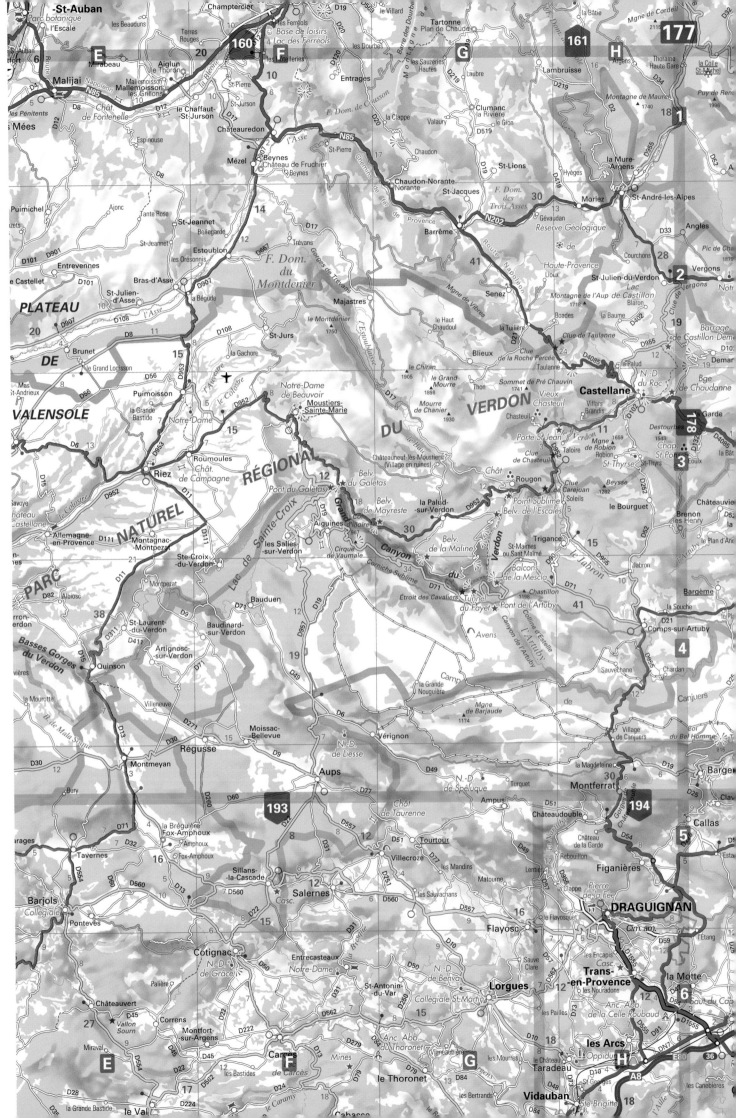

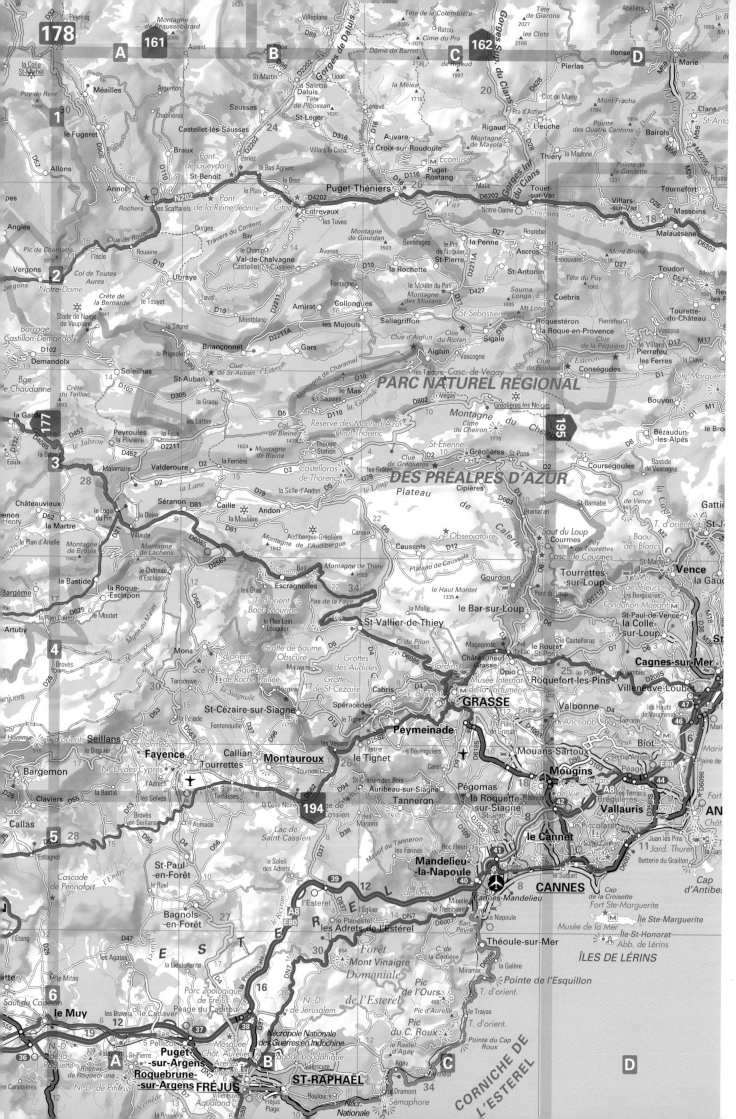

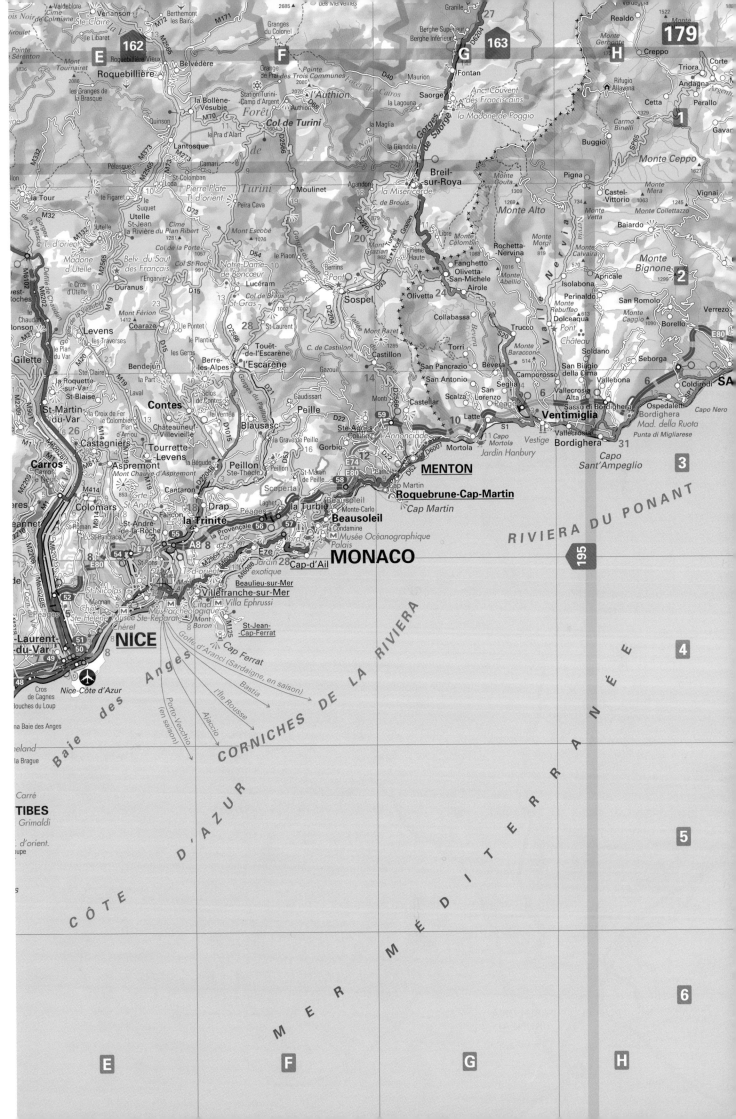

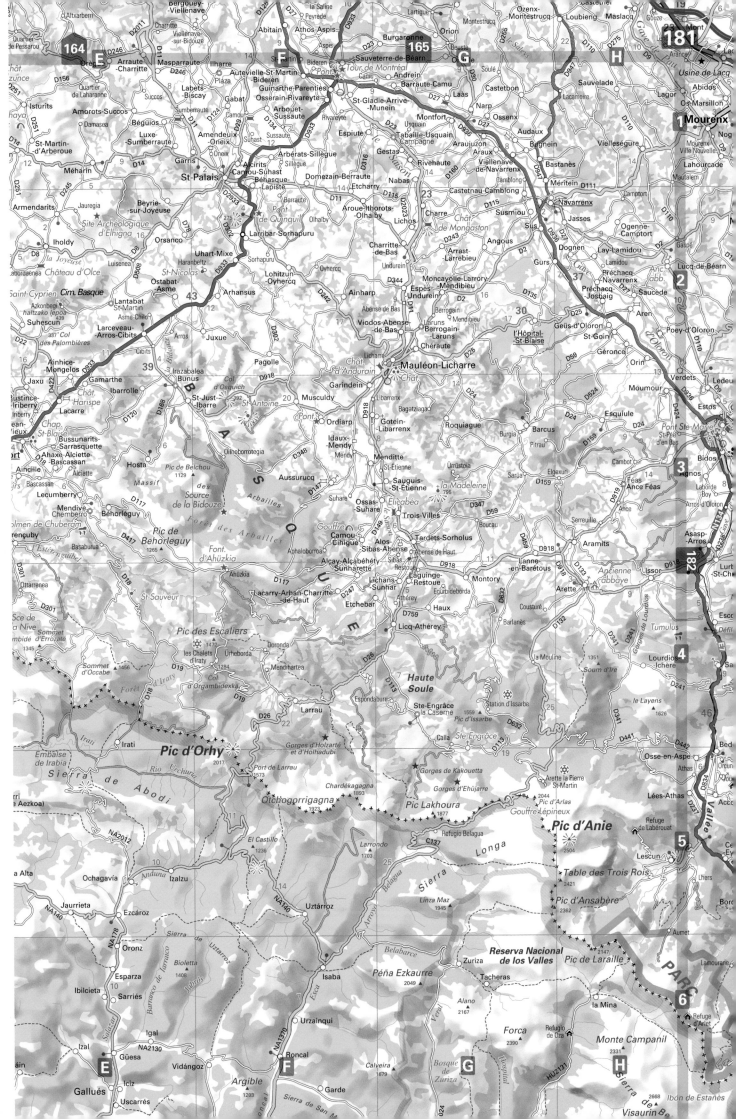

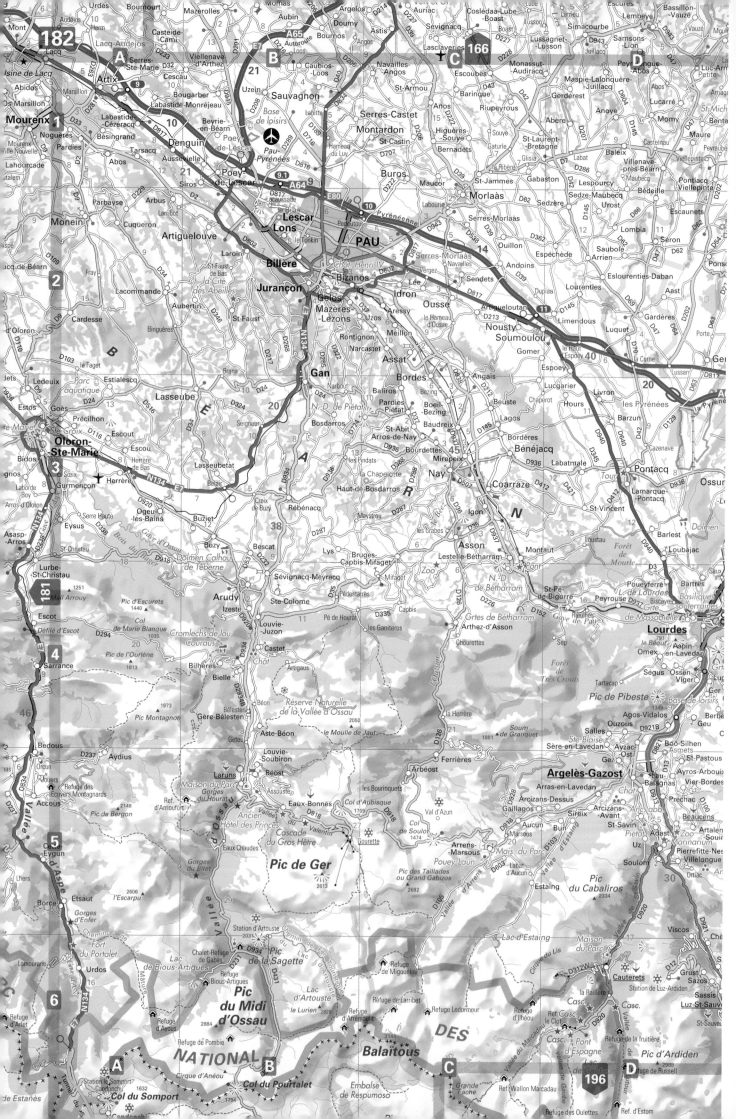

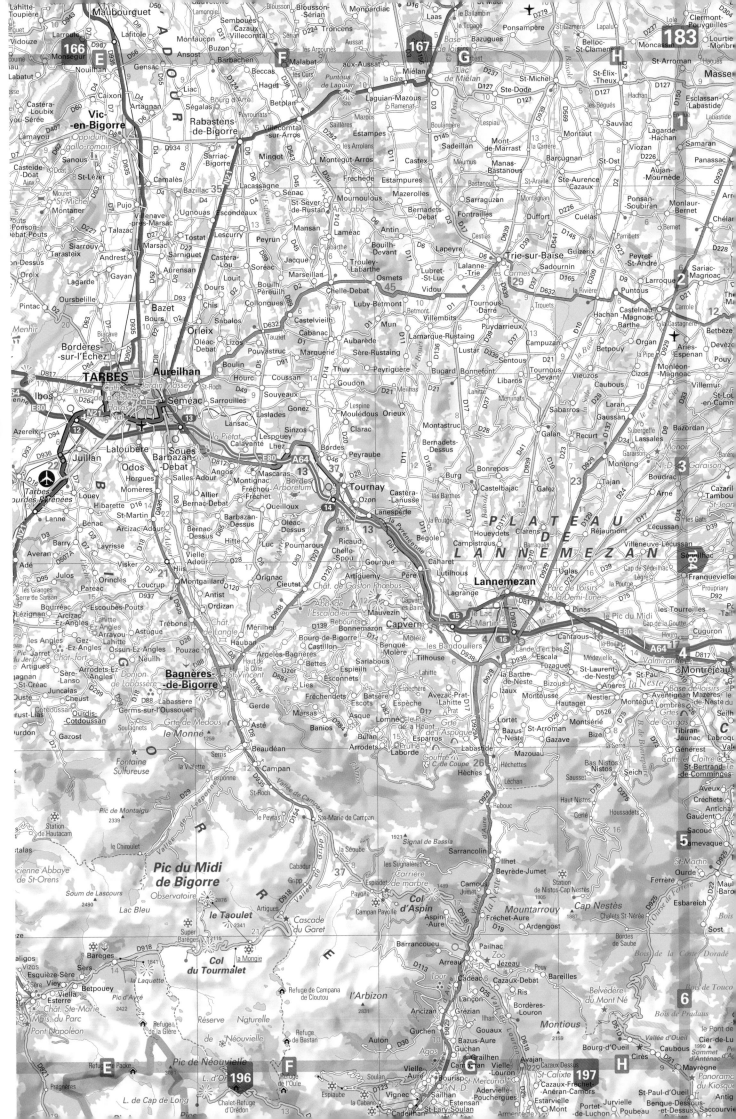

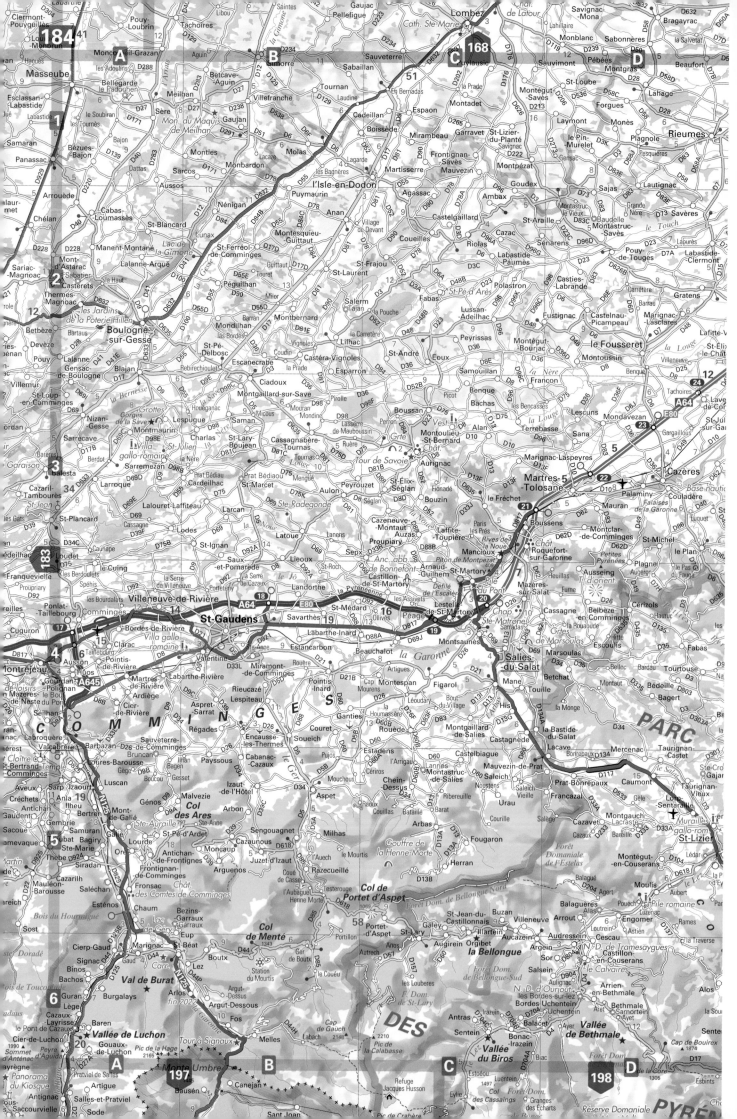

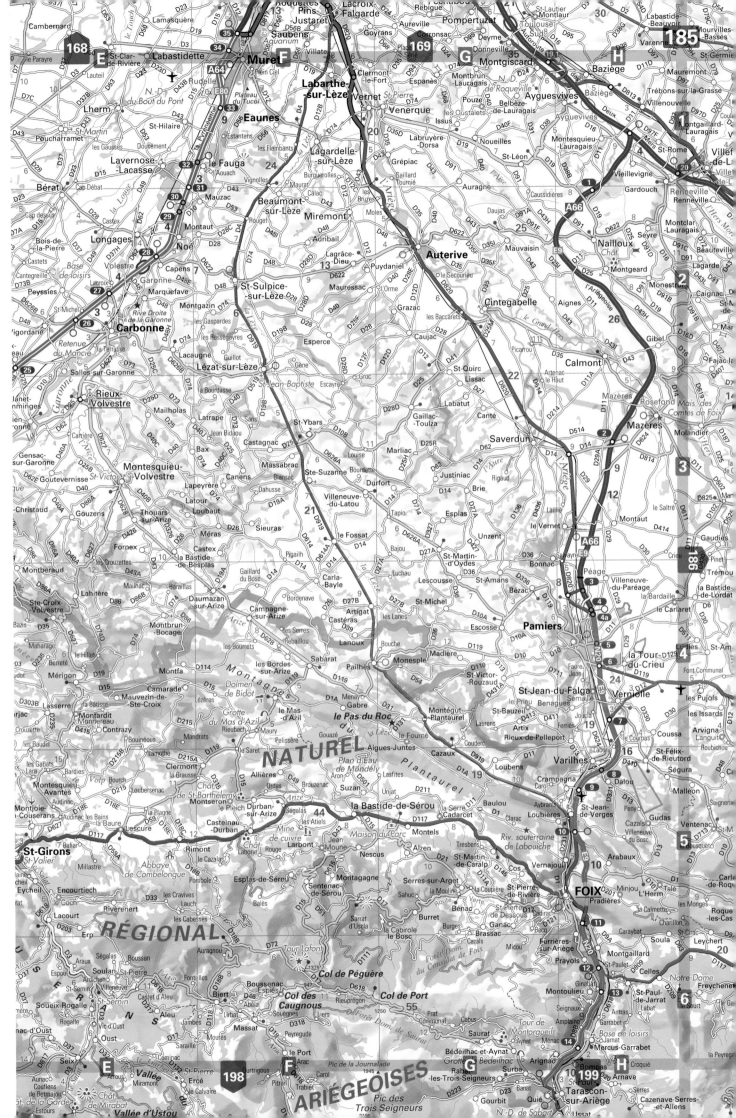

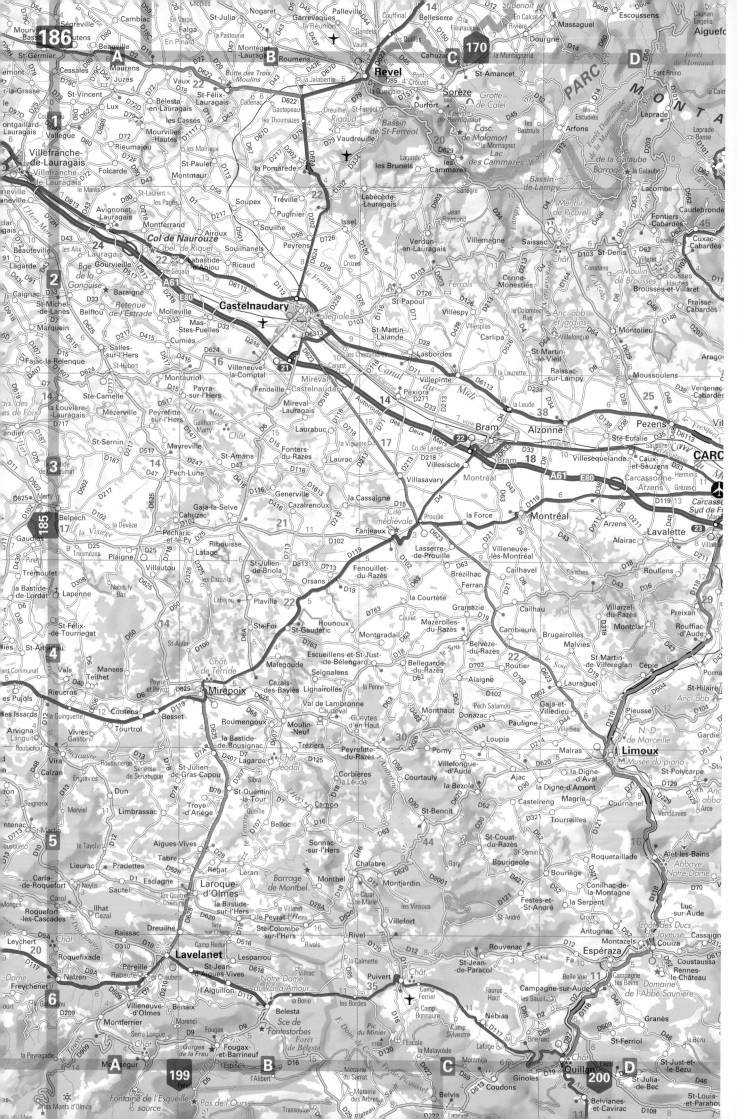

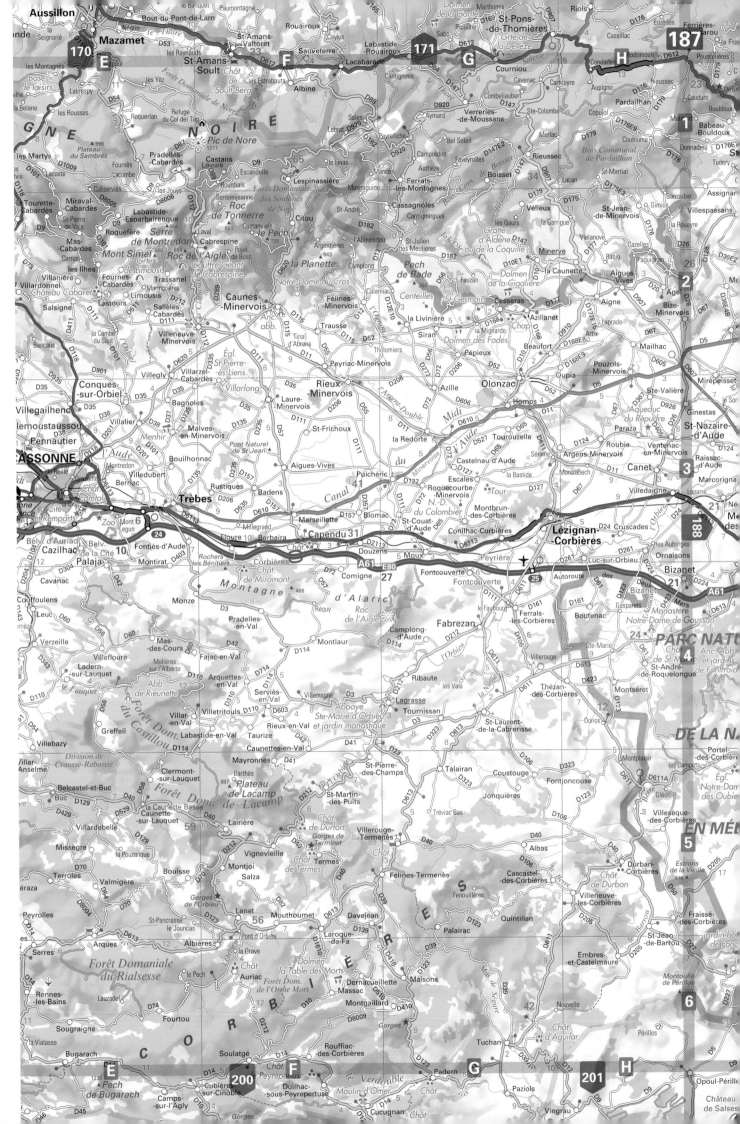

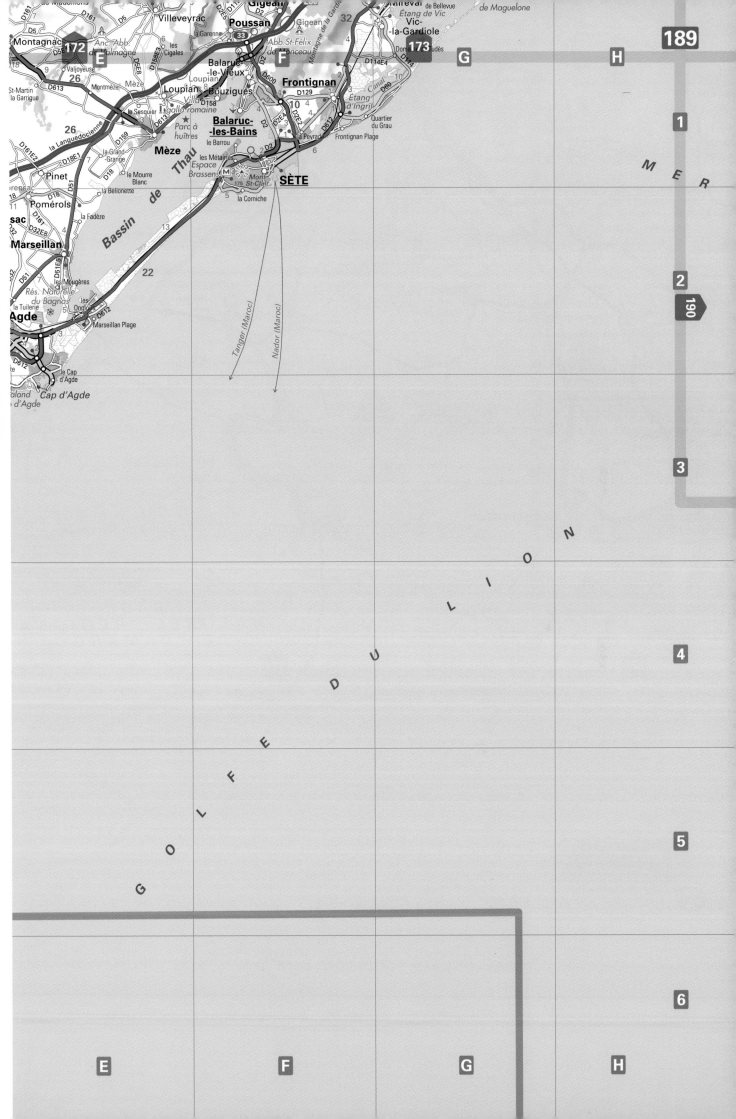

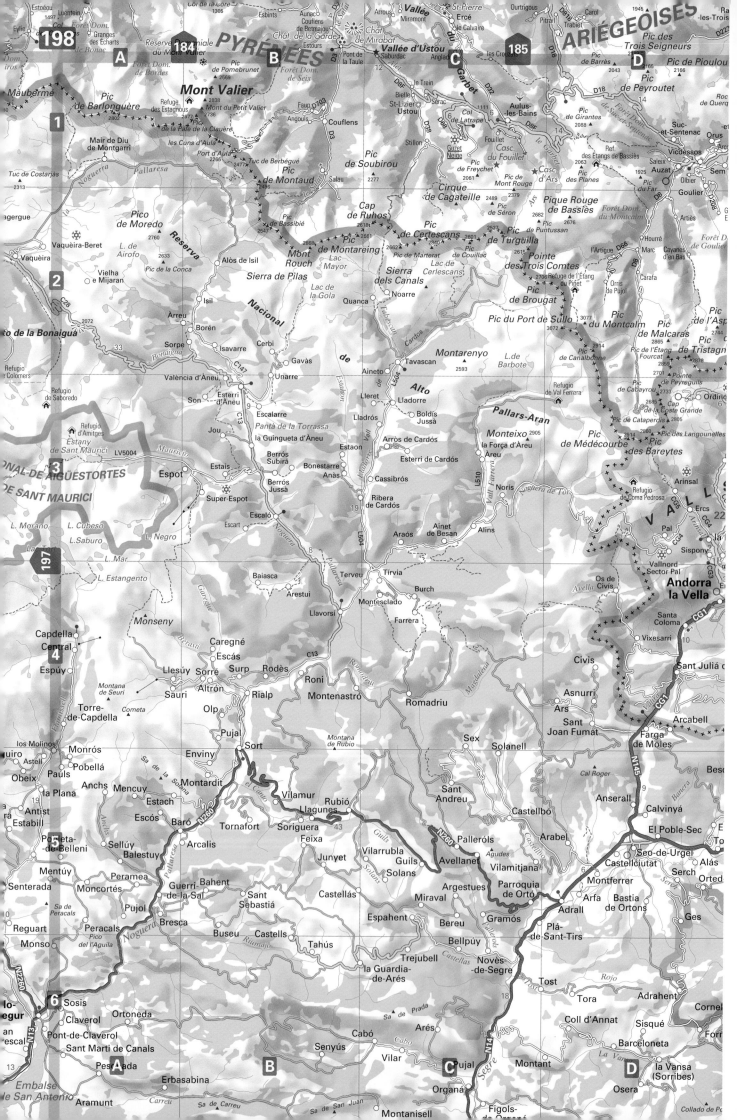

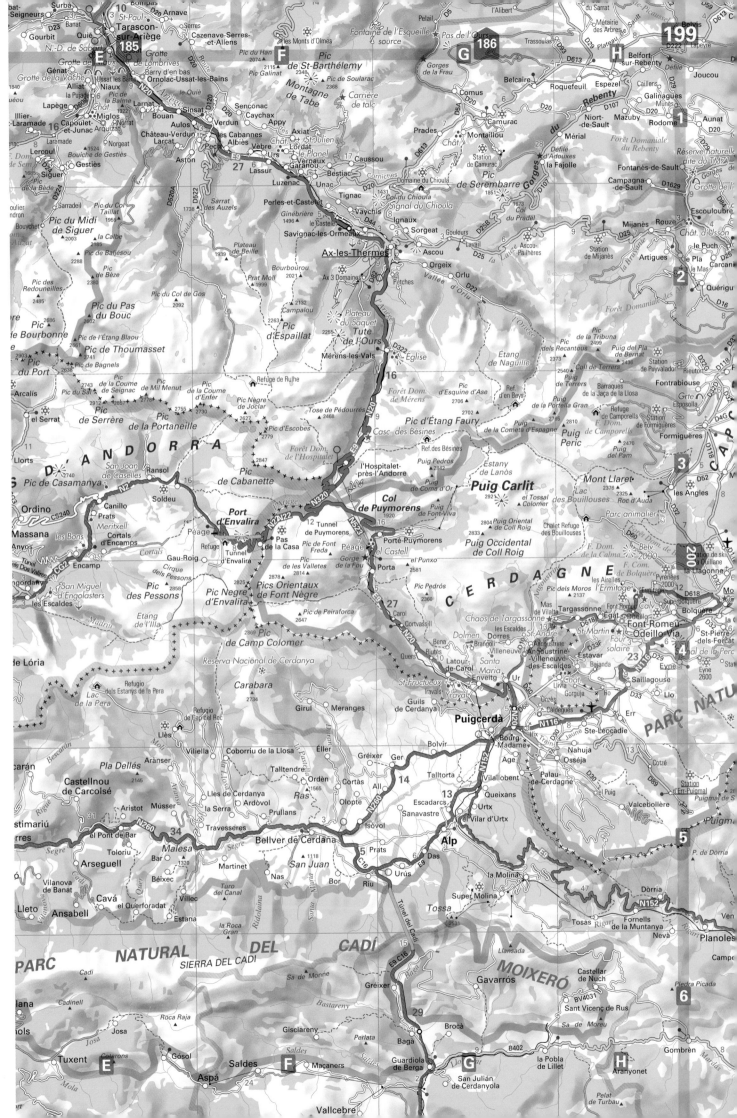

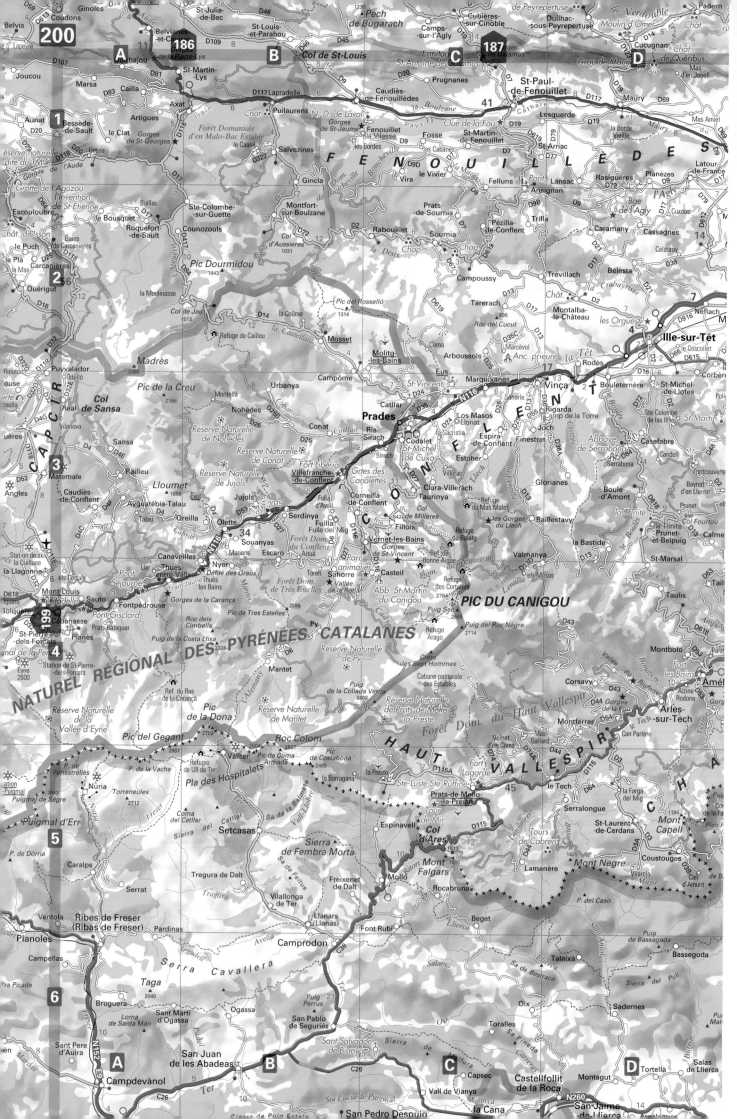

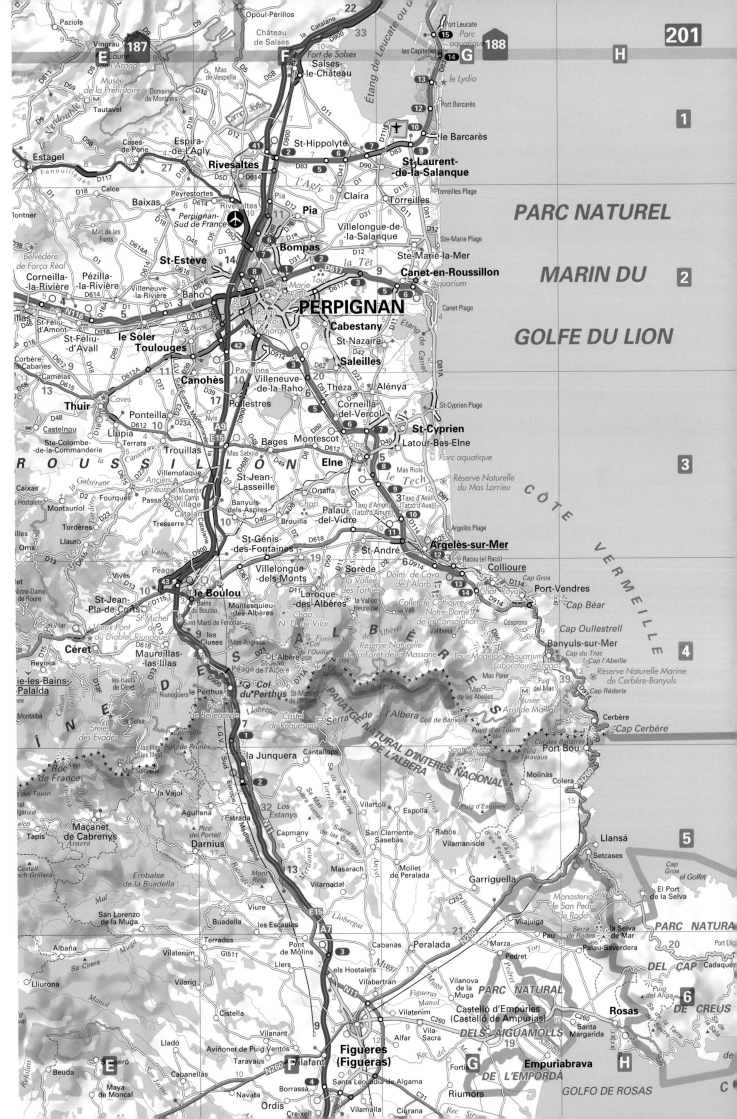

A   B   C   D

1

2

PARC NATUREL MARIN DU CAP CORSE

3

4

Marseille

Toulon (en saison)

Nice

Savone (Italie, en saison)

Livourne (Italie, en saison)

Punta di l'Acciolu

Tour

Ogliast

T30
9

Phare de la Pietra   l'Île-   Tour   Tour
Rousse   de Saleccia   Losari

Losari

D513   D113   D363   304   Monte Négru

Punta di Vallitone   D63   Parc botanique   Monte Négru
Marine de Davia   20   Monticello
Punta di Varcale   Collegiale   Occiglioni   D63   8   T301
Corbara   Santa-Reparata   -di-Balagna
Marine   Algajola   11   Citadelle   D15   de Còrbara   Pigna   Couvent
de Sant'Ambrogio   10   Sant'Antonino   D113   Belgodère   D185   Palasca
Punta Spano   Tour   D71   D551   Aregno   Costa   D63   D71   Tocconi
Tour   7   Lumio   D413   Couvent de Tuani
la Revellata   Punta   Lavatoggio   8   Occhiatana   D963   D301   7
Caldanu   Bocca   509   D13   Cateri   Ville-di-Paraso
Grotte   Citadelle   San Petru   di Salvi   Avapessa   31   Speloncato   5
des Veaux Marins   D81B   Golfe   T30   D151   D71   9   Nessa   17   D63   Pioggiola
Calvi   de Calvi   10   B   A   L   A   G   N   E   D963   Olmi Cappella
1   San Raineru   17   D663   Feliceto   D63
N.-D.   D151   D451   Muro   Vallic
de la Serra   Petra   8   Cassano   San Parteo   D963
Maio   Montemàggiore   Zilia   1680   Mausoléo
Punta di Cantaleli   Montegrosso   Anc. Couvent   Monte
725   Priugio   d'Alzi Pratu   Grosso
Capo Cavallo   Sémaphore   15   Calvi-   9   Santa Restitua   1937   Monte Padru
295   -Sainte-Catherine   Moncale   Calenzana   2393
Torre Truccia   D81B   7   Tarazone   Capu   Cima
801   Monte   a u Dente   di a Statoghia
Truccia   Suare   D251   la Figarella   2029   2304
30   Torre   Cintu   2143   Asco   Gorge
Mozza   27   D81   Refuge   Monte Corona   Capu   2145   Pont génois
Capu di a Mursetta   l'Argentella   Chaos de   Ladroncellu   13
B   Pieve   C   Bocca Rezza   Cirque   D
15   Capu   16   Amacu   Frassigna   de Bonifatu
di l'Argentella   Refuge
Punta di Ciuttone

A   204   B   C   D

6

A

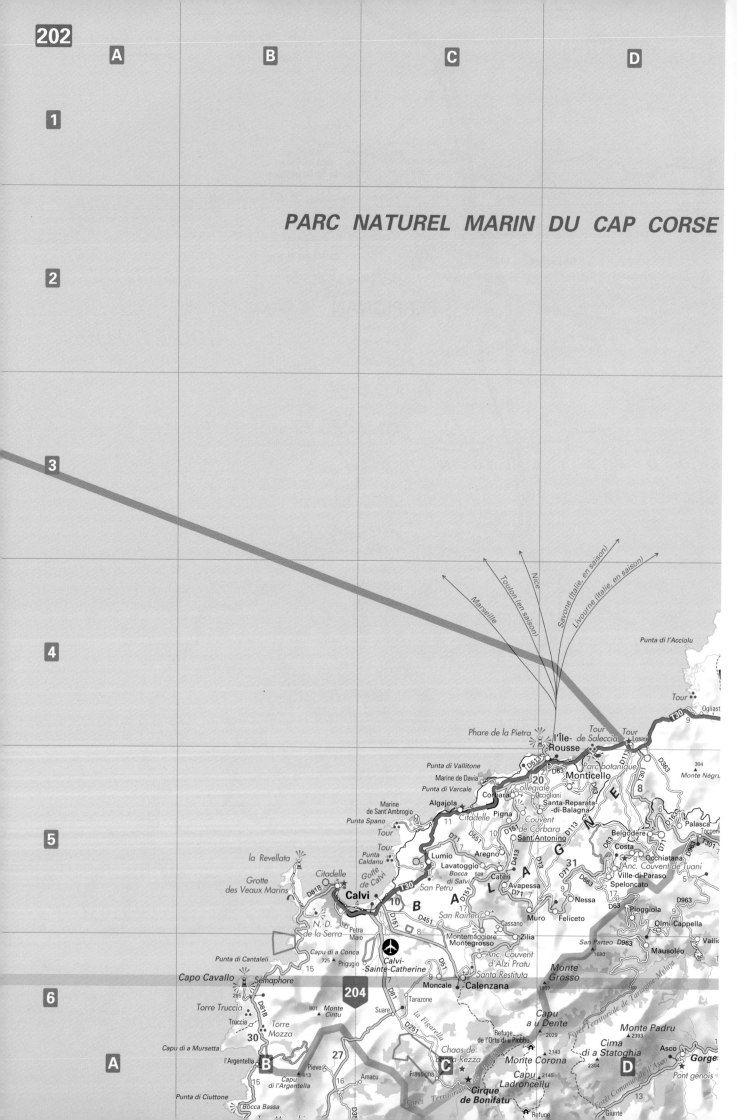

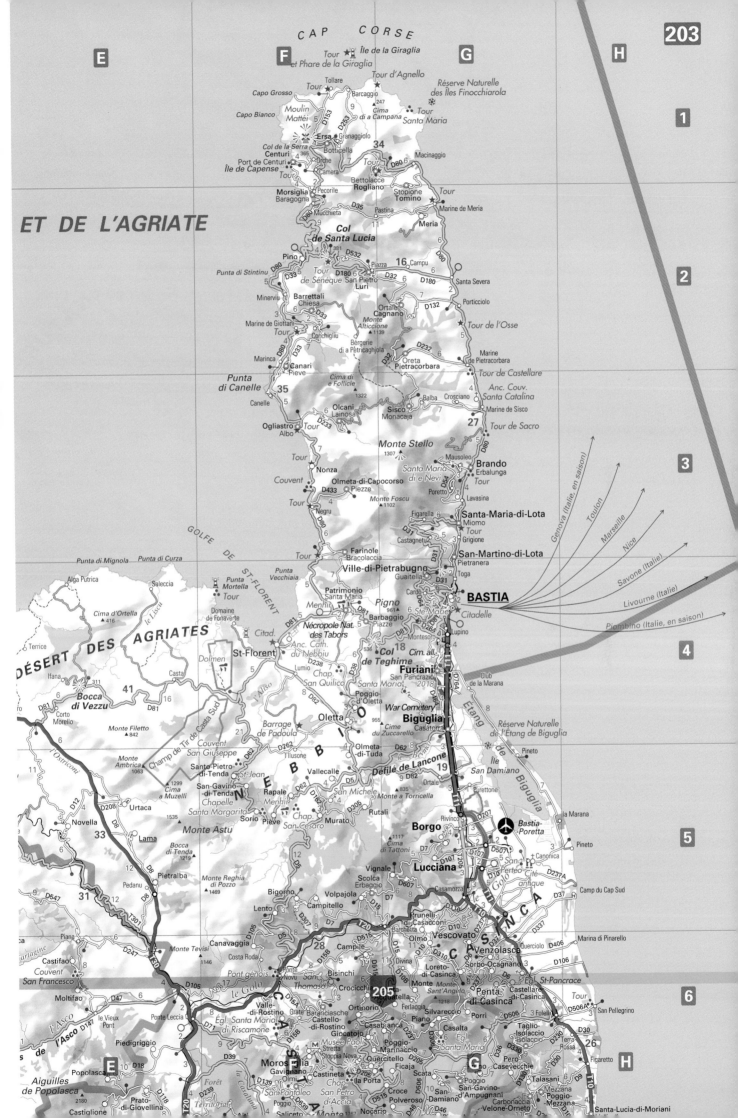

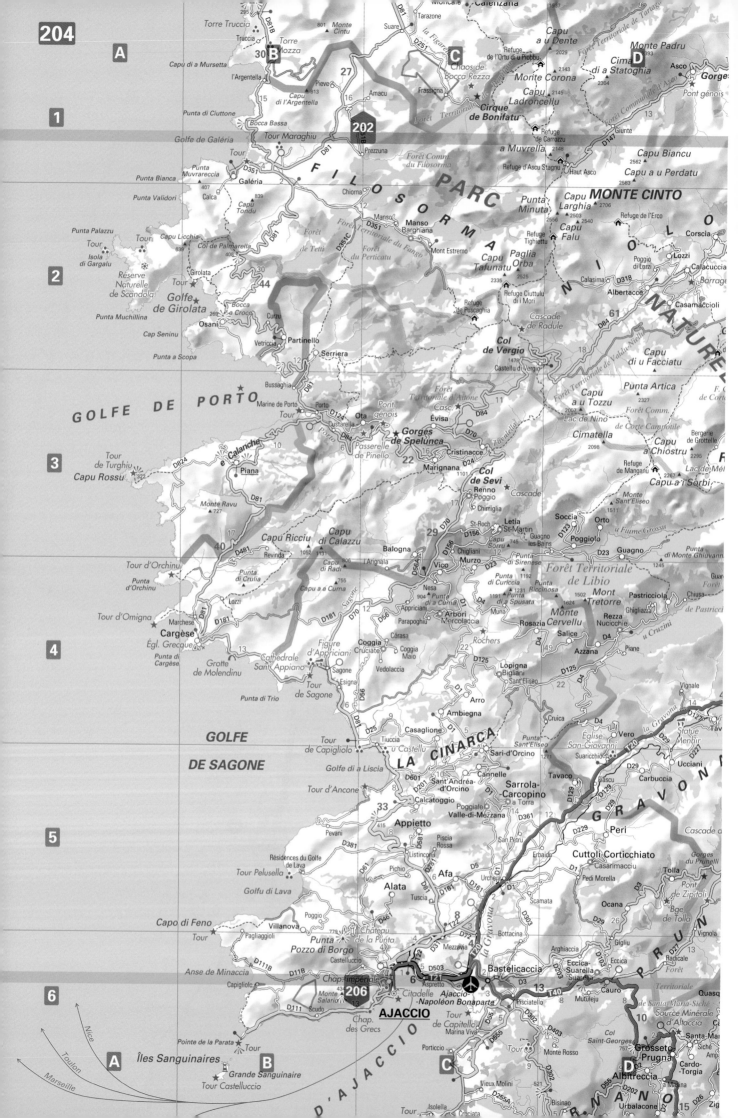

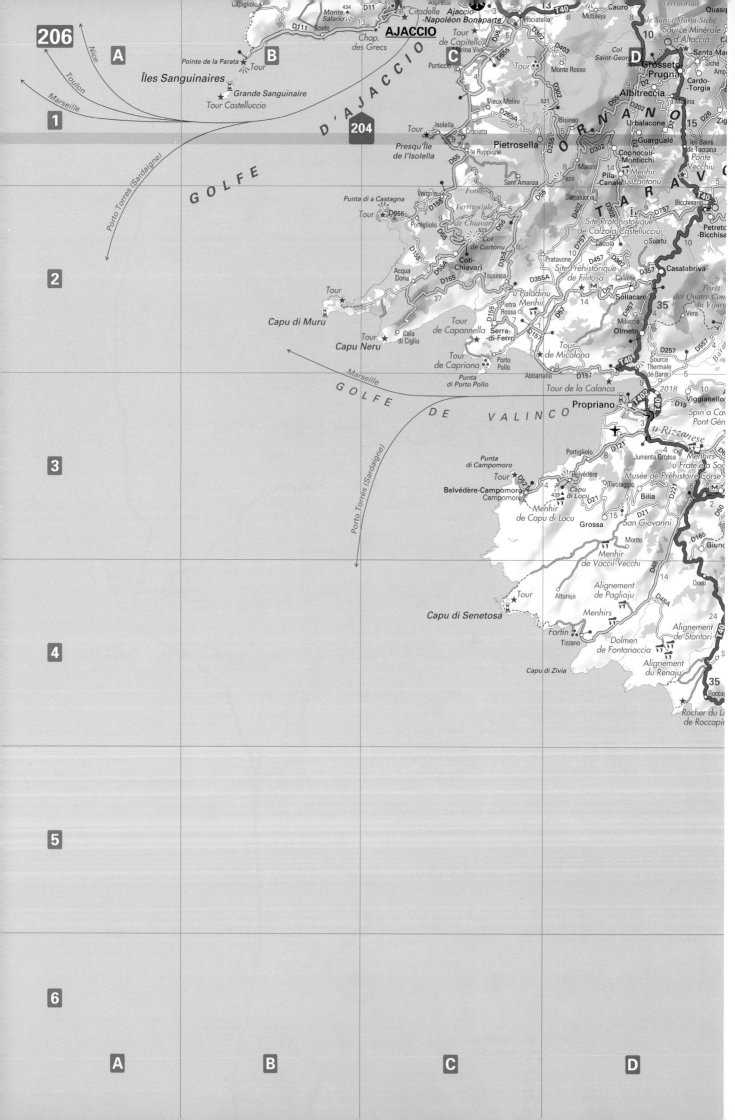

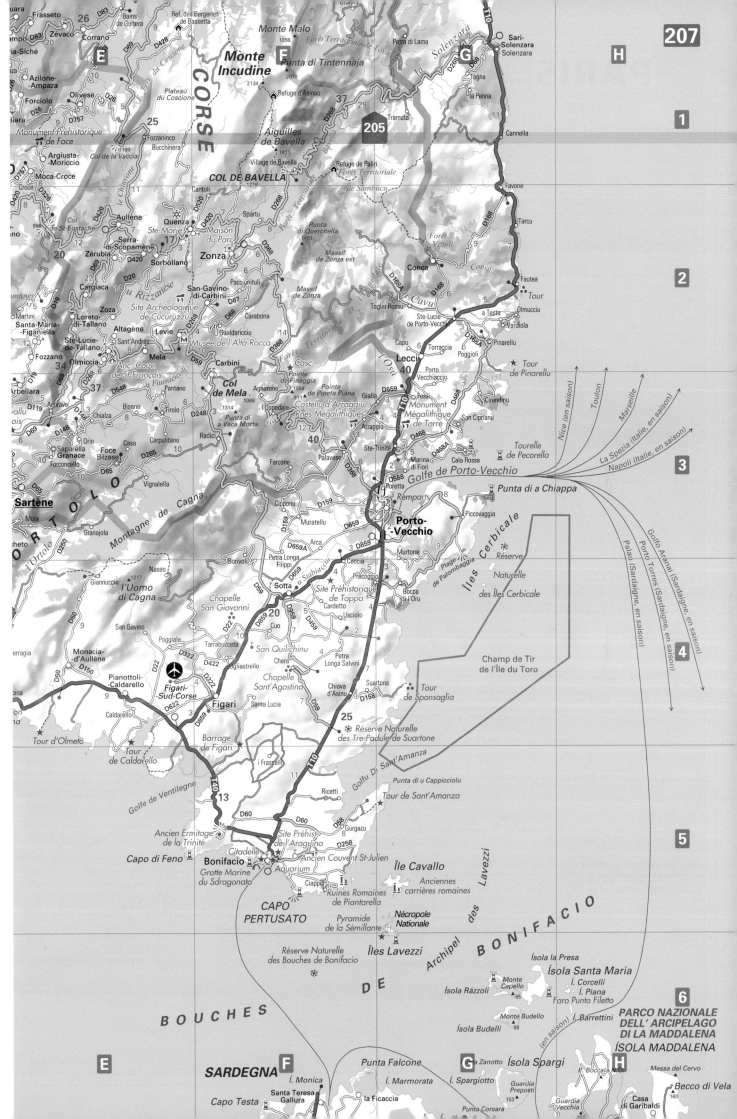

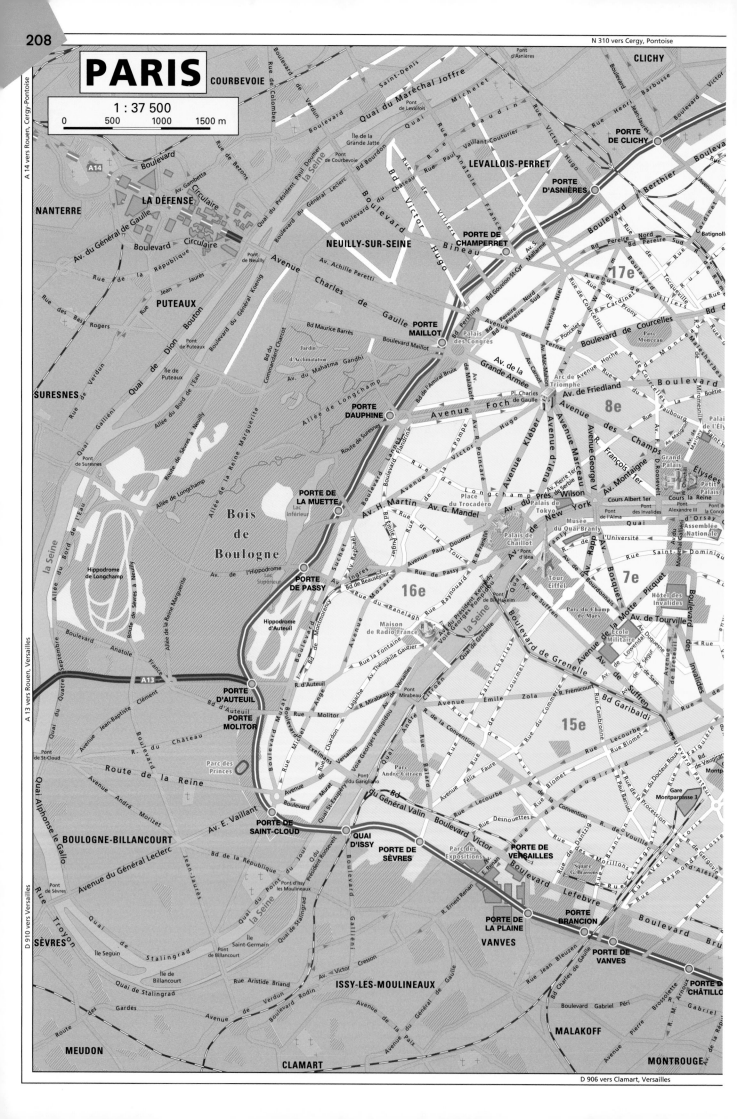

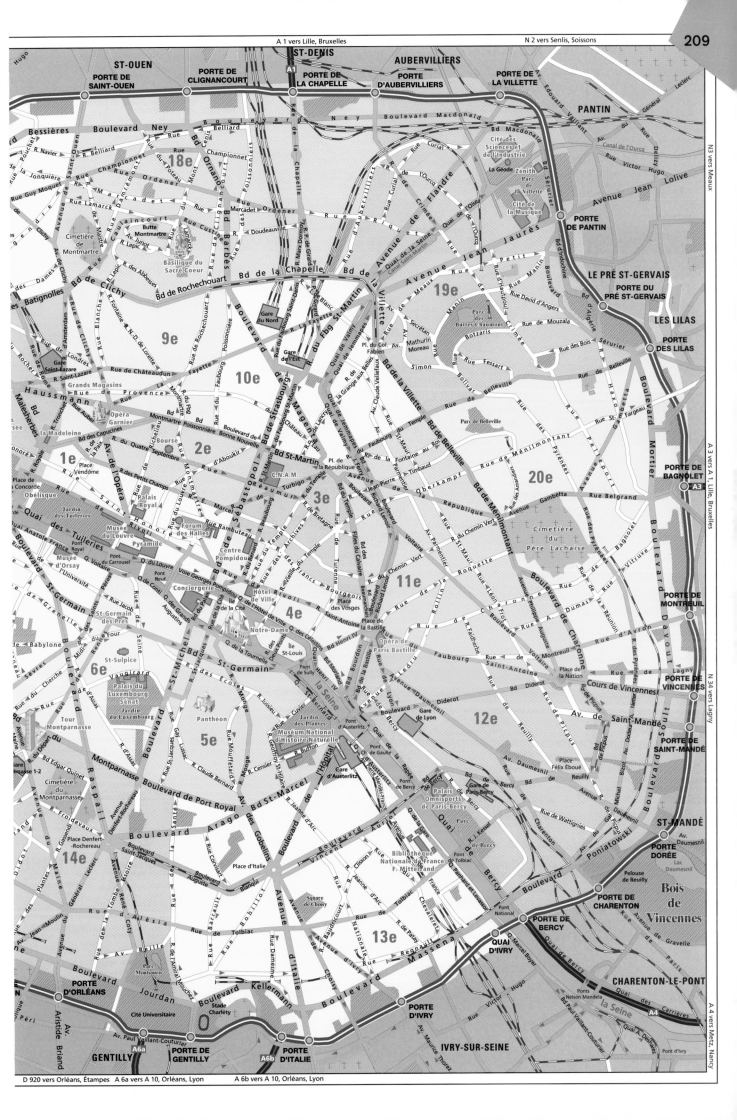

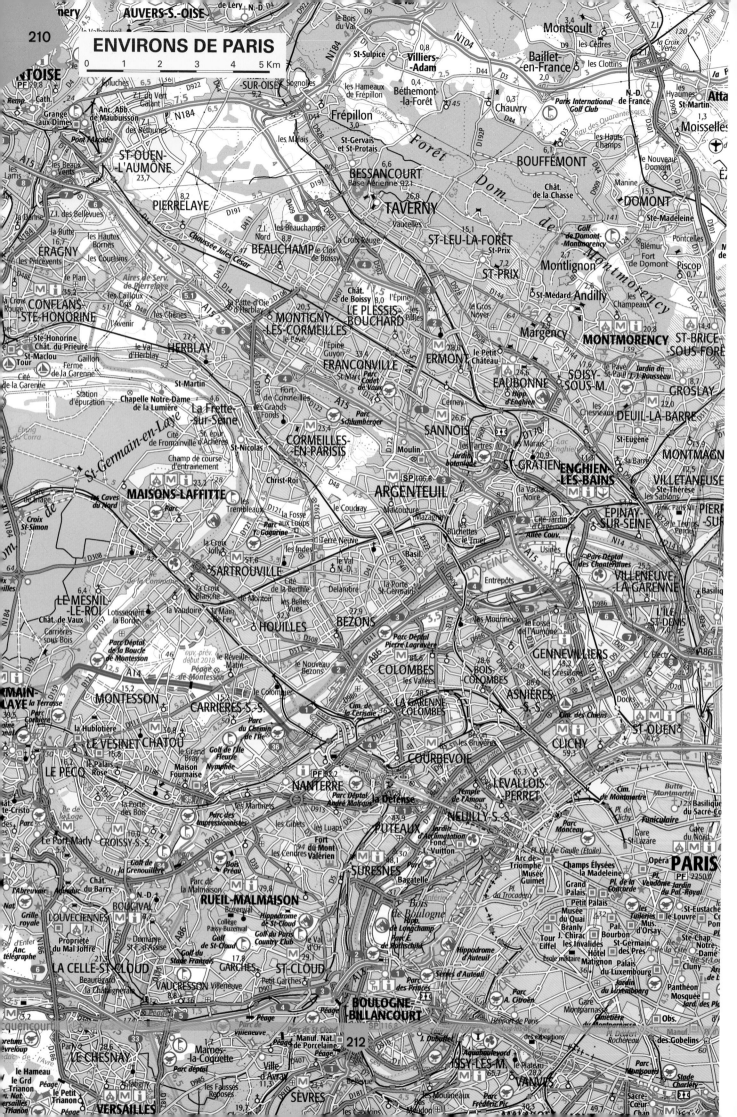

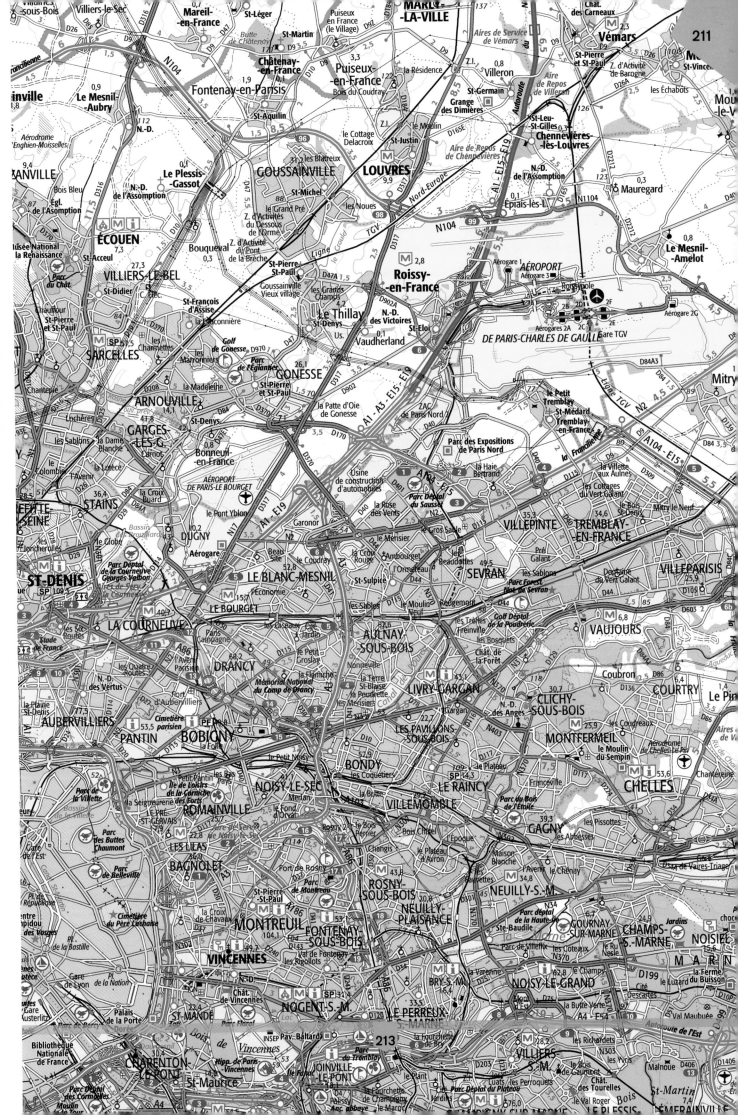

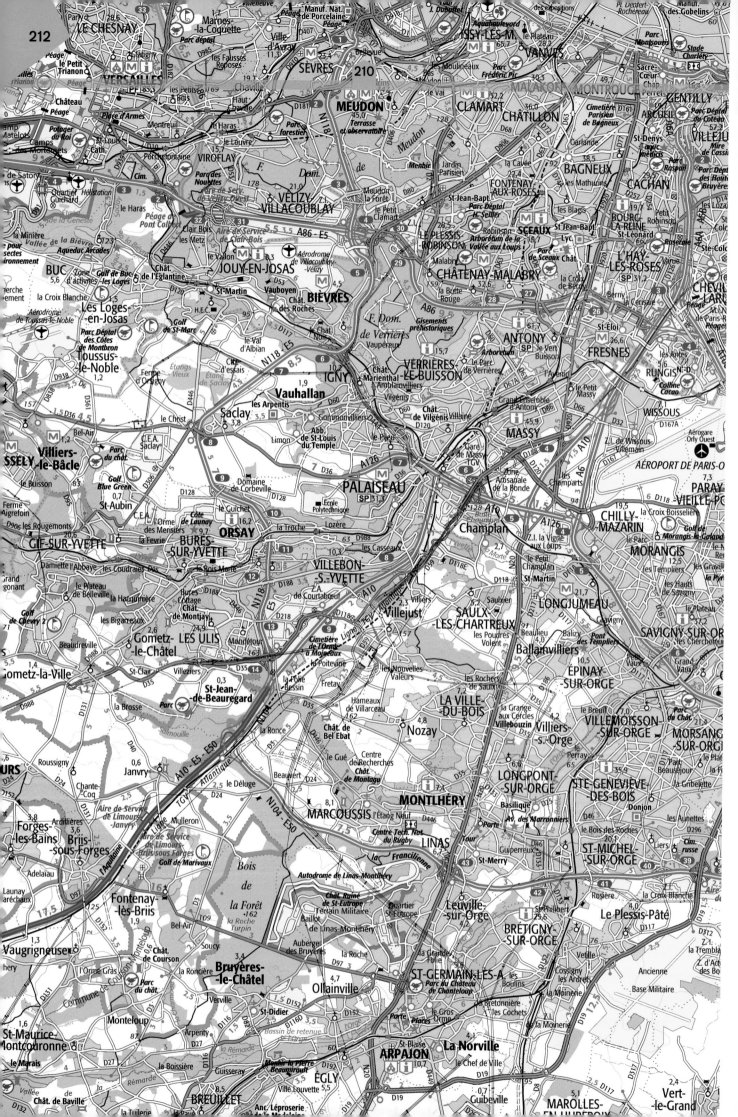

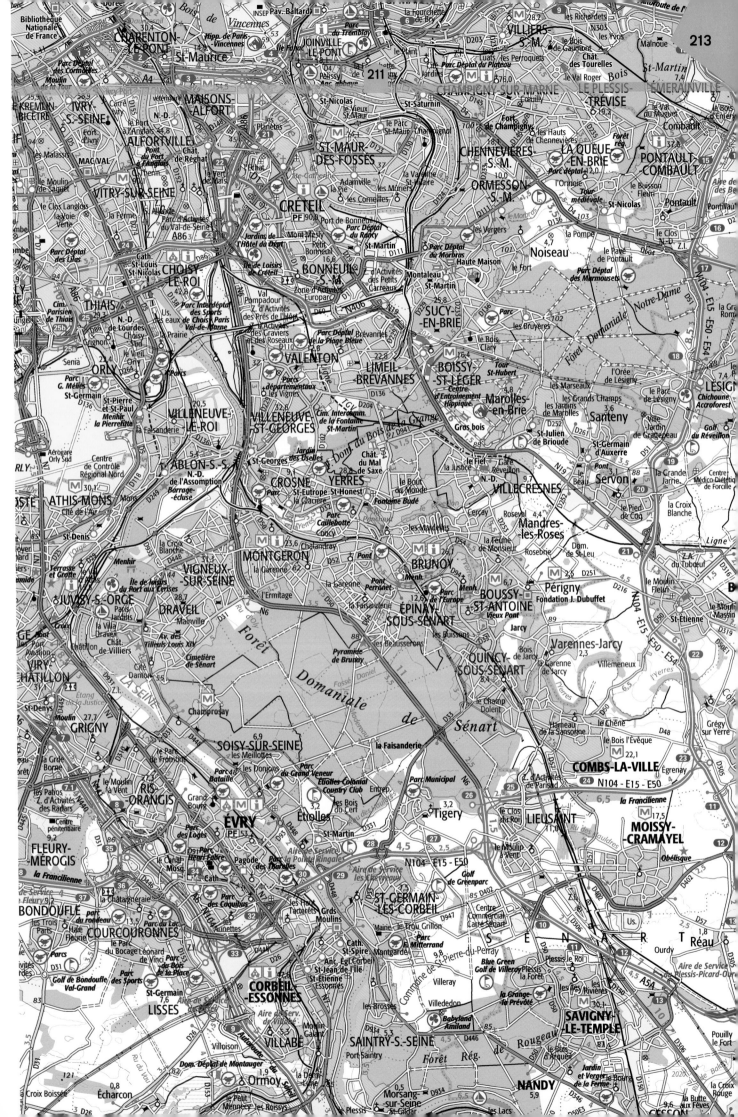

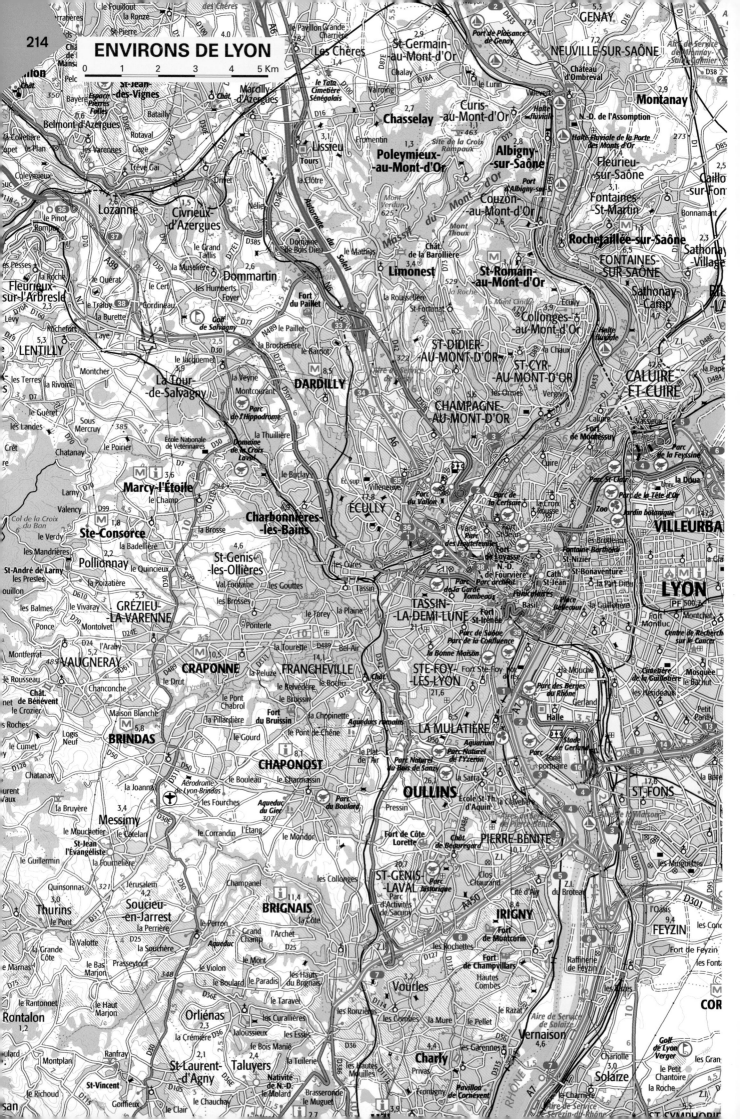

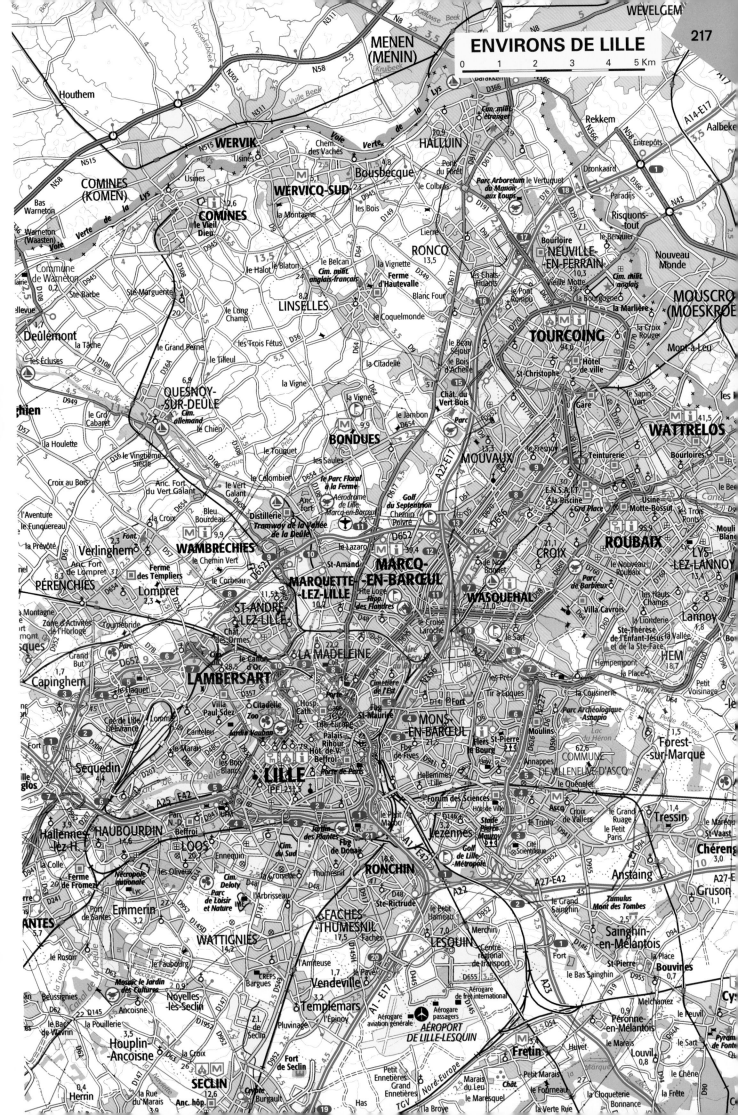

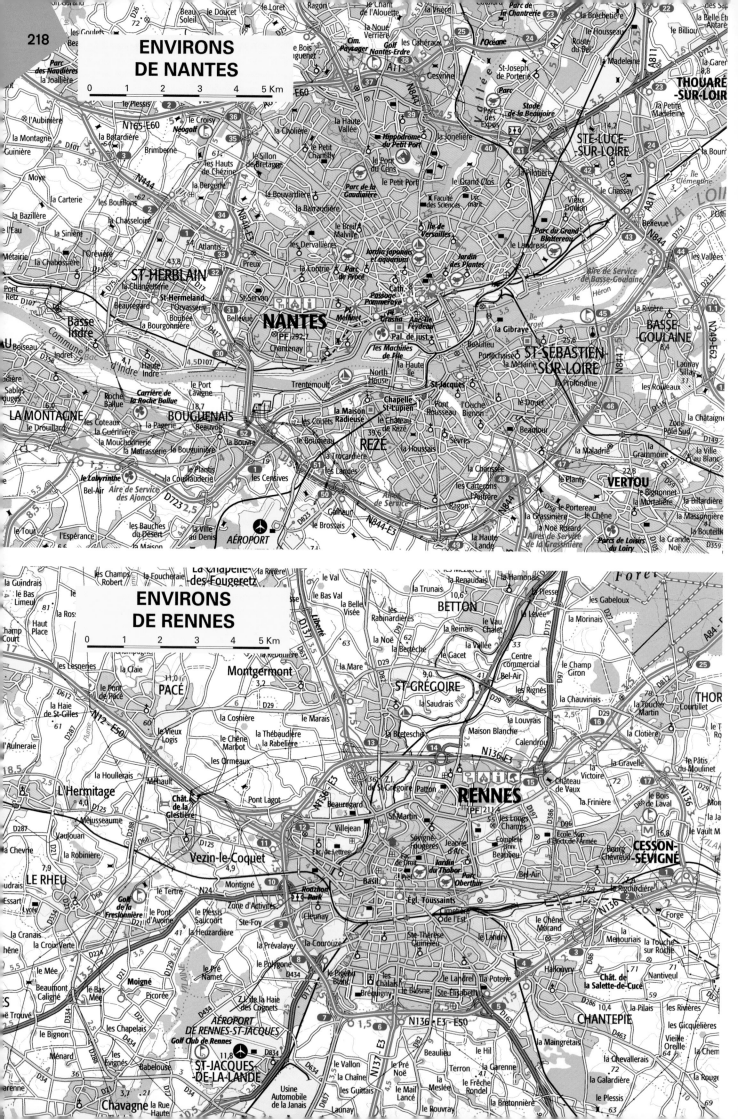

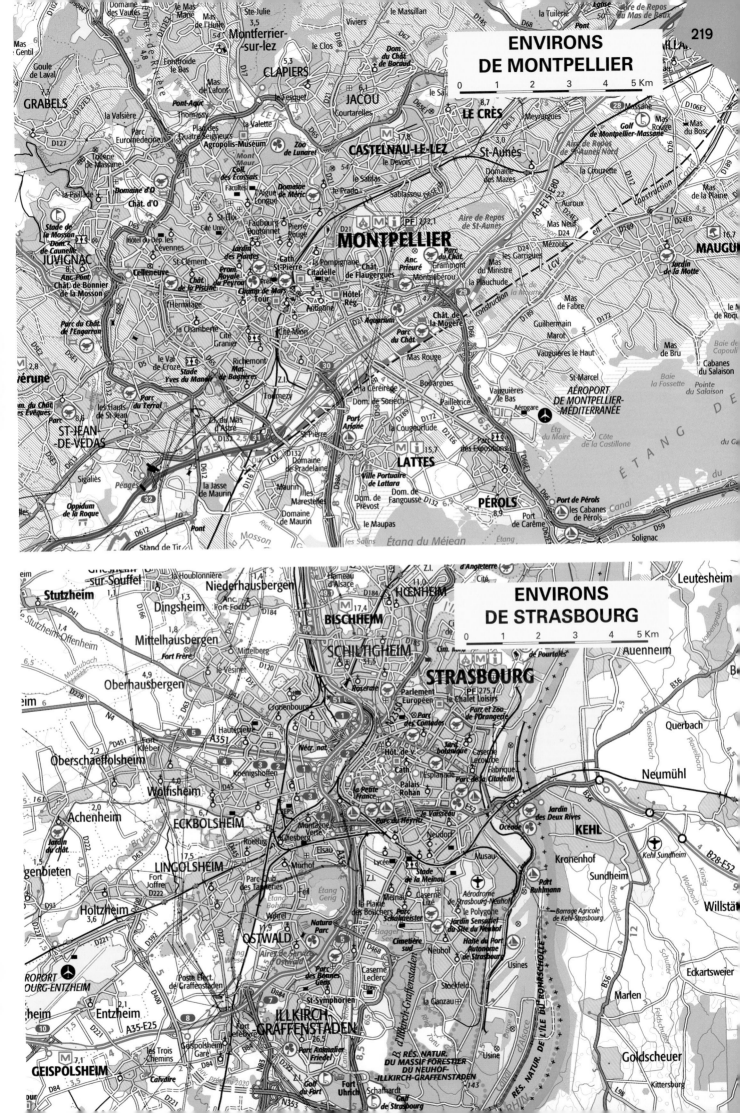

ENVIRONS
DE MONTPELLIER

0   1   2   3   4   5 Km

ENVIRONS
DE STRASBOURG

0   1   2   3   4   5 Km

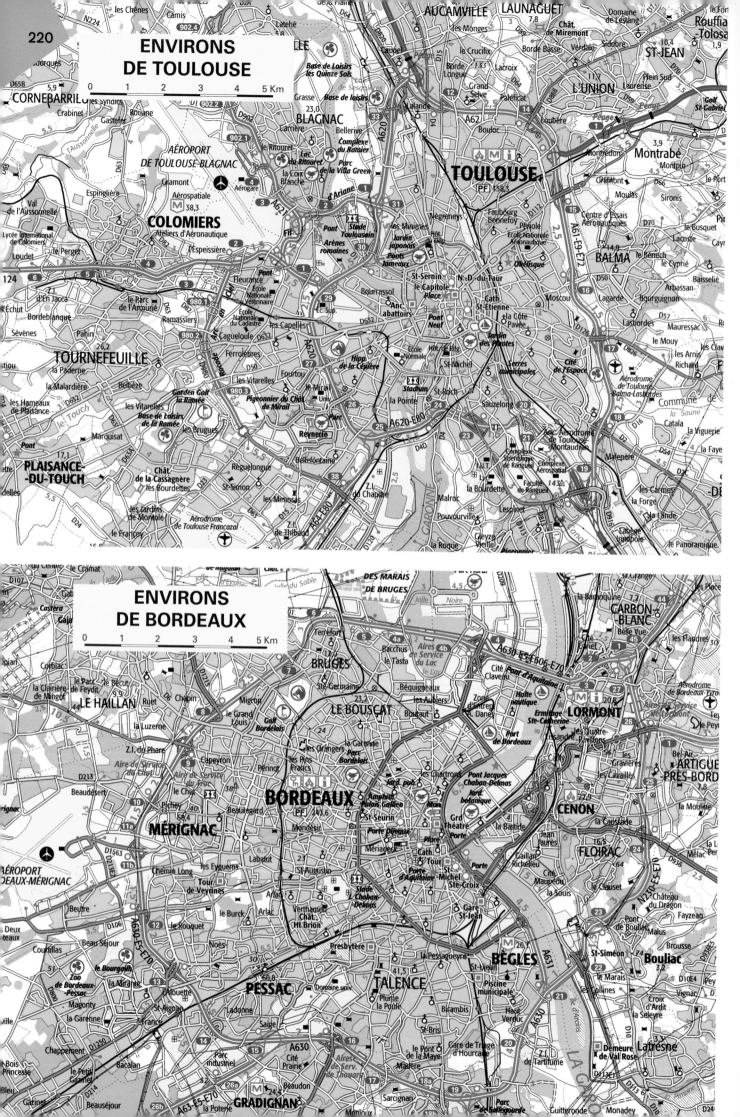

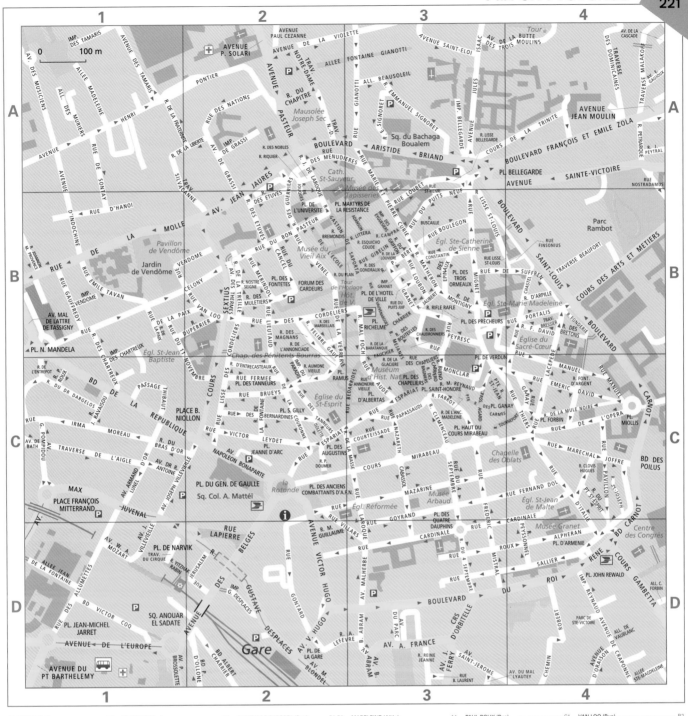

ADANSON (Rue) B3
AGARD (Passage) C3
AIGLE D'OR (Traverse de l') C3
ALBERT CHARRIER (Boulevard) D2
ALBERTAS (Place d') C3
ALLUMETTES (Rue des) C3
ANCIENNE MADELEINE (Rue de l') C3
ANCIENS COMBATTANTS D'A.F.N.
  (Place des) C2
ANDRE LEFEVRE (Rue) D2-D3
ANNONCIADE (Rue de l') C3
ANNONERIE VIEILLE (Rue) C3
ARBILLE (Rue d') B4
ARISTIDE BRIAND (Boulevard) A2-A3
ARMAND LUNEL (Avenue) C1
ARMENIE (Place d') D4
ARTS ET METIERS (Cours des) B4
AUDE (Rue d') C3
AUGUSTINS (Place des) C3
AUMONE VIEILLE (Rue) C2
BAGNIERS (Rue des) C3
BARATANQUE (Rue de la) B3
BARTHELEMY NIOLLON (Place) C2
BATH (Avenue de) C1
BEAUFORT (Traverse) B4
BEAUSOLEIL (Allée) A3
BEDARRIDES (Rue) C3
BELGES (Avenue des) D1-C2
BELLEGARDE (Impasse) A3
BELLEGARDE (Place) A3
BENJAMIN ABRAM (Avenue) D3
BERNARDINES (Rue des) C2
BON PASTEUR (Rue du) B2
BONIFACE LAURENT (Rue) D3
BOUGLEON (Rue) B3
BOUTEILLES (Rue des) B3
BRAS D'OR (Rue du) C1-C2
BREMONDIS (Traverse) B2-B3
BRESSIER (Traverse) B4
BRETONS (Rue des) B4
BRUEYS (Rue) C2
BUENO CARRIERO (Rue) C3
BUSCAILLE (Rue) B3
BUTTE DES TROIS MOULINS
  (Avenue de la) A3-A4
CAMPRA (Rue) B3
CANCEL (Rue du) B2
CARDEURS (Forum des) B2
CARDINALE (Rue) D2-C4
CARMES (Petite rue des) C3-C4
CARNOT (Boulevard) B4-D4
CASCADE (Avenue de la) A4
CELONY (Rue) B1-B2

CHABRIER (Rue) B3
CHAPELIERS (Place des) C3
CHAPELIERS (Rue des) B3-C3
CHAPITRE (Rue du) A2
CHARTREUX (Impasse des) B1-C1
CHARTREUX (Rue des) B1-C1
CHASTEL (Rue) B3
CHAUDRONNIERS (Rue des) B3
CIRQUE (Traverse du) D1
CLAUDE FORBIN (Allée) D4
CLEMENCEAU (Rue) C3
CLOVIS HUGUES (Rue) C4
CONSTANTIN (Rue) B3
CORDELIERS (Rue des) B2-B3
COURONNE (Rue de la) C2
COURTEISSADE (Rue) C3
CRAPONNE (Avenue de) D4
DOCTEUR DARGELOS (Rue du) C1
DOCTEUR RENEE ANTOINE (Avenue) . . C1
DOMINICAINES (Traverse des) A4
DUPERRIER (Rue) B1-B2
ECOLE (Rue de l') B2
EMERIC DAVID (Rue) C3-C4
EMILE GAUJOUX (Avenue) A4
EMILE TAVAN (Rue) B1
EMMANUEL SIGNORET (Rue) A3
ENTRECASTEAUX (Rue d') C2
ENTREPOT (Rue de l') C1
EPINAUX (Rue des) B3
ESPARIAT (Rue) C2-C3
ESQUICHO COUDE (Rue) B2
ETUVES (Rue des) A2-B2
EUROPE (Avenue de l') D1
EYGUESIERS (Impasse des) B3
FABROT (Rue) C3
FAUCHIER (Rue) B3-C3
FELIBRE GAUT (Rue) B2-C2
FELICIEN DAVID (Rue) B4
FERNAND DOL (Rue) C3-C4
FINSONIUS (Rue) B4
FONDERIE (Rue) B4
FONTAINE (Rue de la) C2
FONTAINE D'ARGENT (Rue) C3
FONTAINE GIANOTTI (Allée) A2-A3
FONTETES (Rue des) B2
FORBIN (Place) C4
FRANÇOIS ET EMILE ZOLA (Bd) . . . A3-A4
FRANÇOIS MITTERRAND (Place) C1
FRATERNITE (Rue de la) A1-A2
FREDERIC MISTRAL (Rue) D3-D3
GAMBETTA (Cours) D4
GANAY (Place) C4
GANAY (Rue) C4
GARE (Place de la) D2

GASTON DE SAPORTA (Rue) B2-B3
GAUFFREDY (Rue) B1
GENERAL DE GAULLE (Place du) C2
GEORGES POMPIDOU (Avenue) C1
GIBELIN (Rue) B3
GLACIERE (Rue de la) D2-D3
GONDRAUX (Rue des) B3
GONTARD (Rue) C2-D2
GOYRAND (Rue) C2-D3
GRANET (Impasse) B3
GRANET (Rue) B3
GRASSI (Avenue de) A2-B2
GRASSI (Impasse de) A2
GRIFFON (Rue du) B2
GUERRIERS (Rue des) A2-B2
GUSTAVE DESPLACES (Impasse) D2
GUSTAVE DESPLACES (Rue) D2
HANOI (Rue d') B1
HAUT DU COURS MIRABEAU (Place) . . C3
HENRI PONTIER (Avenue) A1-A2
INDOCHINE (Avenue d') A1-B1
ISOLETTE (Rue) C2
ITALIE (Rue d') C4-D4
JACQUES DE LAROQUE (Rue) A2-B2
JAUBERT (Rue) B3
JEAN DE LA FONTAINE (Allée) D1
JEAN JAURES (Avenue) A2-B2
JEAN MOULIN (Avenue) A4
JEAN PEYTRAL (Rue) A4
JEAN-MICHEL JARRET (Rue) D1
JEANNE D'ARC (Place) C2
JERUSALEM (Rue) D1
JOANNON MARCEL PROVENCE (Rue) . . B1
JOSEPH CABASSOL (Rue) C3-D3
JOSEPH RAVAISOU (Rue) C1
JOSEPH VILLEVIEILLE (Avenue) . . . D1-D2
JOQUES (Rue des) A2-B2
JULES FERRY (Avenue) A3
JULES ISAAC (Avenue) A3
LACEPEDE (Rue) B4-C4
LAPIERRE (Rue) D1-D2
LAROQUE (Rue de) B2
LIBERTE (Rue de la) A1-A2
LIEUTAUD (Rue) B2-C2
LISSE BELLEGARDE (Rue) A3-B3
LISSE DES CORDELIERS (Rue) B3
LISSE SAINT-LOUIS (Rue) B3-B4
LITTERA (Rue des) B3
LOUBET (Avenue) A3-B3
LOUBON (Rue) B3
LOUVIERE (Rue de la) B3

MADELEINE (Allée) A1
MAGNANS (Rue des) B2-C2
MALAKOFF (Traverse) A4
MALHERBE (Avenue) C4
MANUEL (Rue) B3-C4
MARCEL GUILLAUME (Rue) D2-D3
MARECHAL DE LATTRE DE TASSIGNY
  (Avenue) B1
MARECHAL FOCH (Rue) B3-C3
MARECHAL JOFFRE (Rue) C4
MARECHAL LYAUTEY (Avenue du) D3
MARIE ET PIERRE CURIE (Rue) A3-B3
MARIUS REYNAUD (Rue) C3
MARSEILLAIS (Rue des) B2-B3
MARTYRS DE LA RESISTANCE (Place) . . B3
MASSE (Rue de la) C2-C3
MATHERON (Rue) B3
MAURICE BLONDEL (Avenue) D2
MAX JUVENAL (Avenue) C1-D1
MAZARINE (Rue) C2-C3
MEJANES (Rue) B3-C3
MENUDIERES (Rue des) A2-A3
MERINDOL (Rue) B2
MIGNET (Rue) A3-B3
MIOLLIS (Place) C4
MIRABEAU (Cours) C2-C3
MOLLE (Rue de la) B1-B2
MONCLAR (Rue) B3-C3
MONTIGNY (Rue de) B3
MULE NOIRE (Rue de la) C4
MULETIERS (Rue des) B2
MURIERS (Allée des) A1
MUSICIENS (Allée des) A1
NAPOLEON BONAPARTE (Avenue) C2
NARVIK (Place de) D1
NATIONS (Rue des) A2
NAZARETH (Rue) C2
NELSON MANDELA (Place) B1
NOBLES (Rue des) A2
NOSTRADAMUS (Rue) A4-B4
NOSTRE SEIGNE (Rue) B2
NOTRE-DAME (Traverse) A1-A2
OPERA (Rue de l') C4
ORAISON (Avenue d') D4
ORBITELLE (Cours d') D3
PAIX (Rue de la) B1-B2
PAPASSAUDI (Rue) C3
PARADIS (Impasse du) C2
PARC (Avenue du) C4
PASTEUR (Avenue) B3
PAUL BERT (Rue) B3
PAUL CEZANNE (Avenue) A2
PAUL D'OLLONE (Boulevard) A2
PAUL DOUMER (Rue) C2

PAUL ROUX (Rue) C1
PAVILLON (Rue) C4-D4
PETIT BARTHELEMY (Avenue du) D1
PETIT SAINT-ESPRIT (Rue du) C4-C4
PETRARQUE (Rue de) A4
PEYRESC (Rue) B3
PEYSSONNEL (Rue) C4-D4
PHILIPPE SOLARI (Avenue) A2
PIERRE BROSSOLETTE (Avenue) D1
PLAN (Rue du) B2-B3
POILUS (Boulevard des) C4
PORTALIS (Rue) B3-B4
PRECHEURS (Place des) B3
PUITS JUIF (Rue du) B3
PUITS NEUF (Rue du) A3-B3
QUATRE DAUPHINS (Place des) D3
4 SEPTEMBRE (Rue du) C3-D3
RAMUS (Place) C3
REINE JEANNE (Rue) D3
REPUBLIQUE (Boulevard de la) C1-C2
REYNAUD (Impasse) D4
RICHELME (Place) B3
RIFLE RAFLE (Rue) B3
RIQUIER (Rue) A2
ROBERT (Chemin) D4
ROI RENE (Boulevard du) D2-D4
ROUX ALPHERAN (Rue) D3-D4
SAINT-ELOI (Avenue) A3
SAINT-HENRI (Rue) A3-B3
SAINT-HONORE (Place) C3
SAINT-JEAN (Petite rue) C3-C4
SAINT-JEROME (Avenue) A3
SAINT-JOSEPH (Rue) C4
SAINT-LOUIS (Boulevard) B3-B4
SAINTE-MAGDELEINE (Allée) D4
SAINTE-VICTOIRE (Avenue) A3-A4
SAINTE-VICTOIRE (Parc de) D4
SALLIER (Rue) D3-D4
SERAPHIN GILLY (Place) C2
SEXTIUS (Cours) B2-C2
SILVACANE (Traverse) A1-B2
SONTAY (Rue de) A1-B1
SUFFREN (Rue de) B3-B4
TAMARIS (Avenue des) A1
TAMARIS (Impasse des) A1
TANNEURS (Place des) C2
TANNEURS (Rue des) C2
THERMES (Avenue des) B2
THIBAUT (Passage) C1
THIERS (Rue) C3-C4
TOURNEFORT (Rue) C3-C4
TREILLE (Rue de la) B2
TRINITE (Cours de la) A3-A4
TROIS ORMEAUX (Place des) B3
UNIVERSITE (Place de l') B2

VAN LOO (Rue) B2
VAUBLANC (Allée de) D4
VAUVENARGUES (Rue) B3
VENDOME (Impasse) B1
VENDOME (Rue) B1-B2
VENEL (Rue) B2
VERDUN (Place de) B3
VERRERIE (Rue de la) B2-C3
VICTOR COQ (Boulevard) D1
VICTOR HUGO (Avenue) C2-D2
VICTOR LEYDET (Rue) C2
VILLARS (Rue) C2-D3
VIOLETTE (Avenue de la) A2-A3
WOLFGANG-AMADEUS MOZART
  (Avenue) C1-D1
YITZHAK RABIN (Rue) D1-D2
YVES MONTAND (Allées) D1

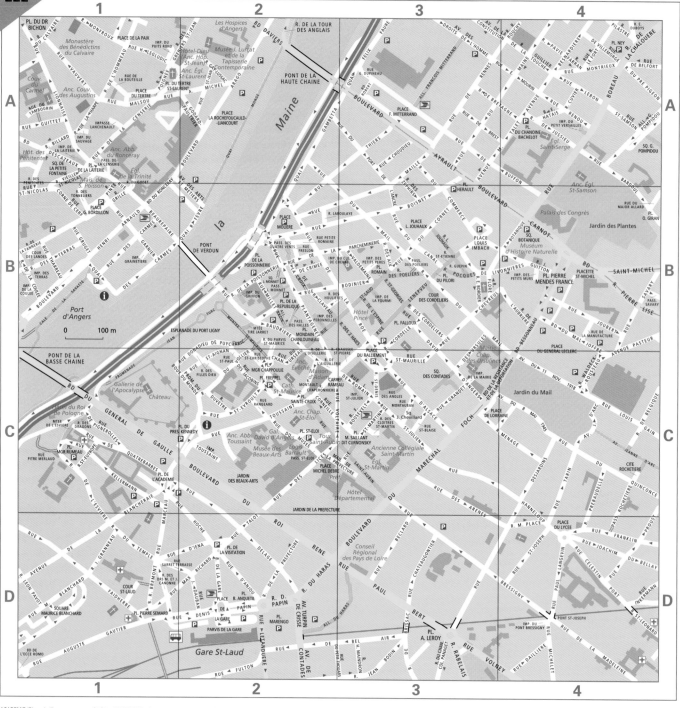

ACADEMIE (Place de l') C1-C2
AIGUILLERIE (Rue de l') C2
AIX (Rue d') B3
ALSACE (Rue d') C3
ANDRE LEROY (Place) D3
ANGLES (Rue des) C3
ANJOU (Rue d') D2
ARAGO (Boulevard) A1-A2
ARENES (Rue des) C3-D4
ARTS ET METIERS (Avenue des) ... A1-B2
AUBRIERE (Rue de l') B4
AUGUSTE GAUTIER (Rue) D1
AUGUSTE MICHEL (Place) A1-A2
AYRAULT (Boulevard) A3
BARDOUL (Rue) A4-B4
BASSE CHAINE (Pont de la) C1
BAUDRIERE (Rue) B2
BEAUREPAIRE (Rue) A1-B1
BEAUX-ARTS (Jardin des) C2
BECLARD (Rue) C3
BEL AIR (Rue de) D2-D3
BELFORT (Rue de) A4
BELGIQUE (Rue de) C4
BELLE POIGNEE (Rue) A1
BERNARD ANQUETIL (Place) B2
BESNARDIERE (Avenue) A4
BESSONNEAU (Boulevard) B4-C4
BILLARD (Rue) A1
BLANCHERAIE (Avenue de la) A1
BODINIER (Rue) B2-B3
BOISNET (Rue) B2-B3
BOREAU (Rue) A4
BOTANIQUE (Rue) B4
BOTANIQUE (Square) B4
BOUT DU MONDE (Promenade du) . C1-C2
BOUTEILLE (Rue de la) A2
BRESSIGNY (Rue) C3-D4
BREST (Rue de) A3-A4
BRETAGNE (Rue de) A3-A4
BRISSAC (Rue de) D3
BUFFON (Rue de) A4
CALVAIRE (Rue du) A1
CANAL (Rue du) B3
CARMES (Quai des) B1
CARMES (Rue des) B1
CARNOT (Boulevard) B3
CELESTIN PORT (Rue) D4
CENSERIE (Passage de la) A1
CENSERIE (Rue de la) A1
CHALOUERE (Rue de la) A4
CHANOINE BACHELOT (Rue du) .. A3
CHANOINE COLONEL PANGET (Rue du) . D3
CHANOINE URSEAU (Rue du) ... B2-C2
CHAPERONNIERE (Rue) C2
CHATEAUGONTIER (Rue) D3
CHAUSSEE SAINT-PIERRE (Rue) . C2-C3
CHEVREUL (Rue) B3-B4
CHOUDIEU (Rue) A3

CLAVEAU (Rue) B2
CLOITRES SAINT-MARTIN (Rue des) .. C3
COMMERCE (Rue du) A3-B3
CONSTITUTION (Avenue de la) A3-A4
CONTADES (Avenue de) D2
CONTADES (Square des) C2
CORDELIERS (Cour des) B3
CORDELIERS (Rue des) B3
CORNEILLE (Rue) C2-C3
CORNE DE CERF (Rue) B2
CORNET (Rue du) B3
COULEE (Rue de la) B1
CRIMEE (Rue de) B1
CROIX (Rue de la) B2
CUL DE CHEVAL (Impasse du) . B2-B3
CUVIER (Rue) A4
DAILLIERE (Rue) A4
DAVID D'ANGERS (Rue) B3-C3
DAVIERS (Boulevard) A2
DELAGE (Rue) A2
DENIS PAPIN (Rue) D1-D2
DESCAZEAUX (Boulevard) A1
DESJARDINS (Rue) D3-C4
DEUX HAIES (Rue des) B2-B3
DOCTEUR BICHON (Place du) A1
DOCTEURS M. ET J. CANONNE (Rue des) . D2
DONADIEU DE PUYCHARIC (Rue) . C1-B2
DRAGONS (Rue des) C1
DROITS DE L'HOMME (Avenue des) . A3
DU PETIT THOUARS (Rue) D2-D3
DUVETRE (Rue) C1
ECCE HOMO (Rue) D1
EMILE BORDIER (Rue) B3
EMILE HATAIS (Rue) A4
ERNEST DUBOYS (Rue) A4
ERNEST MOURIN (Rue) A3-A4
ESPINE (Rue de l') C1
ESVIERE (Montée de l') C1
ESVIERE (Rue de l') C1-D1
FAIDHERBE (Rue) D1
FALLOUX (Place) C3
FARRAN (Rue) A4
FELIX FAURE (Quai) A2
FILLES DIEU (Rue des) C2
FLORE (Rue) B3
FOURMI (Impasse de la) B2
FRANCOIS MITTERRAND (Allée) . A3
FRANCOIS MITTERRAND (Place) . A3
FRANKLIN (Rue) D4
FRANKLIN ROOSEVELT (Rue) C2
FREPPEL (Place) C2
FRESLON (Rue) B2
FULTON (Rue) D2
GABRIEL DUPINEAU (Rue) A3
GAMBETTA (Quai) B2-B3
GARE (Parvis de la) D2

GARE (Place de la) D2
GARE (Rue de la) C3
GARNIER (Rue) B1
GAY-LUSSAC (Rue) A1-A2
GENERAL DE GAULLE (Boulevard du) . C1-C2
GENERAL LECLERC (Rue du) ... B4-C4
GEORGES POMPIDOU (Allée) A4
GEORGES POMPIDOU (Square) ... A4
GODARD-FAULTRIER (Rue) A2
GODET (Rue) A2
GRAINETIERE (Impasse) B1
GRANDET (Rue) A2
GREGOIRE BORDILLON (Place) .. C1-B2
GRENIERS SAINT-JEAN (Rue des) . A1-A2
GRIFFON (Impasse du) B2
GRILLE (Rue) B2
GRUGET (Rue) B1
GUEPIN (Rue) B2
GUILLIER DE LA TOUCHE (Rue) ... A4
GUITTET (Rue) A1
HALLES (Passage des) B2
HANNELOUP (Rue) C3-D4
HARAS (Allée du) D3
HARAS (Rue du) D2
HARPE (Rue de la) B2
HAUTE CHAINE (Pont de la) A2
HENRI ARNAULD (Boulevard) B1
HENRI LEGLUDIC (Rue) B1
HERAULT (Place) B2
HIPPOLYTE MAINDRON (Rue) A4
HOCHE (Rue) C1-D2
HOMMEAU (Rue de l') B2
HOULIERES (Rue des) B2-B3
8 MAI 1945 (Avenue du) C3-C4
IENA (Rue d') D1-D2
INKERMANN (Rue) D1
JACOBINS (Rue des) C2
JACQUES GRANNEAU (Rue) B1
JEAN BODIN (Rue) D3
JEAN MONNET (Passage) C1
JEAN MONNET (Square) C1
JEAN TURC (Promenade) C1-C2
JEANNE D'ARC (Avenue) A4
JOACHIM DU BELLAY (Rue) D4
JOUBERT (Rue) B4
JULES DAUBAN (Rue) D2
JULES GUITTON (Rue) A2
JUSSIEU (Rue de) A4
KELLERMANN (Rue) C1
LABOULAYE (Rue) B2
LAITERIE (Impasse de la) A1
LAITERIE (Rue de la) A1
LANCHENAULT (Impasse) A1
LANDES (Rue des) B1
LEBON (Rue) B3
LENEPVEU (Rue) B3
LEON JOUHAUX (Place) B3
LEON JOUHAUX (Rue) A3-B3

LEON PAVOT (Rue) D1
LETANDUERE (Rue) D2
LICES (Rue des) C2-C3
LIONNAISE (Rue) A1
LORRAINE (Place de) C3-C4
LOUIS DE ROMAIN (Rue) C3
LOUIS GAIN (Rue) C4
LOUIS IMBACH (Place) B3
LYCEE (Rue du) D4
MADELEINE (Rue de la) D4
MAIL (Rue du) B2-B3
MAILLE (Rue) B2-A3
MAINE (Rue de) A3-A4
MAIRIE (Impasse de la) B2
MAJOR ALLARD (Rue du) B4
MALSOU (Rue) A2
MANUFACTURE (Rue de la) B4
MARCEAU (Rue) C1
MARECHAL FOCH (Boulevard du) . D2-C3
MARECHAL JOFFRE (Boulevard du) . B4-C4
MARENGO (Rue) D2
MARIE PLACE (Rue) C4
MARIE TALET (Avenue) A3-A4
MAURICE BLANCHARD (Rue) C4
MAURICE BLANCHARD (Square) . C4
MAURICE SAILLANT DIT CURNONSKY (Place) . C3

MAX RICHARD (Rue) D1-D2
MENAGE (Rue) C3
MICHELET (Rue) C1-D2
MICHELET (Place) D2
MILLET (Place du) B3-C3
MOLIERE (Place) B2
MONDAIN CHANLOUINEAU (Place) . B2
MONFROUX (Rue) A1
MONGE (Rue) A2-B2
MONSEIGNEUR CHAPPOULIE (Place) . C3
MONSEIGNEUR RUMEAU (Place) . C1
MONTAUBAN (Rue) C3
MONTAULT (Rue) C3
MONTRIEUX (Rue) A4
MUSEE (Rue) C2
NEY (Place) A4
OISELLERIE (Rue de l') B2-C2
OLIVIER GIRAN (Rue) A4
11 NOVEMBRE 1918 (Avenue du) . C3
PAIX (Place de la) A1
PARCHEMINERIE (Rue de la) .. B2-B3
PARVIS SAINT-MAURICE (Rue du) . C3
PASTEUR (Avenue) B4-C4
PAUL BERT (Rue) D2-D3
PAUL LANGEVIN (Rue) D4
PAVIE (Rue) A4
PENITENTES (Rue des) A1
PERONNELLES (Rue des) B2
PETIT VERSAILLES (Impasse du) . A4
PETITE FONTAINE (Square de la) . A1
PETITE ROMAINE (Rue) B2
SAINT-DENIS (Rue) C3

PETITS MURS (Impasse des) B4
PETITS PERES (Impasse des) B3
PIERRE LISE (Rue) B4
PIERRE MENDES FRANCE (Place) . B4
PIERRE SEMARD (Place) D1
PIGNEROLLES (Rue de) C1
PILASTRE (Rue) A4
PILORI (Place du) B3
PINTE (Place de) A1-B1
PITRE MERLAUD (Rue) C1
PLANTAGENET (Rue) B2-C2
POCQUET DE LIVONNIERES (Rue) . B3-B4
POELIERS (Passage des) B3
POELIERS (Rue des) B3
POISSONNERIE (Impasse de la) .. B2
POISSONNERIE (Rue de la) B2
PONT BRESSIGNY (Impasse du) .. D4
PORT DE L'ANCRE (Rue du) ... A2-B3
PORT LIGNY (Esplanade du) .. C1-B2
PRE PIGEON (Rue du) A4
PREBAUDELLE (Rue) C4-D4
PREFECTURE (Jardin de la) C2
PREFECTURE (Mail de la) C2-C3
PRESIDENT KENNEDY (Place du) . C1-C2
PROUST (Rue) C4-D4
PUITS ROND (Impasse du) A1
QUATRE VENTS (Passage des) .. B2
QUATREBARBES (Rue de) C1
QUINCONCE (Rue du) C4
RABELAIS (Rue) D3
RALLIEMENT (Place du) B3-C3
RAMEAU (Carrefour) C2
RANGEARD (Rue) C2
RENE BAZIN (Allée) B2
RENE BREMONT (Rue) D1
RENE ROUCHY (Rue) A4
RENNES (Rue de) A4
RENOU (Rue) A4
REPUBLIQUE (Place de la) B2
RESISTANCE ET DE LA DEPORTATION
(Boulevard de la) C3-C4
ROBERT (Rue) C3-C4
ROBERT FEVRE (Quai) B1-B2
ROBERT LE FORT (Rue) B3
ROCHEFOUCAULD-LIANCOURT
(Place) A1-B2
ROCHETIERE (Cité) C4
ROCHETIERE (Passage) C4-D4
ROE (Rue de la) B3
ROI RENE (Boulevard du) C1-D2
ROMAIN (Place de la) C3
RONCERAY (Boulevard du) A1-B1
SAINT-AIGNAN (Rue) C2
SAINT-AUBIN (Rue du) C3
SAINT-BLAISE (Rue) C3
SAINT-CHRISTOPHE (Rue) C3

SAINTE-CROIX (Place) C2
SAINT-ELOI (Passage) C2
SAINT-ELOI (Place) C2
SAINT-ETIENNE (Rue) B3
SAINT-EUTROPE (Rue) C2
SAINT-EVROULT (Rue) B3
SAINT-GEORGES (Rue) B3
SAINT-JEAN (Rue) A2
SAINT-JOSEPH (Rue) D4
SAINT-JULIEN (Impasse) C3
SAINT-JULIEN (Rue) C3
SAINT-LAUD (Cour) D1
SAINT-LAUD (Rue) B2-B3
SAINT-LEONARD (Rue) D4
SAINT-MARTIN (Rue) C3
SAINT-MAURICE (Montée) B2-C2
SAINT-MICHEL (Boulevard) ... B3-C3
SAINT-MICHEL (Placette) B4
SAINT-NICOLAS (Rue) B1
SAINT-PAUL (Rue) B2-C2
SAINT-SAMSON (Rue) A4
SARRETTERRASSE (Rue) D1-D2
SAUVAGE (Impasse du) A1
SAVARY (Passage) C4
SAVARY (Cale de la) B1
SAVATTE (Cale de la) B4-C4
ST-JOSEPH (Pont) D4
TALOT (Rue) C2
TAMBOURIN (Rue des) C2-D2
TANNERIE (Rue de la) A1
TARIN (Rue) C4-D4
TEMPLE (Rue du) D1
TERRAS (Impasse des) B1
TERRAS (Rue des) B1
TERTRE (Rue du) A2
TERTRE SAINT-LAURENT (Place du) . A1-A2
THARREAU (Rue) A4
THIERS (Rue) B2-A3
TIRE JARRET (Montée) B2
TIREMONT (Rue des) A1-B1
TONNELIERS (Rue des) B1
TOUR DES ANGLAIS (Rue de la) .. A2
TOUSSAINT (Impasse) C2
TOUSSAINT (Rue) C2
TURPIN DE CRISSE (Avenue) .. B3-C3
URSULES (Rue des) C3
VALDEMAINE (Rue) A4
VAUVERT (Rue) B2
VIEILLE SAINT-NICOLAS (Rue) ... A1-B1
VILLEMORGE (Rue de) A4
VISITATION (Place de la) C2
VOLLIER (Rue de) B2-C2
VOLNEY (Rue) D3-D4
VOLTAIRE (Rue) C2-C3
WALDECK-ROUSSEAU (Rue) C4
ZEPHIRS (Rue des) A3-B3

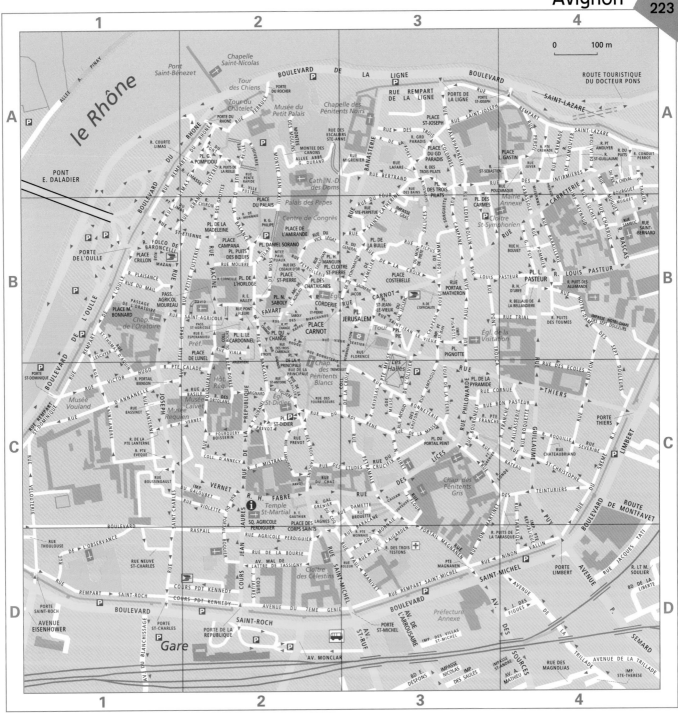

ABBE GEORGES DURAND (Allée)........A2
AGRICOL MOUREAU (Passage)........B2
AGRICOLE PERDIGUIER (Rue)........D2
AGRICOLE PERDIGUIER (Square)........C2
AIGARDEN (Rue de l')........C3-D3
AMELIER (Rue de l')........B3
AMIRANDE (Place de l')........A2
AMPHOUX (Rue)........B3-C3
ANNANELLE (Rue d')........C1
ANSELME MATHIEU (Avenue)........D4
ANTOINE PINAY (Allée)........A1
ARCADE DE L'AGNEAU (Rue)........B2
ARGENTIERE (Rue)........B2
ARROUSAIRE (Avenue de l')........D3
ARMAND DE PONTMARTIN (Rue)........B3
ARTAUD (Rue)........B3
BAINS (Rue des)........B3
BALANCE (Rue de la)........A2-B2
BANASTERIE (Rue)........B2-A3
BANCASSE (Rue)........B2
BARACANE (Rue)........B4
BARAILLERIE (Rue)........B4
BASILE (Rue)........C1-C2
BASSINET (Rue)........C1
BELLAUD DE LA BELLANDIERE (Rue)........B2
BERNHEIM LYON (Rue)........A3
BERTRAND (Rue)........A3
BLANCHISSAGE (Avenue du)........D1
BON MARTINET (Rue)........C3-C4
BON PASTEUR (Rue)........C3
BONNETERIE (Rue)........B2-C2
BOUQUERIE (Rue)........B2-C2
BOURGNEUF (Rue)........C2
BOURGUET (Rue)........A4-B4
BOURSE (Rue de la)........D2
BOUSSINGAULT (Rue)........C2
BROUETTE (Rue)........B4-C4
BUFFON (Rue)........A3
BULLE (Place de la)........B3
CABASSOLE (Rue)........B2
CAMPANA (Place)........B2
CAMPANE (Rue)........A3-B3
CANONS (Montée des)........A2
CARMES (Place des)........B3
CARNOT (Place)........B3
CARNOT (Rue)........B3
CARRETERIE (Rue)........B3-A4
CASSAN (Rue)........B3
CHANGE (Place du)........B2
CHANGE (Rue du)........B2-B3
CHAPEAU ROUGE (Rue)........A4-B4
CHARRUE (Rue)........C2
CHAT (Rue du)........C2
CHATAIGNES (Place des)........B2
CHATEAUBRIAND (Rue)........C3
CHIRON (Rue)........B2
58EME R.I. (Rue du)........C4-D4
CISEAUX D'OR (Rue des)........B2
CLOITRE SAINT-PIERRE (Place)........B2
COLLEGE D'ANNECY (Rue)........C2
COLLEGE DE LA CROIX (Rue)........B2
COLLEGE DU ROURE (Rue)........B2
CONDUIT PERROT (Rue)........A4
COQ (Rue du)........B2
CORDERIE (Rue)........B2
CORNEILLE (Rue)........B2
CORNUE (Rue)........C3-C4
CORPS SAINTS (Place des)........C2
COSTEBELLE (Rue)........B3
COURTE LIMAS (Rue)........A2
CREMADE (Rue)........A4
CROIX (Rue de la)........B2
DAMETTE (Rue)........C2-C3
DANIEL SORANO (Place)........B2
DOCTEUR PONS (Route touristique du)........A4
DOREE (Rue)........B2-C2
CRUCIFIX (Rue du)........C3
ECOLES (Rue des)........C4
EDMOND HALLEY (Rue)........B2
EDOUARD DALADIER (Pont)........A1-B1
EISENHOWER (Avenue)........D1
EMILE DESFONS (Boulevard)........D1
EMILE ESPERANDIEU (Rue)........B2
ESCALIERS SAINTE-ANNE (Rue des)........A2-A3
ETROITE (Rue)........C2
ETUDES (Rue des)........C2-C3
FAVART (Rue)........B2
FELICIEN DAVID (Rue)........C3
FELIX GRAS (Rue)........C1-B2
FER A CHEVAL (Rue du)........A2
FERRUCE (Rue)........A2
FIGUIERE (Rue)........B3
FLORENCE (Rue)........B3
FOLCO DE BARONCELLI (Rue)........B1
FORET (Rue de la)........A3-B3
FOUR (Rue du)........A3-B3
FOUR DE LA TERRE (Rue)........B3-C3
FOURBISSEURS (Rue des)........B2
FRANCHE (Rue)........C3
FREDERIC MISTRAL (Rue)........C2-C3
GAL (Rue)........B3
GALANTE (Rue)........B2
GALOUBET (Impasse du)........C1-C2
GEORGES POMPIDOU (Place)........A2
GENERAL LECLERC (Rue)........B3
GEORGES TAULIER (Avenue)........A4-B4
GERARD PHILIPE (Rue)........A3
GRAND PARADIS (Place de)........A3
GRAND PARADIS (Rue)........A3
GRANDE FUSTERIE (Rue)........B1-A2
GRANDE MEUSE (Rue)........B3
GRANDE MONNAIE (Rue)........C3-D3
GRENIER (Galerie)........C2-C3
GRIFFONS (Rue des)........C2
GRIVOLAS (Rue)........C3
GROTTES (Rue des)........A2-B2
GUILLAUME PUY (Rue)........B4-D4
HENRI BOUVET (Rue)........B3
HENRI FABRE (Rue)........C2
HENRI MANGUIN (Place)........B3
HONORE D'URFE (Rue)........B3
HORACE VERNET (Rue)........C1-C2
HORLOGE (Place de l')........B2
INFIRMIERES (Rue des)........A3-A4
JACOB (Rue)........B3
JACQUES TATI (Rue)........D4
JEAN XXIII (Montée)........A2
JEAN DES FIGUES (Rue)........C4
JEAN VILAR (Rue)........B2
JEAN-PIERRE GRAS (Impasse)........B3
JERUSALEM (Place)........B2
JOSEPH VERNET (Rue)........C1-B2
JOYEUSE (Rue)........C3
JUIVERIE (Rue)........C3
JULES FLOUR (Rue)........B3
JUVER (Rue)........A4
LABOUREUR (Rue)........A4
LAFARE (Rue)........A3
LAGNES (Rue)........D2-C3
LANTERNE (Rue)........C1
LEDRU ROLLIN (Rue)........A3-B3
LIBERTE (Boulevard de la)........D4
LICES (Rue des)........B4
LIGNE (Boulevard de la)........A2-A3
LIGNE (Rue de la)........A2-A3
LIGNE (Porte de la)........A3
LIMAS (Rue)........B1-A2
LIMASSET (Rue)........A2
LIMBERT (Boulevard)........C4-D4
LIMBERT (Porte)........D4
LONDE (Rue)........C3-C4
LOUIS GASTIN (Place)........A4
LOUIS LE CARDONNEL (Place)........B2
LOUIS PASTEUR (Rue)........B4
LOUIS PASTEUR (Boulevard)........B3-A4
LT MARCEL SOULIER (Rue)........D4
LUCHET (Rue)........A4-B4
LUNEL (Rue de)........B2
MADELEINE (Place de la)........B2
MAGNANEN (Porte)........D3
MAGNOLIAS (Rue des)........D4
MAIL (Rue du)........B1
MARCHANDS (Rue des)........B2
MARECHAL DE LATTRE DE TASSIGNY (Avenue)........D2
MASSE (Rue de la)........C3
MAURICE BONNARD (Place)........B1
MAZAN (Rue)........B1
MIGNARD (Rue)........B2
MIGNENIER (Rue)........A3
MIGRENIER (Rue)........A3
MOLIERE (Rue)........B3
MONCLAR (Avenue)........D2
MONNAIE (Rue de la)........B2
MONS (Rue de)........B3
MONT DE PIETE (Rue du)........B3
MONTFAVET (Route de)........C4
MOULINS (Montée des)........A2
MUGUET (Rue)........A4-B4
NEUVE SAINT-CHARLES (Rue)........C1-D1
NICOLAS (Impasse)........D3
NICOLAS LESCUYER (Rue)........B1
NICOLAS SABOLY (Place)........B2
NINON VALLIN (Rue)........D3-D4
NOEL BIRET (Rue)........B2
NOTRE-DAME DES SEPT DOULEURS (Impasse)........B4
NOTRE-DAME DES SEPT DOULEURS (Rue)........B4-C4
OBSERVANCE (Rue de l')........C1-D1
OFFICIALITE (Rue de l')........B2
OLIVIER (Rue de l')........B3-C3
ORATOIRE (Passage de l')........B1
ORIFLAMME (Rue de l')........B3
ORTOLANS (Rue des)........C2
OULLE (Boulevard de l')........B1-C1
OULLE (Porte de l')........B1
PAILLASSERIE (Rue)........A2
PALAIS (Place du)........A2
PALAPHARNERIE (Rue)........A3
PAUL MANIVET (Rue)........D2-D3
PAUL PUAUX (Montée)........B3
PAUL SAIN (Rue)........B3-C3
PAVOT (Rue)........C2
PENTE RAPIDE (Rue)........A2
PERSIL (Rue)........A4
PETIT AMOUYER (Rue)........A4
PETIT CHANGE (Rue)........B2
PETIT CREMADE (Rue)........A4
PETIT GRENIER (Rue)........C2
PETIT LIMAS (Rue du)........A1-B2
PETIT MUGUET (Rue)........B4
PETIT REPUBLIQUE (Impasse)........C4-D4
PETIT SAINT-JEAN (Impasse)........B3
PETITE CALADE (Rue)........C1-C2
PETITE CREMADE (Rue)........A4
PETITE FRANCHE (Rue)........C3-C4
PETITE FUSTERIE (Rue)........B2
PETITE LANTERNE (Rue)........C1
PETITE MEUSE (Rue)........B3-C3
PETITE MONNAIE (Rue)........C3-D3
PETITE REILLE (Rue)........B2
PETITE REPUBLIQUE (Impasse)........C4-D4
PETITE SAUNERIE (Rue)........B2-B3
PETRAMALE (Rue)........C3
PEYROLLERIE (Rue)........B2
PHILONARDE (Rue)........B3
PICPUS (Rue)........B3
PIE (Place)........B3
PIERRE SEMARD (Avenue)........D4
PIGNOTTE (Impasse)........B3
PIGNOTTE (Place)........B3
PLAISANCE (Rue)........B1
POMMIER (Rue)........B4
PONT (Rue du)........A2
PONT FLEURI (Rue)........B2
PONT TROUCA (Rue)........B3-C4
PORTAIL BIENSON (Rue)........C1
PORTAIL BOQUIER (Rue du)........C2-D2
PORTAIL MAGNANEN (Rue)........C3-D3
PORTAIL MATHERON (Rue)........B3
PORTAIL PEINT (Place du)........C3
PORTE EVEQUE (Rue)........C2
POURQUERY BOISSERIN (Rue)........C2
POUZARAQUE (Rue)........A4
PRESIDENT KENNEDY (Cours)........D1-D2
PREVOT (Rue)........C2
PRINCIPALE (Place de la)........B2-C2
PRINCIPALE (Rue de la)........B2-C2
PRIVADE (Rue)........A4-B4
PUITS (Rue du)........A4
PUITS DE LA REILLE (Rue)........A2
PUITS DE LA TARASQUE (Rue)........C4-D4
PUITS DES ALLEMANDS (Rue)........B2
PUITS DES BOEUFS (Place)........B2
PUITS DES TOUMES (Rue)........B4
PYRAMIDE (Place de la)........C3
RACINE (Rue)........B2
RAPPE (Rue)........B2
RASCAS (Rue)........B4
RASPAIL (Boulevard)........C1-D2
RATEAU (Rue)........C3
REMPART DE LA LIGNE (Rue)........A3
REMPART DE L'OULLE (Rue)........B1-C1
REMPART DU RHONE (Rue)........A1-A2
REMPART SAINT-LAZARE (Rue)........A3-A4
REMPART SAINT-MICHEL (Rue)........D3
REMPART SAINT-ROCH (Rue)........D1
REMPART SAINT-DOMINIQUE (Rue)........C1
REPUBLIQUE (Rue de la)........C2-D2
REPUBLIQUE (Porte de la)........D2
REYNAUD (Impasse)........A4-B4
RHONE (Boulevard du)........B1-A2
RHONE (Rue du)........A2
ROCHER (Porte du)........A2
ROI RENE (Rue du)........B3-C3
ROQUILLE (Rue)........C4
ROUGE (Rue du)........B2
SABOLY (Rue)........B2
SAINT-AGRICOLE (Passage)........B2
SAINT-AGRICOLE (Rue)........B2
SAINT-ANDRE (Impasse)........D3-D4
SAINT-ANTOINE (Rue)........B2
SAINT-BERNARD (Rue)........B4
SAINT-CHARLES (Porte)........C1-D1
SAINT-CHARLES (Rue)........C1-D1
SAINT-CHRISTOPHE (Rue)........C3-C4
SAINT-DIDIER (Place)........C2
SAINT-DOMINIQUE (Porte)........C1
SAINT-ETIENNE (Rue)........B1-B2
SAINT-GUILLAUME (Rue)........C4
SAINT-JEAN LE VIEUX (Place)........B3
SAINT-JEAN LE VIEUX (Rue)........B3
SAINT-JOSEPH (Place)........A3
SAINT-JOSEPH (Porte)........A4
SAINT-JOSEPH (Rue)........A3-A4
SAINT-LAZARE (Boulevard)........A3-A4
SAINT-MICHEL (Boulevard)........D3-D4
SAINT-MICHEL (Porte)........D3
SAINT-PIERRE (Place)........B2
SAINT-PIERRE (Rue)........B2
SAINT-ROCH (Boulevard)........D1-D3
SAINT-ROCH (Porte)........D1
SAINT-RUF (Avenue)........D3
SAINT-SEBASTIEN (Rue)........A3
SAINT-THOMAS D'AQUIN (Rue)........B1-C1
SAINTE-CATHERINE (Rue)........A3-B3
SAINTE-PERPETUE (Rue)........B3
SAINTE-THERESE (Impasse)........D4
SALUCES (Rue)........B3
SAMBUC (Rue)........B4
SARRAILLERIE (Rue de la)........C2
SAULES (Impasse des)........D3
7EME GENIE (Avenue du)........D2-D3
SEVERINE (Rue)........C4
SORGUETTE (Rue)........C4
SOURCES (Avenue des)........D3-D4
TARASQUE (Rue)........C4-D4
TAULIGNAN (Rue)........B2
TEINTURIERS (Rue des)........C3-C4
THEODORE AUBANEL (Rue)........B2
THEOPHILE GAUTHIER (Rue)........C2
THIERS (Porte)........C3
THIERS (Rue)........B3-C4
THOULOUSE (Rue)........D1
TOUR (Rue de la)........A4
TREMOULET (Rue)........A4
TRIAL (Rue)........B3-B4
TRILLADE (Avenue de la)........D4
TROIS CARREAUX (Rue des)........A3
TROIS COLOMBES (Rue des)........A3
TROIS FAUCONS (Rue des)........C2
TROIS PILATS (Rue des)........A3
TROIS TESTONS (Rue des)........B2-B3
TROIS-PILATS (Place des)........A3
VELOUTERIE (Rue)........C1-D1
VIALA (Rue)........B2
VICE LEGAT (Rue du)........B2-B3
VICTOR HUGO (Rue)........C1
VIEILLE POSTE (Rue)........A2
VIENEUVE (Rue)........B4
VIEUX SEXTIER (Rue du)........B2-B3
VILLAS ST-MICHEL (Impasse des)........D3
VIOLETTE (Rue)........C1-C2

Bordeaux

ABBE DE L'EPEE (Rue) A1-B1
ALAUDETTES (Rue) B2
ALBRET (Cours d') C1-D1
ALLAMANDIERS (Rue des) D4
ALSACE LORRAINE (Cours d') C2-C4
ANATOLE FRANCE (Cours) D1
ANDRE LHOTE (Square) C1
ARGENTIERS (Passage des) C3
ARGENTIERS (Rue des) C3
ARNAUD MIQUEU (Rue) C3
AUSONE (Rue) C4
AYRES (Rue des) D2-D3
BAHUTIERS (Rue des) C3
BARBOT (Impasse) A1
BASQUES (Place des) C3
BEAUBADAT (Rue) B1
BELFORT (Rue) C1-D1
BERTHUS (Impasse) B1
BIR HAKEIM (Place) D4
BIROUETTE (Impasse) C2-D2
BLANC DUTROUILH (Rue) A2
BOETIE (Rue de la) C1
BONNAFFE (Rue) C1
BONNIER (Impasse) C1
BOUQUIERE (Impasse) C3
BOUQUIERE (Rue) D3
BOURSE (Place de la) B3
BRISTOL (Allée de) A3
BUFFON (Rue) B2
BUHAN (Rue) D4
CABIROL (Rue) D1
CAILHAU (Porte) C4
CAILLABET (Impasse) C4
CAMILLE JULLIAN (Place) C3
CAMILLE PELLETAN (Place) D3
CAMILLE SAUVAGEAU (Rue) D4
CANCERA (Rue) C3
CANIHAC (Rue) C1
CANTELOUP (Place) D4
CAPERANS (Rue des) B3-C3
CARPENTEYRE (Rue) D4
CASTEJA (Rue) B1
CASTELMORON (Rue) C1
CASTELNAU D'AUROS (Rue) B2-C2
CASTILLON (Rue) B2
CERF VOLANT (Rue du) C3
CHAI DES FARINES (Rue des) C3-C4
CHAMP DE MARS (Place du) A2
CHAPEAU ROUGE (Cours du) B2-B3
CHAPELLE SAINT-JEAN (Rue de la) C3
CHARLES DE GAULLE (Esplanade) C1-D1
CHARLES GRUET (Place) A1
CHARLES LAMOUREUX (Rue) B3

CHARTRES (Allée de) A2-A3
CHATEAU D'EAU (Rue du) B1-C1
CHATEAU TROMPETTE (Rue du) A2
CHEVERUS (Rue) A2
CLAUDE BONNIER (Rue) C1
CLOITRE (Rue du) D4
COLISEE (Rue du) A1
COLONEL RAYNAL (Place du) C1
COMBE (Rue) C3
COMEDIE (Place de la) B2-B3
COMMANDANT ARNOULD (Rue du) C2-D2
CONDE (Rue de) B3
CONDILLAC (Rue) A2-B2
COQUILLE (Rue de la) C3-C4
CORCELLE (Rue) C4
CORDELIERS (Rue des) D3-D4
COUR DES AIDES (Rue de la) C3-C4
COURBIN (Rue) C3
CREON (Rue de) C2
CURSOL (Rue de) D2
DABADIE (Rue) D2-D3
DARNAL (Impasse) B1
DARNAL (Rue) B1
DESFOURNIEL (Rue) D1
DEVISE (Rue de la) C3
DIDEROT (Rue) B2
DIEU (Rue) B3
DOCTEUR ALBERT BARRAUD (Rue du) A1
DOCTEUR CHARLES NANCEL PENARD
        (Rue du) B1-C1
DOCTEUR LANOU (Square) A4
DOUANE (Quai de la) B4-C4
DROITS DE L'HOMME (Parvis des) D1
DUBURG (Rue) D4
DUCRU (Rue) D2
DUDON (Rue) C1-D1
DUFAU (Rue) C1
DUFFOUR-DUBERGIER (Impasse) C2-D2
DUFFOUR-DUBERGIER (Rue) C2-D2
EDMOND MICHELET (Rue) C1-C2
ELISEE RECLUS (Rue) C2
EMILE DUPLOYE (Rue) C2
EMILE FOURCAND (Rue) A2
ENGHIEN (Rue d') A2
ENTRE 2 MURS (Rue) B3
ESPRIT DES LOIS (Rue) B3
ETUVES (Passage de l') D2
FAURE (Impasse) D3
FAURES (Rue des) D4
FAUSSETS (Rue des) B3-C3
FENELON (Rue) B2
FENOUIL (Impasse) A1
FERME DE RICHEMONT (Place de la) D3
FERNAND LAFARGUE (Place) C3
FERNAND MARIN (Rue) C3-D3
FERNAND PHILIPPART (Rue) B3
FONDAUDEGE (Rue) B1

FOURS (Rue des) D4
FOY (Rue) A3
FRANCOIS BUGNICOURT (Rue) D4
FRANKLIN (Rue) B1-C1
LEO DROUYN (Rue) C1
FRERES BONIE (Rue des) D1-C2
FUSTERIE (Rue de la) B3
GABILLON (Rue) D4
GABRIEL (Place) B3
GALIENE (Rue) A1
GAMBETTA (Place) B1
GASPARD PHILIPPE (Rue) C3
GENSAN (Rue) D4
GENSONNE (Rue) D4
GEORGES BONNAC (Rue) B1-C1
GEORGES CLEMENCEAU (Cours) B1-A2
GEORGES DE PORTO RICHE (Place) B3
GOBINEAU (Rue) C1
GOURGUE (Cours du) A3
GOUVEA (Rue) D3
GRAND RABIN JOSEPH COHEN
        (Rue du) D2-D3
GRANDS HOMMES (Place des) B2
GRASSI (Rue de) B2
GRAVE (Quai de) D4
GUERIN (Rue) C2
GUIENNE (Rue de) D3
GUILLAUME BROCHON (Rue) C1
GUIRAUDE (Impasse) C3
GUIRAUDE (Rue) C2-C3
HA (Rue) C2
HALLE (Rue de la) C4
HERBES (Rue des) C4
HONORE TESSIER (Rue) D3
HOPITAL (Passage de l') D2
HOTEL DE VILLE (Rue de l') C1
HUGLA (Rue) D3-D4
HUGUERIE (Rue) A1-A2
HUSTIN (Impasse) A2
HUSTIN (Rue) A2
INTENDANCE (Cours de l') B1-B2
JACQUES LEMOINE (Rue) C3
JEAN BUREAU (Rue) D3
JEAN BURGUET (Rue) D2
JEAN FLEURET (Square) D1
JEAN JAURES (Place) B3
JEAN MOULIN (Place) C2
JEAN-JACQUES BEL (Rue) B3
JEAN-JACQUES ROUSSEAU (Rue) A2-B2
JOSEPH DE CARAYON LATOUR (Rue) C1-D1
JOUANNET (Rue) B3
JUDAIQUE (Rue) B1
KATER (Rue) D1
LABIRAT (Rue) D2
LACORNEE (Rue) D1
LAFAURIE MONBADON (Rue) A1-B1
LAFAYETTE (Rue) B3
LALANDE (Rue) D2
LALIMENT (Passage) B1
LALIMENT (Rue) B1
PARLEMENT (Place du) B3-C3

LAURIERS (Rue des) B3
LEBRUN (Rue) A1
LECOCQ (Rue) D1
PARLEMENT SAINTE-CATHERINE (Rue) C2-C3
PARLEMENT SAINT-PIERRE (Rue) C3
PASSAGE SAINT-GEORGES (Impasse du) C3
PASSAGE SAINT-GEORGES (Rue du) C3
PASSICOS (Square) A1
PASTEUR (Cours) D2
PAUL BERT (Rue) D2-D3
PAUL LOUIS LANDE (Rue) D2
PAUL PAINLEVE (Rue) B3
PERE DEUZAIDE (Rue) C1
PERE LOUIS JABRUN (Rue du) C2
PETITS CAPERANS (Rue des) B3
PEY BERLAND (Place) C2
PIERLOT (Rue) C1
LEUPOLD (Rue) B3-C3
LEYTEIRE (Rue) D2
LHOTE (Rue) C1
LIBERATION (Cours de la) D1
LIGIER (Rue) D1
LOS ANGELES (Allée de) A2
LOUIS (Rue) B3
LOUIS DE FOIX (Rue) C1
LOUIS XVIII (Quai) A3-B3
LOUP (Rue du) C2-C3
LURBE (Rue de) B1
MABLY (Rue) A2-B2
MAISON DAURADE (Rue de la) B2-B3
MARCHAL FOCH (Cours du) A3
MARECHAL JOFFRE (Rue du) C2-D2
MARECHAL JUIN (Cours du) D1
MARECHAL LYAUTEY (Quai du) B3-A4
MARENGO (Rue) C1
MARGAUX (Impasse) C2
MARGAUX (Rue) C2
MARTIGNAC (Rue) C1
MARTYRS DE LA RESISTANCE (Place des) B1
MAUBEC (Impasse) D4
MAUBEC (Rue) D4
MAUCOUDINAT (Rue) C3
MAUCOUYADE (Impasse) C3-D3
MAURIAC (Impasse) D4
MAURIAC (Rue) D4
MAURICE LANOIRE (Rue) D2
MAUTREC (Rue) B2
MENUTS (Rue des) D4
MERCI (Impasse de la) C3
MERCI (Rue de la) C3
MERIGNAC (Rue de) B3-C3
METIVIER (Rue) B3
MEYNARD (Place) D4
MILLANGES (Rue) C3
MINIMETTES (Impasse des) D2
MIRAIL (Rue du) D3
MONTAIGNE (Rue) C2
MONTBAZON (Rue) C1
MONTESQUIEU (Rue) B1-B2
MOUNEYRA (Rue) D1
MUGUET (Rue du) C4-D4
MULET (Rue du) C3
MUNICH (Allée de) A2-A3
NEUVE (Rue) D3
NUYENS (Rue) A4
OBSERVANCE (Rue de l') D3
ORLEANS (Allée d') A3
PALAIS (Place du) C4
PALAIS GALLIEN (Rue du) A1
PALAIS OMBRIERE (Rue du) C3-C4
PALANQUES (Rue des) D3

PIERRE (Pont de) C4-D4
PIERRE CHARRON (Rue) B1-C1
PIERRE DE COUBERTIN (Rue) D3
PILET (Rue) D2
PILIERS DE TUTELLE (Rue des) B3-C3
PLATEFORME (Rue de la) A1
POITEVIN (Rue) A1
POITEVINE (Impasse) A1
PONT DE LA MOUSQUE (Rue du) B3
PONTETS (Rue des) D4
POQUELIN MOLIERE (Rue) C2
PORTE BASSE (Rue de la) C2-D2
PORTE CAILHAU (Rue de la) C4
PORTE DES PORTANETS (Rue) C4
PORTE DIJEAUX (Rue de la) B1-B2
PORTE SAINT-JEAN (Rue de la) D1
PROFESSEUR DEMONS (Rue du) A1
PUITS DESCAZEAUX (Rue du) C3
PUITS DESCUJOLS (Rue du) B3
PUY PAULIN (Rue) B2
QUAI BOURGEOIS (Rue) C3
QUEYRIES (Quai des) A4-B4
QUINCONCES (Place des) A3
RAVEZ (Rue) C3-D3
RAYMOND COLOM (Rue) D2
REMPARTS (Rue des) B1-C2
RENIERE (Rue) D3-D4
REPUBLIQUE (Place de la) D1
RICHELIEU (Quai) C4-D4
ROBERT PICQUE (Passage) A1
ROHAN (Rue) C2
ROLLAND (Rue) B1
ROUSSELLE (Rue de la) C4-D4
RUAT (Rue) B2-C2
RUE NEUVE (Impasse) D3
SAIGE (Rue) B2
SAINT-CHRISTOLY (Place) B2
SAINTE-CADENNE (Impasse) D4
SAINTE-CATHERINE (Rue) C2-C3
SAINTE-COLOMBE (Rue) C3
SAINTE-EULALIE (Place) D2
SAINT-ELOI (Rue) D3
SAINT-FORT (Rue) A1
SAINT-FRANCOIS (Rue) D3-D4

SAINT-JAMES (Impasse) D3
SAINT-JAMES (Rue) D3
SAINT-JOHN PERSE (Square) C1-D1
SAINT-LAZARE (Impasse) B1
SAINT-PAUL (Impasse) D3
SAINT-PIERRE (Impasse) C3
SAINT-PIERRE (Place) C3
SAINT-PROJET (Impasse) C3
SAINT-PROJET (Place) C2-C3
SAINT-REMI (Rue) B2-B3
SAINT-SERNIN (Rue) B1-C1
SAINT-SIMEON (Rue) C3
SALINIERES (Quai des) D4
SANSAS (Rue) A1
SARGET (Passage) B2
SAU (Rue de la) D4
SERPOLET (Rue du) C3
SERVANDONI (Rue) D1
SEZE (Rue de) A2
SOLEIL (Rue du) D4
TANNERIES (Impasse des) A1
TASTET (Rue) D1
TEMPLE (Rue du) B2-C2
TEULERE (Rue) D3
THIAC (Rue) B1
TOULOUSE-LAUTREC (Rue) C1
TOUR DE GASSIES (Passage de la) C3
TOUR DE GASSIES (Rue de la) C3
TOUR DU PIN (Rue de la) D4
TOURNON (Cours de) A2
TOURNY (Allée de) A2-B2
TOURNY (Place) A2
TOUSSAINT LOUVERTURE (Square) A4
30 JUILLET (Cours du) A2-B3
3 CHANDELIERS (Rue des) C3
3 CONILS (Rue des) C3
TURENNE (Rue de) A1
TUSTAL (Rue) C3
ULYSSE DESPAUX (Rue) D4
VACHE (Rue de la) C3
VAUBAN (Rue) A3
VERDUN (Cours de) A2
VERTEUIL (Rue) C1
VEYRINES (Rue) D2
VICTOIRE AMERICAINE (Impasse) A2
VICTOIRE AMERICAINE (Rue) A2
VICTOR HUGO (Cours) D2-D4
VIEILLE TOUR (Impasse de la) B1-B2
VIEILLE TOUR (Rue de la) B1-B2
VIEUX MARCHE (Rue du) D4
VILLE DE MIRMONT (Rue de la) A1-A2
VILLENEUVE (Rue) C1
VINET (Place) C3
VINET (Square) C3
VITAL CARLES (Rue) B2-C2
VOLTAIRE (Rue) B2

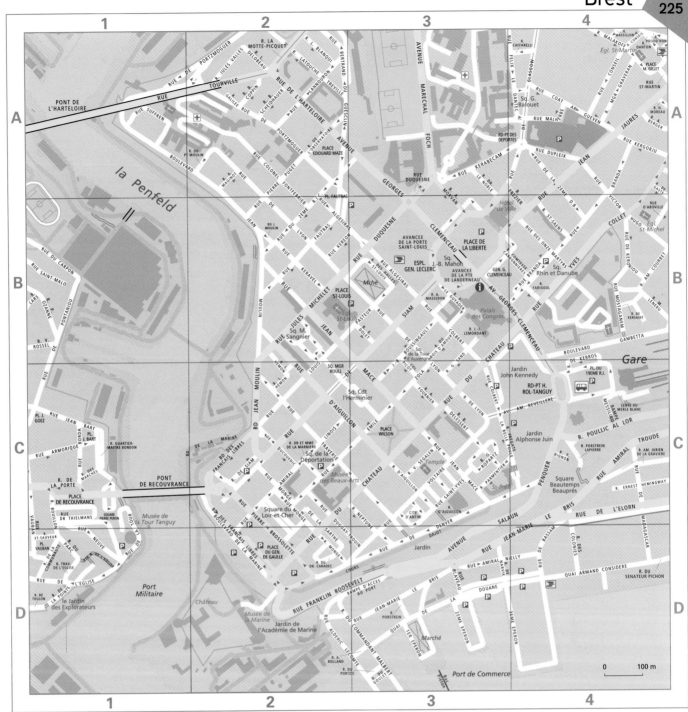

0   100 m

Brest

ABOVILLE (Rue d') B4
ACCES AU PORT (Rampe d') D2-D3
AIGUILLON (Rue d') B2-C3
ALAIN FOURNIER (Rue) C3
ALBERT ROLLAND (Rue) D3
ALDERIC LECOMTE (Rue) D2-D3
ALEXANDRE MASSERON (Rue) B3
ALGESIRAS (Rue) B2-B3
AMIRAL COURBET (Rue) B4
AMIRAL JURIEN DE LA GRAVIERE
   (Rue) C4
AMIRAL LINOIS (Rue) C2-D2
AMIRAL NIELLY (Rue) D3-D4
AMIRAL REVEILLERE (Avenue) C3-C4
AMIRAL RONARC'H (Rue) D1
AMIRAL TROUDE (Rue) C4
ANDRE BERGER (Rue) A4
ANDRE MAGINOT (Rue) A2
ANTIN (Cité d') C3-D3
ARMAND CONSIDERE (Quai) D4
ARMORIQUE (Rue) C1
AUGUSTIN MORVAN (Rue) A3-B3
BAC PIETON D3
BASSAM (Rue de) C4-D4
BENJAMIN DELESSERT (Rue) C3
BERNARD SCHEIDHAUER (Rue) A2
BERTRAND DU GUESCLIN (Rue) A2
BLAVEAU (Rue) D3
BOIS D'AMOUR (Rue du) B3
BORDA (Rue) C1
BOUILLON (Rue) C1-D1
BRANDA (Rue) A4-B4
CAFFARELLI (Rue) A4
CARPON (Rue du) B1
CHATEAU (Rue du) D2-B4
COAT AR GUEVEN (Rue) A4
COLBERT (Rue) B3-C3
COLONEL FONTFERRIER (Rue) A2-B2
COLONEL PICOT (Rue) B3-C3
COLONIES (Rue des) C4-D4
COMMANDANT MALBERT (Rue du) . . . D2-D3
COMMUNAUTE (Rue de la) D1
COMTESSE CARBONNIERES (Rue) . . . B3-B4
CONSEIL (Rue du) A4
DAJOT (Cours) D2-C3
DANTON (Rue) A4
DENVER (Rue de) C2-C4
DEPORTES (Rond-point des) A3
2EME D.B. (Rue de la) A4-B4
2EME EPERON D3
2EME R.I.C. (Rue du) B2-A3
19EME R.I. (Place de la) C4
DOCTEUR CARADEC (Rue du) D2
DOCTEUR ET MADAME DE LA MARNIERE
   (Rue) C2

DOCTEUR LE NOBLE (Rue) A3-B3
DOCTEUR THIELMANS (Rue) C1
DOUANE (Quai de la) D3-D4
DUCOUEDIC (Rue) C2
DUGUAY-TROUIN (Rue) C2-D3
DUPLEIX (Rue) A4
DUQUESNE (Rue) B2-A3
EDOUARD MAZE (Place) A2
EGLISE (Petite rue de l') D1
EGLISE (Rue de l') D1
ELORN (Rue de l') C4
EMILE ZOLA (Rue) C2-C3
ERNEST HEMINGWAY (Rue) C4
ETIENNE DOLET (Rue) B3
FARIGOUL (Rue) B4
FAUTRAS (Place) A2-B2
FAUTRAS (Rue) B2
FELIX LE DANTEC (Rue) A4
FRANCAIS LIBRES (Boulevard des) . . . C2-D2
FRANKLIN ROOSEVELT (Rue) D2-D3
FREDERIC LE GUYADER (Rue) B3
FREGATE LA BELLE POULE (Rue) C3-C4
FREZIER (Rue) A3-B4
GALILEE (Rue) A2
GAMBETTA (Boulevard) B4
GASTE (Rue de) A4
GENERAL DE GAULLE (Place du) D2
GENERAL GEORGES CLEMENCEAU (Rue) . . B3
GENERAL LECLERC (Esplanade) B3
GEORGE SAND (Rue) B3-C3
GEORGES CLEMENCEAU (Avenue) . . . B3-A4
GLASGOW (Rue de) A3-A4
GOULET (Rue du) D3
GUY ROPARTZ (Rue) C3
HALLES SAINT-LOUIS (Rue des) B2-B3
HARTELOIRE (Pont de l') A1
HARTELOIRE (Rue de l') A2
HENRI MOREAU (Rue) A4
HENRI ROL-TANGUY (Rond-point) C4
JEAN BART (Place) C1
JEAN BART (Rue) C1
JEAN JAURES (Rue) B3-A4
JEAN MACE (Rue) B2-C3
JEAN MOULIN (Boulevard) A1-C2
JEAN-BAPTISTE BOUSSINGAULT
   (Rue) B3-C3
JEAN-JULIEN LEMORDANT (Rue) B3
JEAN-MARIE LE BRIS (Rue) D3-C4
JOSEPH GOEZ (Place) C1
JULES MICHELET (Rue) B2
JULES VALLES (Rue) A2
KERABECAM (Rue) A3-A4
KERAVEL (Rue) B2
KEREON (Rue) B2-B3
KERGORJU (Rue) A4

KERORIOU (Rue de) B4
KERROS (Rue de) B4-C4
KERSAINT (Rue de) B4
LANNOURON (Rue) A2
LARS (Rue de) B1
LATOUCHE TREVILLE (Rue) A2
LIBERTE (Place de la) B3
LOIR ET CHER (Square du) C2-D2
LOUIS BLANQUI (Rue) A2
LOUIS DELOBEAU (Rue) A2
LOUIS HEMON (Rue) B2-C2
LOUIS PASTEUR (Rue) B2-B3
LYON (Rue de) A2-C3
MADAGASCAR (Rue de) C4-D4
MALAKOFF (Rue) A4
MALHERBE (Rue) A4
MARCHES (Rue des) C1
MARECHAL FOCH (Avenue) A3
MARENGO (Rue) A4
MARIE LENERU (Rue) A3
MARINE (Boulevard de la) C1-D2
MASSILLON (Rue) B2
MAURICE GILLET (Place) A4
MERLE BLANC (Sente du) C3
MESSILIAU (Rampe) C4
MONGE (Rue) C2-D2
MONSEIGNEUR GRAVERAN (Rue) A4
MONSEIGNEUR ROULL (Square) B2-C2
MOSTAGANEM (Rue) B4
MOTTE PICQUET (Rue la) A2
NARVIK (Rue de) C4
NEPTUNE (Rue) C2-D3
NEUVE (Rue) C1-D1
OBSERVATOIRE (Rue de l') A2
11 MARTYRS (Rue des) B4
PARC (Rue du) D1
PARMENTIER (Rue) C3-C4
PETIT MOULIN (Rue du) A2
PIERRE BROSSOLETTE (Rue) C2-D2
PIERRE OZANNE (Rue) B1
PIERRE PERON (Square) C1
PIERRE PUGET (Rue) A2-B2
POINTE (Rue de la) D1
PONTANIOU (Rue de) B1-C1
PORSTREIN (Rue) D3
PORSTREIN LAPIERRE (Rue) C3
PORTE (Rue de la) C1
PORTE DE LANDERNEAU
   (Avancée de la) B3
PORTE SAINT-LOUIS (Avancée de la) . . . B3
PORTZIC (Rue du) D3
PORTZMOGUER (Rue de) A1-A2
POULLIC AL LOR (Rue de) C4
1ER EPERON D3
PROUD'HON (Rue) A4

QUARTIER MAITRE BONDON (Rue) C1
RECOUVRANCE (Place de la) C1
RECOUVRANCE (Pont de) C2
REMY COPPIN (Rue) A2
REPUBLIQUE (Rue de la) B4
SAINT-LOUIS (Place) B3
SAINT-MALO (Rue) B1
SAINT-MARTIN (Rue) A4
SAINT-SAENS (Rue) B4
SAINT-SAUVEUR (Rue) D1
SALAUN PENQUER (Avenue) D3-C4
SARTHE (Rue de la) C2-D2
SENATEUR PICHON (Rue du) D4
SIAM (Rue de) B2-B3
SUFFREN (Rue de) A1
TOULON (Rue de) D1
TOUR (Rue de la) C1-D1
TOURVILLE (Rue) A1-A2
TRAVERSE (Rue) C2-D3
TRAVERSE DE L'EGLISE (Rue) D1
3EME EPERON D3-D4
VAUBAN (Place) D1
VAUBAN (Rue) C1-D1
VICTOR HUGO (Rue) A4-B4
VICTOR ROSSEL (Rue) B1
VICTOR SEGALEN (Rue) C3
VOLTAIRE (Rue) C3
WILSON (Place) C3
YVES BIGNON (Rue) C4
YVES COLLET (Rue) A4-B4

Caen

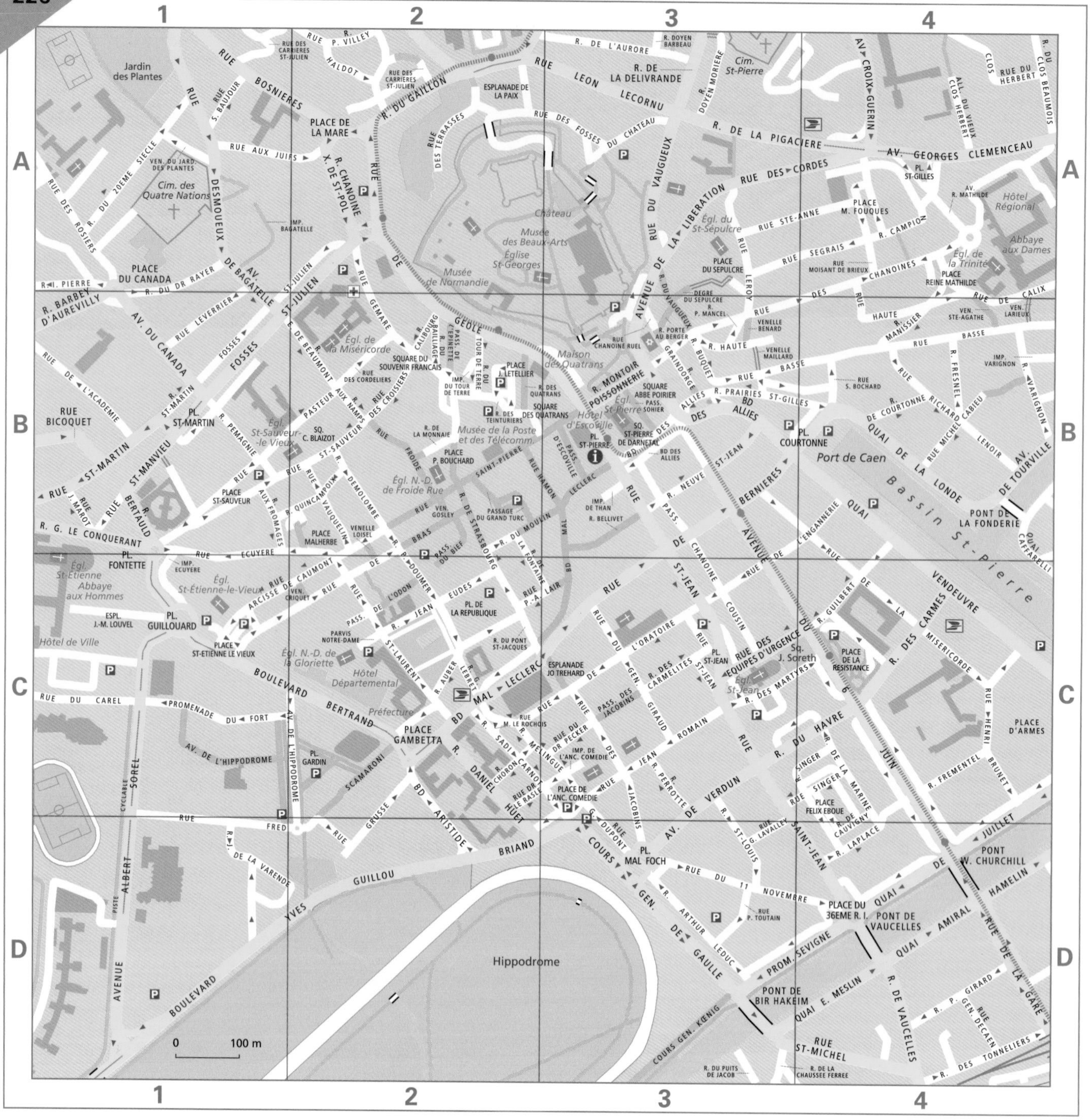

ABBE POIRIER (Square) B3
ACADEMIE (Rue de l'). B1
ALBERT SOREL (Avenue). C1-D1
ALLIES (Boulevard des) B3
AMIRAL HAMELIN (Quai). D4
ANCIENNE COMEDIE (Impasse de l') . . . C3
ANCIENNE COMEDIE (Place de l'). C3
ARCISSE DE CAUMONT (Rue). C1-C2
ARISTIDE BRIAND (Boulevard) C2-D3
ARMES (Place d') C4
ARTHUR LEDUC (Rue) D3
AUBER (Rue) C2
AURORE (Rue de l') A2-A3
BAGATELLE (Avenue de) A1-B1
BAGATELLE (Impasse) A1
BAILLIAGE (Rue du) B2
BARBEY D'AUREVILLY (Rue) A1-B1
BASSE (Rue) B3-B4
BELLIVET (Rue) B3
BENARD (Venelle). B3
BERNIERES (Rue de) B3-C3
BERTAULD (Rue). B1
BERTRAND (Boulevard) C1-C2
BICOQUET (Rue). B1
BIEF (Passage du) B2-C2
BIR HAKEIM (Pont de) D3
BOSNIERES (Rue). A1-A2
BRAS (Rue de). C1-B2
BUQUET (Rue). B3
CAFFARELLI (Quai). B4-C4
CALIBOURG (Rue) B2
CALIX (Rue de) A4-B4
CAMILLE BLAIZOT (Square) B1
CAMPION (Rue) A4
CANADA (Avenue du) A1-B1
CANADA (Place du) A1
CAREL (Rue du). C1
CARMELITES (Rue des) C3
CARMES (Rue des). C4
CARRIERES SAINT-JULIEN
(Rue des). A1-A2
CAUVIGNY (Rue de) C4-D4
CHANOINE COUSIN (Passage) B3-C3
CHANOINE RUEL (Rue) B3
CHANOINE XAVIER DE SAINT-POL
(Rue) A2
CHANOINES (Rue des). B3-A4
CHAUSSEE FERREE (Rue de la). D3
CHORON (Rue) C2
CLOS BEAUMOIS (Rue du) A4
CLOS HERBERT (Rue du) A4
CORDELIERS (Rue des) B2
CORDES (Rue des) A3-A4
COURTONNE (Place) B3-B4
COURTONNE (Rue de) B4
CRIQUET (Venelle) C2
CROISIERS (Rue des) B2
CROIX GUERIN (Avenue) A4
DANIEL HUET (Rue) C2-D2
DELIVRANDE (Rue de la) A3
DEMOLOMBE (Rue) B2
DESMOUEUX (Rue) A1
DOCTEUR LE RASLE (Rue). C2-C3
DOCTEUR PECKER (Rue du) C3
DOCTEUR RAYER (Rue du) A1-B1
DOYEN BARBEAU (Rue). A3
DOYEN MORIERE (Rue) A3
ECUYERE (Impasse) B1-C1
ECUYERE (Rue). B1-C2
ELIE DE BEAUMONT (Rue) B1-B2
ENGANNERIE (Rue de l') C3-B4
EPINETTE (Passage de l'). B2
EQUIPES D'URGENCE (Rue des). C3-C4
ESCOVILLE (Passage d'). B3
EUGENE MESLIN (Quai) D3-D4
FELIX EBOUE (Place) C4-D4
FONDERIE (Pont de la) B4
FONTAINE (Rue de la) B2-C3
FONTETTE (Place). B1
FORT (Promenade du) C1-C2
FOSSES DU CHATEAU (Rue des) . . . A2-A3
FRED SCAMARONI (Rue). D1-C2
FREMENTEL (Rue) C4
FRESNEL (Rue) B4
FROIDE (Rue). B2
FROMAGES (Rue aux) B1
GABRIEL DUPONT (Rue) C3-D3
GAILLON (Rue du) A2
GAMBETTA (Place). C2
GARDIN (Place). C2
GARE (Rue de la) D4
GASTON LAVALLEY (Rue) C3-D3
GEMARE (Rue) A2-B2
GENERAL DE GAULLE (Cours) D3
GENERAL DECAEN (Rue). D4
GENERAL GIRAUD (Rue du) C3
GENERAL KŒNIG (Cours). D3
GEOLE (Rue de) A2-B3
GEORGES CLEMENCEAU (Avenue) A4
GEORGES LEBRET (Rue) C2
GOSLEY (Venelle). B2
GRAINDORGE (Rue). B3
GRAND TURC (Passage du) B2
GRUSSE (Rue). C2-D2
GUILBERT (Rue) B4-C4
GUILLAUME LE CONQUERANT (Rue) . . B1
GUILLOUARD (Place) C1
HALDOT (Rue). A2
HAMON (Rue) .B2-B3
HAUTE (Rue). B3-A4
HAVRE (Rue du) C3-C4
HENRI BRUNET (Rue). C4
HIPPODROME (Avenue de l'). D1-C2
ISIDORE PIERRE (Rue) A1
JACOBINS (Passage des). C3
JACOBINS (Rue des) C3-D3
JARDIN DES PLANTES (Venelle du) A1
JEAN DE LA VARENDE (Rue). D1-D2
JEAN EUDES (Rue). C2
JEAN LETELLIER (Place) B2
JEAN MAROT (Rue) B1
JEAN ROMAIN (Rue) C3
JEAN-MARIE LOUVEL (Esplanade) C1
JO TREHARD (Esplanade). C3
JUIFS (Rue aux) A1-A2
JUILLET (Quai de). C4-D4
LAPLACE (Rue) C4-D4
LARIEUX (Venelle) A4-B4
LEON LECORNU (Rue) A2-A3
LEROY (Rue) A3-B3
LEVERRIER (Rue) A1-B1
LIBERATION (Avenue de la). A3-B3
LOISEL (Venelle) B2-C2
LONDE (Quai de la). B4
MAILLARD (Venelle). B3
MALHERBE (Place) C2
MANISSIER (Rue) B4
MARE (Place de la) A2
MARECHAL FOCH (Place) D3
MARECHAL LECLERC (Boulevard) . . .C2-B3
MARINE (Rue de la) C4-D4
MARTHE LE ROCHOIS (Rue) C2
MARTYRS (Rue des). C3-C4
MAURICE FOUQUES (Place) A4
MELINGUE (Rue) C2-C3
MICHEL CABIEU (Rue) B4
MISERICORDE (Rue de la) B3-C4
MOISANT DE BRIEUX (Rue) A4
MONNAIE (Rue de la). B2
MONTOIR POISSONNERIE (Rue). B3
MOULIN (Rue du) B2-B3
NAMPS (Rue aux). B2
NEUVE SAINT-JEAN (Rue). B3
NOTRE-DAME (Parvis) C2
ODON (Passage de l'). C2
11 NOVEMBRE (Rue du) D3-D4
ORATOIRE (Rue de l') C2-C3
PAIX (Esplanade de la) A2
PASTEUR (Rue) B1-B2
PAUL DOUMER (Rue) B2-C2
PAUL TOUTAIN (Rue) D3
PEMAGNIE (Rue). B1
PIERRE AIME LAIR (Rue) C2-C3
PIERRE BOUCHARD (Place). B2
PIERRE GIRARD (Rue) D4
PIERRE MANCEL (Rue). B3
PIERRE VILLEY (Rue). A2
PIGACIERE (Rue de la) A3-A4
PISTE CYCLABLE C1-D1
PONT SAINT-JACQUES (Rue du). C2-C3
PORTE AU BERGER (Rue) B3
PRAIRIES SAINT-GILLES (Rue). B3-B4
PUITS DE JACOB (Rue du). D3
QUATRANS (Rue des) B2
QUATRANS (Square des). B2
QUINCAMPOIX (Rue) B1-B2
REINE MATHILDE (Avenue) A4
REINE MATHILDE (Place). A4
RENE PERROTTE (Rue). C3
REPUBLIQUE (Place de la) C2
RESISTANCE (Place de la) C4
RICHARD LENOIR (Rue) B4
ROSIERS (Rue des). A1
SADI CARNOT (Rue). C2-C3
SAINT-ETIENNE LE VIEUX (Place) C1
SAINT-GILLES (Place) A4
SAINT-JEAN (Place) C3
SAINT-JEAN (Rue). B3-D4
SAINT-JULIEN (Fossés) B1-A2
SAINT-LAURENT (Rue) C2
SAINT-LOUIS (Rue) C3-D3
SAINT-MANVIEU (Rue). B1
SAINT-MARTIN (Place) B1
SAINT-MARTIN (Rue) B1
SAINT-MICHEL (Rue). D3-D4
SAINT-PIERRE (Place) B3
SAINT-PIERRE (Rue) B2-B3
SAINT-PIERRE DE DARNETAL (Square) . B3
SAINT-SAUVEUR (Place) B1
SAINT-SAUVEUR (Rue). B1-B2
SAINTE-AGATHE (Venelle). B4
SAINTE-ANNE (Rue). A3-A4
SAMUEL BOCHARD (Rue) B4
SEGRAIS (Rue) A3-A4
SEPULCRE (Degré du) A3-B3
SEPULCRE (Place du) A3
SEVIGNE (Promenade). D3-D4
SINGER (Rue) C3-C4
6 JUIN (Avenue du) B3-D4
SOHIER (Passage). B3
SOPHRONYME BAUJOUR (Rue). A1
SOUVENIR FRANCAIS(Square du) B2
STRASBOURG (Rue de) B2-C2
TEINTURIERS (Rue des) B2
TERRASSES (Rue des) A2
THAN (Impasse de). B3
TONNELIERS (Rue des) D4
TOUR DE TERRE (Impasse du). B2
TOUR DE TERRE (Rue du). B2
TOURVILLE (Avenue de). B4
36EME REGIMENT D'INFANTERIE
(Place du) D4
VARIGNON (Impasse). B4
VARIGNON (Rue) B4
VAUCELLES (Pont de). D4
VAUCELLES (Rue de) D4
VAUGUEUX (Rue du) A3-B3
VAUQUELIN (Rue). B2
VENDEUVRE (Quai) B3-C4
VERDUN (Avenue de). C3-D3
VIEUX CLOS HERBERT (Allée du) A4
20EME SIECLE (Rue du). A1
WINSTON CHURCHILL (Pont) D4
YVES GUILLOU (Boulevard) D1-D2

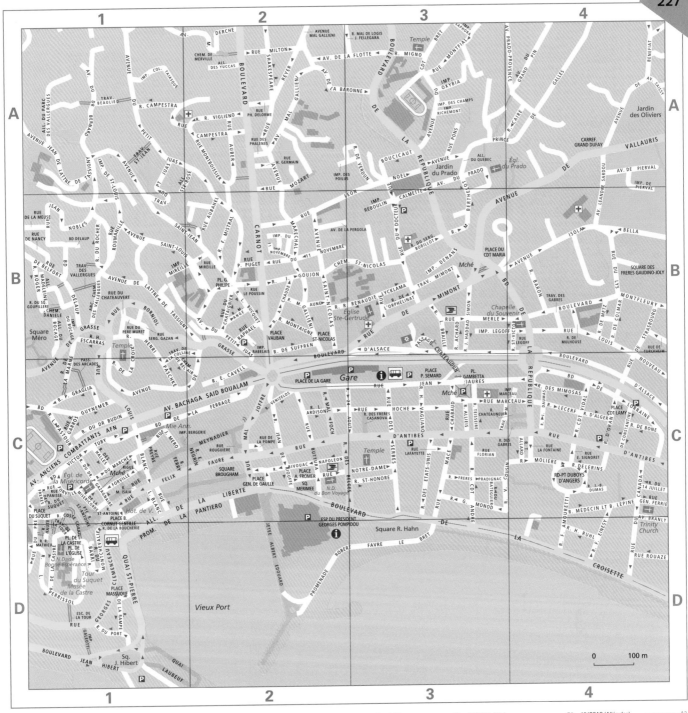

Cannes

227

ACHARD (Rue) B3
ALBERT EDOUARD (Jetée) C2-D2
ALBERT FROMER (Place) C2
ALGER (Rue d') C4
ALLIEIS (Rue) C3
ALSACE (Boulevard d') C2-B4
ANCIENS COMBATTANTS A F N (Avenue) C1
ANDRE CHAUDE (Rue) B2
ANTIBES (Rue d') C2-C4
ARCADES (Passage des) C1
AUBANEL (Rue) B2
AUBER (Rue) A2-B2
B. CORNUT GENTILLE (Place) D1
BACHAGA SAID BOUALAM (Avenue) C1-C2
BARON (Rue) B4
BARONNE (Avenue de la) A2-A3
BARRI (Rue du) D1
BATEGUIER (Rue du) C4
BEAULIEU (Traverse) A1
BEL AIR (Chemin de) B1-C2
BELFORT (Rue de) B1
BELGES (Rue) C2-C3
BENEFIAT (Avenue de) A4
BERGERIE (Impasse) C1
BIVOUAC NAPOLEON (Rue) C2
BOCAGE (Allée du) B1-C1
BOCAGE (Impasse du) B1
BONE (Rue de) C4
BORNIOL (Rue) B1-B2
BOUCHERIE (Rue de la) C1-D1
BOUCICAUT (Rue) A3
BRANLY (Avenue) C4-D4
BROUGHAM (Square) C2
BUTTURA (Rue) C2
CAIRE (Rue) A3-A4
CAMPESTRA (Rue) A1-A2
CANADA (Rue de) C4-D4
CARNOT (Boulevard) A2-C2
CASTRE (Place de la) D1
CASTRE (Rue de la) D1
CHABAUD (Rue) C3
CHAMPS (Impasse des) A3
CHATAIGNIER (Rue du) B2
CHATEAUDUN (Passage) B3-C3
CHATEAUNEUF (Rue) C3-C4
CHATEAUVERT (Rue du) B2
COLLINE (Traverse de la) C1-B2
COLMAR (Rue) B4
COLONEL TAJASQUE (Impasse) A1
COMMANDANT ANDRE (Rue) C3-D3
COMMANDANT BRET (Avenue du) A1
COMMANDANT LAMY (Place) C4
COMMANDANT MARIA (Place du) B3

COMMANDANT VIDAL (Rue) C4
CONSTANTINE (Rue de) C4
COSTE CORAIL (Rue) C1-D1
CROISETTE (Boulevard de la) C2-D4
CROIX (Rue de la) B1-C1
DANIELE (Chemin) B1
DELAUP (Boulevard) B1
DENANS (Impasse) B3
DIX-HUIT JUIN (Place du) C2
DOCTEUR BERNARD (Avenue du) A1
DOCTEUR BUDIN (Rue du) C1
DOCTEUR CALMETTE (Rue du) A3-B3
DOCTEUR P GAZAGNAIRE (Rue du) C1
DUBOYS D'ANGERS (Rond-point) C4
EDITH CAVELL (Rue) C2
ÉGLISE (Place de l') D1
EMILE NEGRIN (Rue) C4
EMMANUEL SIGNORET (Rue) C1
ETATS-UNIS (Rue des) C3
FELIX FAURE (Rue) C1-C2
FERRAGE (Boulevard de la) C1-C2
FERRY (Rue) C1
FLORIAN (Rue) C3
FLOTTE (Avenue de la) A2-A3
FONTAINE (Rue de la) C2
FORVILLE (Rue) C1
FRANCOIS EINESY (Rue) C4-D4
FREDERIC AMOURETTI (Rue) C4-D4
FREDERIC MISTRAL (Rue) B2
FRERES (Rue des) C1
FRERES CASANOVA (Rue des) C3
FRERES GAUDINO-JOLY (Square des) B4
FRERES PRADIGNAC (Rue) C3
GABRES (Rue des) C4
GABRES (Traverse des) B4
GALEOTTI (Impasse) D1
GAMBETTA (Place) C2
GARE (Place de la) C2
GENERAL DE GAULLE (Place) C2
GENERAL FERRIE (Rue) C2
GEORGES CLEMENCEAU (Rue) A3-B3
GEORGES POMPIDOU (Esplanade) D1
GERARD MONOD (Rue) C3
GERARD PHILIPE (Place) C2
GRAND DUFAY (Carrefour) A4
GRAND PIN (Avenue du) A4
GRASSE (Avenue de) C1-B2
GUYNEMER (Boulevard) C1
HALLES (Rue des) C1
HAUTE (Rue) C1-D1
HELENE VAGLIANO (Rue) C3
HENRI GERMAIN (Rue) A2
HENRI PASCHKE (Rue) B1-C1
HENRI RUHL (Rue) D4
HOCHE (Rue) C2-C3

HONORE ESCARRAS (Rue) B1
HOTEL DE VILLE (Place de l') C1-D1
ISOLA BELLA (Avenue) B3-B4
JEAN DAUMAS (Rue) C2
JEAN DE LATTRE DETASSIGNY (Avenue) A1-B1
JEAN DE RIOUFFE (Rue) C2
JEAN GOUJON (Rue) B2
JEAN HADDAD SIMON (Rue) B3
JEAN HIBERT (Boulevard) D1
JEAN JAURES (Rue) C2-C4
JEAN MERO (Rue) C1
JEAN NOBLES (Rue) C1
JEAN-BAPTISTE DUMAS (Rue) C3
LAFAYETTE (Rue) B1-B2
LATTRE DE TASSIGNY (Avenue de) B1-B2
LAUBEUF (Quai) D1-D2
LEANDRE SARDOU (Avenue) A4-B4
LECERF (Rue) C4
LEGOFF (Impasse) B3-B4
LEGOFF (Rue) B4
LEON NOEL (Rue) B2-A3
LEOPOLD BUCQUET (Rue) B2
LERINS (Rue de) C3
LIBERTE (Allée de la) D1-C2
LORRAINE (Boulevard de) C2
LOUIS ARDISON (Rue) C2
LOUIS BLANC (Rue) B1-C1
LOUIS BRAILLE (Rue) B3
LOUIS NOUVEAU (Rue) B4-C4
LOUIS PASTOUR (Rue) C1
LOUIS PERRISSOL (Rue) D1
LYCKLAMA (Rue du) B3
LYS (Rue du) B4
MACE (Rue) C3-D3
MADELEINE (Allée) B1
MAL DE LOGIS J FELLEGARA (Rue) A3
MARCEAU (Impasse) C3
MARCEAU (Rue) C3-C4
MARCEAU (Traverse) C3
MARECHAL FERRIE (Avenue du) C1
MARCELLIN BERTHELOT (Rue) A3-B3
MARCHE FORVILLE (Rue du) C1
MARECHAL FOCH (Rue) C2
MARECHAL GALLIENI (Avenue) A2-C2
MARECHAL JOFFRE (Rue) C2
MARIUS AUNE (Rue) B1
MARIUS ISAIA (Rue) C1
MARNE (Rue de la) B1-C1
MASSUQUE (Place) D1
MAURICE DERCHE (Avenue) A1-A2
MEDECIN LT B. LEPINE (Rue) C4
MERIMEE (Square) C3
MERLE (Rue de) B3-B4
MERVILLE (Chemin de) A2
METZ (Rue de) B4

MEUSE (Rue de la) B1
MEYNADIER (Rue) C1-C2
MICHEL ANGE (Rue) C4
MIGNO (Rue) A3
MILTON (Rue) A2
MIMONT (Rue de) B2-B3
MIMONT (Traverse) B3
MIMOSAS (Rue des) C4
MIREILLE (Impasse) B1-B2
MIREILLE (Rue) B2
MISERICORDE (Rue de la) C1
MOLIERE (Rue) C3
MONTAIGNE (Rue) B2
MONTBOISSIER (Rue) A2
MONTCHEVALIER (Rue) C1
MONTFIAL (Rue) A3
MONTFLEURY (Boulevard) B4
MOZART (Rue) A2
MULHOUSE (Rue de) B4
NANCY (Rue de) B1
NOTRE-DAME (Rue) C2-C3
ONZE NOVEMBRE (Impasse du) B2
ONZE NOVEMBRE (Rue du) B2
ORAN (Rue d') C4
ORPHELINAT (Rue de l') B3
OXYBIA (Impasse) A3
PANISSE (Rue) C1
PANTIERO (Promenade de la) D1-C2
PARC DES VALLERGUES (Allée du) A1
PAUL MERO (Square) B1-C1
PERE MURET (Rue du) B1
PERGOLA (Avenue de la) B2-B3
PETIT JUAS (Avenue du) A1-C2
PETIT JUAS (Traverse du) A1-B1
PHALENES (Rue des) A2
PHILIBERT DELORME (Rue) A2
PIERRE GRAGLIA (Rue) B2
PIERRE PUGET (Rue) B2
PIERRE SEMARD (Place) C2
PIERVAL (Avenue de) A4
PIERVAL (Impasse de) A4-B4
POILUS (Impasse des) A3
POMPE (Rue de la) C2
PONS (Rue) A3
PORT (Rue du) D1
POUSSIN (Rue le) B2
PRADO (Avenue du) A4
PRADO-PROVENCE (Avenue) A4
PRE (Rue du) C1-D1
PREYRE (Rue) D1
PRINCE DE GALLES (Avenue) A3-A4
QUATORZE JUILLET (Rue du) C4
QUEBEC (Allée du) A3
RABELAIS (Impasse) B2
RAMPE (Rue) D1

RAPHAEL (Rue) B2
RAYMOND MATHIEU (Rue) C1-D1
REBOULIN (Impasse) B3
RENE VIGLIENO (Rue) A2
REPUBLIQUE (Boulevard de la) A3-C4
REYER (Rue) A2
RICHEMONT (Impasse) A3
RIGUE (Rue) C1
ROBERT FAVRE LE BRET (Promenade) D2-D3
ROCHER (Rue du) B1
ROGER (Rue) B1
ROGER RENAUDIE (Rue) B2-B3
ROLAND GARROS (Rue) C1
ROUAZE (Rue) D4
ROUGUIERE (Rue) C2
ROUMANILLE (Rue) B1
SAINT-ANTOINE (Petite rue) C1-D1
SAINT-ANTOINE (Rue) C1
SAINTE-ROSE (Allée) B1-A2
SAINT-HONORE (Rue) C3
SAINT-JEAN (Avenue) A1-B2
SAINT-JEAN (Traverse) A1
SAINT-LOUIS (Avenue) B1-B2
SAINT-LOUIS (Impasse de) A1-B1
SAINT-NICOLAS (Avenue) B2
SAINT-NICOLAS (Chemin) B2-B3
SAINT-PIERRE (Quai) D1
SAINT-VICTOR (Rue) B4
SAISSY (Avenue) A4
SERBES (Rue des) C3
SERGENT BOBILLOT (Rue du) B3
SERGENT GAZAN (Rue) B1
SHAKESPEARE (Rue) A2
SQUARE GOUPILLERE (Rue du) B1
ST-NICOLAS (Place) B2
STRASBOURG (Rue de) B4-C4
SUFFREN (Rue de) B2
SUQUET (Place du) C1
SUQUET (Rue du) C1
TEISSEIRE (Rue) C3
TONY ALLARD (Rue) C4
TOUR (Escalier de la) C1-D1
TURCKHEIM (Rue de) B4
VALLAURIS (Avenue de) B3-A4
VALLERGUES (Ancien chemin des) B1
VALLERGUES (Traverse des) B1
VAUBAN (Place) B2
VENIZELOS (Rue) A2-A3
VERDUN (Rue de) A2-A3
VICTOR COUSIN (Rue) C3-C4
VICTOR TUBY (Boulevard) C1
VINGT-QUATRE AOUT (Rue) C2-C3

YUCCAS (Allée des) A2

Clermont-Ferrand

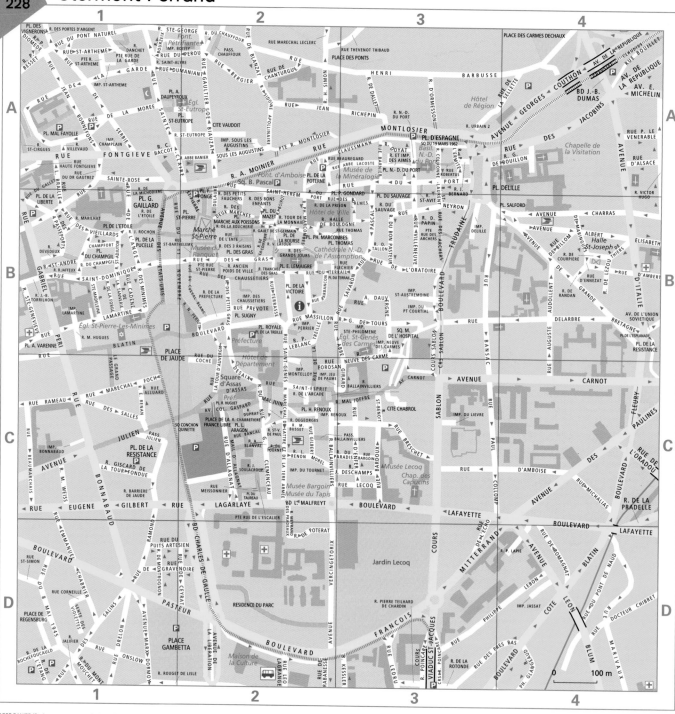

ABBE BANIER (Rue) A1-A2
ABBE DAUPEYROUX (Place) A1
ABBE GIRARD (Rue) B2-C3
ABBE LACOSTE (Rue) A2-A3
AIMES (Rue des) A3
ALEXANDRE VARENNE (Place) B1
ALLAGNAT (Mail d') C2
ALLAGNAT (Rue d') C2
ALLUARD (Rue) C2
ALSACE (Rue d') A4
AMBERT (Rue d') B4
AMBOISE (Rue d') C3-C4
ANCIEN POIDS DE VILLE (Rue) B2
ANDRE MOINIER (Rue) A2-A3
ANGE (Rue de l') A1-B1
ANTOINE DAUVERNE (Rue) B3
ARCADE (Rue de l') B3
ARCHERS (Petite rue des) B3
ARCHERS (Rue des) B3
ARTAUD BLANVAL (Rue) C2
ASSAS (Rue d') C2
AUGUSTE AUDOLLENT (Rue) B4-C4
BALLAINVILLIERS (Passage) C2
BALLAINVILLIERS (Rue) C2-C3
BANCAL (Rue) C2
BANSAC (Rue) B3-C3
BARBANCON (Rue) B2
BARDOUX (Rue) B2
BARGOIN (Rue) C2
BARNIER (Rue) A3
BARRIERE DE JAUDE (Rue) C1
BEAUMARCHAIS (Rue) C1
BEAUREGARD (Rue) A2
BERGIER (Rue) A2
BILLOM (Rue de) B4
BLANZAT (Rue de) B1
BLATIN (Rue) B1-C1
BOHEMES (Rue des) B2-B3
BOIROT (Rue) B2
BOISSY (Impasse) A1
BON PASTEUR (Rue du) C1
BONNABAUD (Impasse) C1
BONNABAUD (Rue) B1-D1
BONS ENFANTS (Rue des) A2-B2
BOUCHERIE (Rue de la) B2
BOUILLET (Rue) A4
BOURSE (Place de la) B2
BOURZEIX (Rue) C2
BRESCHET (Rue) C3
CADENE (Rue) B2
CARMES DECHAUX (Place des) A4
CARNOT (Avenue) C3-C4
CEYRAT (Rue de) D2
CHABROL (Cité) C2
CHAMPFORT (Rue) B1
CHAMPGIL (Place du) B1
CHAMPGIL (Rue du) B1

CHAMPLAIN (Impasse) A1
CHANTURGUE (Rue de) A2
CHARLES DE GAULLE (Boulevard) . C2-D2
CHARRAS (Avenue) B3-B4
CHARRETIERE (Rue) C3
CHAUFFOUR (Passage) A2
CHAUFFOUR (Rue du) A2
CHAUSSETIERS (Impasse des) B2
CHAUSSETIERS (Rue des) B2
CHEVAL BLANC (Rue du) B2
CLAUDE BACCOT (Rue) A1
CLAUDIUS (Chaussée) A1
CLAUSSMANN (Rue) B2-A3
COCHE (Rue du) C2
COIFFERIE (Rue de la) C2
COLONEL GASPARD (Avenue) C2
CONCHON QUINETTE (Square) C1
CORNEILLE (Rue) D1
COTE BLATIN (Boulevard) D3-D4
COURONNE (Rue de la) A3
COURPIERE (Rue de) B4
DALLET (Rue de) A3
DANCHET (Rue) A1
DEGEORGES (Rue) C2
DELARBRE (Rue) B3-B4
DELILLE (Impasse) B3
DELILLE (Place) B3
DENIS PAPIN (Rue) A4
DESAIX (Boulevard) B2-C2
DEUX MARCHES (Rue des) B2
DEVEDEUX (Rue) B1
19 MARS 1962 (Rue du) A4-B4
DOCTEUR CHIBRET (Rue) D4
DOCTEUR GAUTREZ (Rue) A2
DOYAT (Rue) A3
DRELON (Rue) D1
DULAURE (Rue) A2-A3
DUMANIANT (Rue) A1-A2
DUPRAT (Rue) C2
ECHO (Rue de l') C3-D3
EDMOND LEMAIGRE (Place) B2
EDOUARD MICHELIN (Avenue) B4
EMMANUEL CHABRIER (Rue) C1-D1
ENFER (Rue d') C2
ENNEZAT (Rue d') B4
ENTE (Rue de l') B2
ERNEST RENAN (Rue) C1
ESCALIER (Petite rue de l') ... C2
ESPAGNE (Place d') A3
ESPLANADE (Place de l') B4
ETATS UNIS (Avenue des) B1
ETOILE (Place de l') B1
ETOILE (Rue de l') B1
EUGENE GILBERT (Rue) C1
FLECHIER (Rue) B2
FLEURY (Boulevard) B4-D4
FONTGIEVE (Rue) A1

FORGE (Rue de la) B1
FORGSAN (Rue) C2-C3
FRANCE LIBRE (Place de la) C1
FRANCIS PONGE (Place) C2
FRANCOIS MITTERRAND (Bd) D2-D4
GABRIEL PERI (Rue) B1
GALLET (Rue du) A1-B1
GAMBETTA (Place) D1
GARDE (Petite rue de la) A1
GARDE (Rue de la) A1
GAULT DE ST-GERMAIN (Rue) B2
GAULTIER DE BIAUZAT (Rue) C2
GEORGES CLEMENCEAU (Rue) C2
GEORGES COUTHON (Avenue) A3-A4
GILBERT GAILLARD (Place) B1
GILBERT MOREL (Rue) C2
GIRARD DE LA TOUR FONDUE (Rue) C1
GODEFROY DE BOUILLON (Rue) ... B3
GRANDE BRETAGNE (Avenue de).. C4
GRANDS JOURS (Rue des) B2
GRAS (Place des) B2
GRAS (Rue des) B1-B2
GRAVENOIRE (Rue de) D1-D2
GREGOIRE DE TOURS (Rue) B2-B3
HALLE DE BOULOGNE (Rue de) ... B2
HAUTE FONTGIEVE (Rue) A1
HENRI BARBUSSE (Rue) A2-A4
HENRI SIMON (Rue) A2
HIPPOLYTE RENOUX (Rue) C2
ITALIE (Avenue d') A4-B4
JACOBINS (Rue des) A3-A4
JACQUES BERNARD (Rue) C3
JALIFIER (Rue) D1
JASSAT (Impasse) D4
JAUDE (Place de) C1-C2
JEAN BONNEFONS (Rue) A1
JEAN DESCHAMPS (Rue) C2-C3
JEAN RICHEPIN (Rue) A2-A3
JEAN ROCHON (Rue) A2
JEAN SOULACROUP (Rue) C2
JEAN-BAPTISTE DUMAS (Boulevard) A4
JEU DE PAUME (Impasse) C2
JULIEN (Avenue) C1
JULIEN (Passage) C1
KESSLER (Rue) D3
LAFAYETTE (Boulevard) C3
LAGARLAYE (Rue) C1-C2
LAMARTINE (Impasse) B1
LAMARTINE (Rue) B1
LE GRAND PASSAGE B1-C1
LECOQ (Rue) C2
LEDRU (Rue) D3
LEON BLUM (Avenue) C4-D4
LEON MALFREYT (Boulevard) C2
LEZOUX (Rue de) B4

LIBERATION (Avenue de la) D2
LIBERTE (Place de la) B3
LIEVRE (Impasse du) B3
LOUIS ARAGON (Place) C1
LOUIS BRAILLE (Rue) A1-B1
LOUIS RENON (Rue) C2
MARCHE AUX POISSONS (Place) .. B2
MARECHAL DE LATTRE ET DE LA 1ERE
  ARMEE (Rue) C2
MARECHAL FAYOLLE (Place) A1
MARECHAL FOCH (Rue) C2
MARECHAL JOFFRE (Rue) C2-C3
MARECHAL LECLERC (Rue) A2
MARILHAT (Rue) B1
MARINGUES (Rue de) B4
MARIVAUX (Rue) D1
MARX DORMOY (Avenue) D1
MASSILLON (Rue) B2
MAURICE BUSSET (Rue) C2
MAURICE WEISS (Rue) B2
MAZET (Place) B2
MEISSONNIER (Rue) C2
MEYRAND DE PRADEAUX (Rue) C2-D2
MICHALIAS (Rue) C4
MICHEL DE L'HOSPITAL (Square) . B3
MICHEL HUGUES (Rue) B1
MICHODIERE (Rue de la) A1-B1
MINIMES (Rue des) B1
MONT MOUCHET (Rue du) D1
MONTELLOY (Impasse) C2
MONTLOSIER (Petite rue) A2-A3
MONTLOSIER (Rue) A2-A3
MONTROGNON (Rue de) C2
MOREE (Rue de la) A1
NESTOR PERRET (Rue) C2
NEUVE DES CARMES (Impasse) ... B3-C3
NEUVE DES CARMES (Rue) B3-C3
NEYRON (Rue) B3
NOTRE DAME DU PORT (Place) ... A3
NOTRE DAME DU PORT (Rue) A3
OMERTAILLON (Rue) B3
ONSLOW (Rue) D1
11 NOVEMBRE (Rue du) C4
ORADOU (Rue de l') C4
ORATOIRE (Rue de l') B3
ORMESSON (Rue d') A3
PARADIS (Rue du) C2-C3
PARC (Résidence du) D2
PASCAL (Rue) A3-B3
PASTEUR (Boulevard) D1-D2
PAUL COLLOMP (Rue) C3
PAUL DIOMEDE (Rue) A1
PAUL GONDARD (Place) B3
PAUL LAPIE (Rue) D3
PAUL LEBLANC (Rue) C2
PAULINES (Avenue des) C4
PEROU (Rue du) A1-A2

PERRIER (Impasse) B2
PETIT COURTIAL (Impasse du) .. B3
PETITS FAUCHERS (Rue des) A2-B2
PETITS GRAS (Rue des) B2
PHILIPPE GLANGEAUD (Rue) D4
PHILIPPE LEBON (Rue) C3
PHILIPPE MARCOMBES (Impasse) . D3-D4
PHILIPPE MARCOMBES (Rue) B1
PIERRE BESSET (Rue) B2
PIERRE LE VENERABLE (Rue) A4
PIERRE L'ERMITE (Rue) A3
PIERRE TEILHARD DE CHARDIN (Rue) D3
PONT DE NAUD (Rue du) D4
PONT NATUREL (Rue du) A1
PONTS (Place des) A2
PORT (Rue du) B2-A3
PORTES D'ARGENT (Rue des) A1
POTERAT (Rue de) D2
POTERNE (Place de la) A3
PREFECTURE (Rue de la) B2
PRES BAS (Rue des) D3-D4
PREVOTE (Rue) B2
PRISON (Rue de la) B3
PUCELLE (Place de la) B1
PUITS ARTESIEN (Rue du) D1-D2
4 PASSEPORTS (Rue des) D1
RABANESSE (Rue de) D2
RAMEAU (Rue) B1
RAMOND (Rue) C1-D1
RANDAN (Rue de) B3
RAYMOND POINCARE (Cours) D3
REGENSBURG (Place de) D1
RENOUX (Impasse) C2
REPUBLIQUE (Avenue de la) A4
RESISTANCE (Place de la) C2-B4
RIBEYRE JAFFEUX (Rue) B1
ROBERT HUGUET (Place) C2
ROBERTUS (Rue) A3
ROCHEFOUCAULD (Rue de la) D1
ROMAGNAT (Rue de) C4-D4
ROTONDE (Rue de la) D3
ROYALE (Place) D1-D2
SABLON (Cours) B3-D3
SAINT-ADJUTOR (Rue) B1
SAINT-ALYRE (Rue) A2
SAINT-ANDRE (Rue) D2
SAINT-ARTHEME (Impasse) A1
SAINT-ARTHEME (Petite rue) ... A1
SAINT-ARTHEME (Rue) A1
SAINT-ASTREMOINE (Impasse) ... B3
SAINT-AVIT (Rue) A3-B3
SAINT-BARTHELEMY (Rue) B2
SAINT-BENOIT (Rue) C3
SAINT-CIRGUES (Rue) A1
SAINT-DOMINIQUE (Rue) B1
SAINT-ESPRIT (Rue) C2

SAINT-EUTROPE (Place) A2
SAINT-EUTROPE (Rue) A1-A2
SAINT-GENES (Rue) B2-C2
SAINT-HEREM (Rue) A2-B2
SAINT-LAURENT (Rue) A3-B3
SAINT-PIERRE (Petite rue) B2
SAINT-PIERRE (Place) B2
SAINT-PIERRE (Rue) A2-B2
SAINT-SIMON (Rue) D1
SAINT-VINCENT DE PAUL (Rue) .. A4
SAINTE-CLAIRE (Rue) A1-A2
SAINTE-GENEVIEVE (Rue) B1
SAINTE-GEORGE (Rue) A1-A2
SAINTE-MADELEINE (Rue) B1
SAINTE-PHILOMENE (Impasse) ... B1
SAINTE-ROSE (Rue) A1-B1
SAVARON (Rue) B2-B3
SELLETTE (Rue de la) A3-A4
SERBIE (Rue de) A1
SIDOINE APOLLINAIRE (Rue) A2
SOUS LES AUGUSTINS (Impasse) . A2
SOUS LES AUGUSTINS (Rue) A2
SUGNY (Place) B2
TANNERIE (Rue de la) B1
TAUREAU (Place du) C2
TERRAIL (Place du) B3
TERRAIL (Rue du) B2-B3
TERRASSE (Rue de la) C2
THEVENOT THIBAUD (Rue) A2-A3
THIERS (Rue de) B4
THOMAS (Place) B2
THOMAS (Rue) B2-B3
TOUR D'AUVERGNE (Rue la) B2-C2
TOUR DE LA MONNAIE (Rue) B2
TOURNET (Impasse du) C2
TOURNET (Rue du) C2
TRANCHEE DES GRAS (Rue) B2
TREILLE (Place de la) B2-C2
3 RAISINS (Rue des) B2
TRUDAINE (Boulevard) B3
UNION SOVIETIQUE (Avenue de l') B4
URBAIN 2 (Rue) A3
VAUDOIT (Cité) A2
VERCINGETORIX (Avenue) C2-D2
VERDIER LATOUR (Rue) A2-B2
VIADUC SAINT-JACQUES (Rue) ... D3
VICTOIRE (Place de la) B2
VICTOR HUGO (Rue) A4
VIEILLARDS (Rue des) B1
VIGNERONS (Place des) A1
VILLENEUVE (Rue) A3-B3
VILLEVAUD (Rue) A1
VIOLETTES (Sente des) D1

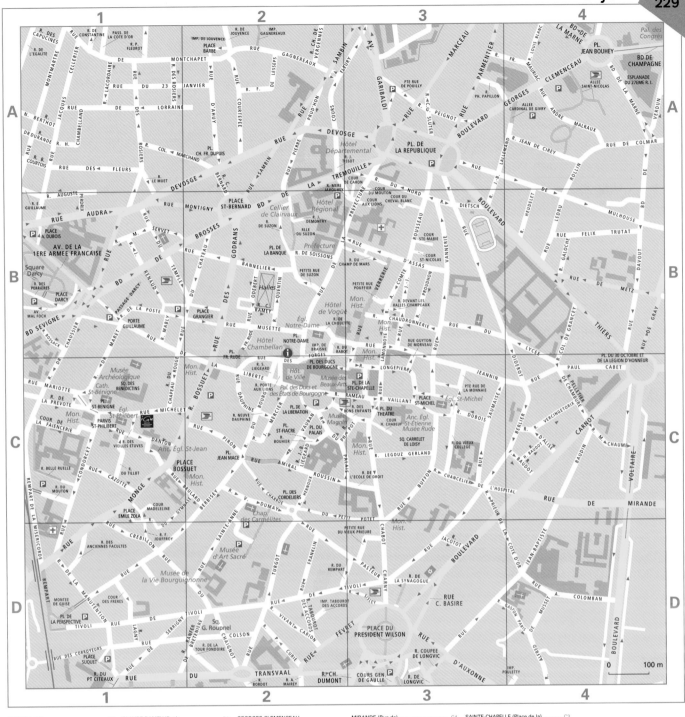

AHUY (Rue d')......................A2
ALFRED DE MUSSET (Rue)..........D4
ALISE (Rue)........................C4
ALPHONSE MAIREY (Rue)..........D2
AMIRAL ROUSSIN (Rue)........C2-C3
ANCIENNES FACULTES (Rue des)....C1
ANDRE COLOMBAN (Rue)............D4
ANDRE MALRAUX (Rue)............A4
ASSAS (Rue d')..................B2-B3
AUDRA (Rue)........................B1
AUGUSTE COMTE (Rue)............B3
AUGUSTE DUBOIS (Place)..........B1
AUGUSTE PERDRIX (Rue)........A1-B1
AUXONNE (Rue d')..................D3
BANNELIER (Rue)................B1-B2
BANQUE (Place de la)..............B2
BARBE (Place)......................B1
BELLE RUELLE (Rue)................C1
BENEDICTINS (Square des)..........C1
BERBISEY (Rue)..................D1-C2
BERLIER (Rue)....................D3-C4
BERNARD COURTOIS (Rue)..........A1
BONS ENFANTS (Rue des)........C2-C3
BORDOT (Rue)......................D2
BOSSACK (Rue)......................B1
BOSSUET (Place)................C1-C2
BOSSUET (Rue)......................C2
BOUHIER (Rue)......................C2
BOURG (Rue du)....................C2
BRAISNE (Impasse de)..............B2
BROSSES (Boulevard de)........B1-B2
BRULARD (Rue)..................C1-C2
BUFFON (Rue)....................C3-D3
CAPUCINES (Rue des)..............A1
CARDINAL DE GIVRY (Allée)........A4
CARNOT (Boulevard)............D3-C4
CARON (Cour de)................A3-B3
CARRELET DE LOISY (Square)......C3
CAZOTTE (Rue)......................C1
CHABOT CHARNY (Rue)..........C3-D3
CHAIGNOT (Rue du)................C4
CHAMP DE MARS (Rue du)......B2-B3
CHAMPAGNE (Boulevard de)........A4
CHANCELIER DE L'HOSPITAL (Rue)..C3-C4
CHAPEAU ROUGE (Rue du)......B1-C1
CHARLES DE VERGENNES (Rue)......A2
CHARLES DUMONT (Rue)............C2
CHARLES FRANCOIS DUPUIS (Place)....A2
CHARRUE (Rue)......................C2
CHATEAU (Rue du)..............B1-B2
CHAUDRONNERIE (Rue)..............B3
CHEVAL BLANC (Cour du)..........B3
CHOUETTE (Rue de la)..........B2-B3
CLAUDE BASIRE (Rue)..............D3
CLAUDE BERNARD (Rue)........A2-B2

CLAUDE RAMEY (Rue)..............B2
CLAUS SLUTER (Rue)................A3
COLMAR (Rue de)..................A4
COLONEL DE GRANCEY (Rue)....B4-C4
COLONEL MARCHAND (Rue)......A1-A2
COLSON (Rue)....................D1-D2
CONSTANTINE (Rue de)............A1
CORDELIERS (Place des)............C2
CORROYEURS (Rue des)............D1
COTE D'OR (Passage de la)........A1
COUPEE DE LONGVIC (Rue)........D3
COURTEPEE (Rue)..................A2
CREBILLON (Rue)................C1-D1
DANTON (Rue)......................C1
DARCY (Passage)....................B1
DARCY (Place)......................B1
DAUPHINE (Rue)....................C2
DAVOUT (Rue)......................B4
DEVANT LES HALLES CHAMPEAUX
DEVOSGE (Rue)..................B1-A3
DIDEROT (Rue)..................A3-C4
DIETSCH (Rue)......................B3
DOCTEUR CHAUSSIER (Rue)....B1-C1
DOCTEUR DURANDE (Rue)..........A1
DOCTEUR MARET (Rue)........B1-C1
DUBOIS (Rue)......................C3
DUCS DE BOURGOGNE
(Place des)....................B2-C3
ECOLE DE DROIT (Rue de l')....C2-C3
EGALITE (Rue de l')................A1
EMILE ZOLA (Place)................C1
EUGENE GUILLAUME (Rue)..........B1
FAIENCERIE (Cour de la)..........C1
FELIX TRUTAT (Rue)................B2
FERDINAND DE LESSEPS (Rue)......A2
FEVRET (Rue)....................D2-D3
FLEURS (Rue des)..................A1
FLEUROT (Rue)......................A3
FLEURY (Cours)..................A2-A3
FORGES (Rue des)..............B2-C2
FRANCOIS BAUDOT (Rue)..........C4
FRANCOIS JOUFFROY (Rue)....C1-D1
FRANCOIS MAURIAC (Rue)......A3-A4
FRANCOIS RUDE (Place)........B2-C2
FRANCOIS RUDE (Rue)..............B2
FRANKLIN (Rue)....................A3
FRERES (Cour des)................D1
GABRIEL PEIGNOT (Rue)............C1
GAGNEREAUX (Impasse)............A2
GAGNEREAUX (Rue)................A2
GALOCHE (Cour du)................B4
GARIBALDI (Avenue)................A3
GASTON PARIS (Rue)............D3-D4
GENERAL DE GAULLE (Cours)......D3

GEORGES CLEMENCEAU
(Boulevard)....................A3-A4
GODRANS (Rue des)............B2-C2
GRANGIER (Place)..............B1-B2
GRAY (Rue de)..................B4-C4
GUILLAUME (Porte)................B1
GUYTON DE MORVEAU (Rue)....B2-B3
GYMNASE (Rue du)..............D1-C2
HENRI BAUDOT (Rue)..............C2
HENRI CHABEUF (Cour)............C3
HENRY CHAMBELLAND (Rue)........A1
HERNOUX (Rue)....................C2
HEUDELET (Rue)................A4-B4
JACOTOT (Rue)......................D3
JACQUES CELLERIER (Rue)......A1-B1
JAMES DEMONTRY (Rue)............B2
JEAN BOUHEY (Place)..............A4
JEAN DE CIREY (Rue)..............A4
JEAN MACE (Place)................C2
JEAN RENAUD (Rue)................B2
JEAN-BAPTISTE BAUDIN (Rue)....D3-C4
JEAN-BAPTISTE LALLEMAND (Rue)....B3-B4
JEAN-BAPTISTE LIEGEARD (Rue)....B3
JEAN-JACQUES ROUSSEAU (Rue)....B3-C4
JEANNIN (Rue)..................B3-C4
JOSEPH TISSOT (Rue)..............A2
JOUVENCE (Impasse de)............A2
JOUVENCE (Rue de)................A2
JULES VIOLLE (Rue)................
LACORDAIRE (Rue)................A1
LAGNY (Rue)........................D1
LAMONNOYE (Rue)..............B3-C3
LEDRU ROLLIN (Rue)............A4-B4
LEGOUZ GERLAND (Rue)............C3
LIBERATION (Place de la)......B1-C2
LIONS (Cour aux)..................B3
LONGEPIERRE (Rue)................B3
LONGVIC (Rue de)................D3
LOUIS BLANC (Rue)................A4
LYCEE (Rue du)................B3-C4
MABLY (Rue)........................B1
MADELEINE (Cour)................B3
MANUTENTION (Rue de la)........D1
MARCEAU (Rue)....................A3
MARECHAL FOCH (Avenue)........B1
MARIOTTE (Rue)....................C1
MARNE (Boulevard de la)..........A4
MAURICE CHAUME (Rue)............C4
MERE JAVOUHEY (Rue)..........A2-B3
METZ (Rue de)......................B4
MICHEL SERVET (Rue)..........B1-B2
MICHELET (Rue)................C1-C2

MIRANDE (Rue de)................C4
MISERICORDE (Rempart de la)....C1-D1
MONGE (Rue)....................C1-D1
MONNAIE (Petite rue de la)......C3
MONTCHAPET (Rue de)..........A1-A2
MONTIGNY (Rue)................B1-B2
MONTMARTRE (Rue)................A1
MOUTON (Cour du)..............A3-B3
MOUTON (Rue)......................C1
MUET (Rue le)......................A1
MULHOUSE (Rue de)............A3-B4
MUSETTE (Rue)....................B2
NEUVE DAUPHINE (Rue)............C2
NICOLAS BERTHOT (Rue)..........A1
NORD (Rue du)..................A3-B3
NOTRE DAME (Place)............B2-C2
ODEBERT (Rue)....................B2
PALAIS (Place du)................C2
PALAIS (Rue du)................C2-C3
PARMENTIER (Rue)................A3
PASTEUR (Rue)..................C2-D3
PAUL CABET (Rue)................C4
PELLETIER DE CHAMBURE (Rue)....C3
PERRIERES (Rue des)..............B1
PERSPECTIVE (Place de la)........D1
PETIT CITEAUX (Rue du)..........D1
PETIT POTET (Rue du)..........C2-C3
PHILIBERT PAPILLON (Rue)......A3-A4
PHILIPPE POT (Rue)............C2-C3
PIERRE CURIE (Rue)................D2
PIERRE FLEUROT (Rue)............A1
PIERRE PRUD'HON (Rue)..........A2
PIRON (Rue)........................C2
PORTE AUX LIONS (Rue)............C2
POSTE (Rue de la)................B1
POUFFIER (Petite rue de)..........B1
POUILLY (Petite rue de)..........A3
POULETTY (Impasse)................D4
PREFECTURE (Rue de la)........B2-A3
1ERE ARMEE FRANCAISE
(Avenue de la)....................B1
PRESIDENT WILSON (Place du)....D3
PREVOTE (Rue de la)..............C1
PRIEUR DE LA COTE D'OR (Rue)....C3-D4
PROUDHON (Rue)..................B3
QUENTIN (Rue)....................B2
RABOT (Rue du)....................B2
RAMEAU (Rue)..................C2-C3
RANFER DE BRETENIERE (Rue)....D1-D2
REMPART (Rue du)..............D2-D3
REPUBLIQUE (Place de la)........A3
ROSIERS (Rue des)..............A1-B1
SAINT-BENIGNE (Place)............C1
SAINT-BERNARD (Place)............B1
SAINTE-ANNE (Rue)............C2-D2

SAINTE-CHAPELLE (Place de la)....C3
SAINTE-MARIE (Cour)..............B3
SAINT-FIACRE (Place)..............C2
SAINT-MICHEL (Place)..............C3
SAINT-NICOLAS (Allée)............A4
SAINT-NICOLAS (Cour)............B3
SAINT-PHILIBERT (Parvis)........C1
SAMBIN (Rue)..................B2-A3
SAUMAISE (Rue)..................C3
SERRIGNY (Rue de)............D1-D2
SEVIGNE (Boulevard)..............B1
SISLEY (Rue)....................D2-D3
SOISSONS (Rue de)................B2
STEPHEN LIEGEARD (Rue)..........C2
SUQUET (Place)....................D1
SUZON (Petite rue de)............B2
SUZON (Rue du)....................B2
SUZON (Ruelle du)................B2
TABOUROT DES ACCORDS (Impasse)....D2
TABOUROT DES ACCORDS (Rue)....D2
TEMPLE (Rue du)................B1-B2
THEATRE (Rue du)................C3
THIERS (Boulevard)............A3-C4
TILLOT (Rue du)..................C1
TIVOLI (Rempart)..................D1
TIVOLI (Rue de)................D1-D3
TOUR FONDOIRE (Rue de la)......D1
TRANSVAAL (Rue du)............D1-D3
TREMOUILLE (Boulevard de la)....B2-A3
30 OCTOBRE ET DE LA LEGION
D'HONNEUR (Place du)............C4
TURGOT (Rue)..................C2-D2
VAILLANT (Rue)....................C3
VANNERIE (Rue)................B3-C3
VAUBAN (Rue)......................C3
VERCINGETORIX (Rue)..............C3
VERDUN (Boulevard de)........A4-B4
VERRERIE (Rue)................B3-C3
VICTOR DUMAY (Rue)..............C2
VIEILLES ETUVES (Rue)............C1
VIEUX COLLEGE (Rue du)..........C3
VIEUX PRIEURE (Petite rue du)....D3
27EME REGIMENT D'INFANTERIE
(Esplanade du)....................A4
23 JANVIER (Rue du)............A1-A2
VIVANT CARION (Rue)..............D2
VOLTAIRE (Boulevard)..........C4-D4

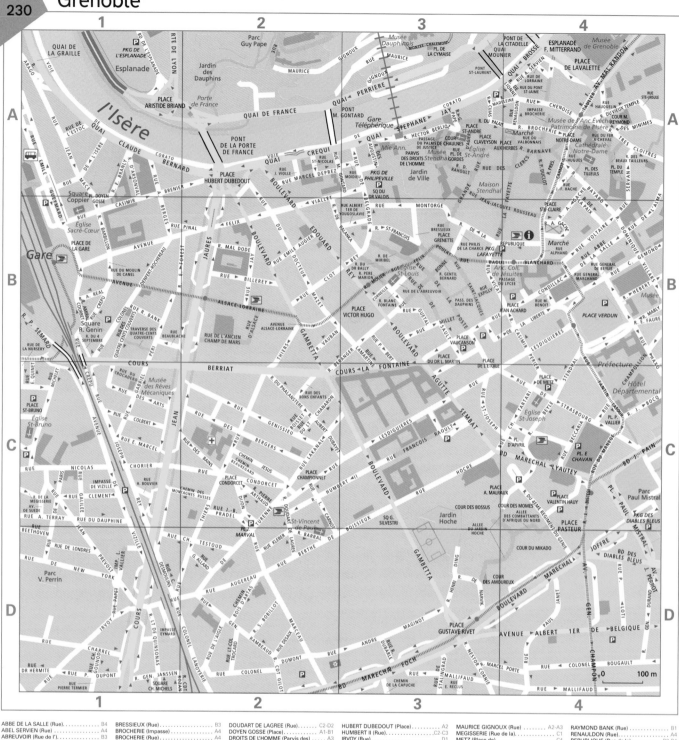

ABBE DE LA SALLE (Rue) B4
ABEL SERVIEN (Rue) A4
ABREUVOIR (Rue de l') B3
AGIER (Rue) A3
AGUTTE SEMBAT (Boulevard) B3-C3
AIGLE (Rue de l') D2
ALBERT 1ER DE BELGIQUE
(Avenue) D3-D4
ALEXANDRE 1ER DE YOUGOSLAVIE
(Rue) B2-B3
ALMA (Rue de l') A4-B4
ALPHAND (Rue) B4
ALPHONSE TERRAY (Rue) C1
ALSACE (Rue d') B2
ALSACE LORRAINE (Avenue) B1-B2
AMIRAL COURBET (Rue) A3
AMOUREUX (Cour des) D3
ANCIEN CHAMP DE MARS (Rue de l') .. B2
ANDRE MAGINOT (Rue) D2-D3
ANDRE MALRAUX (Place) C3-C4
ANDRE REAL (Rue) B1
APVRIL (Place d') C1
ARAGO (Rue) A1
ARISTIDE BERGES (Rue) A1-B1
ARISTIDE BRIAND (Place) A1
ARSONVAL (Rue d') A1-B1
ARTS (Rue des) C1
AUBERT DUBAYET (Rue) C2-C3
AUGEREAU (Rue) D2
AUGUSTE GACHE (Rue) A4
AUGUSTINS (Rue des) A3
BAINS (Rue des) C1
BARBILLON (Rue) B1
BARNAVE (Rue) B1
BARRAL (Rue) B2
BAYARD (Rue) A4-B4
BEAUBLACHE (Rue) B1
BEAUREGARD (Chemin) C2
BEAUX TAILLEURS (Rue des) A4
BECCARIA (Rue) C4
BEETHOVEN (Rue) D1
BELGRADE (Rue de) A3-B3
BERANGER (Rue) C2-B3
BERGERS (Rue des) C2
BERRIAT (Cours) B1-C2
BERTHE DE BOISSIEUX (Rue) D2-C3
BERULLE (Place de) A3
BEYLE STENDHAL (Rue) B4-C4
BILLERY (Rue) B2
BOIS D'ARTAS (Chemin) D2
BOISSET (Rue) B1
BONNE (Rue de) B3
BONS ENFANTS (Rue des) C3
BOSSUS (Cour des) C3

BRESSIEUX (Rue) B3
BROCHERIE (Impasse) A4
BROCHERIE (Rue de la) A4
CAMILLE DESMOULINS (Rue) D1
CAPUCHE (Chemin de la) D4
CASIMIR BRENIER (Rue) B1-A2
CASIMIR PERIER (Rue) B4-C4
CHALEMONT (Montée) A3
CHAMPIONNET (Place) C2
CHAMPOLLION (Rue) B4-C4
CHARLES GOUNOD (Rue) D1
CHARLES MICHELS (Square) D1
CHARLES TARTARI (Rue) C3
CHARLES TESTOUD (Rue) D1-D2
CHARREL (Rue) D1
CHAULNES (Cour de) A3
CLAUDE BERNARD (Quai) A1-A2
CLAUDE BROSSE (Quai) A3
CLAVEYSON (Place) A3
CLEMENT (Rue) C1
CLERCS (Rue des) A3-A4
CLOT BEY (Rue) B2-B3
COLBERT (Rue) C1
COLONEL BOUGAULT (Rue) D4
COLONEL DENFERT ROCHEREAU
(Rue) B1
COLONEL DUMONT (Rue) D1
COLONEL LANOYERIE (Rue) D1
COMBATTANTS D'AFRIQUE DU NORD
(Allée des) C4-D4
COMMANDANT GILOT (Rue) D4
COMMANDANT ROZAN (Rue) D1
CONDILLAC (Rue) B3-B4
CONDORCET (Place) C2
CONDORCET (Rue) C1-C2
CORATO (Voie de) A1-A4
CORNEILLE (Rue) B3
CORNELIE GEMOND (Rue) B3
CREPU (Rue) B1-C1
CREQUI (Quai) A3-B3
CUJAS (Rue) B2
CYMAISE (Place de la) A3
DAUPHINE (Rue du) D2
DAUPHINS (Passage des) B3
DESAIX (Rue) B3
DIABLES BLEUS (Boulevard des) D4
DIODORE RAHOULT (Rue) A4
DOCTEUR BALLY (Rue du) B3
DOCTEUR HERMITE (Rue du) A4
DOCTEUR LEON MARTIN (Rue du) ..B3-C3
DOCTEUR MAZET (Rue du) A2-B2
DOCTEUR VALOIS (Square du) B3
DOMINIQUE VILLARS (Rue) B4

DOUDART DE LAGREE (Rue) C2-D2
DOYEN GOSSE (Place) A1-B1
DROITS DE L'HOMME (Parvis des) A3
EDGAR QUINET (Rue) D1
EDOUARD BRANLY (Rue) A1
EDOUARD REY (Boulevard) D2
ELISEE RECLUS (Rue) D3
EMILE AUGIER (Rue) B2
EMILE GUEYMARD (Rue) A1
ESPLANADE (Boulevard de l') A1
ESTOC (Rue de l') A1
ETIENNE FOREST (Rue) A1-B1
ETIENNE MARCEL (Rue) A1-B2
ETOILE (Place de l') B3-C3
EUGENE FAURE (Rue) B4
EXPILLY (Impasse) C1
EYMARD (Impasse) D3
FANTIN LATOUR (Rue) B4-C4
FELIX POULAT (Rue) B3
FELIX VIALLET (Avenue) B1-B3
FER A CHEVAL (Rue du) A4
FONTAINE (Cours la) C2-B3
FRANCE (Quai de) A2
FRANCOIS MITTERRAND (Esplanade) ... A4
FRANCOIS RAOULT (Rue) A4
FREDERIC TAULIER (Rue) A4
GABRIEL PERI (Rue) B1-C1
GALILEE (Rue) C1
GAMBETTA (Boulevard) A2-D3
GARE (Place de la) B1
GENERAL CHAMPON (Avenue) D4
GENERAL DE BEYLIE (Rue) B4
GENERAL DURAND (Rue) D1
GENERAL JANSSEN (Rue) D1
GENERAL MARCHAND (Rue) B4
GENERAL RAMBEAUD (Rue) D2
GENISSIEU (Rue) C2
GENTIL BERNARD (Rue) B3
GODEFROY SILVESTRI (Square) D3
GORDES (Rue de) A3
GRAILLE (Quai de la) A1
GRANDE RUE A3-B3
GRENETTE (Place) B3
GUETAL (Rue) B3
GUSTAVE RIVET (Place) D3
GUY ALLARD (Rue) D2
GUY PAPE (Rue) A2
HAUQUELIN (Rue) D3-D4
HAXO (Rue) B4-C4
HEBERT (Rue) B3
HECTOR BERLIOZ (Rue) A3
HENRI DING (Rue) B3-C3
HERBES (Place aux) A3-A4
HIPPOLYTE BOUVIER (Rue) C1
HOCHE (Rue) C3

HUBERT DUBEDOUT (Place) A2
HUMBERT II (Rue) C2-C3
IRVOY (Rue) D1
ISERE (Rue de l') A1
JACQUELINE MARVAL (Place) C2-D2
JARDIN HOCHE (Allée du) C3-D4
JAY (Rue) B2
JEAN ACHARD (Place) B3-B4
JEAN BISTESI (Rue) C4-D4
JEAN BOCQ (Rue) C4
JEAN JAURES (Cours) D1-A2
JEAN MACE (Rue) A1-B1
JEAN PAIN (Boulevard) C4
JEAN PERROT (Rue) D4
JEAN PREVOST (Rue) C1-D1
JEAN-BAPTISTE PRADEL (Rue) C1
JEAN-FRANCOIS HACHE (Rue) A4
JEAN-JACQUES ROUSSEAU (Rue) ...A3-B4
JESUS (Chemin) C2
JOSEPH REY (Rue) B1-D1
JULES VIOLLE (Rue) A2
KLEBER (Rue) D2
LAFAYETTE (Rue) B3-B4
LAKANAL (Rue) C2-C3
LAMARTINE (Rue) B3-C3
LAVALETTE (Place de) A4
LAZARE CARNOT (Rue) C2-D2
LESDIGUIERES (Rue) B3
LIBERTE (Rue de la) B3-B4
LIEUTENANT CHANARON (Rue du) ...C2-C3
LIEUTENANT DE QUINSONAS (Rue) D1
LIEUTENANT-COLONEL TROCARD
(Rue) ....
LIONNE (Rue de) A4
LONDRES (Rue de) D1
LORRAINE (Rue de) A4
LOUIS VALLIER (Impasse) D1
LYCEE (Rue du) B4
LYON (Route de) A1
MABLY (Rue) B4
MADELEINE (Rue) A3
MALLIFAUD (Rue) D3-D4
MANEGE (Rue du) D2
MARCEAU (Rue) B1
MARCEL BENOIT (Rue) B4
MARCEL DEPREZ (Rue) B2
MARCEL PORTE (Rue) D3
MARCEL REYMOND (Cour) D4
MARECHAL DODE (Rue) B2
MARECHAL FOCH (Boulevard) D2-D3
MARECHAL JOFFRE (Boulevard) ...C3-D4
MARECHAL LYAUTEY (Boulevard) ..C3-C4
MARECHAL RANDON (Avenue) A4
MARIUS GONTARD (Pont) A2
MARIUS GONTARD (Rue) A2-A3

MAURICE GIGNOUX (Rue) A2-A3
MEGISSERIE (Rue de la) C1
METZ (Place de) C4
MICHELET (Rue) C4
MIKADO (Cour du) D4
MILLET (Rue) B3
MINIMES (Rue des) A4
MIRIBEL (Rue de) B3
MOIDIEU (Rue) A2-A3
MOLIERE (Rue) C4
MOMES (Cour des) C4
MONTAGNES RUSSES
(Chemin des) C1-C2
MONTORGE (Rue) B3
MOULIN DE CANEL (Rue du) B1
MOUNIER (Quai) A3
NARVIK (Rue de) D3
NESTOR CORNIER (Rue) D3
NEW YORK (Rue de) D1
NICOLAS CHORIER (Rue) C1
NOTRE-DAME (Place) A4
NURSERY (Rue de la) B1-C1
PAIX (Rue de la) A4-B4
PALAIS (Rue du) A3-A4
PALAIS DE JUSTICE (Passage du) A3
PALANKA (Rue) A2-B3
PAPET (Rue) A3
PARIS (Rue de) C1
PASTEUR (Place) C1-D1
PAUL BERT (Rue) B3-B4
PAUL DIJON (Rue) C2
PAUL JANET (Rue) D4
PAUL MISTRAL (Place) C4-D4
PERE MARION (Rue) B3
PERRIERE (Quai) A2-A3
PHALANSTERE (Rue du) C2
PHILIS DE LA CHARCE (Rue) B3
PIERRE ARTHAUD (Rue) C2
PIERRE DUCLOT (Rue) A4
PIERRE DUPONT (Rue) D1
PIERRE LOTI (Rue) D4
PIERRE SEMARD (Rue) B1
PIERRE TERMIER (Rue) D1
PINAL (Rue) B1-B2
PONT SAINT-JAIME (Rue de) A4
PORTE DE FRANCE (Pont de la) A2
POSTE (Rue de la) B3
PRESIDENT CARNOT (Rue) A4
PRES DE FRANCE (Pont de la) ....
400 COUVERTS (Rue des) B1-C1
4 SEPTEMBRE (Rue du) B1
4EME REGIMENT DU GENIE
(Rue du) C4-D4
400 COUVERTS (Traverse des) ....
RAOUL BLANCHARD (Rue) B3-B4

RAYMOND BANK (Rue) B1
RENAULDON (Rue) A4
REPUBLIQUE (Rue de la) B3-B4
ROBERT DUBARLE (Rue) D3
SAINT-ANDRE (Place) A3
SAINT-BRUNO (Place) C1
SAINTE-CLAIRE (Place) A4-B4
SAINTE-URSULE (Rue) A4
SAINT-FRANCOIS (Rue) B3
SAINT-HUGUES (Rue) A4
SAINT-JACQUES (Rue) B3
SAINT-JOSEPH (Rue) C3-C4
SAINT-LAURENT (Pont) A3-A4
SAINT-NICOLAS (Rue) A2
SAULT (Rue de) B3
SERGENT BOBILLOT (Rue) D3
SERVAN (Rue) A4-B4
STALINGRAD (Rue de) D3
STEPHANE JAY (Quai) A2-A4
STRASBOURG (Rue de) C3-C4
SUEDE (Avenue de) C1
TEMPLE (Place du) A4
THIERS (Rue) D1-B2
TILLEULS (Place des) A4
TRES CLOITRES (Rue) A3-A4
TROCADERO (Rue du) C1
TURENNE (Rue de) D1-C2
VALBONNAIS (Rue du) B1
VALENTIN HAUY (Place) C4
VAUBAN (Rue) B2-B3
VAUCANSON (Place) B3
VERDUN (Place) B4
VICAT (Rue) A3
VICTOR HUGO (Place) B2-B3
VIEUX TEMPLE (Rue du) A4
VIZILLE (Avenue de) B1-D1
VIZILLE (Impasse de) C1
VOLTAIRE (Rue) B4

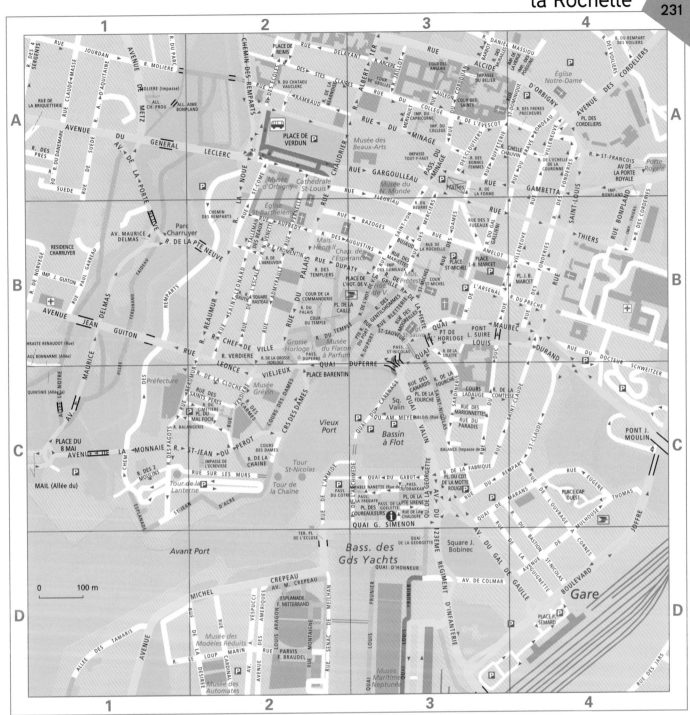

ABLOIS (Rue d') C3
ABREUVOIR (Rue de l') B2
ADMYRAULT (Rue) C3
AIMABLE NANETTE (Rue de l') A1
AIME BONPLAND (Allée) A1
ALBERT 1ER (Rue) A3
ALCIDE D'ORBIGNY (Rue) A3-A4
ALIENOR D'AQUITAINE (Rue) A1
AMELOT (Rue) B3-B4
AMERIGO VESPUCCI (Avenue) D2
AMERIQUES (Avenue) D2
AMIRAL MEYER (Quai) C3
AMOS BARBOT (Rue) A3
ANGLAIS (Cour des) A3
ARCERE (Rue) A3
ARCHIMEDE (Rue de l') C3
ARMIDE (Rue de l') D2-C3
ARSENAL (Rue de l') B3
AUFREDY (Rue) B2
AUGUSTINS (Rue des) B2-B3
BALANCE (Impasse de la) C3
BALANGERIE (Rue) C1-C2
BARENTIN (Place) C2
BASTION SAINT-NICOLAS (Rue du) C3-D4
BAZOGES (Rue) B2-B3
BEARNOISE (Rue de la) A2
BELIER (Impasse du) A3
BEURRE (Rue du) B3
BLETTERIE (Rue) B3
BONNES FEMMES (Rue des) A3
BONPLAND (Impasse) A4
BONPLAND (Rue) A4-B4
BRAVE RONDEAU (Rue du) B3-A4
BRIQUETTERIE (Rue de la) A1
BUFFETERIE (Rue) A3-A4
BUJAUD (Rue) B3
CAILLE (Palce de la) B2
CANARDS (Rue des) C3
CAP OUEST (Place) C4
CAPRICORNE (Impasse du) A3
CARDINAL (Rue) D2
CARENAGE (Quai du) C3
CARMES (Rue des) C2
123EME REGIMENT D'INFANTERIE
(Avenue du) C3-D3
CHAINE (Rue de la) C3
CHALOUPE (Rue de la) C3
CHARLES PROU (Allée) A1
CHARRUYER (Résidence) B1
CHATEAU VAUCLERC (Rue du) A2
CHAUDRIER (Rue) B2-A3
CHEF DE VILLE (Rue) B2
CIMETIERE (Rue du) C2
CLAUDE MASSE (Rue) A1
CLOCHE (Rue de la) C2

CLOUTIERS (Rue des) A3
COLLEGE (Impasse du) A3
COLLEGE (Rue du) A3
COLMAR (Avenue de) D3-D4
COMMANDANT DE LA MOTTE ROUGE
(Place du) C3
COMMANDERIE (Cour de la) B2
COMTESSE (Rue de la) C3-C4
CORDELIERS (Avenue des) A4
CORDELIERS (Place des) A4
CORDERIES (Rue des) A4-B4
CORDOUAN (Rue du) A3
COUREAULEURS (Place des) C3
COTRE (Passage du) D1-D2
CREPEAU (Avenue) D1-D2
DAMES (Cours des) C3
DAMES (Rue des) B3
DANIEL MASSIOU (Rue) A3-A4
DANEMARK (Rue de) A1
DELAYANT (Rue) A2-A3
DESIREE (Rue) D1-D2
DOCTEUR SCHWEITZER (Rue du) B4
DRAKKAR (Passage du) B3-C3
DUC (Rue du) B3-C3
DUPATY (Rue) B2-B3
DUPERRE (Passage) B2-C2
DUPERRE (Quai) C2-C3
ECHELLE CHAUVIN (Rue) A3-A4
ECHELLE DE LA COURONNE (Rue) A4
ECLUSE (Terre plein de l') C2-D2
ECOLES (Rue des) A2
ECREVISSE (Impasse de l') C2
ESCALE (Rue de l') B2
EUGENE FROMENTIN (Rue) B2
EUGENE THOMAS (Rue) C4
EVESCOT (Rue de l') A3-A4
FABRIQUE (Rue de la) C4
FAGOTS (Rue des) B3
FERDINAND FAIDEAU (Allée) A1-C1
FERNAND BRAUDEL (Parvis) D2
FERTE (Rue de la) B3
FLEURIAU (Rue) A2-B3
FONDERIES (Rue des) A4-B4
FORME (Rue de la) A3-B3
FOURCHE (Place de la) C3
FOURCHE (Rue de la) C3
FREGATE (Passage de la) C3
FRERES PRECHEURS (Rue des) A4
GABUT (Quai du) C3
GAMBETTA (Rue) A3-B4
GARGOULLEAU (Rue) A2-A3
GEMEAUX (Rue des) B2
GENERAL DE GAULLE (Avenue du) C3-D3

GENERAL GALLIENI (Rue du) B3
GENERAL LECLERC (Avenue de) A1-A2
GENTILSHOMMES (Rue des) B3
GEORGES SIMENON (Quai) C3
GEORGETTE (Quai de la) C3-D3
GOELETTE (Passage de la) C3
GRILLE (Rue de la) B3
GROLLES (Cour de) C3
GROSSE HORLOGE (Rue de la) B2-C2
GUIGNETTE (Rue de la) C3-D4
HONNEUR (Quai d') D3
HORLOGE (Pont de l') B3
HOTEL DE VILLE (Place de l') B3
HOTEL DE VILLE (Rue de l') B3
ITOUT Y FAUT (Impasse) A3
JAILLOT (Rue) A3
JARS (Rue des) D4
JEAN BAPTISTE MARCET (Place) B4
JEAN GUITON (Avenue) B1
JEAN GUITON (Impasse) B1
JEAN MOULIN (Pont) C2
JEAN-BAPTISTE MARCET (Place) B3
JOFFRE (Boulevard) D3-C4
JOURDAN (Rue) A1
LA ROCHELLE (Rue de) B3
LADAUGE (Cours) C3
LEONCE VIELJEUX (Rue) B1-C2
LOUIS ARAGON (Rue) D2
LOUIS DURAND (Quai) C3-B4
LOUIS PRUNIER (Quai) D3
LOUIS SUIRE (Pont) C3
LOUP MARIN (Rue le) D1-D2
MAIL (Allée du) C1
MARANS (Quai de) C3-C4
MARECHAL FOCH (Place du) C2
MARIETTES (Rue des) B3
MARIONNETTES (Rue des) C3
MAUBEC (Quai) C3-B4
MAURICE DELMAS (Avenue) B1-C1
MERCIERS (Rue des) A3-B3
MERVAULT (Rue) A3
METZ (Avenue de) A1
MICHEL CREPEAU (Avenue) D1-D2
MINAGE (Passage du) A3
MINAGE (Rue du) A3
MOLIERE (Impasse) A1
MOLIERE (Rue) A1
MONNAIE (Avenue de la) C1
MONTAGNE (Rue) D2
MOUREILLES (Rue des) B3
MULHOUSE (Avenue de) C4-D4
MURAILLES (Rue des) A3
NICOLAS VENETTE (Rue) B3
NORVEGE (Rue de) B1

NOTRE (Allée le) B1-C1
NOUE (Rue la) A2-B2
OUVRAGE A CORNES (Rue de l') C4-D4
PALAIS (Rue du) B3
PARADIS (Rue du) C3
PARC (Rue du) A1
PAUL BONNARME (Allée) B1-C1
PAUL GARREAU (Rue) B1
PAULEON (Rue) A2-B2
PERNELLE (Rue) B3
PETITE SIRENE (Place de la) C3
PIERRE SEMARD (Place) D4
POISSONS (Impasse des) A4
PORT (Petite rue du) C2-B3
PORT (Rue du) B3-C3
PORTE NEUVE (Avenue de la) A1-B2
PORTE NEUVE (Rue de la) B1-B2
PORTE ROYALE (Avenue de la) A4
PRECHE (Rue du) B3-B4
PRES (Rue des) A1
QUINTINIE (Allée la) C1
4 SERGENTS (Rue des) A1
RAMBAUD (Rue) A2-A3
RASTEAU (Square) B2
REAUMUR (Rue) C1-B2
REIMS (Place de) A2
REMPART DES VOILIERS (Rue du) A4
REMPART SAINT-CLAUDE (Rue du) C3-C4
REMPARTS (Chemin des) C1-A2
RENE GAUTIER (Rue) B2
SAINT-CLAUDE (Rue) C3-B4
SAINT-COME (Rue) A2-B2
SAINT-DOMINIQUE (Rue) A4
SAINT-FRANCOIS (Rue) A4
SAINT-JEAN D'ACRE (Esplanade) D1-C2
SAINT-JEAN DU PEROT (Rue) C1-C2
SAINT-LEONARD (Rue) B2
SAINT-LOUIS (Rue) A4-B4
SAINT-MICHEL (Cour) B3
SAINT-MICHEL (Place) B3
SAINT-MICHEL (Rue) B3
SAINT-NICOLAS (Passerelle) B3
SAINT-NICOLAS (Rue) B3-C3
SAINT-SAUVEUR (Rue) B3
SAINT-YON (Rue) A3-B3
SAINTES CLAIRES (Rue des) A2-A3
SARDINERIE (Rue) B3-C3
SENAC DE MEILHAN (Rue) D2
SOLETTE (Rue de la) B3-C3
SUR LES MURS (Rue) C1-C2
TALLEMANT DES REAUX (Rue) B3
TAMARIS (Allée des) D1

TEMPLE (Cour du) B2
TEMPLE (Rue du) B2-B3
TEMPLIERS (Rue des) B2
THEOPHRASTE RENAUDOT (Rue) C1
THIERS (Impasse) B4
THIERS (Rue) A3-B4
3 FUSEAUX (Rue des) B3
VALIN (Quai) C3
VERDIERE (Rue) B2-C2
VERDUN (Place de) A2
VIERGE (Impasse de la) A3-A4
VILLENEUVE (Rue des) B3-A4
VOILIERS (Rue des) A4

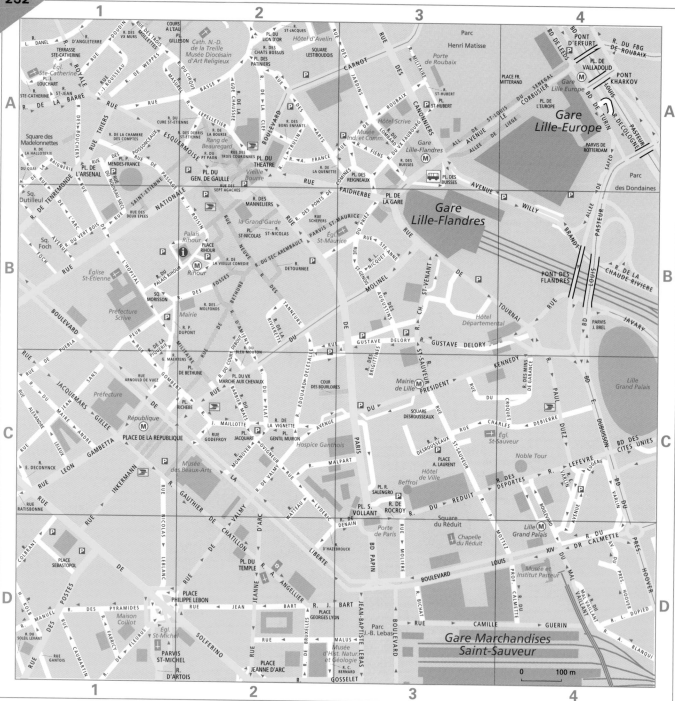

A FIENS (Rue) A3
A L'EAU (Cours) A2
ALEXANDRE DESROUSSEAUX (Rue). . C3
ALEXANDRE LELEUX (Rue). C1
AMIENS (Rue d') B2-C2
ANATOLE FRANCE (Rue) A2
ANGLETERRE (Rue d') A1
ARC (Rue de l') A1-B1
ARNOULD DE VUEZ (Rue) C1
ARSENAL (Place de l') A1
ARTOIS (Rue d') D1
ARTS (Rue des) A2
AUGUSTE ANGELLIER (Rue) D2
AUGUSTE BLANQUI (Rue) D4
AUGUSTIN LAURENT (Place) C3
AUGUSTINS (Rue des) B3
BAIGNERIE (Rue de la) A1-B1
BARBIER MAES (Rue du) C1
BARRE (Rue de la) A1
BASSE (Rue) A1-A2
BETHUNE (Place de) C2
BETHUNE (Rue de) B2-C2
BICHAT (Rue) D3
BLEU MOUTON (Rue du) C2
BONS ENFANTS (Rue des) A2
BOUCHERS (Rue des) A1
BOURLOIRES (Cour des) C2-C3
BOURSE (Rue de la) A2
BRIGITTINES (Rue des) B3-C3
BRUXELLES (Rue de) D2
BUISSES (Place des) A3
BUISSES (Rue des) A3
CAMILLE GUERIN (Rue) D3-D4
CANONNIERS (Rue des) A2-A3
CARNOT (Boulevard) A2-A3
CAUMARTIN (Rue) D1
CHAMBRE DES COMPTES (Rue de la) . A1
CHARLES DEBIERRE (Rue). C3-C4
CHARLES ST-VENANT (Rue) B3
CHATS BOSSUS (Rue) A2
CHAUDE RIVIERE (Rue de la) B2
CIRQUE (Rue du) A1-A2
CITES UNIES (Boulevard des) C4
CLAUDE BERNARD (Rue) D2
CLEF (Rue de la) A2
COLBRANT (Rue) D1
COLOGNE (Rue de) A4
COURT DEBOUT (Rue du) B2-C2
CROQUET (Rue du) C3-C4
CURE ST-ETIENNE (Rue du) A2
DEBRIS ST-ETIENNE (Rue des) A2
DENAIN (Rue de) C2
DEPORTES (Rue des) C3-C4
DESROUSSEAUX (Square) C3
DETOURNEE (Rue) B2

DEUX EPEES (Rue des) B1
DOCTEUR CALMETTE (Rue du). D4
DOUDIN (Rue). A1
EDOUARD DELESALLE (Rue). C2
EMILE DUBUISSON (Boulevard) B4-C4
ERFURT (Pont d') A4
ERNEST DECONYNCK (Rue) C1
ESQUERMOISE (Rue). A2
EUGENE VARLIN (Avenue) C4-D4
EUGENE VARLIN (Rue) C4
EUROPE (Place de l') A4
FABRICY (Rue) D1
FAIDHERBE (Rue) A2-B3
FAUBOURG DE ROUBAIX (Rue du) . . . A4
FLANDRES (Pont des) B4
FLEURUS (Rue de) D1
FOCH (Avenue) B1-B2
FOSSES (Rue des) B1-B2
FRANÇOIS MITTERAND (Place) A4
FREDERIC MOTTEZ (Rue). C3-C4
GANTOIS (Rue) D1
GARE (Place de la) B3
GAUTHIER DE CHATILLON (Rue) . . . C1-D2
GENERAL DE GAULLE (Place du) A2-B2
GENTIL MUIRON (Place) C2
GEORGES LYON (Rue) D3
GEORGES MAERTENS (Rue). B1-C1
GILLESON (Place) A1-A2
GODEFROY (Rue) C2
GOMBERT (Rue) C2
GOSSELET (Rue) D2-D3
GRANDE CHAUSSEE (Rue de la). A2
GUSTAVE DELORY (Rue). B2-B4
HALLOTERIE (Rue de la) A1
HAZEBROUCK (Rue d'). D2-D3
HENRI KOLB (Rue) D1
HOPITAL MILITAIRE (Rue de l') A1-C2
INKERMANN (Rue) C1-D1
JACQUART (Rue) C2
JACQUEMARS GIELEE (Rue). B1-C1
JACQUES BREL (Parvis) B4
JACQUES LOUCHART (Rue) A1
JARDINS (Rue des) A2-A3
JAVARY (Rue) C4
JEAN BART (Rue) C2-D2
JEAN ROISIN (Rue) B2
JEAN SANS PEUR (Rue) B1-C1
JEAN-BAPTISTE LEBAS (Boulevard) . . C3
JEAN-JACQUES ROUSSEAU (Rue) A1
JEANNE D'ARC (Place) C2-D2
JEANNE D'ARC (Rue) C2-D2
JEANNE MAILLOTTE (Rue) C1
KHARKOV (Place) A4
LE CORBUSIER (Avenue) B3-B4
LEEDS (Boulevard de) A4

LEFEVRE (Rue) C4
LEON GAMBETTA (Rue). C1
LEON TRULIN (Rue) A2
LEONARD DANEL (Rue) A1
LEPELLETIER (Rue) A2
LESTIBOUDOIS (Square) A2
LIBERTE (Boulevard de la) B1-D3
LIEGE (Allée de) A3-A4
LION D'OR (Place du) A2
LOMBARD (Rue du) A3
LOUIS DUPIED (Rue) D4
LOUIS NICQUET (Rue) B3
LOUIS PASTEUR (Boulevard) A4-B4
LOUIS XIV (Boulevard) D3-D4
LYDERIC (Rue) C2-D2
MAIRE ANDRE (Rue du) C1
MALPART (Rue) C2-C3
MALUS (Rue) D2-D3
MANNELIERS (Rue des) A2-B2
MANUEL (Rue) D1
MARECHAL VAILLANT (Bd du) C4-D4
MARECHAL VAILLANT (Rue du) D4
MASUREL (Rue) A1-A2
MILITAIRE (Rue) A3
MOLFONDS (Rue des) B2
MOLIERE (Rue) C3-D3
MOLINEL (Rue du) C2-B3
MONNOYER (Rue) B2
MORISSON (Square) B1
MOULINS DE GARANCE (Rue des) . . .B4-C4
NATIONALE (Rue) B1-A2
NEUVE (Rue) B2
NICOLAS LEBLANC (Rue) C1-D1
NOUVEAU SIECLE (Rue du) A1-B1
OVIGNEUR (Rue du) C2
PALAIS RIHOUR (Rue de l') B1-B2
PAPIN (Rue) D3
PARIS (Rue de) B2-C3
PASSAGE (Rue du) A2
PATINIERS (Place des) A2
PAUL DUEZ (Rue) B4-C4
PETIT PAON (Rue du) A2
PHILIPPE LEBON (Place) D1
PIERRE DUPONT (Rue). B1
PIERRE MENDES-FRANCE (Place) . . .B1-C1
PIQUERIE (Rue de la) C2
PLAT (Rue du) C2
POISSONCEAUX (Rue des) A2
PONTS DE COMINES (Rue des) B2-A3
POSTES (Rue des) C1
PRESIDENT HOOVER (Avenue du) . . . D4
PRESIDENT HOOVER (Bd du) D4
PRESIDENT KENNEDY (Avenue du) . . C4-D2
PRIEZ (Rue) B2
PROFESSEUR CALMETTE (Rue du) . . . D3

PUEBLA (Rue de) B1-C1
PYRAMIDES (Rue des) D1
QUAI (Rue du) A1
QUENETTE (Rue de la) A2-A3
RATISBONNE (Rue) C1
REDUIT (Rue du) C3
REIGNEAUX (Place des) A3
REPUBLIQUE (Place de la) C1-C2
RICHEBE (Place) C1-C2
RIHOUR (Place) B2
RIVIERETTE (Rue de la) B2
ROCROY (Rue de) C3-D3
ROGER SALENGRO (Place) C3-D3
ROTTERDAM (Parvis de) A4
ROUBAIX (Rue de) A2-A3
ROYALE (Rue) A1
SAFED (Allée de) A4-B4
SAINT-ETIENNE (Rue) B1-A2
SAINT-GENOIS (Rue) B3
SAINT-HUBERT (Place) A3
SAINT-HUBERT (Rue) A3
SAINT-JACQUES (Rue) A2
SAINT-JEAN (Rue) A1
SAINT-LOUIS DU SENEGAL (All. de) . .A3-A4
SAINT-MAURICE (Parvis) B2-B3
SAINT-MICHEL (Parvis) D1
SAINT-NICOLAS (Place) B2
SAINT-NICOLAS (Rue) B2
SAINT-SAUVEUR (Rue) B3-C3
SAINTE-ANNE (Rue) B3
SAINTE-CATHERINE (Rue) A1
SAINTE-CATHERINE (Terrasse) A1
SCHEPERS (Rue). B2
SEBASTOPOL (Place) C1-D1
SEC AREMBAULT (Rue du) C1-D1
SEPT AGACHES (Rue des) B2
SIMON VOLLANT (Place) C3-D3
SOLEIL LEVANT (Rue du) D1
SOLFERINO (Rue) C1-D2
TANNEURS (Rue des) B2
TEMPLE (Place du) D2
TENREMONDE (Rue de) A1-B1
THEATRE (Place du) A2-B2
THIERS (Rue) A1
TOURNAI (Rue de) B3-B4
TROIS COURONNES (Rue des) A2
TROIS MOLLETTES (Rue des) A1
TURIN (Boulevard de) A4
VALLADOLID (Place de) A4
VALMY (Rue de) C2-D2
VERT BOIS (Rue du) B1
VIEILLE COMEDIE (Rue de la) B2
VIEUX FAUBOURG (Rue du) A3
VIEUX MARCHE AUX CHEVAUX
    (Place du) C2

VIEUX MURS (Rue des) A1
VIGNETTE (Rue de la). C2
WATTEAU (Rue) C2-D2
WEPPES (Rue des) A1
WILLY BRANDT (Avenue). A3-B4

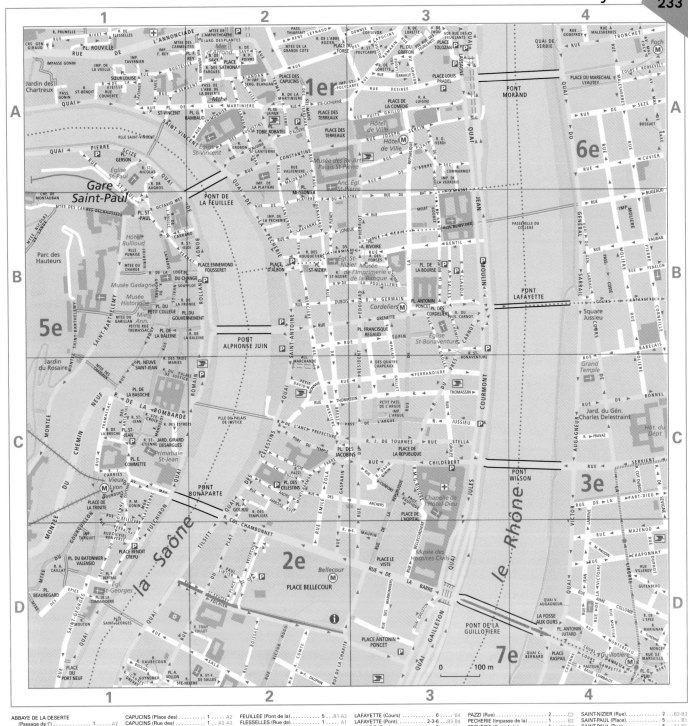

ABBAYE DE LA DESERTE
(Passage de l') . . . 1 . . . A2
ABBE ROZIER (Rue de l') . . . 1 . . . A2-A3
ADOLPHE MAX (Avenue) . . . 5 . . . C1
AIME COLLOMB (Rue) . . . 3 . . . D4
ALBON (Place d') . . . 1-2 . . . B2
ALEXANDRE LUIGINI (Rue) . . . 1 . . . A2
ALGERIE (Rue d') . . . 1 . . . A3
ALPHONSE FOCHIER (Rue) . . . 2 . . . C1-D1
ALPHONSE JUIN (Pont) . . . 5 . . . B2
AMBOISE (Rue) . . . 5 . . . A2
AMPHITHEATRE (Montée de l') . . . 1 . . . A2
ANCIENNE PREFECTURE
(Rue de l') . . . 2 . . . C2
ANDRE LASSAGNE (Quai) . . . 1 . . . A3
ANGILE (Rue de l') . . . 5 . . . B1
ANNONCIADE (Rue de l') . . . 1 . . . A2
ANTOINE RIVOIRE (Place) . . . 2 . . . B3
ANTOINE SALLES (Rue) . . . 2 . . . B3
ANTOINE VOLLON (Rue) . . . 2 . . . D1
ANTONIN GOURJU (Place) . . . 2 . . . C1
ANTONIN JUTARD (Place) . . . 3 . . . D4
ANTONIN PONCET (Place) . . . 2 . . . D2-B3
ANTONINS (Rue des) . . . 5 . . . C1
ARBRE SEC (Rue de l') . . . 1 . . . A3
ARCHERS (Rue des) . . . 2 . . . C2-C3
ARGUE (Impasse de l') . . . 2 . . . B2
ARGUE (Passage de l') . . . 2 . . . C2-C3
ARMAND CAILLAT (Rue) . . . 2 . . . C2
AUGUSTE COMTE (Rue) . . . 2 . . . D2
AUGUSTINS (Rue des) . . . 1 . . . A2
BALEINE (Impasse de la) . . . 5 . . . B1
BALEINE (Rue de la) . . . 5 . . . B1-B2
BARRE (Rue de la) . . . 2 . . . D3
BASOCHE (Place de la) . . . 5 . . . C1
BASSE COMBALOT (Rue) . . . 7 . . . D4
BAT D'ARGENT (Rue du) . . . 1-2 . . . A3-B3
BATONNIER VALENSIO
(Place du) . . . 5 . . . D1
BEAUREGARD (Place) . . . 5 . . . D1
BELLECORDIERE (Rue) . . . 2 . . . C3-D3
BELLECOUR (Place) . . . 2 . . . D2-D3
BELLIEVRE (Rue) . . . 5 . . . D1
BENOIT CREPU (Place) . . . 5 . . . D1
BOEUF (Rue du) . . . 5 . . . B1
BOISSAC (Rue) . . . 2 . . . C2
BOMBARDE (Rue de la) . . . 5 . . . C1-C2
BONAPARTE (Pont) . . . 2 . . . C1-C2
BONDY (Quai de) . . . 5 . . . A1-B2
BONNEL (Rue de) . . . 3 . . . C4
BOSSUET (Rue) . . . 6 . . . A4
BOUQUETIERS (Rue des) . . . 1-2 . . . B2
BOURSE (Place de la) . . . 2 . . . B3
BOURSE (Rue de la) . . . 1-2 . . . B3
BOUTEILLE (Rue) . . . 1 . . . A1-A2
BRECHE (Rue de la) . . . 5 . . . C1
BREST (Rue de) . . . 2 . . . B2-C2
BUGEAUD (Rue) . . . 6 . . . A4-B4

CAPUCINS (Place des) . . . 1 . . . A2
CAPUCINS (Rue des) . . . 1 . . . A2-A3
CARMELITES (Montée des) . . . 1 . . . A2
CARMES DECHAUSSEES
(Montée des) . . . 5 . . . B1
CAVENNE (Rue) . . . 7 . . . D4
CELESTINS (Place des) . . . 2 . . . C2
CELESTINS (Quai des) . . . 2 . . . C2
CHAMPIER (Rue) . . . 2 . . . B3
CHANGE (Montée du) . . . 5 . . . B1
CHANGE (Place du) . . . 5 . . . B1
CHAPONNAY (Rue) . . . 3 . . . D4
CHARITE (Rue de la) . . . 2 . . . C2
CHARLES DULLIN (Rue) . . . 2 . . . C2
CHAVANNE (Rue) . . . 1 . . . B2
CHAZEAUX (Montée des) . . . 5 . . . B1
CHEMIN NEUF (Montée du) . . . 5 . . . C1-D1
CHILDEBERT (Rue) . . . 2 . . . C3
CLAUDE BERNARD (Quai) . . . 7 . . . D4
CLAUDIA (Rue) . . . 2 . . . B3
CLOTILDE BIZOLON (Rue) . . . 2 . . . D1
COLLEGE (Passerelle du) . . . 2 . . . B3-B4
COLONEL CHAMBONNET (Rue) . . . 2 . . . C2-C2
COMEDIE (Place de la) . . . 1 . . . A3
COMMANDANT DUBOIS (Rue) . . . 3 . . . C4
COMMANDERIE (Rue de la) . . . 5 . . . D1
COMMARMOT (Rue) . . . 1 . . . A3
CONFORT (Rue du) . . . 2 . . . C3
CONSTANTINE (Rue) . . . 1 . . . A3
CORDELIERS (Place des) . . . 2 . . . B3
COSTE (Passage) . . . 6 . . . B4
COUSTOU (Rue) . . . 1 . . . A2
COUVERTE (Rue) . . . 5 . . . A1
COYSEVOX (Rue) . . . 1 . . . A2
CUVIER (Rue) . . . 6 . . . A4
DAVID GIRIN (Rue) . . . 2 . . . A3
DESIREE (Rue) . . . 1 . . . A3
DOCTEUR AUGROS (Rue) . . . 5 . . . A1
DONNEE (Rue) . . . 1 . . . A3
DOYENNE (Avenue du) . . . 5 . . . C1
DOYENNE (Rue du) . . . 5 . . . B1-C1
DUBOIS (Rue) . . . 2 . . . B2-B3
DUPHOT (Rue) . . . 3 . . . D4
EDOUARD COMMETTE (Rue) . . . 5 . . . C1
EMILE ZOLA (Rue) . . . 2 . . . A1
ENNEMOND FOUSSERET (Place) . . . 5 . . . B2
EPEE (Rue de l') . . . 3 . . . D4
EPIES (Montée des) . . . 5 . . . D1
ESTREES (Rue des) . . . 5 . . . C1
FARGUES (Rue des) . . . 1 . . . A2
FENELON (Rue) . . . 6 . . . A4
FERNAND REY (Impasse) . . . 1 . . . A1-A2
FERNAND REY (Place) . . . 1 . . . A1-A2
FERNAND REY (Rue) . . . 1 . . . A2
FERRACHAT (Rue) . . . 5 . . . D1
FERRANDIERE (Rue) . . . 2 . . . C2-C3
FEUILLANTS (Grande rue des) . . . 1 . . . A3
FEUILLANTS (Petite rue des) . . . 1 . . . A3

FEUILLEE (Pont de la) . . . 5 . . . B1-A2
FLESSELLES (Rue de) . . . 1 . . . A1
FORCES (Rue des) . . . 2 . . . B3
FOREZ (Place du) . . . 1 . . . A2
FRANCISQUE REGAUD (Place) . . . 2 . . . B3
FRANCOIS BERTRAS (Place) . . . 5 . . . D1
FRANCOIS DAUPHIN (Rue) . . . 2 . . . D2
FRANCOIS VERNAY (Rue) . . . 5 . . . B1-B2
FRANKLIN ROOSEVELT (Cours) . . . 6 . . . A4
FROMAGERIE (Rue de la) . . . 1-2 . . . B2-B3
FRONDE (Rue de la) . . . 5 . . . B1
FULCHIRON (Quai) . . . 5 . . . C1-D1
GABRIEL PERI (Place) . . . 7 . . . D4
GABRIEL RAMBAUD (Place) . . . 1 . . . A2
GADAGNE (Rue de) . . . 5 . . . B1
GAILLETON (Quai) . . . 2 . . . D3
GAMBETTA (Cours) . . . 3-7 . . . D4
GARET (Rue du) . . . 1 . . . A3-B3
GARILLAN (Montée du) . . . 5 . . . B1
GASPARD ANDRE (Rue) . . . 2 . . . C2
GASPARIN (Rue) . . . 2 . . . C2-D2
GENERAL GIRAUD (Cours) . . . 1 . . . A2
GENERAL SARRAIL (Quai du) . . . 6 . . . A4-B4
GENTIL (Rue) . . . 2 . . . B3
GERBE (Rue) . . . 2 . . . B3
GERSON (Place) . . . 5 . . . A1
GIRARD DESARGUES (Jardin) . . . 5 . . . C1
GIUSEPPE VERDI (Rue) . . . 1 . . . A3
GODEFROY (Rue) . . . 6 . . . A4
GONIN (Impasse) . . . 1 . . . A1
GONIN (Passage) . . . 1 . . . A1
GOURGUILLON (Montée du) . . . 5 . . . C1-D1
GOUVERNEMENT (Place du) . . . 5 . . . B1
GRANDE COTE (Montée de la) . . . 1 . . . A2
GRENETTE (Rue) . . . 2 . . . B2-B3
GRIFFON (Place du) . . . 1 . . . A3
GRIFFON (Rue du) . . . 1 . . . A2-A3
GROBON (Rue) . . . 1 . . . A2
GROLEE (Rue) . . . 2 . . . B3
GUILLOTIERE (Pont de la) . . . 2-3-7 . . . D3-D4
GUTENBERG (Rue) . . . 3 . . . D4
GUYNEMER (Rue) . . . 2 . . . D1
HENRI GERMAIN (Rue) . . . 2 . . . B3
HIPPOLYTE FLANDRIN (Rue) . . . 1 . . . A2
HOPITAL (Place de l') . . . 2 . . . C3-D3
JACOBINS (Place des) . . . 2 . . . C2-C3
JARDIN DES PLANTES (Rue du) . . . 1 . . . A2
JEAN CARRIES (Rue) . . . 5 . . . D1
JEAN DE TOURNES (Rue) . . . 2 . . . C3
JEAN FABRE (Rue) . . . 2 . . . C2
JEAN LARRIVE (Rue) . . . 3 . . . C4-D4
JEAN MOULIN (Quai) . . . 1-2 . . . A3-B3
JEANNES DREVET (Rue) . . . 2 . . . C1
JOSEPH SERLIN (Rue) . . . 1 . . . A3
JUIVERIE (Rue) . . . 5 . . . B1
JULES COURMONT (Quai) . . . 2 . . . B3-D3
JUSSIEU (Rue) . . . 2 . . . C3-D3
LA FOSSE AUX OURS (Rue de) . . . 3 . . . C4-D4

LAFAYETTE (Cours) . . . 6 . . . B4
LAFAYETTE (Pont) . . . 2-3-6 . . . B3-B4
LAINERIE (Rue de la) . . . 5 . . . B1
LANTERNE (Rue) . . . 1 . . . A2-B2
LIBERTE (Cours de la) . . . 3 . . . B4-D4
LOGE (Rue de la) . . . 5 . . . B1-B2
LONGUE (Rue) . . . 1 . . . B2-B3
LORETTE (Rue de) . . . 1 . . . A3
LOUIS CARRAND (Rue) . . . 5 . . . B1-B2
LOUIS PRADEL (Place) . . . 1 . . . A3
LOUIS VITET (Rue) . . . 2 . . . C2
MAJOR MARTIN (Rue) . . . 1 . . . A2-B2
MALESHERBES (Rue) . . . 6 . . . A4
MANDELOT (Rue) . . . 5 . . . B1
MARCEL GABRIEL RIVIERE (Rue) . . . 2 . . . C3
MARCHANDE (Allée) . . . 1 . . . A3
MARCHE (Rue du) . . . 1 . . . A3
MARECHAL DE SAXE (Avenue) . . . 3 . . . A4
MARECHAL FOCH (Avenue) . . . 6 . . . A4
MARECHAL LYAUTEY (Place) . . . 6 . . . A4
MARIGNAN (Rue) . . . 3 . . . D4
MARIUS AUDIN (Rue) . . . 3 . . . D4
MARIUS GONIN (Rue) . . . 5 . . . C1-D1
MARRONNIERS (Rue des) . . . 2 . . . D3
MARSEILLE (Rue de) . . . 7 . . . D4
MARTINIERE (Rue de la) . . . 1 . . . A1-A2
MAZENOD (Rue) . . . 3 . . . C4
MEISSONIER (Rue) . . . 1 . . . B2
MENESTRIER (Passage) . . . 1 . . . A2
MERCIERE (Rue) . . . 2 . . . B2-C2
MGR LAVARENNE (Rue) . . . 5 . . . C1-D1
MOLIERE (Impasse) . . . 6 . . . A4
MOLIERE (Rue) . . . 3-6 . . . A4-C4
MONCEY (Rue) . . . 3 . . . C4
MONNAIE (Rue) . . . 2 . . . C2
MONTAUBAN (Chemin de) . . . 5 . . . A1
MONTCHARMONT (Rue) . . . 2 . . . C3
MONTEBELLO (Rue) . . . 3 . . . D4
MORAND (Pont) . . . 1 . . . A3-A4
MOULIN (Rue du) . . . 2 . . . B3
MOURGUET (Rue) . . . 5 . . . B1
MOUTON (Rue) . . . 1 . . . A3
MULET (Rue) . . . 1 . . . B3
NEUVE (Rue) . . . 1-2 . . . B2-B3
NICOLAS DE LANGE (Montée) . . . 1 . . . A2
OCTAVIO MEY (Rue) . . . 5 . . . B1
ORAN (Rue d') . . . 1 . . . A2
PAIX (Rue de la) . . . 1 . . . A2
PALAIS DE JUSTICE
(Passerelle du) . . . 2 . . . C1-C2
PALAIS DE JUSTICE (Rue du) . . . 5 . . . C1
PAREILLE (Rue) . . . 1 . . . A2
PART-DIEU (Rue de la) . . . 3 . . . A4
PAUL BERT (Rue) . . . 3 . . . D4
PAUL CHENAVARD (Rue) . . . 1 . . . A2-B2
PAUL LINTIER (Rue) . . . 2 . . . D2

PAZZI (Rue) . . . 2 . . . C2
PECHERIE (Impasse de la) . . . 1 . . . B2
PECHERIE (Quai de la) . . . 1 . . . A2-B2
PETIT COLLEGE (Place du) . . . 5 . . . B1
PETIT COLLEGE (Rue du) . . . 5 . . . B1
PETIT DAVID (Rue) . . . 2 . . . B2-B3
PETIT PASSAGE DE L'ARGUE . . . 2 . . . C3
PIERRE CORNEILLE (Rue) . . . 3-6 . . . A4-C4
PIERRE POIVRE (Rue) . . . 1 . . . A2
PIERRE SCIZE (Quai) . . . 5 . . . A1
PIZAY (Rue) . . . 1 . . . A3
PLAT (Rue du) . . . 2 . . . D1-D2
PLATIERE (Impasse de la) . . . 1 . . . A2-B2
PLATIERE (Rue de la) . . . 1 . . . B2
PLATRE (Rue du) . . . 1 . . . B2-B3
PLENEY (Rue) . . . 1 . . . B2
PORT DU TEMPLE (Rue) . . . 2 . . . B2
PORT NEUF (Place du) . . . 5 . . . D1
POULAILLERIE (Rue de la) . . . 2 . . . B2-B3
PRAVAZ (Rue) . . . 3 . . . C4
PRESIDENT CARNOT (Rue) . . . 2 . . . B3-C3
PRESIDENT EDOUARD HERRIOT
(Rue) . . . 1-2 . . . A3-D3
PROFESSEUR LOUIS PAUFIQUE
(Rue) . . . 2 . . . C3
PRUNELLE (Rue) . . . 1 . . . A1
PUITS GAILLOT (Rue) . . . 1 . . . A3
PUNAISE (Rue) . . . 5 . . . B1
QUATRE CHAPEAUX (Rue des) . . . 2 . . . B3-C3
RABELAIS (Rue) . . . 3 . . . B4-C4
RASPAIL (Place) . . . 7 . . . D4
RENE LEYNAUD (Rue) . . . 1 . . . A2
REPUBLIQUE (Place de la) . . . 2 . . . B3-C3
REPUBLIQUE (Rue de la) . . . 1-2 . . . A3-D3
RIVET (Rue) . . . 1 . . . A1
ROMAIN ROLLAND (Quai) . . . 5 . . . C1-D2
ROMARIN (Rue) . . . 1 . . . A2
ROUVILLE (Place) . . . 1 . . . A1
SAINT-ANTOINE (Quai) . . . 2 . . . B2-C2
SAINT-BARTHELEMY (Montée) . . . 5 . . . B1-C1
SAINT-BENOIT (Rue) . . . 1 . . . A1
SAINT-BONAVENTURE (Rue) . . . 2 . . . B3
SAINT-CLAUDE (Rue) . . . 1 . . . A3
SAINTE-CATHERINE (Rue) . . . 1 . . . A2-A3
SAINTE-CROIX (Rue) . . . 5 . . . C1
SAINTE-HELENE (Rue) . . . 2 . . . D1-D2
SAINT-ELOI (Rue) . . . 5 . . . B1-B2
SAINTE-MARIE DES TERREAUX
(Rue) . . . 1 . . . A2
SAINT-ETIENNE (Rue) . . . 5 . . . C1
SAINT-EXUPERY (Rue) . . . 2 . . . D1-D2
SAINT-FRANCOIS DE SALLES
(Rue) . . . 2 . . . C1-C2
SAINT-GEORGES (Passerelle) . . . 5 . . . C1-D1
SAINT-GEORGES (Rue) . . . 5 . . . C1-D1
SAINT-JEAN (Rue) . . . 5 . . . B1-C1
SAINT-NICOLAS (Rue) . . . 1 . . . A1
SAINT-NIZIER (Rue) . . . 1-2 . . . B2

SAINT-NIZIER (Rue) . . . 2 . . . B2-B3
SAINT-PAUL (Place) . . . 5 . . . B1
SAINT-PAUL (Rue) . . . 5 . . . A1-B1
SAINT-POLYCARPE (Impasse) . . . 1 . . . A2-A3
SAINT-POLYCARPE (Rue) . . . 1 . . . A3
SAINT-VINCENT (Passerelle) . . . 5 . . . A1
SAINT-VINCENT (Place) . . . 1 . . . A1
SAINT-VINCENT (Quai) . . . 1 . . . A1-A2
SALA (Rue) . . . 2 . . . D1-D2
SATHONAY (Place) . . . 1 . . . A2
SAVOIE (Rue de) . . . 2 . . . C2
SAVY (Rue de) . . . 1 . . . A2
SERBIE (Quai de) . . . 6 . . . A4
SERGENT BLANDAN
(Impasse du) . . . 1 . . . A1
SERGENT BLANDAN (Rue) . . . 1 . . . A1-A2
SERVIENT (Rue) . . . 3 . . . C4
SEVIGNE (Rue de) . . . 3 . . . C4-D4
SEZE (Rue de) . . . 6 . . . A4
SIMON MAUPIN (Rue) . . . 2 . . . D2-D3
SŒUR LOUISE (Place) . . . 5 . . . C1
SOUFFLOT (Rue) . . . 5 . . . B1
STELLA (Rue) . . . 2 . . . C3
TAVERNIER (Impasse) . . . 1 . . . A3
TAVERNIER (Rue) . . . 1 . . . A3
TEMPLIERS (Rue des) . . . 2 . . . C2
TERME (Rue) . . . 1 . . . A2
TERRAILLE (Rue) . . . 1 . . . A2
TERREAUX (Place des) . . . 1 . . . A2-A3
THIAFFAIT (Passage) . . . 1 . . . A2
THIMONNIER (Rue) . . . 1 . . . A2
THOMASSIN (Rue) . . . 2 . . . C2-C3
THOU (Rue de) . . . 1 . . . A3
TILSITT (Quai) . . . 2 . . . C1-D2
TOBIE ROBATEL (Place) . . . 1 . . . A2
TOLOZAN (Place) . . . 1 . . . A3
TONY TOLLET (Rue) . . . 2 . . . D1-D2
TRAMASSAC (Rue) . . . 5 . . . C1
TREMASSAC (Petite rue) . . . 5 . . . B1
TRINITE (Place de la) . . . 5 . . . C1
TROIS MARIES (Rue des) . . . 5 . . . B1
TRONCHET (Rue) . . . 6 . . . A4
TUPIN (Rue) . . . 2 . . . B2-B3
TURENNE (Rue) . . . 3 . . . D4
TURQUET (Impasse) . . . 5 . . . D1
VALFENIERE (Rue) . . . 1 . . . A2-B2
VAUBAN (Rue) . . . 6 . . . B4
VAUBECOUR (Rue) . . . 2 . . . D1
VERRERIE (Impasse de la) . . . 1 . . . A3
VICTOIRE (Rue de la) . . . 3 . . . D4
VICTOR AUGAGNEUR (Quai) . . . 3 . . . B4-C4
VICTOR HUGO (Rue) . . . 2 . . . D2
VIEILLE (Impasse de la) . . . 1 . . . A1
VIEILLE (Rue) . . . 1 . . . A2
VIEL RENVERSE (Rue du) . . . 5 . . . D1
VILLEROY (Rue) . . . 3 . . . D4
VISTE (Place le) . . . 2 . . . D3
WILSON (Pont) . . . 2 . . . C3-C4

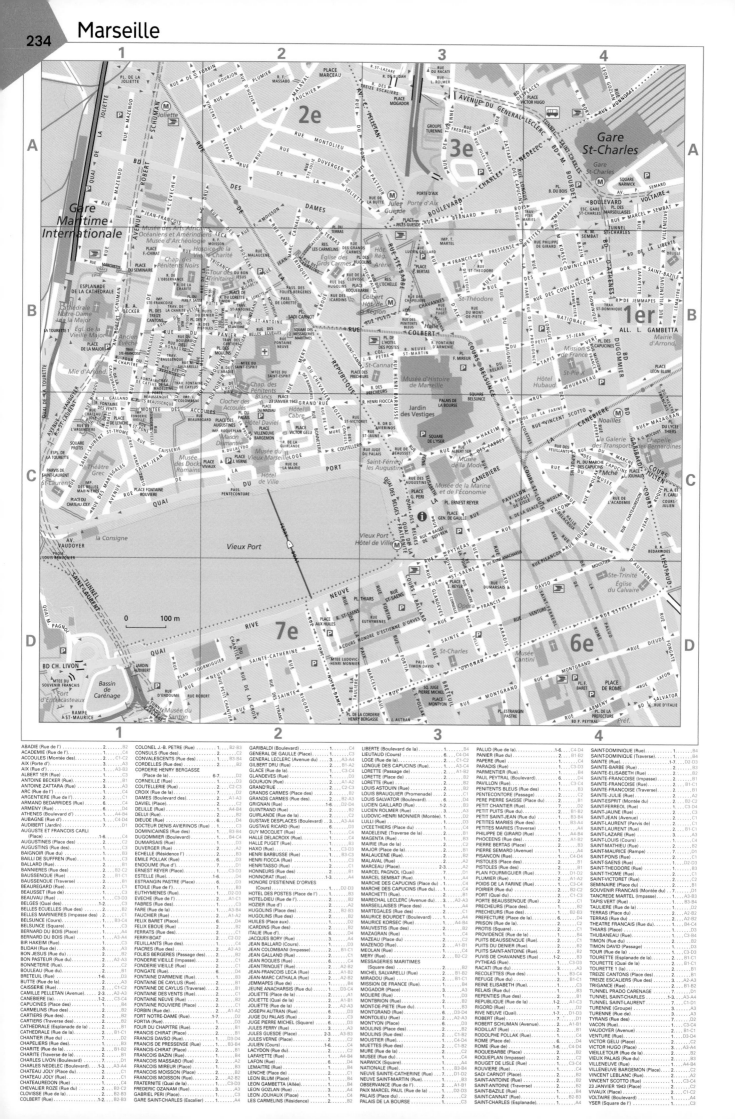

ABADIE (Rue de l') ... 2 ... B2
ACADEMIE (Rue de l') ... 1 ... C4
ACCOULES (Montée des) ... 2 ... C1-C2
AIX (Porte d') ... 3 ... A3-B3
AIX (Rue d') ... 2 ... A3-B3
ALBERT 1ER (Rue) ... 1 ... C3
ANTOINE BECKER (Rue) ... 2 ... B1
ANTOINE ZATTARA (Rue) ... 3 ... A4
ARC (Rue de l') ... 1 ... D2
ARGENTIERE (Rue de l') ... 2 ... C1
ARMAND BEDARRIDES (Rue) ... 1 ... C1
ARMENY (Rue) ... 6 ... D4
ATHENES (Boulevard d') ... 1 ... A4-B4
AUBAGNE (Rue d') ... 1 ... C4-D4
AUDIBERT (Jardin) ... D1
AUGUSTE ET FRANCOIS CARLI (Place) ... 1-6 ... C4
AUGUSTINES (Place des) ... 2 ... C1-C2
AUGUSTINS (Rue des) ... 1 ... B3
BAIGNOIR (Rue du) ... 1 ... B3
BAILLI DE SUFFREN (Rue) ... 1 ... C3
BALLARD (Rue) ... 2 ... B1
BANNIERES (Rue des) ... 2 ... B2-C2
BAUSSENQUE (Rue) ... 2 ... B1-C1
BAUSSENQUE (Traverse) ... 2 ... C1
BEAUREGARD (Rue de) ... 1 ... C3
BEAUVAU (Rue) ... 1 ... C4
BELGES (Quai des) ... 1-2 ... C3
BELLES ECUELLES (Rue des) ... 2 ... B2
BELLES MARINIERES (Impasse des) ... 2 ... C1
BELSUNCE (Cours) ... B3-C4
BELSUNCE (Rue) ... 1 ... B4
BERNARD DU BOIS (Place) ... 1 ... A4
BERNARD DU BOIS (Rue) ... 1 ... A3-A4
BIR HAKEIM (Rue) ... 1 ... C3
BLIDAH (Rue de) ... 3 ... A3
BON JESUS (Rue du) ... 2 ... B2
BON PASTEUR (Rue du) ... 2 ... A2-B3
BONNETERIE (Rue) ... 2 ... C2
BOULEAU (Rue du) ... 1 ... B3
BRETEUIL (Rue) ... 1-6 ... D4
BUTTE (Rue de la) ... 2 ... A4
CAISSERIE (Rue) ... 2 ... C1-C2
CAMILLE PELLETAN (Avenue) ... 2-3 ... A2-A3
CANEBIERE (la) ... 1-2 ... C3-C4
CAPUCINES (Place des) ... B4
CARMELINS (Rue des) ... 2 ... B2
CARTIERS (Rue des) ... 2 ... B2
CARTIERS (Traverse des) ... 2 ... B2
CATHEDRALE (Esplanade de la) ... 2 ... B1
CATHEDRALE (Rue) ... 2 ... B1-C1
CHANTIER (Rue du) ... 7 ... D1
CHAPELIERS (Rue des) ... 1 ... B3
CHARITE (Rue de la) ... 2 ... B1-B2
CHARITE (Traverse de la) ... 2 ... B2
CHARLES LIVON (Boulevard) ... 7 ... D1
CHARLES NEDELEC (Boulevard) ... A3-A4
CHATEAU JOLY (Rue du) ... 2 ... C1
CHATEAU JOLY (Place) ... 2 ... C1
CHATEAUREDON (Rue du) ... 1 ... C4
CHEVALIER ROZE (Rue du) ... 2 ... B2-C2
CLOVISSE (Rue de la) ... 2 ... B2
COLBERT (Rue de) ... 1-2 ... B3

COLONEL J.-B. PETRE (Rue) ... 1 ... B2-B3
CONSULS (Rue des) ... 2 ... C2
CONVALESCENTS (Rue des) ... 1 ... B3-B4
CORDELLES (Rue des) ... 2 ... C1
CORDERIE HENRY BERGASSE (Place de la) ... 6-7 ... D2
CORNEILLE (Rue) ... 1 ... C3
COUTELLERIE (Rue de la) ... 2 ... C2
CROIX (Rue de la) ... 2 ... C2-C3
DAMES (Boulevard des) ... 2 ... A1-A2
DAVIEL (Place) ... 2 ... C2
DELILLE (Rue) ... 1 ... A4-B4
DELUI (Rue) ... 2 ... B2
DIEUDE (Rue) ... 6 ... D4
DOCTEUR DENIS AVIERINOS (Rue) ... 1 ... C3
DOMINICAINES (Rue des) ... 1 ... B3-B4
DUGOMMIER (Boulevard) ... 1 ... B4-C4
DUMARSAIS (Rue) ... 2 ... D3
DUVERGER (Rue) ... 2 ... A2
ECHELLE (Résidence l') ... 1 ... B4
EMILE POLLAK (Rue) ... 2 ... C1
ENDOUME (Rue d') ... 7 ... D1
ERNEST REYER (Rue) ... 1 ... C3-D3
ESTELLE (Rue) ... 1 ... C4
ESTRANGIN PASTRE (Place) ... 1-6 ... D4
ETOILE (Rue de l') ... 1 ... C3
EUTHYMENES (Rue) ... 1 ... D2-D3
EVECHE (Rue de l') ... 2 ... A1-C1
FABRE (Rue de) ... 1 ... C4
FAUCHIER (Rue) ... 2 ... A1-A2
FELIX BARET (Place) ... 6 ... D4
FELIX EBOUE (Rue) ... 2 ... C1
FERRATS (Rue des) ... 2 ... C1
FEUILLANTS (Rue des) ... 1 ... C4
FIACRES (Rue des) ... 2 ... A2-A3
FOLIES BERGERES (Passage des) ... 2 ... B3-B4
FONDERIE VIEILLE (Impasse) ... 2 ... C1
FONDERIE VIEILLE (Rue) ... 2 ... C1
FONGATE (Rue) ... 1 ... C4
FONTAINE D'ARMENIE (Rue) ... 2 ... B3
FONTAINE DE CAYLUS (Rue) ... 2 ... B1
FONTAINE DES VENTS (Rue) ... 2 ... B2
FONTAINE NEUVE (Rue) ... 2 ... B2
FONTAINE ROUVIERE (Place) ... 2 ... C1
FORBIN (Rue) ... 2 ... A1-A2
FORT NOTRE-DAME (Rue) ... 1-7 ... D2
FORTIA (Rue) ... 1 ... D2
FOUR DU CHAPITRE (Rue) ... 2 ... B1
FRANCIS CHIRAT (Place) ... 2 ... B1
FRANCIS DAVSO (Rue) ... 1 ... D3-D4
FRANCIS DE PRESSENSE (Rue) ... 2 ... B3-B4
FRANCOIS BAZIN (Rue) ... 1 ... B4
FRANCOIS CHIRAT (Rue) ... 2 ... B1
FRANCOIS MASSABO (Rue) ... 2 ... A2
FRANCOIS MIREUR (Rue) ... 1 ... C4
FRANCOIS MOISSON (Rue) ... 2 ... A2-B2
FRATERNITE (Rue de la) ... 1 ... C3-D3
FREDERIC OZANAM (Rue) ... 3 ... A3
GABRIEL PERI (Rue) ... 1 ... C4
GARE SAINT-CHARLES (Escalier) ... A4

GARIBALDI (Boulevard) ... 1 ... C4
GENERAL DE GAULLE (Place) ... 1 ... C3
GENERAL LECLERC (Avenue du) ... 3 ... A3-A4
GILBERT DRU (Rue) ... 2 ... B1-A2
GLACE (Rue de la) ... 1 ... A3-A4
GLANDEVES (Rue) ... 1 ... C4
GOURJON (Rue) ... 2 ... A1-A2
GRAND'RUE ... 2 ... C2-C3
GRANDS CARMES (Place des) ... 2 ... B2
GRANDS CARMES (Rue des) ... 2 ... B2
GRIGNAN (Rue) ... 1-6 ... D3-D4
GUINTRAND (Rue) ... 2 ... C1
GUIRLANDE (Rue de la) ... 2 ... C2
GUSTAVE DESPLACES (Boulevard) ... 3 ... A3-A4
GUSTAVE RICARD (Rue) ... 6 ... D4
GUY MOCQUET (Rue) ... 1 ... B4
HALLE DELACROIX (Rue) ... 1 ... C4
HALLE PUGET (Rue) ... 1 ... C4
HAXO (Rue) ... 1 ... C3-D3
HENRI BARBUSSE (Rue) ... 1 ... B3-C3
HENRI FIOCCA (Rue) ... 2 ... B3
HENRITOSSA (Rue) ... 2 ... A2
HOMME D'ESTIENNE D'ORVES (Cours) ... 1 ... D2-D3
HOTEL DES POSTES (Place de l') ... 1 ... B3
HOTEL-DIEU (Place de l') ... 2 ... C2
HOZIER (Rue d') ... 2 ... A2
HUGOLINS (Rue des) ... 2 ... B2-B3
HUILES (Place aux) ... 1 ... D2
ICARDINS (Rue des) ... 2 ... B2
ITALIE (Rue d') ... 6 ... C4-D4
JACQUES BORY (Rue) ... 1 ... C4
JEAN BALLARD (Cours) ... 1 ... D2
JEAN COLOMBANI (Impasse) ... 2 ... B1-C1
JEAN GALLAND (Rue) ... 2 ... C1
JEAN ROQUES (Rue) ... 6 ... D4
JEAN TRINQUET (Rue) ... 2 ... A2
JEAN-FRANCOIS LECA (Rue) ... 2 ... A1-B2
JEAN-MARC CATHALA (Rue) ... 2 ... A2-B2
JEMMAPES (Rue de) ... 1 ... B4
JEUNE ANACHARSIS (Rue du) ... 1 ... D3-D4
JOLIETTE (Place de la) ... 2 ... A1
JOLIETTE (Quai de la) ... 2 ... A1-B1
JOLIETTE (Rue de la) ... 2 ... A1-B1
JOSEPH AUTRAN (Rue) ... 6 ... D3
JUGE DU PALAIS (Rue) ... 2 ... C2
JULES FERRY (Rue) ... 1 ... C4
JULES GUESDE (Place) ... 2-3 ... A3-B3
JULES VERNE (Place) ... 2 ... C2
JULIEN (Cours) ... 1-6 ... C4
LACYDON (Rue du) ... 2 ... C2
LAFAYETTE (Rue) ... 1 ... A4-B4
LAFON (Rue) ... 6 ... D4
LEMAITRE (Rue) ... 1 ... B4
LENCHE (Place de) ... 2 ... C1
LEON BLUM (Place) ... 1 ... B4
LEON GAMBETTA (Allée) ... 1 ... B4
LEON GOZLAN (Rue) ... 1 ... A4
LEON JOUHAUX (Rue) ... 1 ... B4-C4
LES CARMELINS (Résidence) ... 2 ... B2

LIBERTE (Boulevard de la) ... 1 ... B4
LIEUTAUD (Cours) ... 6 ... C4-D4
LOGE (Rue de la) ... 2 ... C2
LONGUE DES CAPUCINS (Rue) ... 1 ... A3-C4
LORETTE (Passage de) ... 2 ... A1-B2
LORETTE (Rue de) ... 2 ... B2
LORETTE (Rue) ... 2 ... B2
LOUIS ASTOUIN (Rue) ... 2 ... B2
LOUIS BRAUQUIER (Promenade) ... 2 ... C1
LOUIS SALVATOR (Boulevard) ... 6 ... D4
LUCIEN GAILLARD (Rue) ... 1 ... D2
LUCIEN ROLMER (Rue) ... 3 ... A3
LUDOVIC-HENRI MONNIER (Montée) ... 1 ... D2
LULLI (Rue) ... 1 ... C4
LYCEE THIERS (Place du) ... 1 ... B4
MADELEINE (Traverse de la) ... 1 ... C4
MAGENTA (Rue) ... 1 ... B3
MAIRIE (Place de la) ... 2 ... C2
MAJOR (Place de la) ... 2 ... B1
MALAUCENE (Rue) ... 2 ... B2
MALAVAL (Rue) ... 2 ... A2
MARCEAU (Place) ... 2-3 ... A2
MARCEL PAGNOL (Quai) ... 7 ... D1
MARCEL SEMBAT (Rue) ... 1 ... A4
MARCHE DES CAPUCINS (Place du) ... 1 ... C4
MARCHE DES CAPUCINS (Rue du) ... 1 ... C4
MARCHETTI (Rue) ... 1 ... C3
MARECHAL LECLERC (Avenue du) ... 3 ... A3-A4
MARSEILLAISES (Place des) ... 1 ... A4
MARTEGALES (Rue des) ... 2 ... C1
MAURICE BOURDET (Boulevard) ... 2 ... A1
MAURICE KORSEC (Rue) ... 1 ... C4
MAUVESTIS (Rue des) ... 2 ... B2
MAZARGUES (Rue) ... 1 ... C4
MAZEAU (Rue) ... 1 ... D2
MAZENOD (Rue) ... 2 ... A1-B1
MEOLAN (Rue) ... 1 ... C4
MERY (Rue) ... 2 ... C2
MESSAGERIES MARITIMES (Square des) ... 2 ... A2
MICHEL SALVARELLI (Rue) ... 2 ... B1-B2
MIRADOU (Rue) ... 2 ... C1
MISSION DE FRANCE (Rue) ... 1 ... B4
MOGADOR (Rue) ... 3 ... A3
MOLIERE (Rue) ... 1 ... C3
MONTBRION (Rue) ... 2 ... D3
MONT-DE-PIETE (Rue du) ... 1 ... B3
MONTGRAND (Rue) ... 6 ... D4
MONTOLIEU (Rue) ... 2 ... A2-A3
MONTYON (Rue) ... 6 ... D4
MOULINS (Place des) ... 2 ... C1-C2
MOULINS (Rue des) ... 2 ... C1
MOUSTIER (Rue) ... 1 ... C4
MUETTES (Rue des) ... 2 ... C1-C2
MUSEE (Rue du) ... 1 ... C4
NARWICK (Square) ... A4
NATIONALE (Rue) ... 1 ... B3-B4
NEUVE SAINTE-CATHERINE (Rue) ... 7 ... D1-D2
NEUVE SAINT-MARTIN (Rue) ... 1 ... B3-C3
OBSERVANCE (Rue de l') ... 2 ... B1
OPERA (Place de l') ... 1 ... D3
PAIX MARCEL PAUL (Rue de la) ... 1 ... C4
PALAIS (Rue du) ... 2 ... C2
PALAIS DE LA BOURSE (Esplanade) ... 1 ... C3

PALUD (Rue de la) ... 1-6 ... C4-D4
PANIER (Rue du) ... 2 ... B1-B2
PAPERE (Rue) ... 1 ... B4
PARADIS (Rue) ... 1 ... C3-D3
PARMENTIER (Rue) ... 1 ... B4
PAUL PEYTRAL (Boulevard) ... 6 ... D4
PAVILLON (Rue) ... 1 ... C4
PENITENTS BLEUS (Rue des) ... 1 ... B3
PENTECONTORE (Passage) ... 2 ... C2
PERE PIERRE SAISSE (Place du) ... 2 ... B1
PETIT CHANTIER (Rue) ... 7 ... D1
PETIT PUITS (Rue du) ... 2 ... B1-B2
PETIT SAINT-JEAN (Rue du) ... 2 ... B1
PETITES MARIES (Rue des) ... 1 ... B3-B4
PETITES MARIES (Traverse) ... 1 ... B3
PHILIPPE DE GIRARD (Rue) ... 1 ... A4-B4
PHOCEENS (Rue des) ... 2 ... A1-B2
PIERRE BERTAS (Rue) ... 1 ... B3
PIERRE SEMARD (Avenue) ... 1 ... A4
PISANCON (Rue) ... 1 ... C4-D4
PISTOLES (Place des) ... 2 ... B1
PISTOLES (Rue des) ... 2 ... B1
PLAN FOURMIGUIER (Rue) ... 7 ... D2
PLUMIER (Rue) ... 2 ... A1-A2
POIDS DE LA FARINE (Rue du) ... 2 ... C3-C4
POIRIER (Rue du) ... 2 ... B2-C2
PORT (Quai du) ... 2 ... C1-C2
PORTE BEAUSSENQUE (Rue) ... 2 ... B1
PRECHEURS (Place des) ... 1 ... B3
PRECHEURS (Rue des) ... 2 ... B2-B3
PREFECTURE (Place de la) ... 6 ... D4
PRISON (Rue de la) ... 2 ... C2
PROTIS (Square) ... 2 ... C1
PROVIDENCE (Rue de la) ... 1 ... B4
PUITS BEAUSSENQUE (Rue) ... 2 ... B1
PUITS DU DENIER (Rue) ... 2 ... B2
PUITS SAINT-ANTOINE (Rue du) ... 2 ... B2
PUVIS DE CHAVANNES (Rue) ... 1-2 ... B3
PYTHEAS (Rue) ... 1 ... C3-D3
RACATI (Rue) ... 3 ... A3
RECOLETTES (Rue des) ... 1 ... B3-C4
REFUGE (Rue du) ... 2 ... B1-C1
REINE ELISABETH (Rue) ... 1 ... C4
RELAIS (Rue) ... 1 ... B4
REPENTIES (Rue des) ... 2 ... B1
REPUBLIQUE (Rue de la) ... 1-2 ... A1-C3
RIGORD (Rue) ... 7 ... D1
RIVE NEUVE (Quai) ... 1 ... D2-D3
ROBERT (Rue) ... 7 ... D1
ROBERT SCHUMAN (Avenue) ... 2 ... A1-B1
RODILLAT (Rue) ... 2 ... C1
RODOLPHE POLLAK (Rue) ... 1 ... C4
ROME (Rue de) ... 1-6 ... C4-D4
ROQUEBARBE (Impasse) ... 2 ... B2
ROUGET DE L'ISLE (Rue) ... 1 ... C4
ROUVIERE (Rue) ... 2 ... C1
SADI CARNOT (Place) ... 2 ... B2
SAINT-ANTOINE (Rue) ... 2 ... B2
SAINT-ANTOINE (Traverse) ... 2 ... B2
SAINT-BAZILE (Rue) ... 1 ... B4
SAINT-CANNAT (Rue) ... 2 ... B3
SAINT-CHARLES (Esplanade) ... 1 ... A4

SAINT-DOMINIQUE (Rue) ... 1 ... B4
SAINT-DOMINIQUE (Traverse) ... 1 ... B4
SAINTE (Rue) ... 1-7 ... D2-D3
SAINTE-BARBE (Rue) ... 2 ... B3
SAINTE-ELISABETH (Rue) ... 2 ... B3
SAINTE-FRANCOISE (Impasse) ... 2 ... B1
SAINTE-FRANCOISE (Rue) ... 2 ... B1-C1
SAINTE-FRANCOISE (Traverse) ... 2 ... B1
SAINTE-JULIE (Rue) ... 2 ... A2
SAINT-ESPRIT (Montée du) ... 2 ... B2-C2
SAINT-FERREOL (Rue) ... 1 ... C3-D4
SAINT-JAUME (Rue du) ... 2 ... B1
SAINT-JEAN (Rue) ... 2 ... C1
SAINT-LAURENT (Parvis de) ... 2 ... C1
SAINT-LAURENT (Rue) ... 2 ... B1-C1
SAINT-LAZARE (Rue) ... 3 ... A3
SAINT-LOUIS (Cours) ... 1 ... C4
SAINT-MATHIEU (Rue) ... 2 ... C1
SAINT-MAURICE (Rampe) ... 7 ... D1
SAINT-PONS (Rue) ... 2 ... C1
SAINT-SAENS (Rue) ... 1 ... D2-D3
SAINT-THEODORE (Rue) ... 1 ... B3
SAINT-THOME (Rue) ... 2 ... C1
SAINT-VICTORET (Rue) ... 2 ... C1
SEMINAIRE (Rue) ... 2 ... C1
SOUVENIR FRANCAIS (Montée du) ... 7 ... D1
TANCREDE MARTEL (Impasse) ... 1 ... A3-B3
TAPIS VERT (Rue) ... 1 ... B4
TAULIERE (Rue de la) ... 1 ... D2
TERRAS (Rue des) ... 2 ... A2-B2
TERRAS (Rue du) ... 2 ... B2
THEATRE FRANCAIS (Rue du) ... 1 ... B4-C4
THIARS (Place) ... 1 ... D2
THUBANEAU (Rue) ... 1 ... C3-B4
TIMON (Rue) ... 2 ... C1
TIMON DAVID (Passage) ... 6 ... D4
TOUR (Rue de la) ... 2 ... C1
TOURETTE (Esplanade de la) ... 2 ... B1-C1
TOURETTE (Quai de la) ... 2 ... B1-C1
TOURETTE 1 (la) ... 2 ... C1-C2
TREIZE CANTONS (Rue des) ... 2 ... B2
TREIZE ESCALIERS (Rue des) ... 3 ... A2-A3
TRIGANCE (Rue) ... 2 ... B1-B2
TUNNEL PRADO CARENAGE ... D1
TUNNEL SAINT-CHARLES ... 1-3 ... C3-A4
TUNNEL SAINT-LAURENT ... C1-D1
TURENNE (Groupe) ... 3 ... A3
TYRANS (Rue des) ... 2 ... D2
VACON (Rue) ... 1 ... C3-C4
VAUDOYER (Avenue) ... 2 ... B1-C1
VENTURE (Rue) ... 1 ... C4
VICTOR GELU (Rue) ... 2 ... C2
VICTOR HUGO (Place) ... 3 ... A3-A4
VIEILLE TOUR (Rue de la) ... 2 ... B2
VIEUX PALAIS (Rue du) ... 2 ... B2
VILLENEUVE (Rue) ... 2 ... A2
VILLENEUVE BARGEMON (Place) ... 2 ... C2
VINCENT LEBLANC (Rue) ... 2 ... A2
VINCENT SCOTTO (Rue) ... 1 ... C3-C4
23 JANVIER 1943 (Place) ... 2 ... C2
VIVAUX (Rue) ... 2 ... C2
VOLTAIRE (Boulevard) ... 1 ... A4
YSER (Square de l') ... 1 ... C4

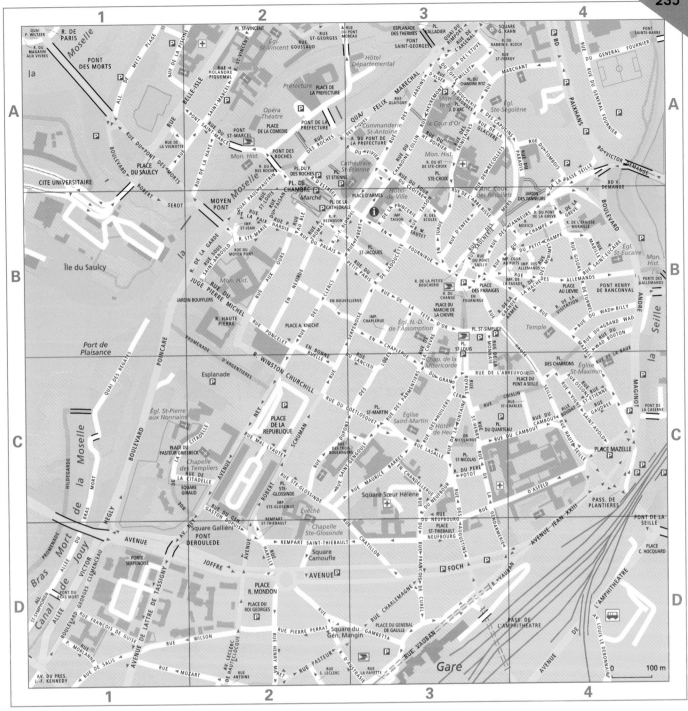

ABBE RISSE (Rue de l') B3
ABREUVOIR (Rue de l') C3-C4
ALGER (Rue d') A3
ALLEMANDS (Impasse des) B4
ALLEMANDS (Porte des) B4
ALLEMANDS (Rue des) B3-B4
AMBROISE THOMAS (Rue) B2
AMPHITHEATRE (Avenue de l') C4-D4
AMPHITHEATRE (Passage de l') D3-D4
ANDRE MAGINOT (Boulevard) A4-C4
ANTOINE (Rue) D2
ARGENTIERES (Promenade d') B1-C2
ARMAND KNECHT (Place) B2
ARMES (Place d') A3-B3
ARSENAL (Rue de l') A3
ASFELD (Rue d') C3-C4
AUGUSTINS (Rue des) C3-D3
AUSTRASIE (Rue d') D2-D3
BASSE SEILLE (Rue de la) A4-B4
BAUE (Rue de la) B4-C4
BELLE-ISLE (Rue) A1-A2
BLE (Rue au) B2
BOUCHERIE SAINT-GEORGES (Rue) C4
BOUDAT (Ruelle) C4
BOUFFLERS (Jardin) B2
BRAS MORT (Allée du) C1-D1
BRAS MORT (Pont du) D1
CAMBOUT (Rue du) C3-C4
CAMILLE HOCQUARD (Place) D4
CAPUCINS (Rue des) A3-A4
CASERNE (Pont de la) B2
CATHEDRALE (Place de la) A2
CHAMBRE (Place de) A2
CHAMPE (Rue du) B3-B4
CHANGE (Rue du) B3
CHANOINE COLLIN (Rue du) A3
CHANOINE RITZ (Place du) A3
CHAPLERUE (Impasse) B3
CHARLEMAGNE (Rue) D3
CHARRONS (Rue des) B4-C4
CHATILLON (Rue) C2-D3
CHEVRE (Rue de la) B3-C3
CHEVREMONT (Rue) B3
CITADELLE (Rue de la) C1-C2
CLERCS (Rue des) B2-C2
COETLOSQUET (Rue du) C2-C3
COFFE MILLET (Rue) C4
COISLIN (Rue) C3-C4
COMEDIE (Place de la) A2
COUR AU PUITS (Impasse) C3
DEROULEDE (Pont) D1
DUPONT DES LOGES (Rue) C2-B3
ECOLES (Rue des) B3
EN BONNE RUELLE B2-C2
EN CHANDELLERUE C3

EN CHAPLERUE B3-C3
EN FOURNIRUE B3
EN JURUE B3
EN NEXIRUE B2
EN NICOLAIRUE C3
EN NOUVELLERUE B2-B3
EPAISSE MURAILLE (Rue de l') B4
ESTREES (Rue d') A2-B2
ETUVE (Rue de l') A3
FABERT (Rue) B2-B3
FAISAN (Rue du) A2-B2
FAVADE (Impasse de la) B3-B4
FELIX MARECHAL (Quai) A2-A3
FOCH (Avenue) D2-D3
FONTAINE (Rue de la) C3
FOUR DU CLOITRE (Rue du) A3-B3
FRANCOIS DE CUREL (Rue) D3
FRANCOIS DE GUISE (Rue) D1
GAMBETTA (Rue) D2-D3
GARDE (Rue de la) B2
GAUDREE (Rue) C4
GENDARMERIE (Rue de la) C3-D3
GENERAL DE GAULLE (Place du) D3
GENERAL FOURNIER (Rue) A4
GENERAL GASTON DUPUIS (Rue du) C2-D2
GEORGES CLEMENCEAU (Boulevard) D1
GIRAUD (Square) C2
GISORS (Rue de la) B4
GLACIERE (Rue de la) A3-A4
GLATIGNY (Rue de) A3
GOUSSAUD (Rue) A2
GRAND CERF (Rue du) B3-B4
GRAND WAD (Rue du) B4
GRANDE ARMEE (Rue de la) B3-B4
GREVE (Rue de la) B4
GUSTAVE KAHN (Square) A1
HACHE (Rue de la) B4
HARELLE (Rue) D2
HAUT DE SAINTE-CROIX (Rue du) A3
HAUT POIRIER (Rue du) A3
HAUTE PIERRE (Rue) B2
HAUTE SEILLE (Rue) B3-C4
HAYE (Rue de la) A2-B2
HENRY DE RANCONVAL (Pont) B4
HILDEGARDE (Promenade) C1-D1
HOLANDRE PIQUEMAL (Rue) A2
HUILIERS (Rue des) C3
JACQUES-FRANCOIS BLONDEL (Rue) B2-B3
JARDINS (Rue des) A3
JEAN XXIII (Avenue) C4-D4
JEANNE D'ARC (Place) A3

JOFFRE (Avenue) D1-D2
JUGE PIERRE MICHEL (Rue du) B2
LADOUCETTE (Rue de) B3-C3
LANCIEU (Rue du) B2-C3
LA FAYETTE (Rue) D3
LASALLE (Rue) C3
LATTRE DE TASSIGNY (Avenue de) D1
LECLERC DE HAUTECLOCQUE (Avenue) D2
LIEVRE (Place au) B4
LOUIS LE DEBONNAIRE (Avenue) D4
MABILLE (Rue) B4
MAGASIN AUX VIVRES (Rue du) A1
MARCHANT (Rue) A3-A4
MARCHE DE LA CHEVRE (Place du) B3
MARECHAL LYAUTEY (Rue) C2
MARIE SAUTET (Rue) B3
MAURICE BARRES (Rue) C2-C3
MAZELLE (Place) B4
MAZELLE (Rue) B3-C4
METZ PLAGE (Allée de) A1
MEXICO (Rue) B4
MINIMES (Rue des) B4
MONNAIE (Rue de la) B3-C3
MORTS (Pont des) A1
MOYEN PONT B2
MOYEN PONT (Rue du) B2
MOZART (Rue) D1-D2
MURS (Rue des) B3-B4
NEUFBOURG (Rue du) C3-D3
NEY (Avenue) D1-C3
OSSONS (Rue aux) C4
OURS (Rue aux) B2
PAIX (Rue de la) B2
PAIXHANS (Boulevard) A4
PALAIS (Rue du) B3
PARADIS (Rue du) A4
PARAIGES (Place des) B3
PARIS (Rue de) A1
PARMENTIERS (Rue des) C3
PASTEUR (Rue) D2
PASTEUR GRIESBECK (Place du) C2
PAUL BEZANSON (Rue) B2-B3
PAUL VAUTRIN (Quai) A2-B2
PAUL WILTZER (Quai) A1
PERE POTOT (Rue du) C3
PETIT CHAMPE (Rue au) B4
PETIT PARIS (Rue du) B2-B3
PETITE BOUCHERIE (Rue de la) B3
PIERRE HARDIE (Rue) B2
PIERRE MORLANNE (Rue) D1
PIERRE PERRAT (Rue) D1
PIQUES (Rue aux) A2-A3
PISCINE (Rue de la) A1-A2
PLANTIERES (Passage de) C4

POINCARE (Boulevard) D1-B2
PONCELET (Rue) B2
PONT A SEILLE (Place du) C4
PONT DE LA GREVE (Rue du) B4
PONT DES MORTS (Rue du) A1-B2
PONT DES MORTS (Place du) A1
PONT DES ROCHES (Place du) A2
PONT DES ROCHES (Rue du) A2
PONT MOREAU (Rue du) A2-A3
PONT SAILLY (Rue du) B3
PONT SAINT-MARCEL (Rue du) A1-A2
PREFECTURE (Place de la) A2-A3
PREFECTURE (Pont de la) A2-A3
PRESIDENT J.F. KENNEDY (Avenue du) D1
PRINCERIE (Rue de la) B3
QUARTEAU (Place du) C3
RABBIN ELIE BLOCH (Rue) A3
RAYMOND MONDON (Place) D2
RECOLLETS (Rue des) B3-A4
REGATES (Quai des) B1-C1
REPUBLIQUE (Place de la) C3
RIMPORT (Rue) A3
ROBERT SCHUMAN (Avenue) C2-D2
ROBERT SEROT (Boulevard) A1-B2
ROCHES (Pont des) A2
ROCHES (Rue des) A2
ROI GEORGE (Place du) D2
ROYALE (Rue) C3
SAINT-CHARLES (Rue) C4
SAINT-ETIENNE (Place) B2-A3
SAINT-ETIENNE (Rue) A3
SAINT-EUCAIRE (Rue) B4
SAINT-FERROY (Rue) A3
SAINT-GENGOULF (Rue) C2-C3
SAINT-GEORGES (Pont) A2
SAINT-GEORGES (Rue) A2
SAINT-HENRY (Rue) C3
SAINT-JACQUES (Place) B3
SAINT-JEAN (Impasse) B2
SAINT-LOUIS (Place) B3-C3
SAINT-LOUIS (Rue) B3-C3
SAINT-MARCEL (Pont) A2
SAINT-MARCEL (Rue) A1-A2
SAINT-MARTIN (Place) C3
SAINT-NICOLAS (Place) C3
SAINT-SIMPLICE (Place) B3
SAINT-SYMPHORIEN (Allée) D1
SAINT-THIEBAULT (Place) C3
SAINT-THIEBAULT (Rempart) C2-D3
SAINT-VINCENT (Place) A2
SAINT-VINCENT (Rue) A2
SAINTE-CROIX (Place) A3
SAINTE-GLOSSINDE (Impasse) C2
SAINTE-GLOSSINDE (Place) C2

SAINTE-GLOSSINDE (Rue) C2
SAINTE-MARIE (Rue) B2
SALIS (Rue de) D1
SAULCY (Place du) A1
SAULNERIE (Rue) B3
SEBASTIEN LECLERC (Rue) D2
SEILLE (Pont de la) D4
SERPENOISE (Porte) D1
SERPENOISE (Rue) C2-B3
SOUS SAINT-ARNOULD (Rue) B2
TAISON (Impasse) A3
TAISON (Rue) A3-B3
TANNEURS (Jardin des) B4
TANNEURS (Rue des) B3-B4
TETE D'OR (Rue de la) B3
THERMES (Esplanade des) A3
TOMBOIS (Rue) A4
TRINITAIRES (Rue des) C2-C3
TURMEL (Rue de) B4
UNIVERSITAIRE (Cité) A1-B1
VALLADIER (Place) A3
VAUBAN (Rue) D3-D4
VICTOR DEMANGE (Boulevard) A4-B4
VICTOR HEGLY (Allée) C1-D1
VIGNE SAINT-AVOLD (Rue) A1-A2
VIGNOTTE (Rue de la) A1-A2
VISITATION (Rue de la) A2-A3
VIVIER (Rue du) A3
WAD BILLY (Rue) B4
WAD BOUTON (Rue du) B4-C4
WILSON (Rue) D1-D2
WINSTON CHURCHILL (Rue) B2-C2

Montpellier

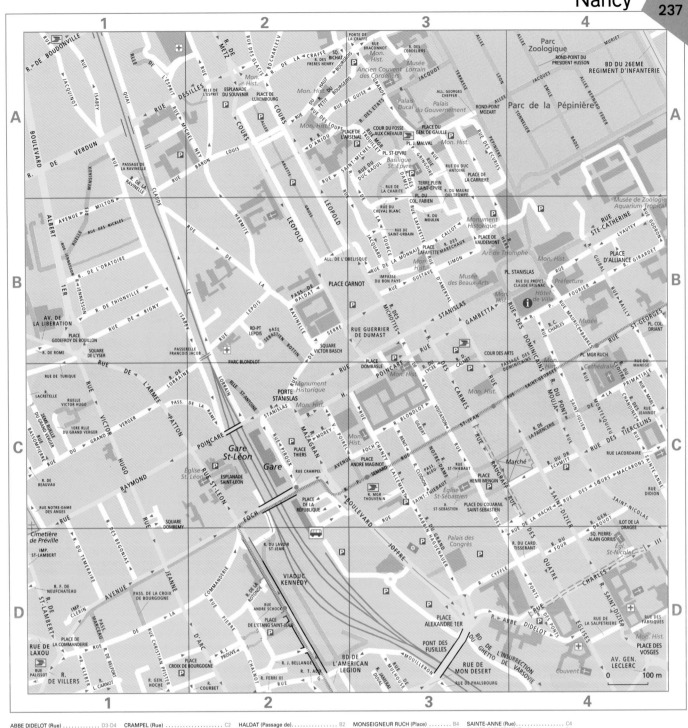

ABBE DIDELOT (Rue) D3-D4
ACQUES MURIET (Allée) A4
ALBERT 1ER (Boulevard) A1-B1
ALEXANDRE 1ER (Place) D3
ALLIANCE (Place d') B4
AMERICAN LEGION (Boulevard de l') . . . D2
AMERVAL (Rue d') B3
ANDRE MAGINOT (Place) C3
ANDRE SCHOCK (Rue) D2
ARLETTE GRUSS (Allée) A2-B2
ARMEE PATTON (Rue de l') B1-C2
ARSENAL (Place de l') A2-A3
ARTS (Cours des) C3-C4
BAILLY (Rue) B4
BARON LOUIS (Rue) A1-A2
BASSOMPIERRE (Rue) C1
BEAUVAU (Rue de) C1
BEGONIAS (Rue des) C1-D1
BELFORT (Rue de) D1
BENIT (Rue) C3
BERNARD FEDER (Allée) A4
BICHAT (Rue) A2
BLEU (Passage) C3
BLONDLOT (Parc) B2
BLONDLOT (Rue) C3
BON PAYS (Impasse du) B3
BOUDONVILLE (Rue de) A1
BRACONNOT (Rue) A3
CALLOT (Rue) B3
CARDINAL TISSERANT (Rue du) D4
CARMES (Rue des) B3-C3
CARNOT (Place) B2
CARRIERE (Place de la) A3-B4
CHANOINES (Rue des) C4
CHANZY (Rue) C3
CHARITE (Rue de la) A3
CHARLES III (Rue) D4
CHARLES V (Boulevard) A2
CHEVAL BLANC (Rue du) B3
CHRISTIAN PFISTER (Rue) D1
CLAUDE CHARLES (Rue) C4
CLAUDE LE LORRAIN (Quai) A1-C2
CLERIN (Impasse) D1
CLODION (Rue) C3
CLOITRE (Rue du) B4-C4
COLONEL DRIANT (Place) B4
COLONEL FABIEN (Place du) A3-B3
COMMANDERIE (Place de la) D1
COMMANDERIE (Rue de la) D1-C2
CORDELIERS (Rue des) A3
COUARAIL SAINT-SEBASTIEN
(Place de) C3
COURBET (Rue) D2
CRAFFE (Porte de la) A2-A3
CRAFFE (Rue de la) A2

CRAMPEL (Rue) C2
CROIX DE BOURGOGNE
(Passage de la) D1
CROIX DE BOURGOGNE (Place) . . . D1-D2
CYFFLE (Rue) D3-D4
DAMES (Rue des) A3
DESILLES (Rue) A1-A2
2EME RUELLE DU GRAND VERGER . . . C1
DIDION (Rue) C4
DOCTEUR SCHMITT (Rue du) C4
DOMBASLE (Place) B3-C3
DOMINICAINS (Passage des) C3-B4
DOMINICAINS (Rue des) B4-C4
DOMINIQUE CALMET (Rue) B3-C3
DOMREMY (Square) C1
DRAGEE (Ilot de la) C4-D4
DUC ANTOINE (Rue du) A3
DUC RAOUL (Rue) A3
ECURIES (Rue des) A3
EMILE BADEL (Allée) A4
ESPRIT (Ruelle de l') A1-A2
ETANG SAINT-JEAN (Place de l') D2
ETATS (Rue des) A3
FABRIQUES (Rue des) D4
FAIENCERIE (Rue de la) C4
FERRI III (Rue) B3
FOCH (Avenue) D1-C3
FOSSE AUX CHEVAUX (Cour du) A3
FOUR (Rue du) D4
FRANCOIS DE NEUFCHATEAU (Rue) . . D1
FRANCOIS JACOB (Passage) B2
FRERES HENRY (Rue des) A2
FUSILLES (Pont des) D3
GABRIEL MOUILLERON (Rue) D2-D3
GAMBETTA (Rue) B3-B4
GENERAL DE GAULLE (Place du) A3
GENERAL DROUOT (Rue) C4-D4
GENERAL HOCHE (Rue) D1
GENERAL LECLERC (Avenue) D4
GEORGES CHEPFER (Allée) A3
GILBERT (Rue) C3
GIRARDET (Rue) B4
GLACIS (Rue des) A2
GODEFROY DE BOUILLON (Place) B1
GODRON (Rue) B4
GRAND RABBIN HAGUENAUER
(Rue du) C3-D3
GRAND VERGER (1ERE ruelle du) C1
GRAND VERGER (Rue du) C1
GRANDE RUE A3-B3
GUERRIER DE DUMAST (Rue) B2-B3
GUIBAL (Rue) C4
GUISE (Rue de) A2-A3
GUSTAVE SIMON (Rue) B3
HACHE (Rue de la) D3-C4

HALDAT (Passage de) B2
HAUT BOURGEOIS (Rue du) A2-A3
HENRI MENGIN (Place) C3
HENRI POINCARE (Rue) C2-B3
HERE (Rue) B3-B4
HERMITE (Rue) A2-B2
INSURRECTION DU GHETTO
DE VARSOVIE (Boulevard de l') . . . D3-D4
ISABEY (Rue) A1-C2
JACQUARD (Rue) A2-B3
JACQUES BELLANGE (Rue) C2
JACQUES MURIET (Allée) A3-A4
JACQUINOT (Rue) A1
JACQUOT (Rue) A3
JAMERAI DUVAL (Rue) D3
JEAN PROUVE (Rue) D2
JEANNE D'ARC (Rue) C1-D2
JEANNOT (Rue) C3
JENNESSON (Rue) B1
JOFFRE (Boulevard) C2-D3
JOSEPH MALVAL (Place) A3
KENNEDY (Viaduc) C2-D2
KLEBER (Rue) D1
LACORDAIRE (Rue) C4
LACRETELLE (Rue) C1
LAFAYETTE (Place) B3
LAFAYETTE (Rue) B3
LAVOIR SAINT-JEAN (Rue du) C2
LAXOU (Rue de) D1
LAZARE CARNOT (Rue) C1-C2
LEONTONNELIER (Allée) A3-A4
LEOPOLD (Cours) A2-B3
LEOPOLD LALLEMENT (Rue) B2
LEPOIS (Rond-point) B2
LIBERATION (Avenue de la) B1
LORRAINE (Rue de) C1-C2
LOUPS (Rue des) A2
LUXEMBOURG (Place de) A2
LYAUTEY (Rue) B4
LYCEE (Rue du) B3
MABLY (Rue) A3
MANEGE (Rue du) B4-C4
MARCEAU (Passage) D1
MARECHAUX (Rue des) B3
MAURE QUITROMPE (Rue du) A3-B3
MAURICE BARRES (Rue) B4
MAZAGRAN (Rue) C2
MENSIAUX (Ruelle des) A1-B1
METZ (Rue de) A2
MICHEL NEY (Rue) A1-A2
MICHOTTES (Rue des) B3
MILTON (Avenue) A1-B1
MON DESERT (Rue de) C3-D4
MONNAIE (Rue de la) B3

MONSEIGNEUR RUCH (Place) B4
MONSEIGNEUR THOUVENIN (Rue) . . . C3
MONSEIGNEUR TROUILLET (Rue) A3
MONTESQUIEU (Rue) B4-C4
MOREY (Rue) C2
MOULIN (Rue du) B3
MOZART (Rond-point) A3
MULHOUSE (Rue de) D3
NICKLES (Rue des) B1
NOTRE-DAME (Rue) C3
NOTRE-DAME DES ANGES (Rue) D1
OBELISQUE (Allée de l') B2-B3
ORATOIRE (Rue de l') B1
PALISSOT (Rue) D1
PEPINIERE (Terrasse) A3-B4
PETIT BOURGEOIS (Rue du) A2-A3
PHALSBOURG (Rue de) D3
PIERRE CHALNOT (Rue) D1
PIERRE FOURIER (Rue) B4
PIERRE GRINGOIRE (Rue) A3
PIERRE SEMARD (Rue) C2-C3
PIERRE-ALAIN GORIUS (Square) D4
PIROUX (Rue) C2
PONT MOUJA (Rue du) B3
PONTS (Rue des) C3-D4
PREFET CLAUDE ERIGNAC (rue du) . . . B4
PRESIDENT HUSSON (Rond-point du) . . A4
PRIMATIALE (Rue de la) B4
QUATRE EGLISES (Rue des) C3-D4
RAME (Passage de la) C1-C2
RAUGRAFF (Rue) C3
RAVINELLE (Passage de la) A1
RAVINELLE (Rue de la) A1-B2
RAYMOND POINCARE (Rue) D1-C2
RENE D'ANJOU (Rue) C2
REPUBLIQUE (Place de la) C2
RIGNY (Rue de) B1
ROME (Rue de) B1
ROTONDE (Rue de la) C2
SAINT-ANTOINE (Ruelle) C2
SAINT-DIZIER (Rue) B3-D4
SAINT-EPVRE (Place) A3
SAINT-EPVRE (Terre-plein) A3
SAINT-GEORGES (Rue) C3-B4
SAINT-JEAN (Rue) C3
SAINT-JULIEN (Rue) B4-C4
SAINT-LAMBERT (Impasse) D1
SAINT-LAMBERT (Rue de) D1
SAINT-LEON (Esplanade) C2
SAINT-LEON (Rue) C2
SAINT-MICHEL (Rue) A2-A3
SAINT-NICOLAS (Rue) C4-D4
SAINT-SEBASTIEN (Rue de) C3
SAINT-THIEBAUT (Rue) C3
SAINT-URBAIN (Rue de) B3

SAINTE-ANNE (Rue) C4
SAINTE-CATHERINE (Rue) B4
SALPETRIERE (Rue de la) D4
SEBASTIEN BOTTIN (Passage de la) . . B2-C2
SERRE (Rue de) B2-C2
SŒURS MACARONS (Rue des) C4
SOURCE (Rue de la) A3-B3
SOUVENIR (Esplanade du) A2
STANISLAS (Place) B4
STANISLAS (Porte) C2
STANISLAS (Rue) C2-B3
TEMERAIRE (Rue du) C1-D1
THIERRY ALIX (Rue) D2
THIERS (Place) C2
THIONVILLE (Rue de) B1
TIERCELINS (Rue des) C4
TURIQUE (Rue de) B1-C1
VAUDEMONT (Place de) B3
VERDUN (Rue de) A1
VICTOR BASCH (Square) B2
VICTOR HUGO (Rue) B1-C1
VICTOR HUGO (Ruelle) C1
VICTOR POIREL (Rue) C2-C3
VILLERS (Rue de) D1
26EME REGIMENT D'INFANTERIE
(Boulevard du) A4
VISITATION (Rue de la) B3-C3
VOSGES (Place des) D4
YSER (Square de l') B1

Nantes

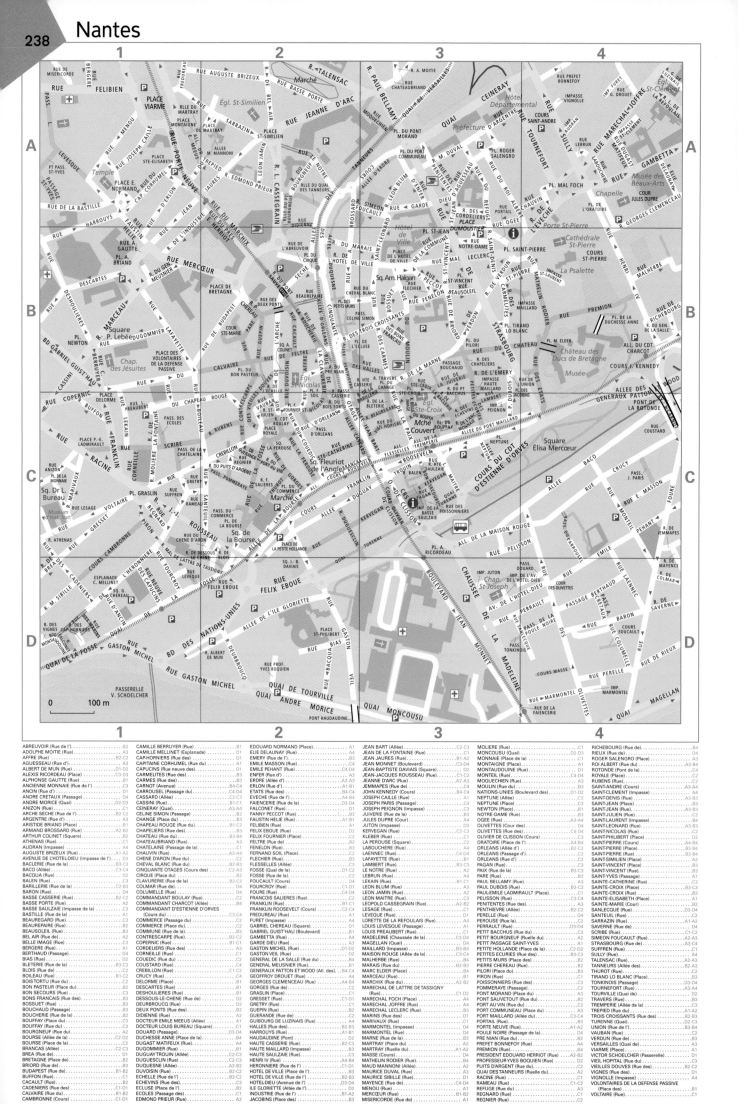

ABREUVOIR (Rue de l').........................B2
ADOLPHE MOITIE (Rue)........................A3
AFFRE (Rue d')............................B2-C2
AGUESSEAU (Rue d').........................A3
ALBERT DE MUN (Rue)....................D1-D2
ALEXIS RICORDEAU (Place)...............C3-C3
ALPHONSE GAUTTE (Rue)...................B1
ANCIENNE MONNAIE (Rue de l')............C3
ANCIN (Rue d')...............................D1
ANDRE CRETAUX (Passage)..................D4
ANDRE MORICE (Quai)...................D2-D3
ANIZON (Rue)................................C1
ARCHE SECHE (Rue de l')................B2-C2
ARGENTRE (Rue d')............................B1
ARISTIDE BRIAND (Place)......................B1
ARMAND BROSSARD (Rue).................A2-B2
ARTHUR COLINET (Square)....................B2
ATHENAS (Rue)...............................C1
AUDRAN (Impasse)............................A3
AUGUSTE BRIZEUX (Rue)..................A1-A2
AVENUE DE L'HOTEL-DIEU (Impasse de l')...D3
BACLERIE (Rue de la)....................B3-C3
BACO (Allée).............................C3-C4
BACOUA (Rue)................................D2
BALEN (Rue)..................................C3
BARILLERIE (Rue de la)..................C2-B3
BARON (Rue).................................D4
BASSE CASSERIE (Rue).......................B3
BASSE PORTE (Rue de la)....................A2
BASSE SAULZAIE (Impasse de la)...........C3
BASTILLE (Rue de la).........................A1
BEAUREGARD (Rue)...........................D1
BEAUREPAIRE (Rue)...........................B2
BEAUSOLEIL (Rue)............................B3
BEL AIR (Rue)..............................A2
BELLE IMAGE (Rue)........................B2-C2
BERGERE (Rue).............................A1
BERTHAUD (Passage).........................D4
BIAS (Rue)..................................D2
BLETERIE (Rue de la)....................B3-C3
BLOIS (Rue de)..............................C2
BOILEAU (Rue)............................B1-C2
BOISTORTU (Rue)............................B1
BON PASTEUR (Rue du).......................B2
BON SECOURS (Rue)..........................B1
BONS FRANCAIS (Rue des)....................B3
BOSSUET (Rue)...............................B3
BOUCHAUD (Passage).........................B3
BOUCHERIE (Rue de la)......................B3
BOUFFAY (Place du).........................C3
BOUFFAY (Rue du)...........................C3
BOURGNEUF (Rue du).........................A2
BOURSE (Place de la)....................C2-C2
BOURSE (Rue de la)......................C2-C2
BRANCAS (Allée)............................A2
BREA (Rue de)..............................D1
BRETAGNE (Place de).........................B1
BRIORD (Rue de)............................B1-B2
BUDAPEST (Rue de)........................B1-B2
BUFFON (Rue)...............................B2
CACAULT (Rue)...............................C3
CADENIERS (Rue des)....................C1-D1
CALVAIRE (Rue du).......................B1-B2
CAMBRONNE (Cours)......................C1-D1

CAMILLE BERRUYER (Rue)....................B1
CAMILLE MELLINET (Esplanade)..............D1
CAP-HORNIERS (Rue des).....................B3
CAPITAINE CORHUMEL (Rue du)...............A1
CAPUCINS (Rue neuve des)...................D1
CARMELITES (Rue des).......................B3
CARMES (Rue des)............................B3
CARNOT (Avenue)........................B4-C4
CARROUSEL (Passage du)....................C3
CASSARD (Allée)..........................C2-C3
CASSINI (Rue)............................B1-C1
CEINERAY (Quai)........................A3-A3
CELINE SIMON (Passage).....................B2
CHANGE (Rue du)............................B3
CHAPEAU ROUGE (Rue du)................B1-C2
CHAPELIERS (Rue des).......................B3
CHATEAU (Rue du)........................B3-B4
CHATEAUBRIAND (Rue)........................A3
CHATELAINE (Passage de la)................B2
CHAUVIN (Rue)..............................A4
CHENE D'ARON (Rue du)......................B3
CHEVAL BLANC (Rue du)...................B2-B3
CINQUANTE OTAGES (Cours des)...........C2-A3
CIRQUE (Place du)...........................B2
CLAVURERIE (Rue de la)..................B2-C2
COLMAR (Rue de)............................D4
COLUMELLE (Rue)............................D4
COMMANDANT BOULAY (Rue)..................C4
COMMANDANT CHARCOT (Rue)..................B4
COMMANDANT D'ESTIENNE D'ORVES
  (Cours du)...........................C3-C4
COMMERCE (Passage du)......................C2
COMMERCE (Place du)........................C2
COMMUNE (Rue de la)........................A3
CONTRESCARPE (Rue de la)...............B2-C2
COPERNIC (Rue)..........................B1-C1
CORDELIERS (Rue des).......................C1
CORNEILLE (Rue)............................C1
COUEDIC (Rue du)...........................C1
COUSTARD (Rue)............................C4
CREBILLON (Rue)............................C1
CRUCY (Rue)................................C4

EDOUARD NORMAND (Place)....................A1
ELIE DELAUNAY (Rue)........................A4
EMERY (Rue de l')..........................B3
EMILE MASSON (Rue).........................C4
EMILE PEHANT (Rue).....................C4-D4
ENFER (Rue d').............................B3
ERDRE (Allée d')........................A2-A3
ERLON (Rue d')..........................A1-B1
ETATS (Rue des)..........................B4-C4
EVECHE (Rue de la)......................A4-B4
FAIENCERIE (Rue de la)..................D3-D4
FALCONET (Rue).............................A4
FANNY PECCOT (Rue).........................B3
FELIBIEN (Rue)..........................A1-B1
FELIX EBOUE (Rue)..........................D2
FELIX FOURNIER (Place).....................C3
FELTRE (Rue de)............................B2
FENELON (Rue)..............................B3
FERNAND SOIL (Place).......................C3
FLECHIER (Rue).............................B3
FLESSELLES (Allée).........................C3
FOSSE (Quai de la)......................D1-D2
FOUCAULT (Cours)...........................D4
FOURCROY (Rue)..........................C4-D4
FOURE (Rue)................................C4
FRANCOIS SALIERES (Rue)....................C4
FRANKLIN (Rue)............................C1-C2
FRANKLIN ROOSEVELT (Cours)..............C2-C4
FREDUREAU (Rue).............................A1
FURET (Impasse)..............................A4

GABRIEL CHEREAU (Square)....................B2
GAMBETTA (Rue)..............................A4
GARDE DIEU (Rue)...........................A3
GASTON MICHEL (Rue)....................D1-D2
GASTON VEIL (Rue)...........................D2
GENERAL DE LA SALLE (Rue du)...............B4
GENERAL MEUSNIER (Rue).....................B4
GENERAUX PATTON ET WOOD (All. des)......B4-C4
GEOFFROY DROUET (Rue)......................A4
GEORGES CLEMENCEAU (Rue)................A4-B2
GORGES (Rue de)............................C2
GRASLIN (Place)............................C1
GRESSET (Rue).............................C1-D2
GRETRY (Rue)...............................C1
GUEPIN (Rue)...............................B2
GUERANDE (Rue de)..........................B2
GUIBOURG DE LUZINAIS (Rue).................D1

HALLES (Rue des).......................B2-B3
HARROUYS (Rue)..............................B1
HAUDAUDINE (Pont)..........................D2
HAUTE CASSERIE (Rue).......................B3
HAUTE MAILLARD (Impasse)...................B3
HAUTE SAULZAIE (Rue).......................C3
HENRI IV (Rue)..........................A4-B4
HERONNIERE (Rue de la).....................C1
HOTEL DE VILLE (Place de l')...............B3
HOTEL DE VILLE (Rue de l').................B3
HOTEL-DIEU (Avenue de l')..............D3-D4
ILE GLORIETTE (Allée de l').................D2
INDUSTRIE (Rue de l')...................B1-B2
JACOBINS (Place des)......................C3

JEAN BART (Allée)........................C2-C3
JEAN DE LA FONTAINE (Rue)..................C1
JEAN JAURES (Rue)..........................A2
JEAN MONNET (Boulevard)................B1-A2
JEAN-BAPTISTE DAVIAIS (Square)..........C3-D4
JEAN-JACQUES ROUSSEAU (Rue)............C1-C2
JEANNE D'ARC (Rue).....................A2-A3
JEMMAPES (Rue de)..........................D4
JOHN KENNEDY (Cours)...................B4-C4
JOSEPH CAILLE (Rue)........................A1
JOSEPH PARIS (Rue).........................C4
JOSEPH PEIGNON (Impasse)...................C3
JUIVERIE (Rue de la).......................B3
JULES DUPRE (Cour).........................A4
JUTON (Impasse).............................D3
KERVEGAN (Rue)..........................C3-C4
KLEBER (Rue)...............................C4
LA PEROUSE (Square).........................C2
LABOUCHERE (Rue)...........................A4
LAENNEC (Rue)..............................C4
LAFAYETTE (Rue)............................B1
LAMBERT (Rue)............................B3-C3
LE NOTRE (Rue)..............................C2
LEBRUN (Rue)...............................A4
LEKAIN (Rue)...............................B1
LEON BLUM (Rue)............................A3
LEON JAMIN (Rue)...........................A2
LEON MAITRE (Rue)..........................A3
LEOPOLD CASSEGRAIN (Rue)...............A2-B2
LESAGE (Rue)...............................C1
LEVEQUE (Rue)..............................D1
LORETTE DE LA REFOULAIS (Rue)..............A1
LOUIS LEVESQUE (Passage)................D3-D4
LOUIS PREAUBERT (Rue)......................C1
MADELEINE (Chaussée de la)..............C3-D4
MAGELLAN (Quai)............................A1
MAILLARD (Impasse)......................B3-B4
MAISON ROUGE (Allée de la).............B3-C3
MALHERBE (Rue).............................B4
MARAIS (Rue du)............................B3
MARC ELDER (Place).........................B4
MARCEAU (Rue)..............................B1
MARCHIX (Rue du)........................A1-A2
MARECHAL DE LATTRE DE TASSIGNY
  (Rue).................................C1-D2
MARECHAL FOCH (Place)......................A3
MARECHAL JOFFRE (Rue)......................A4
MARECHAL LECLERC (Rue).....................A3
MARIVAUX (Rue).............................C1
MARMONTEL (Impasse)........................D4
MARMONTEL (Rue)............................D4
MARNE (Rue de la)..........................B3
MARTRAY (Place du).........................A2
MARTRAY (Ruelle du)........................A2
MASSE (Cours)...............................D4
MATHELIN RODIER (Rue)......................B4
MAUD MANNONI (Allée)....................A2-B2
MAURICE DUVAL (Rue)........................A3
MAURICE SIBILLE (Rue)......................A3
MAYENCE (Rue de)...........................D4
MENOU (Rue)................................A1
MERCOEUR (Rue)..........................B1-B2
MISERICORDE (Rue de).......................A1

MOLIERE (Rue)..............................C1
MONCOUSU (Quai)........................D2-D3
MONNAIE (Place de la)......................C1
MONTAIGNE (Place)..........................A1
MONTAUDOUINE (Rue du)......................D1
MONTEIL (Rue)...........................C4-D4
MOQUECHIEN (Rue)...........................A3
MOULIN (Rue du)............................B3
NATIONS-UNIES (Boulevard des)..........D1-D2
NEPTUNE (Allée)............................C3
NEPTUNE (Rue)..............................C3
NEWTON (Place)..............................B1
NOTRE-DAME (Rue)...........................A3
OGEE (Rue).................................A3-A4
OLIVETTES (Cour des).......................D4
OLIVETTES (Rue des).....................C4-D4
OLIVIER DE CLISSON (Cours).................C3
ORATOIRE (Place de l')..................A4-B4
ORLEANS (Allée d')......................B2-C2
ORLEANS (Passage d')........................B3
ORLEANS (Rue d')...........................C2
PAGAN (Rue)................................C3
PAIX (Rue de la).........................B3-C3
PAUL BELLAMY (Rue).........................A3
PAUL DUBOIS (Rue)......................B3-C3
PAUL-EMILE LADMIRAULT (Place)..............C1
PELISSON (Rue).............................D3
PENITENTES (Rue des)....................C3-C4
PENTHEVRE (Allée).......................B2-C2
PERELLE (Rue)..............................D4
PEROUSE (Rue de la)........................C2
PETIT BACCHUS (Rue)........................B3
PETIT BOURGNEUF (Ruelle du)................A2
PETIT PASSAGE SAINT-YVES...................A1
PETITE HOLLANDE (Place de la)..........C2-D2
PETITES ECURIES (Rue des)..............B3-C3
PETITS MURS (Place des)....................B3
PIERRE CHEREAU (Rue).......................C3
PILORI (Place du)..........................B3
PIRON (Rue)................................C1
POISSONNIERS (Rue des).....................C4
PONT MORAND (Place du)......................A3
PONT SAUVETOUT (Rue du)....................B3
PORT AU VIN (Rue du).......................C2
PORT COMMUNEAU (Rue du)....................A3
PORT MAILLARD (Allée du)...............C3-C4
PORTAIL (Rue du)...........................A4
PORTE NEUVE (Rue).......................A1-A2
POULE NOIRE (Passage de la)................D4
PRE NIAN (Rue du)..........................B2
PREFET BONNEFOY (Rue)......................A3
PREMION (Rue)..............................B4
PRESIDENT EDOUARD HERRIOT (Rue)........A2-B2
PROFESSEUR YVES BOQUIEN (Rue)..............D2
PUITS D'ARGENT (Rue du)....................C1
QUAI DES TANNEURS (Ruelle du)..............A2
RACINE (Rue)...............................C1
RAMEAU (Rue)...............................C1
REFUGE (Rue du)............................A3
REGNARD (Rue)..............................B3
REGNIER (Rue)..............................C2

RICHEBOURG (Rue de)........................B4
RIEUX (Rue de).............................D4
ROGER SALENGRO (Place).....................A3
ROI ALBERT (Rue du)........................A4
ROTONDE (Pont de la).......................C4
ROYALE (Place).............................C2
RUBENS (Rue)...............................C2
SAINT-ANDRE (Cours)....................A3-A4
SAINT-CLEMENT (Impasse)................A3-A4
SAINT-DENIS (Rue).......................A3-B3
SAINT-JEAN (Rue)..........................A3-B3
SAINT-JEAN (Place)..........................B3
SAINT-JEAN (Rue)...........................B3
SAINT-JULIEN (Rue).........................B3
SAINT-LAURENT (Impasse)....................B3
SAINT-LEONARD (Rue)........................B3
SAINT-NICOLAS (Rue)........................C1
SAINT-PHILIBERT (Place)....................D2
SAINT-PIERRE (Cours)....................A4-B4
SAINT-PIERRE (Place).......................B4
SAINT-SIMILIEN (Rue).......................A2
SAINT-VINCENT (Rue)........................B3
SAINT-VINCENT (Place)......................B3
SAINT-YVES (Passage).......................A1
SAINTE-CATHERINE (Rue).....................C3
SAINTE-CROIX (Place)....................C3-C3
SAINTE-CROIX (Rue).........................C3
SAINTE-ELISABETH (Place)...................A1
SAINTE-MARIE (Cour)........................C2
SANLECOLE (Rue)..........................D3-D4
SANTEUIL (Rue)..............................C1
SARRAZIN (Rue)..........................A1-A2
SAVERNE (Rue de)...........................D4
SCRIBE (Rue)............................C1-C2
SIMEON FOUCAULT (Rue)......................A3
STRASBOURG (Rue de)....................A3-C4
SUFFREN (Rue)..............................C1
SULLY (Rue)................................A4
TALENSAC (Rue)..........................A2-A3
TANNEURS (Allée des)....................A2-A3
THUROT (Rue)...............................B3
TIRAND LO BLANC (Place)....................B3
TONKINOIS (Passage)....................D3-D4
TOURNEFORT (Rue)...........................A4
TOURVILLE (Quai de)........................D2
TRAVERS (Rue)..............................B3
TREMPERIE (Allée de la)....................C3
TREPIED (Rue du)........................A1-A2
TROIS CROISSANTS (Rue des).............B2-B3
TURENNE (Quai)..........................C2-D2
UNION (Rue de l')..........................B3
VAUBAN (Rue)...............................B2
VERDUN (Rue de)............................B3
VERSAILLES (Quai de).......................A3
VIARME (Place)..............................A1
VICTOR SCHOELCHER (Passerelle).............D1
VIEIL HOPITAL (Rue du).....................C3
VIEILLES DOUVES (Rue des)..............B2-C2
VIGNES (Rue des)...........................D1
VIGNOLLE (Impasse).........................A4
VOLONTAIRES DE LA DEFENSE PASSIVE
  (Place des)...............................B1
VOLTAIRE (Rue).............................C1

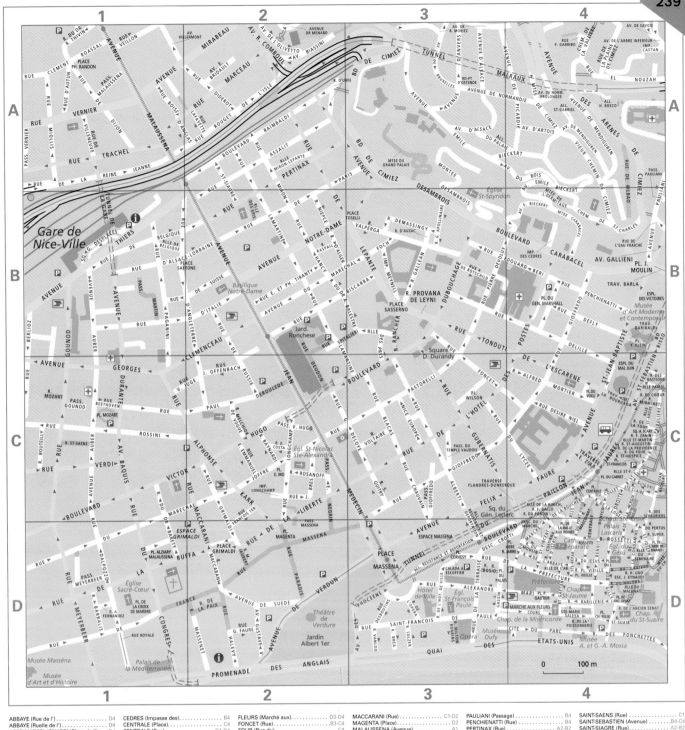

ABBAYE (Rue de l') D4
ABBAYE (Ruelle de l') B3-B4
ABBE MARCEL ISNARDI (Place de l') . . . D4
ABBE ROBERT JARRE (Placette) D4
ADOLPHE DE ROTSCHILD (Rue) B3
ALBERTI (Rue) C3
ALEXANDRE MARI (Rue) D3-D4
ALFRED MORTIER (Rue) C4
ALGER (Rue d') B2
ALPHONSE KARR (Rue) C1-D2
ALSACE (Avenue d') A1
ALSACE-LORRAINE (Rue d') B1-B2
ALZIARY MALAUSSENA (Place) D1
ANCIEN SENAT (Place de l') D4
ANCIEN SENAT (Rue de l') D4
ANGLAIS (Promenade des) D1-D3
ANGLETERRE (Rue d') B1-C2
ANTONIO FERNANDEZ (Rue) D1
ANVERS (Avenue d') A3
ARBRE INFERIEUR (Avenue de l') A4
ARENES DE CIMIEZ (Avenue des) A4-B4
ARTOIS (Avenue d') A3
ASSALIT (Rue) A2-B2
AUBER (Avenue) B1-C1
AUGUSTE ICART (Square) C1
AUTUN (Rue d') A1
AUZAC (Rue d') B3
BAQUIS (Avenue) C1
BARILLERIE (Rue) D4
BARLA (Traverse) B4
BARRALIS (Rue des) D1
BASTIONS (Rue des) C4
BEETHOVEN (Rue) C1
BELGIQUE (Rue de) B1-B2
BELGIQUE (Ruelle de) B1
BENOIT BUNICO (Rue) C4-D4
BERLIOZ (Rue) B1-C1
BIASSINI (Avenue) A2
BILBAO (Rue de) A4-B4
BISCARRA (Rue) B2-B3
BLACAS (Rue) B2-C2
BOIS (Avenue du) A3-A4
BOISSY D'ANGLAS (Rue) A1-A2
BOUCHERIE (Rue de la) C4-D4
BOUCHERIE (Ruelle de la) D4
BOURGADA (Traverse de la) B4
BOUTEILLY (Rue) C1
BREA (Rue) D3
BRUXELLES (Avenue de) A3
BUFFA (Rue de la) D1-D2
CALADA AUGUSTE ESCOFFIER (Rue) D3
CARABACEL (Boulevard) B3-B4
CARABACEL (Montée) B4
CARRET (Rue) C4
CASTAN (Impasse) A4

CEDRES (Impasse des) B4
CENTRALE (Place) B3-C4
CENTRALE (Rue) C4-D4
CHARLES FELIX (Place) D4
CHATEAU (Montée du) D4
CHATEAU (Rue du) D4
CHAUVAIN (Rue) C3-D3
CHŒUR (Rue du) C4
CIMIEZ (Boulevard de) A2-A3
CIMIEZ (Vieux chemin de) A4-B4
CLEMENT ROASSAL (Rue) A1
COLLET (Rue du) C4
COLONNA D'ISTRIA (Rue) C4-D4
CONDAMINE (Rue de la) B4
CONGRES (Rue du) C1-D1
CORVESY (Rue) C2
CROIX (Rue de la) C4-D4
CROIX DE MARBRE (Place de la) D1
CROTTI (Descente) D3-D4
DALPOZZO (Rue) C1-D1
DEFLY (Rue) B4
DELILLE (Rue) B3-C3
DESAMBROIS (Avenue) A2-B3
DESAMBROIS (Montée) A3-B3
DESBOUTINS (Rue) B1
DESIRE NIEL (Rue) C4
DEUDON (Rue) B2-C2
DIDEROT (Rue) A1-A2
DIJON (Rue de) A1
DOCTEUR ALBERT BALESTRE
     (Rue du) B2-B3
DOCTEUR BARETY (Rue du) C1-D1
DOCTEUR MENARD (Avenue) A1-B2
DOCTEUR ROBERT MORIEZ
     (Avenue) A3-A4
DOCTEUR ROBERT THIVIN (Rue du) A1
DROITE (Rue) C4-D4
DUBOUCHAGE (Boulevard) C2-B3
DURANTE (Avenue) B1-C1
EAU FRAICHE (Rue de l') B4
EDOUARD BERI (Rue) B3-B4
EL NOUZAH (Rue) A4
EMILE BIECKERT (Avenue) A3-B4
EMILE NEGRIN (Passage) D2-D2
EMILE ZOLA (Traverse) C2
EMMA ET PHILIPPE TIRANTY (Rue) B2
EMMANUEL BRIDAULT (Avenue) A1
EMMANUEL COSTA (Rue) C2
EPIS (Ruelle des) B2
ETATS-UNIS (Quai des) D3-D4
EUGENE EMMANUEL (Rue) C1
EUGENE MO (Place) C2
FELIX FAURE (Avenue) C3-D3
FLANDRES-DUNKERQUE (Traverse) C4-C3

FLEURS (Marché aux) D3-D4
FONCET (Rue) C4
FOUR (Rue du) C4
FRANCE (Rue de) D1-D2
FRANCIS GALLO (Rue) C4
FRANCOIS 1ER (Rue) C2-D2
FRANCOIS ZANIN (Rue) C4
GABRIEL FAURE (Rue) B3
GALLEAN (Rue) B3
GALLIENI (Avenue) B4
GARIBALDI (Traverse) B4
GENERAL MARSHALL (Place du) B4
GEORGES CLEMENCEAU (Avenue) . . .C1-B2
GIOFFREDO (Passage) C3
GIOFFREDO (Rue) C3-B4
GOUNOD (Passage) C1
GOUNOD (Rue) B1-D1
GRAND PALAIS (Montée du) A3
GRIMALDI (Place) D2
GRIMALDI (Rue) C2-D2
GUBERNATIS (Rue) B3-C4
GUIGONIS (Rue) C4
GUILLAUME APOLLINAIRE (Rue) B3
GUSTAVE DELOYE (Rue) C2-C3
GUSTAVE DESPLACES (Square) B1
GUSTAVE V (Avenue) D2
HALEVY (Rue) D2
HALLE AUX HERBES (Place de la) D4
HALLE AUX HERBES (Ruelle de la) C4-D4
HANCY (Rue) C2
HENRI BOSCO (Allée) A4
HERMITAGE (Montée de l') B4
HONORE UGO (Rue) B4
HOTEL DE VILLE (Rue de l') D3
HOTEL DES POSTES (Rue de l') C2-B4
ITALIE (Rue d') B1-B2
JACQUES OFFENBACH (Rue) C2
JEAN JAURES (Boulevard) D3-C4
JEAN MEDECIN (Avenue) A1-C3
JEAN MOULIN (Place de l') B4
JESUS (Place du) C4
JESUS (Rue du) D4
JOSEPH BRES (Rue) C4
JOUAN NICOLAS (Rue) D4
JULES EYNAUDI (Escalier) B3
JULES GILLY (Traverse) D4
LAFAYETTE (Rue) A2
LAMARTINE (Rue) A2-C3
LEPANTE (Rue de) A2-B3
LIBERTE (Rue de la) C2-D2
LOGE (Rue de la) C4-D4
LONGCHAMP (Impasse) C2
LONGCHAMP (Rue) C2-D2
LOUIS GASSIN (Rue) D3
LYCEE (Rue du) C3-C4

MACCARANI (Rue) C1-D2
MAGENTA (Place) D2
MALAUSSENA (Avenue) A1
MALAUSSENA (Passage) A1
MALONAT (Rue du) D4
MALONAT (Ruelle du) D4
MARCEAU (Rue) A1-A2
MARCHE (Descente du) D4
MARCHE (Rue du) D4
MARECHAL FOCH (Avenue du) B2-B3
MARECHAL JOFFRE (Rue) D1-C2
MARECHAL JUIN (Esplanade du) B4-C4
MARTIN (Passage) B1
MASCOINAT (Rue) C4-D4
MASSENA (Espace) C3-D3
MASSENA (Passage) C2-D2
MASSENA (Place) D2-D3
MASSENA (Rue) D2-D3
MASSENET (Rue) D2
MASSINGY (Rue de) D2
MAURICE JAUBERT (Rue) D2
MELCHIOR DE VOGUE (Rue) B3
MENDIGUREN (Avenue de) A4
MEYERBEER (Passage) D1
MEYERBEER (Rue) D1
MEYNELL (Impasse) B3
MILTON ROBBINS (Rue) A1
MIOLLIS (Rue) A1
MIRABEAU (Avenue) A1-A2
MIRALHETI (Rue) C4
MIRON (Rue) A2-B2
MIRON-LEPANTE (Ruelle) B3
MOULIN (Rue du) D4
MOZART (Place) C1
MOZART (Rue) C1-C2
NICE EUROPE (Rue) C3
NIEPCE (Rue) B2-C2
NORMANDIE (Avenue de) A3-A4
NORMANDIE PROLONGEE (Av. de) A4
NOTRE-DAME (Avenue) B2-B3
OLIVETTO (Avenue de l') A2
OPERA (Rue de l') D4
OSTENDE (Rond-point d') A3
PAGANINI (Rue) B1-C1
PAIROLIERE (Rue) C4
PAIROLIERE (Ruelle) C4
PAIX (Rue de la) D2
PALAIS (Allée du) D4
PALAIS (Place du) D4
PARADIS (Rue) D2
PARC (Cité du) D3-D4
PARIS (Rue de) B2-A3
PASTORELLI (Rue) C2-C3
PAUL DEROULEDE (Rue) C1-C2
PAULIANI (Avenue) A4-B4

PAULIANI (Passage) B4
PENCHIENATTI (Rue) B4
PERTINAX (Rue) A2-B2
PERTUS (Rue du) D4
PHILIPPE RANDON (Place) A1
PHOCEENS (Avenue des) D3
PICARDIE (Avenue de) A3-A4
PIERRE DEVOLUY (Rue) B3-B4
PIERRE GARRIBO (Rue) A4
PIERRE GAUTIER (Place) D4
PLACE VIEILLE (Rue) D4
PLAINE DE CIMIEZ (Rue de la) A4
POISSONNERIE (Rue de la) D4
PONCHETTES (Rue des) D4
PONT VIEUX (Rue du) C4-D4
PONTIN (Rue du) D4
PREFECTURE (Rue de la) D3-D4
PRES (Ruelle des) C4
PROVANA DE LEYNI (Rue) B3
PROVIDENCE (Rue de la) A4
RAIMBALDI (Boulevard) A1-A2
RANCHER (Rue) B3-C3
RAOUL BOSIO (Rue) D3
RASPAIL (Rue) B2
RAYMOND COMBOUL (Avenue) C4
RAYNARDI (Rue) C4
REINE JEANNE (Rue de la) A1
RESISTANCE ET DEPORTATION
     (Allée) C3-D4
RISSO (Boulevard) B4-C4
ROSANOFF (Rue) C2
ROSSETTI (Place) D4
ROSSETTI (Rue) C4-D4
ROSSINI (Rue) C1-C2
ROUGET DE L'ISLE (Rue) C2-C2
ROYALE (Rue) D1
RUSSIE (Rue de) B2-C2
SACHA GUITRY (Rue) C1-C2
SAETONE (Place) B1
SAINT-ANDRE (Ruelle) C4
SAINT-AUGUSTIN (Rue) C4
SAINT-CHARLES (Chemin de) B4
SAINTE-CLAIRE (Rue) B4
SAINTE-MARIE (Avenue) C4
SAINTE-REPARATE (Rue) D4
SAINT-FRANCOIS (Place) C4
SAINT-FRANCOIS (Rue) C4
SAINT-FRANCOIS DE PAULE (Rue) D3
SAINT-GABRIEL (Allée) A4
SAINT-GAETAN (Rue) C1
SAINT-HOSPICE (Rue) C4
SAINT-JEAN-BAPTISTE (Avenue) B4-C4
SAINT-JOSEPH (Rue) C1
SAINT-MARTIN (Ruelle) C4

SAINT-SAENS (Rue) C1
SAINT-SEBASTIEN (Avenue) B4-C4
SAINT-SIAGRE (Rue) A2-B2
SAINT-SUAIRE (Rue) D4
SAINT-VINCENT (Rue) C4
SALEYA (Cours) D3-D4
SASSERNO (Place) B3
SAVOIE (Avenue de) A4
SEMINAIRE (Ruelle du) C4
SERRURIERS (Rue des) C4-D4
SPITALIERI (Rue) B2-B3
SUEDE (Avenue de) D2
SUISSE (Rue de) B1-B2
SULZER (Rue) C2
SUPERIEURE (Rue) D4
TERRASSE (Rue de la) D3
THIERS (Avenue) B1-B2
TONDUTI DE L'ESCARENE (Rue) B3-C4
TOSELLI (Place) B3
TOUR (Rue de la) C4
TRACHEL (Rue) A1
TUNNEL DE LA GARE A1-B1
TUNNEL DU PAILLON D3-B4
TUNNEL MALRAUX A3-A4
URFE (Rue d') A2
VALLIERE (Chemin de la) A4
VALPERGA (Rue) A3
VANLOO (Rue) A3
VEILLON (Rue) A1
VERDI (Rue) C1
VERDUN (Avenue de) D2-D3
VERNIER (Passage) A1
VERNIER (Rue) A1
VICTOIRES (Esplanade des) B4
VICTOR HUGO (Boulevard) D1-D3
VICTOR HUGO (Passage) C2
VICTOR JUGE (Rue) C1-C2
VIEILLE (Rue) D4
VILLENEUVE (Rue de) A1
VILLERMONT (Avenue) A1
VOEU (Place du) C2
VOLTAIRE (Rue) C4
WILSON (Place) C3
YVES KLEIN (Place) B4

ABATTOIR (Rue de l') D1
ABBE DE SAUVAGES (Rue de l') B2
ADRIEN (Rue) A2
AGAU (Rue de l') A2
AGRIPPA (Rue) A1-B1
ALBENAS (Rue d') A2
ALEXANDRE DUCROS (Rue) C2-C3
ALEXANDRE PIEYRE (Rue) D1
ALPHONSE DAUDET (Boulevard) B2
AMIRAL COURBET (Boulevard) B3-A4
ANATOLE FRANCE (Rue) A4
ANCIENNE POSTE (Rue de l') A3-B3
ANDRE MALRAUX (Place) A3
ANGOULEME (Rue d') A4-B4
ANTOINE CHAMPROUX (Rue) D1
ANTONIN (Square) A2
AQUEDUC (Impasse) D2
AQUEDUC (Rue de l') D2
AQUITAINE (Rue d') A4
ARC DUGRAS (Rue de l') A3-B3
ARENES (Boulevard des) C3
ARENES (Place des) C3
ARENES (Rue des) B3-C3
ARISTIDE BRIAND (Place) B1
ARLIER (Rue d') B3
ASPIC (Plan de l') B2-C3
ASPIC (Rue de l') B2-C2
ASSAS (Place d') B2
AUGUSTE (Rue) A2-B2
AUGUSTE PELLET (Rue) B3
BACHALAS (Rue) A3
BADUEL (Rue) A3
BALORE (Rue) A2
BAT D'ARGENT (Rue du) A3
BAUDIN (Rue) A3
BAYARD (Rue) C3-C4
BEAUCAIRE (Rue de) A4
BECDELIEVRE (Rue) C1-B2
BELLECROIX (Rue) B3
BENEDICTINS (Rue des) A1-A2
BENOIT MALON (Rue) B1-C1
BERNARD ATON (Rue) D3-C4
BERNARD LAZARE (Rue) A2
BERNIS (Rue) B2-B3
BIENFAISANCE (Rue de la) C1
BIGOT (Rue) C2-C3
BOISSY D'ANGLAS (Rue) C4
BONS ENFANTS (Rue des) A4
BOSSUET (Rue) D3
BOUCARIE (Rue de la) A2
BOURDALOUE (Rue) D2-C3
BOURGOGNE (Rue de) A3
BRICONNET (Rue) C3
BRIDAINE (Rue) C3
BROQUIERS (Rue des) B3
BRUEYS (Rue) D1-D2
BRUXELLES (Boulevard de) C3
CADEREAU (Rue du) B1

CAISSARGUES (Rue de) D4
CALADE (Place de la) B2
CALADE (Rue de la) B2
CALQUIERES (Impasse des) B3-B4
CALQUIERES (Rue des) B3-B4
CARDINAL DE CABRIERES (Rue) B4
CARNOT (Avenue) B4-C4
CART (Rue) C3-D3
CASERNETTE (Rue de la) D1
CEDRES (Rue des) D1
CHAFFOY (Rue) A2
CHAPELIERS (Rue des) B3
CHAPITRE (Place du) B3
CHAPITRE (Rue du) B3
CHARLEMAGNE (Rue) D2-D3
CHARLES BABUT (Rue) A3-B3
CHARLES MARTEL (Rue) D2-D3
CHASSAINTES (Rue de) B1-B2
CHATEAU (Place du) A3
CHATEAU FADAISE (Rue) B2-C2
CHILDEBERT (Rue) D2
CIRQUE ROMAIN (Rue du) D1-D2
CITE DOCTEUR REBOUL (Rue) B2
CITE FOULC (Rue de la) C3-D3
CLAUDE BROUSSON (Rue) B2
CLERISSEAU (Rue) A2-A3
CLOVIS (Rue) D2
COLBERT (Rue) A2-A3
CONDE (Rue de) A4
CORCOMAIRE (Rue) A3
CORCONNE (Rue) B2
CORNEILLE (Rue) B2
COURONNE (Rue de la) B3
COURT DE GEBELIN (Rue) D3-D4
COURTIEU (Rue du) A2
CREBILLON (Rue) A1-B1
CREMIEUX (Rue) B3
CURATERIE (Rue) B3
DAGOBERT (Rue) D2
DELON SOUBEYRAN (Rue) C1-D1
DEPARCIEUX (Rue) D3
DEYRON (Rue) B2
DHUODA (Rue) D1-D2
DOCTEUR CALMETTE (Impasse du) . . . D4
DOCTEUR CALMETTE (Rue) D4
DOREE (Rue) B3
DU GUESCLIN (Place) C3
DU GUESCLIN (Rue) C3
DUMAS (Rue) A3
DUMONT D'URVILLE (Rue) D1-D2
ECLUSE (Impasse de l') B3
ECLUSE (Rue de l') A4-B4
ECOLE VIEILLE (Rue de l') B3
EMILE JAMAIS (Rue) C1-C2
EMILE ZOLA (Rue) C1
ENCLOS REY (Rue) A4
ERNEST RENAN (Rue) B1
ESCLAFIDOUS (Place des) A3

ETIENNE SAINTENAC (Boulevard) . . . A3-A4
ETOILE (Rue de l') B2-B3
FENELON (Rue) B4
FERNAND PELLOUTIER (Rue) C1-B2
FERRAGE (Rue de la) A3
FEUCHERES (Avenue) C4
FLAMANDE (Rue) A4
FLECHIER (Rue) A3
FLORIAN (Rue) C1
FLOTTES (Rue des) A2-B2
FONTAINE (Quai de la) B1-A2
FORT (Montée du) A2
FORT (Rue du) A2
FOURBISSEURS (Rue des) B3
FRANÇOIS 1ER (Rue) D1-D2
FREDERIC MISTRAL (Rue) D1
FREDERIC PAULHAN (Rue) D4
FRERES MINEURS (Rue des) B2
FRESQUE (Rue) B2-B3
GABRIEL PERI (Place) A4
GAL PERRIER (Rue) B2-B3
GAMBETTA (Boulevard) A2-A3
GARANCE (Rue de la) A3
GASTON BOISSIER (Rue) B1-B2
GASTON MARUEJOLS (Rue) C4
GAUDE (Rue de) A3
GAUTHIER (Rue) A2-A3
GENERAC (Rue de) D2
GEORGES POMPIDOU (Avenue) C1-D1
GERGONNE (Rue) B2
GODIN (Rue) B2
GRAND COUVENT (Place du) A2
GRAND COUVENT (Rue du) A2-B2
GRAND RUE B3
GRAND TEMPLE (Place du) B4
GRAVEROL (Rue) A3
GREFFES (Rue des) B3
GRETRY (Rue) B1-B2
GRIZOT (Rue) B3-B4
GUERIN (Passage) A3-A4
GUILLEMETTE (Rue) C4
GUIRAN (Rue) A3
GUIZOT (Rue) A2-A3
HALLES (Rue des) A3-B3
HENRI BATAILLE (Rue) D1
HENRI ESPERANDIEU (Rue) D1
HENRI IV (Rue) D1-D2
HENRI REVOIL (Rue) D1
HERBES (Place aux) B3
HORLOGE (Place de l') B2
HORLOGE (Rue de l') B2-B3
HOTEL DE VILLE (Place de l') B3
HOTEL DE VILLE (Rue de l') B3
HOTEL DIEU (Rue de l') C1-C2
HUBERT ROUGER (Rue) C2
HUGUES CAPET (Rue) C1-C2
IMBERT (Rue) A3

ISABELLE (Rue) C1
JARDINS (Rue des) B4
JEAN JAURES (Avenue) B1-D1
JEAN REBOUL (Rue) C2
JEAN ROBERT (Place) A4
JEANNE D'ARC (Rue) C3-C4
JULES GUESDE (Place) B1
LA PLACETTE C1
LAMPEZE (Rue de la) A2
LEONCE GUIRAUD (Rue) C3
LEOPOLD MORICE (Rue) C1
LIBERATION (Boulevard de la) B3-C3
LITTRE (Rue) A3
LOMBARDS (Rue des) A3-B3
LOUIS LAGET (Rue) C1-C2
LOUIS RAOUL (Rue) B2
LOUVRE (Petite rue du) B4-C4
LOYE (Rue de) D4
LUXEMBOURG (Impasse du) B4
MADELEINE (Place de la) B2
MADELEINE (Rue de la) B2-B3
MAGAILLE (Rue) D4
MAIL (Rue du) C1-C2
MAISON CARREE (Place de la) B2
MAISON CARREE (Rue de la) B2
MARCHANDS (Rue des) B3
MARCHE (Impasse du) B3
MARCHE (Rue du) B3
MARESCHAL (Rue) B1-B2
MARRONNIERS (Rue des) D4
MASSILLON (Rue) D3
MATHIEU LACROIX (Rue) B2
MAUBET (Rue) B2
MENARD (Rue) A2
MOLIERE (Rue) B2
MONJARDIN (Rue) B4-C4
MONNAIE (Rue de la) B2-B3
MONT DUPLAN (Avenue du) A4
MONTCALM (Rue) D2
MURIER D'ESPAGNE (Passage du) A3
MURIER D'ESPAGNE (Rue du) A3
NANTILLE (Rue) C2
NATIONALE (Rue) A3
NATOIRE (Boulevard) D4
NERVA (Rue) A2
NOTRE DAME (Rue) B4
ONU (Place de l') D4
11 NOVEMBRE 1918 (Rue du) C3
ORANGERS (Rue des) A3
ORATOIRE (Place de l') C2
PABLO PICASSO (Place) A1
PAIX (Rue de la) D1
PAPIN (Rue) A4
PARISIERE (Rue) A2-A3
PASTEUR (Rue) A2
PATINES (Rue des) B3
PECOLET (Rue) C4
PEPIN LE BREF (Rue) D2

PETITS SOULIERS (Rue des) B3
PHARAMOND (Rue) D2-D3
PIERRE SEMARD (Rue) A4
PITIE (Rue de la) C1-C2
PLANAS (Rue du) D3
PLOTINE (Rue) A2
POISE (Rue) B3
POISSONNERIE (Rue de la) B3
PORTE D'ALES (Rue) A3
PORTE DE FRANCE (Place de la) C2
PORTE DE FRANCE (Rue) B2-C2
PRADIER (Rue) B4-C4
PRAGUE (Boulevard de) C3-B4
PRESTON (Rue de) B4
PREVOTE (Rue de la) B3
QUATREFAGES (Rue des) D4
QUESTEL (Place) B2
RABAUD ST-ETIENNE (Rue) B2
RACINE (Rue) B2
RANDON (Impasse) B2
RANGUEIL (Rue de la) B3
RAYMOND MARC (Rue) D3-C4
REGALE (Rue) B3-C3
REPUBLIQUE (Rue de la) D2-C3
REVOLUTION (Place de la) A2
RICHELIEU (Rue) A4
RIVAROL (Rue) A3
ROBERT (Rue) A3
ROUGET DE LISLE (Rue) A1-A2
ROUSSY (Rue) B4-C4
RUFFI (Rue) C3-D3
RULMAN (Rue) A1
SAINT-ANTOINE (Rue) C2-B3
SAINT-CASTOR (Rue) A3-B3
SAINT-CHARLES (Place) A3
SAINT-CHARLES (Rue) C1-C2
SAINT-DOMINIQUE (Rue) B1
SAINT-FRANÇOIS (Rue) C2
SAINT-GILLES (Rue de) D2-D3
SAINT-LAURENT (Rue) B1
SAINT-MARC (Rue) B4
SAINT-MATHIEU (Rue) B2-C2
SAINT-REMI (Rue) B3
SAINT-THOMAS (Rue) B3
SAINT-YON (Rue) B3
SAINTE-AGNES (Rue) C1
SAINTE-ANNE (Rue) C1
SAINTE-CATHERINE (Rue) C1
SAINTE-EUGENIE (Rue) B3
SAINTE-EUGENIE (Ruelle) B3
SAINTE-FELICITE (Rue) D4
SAINTE-MARGUERITE (Rue) B3-B2
SAINTE-URSULE (Rue) C2-C3
SALAMANDRE (Place de la) B3
SALAMANDRE (Rue de la) A2-B3
SAURIN (Rue) A3
SAUVE (Rue de) B1
SCATISSE (Rue) C4-D4

SEGUIER (Rue) A4-B4
SERGENT TRIAIRE (Boulevard) D3-C4
SERVIE (Rue) C4
SEVERINE (Impasse) D1
SEVERINE (Place) D1
SUFFREN (Rue) C2
SUGER (Rue) D2-D3
TALABOT (Boulevard) C4
TEDENAT (Rue) B2-C2
TERRAUBE (Rue) D4
THEODORE AUBANEL (Rue) D2
THIERRY (Rue) D2
THOUMAYNE (Rue) B2
TILLEULS (Rue des) B1-D1
TITUS (Rue) A1
TONDEURS (Rue des) A3-B3
TOUR DE L'EVEQUE (Rue de la) D3
TOUR MAGNE (Rue de la) A1
TRAJAN (Rue) A1-A2
TRAUCAT (Rue) C2
TRAVERSIERE (Rue) B3
TRELYS (Rue) B3
TRESORERIE (Rue de la) B3
TROIS MAURES (Rue des) C2-C3
TURENNE (Rue) A4
TURGOT (Rue) B4
VACHER (Plan) A4
VAISSETTE (Rue) A1-A2
VAUBAN (Rue) D1-D2
VERDET (Rue) B4
VERDUN (Rue de) D1
VESPASIEN (Rue) A2
VICTOR HUGO (Boulevard) B2-C3
VIDAL (Rue) A2
VIEILLE TRIPERIE (Rue) A2
VIERGE (Rue de la) A3
VIERNE (Pont de) B1-B1
VILLEPERDRIX (Rue) C2
VINCENT FAITA (Rue) A4
VIOLETTE (Rue de la) B3
VOLTAIRE (Rue) A2
VOULAND (Rue) B2
XAVIER SIGALON (Rue) A3

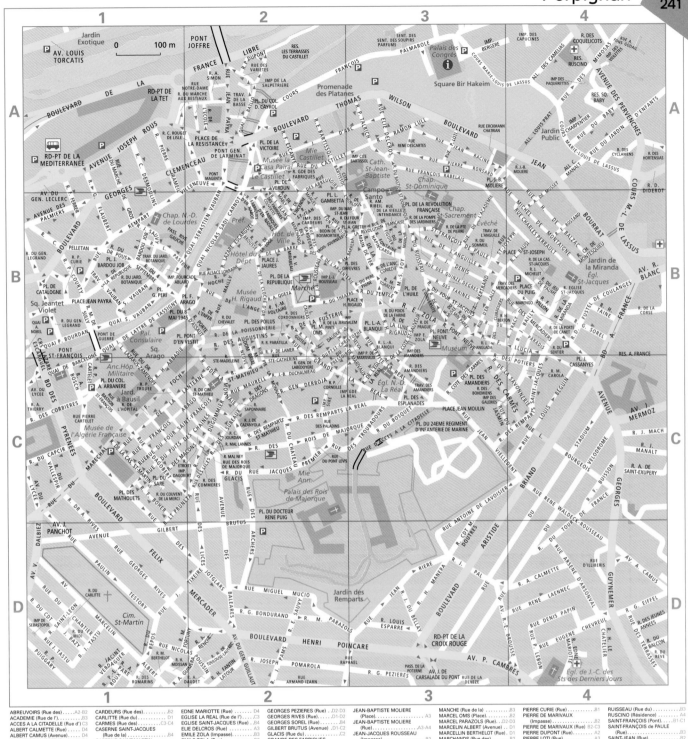

ABREUVOIRS (Rue des) A2-B2
ACADEMIE (Rue de l') B3
ACCES A LA CITADELLE (Rue d') C3-C4
ALBERT CALMETTE (Rue) D4
ALBERT CAMUS (Avenue) C4
ALFRED DE MUSSET (Rue) ..A4-B4
ALFRED NOBEL (Quai) B1
ALPHONSE DAUDET (Rue) D2
ALPHONSE SIMON (Rue) A2
ALSACE LORRAINE (Rue).......B2
AMANDIERS (Impasse des) ..B3-C3
AMANDIERS (Place des) C3
AMANDIERS (Rue des).......B3-C3
AMANDIERS (Traverse des) C3
AMBROISE PARE (Rue) B2
AMIRAL BARRERA (Rue) D2-B3
AMIRAL RIBEIL (Rue).........B3
ANATOLE FRANCE (Rue) ...B4-C4-C4
ANATOLE FRANCE (Rés.) C4-C4
ANCIENNE COMEDIE (Rue de l') B3
ANDRE BOSCH (Rue) A4
ANDRE FONS GODAIL (Rue) A4
ANDRE GRETRY (Place) B3
ANGE (Rue de l') B2
ANGEL GUIMERA (Rue) D1-D2
ANGUILLE (Rue de l') B3
ANGUILLE (Traverse de l') B3
ANTOINE DE LAVOISIER
 (Rue)..................D3-C4
ANTOINE DE SAINT-EXUPERY
 (Rue)......................C4
ANTOINE QUEYA (Rue)........C4
ARCHERS (Rue des) C2-D2
ARGENTIERE (Rue de l') ...B2-B3
ARISTIDE BRIAND (Bd) D3-C4
ARMAND IZARN (Rue) D2
ARSENE D'ARSONVAL (Rue) C4
AUGUSTE RENOIR (Rue) C1
AUGUSTIN THIERRY (Rue) C1
AUGUSTINS (Rue des) C2
BABY (Rue du) A4
BALCON (Rue du) B4
BALEARES (Avenue des) ...C2-C2
BARCELONE (Quai de) D1-C1
BARRE (Rue de la) A2
BASSE (Traverse de la) A2
BASTION SAINT-DOMINIQUE
 (Rue)....................A3-B3
BASTION SAINT-FRANCOIS
 (Rue)......................B1
BERGERE (Impasse) A3-A4
BODIN DE BOISMORTIER Place)B2
BOHEMIENS (Rue des)......B4-C4
BOSQUET (Rue du) C1
CAMELIAS (Allée des) A4
CAMILLE DESMOULINS
 (Rue)..................A1-B1
CAMILLE JOURDAN (Rue) C1
CAMILLE PELLETAN (Rue) C2
CAPCIR (Rue du) C1
CAPUCINES (Impasse des) A4
CARDEURS (Impasse des) B2

CARDEURS (Rue des) B2
CARLITTE (Rue du) D1
CARMES (Rue des)........C3-C4
CASERNE SAINT-JACQUES
 (Rue de la) B2
CASERNE SAINT-MARTIN
 (Rue de la) B1
CASTILLET (Rue du) A2-A3
CATALOGNE (Place de) B2
CELESTIN MANALT (Allée) A4
CHANTIER (Rue du) D1
CHARLES DE MONTESQUIEU
 (Rue).....................A4
CHARLES PERRAULT (Rue) B4
CHATEAU (Rue du) C2
CHEVALET (Rue du) C2
CIMETIERE SAINT-MATHIEU
 (Rue).....................C2
CITE BARTISSOL (Impasse) ..A2-A3
CITE BARTISSOL (Rue) A2-B2
CLAUDE ROUGET DE LISLE
 (Rue)....................A2
CLOCHE D'OR (Rue de la) B2
COLONEL ALFRED ARBANERE
 (Rue)....................B2
COLONEL DOMINIQUE CAYROL
 (Rue)....................A2
COMMANDANT JEAN BAZY
 (Rue)....................D1
COMMANDANT MICHEL DOUTRES
 (Rue)..................C3-D3
COMMERES (Rue des) C1-C2
COQUELICOTS (Impasse des) ..A4
CORBIERES (Rue des) C2
CORDONNIERS (Rue des) B2
CORSE (Rue de la) B4
COTE DES CARMES (Rue) C3
COTE SAINT-SAUVEUR
 (Rue de la)............B3-C3
COUVENT DE LA MERCI
 (Rue du) C1
CROIX ROUGE
 (Rond-Point de la) D3
CUIRASSIERS (Rue des) B3
CYCLAMENS (Rue des) A4
DAGOBERT (Impasse) C1
DAGOBERT (Rue) C1-C2
DENIS DIDEROT (Rue)......B4-A4
DENIS FUSTEL DE COULANGES
 (Rue).....................B4
DENIS PAPIN (Rue) D4
DEVEZE (Rue de la) D3
DOCTEUR ALFRED RIVES
 (Rue).................C1-D1
DOCTEUR LUDWIG LAZARUS
 ZAMENOFF (Rue du)....B1-C1
DOCTEUR POUS (Rue du) B1
DOCTEUR RENE PUIG (Place du)D2
DRAGONS (Rue des) C2
ECOLE (Rue de l') A1
EDMOND BARTISSOL (Rue) A2
EDMOND ROSTAND (Rue) B4

EDNE MARIOTTE (Rue) D4
EGLISE LA REAL (Rue de l') C3
EGLISE SAINT-JACQUES (Rue) ..B4
ELIE DELCROS (Rue) A3
EMILE ZOLA (Impasse) B2
EMILE ZOLA (Rue) B3
EMMANUEL BROUSSE (Rue) B2
EN CALCE (Rue d') B2
ENFER (Rue de l') B2
ERCKMANN CHATRIAN (Rue) ...A3
ESPLANADES (Place des) C3
ETROITE (Rue) C2
EUGENE CHEVREUL (Rue) D4
EUGENE SAUVY (Rue) D2
FABRIQUES COUVERTES
 (Rue des) B2
FABRIQUES D'EN NABOT (Rue) ..B2
FABRIQUES D'EN NADALS (Rue) ..B2
FARINES (Rue des) B3
FELIX MERCADER (Bd).....C1-D2
FERDINAND BUISSON (Rue) C4
FIGUIER (Rue du) B2
FONT FROIDE (Rue) B2-B3
FONTAINE NAPINCARDA (Rue) ..B3
FONTAINE NEUVE (Rue) ...B3-C3
FONTAINE SAINT-FRANCOIS
 (Rue).....................B1
FOUR SAINT-JACQUES (Rue du) .B2
FOUR SAINT-JEAN (Rue du) B2
FOURCADE ABLARD (Impasse) ..B1
FRANCE LIBRE (Bd de la) ...A1-A2
FRANCISCO FERRER (Rue).......A4
FRANÇOIS ARAGO (Place) C2
FRANÇOIS ARAGO (Rue) ...C1-C2
FRANÇOIS BATLLO (Quai) A1-C2
FRANÇOIS LLUCIA (Rue) ...B3-B4
FRANÇOIS PALMAROLE
 (Cours).................A2-A3
FRANÇOIS RABELAIS (Rue) A3
FRANÇOIS VILLON (Rue) B4
FRANÇOIS-MARIE VOLTAIRE
 (Rue).....................B2
FREDERIC ESCANYE (Rue) D2
FUSTERIE (Rue de la) B2
GABRIEL DE MABLY (Rue) B2-B3
GABRIEL PERI (Rue) B2
GALERIES (Impasse des) C4
GENERAL DE LABEDOYERE
 (Rue).....................C2
GENERAL DE LARMINAT (Pont) ..A2
GENERAL DERROJA (Rue) C2
GENERAL GUILLAUT
 (Rue)....................C2
GENERAL LECLERC (Avenue du)A1
GENERAL LEROY (Rue) B1
GEORGES BONDURAND (Rue) ...D2
GEORGES CLEMENCEAU
 (Boulevard) A1-B2
GEORGES GUYNEMER
 (Avenue)...............C4-D4

GEORGES PEZIERES D2-D3
GEORGES RIVES (Rue).....D1-D2
GEORGES SOREL (Rue).........B4
GILBERT BRUTUS (Avenue) .D1-C2
GLACIS (Rue du) C2
GRANDE DES FABRIQUES
 (Rue)....................A2-B2
GRANDE LA MONNAIE (Rue) ...B2
GRANDE LA REAL (Impasse) A1-B1
GRANDE LA REAL (Rue) B2-C3
GUERRE (Pont de) B1
GUILLAUME DAUDER DE SELVA
 (Rue)....................B2
GUSTAVE EIFFEL (Rue) D4
GUSTAVE FLAUBERT (Rue) ..A1-B1
HENRI ABBADIE (Rue) C1-B2
HENRI BERTON (Rue) B3-B4
HENRI DE TOULOUSE LAUTREC
 (Rue).....................C4
HENRI FANTIN LATOUR (Rue) ..D2
HENRI LE CHATELIER (Rue) D4
HENRI MOISSAN (Rue) D1
HIPPOLYTE TAINE (Rue) B3
HOCHE (Rue)...............B2
HONORE DE BALZAC (Rue) ...A4-B4
HOPITAL (Rue de l') C1-C2
HORLOGE (Rue de l') B2
HORTENSIAS (Rue des) A4
HUILE (Rue de l') B3
8 MAI 1945 (Rue du) B2
HYACINTHE MANERA (Rue) D3
HYACINTHE RIGAUD (Rue) B2
ILLIBERIS (Rue d') C2
INCENDIE (Rue de l') B2
JACINT VERDAGUER (Rue) D1
JACQUES DUGOMMIER (Rue) ...D1
JACQUES MACH (Rue) C4
JACQUES MANUEL (Rue) A2-B2
JACQUES PREMIER (Rue) C2
JARDIN BOTANIQUE
 (Traverse du) B1
JARDIN D'ENFANTS (Rue) A1
JASMIN (Rue du) C3-C4
JEAN BAILLY (Rue) B3
JEAN BOURRAT (Boulevard) ..A3-B4
JEAN DE CAZANYOLA (Rue) C2
JEAN DE LATTRE DE TASSIGNY
 (Quai)....................A2
JEAN JAURES (Rue) B2
JEAN MANALT (Rue) B4
JEAN MERMOZ (Avenue) C4
JEAN MOULIN (Rue) B2
JEAN PAYRA (Place) B2
JEAN PAYRA (Rue) B2
JEAN RACINE (Rue) A3
JEAN VIELLEDENT (Rue) C2
JEAN-BAPTISTE DUCHALMEAU
 (Rue)....................C2
JEAN-BAPTISTE MOLIERE

JEAN-BAPTISTE MOLIERE
 (Place) A3
JEAN-BAPTISTE MOLIERE
 (Rue)....................A3-A4
JEAN-JACQUES ROUSSEAU
 (Impasse).................B2
JEAN-JACQUES ROUSSEAU
 (Rue).....................B2
JEANNE D'ARC (Rue) A1-B1
JERUSALEM (Impasse) B2-B3
JEU DE PAUME (Rue d') B4
JEUNES ANNEES (Rue des) D4
JOACHIM DU BELLAY (Rue) D3
JOFFRE (Pont) A2
JOSEPH ANGLADA (Rue) B3
JOSEPH BERTRAND (Rue) B3
JOSEPH CASSANYES (Place) ...B4
JOSEPH CHARPENTIER (Imp.) ...A4
JOSEPH DENIS (Rue) B3
JOSEPH PAL (Rue) D3-D4
JOSEPH POMAROLA (Rue) D3
JOSEPH ROUS (Avenue) A1-A2
JOSEPH SAUVY (Rue) B2
JOSEPH SIRE (Impasse) B2
JOSEPH TASTU (Rue) C1
JOSEPH THIXIERE (Rue) D2
JOTGLARS (Rue des) C1-D2
JULES CARSALADE DU PONT
 (Avenue).................D3
JULES MICHELET (Rue) B4
JULES PAMS (Rue) D2
JULIEN ANGLADA (Rue) B2-C2
JULIEN PANCHOT (Rue) D1
JUSTIN BARDOU JOB (Rue) A1
JUSTIN BARDOU JOB (Rue) ..A1-B1
LANTERNE (Rue de la) C2
LAZARE ESCARGUEL (Cours) C1-C2
LAZARE ESCARGUEL (Rue) C2
LEON BOURGEOIS (Rue) C4
LEON GAMBETTA (Place) B2
LEVIS (Rue du Pont) C2-D2
LICES (Rue des) C2
LIEUTENANT PRUNETA
 (Rue)....................D1-C2
LOGE (Rue de la) B2
LOUIS AUGUSTE BLANQUI
 (Rue).....................B3-C3
LOUIS BAUSIL (Rue) C4
LOUIS BEGUIN (Rue) D1
LOUIS BLANC (Rue) B2
LOUIS CAULAS (Rue) D1
LOUIS ESPARRE (Rue) D3
LOUIS PASTEUR (Rue) B1-B2
LOUIS PRAT (Allée) A4
LOUIS TORCATIS (Avenue) A1
LOUIS-AUGUSTE BLANQUI
 (Place)...................B3
LUNE (Rue de la) B2-C2
LYCEE (Avenue du) C1
MACONS (Rue des) C2
MAGENTA (Pont) A2
MAILLY (Rue) B2
MAIN DE FER (Rue de la) B3

MANCHE (Rue de la) B3
MARCEL OMS (Place) D2
MARCEL PARAZOLS (Rue) ...D2-D3
MARCELIN ALBERT (Rue) C3
MARCELIN ALBERT (Avenue) ...C1
MARCELLIN BERTHELOT (Rue) ..D4
MARCHANDS (Rue des) B2
MARCHE AUX BESTIAUX
 (Rue).....................A1-A2
MARCHE DE GROS (Rue) A1-B1
MARECHAL FERDINAND FOCH
 (Rue)....................C1-B2
MARECHAL LANNES (Rue) C2
MARECHAL NEY (Rue) C2
MARENGO (Rue) B3-B4
MARIANO FORTUNY (Rue) B2
MARIE LOUIS DE LASSUS
 (Cours)..................A3-B4
MAS SAINT-JEAN (Impasse du) .B3
MATHOUETS (Place des) C1
MAUREIL (Rue de la) C2
MAXIMILIEN DE SULLY (Rue) ...B1
MAXIMILIEN SEBASTIEN FOY
 (Rue).....................B1
MEDITERRANEE
 (Rond-point de la) A1
MERCADIERS (Rue des) B3
MERCADIERS (Traverse des) ..B3-B4
MICHEL CAROLA (Rue) B4-C4
MICHEL DE MONTAIGNE
 (Rue).....................C1-C2
MICHEL DOM BRIAL (Rue) ..B2-C2
MICHEL TORRENT (Rue) C2
MIDI (Rue du) C1
MIGUEL MUCIO (Rue) D2-D3
MIMOSAS (Rue des) A4
MIRANDA (Rue de la) B4
MOULIN PARES (Rue) C4
MUSEE (Rue du) B2
NEUVE (Rue) B2-C2
NICOLAS POUSSIN (Rue) D1-D2
NICOLAS SADI CARNOT (Rue) ..B1-B2
NOTRE-DAME (Place de) A2
ORFEVRES (Rue des) B2
PALADINS (Rue des) C2
PALMIERS (Rue des) B1
PAQUERETTES (Impasse des) ...A4
PARADIS (Rue du) B3
PARFUMS (Sentier des) A3
PAUL COURTY (Rue) B1
PAUL DE LAMER (Rue) C4
PAULIN TESTORY (Rue) D1
PERE PIGNE (Rue) B2
PERVENCHES (Avenue des) A4
PETIT JEAN SAINT-CHRISTOPHE
 (Place)...................B2
PETITE LA MONNAIE (Rue) B2
PETITE LA REAL (Rue) B2-C2
PHILIPPE LEBON (Rue) D4
PIERRE BOURDAN (Quai) B1
PIERRE CAMBRES (Rue) C3-D4
PIERRE CARTELET (Rue) B1-C1
PIERRE CORNEILLE (Rue) ...C2-C3

PIERRE CURIE (Rue) B1
PIERRE DE MARIVAUX
 (Impasse)................B4
PIERRE DE MARIVAUX (Rue) B2-C3
PIERRE DUPONT (Rue) A2
PIERRE LOTI (Rue) D1
PIERRE PUIGGARY (Rue) C1
PIERRE RAMEIL (Rue) B3
PIERRE RONSARD (Rue) A3
PIERRE TALRICH (Rue) A3
PIERRE TROUEE (Rue) C1-C2
PIERRE-EMILE ROUX (Rue) C2
PINTE (Rue de la) B3
POIDS DE LA FARINE (Rue du) ..B3
POLLUS (Place des) B3
POMPE DES JARDINIERS
 (Cours)...................B4
PONT D'EN VESTIT (Place) B2
PORTE D'ASSAUT (Rue) B2
PORTE DE CANET (Rue de la) ..B4
PORTE DE PIERRE (Rue de la) ..B4
POTERNE (Passage de la) C2
POTIERS (Rue des) B3-C4
PRAGUE (Rue de) B3
PRESSOIR (Rue de) B2-B3
PUIG (Place du) B3
PUITS DES CHAINES
 (Rue de la)..............C1-C2
PYRENEES (Boulevard des) C1
4 SEPTEMBRE (Rue du) B2
QUINZE DEGRES (Rue des) B2
RAMON LULL (Rue) A3
RAPHAEL (Rue) D2-D3
REMPART VILLENEUVE (Rue) B1-A2
REMPARTS LA REAL
 (Rue de la)..............B3-B4
REMPARTS SAINT-JACQUES
 (Rue de la) C3-B4
REMPARTS SAINT-MATHIEU
 (Rue de la)..............B2-C2
RENE DESCARTES (Rue) A3
RENE LAENNEC (Rue) C4
RENE PARATILLA (Rue) B4
RENE WALDECK-ROUSSEAU
 (Rue)....................C4-D4
REPOS (Impasse du) C1
REPUBLIQUE (Place de la) B2
RESISTANCE (Place de la) A2
REVE (Rue du) D4
REVOLUTION FRANCAISE
 (Rue).....................B2
REVOLUTION FRANCAISE
 (Place)..................B2
RIVE GAUCHE (Passage) B1-B2
ROBERT-EMMANUEL BROUSSE
 (Rue)....................B2
ROIS DE MAJORQUE
 (Rue des) C2
ROMARINS (Rue des) C1
ROSETTE BLANC (Avenue) B4

RUISSEAU (Rue du) B3
RUSCINO (Résidence) A4
SAINT-FRANÇOIS (Pont) B1-C1
SAINT-FRANÇOIS de PAULE
 (Rue).....................B3
SAINT-JEAN (Rue) B2
SAINT-JOSEPH (Place) B3
SAINT-JOSEPH (Rue) B2-C3
SAINT-LEON (Rue) D1
SAINT-MATHIEU (Rue) B2-C2
SAINTE-CATHERINE (Rue) C3
SAINTE-MADELEINE (Rue) ..B2-C2
SALPETRIERE (Impasse de la) ..A2
SAPONNAIRE (Rue) C2
SARE (Place du) C2
SAVONNERIE (Rue de la) B3
SEBASTIEN VAUBAN (Quai) ..B1-B2
SEBASTIEN VAUBAN (Rue) B2
SEBASTIEN VAUBAN (Traverse) .B2
SEBASTOPOL (Impasse del) C1
SENTIER (Rue du) B4
SOMMEIL (Rue du) B3
SOUPIRS (Sentier des) A3
SQUARE BABY (Résidence) A4
STADIUM (Rue du) D3-C4
SUREAUX (Rue des) C2
TEMPLE (Rue du) B2
TERRASSES (Rue des) A2
TERRASSES DU CASTILLET
 (Résidence les) A2
TET (Rond-Point de la) A2
THEATRE (Rue du) B2
THEODORE GUITER (Rue) B3
THOMAS WILSON (Bd) A2-A3
TOUR DE FRANCE (Rue) B3
TRACY (Rue)..............B3-B4
TROIS JOURNEES (Rue des) D2
TROUBADOURS (Rue des) C3
UNIVERSITE (Rue de l') B2
VALLESPIR (Rue du) C1
VARIETES (Rue des) A2
VELODROME (Rue du) C4
VERDUN (Rue du) A2
VICTOIRE (Place de la) A2
VICTOR DALBIEZ (Avenue) ..C1-D1
VICTOR MIRABEAU (Rue) ...D1-D1
VIEILLE INTENDANCE
 (Rue).....................B2
VIOLETTES (Impasse des) A4

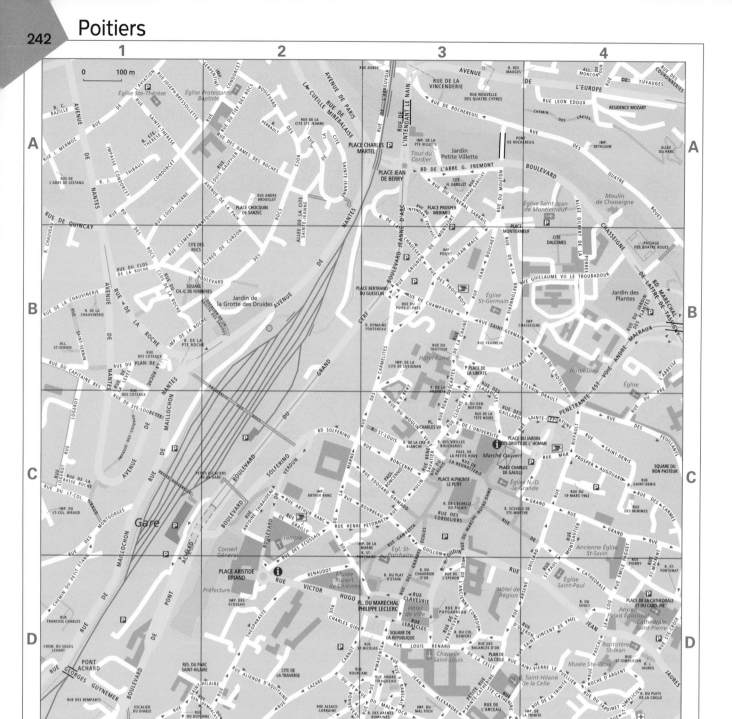

ABBE DE LESTANG (Rue de l') A1
ABBE GEORGES FREMONT (Rue de l') . . . A3
ABREUVOIR (Rue de l') A3
ACHARD (Pont) D1
ALFRED DE CURZON (Rue) B1-B2
ALIENOR D'AQUITAINE (Rue) D2
ALPHONSE LE PETIT (Place) C3
ALSACE-LORRAINE (Rue) D2-D3
ANCIENNE COMEDIE (Rue de l') C3-D3
ANDRE BROUILLET (Rue) A2
ANDRE TIRAQUEAU (Rue) D2
ANTOINE THIBAUDEAU (Rue) C2
ARCEAU (Rue de l') A3
ARENES ROMAINES (Rue des) D3
ARISTIDE BRIAND (Place) D2
ARSENE ORILLARD (Rue) D3-C4
ARTHUR RANC (Impasse) C2
ARTHUR RANC (Rue) C2
AUBER (Rue) A3
AVIATION (Rue de l') A1
BALANCES D'OR (Rue des) D3
BASSE ROCHE (Rue de la) C1
BERTRAND DU GUESCLIN (Place) B3
BETHLEEM (Impasse) A4
BON PASTEUR (Square du) C4
BONCENNE (Passage) C2
BONCENNE (Rue) C2-C3
BOURBEAU (Rue) C2
BOURCANI (Rue) D2-D3
BRETONNERIE (Rue de la) B3
CAMILLE BAZILLE (Rue) A1
CAPITAINE BES (Rue du) B1-C1
CARMELITES (Rue des) C2-B3
CARMES (Rue des) C4
CATHEDRALE (Rue de la) C3-D4
CATHEDRALE ET DU CARDINAL PIE
(Place de la) D4
CELLE (Plan de la) D3
CELLE (Rue de la) D3
CHAINE (Rue de la) B3
CHAMPAGNE (Rue de) B3
CHARLES DE GAULLE (Place) C3
CHARLES GIDE (Rue) D2-D3
CHARLES MARTEL (Place) A3
CHARLES VII (Place) C3
CHARLES-ELIE DE FERRIERES
(Square) .B1-B2
CHASSEIGNE (Boulevard) A3-B4
CHASSEIGNE (Impasse) B4
CHAUDRON D'OR (Rue du) C3
CHAUSSEE (Rue de la) A3-B3
CHAUVEAU (Rue) B1
CHAUVINERIE (Rue de la) B1
CHOCQUIN DE SARZEC (Place) A2
CITE DE LUSIGNAN (Rue de la) B3

CITE SAINTE-JEANNE (Allée de la) . . A2-B2
CITE SAINTE-JEANNE (Rue de la) A2
CLAVEURIER (Rue) D3
CLEMENT JANNEQUIN (Rue) B1-A2
CLOCHE PERSE (Rue) B3-C3
CLOS DE LA ROCHE (Rue du) B1
COLONEL DENFERT (Rue du) D3
CONDORCET (Impasse) A1
CONDORCET (Rue) A1-A2
CORDELIERS (Rue des) C3
COTEAUX (Impasse des) C1
COTEAUX (Rue des) B1-C1
COURONNERIES (Rue des) A4
CRETES (Chemin des) A4
CROIX BLANCHE (Rue de la) C2
CUEILLE MIREBALAISE (Rue de la) . .A2-A3
DALESMES (Cité) A4-B4
DAMES DES ROCHES (Rue des) A2
DIABLE (Escalier du) D1
19 MARS 1962 (Rue du) C4
DOMAINE FONTENEAU (Rue) B3
DOYENNE (Rue du) D1
ECHELLE DU PALAIS (Rue de l') C3
ECOSSAIS (Impasse des) D2
ECOSSAIS (Rue des) C2-D2
EDOUARD GRIMAUD (Rue) C2-C3
EMILE FAGUET (Rue) C4-D4
EPERON (Rue de l') D3
EUROPE (Avenue de l') A3-A4
FEUILLANTS (Rue des) C4
FIEF DES ROCS (Rue du) A2
FLAGEOLLES (Rue des) B3-C3
FRANCOIS CHARLES (Rue) D1
FRANCOIS RABELAIS (Rue) C2
FRANKLIN (Rue) B3
GAILLARDS (Rue des) C3-C4
GAMBETTA (Rue) C3
GASTON HULIN (Rue) C3
GENERAL BERTON (Rue du) B3-C3
GENERAL DEMARCAY (Rue du) D1-D2
GENERAL SARRAIL (Rue du) A3
GEORGES GUYNEMER (Rue) D1
GILBERT DE LA PORREE (Allée) A4-B4
GRAND CERF (Boulevard du) C1-C2
GRAND RUE C4
GRANDES ECOLES (Rue des) C3
GRIGNON DE MONTFORT (Rue) A3-B3
GROTTE DES DRUIDES (Escalier de la) . B2
GUILLAUME VII LE TROUBADOUR
(Rue) B3-B4
HENRI OUDIN (Rue) C3-D3
HENRI PETONNET (Rue) C2-C3
HONORE GABILLET (Cité) A3
HONORE GABILLET (Rue) A3
HOTEL-DIEU (Rue de l') B4-C4

INTENDANT FOUCAULT (Rue de l') . . A3-B3
INTENDANT LE NAIN (Rue de l') A2
JACQUES DE GRAILLY (Rue) C3
JACQUES THIBAULT (Rue) A1
JARDIN DES DROITS DE L'HOMME
(Place du) C3
JARDINET (Rue du) B4
JEAN ALEXANDRE (Rue) D4
JEAN BOUCHET (Rue) B3
JEAN DE BERRY (Place) A3
JEAN JAURES (Rue) C3-D4
JEAN MACE (Rue) A3-B3
JEAN MERMOZ (Rue) A1
JEANNE D'ARC (Boulevard) A3-B3
JOSEPH BRESSOLLETTE (Rue) A1-B1
LAZARE CARNOT (Rue) D2-D3
LEBASCLES (Rue) D3
LEON EDOUX (Rue) A1
LEON PERRAULT (Rue) A4
LEVEE (Rue de la) B1-C1
LIBERTE (Place de la) B3
LIEUTENANT-COLONEL BIRAUD
(Impasse du) C1
LIEUTENANT-COLONEL BIRAUD
(Rue du) C1
LOGEROT (Rue) B1-C1
LOUIS GAUFFIER (Rue) A2
LOUIS RENARD (Rue) D3
LOUIS VIERNE (Rue) A1-B1
MAGENTA (Rue de) D3
MAILLOCHON (Rue de) B1-D1
MARCHE NOTRE-DAME (Rue du) C3
MARECHAL DE LATTRE DE TASSIGNY
(Boulevard) B4
MARECHAL FOCH (Impasse du) C3
MARECHAL FOCH (Rue du) D2-D3
MARECHAL PHILIPPE LECLERC
(Place du) C3
MARNE (Impasse de la) C2-C3
MARNE (Rue de la) C3
MAUGES (Allée des) A4
MINIMES (Rue des) C4
MONCONTOUR (Allée de) A4
MONSEIGNEUR PROSPER AUGOUARD
(Place du) A3
MONTGAUTIER (Rue) C4-D4
MONTGAUTIER (Rue) C1-D1
MONTIERNEUF (Place) A3
MOULIN A VENT (Rue du) B3-C3
MOUTON (Rue du) A3
MOZART (Résidence) A4
NANTES (Avenue de) C1-A3
NOUVELLE DES QUATRE CYPRES
(Rue) A3

OLERON (Rue d') D3-D4
PAIX (Avenue de la) A1-B2
PALAIS (Rue du) C3
PARC (Allée du) A4
PARC SAINT-HILAIRE (Résidence du) . . D1
PARIS (Avenue de) A2-A3
PASCAL LE COQ (Rue) D4
PAUL BERT (Rue) B3-C3
PAUL GUILLON (Rue) C3
PENETRANTE EST
VOIE ANDRE MALRAUX B4-C4
PENTHIEVRE (Rue de) D3
PETIT BONNEVEAU (Rue) D2-D3
PETIT ETANG (Chemin du) C1-D1
PETITE PASSERELLE (Rue) C1
PETITE ROCHE (Rue de la) B1
PETITE ROUE (Passage de la) C1
PETITE VILLETTE (Impasse de la) A3
PETITS ESCALIERS DE LA GARE (Rue) . C2
PIERRE RAT (Rue) B3-B4
PIORRY (Rue) B4
PLAN DE LA ROCHE (Rue du) B1
PLAT D'ETAIN (Rue du) C3
POIZET (Impasse) B3
PONT ACHARD (Boulevard de) C1-D1
PRE L'ABBESSE (Rue du) B4-C4
PREVOTE (Rue de la) C3
PROSPER MERIMEE (Place) A3
PUITS CI-PRES (Rue des) B3
PUITS DE LA CAILLE (Rue du) D4
PUYGARREAU (Rue du) C3
QUATRE ROUES (Passage des) B4
QUATRE ROUES (Rue des) A3-B4
QUINCAY (Rue de) A1-B1
REGRATTERIE (Rue de la) C3
REMPARTS (Rue des) D1
RENE DESCARTES (Rue) B3-C3
RENE SAVATIER (Rue) C3
REPUBLIQUE (Square de la) D3
RIFFAULT (Rue) C4
ROCHE (Impasse de la) B1-B2
ROCHE (Rue de la) B1-B2
ROCHE D'ARGENT (Rue) D4
ROCHEREUIL (Pont de) A3
ROCHEREUIL (Rue de) A3
ROCS (Boulevard des) B1-B2
ROCS (Cité des) B1
ROCS (Passerelle des) B1-C2
SAINT-DENIS (Rue) C3
SAINT-FORTUNAT (Rue) D4
SAINT-GERMAIN (Rue) B3-B4
SAINT-HILAIRE (Rue) D1-D2
SAINT-LOUIS (Rue) C3
SAINT-MAIXENT (Rue) C4-D4
SAINT-NICOLAS (Rue) D3

SAINT-PAUL (Rue) D4
SAINT-PIERRE LE PUELLIER (Rue) . . .D3-D4
SAINT-PORCHAIRE (Rue) D2-C3
SAINT-SERNIN (Allée) B1
SAINT-SERNIN (Rue) B1
SAINT-SIMPLICIEN (Rue) D4
SAINT-VINCENT DE PAUL (Rue) D3-D4
SAINTE-CATHERINE (Petite rue) D3
SAINTE-CATHERINE (Rue) D3
SAINTE-CROIX (Rue) D4
SAINTE-LOUBETTE (Rue de) C3
SAINTE-OPPORTUNE (Rue) C3-C4
SAINTE-THERESE (Rue) A1
SCEVOLE DE SAINTE-MARTHE C3-C4
SERPENTINE (Impasse) A2
SOLEIL LEVANT (Chemin du) D1
SOLFERINO (Boulevard) C1-C2
SOUCI (Rue du) D4
SYLVAIN DRAULT (Rue) B3-C4
TETE NOIRE (Rue de la) C3
THEOPHRASTE RENAUDOT (Rue) . . .D2-D3
TIFFAUGES (Rue de) A4
TRAVERSE (Cité de la) D2
TRINITE (Impasse de la) D4
TRINITE (Rue de la) D3-D4
TROIS ROIS (Rue des) B3
TROTTOIR (Rue du) B3
UNIVERSITE (Rue de l') C3
VERDUN (Boulevard de) C2-D2
VICTOR HUGO (Rue) D2-D3
VIEILLES BOUCHERIES (Rue des) C3
VINCENDERIE (Rue de la) A3

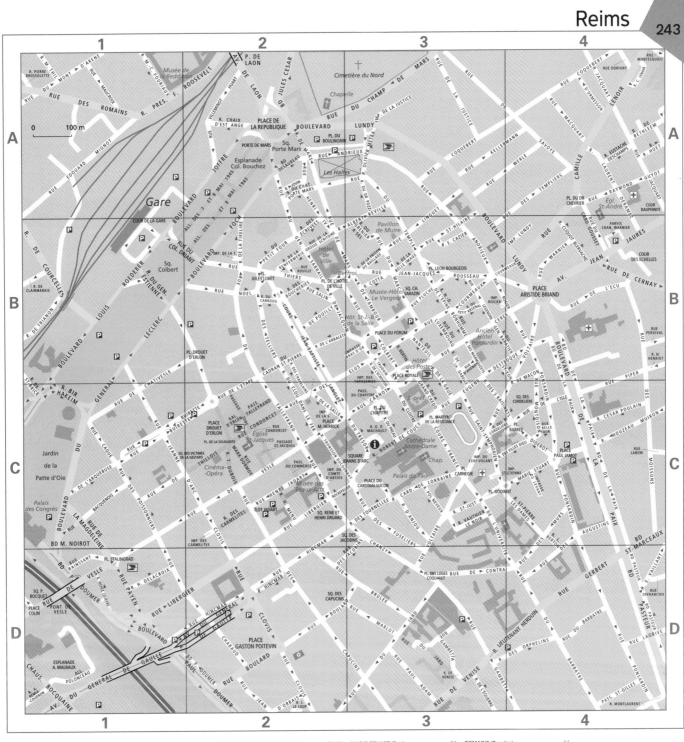

ALBERT REVILLE (Rue) B2-A3
ANATOLE FRANCE (Cours) C3
ANDRE MALRAUX (Esplanade) D1
ANDRIEUX (Rue) A2-B3
ANJOU (Rue d') C3
ARBALETE (Rue de l') C3
ARISTIDE BRIAND (Place) B4
ARLETTE REMIA-COUDRON (Rue) D1
ARQUEBUSE (Rue de l') C1
AUGUSTINS (Rue des) C4-D4
AVENAY (Rue d') B3
BACQUENOIS (Rue) C1
BARBATRE (Rue) D4
BARREE (Place) C3-C4
BELLE IMAGE (Rue de la) B3
BELLE TOUR (Rue) C4
BERTIN (Rue) B3
BETHLEEM (Rue de) A4
BIR HAKEIM (Rue) C1
BOCQUAINE (Chaussée) D1
BONHOMME (Rue) B3
BOUCHERIES (Rue des) D2-D3
BOULARD (Rue) D2
BOULINGRIN (Place du) A2-A3
BRAS D'OR (Impasse) B2-B3
BRULEE (Rue) D2-D3
BUIRETTE (Rue) C1-C2
CADRAN SAINT-PIERRE (Rue du) B2
CAMILLE LENOIR (Rue) A4-B4
CAPUCINS (Rue des) D2
CAPUCINS (Square des) D2
CAQUE (Rue) C1
CARDINAL DE LORRAINE (Rue) C3
CARDINAL GOUSSET (Rue du) A4-B4
CARDINAL LUCON (Place du) C3
CARMELITES (Impasse des) C2
CARMELITES (Rue des) C2
CARNEGIE (Place) C3
CARNOT (Rue) C3
CARROUGE (Rue du) B2
CERES (Rue) B3-B4
CERF-VOLANT (Impasse du) C3
CERNAY (Rue de) B4
CESAR POULAIN (Rue) C4
CHABAUD (Rue) C1-D2
CHAIX D'EST ANGE (Rue) A2-A3
CHAMP DE MARS (Rue du) A2-A3
CHANOINE WARNIER (Parvis) B3
CHANZY (Rue) C2-D3
CHAPELAINS (Rue des) B2-C2
CHAPITRE (Passage du) C3
CHAPITRE (Place du) C3
CHARLES SARAZIN (Square) B3
CHATEAU PORTE MARS (Rue du) A2
CHATIVESLE (Rue de) C1-B2

CLAIRMARAIS (Rue de) B1
CLIQUOT BLERVACHE (Rue) B4
CLOITRE (Rue du) C3
CLOU DANS LE FER (Rue du) B2-C2
CLOVIS (Rue) C2-D2
COLBERT (Rue) B2-B3
COLIN (Place) D1
COLONEL DRIANT (Rue du) B1-B2
COMMERCE (Passage du) C2
COMTE D'ARTOIS (Impasse du) C2
CONDORCET (Rue) C2
CONTRAI (Rue du) D3-D4
COQUEBERT (Rue) C2
CORDELIERS (Rue des) A3-A4
CORDELIERS (Square des) C4
COTTA (Rue) B3
COURCELLES (Rue de) B1
COURMEAUX (Rue) B3-B4
DAUPHINOT (Cour) A4-B4
DEFRANCOIS (Rue) D4
DESAUBEAU (Boulevard) A2
DIDEROT (Rue) C4
DOCTEUR CHEVRIER (Place du) A4
DOCTEUR JACQUIN (Rue du) B2-B3
DOCTEUR POZZI (Rue du) A3
DORIGNY (Rue) A4
DROUET D'ERLON (Place) B1-C2
ECHELLES (Cour des) B2
ECREVEES (Rue des) B2
ECREVISSE (Rue de l') B3-C3
ECU (Rue de l') B4
EDOUARD MIGNOT (Rue) A1
EDOUARD VAILLANT (Rue) D3
ELUS (Rue des) C2-B3
EMILE CAZIER (Rue) B3
EQUERRE (Rue de l') D3
ERLON (Galerie d') C2
ETAPE (Rue de l') B2-C2
EUGENE DESTEUQUE (Rue) C3-D4
EUSTACHE DESCHAMPS (Rue) A4
FILLES DIEU (Rue des) C3-C4
FOCH (Boulevard) B1-A2
FORUM (Place du) B3
FUSELIERS (Rue des) C3-C3
GABELLE (Rue de la) C2
GAMBETTA (Rue) D3-D4
GARE (Cour de la) B1
GASTON POITEVIN (Place) D2
GENERAL BARATIER (Rue du) B3-B4
GENERAL DE GAULLE (Avenue du) D1-D2
GENERAL ESTIENNE (Rue du) B1
GENERAL LECLERC (Boulevard du) B1-D1
GENERAL SARRAIL (Rue du) A2-B2
GERBERT (Rue) C3-D4
GODINOT (Place) C3-C4

GRAND CREDO (Rue du) B3-C3
GRENIER A SEL (Rue du) B3
GROSSE ECRITOIRE (Rue de la) B2
GRUE (Rue de la) B3
GUILLAUME DE MACHAULT (Rue) C3
HENRI DELACROIX (Rue) C1
HENRI IV (Rue) A2-B2
HENRI JADART (Rue) C2
HENRI MENU (Rue) C2
HINCMAR (Rue) D1-C3
HOTEL DE VILLE (Place de l') B2-B3
HOUZEAU MUIRON (Rue) B3
ILOT JADART C2
IRENEE LELIEVRE (Rue) D1
ISLE (Rue de l') C4
JACOBINS (Rue des) D2-C3
JACOBINS (Square des) C3
JACQUART (Rue) A4
JEAN D'ORBAIS (Rue) C3
JEAN JAURES (Avenue) B4
JEAN LE LOUP (Rue) C3
JEAN-BAPTISTE LANGLET (Cours) B2-C3
JEAN-JACQUES ROUSSEAU (Rue) B3-B4
JEANNE D'ARC (Rue) B1-C2
JEANNE D'ARC (Square) C2
JOFFRE (Boulevard) B1-A2
JOVIN (Rue) A2
JULES CESAR (Boulevard) A2
JULES LOBET (Place) B3
JUSTICE (Impasse de la) A3
JUSTICE (Rue de la) A3-A4
KELLERMANN (Rue) A4
LABORI (Rue) C4
LAGRIVE (Rue) D4
LAON (Avenue de) A2
LAON (Pont de) A2
LAURENT DERAMEZ (Rue) A4-B4
LEGENDRE (Rue) B3
LEON BOURGEOIS (Place) B3
LEVANT (Impasse du) C4
LIBERGIER (Rue) D1-C2
LIEUTENANT HERDUIN (Rue du) D3-D4
LINGUET (Rue) A3-B3
LOGES COQUAULT (Place des) C3
LOUIS BERTON (Rue) C4-D4
LOUIS ROEDERER (Boulevard) B1-C1
LUNDY (Boulevard) A2-B4
LUNDY (Impasse) B4
LUXEMBOURG (Rue de) B3
MACON (Rue de) B4-C4
MACQUART (Rue) A4
MAGDELEINE (Rue de la) C1-D1
MARC (Rue) B2
MARCEL THIL (Rue) A1

MARIE STUART (Rue) C4
MARIE-CLEMENCE FOURIAUX (Rue) . . . A1
MARLOT (Rue) D2-D3
MARMOUZETS (Rue des) B3
MARS (Porte de) A2
MARS (Rue de) A2-B3
MARTYRS DE LA RESISTANCE (Place) . . C3
MARX DORMOY (Rue) C2
MAURICE NOIROT (Boulevard) C1-D1
MOISSONS (Rue des) B4-C4
MONT D'ARENE (Rue du) A1
MONTESQUIEU (Rue) A4
MONTLAURENT (Rue) D4
MONTOISON (Rue de) B4-C4
MURS (Rue des) C4-D4
MYRON HERRICK (Place) C2-C3
NANTEUIL (Rue de) B3
NICOLAS HENRIOT (Rue) B4
NOEL (Rue) B2
NOTRE DAME DE L'EPINE (Rue) A3
OLIVIER METRA (Rue) A3
ORMESSON (Rue d') A4
ORPHELINS (Rue des) D3-D4
PAIX (Boulevard de la) B4-D4
PASTEUR (Boulevard) D4
PAUL ADAM (Rue) D3
PAUL BOCQUET (Square) D1
PAUL DOUMER (Boulevard) D1-D2
PAUL JAMOT (Place) C4
PERSEVAL (Rue) B4
PETIT ARSENAL (Rue du) B2
PETIT FOUR (Rue du) B2
PIERRE BROSSOLETTE (Rue) A1
PIPER (Rue) B4-C4
PLUCHE (Rue) B3
POISSONNIERS (Rue des) C1
POL NEVEUX (Rue) B2
POLONCEAU (Allée) D1
PONSARDIN (Rue) B4-C4
POUILLY (Rue de) B2
PREAU (Rue du) A3
PRESIDENT F ROOSEVELT (Rue) A1-A2
PRISON DU BAILLAGE (Rue de la) B3
RAINSSANT (Rue) D1
RAYMOND GUYOT (Rue) A4
RENE ET HENRI DRUARD (Square) C2
RENE HUET (Rue) A4
RENFERMERIE (Rue de la) A2
REPUBLIQUE (Place de la) A2
ROBERT DE COUCY (Rue) C3
ROCKEFELLER (Rue) C2-C3
ROGIER (Impasse) B3-B4
ROGIER (Rue) B3-B4

ROMAINS (Rue des) A1
ROUILLE (Rue) B2
ROYALE (Place) B3-C3
SAINT-BRICE (Rue de) B1-C1
SAINT-ETIENNE (Impasse) C3
SAINT-GILLES (Passage) D4
SAINT-HILAIRE (Rue) A3-B3
SAINT-JACQUES (Passage) C2
SAINT-JUST (Rue) C3
SAINT-MARCEAUX (Boulevard) C4-D4
SAINT-PIERRE LES DAMES (Rue) C3-C3
SAINT-SYMPHORIEN (Rue) C3
SAINT-YON (Rue) B3-B4
SALIN (Rue) B2
SALLE (Impasse de la) C2
SALLE (Rue de la) C2
SAVOYE (Rue de) A3-A4
7 ET 8 MAI 1945 (Allée des) B1-A2
SOLIDARITE (Place de la) C2
STALINGRAD (Place) D1
SUBE (Passage) C2
TALLEYRAND (Passage) C2
TALLEYRAND (Rue de) B2-C2
TAMBOUR (Rue du) B3
TAPISSERIES (Impasse des) C3
TELLIERS (Rue des) B3
TEMPLE (Rue du) A2-B3
TEMPLIERS (Rue des) B3-A4
THEODORE DUBOIS (Rue) B2
THIERS (Rue) B2
THILLOIS (Rue de) C1-C2
TIRELIRE (Impasse de la) B2
TIRELIRE (Rue de la) A2-B2
TOURNELLES (Rue des) C3
TRESOR (Rue du) B3
TRIANON (Rue de) B1
TROIS RAISINETS (Rue des) B3-C4
TRONSSON DUCOUDRAY (Rue) C2-C3
TRUDAINE (Rue) B3
UNIVERSITE (Rue de l') C3-D4
VAUTHIER LE NOIR (Rue) C3
VENISE (Rue de) D3
VESLE (Pont de) D1
VESLE (Rue de) D1-C2
VICTIMES DE LA GESTAPO
(Square des) C2
VILLEMINOT HUART (Rue) A2
VOLTAIRE (Rue) D3-B4
WARNIER (Rue) B4
WERLE (Rue) A3-A4

Rennes

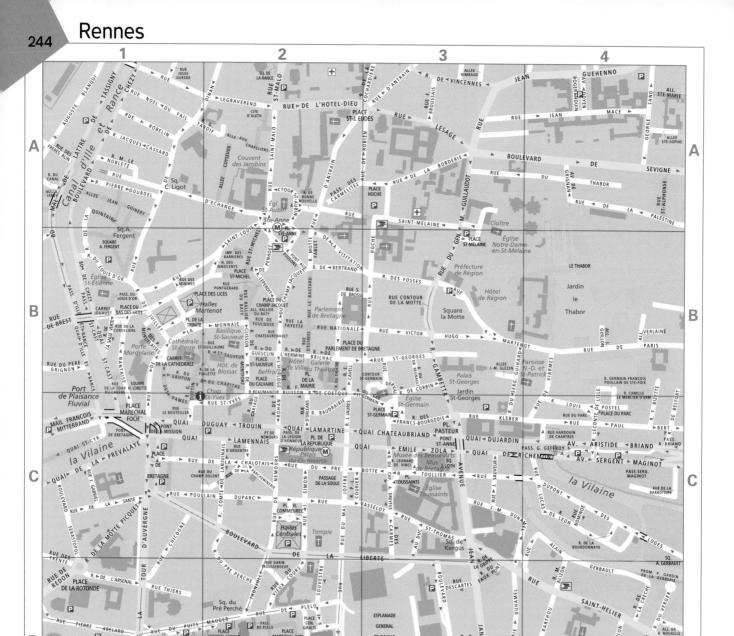

ALAIN FERGENT (Square) B1
ALAIN GERBAULT (Rue) C3-D4
ALAIN GERBAULT (Square) D4
ALBERT AUBRY (Rue) D3
ALBERT EINSTEIN (Mail) D2
ALETH (Cité d') A2
ALFRED JARRY (Allée) A1
ALLIES (Cours des) D2-D3
ALMA (Rue de l') D2
ANNE CATHERINE (Mail) D1
ANTRAIN (Rue d') B2-A3
ARGENTRE (Rue d') C2
ARISTIDE BRIAND (Avenue) C4
ARISTIDE BRIAND (Passage) C4
ARSENAL (Rue de l') D1
BARBOTIERE (Rue de la) C4
BARRIERES (Impasse des) B2
BAS DES LICES (Place du) B1
BASTARD (Rue) B2
BAUDRAIRIE (Rue) C2
BEAUMANOIR (Rue) B2
BEAUMONT (Boulevard de) D3
BELFORT (Rue de) B4-C4
BERTRAND (Rue de) B2-B3
BONNE NOUVELLE (Rue de) A3
BORDERIE (Rue de la) A3
BOURDONNAYE (Rue de la) C4
BOUTEILLER (Rue le) C1
BREST (Rue de) B1
BRETAGNE (Place de) B1
BRETAGNE (Pont de) C1
BRILHAC (Rue de) B2
CALVAIRE (Place du) B2
CAMILLE LE MERCIER D'ERM (Rue) . . B4-C4
CANAL (Impasse du) A1
CAP ALFRED DREYFUS (Rue) C3
CAPITAINE MAIGNAN (Rue du) D2
CARMELITES (Passage des) A2
CARMES (Rue des) C3
CARREFOUR JOUAUST (Rue) B1
CARTAGE (Rue) B2-C2
CATHEDRALE (Carrefour de la) B2
CHALOTAIS (Rue de la) C1-C2
CHAMP DE MARS (Esplanade du) . . D2-D3
CHAMP DOLENT (Rue du) C1-C2
CHAMP JACQUET (Place du) B2
CHAMP JACQUET (Rue du) B2
CHAPELIERS (Ruelle aux) A2
CHAPITRE (Rue du) B1-B2
CHATEAUBRIAND (Quai) C2-C3
CHATEAURENAULT (Rue du) B2
CHEVAUX (Ruelle aux) A2
CHEZY (Boulevard de) A1-B1
CHICOGNE (Rue) C1-D1

50EME REGIMENT D'ARTILLERIE
(Place du) D2
CLISSON (Rue de) B2
COCHARDIERE (Rue de la) A3
COETQUEN (Rue de) B2
COLOMBES (Place des) D1-D2
COLOMBIER (Place du) D2
COMTE DE LANJUINAIS (Rue) B3
CONTOUR DE LA MOTTE (Rue) B3
CONTOUR DE SAINT-AUBIN (Rue) . . . A2
CORBIN (Rue de) B3-C3
CORDELIERE (Rue de la) B1
COUEDIC (Passage du) D1
COYSEVOX (Allée) A2
CRECHE (Rue de la) C4
DAMES (Rue des) B1-C1
DERVAL (Rue) B3-C3
DESCARTES (Rue) D3
DINAN (Rue de) A1
10EME D'ARTILLERIE (Rue du) D2
DOCTEUR FRANCIS JOLY (Rue du) . . D1-D2
DOCTEUR REGNAULT (Rue du) B2
DOCTEUR ROGER NOUAILLE (Rue) . . B2
DOCTEUR ROUX (Rue) D1
DOYEN ROGER HOUIN (Avenue) C4
DUC (Rue du) C3-D3
DUGUAY TROUIN (Quai) C1-C2
DUJARDIN (Quai) C3-C4
DUPONT DES LOGES (Rue) C3-C4
ECHANGE (Rue d') A1-A2
EDITH CAVELL (Rue) D1
EMILE SOUVESTRE (Rue) C2-D2
EMILE SOUVESTRE (Square) D2
EMILE ZOLA (Quai) C3
ESTREES (Rue d') B2
FAUX PONT (Rue du) C3
FERDINAND BUISSON (Rue) B2
FOSSES (Rue des) B3
FRANCAIS LIBRES (Avenue des) D4
FRANCOIS BIZETTE (Rue) B4-C4
FRANCOIS BROUSSAIS (Rue) A3
FRANCOIS MITTERRAND (Mail) C1
FRANCS-BOURGEOIS (Rue) B4-C4
FRERES BLIN (Rue des) A1
GAMBETTA (Rue) B3-C3
GARE (Place de la) D3
GARIN TROUSSEBOEUF (Rue) C2
GASTON TARDIF (Rue) A1
GENERAL DE GAULLE (Esplanade) . . D2-D3
GENERAL GIRAUD (Rue) C1
GENERAL KOENIG (Place) D1-D2
GENERAL MAURICE GUILLAUDOT
(Rue du) A3-B3
GEORGE SAND (Rue) A4
GEORGES DOTTIN (Rue) B1-C1

GERMAIN-FRANCOIS POULLAIN DE
SAINTE-FOIX (Rue) B4
GRIFFON (Rue du) B2
GRIGNAN (Avenue de) A4
GRIPPE (Rue de la) C3-D3
GUESCLIN (Rue du) B2
GURVAND (Rue) D2-D3
GUSTAVE GEFFROY (Passage) C4
HARDOUIN DE CHARTRES (Rue) C4
HERMINE (Rue de l') B2
HIPPOLYTE LUCAS (Rue) B1
HOCHE (Place) B1
HOCHE (Rue) A3-B3
HONORE COMMEUREC (Place) C2
HORLOGE (Rue de l') C1-B2
HOTEL DIEU (Rue de l') A2-A3
HYACINTHE LORETTE (Square) B1
ILLE ET RANCE (Passage d') B1
ILLE ET RANCE (Quai d') B1-C1
INNOCENTS (Rue des) B2
ISLY (Rue d') C2
JACQUES CASSARD (Rue) A1
JACQUES GABRIEL (Rue) C3
JACQUES-MARIE GLEZEN (Allée) B2
JEAN GUEHENNO (Rue) A3-A4
JEAN GUIHERY (Allée) A1
JEAN JANVIER (Avenue) C3-D3
JEAN MACE (Rue) A3-A4
JEAN MILON (Rue) C4
JEAN-MARIE DUHAMEL (Rue) D3-C4
JEANNE GUILLON (Allée) B4
JOSEPH LOTH (Square) B1
JOSEPH SAUVEUR (Rue) C2
JUILLET (Rue du) B1
JULES GUESDE (Rue) A1
JULES SIMON (Rue) C2
KLEBER (Rue) C3-C4
LA FAYETTE (Rue) B2
LAMARTINE (Quai) C2
LAMENNAIS (Quai) C1-C2
LE THABOR B3-A4
LECONTE DE LISLE (Rue) B4-C4
LEGION D'HONNEUR (Passage de la) . . C4
LEGRAVEREND (Rue) A1-A2
LEON (Rue de) C4
LEONARD DE VINCI (Rue) C2
LEPERDIT (Rue) B2
LESAGE (Rue) A3
LIBERTE (Boulevard de la) C1-D3
LICES (Place des) C2-D2
LOUIS BARTHOU (Avenue) D3
LOUIS D'OR (Passage du) B1
LOUIS POSTEL (Rue) C4
MAGENTA (Boulevard) D3

MAIRIE (Place de la) B2
MARECHAL DE LATTRE DE TASSIGNY
(Boulevard) A1-B1
MARECHAL FOCH (Place) C1
MARECHAL JOFFRE (Rue du) C2
MARECHAL JUIN (Place) D2
MARIE ALIZON (Rue) C4-D4
MARTENOT (Rue) B3-B4
MARTYRS DE LA RESISTANCE
(Square des) D2
MICHEL LE NOBLETZ (Rue) A1
MINIMES (Rue des) B1
MISSION (Pont de la) C1
MONNAIE (Rue de la) C1-B2
MONTFORT (Rue de) B2
MOTTE (Square de la) B3
MOTTE FABLET (Rue) B2
MOTTE PICQUET (Rue de la) C1-D1
NANTAISE (Rue) B1-C1
NATIONALE (Rue) B2-B3
NEMOURS (Pont de) C2
NEMOURS (Rue de) C2
NOEL DU FAIL (Rue) A1
NOMINOE (Rue) C4
ORLEANS (Rue d') C2
PALESTINE (Rue de) A4
PAPIERTIMBRE (Rue du) D1
PARC (Place du) C4
PARC (Rue du) C4
PARCHEMINERIE (Rue de la) C2
PARIS (Rue de) B4
PARLEMENT DE BRETAGNE
(Place du) B2-B3
PASTEUR (Place) C3
PAUL BERT (Rue) C4
PAUL LOUIS COURIER (Rue) C2
PENHOET (Rue de) B2
PERE GRIGNON (Rue du) B1
PIERRE ABELARD (Rue) D1
PIERRE GARDIN DE LA GERBERIE
(Promenade) D4
PIERRE GOURDEL (Rue) A1
PIERRE HENRI TEITGEN (Rue) D4
PLELO (Passage de) C2
PLELO (Rue de) C2
PONT AUX FOULONS (Rue) B2
PORTES MORDELAISES (Rue des) . . . B2
POULLAIN DUPARC (Rue) C1-C2
PRE BOTTE (Rue du) C3
PRE PERCHE (Rue du) C2-D2
PREVALAYE (Quai de la) C1
PSALETTE (Rue de la) B1-B2
PUITS MAUGER (Passage du) D1-D2
PUITS MAUGER (Rue du) D2

QUINTAINE (Rue de la) A1-B1
RALLIER DU BATY (Allée) B2
RALLIER DU BATY (Rue) B2
RANCE (Square de la) A2
RAPHAEL BINET (Cours) D1
REDON (Rue de) D1
RENE LAENNEC (Boulevard) D4
RENE LEHERPEUX (Passage) D4
REPUBLIQUE (Place de la) C2
RICHEMONT (Quai de) C3-C4
RIMBAUD (Allée) A3
ROBELIN (Rue) A1
ROBIEN (Rue de) A2-A3
ROHAN (Rue de) B2-C2
ROI ARTHUR (Place du) D2
ROTONDE (Place de la) D1
SAINT-ALPHONSE (Rue) A4
SAINT-ANNE (Pont) A4
SAINT-CAST (Passage) B1
SAINT-CAST (Quai) B1-C1
SAINT-CYR (Quai) C1
SAINTE-ANNE (Place) A2-B2
SAINTE-MARIE (Allée) A4
SAINTE-SOPHIE (Allée) A4
SAINT-GEORGES (Rue) B3
SAINT-GERMAIN (Contour) B3-C3
SAINT-GERMAIN (Place) C3
SAINT-GUILLAUME (Rue) B1-B2
SAINT-HELIER (Rue) C3-D4
SAINT-JEAN EUDES (Place) A2
SAINT-LOUIS (Rue) B1-A2
SAINT-MALO (Rue) A2-B2
SAINT-MELAINE (Place) A3-B3
SAINT-MELAINE (Rue) A2-A3
SAINT-MICHEL (Place) B2
SAINT-MICHEL (Rue) A2-B2
SAINT-SAUVEUR (Rue) B1-B2
SAINT-THOMAS (Rue) C4
SAINT-YVES (Rue) C1-B2
SALOMON DE BROSSE (Rue) B2-B3
SANTE (Rue de la) C1
SEBASTOPOL (Boulevard) C1-D1
SERGENT GUIHARD (Rue du) B3-C3
SERGENT MAGINOT (Avenue) C4
SERGENT MAGINOT (Passage) C4
SEVIGNE (Boulevard de) A3-A4
SOLFERINO (Boulevard) D3-D4
SOULE (Rue de la) C3
THABOR (Rue du) A3-A4
THEATRE (Rue du) B2
THEOPHILE BRIANT (Rue) D2
THIERS (Rue) D1
TOULLIER (Rue) C3

TOULOUSE (Rue de) B2
TOUR D'AUVERGNE
(Boulevard de la) C1-D1
TOUR DU CHESNE (Rue de la) B1
TOUSSAINTS (Place) C3
TRENTE (Rue des) D1
TRINITE (Place de la) B1
TRONJOLLY (Rue) C2-D2
VASSELOT (Rue) C2-C3
VAU SAINT-GERMAIN (Rue du) B2-C3
VERGER (Rue du) D4
VERLAINE (Allée) B4
VIARMES (Rue des) B4-C4
VICTOR HUGO (Rue) B3
VIEUX COURS (Rue du) C2-D2
VINCENNES (Rue de) A3
VISITATION (Rue de la) B2-B3

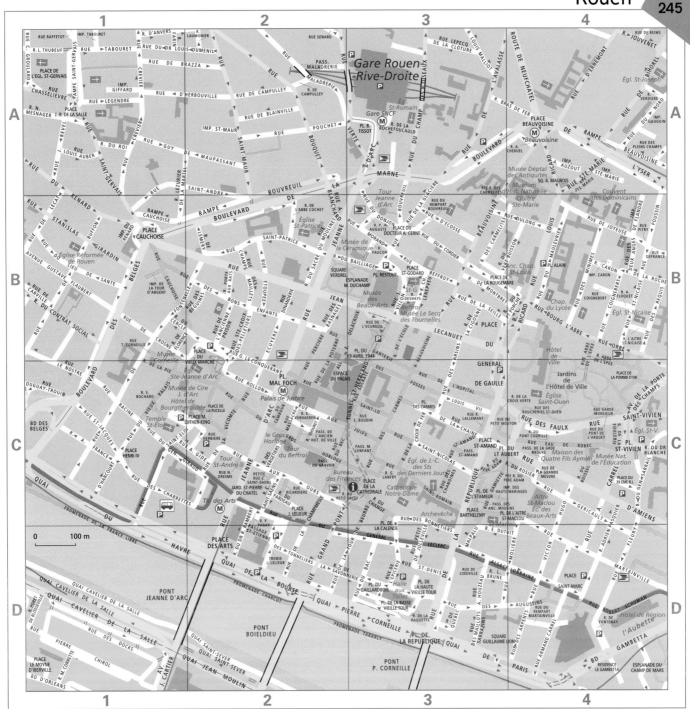

ABBE COCHET (Rue de l') ... B2
ABBE DE L'EPEE (Rue) ... B4-C4
ADOLPHE CHERUEL (Rue) ... A4
ADRIEN AUZOUT (Impasse) ... A4
ADRIEN PASQUIER (Rue) ... C4-D4
AIMABLE FLOQUET (Rue) ... B4
AITRE SAINT-MACLOU (Place de l') ... C4
AITRE SAINT-NICAISE (Rue l') ... B4
ALAIN (Place) ... B4
ALAIN BLANCHARD (Rue) ... A2-B2
ALSACE-LORRAINE (Rue) ... D3-D4
AMBROISE FLEURY (Rue) ... C4-D4
AMIENS (Rue d') ... C3-D4
ANATOLE FRANCE (Rue) ... C1
ANCIEN HOTEL DE VILLE
(Passage de l') ... C2
ANCIENNE PRISON (Rue de l') ... C2
ANCIENS MOULINS (Passage des) ... C3
ANDRE GIDE (Rue) ... C1-C2
ANDRE MAUROIS (Square) ... A4
ANVERS (Rue d') ... C2
ARMAND CARREL (Rue) ... C4-D4
ARPENTS (Rue des) ... B3-C3
ARSINS (Rue des) ... C3
ARTS (Place des) ... D2
AUGUSTE HOUZEAU (Rue) ... C3
AUGUSTINS (Rue des) ... A3-D3
AVALASSE (Rue de l') ... A3
BAC (Rue du) ... D3
BAILLIAGE (Rue du) ... B2-B3
BARTHELEMY (Place) ... C3
BASNAGES (Rue des) ... B2
BASSE VIEILLE TOUR (Place de la) ... D3
BEAUVOISINE (Rue) ... A4-B4
BEAUVOISINE (Rampe) ... A4
BEC (Rue du) ... C2-C3
BEFFROY (Rue) ... B3
BEGUINES (Rue des) ... B4
BELGES (Boulevard des) ... B1-C1
BERNARD TISSOT (Place) ... A4
BIHOREL (Rue) ... A4
BLAINVILLE (Rue de) ... A2
BOIELDIEU (Pont) ... D2
BONNETIERS (Rue des) ... C4
BONS ENFANTS (Rue des) ... B1-B2
BOUCHERIES SAINT-OUEN (Rue des) ... C4
BOUQUET (Rue) ... A2
BOURG L'ABBE (Rue) ... B4
BOURSE (Quai de la) ... D2
BOUVREUIL (Rue) ... B1-A2
BOUVREUIL (Rue) ... A3-B3
BRAS DE FER (Rue) ... A3-A4
BRAZZA (Rue de) ... A1-A2
BUFFON (Rue de) ... B1

CALENDE (Place de la) ... C3-D3
CAMILLE SAINT-SAENS (Petite rue) ... C2
CAMILLE SAINT-SAENS (Rue) ... C2
CAMPULLEY (Rue de) ... A2
CARMELITES (Petite rue des) ... B3-B4
CARMELITES (Rue des) ... B3-B4
CARMES (Place des) ... C3
CARMES (Rue des) ... C3
CARON (Impasse) ... B4
CARVILLE (Rue de) ... B1
CAUCHOISE (Place) ... B1
CAUCHOISE (Rampe) ... B1
CAUCHOISE (Rue) ... B1-B2
CAVELIER DE LA SALLE (Quai) ... D1
CERCLE (Rue du) ... B1-B2
CHAINE (Rue de la) ... C3
CHAMP DE MARS (Esplanade du) ... D4
CHAMP DES OISEAUX (Rue du) ... A3
CHAMPMESLE (Rue de la) ... C2-D2
CHAMPS MAILLETS (Rue des) ... B3
CHANGE (Rue du) ... C3
CHANOINES (Rue des) ... C3
CHARCOT (Promenade) ... D2
CHARLES LENEPVEU (Rue) ... B3
CHARRETTES (Rue des) ... C1-C2
CHASSELIEVRE (Rue) ... A1
CIDEVILLE (Rue de) ... B1
CIGOGNE (Rue de la) ... B3
CLAUDE GROULARD (Rue) ... A1
COIGNEBERT (Rue) ... B4
CONTRAT SOCIAL (Rue du) ... B1
CORDIER (Rue du) ... B4
CREVIER (Rue) ... A1-B1
CROIX DE FER (Rue de la) ... C3
CROIX VERTE (Rue de la) ... C3
CROSNE (Rue de) ... B1-B2
DAMIETTE (Rue) ... C4
DEFRANCE (Rue) ... B4
DESHAYS (Rue) ... B3
2 ANGES (Rue des) ... B4
DINANDERIE (Rue) ... C3
DOCKS (Rue des) ... D1
DOCTEUR ALFRED CERNE (Place du) ... B3
DOCTEUR LOUIS DUMENIL
(Rue du) ... A1-A2
DOCTEUR ROBERT RAMBERT
(Rue du) ... C2-D2
DONJON (Rue du) ... A3-B3
DUGUAY TROUIN (Rue) ... C1
DULONG (Rue) ... B3-B4
EAU DE ROBEC (Rue du) ... C4

ECOLE (Rue de l') ... B3-C3
ECOSSE (Rue d') ... B3
ECUREUIL (Rue de l') ... B3
ECUYERE (Rue) ... B2-C2
EGLISE SAINT-GERVAIS (Place de l') ... A1
EMILE VERHAEREN (Rue) ... C3
EPICERIE (Rue d') ... D3
ERNEMONT (Rue de l') ... A4
ESPACE DU PALAIS ... C2
ETAMEUR (Place de l') ... C3
ETOUPEE (Rue) ... B2
EUGENE BOUDIN (Rue) ... C3
EUGENE DELACROIX (Allée) ... C2-B3
EUGENE DUTUIT (Rue) ... D3-D4
FARDEAU (Rue du) ... C3
FARIN (Rue) ... A2
FAUCON (Rue au) ... B3
FAULX (Rue des) ... C4
FLANDRE (Impasse de) ... B4
FLORENCE (Rue de) ... B1-B2
FONTENAY (Rue de) ... D4
FONTENELLE (Rue de) ... C1-B2
FOSSES LOUIS VIII (Rue des) ... B2-C3
FOULERIE (Rue de la) ... C4
FRANCE LIBRE (Promenade de la) ... C1-D2
GAILLARDBOIS (Rue) ... C4
GAMBETTA (Boulevard) ... D4
GAMBETTA (Résidence le) ... D4
GANTERIE (Rue) ... B3-C3
GARDE MONSIEUR (Rue) ... C4
GAUGUIN (Impasse) ... A4
GENERAL DE GAULLE (Place du) ... C1-B3
GENERAL GIRAUD (Rue du) ... C1-C2
GENERAL LECLERC (Rue du) ... C2-D3
GENERAL SARRAIL (Rue du) ... C4
GEORGES LANFRY (Rue) ... C4-D4
GERICAULT (Rue) ... C4-D4
GIFFARD (Impasse) ... A1
GLACIERE (Rue) ... A3-B3
GRAND PONT (Rue) ... C2-D2
GRANDE MESURE (Passage de la) ... C4
GRANDE MESURE (Rue de la) ... C4
GRAVIER (Passage du) ... C3
GROS HORLOGE (Rue du) ... C2-C3
GUILLAUME LE CONQUERANT
(Rue) ... B2-C2
GUILLAUME LION (Square) ... C1-D2
GUSTAVE FLAUBERT (Avenue) ... B1
GUY DE MAUPASSANT (Rue) ... A2

HERBOUVILLE (Rue d') ... A1-A2
HOPITAL (Rue de l') ... C3
JACQUES CARTIER (Avenue) ... D1
JACQUES LELIEUR (Place) ... D2
JACQUES LELIEUR (Trémie) ... C2-D2
JACQUES VILLON (Rue) ... B3
JEAN LECANUET (Rue) ... B1-B3
JEAN MOULIN (Quai) ... D1-D2
JEAN REVEL (Rue) ... A1
JEAN-BAPTISTE DE LA SALLE (Place) ... A1
JEANNE D'ARC (Pont) ... D1-D2
JEANNE D'ARC (Rue) ... D2-A3
JOUVENET (Rue) ... A4
JOYEUSE (Rue de) ... B4
JUIFS (Rue aux) ... C2-C3
LAUMONIER (Rue) ... A2
LECAT (Rue de) ... A1-B1
LEGENDRE (Rue) ... A1
LEMERY (Rue de) ... B3
LEPECQ DE LA CLOTURE (Rue) ... A3
LIEU DE SANTE (Rue) ... B1
LIEUTENANT DE LA MARTEL (Rue) ... B1-A2
LIEUTENANT AUBERT (Place du) ... C3-C4
LOUIS AUBER (Rue) ... A1
LOUIS BRUNE (Rue) ... D3
LOUIS MALLIOT (Rue) ... A3
LOUIS RICARD (Rue) ... B3
LOUIS THUBEUF (Rue) ... A1
MAILLOTS SARRAZINS (Rue des) ... D3
MALADRERIE (Passage) ... A2
MALADRERIE (Rue de la) ... A2-A3
MALPALU (Rue) ... C3-D3
MARCEL DUCHAMP (Esplanade) ... B3
MARECHAL FOCH (Place) ... C2
MARNE (Boulevard de la) ... B1-A3
MARTAINVILLE (Rue) ... C3-D4
MARTIN LUTHER-KING (Place) ... C1-C2
MASSACRE (Rue) ... C3
MAULEVRIER (Rue du) ... B4
MAURICE LENFANT (Passage) ... C3
MAURICE CORRETTE (Rue) ... C4
MINIMES (Rue des) ... B4
MOLIERE (Rue) ... D3-C4
MONTBRET (Rue de) ... B3-B4
MORAND (Rue) ... B2-B3
MOULINET (Rue) ... B2
MOYNE D'IBERVILLE (Place le) ... D1
NEUFCHATEL (Route de) ... A4
NICOLAS MESNAGER (Rue) ... A4
NICOLE ORESME (Rue) ... C3
NORD (Rue du) ... A4
NOSTRE (Rue le) ... C1
ORBE (Rue) ... B4-C4
ORLEANS (Boulevard d') ... D1
OURS (Rue aux) ... C3

PARIS (Quai de) ... D3-D4
PAUL PARAY (Rue) ... C2-D2
PERCIERE (Rue) ... B2-C2
PERE ADAM (Petite rue du) ... C3
PERE ADAM (Rue du) ... C3
PETIT DE JULLEVILLE (Rue) ... C3-D3
PETIT MOUTON (Rue du) ... C3-C4
PETIT PORCHE (Rue du) ... B3-B4
PETIT SALUT (Rue du) ... C2-C3
PHILIPPE AUGUSTE (Rue) ... B3
PIE (Rue de la) ... B1-C1
PIERRE CHIROL (Rue) ... D1
PIERRE CORNEILLE (Pont) ... D3
PIERRE CORNEILLE (Quai) ... D2-D3
PITRY (Rue) ... B2
PLEINS CHAMPS (Rue des) ... A4
POMME D'OR (Place de la) ... C4
PONT CODRILLE (Rue du) ... C4
PONT DE L'ARQUET (Rue du) ... C4
PORET DE BLOSSEVILLE (Rue) ... D1
PORTE AUX RATS (Rue) ... B2
PORTE DES CHAMPS (Avenue de la) ... C4
POTERNE (Rue de la) ... D3
POUCHET (Rue) ... A2-A3
POUSSIN (Rue) ... A4-B4
PUCELLE D'ORLEANS (Place de la) ... C2
QUEBEC (Rue) ... B3
RACINE (Rue) ... C1
RAFFETOT (Rue) ... A1
RAQUETTE (Rue de la) ... D4
REIMS (Rue de) ... A4
REMPART BOUVREUIL (Rue du) ... A3
REMPART MARTAINVILLE (Rue du) ... C4
RENARD (Rue) ... A1-B1
RENARD (Impasse du) ... B1
REPUBLIQUE (Rue de la) ... C3-D3
REQUIS (Rue des) ... B4
RESTOUT (Rue) ... B3
RICARDIERE (Rue) ... C4
RICHARD LALLEMANT (Rue) ... C4
ROBERT SCHUMAN (Rue) ... D4
ROCHE (Rue de la) ... B4
ROCHEFOUCAULD (Rue de la) ... A3
ROI (Rue du) ... A1
ROLLON (Rue) ... C2
ROSIER (Rue du) ... C3-C4
ROUGEMARE (Place de la) ... B3-B4
RUISSEL (Rue du) ... C3
SACRE (Rue) ... B2
SAINT-AMAND (Passage) ... C3
SAINT-AMAND (Rue) ... C3
SAINT-ANDRE (Rue) ... A1-B2
SAINT-DENIS (Rue) ... C4

SAINT-ELOI (Rue) ... C1-C2
SAINT-ETIENNE DES TONNELIERS
(Passage) ... D2
SAINT-GERVAIS (Rampe) ... A1
SAINT-GERVAIS (Rue) ... A1-B1
SAINT-GODARD (Place) ... B3
SAINT-HERBLAND (Tunnel) ... C2-B3
SAINT-JACQUES (Rue) ... C1
SAINT-LO (Rue) ... C2-C3
SAINT-MARC (Place) ... D4
SAINT-MAUR (Impasse) ... A2
SAINT-MAUR (Rue) ... A2-B2
SAINT-NICAISE (Rue) ... B4
SAINT-NICOLAS (Rue) ... C3
SAINT-PATRICE (Rue) ... B2
SAINT-PIERRE DU CHATEL (Jardin) ... C2
SAINT-ROMAIN (Rue) ... C3
SAINT-SEVER (Quai) ... D1-D2
SAINT-VIVIEN (Place) ... C4
SAINT-VIVIEN (Rue) ... C4
SAINTE-CROIX-DES-PELLETIERS (Rue) ... B2
SAINTE-MARIE (Impasse) ... A4
SAINTE-MARIE (Rampe) ... A4
SAMUEL BOCHARD (Rue) ... C1
SAVONNERIE (Rue de la) ... D2-D3
SEILLE (Rue de la) ... B3
SENARD (Rue) ... A2
SOCRATE (Rue) ... C2
STANISLAS GIRARDIN (Rue) ... B1
TABARLY (Promenade) ... D2-D3
TABOURET (Impasse) ... A1
TABOURET (Rue) ... A1
TAMBOUR (Rue du) ... C2
THOMAS CORNEILLE (Rue) ... B1-C1
THOURET (Rue) ... C2
TOUR D'ARGENT (Impasse de la) ... B1
TOUR DE BEURRE (Rue de la) ... D2-D3
39EME R.I. (Place du) ... C4
VERDIERE (Rue) ... A4
VERDREL (Square) ... B2
VERGETIERS (Rue des) ... C3
VERT BUISSON (Rue du) ... B3-B4
VERTE (Rue) ... A2-A3
VICOMTE (Rue de la) ... C3
VICTOR HUGO (Rue) ... C4-D4
VIEUX MARCHE (Place du) ... C1-C2
VIEUX PALAIS (Rue du) ... C2
YSER (Boulevard de l') ... A3-A4

Strasbourg

0   100 m

ABATTOIR (Pont de l')....... C1
ABREUVOIR (Passerelle de l') . C4
ABREUVOIR (Ruelle de l')..... C4
ADELE RITON (Rue)....... A1-A3
ADOLPHE SEYBOTH (Rue)..... C1
AGNEAU (Ruelle de l')....... D3
AIL (Rue de l')............. C2
AIMANT (Rue de l')......... C2
ANCIENNE GARE (Rue de l') .. B2
ANCIENNE SYNAGOGUE
  (Square de l')............ B2
ANCRE (Impasse de l')....... D4
ANDRE ET PAUL HORN
  (Passage)............. B3-C3
ARBRE VERT (Rue de l')...... C3
ARC EN CIEL (Rue de l')... B4-C4
ARGILE (Rue de l')......... C2
AUBETTE (Cours de l').... C2-C3
AUGUSTE LAMEY (Rue)...... A4
AUSTERLITZ (Petite rue d') ... D4
AUSTERLITZ (Rue d')....... C4
AUSTERLITZ (Rue d')....... D4
AVEUGLES (Rue des)........ C2
BAIN AUX PLANTES
  (Impasse du)............ C2
BAIN AUX PLANTES (Rue du) . C2
BAIN AUX ROSES (Rue du) ... C2
BAIN FINKWILLER (Rue du)... D2
BALDUNG GRIEN (Rue)...... A4
BATELIERS (Quai des).... C4-D4
BATELIERS (Rue des)....... D4
BENJAMIN KUGLER (Rue).... D1
BENJAMIN ZIX (Place)....... D2
BERNE (Rue de)........... D4
BIERE (Impasse de la)....... B3
BISCHEIM (Impasse de)..... B3
BISCHWILLER (Rue de).... A2-A4
BITCHE (Rue de)........... A4
BŒUFS (Cours des)........ D4
BŒUFS (Rue des).......... D4
BONNES GENS (Impasse des)
BONNES GENS (Rue des) . A2-B2
BOTTELEURS (Rue des)...... D2
BOUCHERS (Rue des)....... D4
BOUCLIER (Rue du)........ C2
BOUXWILLER (Rue de).... A1-A2
BRIGADE ALSACE-LORRAINE
  (Rue de la)............. D4
BROGLIE (Place)........ B3-B4
BROGLIE-MESANGE (Passage) . B3
BRUCHE (Rue de la)....... C3-D3
BRULEE (Rue)........... C3-B4
CATHEDRALE
CATHEDRALE (Place de la). C3-C3
CHAINE (Rue de la)........ C3
CHAINE D'OR (Place de la)... C3
CHANDELLES (Rue des)...... C3
CHAPON (Rue du)......... C4

CHARLES ALTORFFER (Quai). C1
CHARLES FREY (Quai)...... D3
CHARPENTIERS
  (Impasse des)........ B4-C4
CHARPENTIERS (Rue des). B4-C4
CHAUDRON (Rue du)....... C4
CHEVEUX (Rue des)....... C2
CHEVREUIL (Rue du)....... A3
CIEL (Rue du)............. C4
CIGOGNES (Rue des).... A2-A3
CLARISSES (Rue des)....... C2
CLAUDE CHAPPE (Rue)..... A1
CLEMENCEAU (Boulevard) A2-A3
CLEMENT (Place).......... B2
CLEMENT (Rue)........... B2
CLEMENT (Rue du)........ B2
COIN BRULE (Rue du)...... C2
COMEDIE (Rue de la)....... B4
COQ (Rue du)............ B2
CORBEAU (Impasse du)..... D4
CORBEAU (Pont du)....... D4
CORBEAU (Quai du)....... D4
CORDIERS (Rue des)....... C4
CORDONNIERS (Rue des). C3-D3
CORNEILLE (Impasse de la) .. B3
CORNETS (Impasse des)..... C3
COUPLES (Rue des)........ B2
COURSE (Petite rue de la).... C1
COURSE (Rue de la)........ C1
COURTINE (Rue de la)...... C1
COUVERTS (Rue des)....... C2
CROIX (Rue de la)......... D2
CRONENBOURG-STRASBOURG-
  NORD (Echangeur de l')... A1
CUILLER A POT (Ruelle de la) . D2
CYGNE (Place du)......... D2
CYGNE (Rue du)........... D2
DEMI-LUNE (Rue de la)..... C3
DENTELLES (Petite rue des) .. C2
DENTELLES (Rue des).... C2-C3
DESAIX (Quai).......... C1-C2
DESERTE (Rue)........... C2
DEVIDOIR (Rue du)........ C2
DINSENMUHLE (Pont de la).. D2
DIVISION LECLERC
  (Rue de la)........... D3-D3
DOME (Rue du).......... C3-D3
DOMINICAINS (Rue des).... C3
DOUANE (Rue de la).... D3-D4
DRAGON (Rue du)........ D2
DRAPIERS (Rue des)....... C3
DRULINGEN (Rue de)....... A3
ECARLATE (Rue de l')...... D3
ECHASSES (Impasse des)... C4
ECHASSES (Rue des)....... C4
ECREVISSE (Impasse de l').. B3
ECRIVAINS (Rue des)....... C3
ECURIE (Rue de l')........ D3
EGLISE (Petite rue de l')..... B3

EGLISE (Rue de l').......... B3
EHRMANN (Rue)........... A4
EPINE (Rue de l')........ C3-D3
ESCARPEE (Rue de l')...... C3
ESPRIT (Ruelle de l')....... D3
ETAL (Rue de l')........ D3-D3
ETUDIANTS (Place des)..... C3
ETUDIANTS (Rue des).... B3-C3
FAISAN (Rue du).......... C4
FARINE (Rue de la)...... D3-D4
FAUBOURG DE PIERRE
  (Place du)............. A3
FAUBOURG DE PIERRE
  (Pont du)............. A3
FAUBOURG DE PIERRE
  (Rue du)............ A2-B3
FAUBOURG DE SAVERNE
  (Rue de la)........... B1-C2
FAUBOURG NATIONAL
  (Rue du)............. C1
FAUX REMPART
  (Passerelle du)........ B3
FEU (Rue du)........... B1-B2
FIL (Rue du)............. B2
FINKMATT (Quai)......... A2
FINKMATT (Rue)......... A2-B2
FINKWILLER (Place)....... D2
FINKWILLER (Quai)..... D2-D3
FINKWILLER (Rue)........ D2
FONDERIE (Impasse de la)... B3
FONDERIE (Petite rue de la).. B3
FONDERIE (Pont de la)..... B3
FONDERIE (Rue de la).... B3-B4
FORT (Rue du).......... A3-B3
FOSSE DES TAILLEURS..... C3
FOSSE DES TANNEURS..... C2
FOSSE DES TREIZE........ A3
FRANCS-BOURGEOIS
  (Rue des)............ C2-C3
FREDERIC PITON (Rue).... C2
FRERE MEDARD (Place du). C4
FRERES (Rue des)......... C3
FRERES MATTHIS (Pont des) .D1
FRERES MATTHIS (Rue des) . D1
FRIESE (Rue)............ A2
FUMIER (Ruelle du)....... D2
GARE (Place de la)..... B1-C1
GENERAL DE CASTELNAU
  (Rue du)............ B4-B4
GENERAL FRERE (Rue du).. A3
GENERAL GANIVAL (Rue du) . D1
GENERAL RAPP (Rue du).... A4
GEORGES FRANKHAUSER
  (Passage)............. D1
GEORGES WODLI (Rue)... A1-B1
GLACIERES (Rue des)...... D2
GLOXIN (Rue de)........ A2-A3

GRAND RUE........... C1-C3
GRANDE BOUCHERIE
  (Impasse de la)......... D4
GRANDE BOUCHERIE
  (Place de la)........... D4
GRANDE ECLUSE
  (Impasse de la)......... D1
GRANDES ARCADES
  (Rue des)............ B3-C3
GRANGE (Rue de la).... C2-C3
GRAUMANN (Rue)........ A3
GRENIERS (Rue des)....... D2
GUNTHER (Impasse)....... D4
GUSTAVE DORE (Rue)...... C3
GUSTAVE-ADOLPHE HIRN
  (Rue de la).......... C4-D4
GUTENBERG (Place)....... C3
GUTENBERG (Rue)........ C3
HACHE (Rue de la)........ C3
HAGUENAU (Place de)..... A2
HAGUENAU (Rue de)...... A2
HALLEBARDES (Rue des)... C3
HALLES (Place des).... A2-B2
HALLES (Rue des)...... A2-B2
HANNETONS (Rue des).... C2
HANNONG (Rue)......... B2
HANS JEAN ARP (Place).. C1-D1
HAUTE MONTEE
  (Rue de la).......... B2-B3
HENRY DUNANT (Place).... D1
HOMME DE FER
  (Place de l')......... B2-B3
HOPITAL (Place de l').... D3-D3
HOUBLON (Rue du)....... D1
HUMANN (Rue)........ D1-D2
INGWILLER (Rue d')....... A2
JACQUES STURM (Rue)... B3-B4
JARDIN AUX ROSES
  (Impasse du)........... B2
JARDINIERS (Rue des)..... C2
JARDINS (Rue des)........ C3
JEAN STURM (Rue)........ B3
JEU DES ENFANTS (Rue du).. C2
JOSEPH MASSOL (Rue).... B4
JUIFS (Rue des)........ B3-B4
KAGENECK (Rue de).... B1-C1
KELLERMANN (Quai).... B2-B3
KIRSCHLEGER (Rue)...... C1
KLEBER (Place).......... C2-C3
KLEIN (Rue)............ D4
KUHN (Rue)........... B1-B2
KUSS (Pont).............C1
KUSS (Rue)............. C1
LANTERNE (Rue de la)..... C3
LENTILLES (Rue des)...... C3
LEZAY MARNESIA (Quai)... B4
LOUIS APFFEL (Rue)....... A4
LOUISE WEISS (Square).... D2

LOUVETEAU (Impasse du). A2-A3
MACONS (Impasse des).... B4
MAGASINS (Petite rue des) .. A1
MAGASINS (Rue des).... A1-A2
MAI (Impasse du)......... A3
MAIRE KUSS (Rue du)... C1-C2
MARAIS KAGENECK (Rue) . B1
MARAIS VERT (Rue du)... A1-B2
MARAIS VERT-WODLI (Tunnel) B1
MARBACH (Rue)........ B2-B3
MARC BLOCH (Quai)...... D1
MARCHE (Pont du)....... B2
MARCHE (Rue du)...... B2-C2
MARCHE AUX CHEVAUX DE
  LAIT (Place du)...... C4-D4
MARCHE AUX POISSONS
  (Place du).......... C3-D3
MARCHE GAYOT (Place du). C4
MARCHE NEUF (Place du)... C3
MARECHAL FOCH (Rue du). A3-A4
MARIE LESZCZYNSKA (Place) D3
MARKOS BOTZARIS (Square) B4
MARMOULIN (Rue de la)... C3
MARSEILLAISE (Avenue de la) B4
MARTIN BUCER (Rue)...... C1
MARTIN LUTHER (Rue).... D3
MATHIAS MERIAN (Place)... C3
MATHISS (Quai).......... D1
MERCIERE (Rue)....... C3-C4
MESANGE (Rue de la)...... B3
METZ (Boulevard de)...... C1
MEUNIERS (Place des)..... C2
MEUNIERS (Rue des)...... C2
MINEURS (Rue des)..... B2-A3
MIROIR (Rue du)......... C2
MODESTE SCHICKELE (Rue). C4
MOLL (Rue).............. B1
MOLSHEIM (Rue de)....... B2
MONNAIE (Rue de la).... D2-D3
MOULIN ZORN (Cour du).. D1
MOULINS (Passerelle des)... D2
MOULINS (Pont des)....... D2
MOULINS (Ponts des)...... C2
MOULINS (Rue des)..... C2-D2
MOULINS (Square des)..... D2
NATIONAL (Pont)........ C1
NOYER (Rue du).......... B2
NUEE BLEUE (Rue de la)... B3
OBERLIN (Rue).......... A4
OBERNAI (Rue d')........ D1
OR (Rue d')............. C3
ORFEVRES (Impasse des)... C3
ORFEVRES (Place des)..... C3
ORPHELINS (Place des).... D4
ORPHELINS (Rue des)..... D4
OUTRE (Rue de l')........ C3

PAON (Rue du).......... D3
PAQUES (Rue de)........ B2
PARCHEMIN (Rue du)..... B4
PARIS (Pont de)......... B2
PARIS (Quai de)...... B2-C2
PATRE (Ruelle du)....... D2
PAUL MULLER SIMONIS (Rue) A3
PAUL REISS (Rue)........ A3
PELLETIERS (Rue des)..... C2
PENITENTS (Impasse des)... D4
PETIT BROGLIE (Place du)... B4
PETITE FRANCE
  (Quai de la)......... D1-C2
PHALSBOURG (Rue de).... A3
PIE (Impasse de la)....... A3
PIERRE BUCHER (Rue)..... B4
PIERRES (Impasse des). B4-C4
POMME DE PIN
  (Passage de la)........ C3
PONT SAINT-MARTIN (Rue du) D2
POSTE (Pont de la)....... B4
POUMON (Rue du)....... C3
PREMIERE ARMEE
  (Rue de la)......... D3-D4
PRESIDENT POINCARE
  (Boulevard du)........ A2
PRESIDENT WILSON
  (Boulevard du)...... B1-A2
PUCELLES (Rue des)..... C3
PUITS (Rue du)......... C3
QUARTIER BLANC
  (Place du).......... D1-D2
QUESTION (Rue de la).... D2
RAPE (Rue de la)........ D2
RATEAU (Impasse du).... D2
RECOLLETS (Rue des)..... B4
REMPART (Rue du)...... C1
REPUBLIQUE (Place de la). A4-B4
ROHAN (Rue de)........ C4
ROSES (Ruelle des)...... C2
SABLE (Quai du)........ C4
SAINT-ARBOGAST (Rue)... A3
SAINT-ETIENNE (Rue)..... C4
SAINT-JEAN (Quai)...... C1-B2
SAINT-LEON (Rue)....... A3
SAINT-LOUIS (Rue)...... D3
SAINT-MARC (Rue)...... D2
SAINT-MARTIN (Pont).... D2
SAINT-MEDARD (Ruelle)... C4
SAINT-MICHEL (Rue)..... C1
SAINT-NICOLAS (Cour)... D3
SAINT-NICOLAS (Pont)... D3
SAINT-NICOLAS (Rue).. D3-D4
SAINT-PIERRE LE JEUNE (Pl.) B3
SAINT-PIERRE LE JEUNE (Rue) B3

SAINT-PIERRE LE VIEUX
  (Place)............. C2
SAINT-THOMAS (Place).... D3
SAINT-THOMAS (Pont).... D3
SAINT-THOMAS (Rue)..... D3
SAINTE-AURELIE (Impasse).. C1
SAINTE-BARBE (Impasse)... C1
SAINTE-BARBE (Rue)...... C1
SAINTE-ELISABETH (Impasse) D3
SAINTE-ELISABETH (Rue) . D2-D3
SAINTE-HELENE (Rue).... C2-C3
SAINTE-MADELEINE (Imp.).. C4
SAINTE-MADELEINE (Pont).. C4
SAINTE-MADELEINE (Rue).. C4
SAINTE-MARGUERITE
  (Rue).............. C1-D1
SAINTE-MARGUERITE (Ruelle) C1
SAINTE-ODILE (Rue)..... A3-A4
SALZMANN (Rue)....... C3-D3
SARREBOURG (Rue de).... A1
SARREGUEMINES (Rue de).. A3
SAUMON (Rue du)....... C3
SAVERNE (Pont de)...... B2
SAVERNE-WODLI (Tunnel). B1-B2
SAVON (Rue du)........ C3
SCHOEPFLIN (Quai)... B3-B4
SCHWENDI (Rue)....... B4
SEBASTOPOL (Rue de)... B2
SEDILLOT (Rue)........ D4
SELLENICK (Rue)...... A3-A4
SENGENWALD (Rue)..... D4
SEPT HOMMES (Rue des)... C3
SERRURIERS (Rue des).. C3-D3
SŒURS (Rue des)....... D3
SOLEURE (Rue de)...... D4
SOPHIE TAEUBER ARP
  (Place)............ B3-C3

TRIPIERS (Place des).... C3-D3
TROIS GATEAUX (Rue des) . C4
TURCKHEIM (Quai).... C1-D1
TURENNE (Rue de)...... A4
VEAUX (Rue des)....... C4
VICTOR SCHOELCHER (Av.). B4
VIEIL HOPITAL (Rue du)... C3
VIEUX MARCHE AUX GRAINS
  (Rue du)............ C3
VIEUX MARCHE AUX POISSONS
  (Rue du)........... C3-D4
VIEUX MARCHE AUX VINS
  (Petite rue du)........ C2
VIEUX MARCHE AUX VINS
  (Place du).......... C2
VIEUX MARCHE AUX VINS
  (Rue du).......... B2-C2
VIEUX SEIGLE (Rue du)... C3
VIGNETTE (Rue de la)..... C2
22 NOVEMBRE (Rue du). C2-C3
VOSGES (Place des).... A3-A4
WALTER BENJAMIN (Passage) B3
WASSELONNE (Rue de).... D1
WISSEMBOURG (Rue de)... C1
WODLI-SEBASTOPOL
  (Tunnel)........... A1-B2
WODLI-WILSON (Tunnel).. A1
WOERTHEL (Quai du)..... D2

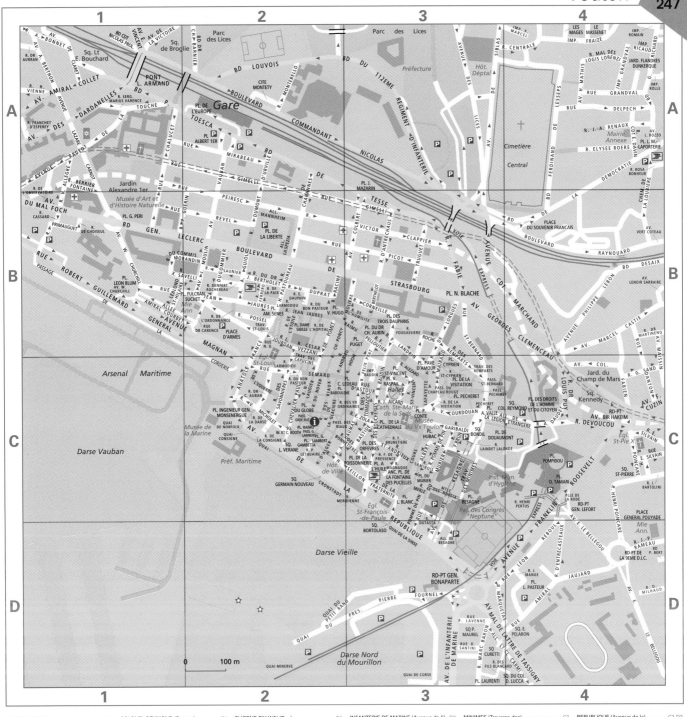

A L'HUILE (Place). C3
A. VALLE (Place) C3
ADOLPHE GUIOL (Rue) B2
ALBERT (Place). C3
ALBERT 1ER (Place) A2
ALEZARD (Rue) B3-C3
ALGER (Rue d') C2-C3
ALPHONSE DAUDET (Rue) C4
AMIRAL COLLET (Avenue) A1
AMIRAL COURBET (Allée) B1-B2
AMIRAL JAUJARD (Rue) D3-D4
AMIRAL SENES (Place) B2
ANATOLE FRANCE (Rue) B2-C2
ANCIENNE PLACE DE LA FONTAINE DES
   PUCELLES C3
ANTOINE BONNET (Rue) A1
ANTRECHAUS (Rue d'). B3
ARMES (Place d'). B2-C2
ASTOUR (Rue d'). C3
AUGUSTE BERTHON (Avenue) A1
AUGUSTIN DAUMAS (Rue) C2-C3
BABOULENE (Place). C2
BASTIDE (Rue) C3
BAUDIN (Impasse). C3
BAUDIN (Rue) B3-C3
BERRIER FONTAINE (Rue) A1-B1
BERTHELOT (Rue). B2
BESAGNE (Allée de) D3
BESAGNE (Avenue de). C3-D3
BESAGNE (Place). C3
BIR HAKEIM (Rond-point) C4
BONDIL (Square) C3
BONNETIERES (Rue des) C2-C3
BORTOLASO (Square) C3-D3
BOUCHERIES (Rue des) C2
CAMILLE LEDEAU (Place) C2-C3
CAPUCINS (Traverse des) C2
CASSARD (Rue) B1
CATHEDRALE (Place de la) C3
CENTRALE (Rue). A3-A4
CESAR VEZZANI (Rue) B2
CHABANNES (Rue de). A2-B2
CHALUCET (Rue) A1-B1
CHAPEAU ROUGE (Passage du) C3
CHARLES PONCY (Rue) B2-C2
CHEVALIER PAUL (Rue) B1
CHOISEUL (Rue de) B1
CLARET (Avenue de) A1
COLBERT (Avenue). B2
COLONEL DESIRE LUCCA
   (Square du) D3-D4
COLONEL FABIEN (Avenue). C4

COLONEL REYMOND (Square) C4
COMMANDANT EMMANUEL DAVIN
   (Rue) A4
COMMANDANT MARCHAND
   (Rue) B3-B4
COMMANDANT NICOLAS
   (Boulevard) A2-A3
COMMANDANT NICOLAS PROLONGEE
   (Boulevard) A1
COMMISSAIRE MORANDIN
   (Rue du) B1-B2
CONSIGNE (Quai) C2
CONSIGNE (Rue de la) C2
CORDERIE (Passage de la) B1-C2
CORNEILLE (Rue) B3
CORSE (Quai de). C2
CRONSTADT (Quai) C2-D3
CURETTI (Square). C3
CYPRIEN (Place) C3
DAME SIBILLE (Place) C3
DANTON (Rue) B2
DARDANELLES (Avenue des) A1
DARIUS MILHAUD (Rue) D4
DARSE (Rue de la) C2
DELPECH (Rue). A4
DEMOCRATIE (Boulevard de la). B3-A4
DENFERT ROCHEREAU (Rue) B2
DESAIX (Boulevard). B4
DOCTEUR AURRAN (Rue). A1
DOCTEUR CAMILLE AUBAN (Rue) C3
DOCTEUR CARENCE (Rue) C2
DOCTEUR CHARLES AUBIN (Place du) . . B3
DOCTEUR CHARLES BARNIER
   (Boulevard). A2
DOCTEUR JEAN BERTHOLET (Rue du) . . B2
DOCTEUR LOUIS PUY (Rue) C4
DOCTEUR MARTINENQ (Rue) C4
DOMINIQUE SANTINI (Rue). D3
DOUAUMONT (Place de) C3-C4
DROITS DE L'HOMME ET DU CITOYEN
   (Place des) C3
DUGOMMIER (Rue) B2
DUMONT D'URVILLE (Rue) A2-B2
DUTASTA (Rue) C2-C3
EDOUARD LE BELLEGOU (Rue) C4-D4
ELYSEE ROERE (Rue) A4
EMILE VINCENT (Avenue) A1
EMILE ZOLA (Rue) C2
ENTRECASTEAUX (Rue d') D4
EQUERRE (Rue de l') C2
ETIENNE DAUPHIN (Rue) B2
ETIENNE PELABON (Square). C2
ETOILE (Rue de l'). B2

EUGENE SILVAIN (Rue) C4
EUROPE (Place de l') A2
EXPRESS (Voie) B3-D4
FELIX BRUN (Rue) C3
FELIX PYAT (Rue) B3-B4
FERDINAND BRUNETIERE (Rue). C3
FERDINAND DE LESSEP
   (Boulevard). A3-B4
FERDINAND PELLOUTIER (Rue) B3
FILS BLANCARD (Rue des) C3
FLANDRES DUNKERQUE (Jardin). A4
FOUGASSIERE (Rue) B3
FRAIZE (Impasse) A3
FRANCHET D'ESPEREY (Rue) A1
FRANCIS DE PRESSENCE (Rue) C3
FRANCOIS CUZIN (Avenue). C4
FRANCOIS FABIE (Rue) B3
FRANCOIS MARCEL (Impasse) A3-A4
FRANKLIN ROOSEVELT (Avenue) D3-C4
FRATERNITE (Rue de la). C3
FULCRAN SUCHET (Place). B2
GABRIEL PERI (Place). B1
GAMBETTA (Place) C3
GARIBALDI (Rue) C3
GENERAL BONAPARTE (Rond-point) C4
GENERAL LECLERC (Boulevard). B1-B2
GENERAL LEFORT (Rond-point) C4
GENERAL MAGNAN (Avenue) B1-C2
GENERAL POUYADE (Place) C4
GEORGE SAND (Rue) C4
GEORGES CLEMENCEAU (Avenue) B4
GEORGES RICHARD (Boulevard) A4
GERMAIN NOUVEAU (Square) C4
GIMELLI (Rue) A1-B3
GLACIERE (Rue de la). C3
GLOBE (Place du) C2
GRANDE RUE (Passage). C3
GRANDVAL (Impasse). A4
GRANDVAL (Rue) A4
GUSTAVE LAMBERT (Passage) C2
GUSTAVE LAMBERT (Place) C2
HENRI MATHIS (Avenue). A4
HENRI PASTOUREAU (Rue) B3
HENRI PERTUS (Rue) C4
HENRI POINCARE (Rue) C4-D4
HENRI SEILLON (Rue) C3-C4
HENRI VIENNE (Rue) A1
HIPPOLYTE DUPRAT (Rue). B2
HOCHE (Rue). B3-C3
HOPITAL (Rue de l') B3
HOREIA (Montée de l') C3
HUBAC (Place) C3
HUMILITE (Rue de l') B3

INFANTERIE DE MARINE (Avenue de l'). D3
INGENIEUR GENERAL MONSENERGUE
   (Place). C2
JEAN AICARD (Rue) A1-A2
JEAN BARTOLINI (Rue) C4
JEAN JAURES (Rue). B1-B2
JEAN MOULIN (Avenue) B2
JEAN-PHILIPPE RAMEAU (Rue). C4
JOSE MANGE (Rue) D4
JULES MAZARIN (Place) B3
JULES MURAIRE DIT RAIMU (Rue). . . .B2-B3
JULES-ALEXANDRE RENAUX (Rue). A4
L. BLANC (Place) C3
LAFAYETTE (Cours) C3
LAINDET LALONDE (Rue) C3
LAMINOIS (Rue) C3
LARMODIEU (Rue) B2-C2
LAURENTI (Place). C3
LAZARE CARNOT (Avenue) A1-B1
LE MASSENET A4
LEBLOND SAINT-HILAIRE (Rue). B1-B2
LEGION ETRANGERE (Allée de la) C3-C4
LENOIR SARRAIRE (Avenue) B4
LEON BLUM (Place) B1
LEON REBOUL (Rue) D3-D4
LEON VERANE (Square) C4
LES MAGES. A4
LIBERTE (Place de la) B2
LICES (Avenue des) A3-B3
LIEUTENANT COLONEL CARMI
   (Allée) D3-D4
LORGUES (Rue de) B3-C3
LOUBIERE (Chemin de la) A4-B4
LOUIS ARMAND (Pont) A1
LOUIS BOZZO (Avenue) A1
LOUIS JOURDAN (Rue) A2
LOUIS PASTEUR (Rue) D4
LOUIS-MARTIAL LAPORTERIE (Place) . . . A4
LOUVOIS (Boulevard). A2
MAGNAQUE (Rue) C2
MAIRAUD (Rue). B3-C3
MAISSIN (Avenue) B4-C4
MANNHEIM (Allée). B2
MARC BARON (Rue) B4
MARCEL CASTIE (Avenue) B4
MARECHAL DE LATTRE DE TASSIGNY
   (Avenue) D3-D4
MARECHAL DES LOGIS LORENZI (Rue). . A4
MARECHAL FOCH (Avenue du) A1
MARQUETAS (Rue) D3-D4
MERIDIENNE (Rue) C3
MERLE (Rue) C3
MINERVE (Quai) D2

MINIMES (Traverse des) C3
MIRABEAU (Rue) A1-A2
MOLIERE (Rue) B2-B3
MONTEBELLO (Rue) A2
MONTETY (Cité) A2
MURIER (Place du) C3
MURIER (Rue du). C3-D3
9EME D.I.C. (Rond-point de la) D4
NICOLAS LAUGIER (Place) C3
NOEL BLACHE (Place) B3
NORFOLK (Quai de) C2
NOTRE DAME (Rue) B2
NOYER (Rue du) C3
OBSERVATOIRE (Rue de l') A1-B1
OLIVE TAMARI (Place). C4
112EME REGIMENT D'INFANTERIE
   (Boulevard du) A2-B3
ORDONNANCE (Rue de l') B2
ORFEVRES (Place des) C3
PAIX (Rue de la) B2
PAUL BERT (Boulevard) D4
PAUL CONTE (Place). C3
PAUL LANDRIN (Rue) B3-C3
PAUL MAUREL (Square) C4
PAULIN GUERIN (Rue) B1-B2
PAVE D'AMOUR (Place) C3
PECHERET (Passage) C3
PECHERET (Place) C3
PECHERET (Rue). C3
PEIRESC (Rue) A1-B2
PETIT RANG (Quai du) D2-D3
PHILIPPE LEBON (Avenue) B4-C4
PICOT (Rue) B2-B3
PIERRE LAVENNE (Rue) D3
PIERRE LETHUAIRE (Rue) C2
PIERRE SEMARD (Rue). C2
PIERRE TOESCA (Boulevard) A1-A2
POISSONNERIE (Place de la) C3
POMET (Rue du) B2-C2
POMME DE PIN (Rue) C2-C3
POMPIDOU (Place) C3
POSSEL (Rue) B2
PRESIDENT PIERRE FOURNEL
   (Quai du) D2-D3
PRIMAUGUET (Rue) B1
PROSPER FERRERO (Rue) B2
PUGET (Place) B2
RACINE (Rue) B3
RAGEOT DE LATOUCHE (Avenue) A1
RAIMU (Rue) B2
RAYNOUARD (Boulevard) B3-B4
REMPARTS (Rue des). B3-C3
REMPARTS (Traverse des) C3

REPUBLIQUE (Avenue de la) C2-D3
REVEL (Rue). B1-B2
RIAUX (Passage des) C3
RIAUX (Rue des) C2
RICAUD (Impasse) A4
RICHARD ANDRIEU (Rue) C2-B3
ROBERT GUILLEMARD (Rue). B1
ROCHE (Rue) B3-C3
RODE (Passerelle de la) C4
ROGER DEVOUCOUX (Avenue). C4
ROLLE (Impasse). A4
ROMAIN (Impasse). A4
ROSA BONHEUR (Rue). A4
SAINT-ANDRIEUX (Rue) C3
SAINT-BERNARD (Passage) C3
SAINT-BERNARD (Rue). B3-C3
SAINT-CYPRIEN (Rue). C3
SAINT-LOUIS (Traverse) B2
SAINT-VINCENT (Place) C3
SAINT-VINCENT (Rue). C3
SAUNIER (Rue) B2
SAVONNIERES (Rue des) C2
SERGENT MARIUS VARENCE (Rue) A1
SIBLAS (Avenue de) A3-B3
SINSE (Quai de la) D3
SOUVENIR FRANCAIS (Place du) B3-B4
SPEZIA (Allée la.). A4
ST-PIERRE (Square) C3
STRASBOURG (Boulevard de) B2-B3
TESSE (Boulevard de) A2-B3
TOMBADES (Rue des) C3
TROIS DAUPHINS (Place des) B3
TRUGUET (Rue) B3
VAUBAN (Avenue) A2-B2
VERT COTEAU (Avenue de la) A4
VICTOIRE (Avenue de la) A1
VICTOR CLAPPIER (Rue). B2-B3
VICTOR HUGO (Place). B2-B3
VICTOR MICHELET (Rue) C3
VIEUX ORDINAIRES (Rue des) C2-C3
VINCENT ALLEGRE (Rue) A1-B1
VINCENT COURDOUAN (Rue). C3
VINCENT RASPAIL (Place). C3
VISITATION (Place de la) C3
VISITATION (Rue de la). C3
WILLIAM ET CATHERINE BOOTH
   (Square) C2
WINSTON CHURCHILL (Avenue) C2
XAVIER SAVELLI (Rue). B1-B2

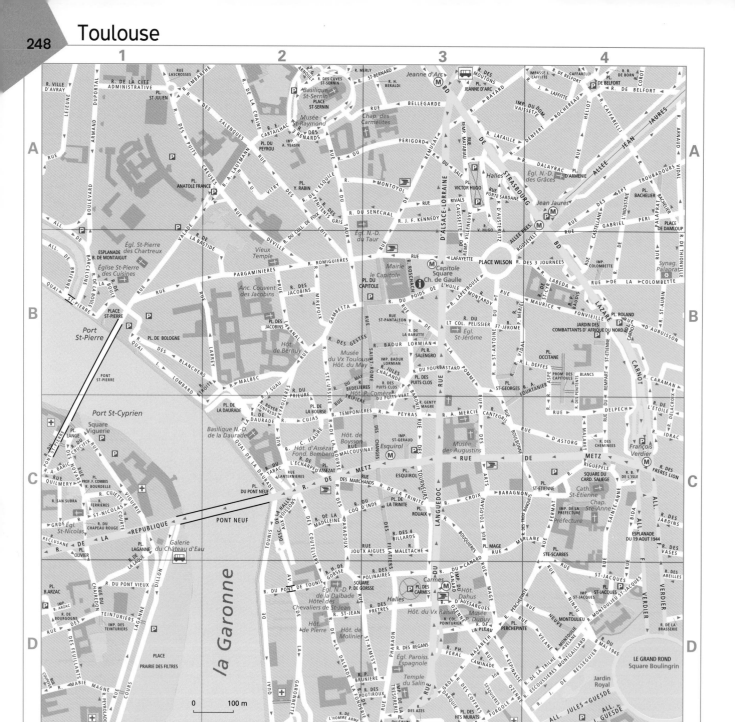

ABEILLES (Rue des) D4
ALBERT LAUTMANN (Rue) A2
ALEXANDRE FOURTANIER (Rue) . . . B3-B4
ALEXANDRE YERSIN (Impasse) A2
ALSACE-LORRAINE (Rue d') A3-C3
ANATOLE FRANCE (Place) A1-A2
ANTONIN MERCIE (Rue) C3
ARMAND DUPORTAL (Boulevard) . . A1-B1
ARMENIE (Place d') A4
ARNAUD BARIC (Rue) C2
ARNAUD VIDAL (Rue) A4
ARTS (Place d') B3-C3
ASSEZAT (Rue d') C3-C4
ASTORY (Rue d') C3-C4
AUBUISSON (Rue d') B4
AUSSARGUES (Rue d') A4
AUSTERLITZ (Rue d') A3
AZES (Rue des) D3
BACHELIER (Place) A4
BACHELIER (Rue) A4
BAOUR LORMIAN (Impasse) B3
BAOUR LORMIAN (Rue) B3
BARCELONE (Allée de) A1-B1
BARONIE (Rue) B3-C3
BARUTTE (Rue de la) B3
BASTIDE (Rue de la) B1-B2
BAYARD (Rue) A3-A4
BEDELIERES (Rue) B2-B3
BELFORT (Place de) A4
BELFORT (Rue de) A4
BELLEGARDE (Rue) A2-A3
BENOIT ARZAC (Place) D1
BENOIT ARZAC (Impasse) D1
BERTRAND DE BORN (Rue) A4
BERTRAND DE L'ISLE (Rue) C4
BERTRAND DE MONTAIGUT
(Esplanade) B1
BIDA (Rue) C4-D4
BLANCHERS (Rue des) B1-B2
BOLOGNE (Place de) B1-B2
BOULBONNE (Rue) C3-C4
BOULE (Rue de la) B1
BOUQUIERES (Rue) C3
BOURDELLE (Rue) C1
BOURGOGNE (Rue de) D1
BOURSE (Place de la) C2
BOURSE (Rue de la) C2
BOYER FONFREDE (Rue) C2
BRASSERIE (Rue de la) D4
BRIENNE (Allée de) B1
CAFFARELLI (Rue) A4
CAMINADE (Rue) D3
CANARD (Impasse du) D1
CANARD (Rue) C3-D3
CANTEGRIL (Rue) C3

CAPITOLE (Place du) B2-B3
CAPITOULS (Promenade des) B4-C4
CARAMAN (Rue) B4
CARDINAL SALIEGE (Square du) C4
CARMES (Place des) C3
CASTELLANE (Rue) A4-B4
CAUSSETTE (Rue) A3-B3
CHAINE (Rue de la) A2
CHAIREDON (Rue du) D1
CHANGES (Rue des) C2
CHAPEAU ROUGE (Rue du) C1
CHEMINEES (Rue des) C3
CITE ADMINISTRATIVE (Rue de la) . . . A1
CLEMENCE ISAURE (Rue) C2
COFFRES (Rue des) D3
COLLEGE DE FOIX (Rue du) A2-B2
COLOMBETTE (Impasse) B4
COLOMBETTE (Rue de la) B4
COLONEL POINTURIER (Rue) D3
COMBATTANTS D'AFRIQUE DU NORD
(Jardin des) B4
COQ D'INDE (Rue du) C2-C3
COROT (Rue) A4
COUPEFER (Rue) D1
COURTE (Rue) C1
COUTELIERS (Rue des) C2-C3
CROIX BARAGNON (Rue) C3-C4
CRUCIFIX (Rue du) C1
CUJAS (Rue) C2
CUJETTE (Rue) C2
CUVES SAINT-SERNIN (Rue des) A2
DALAYRAC (Rue) A3-A4
DALBADE (Rue de la) D2
DAMLOUP (Place de) A4-B4
DARQUIE (Rue) D3
DAURADE (Place de la) B2-C2
DAURADE (Quai de la) C2
DAURADE (Rue de la) C2
DELACROIX (Rue) B4-C4
DELPECH (Rue) B4
DENFERT ROCHEREAU (Rue) A3-A4
DEVILLE (Rue) A2-B2
DILLON (Cours) C1-D1
ECHARPE (Rue de l') C2
EMBARTHE (Rue) A1-A2
EMILE CARTAILHAC (Rue) A2
ESCOUSSIERES MONTGAILLARD
(Rue) D3-D4
ESPINASSE (Rue) D3-D4
ESQUILE (Rue de l') A3
ESQUIROL (Place) C3
ETOILE (Rue de l') B4
ETROITE (Rue) C1-B2
FERMAT (Rue) C4

FERRIERES (Rue) C1
FEUILLANTS (Rue des) D1
FILATERS (Rue des) A2-B2
FONDERIE (Rue de la) D2-D3
FOURBASTARD (Rue du) B3
FRANCOIS VERDIER (Allée) C4-D4
FRERES LION (Rue des) C4
FURGOLE (Rue) C1
GABRIEL PERI (Rue) A4-B4
GAMBETTA (Rue) B2
GARONNETTE (Avenue de la) C2-C2
GATIEN ARNOULT (Rue) A2
GENTY MAGRE (Rue) C3
GESTES (Rue des) B2
GRAND ROND (du) D4
HALLE AUX POISSONS
(Descente de la) C2-C2
HAUTS MURATS (Place des) D3
HELIOT (Rue) A4
HENRI BERALDI (Rue) A3
HENRI DE GORSSE (Rue) D2
HOMME ARME (Rue de l') D2
8 MAI 1945 (Rue du) C4
IDRAC (Rue) C4
IMPASSE DU DOMAINE
VAISSETE A3-A4
INDUSTRIE (Rue de l') A4-B4
JACOBINS (Place des) B2
JACOBINS (Rue des) B2-B2
JACQUES LAFFITTE (Impasse) A3-A4
JACQUES LAFFITTE (Rue) A3-A4
JARDINS (Rue des) C4
JEAN JAURES (Allée) A4
JEAN SUAU (Rue) B2-C2
JEANNE D'ARC (Place) A3
JOHN FITZGERALD KENNEDY (Rue) . A3
JOUTX AIGUES (Rue) C2-C3
JULES CHALANDE (Rue) B3-B3
JULES DE RESSEGUIER (Rue) A3
JULES GUESDE (Allée) D4
LABEDA (Rue) B4
LAFAILLE (Rue) A3
LAFAYETTE (Rue) B3
LAGANNE (Place) C1-C1
LAKANAL (Rue) B2
LANGE (Rue) C1
LANGUEDOC (Rue du) C3-C3
LANTERNIERES (Rue) C2
LAPEYROUSE (Rue) B4
LAQUE (Rue de la) C1-D1
LARREY (Rue) B1-B2
LASCROSSES (Rue) A1
LAZARE CARNOT (Boulevard) A4-C4
LEJEUNE (Rue) A1

LIEUTENANT COLONEL PELISSIER
(Rue du) B3
LOIS (Rue des) A2-B2
LOUIS DEFFES (Rue) B3-B4
LUCIEN LOMBARD (Quai) C1-B2
MADELEINE (Rue de la) C1
MAGE (Place) C3
MAGE (Rue) C3-D3
MALARET (Rue) C4
MALBEC (Rue) B2
MALCOUSINAT (Rue) C2
MALETACHE (Rue) C3
MARCHANDS (Rue des) C2-C3
MARIE MAGNE (Rue) D1
MAURICE FONVIEILLE (Rue) B3-B4
MAY (Rue du) B2-B3
MERLANE (Rue) C4-C4
MERLY (Rue) A2
METZ (Rue de) C2-C4
MIREPOIX (Rue) B2
MONTARDY (Rue) B3
MONTOULIEU (Place) D4
MONTOULIEU SAINT-JACQUES (Rue) . D4
MONTOULIEU VELANE (Rue) D4
MOUTONS (Rue des) A2-A3
NAZARETH (Grande rue) C4
NEUF (Pont) C1-C2
NEUVE (Rue) D3-D4
NINAU (Rue) C4
NOVARS (Rue des) A3
OCCITANE (Place) B4
OLIVIER (Place) C1-D1
OZENNE (Rue) C4
PALAPRAT (Rue) A4-A4
PARADOUX (Rue des) C2-D2
PARGAMINERES (Rue) B1-B2
PAUL MERIEL (Rue) B4
PAUL VIDAL (Rue) B4
PENITENTS BLANCS (Rue des) B4-C4
PENITENTS GRIS (Rue des) C4
PERCHEPINTE (Place) D3
PERCHEPINTE (Rue) D3-D4
PERIGORD (Rue du) A2-A3
PEYRAS (Rue) C3
PEYROLADE (Rue) D1
PEYROLIERES (Rue) B2-C2
PEYROU (Place du) A2
PHARAON (Rue) D3
PHILIPPE FERAL (Rue) C4
PIERRE BAUDIS (Rue) B4
PIERRE BRUNIERE (Rue) D2
PIERRE DE GORSSE (Square) D2
PLEAU (Rue de la) D3
POIDS DE L'HUILE (Rue du) B3

POLINAIRES (Rue des) D2-D3
POMME (Rue de la) B3-C3
PONT DE TOUNIS (Rue du) D2
PONT NEUF (Place du) C2
PONT SAINT-PIERRE (Rue du) C1
PONT VIEUX (Rue du) D2
PORTE SARDANE (Rue) A3-A4
POUTIROUX (Rue des) D2-D3
PRAIRIE DES FILTRES (Place) D1
PREFECTURE (Impasse de la) C4
PRESIDENT ROOSEVELT (Allée) . . . B3-A4
PRETRES (Rue des) D3
PRIEURE (Rue du) B2-C2
PROFESSEUR FRANCOIS COMBES
(Place) C1
PUITS CLOS (Place des) C3
PUITS CLOS (Rue des) B3-C3
PUITS CREUSES (Rue des) A1-A2
PUITS VERT (Rue des) B3-C3
QUILMERY (Rue) C1
RECLUSANE (Rue) C1
REGANS (Rue des) D3
REMPART MATABIAU (Rue) A3
REMPART SAINT-ETIENNE (Rue) C4
REMPART VILLENEUVE (Rue du) . . . A3-B3
REMUSAT (Rue de) A3-B3
RENEE ASPE (Rue) B4-C4
REPUBLIQUE (Rue de la) C1
RIGUEPELS (Rue) C4
RIVALS (Rue) A3
ROGER SALENGRO (Place) B3
ROLAND (Place) B4
ROMIGUIERES (Rue) B2
ROSCHACH (Rue) B3
ROUAIX (Place) C3
SAINT-ANTOINE DUT (Rue) B3
SAINT-AUBIN (Rue) B4
SAINT-BERNARD (Rue) A2-A3
SAINT-CYR (Rue) A3
SAINT-ANNE (Rue) C4
SAINT-SERNIN (Place) A3
SAINTE-SCARBES (Place) C4-D4
SAINTE-ETIENNE (Rue) C4
SAINTE-URSULE (Rue) B2-C2
SAINT-GEORGES (Place) B3-C3
SAINT-GERAUD (Impasse) C3
SAINT-JACQUES (Impasse) D4
SAINT-JACQUES (Rue) D4
SAINT-JEAN (Rue) D2-D3
SAINT-JEROME (Rue) B4
SAINT-JULIEN (Rue) A1
SAINT-NICOLAS (Grande rue) C1
SAINT-PANTALEON (Rue) B3
SAINT-PIERRE (Place) B1

SAINT-PIERRE (Pont) B1-C1
SAINT-PIERRE (Quai) B1
SAINT-REMESY (Rue) D2-D3
SAINT-ROME (Rue) B3-C3
SAINT-SERNIN (Place) A3
SALE (Rue du) A3
SALENQUES (Rue des) A1-A2
SALIN (Place du) D3
SAN SUBRA (Rue) C1
SENECHAL (Rue du) A2-A3
SEPTTROUBADOURS (Rue des) A4-B4
SESQUIERES (Rue des) D3
STRASBOURG (Boulevard de) A3-A4
TABAC (Rue du) C1
TAUR (Rue du) A2-B2
TEINTURIERS (Impasse des) D1
TEMPONIERES (Rue) C2
TEINTURIERS (Rue des) D1
THIONVILLE (Rue) B4
TOLOSANE (Rue) C3
TOUNIS (Quai de) C2-D2
TOURNEURS (Rue des) C3
TRESORERIE (Impasse de la) D3
TRILHE (Rue de la) D4
TRINITE (Place de la) C3
TRINITE (Rue de la) C3
TRIPIERE (Rue) B2-C3
TROIS BANQUETS (Rue des) C3
3 JOURNEES (Rue des) B3-B4
3 RENARDS (Rue des) A2
URBAIN VITRY (Rue) A2
VALADE (Rue) B1-A2
VASES (Rue des) D4
VELANE (Rue) D3-D4
VICTOR HUGO (Place) A3
VICTOR HUGO (Rue) A3
VIGUERIE (Rue) C1
VILLE D'AVRAY (Rue) A1
WILSON (Place) B3
YITZHAK RABIN (Place) A2

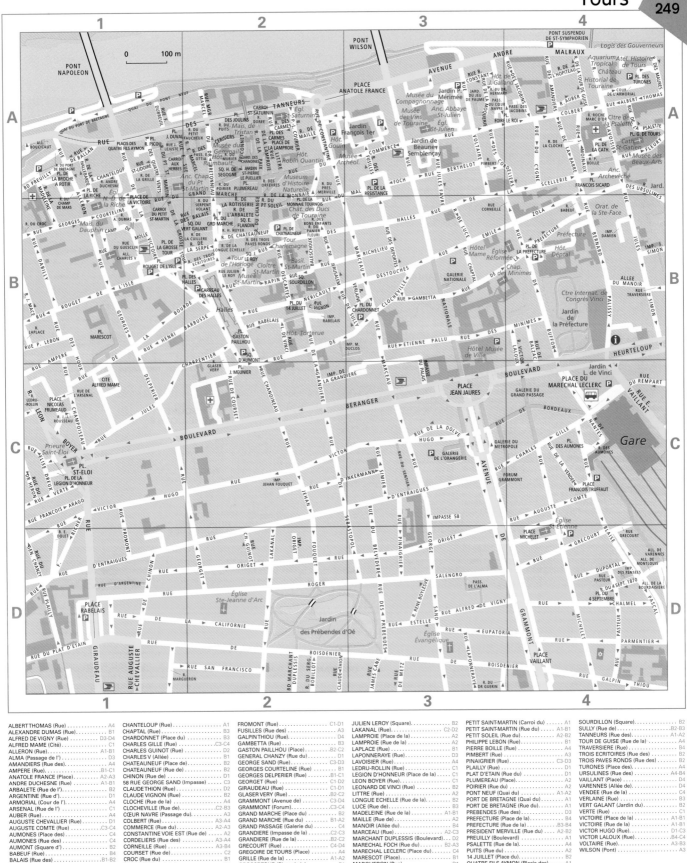

ALBERT THOMAS (Rue) A4
ALEXANDRE DUMAS (Rue) B1
ALFRED DE VIGNY (Rue) D3-D4
ALFRED MAME (Cité) C1
ALLERON (Rue) A1-B1
ALMA (Passage de l') D3
AMANDIERS (Rue des) A4
AMPERE (Rue) B1-C1
ANATOLE FRANCE (Place) A2-A3
ANDRE DUCHESNE (Rue) A1-B1
ARBALETE (Rue de l') B2
ARGENTINE (Rue d') D1
ARMORIAL (Cour de l') A4
ARSENAL (Rue de l') C1
AUBER (Rue) C1
AUGUSTE CHEVALLIER (Rue) D1
AUGUSTE COMTE (Rue) C3-C4
AUMONES (Rue des) A3-A4
AUMONES (Place des) C4
AUMONT (Square d') B2
BABEUF (Rue) A4
BALAIS (Rue des) B1-B2
BALESCHOUX (Rue) B2
BALLAN (Rue) A1
BALZAC (Rue) B4-C4
BARRE (Rue de la) A4
BEAUNE SEMBLANCAY (Jardin de) . . . A3
BELVEDERE (Rue) C3-D3
BENJAMIN CONSTANT (Rue) A3
BERANGER (Boulevard) C1-C3
BERNARD PALISSY (Rue) B4
BERTHELOT (Rue) A3
BLAISE PASCAL (Rue) C4-D4
BOISDENIER (Rue de) D1-D4
BONS ENFANTS (Rue des) B2
BORDEAUX (Rue de) C3-C4
BOUCICAUT (Allée) A1
BOURDAISIERE (Allée de la) D4
BOURDE (Rue de la) C1-B2
BRICONNET (Rue) A2
BROCHE A ROTIR (Passage de la) A1
BUFFON (Rue) B4
CALIFORNIE (Rue) D1-D2
CAMP DE MOLLE (Rue) B1
CAPUCINS (Rue) A4
CARMES (Place des) A2
CARMES (Rue des) A1-A2
CATHEDRALE (Place de la) A4
CERISIERS (Rue des) A2
CHALMEL (Rue) D4
CHAMP DE MARS (Rue du) A1
CHAMPOISEAU (Rue) B1
CHANGE (Rue du) A2-B2
CHANGINEAU (Rue) C2
CHANOINES (Jardin des) A2

CHANTELOUP (Rue) A1
CHAPTAL (Rue) A3
CHARDONNET (Place du) B3
CHARLES GILLE (Rue) C3-C4
CHARLES GUINOT (Rue) D2
CHARLES V (Allée) B1
CHATEAUNEUF (Place de) B2
CHATEAUNEUF (Rue de) B2
CHINON (Rue de) D1
CLAUDE THION (Rue) D2
CLAUDE VIGNON (Rue) B2
CLOCHE (Rue de la) A4
CLOCHEVILLE (Rue de) C2-B3
COLBERT (Rue) A3-A4
COMMERCE (Rue du) A2-A3
CONSTANTINE VOIE EST (Rue de) . . C2-C3
CORDELIERS (Rue des) A3-A4
CORNEILLE (Rue) A3-B4
COURSET (Rue de) C2
CROC (Rue du) B1
CUILLERE (Rue de la) B2
CYGNE (Rue du) A4
DABILLY (Rue) B1
DAMIEN (Impasse) B4
DEPORTES (Rue des) B3
DESCARTES (Rue) B3
DOCTEUR (Rue du) A3
DOCTEUR BRETONNEAU (Rue du) . . . C1
DOCTEUR GUERIN (Rue du) D3
DOCTEUR HERON (Rue du) C3
DOLVE (Rue de la) C3
DOREE (Rue) A2
DUPORTAL (Rue) D4
EDOUARD VAILLANT (Rue) D4
ELISE DREUX (Rue) C1
EMILE OTTIA (Passage) A2
EMILE ZOLA (Rue) B3-B4
ENTRAIGUES (Rue d') D1-C3
ESTELLE (Rue) D4
ETIENNE DOLET (Rue) C1-D1
ETIENNE MARCEL (Rue) A1-A2
ETIENNE PALLU (Rue) B3
EUGENE FLANDIN (Square) A2
EUGENE SUE (Rue) A1-A2
EUPATORIA (Rue) D3-D4
FERDINAND DUBREUIL (Rue) A2
FLEURY (Rue) A4
FOIRE LE ROI (Place) A4
FRANCOIS 1ER (Jardin) A2-A3
FRANCOIS ARAGO (Rue) C1
FRANCOIS RICHER (Rue) C1-D1
FRANCOIS SICARD (Place) A4-B4
FRANCOIS TRUFFAUT (Place) C4

FROMONT (Rue) C1-D1
FUSILLES (Rue des) A3
GALPIN THIOU (Rue) D4
GAMBETTA (Rue) B3
GASTON PAILLHOU (Place) B2-C2
GENERAL CHANZY (Rue du) C3
GEORGE SAND (Rue) C3-D3
GEORGES COURTELINE (Rue) B1
GEORGES DELPERIER (Rue) B1-C1
GEORGET (Rue) C1-D2
GIRAUDEAU (Rue) C1-D1
GLASER VERY (Rue) C2-C2
GRAMMONT (Avenue de) C3-D4
GRAMMONT (Forum) C3-C4
GRAND MARCHE (Place du) B2
GRAND MARCHE (Rue du) B1-B2
GRAND PASSAGE (Galerie du) C4
GRANDIERE (Impasse de la) C2-C3
GRANDIERE (Rue de la) B2-C2
GRECOURT (Rue) C4-D4
GREGOIRE DE TOURS (Place) A4
GRILLE (Rue de la) A1-A2
GROSSE TOUR (Place de la) B1
GROSSE TOUR (Rue de la) B1-B2
GUESCLIN (Rue du) B1
HALLEBARDE (Rue de la) B2
HALLES (Carreau des) B2
HALLES (Place des) B2
HALLES (Rue des) B2-B3
HENRI BARBUSSE (Rue du) A3
HENRI DE SEGOGNE (Square) A2
HENRI ROYER (Rue) B2
HERBES (Carroi aux) A1
HEURTELOUP (Boulevard) C3-B4
HOPITEAU (Rue de l') A4
HOUX (Rue des) B1-C1
INKERMANN (Rue d') C3
JACOBINS (Passage des) A4
JAMES CANE (Rue) D3
JEAN JAURES (Place) B3
JEAN LEJUSTE (Rue) A1
JEAN MACE (Rue) C1
JEAN MEUNIER (Place) C2
JEAN-JACQUES ROUSSEAU (Rue) . . . B1
JEHAN FOUQUET (Rue) C2-D2
JERUSALEM (Rue de) B3
JEU DE PAUME (Jardin) A3
JOULINS (Place des) A2
JULES CHARPENTIER (Rue) C1-B2
JULES FAVRE (Rue) A3-B3
JULES MOINAUX (Rue) B4
JULES SIMON (Rue) B4
JULIEN LE ROY (Rue) B2

JULIEN LEROY (Square) B2
LAKANAL (Rue) C2-D2
LAMPROIE (Place de la) A2
LAMPROIE (Rue de la) A2
LAPLACE (Rue) B1
LAPONNERAYE (Rue) B1
LAVOISIER (Rue) A4
LEDRU-ROLLIN (Rue) C1
LEGION D'HONNEUR (Place de la) . . . C1
LEON BOYER (Rue) C1
LEONARD DE VINCI (Rue) B2
LITTRE (Rue) C1
LONGUE ECHELLE (Rue de la) B2
LUCE (Rue de) B3
MADELEINE (Rue de la) A1-B1
MAILLE (Rue de) A4
MANOIR (Allée du) B4
MARCEAU (Rue) A2-C3
MARCHANT DUPLESSIS (Boulevard) . . D2
MARECHAL FOCH (Rue) B2-B3
MARECHAL LECLERC (Place du) C4
MARESCOT (Place) B1
MARGUERON (Rue) D1
MAURES (Rue des) A2
METROPOLE (Galerie du) C3-C4
METZ (Rue de) D3
MICHEL DUCLOS (Impasse) B2-B3
MICHELET (Rue) D3-D4
MICHELET (Place) C4-D4
MINIMES (Rue des) B3-B4
MONNAIE (Rue de la) B2
MONNAIE TOURNOIS (Place de la) . . . B2
MONSEIGNEUR MARCEL (Rue) A2
MONTLOUIS (Allée de) A2
MOQUERIE (Rue de la) A2
MURIER (Rue du) A1
NANTES (Rue de) B2-B3
NAPOLEON (Pont) A1
NATIONALE (Galerie) B3
NATIONALE (Rue) A3-C3
NERICAULT DESTOUCHES (Rue) . . . B2-B3
NICOLAS FRUMEAUD (Place) C1
ORANGERIE (Galerie de l') C3
ORFEVRES (Rue des) A2
ORIGET (Rue) C1-C3
ORLEANS (Quai d') A3-A4
PAIX (Rue de la) A2
PALAIS (Impasse du) B3
PANIER FLEURI (Rue du) B2
PARMENTIER (Rue) D4
PASTEUR (Rue) D4
PAUL-LOUIS COURIER (Rue) A2
PENSEES (Impasse des) D4
PETIT FAUCHEUX (Rue du) A2

PETIT SAINT-MARTIN (Carroi du) A1
PETIT SAINT-MARTIN (Rue du) A1-B1
PETIT SOLEIL (Rue du) A2-B2
PHILIPPE LEBON (Rue) B1
PIERRE BOILLE (Rue) B4
PIMBERT (Rue) A4
PINAIGRIER (Rue) C3-D3
PLAILLY (Rue) D1
PLAT D'ETAIN (Rue du) D1
PLUMEREAU (Place) A2
PORIER (Rue du) A2
PONT NEUF (Quai du) A1-A2
PORT DE BRETAGNE (Quai du) A1
PORT DE BRETAGNE (Rue du) A1
PREBENDES (Rue des) D3
PREFECTURE (Place de la) B3
PREFECTURE (Rue de la) B3-B4
PRESIDENT MERVILLE (Rue du) . . . A2-B2
PREUILLY (Boulevard) A1
PSALETTE (Rue de la) A4
PUITS (Rue du) A2
14 JUILLET (Place du) B2
QUATRE FILS AYMON (Placis des) . . . A1
4 SEPTEMBRE (Place du) D4
4 SEPTEMBRE (Rue du) D4
QUATRE VENTS (Rue des) A1-B1
RABELAIS (Impasse) B2
RABELAIS (Place) D1
RABELAIS (Rue) B2
RAPIN (Rue) B2
REMPART (Rue du) C4
RENE BOYLESVE (Rue) C4
RESISTANCE (Place de la) A3-B3
RICHE (Rue de la) A1-B1
RICHELIEU (Rue) B2-B3
ROBERT PICOU (Place) A1
ROCHE MARC D'OR (Rue) A4
ROGER SALENGRO (Rue) D1-D4
ROTISSERIE (Rue de la) B2
ROUGET DE L'ISLE (Place) B1
ROUGET DE L'ISLE (Rue) B1
SAINT-ELOI (Place) C1
SAINT-ISIDORE (Rue) A1
SAINT-PIERRE PUELLIER (Jardin) A2
SAINT-SATURNIN (Carroi) A2
SAINT-SYMPHORIEN
 (Pont suspendu de) A4
SAN FRANCISCO (Rue) D1-D2
SCELLERIE (Rue de la) B3-A4
SEBASTOPOL (Rue de) C2-C3
SENTIER (Rue du) C3
SERGENT BOBILLOT (Rue du) C3
SERPE (Rue de la) B1-B2
SERPENT VOLANT (Rue du) A2-B2
SIMIER (Rue) B2

SOURDILLON (Square) B2
SULLY (Rue de) B2-B3
TANNEURS (Rue des) A1-A2
TOUR DE GUISE (Rue de la) A4
TRAVERSIERE (Rue) B4
TROIS ECRITOIRES (Rue des) B2
TROIS PAVES RONDS (Rue des) B2
TURONES (Rue des) A4
URSULINES (Rue des) A4-B4
VAILLANT (Place) D4
VARENNES (Allée de) D4
VENDEE (Rue de la) C4
VERLAINE (Rue) B3
VERT GALANT (Jardin du) B2
VERTE (Rue) C1
VICTOIRE (Place de la) A1-B1
VICTOIRE (Rue de la) A1-B1
VICTOR HUGO (Rue) D1-C3
VICTOR LALOUX (Rue) B4-C4
VOLTAIRE (Rue) A3-B3
WILSON (Pont) A3

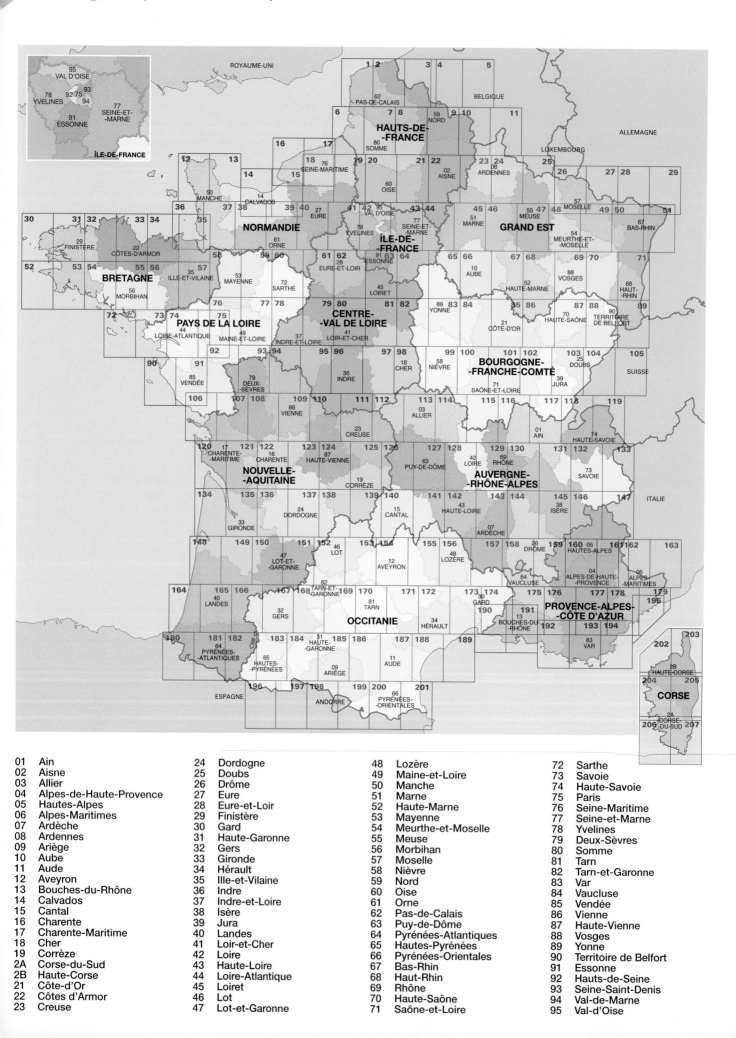

01	Ain	24	Dordogne	48	Lozère	72	Sarthe
02	Aisne	25	Doubs	49	Maine-et-Loire	73	Savoie
03	Allier	26	Drôme	50	Manche	74	Haute-Savoie
04	Alpes-de-Haute-Provence	27	Eure	51	Marne	75	Paris
05	Hautes-Alpes	28	Eure-et-Loir	52	Haute-Marne	76	Seine-Maritime
06	Alpes-Maritimes	29	Finistère	53	Mayenne	77	Seine-et-Marne
07	Ardèche	30	Gard	54	Meurthe-et-Moselle	78	Yvelines
08	Ardennes	31	Haute-Garonne	55	Meuse	79	Deux-Sèvres
09	Ariège	32	Gers	56	Morbihan	80	Somme
10	Aube	33	Gironde	57	Moselle	81	Tarn
11	Aude	34	Hérault	58	Nièvre	82	Tarn-et-Garonne
12	Aveyron	35	Ille-et-Vilaine	59	Nord	83	Var
13	Bouches-du-Rhône	36	Indre	60	Oise	84	Vaucluse
14	Calvados	37	Indre-et-Loire	61	Orne	85	Vendée
15	Cantal	38	Isère	62	Pas-de-Calais	86	Vienne
16	Charente	39	Jura	63	Puy-de-Dôme	87	Haute-Vienne
17	Charente-Maritime	40	Landes	64	Pyrénées-Atlantiques	88	Vosges
18	Cher	41	Loir-et-Cher	65	Hautes-Pyrénées	89	Yonne
19	Corrèze	42	Loire	66	Pyrénées-Orientales	90	Territoire de Belfort
2A	Corse-du-Sud	43	Haute-Loire	67	Bas-Rhin	91	Essonne
2B	Haute-Corse	44	Loire-Atlantique	68	Haut-Rhin	92	Hauts-de-Seine
21	Côte-d'Or	45	Loiret	69	Rhône	93	Seine-Saint-Denis
22	Côtes d'Armor	46	Lot	70	Haute-Saône	94	Val-de-Marne
23	Creuse	47	Lot-et-Garonne	71	Saône-et-Loire	95	Val-d'Oise

A

Aast (64).......182 D2
Abainville (55).......68 B1
Abancourt (59).......8 D3
Abancourt (60).......19 G2
Abaucourt (54).......48 D3
Abaucourt-Hautecourt (55).......25 F6
Abbans-Dessous (25).......103 F2
Abbans-Dessus (25).......103 F2
Abbaretz (44).......74 D2
Abbécourt (02).......21 H3
Abbecourt (60).......20 B5
Abbenans (25).......88 A4
Abbeville (80).......6 D4
Abbéville-la-Rivière (91).......63 F3
Abbéville-lès-Conflans (54).......25 H6
Abbeville-Saint-Lucien (60).......20 B3
Abbévillers (25).......88 D5
Abeilhan (34).......188 C1
Abelcourt (70).......87 H2
Abère (64).......182 D1
l'Abergement-Clémenciat (01).......116 C5
l'Abergement-de-Cuisery (71).......116 C1
l'Abergement-de-Varey (01).......117 F6
Abergement-la-Ronce (39).......102 C2
Abergement-le-Grand (39).......102 D4
Abergement-le-Petit (39).......103 E4
Abergement-lès-Thésy (39).......103 F4
l'Abergement-Sainte-Colombe (71).......101 H5
Abidos (64).......182 A1
Abilly (37).......95 E4
Abitain (64).......165 E6
Abjat-sur-Bandiat (24).......123 F4
Ablain-Saint-Nazaire (62).......8 B1
Ablaincourt-Pressoir (80).......8 B6
Ablainzevelle (62).......8 B3
Ablancourt (51).......46 A4
Ableiges (95).......42 B2
les Ableuvenettes (88).......69 G4
Ablis (78).......62 D1
Ablon (14).......15 F3
Ablon-sur-Seine (94).......42 D5
Aboën (42).......128 D6
Aboncourt (54).......69 E2
Aboncourt (57).......26 C4
Aboncourt-Gesincourt (70).......87 F2
Aboncourt-sur-Seille (57).......48 D4
Abondance (74).......119 F4
Abondant (28).......41 F4
Abos (64).......182 A1
Abreschviller (57).......50 A5
Abrest (03).......114 A6
Les Abrets en Dauphiné (38).......131 F5
Abriès (05).......147 G5
Abscon (59).......9 E2
l'Absie (79).......92 D6
Abzac (16).......109 G5
Abzac (33).......135 H4
Accolans (25).......88 A4
Accons (07).......143 F5
Accous (64).......182 A5
Achain (57).......49 F3
Les Achards (85).......91 E5
Achen (57).......50 A1
Achenheim (67).......50 D5
Achères (18).......97 H1
Achères (78).......42 B3
Achères-la-Forêt (77).......63 H3
Achery (02).......22 A2
Acheux-en-Amiénois (80).......7 H4
Acheux-en-Vimeu (80).......6 C4
Acheville (62).......8 B1
Achey (70).......86 C4
Achicourt (62).......8 B2
Achiet-le-Grand (62).......8 B4
Achiet-le-Petit (62).......8 B4
Achun (58).......99 H2
Achy (60).......20 A3
Acigné (35).......57 G2
Aclou (27).......40 B1
Acon (27).......40 D4
Acq (62).......8 A2
Acqueville (14).......38 C2
Acquigny (27).......41 E1
Acquin-Westbécourt (62).......2 A4
Acy (02).......22 B5
Acy-en-Multien (60).......43 G2
Acy-Romance (08).......23 G4
Adaincourt (57).......49 E2
Adainville (78).......41 G5
Adam-lès-Passavant (25).......87 H6
Adam-lès-Vercel (25).......104 A1
Adamswiller (67).......50 B3
Adast (65).......182 D5
Adé (65).......183 E3
Adelange (57).......49 F2
Adelans-et-le-Val-de-Bithaine (70).......87 H2
Aderville-Pouchergues (65).......197 E1
Adilly (79).......93 F6
Adinfer (62).......8 A3
Adissan (34).......172 C6
les Adjots (16).......108 D6
Adon (45).......82 B2
les Adrets (38).......146 A1
les Adrets-de-l'Estérel (83).......178 B5
Adriers (86).......109 H4
Afa (2A).......204 C5
Affieux (19).......125 E5
Affléville (54).......25 H5

Affoux (69).......129 F2
Affracourt (54).......69 G1
Affringues (62).......1 H4
Agassac (31).......184 C2
Agde (34).......188 D2
Agel (34).......187 H2
Agen (47).......151 F5
Agen-d'Aveyron (12).......154 D4
Agencourt (21).......101 H2
Agenville (80).......7 F3
Agenvillers (80).......7 E3
les Ageux (60).......20 D5
Ageville (52).......68 B5
Agey (21).......101 F1
Aghione (2B).......205 G4
Agincourt (54).......48 D1
Agmé (47).......150 D3
Agnac (47).......150 D1
Agnat (43).......141 H1
Agneaux (50).......37 F1
Agnetz (60).......20 C5
Agnez-lès-Duisans (62).......8 A2
Agnières (62).......8 A2
Agnin (38).......144 A1
Agnos (64).......181 H3
Agny (62).......8 B3
Agon-Coutainville (50).......36 D1
Agonac (24).......137 F1
Agonès (34).......173 E3
Agonges (03).......113 G1
Agos-Vidalos (65).......182 D4
Agris (16).......122 D3
Agudelle (17).......121 F6
Aguessac (12).......155 F6
Aguilcourt (02).......23 E4
Aguts (81).......170 A6
Agy (14).......13 H5
Ahaxe-Alciette-Bascassan (64).......181 E3
Ahetze (64).......164 A6
Ahéville (88).......69 G3
Ahuillé (53).......58 C5
Ahun (23).......111 H6
Ahuy (21).......85 H4
Aibes (59).......10 B3
Aibre (25).......88 B4
Aïcirits-Camou-Suhast (64).......181 F1
Aiffres (79).......107 H4
Aigaliers (30).......174 A1
l'Aigle (61).......40 A4
Aiglemont (08).......24 B1
Aiglepierre (39).......103 E3
Aigleville (27).......41 F2
Aiglun (04).......177 E1
Aiglun (06).......178 C2
Aignan (32).......167 E4
Aignay-le-Duc (21).......85 F3
Aigne (34).......187 H2
Aigné (72).......60 A5
Aignes (31).......185 G2
Aigneville (80).......6 C4
Aigny (51).......45 G2
Aigonnay (79).......108 A3
Aigre (16).......122 B2
Aigrefeuille (31).......169 G6
Aigrefeuille-d'Aunis (17).......107 E5
Aigrefeuille-sur-Maine (44).......74 D6
Aigremont (30).......173 H2
Aigremont (52).......68 D5
Aigremont (78).......42 B3
Aigremont (89).......84 A3
Aiguebelette-le-Lac (73).......131 G5
Aiguebelle (73).......132 C5
Aigueblanche (73).......132 D5
Aiguefonde (81).......170 D6
Aigueperse (63).......127 F1
Aigueperse (69).......115 G4
Aigues-Juntes (09).......185 G4
Aigues-Mortes (30).......174 A6
Aigues-Vives (09).......186 B5
Aigues-Vives (11).......187 F3
Aigues-Vives (30).......173 H4
Aigues-Vives (34).......187 H2
Aiguèze (30).......157 H5
Aiguilhe (43).......142 C4
Aiguilles (05).......147 G6
l'Aiguillon (09).......186 B6
Aiguillon (47).......150 D4
l'Aiguillon-sur-Mer (85).......106 B3
l'Aiguillon-sur-Vie (85).......90 D4
Aiguines (83).......177 F3
Aigurande (36).......111 G3
Ailhon (07).......157 G2
Aillant-sur-Milleron (45).......82 C2
Aillas (33).......150 A3
Ailleux (42).......128 C3
Aillevans (70).......87 H3
Ailleville (10).......67 E3
Aillevillers-et-Lyaumont (70).......69 H6
Aillianville (52).......68 B2
Aillières-Beauvoir (72).......60 B2
Aillon-le-Jeune (73).......132 A4
Aillon-le-Vieux (73).......132 A4
Ailloncourt (70).......87 H2
Ailly (27).......41 E1
Ailly-le-Haut-Clocher (80).......7 E4
Ailly-sur-Noye (80).......20 C1
Ailly-sur-Somme (80).......7 F6
Aimargues (30).......173 H5
Aime-la-Plagne (73).......133 E4
Ainay-le-Château (03).......98 B6
Ainay-le-Vieil (18).......97 H6
Aincille (64).......181 E3
Aincourt (95).......41 H2
Aincreville (55).......24 D5
Aingeray (54).......48 B4

Aingeville (88).......68 D4
Aingoulaincourt (52).......68 A1
Ainharp (64).......181 F2
Ainhice-Mongelos (64).......181 E3
Ainhoa (64).......180 C1
Ainvelle (70).......87 G1
Ainvelle (88).......69 E5
Airaines (80).......7 E5
Aire (08).......23 F4
Aire-sur-la-Lys (62).......2 B5
Aire-sur-l'Adour (40).......166 B4
Airel (50).......13 F6
les Aires (34).......172 A6
Airion (60).......20 C4
Airon-Notre-Dame (62).......6 C1
Airon-Saint-Vaast (62).......6 C1
Airoux (11).......186 B2
Airvault (79).......93 G5
Aiserey (21).......102 A2
Aisey-et-Richecourt (70).......87 E1
Aisey-sur-Seine (21).......85 E2
Aisonville-et-Bernoville (02).......9 F5
Aïssey (25).......87 H6
Aisy-sous-Thil (21).......84 C5
Aisy-sur-Armançon (89).......84 C3
Aiti (2B).......205 F1
Aiton (73).......132 B4
Aix (19).......126 A4
les Aix-d'Angillon (18).......98 A2
Aix-en-Ergny (62).......1 H5
Aix-en-Issart (62).......1 G6
Aix-en-Provence (13).......192 B1
Aix-la-Fayette (63).......127 H5
Aix-les-Bains (73).......131 H3
Aix-Noulette (62).......8 A1
Aix-Villemaur-Pâlis (10).......65 G4
Aixe-sur-Vienne (87).......124 A3
Aizac (07).......157 F1
Aizanville (52).......67 G5
Aize (36).......96 C2
Aizecourt-le-Bas (80).......8 C5
Aizecourt-le-Haut (80).......8 C5
Aizelles (02).......22 D4
Aizenay (85).......91 F4
Aizier (27).......15 H2
Aizy-Jouy (02).......22 B4
Ajac (11).......186 C5
Ajaccio (2A).......204 C6
Ajain (23).......111 H5
Ajat (24).......137 H3
Ajoncourt (57).......48 D3
Ajoux (07).......143 G6
Alaigne (11).......186 C4
Alaincourt (02).......22 A1
Alaincourt (70).......69 F6
Alaincourt-la-Côte (57).......48 D3
Alairac (11).......186 D3
Alan (31).......184 C3
Alando (2B).......205 F2
Alata (2A).......204 C5
Alba-la-Romaine (07).......157 H2
Alban (81).......171 E3
Albaret-le-Comtal (48).......141 F5
Albaret-Sainte-Marie (48).......141 G5
Albas (11).......187 G5
Albas (46).......152 B3
Albé (67).......71 F2
Albefeuille-Lagarde (82).......169 E1
l'Albenc (38).......145 E2
Albepierre-Bredons (15).......140 D3
L'Albère (66).......201 F4
Albert (80).......8 A5
Albertacce (2B).......204 D2
Albertville (73).......132 C3
Albestroff (57).......49 G3
Albi (81).......170 C2
Albiac (46).......139 E6
Albias (82).......169 F1
Albières (11).......187 F6
Albiès (09).......199 F1
Albiez-le-Jeune (73).......146 C2
Albiez-Montrond (73).......146 C2
Albignac (19).......138 D3
Albigny-sur-Saône (69).......130 A2
Albine (81).......187 F1
Albitreccia (2A).......206 D1
Albon (26).......144 A2
Albon-d'Ardèche (07).......143 F6
Alboussière (07).......143 H5
les Albres (12).......153 H4
Albussac (19).......139 E3
Alby-sur-Chéran (74).......132 A2
Alçay-Alçabéhéty-Sunharette (64).......181 F4
Aldudes (64).......180 C3
Alembon (62).......1 G3
Alençon (61).......60 A2
Alénya (66).......201 F3
Aléria (2B).......205 H4
Alès (30).......157 E6
Alet-les-Bains (11).......186 D5
Alette (62).......1 G6
Aleu (09).......185 E6
Alex (74).......132 B1
Alexain (53).......58 C3
Aleyrac (26).......158 C3
Alfortville (94).......42 D4
Algajola (2B).......202 C5
Algans (81).......170 A5
Algolsheim (68).......71 G5
Algrange (57).......26 B3
Alièze (39).......117 G1
Alignan-du-Vent (34).......188 D1
Alincourt (08).......23 G4
Alincthun (62).......1 G4

Alise-Sainte-Reine (21).......84 D4
Alissas (07).......158 A1
Alix (69).......129 H2
Alixan (26).......144 C4
Alizay (27).......18 D5
Allain (54).......48 B6
Allaines (80).......8 C5
Allaines-Mervilliers (28).......62 D4
Allainville (28).......41 E5
Allainville (78).......62 D2
Allaire (56).......73 H1
Allamont (54).......48 A1
Allamps (54).......48 A6
Allan (26).......158 B3
Allanche (15).......141 E2
Alland'Huy-et-Sausseuil (08).......24 A3
Allarmont (88).......70 D1
Allas-Bocage (17).......121 F6
Allas-Champagne (17).......121 G5
Allas-les-Mines (24).......137 H6
Allassac (19).......138 C2
Allauch (13).......192 B3
Allègre (43).......142 B2
Allègre-les-Fumades (30).......157 F6
Alleins (13).......175 G4
Allemagne-en-Provence (04).......177 E3
Allemanche-Launay-et-Soyer (51).......45 E6
Allemans (24).......136 C1
Allemans-du-Dropt (47).......150 D2
Allemant (02).......22 B4
Allemant (51).......45 E5
Allemond (38).......146 A3
Allenay (80).......6 B4
Allenc (48).......156 B3
Allenjoie (25).......88 D4
Allennes-les-Marais (59).......3 F6
Allerey (21).......101 E2
Allerey-sur-Saône (71).......101 H4
Alleriot (71).......101 H5
Allery (80).......7 E6
Alles-sur-Dordogne (24).......137 G5
Alleuze (15).......141 F5
Allevard (38).......132 A6
Allèves (74).......132 A3
Allex (26).......144 C5
Alleyrac (43).......142 D5
Alleyras (43).......142 B5
Alleyrat (19).......125 H5
Alleyrat (23).......125 G1
Allez-et-Cazeneuve (47).......151 F4
Alliancelles (51).......46 C4
Alliat (09).......199 E1
Allibaudières (10).......45 F6
Allichamps (52).......46 C6
Allier (65).......183 F3
Allières (09).......185 F5
les Alliés (25).......104 A3
Alligny-Cosne (58).......82 C5
Alligny-en-Morvan (58).......100 C1
Allineuc (22).......33 F6
Allinges (74).......119 E3
Allogny (18).......97 G1
Alloinay (79).......108 B5
Allondans (25).......88 C4
Allondaz (73).......132 C3
Allondrelle-la-Malmaison (54).......25 F3
Allonne (60).......20 B5
Allonne (79).......107 H1
Allonnes (28).......62 C3
Allonnes (49).......77 H6
Allonnes (72).......60 A6
Allons (04).......178 A1
Allons (47).......150 A5
Allonville (80).......7 G5
Allonzier-la-Caille (74).......118 B6
Allos (04).......161 F5
Allouagne (62).......2 B6
Alloue (16).......109 F6
Allouis (18).......97 F2
Allouville-Bellefosse (76).......18 A3
les Allues (73).......132 D6
les Alluets-le-Roi (78).......42 A3
Alluy (58).......99 G3
Alluyes (28).......62 A4
Ally (15).......139 H3
Ally (43).......141 G3
Almayrac (81).......170 C1
Almenêches (61).......39 F5
Almont-les-Junies (12).......154 A2
Alos (09).......184 D6
Alos (81).......170 A2
Alos-Sibas-Abense (64).......181 G3
Aloxe-Corton (21).......101 G3
Alquines (62).......1 H4
Alrance (12).......154 D6
Alsting (57).......27 G4
Altagène (2A).......207 E2
Alteckendorf (67).......50 D3
Altenach (68).......89 E3
Altenheim (67).......50 C4
Althen-des-Paluds (84).......175 F2
Altiani (2B).......205 F3
Altier (48).......156 C3
Altillac (19).......139 E4
Altkirch (68).......89 F3
Altorf (67).......50 D6
Altrippe (57).......49 G2
Altviller (57).......27 F5
Altwiller (67).......49 H3
Aluze (71).......101 F5
Alvignac (46).......138 D4
Alvimare (76).......16 D4
Alzen (09).......185 G5
Alzi (2B).......205 F2

Alzing (57).......27 E4
Alzon (30).......172 C2
Alzonne (11).......186 D3
Amage (70).......88 A1
Amagne (08).......23 H3
Amagney (25).......87 G6
Amailloux (79).......93 F5
Amance (10).......66 D3
Amance (54).......48 D4
Amance (70).......87 F1
Amancey (25).......103 G3
Amancy (74).......118 D6
Amange (39).......102 D2
Amanlis (35).......57 G4
Amanty (55).......68 C1
Amanvillers (57).......26 B5
Amanzé (71).......115 F4
Amarens (81).......170 A1
Amathay-Vésigneux (25).......103 H3
Amayé-sur-Orne (14).......14 B5
Amayé-sur-Seulles (14).......38 A1
Amazy (58).......83 G6
Ambacourt (88).......69 F2
Ambarès-et-Lagrave (33).......135 F4
Ambax (31).......184 C2
Ambazac (87).......124 C1
Ambel (38).......145 H6
Ambenay (27).......40 B4
Ambérac (16).......122 B2
Ambérieu-en-Bugey (01).......130 D1
Ambérieux (69).......129 H1
Ambérieux-en-Dombes (01).......130 B1
Ambernac (16).......123 E1
Amberre (86).......94 A5
Ambert (63).......128 B5
Ambès (33).......135 F4
Ambeyrac (12).......153 G3
Ambialet (81).......170 D2
Ambiegna (2A).......204 C4
Ambierle (42).......114 D6
Ambiévillers (70).......69 G6
Ambillou (37).......78 C5
Ambilly (74).......118 C4
Amblainville (60).......20 B6
Amblans-et-Velotte (70).......87 H2
Ambleny (02).......21 H5
Ambléon (01).......131 F3
Ambleteuse (62).......1 F3
Ambleville (16).......121 H5
Ambleville (95).......41 H1
Ambloy (41).......79 F2
Ambly-Fleury (08).......23 H4
Ambly-sur-Meuse (55).......47 G2
Amboise (37).......79 F5
Ambon (56).......73 E2
Ambonil (26).......144 B6
Ambonnay (51).......45 G2
Ambonville (52).......67 G3
Ambrault (36).......97 E5
Ambres (81).......169 H4
Ambricourt (62).......2 A6
Ambrief (02).......22 B5
Ambrières (51).......46 C6
Ambrières-les-Vallées (53).......58 D2
Ambrines (62).......7 H2
Ambronay (01).......117 E6
Ambrugeat (19).......125 G5
Ambrumesnil (76).......17 G2
Ambrus (47).......150 C5
Ambutrix (01).......130 D1
Amécourt (27).......19 G5
Amel-sur-l'Étang (55).......25 G6
Amelécourt (57).......49 E3
Amélie-les-Bains-Palalda (66).......200 D4
Amendeuix-Oneix (64).......181 F1
Amenoncourt (54).......49 G5
Amenucourt (95).......41 G1
Ames (62).......2 C6
Amettes (62).......2 B6
Ameugny (71).......116 A2
Ameuvelle (88).......69 E6
Amfreville (14).......14 C4
Amfreville-la-Mi-Voie (76).......18 D4
Amfreville-les-Champs (27).......19 E5
Amfreville-les-Champs (76).......17 F4
Amfreville-Saint-Amand (27).......18 B6
Amfreville-sous-les-Monts (27).......18 D5
Amfreville-sur-Iton (27).......40 D1
Amfroipret (59).......9 G2
Amiens (80).......7 G6
Amifontaine (02).......23 E4
Amigny (50).......13 E6
Amigny-Rouy (02).......22 A3
Amillis (77).......43 H5
Amilly (28).......62 C2
Amilly (45).......64 B6
Amions (42).......128 D2
Amirat (06).......178 B2
Ammerschwihr (68).......71 F4
Amné (72).......59 H5
Amnéville (57).......26 B4
Amoncourt (70).......87 F2
Amondans (25).......103 G2
Amont-et-Effreney (70).......88 A1
Amorots-Succos (64).......181 E1
Amou (40).......165 G5
Ampilly-le-Sec (21).......85 E2
Ampilly-les-Bordes (21).......85 E3
Ampoigné (53).......76 C1
Amponville (77).......63 H3

Ampriani (2B).......205 G2
Ampuis (69).......130 A5
Ampus (83).......177 G5
Amuré (79).......107 G4
Amy (60).......21 F2
Anais (16).......122 C3
Anais (17).......107 E4
Anan (31).......184 B2
Ance Féas (64).......181 H3
Anceaumeville (76).......18 C3
Ancelle (05).......160 C1
Ancemont (55).......47 F2
Ancenis (44).......75 E4
Ancerville (55).......46 D6
Ancerville (57).......48 D2
Ancerviller (54).......49 G6
Ancey (21).......85 F6
Anchamps (08).......11 E5
Anché (37).......94 B2
Anché (86).......108 D3
Anchenoncourt-et-Chazel (70).......87 F1
Ancienville (02).......21 H6
Ancier (70).......86 D5
Ancinnes (72).......60 A2
Ancizan (65).......183 G6
les Ancizes-Comps (63).......126 D2
Ancône (26).......158 A2
Ancourt (76).......17 H2
Ancourteville-sur-Héricourt (76).......17 E4
Ancretiéville-Saint-Victor (76).......17 F4
Ancretteville-sur-Mer (76).......16 D3
Ancteville (50).......36 D1
Anctoville-sur-Boscq (50).......36 D3
Ancy (69).......129 G2
Ancy-Dornot (57).......48 C2
Ancy-le-Franc (89).......84 B2
Ancy-le-Libre (89).......84 B2
Andainville (80).......6 D6
Andance (07).......144 A2
Andancette (26).......144 A2
Andé (27).......18 D6
Andechy (80).......21 E2
Andel (22).......33 H5
Andelain (02).......22 A4
Andelaroche (03).......114 C4
Andelarre (70).......87 F3
Andelarrot (70).......87 F3
Andelat (15).......141 E4
Andelnans (90).......88 C3
Andelot-Blancheville (52).......68 A3
Andelot-en-Montagne (39).......103 F4
Andelot-Morval (39).......117 F3
Andelu (78).......41 H3
les Andelys (27).......19 E6
Andernay (55).......46 D4
Andernos-les-Bains (33).......134 B6
Anderny (54).......25 H5
Andert-et-Condon (01).......131 F2
Andeville (60).......20 B6
Andillac (81).......170 A2
Andilly (17).......106 D4
Andilly (54).......48 B4
Andilly (74).......118 B6
Andilly (95).......42 C2
Andilly-en-Bassigny (52).......68 C6
Andiran (47).......150 C6
Andlau (67).......71 F2
Andoins (64).......182 C2
Andolsheim (68).......71 F4
Andon (06).......178 B3
Andonville (45).......63 E3
Andornay (70).......88 B3
Andouillé (53).......58 C4
Andouillé-Neuville (35).......57 F1
Andouque (81).......170 D2
Andrein (64).......181 G1
Andres (62).......1 G3
Andrest (65).......183 E2
Andrésy (78).......42 B3
Andrezel (77).......43 F6
Andrézieux-Bouthéon (42).......129 E5
Andryes (89).......83 F4
Anduze (30).......173 G1
Anères (65).......183 H4
Anet (28).......41 F4
Angaïs (64).......182 C2
Angé (41).......79 H6
Angeac-Champagne (16).......121 G4
Angeac-Charente (16).......122 A4
Angecourt (08).......24 C2
Angeduc (16).......122 A5
Angely (89).......84 A4
Angeot (90).......88 D2
Angers (49).......76 D4
Angerville (14).......14 D4
Angerville (91).......63 E3
Angerville-Bailleul (76).......16 C4
Angerville-la-Campagne (27).......40 D2
Angerville-la-Martel (76).......16 D3
Angerville-l'Orcher (76).......15 F1
Angervilliers (91).......42 B6
Angeville (82).......168 C2
Angevillers (57).......26 B3
Angicourt (60).......20 D5
Angiens (76).......17 E2
Angirey (70).......86 D5
Angivillers (60).......20 D4
Anglards-de-Saint-Flour (15).......141 F4
Anglards-de-Salers (15).......140 A2
Anglars (46).......153 F1
Anglars-Juillac (46).......152 B3
Anglars-Nozac (46).......138 B6

Anglars-Saint-Félix (12)...... 153 H4
Anglefort (01) 131 G1
Anglemont (88) 70 B2
Angles (04) 177 H2
les Angles (30) 174 D2
les Angles (65) 183 E4
les Angles (66) 199 H3
Anglès (81) 171 E6
Angles (85) 106 B2
les Angles-sur-Corrèze (19)... 139 E1
Angles-sur-l'Anglin (86) 95 F6
Anglesqueville-la-Bras-
Long (76) 17 E3
Anglesqueville-
l'Esneval (76) 16 B4
Anglet (64) 164 B6
Angliers (17) 107 E4
Angliers (86) 94 A3
Anglure (51) 45 E6
Anglure-sous-Dun (71) 115 G4
Angluzelles-et-
Courcelles (51) 45 E6
Angoisse (24) 124 A6
Angomont (54) 49 H6
Angos (65) 183 F3
Angoulême (16) 122 C4
Angoulins (17) 106 D5
Angoumé (40) 164 D4
Angous (64) 181 G2
Angoustrine-Villeneuve-
des-Escaldes (66) 199 G4
Angoville (14) 38 C3
Angres (62) 8 B1
Angresse (40) 164 C4
Angrie (49) 76 B3
Anguilcourt-le-Sart (02) 22 B2
Angy (60) 20 C5
Anhaux (64) 180 D3
Anhiers (59) 8 D1
Aniane (34) 172 D5
Aniche (59) 9 E2
Anisy (14) 14 B4
Anizy-le-Château (02) 22 B4
Anjeux (70) 87 G1
Anjou (38) 144 B1
Anjouin (36) 96 D2
Anjoutey (90) 88 D2
Anla (65) 184 A6
Anlezy (58) 99 G4
Anlhiac (24) 138 A1
Annay (58) 82 C4
Annay (62) 8 B1
Annay-la-Côte (89) 84 A4
Annay-sur-Serein (89) 84 A2
Annebault (14) 15 E4
Annecy (74) 132 B1
Annelles (08) 23 G4
Annemasse (74) 118 C4
Annéot (89) 84 A4
Annepont (17) 121 E2
Annequin (62) 2 D6
Annesse-et-Beaulieu (24) 137 E2
Annet-sur-Marne (77) 43 F3
Anneux (59) 8 D3
Anneville-Ambourville (76) 18 B4
Anneville-en-Saire (50) 13 E2
Annéville-la-Prairie (52) 67 H4
Anneville-sur-Mer (50) 12 C6
Anneville-sur-Scie (76) 17 G2
Anneyron (26) 144 B2
Annezay (17) 107 F6
Annezin (62) 2 D6
Annœullin (59) 3 E6
Annoire (39) 102 B4
Annois (02) 21 H2
Annoisin-Chatelans (38) 130 D3
Annoix (18) 97 H4
Annonay (07) 143 H2
Annonville (52) 68 A2
Annot (04) 178 A2
Annouville-Vilmesnil (76) 16 C4
Annoux (89) 84 B3
Annoville (50) 36 D2
Anor (59) 10 B5
Anos (64) 182 C1
Anost (71) 100 B3
Anould (88) 70 B4
Anoux (54) 25 H5
Anoye (64) 182 D1
Anquetierville (76) 18 A3
Anrosey (52) 86 D1
Ansac-sur-Vienne (16) 123 F1
Ansacq (60) 20 C5
Ansan (32) 168 A4
Ansauville (54) 48 A4
Ansauvillers (60) 20 C3
Anse (69) 129 H1
Ansignan (66) 200 C2
Ansost (65) 183 F1
Ansouis (84) 176 A4
Anstaing (59) 3 G5
Antagnac (47) 150 B4
Anterrieux (15) 141 E6
Anteuil (25) 88 B5
Antezant-la-Chapelle (17) 107 H6
Anthé (47) 151 H4
Anthelupt (54) 49 E6
Anthenay (51) 44 D1
Antheny (08) 10 C6
Antheuil (21) 101 F2
Antheuil-Portes (60) 21 E4
Anthien (58) 83 H6
Anthon (38) 130 C3
Anthy-sur-Léman (74) 118 D3
Antibes (06) 178 D5
Antichan (65) 184 A5
Antichan-de-
Frontignes (31) 184 A5

Antignac (15) 140 B1
Antignac (31) 197 F1
Antigny (85) 92 C6
Antigny (86) 109 H2
Antigny-la-Ville (21) 101 E2
Antilly (57) 26 C5
Antilly (60) 43 G1
Antin (65) 183 G2
Antisanti (2B) 205 G3
Antist (65) 183 F4
Antogny-le-Tillac (37) 94 D3
Antoigné (49) 93 G2
Antoingt (63) 127 F5
Antonne-et-Trigonant (24)...137 G2
Antony (92) 42 C5
Antraigues-sur-Volane (07)...157 G1
Antrain (35) 35 G5
Antran (86) 94 D4
Antras (09) 184 C6
Antras (32) 167 G4
Antrenas (48) 155 G2
Antugnac (11) 186 D5
Antully (71) 100 D4
Anvéville (76) 17 E4
Anville (16) 122 A2
Anvin (62) 7 G1
Any-Martin-Rieux (02) 10 C6
Anzat-le-Luguet (63) 141 E1
Anzeling (57) 26 D4
Anzême (23) 111 G4
Anzex (47) 150 C5
Anzin (59) 9 F2
Anzin-Saint-Aubin (62) 8 B2
Anzy-le-Duc (71) 115 E4
Aoste (38) 131 F4
Aougny (51) 44 D1
Aouste (08) 23 G1
Aouste-sur-Sye (26) 158 C1
Aouze (88) 69 E2
Apach (57) 26 D2
Apchat (63) 141 F1
Apchon (15) 140 C2
Apinac (42) 142 D1
Appelle (81) 170 A5
Appenai-sous-Bellême (61).... 60 D2
Appenans (25) 88 B5
Appeville (50) 12 D5
Appeville-Annebault (27) 18 A5
Appietto (2A) 204 C5
Appilly (60) 21 H3
Appoigny (89) 83 F1
Apprieu (38) 131 E6
Appy (09) 199 F1
Apremont (01) 117 G4
Apremont (08) 24 C6
Apremont (60) 20 D6
Apremont (70) 86 C5
Apremont (73) 131 H5
Apremont (85) 91 E3
Apremont-la-Forêt (55) 47 H4
Apremont-sur-Allier (18) 98 D4
Aprey (52) 86 A2
Apt (84) 176 A3
Arabaux (09) 185 H5
Arâches-la-Frasse (74) 119 F6
Aragnouet (65) 196 D1
Aragon (11) 187 E2
Aramits (64) 181 H3
Aramon (30) 174 D3
Aranc (01) 117 F6
Arancou (64) 165 E6
Arandas (01) 131 E2
Arandon-Passins (38) 131 E3
Araujuzon (64) 181 G1
Araules (43) 143 E3
Araux (64) 181 G1
Arbanats (33) 149 G1
Arbas (31) 184 C5
Arbecey (70) 87 E2
Arbellara (2A) 207 E3
Arbent (01) 117 G4
Arbéost (65) 182 C5
Arbérats-Sillègue (64) 181 F1
Arbigny (01) 116 C2
Arbigny-sous-
Varennes (52) 86 C1
Arbin (73) 132 A5
Arbis (33) 149 H1
Arblade-le-Bas (32) 166 C4
Arblade-le-Haut (32) 166 D4
Arbois (39) 103 E4
Arbon (31) 184 B5
Arbonne (64) 164 B6
Arbonne-la-Forêt (77) 63 H2
Arboras (34) 172 D4
Arbori (2A) 204 C4
Arbot (52) 85 G1
Arbouans (25) 88 C4
Arboucave (40) 166 A5
Arbouet-Sussaute (64) 181 F1
Arbourse (58) 99 E1
Arboussols (66) 200 C2
Arboys en Bugey (01) 131 F3
l'Arbresle (69) 129 G2
Arbrissel (35) 57 H4
Arbus (64) 182 A2
Arbusigny (74) 118 C5
Arc-en-Barrois (52) 67 G6
Arc-et-Senans (25) 103 E3
Arc-lès-Gray (70) 86 C5
Arc-sous-Cicon (25) 104 A2
Arc-sous-Montenot (25) 103 F4
Arc-sur-Tille (21) 86 A6
Arçais (79) 107 F3
Arcambal (46) 152 D3
Arcangues (64) 164 B6

Arçay (18) 97 G4
Arçay (86) 93 H3
Arceau (21) 86 A5
Arcenant (21) 101 G2
Arcens (07) 143 F5
Arces (17) 120 D4
Arces-Dilo (89) 65 G5
Arcey (21) 101 G1
Arcey (25) 88 B4
Archail (04) 160 D6
Archamps (74) 118 C5
Archelange (39) 102 C2
Arches (15) 140 A1
Arches (88) 70 A4
Archettes (88) 70 A4
Archiac (17) 121 G5
Archignac (24) 138 B4
Archignat (03) 112 C3
Archigny (86) 94 D6
Archingeay (17) 121 E1
Archon (02) 23 F1
Arcinges (42) 115 F5
Arcins (33) 134 D3
Arcis-le-Ponsart (51) 22 C6
Arcis-sur-Aube (10) 66 B1
Arcizac-Adour (65) 183 E3
Arcizac-Ez-Angles (65) 183 E4
Arcizans-Avant (65) 182 D5
Arcizans-Dessus (65) 182 D5
Arcomps (18) 97 H6
Arçon (25) 104 A3
Arçon (42) 128 C1
Arçonnay (72) 60 A2
Arconsat (63) 128 B2
Arconville (10) 67 F4
les Arcs (83) 194 A2
Arcueil (94) 42 D4
Arcy-Sainte-Restitue (02) 22 B6
Arcy-sur-Cure (89) 83 H4
Ardelles (28) 61 G1
Ardelu (28) 62 D3
Ardenais (18) 112 B1
Ardenay-sur-Mérize (72) 60 C6
Ardengost (65) 183 G5
Ardentes (36) 96 D6
Ardes (63) 127 F6
Ardeuil-et-
Montfauxelles (08) 24 B6
Ardiège (31) 184 A4
les Ardillats (69) 115 H5
Ardilleux (79) 108 B5
Ardillières (17) 107 E5
Ardin (79) 107 G2
Ardizas (32) 168 C4
Ardoix (07) 143 H2
Ardon (39) 103 F5
Ardon (45) 80 D2
Ardouval (76) 17 H3
Aregno (2B) 202 C5
Areines (41) 79 G2
Arelaune-en-Seine (76) 18 B4
Aren (64) 181 H2
Arengosse (40) 165 G1
Arenthon (74) 118 D5
Arès (33) 134 B6
Aresches (39) 103 F4
Aressy (64) 182 C2
Arette (64) 181 H4
Arfeuille-Châtain (23) 112 C6
Arfeuilles (03) 114 C5
Arfons (81) 186 D1
Argagnon (64) 165 G6
Arganchy (14) 13 H6
Argançon (10) 67 E3
Argancy (57) 26 C5
Argein (09) 184 C6
Argelès-Bagnères (65) 183 F4
Argelès-Gazost (65) 182 D5
Argelès-sur-Mer (66) 201 G3
Argeliers (11) 188 A2
Argelliers (34) 173 E4
Argelos (40) 165 H5
Argelos (64) 166 B6
Argelouse (40) 149 E4
Argences (14) 14 D5
Argences en Aubrac (12) 140 C6
Argens-Minervois (11) 187 G3
Argent-sur-Sauldre (18) 81 G4
Argentan (61) 39 E4
Argentat-sur-
Dordogne (19) 139 F3
Argentenay (89) 84 B2
Argenteuil (95) 42 C3
Argenteuil-sur-
Armançon (89) 84 B2
l'Argentière-la-Bessée (05)...147 E6
Argentières (77) 43 G6
Argentine (73) 132 C5
Argenton (47) 150 B4
Argenton-l'Église (79) 93 G3
Argenton-Notre-Dame (53)... 76 D2
Argenton-sur-Creuse (36) 111 E1
Argentonnay (79) 93 F3
Argentré (53) 58 D4
Argentré-du-Plessis (35) 58 A5
Argenvières (18) 98 C2
Argenvilliers (28) 61 F3
Argers (51) 46 C2
Arget (64) 165 H5
Argiésans (90) 88 C3
Argillières (70) 86 D3
Argilliers (30) 174 C2
Argilly (21) 101 H3
Argis (01) 131 E1
Argiusta-Moriccio (2A) 207 E1
Argœuves (80) 7 F5

Argol (29) 31 E6
Argonay (74) 132 B1
Argoules (80) 6 D2
Arguel (76) 19 F3
Arguel (25) 103 F1
Arguel (80) 6 D6
Arguenos (31) 184 B5
Argut-Dessous (31) 184 B6
Argy (36) 96 A4
Arhansus (64) 181 F2
Aries-Espénan (65) 183 H2
Arifat (81) 170 D4
Arignac (09) 185 G6
Arinthod (39) 117 G3
Arjuzanx (40) 165 F1
Arlanc (63) 128 B6
Arlay (39) 102 D5
Arlebosc (07) 143 H4
Arlempdes (43) 142 C5
Arles (13) 174 C5
Arles-sur-Tech (66) 200 D4
Arlet (43) 141 H3
Arleuf (58) 100 B3
Arleux (59) 8 D2
Arleux-en-Gohelle (62) 8 B2
Arlos (31) 184 B6
Armaillé (49) 76 A2
Armancourt (60) 21 E5
Armancourt (80) 21 E2
Armaucourt (54) 48 D4
Armbouts-Cappel (59) 2 B2
Armeau (89) 65 E5
Armendarits (64) 181 E2
Armentières (59) 3 E4
Armentières-en-Brie (77) 43 H3
Armentières-sur-Avre (27).... 40 B5
Armentières-sur-
Ourcq (02) 44 B1
Armentieux (32) 167 E6
Armes (58) 83 F5
Armillac (47) 150 D2
Armissan (11) 188 B3
Armix (01) 131 F2
Armous-et-Cau (32) 167 E5
Armoy (74) 119 E3
Arnac (15) 139 H4
Arnac-la-Poste (87) 110 D4
Arnac-Pompadour (19) 124 B6
Arnac-sur-Dourdou (12) 171 H4
Arnage (72) 60 A6
Arnancourt (52) 67 G2
Arnas (69) 116 A6
Arnaud-Guilhem (31) 184 C4
Arnave (09) 185 H6
Arnaville (54) 48 B2
Arnay-le-Duc (21) 101 E2
Arnay-sous-Vitteaux (21) 84 D5
Arnayon (26) 159 E3
Arné (65) 183 H3
Arnéguy (64) 180 D3
Arnèke (59) 2 C3
Arnicourt (08) 23 G3
Arnières-sur-Iton (27) 40 D2
Arnos (64) 165 H6
Arnouville (95) 42 D3
Arnouville-lès-Mantes (78).... 41 H3
Aroffe (88) 69 E2
Aromas (39) 117 F4
Aron (53) 59 E3
Aroue-Ithorots-
Olhaïby (64) 181 F2
Aroz (70) 87 F3
Arpaillargues-et-
Aureillac (30) 174 B2
Arpajon (91) 42 C6
Arpajon-sur-Cère (15) 140 B5
Arpavon (26) 159 E4
Arpenans (70) 87 H3
Arpheuilles (18) 98 A5
Arpheuilles (36) 95 H4
Arpheuilles-Saint-
Priest (03) 112 D5
Arphy (30) 172 D2
Arquenay (53) 59 E5
Arques (11) 187 E5
Arques (12) 154 D5
les Arques (46) 152 B2
Arques (62) 8 B2
Arques-la-Bataille (76) 17 G2
Arquettes-en-Val (11) 187 F4
Arquian (58) 82 C4
Arracourt (54) 49 E4
Arradon (56) 72 D1
Arraincourt (57) 49 E2
Arrancourt (91) 63 F3
Arrancy (02) 22 D4
Arrancy-sur-Crusne (55) 25 G3
Arrans (21) 84 C3
Arras (62) 8 B2
Arras-en-Lavedan (65) 182 D5
Arras-sur-Rhône (07) 144 A3
Arrast-Larrebieu (64) 181 G2
Arraute-Charritte (64) 181 E1
Arraye-et-Han (54) 48 D3
Arrayou-Lahitte (65) 183 E4
Arre (30) 172 D2
Arreau (65) 183 G6
Arrelles (10) 66 C5
Arrembécourt (10) 67 E1
Arrènes (23) 111 E6
Arrens-Marsous (65) 182 C5
Arrentès-de-Corcieux (88) 70 C4
Arrentières (10) 67 E3
Arrest (80) 6 C4
Arreux (08) 11 E6
Arriance (57) 49 E2

Arricau-Bordes (64) 166 C6
Arrien (64) 182 D2
Arrien-en-Bethmale (09) 184 D6
Arrigas (30) 172 D2
Arrigny (51) 46 B6
Arro (2A) 204 C4
Arrodets (65) 183 G4
Arrodets-Ez-Angles (65) 183 E4
Arromanches-les-
Bains (14) 14 A3
Arronnes (03) 114 B6
Arronville (95) 42 B1
Arros-de-Nay (64) 182 C3
Arrosès (64) 166 C5
Arrouède (32) 184 A2
Arrout (09) 184 D5
Arry (57) 48 C2
Arry (80) 6 C2
Ars (16) 121 G4
Ars (23) 125 G1
Ars-en-Ré (17) 106 A4
Ars-Laquenexy (57) 26 C5
Ars-les-Favets (63) 113 E5
Ars-sur-Formans (01) 130 A1
Ars-sur-Moselle (57) 48 C1
Arsac (33) 135 E4
Arsac-en-Velay (43) 142 C4
Arsague (40) 165 G5
Arsans (70) 86 D5
Arsonval (10) 67 E3
Arsure-Arsurette (39) 103 G5
les Arsures (39) 103 E3
Arsy (60) 21 E5
Art-sur-Meurthe (54) 48 D5
Artagnan (65) 183 E1
Artaise-le-Vivier (08) 24 C3
Artaix (71) 115 E4
Artalens-Souin (65) 182 D5
Artannes-sur-Indre (37) 94 D1
Artannes-sur-Thouet (49) 93 H1
Artas (38) 130 C5
Artassenx (40) 166 A3
Artemare (01) 131 F2
Artemps (02) 21 H1
Artenay (45) 62 D5
Arthaz-Pont-Notre-
Dame (74) 118 C5
Arthel (58) 99 F1
Arthémonay (26) 144 C3
Arthenac (17) 121 G5
Arthès (81) 170 C2
Arthez-d'Armagnac (40) 166 B2
Arthez-d'Asson (64) 182 C4
Arthez-de-Béarn (64) 165 H6
Arthezé (72) 77 G2
Arthies (95) 41 H2
Arthon (36) 96 C6
Arthonnay (89) 66 C6
Arthun (42) 128 D3
Artigat (09) 185 F4
Artignosc-sur-Verdon (83) ...177 E4
Artigue (31) 184 A6
Artigueloutan (64) 182 C2
Artiguelouve (64) 182 B2
Artiguemy (65) 183 F4
Artigues (09) 199 H2
Artigues (11) 200 A1
Artigues (65) 183 E4
Artigues (83) 176 C5
les Artigues-de-Lussac (33)...135 H4
Artigues-près-
Bordeaux (33) 135 F5
Artins (41) 79 E2
Artix (09) 185 G4
Artix (64) 182 A1
Artolsheim (67) 71 G3
Artonne (63) 127 F1
Artres (59) 9 F2
Artzenheim (68) 71 G4
Arudy (64) 182 B4
Arue (40) 166 B1
Arvert (17) 120 B3
Arveyres (33) 135 G5
Arvieu (12) 154 C5
Arvieux (05) 147 F6
Arvigna (09) 186 A4
Arvillard (73) 132 A5
Arville (41) 61 F5
Arville (77) 63 H4
Arvillers (80) 21 E1
Arx (40) 150 B6
Arzacq-Arraziguet (64) 166 A5
Arzal (56) 73 F2
Arzano (29) 54 C4
Arzay (38) 130 C6
Arzembouy (58) 99 F1
Arzenc-d'Apcher (48) 141 F6
Arzenc-de-Randon (48) 156 B2
Arzens (11) 186 D3
Arzillières-Neuville (51) 46 B6
Arzon (56) 72 C1
Arzviller (57) 50 A4
Asasp-Arros (64) 182 A3
Ascain (64) 180 B1
Ascarat (64) 180 D3
Aschbach (67) 51 F2
Aschères-le-Marché (45) 63 E5
Asco (2B) 202 D6
Ascou (09) 199 G2
Ascoux (45) 63 F5
Ascros (06) 178 C2
Asfeld (08) 23 F4
Aslonnes (86) 109 E2
Asnan (58) 83 F6
Asnans-Beauvoisin (39) 102 C4
Asnelles (14) 14 A3
Asnières (27) 15 G4
Asnières-en-Bessin (14) 13 G4

Asnières-en-
Montagne (21) 84 C3
Asnières-en-Poitou (79) 108 B5
Asnières-la-Giraud (17) 121 F1
Asnières-lès-Dijon (21) 85 H5
Asnières-sous-Bois (89) 83 G5
Asnières-sur-Blour (86) 109 H5
Asnières-sur-Nouère (16) 122 B3
Asnières-sur-Oise (95) 42 D1
Asnières-sur-Saône (01) 116 C3
Asnières-sur-Seine (92) 42 C3
Asnières-sur-Vègre (72) 77 G3
Asnois (58) 83 G5
Asnois (86) 109 E5
Aspach (57) 49 H5
Aspach (68) 89 F3
Aspach-le-Bas (68) 89 F3
Aspach-Michelbach (68) 89 E1
Aspères (30) 173 G3
Asperjoc (07) 157 G1
Aspet (31) 184 B5
Aspin-Aure (65) 183 G5
Aspin-en-Lavedan (65) 182 D4
Aspiran (34) 172 C6
Aspremont (05) 159 H3
Aspremont (06) 179 E3
les Aspres (61) 40 A5
Aspres-lès-Corps (05) 146 A6
Aspres-sur-Buëch (05) 159 H2
Aspret-Sarrat (31) 184 B4
Asprières (12) 153 H3
Asque (65) 183 F4
Asques (33) 135 F4
Asques (82) 168 C2
Asquins (89) 83 H5
Assac (81) 171 E2
Assainvillers (80) 21 E3
Assais-les-Jumeaux (79) 93 H5
Assas (34) 173 F4
Assat (64) 182 C2
Assay (37) 94 B2
Assé-le-Bérenger (53) 59 F4
Assé-le-Boisne (72) 59 H3
Assé-le-Riboul (72) 60 A4
Assenay (10) 66 B4
Assencières (10) 66 B2
Assenoncourt (57) 49 G4
Asserac (44) 73 F3
Assevent (59) 10 A2
Assevillers (80) 8 B6
Assier (46) 153 F1
Assieu (38) 130 A6
Assignan (34) 187 H1
Assigny (18) 82 B5
les Assions (07) 157 E4
Assis-sur-Serre (02) 22 B2
Asson (64) 182 C3
Asswiller (67) 50 B3
Astaffort (47) 168 A1
Astaillac (19) 139 E5
Asté (65) 183 F4
Aste-Béon (64) 182 B4
Astet (07) 157 E1
Astillé (53) 58 C6
Astis (64) 166 B6
Aston (09) 199 F1
Astugue (65) 183 E4
Athée (21) 102 C1
Athée (53) 58 B6
Athée-sur-Cher (37) 79 F6
Athesans-
Étroitefontaine (70) 88 A3
Athie (21) 84 C4
Athie (89) 84 A4
Athienville (54) 49 E5
Athies (62) 8 B2
Athies (80) 8 C6
Athies-sous-Laon (02) 22 C3
Athis (51) 45 G2
Athis-Mons (91) 42 D5
Athis-Val de Rouvre (61) 38 B4
Athos-Aspis (64) 181 F1
Attainville (95) 42 D2
Attancourt (52) 67 G1
les Attaques (62) 1 H2
Attenschwiller (68) 89 G3
Attiches (59) 3 F6
Attichy (60) 21 G4
Attignat (01) 116 D4
Attignat-Oncin (73) 131 G5
Attignéville (88) 68 D2
Attigny (08) 24 A4
Attigny (88) 69 F5
Attilloncourt (57) 49 E4
Attilly (02) 8 D6
Attin (62) 1 F6
Atton (54) 48 C3
Attray (45) 63 E5
Attricourt (70) 86 B4
Aubagnan (40) 166 A4
Aubagne (13) 192 C4
Aubaine (21) 101 F2
Aubais (30) 173 H4
Aubarède (65) 183 F2
Aubas (24) 138 A3
Aubazat (43) 141 H3
Aubazines (19) 138 D3
Aube (57) 48 D2
Aube (61) 40 A5
Aubéguimont (76) 19 G2
Aubenas (07) 157 G2
Aubenas-les-Alpes (04) 176 C2
Aubenasson (26) 158 D1
Aubencheul-au-Bac (59) 8 D3
Aubencheul-aux-Bois (02) 9 E5
Aubenton (02) 10 B6
Aubepierre-Ozouer-le-
Repos (77) 43 G6

Aubepierre-sur-Aube (52).....85 G1
Auberchicourt (59).....8 D2
Aubercourt (80).....20 D1
Aubergenville (78).....42 A3
Aubérive (51).....23 G6
Auberive (52).....85 H2
Auberives-en-Royans (38).....144 D3
Auberives-sur-Varèze (38).....130 A6
Aubermesnil-aux-Érables (76).....19 F1
Aubermesnil-Beaumais (76).....17 G2
Aubers (59).....3 E5
Aubertin (64).....182 B2
Auberville (14).....14 D3
Auberville-la-Manuel (76).....16 D2
Auberville-la-Renault (76).....16 C4
Aubervilliers (93).....42 D3
Aubeterre (10).....66 B2
Aubeterre-sur-Dronne (16).....136 B1
Aubiac (33).....149 H3
Aubiac (47).....151 E6
Aubiat (63).....127 F1
Aubière (63).....127 F3
Aubiet (32).....168 A5
Aubignan (84).....175 F1
Aubignas (07).....158 A2
Aubigné (35).....57 F1
Aubigné (79).....108 B6
Aubigné-Racan (72).....78 B3
Aubigné-sur-Layon (49).....93 E1
Aubignosc (04).....160 B6
Aubigny (03).....98 D6
Aubigny (14).....38 D3
Aubigny (79).....93 G5
Aubigny (80).....7 H6
Aubigny-au-Bac (59).....8 D3
Aubigny-aux-Kaisnes (02).....21 H1
Aubigny-en-Artois (62).....8 A2
Aubigny-en-Laonnois (02).....22 D4
Aubigny-en-Plaine (21).....102 A2
Aubigny-la-Ronce (21).....101 F3
Aubigny-Les Clouzeaux (85).....91 G5
Aubigny-les-Pothées (08).....23 H1
Aubigny-lès-Sombernon (21).....85 E6
Aubigny-sur-Nère (18).....81 G5
Aubilly (51).....22 D6
Aubin (12).....154 A3
Aubin (64).....166 A6
Aubin-Saint-Vaast (62).....7 E1
Aubinges (18).....98 A1
Auboncourt-Vauzelles (08).....23 H3
Aubonne (25).....104 A3
Aubord (30).....174 A4
Auboué (54).....26 A4
Aubous (64).....166 C5
Aubres (26).....158 D4
Aubréville (55).....46 D1
Aubrives (08).....11 F4
Aubrometz (62).....7 F2
Aubry-du-Hainaut (59).....9 F2
Aubry-le-Panthou (61).....39 G4
Aubure (68).....71 E3
Aubussargues (30).....174 A2
Aubusson (23).....125 G5
Aubusson (61).....38 B4
Aubusson-d'Auvergne (63)...128 A3
Aubvillers (80).....20 D2
Auby (59).....8 C1
Aucaleuc (22).....34 C5
Aucamville (31).....169 F5
Aucamville (82).....168 D3
Aucazein (09).....184 C5
Aucelon (26).....159 E2
Aucey-la-Plaine (50).....35 G6
Auch (32).....167 H5
Auchay-sur-Vendée (85)...107 E2
Auchel (62).....2 C6
Auchonvillers (80).....8 A4
Auchy-au-Bois (62).....2 B6
Auchy-la-Montagne (60).....20 B3
Auchy-lès-Hesdin (62).....7 F1
Auchy-les-Mines (62).....3 E6
Auchy-les-Orchies (59).....3 G6
Aucun (65).....182 C5
Audaux (64).....181 G1
Audelange (39).....102 D2
Audeloncourt (52).....68 C5
Audembert (62).....1 F3
Audenge (33).....148 C1
Audes (03).....112 C2
Audeux (25).....103 F1
Audeville (45).....63 F3
Audierne (29).....52 D2
Audignicourt (02).....21 H4
Audignies (59).....9 H2
Audignon (40).....165 H4
Audigny (02).....9 G6
Audincourt (25).....88 C4
Audincthun (62).....2 A5
Audinghen (62).....1 F3
Audon (40).....165 F3
Audouville-la-Hubert (50)...13 E4
Audrehem (62).....1 H3
Audressein (09).....184 D6
Audresselles (62).....1 F3
Audrieu (14).....14 A4
Audrix (24).....137 G5
Audruicq (62).....2 A3
Audun-le-Roman (54).....26 A3
Audun-le-Tiche (57).....26 A2
Auenheim (67).....51 G3
Auffargis (78).....42 A5
Auffay (76).....17 G4
Aufferville (77).....63 H4
Auffreville-Brasseuil (78)...41 H3

Auflance (08).....25 E2
Auga (64).....166 B6
Augan (56).....56 B4
Auge (08).....10 C6
Auge (23).....112 B4
Augé (79).....108 A2
Auge-Saint-Médard (16)...122 A2
Augea (39).....117 F1
Auger-Saint-Vincent (60)...21 F6
Augerans (39).....102 D3
Augères (23).....111 F6
Augerolles (63).....128 A3
Augers-en-Brie (77).....44 B5
Augerville-la-Rivière (45)...63 G3
Augicourt (70).....87 E2
Augignac (24).....123 F4
Augirein (09).....184 C5
Augisey (39).....117 F1
Augnat (63).....127 F6
Augnax (32).....168 A4
Augne (87).....125 E3
Augny (57).....48 C2
Auguaise (61).....40 A5
Augy (02).....22 B5
Augy (89).....83 G2
Augy-sur-Aubois (18).....98 B5
Aujac (17).....121 G2
Aujac (30).....156 D4
Aujan-Mournède (32).....183 H1
Aujargues (30).....173 H4
Aujeurres (52).....86 A2
Aujols (46).....152 D4
Aulan (26).....159 F5
Aulas (30).....172 D2
Aulhat-Flat (63).....127 G5
Aullène (2A).....207 E2
Aulnat (63).....127 F3
Aulnay (10).....66 D1
Aulnay (17).....107 H6
Aulnay (86).....94 A4
Aulnay-la-Rivière (45).....63 G4
Aulnay-l'Aître (51).....46 A4
Aulnay-sous-Bois (93).....43 E3
Aulnay-sur-Iton (27).....40 D2
Aulnay-sur-Marne (51).....45 G2
Aulnay-sur-Mauldre (78)...42 A3
les Aulneaux (72).....60 B2
Aulnois (88).....68 D3
Aulnois-en-Perthois (55)...47 E6
Aulnois-sous-Laon (02).....22 C3
Aulnois-sous-Seille (57).....48 D3
Aulnoy (77).....43 H4
Aulnoy-lez-Valenciennes (59).....9 F2
Aulnoy-sur-Aube (52).....85 H1
Aulnoye-Aymeries (59).....9 H3
Aulon (23).....111 F6
Aulon (31).....184 B3
Aulon (65).....183 G6
Aulos (09).....199 F1
Ault (80).....6 B4
Aulus-les-Bains (09).....198 C1
Aulx-lès-Cromary (70).....87 G5
Aumagne (17).....121 G2
Aumale (76).....19 G1
Aumâtre (80).....6 D6
Aumelas (34).....172 D5
Auménancourt (51).....23 E5
Aumerval (62).....2 B6
Aumes (34).....188 D1
Aumessas (30).....172 D2
Aumetz (57).....26 A3
Aumeville-Lestre (50).....13 E3
Aumont (39).....102 D4
Aumont (80).....7 E6
Aumont-en-Halatte (60).....20 D6
Aumur (39).....102 B3
Aunac-sur-Charente (16)...122 C1
Aunat (11).....199 H1
Aunay-en-Bazois (58).....99 H2
Aunay-les-Bois (61).....39 G6
Aunay-sous-Auneau (28)...62 D2
Aunay-sous-Crécy (28).....41 E5
Auneau-Bleury-Saint-Symphorien (28).....62 C2
Auneuil (60).....20 A5
Aunou-le-Faucon (61).....39 E5
Aunou-sur-Orne (61).....39 F5
Auppegard (76).....17 G3
Aups (83).....177 F5
Auradé (32).....168 C6
Auradou (47).....151 G4
Auragne (31).....185 G1
Auray (56).....55 E6
Aure (08).....24 A6
Aure sur Mer (14).....13 H5
Aurec-sur-Loire (43).....143 E1
Aureil (87).....124 C3
Aureilhan (40).....148 B5
Aureilhan (65).....183 E3
Aureille (13).....175 F4
Aurel (26).....159 E1
Aurel (84).....159 F6
Aurensan (32).....166 C5
Aurensan (65).....183 E2
Aureville (31).....169 F6
Auriac (11).....187 F6
Auriac (19).....139 G2
Auriac (64).....166 B6
Auriac-du-Périgord (24)...138 A3
Auriac-Lagast (12).....154 C6
Auriac-l'Église (15).....141 F2
Auriac-sur-Dropt (47).....150 C1
Auriac-sur-Vendinelle (31)...169 H6
Auriat (23).....124 D2
Auribail (31).....185 F2
Auribeau (84).....176 A3
Auribeau-sur-Siagne (06)...178 C5

Aurice (40).....165 H3
Auriébat (65).....167 E6
Aurières (63).....126 D4
Aurignac (31).....184 C3
Aurillac (15).....140 A5
Aurimont (32).....168 B5
Aurin (31).....169 G6
Auriol (13).....192 C3
Auriolles (33).....136 B6
Auris (38).....146 B3
Aurons (13).....175 G5
Auros (33).....150 A3
Aurouër (03).....99 E6
Auroux (48).....156 C1
Aussac (81).....170 B3
Aussac-Vadalle (16).....122 C2
Ausseing (31).....184 D4
Aussevielle (64).....182 B1
Aussillon (81).....170 D6
Aussois (73).....147 F2
Ausson (31).....184 A4
Aussonce (08).....23 G5
Aussonne (31).....169 E5
Aussos (32).....184 A1
Aussurucq (64).....181 F3
Autainville (41).....80 A1
Autechaux (25).....87 H5
Autechaux-Roide (25).....88 C5
les Autels (02).....23 F1
les Autels-Villevillon (28)...61 F4
Auterive (31).....185 G2
Auterive (32).....167 H5
Auterive (82).....168 C3
Auterrive (64).....165 E6
Autet (70).....86 D4
Auteuil (60).....20 A5
Auteuil (78).....41 H4
Auteville-Saint-Martin-Bideran (64).....181 F1
Authe (08).....24 B4
Autheuil-Authouillet (27)...41 E1
Autheuil-en-Valois (60).....43 H1
Autheux (80).....7 F4
Authevernes (27).....19 G6
Authezat (63).....127 F4
Authie (14).....14 B4
Authie (80).....7 H4
Authieule (80).....7 G4
les Authieux (27).....41 E3
les Authieux-du-Puits (61)...39 G5
Authieux-Ratiéville (76)...18 D3
les Authieux-sur-Calonne (14).....15 F4
les Authieux-sur-le-Port-Saint-Ouen (76).....18 D5
Authiou (58).....99 F1
Authoison (70).....87 G4
Authon (04).....160 C5
Authon (41).....79 F3
Authon-du-Perche (28)...61 F4
Authon-Ébéon (17).....121 G2
Authon-la-Plaine (91).....62 D2
Authou (27).....18 A6
Authuille (80).....8 A4
Authume (39).....102 C2
Authumes (71).....102 B4
Autichamp (26).....158 C1
Autignac (34).....172 B6
Autigny (76).....17 F3
Autigny-la-Tour (88).....68 D2
Autigny-le-Grand (52).....67 H1
Autigny-le-Petit (52).....67 H1
Autingues (62).....1 H3
Autoire (46).....139 E5
Autoreille (70).....87 E5
Autouillet (78).....41 H4
Autrac (43).....141 F1
Autrans-Méaudre en Vercors (38).....145 F3
Autrèche (37).....79 F4
Autrechêne (90).....88 D3
Autrêches (60).....21 H4
Autrecourt-et-Pourron (08)...24 C3
Autrécourt-sur-Aire (55)...47 E2
Autremencourt (02).....22 D2
Autrepierre (54).....49 G5
Autreppes (02).....9 H6
Autretot (76).....17 E4
Autreville (02).....21 H3
Autreville (88).....69 E1
Autréville-Saint-Lambert (55).....24 D3
Autreville-sur-la-Renne (52)...67 G5
Autreville-sur-Moselle (54)...48 C4
Autrey (54).....48 C6
Autrey (88).....70 B3
Autrey-le-Vay (70).....87 H4
Autrey-lès-Cerre (70).....87 H3
Autrey-lès-Gray (70).....86 C4
Autricourt (21).....67 E6
Autruche (08).....24 C4
Autruy-sur-Juine (45).....63 E3
Autry (08).....24 B6
Autry-Issards (03).....113 G2
Autry-le-Châtel (45).....82 A4
Autun (71).....100 D4
Auty (82).....152 C6
Auvare (06).....178 C1
Auve (51).....46 B2
Auvernaux (91).....63 H1
Auvers (43).....141 H4
Auvers (50).....13 E5
Auvers-le-Hamon (72).....59 F6
Auvers-Saint-Georges (91)...63 F1
Auvers-sous-Montfaucon (72).....59 H5

Auvers-sur-Oise (95).....42 C2
Auvet-et-la-Chapelotte (70)...86 C4
Auvillar (82).....168 B1
Auvillars (14).....15 E4
Auvillars-sur-Saône (21)...102 A3
Auvillers-les-Forges (08)...10 C6
Auvilliers (76).....19 F1
Auvilliers-en-Gâtinais (45)...63 H6
aux-Aussat (32).....183 G1
aux Marais (60).....20 A5
Auxais (50).....13 E6
Auxange (39).....102 D2
Auxant (21).....101 F2
Auxelles-Bas (90).....88 C2
Auxelles-Haut (90).....88 C2
Auxerre (89).....83 F2
Auxey-Duresses (21).....101 F3
Auxi-le-Château (62).....7 F3
Auxon (10).....66 A5
Auxon (70).....87 G3
Auxonne (21).....102 C1
les Auxons (25).....87 F6
Auxy (45).....63 H5
Auxy (71).....100 D4
Auzainvilliers (88).....69 E3
Auzances (23).....126 B1
Auzas (31).....184 C3
Auzat (09).....198 D1
Auzat-la-Combelle (63)...127 G6
Auzebosc (76).....18 A3
Auzelles (63).....127 H4
Auzers (15).....140 B2
Auzet (04).....160 D4
Auzeville-Tolosane (31)...169 F6
Auzielle (31).....169 F6
Auzits (12).....154 A3
Auzon (43).....141 G1
Auzouer-en-Touraine (37)...79 F4
Auzouville-l'Esneval (76)...17 F4
Auzouville-sur-Ry (76).....19 E4
Auzouville-sur-Saône (76)...17 F3
Availles-en-Châtellerault (86)...94 D5
Availles-Limouzine (86)...109 G5
Availles-sur-Seiche (35)...58 A5
Availles-Thouarsais (79)...93 G4
Avajan (65).....183 G6
Avallon (89).....84 A5
les Avanchers-Valmorel (73).....132 D5
Avançon (05).....160 C2
Avançon (08).....23 F4
Avanne-Aveney (25).....103 F1
Avant-lès-Marcilly (10).....65 F2
Avant-lès-Ramerupt (10)...66 C2
Avapessa (2B).....202 C5
Avaray (41).....80 B2
Avaux (08).....23 F4
Aveize (69).....129 G4
Aveizieux (42).....129 G5
Avelanges (21).....85 H4
Avelesges (80).....7 E6
Avelin (59).....3 F6
Aveluy (80).....8 A5
Avenas (69).....116 A5
Avenay (14).....14 B5
Avenay-Val-d'Or (51).....45 F2
Avène (34).....172 A4
Les Avenières Veyrins-Thuellin (38).....131 F4
Avensac (32).....168 B3
Avensan (33).....134 D3
Aventignan (65).....183 H4
Averan (65).....183 E3
Averdoingt (62).....7 H2
Averdon (41).....79 H3
Avermes (03).....113 H1
Avernes (95).....42 A2
Avernes-Saint-Gourgon (61).....39 G3
Avéron-Bergelle (32).....167 E4
Averton (53).....59 G2
Avesnelles (59).....10 A4
Avesnes (62).....1 H6
Avesnes-Chaussoy (80)...6 D6
Avesnes-en-Bray (76).....19 G4
Avesnes-en-Saosnois (72)...60 C3
Avesnes-en-Val (76).....6 B5
Avesnes-le-Comte (62).....7 H2
Avesnes-le-Sec (59).....9 E3
Avesnes-les-Aubert (59)...9 E3
Avesnes-lès-Bapaume (62)...8 A4
Avesnes-sur-Helpe (59)...10 A4
Avessac (44).....74 A1
Avessé (72).....59 F6
Aveux (65).....183 H5
Avezac-Prat-Lahitte (65)...183 G4
Avezan (32).....168 B3
Avèze (30).....172 D2
Avèze (63).....126 B5
Avignon (84).....175 E2
Avignon-lès-Saint-Claude (39).....118 A3
Avignonet (38).....145 G4
Avignonet-Lauragais (31)...186 A2
Avillers (54).....25 H5
Avillers (88).....69 G3
Avillers-Sainte-Croix (55)...47 H2
Avilley (25).....87 H5
Avilly-Saint-Léonard (60)...43 E1
Avion (62).....8 B1
Avioth (55).....25 E3
Avirey-Lingey (10).....66 C5
Aviron (27).....40 D2
Avize (51).....45 F3
Avocourt (55).....24 D6

Avoine (37).....94 B1
Avoine (61).....39 E5
Avoise (72).....77 G1
Avolsheim (67).....50 D6
Avon (77).....64 A2
Avon (79).....108 C3
Avon-la-Pèze (10).....65 G2
Avon-les-Roches (37).....94 C2
Avondance (62).....2 A6
Avord (18).....98 A3
Avosnes (21).....85 E6
Avoudrey (25).....104 A2
Avrainville (54).....48 B4
Avrainville (88).....69 G2
Avrainville (91).....63 F1
Avranches (50).....35 H3
Avranville (88).....68 C2
Avrechy (60).....20 C4
Avrecourt (52).....68 C6
Avrée (58).....100 A5
Avremesnil (76).....17 F2
Avreuil (10).....66 A5
Avricourt (54).....49 G5
Avricourt (57).....49 G5
Avricourt (60).....21 F2
Avrieux (73).....147 F2
Avrigney-Virey (70).....87 E6
Avrigny (60).....20 D5
Avril (54).....26 A4
Avril-sur-Loire (58).....99 F5
Avrillé (49).....76 D4
Avrillé (85).....91 F6
Avrillé-les-Ponceaux (37)...78 B5
Avrilly (03).....114 D4
Avrilly (61).....38 A6
Avroult (62).....2 A5
Avy (17).....121 F4
Awoingt (59).....9 E3
Ax-les-Thermes (09).....199 G2
Axat (11).....200 B1
Axiat (09).....199 F1
Aÿ-Champagne (51).....45 F2
Aÿ-sur-Moselle (57).....26 C4
Ayat-sur-Sioule (63).....113 E6
Aydat (63).....127 E4
Aydie (64).....166 C5
Aydius (64).....182 A5
Aydoilles (88).....70 A3
Ayen (19).....138 B2
Ayencourt (80).....20 D3
Ayette (62).....8 A3
Ayguatébia-Talau (66).....200 A3
Ayguemorte-les-Graves (33).....135 F6
Ayguesvives (31).....185 H1
Ayguetinte (32).....167 G3
Ayherre (64).....180 D1
Ayn (73).....131 G4
Aynac (46).....139 E6
Ayron (86).....94 A6
Ayros-Arbouix (65).....182 D5
Ayse (74).....118 D5
Ayssènes (12).....171 G1
Aytré (17).....106 D5
les Ayvelles (08).....24 B2
Ayzac-Ost (65).....182 D4
Ayzieu (32).....166 D3
Azannes-et-Soumazannes (55)...25 F5
Azas (31).....169 G4
Azat-Châtenet (23).....111 F6
Azat-le-Ris (87).....110 B4
Azay-le-Brûlé (79).....108 A3
Azay-le-Ferron (36).....95 G5
Azay-le-Rideau (37).....94 C1
Azay-sur-Cher (37).....79 E6
Azay-sur-Indre (37).....95 F1
Azay-sur-Thouet (79).....93 F6
Azé (41).....79 F1
Azé (53).....76 D1
Azé (71).....116 B3
Azelot (54).....48 D6
Azerables (23).....110 D3
Azerailles (54).....70 B1
Azerat (24).....138 A3
Azérat (43).....141 G1
Azereix (65).....183 E3
Azet (65).....196 D1
Azeville (50).....13 E3
Azillanet (34).....187 G2
Azille (11).....187 G3
Azilone-Ampaza (2A).....207 E1
Azincourt (62).....7 F1
Azolette (69).....115 G5
Azoudange (57).....49 G4
Azur (40).....164 C3
Azy (18).....98 B2
Azy-le-Vif (58).....99 E5
Azy-sur-Marne (02).....44 B2
Azzana (2A).....204 D4

B

Baâlon (55).....25 E4
Baâlons (08).....24 A3
Babeau-Bouldoux (34)...188 A1
Babœuf (60).....21 G3
Baby (77).....65 E2
Baccarat (54).....70 B1
Baccon (45).....80 B1
Bach (46).....153 E4
Bachant (59).....9 H3
Bachas (31).....184 C3

la Bachellerie (24).....138 A3
Bachivillers (60).....20 A6
Bachos (31).....184 A6
Bachy (59).....3 G6
Bacilly (50).....35 G3
Baconnes (51).....45 H1
la Baconnière (53).....58 C4
Bacouël (60).....20 C3
Bacourt (57).....49 E3
Bacquepuis (27).....40 D2
Bacqueville (27).....19 E5
Bacqueville-en-Caux (76)...17 G3
Badailhac (15).....140 C5
Badaroux (48).....156 A3
Badecon-le-Pin (36).....111 E2
Badefols-d'Ans (24).....138 A2
Badefols-sur-Dordogne (24).....137 F5
Baden (56).....72 C1
Badens (11).....187 F3
Badevel (25).....88 D4
Badménil-aux-Bois (88)...70 A3
Badonviller (54).....70 C1
Badonvilliers-Gérauvilliers (55).....47 H6
Baerendorf (67).....50 A3
Baerenthal (57).....50 D2
la Baffe (88).....70 A4
Baffie (63).....128 C6
Bagard (30).....173 G1
Bagas (33).....150 A1
Bâgé-en-Quercy (46).....152 B4
Bâgé-la-Ville (01).....116 C4
Bâgé-le-Châtel (01).....116 C4
Bagert (09).....184 D4
Bages (11).....188 A4
Bages (66).....201 F3
Bagiry (31).....184 A5
Bagnac-sur-Célé (46).....153 H1
Bagnaux (89).....65 G4
Bagneaux-sur-Loing (77)...64 C4
Bagnères-de-Bigorre (65)...183 F4
Bagnères-de-Luchon (31)...197 F1
Bagneux (02).....22 A4
Bagneux (03).....113 G1
Bagneux (36).....96 C3
Bagneux (51).....65 H1
Bagneux (54).....48 B6
Bagneux (92).....42 C4
Bagneux-la-Fosse (10)...66 C6
Bagnizeau (17).....121 G1
Bagnoles (11).....187 E3
Bagnoles de l'Orne Normandie (61).....38 C6
Bagnolet (93).....42 D4
Bagnols (63).....126 C5
Bagnols (69).....129 G2
Bagnols-en-Forêt (83)...178 B5
Bagnols-sur-Cèze (30)...158 A6
Bagnot (21).....102 A3
Baguer-Morvan (35).....35 G5
Baguer-Pican (35).....35 F4
Baho (66).....201 E2
Bahus-Soubiran (40).....166 B4
Baigneaux (28).....62 D5
Baigneaux (33).....135 H6
Baignes (70).....87 F3
Baignes-Sainte-Radegonde (16).....121 H6
Baigneux-les-Juifs (21)...85 E4
Baigts (40).....165 G4
Baigts-de-Béarn (64).....165 F6
Baillargues (34).....173 G5
Baillé (35).....35 H6
Bailleau-Armenonville (28)...62 C1
Bailleau-le-Pin (28).....62 A2
Bailleau-l'Évêque (28).....62 A1
Baillestavy (66).....200 C3
Baillet-en-France (95).....42 C2
Bailleul (59).....2 D4
Bailleul (61).....39 E4
le Bailleul (72).....77 G2
Bailleul (80).....6 D5
Bailleul-aux-Cornailles (62)...7 H2
Bailleul-la-Vallée (27).....15 G4
Bailleul-le-Soc (60).....20 D4
Bailleul-lès-Pernes (62)...2 B6
Bailleul-Neuville (76).....19 E1
Bailleul-Sir-Berthoult (62)...8 B2
Bailleul-sur-Thérain (60)...20 B5
Baillolet (76).....19 E1
Baillou (41).....61 G6
Bailly (60).....21 G4
Bailly (78).....42 B4
Bailly-aux-Forges (52)...67 G1
Bailly-en-Rivière (76).....6 A4
Bailly-le-Franc (10).....67 E1
Bailly-Romainvilliers (77)...43 G4
Bain-de-Bretagne (35).....57 F2
Baincthun (62).....1 F4
Bainghen (62).....1 G4
Bains (43).....142 B4
Bains-sur-Oust (35).....56 C6
Bainville-aux-Miroirs (54)...69 G1
Bainville-aux-Saules (88)...69 F4
Bainville-sur-Madon (54)...48 C6
Bairols (06).....178 D1
Bairon et ses environs (08)...24 B3
Bais (35).....57 H4
Bais (53).....59 F3
Baisieux (59).....3 G5
Baissey (52).....86 A2
Baives (59).....10 B4
Baix (07).....158 A1

Baixas (66) ... 201 E2
Baizieux (80) ... 7 H5
le Baizil (51) ... 45 E3
Bajamont (47) ... 151 F5
Bajonnette (32) ... 168 A3
Bajus (62) ... 7 H1
Balacet (09) ... 184 C6
Baladou (46) ... 138 C5
Balagny-sur-Thérain (60) ... 20 C5
Balaguères (09) ... 184 D5
Balaguier-d'Olt (12) ... 153 G3
Balaguier-sur-Rance (12) ... 171 E3
Balaiseaux (39) ... 102 C3
Balaives-et-Butz (08) ... 24 B2
Balan (01) ... 130 C2
Balan (08) ... 24 C2
Balanod (39) ... 117 E2
Balansun (64) ... 165 G6
Balanzac (17) ... 120 D3
Balaruc-le-Vieux (34) ... 189 F1
Balaruc-les-Bains (34) ... 189 F1
Balâtre (80) ... 21 F2
Balazé (35) ... 58 A4
Balazuc (07) ... 157 G3
Balbigny (42) ... 129 E2
Balbins (38) ... 130 D6
Balbronn (67) ... 50 C5
Baldenheim (67) ... 71 G3
Baldersheim (68) ... 89 F1
la Baleine (50) ... 37 E2
Baleix (64) ... 182 D1
Balesta (31) ... 184 A3
Baleyssagues (47) ... 150 C1
Balgau (67) ... 71 G6
Balham (08) ... 23 F4
Balignac (82) ... 168 B2
Baligicourt (10) ... 66 D1
Bâlines (27) ... 40 C5
Balinghem (62) ... 1 H3
Baliracq-Maumusson (64) ... 166 B5
Baliros (64) ... 182 C3
Balizac (33) ... 149 G3
Ballainvilliers (91) ... 42 C5
Ballaison (74) ... 118 D3
Ballan-Miré (37) ... 78 D6
Ballancourt-sur-Essonne (91) ... 63 G1
Ballans (17) ... 121 H2
Ballay (08) ... 24 B4
Balledent (87) ... 110 C5
Balleroy-sur-Drôme (14) ... 13 G6
Ballersdorf (68) ... 89 E3
Balléville (88) ... 69 E2
Ballon (17) ... 106 D5
Ballon-Saint Mars (72) ... 60 B4
Ballons (26) ... 159 G5
Ballore (71) ... 115 G2
Ballots (53) ... 58 B6
Balloy (77) ... 64 D2
Balma (31) ... 169 F5
la Balme (73) ... 131 G3
la Balme-de-Sillingy (74) ... 132 A1
la Balme-de-Thuy (74) ... 132 B1
la Balme-d'Épy (39) ... 117 F3
la Balme-les-Grottes (38) ... 130 D2
Balnot-la-Grange (10) ... 66 C6
Balnot-sur-Laignes (10) ... 66 D5
Balogna (2A) ... 204 C3
Balot (21) ... 84 D2
Balschwiller (68) ... 89 E2
Balsièges (48) ... 156 A3
Baltzenheim (68) ... 71 G4
Balzac (16) ... 122 B3
Bambecque (59) ... 2 C2
Bambiderstroff (57) ... 27 E5
Ban-de-Laveline (88) ... 70 D3
Ban-de-Sapt (88) ... 70 D2
le Ban-Saint-Martin (57) ... 26 B5
Ban-sur-Meurthe-Clefcy (88) ... 70 D4
Banassac-Canilhac (48) ... 155 G4
Banca (64) ... 180 C3
Bancigny (02) ... 23 E1
Bancourt (62) ... 8 C4
Bandol (83) ... 192 D5
Baneins (01) ... 116 C5
Baneuil (24) ... 137 F5
Bangor (56) ... 72 A3
Banios (65) ... 183 F4
Banize (23) ... 125 F2
Bannalec (29) ... 54 A3
Bannans (25) ... 103 H4
Bannay (18) ... 82 B6
Bannay (51) ... 44 D4
Bannay (57) ... 26 D5
Banne (07) ... 157 E4
Bannegon (18) ... 98 B5
Bannes (46) ... 139 F6
Bannes (51) ... 45 E4
Bannes (52) ... 86 B1
Bannes (53) ... 59 F5
Banneville-la-Campagne (14) ... 14 C5
Bannières (81) ... 169 H5
Bannoncourt (55) ... 47 G3
Bannost-Villegagnon (77) ... 44 A5
Banogne-Recouvrance (08) ... 23 F3
Banon (04) ... 176 B1
Banos (40) ... 165 H4
Bans (39) ... 102 D3
Bansat (63) ... 127 G6
Bantanges (71) ... 116 D1
Banteux (59) ... 8 D4
Banthelu (95) ... 41 H1
Bantheville (55) ... 24 D5
Bantigny (59) ... 8 D3
Bantouzelle (59) ... 8 D4
Bantzenheim (68) ... 89 G1

Banvillars (90) ... 88 C3
Banville (14) ... 14 B3
Banvou (61) ... 38 B5
Banyuls-dels-Aspres (66) ... 201 F3
Banyuls-sur-Mer (66) ... 201 G4
Baon (89) ... 84 B1
Baons-le-Comte (76) ... 17 E4
Bapaume (62) ... 8 B4
Bar (19) ... 139 E1
Bar-le-Duc (55) ... 47 E4
Bar-lès-Buzancy (08) ... 24 C4
Bar-sur-Aube (10) ... 67 F4
le Bar-sur-Loup (06) ... 178 C4
Bar-sur-Seine (10) ... 66 D5
Baracé (49) ... 77 F3
Baraigne (11) ... 186 A2
Baraize (36) ... 111 E2
Baralle (62) ... 8 C3
Baraqueville (12) ... 154 B5
Barastre (62) ... 8 C4
Baratier (05) ... 161 E2
Barbachen (65) ... 183 F1
Barbaggio (2B) ... 203 F4
Barbaira (11) ... 187 F3
Barbaise (08) ... 24 A2
Barbas (54) ... 49 G6
Barbaste (47) ... 150 D6
Barbâtre (85) ... 90 B1
Barbazan (31) ... 184 A5
Barbazan-Debat (65) ... 183 F3
Barbazan-Dessus (65) ... 183 F3
la Barben (13) ... 175 G6
Barbentane (13) ... 174 D3
Barberaz (73) ... 131 H4
Barberey-Saint-Sulpice (10) ... 66 A3
Barberier (03) ... 113 H5
Barbery (14) ... 38 C2
Barbery (60) ... 21 E6
Barbeville (14) ... 13 H5
Barbey (77) ... 64 C2
Barbey-Seroux (88) ... 70 C4
Barbezières (16) ... 122 A1
Barbezieux-Saint-Hilaire (16) ... 121 H5
Barbières (26) ... 144 C4
Barbirey-sur-Ouche (21) ... 101 F1
Barbizon (77) ... 63 H2
Barbonne-Fayel (51) ... 44 D6
Barbonville (54) ... 48 D6
le Barboux (25) ... 104 C2
Barbuise (10) ... 65 F1
Barby (08) ... 23 G3
Barby (73) ... 132 A4
Barc (27) ... 40 B2
le Barcarès (66) ... 201 G1
Barcelonne (26) ... 144 C5
Barcelonne-du-Gers (32) ... 166 C4
Barcelonnette (04) ... 161 F3
Barchain (57) ... 49 H5
Barcillonnette (05) ... 160 A3
Barcugnan (32) ... 183 G1
Barcus (64) ... 181 G3
Barcy (77) ... 43 G2
Bard (42) ... 128 D5
Bard-le-Régulier (21) ... 100 D2
Bard-lès-Époisses (21) ... 84 C4
Bard-lès-Pesmes (70) ... 86 D6
la Barde (17) ... 136 A3
Bardenac (16) ... 136 A1
Bardigues (82) ... 168 B1
le Bardon (45) ... 80 C1
Bardos (64) ... 164 D6
Bardou (24) ... 137 F6
Bardouville (76) ... 18 B4
Barèges (65) ... 183 E6
Bareilles (65) ... 183 G6
Barembach (67) ... 71 E1
Baren (31) ... 184 A6
Barentin (76) ... 18 C3
Barenton (50) ... 37 H6
Barenton-Bugny (02) ... 22 C2
Barenton-Cel (02) ... 22 C2
Barenton-sur-Serre (02) ... 22 C2
Barésia-sur-l'Ain (39) ... 117 G1
Barfleur (50) ... 13 E1
Bargème (83) ... 178 A4
Bargemon (83) ... 178 A5
Barges (21) ... 101 H1
Barges (43) ... 142 C6
Barges (70) ... 87 E1
Bargny (60) ... 43 G1
Barie (33) ... 150 A2
les Barils (27) ... 40 B5
Barinque (64) ... 182 C1
Barisey-au-Plain (54) ... 69 E1
Barisey-la-Côte (54) ... 48 A6
Barisis-aux-Bois (02) ... 22 A3
Barizey (71) ... 101 F5
Barjac (09) ... 184 D4
Barjac (30) ... 157 G5
Barjac (48) ... 156 A2
Barjols (83) ... 177 E5
Barjon (21) ... 85 G3
Barjouville (28) ... 62 B2
Barles (04) ... 160 D5
Barlest (65) ... 182 D3
Barleux (80) ... 8 C6
Barlieu (18) ... 82 A5
Barlin (62) ... 8 A1
Barly (62) ... 7 H3
Barly (80) ... 7 G3
Barmainville (28) ... 62 D3
Barnas (07) ... 157 E1
Barnave (26) ... 159 E1
Barnay (71) ... 100 D2
Barneville-Carteret (50) ... 12 B4
Barneville-la-Bertran (14) ... 15 F3

Barneville-sur-Seine (27) ... 18 B5
les Baroches (54) ... 26 A4
Baromesnil (76) ... 6 B5
Baron (30) ... 174 A1
Baron (33) ... 135 G5
Baron (60) ... 43 F1
Baron (71) ... 115 F2
Baron-sur-Odon (14) ... 14 B5
la Baronnie (27) ... 41 E3
Barou-en-Auge (14) ... 39 E3
Baroville (10) ... 67 F4
le Barp (33) ... 149 E1
Barquet (27) ... 40 C2
Barr (67) ... 71 G1
Barrais-Bussolles (03) ... 114 C4
Barran (32) ... 167 G5
Barrancoueu (65) ... 183 G6
Barras (04) ... 160 C6
Barraute-Camu (64) ... 181 G1
Barraux (38) ... 132 A6
la Barre (39) ... 102 D2
la Barre (70) ... 87 G5
la Barre (81) ... 171 G4
la Barre-de-Monts (85) ... 90 C2
la Barre-de-Semilly (50) ... 37 G1
Barre-des-Cévennes (48) ... 156 B5
Barrême (04) ... 177 G2
Barret (16) ... 121 H5
Barret-de-Lioure (26) ... 159 F6
Barret-sur-Méouge (05) ... 159 H5
Barretaine (39) ... 103 E5
Barrettali (2B) ... 203 F2
Barriac-les-Bosquets (15) ... 139 H3
Barro (16) ... 108 D6
Barrou (37) ... 95 E4
le Barroux (84) ... 158 D6
Barry (65) ... 183 E3
Barry-d'Islemade (82) ... 169 E1
Bars (24) ... 137 H3
Bars (32) ... 167 F6
Barsac (26) ... 159 E1
Barsac (33) ... 149 G2
Barst (57) ... 27 F6
Bart (25) ... 88 C4
Bartenheim (68) ... 89 G3
Barthe (65) ... 183 H2
la Barthe-de-Neste (65) ... 183 G4
Bartherans (25) ... 103 F3
les Barthes (82) ... 168 D1
Bartrès (65) ... 182 D4
Barville (27) ... 15 G5
Barville (61) ... 60 C1
Barville (88) ... 68 D2
Barville-en-Gâtinais (45) ... 63 G5
Barzan (17) ... 120 D5
Barzun (64) ... 182 D3
Barzy-en-Thiérache (02) ... 9 G4
Barzy-sur-Marne (02) ... 44 C2
Bas-en-Basset (43) ... 142 D1
Bas-et-Lezat (63) ... 127 G1
Bas-Lieu (59) ... 10 A4
Bas-Mauco (40) ... 165 H3
Le Bas Ségala (12) ... 153 H4
Bascons (40) ... 166 A3
Bascous (32) ... 167 E3
Baslieux (54) ... 25 H4
Baslieux-lès-Fismes (51) ... 22 C5
Baslieux-sous-Châtillon (51) ... 45 E1
Basly (14) ... 14 B4
Bassac (16) ... 122 A4
Bassan (34) ... 188 C1
Bassanne (33) ... 150 A2
Basse-Goulaine (44) ... 74 D5
Basse-Ham (57) ... 26 C3
Basse-Rentgen (57) ... 26 C2
la Basse-Vaivre (70) ... 69 F6
la Bassée (59) ... 3 E6
Bassemberg (67) ... 71 F2
Basseneville (14) ... 14 D4
Bassens (33) ... 135 F5
Bassens (73) ... 131 H4
Bassercles (40) ... 165 H5
Basses (86) ... 94 A3
Basseux (62) ... 8 A3
Bassevelle (77) ... 44 B3
Bassignac (15) ... 140 A1
Bassignac-le-Bas (19) ... 139 E4
Bassignac-le-Haut (19) ... 139 G2
Bassigney (70) ... 87 G1
Bassillac et Auberoche (24) ... 137 G2
Bassillon-Vauzé (64) ... 166 D6
Bassing (57) ... 49 G3
Bassoles-Aulers (02) ... 22 A3
Bassoncourt (52) ... 68 C5
Bassou (89) ... 83 F1
Bassoues (32) ... 167 F5
Bassu (51) ... 46 B4
Bassuet (51) ... 46 B4
Bassurels (48) ... 156 B4
Bassussarry (64) ... 164 B6
Bassy (74) ... 131 G1
Bastanès (64) ... 181 G1
Bastelica (2A) ... 205 E5
Bastelicaccia (2A) ... 204 C6
Bastennes (40) ... 165 G4
Bastia (2B) ... 203 G4
la Bastide (66) ... 200 D3
la Bastide (83) ... 178 A4
la Bastide-Clairence (64) ... 164 D5
la Bastide-de-Besplas (09) ... 185 E3
la Bastide-de-Bousignac (09) ... 186 B5
la Bastide-de-Lordat (09) ... 185 H4
la Bastide-de-Sérou (09) ... 185 F5
la Bastide-d'Engras (30) ... 174 B1

la Bastide-des-Jourdans (84) ... 176 B3
la Bastide-du-Salat (09) ... 184 C4
la Bastide-Pradines (12) ... 172 A2
la Bastide-Puylaurent (48) ... 156 D2
la Bastide-Solages (12) ... 171 E2
la Bastide-sur-l'Hers (09) ... 186 B5
la Bastidonne (84) ... 176 B4
le Bastit (46) ... 153 E1
Basville (23) ... 126 A2
la Bataille (79) ... 108 B5
Bathelémont (54) ... 49 E5
Bathernay (26) ... 144 B2
la Bâthie (73) ... 132 D4
la Bâtie-des-Fonds (26) ... 159 G3
la Bâtie-Montgascon (38) ... 131 F4
la Bâtie-Montsaléon (05) ... 159 H3
la Bâtie-Neuve (05) ... 160 C2
la Bâtie-Rolland (26) ... 158 B2
la Bâtie-Vieille (05) ... 160 C2
les Bâties (70) ... 87 E4
Batilly (54) ... 26 A5
Batilly-en-Gâtinais (45) ... 63 G5
Batilly-en-Puisaye (45) ... 82 B4
Bats (40) ... 166 A4
Batsère (65) ... 183 G4
Battenans-les-Mines (25) ... 87 H5
Battenans-Varin (25) ... 88 C6
Battenheim (68) ... 89 F1
Battexey (88) ... 69 G2
Battigny (54) ... 69 E1
Batz-sur-Mer (44) ... 73 F4
Batzendorf (67) ... 51 E4
Baubigny (21) ... 101 F3
Baubigny (50) ... 12 B3
la Bauche (73) ... 131 G5
Baud (56) ... 55 E4
Baudement (51) ... 45 E6
Baudemont (71) ... 115 F4
Baudignan (40) ... 150 B6
Baudignécourt (55) ... 47 G6
Baudinard-sur-Verdon (83) ... 177 F4
Baudoncourt (70) ... 87 H2
Baudonvilliers (55) ... 46 D5
Baudre (50) ... 37 G1
Baudrecourt (52) ... 67 G2
Baudrecourt (57) ... 49 E2
Baudreix (64) ... 182 C3
Baudrémont (55) ... 47 F4
Baudres (36) ... 96 B3
Baudreville (28) ... 62 D3
Baudricourt (88) ... 69 F3
Baudrières (71) ... 101 H6
Bauduen (83) ... 177 F4
Baugé-en-Anjou (49) ... 77 G4
Baugy (18) ... 98 B3
Baugy (60) ... 21 E4
Baugy (71) ... 115 E4
Baulay (70) ... 87 F2
Baule (45) ... 80 C2
Baule-Escoublac (44) ... 73 F4
Baulme-la-Roche (21) ... 85 F6
Baulne (91) ... 63 G1
Baulny (55) ... 24 C6
Baulon (35) ... 56 D4
Baulou (09) ... 185 G5
la Baume (74) ... 119 E4
la Baume-Cornillane (26) ... 144 C6
la Baume-de-Transit (26) ... 158 B4
la Baume-d'Hostun (26) ... 144 D4
Baume-les-Dames (25) ... 87 H5
Baume-les-Messieurs (39) ... 102 D6
Baupte (50) ... 12 D5
Baurech (33) ... 135 F6
la Baussaine (35) ... 56 D1
Bauvin (59) ... 3 E6
les Baux-de-Breteuil (27) ... 40 B3
les Baux-de-Provence (13) ... 175 E4
les Baux-Sainte-Croix (27) ... 40 D3
Bauzy (41) ... 80 B4
Bavans (25) ... 88 C4
Bavay (59) ... 9 H2
Bavelincourt (80) ... 7 H5
Bavent (14) ... 14 C4
Baverans (39) ... 102 D2
Bavilliers (90) ... 88 C3
Bavinchove (59) ... 2 C3
Bavincourt (62) ... 7 H3
Bax (31) ... 185 E3
Bay (70) ... 86 D6
Bay-sur-Aube (52) ... 85 H2
Bayard-sur-Marne (52) ... 47 E6
Bayas (33) ... 135 H3
Baye (29) ... 54 B4
Baye (51) ... 44 D4
Bayecourt (88) ... 70 A3
Bayel (10) ... 67 F4
Bayencourt (80) ... 8 A4
Bayenghem-lès-Éperlecques (62) ... 2 A3
Bayenghem-lès-Seninghem (62) ... 1 H4
Bayet (03) ... 113 H4
Bayeux (14) ... 13 H5
Bayon (54) ... 69 G1
Bayon-sur-Gironde (33) ... 135 E3
Bayonne (64) ... 164 B6
Bayons (04) ... 160 C4
Bayonville (08) ... 24 C4
Bayonville-sur-Mad (54) ... 48 B2
Bayonvillers (80) ... 8 A6
Bazac (16) ... 136 A2
Bazaiges (36) ... 111 E2
Bazailles (54) ... 25 H4
Bazainville (78) ... 41 G4

Bazancourt (51) ... 23 F5
Bazancourt (60) ... 19 G3
Bazarnes (89) ... 83 G3
Bazas (33) ... 149 H3
Bazauges (17) ... 121 H1
Bazegney (88) ... 69 G3
Bazeilles (08) ... 24 C2
Bazeilles-sur-Othain (55) ... 25 F3
Bazelat (23) ... 111 E3
Bazemont (78) ... 42 A3
Bazens (47) ... 150 D5
Bazentin (80) ... 8 B5
Bazenville (14) ... 14 A3
Bazet (65) ... 183 E2
la Bazeuge (87) ... 110 B4
Bazian (32) ... 167 F4
Bazicourt (60) ... 21 E5
Baziège (31) ... 185 H1
Bazien (88) ... 70 B2
Bazillac (65) ... 183 E2
Bazincourt-sur-Epte (27) ... 19 G5
Bazincourt-sur-Saulx (55) ... 47 E5
Bazinghen (62) ... 1 F3
Bazinval (76) ... 6 B5
la Bazoche-Gouet (28) ... 61 F4
Bazoches (58) ... 83 H6
Bazoches-au-Houlme (61) ... 38 D4
Bazoches-en-Dunois (28) ... 62 B5
Bazoches-lès-Bray (77) ... 64 D2
Bazoches-les-Gallerandes (45) ... 63 E4
Bazoches-les-Hautes (28) ... 62 D4
Bazoches-sur-Guyonne (78) ... 42 A4
Bazoches-sur-Hoëne (61) ... 39 H6
Bazoches-sur-le-Betz (45) ... 64 C5
Bazoches-sur-Vesles (02) ... 22 C5
la Bazoge (72) ... 60 A5
la Bazoge-Montpinçon (53) ... 59 E3
Bazoges-en-Paillers (85) ... 92 A4
Bazoges-en-Pareds (85) ... 92 B6
Bazoilles-et-Ménil (88) ... 69 F3
Bazoilles-sur-Meuse (88) ... 68 D3
Bazolles (58) ... 99 G2
Bazoncourt (57) ... 48 D2
la Bazoque (14) ... 13 G6
la Bazoque (61) ... 38 B4
Bazoques (27) ... 15 H5
Bazordan (65) ... 183 H3
la Bazouge-de-Chemeré (53) ... 59 E5
la Bazouge-des-Alleux (53) ... 58 D4
la Bazouge-du-Désert (35) ... 58 B1
Bazougers (53) ... 59 E5
Bazouges Cré sur Loir (72) ... 77 G2
Bazouges-la-Pérouse (35) ... 35 F5
Bazuel (59) ... 9 G4
Bazugues (32) ... 183 G1
Bazus (31) ... 169 F4
Bazus-Aure (65) ... 183 G6
Bazus-Neste (65) ... 183 G4
le Béage (07) ... 142 D5
Béalcourt (80) ... 7 F3
Béalencourt (62) ... 7 F1
Béard (58) ... 99 E5
Béard-Géovreissiat (01) ... 117 G5
Beaubec-la-Rosière (76) ... 19 F2
Beaubery (71) ... 115 G3
Beaubray (27) ... 40 C3
Beaucaire (30) ... 174 D3
Beaucaire (32) ... 167 G3
Beaucamps-le-Jeune (80) ... 19 G1
Beaucamps-le-Vieux (80) ... 6 D6
Beaucamps-Ligny (59) ... 3 E5
Beaucé (35) ... 58 A2
Beauce la Romaine (41) ... 80 B1
Beaucens (65) ... 182 D5
le Beaucet (84) ... 175 G2
Beauchalot (31) ... 184 C4
Beauchamp (95) ... 42 C2
Beauchamps (50) ... 37 E3
Beauchamps (80) ... 6 B5
Beauchamps-sur-Huillard (45) ... 63 G6
Beauchastel (07) ... 144 A6
Beauche (28) ... 40 C5
Beauchemin (52) ... 86 A1
Beauchêne (41) ... 61 F6
Beauchery-Saint-Martin (77) ... 44 B6
Beauclair (55) ... 24 D4
Beaucoudray (50) ... 37 F2
Beaucourt (90) ... 88 D4
Beaucourt-en-Santerre (80) ... 20 D1
Beaucourt-sur-l'Ancre (80) ... 8 A4
Beaucourt-sur-l'Hallue (80) ... 7 H5
Beaucouzé (49) ... 76 D4
Beaucroissant (38) ... 145 E1
Beaudéan (65) ... 183 F4
Beaudéduit (60) ... 20 A2
Beaudignies (59) ... 9 G3
Beaudricourt (62) ... 7 G3
Beaufai (61) ... 39 H4
Beaufay (72) ... 60 C4
Beauficel (50) ... 37 G4
Beauficel-en-Lyons (27) ... 19 F4
Beaufin (38) ... 146 A6
Beaufort (31) ... 184 D1
Beaufort (34) ... 187 G2
Beaufort (38) ... 144 C1
Beaufort (39) ... 117 F1
Beaufort (73) ... 132 D3
Beaufort-Blavincourt (62) ... 7 H2
Beaufort-en-Anjou (49) ... 77 F5
Beaufort-en-Argonne (55) ... 24 D4
Beaufort-en-Santerre (80) ... 21 E1
Beaufort-sur-Gervanne (26) ... 144 C6

Beaufou (85) ... 91 F3
Beaufour-Druval (14) ... 15 E4
Beaufremont (88) ... 68 D3
Beaugas (47) ... 151 F3
Beaugeay (17) ... 120 C1
Beaugency (45) ... 80 B2
Beaugies-sous-Bois (60) ... 21 G2
Beaujeu (04) ... 160 D5
Beaujeu (69) ... 115 H5
Beaujeu-Saint-Vallier-Pierrejux-et-Quitteur (70) ... 86 D4
Beaulencourt (62) ... 8 B4
Beaulieu (07) ... 157 F4
Beaulieu (15) ... 126 B6
Beaulieu (21) ... 85 F2
Beaulieu (34) ... 173 G4
Beaulieu (36) ... 110 C3
Beaulieu (38) ... 145 E2
Beaulieu (43) ... 142 C3
Beaulieu (58) ... 99 G1
Beaulieu (61) ... 40 B5
Beaulieu (63) ... 127 G6
Beaulieu-en-Argonne (55) ... 46 D2
Beaulieu-les-Fontaines (60) ... 21 F2
Beaulieu-lès-Loches (37) ... 95 G2
Beaulieu-sous-la-Roche (85) ... 91 F4
Beaulieu-sous-Parthenay (79) ... 108 A1
Beaulieu-sur-Dordogne (19) ... 139 E4
Beaulieu-sur-Layon (49) ... 76 D6
Beaulieu-sur-Loire (45) ... 82 B4
Beaulieu-sur-Mer (06) ... 179 F4
Beaulieu-sur-Oudon (53) ... 58 B5
Beaulieu-sur-Sonnette (16) ... 122 D1
Beaulon (03) ... 114 C1
Beaumais (14) ... 39 E3
Beaumarchés (32) ... 167 E5
Beaumé (02) ... 10 B6
la Beaume (05) ... 159 G2
Beauménil (88) ... 70 B4
Beaumerie-Saint-Martin (62) ... 6 D1
Beaumes-de-Venise (84) ... 158 C6
Beaumesnil (14) ... 37 G3
Beaumettes (84) ... 175 G3
Beaumetz (80) ... 7 F4
Beaumetz-lès-Aire (62) ... 2 A6
Beaumetz-lès-Cambrai (62) ... 8 C4
Beaumetz-lès-Loges (62) ... 8 A3
Beaumont (07) ... 157 E3
Beaumont (19) ... 125 E6
Beaumont (32) ... 167 F2
Beaumont (43) ... 141 G1
Beaumont (54) ... 48 A4
Beaumont (63) ... 127 F3
Beaumont (74) ... 118 B5
Beaumont (89) ... 83 F1
Beaumont-de-Lomagne (82) ... 168 C3
Beaumont-de-Pertuis (84) ... 176 C4
Beaumont-du-Gâtinais (77) ... 63 H5
Beaumont-du-Lac (87) ... 125 E3
Beaumont-du-Ventoux (84) ... 158 D6
Beaumont-en-Argonne (08) ... 24 C3
Beaumont-en-Auge (14) ... 15 E4
Beaumont-en-Beine (02) ... 21 H2
Beaumont-en-Cambrésis (59) ... 9 F4
Beaumont-en-Diois (26) ... 159 F2
Beaumont-en-Verdunois (55) ... 25 F6
Beaumont-en-Véron (37) ... 94 B1
Beaumont-Hamel (80) ... 8 A4
Beaumont-la-Ferrière (58) ... 99 E2
Beaumont-le-Hareng (76) ... 17 H4
Beaumont-le-Roger (27) ... 40 B2
Beaumont-les-Autels (28) ... 61 F3
Beaumont-les-Nonains (60) ... 20 A5
Beaumont-lès-Randan (63) ... 127 G1
Beaumont-lès-Valence (26) ... 144 B5
Beaumont-Louestault (37) ... 78 D4
Beaumont-Monteux (26) ... 144 B4
Beaumont-Pied-de-Bœuf (53) ... 59 E6
Beaumont-Pied-de-Bœuf (72) ... 78 C2
Beaumont Saint-Cyr (86) ... 94 C5
Beaumont-Sardolles (58) ... 99 F4
Beaumont-sur-Dême (72) ... 78 D3
Beaumont-sur-Grosne (71) ... 101 G6
Beaumont-sur-Lèze (31) ... 185 F2
Beaumont-sur-Oise (95) ... 42 C1
Beaumont-sur-Sarthe (72) ... 60 A3
Beaumont-sur-Vesle (51) ... 45 G1
Beaumont-sur-Vingeanne (21) ... 86 B5
Beaumont-Village (37) ... 95 H2
Beaumont (21) ... 40 B1
Beaumontois en Périgord (24) ... 137 F6
Beaumotte-Aubertans (70) ... 87 G5
Beaumotte-lès-Pin (70) ... 87 E6
Beaune (21) ... 101 G3
Beaune-d'Allier (03) ... 113 E4
Beaune-la-Rolande (45) ... 63 G5
Beaune-sur-Arzon (43) ... 142 B2
Beaunotte (21) ... 85 F3
Beaupont (01) ... 117 E3
Beaupouyet (24) ... 136 C4
Beaupréau-en-Mauges (49) ... 75 G5

Beaupuy (31) 169 F5
Beaupuy (32) 168 C5
Beaupuy (47) 150 C2
Beaupuy (82) 168 D3
Beauquesne (80) 7 G4
Beaurain (59) 9 F3
Beaurains (62) 8 B3
Beaurains-lès-Noyon (60) 21 G3
Beaurainville (62) 7 E1
Beaurecueil (13) 192 C2
Beauregard (01) 129 H1
Beauregard (46) 153 F4
Beauregard-Baret (26) 144 C4
Beauregard-de-
Terrasson (24) 138 A3
Beauregard-et-Bassac (24) . 137 E4
Beauregard-l'Évêque (63) ... 127 G3
Beauregard-Vendon (63) 127 F1
Beaurepaire (38) 144 C1
Beaurepaire (60) 20 D6
Beaurepaire (76) 16 B4
Beaurepaire (85) 92 A3
Beaurepaire-en-
Bresse (71) 102 C6
Beaurepaire-sur-
Sambre (59) 9 H4
Beaurevoir (02) 9 E5
Beaurières (26) 159 G2
Beaurieux (02) 22 C5
Beaurieux (59) 10 B3
Beauronne (24) 136 D3
Beausemblant (26) 144 A4
Beausite (55) 47 E3
Beausoleil (06) 179 F3
Beaussais-sur-Mer (22) 34 C4
Beaussais-Vitré (79) 108 B4
Beaussault (76) 19 F2
le Beausset (83) 192 D4
Beauteville (31) 186 A2
Beautheil (77) 43 H5
Beautiran (33) 149 G1
Beautor (02) 22 A2
Beautot (76) 17 G4
Beauvain (61) 38 C6
Beauvais (60) 20 B4
Beauvais-sur-Matha (17) ... 121 H2
Beauvais-sur-Tescou (81) ... 169 G3
Beauval (80) 7 G4
Beauval-en-Caux (76) 17 G3
Beauvallon (26) 144 B5
Beauvène (07) 143 G5
Beauvernois (71) 102 C5
Beauvezer (04) 161 F6
Beauville (31) 186 A1
Beauville (47) 151 G5
Beauvilliers (28) 62 C3
Beauvilliers (89) 84 B5
Beauvoir (50) 35 G4
Beauvoir (60) 20 C3
Beauvoir (77) 43 G6
Beauvoir (89) 83 E2
Beauvoir-de-Marc (38) 130 C6
Beauvoir-en-Lyons (76) 19 F4
Beauvoir-en-Royans (38) ... 144 D3
Beauvoir-sur-Mer (85) 90 C2
Beauvoir-sur-Niort (79) 107 H5
Beauvoir-Wavans (62) 7 F1
Beauvois (62) 7 F1
Beauvois-en-
Cambrésis (59) 9 E4
Beauvois-en-
Vermandois (02) 8 D6
Beauvoisin (26) 159 E5
Beauvoisin (30) 174 A4
Beaux (43) 142 D2
Beauzac (43) 142 D2
Beauzelle (31) 169 E5
Beauziac (47) 150 B4
Bébing (57) 49 H4
Beblenheim (68) 71 F4
Bec-de-Mortagne (76) 16 C4
le Bec-Hellouin (27) 18 A6
le Bec-Thomas (27) 18 C6
Beccas (32) 183 F1
Béceleuf (79) 107 G2
Béchamps (54) 25 H6
Bécherel (35) 56 D1
Bécheresse (16) 122 B5
Béchy (57) 48 D2
Bécon-les-Granits (49) 76 C4
Bécordel-Bécourt (80) 8 A5
Bécourt (62) 1 G5
Becquigny (02) 9 F5
Becquigny (80) 21 E2
Bédarieux (34) 172 B5
Bédarrides (84) 175 E1
Beddes (18) 112 A1
Bédéchan (32) 168 B5
Bédée (35) 56 D2
Bédeilhac-et-Aynat (09) 185 G6
Bédeille (09) 184 D4
Bédeille (64) 182 D2
Bedenac (17) 135 G2
Bédoin (84) 158 D6
Bédouès-Cocurès (48) 156 B4
Bedous (64) 182 A5
Béduer (46) 153 G2
Beffes (18) 98 C3
Beffia (39) 117 F2
Beffu-et-le-
Morthomme (08) 24 C4
Bégaar (40) 165 F3
Bégadan (33) 120 C6
Béganne (56) 73 G1
Bégard (22) 32 D3
Bègles (33) 135 E5
Begnécourt (88) 69 G4
Bégole (65) 183 G3

Bégrolles-en-Mauges (49) 92 B1
la Bégude-de-Mazenc (26) .. 158 C2
Bègues (03) 113 G5
Béguey (33) 149 G1
Béguios (64) 181 E1
Béhagnies (62) 8 B4
Béhasque-Lapiste (64) 181 F1
Béhen (80) 6 D4
Béhencourt (80) 7 H5
Béhéricourt (60) 21 G3
Behonne (55) 47 E4
Béhorléguy (64) 181 E3
Béhoust (78) 41 H4
Behren-lès-Forbach (57) 27 G5
Béhuard (49) 76 D5
Beignon (56) 56 C4
Beillé (72) 60 C5
Beine (89) 83 G2
Beine-Nauroy (51) 23 F6
Beinheim (67) 51 G3
Beire-le-Châtel (21) 86 A5
Beire-le-Fort (21) 102 B1
Beissat (23) 125 H3
Bélâbre (36) 110 B2
Belan-sur-Ource (21) 67 E6
Bélarga (34) 172 D6
Bélaye (46) 152 B3
Belberaud (31) 169 G6
Belbeuf (76) 18 D5
Belbèze-de-Lauragais (31) .. 185 G1
Belbèze-en-
Comminges (31) 184 D4
Belbèze-en-Lomagne (82) .. 168 C3
Belcaire (11) 199 G1
Belcastel (12) 154 A4
Belcastel (81) 169 H5
Belcastel-et-Buc (11) 187 E5
Belcodène (13) 192 C2
Bélesta (09) 186 B6
Bélesta (66) 200 D2
Bélesta-en-Lauragais (31) .. 186 A1
Beleymas (24) 137 E4
Belfahy (70) 88 B1
Belfays (25) 88 D6
Belflou (11) 186 A2
Belfonds (61) 39 F6
Belforêt-en-Perche (61) 60 D2
Belfort (90) 88 C3
Belfort-du-Quercy (46) 152 D5
Belfort-sur-Rebenty (11) ... 199 H1
Belgeard (53) 59 E3
Belgentier (83) 193 F4
Belgodère (2B) 202 D5
Belhade (40) 149 E4
Belhomert-
Guéhouville (28) 61 G1
le Béliou (25) 104 C2
Béligneux (01) 130 C2
Belin-Béliet (33) 148 D2
Bélis (40) 166 A1
Bellac (87) 110 B5
Bellaffaire (04) 160 C3
Bellaing (59) 9 F2
Bellancourt (80) 7 E4
Bellange (57) 49 F3
Bellavilliers (61) 60 C2
le Bellay-en-Vexin (95) 42 A1
Belle-Église (60) 42 C1
Belle-et-Houllefort (62) 1 F4
Belle Vie en Auge (14) 14 D5
Belleau (02) 44 B2
Belleau (54) 48 C4
Bellebat (33) 135 H6
Bellebrune (62) 1 G4
Bellechassagne (19) 125 H4
Bellechaume (89) 65 G5
Bellecombe (39) 118 A3
Bellecombe-en-
Bauges (73) 132 B3
Bellecombe-Tarendol (26) . 159 E4
Bellefond (21) 85 H5
Bellefond (33) 135 H6
Bellefonds (86) 94 D6
Bellefont-La Rauze (46) 152 C3
Bellefontaine (39) 118 B1
Bellefontaine (88) 69 H5
Bellefontaine (95) 42 D2
Bellefosse (67) 71 E1
Bellegarde (30) 174 C4
Bellegarde (32) 184 A1
Bellegarde (45) 63 G6
Bellegarde-du-Razès (11) .. 186 C4
Bellegarde-en-Diois (26) ... 159 F2
Bellegarde-en-Forez (42) .. 129 E4
Bellegarde-en-Marche (23) . 125 H1
Bellegarde-Marsal (81) 170 D3
Bellegarde-Poussieu (38) .. 144 B1
Bellegarde-Sainte-
Marie (31) 168 D4
Bellegarde-sur-
Valserine (01) 118 A5
Belleherbe (25) 88 B6
Bellemagny (68) 89 E2
Bellême (61) 60 D2
Bellenaves (03) 113 G5
Bellencombre (76) 17 H4
Bellaneuve (21) 86 A6
Bellenglise (02) 9 E6
Bellengreville (14) 14 C5
Bellengreville (76) 17 H2
Bellenod-sur-Seine (21) 85 E3
Bellenot-sous-Pouilly (21) . 101 E1
Belleray (50) 47 F1
Bellerive-sur-Allier (03) 114 A6
Belleroche (42) 115 G5
Belles-Forêts (57) 49 H4
Bellesserre (81) 170 B4

Bellesserre (31) 168 D4
Belleu (02) 22 A5
Belleuse (80) 20 B2
Bellevaux (74) 119 E4
Bellevesvre (71) 102 C5
Bellevigne (16) 122 A5
Bellevigne-en-Layon (49) ... 77 E6
Bellevigny (85) 91 G3
Belleville (54) 48 C4
Belleville (79) 107 G5
Belleville (69) 116 B6
Les Belleville (73) 132 D6
Belleville-en-Caux (76) 17 G4
Belleville-et-Châtillon-sur-
Bar (08) 24 B4
Belleville-sur-Loire (18) 82 B4
Belleville-sur-Meuse (55) ... 47 F1
Bellevue-la-Montagne (43) . 142 B2
Belley (01) 131 F3
Belleydoux (01) 117 H4
Bellicourt (02) 9 E5
la Bellière (61) 39 E5
la Bellière (76) 19 F3
Bellignat (01) 117 G4
Belligny (51) 9 H2
Bellignies (59) 9 H2
la Belliole (89) 64 D4
Belloc (09) 186 B5
Belloc-Saint-Clamens (32) . 183 H1
Bellocq (64) 165 F5
Bellon (16) 136 B1
Bellone (62) 8 C2
Bellou (14) 15 E6
Bellou-en-Houlme (61) 38 B5
Bellou-le-Trichard (61) 60 D3
Belloy (60) 21 E3
Belloy-en-France (95) 42 D2
Belloy-en-Santerre (80) 8 C6
Belloy-Saint-Léonard (80) 6 D6
Belloy-sur-Somme (80) 7 F5
Belluire (17) 121 F5
Belmesnil (76) 17 G3
Belmont (25) 104 A1
Belmont (32) 167 F4
Belmont (38) 131 E5
Belmont (39) 102 D3
Belmont (52) 86 C2
Belmont (67) 71 E1
Belmont (70) 88 A1
Belmont-Bretenoux (46) 139 F5
Belmont-d'Azergues (69) .. 129 H2
Belmont-de-la-Loire (42) .. 115 G5
Belmont-lès-Darney (88) 69 F5
Belmont-Luthézieux (01) ... 131 F2
Belmont-Sainte-Foi (46) ... 153 E5
Belmont-sur-Buttant (88) ... 70 B3
Belmont-sur-Rance (12) 171 G3
Belmont-sur-Vair (88) 69 E3
Belmont-Tramonet (73) 131 F5
Belonchamp (70) 88 B2
Belpech (11) 186 A3
Belrain (55) 47 F3
Belrupt (88) 69 F5
Belrupt-en-Verdunois (55) . 47 G1
Bélus (40) 165 E5
Belval (08) 24 A1
Belval (50) 37 E1
Belval (88) 70 D1
Belval-Bois-des-
Dames (08) 24 C4
Belval-en-Argonne (51) 46 D3
Belval-sous-Châtillon (51) .. 45 E1
Belvédère (06) 179 E1
Belvédère-
Campomoro (2A) 206 C3
Belverne (70) 88 B3
Belvès-de-Castillon (33) ... 136 A5
Belvèze (82) 152 A4
Belvèze-du-Razès (11) 186 C4
Belvézet (30) 174 B1
Belvianes-et-Cavirac (11) . 200 A1
Belvis (11) 199 H1
Belvoir (25) 88 B6
Belz (56) 54 D6
Bémécourt (27) 40 C4
Bénac (09) 185 G5
Bénac (65) 183 E3
Benagues (09) 185 H4
Bénaix (09) 186 B6
Bénaménil (54) 49 F6
Bénarville (76) 16 D4
Benassay (86) 108 C1
Benay (02) 22 A1
Benayes (19) 124 C5
Bendejun (06) 179 E2
Bendorf (68) 89 F4
Bénéjacq (64) 182 C3
Benerville-sur-Mer (14) 15 E3
Bénesse-lès-Dax (40) 165 E4
Bénesse-Maremne (40) ... 164 C4
Benest (16) 109 F6
Bénestroff (57) 49 G3
Bénesville (76) 17 F3
Benet (85) 107 G3
Beneuvre (21) 85 G3
Bénévent-l'Abbaye (23) 111 E5
Beney-en-Woëvre (55) 48 A3
Benfeld (67) 71 G2
Bengy-sur-Craon (18) 98 B3
Bénifontaine (62) 3 E6
Béning-lès-Saint-
Avold (57) 27 F5
la Bénisson-Dieu (42) 115 E5
Bénivay-Ollon (26) 158 D5
Bennecourt (78) 41 G2
Benney (54) 69 G1
Bennwihr (68) 71 F4

Bénodet (29) 53 F4
Benoisey (21) 84 D4
Benoîtville (50) 12 B3
Benon (17) 107 E4
Bénonces (01) 131 E2
Bénouville (14) 14 C4
Bénouville (76) 16 B3
Benque (31) 184 C3
Benque-Dessous-et-
Dessus (31) 197 F1
Benqué-Molère (65) 183 G4
Benquet (40) 166 A3
Bentayou-Sérée (64) 182 D1
Bény (01) 117 E4
Bény-sur-Mer (14) 14 B3
Béon (01) 131 G2
Béon (89) 65 E6
Béost (64) 182 B5
Bérat (31) 185 E2
Béraut (32) 167 G2
Berbérust-Lias (65) 182 D4
Berbezit (43) 142 A2
Berbiguières (24) 137 H6
Bercenay-en-Othe (10) 66 A4
Bercenay-le-Hayer (10) 65 G3
Berche (25) 88 C4
Berchères-les-Pierres (28) . 62 B2
Berchères-Saint-
Germain (28) 62 B1
Berchères-sur-Vesgre (28) . 41 G4
Berck (62) 6 C1
Bercloux (17) 121 F2
Berd'huis (61) 61 E2
Berdoues (32) 167 G6
Bérelles (59) 10 B3
Bérengeville-la-
Campagne (27) 40 D1
Berentzwiller (68) 89 F4
Bérenx (64) 165 F6
Béréziat (01) 116 C3
Berfay (72) 61 E6
Berg (67) 50 A3
Berg-sur-Moselle (57) 26 C2
Berganty (46) 153 E3
Bergbieten (67) 50 C6
Bergerac (24) 136 D5
Bergères (10) 67 E4
Bergères-lès-Vertus (51) 45 F4
Bergères-sous-
Montmirail (51) 44 C4
Bergesserin (71) 115 H3
Bergheim (68) 71 F3
Bergholtz (68) 71 F6
Bergholtzzell (68) 71 E6
Bergicourt (80) 20 A1
Bergnicourt (08) 23 G4
Bergonne (63) 127 F5
Bergouey (40) 165 G5
Bergouey-Viellenave (64) . 165 E6
Bergueneuse (62) 2 B6
Bergues (59) 2 C2
Bergues-sur-Sambre (02) 9 G5
Berhet (22) 32 D2
Bérig-Vintrange (57) 49 F2
Bérigny (50) 13 G6
Berjou (61) 38 B3
Berlaimont (59) 9 H3
Berlancourt (60) 21 G2
Berlancourt (02) 22 D1
Berlats (81) 171 E4
Berlencourt-le-Cauroy (62) . 7 H2
Berles-au-Bois (62) 8 A3
Berles-Monchel (62) 7 H2
la Berlière (08) 24 C3
Berling (57) 50 B4
Berlise (02) 23 F2
Berlou (34) 188 A1
Bermerain (59) 9 F3
Berméricourt (51) 23 E5
Bermeries (59) 9 G2
Bermering (57) 49 F3
Bermesnil (80) 6 D6
Bermicourt (62) 7 F1
Bermont (90) 88 D3
Bernac (16) 108 D6
Bernac (81) 170 B2
Bernac-Debat (65) 183 E3
Bernac-Dessus (65) 183 E3
Bernadets (64) 182 C1
Bernadets-Debat (65) 183 G2
Bernadets-Dessus (65) 183 G3
le Bernard (85) 91 F6
la Bernardière (85) 91 H1
Bernardswiller (67) 71 F1
Bernardvillé (67) 71 F2
Bernâtre (80) 7 F3
Bernaville (80) 7 F4
Bernay (27) 15 H5
Bernay-en-
Champagne (72) 59 H5
Bernay-en-Ponthieu (80) 6 D2
Bernay-Saint-Martin (17) .. 107 G6
Bernay-Vilbert (77) 43 G5
Berné (56) 54 C3
Bernécourt (54) 48 A4
Bernède (32) 166 C4
la Bernerie-en-Retz (44) 73 H6
Bernes (80) 8 D6
Bernes-sur-Oise (95) 42 C1
Bernesq (14) 13 G5
Berneuil (16) 122 A6
Berneuil (17) 121 E4
Berneuil (80) 7 F4
Berneuil (87) 110 B6
Berneuil-en-Bray (60) 20 A5
Berneuil-sur-Aisne (60) 21 G4
Berneville (62) 8 A2
Bernex (74) 119 F3

Bernienville (27) 40 D2
Bernières (76) 16 D4
Bernières-d'Ailly (14) 39 E2
Bernières-sur-Mer (14) 14 B3
Bernieulles (62) 1 G6
Bernin (38) 145 H1
Bernis (30) 174 A4
Bernolsheim (67) 51 E4
Bernon (10) 66 A6
Bernos-Beaulac (33) 149 H4
Bernot (02) 9 F6
Bernouil (89) 84 A1
Bernouville (27) 19 G5
Bernwiller (68) 89 E2
Berny-en-Santerre (80) 8 B6
Berny-Rivière (02) 21 H5
Bérou-la-Mulotière (28) 40 D5
Berrac (32) 167 H1
le Bersac (05) 159 H3
Bersac-sur-Rivalier (87) ... 110 D6
Bersaillin (39) 102 D4
Bersée (59) 3 G6
Bersillies (59) 10 A2
Berson (33) 135 E3
Berstett (67) 50 D5
Berstheim (67) 51 E4
Bert (03) 114 C4
Bertangles (80) 7 G5
Bertaucourt-Epourdon (02) . 22 A3
Berteaucourt-les-
Dames (80) 7 F4
Berteaucourt-lès-
Thennes (80) 20 D1
Bertheauville (76) 16 D3
Berthecourt (60) 20 B5
Berthegon (86) 94 B4
Berthelange (25) 103 E1
Berthelming (57) 49 H4
Berthen (59) 2 D4
Berthenay (37) 78 C6
Berthenicourt (02) 22 A1
la Berthenoux (36) 97 E6
Berthez (33) 150 A3
Bertholène (12) 154 D4
Berthouville (27) 15 H5
Bertignat (63) 128 B4
Bertignolles (10) 66 D5
Bertincourt (62) 8 C4
Bertoncourt (08) 23 G3
Bertrambois (54) 49 H5
Bertrancourt (80) 7 H4
Bertrange (57) 26 B4
Bertre (81) 170 A5
Bertren (65) 184 A5
Bertreville (76) 16 D3
Bertreville-Saint-Ouen (76) . 17 G3
Bertric-Burée (24) 136 D1
Bertrichamps (54) 70 C1
Bertricourt (02) 23 E5
Bertrimont (76) 17 G4
Bertrimoutier (88) 70 D3
Bertry (59) 9 F4
Béru (89) 84 A2
Béruges (86) 108 D1
Bérulle (10) 65 G4
Bérus (72) 60 A2
Berville (76) 17 F4
Berville (95) 42 B1
Berville-la-Campagne (27) . 40 C2
Berville-sur-Mer (27) 15 G2
Berville-sur-Seine (76) 18 B4
Berviller-en-Moselle (57) ... 27 E4
Berzé-la-Ville (71) 116 A3
Berzé-le-Châtel (71) 116 A3
Berzème (07) 157 H2
Berzieux (51) 46 C1
Berzy-le-Sec (02) 22 A5
la Besace (08) 24 C3
Besain (39) 103 E5
Besançon (25) 103 F1
Bésayes (26) 144 C4
Bescat (64) 182 B3
Bésignan (26) 159 E4
Bésingrand (64) 182 A1
Beslon (50) 37 F3
Besmé (02) 21 H3
Besmont (02) 10 B6
Besnans (70) 87 G5
Besné (44) 73 H3
Besneville (50) 12 C4
Besny-et-Loizy (02) 22 C3
Bessac (16) 122 A6
Bessais-le-Fromental (18) .. 98 B6
Bessamorel (43) 142 D3
Bessan (34) 188 D2
Bessancourt (95) 42 C1
Bessans (73) 147 G1
Bessas (07) 157 F4
le Bessat (42) 143 F1
Bessay (85) 106 C1
Bessay-sur-Allier (03) 113 H3
Besse (15) 140 A3
Bessé (16) 122 B1
Besse (24) 152 A1
Besse (38) 145 H3

Besse-et-Saint-
Anastaise (63) 127 E5
Bessé-sur-Braye (72) 79 E1
Besse-sur-Issole (83) 193 G3
Bessède-de-Sault (11) 200 A1
Bessèges (30) 157 E5
Bessenay (69) 129 G3
Bessens (82) 169 E3
Besset (09) 186 A4
Bessey (42) 129 H6
Bessey-en-Chaume (21) ... 101 F2
Bessey-la-Cour (21) 101 F2
Bessey-lès-Cîteaux (21) ... 102 A2
la Besseyre-Saint-
Mary (43) 141 H4
Bessières (31) 169 G3
Bessines (79) 107 G3
Bessines-sur-
Gartempe (87) 110 D6
Bessins (38) 144 D2
Besson (03) 113 H2
Bessoncourt (90) 88 D3
Bessonies (46) 139 G6
les Bessons (48) 141 G6
Bessuéjouls (12) 154 D3
Bessy (10) 66 A1
Bessy-sur-Cure (89) 83 G3
Bestiac (09) 199 F1
Bétaille (46) 139 E5
Betaucourt (70) 87 E1
Betbèze (65) 184 A2
Betbezer-d'Armagnac (40) . 166 C2
Betcave-Aguin (32) 184 B1
Betchat (09) 184 D4
Bétête (23) 111 H3
Béthancourt-en-Valois (60) . 21 F6
Béthancourt-en-Vaux (02) . 21 H3
Béthelainville (55) 47 F1
Béthemont-la-Forêt (95) 42 C2
Béthencourt (59) 9 F4
Béthencourt-sur-Mer (80) 6 B4
Béthencourt-sur-
Somme (80) 21 G1
Bétheniville (51) 23 G5
Bétheny (51) 23 E6
Béthincourt (55) 25 E6
Béthines (86) 110 A2
Béthisy-Saint-Martin (60) .. 21 F6
Béthisy-Saint-Pierre (60) ... 21 F5
Bethmale (09) 184 D6
Bethon (51) 44 D6
Béthon (72) 60 A2
Bethoncourt (25) 88 C4
Béthonsart (62) 7 H1
Béthonvilliers (28) 61 F4
Bethonvilliers (90) 88 D2
Béthune (62) 2 D6
Bétignicourt (10) 66 D2
Beton-Bazoches (77) 44 A5
Betoncourt-lès-Brotte (70) . 87 H2
Betoncourt-Saint-
Pancras (70) 69 G4
Betoncourt-sur-Mance (70) . 86 D1
Bétous (32) 166 D4
Betplan (32) 183 F1
Betpouey (65) 183 E6
Betpouy (65) 183 H2
Bétracq (64) 166 D6
Betschdorf (67) 51 F2
Bettainvillers (54) 26 A4
Bettancourt-la-Ferrée (52) . 46 D5
Bettancourt-la-Longue (51) . 46 C4
Bettange (57) 26 D4
Bettant (01) 130 D1
Bettborn (57) 50 A4
Bettegney-Saint-Brice (88) . 69 G3
Bettelainville (57) 26 C4
Bettembos (80) 19 H1
Bettencourt-Rivière (80) 7 F5
Bettencourt-Saint-
Ouen (80) 7 F5
Bettendorf (68) 89 F3
Bettes (65) 183 F4
Bettignies (59) 10 A2
Betting (57) 27 F5
Bettlach (68) 89 G4
Betton (35) 57 F2
Betton-Bettonet (73) 132 B5
Bettoncourt (88) 69 G2
Bettrechies (59) 9 G2
Bettviller (57) 28 A5
Bettwiller (67) 50 B3
Betz (60) 43 G1
Betz-le-Château (37) 95 F3
Beugin (62) 7 H1
Beugnâtre (62) 8 B4
Beugneux (02) 22 B6
Beugnies (59) 10 A3
le Beugnon (79) 107 H1
Beugnon (89) 65 H6
Beugny (62) 8 C4
Beuil (06) 162 B6
le Beulay (88) 70 D2
Beulotte-Saint-Laurent (70) . 88 B1
Beure (25) 103 F1
Beurey (10) 66 D4
Beurey-Bauguay (21) 100 D1
Beurey-sur-Saulx (55) 46 D4
Beurières (63) 128 B6
Beurizot (21) 84 D6
Beurlay (17) 120 D2
Beurville (52) 67 F3
Beussent (62) 1 G6
Beuste (64) 182 C3
Beutal (25) 88 B4
Beutin (62) 1 F6
Beuvardes (02) 44 C1
Beuveille (54) 25 G4

Beuvezin (54) 69 E2
Beuvillers (14) 15 F5
Beuvillers (54) 26 A3
Beuvrages (59) 9 F1
Beuvraignes (80) 21 F2
Beuvrequen (62) 1 F3
Beuvrigny (50) 37 G2
Beuvron (58) 83 F6
Beuvron-en-Auge (14) 14 D4
Beuvry (62) 2 D6
Beuvry-la-Forêt (59) 9 E1
Beux (57) 48 D2
Beuxes (86) 94 B2
Beuzec-Cap-Sizun (29) 52 D2
Beuzeville (27) 15 G3
Beuzeville-la-Bastille (50) 12 D4
Beuzeville-la-Grenier (76) 15 G1
Beuzeville-la-Guérard (76) 16 D3
Beuzevillette (76) 15 H1
Bévenais (38) 131 E6
Beveuge (70) 88 A4
Béville-le-Comte (28) 62 C2
Bévillers (59) 9 E3
Bevons (04) 160 A6
Bévy (21) 101 G2
Bey (01) 116 B5
Bey (71) 101 H5
Bey-sur-Seille (54) 48 D4
Beychac-et-Caillau (33) 135 G5
Beylongue (40) 165 F2
Beynac (87) 124 A3
Beynac-et-Cazenac (24) 138 A5
Beynat (19) 139 E3
Beynes (04) 177 F1
Beynes (78) 42 A4
Beynost (01) 130 B2
Beyrède-Jumet (65) 183 G5
Beyren-lès-Sierck (57) 26 C2
Beyrie-en-Béarn (64) 182 B1
Beyrie-sur-Joyeuse (64) 181 E2
Beyries (40) 165 H5
Beyssac (19) 138 C1
Beyssenac (19) 124 B6
le Bez (81) 171 E5
Bez-et-Esparon (30) 172 D2
Bézac (09) 185 G4
Bezalles (77) 44 A5
Bézancourt (76) 19 F4
Bezange-la-Grande (54) 49 E4
Bezange-la-Petite (57) 49 F4
Bezannes (51) 23 E6
Bézaudun-les-Alpes (06) 178 D3
Bézaudun-sur-Bîne (26) 158 D2
Bezaumont (54) 48 C3
Bèze (21) 86 A5
Bézenet (03) 113 E4
Bézéril (32) 168 B6
Béziers (34) 188 C2
Bezinghem (62) 1 G5
Bezins-Garraux (31) 184 A5
la Bezole (11) 186 C5
Bezolles (32) 167 F3
Bezons (95) 42 C3
Bezonvaux (55) 25 F6
Bezouce (30) 174 C3
Bézouotte (21) 86 B5
Bézu-la-Forêt (27) 19 G4
Bézu-le-Guéry (02) 44 A2
Bézu-Saint-Éloi (27) 19 G5
Bézu-Saint-Germain (02) 44 B1
Bézues-Bajon (32) 184 A1
Biache-Saint-Vaast (62) 8 C2
Biaches (80) 8 C6
Bians-les-Usiers (25) 103 H3
Biard (86) 109 E1
Biarne (39) 102 C2
Biarre (80) 21 F2
Biarritz (64) 164 B6
Biarrotte (40) 164 C6
Biars-sur-Cère (46) 139 E5
Bias (40) 148 A5
Bias (47) 151 F4
Biaudos (40) 164 C5
Bibiche (57) 26 D3
Biblisheim (67) 51 E3
Bibost (69) 129 G3
Bichancourt (02) 21 H3
Biches (58) 99 G3
Bickenholtz (57) 50 B4
Bicqueley (54) 48 B6
Bidache (64) 164 D6
Bidarray (64) 180 D2
Bidart (64) 164 A6
Bidestroff (57) 49 G3
Biding (57) 49 G1
Bidon (07) 157 H4
Bidos (64) 182 A3
Biécourt (88) 69 E3
Biederthal (68) 89 G4
Bief (25) 88 C6
Bief-des-Maisons (39) 103 G6
Bief-du-Fourg (39) 103 G5
Biefmorin (39) 102 D4
Biefvillers-lès-Bapaume (62) 8 B4
Bielle (64) 182 B4
Biencourt (80) 6 C5
Biencourt-sur-Orge (55) 47 F6
Bienville (60) 21 F4
Bienville-la-Petite (54) 49 E5
Bienvillers-au-Bois (62) 8 A3
Biermes (08) 23 G4
Biermont (60) 21 E3
Bierné (53) 77 E1
Bierne (59) 2 C2
Bierre-lès-Semur (21) 84 C3
Bierry-les-Belles-
Fontaines (89) 84 B4
Biert (09) 185 F6

Bierville (76) 18 D3
Biesheim (68) 71 G5
Biesles (52) 68 A5
Bietlenheim (67) 51 E4
Bieujac (33) 150 A1
Bieuxy (02) 22 A4
Bieuzy (56) 55 E3
Biéville (50) 37 H1
Biéville-Beuville (14) 14 C4
Bièvres (02) 22 C4
Bièvres (08) 25 E3
Bièvres (91) 42 C5
Biffontaine (88) 70 C3
Biganos (33) 148 C1
Bignac (16) 122 B3
Bignan (56) 55 G4
Bignay (17) 121 F1
Bignicourt (08) 23 H5
Bignicourt-sur-Marne (51) 46 B5
Bignicourt-sur-Saulx (51) 46 C4
le Bignon (44) 74 D6
le Bignon-du-Maine (53) 58 D6
le Bignon-Mirabeau (45) 64 C4
Bignoux (86) 109 F1
Bigorno (2B) 203 F5
la Bigottière (53) 58 C3
Biguglia (2B) 203 G4
Bihorel (76) 18 D4
Bihucourt (62) 8 B4
Bilhac (19) 139 E5
Bilhères (64) 182 B4
Bilia (2A) 206 D3
Bilieu (38) 131 F6
Billancelles (28) 61 H1
Billancourt (80) 21 F2
les Billanges (87) 124 D1
les Billaux (33) 135 G4
Billé (35) 57 H1
Billecul (39) 103 G5
Billère (64) 182 B2
Billey (21) 102 C2
Billezois (03) 114 B5
Billiat (01) 117 H6
Billième (73) 131 G3
Billière (31) 197 F1
Billiers (56) 73 F2
Billio (56) 55 G4
Billom (63) 127 G3
Billy (03) 114 A4
Billy (41) 80 B6
Billy-Berclau (62) 3 E6
Billy-Chevannes (58) 99 F3
Billy-le-Grand (51) 45 G1
Billy-lès-Chanceaux (21) 85 F4
Billy-Montigny (62) 8 C1
Billy-sous-
Mangiennes (55) 25 G5
Billy-sur-Aisne (02) 22 A5
Billy-sur-Oisy (58) 83 F5
Billy-sur-Ourcq (02) 22 A6
Biltzheim (68) 71 F5
Bilwisheim (67) 50 D4
Bimont (62) 1 G6
Binarville (51) 24 C6
Binas (41) 80 A1
Bindernheim (67) 71 H2
Binges (21) 86 A6
Binic-Étables-sur-Mer (22) 33 G3
Bining (57) 50 B1
Biniville (50) 12 D4
Binos (31) 184 A6
Binson-et-Orquigny (51) 45 E2
Bio (46) 139 E6
Biol (38) 131 E5
la Biolle (73) 131 H3
Biollet (63) 126 C1
Bioncourt (57) 48 D4
Bionville (54) 70 D1
Bionville-sur-Nied (57) 26 D5
Biot (06) 178 D4
le Biot (74) 119 F4
Bioule (82) 169 F1
Bioussac (16) 108 D6
Biozat (03) 113 H6
Birac (16) 122 A4
Birac (33) 150 A3
Birac-sur-Trec (47) 150 C3
Biran (32) 167 G4
Biras (24) 137 E1
Biriatou (64) 180 A1
Birieux (01) 130 B1
Biron (17) 121 F4
Biron (24) 151 G2
Biron (64) 165 G6
Biscarrosse (40) 148 B3
Bischheim (67) 51 E5
Bischholtz (67) 50 D3
Bischoffsheim (67) 50 D6
Bischwihr (68) 71 G4
Bischwiller (67) 51 F4
Bisel (68) 89 F4
Bisinchi (2B) 203 F6
Bislée (55) 47 G3
Bissert (67) 49 H2
Bisseuil (51) 45 F2
Bissey-la-Côte (21) 85 F1
Bissey-la-Pierre (21) 84 D1
Bissey-sous-Cruchaud (71) 101 F6
Bissezeele (59) 2 C2
Bissy-la-Mâconnaise (71) 116 B2
Bissy-sous-Uxelles (71) 116 A1
Bissy-sur-Fley (71) 101 F5
Bisten-en-Lorraine (57) 27 E5
Bistroff (57) 49 F2
Bitche (57) 28 B5
Bitry (58) 82 C5
Bitry (60) 21 G4
Bitschhoffen (67) 50 D3
Bitschwiller-lès-Thann (68) 89 E1
Bivès (32) 168 B3

Biviers (38) 145 G2
Bivilla-la-Baignarde (76) 17 G3
Bivilla-la-Rivière (76) 17 F3
Bizanet (11) 187 H4
Bizanos (64) 182 B2
Bize (52) 86 D1
Bize (65) 183 H4
Bize-Minervois (11) 187 H2
Bizeneuille (03) 112 D3
Biziat (01) 116 C5
Bizonnes (38) 131 E6
le Bizot (25) 104 C2
les Bizots (71) 100 D5
Bizou (61) 61 E1
Bizous (65) 183 H4
Blacé (69) 116 A6
Blacourt (60) 19 H4
Blacqueville (76) 18 B3
Blacy (51) 46 A5
Blacy (89) 84 B4
Blaesheim (67) 50 D6
Blagnac (31) 169 E5
Blagny (08) 24 D2
Blagny-sur-Vingeanne (21) 86 B5
Blaignac (33) 150 A2
Blaignan (33) 134 D1
Blain (44) 74 B3
Blaincourt-lès-Précy (60) 20 C6
Blaincourt-sur-Aube (10) 66 D2
Blainville-Crevon (76) 19 E4
Blainville-sur-l'Eau (54) 49 E6
Blainville-sur-Mer (50) 36 D1
Blainville-sur-Orne (14) 14 C4
Blairville (62) 8 B3
Blaise-sous-Arzillières (51) 46 B5
Blaison-Saint-Sulpice (49) 77 F5
Blaisy (52) 67 G4
Blaisy-Bas (21) 85 F6
Blaisy-Haut (21) 85 F6
Blajan (31) 184 A2
Blamont (25) 88 C5
Blâmont (54) 49 G6
Blan (31) 170 B6
le Blanc (36) 110 B1
le Blanc-Mesnil (93) 42 D3
Blancafort (18) 81 H4
Blancey (21) 84 D6
Blancfossé (60) 20 B2
Blanche-Église (57) 49 F4
Blanchefosse-et-Bay (08) 23 F1
Blancherupt (67) 71 E1
Blandainville (28) 61 H3
Blandas (30) 172 D3
Blandin (38) 131 E5
Blandouet-St Jean (53) 59 F5
Blandy (77) 64 B1
Blandy (91) 63 F3
Blangerval-
Blangermont (62) 7 F2
Blangy-le-Château (14) 15 F4
Blangy-sous-Poix (80) 20 A1
Blangy-sur-Bresle (76) 6 C5
Blangy-sur-Ternoise (62) 7 F1
Blangy-Tronville (80) 7 H6
Blannay (89) 83 H4
Blanot (21) 100 C2
Blanot (71) 116 A2
Blanquefort (32) 168 B5
Blanquefort (33) 135 E4
Blanquefort-sur-
Briolance (47) 151 H2
Blanzac (43) 142 C3
Blanzac (87) 110 B5
Blanzac-lès-Matha (17) 121 G2
Blanzaguet-Saint-
Cybard (16) 122 C5
Blanzat (63) 127 E2
Blanzay (86) 108 D4
Blanzay-sur-Boutonne (17) 107 H6
Blanzée (55) 47 G1
Blanzy (71) 100 D6
Blanzy-la-Salonnaise (08) 23 F4
Blanzy-lès-Fismes (02) 22 C5
Blargies (60) 19 G2
Blarians (25) 87 G5
Blaringhem (59) 2 B4
Blars (46) 153 E2
Blaru (78) 41 F2
Blasimon (33) 136 A6
Blaslay (86) 94 C2
Blassac (43) 141 H3
Blaudeix (23) 111 H5
Blausasc (06) 179 F3
Blauvac (84) 175 G1
Blauzac (30) 174 B2
Blavignac (48) 141 G5
Blavozy (43) 142 D4
Blay (14) 13 G5
Blaye (33) 135 E3
Blaye-les-Mines (81) 170 C1
Blaymont (47) 151 G5
Blaziert (32) 167 G2
Blécourt (52) 67 H2
Blécourt (59) 8 D3
Bleigny-le-Carreau (89) 83 G2
Blémerey (54) 49 G6
Blémerey (88) 69 F2
Blendecques (62) 2 B4
Bléneau (89) 82 C3
Blennes (77) 64 C3
Blénod-lès-Pont-à-
Mousson (54) 48 C3
Blénod-lès-Toul (54) 48 A6
Bléquin (62) 1 H5
Blérancourt (02) 21 H4
Bléré (37) 79 F6
Bléruais (35) 56 C2
Blésignac (33) 135 G6
Blesle (43) 141 F1

Blesme (51) 46 C5
Blesmes (02) 44 C2
Blessac (23) 125 G1
Blessonville (52) 67 G5
Blessy (62) 2 B5
Blet (18) 98 B4
Bletterans (39) 102 C5
Bleurville (88) 69 E5
Blevaincourt (88) 68 D4
Blèves (72) 60 C1
Blicourt (60) 20 A3
Blienschwiller (67) 71 F2
Blies-Ébersing (57) 27 H5
Blies-Guersviller (57) 27 H5
Bliesbruck (57) 28 A5
Bligny (10) 66 D2
Bligny (51) 45 E1
Bligny-le-Sec (21) 85 F5
Bligny-lès-Beaune (21) 101 G3
Bligny-sur-Ouche (21) 101 F2
Blincourt (60) 21 E5
Blingel (62) 7 F1
Blismes (58) 100 A2
Blodelsheim (68) 71 G6
Blois (41) 79 H4
Blois-sur-Seille (39) 102 D5
Blomac (11) 187 F3
Blomard (03) 113 F4
Blombay (08) 23 H1
Blond (87) 110 A6
Blondefontaine (70) 87 E1
Blonville-sur-Mer (14) 15 E3
Blosseville (76) 17 E2
Blosville (50) 13 E4
Blot-l'Église (63) 113 F6
Blotzheim (68) 89 G3
Blou (49) 77 H5
Blousson-Sérian (32) 167 E6
la Bloutière (50) 37 F3
Bloye (74) 131 H2
Bluffy (74) 132 B2
Blumeray (52) 67 F2
Blussangeaux (25) 88 B5
Blussans (25) 88 B5
Blye (39) 117 G1
Blyes (01) 130 D2
le Bô (14) 38 C3
Bobigny (93) 42 D3
Bobital (22) 34 C5
le Bocasse (76) 18 C3
Bocognano (2A) 205 E4
Bocquegney (88) 69 G3
le Bodéo (22) 33 F6
Bodilis (29) 31 G3
Boé (47) 151 F6
Boëcé (61) 60 C1
Boëge (74) 118 D4
Boeil-Bezing (64) 182 C3
Boën-sur-Lignon (42) 128 D3
Bœrsch (67) 71 F1
Boeschepe (59) 2 D3
Boëseghem (59) 2 C5
Bœsenbiesen (67) 71 G3
Boesse-le-Sec (72) 60 D4
Bœsses (45) 63 G4
Bœurs-en-Othe (89) 65 G4
Boffles (62) 7 F3
Boffres (07) 143 H5
Bogève (74) 118 D4
Bogny-sur-Meuse (08) 11 F6
Bogy (07) 144 A2
Bohain-en-
Vermandois (02) 9 F5
Bohal (56) 56 A5
Bohars (29) 30 D4
Bohas-Meyriat-Rignat (01) 117 F5
Boigneville (91) 63 G3
Boigny-sur-Bionne (45) 81 E1
Boinville-en-Mantois (78) 41 H3
Boinville-en-Woëvre (55) 25 G6
Boinville-le-Gaillard (78) 62 D1
Boinvilliers (78) 41 G3
Boiry-Becquerelle (62) 8 B3
Boiry-Notre-Dame (62) 8 C2
Boiry-Saint-Martin (62) 8 B3
Boiry-Sainte-Rictrude (62) 8 B3
le Bois (73) 132 D5
Bois-Anzeray (27) 40 B3
Bois-Arnault (27) 40 B4
Bois-Bernard (62) 8 C1
Bois-Colombes (92) 42 C3
Bois-d'Amont (39) 118 B1
Les Bois d'Anjou (49) 77 G4
Bois-d'Arcy (78) 42 B4
Bois-d'Arcy (89) 83 G4
Bois-de-Céné (85) 90 D2
Bois-de-Champ (88) 70 C3
Bois-de-Gand (39) 102 C5
Bois-de-la-Pierre (31) 185 E2
Bois-Grenier (59) 3 E5
Bois-Guilbert (76) 19 E3
Bois-Guillaume (76) 18 D4
le Bois-Hellain (27) 15 G4
Bois-Héroult (76) 19 E3
Bois-Herpin (91) 63 F2
Bois-Himont (76) 18 A3
Bois-Jérôme-Saint-
Ouen (27) 41 G1
Bois-le-Roi (27) 41 E4
Bois-le-Roi (77) 64 A1
Bois-lès-Pargny (02) 22 C2
Bois-l'Évêque (76) 18 D4
Bois-Normand-près-
Lyre (27) 40 B3

le Bois-Plage-en-Ré (17) 106 B4
le Bois-Robert (76) 17 G2
Bois-Sainte-Marie (71) 115 G4
Boisbergues (80) 7 F3
Boisbreteau (16) 135 H1
Boischampré (61) 39 E5
Boiscommun (45) 63 G5
Boisdinghem (62) 2 A4
Boisdon (77) 44 A5
Boisemont (27) 19 F6
Boisemont (95) 42 B2
Boisgervilly (35) 56 C2
Boisjean (62) 6 D1
le Boisle (80) 7 E2
Boisleux-au-Mont (62) 8 B3
Boisleux-Saint-Marc (62) 8 B3
Boismé (79) 93 E5
Boismont (54) 25 H4
Boismont (80) 6 C3
Boismorand (45) 82 A2
Boisné-La-Tude (16) 122 C5
Boisney (27) 40 A1
Boisredon (17) 135 F1
Boissay (76) 19 E3
la Boisse (01) 130 B2
Boisse (24) 151 F1
Boisse-Penchot (12) 153 H2
Boisseau (41) 79 H2
Boisseaux (45) 63 E3
Boissède (31) 184 B1
Boissei-la-Lande (61) 39 F5
Boisserolles (79) 107 H5
Boisseron (34) 173 H4
Boisset (15) 139 H6
Boisset (34) 187 G1
Boisset (43) 142 D1
Boisset-et-Gaujac (30) 173 G1
Boisset-les-
Prévanches (27) 41 E3
Boisset-Saint-Priest (42) 128 D5
Boissets (78) 41 G4
Boissettes (77) 64 A1
Boisseuil (87) 124 B3
Boisseuilh (24) 138 A1
Boissey (01) 116 C3
Boissey-le-Châtel (27) 18 B6
Boissezon (81) 170 D6
Boissia (39) 117 H1
la Boissière (14) 15 E5
la Boissière (27) 41 F3
la Boissière (34) 173 E5
la Boissière (39) 117 F3
la Boissière (53) 76 B1
la Boissière-de-
Montaigu (85) 92 A3
la Boissière-des-
Landes (85) 91 G5
la Boissière-du-Doré (44) 75 F5
la Boissière-École (78) 41 G5
la Boissière-en-
Gâtine (79) 107 H1
Boissières (30) 174 A4
Boissières (46) 152 C2
Boissise-la-Bertrand (77) 63 H1
Boissise-le-Roi (77) 63 H1
Boissy-aux-Cailles (77) 63 H3
Boissy-en-Drouais (28) 41 E5
Boissy-Fresnoy (60) 43 G1
Boissy-la-Rivière (91) 63 F2
Boissy-l'Aillerie (95) 42 B2
Boissy-Lamberville (27) 15 H5
Boissy-le-Bois (60) 19 H6
Boissy-le-Châtel (77) 44 A4
Boissy-le-Cutté (91) 63 F2
Boissy-le-Repos (51) 44 D4
Boissy-le-Sec (91) 63 E1
Boissy-lès-Perche (28) 40 C5
Boissy-Mauvoisin (78) 41 G3
Boissy-Saint-Léger (94) 43 E5
Boissy-sans-Avoir (78) 41 H4
Boissy-sous-Saint-Yon (91) 63 F1
Boistrudan (35) 57 G4
Boisville-la-Saint-Père (28) 62 C3
Boisyvon (50) 37 F4
Boitron (61) 39 G6
Boitron (77) 44 A3
Bolandoz (25) 103 G3
Bolazec (29) 32 B4
Bolbec (76) 15 G1
Bollène (84) 158 B5
la Bollène-Vésubie (06) 179 F1
Bolleville (76) 15 H1
Bollezeele (59) 2 B3
Bollwiller (68) 71 F6
Bologne (52) 67 H4
Bolozon (01) 117 F5
Bolquère (66) 199 H4
Bolsenheim (67) 71 G1
Bombon (77) 43 G6
Bommes (33) 149 G2
Bommiers (36) 97 E5
Bompas (09) 185 H6
Bompas (66) 201 F2
Bomy (62) 2 A5
Bon-Encontre (47) 151 F6
Bon Repos sur Blavet (22) 55 E1
Bona (58) 99 F3
Bonac-Irazein (09) 184 C6
Bonas (32) 167 G3
Bonboillon (70) 86 D6
Boncé (28) 62 B3
Bonchamp-lès-Laval (53) 58 D5
Boncourt (02) 23 E3
Boncourt (27) 41 E2
Boncourt (28) 41 F4
Boncourt (54) 48 A1
Boncourt-le-Bois (21) 101 H2

Boncourt-sur-Meuse (55) 47 G4
Bondaroy (45) 63 F4
Bondeval (25) 88 C4
Bondigoux (31) 169 F3
les Bondons (48) 156 B4
Bondoufle (91) 42 D6
Bondues (59) 3 F4
Bondy (93) 43 E3
Bongheat (63) 127 H3
le Bonhomme (68) 71 E4
Bonifacio (2A) 207 F5
Bonlier (60) 20 B4
Bonlieu (39) 117 H1
Bonlieu-sur-Roubion (26) 158 B2
Bonloc (64) 180 D1
Bonnac (09) 185 G5
Bonnac (15) 141 F2
Bonnac-la-Côte (87) 124 B1
Bonnal (25) 87 H4
Bonnard (89) 83 F1
Bonnat (23) 111 G4
Bonnay (25) 87 F6
Bonnay (71) 116 A2
Bonnay (80) 7 H5
Bonne (74) 118 D5
Bonnebosq (14) 15 E4
Bonnecourt (52) 68 C6
Bonnée (45) 81 G2
Bonnefamille (38) 130 C4
Bonnefoi (61) 40 A5
Bonnefond (19) 125 F5
Bonnefont (65) 183 G3
Bonnefontaine (39) 103 E5
Bonnegarde (40) 165 G5
Bonnelles (78) 42 B6
Bonnemain (35) 35 E5
Bonnemaison (14) 38 B2
Bonnemazon (65) 183 F4
Bonnencontre (21) 102 A2
Bonnes (16) 136 B2
Bonnes (86) 109 G1
Bonnesvalyn (02) 44 B1
Bonnet (55) 68 B1
Bonnétable (72) 60 C4
Bonnétage (25) 104 C1
Bonnetan (33) 135 F5
Bonneuil (16) 121 H4
Bonneuil (36) 110 C3
Bonneuil-en-France (95) 42 D3
Bonneuil-en-Valois (60) 21 G6
Bonneuil-les-Eaux (60) 20 B2
Bonneuil-Matours (86) 94 D6
Bonneuil-sur-Marne (94) 43 E4
Bonneval (28) 62 A4
Bonneval (43) 142 B1
Bonneval (73) 132 D5
Bonneval-sur-Arc (73) 133 G6
Bonnevaux (25) 103 H5
Bonnevaux (30) 157 E4
Bonnevaux (74) 119 F3
Bonneveau (41) 79 E2
Bonnevent-Velloreille (70) 87 E5
Bonneville (16) 122 A2
la Bonneville (50) 12 D4
Bonneville (74) 118 D5
Bonneville (80) 7 G4
Bonneville-Aptot (27) 18 A6
Bonneville-et-Saint-Avit-
de-Fumadières (24) 136 B5
Bonneville-la-Louvet (14) 15 G4
la Bonneville-sur-Iton (27) 40 D2
Bonneville-sur-
Touques (14) 15 E3
Bonnières (60) 20 A4
Bonnières (62) 7 G3
Bonnières-sur-Seine (78) 41 G2
Bonnieux (84) 175 H3
Bonningues-lès-Ardres (62) 1 H3
Bonningues-lès-Calais (62) 1 G3
Bonnœil (14) 38 C3
Bonnœuvre (44) 75 F2
Bonnut (64) 165 G5
Bonny-sur-Loire (45) 82 B4
Bono (56) 55 E6
Bonrepos (65) 183 G3
Bonrepos-Riquet (31) 169 G5
Bonrepos-sur-
Aussonnelle (31) 168 D6
Bons-en-Chablais (74) 118 D4
Bons-Tassilly (14) 38 D2
Bonsecours (76) 18 D4
Bonsmoulins (61) 40 A5
Bonson (06) 179 E2
Bonson (42) 129 E5
Bonvillard (73) 132 C4
Bonvillaret (73) 132 C4
Bonviller (54) 49 E5
Bonvillers (60) 20 C3
Bonvillet (88) 69 F5
Bony (02) 8 D5
Bonzac (33) 135 H4
Bonzée (55) 47 G1
Boô-Silhen (65) 182 D5
Boofzheim (67) 71 H2
Boos (40) 18 D5
Boostzheim (67) 71 G3
Boqueho (22) 33 F4
Bor-et-Bar (12) 153 G6
Boran-sur-Oise (60) 42 D1
Borce (64) 182 A5
Bord-Saint-Georges (23) 112 B4
Bordeaux (33) 135 E5
Bordeaux-en-Gâtinais (45) 63 H5
Bordeaux-Saint-Clair (76) 16 B4
Bordères (64) 182 C3
Bordères-et-
Lamensans (40) 166 B3

Bordères-Louron (65) 183 G6
Bordères-sur-l'Échez (65) ... 183 E2
les Bordes (36) 97 E3
les Bordes (45) 81 G2
Bordes (64) 182 C2
Bordes (65) 183 F3
les Bordes (71)............... 101 H4
les Bordes (89) 65 E5
Bordes-de-Rivière (31)....... 184 A4
les Bordes-sur-Arize (09) ... 185 F4
Bordes-Uchentein (09)....... 184 D6
Bordezac (30)................. 157 E5
Bords (17) 120 D1
Borée (07) 143 E5
Boresse-et-Martron (17) 136 A1
Borest (60) 43 F1
Borey (70) 87 H3
Borgo (2B) 203 G5
Bormes-les-Mimosas (83) ... 193 H5
le Born (31) 169 F3
le Born (48) 156 B2
Bornambusc (76) 16 C4
Bornay (39) 117 F1
Borne (07) 156 D2
Borne (43) 142 B3
Bornel (60) 42 C1
Boron (90) 88 D3
Borre (59) 2 D4
Borrèze (24) 138 B4
Bors (16) 135 H1
Bors (16) 136 B1
Bort-les-Orgues (19) 126 B6
Bort-l'Étang (63) 127 H3
Borville (54) 69 H1
le Bosc (09) 185 G5
le Bosc (34) 172 C4
Bosc-Bérenger (76) 17 H4
Bosc-Bordel (76) 19 E3
le Bosc du Theil (27) 18 B6
Bosc-Édeline (76) 19 E3
Bosc-Guérard-Saint-
  Adrien (76).................. 18 D3
Bosc-Hyons (76) 19 G4
Bosc-le-Hard (76) 17 H4
Bosc-Mesnil (76) 19 E2
le Bosc-Renoult (61) 39 G3
Boscamnant (17) 136 A2
Bosdarros (64) 182 B3
Bosgouet (27) 18 B5
Bosjean (71) 102 B5
Bosmie-l'Aiguille (87) 124 A3
Bosmont-sur-Serre (02) 22 D2
Bosmoreau-les-Mines (23) .. 125 E1
Bosquel (80) 20 B1
Bosquentin (27) 19 F4
Bosrobert (27) 18 A6
Bosroger (23) 125 H1
Bosroumois (27) 18 B5
Bossancourt (10) 67 E3
Bossay-sur-Claise (37) 95 F5
la Bosse (25) 104 C2
la Bosse (72) 60 D4
la Bosse-de-Bretagne (35) .. 57 F5
Bossée (37) 95 E2
Bosselshausen (67) 50 D3
Bossendorf (67) 50 D4
Bosset (24) 136 D4
Bossey (74) 118 C5
Bossieu (38) 130 C6
Bossugan (33) 136 A6
Bossus-lès-Rumigny (08) ... 10 C6
Bost (03).................... 114 B5
Bostens (40) 166 B2
Bosville (76) 17 E3
Botans (90) 88 C3
Botmeur (29) 31 H5
Botsorhel (29)................ 32 B4
les Bottereaux (27) 40 A3
Bou (45) 81 E1
Bouafle (78) 42 A3
Bouafles (27) 19 E6
Bouan (09) 199 E1
Bouaye (44) 74 B5
Boubers-lès-Hesmond (62) .. 1 H6
Boubers-sur-Canche (62) ... 7 F2
Boubiers (60)................. 19 H6
Bouc-Bel-Air (13) 192 B2
Boucagnères (32) 167 H5
Boucau (64) 164 B5
Boucé (03).................... 114 A4
Boucé (61)................... 39 E5
le Bouchage (16) 109 E6
le Bouchage (38) 131 E4
Bouchain (59)................. 9 E2
Bouchamps-lès-Craon (53) .. 76 B1
le Bouchaud (03) 114 D2
Bouchavesnes-Bergen (80) .. 8 C5
Bouchemaine (49) 76 D5
Boucheporn (57) 27 E5
Bouchet (26) 158 B5
le Bouchet-Mont-
  Charvin (74)................. 132 C2
le Bouchet-Saint-
  Nicolas (43) 142 B5
Bouchevilliers (27) 19 G4
Bouchoir (80) 21 E1
Bouchon (80) 7 E5
Bouchy-Saint-Genest (51).. 44 C6
Boucieu-le-Roi (07) 143 H4
Bouclans (25)................. 103 H1
Boucoiran-et-Nozières (30) .. 173 H2
Boucq (54) 48 A4
Boudes (63) 127 F6
Boudeville (76) 17 F3
Boudou (82) 168 C1
Boudrac (31) 183 H3
Boudreville (21) 67 F6
Boudy-de-Beauregard (47).. 151 F2
Boué (02) 9 G5
Bouée (44) 74 A4
Boueilh-Boueilho-
  Lasque (64).................. 166 B5
Bouelles (76) 19 F2
Bouër (72) 60 D5
Bouère (53) 77 E1
Bouessay (53) 77 F1
Bouesse (36) 111 F1
Boueux (16) 122 D4
la Bouëxière (35) 57 G2
Bouffémont (95) 42 C2
Boufféré (85) 91 H2
Bouffignereux (02) 22 D5
Boufflers (80) 7 E2
Bouffry (41) 61 G6
Bougainville (80) 7 E6
Bougarber (64) 182 B1
Bougé-Chambalud (38) 144 B1
Bouges-le-Château (36) 96 C3
Bougey (70) 87 E2
Bougival (78) 42 B4
Bouglainval (28) 41 F6
Bougligny (77) 64 A4
Bouglon (47) 150 B4
Bougneau (17) 121 F4
Bougnon (70) 87 F2
Bougon (79) 108 B3
Bougue (40) 166 B2
Bouguenais (44) 74 C5
Bougy (14) 14 A5
Bougy-lez-Neuville (45) 63 E5
Bouhans (71) 102 B5
Bouhans-et-Feurg (70) 86 C4
Bouhans-lès-Lure (70) 87 H2
Bouhans-lès-
  Montbozon (70).............. 87 H4
Bouhet (17) 107 E5
Bouhey (21) 101 F1
Bouhy (58) 82 D5
Bouilh-Devant (65) 183 F2
Bouilh-Péreuilh (65) 183 F2
Bouilhonnac (11) 187 E3
Bouillac (12) 153 H2
Bouillac (24) 137 G6
Bouillac (82) 168 D3
la Bouilladisse (13) 192 C3
Bouillancourt-en-Séry (80) .. 6 C5
Bouillancourt-la-
  Bataille (80)................. 20 D2
Bouillancy (60) 43 G1
Bouilland (21) 101 G2
Bouillargues (30) 174 B3
la Bouille (76) 18 B5
Bouillé-Courdault (85) 107 F3
Bouillé-Loretz (79) 93 F2
Bouillé-Ménard (49) 76 B2
la Bouillie (22) 34 A4
le Bouillon (61) 39 F6
Bouillon (64) 166 A6
Bouillonville (54) 48 A3
Bouilly (10) 66 A4
Bouilly (51) 45 E1
Bouilly-en-Gâtinais (45) 63 F5
Bouin (79) 108 C5
Bouin (85) 90 C1
Bouin-Plumoison (62) 7 E1
Bouisse (11) 187 E5
Bouix (21) 84 D1
Boujailles (25) 103 G4
Boujan-sur-Libron (34) 188 C2
Boulages (10) 45 E6
Boulaincourt (88) 69 F2
Boulancourt (77) 63 G3
Boulange (57) 26 A3
Boulaur (32) 168 A6
le Boulay (37) 79 E3
Boulay-les-Barres (45) 62 C6
Boulay-les-Ifs (53) 59 G2
le Boulay-Morin (27) 41 E2
Boulay-Moselle (57) 26 D5
la Boulaye (71) 100 C6
Boulazac Isle Manoire (24) .. 137 F2
Boulbon (13) 174 D3
Boulc (26).................... 159 G1
Boule-d'Amont (66) 200 D3
Bouleternère (66) 200 D3
Bouleurs (77) 43 G4
Bouleuse (51) 22 D6
Bouliac (33) 135 F5
Boulieu-lès-Annonay (07).. 143 H2
Bouligneux (01) 116 C6
Bouligney (70) 69 G6
Bouligny (55) 25 H5
Boulin (65) 183 F2
Boullarre (60) 43 H1
le Boullay-les-Deux-
  Églises (28)................. 41 E6
Boullay-les-Troux (91) 42 B5
le Boullay-Mivoye (28)...... 41 F6
le Boullay-Thierry (28)...... 41 F6
Boulleret (18) 82 B5
Boulleville (27) 15 G3
Bouloc (31) 169 F4
Bouloc-en-Quercy (82)...... 152 A5
Boulogne-Billancourt (92).. 42 C4
Boulogne-la-Grasse (60).... 21 E3
Boulogne-sur-Gesse (31).... 184 A2
Boulogne-sur-Helpe (59)... 9 H4
Boulogne-sur-Mer (62)..... 1 F4
Bouloire (72) 60 D6
Boulon (14) 38 C2
Boulot (70) 87 F6
le Boulou (66) 201 E4
Boult (70) 87 F5
Boult-aux-Bois (08) 24 B4
Boult-sur-Suippe (51)....... 23 F5
le Boulvé (46) 152 A4
le Boulvé (85) 92 B5
Bouquehault (62) 1 G3
Bouquelon (27) 15 H3
Bouquemaison (80) 7 G3
Bouquemont (55) 47 G2
Bouquet (30) 157 F6
Bouquetot (27) 18 B5
Bouqueval (95) 42 D2
Bouranton (10) 66 B3
Bouray-sur-Juine (91) 63 G1
Bourbach-le-Bas (68) 88 D1
Bourbach-le-Haut (68)...... 88 D1
Bourberain (21) 86 B4
Bourbévelle (70) 69 E6
Bourbon-Lancy (71) 114 C1
Bourbon-
  l'Archambault (03).......... 113 F1
Bourbonne-les-Bains (52).. 68 D6
la Bourboule (63) 126 C5
Bourbourg (59) 2 A2
Bourbriac (22) 33 E4
Bourcefranc-le-
  Chapus (17)................. 120 B2
Bourcq (08) 24 A5
Bourdainville (76) 17 F4
Bourdalat (40) 166 C3
Bourdeau (73) 131 H3
Bourdeaux (26) 158 D2
Bourdeilles (24) 137 E1
le Bourdeix (24) 123 E4
Bourdelles (33) 150 B2
Bourdenay (10) 65 G3
le Bourdet (79) 107 G4
Bourdettes (64) 182 C3
la Bourdinière-Saint-
  Loup (28) 62 A3
Bourdon (80) 7 E5
Bourdonnay (57) 49 G4
Bourdonné (78) 41 G5
Bourdons-sur-Rognon (52).. 68 B4
Bourecq (62) 2 C5
Bouresches (02) 44 B2
Bouresse (86) 109 G3
Bouret-sur-Canche (62) 7 G2
Boureuilles (55) 24 C6
Bourg (33) 135 E3
le Bourg (46) 153 F1
Bourg (52) 86 B2
Bourg-Achard (27) 18 B5
Bourg-Archambault (86).... 110 A3
Bourg-Argental (42) 143 G1
Bourg-Beaudouin (27) 19 E5
Bourg-Blanc (29) 30 D4
Bourg-Bruche (67) 71 E2
Bourg-Charente (16) 121 H3
Bourg-de-Bigorre (65) 183 F4
Bourg-de-Péage (26) 144 C4
Bourg-de-Sirod (39) 103 F5
Bourg-de-Visa (82) 151 H5
Bourg-des-Comptes (35) ... 57 E4
Bourg-des-Maisons (24) ... 136 D1
le Bourg-d'Hem (23) 111 F4
le Bourg-d'Oisans (38) 146 A3
Bourg-d'Oueil (31) 183 H6
Bourg-du-Bost (24) 136 C1
le Bourg-Dun (76) 17 F2
Bourg-en-Bresse (01) 117 E5
Bourg-et-Comin (02) 22 C5
Bourg-Fidèle (08) 10 D6
Bourg-la-Reine (92) 42 D4
Bourg-Lastic (63) 126 B4
Bourg-le-Comte (71) 115 E4
Bourg-le-Roi (72) 60 A2
Bourg-lès-Valence (26) 144 B5
Bourg-l'Évêque (49) 76 B3
Bourg-Madame (66) 199 G4
Bourg-Saint-Andéol (07) .. 158 A4
Bourg-Saint-Bernard (31).. 169 H5
Bourg-Saint-
  Christophe (01) 130 C2
Bourg-Saint-Maurice (73).. 133 F4
Bourg-Sainte-Marie (52) ... 68 C4
Bourg-sous-Châtelet (90).. 88 D2
Bourgaltroff (57)............. 49 G3
Bourganeuf (23) 125 E1
Bourgbarré (35) 57 F4
Bourgeauville (14) 15 E4
Bourges (18) 97 G3
le Bourget (93) 42 D3
le Bourget-du-Lac (73) 131 H4
le Bourget-en-Huile (73) .. 132 B5
Bourgheim (67) 71 G1
Bourghelles (59) 3 G5
Bourgnac (24) 136 D4
Bourgneuf (17) 106 D4
Bourgneuf (73) 132 B5
Bourgogne-Fresne (51)..... 23 E5
Bourgoin-Jallieu (38) 130 D4
Bourgon (53) 58 B4
la Bourgonce (88) 70 C2
Bourgougnague (47)........ 150 D2
Bourgs sur Colagne (48)... 155 G3
Bourguébus (14) 14 C5
Bourgueil (37) 78 A6
Bourguenolles (50) 37 E4
le Bourguet (83) 177 H3
Bourguignon (25).............. 88 C5
Bourguignon-lès-
  Conflans (70)................. 87 G1
Bourguignon-lès-la-
  Charité (70) 87 F4
Bourguignon-lès-
  Morey (70) 86 D2
Bourguignon-sous-
  Coucy (02) 21 H3
Bourguignon-sous-
  Montbavin (02) 22 B3
Bourguignons (10) 66 C5
Bourgvallées (50) 37 F1
Bourgvilain (71) 116 A3
Bourideys (33) 149 G4
Bourièges (11) 186 D5
Bourigeole (11) 186 C5
Bourisp (65) 183 G6
Bourlens (47) 151 H4
Bourlon (62) 8 D3
Bourmont-entre-Meuse-et-
  Mouzon (52) 68 C4
Bournainville-
  Faverolles (27) 15 G5
Bournan (37) 95 E3
Bournand (86) 94 A2
Bournazel (12) 154 A3
Bournazel (81) 170 B1
Bourneau (85) 107 F1
Bournel (47) 151 F2
Bourneville-Sainte-
  Croix (27) 15 H3
Bournezeau (85) 92 A6
Bourniquel (24) 137 F6
Bournois (25) 88 A4
Bournoncle-Saint-
  Pierre (43) 141 G1
Bournonville (62) 1 G4
Bournos (64) 166 A6
Bourogne (90) 88 D3
Bourran (47) 150 D4
Bourréac (65) 183 E4
Bourret (82) 168 D2
Bourriot-Bergonce (40) 149 H2
Bourron-Marlotte (77)...... 64 A3
Bourrou (24) 137 E4
Bourrouillan (32) 166 D3
Bours (62) 7 G1
Bours (65) 183 E2
Boursault (51) 45 E2
Boursay (41) 61 F5
Bourscheid (57) 50 B4
Bourseul (22) 34 B5
Bourseville (80) 6 B4
Boursières (70) 87 F3
Boursies (59) 8 C4
Boursin (62) 1 G4
Boursonne (60) 21 G6
Bourth (27) 40 B4
Bourthes (62) 1 G5
Bourville (76) 17 F3
Boury-en-Vexin (60) 19 G6
Bousbach (57) 27 G5
Bousbecque (59) 3 F4
le Bouscat (33) 135 E5
Bousies (59) 9 G3
Bousignies (59) 9 E1
Bousignies-sur-Roc (59)... 10 B2
le Bousquet (11) 200 A2
le Bousquet-d'Orb (34) 172 B5
Boussac (12) 154 B5
Boussac (23) 112 A3
la Boussac (35) 35 F5
Boussac (46) 153 F2
Boussac-Bourg (23) 112 A3
Boussais (79) 93 F4
Boussan (31) 184 C3
Boussay (37) 95 F5
Boussay (44) 92 A2
Bousse (57) 26 C4
Bousse (72) 77 H2
Bousselange (21) 102 B3
Boussenac (09) 185 F6
Boussenois (21) 86 A3
Boussens (31) 184 C3
Bousseraucourt (70) 69 E5
Boussès (47) 150 B6
Bousseviller (57) 28 B5
Boussey (21) 85 E6
Boussicourt (80) 20 D2
Boussières (25) 103 F2
Boussières-en-
  Cambrésis (59) 9 E3
Boussières-sur-
  Sambre (59) 9 H3
Boussois (59) 10 A2
Boussy (74) 131 H2
Boussy-Saint-Antoine (91) .. 43 E5
Boust (57) 26 B2
Boustroff (57) 49 F2
Bout-du-Pont-de-Larn (81).. 170 D6
Boutancourt (08) 24 B2
Boutavent (60) 19 G2
la Bouteille (02) 10 A6
Bouteilles-Saint-
  Sébastien (24) 136 C1
Boutenac (11) 187 H4
Boutenac-Touvent (17) 120 D5
Boutencourt (60) 19 H5
Boutervilliers (91) 63 E2
Bouteville (16) 121 H4
Boutiers-Saint-Trojan (16).. 121 G3
Boutigny (77) 43 G3
Boutigny-Prouais (28) 41 G5
Boutigny-sur-Essonne (91).. 63 G2
Bouttencourt (80) 6 C5
Boutteville (50) 13 E4
Boutx (31) 184 B6
Bouvaincourt-sur-
  Bresle (80) 6 B5
Bouvancourt (51) 22 D5
Bouvante (26) 144 D4
Bouvelinghem (62) 1 H4
Bouvellemont (08) 24 A3
Bouverans (25) 103 H4
Bouvesse-Quirieu (38) 131 E3
Bouvières (26) 158 D3
Bouvignies (59) 9 E1
Bouvigny-Boyeffles (62) ... 8 A1
Bouville (28) 62 B3
Bouville (76) 18 B3
Bouville (91) 63 F2
Bouvincourt-en-
  Vermandois (80) 8 C6
Bouvines (59) 3 G5
Bouvresse (60) 19 G2
Bouvron (44) 74 B3
Bouvron (54) 48 B4
Boux-sous-Salmaise (21)... 85 E5
Bouxières-aux-Bois (88)... 69 G3
Bouxières-aux-Chênes (54) .. 48 D4
Bouxières-aux-Dames (54).. 48 C4
Bouxières-sous-
  Froidmont (54) 48 C3
Bouxurulles (88) 69 G2
Bouxwiller (67) 50 C3
Bouxwiller (68) 89 F4
Bouy (51) 45 H2
Bouy-Luxembourg (10) 66 C2
Bouy-sur-Orvin (10) 65 F3
Bouyon (06) 178 D3
le Bouyssou (46) 153 G1
Bouzais (18) 97 H6
Bouzancourt (52) 67 G3
Bouzanville (54) 69 F2
Bouze-lès-Beaune (21)..... 101 G3
Bouzel (63) 127 G3
Bouzemont (88) 69 G3
Bouzeron (71) 101 F4
Bouzic (24) 152 B1
Bouziès (46) 153 E3
Bouzigues (34) 189 F1
Bouzin (31) 184 C3
Bouzincourt (80) 8 A5
Bouzon-Gellenave (32) 166 D4
Bouzonville (57) 27 E4
Bouzonville-aux-Bois (45).. 63 F5
Bouzy (51) 45 G2
Bouzy-la-Forêt (45) 81 G1
Bovée-sur-Barboure (55) .. 47 G5
Bovel (35) 56 D4
Bovelles (80) 7 F6
Boves (80) 7 G6
Boviolles (55) 47 G5
Boyaval (62) 2 B6
Boyelles (62) 8 B3
Boyer (42) 115 F6
Boyer (71) 116 B1
Boyeux-Saint-Jérôme (01).. 117 F6
Boynes (45) 63 G5
Boz (01) 116 C3
Bozas (07) 143 H4
Bozel (73) 133 E5
Bozouls (12) 154 D3
Brabant-en-Argonne (55) .. 47 E1
Brabant-le-Roi (55) 46 D4
Brabant-sur-Meuse (55) ... 25 E6
Brach (33) 134 C3
Brachay (52) 67 G2
Braches (80) 20 D2
Brachy (76) 17 F3
Bracieux (41) 80 B4
Bracon (39) 103 F4
Bracquetuit (76) 17 H4
Bradiancourt (76) 19 E2
Bragassargues (30) 173 G2
Bragayrac (31) 168 C6
Brageac (15) 139 H2
Bragelogne-Beauvoir (10).. 66 C6
Bragny-sur-Saône (71)..... 101 H4
Braillans (25) 87 F6
Brailly-Cornehotte (80) ... 7 E3
Brain (21) 84 D5
Brain-sur-Allonnes (49) ... 77 H6
Brainans (39) 102 D4
Braine (02) 22 B5
Brains (44) 74 C5
Brains-sur-Gée (72) 59 H5
Brains-sur-les-
  Marches (53) 58 A6
Brainville (50) 36 D1
Brainville (54) 48 A1
Brainville-sur-Meuse (52).. 68 C4
Braisnes-sur-Aronde (60).. 21 F4
Braize (03) 98 A6
Bralleville (54) 69 G2
Bram (11) 186 C3
Bramans (73) 147 E3
Brametot (76) 17 F3
Bramevaque (65) 184 A5
Bran (17) 121 G6
Branceilles (19) 138 D4
Branches (89) 83 F1
Brancourt-en-
  Laonnois (02) 22 B4
Brancourt-le-Grand (02) .. 9 E5
Brandérion (56) 54 D5
Brandeville (55) 25 E4
Brandivy (56) 55 F5
Brando (2B) 203 G3
Brandon (71) 115 H3
Brandonnet (12) 153 H4
Brandonvillers (51) 46 A6
Branges (71) 102 A4
Brangues (38) 131 E3
Brannay (89) 64 D4
Branne (25) 88 A5
Branne (33) 135 H5
Brannens (33) 150 A2
Branoux-les-Taillades (30) .. 156 D5
Brans (39) 102 D1
Bransat (03) 113 H4
Branscourt (51) 22 D6
Bransles (77) 64 B4
Brantes (84) 159 E6
Brantigny (88) 69 G2
Brantôme en Périgord (24) .. 137 F1
Branville (14) 15 E4
Braquis (55) 47 H1
Bras (83) 193 G3
Bras-d'Asse (04) 177 E2
Bras-sur-Meuse (55) 25 E6
Brasc (12) 171 E2
Braselle (82) 44 B2
Braslou (37) 94 C3
Brasparts (29) 31 H6
Brassac (09) 185 G5
Brassac (81) 171 E5
Brassac-les-Mines (63) 127 G6
Brassempouy (40) 165 G5
Brasseuse (60) 21 E6
Brassy (58) 100 A1
Brassy (80) 20 A2
Bratte (54) 48 D4
Braud-et-Saint-Louis (33) .. 135 E1
Brauvilliers (55) 47 E6
Braux (04) 178 A1
Braux (10) 66 D1
Braux (21) 84 D5
Braux-le-Châtel (52) 67 G5
Braux-Saint-Remy (51)..... 46 C2
Braux-Sainte-Cohière (51).. 46 C2
Brax (31) 168 D5
Brax (47) 151 E5
Bray (27) 40 C1
Bray (71) 116 A2
Bray-Dunes (59) 2 C1
Bray-et-Lû (95) 41 G1
Bray-lès-Mareuil (80) 6 D4
Bray-Saint-Aignan (45) 81 G2
Bray-Saint-Christophe (02) .. 21 H1
Bray-sur-Seine (77) 64 D2
Bray-sur-Somme (80) 8 B5
Braye (02) 22 A4
Braye-en-Laonnois (02) ... 22 C4
Braye-en-Thiérache (02) .. 23 E1
Braye-sous-Faye (37) 94 C3
Braye-sur-Maulne (37) 78 B4
Brazey-en-Morvan (21) ... 100 D2
Brazey-en-Plaine (21) 102 B3
Bréal-sous-Montfort (35) .. 56 D3
Bréal-sous-Vitré (35) 58 B4
Bréançon (95) 42 B1
Bréau (77) 64 B1
Bréau-et-Salagosse (30) .. 172 D2
Bréauté (76) 16 C4
Bréban (51) 45 H6
Brebières (62) 8 C2
Brebotte (90) 88 D3
Brécé (35) 57 G3
Brécé (53) 58 C2
Brécey (50) 37 F4
Brech (56) 55 E6
Brechainville (88) 68 B2
Bréchamps (28) 41 F5
Bréchaumont (68) 89 E2
Brèches (37) 78 C4
Breconchaux (25) 87 H6
Brectouville (50) 37 F2
Brécy (02) 44 B1
Brécy (18) 98 A2
Brécy-Brières (08) 24 B5
la Brède (33) 149 F1
Brée (53) 59 E4
Brée-les-Bains (17) 106 B6
Brégnier-Cordon (01) 131 F4
Brégy (60) 43 G2
Bréhain (57) 49 E3
Bréhain-la-Ville (54) 26 A2
Bréhal (50) 36 D3
Bréhan (56) 55 G3
Bréhand (22) 33 H5
Bréhémont (37) 78 B6
Bréhéville (55) 25 E5
Breidenbach (57) 28 B5
le Breil-sur-Mérize (72) ... 60 C5
Breil-sur-Roya (06) 179 G2
la Breille-les-Pins (49) 77 H6
Breilly (80) 7 F5
Breistroff-la-Grande (57) .. 26 C2
Breitenau (67) 71 F2
Breitenbach (67) 71 F2
Breitenbach-Haut-Rhin (68).. 71 F5
Brêles (29)................... 30 C4
Brélidy (22) 33 E3
Brem-sur-Mer (85) 90 D5
Brémenil (54) 49 H6
Brèmes (62) 1 H3
Brémoncourt (54) 69 H1
Bremondans (25) 104 A1
Brémontier-Merval (76) ... 19 G3
Brémoy (14) 37 H2
Brémur-et-Vaurois (21) ... 85 E2
Bren (26) 144 B3
Brenas (34) 172 B5
Brenat (63) 127 G5
Brénaz (01) 131 G1
Brenelle (02) 22 B5
Brengues (46) 153 F2
Brennes (52) 86 A2
Brennilis (29) 31 H5
Brénod (01) 117 G6
Brenon (83) 177 H3
Brenouille (60) 20 D5
Brenoux (48) 156 A4

Brens (01) 131 G3
Brens (81) 170 A3
Brenthonne (74) 118 D4
Breny (02) 44 B1
Brères (25) 103 F2
Bréry (39) 102 D5
Bresdon (17) 122 A2
les Bréseux (25) 88 C6
Bresilley (70) 102 D1
Bresle (17) 7 H5
Bresles (60) 20 B4
Bresnay (03) 113 H3
la Bresse (88) 70 C5
Bresse-sur-Grosne (71) 116 A1
Bressey-sur-Tille (21) 86 A6
Bressieux (38) 144 D1
Bressolles (01) 130 C2
Bressolles (03) 113 H2
Bressols (82) 169 E2
Bresson (38) 145 G3
Bressuire (79) 93 E4
Brest (29) 30 D4
Brestot (27) 18 A5
Bretagne (36) 96 C3
Bretagne (90) 88 D3
Bretagne-
    d'Armagnac (32) 167 E2
Bretagne-de-Marsan (40) 166 A3
Bretagnolles (27) 41 F3
Breteau (45) 82 B3
Breteil (35) 56 D2
Bretenière (21) 102 A1
la Bretenière (25) 87 H5
la Bretenière (39) 102 D2
Bretenières (39) 102 D4
Bretenoux (46) 139 E5
Breteuil (27) 40 C4
Breteuil (60) 20 C2
Brethel (61) 40 A5
Brethenay (52) 67 H4
le Brethon (03) 112 D1
Bretigney (25) 88 B4
Bretigney-Notre-Dame (25) .. 87 H6
Bretignolles (79) 92 D4
Bretignolles-sur-Mer (85) ... 90 D2
Bretigny (21) 85 H5
Brétigny (27) 18 A6
Brétigny (60) 21 H3
Brétigny-sur-Orge (91) 42 C6
Bretoncelles (61) 61 F2
la Bretonnière-la-
    Claye (85) 91 H6
Bretonvillers (25) 104 C1
Brette (26) 159 E2
Brette-les-Pins (72) 60 B6
Bretten (68) 89 E2
Brettes (16) 108 C6
Bretteville (50) 12 D2
Bretteville-du-Grand-
    Caux (76) 16 C4
Bretteville-le-Rabet (14) 38 D2
Bretteville-Saint-
    Laurent (76) 17 F3
Bretteville-sur-Ay (50) 12 C5
Bretteville-sur-Laize (14) 38 C2
Bretteville-sur-Odon (14) 14 B5
Brettnach (57) 27 E4
Bretx (31) 168 D4
Breuches (70) 87 H1
Breuchotte (70) 88 A1
Breugnon (58) 83 F5
le Breuil (03) 114 B5
Breuil (51) 22 D5
le Breuil (51) 44 D3
le Breuil (69) 129 G2
le Breuil (71) 101 E5
Breuil (80) 21 G2
Breuil-Barret (85) 92 D6
le Breuil-Bernard (79) 93 E5
Breuil-Bois-Robert (78) 41 H3
le Breuil-en-Auge (14) 15 F4
le Breuil-en-Bessin (14) 13 G5
Breuil-la-Réorte (17) 107 F6
Breuil-le-Sec (60) 20 D5
Breuil-le-Vert (60) 20 D5
Breuil-Magné (17) 106 D6
le Breuil-sur-Couze (63) 127 G6
Breuilaufa (87) 110 B6
Breuillet (17) 120 C3
Breuillet (91) 42 C6
Breuilpont (27) 41 F3
Breurey-lès-Faverney (70) 87 G2
Breuschwickersheim (67) 50 D5
Breuvannes-en-
    Bassigny (52) 68 C5
Breuvery-sur-Coole (51) 45 H4
Breuville (50) 12 C3
Breux (55) 25 E3
Breux-Jouy (91) 63 F1
Breux-sur-Avre (27) 40 D4
Brévainville (41) 61 H6
Bréval (78) 41 G3
Brevans (39) 102 C2
le Brévedent (14) 15 F4
Brèves (58) 83 G5
les Bréviaires (78) 41 H5
Bréviandes (10) 66 B3
Bréville (16) 121 H2
Bréville-les-Monts (14) 14 C4
Bréville-sur-Mer (50) 36 D3
Brévillers (62) 7 E2
Brévillers (80) 7 G3
Brévilliers (70) 88 C3
Brévilly (08) 24 D2
Brévonnes (10) 66 D2
Bréxent-Énocq (62) 1 F6
Brey-et-Maison-du-
    Bois (25) 103 H5

Brézé (49) 93 H1
Bréziers (05) 160 C3
Brézilhac (11) 186 C4
Brézins (38) 144 D1
Brezolles (28) 40 D5
Brezons (15) 140 D4
Briançon (05) 147 E5
Briançonnet (06) 178 B2
Brianny (21) 84 D5
Briant (71) 115 F4
Briantes (36) 111 H2
Briare (45) 82 A3
Briarres-sur-Essonne (45) 63 G4
Brias (62) 7 G1
Briastre (59) 9 F3
Briatexte (81) 170 A4
Briaucourt (52) 68 A4
Briaucourt (70) 87 G1
Bricon (52) 67 G5
Briconville (28) 62 A1
Bricquebec-en-
    Cotentin (50) 12 C3
Bricquebosq (50) 12 B3
Bricqueville (14) 13 G5
Bricqueville-la-
    Blouette (50) 36 D1
Bricqueville-sur-Mer (50) 36 D2
Bricy (45) 62 C6
Brides-les-Bains (73) 132 D5
la Bridoire (73) 131 G5
Bridoré (37) 95 G3
Brie (02) 22 B3
Brie (09) 185 G3
Brie (16) 122 C3
Brie (35) 57 F4
Brie (79) 93 H4
Brie (80) 8 C6
Brie-Comte-Robert (77) 43 E5
Brié-et-Angonnes (38) 145 G3
Brie-sous-Archiac (17) 121 G5
Brie-sous-Barbezieux (16) .. 122 A6
Brie-sous-Chalais (16) 136 A1
Brie-sous-Matha (17) 121 H2
Brie-sous-Mortagne (17) 120 D5
Briec (29) 53 G2
Briel-sur-Barse (10) 66 C4
Brielles (35) 58 A5
Brienne (71) 116 C1
Brienne-la-Vieille (10) 66 D2
Brienne-le-Château (10) 66 D2
Brienne-sur-Aisne (08) 23 E4
Briennon (42) 115 E5
Brienon-sur-
    Armançon (89) 65 G6
Brières-les-Scellés (91) 63 F2
Brieuil-sur-Chizé (79) 108 A5
Brieulles-sur-Bar (08) 24 B4
Brieulles-sur-Meuse (55) 24 D5
Brieux (61) 39 E4
Briffons (63) 126 C4
Brignac (34) 172 D5
Brignac (56) 56 A2
Brignac-la-Plaine (19) 138 D2
Brignais (69) 129 H4
Brignancourt (95) 42 A1
Brignemont (31) 168 C4
Brignoles (83) 193 F2
Brignon (30) 174 A2
le Brignon (43) 142 C5
la Brigue (06) 163 F6
Briguel-le-Chantre (86) 110 B3
Brigueuil (16) 123 G1
Briis-sous-Forges (91) 42 B6
Brillac (16) 109 H6
la Brillanne (04) 176 D2
Brillecourt (10) 66 C1
Brillevast (50) 12 D2
Brillon (59) 9 E1
Brillon-en-Barrois (55) 47 E5
Brimeux (62) 6 D1
Brimont (51) 23 E5
Brin-sur-Seille (54) 48 D4
Brinay (18) 97 F2
Brinay (58) 99 H3
Brinckheim (68) 89 G3
Brindas (69) 129 H3
Bringolo (22) 33 F4
Brinon-sur-Beuvron (58) 99 F1
Brinon-sur-Sauldre (18) 81 F4
Briod (39) 102 D6
Briollay (49) 77 E3
Brion (01) 117 G5
Brion (36) 96 C4
Brion (38) 144 D1
Brion (48) 155 F1
Brion (71) 100 C4
Brion (86) 109 F3
Brion (89) 65 F6
Brion-près-Thouet (79) 93 G2
Brion-sur-Ource (21) 85 E1
la Brionne (23) 111 F5
Brionne (27) 18 A6
Briord (01) 131 E3
Briosne-lès-Sables (72) 60 C4
Briot (60) 19 H2
Brion (41) 80 A2
Brioude (43) 141 G2
Brioux-sur-Boutonne (79) .. 108 A5
Briouze (61) 38 C5
Briquemesnil-
    Floxicourt (80) 7 F6
Briquenay (08) 24 B4
Briscous (64) 164 C6
Brison-Saint-Innocent (73) .. 131 H3
Brissac (34) 173 E3
Brissac Loire Aubance (49) ... 77 E5
Brissay-Choigny (02) 22 A2
Brissy-Hamégicourt (02) 22 A1

Brive-la-Gaillarde (19) 138 C3
Brives (36) 97 E5
Brives-Charensac (43) 142 C4
Brives-sur-Charente (17) 121 F3
Brivezac (19) 139 E4
Brix (50) 12 C2
Brixey-aux-Chanoines (55) ... 68 D1
Brizambourg (17) 121 F2
Brizay (37) 94 C2
Brizeaux (55) 46 D2
Brizon (74) 119 E6
le Broc (06) 179 E3
le Broc (63) 127 G5
Brocas (40) 166 A1
Brochon (21) 101 H1
Brocourt (80) 6 D6
Brocourt-en-Argonne (55) 47 E1
Broglie (27) 40 A2
Brognard (25) 88 C4
Brognon (08) 10 C5
Brognon (21) 86 A5
Broin (21) 102 A2
Broindon (21) 101 H1
Broissia (39) 117 F3
Brombos (60) 19 H2
Bromeilles (45) 63 H4
Brommat (12) 140 C6
Bromont-Lamothe (63) 126 D2
Bron (69) 130 B3
Bronvaux (57) 26 B5
Broons (22) 34 B6
la Broque (67) 71 E1
Broquiers (60) 19 H2
Broquiès (12) 171 F2
Brossac (16) 136 A1
Brossainc (07) 143 H1
Brossay (49) 93 G1
la Brosse-Montceaux (77) 64 C3
Brosses (89) 83 G4
Brosville (27) 40 D1
Brotte-lès-Luxeuil (70) 87 H2
Brotte-lès-Ray (70) 86 D3
Brou (28) 61 G4
Brou-sur-Chantereine (77) 43 E4
Brouains (50) 37 G4
Broualan (35) 35 F5
Brouchaud (24) 137 H2
Brouchy (80) 21 G2
Brouck (57) 26 D5
Brouckerque (59) 2 D2
Brouderdorff (57) 50 A5
Broué (28) 41 F5
Brouennes (55) 25 E3
le Brouilh-Monbert (32) 167 G4
Brouilla (66) 201 F3
Brouillet (51) 22 D6
Brouqueyran (33) 149 H3
la Brousse (17) 121 G1
la Brousse (23) 126 B1
Brousse (63) 127 H4
Brousse (81) 170 B4
Brousse-le-Château (12) 171 F2
Brousses-et-Villaret (11) 186 D2
Brousseval (52) 67 G1
Broussey-en-Blois (55) 47 G5
Broussey-Raulecourt (55) 47 H4
Broussy-le-Grand (51) 45 E4
Broussy-le-Petit (51) 45 E4
Broût-Vernet (03) 113 H5
Brouvelieures (88) 70 B3
Brouville (54) 70 B1
Brouviller (57) 50 A4
Brouy (91) 63 F3
Brouzet-lès-Alès (30) 157 F6
Brouzet-lès-Quissac (30) ... 173 G3
les Brouzils (85) 91 H2
Broxeele (59) 2 B3
Broye (71) 100 D4
Broye-Aubigney-
    Montseugny (70) 86 C6
Broye-les-Loups-et-
    Verfontaine (70) 86 B5
Broyes (51) 44 D5
Broyes (60) 20 D3
Broze (81) 170 A2
Brû (88) 70 B2
Bruailles (71) 117 E1
Bruay-la-Buissière (62) 2 C6
Bruay-sur-l'Escaut (59) 9 F1
Bruc-sur-Aff (35) 56 C5
Brucamps (80) 7 E4
Bruch (47) 150 D5
Brucheville (50) 13 E4
Brue-Auriac (83) 193 E1
Bruebach (68) 89 F2
Brueil-en-Vexin (78) 41 H2
Bruère-Allichamps (18) 97 H5
la Bruère-sur-Loir (72) 78 B3
la Bruffière (85) 92 A3
Brugairolles (11) 186 C4
le Brugeron (63) 128 B3
Bruges (33) 135 E5
Bruges-Capbis-
    Mifaget (64) 182 C3
Brugheas (03) 114 A6
Brugnac (47) 151 E3
Brugnens (32) 168 A3
Brugny-Vaudancourt (51) 45 E2
la Bruguière (30) 174 B1
Bruguières (31) 169 F4
Bruille-lez-
    Marchiennes (59) 9 E2
Bruille-Saint-Amand (59) 9 F1
Bruis (05) 159 F3
Brûlain (79) 108 A4
Brûlange (57) 49 E2

la Brûlatte (53) 58 B4
Bruley (54) 48 A5
Brullemail (61) 39 G5
Brullioles (69) 129 G3
Brûlon (72) 59 G6
Brumath (67) 51 E4
Brumetz (02) 44 A2
Brunehamel (02) 23 F1
Brunelles (28) 61 F3
les Brunels (11) 186 C1
Brunembert (62) 1 G4
Brunémont (59) 8 D2
Brunet (04) 177 E2
Bruniquel (82) 169 G1
Brunoy (91) 43 E5
Brunstatt-Didenheim (68) 89 F2
Brunvillers-la-Motte (60) 20 D3
Brusque (12) 171 H4
le Brusquet (04) 160 D6
Brussey (70) 87 E6
Brussieu (69) 129 G3
Brusson (51) 46 B5
Brusvily (22) 34 C6
Brutelles (80) 6 B4
Bruville (54) 26 A5
Brux (86) 108 D4
la Bruyère (70) 88 A1
Bruyères (88) 70 B3
Bruyères-et-
    Montbérault (02) 22 C3
Bruyères-le-Châtel (91) 42 C6
Bruyères-sur-Fère (02) 44 B1
Bruyères-sur-Oise (95) 42 D1
Bruys (02) 22 B6
Bruz (35) 57 E3
Bry (59) 9 G2
Bry-sur-Marne (94) 43 E4
Bû (28) 41 F4
le Bû-sur-Rouvres (14) 38 D2
Buais-les-Monts (50) 37 G6
Buanes (40) 166 A4
Bubertré (61) 40 B4
Bubry (56) 54 D3
Buc (78) 42 B5
Buc (90) 88 C3
Bucamps (60) 20 C3
Bucéels (14) 14 A4
Bucey-en-Othe (10) 65 H3
Bucey-lès-Gy (70) 87 E5
Bucey-lès-Traves (70) 87 F3
Buchelay (78) 41 G3
Buchères (10) 66 B4
Buchy (57) 48 D2
Buchy (76) 19 E3
Bucilly (02) 10 B6
Bucquoy (62) 8 A4
Bucy-le-Long (02) 22 A5
Bucy-le-Roi (45) 62 D5
Bucy-lès-Cerny (02) 22 B3
Bucy-lès-Pierrepont (02) 22 D2
Bucy-Saint-Liphard (45) 62 C6
Budelière (23) 112 C5
Buding (57) 26 C3
Budling (57) 26 C3
Budos (33) 149 G2
Bué (18) 82 B6
Bueil (27) 41 F3
Bueil-en-Touraine (37) 78 D3
Buellas (01) 116 D5
Buethwiller (68) 89 E2
Buffard (25) 103 E3
Buffières (71) 115 H3
Buffignécourt (70) 87 F1
Buffon (21) 84 C3
Bugarach (11) 187 E6
Bugard (65) 183 G2
Bugeat (19) 125 F4
Bugnein (64) 181 G1
Bugnicourt (59) 8 D2
Bugnières (52) 67 H6
Bugny (25) 104 A3
le Bugue (24) 137 G5
Buhl (67) 51 F2
Buhl (68) 71 E6
Buhl-Lorraine (57) 50 A4
Buhy (95) 41 H1
Buicourt (60) 19 H3
Buigny-l'Abbé (80) 7 E4
Buigny-lès-Gamaches (80) 6 C5
Buigny-Saint-Maclou (80) 6 D3
Buire (02) 10 B6
Buire-au-Bois (62) 7 F2
Buire-Courcelles (80) 8 C6
Buire-le-Sec (62) 6 D1
Buire-sur-l'Ancre (80) 8 A5
Buironfosse (02) 9 H5
le Buis (87) 110 C6
Buis-les-Baronnies (26) 159 E5
Buis-sur-Damville (27) 40 D4
Buissard (05) 160 C1
la Buisse (38) 145 F1
la Buissière (38) 132 A6
le Buisson (48) 155 G2
le Buisson (51) 46 C4
le Buisson (51) 158 C5
le Buisson-de-Cadouin (24). 137 G5
Buissoncourt (54) 48 D5
Bujaleuf (87) 124 D3
Bulan (65) 183 F4
Bulat-Pestivien (22) 32 D5
Bulcy (58) 98 D1
Buléon (56) 55 G4
Bulgnéville (88) 69 E4
Bulhon (63) 127 G2
Bullainville (28) 62 B1
Bulle (25) 103 H4
Bullecourt (62) 8 C3
Bulles (60) 20 C4

Bulligny (54) 48 A6
Bullion (78) 42 B6
Bullou (28) 61 H3
Bully (42) 128 D2
Bully (69) 129 G2
Bully (76) 19 E2
Bully-les-Mines (62) 8 B1
Bulson (08) 24 C2
Bult (88) 70 B3
Bun (65) 182 D5
Buncey (21) 85 E2
Buneville (62) 7 G2
Buno-Bonnevaux (91) 63 G2
Bunus (64) 181 E3
Bunzac (16) 122 D3
Buoux (84) 175 H3
Burbach (67) 50 A3
Burbure (62) 2 C6
Burcin (38) 131 E6
Burcy (77) 63 H4
Burdignes (42) 143 G2
Burdignin (74) 118 D4
Bure (55) 68 B1
Buré (61) 60 C1
Bure-les-Templiers (21) 85 G2
Burelles (02) 22 D1
Bures (54) 49 F5
Bures (61) 39 G6
Bures-en-Bray (76) 19 E1
Bures-sur-Yvette (91) 42 C5
Burey (27) 40 C2
Burey-en-Vaux (55) 47 H6
Burey-la-Côte (55) 68 D1
Burg (65) 183 G3
Burgalays (31) 184 A6
Burgaronne (64) 181 G1
le Burgaud (31) 168 D3
Burgille (25) 87 E6
Burgnac (87) 124 A3
Burgy (71) 116 B2
Burie (17) 121 G2
Buriville (54) 49 G6
Burlats (81) 170 D3
Burlioncourt (57) 49 F3
Burnand (71) 116 A1
Burnevillers (25) 88 D5
Burnhaupt-le-Bas (68) 89 E2
Burnhaupt-le-Haut (68) 89 E2
Buros (64) 182 C1
Burosse-Mendousse (64) 166 C6
Burret (09) 185 G5
Bursard (61) 39 F6
Burthecourt-aux-
    Chênes (54) 48 D6
Burtoncourt (57) 26 D4
Bury (60) 20 C5
Burzet (07) 157 F1
Burzy (71) 115 H1
Bus (62) 8 C4
Bus-la-Mésière (80) 21 E2
Bus-lès-Artois (80) 7 H4
Buschwiller (68) 89 G3
Busigny (59) 9 F5
Busloup (41) 79 G1
Busnes (62) 2 C5
Busque (81) 170 A4
Bussac (24) 137 E2
Bussac-Forêt (17) 135 G2
Bussac-sur-Charente (17) ... 121 E2
Bussang (88) 70 C6
le Busseau (79) 107 G1
Busseaut (21) 85 E2
Busséol (63) 127 G4
Busserolles (24) 123 F4
Bussero-et-
    Montenaille (21) 85 G3
Busset (03) 114 B6
Bussiares (02) 44 A2
la Bussière (45) 82 A2
la Bussière (86) 109 H1
Bussière-Badil (24) 123 E4
Bussière-Dunoise (23) 111 F4
Bussière-Galant (87) 123 H4
Bussière-Nouvelle (23) 126 A1
Bussière-Poitevine (87) 110 A3
Bussière-Saint-
    Georges (23) 112 A3
la Bussière-sur-Ouche (21) . 101 F1
Bussières (21) 85 G3
Bussières (42) 129 G2
Bussières (63) 112 D6
Bussières (70) 87 F6
Bussières (71) 116 A3
Bussières (77) 44 A3
Bussières (89) 84 B5
Bussières-et-Pruns (63) 127 F1
Busson (52) 68 B3
Bussu (80) 8 C5
Bussunarits-
    Sarrasquette (64) 181 E3
Bussus-Bussuel (80) 7 E4
Bussy (18) 98 A4
Bussy (60) 21 G3
Bussy-Albieux (42) 128 D3
Bussy-en-Othe (89) 65 F6
Bussy-la-Pesle (21) 85 F6
Bussy-la-Pesle (58) 99 F1
Bussy-le-Château (51) 46 A2
Bussy-le-Grand (21) 85 E4
Bussy-le-Repos (51) 46 C3
Bussy-le-Repos (89) 64 D5
Bussy-lès-Daours (80) 7 H6
Bussy-lès-Poix (80) 20 A1
Bussy-Lettrée (51) 45 G4
Bussy-Saint-Georges (77) 43 F4
Bussy-Saint-Martin (77) 43 F4

Bust (67) 50 B3
Bustanico (2B) 205 F2
Bustince-Iriberry (64) 181 E3
Buswiller (67) 50 D3
Busy (25) 103 F1
Buthiers (70) 87 F6
Buthiers (77) 63 G3
Butot (76) 17 G4
Butot-Vénesville (76) 16 D3
Butry-sur-Oise (95) 42 C2
Butteaux (89) 65 H4
Butten (67) 50 B2
Buverchy (80) 21 G2
Buvilly (39) 103 E4
la Buxerette (36) 111 F2
Buxerolles (21) 85 G2
Buxerolles (86) 109 E1
Buxeuil (10) 66 D5
Buxeuil (36) 96 C2
Buxeuil (86) 95 E3
Buxières-d'Aillac (36) 111 F1
Buxières-lès-Clefmont (52) .. 68 B5
Buxières-les-Mines (03) 113 F2
Buxières-lès-Villiers (52) 67 H5
Buxières-sous-les-
    Côtes (55) 47 H3
Buxières-sous-
    Montaigut (63) 113 E5
Buxy (71) 101 F6
Buysscheure (59) 2 B3
Buzan (09) 184 C5
Buzançais (36) 96 A4
Buzançois (36) 22 A5
Buzancy (08) 24 C4
Buzet-sur-Baïse (47) 150 D5
Buzet-sur-Tarn (31) 169 G4
Buziet (64) 182 B3
Buzignargues (34) 173 G4
Buzon (65) 183 F1
Buzy (64) 182 B3
Buzy-Darmont (55) 47 H1
By (25) 103 F3
Byans-sur-Doubs (25) 103 E2

C

Cabanac (65) 183 F2
Cabanac-Cazaux (31) 184 B5
Cabanac-et-Villagrains (33) .. 149 F2
Cabanac-Séguenville (31) ... 168 C3
la Cabanasse (66) 200 A4
Cabanès (12) 154 A6
Cabanès (81) 170 A4
le Cabanial (31) 170 A6
les Cabannes (09) 199 F1
les Cabannes (13) 175 F3
les Cabannes (81) 170 A1
Cabara (33) 135 H5
Cabariot (17) 120 D1
Cabas-Loumassès (32) 184 A2
Cabasse (83) 193 G2
Cabestany (66) 201 F2
Cabidos (64) 166 A5
Cabourg (14) 14 D4
Cabrerets (46) 153 E3
Cabrerolles (34) 172 A6
Cabrespine (11) 187 E2
Cabrières (30) 174 B3
Cabrières (34) 172 C6
Cabrières-d'Aigues (84) 176 A3
Cabrières-d'Avignon (84) ... 175 G3
Cabriès (13) 192 B2
Cabris (06) 178 C4
Cachan (94) 42 D4
Cachen (40) 166 A1
Cachy (80) 7 H6
Cadalen (81) 170 B3
Cadarcet (09) 185 G5
Cadarsac (33) 135 G5
Cadaujac (33) 135 F6
Cadéac (65) 183 G6
Cadeilhan (32) 168 A3
Cadeilhan-Trachère (65) 196 D1
Cadeillan (32) 184 C1
Cademène (25) 103 G2
Caden (56) 73 G1
Cadenet (84) 175 H4
la Cadière-d'Azur (83) 192 C4
la Cadière-et-Cambo (30) .. 173 F2
Cadillac (33) 149 G2
Cadillac-en-
    Fronsadais (33) 135 G4
Cadillon (64) 166 C6
Cadix (81) 171 E2
Cadolive (13) 192 C3
Cadours (31) 168 C4
Cadrieu (46) 153 F3
Caen (14) 14 B4
Caëstre (59) 2 B3
Caffiers (62) 1 G3
Cagnac-les-Mines (81) 170 C2
Cagnano (2B) 203 G2
Cagnes-sur-Mer (06) 178 D4
Cagnicourt (62) 8 C3
Cagnoncles (59) 9 E3
Cagnotte (40) 165 G6
Cagny (14) 14 C5
Cagny (80) 7 G6
Cahagnes (14) 38 A1
Cahagnolles (14) 13 H6
Cahan (61) 38 C3
Caharet (65) 183 G3
Cahon (80) 6 C4
Cahors (46) 152 C3
Cahus (46) 139 F5

Cahuzac (11) ... 186 A3
Cahuzac (47) ... 151 E1
Cahuzac (81) ... 186 C1
Cahuzac-sur-Adour (32) ... 166 D5
Cahuzac-sur-Vère (81) ... 170 A2
Caignac (31) ... 185 H2
le Cailar (30) ... 174 A5
Cailhau (11) ... 186 C4
Cailhavel (11) ... 186 C4
Cailla (11) ... 200 A1
Caillac (46) ... 152 C3
Caillavet (32) ... 167 F4
Caille (06) ... 178 B3
la Caillère-Saint-Hilaire (85) ... 92 B6
Cailleville (76) ... 17 E2
Caillouël-Crépigny (02) ... 21 H3
Caillouet-Orgeville (27) ... 41 E2
Cailloux-sur-Fontaines (69) ... 130 A2
Cailly (76) ... 18 D3
Cailly-sur-Eure (27) ... 41 E1
la Caine (14) ... 38 B2
Cairanne (84) ... 158 C5
le Caire (04) ... 160 B4
Cairon (14) ... 14 B4
Caisnes (60) ... 21 G3
Caissargues (30) ... 174 B4
Caix (80) ... 21 E1
Caixas (66) ... 200 D3
Caixon (65) ... 183 E1
Cajarc (46) ... 153 F3
Calacuccia (2B) ... 204 D2
Calais (62) ... 1 G2
Calamane (46) ... 152 C3
Calan (56) ... 54 C4
Calanhel (22) ... 32 C5
Calavanté (65) ... 183 E1
Calcatoggio (2A) ... 204 C5
Calce (66) ... 201 E2
Calenzana (2B) ... 202 C6
Calès (24) ... 137 F5
Calès (46) ... 138 C5
Calignac (47) ... 150 D6
Caligny (61) ... 38 B4
Callac (22) ... 32 C5
Callas (83) ... 177 H5
Callen (40) ... 149 F4
Callengeville (76) ... 19 F1
Calleville (27) ... 18 A6
Calleville-les-Deux-Églises (76) ... 17 G4
Callian (32) ... 167 F5
Callian (83) ... 178 B5
Calmeilles (66) ... 200 D3
Calmels-et-le-Viala (12) ... 171 G2
la Calmette (30) ... 174 A2
Calmont (12) ... 154 B5
Calmont (31) ... 185 H2
Calmoutier (70) ... 87 G3
Caloire (42) ... 129 E6
Calonges (47) ... 150 C4
Calonne-Ricouart (62) ... 2 C6
Calonne-sur-la-Lys (62) ... 2 D5
Calorguen (22) ... 34 D5
la Calotterie (62) ... 1 F6
Caluire-et-Cuire (69) ... 130 A3
Calvi (2B) ... 202 B5
Calviac-en-Périgord (24) ... 138 B5
Calvignac (46) ... 153 E3
Calvinet (15) ... 154 B1
Calvisson (30) ... 173 H4
Calzan (09) ... 186 A5
Camalès (65) ... 183 E1
Camarade (09) ... 185 E4
Camarès (12) ... 171 G3
Camaret-sur-Aigues (84) ... 158 B6
Camaret-sur-Mer (29) ... 30 D5
Camarsac (33) ... 135 G5
Cambayrac (46) ... 152 B4
la Cambe (14) ... 13 F4
Cambernard (31) ... 185 E1
Cambernon (50) ... 37 E1
Cambes (33) ... 135 F6
Cambes (46) ... 153 G2
Cambes (47) ... 150 D2
Cambes-en-Plaine (14) ... 14 B4
Cambia (2B) ... 205 F2
Cambiac (31) ... 169 H6
Cambieure (11) ... 186 C4
Camblain-Châtelain (62) ... 2 C6
Camblain-l'Abbé (62) ... 8 A2
Camblanes-et-Meynac (33) ... 135 F6
Cambligneul (62) ... 8 A1
Cambo-les-Bains (64) ... 180 C1
Cambon (81) ... 170 C3
Cambon-et-Salvergues (34) ... 171 G5
Cambon-lès-Lavaur (81) ... 170 A6
Camboulazet (12) ... 154 B5
Camboulit (46) ... 153 G2
Cambounès (81) ... 171 E5
Cambounet-sur-le-Sor (81) ... 170 B6
le Cambout (22) ... 55 H3
Cambrai (59) ... 9 E3
Cambremer (14) ... 15 E5
Cambrin (62) ... 2 D6
Cambron (80) ... 6 D4
Cambronne-lès-Clermont (60) ... 20 C5
Cambronne-lès-Ribécourt (60) ... 21 F4
Camburat (46) ... 153 G2
Came (64) ... 164 D6
Camélas (66) ... 201 E2
Camelin (02) ... 21 H3
Camembert (61) ... 39 F3
Cametours (50) ... 37 E1
Camiac-et-Saint-Denis (33) .. 135 G6

Camiers (62) ... 1 F5
Camiran (33) ... 150 A1
Camjac (12) ... 154 B6
Camlez (22) ... 32 D2
les Cammazes (81) ... 186 C1
Camoël (56) ... 73 F2
Camon (09) ... 186 B5
Camon (80) ... 7 G6
Camors (56) ... 55 E4
Camou-Cihigue (64) ... 181 F3
Camous (65) ... 183 G5
Campagna-de-Sault (11) ... 199 H1
Campagnac (12) ... 155 F4
Campagnac (81) ... 170 A1
Campagnac-lès-Quercy (24) ... 152 B1
Campagnan (34) ... 172 D6
Campagne (24) ... 137 G5
Campagne (34) ... 173 G4
Campagne (40) ... 165 H2
Campagne (60) ... 21 G2
Campagne-d'Armagnac (32) ... 166 D3
Campagne-lès-Boulonnais (62) ... 1 H5
Campagne-lès-Guines (62) ... 1 G3
Campagne-lès-Hesdin (62) ... 6 D1
Campagne-lès-Wardrecques (62) ... 2 B4
Campagne-sur-Arize (09) ... 185 F4
Campagne-sur-Aude (11) ... 186 D6
Campagnolles (14) ... 37 G3
Campan (65) ... 183 F5
Campana (2B) ... 205 F1
Camparan (65) ... 183 G6
Campbon (44) ... 74 A3
Campeaux (60) ... 19 G3
Campénéac (56) ... 56 B4
Campestre-et-Luc (30) ... 172 C2
Campet-et-Lamolère (40) ... 165 H2
Camphin-en-Carembault (59) ... 3 F6
Camphin-en-Pévèle (59) ... 3 G5
Campi (2B) ... 205 G2
Campigneulles-les-Grandes (62) ... 6 C1
Campigneulles-les-Petites (62) ... 6 D1
Campigny (14) ... 13 H5
Campigny (27) ... 15 H3
Campile (2B) ... 203 F6
Campistrous (65) ... 183 G3
Campitello (2B) ... 203 F5
Camplong (34) ... 172 A5
Camplong-d'Aude (11) ... 187 G4
Campneuseville (76) ... 6 C6
Campo (2A) ... 205 E6
Campôme (66) ... 200 B3
Campouriez (12) ... 154 C1
Campoussy (66) ... 200 C2
Campremy (60) ... 20 C3
Camprond (50) ... 37 E1
Camps-en-Amiénois (80) ... 7 E6
Camps-Saint-Mathurin-Léobazel (19) ... 139 F4
Camps-sur-l'Agly (11) ... 187 E6
Camps-sur-l'Isle (33) ... 136 A4
Campsas (82) ... 169 E3
Campsegret (24) ... 137 E5
Campuac (12) ... 154 C2
Campugnan (33) ... 135 E2
Campuzan (65) ... 183 H2
Camurac (11) ... 199 G1
Canale-di-Verde (2B) ... 205 G2
Canals (82) ... 169 E3
Canaples (80) ... 7 F4
Canappeville (27) ... 40 D1
Canapville (14) ... 15 E3
Canapville (61) ... 39 G3
Canari (2B) ... 203 F2
Canaules-et-Argentières (30) ... 173 G2
Canavaggia (2B) ... 203 F6
Canaveilles (66) ... 200 B4
Cancale (35) ... 35 E3
Canchy (14) ... 13 G5
Canchy (80) ... 6 D3
Cancon (47) ... 151 F2
Candas (80) ... 7 G4
Candé (49) ... 75 G2
Candé-sur-Beuvron (41) ... 79 H4
Candes-Saint-Martin (37) ... 94 A1
Candillargues (34) ... 173 H5
Candor (21) ... 21 F3
Candresse (40) ... 165 E4
Canehan (76) ... 6 A5
Canéjan (33) ... 135 E6
Canens (31) ... 185 F3
Canenx-et-Réaut (40) ... 166 A1
Canet (11) ... 187 H3
Canet (34) ... 172 D5
Canet-de-Salars (12) ... 154 D5
Canet-en-Roussillon (66) ... 201 G2
Canettemont (62) ... 7 G2
Cangey (37) ... 79 G5
Caniac-du-Causse (46) ... 153 E2
Canihuel (22) ... 33 E6
Canisy (50) ... 37 F1
Canlers (62) ... 2 A6
Canly (60) ... 21 E5
Cannectancourt (60) ... 21 F3
Cannelle (2A) ... 204 C5
Cannes (06) ... 178 D5
Cannes-Écluse (77) ... 64 C2
Cannes-et-Clairan (30) ... 173 H3
Cannessières (80) ... 6 D5
le Cannet (06) ... 178 D5

Cannet (32) ... 166 D5
le Cannet-des-Maures (83) ... 193 H2
Canny-sur-Matz (60) ... 21 F3
Canny-sur-Thérain (60) ... 19 G3
Canohès (66) ... 201 E2
la Canourgue (48) ... 155 G4
Cans et Cévennes (48) ... 156 B5
Cantaing-sur-Escaut (59) ... 8 D4
Cantaous (65) ... 183 H4
Cantaron (06) ... 179 F3
Canté (09) ... 185 G3
Canteleu (76) ... 18 C4
Canteloup (14) ... 14 D5
Canteloup (50) ... 13 E2
Cantenay-Épinard (49) ... 76 D4
Cantigny (80) ... 20 D2
Cantillac (24) ... 123 E6
Cantin (59) ... 8 D2
Cantoin (12) ... 140 D6
Cantois (33) ... 149 H1
Canville-la-Rocque (50) ... 12 C4
Canville-les-Deux-Églises (76) ... 17 F3
Cany-Barville (76) ... 16 D3
Caorches-Saint-Nicolas (27) ... 40 A2
Caouënnec-Lanvézéac (22) ... 32 D2
Caours (80) ... 6 D4
Cap-d'Ail (06) ... 179 G4
Capavenir Vosges (88) ... 69 H3
Capbreton (40) ... 164 B4
Capdenac (46) ... 153 G2
Capdenac-Gare (12) ... 153 G2
Capdrot (24) ... 151 H1
la Capelle (02) ... 10 A5
Capelle (59) ... 9 F3
la Capelle-Balaguier (12) ... 153 G4
la Capelle-Bleys (12) ... 153 H5
la Capelle-Bonance (12) ... 155 F4
la Capelle-et-Masmolène (30) ... 174 C1
Capelle-Fermont (62) ... 8 A2
la Capelle-lès-Boulogne (62) ... 1 F4
Capelle-les-Grands (27) ... 39 H2
Capelle-lès-Hesdin (62) ... 7 E2
Capendu (11) ... 187 F3
Capens (31) ... 185 E2
Capestang (34) ... 188 B2
Capian (33) ... 135 G6
Capinghem (59) ... 3 F5
Caplong (33) ... 136 B6
Capoulet-et-Junac (09) ... 199 E1
Cappel (57) ... 27 F5
Cappelle-Brouck (59) ... 2 A2
Cappelle-en-Pévèle (59) ... 3 G6
Cappelle-la-Grande (59) ... 2 B2
Cappy (80) ... 8 B6
Captieux (33) ... 149 H4
Capvern (65) ... 183 G4
Caragoudes (31) ... 169 G6
Caraman (31) ... 169 H6
Caramany (66) ... 200 D2
Carantec (29) ... 31 H2
Carantilly (50) ... 37 F1
Carayac (46) ... 153 F3
Carbay (49) ... 57 H6
Carbes (81) ... 170 C5
Carbini (2A) ... 207 F3
Carbon-Blanc (33) ... 135 F5
Carbonne (31) ... 185 E2
Carbuccia (2A) ... 204 D5
Carcagny (14) ... 14 A4
Carcanières (09) ... 200 A2
Carcans (33) ... 134 B3
Carcarès-Sainte-Croix (40) ... 165 G3
Carcassonne (11) ... 187 E3
Carcen-Ponson (40) ... 165 G2
Carcès (83) ... 193 G2
Carcheto-Brustico (2B) ... 205 G1
Cardaillac (46) ... 153 G1
Cardan (33) ... 149 G1
Cardeilhac (31) ... 184 B3
Cardesse (64) ... 182 A2
Cardet (30) ... 173 H1
Cardo-Torgia (2A) ... 206 D1
Cardonnette (80) ... 7 G5
le Cardonnois (80) ... 20 D3
Cardonville (14) ... 13 F4
Cardroc (35) ... 56 D1
Carelles (53) ... 58 C2
Carency (62) ... 8 A1
Carennac (46) ... 139 E5
Carentan les Marais (50) ... 13 E5
Carentoir (56) ... 56 C5
Cargèse (2A) ... 204 B4
Cargiaca (2A) ... 207 E2
Carhaix-Plouguer (29) ... 32 B6
Carignan (08) ... 24 D2
Carignan-de-Bordeaux (33) .. 135 F5
Carisey (89) ... 65 H6
Carla-Bayle (09) ... 185 F4
Carla-de-Roquefort (09) ... 186 A5
le Carlaret (09) ... 185 H4
Carlat (15) ... 140 B5
Carlencas-et-Levas (34) ... 172 B5
Carlepont (60) ... 21 G4
Carling (57) ... 27 F5
Carlipa (11) ... 186 C3
Carlucet (46) ... 152 D1
Carlus (81) ... 170 B3
Carlux (24) ... 138 B5
Carly (62) ... 1 F5
Carmaux (81) ... 170 C1
Carnac (56) ... 72 B1
Carnac-Rouffiac (46) ... 152 B4

Carnas (30) ... 173 G3
Carnetin (77) ... 43 F3
Carneville (50) ... 12 D1
Carnières (59) ... 9 E3
Carnin (59) ... 3 F6
Carnoët (22) ... 32 B5
Carnoules (33) ... 193 G3
Carnoux-en-Provence (13) ... 192 C4
Carnoy (80) ... 8 B5
Caro (56) ... 56 B5
Caro (64) ... 180 D3
Carolles (50) ... 36 D4
Caromb (84) ... 158 D6
Carpentras (84) ... 175 F1
Carpineto (2B) ... 205 G2
Carpiquet (14) ... 14 B4
Carquebut (50) ... 13 E4
Carquefou (44) ... 74 D4
Carqueiranne (83) ... 193 F5
Carrépuis (80) ... 21 F2
Carrère (64) ... 166 B6
Carresse-Cassaber (64) ... 165 E6
Carrières-sous-Poissy (78) ... 42 B3
Carrières-sur-Seine (78) ... 42 C3
Carros (06) ... 179 E3
Carrouges (61) ... 38 D6
Carry-le-Rouet (13) ... 191 H5
les Cars (87) ... 123 H4
Carsac-Aillac (24) ... 138 B6
Carsac-de-Gurson (24) ... 136 B4
Carsan (30) ... 157 H5
Carspach (68) ... 89 E3
Cartelègue (33) ... 135 E2
Carticasi (2B) ... 205 F2
Cartignies (59) ... 9 H4
Cartigny (80) ... 8 C6
Cartigny-l'Épinay (14) ... 13 F5
Carves (24) ... 137 H6
Carville-la-Folletière (76) ... 18 B3
Carville-Pot-de-Fer (76) ... 17 E3
Carvin (62) ... 3 F6
Casabianca (2B) ... 203 G6
Casaglione (2A) ... 204 C4
Casalabriva (2A) ... 206 D2
Casalta (2B) ... 203 G6
Casamaccioli (2B) ... 204 D2
Casanova (2B) ... 205 E3
Cascastel-des-Corbières (11) ... 187 G5
Casefabre (66) ... 200 D3
Caseneuve (84) ... 176 A3
Cases-de-Pène (66) ... 201 E1
Casevecchie (2B) ... 205 G3
Cassagnabère-Tournas (31) ... 184 B3
Cassagnas (48) ... 156 C5
la Cassagne (24) ... 138 B4
Cassagne (31) ... 184 C4
Cassagnes (46) ... 152 A2
Cassagnes (66) ... 200 D2
Cassagnes-Bégonhès (12) ... 154 C6
Cassagnoles (30) ... 173 H2
Cassagnoles (34) ... 187 G2
la Cassaigne (11) ... 186 B3
Cassaigne (32) ... 167 F2
Cassaignes (11) ... 186 D6
Cassaniouze (15) ... 154 B1
Cassel (59) ... 2 C3
Cassen (40) ... 165 F3
Casseneuil (47) ... 151 F3
les Cassés (11) ... 186 B1
Casseuil (33) ... 150 A2
Cassignas (47) ... 151 G5
Cassis (13) ... 192 C4
Casson (44) ... 74 D3
Cassuéjouls (12) ... 154 D1
Cast (29) ... 53 F1
Castagnac (31) ... 185 F3
Castagnède (31) ... 184 C4
Castagnède (64) ... 165 E6
Castagniers (06) ... 179 E3
Castaignos-Souslens (40) ... 165 G5
Castandet (40) ... 166 A3
Castanet (12) ... 154 A5
Castanet (81) ... 170 D2
Castanet (82) ... 153 G6
Castanet-le-Haut (34) ... 171 H5
Castanet-Tolosan (31) ... 169 F6
Castans (11) ... 187 F1
Casteide-Cami (64) ... 182 A1
Casteide-Candau (64) ... 165 H6
Casteide-Doat (64) ... 183 E1
Casteil (66) ... 200 C4
Castel-Sarrazin (40) ... 165 G5
Castelbajac (65) ... 183 G3
Castelbiague (31) ... 184 C4
Castelculier (47) ... 151 F6
Castelferrus (82) ... 168 D2
Castelfranc (46) ... 152 B3
Castelgaillard (31) ... 184 C2
Castelginest (31) ... 169 F4
Casteljaloux (47) ... 150 B4
Castella (47) ... 151 F4
Castellane (04) ... 177 H3
Castellar (06) ... 179 G3
le Castellard-Mélan (04) ... 160 C5
Castellare-di-Casinca (2B) ... 203 G6
Castellare-di-Mercurio (2B) ... 205 F2
le Castellet (04) ... 176 D2
le Castellet (83) ... 192 D4
Castellet (84) ... 176 A3
Castellet-lès-Sausses (04) ... 178 B1
Castello-di-Rostino (2B) ... 203 F6
Castelmary (12) ... 154 A6
Castelmaurou (31) ... 169 F5
Castelmayran (82) ... 168 C1
Castelmoron-d'Albret (33) ... 150 B1

Castelmoron-sur-Lot (47) ... 151 E4
Castelnau-Barbarens (32) ... 168 A5
Castelnau-Chalosse (40) ... 165 G4
Castelnau-d'Anglès (32) ... 167 F5
Castelnau-d'Arbieu (32) ... 168 A3
Castelnau-d'Aude (11) ... 187 G3
Castelnau d'Auzan Labarrère (32) ... 167 E2
Castelnau-de-Guers (34) ... 188 D1
Castelnau-de-Lévis (81) ... 170 B2
Castelnau-de-Mandailles (12) ... 155 E3
Castelnau-de-Médoc (33) ... 134 D3
Castelnau-de-Montmiral (81) ... 170 A2
Castelnau-d'Estrétefonds (31) ... 169 E4
Castelnau-Durban (09) ... 185 F5
Castelnau-le-Lez (34) ... 173 F5
Castelnau-Magnoac (65) ... 183 H2
Castelnau Montratier-Ste Alauzie (46) ... 152 C5
Castelnau-Pégayrols (12) ... 155 E6
Castelnau-Picampeau (31) ... 184 D2
Castelnau-Rivière-Basse (65) ... 166 D5
Castelnau-sur-Gupie (47) ... 150 C2
Castelnau-sur-l'Auvignon (32) ... 167 G2
Castelnau-Tursan (40) ... 166 A4
Castelnau-Valence (30) ... 174 A2
Castelnaud-de-Gratecambe (47) ... 151 F2
Castelnaud-la-Chapelle (24) ... 138 A6
Castelnaudary (11) ... 186 B2
Castelnavet (32) ... 167 E4
Castelner (40) ... 165 H5
Castelnou (66) ... 201 E3
Castelreng (11) ... 186 C5
Castels et Bézenac (24) ... 137 H5
Castelsagrat (82) ... 151 H6
Castelsarrasin (82) ... 168 D1
Castelvieilh (65) ... 183 F3
Castelviel (33) ... 150 A1
le Castéra (31) ... 168 D5
Castéra-Bouzet (82) ... 168 C2
Castéra-Lectourois (32) ... 167 H2
Castéra-Lou (65) ... 183 F2
Castéra-Loubix (64) ... 183 E1
Castéra-Verduzan (32) ... 167 G3
Castéra-Vignoles (31) ... 184 B2
Castéras (09) ... 185 F4
Casterets (65) ... 184 A2
Castéron (32) ... 168 B3
Castet (64) ... 182 A4
Castet-Arrouy (32) ... 168 A2
Castetbon (64) ... 181 G1
Castétis (64) ... 165 G6
Castetnau-Camblong (64) ... 181 G2
Castetner (64) ... 165 G6
Castetpugon (64) ... 166 C5
Castets (40) ... 164 D2
Castets et Castillon (33) ... 150 A2
Castex (09) ... 185 F3
Castex (32) ... 183 G1
Castex-d'Armagnac (32) ... 166 C3
Casties-Labrande (31) ... 184 D2
Castifao (2B) ... 203 E6
Castiglione (2B) ... 205 E1
Castillon (06) ... 179 G2
Castillon (14) ... 13 H6
Castillon (65) ... 183 F4
Castillon (66) ... 166 C6
Castillon-de-Larboust (31) ... 197 F1
Castillon-de-Saint-Martory (31) ... 184 C4
Castillon-Debats (32) ... 167 E4
Castillon-du-Gard (30) ... 174 C2
Castillon-en-Auge (14) ... 39 F2
Castillon-en-Couserans (09) ... 184 D6
Castillon-la-Bataille (33) ... 136 A5
Castillon-Massas (32) ... 167 H4
Castillon-Savès (32) ... 168 C5
Castillonnès (47) ... 151 F1
Castin (32) ... 167 H4
Castineta (2B) ... 205 F2
Castirla (2B) ... 205 E2
Castres (02) ... 21 H1
Castres (81) ... 170 C5
Castres-Gironde (33) ... 149 G1
Castries (34) ... 173 G5
le Cateau-Cambrésis (59) ... 9 F4
Le Catelet (02) ... 9 E5
le Catelier (76) ... 17 G3
Catenay (76) ... 19 E3
Catenoy (60) ... 20 D5
Cateri (2B) ... 202 C6
Catheux (60) ... 20 B2
Catigny (60) ... 21 F2
Catillon-Fumechon (60) ... 20 C4
Catillon-sur-Sambre (59) ... 9 G4
Catllar (66) ... 200 C3
Catonvielle (32) ... 168 C5
Cattenières (59) ... 9 E4
Cattenom (57) ... 26 C3
Catteville (50) ... 12 C4
Catus (46) ... 152 C2
Catz (50) ... 13 E5
Caubeyres (47) ... 150 C5
Caubiac (31) ... 168 C4
Caubios-Loos (64) ... 182 B1
Caubon-Saint-Sauveur (47) ... 150 C2

Caubous (31) ... 183 H6
Caubous (65) ... 183 H3
Caucalières (81) ... 170 D6
la Cauchie (62) ... 8 A3
Cauchy-à-la-Tour (62) ... 2 C6
Caucourt (62) ... 7 H1
Caudan (56) ... 54 C5
Caudebec-lès-Elbeuf (76) ... 18 C6
Caudebronde (11) ... 187 E2
Caudecoste (47) ... 151 F6
Caudiès-de-Conflent (66) ... 200 A4
Caudiès-de-Fenouillèdes (66) ... 200 B1
Caudrot (33) ... 150 A2
Caudry (59) ... 9 F4
Cauffry (60) ... 20 D5
Caugé (27) ... 40 D2
Caujac (31) ... 185 G2
Caulaincourt (02) ... 8 D6
le Caule-Sainte-Beuve (76) ... 19 F1
Caulières (80) ... 19 H1
Caullery (59) ... 9 E4
Caulnes (22) ... 56 C1
Caumont (02) ... 21 H2
Caumont (09) ... 184 D5
Caumont (27) ... 18 B5
Caumont (32) ... 166 C4
Caumont (33) ... 150 B1
Caumont (62) ... 7 E2
Caumont (82) ... 168 C1
Caumont-sur-Aure (14) ... 37 H1
Caumont-sur-Durance (84) ... 175 E3
Caumont-sur-Garonne (47) ... 150 C3
Cauna (40) ... 165 H3
Caunay (79) ... 108 C4
Cauneille (40) ... 165 E5
Caunes-Minervois (11) ... 187 F2
la Caunette (11) ... 187 H2
Caunette-sur-Lauquet (11) ... 187 E5
Caunettes-en-Val (11) ... 187 F4
Caupenne (40) ... 165 G4
Caupenne-d'Armagnac (32) ... 166 D3
la Caure (51) ... 45 E3
Caurel (22) ... 55 E1
Caurel (51) ... 23 F5
Cauro (2A) ... 204 D6
Cauroir (59) ... 9 E3
Cauroy (08) ... 23 H5
Cauroy-lès-Hermonville (51) ... 23 E5
le Causé (82) ... 168 C4
Cause-de-Clérans (24) ... 137 E5
Caussade (82) ... 152 D6
Caussade-Rivière (65) ... 166 D6
Causse-Bégon (30) ... 172 C1
Causse-de-la-Selle (34) ... 173 E4
Causse-et-Diège (12) ... 153 G3
Caussens (32) ... 167 G2
Causses-et-Veyran (34) ... 188 B1
Caussiniojouls (34) ... 172 B6
Caussols (04) ... 178 C3
Caussou (09) ... 199 F1
Cauterets (65) ... 182 D6
Cauverville-en-Roumois (27) ... 18 A5
Cauvicourt (14) ... 38 D2
Cauvignac (33) ... 150 A3
Cauvigny (60) ... 20 B5
Cauville (14) ... 38 B2
Cauville-sur-Mer (76) ... 16 A4
Caux (34) ... 172 C6
Caux-et-Sauzens (11) ... 186 D3
Cauzac (47) ... 151 G5
Cavagnac (46) ... 138 D4
Cavaillon (84) ... 175 F3
Cavalaire-sur-Mer (83) ... 194 A4
la Cavalerie (12) ... 172 B2
Cavan (22) ... 32 D3
Cavanac (11) ... 187 E4
Cavarc (47) ... 151 F1
Caveirac (30) ... 174 A3
Caves (11) ... 188 A6
Cavignac (33) ... 135 G2
Cavigny (50) ... 13 F6
Cavillargues (30) ... 174 C1
Cavillon (80) ... 7 F6
Cavron-Saint-Martin (62) ... 7 E1
Caychax (09) ... 199 F1
Cayeux-en-Santerre (80) ... 21 E1
Cayeux-sur-Mer (80) ... 6 B3
le Caylar (34) ... 172 C3
Caylus (82) ... 153 E5
Cayrac (82) ... 169 F1
Cayres (43) ... 142 B5
Cayriech (82) ... 152 D5
le Cayrol (12) ... 154 D2
Cayrols (15) ... 139 H6
Cazac (31) ... 184 C2
Cazalis (33) ... 149 G4
Cazalis (40) ... 165 G5
Cazalrenoux (11) ... 186 B3
Cazals (46) ... 152 B2
Cazals (82) ... 153 E6
Cazals-des-Baylès (09) ... 186 B4
Cazarilh-Tambourès (31) ... 183 H3
Cazarilh (65) ... 184 A3
Cazarilh-Laspènes (31) ... 197 F1
Cazats (33) ... 149 H3
Cazaubon (32) ... 166 D2
Cazaugitat (33) ... 150 B1
Cazaunous (31) ... 184 B3
Cazaux (09) ... 185 G4
Cazaux-d'Anglès (32) ... 167 F5
Cazaux-Debat (65) ... 183 G6
Cazaux-Fréchet-Anéran-Camors (65) ... 183 G6
Cazaux-Layrisse (31) ... 184 A4
Cazaux-Savès (32) ... 168 C5

Cazaux-Villecomtal (32) 183 F1
Cazavet (09) 184 D5
Cazeaux-de-Larboust (31) 197 F1
Cazedarnes (34) 188 B1
Cazenave-Serres-et-
Allens (09) 199 F1
Cazeneuve (32) 167 E2
Cazeneuve-Montaut (31) 184 C3
Cazères (31) 184 D3
Cazères-sur-l'Adour (40) 166 B3
Cazes-Mondenard (82) 152 B5
Cazevieille (34) 173 F4
Cazideroque (47) 151 H4
Cazilhac (11) 187 E3
Cazilhac (34) 173 E2
Cazillac (46) 138 D4
Cazoulès (24) 138 C5
Cazouls-d'Hérault (34) 172 D6
Cazouls-lès-Béziers (34) 188 B2
Ceaucé (61) 58 D1
Ceaulmont (36) 111 E2
Céaux (50) 35 H4
Céaux-d'Allègre (43) 142 D3
Ceaux-en-Couhé (86) 108 D3
Ceaux-en-Loudun (86) 94 B3
Cébazan (34) 188 A1
Cébazat (63) 127 F2
Ceffonds (52) 67 F1
Ceignes (01) 117 F5
Ceilhes-et-Rocozels (34) 172 A4
Ceillac (05) 161 G1
Ceilloux (63) 127 H4
Ceintrey (54) 69 F1
la Celette (18) 112 C1
la Celle (03) 113 E5
la Celle (18) 97 H5
Cellé (41) 79 E1
la Celle (63) 126 B2
la Celle (83) 193 F3
la Celle-Condé (18) 97 F5
la Celle-Dunoise (23) 111 F4
la Celle-en-Morvan (71) 100 C3
la Celle-Guenand (37) 95 F4
la Celle-les-Bordes (78) 42 A6
Celle-Lévescault (86) 108 D3
la Celle-Saint-Avant (37) 94 D3
la Celle-Saint-Cloud (78) 42 C4
la Celle-Saint-Cyr (89) 65 E6
la Celle-sous-
Chantemerle (51) 44 D6
la Celle-sous-Gouzon (23) 112 A5
la Celle-sur-Loire (58) 82 C5
la Celle-sur-Morin (77) 43 G4
la Celle-sur-Nièvre (58) 99 E1
Cellefrouin (16) 122 D2
Celles (09) 185 H6
Celles (17) 121 G4
Celles (24) 136 D1
Celles (34) 172 C5
Celles-en-Bassigny (52) 68 C6
Celles-lès-Condé (02) 44 C2
Celles-sur-Aisne (02) 22 B5
Celles-sur-Belle (79) 108 A4
Celles-sur-Durolle (63) 128 A2
Celles-sur-Ource (10) 66 D5
Celles-sur-Plaine (88) 70 C1
la Cellette (23) 111 H3
la Cellette (63) 112 D6
Cellettes (16) 122 C2
Cellettes (41) 80 A4
le Cellier (44) 75 E4
Cellier-du-Luc (07) 156 D1
Cellieu (42) 129 G5
Celon (36) 110 D2
Celoux (15) 141 G3
Celsoy (52) 86 C1
Cély (77) 63 H2
Cemboing (70) 87 E1
Cempuis (60) 20 A2
Cénac (33) 135 F6
Cénac-et-Saint-Julien (24) 138 A6
Cenans (70) 87 G5
Cendras (30) 157 E6
le Cendre (63) 127 F3
Cendrecourt (70) 87 E1
Cendrey (25) 87 G5
Cénevières (46) 153 E1
Cenne-Monestiés (11) 186 C2
Cenon (33) 135 F5
Cenon-sur-Vienne (86) 94 D5
Censeau (39) 103 G5
Censerey (21) 100 D1
Censy (89) 84 B3
les Cent-Acres (76) 17 G3
Centrès (12) 154 B6
Centuri (2B) 203 F1
Cenves (69) 116 A4
Cépet (31) 169 F4
Cépie (11) 186 D4
Cepoy (45) 64 A5
Céran (32) 168 A3
Cérans-Foulletourte (72) 77 H1
Cerbère (66) 201 H4
Cerbois (18) 97 F2
Cercié (69) 116 A5
Cercier (74) 118 B6
Cercottes (45) 62 D6
Cercoux (17) 135 H3
le Cercueil (61) 39 E6
Cercy-la-Tour (58) 99 G5
Cerdon (01) 117 F6
Cerdon (45) 81 G3
Cère (40) 166 A1
Céré-la-Ronde (37) 95 H1
Cerelles (37) 78 D4
Cérences (50) 36 D2
Céreste (04) 176 B3
Céret (66) 201 E4

Cerfontaine (59) 10 A2
le Cergne (42) 115 G5
Cergy (95) 42 B2
Cérilly (03) 113 E1
Cérilly (21) 84 D1
Cérilly (89) 65 G4
Cerisé (61) 60 A1
Cerisières (52) 67 H3
Cerisiers (89) 65 F5
Cerisy (80) 8 A6
Cerisy-Belle-Étoile (61) 38 A4
Cerisy-Buleux (80) 6 D5
Cerisy-la-Forêt (50) 13 G6
Cerisy-la-Salle (50) 37 E2
Cerizay (79) 92 D4
Cérizols (09) 184 D4
Cerizy (02) 22 A1
Cernans (39) 103 F4
Cernay (14) 39 G2
Cernay (28) 61 H2
Cernay (68) 89 E1
Cernay (86) 94 B5
Cernay-en-Dormois (51) 24 B6
Cernay-la-Ville (78) 42 A5
Cernay-l'Église (25) 88 C6
Cernay-lès-Reims (51) 23 F6
Cernex (74) 118 B6
Cerniébaud (39) 103 G5
Cernion (08) 23 G1
Cernon (39) 117 G3
Cernon (51) 45 H4
Cernoy (60) 20 D4
Cernoy-en-Berry (45) 82 A4
Cernusson (49) 93 E1
Cerny (91) 63 G1
Cerny-en-Laonnois (02) 22 C4
Cerny-lès-Bucy (02) 22 B3
Céron (71) 114 D4
Cérons (33) 149 G1
les Cerqueux (49) 92 D3
Cerre-lès-Noroy (70) 87 H3
Cers (34) 188 C2
Cerseuil (02) 22 B5
Cersot (71) 101 F6
Certilleux (88) 68 D3
Certines (01) 117 E5
Cervens (74) 118 D4
Cervières (42) 147 F5
Cervières (42) 128 B2
Cerville (54) 48 D5
Cervione (2B) 205 G2
Cervon (58) 99 H1
Cerzat (43) 141 H3
Cesancey (39) 117 F1
Césarches (73) 132 C3
Césarville-Dossainville (45) 63 F3
Cescau (09) 184 D6
Cescau (64) 182 B1
Cesny-aux-Vignes (14) 14 D5
Cesny-Bois-Halbout (14) 38 C2
Cessac (33) 135 H6
Cessales (31) 186 A1
Cesse (55) 24 D3
Cessenon-sur-Orb (34) 188 B1
Cesseras (34) 187 G2
Cesset (03) 113 G4
Cesseville (27) 40 C1
Cessey (25) 103 F2
Cessey-sur-Tille (21) 86 A6
Cessières (02) 22 B3
Cessieu (38) 131 E5
Cesson (77) 63 H1
Cesson-Sévigné (35) 57 F3
Cessoy-en-Montois (77) 64 D1
Cessy (01) 118 B3
Cessy-les-Bois (58) 82 D6
Cestas (33) 135 E6
Cestayrols (81) 170 B2
Ceton (61) 61 E4
Cette-Eygun (64) 182 A5
Cevins (73) 132 D4
Ceyras (34) 172 D5
Ceyrat (63) 127 E3
Ceyreste (13) 192 C4
Ceyroux (23) 111 E6
Ceyssac (43) 142 C4
Ceyssat (63) 126 D3
Ceyzériat (01) 117 E5
Ceyzérieu (01) 131 G2
Cézac (33) 135 F3
Cézac (46) 152 C4
Cezais (85) 107 F1
Cézan (32) 167 G3
Cezay (42) 128 C3
Cézens (15) 140 D4
Cézia (39) 117 G3
Cézy (89) 65 E6
Chabanais (16) 123 F2
Chabanière (69) 129 H5
la Chabanne (03) 128 B1
Chabestan (05) 159 H3
Chabeuil (26) 144 B5
Chablis (89) 83 H2
Châbons (38) 131 E6
Chabottes (05) 160 C1
Chabournay (86) 94 B6
Chabrac (16) 123 F1
Chabreloche (63) 128 B2
Chabrignac (19) 138 B1
Chabrillan (26) 158 C1
Chabris (36) 96 C1
Chacé (49) 93 H1
Chacenay (10) 66 D5
Chacrise (02) 22 B5
Chadeleuf (63) 127 F5
Chadenac (17) 121 F5

Chadenet (48) 156 B3
Chadrac (43) 142 C4
Chadron (43) 142 C5
Chadurie (16) 122 B5
le Chaffal (26) 144 D5
le Chaffaut-Saint-
Jurson (04) 177 F1
Chaffois (25) 103 H4
Chagey (70) 88 C3
Chagnon (42) 129 G5
Chagny (08) 24 A3
Chagny (71) 101 F4
Chahaignes (72) 78 C2
Chahains (61) 38 D6
Chaignay (21) 85 H5
Chaignes (27) 41 F2
Chail (79) 108 B4
Chaillac (36) 110 C3
Chaillac-sur-Vienne (87) 123 G2
Chailland (53) 58 C3
Chaillé-les-Marais (85) 106 D2
Chailles (41) 79 H4
la Chailleuse (39) 117 F1
Chaillevette (17) 120 C3
Chaillevois (02) 22 B4
Chailley (89) 65 G5
Chaillon (55) 47 H3
Chailloué (61) 39 F5
Chailly-en-Bière (77) 64 A2
Chailly-en-Brie (77) 43 H4
Chailly-en-Gâtinais (45) 63 H6
Chailly-lès-Ennery (57) 26 C4
Chailly-sur-Armançon (21) 101 E1
Chainaz-les-Frasses (74) 132 A3
Chaînée-des-Coupis (39) 102 C4
Chaingy (45) 80 C1
Chaintré (71) 116 B4
Chaintreaux (77) 64 B4
Chaintrix-Bierges (51) 45 F3
la Chaise (10) 67 E2
la Chaise-Baudouin (50) 37 F4
la Chaise-Dieu (43) 142 B1
Chaise-Dieu-du-Theil (27) 40 B4
la Chaize-Giraud (85) 90 D4
la Chaize-le-Vicomte (85) 91 H4
Chalabre (11) 186 B5
Chalagnac (24) 137 F3
Chalain-d'Uzore (42) 128 D4
Chalain-le-Comtal (42) 129 E4
Chalaines (55) 47 H6
Chalais (16) 136 B1
Chalais (24) 123 G5
Chalais (36) 110 C2
Chalais (86) 94 A3
Chalamont (01) 130 C1
Chalampé (68) 89 G1
Chalancey (52) 85 H3
Chalancon (26) 159 E3
Chalandray (86) 93 H6
Chalandry (02) 22 C2
Chalandry-Elaire (08) 24 B2
le Chalange (61) 39 G6
le Chalard (87) 124 A6
Chalautre-la-Grande (77) 65 F1
Chalautre-la-Petite (77) 65 E1
Chalaux (58) 84 A6
Chaleins (01) 116 B6
Chalencon (07) 143 G5
les Chalesmes (39) 103 G6
Châlette-sur-Loing (45) 64 A6
Chalette-sur-Voire (10) 66 D2
Chaley (01) 131 E1
Chalèze (25) 87 F6
Chalezeule (25) 87 F6
Chaliers (15) 141 F5
Chalifert (77) 43 F3
Chaligny (54) 48 C5
Chalindrey (52) 86 B2
Chalivoy-Milon (18) 98 B5
Challain-la-Potherie (49) 75 G1
Challans (85) 90 D2
Challement (58) 83 G6
Challerange (08) 24 B5
Challes (72) 60 C6
Challes-la-Montagne (01) 117 F6
Challes-les-Eaux (73) 132 A5
Challet (28) 62 A1
Challex (01) 118 B5
Challignac (16) 122 A6
Challonges (74) 118 A6
Challuy (58) 98 D4
Chalmaison (77) 64 D1
Chalmazel-
Jeansagnière (42) 128 C4
Chalmoux (71) 114 D1
Chalo-Saint-Mars (91) 63 E2
le Chalon (26) 144 C3
Chalon (38) 130 B6
Chalon-sur-Saône (71) 101 G5
Chalonnes-sur-Loire (49) 76 C5
Châlons-du-Maine (53) 58 D4
Châlons-en-
Champagne (51) 45 H3
Châlons-sur-Vesle (51) 23 E6
Châlonvillars (70) 88 C3
Chalou-Moulineux (91) 63 E2
Chaltrait (51) 45 E3
Châlus (63) 127 F6
Châlus (87) 123 H4
Chalvignac (15) 139 H2
Chalvraines (52) 68 B3
Chamadelle (33) 136 A3
Chamagne (88) 69 G2
Chamagnieu (38) 130 C4
Chamalières (63) 127 E3
Chamalières-sur-Loire (43) 142 D3
Chamaloc (26) 145 E6
Chamant (60) 21 E6

Chamarande (91) 63 F1
Chamarandes-
Choignes (52) 68 A5
Chamaret (26) 158 B4
la Chamba (42) 128 B3
Chambain (21) 85 G2
Chambaron sur
Morge (63) 127 F1
Chambeire (21) 86 A6
Chambellay (49) 76 D2
Chambéon (42) 129 E4
Chambérat (03) 112 B3
Chamberaud (23) 111 H6
Chamberet (19) 125 E5
Chambéria (39) 117 G2
Chambéry (73) 131 H4
Chambezon (43) 141 G1
Chambilly (71) 115 E4
Chamblac (27) 40 A2
Chamblanc (21) 102 A3
Chamblay (39) 103 E3
Chambles (42) 129 E6
Chamblet (03) 112 D4
Chambley-Bussières (54) 48 B2
Chambly (60) 42 C1
Chambœuf (21) 101 G1
Chambœuf (42) 129 F5
Chambois (27) 40 D3
Chambolle-Musigny (21) 101 H2
le Chambon (07) 143 F6
Chambon (17) 107 E5
Chambon (18) 97 G5
Chambon (30) 157 E5
Chambon (37) 95 E5
le Chambon-
Feugerolles (42) 129 F6
Chambon-la-Forêt (45) 63 F5
Chambon-le-Château (48) 142 B5
Chambon-Sainte-
Croix (23) 111 F3
Chambon-sur-Dolore (63) 128 A5
Chambon-sur-Lac (63) 126 D5
le Chambon-sur-
Lignon (43) 143 F4
Chambon-sur-Voueize (23) 112 C5
Chambonas (07) 157 E4
Chambonchard (23) 112 C5
la Chambonie (42) 128 B3
Chamboret (87) 124 A1
Chamborigaud (30) 156 D5
Chambornay-lès-
Bellevaux (70) 87 G5
Chambornay-lès-Pin (70) 87 E6
Chambors (60) 19 H6
Chambost-Allières (69) 129 G1
Chambost-
Longessaigne (69) 129 F3
Chamboulive (19) 125 E6
Chambourcy (78) 42 B3
Chambourg-sur-Indre (37) 95 F2
Chambray (27) 41 E2
Chambray-lès-Tours (37) 78 D6
la Chambre (73) 132 C6
Chambrecy (51) 45 E1
Chambretaud (85) 92 B3
Chambrey (51) 49 E4
Chambroncourt (52) 68 B2
Chambry (02) 22 C3
Chambry (77) 43 G2
Chaméane (63) 127 H5
Chamelet (69) 129 G1
Chamery (51) 45 F1
Chamesey (25) 104 C1
Chamesol (25) 88 C5
Chamesson (21) 85 E2
Chameyrat (19) 138 D2
Chamigny (77) 44 A3
Chamilly (71) 101 F4
Chamole (39) 103 E4
Chamonix-Mont-Blanc (74) 133 F1
Chamouillac (17) 135 F1
Chamouille (02) 22 C4
Chamouilley (52) 46 D6
Chamousset (73) 132 B4
Chamoux (89) 83 G5
Chamoux-sur-Gelon (73) 132 B5
Chamoy (10) 66 A5
le Champ-de-la-Pierre (61) 38 D6
Champ-d'Oiseau (21) 84 C4
Champ-Dolent (27) 40 D3
Champ-Haut (61) 39 G5
Champ-Laurent (73) 132 B5
le Champ-près-Froges (38) 145 H1
le Champ-Saint-Père (85) 91 G6
Champ-sur-Barse (10) 66 D4
Champ-sur-Drac (38) 145 G3
Champagnac (15) 140 A1
Champagnac (17) 121 G6
Champagnac-de-
Belair (24) 123 F6
Champagnac-la-
Noaille (19) 139 F1
Champagnac-la-Prune (19) 139 F2
Champagnac-la-
Rivière (87) 123 G3
Champagnac-le-Vieux (43) 141 H1
Champagnat (23) 125 H1
Champagnat (71) 117 E2
Champagnat-le-Jeune (63) 127 H6
Champagne (07) 144 A2
Champagne (17) 120 D6
Champagné (72) 60 B5
Champagne-au-Mont-
d'Or (69) 130 A3

Champagne-en-
Valromey (01) 131 F1
Champagne-et-
Fontaine (24) 122 C6
Champagné-le-Sec (86) 108 D5
Champagné-les-
Marais (85) 106 D3
Champagne-Mouton (16) 122 D1
Champagné-Saint-
Hilaire (86) 109 E3
Champagne-sur-Loue (39) 103 E3
Champagne-sur-Oise (95) 42 C1
Champagne-sur-Seine (77) 64 B2
Champagne-sur-
Vingeanne (21) 86 B5
Champagne-Vigny (16) 122 B5
Champagneux (73) 131 F4
Champagney (25) 103 F1
Champagney (39) 102 C1
Champagney (70) 88 B2
Champagnier (38) 145 G3
Champagnole (39) 103 F5
Champagnolles (17) 121 E5
Champagny (21) 85 F5
Champagny-en-
Vanoise (73) 133 D3
Champagny-sous-
Uxelles (71) 116 A1
Champallement (58) 99 F1
Champanges (74) 119 E3
Champaubert (51) 44 D4
Champcella (05) 147 E6
Champcenest (77) 44 B5
Champcerie (61) 38 D4
Champcevinel (24) 137 F2
Champcevrais (89) 82 C2
Champclause (43) 143 E4
Champcueil (91) 63 G1
Champdeniers-Saint-
Denis (79) 107 H2
Champdeuil (77) 43 F6
Champdieu (42) 128 D4
Champdivers (39) 102 C3
Champdolent (17) 120 D1
Champdor-Corcelles (01) 117 G6
Champdôtre (21) 102 B2
Champdray (88) 70 B4
Champeau-en-Morvan (21) 100 C1
Champeaux (50) 57 H2
Champeaux (50) 36 D4
les Champeaux (61) 39 F3
Champeaux (77) 43 F6
Champeaux-sur-
Sarthe (61) 39 H6
Champeix (63) 127 F5
Champenard (27) 41 E1
la Champenoise (36) 96 D3
Champenoux (54) 48 D4
Champéon (53) 59 E2
Champétières (63) 128 B5
Champey (70) 88 B3
Champey-sur-Moselle (54) 48 C3
Champfleur (72) 60 A2
Champfleury (10) 45 F6
Champfleury (51) 23 E6
Champforgeuil (71) 101 G5
Champfrémont (53) 59 H2
Champfromier (01) 117 H5
Champgenéteux (53) 59 F3
Champguyon (51) 44 C4
Champhol (28) 62 B1
Champien (80) 21 F2
Champier (38) 130 D6
Champignelles (89) 82 C2
Champigneul-
Champagne (51) 45 G3
Champigneul-sur-
Vence (08) 24 A2
Champigneulle (08) 24 C5
Champigneulles (54) 48 C4
Champigneulles-en-
Bassigny (52) 68 C4
Champignol-lez-
Mondeville (10) 67 E4
Champignolles (21) 101 E3
Champignolles (27) 40 B3
Champigny (51) 23 E6
Champigny (89) 64 D3
Champigny-en-Beauce (41) 79 H3
Champigny en
Rochereau (86) 94 A6
Champigny-la-
Futelaye (27) 41 E4
Champigny-lès-
Langres (52) 86 B1
Champigny-sous-
Varennes (52) 86 D1
Champigny-sur-Aube (10) 66 B1
Champigny-sur-Marne (94) 43 E4
Champigny-sur-Veude (37) 94 B2
Champillet (36) 112 A2
Champillon (51) 45 F2
Champis (07) 143 H4
Champlan (91) 42 C5
Champlat-et-
Boujacourt (51) 45 E1
Champlay (89) 65 F6
Champlecy (71) 115 F2
Champlemy (58) 99 F1
Champlin (08) 10 C6
Champlin (58) 99 F1
Champlitte (70) 86 C3
Champlive (25) 87 G6
Champlost (89) 65 G5
Champmillon (16) 122 B4
Champmotteux (91) 63 G3
Champnétery (87) 124 D2
Champneuville (55) 25 E6

Champniers (16) 122 C3
Champniers (86) 109 E4
Champniers-et-
Reilhac (24) 123 F4
Champoléon (05) 146 C6
Champoly (42) 128 C2
Champosoult (61) 39 F3
Champougny (55) 47 H6
Champoulet (45) 82 C3
Champoux (25) 87 G6
Champrenault (21) 85 F5
Champrepus (50) 37 E3
Champrond (72) 61 E5
Champrond-en-Gâtine (28) 61 G2
Champrond-en-
Perchet (28) 61 F3
Champrougier (39) 102 D4
Champs (02) 21 H3
Champs (63) 113 G6
les Champs-Géraux (22) 34 D5
Champs-Romain (24) 123 F5
Champs-sur-Marne (77) 43 E4
Champs-sur-Tarentaine-
Marchal (15) 126 B6
Champs-sur-Yonne (89) 83 G2
Champsac (87) 123 H3
Champsanglard (23) 111 G4
Champsecret (61) 38 B6
Champseru (28) 62 C1
Champsevraine (52) 86 C2
Champtercier (04) 160 C6
Champtocé-sur-Loire (49) 76 C5
Champtonnay (70) 86 D5
Champvans (39) 102 C2
Champvans (70) 86 C5
Champvans-les-
Moulins (25) 103 F1
Champvert (58) 99 G5
Champvoisy (51) 44 D1
Champvoux (58) 98 D2
Chamrousse (38) 145 H3
Chamvres (89) 65 E6
Chanac (48) 155 H3
Chanac-les-Mines (19) 139 E2
Chanaleilles (43) 141 H5
Chanas (38) 144 A1
Chanat-la-Mouteyre (63) 127 E2
Chanay (01) 117 H6
Chanaz (73) 131 G2
Chançay (37) 79 E5
Chancé (35) 57 G3
Chanceaux (21) 85 F4
Chanceaux-près-
Loches (37) 95 F2
Chanceaux-sur-
Choisille (37) 78 D5
Chancelade (24) 137 F2
Chancenay (52) 46 D5
Chancey (70) 86 D6
Chancia (39) 117 G3
Chandai (61) 40 B4
Chandolas (07) 157 F4
Chandon (42) 115 G5
Chanéac (07) 143 F5
Chaneins (01) 116 B6
Chânes (71) 116 B4
Changé (53) 58 C4
Changé (71) 101 F4
Changé (72) 60 B6
Changey (52) 68 B6
Changis-sur-Marne (77) 43 H3
Changy (42) 114 D5
Changy (51) 46 B4
Changy (71) 115 F3
Chaniat (43) 141 H1
Chaniers (17) 121 F3
Channay (21) 84 C1
Channay-sur-Lathan (37) 78 B4
Channes (10) 66 C6
Chanonat (63) 127 F4
Chanos-Curson (26) 144 B4
Chanousse (05) 159 G4
Chanoy (52) 68 A6
Chanoz-Châtenay (01) 116 C5
Chanteau (45) 62 D6
Chantecoq (45) 64 C5
Chantecorps (79) 108 B2
Chanteheux (54) 49 F6
Chanteix (19) 138 D1
Chantelle (03) 113 G4
Chanteloup (35) 57 F4
Chanteloup (50) 36 D3
Chanteloup (79) 93 E5
Chanteloup-en-Brie (77) 43 F4
Chanteloup-les-Bois (49) 92 D2
Chanteloup-les-Vignes (78) 42 B3
Chantelouve (38) 146 A4
Chantemerle (51) 44 D6
Chantemerle-les-Blés (26) 144 B3
Chantemerle-lès-
Grignan (26) 158 B3
Chantemerle-sur-la-
Soie (17) 107 F6
Chantenay-Saint-
Imbert (58) 99 E6
Chantenay-Villedieu (72) 59 G6
Chantepie (35) 57 F3
Chantérac (24) 136 D2
Chanteraine (55) 47 F5
Chanterelle (15) 140 D1
Chantes (70) 87 E3
Chantesse (38) 145 E2
Chanteuges (43) 142 A4
Chantillac (16) 135 G1
Chantilly (60) 42 D1
Chantonnay (85) 92 A6
Chantraine (88) 69 H4
Chantraines (52) 68 A4

Chantrans (25) 103 G3
Chantrigné (53) 59 E2
Chanu (61) 38 A4
Chanville (57) 49 E2
Chaon (41) 81 F4
Chaouilley (54) 69 F1
Chaource (10) 66 B5
Chaourse (02) 23 E2
Chapaize (71) 116 A1
Chapareillan (38) 132 A5
Chapdes-Beaufort (63) 126 D2
Chapdeuil (24) 136 D1
Chapeau (03) 114 B2
Chapeiry (74) 132 A2
Chapelaine (51) 46 A6
la Chapelaude (03) 112 C3
la Chapelle (03) 114 B6
la Chapelle (08) 24 C1
la Chapelle (16) 122 B2
la Chapelle (73) 132 C6
la Chapelle-Agnon (63) 128 A4
la Chapelle-Anthenaise (53) 58 D4
la Chapelle-au-Mans (71) 114 D1
la Chapelle-au-Moine (61) 38 B5
la Chapelle-au-Riboul (53) 59 F2
la Chapelle-Aubareil (24) 138 A4
la Chapelle-aux-Bois (88) 69 H5
la Chapelle-aux-Brocs (19) 138 D3
la Chapelle-aux-Chasses (03) 99 G6
la Chapelle-aux-Choux (72) 78 B3
la Chapelle-aux-Filtzméens (35) 35 E6
la Chapelle-aux-Lys (85) 92 D6
la Chapelle-aux-Naux (37) 78 C6
la Chapelle-aux-Saints (19) 138 D4
la Chapelle-Baloue (23) 111 E3
la Chapelle-Bâton (79) 108 A2
la Chapelle-Bâton (86) 109 E5
la Chapelle-Bayvel (27) 15 G4
la Chapelle-Bertin (43) 142 A2
la Chapelle-Bertrand (79) 93 G6
la Chapelle-Biche (61) 38 A5
la Chapelle-Blanche (22) 56 C1
la Chapelle-Blanche (73) 132 A5
la Chapelle-Blanche-Saint-Martin (37) 95 E2
la Chapelle-Bouëxic (35) 56 D4
la Chapelle-Cécelin (50) 37 F4
la Chapelle-Chaussée (35) 57 E1
la Chapelle-Craonnaise (53) 58 B6
la Chapelle-d'Abondance (74) 119 G3
la Chapelle-d'Alagnon (15) 140 D2
la Chapelle-d'Aligné (72) 77 F2
la Chapelle-d'Angillon (18) 81 G6
la Chapelle-d'Armentières (59) 3 E5
la Chapelle-d'Aunainville (28) 62 D2
la Chapelle-d'Aurec (43) 143 E1
la Chapelle-de-Bragny (71) 116 B2
la Chapelle-de-Brain (35) 56 D6
la Chapelle-de-Guinchay (71) 116 B5
la Chapelle-de-la-Tour (38) 131 E4
la Chapelle-de-Surieu (38) 130 B6
Chapelle-des-Bois (25) 118 B1
la Chapelle-des-Fougeretz (35) 57 E2
la Chapelle-des-Marais (44) 73 G3
la Chapelle-des-Pots (17) 121 F3
la Chapelle-devant-Bruyères (88) 70 C4
Chapelle-d'Huin (25) 103 G4
la Chapelle-du-Bard (38) 132 A6
la Chapelle-du-Bois (72) 60 D4
la Chapelle-du-Bois-des-Faulx (27) 40 D1
la Chapelle-du-Bourgay (76) 17 G3
la Chapelle-du-Châtelard (01) 116 C6
La Chapelle du Lou du Lac (35) 56 D2
la Chapelle-du-Mont-de-France (71) 115 H3
la Chapelle-du-Mont-du-Chat (73) 131 H3
la Chapelle-du-Noyer (28) 61 H5
la Chapelle-en-Lafaye (42) 128 D6
la Chapelle-en-Serval (60) 43 E1
la Chapelle-en-Valgaudémar (05) 146 B5
la Chapelle-en-Vercors (26) 145 E4
la Chapelle-en-Vexin (95) 41 H1
la Chapelle-Enchérie (41) 79 H2
la Chapelle-Erbrée (35) 58 A4
la Chapelle-Faucher (24) 137 F1
la Chapelle-Felcourt (51) 46 C2
la Chapelle-Forainvilliers (28) 41 F5
la Chapelle-Fortin (28) 40 C5
la Chapelle-Gauthier (27) 39 H2
la Chapelle-Gauthier (77) 64 B1
la Chapelle-Geneste (43) 142 B1
la Chapelle-Glain (44) 74 D1
la Chapelle-Gonaguet (24) 137 E2
la Chapelle-Grésignac (24) 122 D6
Chapelle-Guillaume (28) 61 F5
la Chapelle-Hareng (27) 15 G5
la Chapelle-Hermier (85) 91 E1
la Chapelle-Heulin (44) 75 E5
la Chapelle-Hugon (18) 98 C4
la Chapelle-Huon (72) 79 E1

la Chapelle-Iger (77) 43 H6
la Chapelle-Janson (35) 58 B2
la Chapelle-la-Reine (77) 63 H3
la Chapelle-Lasson (51) 45 E6
la Chapelle-Launay (44) 74 A3
la Chapelle-Laurent (15) 141 G3
la Chapelle-lès-Luxeuil (70) 87 H2
la Chapelle-Longueville (27) 41 F1
la Chapelle-Marcousse (63) 127 F6
la Chapelle-Montabourlet (24) 122 D6
la Chapelle-Montbrandeix (87) 123 G4
la Chapelle-Montligeon (61) 60 D1
la Chapelle-Montlinard (18) 98 C2
la Chapelle-Montmartin (41) 96 C1
la Chapelle-Montmoreau (24) 123 F6
la Chapelle-Montreuil (86) 108 D7
la Chapelle-Moulière (86) 94 D6
la Chapelle-Moutils (77) 44 B4
la Chapelle-Naude (71) 116 D1
la Chapelle-Neuve (22) 32 C4
la Chapelle-Neuve (56) 55 F4
la Chapelle-Onzerain (45) 62 B5
la Chapelle-Orthemale (36) 96 B5
la Chapelle-Palluau (85) 91 F3
la Chapelle-Pouilloux (79) 108 C5
la Chapelle-près-Sées (61) 39 F6
la Chapelle-Rablais (77) 64 C1
la Chapelle-Rainsouin (53) 59 E4
la Chapelle-Rambaud (74) 118 C6
Chapelle-Royale (28) 61 G4
la Chapelle-Saint-André (58) 83 E5
la Chapelle-Saint-Aubert (35) 57 H1
la Chapelle-Saint-Aubin (72) 60 A5
la Chapelle-Saint-Étienne (79) 92 D6
la Chapelle-Saint-Fray (72) 60 A4
la Chapelle-Saint-Géraud (19) 139 F4
la Chapelle-Saint-Jean (24) 138 A2
la Chapelle-Saint-Laud (49) 77 F3
la Chapelle-Saint-Laurent (79) 93 E5
la Chapelle-Saint-Laurian (36) 96 D3
la Chapelle-Saint-Luc (10) 66 B3
la Chapelle-Saint-Martial (23) 111 G6
la Chapelle-Saint-Martin (73) 131 G4
la Chapelle-Saint-Martin-en-Plaine (41) 80 A3
la Chapelle-Saint-Maurice (74) 132 B3
la Chapelle-Saint-Mesmin (45) 80 D1
la Chapelle-Saint-Ouen (76) 19 E3
la Chapelle-Saint-Quillain (70) 87 E4
la Chapelle-Saint-Rémy (72) 60 C5
la Chapelle-Saint-Sauveur (71) 102 B5
la Chapelle-Saint-Sépulcre (45) 64 B6
la Chapelle-Saint-Sulpice (77) 64 D1
la Chapelle-Saint-Ursin (18) 97 G3
la Chapelle-Souëf (61) 60 D3
la Chapelle-sous-Brancion (71) 116 B1
la Chapelle-sous-Dun (71) 115 F4
la Chapelle-sous-Orbais (51) 44 D3
la Chapelle-sous-Uchon (71) 100 C5
Chapelle-Spinasse (19) 139 G1
la Chapelle-sur-Aveyron (45) 82 B1
la Chapelle-sur-Chézy (02) 44 B3
la Chapelle-sur-Coise (69) 129 G4
la Chapelle-sur-Dun (76) 17 F2
la Chapelle-sur-Erdre (44) 74 D4
la Chapelle-sur-Furieuse (39) 103 F3
la Chapelle-sur-Loire (37) 94 B1
la Chapelle-sur-Oreuse (89) 65 E3
la Chapelle-sur-Usson (63) 127 H6
la Chapelle-Taillefert (23) 111 G6
la Chapelle-Thècle (71) 116 D1
la Chapelle-Thémer (85) 107 E1
la Chapelle-Thireuil (79) 107 G1
la Chapelle-Thouarault (35) 57 E2
Chapelle-Vallon (10) 66 B2
la Chapelle-Vaupelteigne (89) 83 H1
la Chapelle-Vendômoise (41) 79 H3
la Chapelle-Vicomtesse (41) 61 G6
la Chapelle-Viel (61) 40 A5
la Chapelle-Villars (42) 129 H6
Chapelle-Viviers (86) 109 G2

Chapelle-Voland (39) 102 C5
les Chapelles (73) 133 E4
les Chapelles-Bourbon (77) 43 G5
Chapelon (45) 63 H5
la Chapelotte (18) 81 H6
Chapet (78) 42 A3
Chapois (39) 103 F4
Chaponnay (69) 130 B4
Chaponost (69) 129 H3
Chappes (03) 113 F3
Chappes (08) 23 G3
Chappes (10) 66 C4
Chappes (63) 127 F2
Chaptelat (87) 124 B2
Chaptuzat (63) 113 G6
Charancieu (38) 131 F5
Charantonnay (38) 130 C5
Charavines (38) 131 E6
Charbogne (08) 24 A4
Charbonnat (71) 100 D5
Charbonnier-les-Mines (63) 127 G6
Charbonnières (28) 61 F4
Charbonnières (71) 116 B3
Charbonnières-les-Bains (69) 129 H3
Charbonnières-les-Varennes (63) 127 E2
Charbonnières-les-Vieilles (63) 127 E1
Charbuy (89) 83 F2
la Charce (26) 159 F3
Charcenne (70) 87 E5
Charchigné (53) 59 F2
Charchilla (39) 117 H2
Charcier (39) 117 H1
Chard (23) 126 B1
Chardeny (08) 24 A4
Chardogne (55) 47 E4
Chardonnay (71) 116 B2
Chareil-Cintrat (03) 113 G4
Charencey (21) 85 E5
Charency (39) 103 F5
Charency-Vezin (54) 25 F4
Charens (26) 159 F2
Charensat (63) 126 C1
Charentay (69) 116 A6
Charentenay (89) 83 F3
Charentilly (37) 78 D6
Charenton-du-Cher (18) 98 A6
Charenton-le-Pont (94) 42 D4
Charentonnay (18) 98 C2
Charette (38) 130 D2
Charette-Varennes (71) 102 B4
Charey (54) 48 B2
Charézier (39) 117 H1
Chargé (37) 79 F5
Chargey-lès-Gray (70) 86 C4
Chargey-lès-Port (70) 87 F2
Chariez (70) 87 F3
Charigny (21) 84 D6
la Charité-sur-Loire (58) 98 D2
Charix (01) 117 G5
Charlas (31) 184 B3
Charleval (13) 175 G4
Charleval (27) 19 E5
Charleville (51) 44 D4
Charleville-Mézières (08) 24 A1
Charleville-sous-Bois (57) 26 D5
Charlieu (42) 115 F5
Charly (18) 98 B4
Charly (69) 130 A4
Charly-Oradour (57) 26 C5
Charly-sur-Marne (02) 44 A3
Charmauvillers (25) 88 D6
Charmé (16) 122 B1
la Charme (39) 102 D4
le Charme (45) 82 C2
la Charmée (71) 101 G6
Charmeil (03) 114 A5
le Charmel (02) 44 C1
Charmensac (15) 141 F2
Charmentray (77) 43 F3
Charmes (02) 22 A2
Charmes (03) 113 H6
Charmes (21) 86 B5
Charmes (52) 68 B6
Charmes (88) 69 G2
Charmes-en-l'Angle (52) 67 G2
Charmes-la-Côte (54) 48 A6
Charmes-la-Grande (52) 67 G2
Charmes-Saint-Valbert (70) 86 D2
Charmes-sur-l'Herbasse (26) 144 B3
Charmes-sur-Rhône (07) 144 A5
Charmoille (25) 88 B6
Charmoille (70) 87 F3
Charmois (54) 49 E6
Charmois (90) 88 D3
Charmois-devant-Bruyères (88) 70 A4
Charmois-l'Orgueilleux (88) 69 G4
Charmont (51) 46 C4
Charmont (95) 41 H1
Charmont-en-Beauce (45) 63 E4
Charmont-sous-Barbuise (10) 66 B2
les Charmontois (51) 46 D3
Charmoy (10) 65 G2
Charmoy (71) 100 D5
Charmoy (89) 65 F6
Charnas (07) 143 H1
Charnat (63) 127 H1
Charnay (25) 103 F2
Charnay (69) 129 H2
Charnay-lès-Chalon (71) 102 A4
Charnay-lès-Mâcon (71) 116 B4

Charnècles (38) 145 F1
Charnizay (37) 95 F4
Charnod (39) 117 F3
Charnois (08) 11 F4
Charnoz-sur-Ain (01) 130 D2
Charny (21) 84 D6
Charny (77) 43 F3
Charny-le-Bachot (10) 66 A1
Charny Orée de Puisaye (89) 82 D1
Charny-sur-Meuse (55) 25 E6
Charolles (71) 115 F3
Charols (26) 158 C2
Charonville (28) 61 H3
Chârost (18) 97 F3
Charpentry (55) 24 C6
Charpey (26) 144 C5
Charpont (28) 41 F5
Charquemont (25) 104 D1
Charraix (43) 142 A3
Charras (16) 122 D5
Charre (64) 181 G2
Charrecey (71) 101 F5
Charrey-sur-Saône (21) 102 A2
Charrey-sur-Seine (21) 66 D6
Charrin (58) 99 G5
Charritte-de-Bas (64) 181 G2
Charron (17) 106 D3
Charron (23) 112 C6
Charroux (03) 113 G5
Charroux (86) 109 E5
Chars (95) 42 A1
Charsonville (45) 62 B6
Chartainvilliers (28) 62 B1
Chartèves (02) 44 C2
la Chartre-sur-le-Loir (72) 78 D2
Chartres (28) 62 B2
Chartres-de-Bretagne (35) 57 E3
Chartrettes (77) 64 A1
Chartrier-Ferrière (19) 138 C3
Chartronges (77) 44 A5
Chartuzac (17) 135 F1
Charvieu-Chavagneux (38) 130 C3
Charvonnex (74) 132 B1
Chas (63) 127 G3
Chaserey (10) 66 B6
Chasnais (85) 91 H6
Chasnay (58) 99 E1
Chasné-sur-Illet (35) 57 F2
Chaspinhac (43) 142 C3
Chaspuzac (43) 142 B3
la Chassagne (39) 102 C4
Chassagne (63) 127 E5
Chassagne-Montrachet (21) 101 F4
Chassagne-Saint-Denis (25) 103 G2
Chassagnes (43) 142 A2
Chassagny (69) 129 H4
Chassaignes (24) 136 C2
Chassal (39) 117 H3
Chassant (28) 61 G3
Chasse-sur-Rhône (38) 130 A5
Chasselas (71) 116 A5
Chasselay (38) 144 D2
Chasselay (69) 130 A2
Chassemy (02) 22 B5
Chassenard (03) 114 D3
Chasseneuil (36) 110 D1
Chasseneuil-du-Poitou (86) 94 C6
Chasseneuil-sur-Bonnieure (16) 122 D2
Chassenon (16) 123 F2
Chassey (21) 84 D5
Chassey-Beaupré (55) 68 B1
Chassey-le-Camp (71) 101 F4
Chassey-lès-Montbozon (70) 87 H4
Chassey-lès-Scey (70) 87 F3
Chassiecq (16) 122 D1
Chassiers (07) 157 F2
Chassieu (69) 130 B3
Chassignelles (89) 84 B2
Chassignieu (38) 131 E5
Chassignolles (36) 111 G2
Chassignolles (43) 127 H6
Chassigny (52) 86 B2
Chassigny-sous-Dun (71) 115 F4
Chassillé (72) 59 G5
Chassors (16) 121 H3
Chassy (18) 98 B3
Chassy (71) 115 E1
Chassy (89) 83 E1
le Chastang (19) 139 E3
Chastanier (48) 156 C1
Chasteaux (19) 138 C3
Chastel (43) 141 G3
Chastel-Arnaud (26) 158 D1
Chastel-Nouvel (48) 156 A2
Chastellux-sur-Cure (89) 84 A6
Chastreix (63) 126 C5
la Chataigneraie (85) 92 D6
Chatain (86) 109 E6
Châtaincourt (28) 41 E5
Châtas (88) 70 D2
Château (71) 115 H3
Château-Arnoux-Saint-Auban (04) 160 B6
Château-Bernard (38) 145 F4
Château-Bréhain (57) 49 E3
Château-Chalon (39) 102 D5
Château-Chervix (87) 124 B4
Château-Chinon (58) 100 A3
Château-Chinon (58) 100 A3
le Château-d'Almenêches (61) 39 F1
Château-des-Prés (39) 118 A2
Charnay-sur-Meuse ... le Château-d'Oléron (17) 120 B1

Château-d'Olonne (85) 91 E6
Château-Gaillard (01) 130 D1
Château-Garnier (86) 109 E4
Château-Gontier (53) 76 D1
Château-Guibert (85) 91 H5
Château-la-Vallière (37) 78 B4
Château-l'Abbaye (59) 4 B6
Château-Landon (77) 64 A4
Château-Larcher (86) 109 E3
Château-l'Évêque (24) 137 F2
Château-l'Hermitage (72) 78 A2
Château-Porcien (08) 23 F3
Château-Renard (45) 82 C1
Château-Renault (37) 79 F4
Château-Rouge (57) 27 E4
Château-Salins (57) 49 E4
Château-sur-Allier (03) 98 D5
Château-sur-Cher (63) 112 C6
Château-sur-Epte (27) 19 G6
Château-Thébaud (44) 74 D6
Château-Thierry (02) 44 B2
Château-Verdun (09) 199 F1
Château-Ville-Vieille (05) 147 F6
Château-Voué (57) 49 F3
Châteaubernard (16) 121 G3
Châteaubleau (77) 43 H6
Châteaubourg (07) 144 A4
Châteaubourg (35) 57 G3
Châteaubriant (44) 57 G6
Châteaudouble (26) 144 C5
Châteaudouble (83) 177 H5
Châteaudun (28) 62 A5
Châteaufort (04) 160 B5
Châteaufort (78) 42 B5
Châteaugay (63) 127 F2
Châteaugiron (35) 57 G3
Châteaulin (29) 53 G1
Châteaumeillant (18) 112 A2
Châteauneuf (21) 101 E1
Châteauneuf (42) 129 H5
Châteauneuf (71) 115 F5
Châteauneuf (73) 132 B5
Châteauneuf (85) 90 D2
Châteauneuf-de-Bordette (26) 158 D4
Châteauneuf-de-Gadagne (84) 175 E2
Châteauneuf-de-Galaure (26) 144 C2
Châteauneuf-de-Randon (48) 156 B2
Châteauneuf-de-Vernoux (07) 143 H5
Châteauneuf-d'Entraunes (06) 161 G6
Châteauneuf-d'Ille-et-Vilaine (35) 34 D4
Châteauneuf-d'Oze (05) 160 A3
Châteauneuf-du-Faou (29) 54 A1
Châteauneuf-du-Pape (84) 175 E1
Châteauneuf-du-Rhône (26) 158 A3
Châteauneuf-en-Thymerais (28) 41 E6
Châteauneuf-Grasse (06) 178 C4
Châteauneuf-la-Forêt (87) 124 D3
Châteauneuf-le-Rouge (13) 192 C2
Châteauneuf-les-Bains (63) 126 D1
Châteauneuf-les-Martigues (13) 191 H5
Châteauneuf-Miravail (04) 159 H3
Châteauneuf-sur-Charente (16) 122 A4
Châteauneuf-sur-Cher (18) 97 G5
Châteauneuf-sur-Isère (26) 144 B4
Châteauneuf-sur-Loire (45) 81 F1
Châteauneuf-sur-Sarthe (49) 77 E2
Châteauneuf-Val-de-Bargis (58) 99 E1
Châteauneuf-Val-Saint-Donat (04) 160 B6
Châteauneuf-Villevieille (06) 179 E3
Châteauponsac (87) 110 C5
Châteauredon (04) 177 F1
Châteaurenard (13) 175 E3
Châteauroux (36) 96 C5
Châteauroux-les-Alpes (05) 161 E1
Châteauvert (83) 193 F2
Châteauvieux (05) 160 B3
Châteauvieux (41) 96 A1
Châteauvieux (83) 178 A3
Châteauvieux-les-Fossés (25) 103 H2
Châteauvilain (38) 130 D5
Châteauvillain (52) 67 G5
le Châtel (73) 146 C1
Châtel (74) 119 G4
Châtel-Censoir (89) 83 G4
Châtel-Chéhéry (08) 24 C5
Châtel-de-Joux (39) 117 H2
Châtel-de-Neuvre (03) 113 H4
Châtel-en-Trièves (38) 145 G5
Châtel-Gérard (89) 84 B3
Châtel-Guyon (63) 127 E2
Châtel-Montagne (03) 114 C6
Châtel-Moron (71) 101 F5
Châtel-Saint-Germain (57) 26 B5
Châtel-sur-Moselle (88) 69 H2
Châtelaillon-Plage (17) 106 D6
Châtelain (53) 76 D1
la Châtelaine (39) 103 E4
Châtelard (23) 126 B1
le Châtelard (73) 132 B3
Châtelaudren (22) 33 F4
Chatelay (39) 103 E3
Châtelblanc (25) 103 G6

Châteldon (63) 127 H1
le Châtelet (18) 112 B1
le Châtelet-en-Brie (77) 64 B1
le Châtelet-sur-Meuse (52) 68 C6
le Châtelet-sur-Retourne (08) 23 G4
le Châtelet-sur-Sormonne (08) 10 D6
les Châtelets (28) 40 C5
le Châtelier (39) 102 D4
le Châtelier (51) 46 C3
Châtellenot (21) 101 E1
Châtellerault (86) 94 D5
le Châtellier (35) 58 A1
le Châtellier (61) 38 B5
les Châtelliers-Notre-Dame (28) 61 H2
Châtelneuf (39) 103 F6
Châtelneuf (42) 128 C4
Châtelperron (03) 114 B3
Châtelraould-Saint-Louvent (51) 46 A5
Châtelus (03) 114 C5
Châtelus (38) 145 E3
Châtelus (42) 129 G4
Châtelus-le-Marcheix (23) 124 D1
Châtelus-Malvaleix (23) 111 H4
Châtenay (01) 116 D6
Châtenay (28) 62 D2
Châtenay (38) 144 D1
Châtenay (71) 115 G4
Châtenay-en-France (95) 42 D2
Châtenay-Mâcheron (52) 86 B1
Châtenay-Malabry (92) 42 C5
Châtenay-sur-Seine (77) 64 D2
Châtenay-Vaudin (52) 86 B1
Chatenet (17) 135 G1
le Châtenet-en-Dognon (87) 124 C2
Châteney (70) 87 H2
Châtenois (39) 102 D2
Châtenois (67) 71 F3
Châtenois (70) 87 H2
Châtenois (88) 69 E3
Châtenois-les-Forges (90) 88 C3
Châtenoy (45) 81 G1
Châtenoy (77) 64 A4
Châtenoy-en-Bresse (71) 101 G5
Châtenoy-le-Royal (71) 101 G5
Châtignac (16) 136 A1
Chatignonville (91) 62 D2
Châtillon (03) 113 G2
Châtillon (39) 103 E6
Châtillon (69) 129 H2
Châtillon (86) 108 D3
Châtillon (92) 42 C4
Châtillon-Coligny (45) 82 B2
Châtillon-en-Bazois (58) 99 G3
Châtillon-en-Diois (26) 159 F1
Châtillon-en-Michaille (01) 117 H5
Châtillon-en-Vendelais (35) 58 A3
Châtillon-Guyotte (25) 87 G6
Châtillon-la-Borde (77) 64 B1
Châtillon-la-Palud (01) 130 D1
Châtillon-le-Duc (25) 87 F6
Châtillon-le-Roi (45) 63 E4
Châtillon-lès-Sons (02) 22 C1
Châtillon-Saint-Jean (26) 144 C3
Châtillon-sous-les-Côtes (55) 47 G1
Châtillon-sur-Broué (51) 67 E1
Châtillon-sur-Chalaronne (01) 116 C5
Châtillon-sur-Cher (41) 96 B1
Châtillon-sur-Cluses (74) 119 E5
Châtillon-sur-Colmont (53) 58 D2
Châtillon-sur-Indre (36) 95 H3
Châtillon-sur-Lison (25) 103 F2
Châtillon-sur-Loire (45) 82 A4
Châtillon-sur-Marne (51) 44 D2
Châtillon-sur-Morin (51) 44 C5
Châtillon-sur-Oise (02) 22 B1
Châtillon-sur-Saône (88) 69 E6
Châtillon-sur-Seine (21) 85 E1
Châtillon-sur-Thouet (79) 93 G6
Châtin (58) 100 A2
Châtonnay (38) 130 D5
Chatonrupt-Sommermont (52) 67 H1
Chatou (78) 42 C3
la Châtre (36) 111 H1
la Châtre-Langlin (36) 110 D3
Châtres (10) 65 H1
Châtres (24) 138 A2
Châtres (77) 43 F5
Châtres-la-Forêt (53) 59 E4
Châtres-sur-Cher (41) 96 D1
Châtrices (51) 46 D2
Chattancourt (55) 25 E6
Chatte (38) 144 D2
Chatuzange-le-Goubet (26) 144 C4
Chaucenne (25) 87 E6
Chauchailles (48) 141 F6
Chauché (85) 91 H3
le Chauchet (23) 112 B6
Chauchigny (10) 66 A2
Chauconin-Neufmontiers (77) 43 G3
Chaudardes (02) 22 D5
Chaudebonne (26) 159 E3
Chaudefonds-sur-Layon (49) 76 C6
Chaudefontaine (25) 87 G6
Chaudefontaine (51) 46 C1
Chaudenay (52) 86 C1
Chaudenay (71) 101 G4
Chaudenay-la-Ville (21) 101 F2

Chaudenay-le-Château (21) 101 F2
Chaudeney-sur-Moselle (54) 48 B5
Chaudes-Aigues (15) 141 E6
Chaudeyrac (48) 156 C2
Chaudeyrolles (43) 143 E5
la Chaudière (26) 158 D2
Chaudon (28) 41 F5
Chaudon-Norante (04) 177 G2
Chaudrey (10) 66 C1
Chaudun (02) 22 A5
Chauffailles (71) 115 G5
Chauffayer (05) 146 A6
Chauffecourt (88) 69 F2
Chauffour-lès-Bailly (10) 66 C4
Chauffour-lès-Étréchy (91) 63 F1
Chauffour-sur-Vell (19) 138 D4
Chauffours (28) 62 A2
Chauffourt (52) 68 B6
Chauffry (77) 44 A4
Chaufour-lès-Bonnières (78) 41 F2
Chaufour-Notre-Dame (72) 60 A5
Chaugey (21) 85 G2
Chaulgnes (58) 98 D2
Chaulhac (48) 141 G5
Chaulieu (50) 37 H4
la Chaulme (63) 128 C6
Chaulnes (80) 21 F1
Chaum (31) 184 A5
Chaumard (58) 100 A2
la Chaume (21) 85 F1
Chaume-et-Courchamp (21) 86 B4
Chaume-lès-Baigneux (21) 85 E3
Chaumeil (19) 125 F6
Chaumercenne (70) 86 D6
Chaumergy (39) 102 C4
Chaumes-en-Brie (77) 43 G5
Chaumes-en-Retz (44) 74 A6
Chaumesnil (10) 67 E2
Chaumont (18) 98 B5
Chaumont (52) 67 H4
Chaumont (61) 39 G4
Chaumont (74) 118 A6
Chaumont (89) 64 D3
Chaumont-devant-Damvillers (55) 25 F5
Chaumont-en-Vexin (60) 19 H6
Chaumont-la-Ville (52) 68 D4
Chaumont-le-Bois (21) 67 E6
Chaumont-le-Bourg (63) 128 B6
Chaumont-Porcien (08) 23 F2
Chaumont-sur-Aire (55) 47 F3
Chaumont-sur-Loire (41) 79 G3
Chaumont-sur-Tharonne (41) 80 D4
Chaumontel (95) 42 D1
Chaumot (58) 99 G1
Chaumot (89) 64 D5
Chaumousey (88) 69 H4
Chaumoux-Marcilly (18) 98 B2
Chaumussay (37) 95 F4
la Chaumusse (39) 118 A1
Chaumuzy (51) 45 E1
Chaunac (17) 121 G6
Chaunay (86) 108 D4
Chauny (02) 21 H3
Chauray (79) 107 H3
Chauriat (63) 127 G3
la Chaussade (23) 125 H1
Chaussan (69) 129 H4
la Chaussée (76) 17 G3
la Chaussée (86) 94 A4
la Chaussée-d'Ivry (28) 41 F3
la Chaussée-Saint-Victor (41) 80 A3
la Chaussée-sur-Marne (51) 46 A4
la Chaussée-Tirancourt (80) 7 F4
Chaussenac (15) 139 H3
Chaussenans (39) 103 E5
Chausseterre (42) 128 B2
Chaussin (39) 102 C3
Chaussoy-Epagny (80) 20 C2
Chaussy (45) 63 E4
Chaussy (95) 41 H1
le Chautay (18) 98 C4
Chauvac-Laux-Montaux (26) 159 G4
Chauvé (44) 74 A5
Chauvency-le-Château (55) 25 E3
Chauvency-Saint-Hubert (55) 25 E3
Chauvigné (35) 35 G6
Chauvigny (86) 109 G1
Chauvigny-du-Perche (41) 61 G6
Chauvincourt-Provemont (27) 19 G6
Chauvirey-le-Châtel (70) 86 D2
Chauvirey-le-Vieil (70) 86 D2
Chauvoncourt (55) 47 G3
Chauvry (95) 42 C2
Chaux (21) 101 G2
la Chaux (25) 104 A3
la Chaux (61) 38 D6
la Chaux (71) 102 B5
Chaux (90) 88 C2
Chaux-Champagny (39) 103 F4
Chaux-des-Crotenay (39) 103 F6
la Chaux-du-Dombief (39) 118 A1
Chaux-la-Lotière (70) 87 F5
Chaux-lès-Clerval (25) 88 A5
Chaux-lès-Passavant (25) 104 A1
Chaux-lès-Port (70) 87 F2

Chaux-Neuve (25) 103 G6
Chauzon (07) 157 G3
Chavagne (35) 57 E3
Chavagnes-en-Paillers (85) 91 H2
Chavagnes-les-Redoux (85) 92 B5
Chavanac (19) 125 G4
Chavanat (23) 125 F1
Chavanatte (90) 89 E3
Chavanay (42) 129 H6
Chavanges (10) 67 E1
Chavaniac-Lafayette (43) 142 A3
Chavannaz (74) 118 B6
Chavanne (70) 88 B4
la Chavanne (73) 132 A5
Chavannes (18) 97 G5
Chavannes (26) 144 B3
les Chavannes-en-Maurienne (73) 132 C6
Chavannes-les-Grands (90) 88 D3
Chavannes-sur-l'Étang (68) 88 D3
Chavannes-sur-Reyssouze (01) 116 C3
Chavanod (74) 132 A2
Chavanoz (38) 130 C3
Chavaroux (63) 127 G2
la Chavatte (80) 21 E1
Chaveignes (37) 94 C3
Chavelot (88) 69 H3
Chavenay (78) 42 B4
Chavençon (60) 42 B1
Chavéria (39) 117 G2
Chaveroche (19) 125 H5
Chaveyriat (01) 116 D5
Chavignon (02) 22 A4
Chavigny (02) 22 A4
Chavigny (54) 48 C5
Chavigny-Bailleul (27) 41 E3
Chaville (92) 42 C4
Chavin (36) 111 E2
Chavonne (02) 22 C5
Chavornay (01) 131 G2
Chavot-Courcourt (51) 45 E2
Chavoy (50) 35 H3
Chavroches (03) 114 B3
le Chay (17) 120 D4
Chay (21) 103 F3
Chazay-d'Azergues (69) 129 H2
Chazé-sur-Argos (49) 76 B3
Chazeaux (07) 157 F2
Chazelet (36) 110 D2
Chazelles (15) 141 G3
Chazelles (16) 122 D4
Chazelles (43) 141 H4
Chazelles-sur-Albe (54) 49 G6
Chazelles-sur-Lavieu (42) 128 D5
Chazelles-sur-Lyon (42) 129 F4
Chazemais (03) 112 C2
Chazeuil (21) 86 A4
Chazeuil (58) 99 F1
Chazey-Bons (01) 131 F2
Chazey-sur-Ain (01) 130 D2
Chazilly (21) 101 E2
Chazot (25) 88 B6
Chécy (45) 81 E1
Chédigny (37) 95 G1
Chef-Boutonne (79) 108 B5
Chef-Haut (88) 69 F2
Cheffes (49) 77 E3
Cheffois (85) 92 C6
Cheignieu-la-Balme (01) 131 F2
Cheillé (37) 94 C1
Cheilly-lès-Maranges (71) 101 F4
Chein-Dessus (31) 184 C5
Cheissoux (87) 124 D2
le Cheix (63) 127 F1
Cheix-en-Retz (44) 74 B5
Chélan (32) 184 A2
Chelers (62) 7 H1
Chélieu (38) 131 E5
Chelle-Debat (65) 183 F2
Chelle-Spou (65) 183 F4
Chelles (60) 21 G5
Chelles (77) 43 E4
Chelun (35) 57 H5
Chemaudin et Vaux (25) 103 F1
Chemazé (53) 76 C1
Chemenot (39) 102 D4
Chémeré-le-Roi (53) 59 E6
Chémery (41) 80 A6
Chémery-Chéhéry (08) 24 B3
Chémery-les-Deux (57) 26 D4
Chemilla (39) 117 G3
Chemillé-en-Anjou (49) 92 D1
Chemillé-sur-Dême (37) 78 D3
Chemillé-sur-Indrois (37) 95 H2
Chemilli (61) 60 C2
Chemilly (03) 113 H2
Chemilly (70) 87 F3
Chemilly-sur-Serein (89) 83 H2
Chemilly-sur-Yonne (89) 83 F1
Chemin (39) 102 B3
le Chemin (51) 46 D2
Chemin-d'Aisey (21) 85 E2
Cheminas (07) 144 A3
Cheminon (51) 46 C5
Cheminot (57) 48 C3
Chemiré-en-Charnie (72) 59 G4
Chemiré-le-Gaudin (72) 59 H6
Chemy (59) 3 F6
Chenailler-Mascheix (19) 139 E4
la Chenalotte (25) 104 C2
Chénas (69) 116 A5
Chenay (51) 23 E5
Chenay (72) 60 A1

Chenay (79) 108 C3
Chenay-le-Châtel (71) 114 D5
le Chêne (10) 66 B1
Chêne-Bernard (39) 102 C4
Chêne-en-Semine (74) 118 A6
Chêne-Sec (71) 102 C4
Chenebier (70) 88 B3
Chenecey-Buillon (25) 103 F2
Chênelette (69) 115 H5
Chénérailles (23) 112 A6
Chenereilles (42) 128 D6
Chenereilles (43) 143 E3
Chenevelles (86) 94 D6
Chenevières (54) 49 F6
Chenevrey-et-Morogne (70) 86 D6
Chênex (74) 118 B5
Cheney (89) 84 A1
Chenicourt (54) 48 D3
Chenières (54) 25 H4
Chéniers (23) 111 F3
Cheniers (51) 45 G3
Chenillé-Champteussé (49) 76 D3
Chéniménil (88) 70 B4
Chennebrun (27) 40 B5
Chennegy (10) 65 H4
Chennevières-lès-Louvres (95) 43 E2
Chennevières-sur-Marne (94) 43 E4
Chenois (57) 49 E2
Chenoise (77) 44 A6
Chenon (16) 122 C1
Chenonceaux (37) 79 G6
Chenou (77) 64 A4
Chenôve (21) 85 H6
Chenôves (71) 101 F6
Chens-sur-Léman (74) 118 C3
Chenu (72) 78 B3
Cheny (89) 65 F6
Chepniers (17) 135 G1
Chepoix (60) 20 C3
la Cheppe (51) 46 A2
Cheppes-la-Prairie (51) 46 A4
Cheppy (55) 24 D6
Cheptainville (91) 63 F1
Chepy (51) 46 A3
Chépy (80) 6 C4
Chérac (17) 121 F3
Chérancé (53) 76 B1
Chérancé (72) 60 A3
Chéraute (64) 181 G2
Cherbonnières (17) 121 G1
Cherbourg-en-Cotentin (50) 12 C2
Chérence (95) 41 G2
Chérencé-le-Héron (50) 37 F4
Chéreng (59) 3 G5
les Chères (69) 129 H2
Chérêt (02) 22 C4
Chériennes (62) 7 F2
Cherier (42) 128 C1
Chérigné (79) 108 B5
Chérisay (72) 60 A2
Chérisey (57) 48 D2
Chérisy (28) 41 F5
Chérisy (62) 8 C3
Chérizet (71) 115 H2
Chermignac (17) 121 E3
Chermisey (88) 68 C2
Chermizy-Ailles (02) 22 C4
Chéronnac (87) 123 F3
Chéronvilliers (27) 40 B4
Chéroy (89) 64 C4
Cherré (72) 60 D4
Cherreau (72) 60 D4
Cherrueix (35) 35 F4
Cherval (24) 122 D6
Cherveix-Cubas (24) 138 A1
Cherves (86) 93 H6
Cherves-Châtelars (16) 123 E2
Cherves-Richemont (16) 121 G3
Chervettes (17) 107 F6
Cherveux (79) 108 A2
Chervey (10) 66 D5
Cherville (51) 45 G2
Chéry (18) 97 E2
Chéry-Chartreuve (02) 22 C5
Chéry-lès-Pouilly (02) 22 C2
Chéry-lès-Rozoy (02) 23 F2
Chesley (10) 66 B6
le Chesnay (78) 42 C4
Chesnois-Auboncourt (08) 24 A3
Chesny (51) 48 D2
Chessenaz (74) 118 A6
Chessy (69) 129 G2
Chessy (77) 43 F4
Chessy-les-Prés (10) 66 A6
Chéu (89) 65 H6
Cheuge (21) 86 B5
Cheust (65) 183 E4
Chevagnes (03) 114 B1
Chevagny-les-Chevrières (71) 116 B4
Chevaigné (35) 57 F2
Chevaigné-du-Maine (53) 59 F1
Cheval-Blanc (84) 175 F3
Chevaline (74) 132 B3
la Chevallerais (44) 74 D3
Chevanceaux (17) 135 H1
Chevannay (21) 85 E5
Chevannes (21) 101 G2
Chevannes (45) 64 B5
Chevannes (89) 83 F2
Chevannes (91) 63 G1
Chevannes-Changy (58) 99 F1
Chevennes (02) 22 C1

Chevenon (58) 99 E4
Chevenoz (74) 119 F3
Cheverny (41) 80 A4
Cheveuges (08) 24 B2
Chevières (08) 24 C5
Chevigney (70) 86 C6
Chevigney-lès-Vercel (25) 104 A1
Chevigny-sur-l'Ognon (25) 87 E6
Chevigny (39) 102 C2
Chevigny-en-Valière (21) 101 H3
Chevigny-Saint-Sauveur (21) 86 A6
Chevillard (01) 117 G3
Chevillé (72) 59 G6
Chevillon (52) 67 H1
Chevillon-sur-Huillard (45) 64 A6
la Chevillotte (25) 103 G1
Chevilly (45) 62 D5
Chevilly-Larue (94) 42 D5
Chevinay (69) 129 G3
Chevincourt (60) 21 F4
Chevrainvilliers (77) 64 A4
Chevreaux (39) 117 F2
Chevregny (02) 22 C4
Chèvremont (90) 88 D3
la Chèvrerie (16) 108 D6
Chevresis-Monceau (02) 22 B1
Chevreuse (78) 42 B5
Chèvreville (60) 43 G1
Chevrier (74) 118 A5
Chevrières (38) 144 D2
Chevrières (42) 129 F5
Chevrières (60) 21 E5
Chevroches (58) 83 F5
la Chevrolière (44) 74 C6
Chevrotaine (39) 103 F6
Chevroux (01) 116 C3
Chevroz (25) 87 F6
Chevru (77) 44 A5
Chevry (01) 118 B4
Chevry-Cossigny (77) 43 F5
Chevry-en-Sereine (77) 64 C3
Chevry-sous-le-Bignon (45) 64 B4
Chey (79) 108 C4
Cheylade (15) 140 C2
le Cheylard (07) 143 F5
Cheylard-l'Évêque (48) 156 C2
le Cheylas (38) 132 A6
Cheyssieu (38) 130 A6
Chezal-Benoît (18) 97 F5
la Chèze (22) 55 H2
Chèze (65) 182 D6
Chézeaux (52) 86 D1
Chezelle (03) 113 G6
Chezelles (36) 96 B4
Chezelles (37) 94 C3
Chèzeneuve (38) 130 D5
Chézery-Forens (01) 118 A4
Chézy (03) 114 A1
Chézy-en-Orxois (02) 44 A1
Chézy-sur-Marne (02) 44 B3
Chiatra (2B) 205 G2
Chiché (79) 93 F5
Chichée (89) 83 H2
Chichery (89) 83 F1
Chichey (51) 44 D5
Chichilianne (38) 145 F4
Chicourt (57) 49 E3
Chiddes (58) 100 A5
Chiddes (71) 115 H2
Chidrac (63) 127 F5
Chierry (02) 44 B2
Chieulles (57) 26 C5
Chignin (73) 132 A5
Chigny (02) 9 H6
Chigny-les-Roses (51) 45 F1
Chilhac (43) 141 H3
Chillac (16) 122 A6
Chille (39) 102 D6
Chilleurs-aux-Bois (45) 63 E5
le Chillou (79) 93 G5
Chilly (08) 10 D6
Chilly (74) 118 A6
Chilly (80) 21 E1
Chilly-le-Vignoble (39) 102 C6
Chilly-Mazarin (91) 42 D5
Chilly-sur-Salins (39) 103 F4
Chimilin (38) 131 F4
Chindrieux (73) 131 G2
Chinon (37) 94 B2
Chipilly (80) 8 A6
Chirac (16) 123 F1
Chirac (48) 155 H3
Chirac-Bellevue (19) 125 H6
Chirassimont (42) 129 E2
Chirat-l'Église (03) 113 G5
Chiré-en-Montreuil (86) 94 A6
Chirens (38) 131 F6
Chirmont (80) 20 C2
Chirols (07) 157 F1
Chiroubles (69) 116 A4
Chiry-Ourscamp (60) 21 G3
Chis (65) 183 F2
Chisa (2B) 205 F5
Chissay-en-Touraine (41) 79 G6
Chisseaux (37) 79 G6
Chisséria (39) 117 G3
Chissey-en-Morvan (71) 100 C2
Chissey-lès-Mâcon (71) 116 A2
Chissey-sur-Loue (39) 103 E3
Chitenay (41) 80 A4
Chitray (36) 110 D1
Chitry (89) 83 G2
Chitry-les-Mines (58) 99 G1
Chives (17) 122 A1
Chivres (21) 102 A3
Chivres-en-Laonnois (02) 22 D2

Chivres-Val (02) 22 B5
Chivy-lès-Étouvelles (02) 22 C3
Chizé (79) 107 H5
Chocques (62) 2 C6
Choilley-Dardenay (52) 86 B3
Choisel (78) 42 B5
Choiseul (52) 68 C5
Choisey (39) 102 C3
Choisies (59) 10 A3
Choisy (74) 118 B6
Choisy-au-Bac (60) 21 F4
Choisy-en-Brie (77) 44 A5
Choisy-la-Victoire (60) 20 D5
Choisy-le-Roi (94) 42 D5
Cholet (49) 92 C2
Cholonge (38) 145 G4
Choloy-Ménillot (54) 48 A5
Chomelix (43) 142 C2
Chomérac (07) 158 A1
la Chomette (43) 141 H2
Chonas-l'Amballan (38) 130 A6
Chonville-Malaumont (55) 47 G4
Chooz (08) 11 F4
Choqueuse-les-Bénards (60) 20 A2
Choranche (38) 145 E3
Chorey-les-Beaune (21) 101 G3
Chorges (05) 160 D2
Chouain (14) 14 A4
Chouday (36) 97 E4
Choue (41) 61 F6
Chougny (58) 99 H3
Chouilly (51) 45 F2
Chouppes (86) 94 A5
Chourgnac (24) 137 H2
Choussy (41) 79 H6
Chouvigny (03) 113 F5
Choux (39) 117 H4
les Choux (45) 82 A2
Chouy (02) 21 H6
Chouzé-sur-Loire (37) 94 A1
Chouzelot (25) 103 F2
Choye (70) 86 D5
Chozeau (38) 130 C3
Chuelles (45) 64 C6
Chuffilly-Roche (08) 24 A4
Chuignes (80) 8 B6
Chuignolles (80) 8 B6
Chuisnes (28) 61 H2
Chusclan (30) 158 A6
Chuyer (42) 129 H6
Chuzelles (38) 130 A4
Ciadoux (31) 184 B3
Ciamannacce (2A) 205 E5
Ciboure (64) 180 B1
Cideville (76) 17 F4
Ciel (71) 101 H4
Cier-de-Luchon (31) 184 A6
Cier-de-Rivière (31) 184 A4
Cierges (52) 44 C1
Cierges-sous-Montfaucon (55) 24 D5
Cierp-Gaud (31) 184 A6
Cierrey (27) 41 E2
Cierzac (17) 121 G4
Cieurac (46) 152 D4
Cieutat (65) 183 F4
Cieux (87) 123 H1
Ciez (58) 82 D5
Cigogné (37) 95 F1
Cilly (02) 22 D2
Cinais (37) 94 B2
Cindré (03) 114 B4
Cinq-Mars-la-Pile (37) 78 C6
Cinqueux (60) 20 D5
Cintegabelle (31) 185 G2
Cintheaux (14) 38 D2
Cintray (28) 62 A2
Cintré (35) 56 D3
Cintrey (70) 86 D2
La Ciotat (13) 192 C5
Cipières (06) 178 C3
Ciral (61) 59 G1
Ciran (37) 95 F3
Circourt (88) 69 G3
Circourt-sur-Mouzon (88) 68 D3
Ciré-d'Aunis (17) 107 E6
Cirès (31) 183 H6
Cires-lès-Mello (60) 20 C6
Cirey (70) 87 G5
Cirey-lès-Mareilles (52) 68 A4
Cirey-lès-Pontailler (21) 86 B6
Cirey-sur-Blaise (52) 67 G3
Cirey-sur-Vezouze (54) 49 H6
Cirfontaines-en-Azois (52) 67 G5
Cirfontaines-en-Ornois (52) 68 B1
Cirières (79) 92 D4
Ciron (36) 110 C1
Ciry-le-Noble (71) 115 F1
Ciry-Salsogne (02) 22 B5
Cisai-Saint-Aubin (61) 39 G4
Cisery (89) 84 B4
Cissac-Médoc (33) 134 D2
Cissé (86) 94 B6
Cisternes-la-Forêt (63) 126 C3
Cistrières (43) 142 A1
Citerne (80) 6 D5
Citers (70) 87 H2
Citey (70) 87 E5
Citou (34) 187 F2
Citry (77) 44 A3
Civaux (86) 109 G2
Civens (42) 129 E3
Civrac-de-Blaye (33) 135 F3
Civrac-en-Médoc (33) 120 C6
Civrac-sur-Dordogne (33) 136 A5
Civray (18) 97 E4
Civray (86) 109 E5

Civray-de-Touraine (37) 79 F6
Civray-sur-Esves (37) 95 E3
Civrieux (01) 130 A1
Civrieux-d'Azergues (69) 129 H2
Civry-en-Montagne (21) 85 E6
Civry-la-Forêt (78) 41 G4
Cizancourt (80) 8 C6
Cizay-la-Madeleine (49) 93 G1
Cize (01) 117 F5
Cize (39) 103 F5
Cizely (58) 99 F3
Cizos (65) 183 H2
Clacy-et-Thierret (02) 22 B3
Cladech (24) 137 H6
Claira (66) 201 F2
Clairac (47) 150 D4
Clairavaux (23) 125 G3
Clairefontaine-en-Yvelines (78) 42 A6
Clairegoutte (70) 88 B3
Clairfayts (59) 10 B3
Clairfontaine (02) 10 A5
Clairmarais (62) 2 B4
Clairoix (60) 21 F4
Clairvaux-d'Aveyron (12) 154 B4
Clairvaux-les-Lacs (39) 117 H1
Clairy-Saulchoix (80) 7 F6
Clais (76) 19 F1
Claix (16) 122 B5
Claix (38) 145 G3
Clam (17) 121 F5
Clamanges (51) 45 F4
Clamart (92) 42 C4
Clamecy (02) 22 A4
Clamecy (58) 83 F5
Clamensane (04) 160 B4
Clamerey (21) 84 D5
Clans (06) 178 D1
Clans (70) 87 F3
Clansayes (26) 158 B4
le Claon (55) 46 D1
le Clapier (12) 172 B3
Clapiers (34) 173 F5
Clara-Villerach (66) 200 C3
Clarac (31) 184 A4
Clarac (65) 183 F3
Claracq (64) 166 B6
Clarafond-Arcine (74) 118 A6
Clarbec (14) 15 E4
Clarens (65) 183 G3
Clarensac (30) 174 A3
Claret (04) 160 B4
Claret (34) 173 F3
Clary (59) 9 E4
Classun (40) 166 A4
Clastres (02) 21 H1
Clasville (76) 16 D3
le Clat (11) 200 A1
Claudon (88) 69 F5
le Claux (15) 140 C3
Clavans-en-Haut-Oisans (38) 146 B3
Clavé (79) 108 B2
Claveisolles (69) 115 H6
Clavette (17) 106 D5
Claveyson (26) 144 B2
Clavières (15) 141 G4
Claviers (83) 178 A5
Claville (27) 40 D2
Claville-Motteville (76) 18 D3
Clavy-Warby (08) 23 H1
Claye-Souilly (77) 43 F3
Clayes (35) 57 E2
les Clayes-sous-Bois (78) 42 B4
la Clayette (71) 115 G4
Clayeures (54) 69 H1
Clécy (14) 38 B3
Cléden-Cap-Sizun (29) 52 C2
Cléden-Poher (29) 32 B6
Cléder (29) 31 G2
Clèdes (40) 166 B5
Cleebourg (67) 51 F2
Clef Vallée d'Eure (27) 41 E1
Clefmont (52) 68 C5
les Clefs (74) 132 C2
Cléguer (56) 54 C4
Cléguérec (56) 55 E2
Clelles (38) 145 F5
Clémencey (21) 101 G1
Clémensat (63) 127 F5
Clémery (54) 48 C3
Clémont (18) 81 F4
Clénay (21) 85 H5
Clenleu (62) 1 G6
Cléon (76) 18 C5
Cléon-d'Andran (26) 158 C2
Cleppé (42) 129 E3
Clérac (17) 135 H2
Cléré-du-Bois (36) 95 G4
Cléré-les-Pins (37) 78 B5
Cléré-sur-Layon (49) 93 F2
Clères (76) 18 D3
Clérey (10) 66 B4
Clérey-la-Côte (88) 68 D1
Clérey-sur-Brenon (54) 69 F1
Clergoux (19) 139 F2
Clérieux (26) 144 B3
les Clérimois (89) 65 F4
le Clerjus (88) 69 H6
Clerlande (63) 127 F2
Clermain (71) 115 H3
Clermont (09) 185 F5
Clermont (40) 165 F6
Clermont (60) 20 C5
Clermont (74) 131 H1
Clermont-Créans (72) 77 H2
Clermont-de-Beauregard (24) 137 E4

Clermont-Dessous (47)......... 151 E5
Clermont-d'Excideuil (24)....... 137 H1
Clermont-en-Argonne (55)...... 46 D1
Clermont-Ferrand (63)........... 127 F3
Clermont-le-Fort (31)............ 185 F1
Clermont-les-Fermes (02)........ 23 E2
Clermont-l'Hérault (34).......... 172 C5
Clermont-Pouyguillès (32)...... 167 G6
Clermont-Savès (32)............. 168 C5
Clermont-Soubiran (47)......... 151 G6
Clermont-sur-Lauquet (11)..... 187 B5
Cléron (25)........................ 103 G2
Clerques (62)........................ 1 H3
Cléry (21)............................ 86 C6
Cléry (73)........................... 132 C4
Cléry-en-Vexin (95)............... 42 A1
Cléry-le-Grand (55).............. 24 D5
Cléry-le-Petit (55)................ 24 D5
Cléry-Saint-André (45).......... 80 C2
Cléry-sur-Somme (80)............. 8 B5
Clesles (51)......................... 65 H1
Clessé (71)......................... 116 B3
Clessé (79).......................... 93 E5
Clessy (71)......................... 115 G2
Cléty (62)............................ 2 A5
Cleurie (88)......................... 70 B5
Cleuville (76)....................... 16 D4
Cléville (14)......................... 14 D5
Cléville (76)......................... 16 D4
Clévilliers (28).................... 62 A1
Cleyrac (33)....................... 136 A6
Cleyzieu (01)...................... 131 E2
Clézentaine (88)................... 70 A2
Clichy (92).......................... 42 C3
Clichy-sous-Bois (93)............ 43 E3
Climbach (67)...................... 51 E1
Clinchamp (52).................... 68 B4
Clion (17).......................... 121 F5
Clion (36)........................... 95 H4
Cliousclat (26).................... 158 B1
Cliponville (76).................... 17 E4
Cliron (08)........................... 24 A1
la Clisse (17)...................... 120 D3
Clisson (44)........................ 75 E6
Clitourps (50)...................... 12 D2
Clohars-Carnoët (29)............ 54 B5
Clohars-Fouesnant (29)......... 53 G3
le Cloître-Pleyben (29).......... 31 H6
le Cloître-Saint-
  Thégonnec (29)................. 32 A4
Clomot (21)........................ 101 E2
Clonas-sur-Varèze (38)......... 130 A6
Clos-Fontaine (77)................ 43 H6
la Clotte (17)...................... 135 H3
Clouange (57)....................... 26 B4
Cloué (86)......................... 108 D2
Cloyes-les-Trois-
  Rivières (28)...................... 61 H6
Cloyes-sur-Marne (51).......... 46 B5
Clucy (39).......................... 103 F3
Clugnat (23)....................... 111 H4
Cluis (36).......................... 111 F2
Clumanc (04)...................... 177 G1
Cluny (71)......................... 116 A3
la Clusaz (74).................... 132 C1
la Cluse-et-Mijoux (25)........ 104 A4
les Cluses (66).................... 201 F4
Cluses (74)........................ 119 E6
Clussais-la-
  Pommeraie (79)................ 108 C5
Clux-Villeneuve (71)............ 102 A4
Coadout (22)........................ 33 E4
Coaraze (06)...................... 179 E2
Coarraze (64)..................... 182 C3
Coat-Méal (29)..................... 30 D3
Coatascorn (22)................... 32 D3
Coatréven (22)..................... 32 D2
Cobonne (26)..................... 144 C6
Cobrieux (59)........................ 3 G6
Cocherel (77)...................... 43 H2
Cocheren (57)...................... 27 F5
Coclois (10)........................ 66 C1
Cocquerel (80)...................... 7 E4
Cocumont (47).................... 150 B3
Codalet (66)....................... 200 C3
Codognan (30).................... 174 A4
Codolet (30)....................... 158 A6
Coësmes (35)....................... 57 G5
Coëtlogon (22).................... 55 H2
Coëtmieux (22).................... 33 H5
Cœur de Causse (46)........... 152 D2
Cœuvres-et-Valsery (02)....... 21 H5
Coëx (85)............................ 91 E4
Coggia (2A)....................... 204 C4
Cogna (39)......................... 117 H1
Cognac (16)....................... 121 G3
Cognac-la-Forêt (87)........... 123 H2
Cognat-Lyonne (03)............ 113 H6
Cogners (72)........................ 78 D1
Cognet (38)....................... 145 G5
Cognières (70)..................... 87 H4
Cognin (73)........................ 131 H5
Cognin-les-Gorges (38)........ 145 E2
Cognocoli-Monticchi (2A)..... 206 D1
Cogny (18)......................... 98 A5
Cogny (69)........................ 129 G1
Cogolin (83)....................... 194 A4
Cohade (43)....................... 141 G1
Cohennoz (73).................... 132 D3
Cohiniac (22)....................... 33 F5
Cohons (52)......................... 86 B2
Coiffy-le-Bas (52)................ 68 D6
Coiffy-le-Haut (52).............. 68 D6
Coigneux (80)....................... 7 H4
Coignières (78)..................... 42 A5
Coimères (33)..................... 149 H3
Coin-lès-Cuvry (57).............. 48 C2
Coin-sur-Seille (57).............. 48 C2

Coinces (45)........................ 62 C6
Coinches (88)....................... 70 D3
Coincourt (54)...................... 49 F5
Coincy (02)......................... 44 B1
Coincy (57)......................... 26 C5
Coings (36)......................... 96 C4
Coingt (02).......................... 23 F1
Coirac (33)........................ 150 A1
Coise (69)......................... 129 G4
Coise-Saint-Jean-Pied-
  Gauthier (73).................. 132 B5
Coiserette (39).................... 117 H3
Coisevaux (70)..................... 88 B3
Coisy (80)............................ 7 G5
Coivert (17)....................... 107 H6
Coivrel (60)......................... 20 D3
Coizard-Joches (51)............. 45 E4
Colayrac-Saint-Cirq (47)...... 151 E5
Colembert (62)...................... 1 G4
Coligny (01)....................... 117 E3
Colincamps (80)..................... 8 A4
Collan (89)......................... 83 H1
la Collancelle (58)................ 99 G2
Collandres (15)................... 140 C2
Collandres-
  Quincarnon (27)............... 40 C2
Collanges (63).................... 127 F6
Collat (43)......................... 142 A2
la Colle-sur-Loup (06)......... 178 D4
Collégien (77)...................... 43 F4
Collemiers (89)..................... 64 D4
Colleret (59)......................... 10 B3
le Collet-de-Dèze (48)......... 156 D5
Colletot (27)......................... 15 H3
Colleville (76)...................... 16 C3
Colleville-
  Montgomery (14).............. 14 C4
Colleville-sur-Mer (14)......... 13 G4
Collias (30)........................ 174 B2
Colligis-Crandelain (02)......... 22 C4
Colligny-Maizery (57)........... 26 C5
Colline-Beaumont (62)........... 6 C2
Collioure (66)..................... 201 G4
Collobrières (83)................. 193 H4
Collonge-en-
  Charollais (71)................ 115 H1
Collonge-la-Madeleine (71)... 101 E4
Collonges (01).................... 118 A5
Collonges-au-Mont-
  d'Or (69)........................ 130 A2
Collonges-la-Rouge (19)...... 138 D4
Collonges-lès-Bévy (21)...... 101 G2
Collonges-lès-
  Premières (21)................ 102 B1
Collonges-sous-
  Salève (74)...................... 118 C5
Collongues (06).................. 178 C2
Collongues (65).................. 183 F2
Collorec (29)........................ 32 A6
Collorgues (30)................... 174 A2
Colmar (68)......................... 71 F4
Colmars (04)...................... 161 F5
Colmen (57)......................... 27 E3
Colmesnil-Manneville (76)...... 17 G2
Colmey (54)......................... 25 F4
Colmier-le-Bas (52)............. 85 G2
Colmier-le-Haut (52)........... 85 G2
Colognac (30)..................... 173 F1
Cologne (32)...................... 168 C4
Colomars (06).................... 179 E3
Colombe (38)...................... 131 E6
la Colombe (50).................... 37 F3
Colombé-la-Fosse (10).......... 67 F3
Colombé-le-Sec (10)............ 67 F3
Colombe-lès-Vesoul (70)....... 87 G3
Colombelles (14).................. 14 C4
Colombes (92)...................... 42 C3
Colombey-les-Belles (54)...... 69 E1
Colombey les Deux
  Églises (52)..................... 67 G4
Colombier (03).................... 113 E4
Colombier (21)................... 101 F2
Colombier (24)................... 137 E6
Colombier (42)................... 143 G1
Colombier (70)..................... 87 G3
Colombier-en-
  Brionnais (71)................. 115 G4
Colombier-Fontaine (25)........ 88 B4
Colombier-le-Cardinal (07)... 143 H2
Colombier-le-Jeune (07)...... 143 H4
Colombier-le-Vieux (07)....... 143 H3
Colombier-Saugnieu (69)..... 130 C3
Colombières (14).................. 13 F5
Colombières-sur-Orb (34).... 171 H6
Colombiers (17).................. 121 F4
Colombiers (18).................... 97 H6
Colombiers (34).................. 188 B2
Colombiers (61).................... 60 A1
Colombiers (86).................... 94 C5
Colombiers-du-Plessis (53)..... 58 C2
Colombiers-sur-
  Seulles (14)...................... 14 B3
Colombiès (12)................... 154 A4
Colombotte (70)................... 87 H3
Colomby (50)....................... 12 D3
Colomby-Anguerny (14)........ 14 B4
Colomiers (31)................... 169 E5
Colomieu (01).................... 131 F3
Colondannes (23)............... 111 E4
Colonfay (02)........................ 9 G6
Colonne (39)...................... 102 D4
Colonzelle (26)................... 158 B4
Colpo (56).......................... 55 F5
Colroy-la-Roche (67)............ 71 E2
Coltainville (28)................... 62 B1
Coltines (15)...................... 141 E3
Coly (24).......................... 138 B3

Combaillaux (34)................ 173 F5
Combas (30)...................... 173 H3
la Combe-de-Lancey (38)..... 145 H2
Combeaufontaine (70).......... 87 E2
Combefa (81)..................... 170 B1
Comberanche-et-
  Épeluche (24).................. 136 C1
Comberjon (70)................... 87 G3
Comberouger (82).............. 168 D3
Combertault (21)................ 101 G3
les Combes (25)................. 104 B2
Combes (34)...................... 172 A5
Combes (16)...................... 122 D5
Comblanchien (21)............. 101 G2
Combles (80)........................ 8 B5
Combles-en-Barrois (55)....... 47 E5
Comblessac (35).................. 56 C5
Combleux (45)..................... 81 E1
Combloux (74).................... 133 E1
Combon (27)........................ 40 C1
Combourg (35)..................... 35 E6
Combourtillé (35).................. 57 H1
Combovin (26)................... 144 C5
Combrailles (63)................. 126 C2
Combrand (79)..................... 92 D4
Combray (14)....................... 38 C2
Combre (42)....................... 115 F6
Combres (28)....................... 61 G3
Combres-sous-les-
  Côtes (55)........................ 47 H2
Combressol (19)................. 125 G6
Combret (12)...................... 171 F3
Combreux (45)..................... 63 F6
Combrimont (88).................. 70 D3
Combrit (29)........................ 53 F3
Combronde (63).................. 127 F1
Combs-la-Ville (77)............... 43 E5
la Comelle (71)................... 100 C4
Comigne (11)...................... 187 F4
Comines (59)........................ 3 F4
Commana (29)...................... 31 H5
Commarin (21).................... 101 F1
Commeaux (61)..................... 38 D4
Commelle (38).................... 130 D6
Commelle-Vernay (42)......... 128 D1
Commenailles (39).............. 102 C5
Commenchon (02)................ 21 H2
Commensacq (40)............... 148 D5
Commentry (03)................. 112 D4
Commeny (95)...................... 42 A1
Commequiers (85)................ 90 D3
Commer (53)........................ 58 D3
Commercy (55)..................... 47 H4
Commerveil (72)................... 60 C3
Commes (14)........................ 13 H5
Communay (69).................. 130 A4
Commune nouvelle
  d'Arrou (28)...................... 61 G5
Compains (63).................... 127 E6
Compainville (76)................. 19 F2
Compans (77)...................... 43 F3
le Compas (23)................... 126 B1
Compertrix (51)................... 45 H3
Compeyre (12)................... 155 F6
Compiègne (60)................... 21 F4
Compigny (89)..................... 65 E2
Compolibat (12)................. 153 H4
la Compôte (73)................. 132 B3
Comprégnac (12)............... 171 H1
Compreignac (87).............. 124 B1
Comps (26)....................... 158 D2
Comps (30)........................ 174 C3
Comps (33)........................ 135 E3
Comps-la-Grand-Ville (12)... 154 C5
Comps-sur-Artuby (83)....... 177 H4
le Comté (62)........................ 7 H1
Comus (11)........................ 199 G1
Conan (41).......................... 79 H2
Conand (01)...................... 131 E2
Conat (66)......................... 200 B3
Conca (2A)........................ 207 G2
Concarneau (29).................. 53 G4
Concevreux (02).................. 22 D5
Concèze (19)...................... 138 B1
Conches-en-Ouche (27)........ 40 C3
Conches-sur-Gondoire (77).... 43 F4
Conchez-de-Béarn (64)....... 166 C5
Conchil-le-Temple (62).......... 6 C1
Conchy-les-Pots (60)............ 21 E3
Conchy-sur-Canche (62)........ 7 F2
Concorès (46).................... 152 C1
Concoret (56)...................... 56 B3
Concots (46)...................... 153 E4
Concoules (30)................... 156 D4
Concremiers (36)................ 110 B1
Concressault (18)................. 81 H5
Conciers (41)....................... 80 A2
Condac (16)....................... 108 D6
Condal (71)....................... 117 E2
Condamine (01).................. 117 G5
Condamine (39).................. 102 C6
la Condamine-
  Châtelard (04)................. 161 G3
Condat (15)....................... 140 C1
Condat (46)....................... 138 D4
Condat-en-Combraille (63)... 126 B2
Condat-lès-
  Montboissier (63)............ 127 H5
Condat-sur-Ganaveix (19)... 124 D3
Condat-sur-Trincou (24)...... 123 F6
Condat-sur-Vézère (24)....... 138 A3
Condat-sur-Vienne (87)....... 124 B3
Condé (36).......................... 97 E4
Condé-en-Brie (02)............... 44 C2
Condé-en-Normandie (14)..... 38 B3
Condé-Folie (80).................... 7 E5
Condé-lès-Autry (08)............ 24 B6

Condé-lès-Herpy (08)........... 23 F3
Condé-Northen (57)............. 26 D5
Condé-Sainte-Libiaire (77)..... 43 G3
Condé-sur-Aisne (02)........... 22 B5
Condé-sur-Ifs (14)................ 39 E2
Condé-sur-l'Escaut (59).......... 9 G1
Condé-sur-Marne (51).......... 45 G2
Condé-sur-Risle (27)............ 15 H3
Condé-sur-Sarthe (61).......... 60 A2
Condé-sur-Seulles (14)......... 14 A4
Condé-sur-Suippe (02).......... 23 E4
Condé-sur-Vesgre (78).......... 41 G5
Condé-sur-Vire (50).............. 37 G1
Condeissiat (01)................. 116 D5
Condéon (16)..................... 121 H6
Condes (39)....................... 117 G3
Condes (52)........................ 67 H4
Condette (62)........................ 1 F5
Condezaygues (47)............. 151 H3
Condillac (26).................... 158 B2
Condom (32)...................... 167 G2
Condom-d'Aubrac (12)........ 155 E2
Condorcet (26)................... 158 D4
Condren (02)........................ 22 A2
Condrieu (69)..................... 130 A6
Conflandey (70)................... 87 F2
Conflans-en-Jarnisy (54)....... 48 A1
Conflans-Sainte-
  Honorine (78).................. 42 B2
Conflans-sur-Anille (72)........ 61 E6
Conflans-sur-Lanterne (70)... 87 G1
Conflans-sur-Loing (45)........ 64 B6
Conflans-sur-Seine (51)......... 65 G1
Confolens (16)................... 109 G6
Confolent-Port-Dieu (19)..... 126 B5
Confort (01)....................... 117 H5
Confort-Meilars (29)............. 53 E2
Confracourt (70).................. 87 E3
Confrançon (01)................. 116 D4
Congé-sur-Orne (72)............ 60 B4
Congénies (30)................... 173 H4
Congerville-Thionville (91)..... 63 E2
Congis-sur-
  Thérouanne (77)............... 43 G2
Congrier (53)....................... 76 A1
Congy (51)........................... 45 E4
Conie-Molitard (28).............. 62 A5
Conilhac-Corbières (11)...... 187 G3
Conilhac-de-la-
  Montagne (11)................. 186 D5
Conjux (73)....................... 131 G2
Conlie (72).......................... 59 H4
Conliège (39)..................... 102 D6
Connac (12)....................... 171 F2
Connangles (43)................. 142 A1
Connantray-Vaurefroy (51).... 45 F5
Connantre (51).................... 45 E5
Connaux (30)..................... 174 C1
Conne-de-Labarde (24)....... 137 E6
Connelles (27)..................... 18 D6
Connerré (72)...................... 60 C5
Connezac (24).................... 123 E5
Conniggis (02)..................... 44 C2
Conquereuil (44)................. 74 C1
Conques-en-Rouergue (12)... 154 B2
Conques-sur-Orbiel (11)...... 187 E3
le Conquet (29)................... 30 C5
Conqueyrac (30)................. 173 F2
Cons-la-Grandville (54)......... 25 G4
Consac (17)....................... 121 E6
Conségudes (06)................ 178 D3
Consenvoye (55).................. 25 E5
Consigny (52)...................... 68 B4
Consolation-
  Maisonnettes (25)............ 104 B1
Contalmaison (80)................. 8 B5
Contamine-Sarzin (74)........ 118 B6
Contamine-sur-Arve (74)..... 118 D5
les Contamines-
  Montjoie (74)................... 133 E2
Contault (51)....................... 46 C3
Contay (80).......................... 7 H5
Conte (39)......................... 103 G5
Contes (06)........................ 179 E3
Contes (62)........................... 7 E1
Contescourt (02).................. 21 H1
Contest (53)........................ 58 D3
Conteville (14)..................... 15 G2
Conteville (60)..................... 20 A2
Conteville (76)..................... 19 G2
Conteville (80)...................... 7 F3
Conteville-en-Ternois (62)...... 7 G1
Conteville-lès-
  Boulogne (62).................... 1 F4
Conthil (57)......................... 49 F3
Contigny (03)..................... 113 H3
Contilly (72)........................ 60 C2
Continvoir (37).................... 78 A5
Contoire (80)....................... 20 D2
Contrazy (09)..................... 185 E4
Contré (17)........................ 108 A6
Contre (80).......................... 20 B1
Contréglise (70)................... 87 F1
Contremoulins (76).............. 16 C3
Contres (18)........................ 97 H5
Contres (41)........................ 80 A5
Contreuve (08)..................... 24 A5
Contrevoz (01)................... 131 F2
Contrexéville (88)................ 69 E4
Contrières (50)..................... 36 D2
Contrisson (55)................... 46 D4
Conty (80)........................... 20 B1
Contz-les-Bains (57)............ 26 C2
Conzieu (01)...................... 131 F3
Coole (51)........................... 45 H4
Coolus (51)......................... 45 H3
la Copechagnière (85).......... 91 G3

Copponex (74).................... 118 B6
Coquainvilliers (14).............. 15 F4
Coquelles (62)....................... 1 G2
la Coquille (24)................... 123 H5
Corancez (28)...................... 62 B2
Corancy (58)...................... 100 B2
Coray (29).......................... 53 H2
Corbara (2B)...................... 202 C5
Corbarieu (82).................... 169 E2
Corbas (69)........................ 130 B4
Corbehem (62)...................... 8 C2
Corbeil (51)......................... 46 A6
Corbeil-Cerf (60).................. 20 B6
Corbeil-Essonnes (91).......... 42 D6
Corbeilles (45)..................... 63 H5
Corbel (73)........................ 131 G6
Corbelin (38)...................... 131 F4
Corbenay (70)...................... 69 H6
Corbeny (02)........................ 22 D4
Corbère (66)...................... 200 D2
Corbère-Abères (64)........... 166 C6
Corbère-les-Cabanes (66).... 200 D2
Corberon (21).................... 101 H3
Corbès (30)........................ 173 G1
la Corbière (70).................... 88 A1
Corbières (04).................... 176 C4
Corbières (11).................... 186 B5
Corbigny (58)....................... 99 H1
Corbon (61)........................ 60 D1
Corbonod (01).................... 131 G1
Corbreuse (91)..................... 62 D1
Corcelle-Mieslot (25)........... 87 G5
Corcelles-en-
  Beaujolais (69)................ 116 A5
Corcelles-Ferrières (25)....... 103 E1
Corcelles-les-Arts (21)........ 101 G4
Corcelles-lès-Cîteaux (21).... 102 A2
Corcelles-les-Monts (21)....... 85 G6
Corcieux (88)....................... 70 C4
Corconne (30).................... 173 G3
Corcondray (25).................. 103 E1
Corconne (30).................... 173 G3
Corcoué-sur-Logne (44)........ 91 F1
Corcy (02)............................ 21 H6
Cordebugle (14)................... 15 G5
Cordelle (42)..................... 128 D1
Cordemais (44).................... 74 B4
Cordes-sur-Ciel (81)........... 170 A1
Cordes-Tolosannes (82)...... 168 D2
Cordesse (71).................... 100 D3
Cordey (14)......................... 38 D3
Cordon (74)....................... 133 E1
Cordonnet (70).................... 87 F5
Coren (15)......................... 141 F4
Corenc (38)....................... 145 G2
Corent (63)........................ 127 F4
Corfélix (51)........................ 44 D4
Corgengoux (21)................ 101 H3
Corgnac-sur-l'Isle (24)........ 123 G6
Corgoloin (21).................... 101 G2
Corignac (17)..................... 135 G2
Corlay (22).......................... 33 E6
Corlier (01)........................ 117 F6
Cormainville (28).................. 62 B4
Cormaranche-en-
  Bugey (01)...................... 131 F1
Cormatin (71).................... 116 A2
Corme-Écluse (17).............. 120 D4
Corme-Royal (17)............... 120 D3
Cormeilles (27).................... 15 G4
Cormeilles (60).................... 20 B2
Cormeilles-en-Parisis (95)..... 42 C3
Cormeilles-en-Vexin (95)...... 42 B1
Cormelles-le-Royal (14)........ 14 C5
Cormenon (41)..................... 61 F6
Cormeray (41)..................... 80 A5
Cormery (37)....................... 95 F1
Cormes (72)......................... 61 E4
Cormicy (51)........................ 22 D5
le Cormier (27).................... 41 E3
Cormolain (14)..................... 37 H1
Cormont (62)........................ 1 F5
Cormontreuil (51)................. 23 E6
Cormoranche-sur-
  Saône (01)...................... 116 B4
Cormost (10)........................ 66 B4
Cormot-Vauchignon (21)..... 101 F4
Cormoyeux (51)................... 45 E1
Cormoz (01)....................... 117 E2
Corn (46).......................... 153 F2
Cornac (46)....................... 139 F5
Cornant (89)........................ 64 D5
Cornas (07)....................... 144 A4
Cornay (08)......................... 24 C5
Cornebarrieu (31)............... 169 E5
Corneilhan (34)................... 188 C1
Corneilla-de-Conflent (66)... 200 B3
Corneilla-del-Vercol (66)..... 201 F3
Corneilla-la-Rivière (66)...... 201 E2
Corneillan (32)................... 166 C4
Corneville-la-
  Fouquetière (27)............... 40 B2
Corneville-sur-Risle (27)....... 15 H3
Cornier (74)....................... 118 D6
Cornil (19)......................... 138 D2
Cornillac (26)..................... 159 E4
Cornille (24)....................... 137 F5
Cornillé (35)........................ 57 H3
Cornillé-les-Caves (49)......... 77 F4
Cornillon (30).................... 157 H5
Cornillon-Confoux (13)....... 175 F6
Cornillon-en-Trièves (38).... 145 G5
Cornillon-sur-l'Oule (26)..... 159 E3
Cornimont (88).................... 70 C6
Cornod (39)....................... 117 G4
Cornot (70)......................... 87 E3
Cornus (12)....................... 172 B3
Cornusse (18)..................... 98 B4

Corny (27)........................... 19 E6
Corny-Machéroménil (08)...... 23 H3
Corny-sur-Moselle (57)......... 48 C2
Coron (49).......................... 92 D2
Corpe (85).......................... 91 H6
Corpeau (21)...................... 101 F4
Corpoyer-la-Chapelle (21)..... 85 E4
Corps (38)......................... 146 A5
Corps-Nuds (35).................. 57 F4
Corquilleroy (45)................. 64 A5
Corquoy (18)....................... 97 G4
Corrano (2A)...................... 205 E6
Corravillers (70)................... 70 B6
Corre (70)........................... 69 F6
Corrençon-en-Vercors (38)... 145 F4
Correns (83)....................... 193 F2
Corrèze (19)....................... 139 F1
Corribert (51)....................... 44 D3
Corrobert (51)...................... 44 C3
Corrombles (21)................... 84 C4
Corronsac (31)................... 185 G1
Corroy (51).......................... 45 E5
Corsaint (21)....................... 84 C4
Corsavy (66)...................... 200 D4
Corscia (2B)....................... 204 D2
Corsept (44)........................ 73 H4
Corseul (22)........................ 34 C5
Cortambert (71)................. 116 A2
Corte (2B)......................... 205 E4
Cortevaix (71).................... 116 A2
Cortrat (45)......................... 82 B1
les Corvées-les-Yys (28)....... 61 G2
Corveissiat (01)................. 117 F4
Corvol-d'Embernard (58)....... 99 F1
Corvol-l'Orgueilleux (58)....... 83 E5
Corzé (49)........................... 77 E4
Cos (09)............................ 185 G5
Cosges (39)....................... 102 C5
Coslédaà-Lube-Boast (64)... 166 B6
Cosmes (53)........................ 58 C6
Cosnac (19)....................... 138 D3
Cosne-Cours-sur-Loire (58)... 82 C5
Cosne-d'Allier (03)............. 113 E2
Cosnes-et-Romain (54)......... 25 G3
Cossaye (58)........................ 99 F6
Cossé-en-Champagne (53).... 59 F6
Cossé-le-Vivien (53)............. 58 B6
Cossesseville (14)................. 38 C3
Cosswiller (67)..................... 50 C5
Costa (2B)......................... 202 D5
Costaros (43)..................... 142 C5
les Costes (05)................... 146 A4
les Costes-Gozon (12)........ 171 G2
la Côte (70)......................... 88 B2
la Côte-d'Arbroz (74).......... 119 F4
la Côte-d'Aime (73)............ 133 F5
la Côte-en-Couzan (42)....... 128 C3
la Côte-Saint-André (38)..... 130 D6
le Coteau (42).................... 115 E6
Côteaux du Blanzacais (16)... 122 B5
Coteaux du Lizon (39)......... 117 H3
Les Coteaux
  Périgourdins (24)............. 138 B3
Côteaux-sur-Loire (37)......... 78 B6
Côtebrune (25)..................... 87 H6
les Côtes-d'Arey (38).......... 130 A6
les Côtes-de-Corps (38)...... 145 H5
Coti-Chiavari (2A)............... 206 C2
Cotignac (83)..................... 177 F6
Cottance (42)..................... 129 E3
Cottenchy (80).................... 20 C1
Cottévrard (76)..................... 17 H4
Cottun (14).......................... 13 H5
la Couarde (79).................. 108 B3
la Couarde-sur-Mer (17)..... 106 B4
Couargues (18)................... 98 C1
Coubert (77)........................ 43 F5
Coubeyrac (33).................. 136 B6
Coubisou (12).................... 154 D2
Coubjours (24)................... 138 B2
Coublanc (52)...................... 86 C3
Coublanc (71).................... 115 F5
Coublevie (38).................... 145 F1
Coublucq (64).................... 166 B6
Coubon (43)....................... 142 C4
Coubron (93)....................... 43 E3
Couches (71)...................... 101 E4
Couchey (21)...................... 101 H1
la Coucourde (26).............. 158 B2
Coucouron (07).................. 142 D6
Coucy (02).......................... 23 H4
Coucy-la-Ville (02)............... 22 A3
Coucy-le-Château-
  Auffrique (02)................... 22 A3
Coucy-lès-Eppes (02).......... 22 D3
Couddes (41)....................... 80 A6
Coudehard (61).................... 39 F4
Coudekerque-Branche (59)..... 2 B1
Coudes (63)....................... 127 F4
Coudeville-sur-Mer (50)....... 36 D3
Coudons (11)..................... 186 C6
Coudoux (13)..................... 175 G6
Coudray (27)....................... 19 F5
le Coudray (28).................... 62 B2
Coudray (53)........................ 76 D1
Coudray-au-Perche (28)........ 61 F3
le Coudray-Macouard (49).... 93 G1
le Coudray-
  Montceaux (91)................ 63 H1
Coudray-Rabut (14)............. 15 F4
le Coudray-Saint-
  Germer (60)..................... 19 H4
Le Coudray-sur-Thelle (60)... 20 B5
Coudreceau (28).................. 61 F2
Coudrecieux (72).................. 60 D6
Coudres (27)........................ 41 E4
Coudroy (45)........................ 81 G1
Coudun (60)........................ 21 F4
Coudures (40)..................... 166 A4

Coueilles (31) 184 C2
Couëron (44) 74 C5
Couesmes (37) 78 B4
Couesmes-Vaucé (53) 58 D1
Couffé (44) 75 E3
Couffoulens (11) 186 A6
Couffy (41) 96 B1
Couffy-sur-Sarsonne (19) 126 A4
Couflens (09) 198 B1
Coufouleux (81) 169 H3
Couhé (86) 108 D2
Couilly-Pont-aux-Dames (77) 43 G4
Couin (62) 7 H4
Couiza (11) 186 D6
Couladère (31) 184 D3
Coulaines (72) 60 B5
Coulandon (03) 113 H2
Coulangeron (89) 83 F3
Coulanges (03) 114 D2
Coulanges-la-Vineuse (89) 83 G3
Coulanges-lès-Nevers (58) 99 E3
Coulanges-sur-Yonne (89) 83 F4
Coulans-sur-Gée (72) 59 H5
Coulaures (24) 137 H1
Couleuvre (03) 98 C6
Coulevon (70) 87 G3
Coulgens (16) 122 C2
Coulimer (61) 60 C1
Coullemelle (80) 20 C2
Coullemont (62) 7 H3
Coullons (45) 81 H3
Coulmer (61) 39 G4
Coulmier-le-Sec (21) 84 D2
Coulmiers (45) 62 C6
Coulobres (34) 188 C1
Coulogne (62) 1 G2
Couloisy (60) 21 G5
Coulombiers (72) 60 A3
Coulombiers (86) 108 D2
Coulombs (28) 41 G6
Coulombs-en-Valois (77) 43 H2
Coulomby (62) 1 H4
Coulommes (77) 43 G3
Coulommes-et-Marqueny (08) 24 A4
Coulommes-la-Montagne (51) 23 E6
Coulommiers (77) 43 H4
Coulommiers-la-Tour (41) 79 G2
Coulon (79) 107 G3
Coulonces (61) 39 E4
la Coulonche (61) 38 B5
Coulongé (72) 78 A3
Coulonges (16) 122 B2
Coulonges (17) 121 G4
Coulonges (86) 110 B3
Coulonges-Cohan (02) 22 C6
Coulonges-sur-l'Autize (79) 107 G2
Coulonges-sur-Sarthe (61) 60 C1
Coulonges-Thouarsais (79) 93 F4
Coulonvillers (80) 7 E4
Couloumé-Mondebat (32) 167 E5
Coulounieix-Chamiers (24) 137 F2
Coulours (89) 65 G4
Couloutre (58) 82 D5
Coulouvray-Boisbenâtre (50) 37 F4
Coulx (47) 151 E3
Coume (57) 27 E4
Counozouls (11) 200 A2
Coupelle-Neuve (62) 2 A6
Coupelle-Vieille (62) 2 A6
Coupetz (51) 45 H4
Coupéville (51) 46 B3
Coupiac (12) 171 F2
Coupray (52) 67 G6
Coupru (02) 44 A2
Couptrain (53) 59 F1
Coupvray (77) 43 F3
Couquèques (33) 120 D6
Cour-Cheverny (41) 80 A4
Cour-et-Buis (38) 130 B6
Cour-l'Évêque (52) 67 G6
la Cour-Marigny (45) 81 H1
Cour-Maugis sur Huisne (61) 61 G2
Cour-Saint-Maurice (25) 88 C6
Cour-sur-Loire (41) 80 A3
Courances (91) 63 H2
Courant (17) 107 G6
Courban (21) 85 F1
Courbehaye (28) 62 B4
Courbépine (27) 15 H5
Courbes (02) 22 B2
Courbesseaux (54) 49 E5
Courbette (39) 117 G1
Courbeveille (53) 58 C5
Courbevoie (92) 42 C3
Courbiac (47) 152 A4
Courbillac (16) 121 H3
Courboin (02) 44 A3
Courbouzon (39) 102 D6
Courbouzon (41) 80 B3
Courçais (03) 112 C2
Courçay (37) 95 F1
Courcebœufs (72) 60 B4
Courcelette (80) 8 B4
Courcelles (17) 121 F1
Courcelles (25) 103 F2
Courcelles (45) 63 G5
Courcelles (54) 69 F2
Courcelles (58) 83 E5
Courcelles (90) 89 E4
Courcelles-au-Bois (80) 8 A4
Courcelles-Chaussy (57) 26 D5
Courcelles-de-Touraine (37) 78 B4

Courcelles-en-Barrois (55) 47 G4
Courcelles-en-Bassée (77) 64 C2
Courcelles-en-Montagne (52) 86 A1
Courcelles-Epayelles (60) 21 E3
Courcelles-Frémoy (21) 84 B5
Courcelles-la-Forêt (72) 77 H2
Courcelles-le-Comte (62) 8 B3
Courcelles-lès-Gisors (60) 19 G6
Courcelles-lès-Lens (62) 8 C1
Courcelles-lès-Montbard (21) 84 D4
Courcelles-lès-Montbéliard (25) 88 C4
Courcelles-lès-Semur (21) 84 C5
Courcelles-Sapicourt (51) 22 D6
Courcelles-sous-Châtenois (88) 68 D3
Courcelles-sous-Moyencourt (80) 20 A1
Courcelles-sous-Thoix (80) 20 A2
Courcelles-sur-Aire (55) 47 E3
Courcelles-sur-Blaise (52) 67 G2
Courcelles-sur-Nied (57) 48 D1
Courcelles-sur-Seine (27) 41 F1
Courcelles-sur-Vesle (02) 22 C5
Courcelles-sur-Viosne (95) 42 B2
Courcelles-sur-Voire (10) 66 D1
Courcemain (51) 45 E6
Courcemont (72) 60 B4
Courcerac (17) 121 G2
Courceroy (10) 65 E2
Courchamp (77) 44 B6
Courchamps (02) 44 A1
Courchamps (49) 93 G1
Courchapon (25) 103 E1
Courchaton (70) 88 A4
Courchelettes (59) 8 C2
Courchevel (73) 133 E5
Courcité (53) 59 G3
Courcival (72) 60 C3
Courcôme (16) 122 B1
Courçon (17) 107 E4
Courcoué (37) 94 C3
Courcouronnes (91) 42 D6
Courcoury (17) 121 F3
Courcuire (70) 87 E6
Courcy (14) 39 E2
Courcy (50) 37 E1
Courcy (51) 23 E5
Courcy-aux-Loges (45) 63 F5
Courdemanche (27) 41 E4
Courdemanche (72) 78 D1
Courdemanges (51) 46 A5
Courdimanche (95) 42 B2
Courdimanche-sur-Essonne (91) 63 G2
Couret (31) 184 B4
Courgains (72) 60 B3
Courgeac (16) 122 B6
Courgenard (72) 61 E4
Courgenay (89) 65 F3
Courgent (78) 41 G3
Courgeon (61) 60 D1
Courgeoût (61) 60 C1
Courgis (89) 83 H2
Courgivaux (51) 44 C5
Courgoul (63) 127 E5
Courjeonnet (51) 45 E4
Courlac (16) 136 B1
Courlandon (51) 22 C5
Courlans (39) 102 C6
Courlaoux (39) 102 C6
Courlay (79) 93 E5
Courléon (49) 78 A5
Courlon (21) 85 G3
Courlon-sur-Yonne (89) 64 D3
Courmangoux (01) 117 E3
Courmas (51) 45 E1
Courmelles (02) 22 A5
Courmemin (41) 80 B5
Courmes (06) 178 D3
Courmont (02) 44 C1
Courmont (70) 88 B3
Cournanel (11) 186 D5
Courniou (34) 187 G1
Cournols (63) 127 E4
Cournon (56) 56 C6
Cournon-d'Auvergne (63) 127 F3
Cournonsec (34) 173 E6
Cournonterral (34) 173 E6
la Couronne (16) 122 B4
Courouvre (55) 47 F3
Courpalay (77) 43 G6
Courpiac (33) 135 H6
Courpière (63) 128 A3
Courpignac (17) 135 F1
Courquetaine (77) 43 F5
Courrensan (32) 167 F3
Courrières (62) 8 C1
Courris (81) 170 D2
Courry (30) 157 E5
Cours (47) 151 E4
le Cours (56) 55 H6
Cours (69) 115 G6
Cours (79) 107 H2
Cours-de-Monségur (33) 150 C1
Cours-de-Pile (24) 137 E5
Cours-les-Bains (33) 150 B4
Cours-les-Barres (18) 98 D3
Coursac (24) 137 E3
Coursan (11) 188 B3
Coursan-en-Othe (10) 65 H5
Coursegoules (06) 178 D3
Courset (62) 1 G5
Courseulles-sur-Mer (14) 14 B3
Courson-les-Carrières (89) 83 F4

Courson-Monteloup (91) 42 B6
Courtacon (77) 44 B5
Courtagnon (51) 45 E1
Courtaoult (10) 65 H6
Courtauly (11) 186 C5
Courtavon (68) 89 E4
Courtefontaine (25) 88 D6
Courtefontaine (39) 103 E2
Courteilles (27) 40 C5
Courteix (19) 126 A4
Courtelevant (90) 89 E4
Courtemanche (80) 20 D2
Courtemaux (45) 64 C5
Courtémont (51) 46 C1
Courtemont-Varennes (02) 44 C2
Courtempierre (45) 64 A5
Courtenay (38) 131 E3
Courtenay (45) 64 C5
Courtenot (10) 66 C4
Courteranges (10) 66 C3
Courteron (10) 66 D6
Courtes (01) 116 D2
Courtesoult-et-Gatey (70) 86 D3
Courtetain-et-Salans (25) 88 A6
la Courtète (11) 186 C4
Courteuil (60) 43 E1
Courthézon (84) 175 E1
Courthiézy (51) 44 C2
Courties (32) 167 E5
Courtieux (60) 21 G5
Courtillers (72) 77 F1
Courtils (50) 35 H4
la Courtine (23) 125 H4
Courtisols (51) 46 A3
Courtivron (21) 85 G4
Courtoin (89) 64 D5
Courtois-sur-Yonne (89) 65 E4
Courtomer (61) 39 G6
Courtomer (77) 43 G6
Courtonne-la-Meurdrac (14) 15 F5
Courtonne-les-Deux-Églises (14) 15 G5
Courtrizy-et-Fussigny (02) 22 D3
Courtry (77) 43 E3
Courvaudon (14) 38 B2
Courvières (25) 103 G4
Courville (51) 22 C6
Courville-sur-Eure (28) 61 H2
Courzieu (69) 129 G3
Cousance (39) 117 E2
Cousances-les-Forges (55) 47 E6
Cousances-lès-Triconville (55) 47 F4
Cousolre (59) 10 B3
Coussa (09) 185 H4
Coussac-Bonneval (87) 124 B5
Coussan (65) 183 F3
Coussay (86) 94 B4
Coussay-les-Bois (86) 95 E5
Coussegrey (10) 66 A4
Coussey (88) 68 D2
Coust (18) 98 A6
Coustaussa (11) 186 D6
Coustouge (11) 187 G5
Coustouges (66) 200 D5
Coutances (50) 36 D1
Coutansouze (03) 113 F5
Coutarnoux (89) 84 A4
Coutençon (77) 64 C2
Coutens (09) 186 A4
Couternon (21) 86 A6
Couteuges (43) 141 H2
Coutevroult (77) 43 G4
Couthenans (70) 88 C3
Couthures-sur-Garonne (47) 150 B3
Coutiches (59) 8 D1
Coutières (79) 108 B2
Coutouvre (42) 115 F6
Coutras (33) 135 H3
Couture (16) 122 C1
la Couture (62) 2 D5
la Couture (85) 91 H6
la Couture-Boussey (27) 41 F3
Couture-d'Argenson (79) 108 B6
Couture-sur-Loir (41) 78 D2
Couturelle (62) 7 H3
Coutures (24) 136 D1
Coutures (33) 150 B1
Coutures (82) 168 C2
Couvains (50) 13 F6
la Couvertoirade (12) 172 C3
Couvertpuis (55) 47 F6
Couvignon (10) 67 E4
Couville (50) 12 C2
Couvonges (55) 46 D4
Couvrelles (02) 22 B5
Couvron-et-Aumencourt (02) 22 B2
Couvrot (51) 46 B5
Coux (07) 157 H1
Coux (17) 135 G1
Coux et Bigaroque-Mouzens (24) 137 G6
Couy (18) 98 B2
la Couyère (35) 57 G5
Couze-et-Saint-Front (24) 137 F6
Couzeix (87) 124 B2
Couziers (37) 94 A2
Couzon (03) 113 G1
Couzon-au-Mont-d'Or (69) 130 A2
Couzou (46) 138 D6
Cox (31) 168 C4
Coye-la-Forêt (60) 42 D1
Coyecques (62) 2 A5
Coyolles (02) 21 G6

Coyrière (39) 118 A3
Coyron (39) 117 G2
Coyviller (54) 48 D6
Cozes (17) 120 D4
Cozzano (2A) 205 E5
Crach (56) 72 C1
Crachier (38) 130 D5
Crain (89) 83 F4
Craincourt (57) 48 D3
Craintilleux (42) 129 E5
Crainvilliers (88) 69 E4
Cramaille (02) 22 B6
Cramans (39) 103 E3
Cramant (51) 45 F3
Cramchaban (17) 107 F4
Craménil (61) 38 C2
Cramoisy (60) 20 C6
Cramont (80) 7 E4
Crampagna (09) 185 H5
Crancey (10) 65 G1
Crandelles (15) 140 A5
Crannes-en-Champagne (72) 59 H6
Crans (01) 130 C1
Crans (39) 103 F6
Cransac (12) 154 A3
Crantenoy (54) 69 G1
Cranves-Sales (74) 118 D5
Craon (53) 76 B1
Craon (86) 93 H5
Craonne (02) 22 D4
Craonnelle (02) 22 D4
Crapeaumesnil (60) 21 F2
Craponne (69) 129 H3
Craponne-sur-Arzon (43) 142 C1
Cras (38) 145 E2
Cras (46) 152 D2
Cras-sur-Reyssouze (01) 116 D4
Crastatt (67) 50 C5
Crastes (32) 168 A4
Crasville (27) 18 C6
Crasville (50) 13 E3
Crasville-la-Mallet (76) 17 E3
Crasville-la-Rocquefort (76) 17 F3
la Crau (83) 193 F5
Cravanche (90) 88 C3
Cravans (17) 121 E4
Cravant (45) 80 B2
Cravant-les-Côteaux (37) 94 C2
Cravencères (32) 166 D4
Cravent (78) 41 F2
Crayssac (46) 152 C3
Craywick (59) 2 B2
Crazannes (17) 121 E2
Créances (50) 12 C6
Créancey (21) 101 E1
Crécey-sur-Tille (21) 85 H4
Crèches-sur-Saône (71) 116 B4
Créchets (65) 184 A5
Créchy (03) 114 A4
Crécy-au-Mont (02) 22 A4
Crécy-Couvé (28) 41 E5
Crécy-en-Ponthieu (80) 6 D3
Crécy-la-Chapelle (77) 43 G4
Crécy-sur-Serre (02) 22 C2
Crédin (56) 55 G3
Crégols (46) 153 E3
Crégy-lès-Meaux (77) 43 G3
Créhange (57) 49 F1
Créhen (22) 34 C4
Creil (60) 20 D6
Creissan (34) 188 A2
Creissels (12) 172 A1
Crémarest (62) 1 G4
Cremeaux (42) 128 C2
Crémery (80) 21 F1
Crémieu (38) 130 D3
Crempigny-Bonneguête (74) 131 H1
Cremps (46) 152 D4
Crenans (39) 117 H2
Creney-près-Troyes (10) 66 B3
Crennes-sur-Fraubée (53) 59 F2
Créon (33) 135 G6
Créon-d'Armagnac (40) 166 C1
Créot (71) 101 F4
Crépand (21) 84 C3
Crépey (54) 69 E1
Crépol (26) 144 C2
Crépon (14) 14 A3
Crépy (02) 22 B3
Crépy (62) 2 A6
Crépy-en-Valois (60) 21 F6
Créquy (62) 1 H6
le Crès (34) 173 G5
Cresancey (70) 86 D5
Crésantignes (10) 66 A4
les Cresnays (50) 37 F4
Crespian (30) 173 H3
Crespières (78) 42 A3
Crespin (12) 154 A6
Crespin (59) 9 G1
Crespin (81) 170 A1
Crespinet (81) 170 D2
Crespy-le-Neuf (10) 67 E2
Cressanges (03) 113 G3
la Cresse (12) 155 F6
Cressé (17) 121 H1
Cressensac (46) 138 C4
Cresserons (14) 14 B3
Cresseveuille (14) 15 E4
Cressia (39) 117 F2
Cressin-Rochefort (01) 131 G3
Cressonsacq (60) 20 D4
Cressy (76) 17 H3

Cressy-Omencourt (80) 21 F2
Cressy-sur-Somme (71) 100 A6
Crest (26) 158 C1
le Crest (63) 127 F4
Crest-Voland (73) 132 D2
Creste (63) 127 E5
le Crestet (07) 143 H4
Crestet (84) 158 D5
Crestot (27) 18 C6
Créteil (94) 42 D4
Crêts en Belledonne (38) 132 A6
Creully sur Seulles (14) 14 A3
la Creuse (70) 87 H3
Creuse (80) 7 F6
le Creusot (71) 101 E5
Creutzwald (57) 27 F4
Creuzier-le-Neuf (03) 114 A5
Creuzier-le-Vieux (03) 114 A5
Crevans-et-la-Chapelle-lès-Granges (70) 88 B4
Crevant (36) 111 G2
Crevant-Laveine (63) 127 G2
Crévéchamps (54) 48 D6
Crèvecœur-en-Brie (77) 43 G5
Crèvecœur-le-Grand (60) 20 A3
Crèvecœur-le-Petit (60) 20 D3
Crèvecœur-sur-l'Escaut (59) 9 E4
Creveney (70) 87 H2
Crévic (54) 49 E5
Crevin (35) 57 F4
Crévoux (05) 161 F2
Creys-Mépieu (38) 131 E3
Creyssac (24) 137 E1
Creysse (24) 137 E5
Creysse (46) 138 D5
Creysseilles (07) 143 G6
Creyssensac-et-Pissot (24) 137 F3
Crézançay-sur-Cher (18) 97 G5
Crézancy (02) 44 C2
Crézancy-en-Sancerre (18) 82 A6
Crézières (79) 108 B5
Crézilles (54) 48 B6
Cricquebœuf (14) 15 F3
Cricqueville-en-Auge (14) 14 D4
Cricqueville-en-Bessin (14) 13 F4
Criel-sur-Mer (76) 6 A5
Crillon (60) 19 H3
Crillon-le-Brave (84) 158 D6
Crimolois (21) 102 A1
Crion (54) 49 E5
la Crique (76) 17 H4
Criquebeuf-en-Caux (76) 16 C3
Criquebeuf-la-Campagne (27) 18 C6
Criquebeuf-sur-Seine (27) 18 C5
Criquetot-le-Mauconduit (76) 16 D3
Criquetot-l'Esneval (76) 16 B4
Criquetot-sur-Longueville (76) 17 G3
Criquetot-sur-Ouville (76) 17 F4
Criquiers (76) 19 G2
Crisenoy (77) 43 F6
Crisolles (60) 21 G3
Crissay-sur-Manse (37) 94 C2
Crissé (72) 59 H4
Crissey (39) 102 C2
Crissey (71) 101 G5
Cristinacce (2A) 204 C3
Cristot (14) 14 A4
Criteuil-la-Magdeleine (16) 121 H5
Critot (76) 18 D3
Croce (2B) 205 G1
Crochte (59) 2 B2
Crocicchia (2B) 203 F6
Crocq (23) 126 A2
le Crocq (60) 20 B3
Crocy (14) 39 E3
Crœttwiller (67) 51 G2
Croignon (33) 135 G5
Croisette (62) 7 G2
le Croisic (44) 73 E4
la Croisille (27) 40 C2
la Croisille-sur-Briance (87) 124 D4
Croisilles (14) 38 C2
Croisilles (28) 41 F5
Croisilles (61) 39 G4
Croisilles (62) 8 B3
Croismare (54) 49 F6
Croissy-Beaubourg (77) 43 F4
Croissy-sur-Celle (60) 20 B2
Croissy-sur-Seine (78) 42 B4
le Croisty (56) 54 C2
Croisy (18) 98 B4
Croisy-sur-Andelle (76) 19 E4
Croisy-sur-Eure (27) 41 F2
Croix (59) 3 G4
Croix (90) 88 D4
la Croix-aux-Bois (08) 24 B4
la Croix-aux-Mines (88) 70 D3
la Croix-Blanche (47) 151 F5
la Croix-Caluyau (59) 9 G4
la Croix-Chapeau (17) 106 D5
la Croix-Comtesse (17) 107 G5
la Croix-de-la-Rochette (73) 132 B5
la Croix-du-Perche (28) 61 G3
la Croix-en-Brie (77) 43 H6
la Croix-en-Champagne (51) 46 B2
la Croix-en-Ternois (62) 7 G1
la Croix-en-Touraine (37) 79 F6
la Croix-Fonsomme (02) 9 E6
la Croix-Helléan (56) 56 A4
la Croix-Mare (76) 18 B3
la Croix-Moligneaux (80) 21 G1
la Croix-sur-Gartempe (87) 110 A5
la Croix-sur-Ourcq (02) 44 B1

la Croix-sur-Roudoule (06) 178 C1
la Croix-Valmer (83) 194 B4
Croixanvec (56) 55 F2
Croixdalle (76) 19 E1
la Croixille (53) 58 B3
Croixrault (80) 20 A1
Croizet-sur-Gand (42) 129 E2
Crolles (38) 145 H1
Cromac (87) 110 C3
Cromary (70) 87 F5
Cronat (71) 99 H6
Cronce (43) 141 G3
la Cropte (53) 59 E6
Cropus (76) 17 G3
Cros (30) 173 F2
le Cros (34) 172 C3
Cros (63) 126 B6
Cros-de-Géorand (07) 142 D6
Cros-de-Montvert (15) 139 G4
Cros-de-Ronesque (15) 140 C5
Crosey-le-Grand (25) 88 A5
Crosey-le-Petit (25) 88 A5
Crosmières (72) 77 G2
Crosne (91) 42 D5
Crossac (44) 73 H3
Crosses (18) 98 A3
Crosville-la-Vieille (27) 40 C1
Crosville-sur-Douve (50) 12 D4
Crosville-sur-Scie (76) 17 G3
Crotelles (37) 79 E4
Crotenay (39) 103 E5
Croth (27) 41 F4
le Crotoy (80) 6 C3
Crots (05) 161 E2
Crottes-en-Pithiverais (45) 63 E5
Crottet (01) 116 B4
le Crouais (35) 56 C2
Crouay (14) 13 H5
Crouseilles (64) 166 C6
Croutelle (86) 109 E2
les Croûtes (10) 65 H6
Croutoy (60) 21 G5
Croutes (61) 39 F3
Crouttes-sur-Marne (02) 44 A3
Crouy (02) 22 A5
Crouy-en-Thelle (60) 20 C6
Crouy-Saint-Pierre (80) 7 F5
Crouy-sur-Cosson (41) 80 B3
Crouy-sur-Ourcq (77) 43 H2
le Crouzet (25) 103 G6
Crouzet-Migette (25) 103 G3
la Crouzille (63) 112 D5
Crouzilles (37) 94 C2
Crozant (23) 111 E3
Croze (23) 125 G3
Crozes-Hermitage (26) 144 A3
Crozet (01) 118 B4
le Crozet (42) 114 D5
les Crozets (39) 117 H2
Crozon (29) 30 D6
Crozon-sur-Vauvre (36) 111 G2
Cruas (07) 158 B1
Crucey-Villages (28) 40 D5
Cruchery (41) 79 G2
Cruet (73) 132 A5
Crugey (21) 101 F2
Crugny (51) 22 D6
Cruguel (56) 55 H4
Cruis (04) 176 C1
Crulai (61) 40 A5
Crupies (26) 158 D2
Crupilly (02) 9 H6
Cruscades (11) 187 H3
Cruseilles (74) 118 B6
Crusnes (54) 26 A2
Cruviers-Lascours (30) 173 H2
Crux-la-Ville (58) 99 G2
Cruzille (71) 116 B2
Cruzilles-lès-Mépillat (01) 116 B4
Cruzy (34) 188 A2
Cruzy-le-Châtel (89) 84 C1
Cry (89) 84 C3
Cubelles (43) 142 A4
Cubières (48) 156 C3
Cubières-sur-Cinoble (11) 187 E6
Cubiérettes (48) 156 C3
Cubjac-Auvézère-Val d'Ans (24) 137 G2
Cublac (19) 138 B3
Cublize (69) 129 F1
Cubnezais (33) 135 F3
Cubry (25) 87 H4
Cubry-lès-Faverney (70) 87 G1
Cubzac-les-Ponts (33) 135 F4
Cucharmoy (77) 44 A6
Cuchery (51) 45 E1
Cucq (62) 1 F6
Cucugnan (11) 200 D1
Cucuron (84) 176 A4
Cudos (33) 149 H4
Cudot (89) 64 D6
Cuébris (06) 178 D2
Cuélas (32) 183 H2
Cuers (83) 193 F4
Cuffies (02) 22 A5
Cuffy (18) 98 D4
Cugand (85) 75 E6
Cuges-les-Pins (13) 192 D4
Cugnaux (31) 169 E6
Cugney (70) 86 D5
Cugny (02) 21 H2
Cuguen (35) 35 F5
Cuguron (31) 183 H4
Cuhon (86) 94 A5
Cuignières (60) 20 D4
Cuigy-en-Bray (60) 19 H4

Cuillé (53)........58 A5
Cuinchy (62)........2 D6
Cuincy (59)........8 C1
le Cuing (31)........184 A4
Cuinzier (42)........115 F5
Cuirieux (02)........22 D2
Cuiry-Housse (02)........22 B6
Cuiry-lès-Chaudardes (02)........22 D5
Cuiry-lès-Iviers (02)........23 F1
Cuis (51)........45 F2
Cuise-la-Motte (60)........21 G5
Cuiseaux (71)........117 E2
Cuiserey (21)........86 B5
Cuisery (71)........116 C1
Cuisia (39)........117 F2
Cuisles (51)........44 D1
Cuissai (61)........59 H1
Cuissy-et-Geny (02)........22 C4
Cuisy (55)........24 D6
Cuisy (77)........43 F2
Cuisy-en-Almont (02)........21 H4
Culan (18)........112 B2
Culètre (21)........101 E2
Culey (55)........47 F4
Culey-le-Patry (14)........38 B2
Culhat (63)........127 G2
Culin (38)........130 D5
Culles-les-Roches (71)........116 A1
Culmont (52)........86 B1
Culoz (01)........131 G2
Cult (70)........86 D6
Cultures (48)........155 H3
Cumières (51)........45 E2
Cumières-le-Mort-
    Homme (55)........25 E6
Cumiès (11)........186 A2
Cumont (82)........168 B3
Cunac (81)........170 C2
Cuncy-lès-Varzy (58)........83 F6
Cunèges (24)........136 D6
Cunel (55)........24 D5
Cunelières (90)........88 D3
Cunfin (10)........67 E5
Cunlhat (63)........128 A4
Cuon (49)
Cuperly (51)........45 H2
Cuq (47)........168 A1
Cuq (81)........170 B5
Cuq-Toulza (81)........170 A6
Cuqueron (64)........182 A2
Curac (16)........136 B1
Curan (12)........155 E6
Curbans (04)........160 B3
Curbigny (71)........115 G4
Curçay-sur-Dive (86)........93 H3
Curchy (80)........21 F1
Curciat-Dongalon (01)........116 D2
Curdin (71)........115 E1
Curel (04)........159 G6
Curel (52)........67 H1
Curemonte (19)........139 E4
Cures (72)........59 H5
Curgies (59)........9 G2
Curgy (71)........100 D3
Curienne (73)........132 A4
Curières (12)........155 E2
Curis-au-Mont-d'Or (69)........130 A2
Curley (21)........101 G1
Curlu (80)........8 B5
Curmont (52)........67 G3
Curnier (26)........159 E4
Cursan (33)........135 G2
Curtafond (01)........116 C4
Curtil-Saint-Seine (21)........85 G5
Curtil-sous-Buffières (71)........115 H3
Curtil-sous-Burnand (71)........116 A1
Curtil-Vergy (21)........101 G2
Curvalle (81)........171 E2
Curzay-sur-Vonne (86)........108 C2
Curzon (85)........91 G6
Cusance (25)........88 A6
Cuse-et-Adrisans (25)........87 H4
Cusey (52)........86 B3
Cussac (15)........141 E4
Cussac (87)........123 G3
Cussac-Fort-Médoc (33)........134 D3
Cussac-sur-Loire (43)........142 C4
Cussangy (10)........66 B6
Cussay (37)........95 E3
Cusset (03)........114 A5
Cussey-les-Forges (21)........85 H3
Cussey-sur-Lison (25)........103 F2
Cussey-sur-l'Ognon (25)........87 F6
Cussy (14)........13 H5
Cussy-en-Morvan (71)........100 C2
Cussy-la-Colonne (21)........101 F3
Cussy-le-Châtel (21)........101 E2
Cussy-les-Forges (89)........84 B5
Custines (54)........48 C4
Cusy (74)........132 A3
Cutry (02)........21 H5
Cutry (54)........25 H4
Cuts (60)........21 G3
Cutting (57)........49 G3
Cuttoli-Corticchiato (2A)........204 D5
Cuvat (74)........132 A1
Cuve (70)........69 G6
Cuvergnon (60)........43 H1
Cuverville (14)........14 C4
Cuverville (27)........19 E5
Cuverville (76)........16 B4
Cuverville-sur-Yères (76)........6 B5
Cuves (50)........37 F4
Cuves (52)........68 B5
Cuvier (39)........103 G5
Cuvillers (59)........9 E3
Cuvilly (60)........21 E3
Cuvry (57)........48 C2
Cuxac-Cabardès (11)........186 D2

Cuxac-d'Aude (11)........188 A3
Cuy (60)........21 F3
Cuy (89)........65 E3
Cuy-Saint-Fiacre (76)........19 G3
Cuzac (46)........153 H2
Cuzance (46)........138 C4
Cuzieu (01)........131 F2
Cuzieu (42)........129 E4
Cuzion (36)........111 E2
Cuzorn (47)........151 H2
Cuzy (71)........100 B5
Cys-la-Commune (02)........22 C5
Cysoing (59)........3 G5

D

Dabo (57)........50 B5
Dachstein (67)........50 D6
Dadonville (45)........63 F4
Daglan (24)........152 B1
Dagneux (01)........130 C2
Dagny (77)........44 A5
Dagny-Lambercy (02)........23 E1
Dagonville (55)........47 F4
Dahlenheim (67)........50 D5
Daignac (33)........135 G6
Daigny (08)........24 C2
Daillancourt (52)........67 G3
Daillecourt (52)........68 C5
Dainville (62)........8 B2
Dainville-Bertheléville (55)........68 C2
Daix (21)........85 G6
Dalem (57)........27 E4
Dalhain (57)........49 F3
Dalhunden (67)........51 F4
Dallet (63)........127 F3
Dallon (02)........21 H1
Dalou (09)........185 H5
Dalstein (57)........26 D3
Daluis (06)........178 B1
Damas-aux-Bois (88)........70 A2
Damas-et-Bettegney (88)........69 G3
Damazan (47)........150 C5
Dambach (67)........50 D2
Dambach-la-Ville (67)........71 F2
Dambelin (25)........88 B5
Dambenois (25)........88 C4
Dambenoît-lès-
    Colombe (70)........87 H2
Damblain (88)........68 D5
Damblainville (14)........39 E3
Dambron (28)........62 D5
Dame-Marie (61)........60 D2
Dame-Marie-les-Bois (37)........79 F4
Damelevières (54)........49 E6
Daméraucourt (60)........19 H2
Damerey (71)........101 H5
Damery (51)........45 E2
Damery (80)........21 E2
Damgan (56)........73 E2
Damiatte (81)........170 B5
Damigny (61)........60 A1
Damloup (55)........25 F6
Dammard (02)........44 A1
Dammarie (28)........62 A1
Dammarie-en-Puisaye (45)........82 B3
Dammarie-les-Lys (77)........64 A1
Dammarie-sur-Loing (45)........82 B2
Dammarie-sur-Saulx (55)........47 F6
Dammartin-en-Goële (77)........43 F2
Dammartin-en-Serve (78)........41 G3
Dammartin-les-
    Templiers (25)........87 H6
Dammartin-Marpain (39)........102 D1
Dammartin-sur-Meuse (52)........68 C6
Dammartin-sur-
    Tigeaux (77)........43 G4
Damousies (59)........10 A3
Damouzy (08)........24 A1
Damparis (39)........102 C2
Dampierre (10)........66 C1
Dampierre (39)........103 E2
Dampierre (52)........88 B6
Dampierre-au-Temple (51)........45 H4
Dampierre-en-Bray (76)........19 G3
Dampierre-en-Bresse (71)........102 B5
Dampierre-en-Burly (45)........81 H2
Dampierre-en-Crot (18)........81 H5
Dampierre-en-Graçay (18)........97 E2
Dampierre-en-
    Montagne (21)........85 E5
Dampierre-en-
    Yvelines (78)........42 B5
Dampierre-et-Flée (21)........86 B5
Dampierre-le-Château (51)........46 C2
Dampierre-les-Bois (25)........88 D4
Dampierre-lès-
    Conflans (70)........87 G1
Dampierre-Saint-
    Nicolas (76)........17 H2
Dampierre-sous-
    Bouhy (58)........82 D5
Dampierre-sous-Brou (28)........61 G4
Dampierre-sous-Avre (28)........40 D4
Dampierre-sur-
    Boutonne (17)........107 H6
Dampierre-sur-le-
    Doubs (25)........88 C4
Dampierre-sur-Linotte (70)........87 H3
Dampierre-sur-Moivre (51)........46 A3
Dampierre-sur-Salon (70)........86 D4
Dampjoux (25)........88 C5
Dampleux (02)........21 H6
Dampmart (77)........43 F3
Dampniat (19)........138 D3
Damprichard (25)........88 D6
les Damps (27)........18 D5

Dampvalley-lès-
    Colombe (70)........87 G3
Dampvalley-Saint-
    Pancras (70)........69 G6
Dampvitoux (54)........48 A2
Damrémont (52)........68 D6
Damvillers (55)........25 F5
Damvix (85)........107 F3
Dancé (42)........128 D2
Dancevoir (52)........67 G6
Dancourt (76)........6 B6
Dancourt-Popincourt (80)........21 E2
Dancy (28)........62 A4
Danestal (14)........15 E4
Dangé-Saint-Romain (86)........94 D4
Dangeau (28)........61 H4
Dangers (28)........62 A1
Dangeul (72)........60 B3
Dangolsheim (67)........50 C6
Dangu (27)........19 G6
Dangy (50)........37 F1
Danizy (02)........22 A2
Danjoutin (90)........88 C3
Danne-et-Quatre-
    Vents (57)........50 B4
Dannelbourg (57)........50 B4
Dannemarie (25)........88 D5
Dannemarie (68)........89 E3
Dannemarie (78)........41 G5
Dannemarie-sur-Crète (25)........103 F1
Dannemoine (89)........84 A1
Dannemois (91)........63 H2
Dannes (62)........1 F5
Dannevoux (55)........25 E5
Danzé (41)........79 F1
Daon (53)........76 D2
Daoulas (29)........31 F5
Daours (80)........7 H6
Darazac (19)........139 G3
Darbonnay (39)........102 D5
Darbres (07)........157 H2
Darcey (21)........85 E4
Dardenac (33)........135 G6
Dardez (27)........41 E2
Dardilly (69)........129 H3
Dareizé (69)........129 G2
Dargies (60)........20 A2
Dargnies (80)........6 B4
Dargoire (42)........129 H5
Darmannes (52)........68 A4
Darnac (87)........110 A4
Darnétal (76)........18 D4
Darnets (19)........125 G6
Darney (88)........69 F5
Darney-aux-Chênes (88)........68 D3
Darnieulles (88)........69 H4
Darois (21)........85 G5
Darvault (77)........64 A3
Darvoy (45)........81 E1
Dasle (25)........88 D4
Daubensand (67)........71 H2
Daubeuf-la-Campagne (27)........18 C6
Daubeuf-près-
    Vatteville (27)........19 E6
Daubeuf-Serville (76)........16 D4
Daubèze (33)........150 A1
Dauendorf (67)........50 D3
Daumazan-sur-Arize (09)........185 F4
Dauphin (04)........176 C2
Dausse (47)........151 G4
Daux (31)........169 E4
Dauzat-sur-Vodable (63)........127 F6
Davayat (63)........127 F1
Davayé (71)........116 B4
Davejean (11)........187 F5
Davenescourt (80)........20 D2
Davézieux (07)........143 H2
Davignac (19)........125 G6
Davrey (10)........66 A5
Davron (78)........42 A4
Dax (40)........165 E4
Deauville (14)........15 E3
Deaux (30)........173 H1
Débats-Rivière-d'Orpra (42)........128 C3
Decazeville (12)........154 A2
Dechy (59)........8 D2
Décines-Charpieu (69)........130 B3
Decize (58)........99 F5
Dégagnac (46)........152 C1
Degré (72)........60 A5
Dehault (72)........60 D4
Dehéries (59)........9 E4
Dehlingen (67)........50 B2
Deinvillers (88)........70 A2
Delain (70)........86 D4
Delettes (62)........2 A5
Delincourt (60)........19 H6
Delle (90)........88 D4
Delme (57)........49 E3
Delouze-Rosières (55)........47 G6
Deluz (25)........87 G6
Demandolx (04)........178 A2
Demange-aux-Eaux (55)........47 G6
Demangevelle (70)........69 F6
Demi-Quartier (74)........133 E2
la Demie (70)........87 G3
Demigny (71)........101 G4

Deneuille-les-Mines (03)........113 E3
Deneuvre (54)........70 B1
Denèvre (70)........86 D4
Dénezé-sous-Doué (49)........93 F1
Denezières (39)........117 H1
Denguin (64)........182 A1
Denicé (69)........129 H1
Denier (62)........7 H2
Denipaire (88)........70 D2
Denneville (50)........12 C5
Dennebrœucq (62)........2 A5
Dennevy (71)........101 F4
Denney (90)........88 D3
Denonville (28)........62 D2
Denting (57)........27 E4
Déols (36)........96 C5
Derbamont (88)........69 G3
Dercé (86)........94 B4
Dercy (02)........22 C2
Dernacueillette (11)........187 F6
Dernancourt (80)........8 A5
Derval (44)........74 C1
Désaignes (07)........143 G4
Désandans (25)........88 B4
Descartes (37)........95 E3
le Deschaux (39)........102 C4
Désertines (03)........112 D3
Désertines (53)........58 C1
les Déserts (73)........132 A4
Déservillers (25)........103 G3
Desges (43)........141 H4
Desingy (74)........118 A6
Desmonts (45)........63 H4
Desnes (39)........102 C5
Desseling (57)........49 G4
Dessenheim (68)........71 G5
Destord (88)........70 B3
la Destrousse (13)........192 C3
Destry (57)........49 F2
Desvres (62)........1 G5
Détain-et-Bruant (21)........101 G2
Dissé-sous-Ballon (72)........60 B3
Dissé-sous-le-Lude (72)........78 A3
Détrier (73)........132 A6
le Détroit (14)........38 C3
Dettey (71)........100 C5
Dettwiller (67)........50 C4
Deuil-la-Barre (95)........42 D3
Deuillet (02)........22 A2
Deûlémont (59)........3 F4
les Deux Alpes (38)........146 B4
Deux-Chaises (03)........113 F3
Deux-Évailles (53)........59 E4
les Deux-Fays (39)........102 C4
Deux-Jumeaux (14)........13 G4
Deux Rivières (89)........83 G3
Deux-Verges (15)........141 E6
les Deux-Villes (08)........24 D2
Deuxville (54)........49 E5
Devay (58)........99 G5
Devecey (25)........87 F6
Devesset (07)........143 F4
Devèze (65)........183 H2
Déviat (16)........122 A6
Dévillac (47)........151 G2
Deville (08)........11 E6
Déville-lès-Rouen (76)........18 C4
Devise (80)........8 C6
Dévoluy (05)........160 A1
Devrouze (71)........102 A5
Deycimont (88)........70 B3
Deyme (31)........185 G1
Deyvillers (88)........70 A3
le Dézert (50)........13 E6
Dezize-lès-Maranges (71)........101 F4
D'Huison-Longueville (91)........63 G2
Dhuisy (77)........44 A2
Dhuizel (02)........22 C5
Dhuizon (41)........80 C4
Dhuys et Morin-en-
    Brie (02)........44 C4
Dialan sur Chaîne (14)........38 A2
Diancey (21)........100 D2
Diane-Capelle (57)........49 H4
Diant (77)........64 C3
Diarville (54)........69 F2
Diconne (71)........102 A5
Die (26)........145 E6
Diebling (57)........27 G5
Diebolsheim (67)........71 H2
Diedendorf (67)........50 A3
Dieffenbach-au-Val (67)........71 F2
Dieffenbach-lès-
    Wœrth (67)........51 E2
Dieffenthal (67)........71 F2
Diefmatten (68)........89 E2
Dième (69)........129 F1
Diemeringen (67)........50 B2
Diémoz (38)........130 C4
Diénay (21)........85 H4
Dienne (15)........140 D3
Dienné (86)........109 F2
Diennes-Aubigny (58)........99 G4
Dienville (10)........66 D5
Dieppe (76)........17 G2
Dieppe-sous-
    Douaumont (55)........25 F6
Dierre (37)........79 H4
Dierrey-Saint-Julien (10)........65 H3
Dierrey-Saint-Pierre (10)........65 H3
Diesen (57)........27 E5
Dietwiller (68)........89 G2
Dieudonné (60)........20 B6
Dieue-sur-Meuse (55)........47 F2
Dieulefit (26)........158 D3
Dieulivol (33)........150 C1
Dieulouard (54)........48 C4
Dieupentale (82)........169 E3
Dieuze (57)........49 G4
Diéval (62)........7 H1

Diffembach-lès-
    Hellimer (57)........49 G2
Diges (89)........83 E2
Digna (39)........117 F2
Digne (16)........122 C5
la Digne-d'Amont (11)........186 C5
la Digne-d'Aval (11)........186 D5
Digne-les-Bains (04)........160 C6
Dignonville (88)........70 A3
Digny (28)........61 G1
Digoin (71)........114 D2
Digosville (50)........12 D2
Dijon (21)........85 H6
Dimancheville (45)........63 G4
Dimbsthal (67)........50 C5
Dimechaux (59)........10 A3
Dimont (59)........10 A3
Dinan (22)........34 D5
Dinard (35)........34 D3
Dinéault (29)........31 F6
Dingé (35)........35 F6
Dingsheim (67)........51 E5
Dingy-en-Vuache (74)........118 A5
Dingy-Saint-Clair (74)........132 B1
Dinozé (88)........70 A4
Dinsac (87)........110 B4
Dinsheim-sur-Bruche (67)........50 C6
Dinteville (52)........67 F6
Dio-et-Valquières (34)........172 B5
Dions (30)........174 A2
Diors (36)........96 D5
Diou (03)........114 C2
Diou (36)........97 E3
Dirac (16)........122 C4
Dirinon (29)........31 F5
Dirol (58)........83 G6
Dissangis (89)........84 A4
Dissay (86)........94 C6
Dissay-sous-
    Courcillon (72)........78 C3
Dissé-sous-Ballon (72)........60 B3
Dissé-sous-le-Lude (72)........78 A3
Distré (49)........93 G1
Distroff (57)........26 C3
Diusse (64)........166 C5
Divajeu (26)........158 C1
Divatte-sur-Loire (44)........75 E5
Dives (60)........21 F3
Dives-sur-Mer (14)........14 D4
Divion (62)........2 C6
Divonne-les-Bains (01)........118 C3
Dixmont (89)........65 E3
Dizimieu (38)........130 D3
Dizy (51)........45 F2
Dizy-le-Gros (02)........23 E2
Doazit (40)........165 H4
Doazon (64)........165 H6
Docelles (88)........70 B4
Dœuil-sur-le-Mignon (17)........107 G5
Dognen (64)........181 H2
Dogneville (88)........70 A3
Dohem (62)........2 A5
Dohis (02)........23 F1
Doignies (59)........8 C4
Doingt (80)........8 C6
Doissat (24)........152 A1
Doissin (38)........131 E3
Doix lès Fontaines (85)........107 F3
Doizieux (42)........129 G6
Dol-de-Bretagne (35)........35 E4
Dolaincourt (88)........68 D2
Dolancourt (10)........67 E3
Dolcourt (54)........69 E1
Dole (39)........102 C2
Dolignon (02)........23 E2
Dolleren (68)........88 D1
Dollon (72)........60 D5
Dollot (89)........64 C4
Dolmayrac (47)........151 F4
Dolomieu (38)........131 E4
Dolus-d'Oléron (17)........120 A1
Dolus-le-Sec (37)........95 F2
Dolving (57)........49 H4
Dom-le-Mesnil (08)........24 B2
Domagné (35)........57 G3
Domaize (63)........128 A4
Domalain (35)........57 H4
Domancy (74)........133 E1
Domarin (38)........130 D4
Domart-en-Ponthieu (80)........7 F4
Domart-sur-la-Luce (80)........20 D1
Domats (89)........64 C5
Domazan (30)........174 D2
Dombasle-devant-
    Darney (88)........69 F4
Dombasle-en-Argonne (55)........47 E1
Dombasle-en-Xaintois (88)........69 F3
Dombasle-sur-
    Meurthe (54)........48 D5
Domblain (52)........67 G1
Domblans (39)........102 D5
Dombras (55)........25 F5
Dombrot-le-Sec (88)........69 E4
Dombrot-sur-Vair (88)........69 E3
Domecy-sur-Cure (89)........83 H5
Domecy-sur-le-Vault (89)........83 H5
Doméliers (60)........20 B2
Domène (38)........145 H2
Domérat (03)........112 C3
Domesmont (80)........7 F4
Domessargues (30)........173 H2
Domessin (73)........131 G5
Domèvre-en-Haye (54)........48 B4
Domèvre-sous-
    Montfort (88)........69 F3
Domèvre-sur-Avière (88)........69 H3
Domèvre-sur-Durbion (88)........70 A3
Domèvre-sur-Vezouze (54)........49 G6

Domeyrat (43)........141 H2
Domeyrot (23)........112 A4
Domezain-Berraute (64)........181 F1
Domfaing (88)........70 B3
Domfessel (67)........50 A2
Domfront (60)........20 D3
Domfront-en-
    Champagne (72)........59 H4
Domfront en Poiraie (61)........38 A6
Domgermain (54)........48 A5
la Dominelais (35)........57 E6
Dominois (80)........6 D2
Domjean (50)........37 G2
Domjevin (54)........49 G6
Domjulien (88)........69 F3
Domléger-Longvillers (80)........7 F3
Domloup (35)........57 G3
Dommarie-Eulmont (54)........69 F2
Dommarien (52)........86 B3
Dommartemont (54)........48 D5
Dommartin (01)........116 C3
Dommartin (25)........103 H4
Dommartin (58)........100 A3
Dommartin (69)........129 H2
Dommartin (80)........20 C1
Dommartin-aux-Bois (88)........69 G4
Dommartin-Dampierre (51)........46 C2
Dommartin-la-
    Chaussée (54)........48 A2
Dommartin-la-
    Montagne (55)........47 H2
Dommartin-le-Coq (10)........66 C1
Dommartin-le-Franc (52)........67 G2
Dommartin-le-Saint-
    Père (52)........67 G2
Dommartin-lès-
    Cuiseaux (71)........117 E2
Dommartin-lès-
    Remiremont (88)........70 B5
Dommartin-lès-Toul (54)........48 B5
Dommartin-lès-Vallois (88)........69 F4
Dommartin-Lettrée (51)........45 H5
Dommartin-sous-
    Amance (54)........48 D4
Dommartin-sous-Hans (51)........46 C1
Dommartin-sur-Vraine (88)........69 E2
Dommartin-Varimont (51)........46 C3
Dommary-Baroncourt (55)........25 G5
Domme (24)........138 A6
Dommery (08)........23 H2
Dommiers (02)........21 H5
Domnom-lès-Dieuze (57)........49 G3
Domont (95)........42 D2
Dompaire (88)........69 G3
Dompcevrin (55)........47 G3
Dompierre (60)........20 D3
Dompierre (61)........38 B5
Dompierre (88)........70 A3
Dompierre-aux-Bois (55)........47 G2
Dompierre-
    Becquincourt (80)........8 B6
Dompierre-du-Chemin (35)........58 A3
Dompierre-en-Morvan (21)........84 C5
Dompierre-les-Églises (87)........110 C4
Dompierre-les-Ormes (71)........115 H3
Dompierre-les-Tilleuls (25)........103 H4
Dompierre-sous-
    Sanvignes (71)........115 F1
Dompierre-sur-Authie (80)........7 E2
Dompierre-sur-Besbre (03)........114 C2
Dompierre-sur-
    Chalaronne (01)........116 C5
Dompierre-sur-
    Charente (17)........121 F3
Dompierre-sur-Helpe (59)........9 H4
Dompierre-sur-Mer (17)........106 D4
Dompierre-sur-Mont (39)........117 G1
Dompierre-sur-Nièvre (58)........99 E1
Dompierre-sur-Veyle (01)........116 D6
Dompierre-sur-Yon (85)........91 G4
Dompnac (07)........157 E2
Domprel (25)........104 B1
Dompremy (51)........46 C5
Domprix (54)........25 H5
Domps (87)........125 E4
Domptail (88)........70 B1
Domptail-en-l'Air (54)........69 G1
Domptin (02)........44 B2
Domqueur (80)........7 E4
Domremy-la-Canne (55)........25 G5
Domrémy-la-Pucelle (88)........68 D2
Domrémy-Landéville (52)........68 A2
Domsure (01)........117 E3
Domvallier (88)........69 F3
Domvast (80)........7 E3
Don (59)........3 E6
Donazac (11)........186 C4
Donchery (08)........24 B2
Doncières (88)........70 B2
Doncourt-aux-
    Templiers (55)........47 H2
Doncourt-lès-Conflans (54)........26 A5
Doncourt-lès-
    Longuyon (54)........25 G4
Doncourt-sur-Meuse (52)........68 C4
Dondas (47)........151 G5
Donges (44)........73 H4
Donjeux (52)........67 H2
Donjeux (57)........49 E3
le Donjon (03)........114 C3
Donnay (14)........38 C2
Donnazac (81)........170 A2
Donnelay (57)........49 F4
Donnemain-Saint-
    Mamès (28)........62 A5
Donnemarie-Dontilly (77)........64 D1
Donnement (10)........66 D1
Donnenheim (67)........50 D4

Donnery (45)................81 E1
Donneville (31)............185 G1
Donnezac (33)..............135 F1
Dontreix (23)...............126 B1
Dontrien (51)..................23 G6
Donville-les-Bains (50)....36 D3
Donzac (33)..................149 H1
Donzac (82)..................151 G6
Donzacq (40).................165 G4
le Donzeil (23)...............111 G6
Donzenac (19)...............138 C2
Donzère (26).................158 A3
Donzy (58).....................82 D6
Donzy-le-Pertuis (71).....116 A2
Doranges (63)...............128 A6
Dorans (90)....................88 C3
Dorat (63).....................127 H2
le Dorat (87)................110 B5
Dordives (45).................64 B4
Dore-l'Église (63)...........142 B1
la Dorée (53)..................58 B1
Dorengt (02).....................9 G5
Dorlisheim (67)...............50 D6
Dormans (51)..................44 D2
Dormelles (77)................64 B3
la Dornac (24)...............138 B3
Dornas (07)...................143 F5
Dornecy (58)...................83 G5
Dornes (58)....................99 F6
Dorres (66)....................199 G4
Dortan (01)...................117 G3
Dosches (10)...................66 C3
Dosnon (10)....................45 G4
Dossenheim-
   Kochersberg (67)........50 D5
Dossenheim-sur-
   Zinsel (67)..................50 C3
Douadic (36)...................95 G6
Douai (59)........................8 D2
Douains (27)...................41 F2
Douarnenez (29).............53 E2
Douaumont (55)..............25 F6
Doubs (25)....................104 A4
Doucelles (72).................60 A3
Douchapt (24)................136 D2
Douchy (02)....................21 H1
Douchy-lès-Ayette (62).....8 B3
Douchy-les-Mines (59)......9 E2
Douchy-Montcorbon (45)...64 C6
Doucier (39)..................103 E6
Doucy-en-Bauges (73)....132 B3
Doudeauville (62)..............1 G5
Doudeauville (76)............20 B2
Doudeauville-en-Vexin (27)...19 F5
Doudelainville (80)............6 D5
Doudeville (76)................17 E3
Doudrac (47)..................151 F1
Doue (77)........................44 A4
Doué-en-Anjou (49).........93 F1
Douelle (46)...................152 C3
le Douhet (17)...............121 F2
Douillet (72)....................59 H3
Douilly (80).....................21 G1
Doulaincourt-Saucourt (52)...68 A3
Doulcon (55)...................24 D5
Doulevant-le-Château (52)...67 G2
Doulevant-le-Petit (52)....67 G2
Doulezon (33)................136 A6
le Doulieu (59)..................2 D4
Doullens (80)....................7 G3
Doumely-Bégny (08).........23 G2
Doumy (64)....................166 B6
Dounoux (88)...................69 H4
Dourbies (30).................172 C1
Dourdain (35)..................57 H2
Dourdan (91)...................42 D5
Dourges (62).....................8 C1
Dourgne (81)..................186 C1
Douriez (62).....................6 D2
Dourlers (59)...................10 A3
le Dourn (81).................171 E2
Dournazac (87)...............123 G4
Dournon (39).................103 H4
Dours (65).....................183 F2
Doussard (74)................132 B3
Doussay (86)...................94 B4
Douvaine (74)................118 D3
Douville (24).................137 E4
Douville-en-Auge (14)......14 D4
Douville-sur-Andelle (27)...19 E5
Douvrend (76)...................6 A6
Douvres (01)..................130 D1
Douvres-la-Délivrande (14)...14 B3
Douvrin (62).....................3 E6
Doux (08).......................23 H4
Doux (79).......................93 H5
Douy-la-Ramée (77).........43 G2
Douzains (47).................151 E2
Douzat (16)...................122 B3
la Douze (24).................137 G3
Douzens (11)..................187 F3
Douzillac (24)................136 D3
Douzy (08).......................24 C2
Doville (50)......................12 D4
Doye (39)......................103 G5
Doyet (03)......................113 E4
Dozulé (14).....................14 D4
Dracé (69).....................116 B3
Draché (37).....................94 D3
Drachenbronn-
   Birlenbach (67)............51 F2
Dracy (89).......................83 E2
Dracy-le-Fort (71)..........101 G5
Dracy-lès-Couches (71)...101 E4
Dracy-Saint-Loup (71)....100 D3
Dragey-Ronthon (50).......35 G4
Draguignan (83).............177 H5
Draillant (74)..................118 C3

Draix (04)......................160 D6
Draize (08)......................23 G2
Drambon (21)..................86 B6
Dramelay (39)................117 F3
Drancy (93).....................42 D3
Drap (06)......................179 F3
Dravegny (02).................22 C6
Draveil (91)......................42 D5
Drée (21).........................85 F6
Drefféac (44)..................74 A2
Drémil-Lafage (31).........169 G5
la Drenne (60).................20 B5
le Drennec (29)...............31 E3
Dreuil-lès-Amiens (80)......7 F6
Dreuilhe (09).................186 B5
Dreux (28).......................41 F5
Drevant (18)....................97 H6
Dricourt (08)....................23 H5
Driencourt (80)..................8 C5
Drincham (59)...................2 B2
Drocourt (62)....................8 C1
Drocourt (78)..................41 H2
Droisy (27)......................40 D4
Droisy (74)....................131 H1
Droiturier (03)...............114 C5
Droizy (02)......................22 A6
Drom (01)......................117 E4
Dromesnil (80)..................6 D6
Drosay (76)......................17 E3
Drosnay (51)....................46 B6
Droué (41)........................61 G5
Droue-sur-Drouette (28)...41 H6
Drouges (35)...................57 H5
Drouilly (51)....................46 A4
Droupt-Saint-Basle (10)...66 A1
Droupt-Sainte-Marie (10)...2 D6
Drouville (54)..................49 E5
Drouvin-le-Marais (62)......2 D6
Droux (87)......................110 B5
Drubec (14).....................15 E4
Drucat (80).......................6 D4
Drucourt (27)..................15 G5
Drudas (31)....................168 D4
Druelle Balsac (12).........154 C4
Drugeac (15)..................140 A3
Druillat (01)...................117 E6
Drulhe (12)....................153 H3
Drulingen (67).................50 C3
Drumettaz-Clarafond (73)...131 H4
Drusenheim (67)..............51 F4
Druy-Parigny (58)............99 F5
Druye (37).......................78 C6
Druyes-les-Belles-
   Fontaines (89)..............83 F4
Dry (45)...........................80 C2
Duault (22).......................32 C5
Ducey-les Chéris (50)........35 H4
Duclair (76)......................18 B4
Ducy-Sainte-
   Marguerite (14)............14 A4
Duerne (69)....................129 G4
Duesme (21).....................85 F3
Duffort (32)....................183 G2
Dugny (93).......................42 D3
Dugny-sur-Meuse (55)......47 F1
Duhort-Bachen (40)........166 B4
Duilhac-sous-
   Peyrepertuse (11).......187 F6
Duingt (74)....................132 B2
Duisans (62)......................8 A2
Dullin (73).....................131 G5
Dumes (40)....................165 H4
Dun (09).........................186 A5
Dun-le-Palestel (23)........111 E4
Dun-le-Poëlier (36)...........96 C1
Dun-les-Places (58)........100 B1
Dun-sur-Auron (18)..........98 A4
Dun-sur-Grandry (58).......99 H3
Dun-sur-Meuse (55).........24 D5
Duneau (72).....................60 C5
Dunes (82).....................168 A1
Dunet (36)......................110 C2
Dunière-sur-Eyrieux (07)...143 H6
Dunières (43).................143 F2
Dunkerque (59)..................2 B1
Duntzenheim (67)............50 D4
Duppigheim (67).............50 D6
Duran (32)......................167 H5
Durance (47)..................150 C2
Duranus (06)..................179 E2
Duranville (27).................15 H5
Duras (47)......................150 C1
Duravel (46)...................152 A3
Durban (32)....................167 H6
Durban-Corbières (11).....187 H5
Durban-sur-Arize (09).....185 F5
Durbans (46)..................153 E1
Durcet (61)......................38 C4
Durdat-Larequille (03)....112 D4
Dureil (72).......................77 G1
Durenque (72)................171 F1
Durfort (09)....................185 G3
Durfort (81)....................186 C1
Durfort-et-Saint-Martin-de-
   Sossenac (30).............173 G2
Durfort-Lacapelette (82)...152 A6
Durlinsdorf (68)...............89 F4
Durmenach (68)...............89 F4
Durmignat (63)...............113 G5
Durnes (25)....................103 H2
Durningen (67).................50 D5
Durrenbach (67)...............51 E3
Durrenentzen (68)............71 G4
Durstel (67).....................50 B3
Durtal (49).......................77 F3
Durtol (63).....................127 E3
Dury (02)........................21 H1

Dury (62)..........................8 C3
Dury (80)..........................7 G6
Dussac (24)....................123 H6
Duttlenheim (67).............50 D6
Duvy (60)........................21 F6
Duzey (55)......................25 G5
Dyé (89)...........................83 H1
Dyo (71).........................115 F3

E

Eancé (35)......................57 H5
Eaubonne (95).................42 C3
Eaucourt-sur-Somme (80)...6 D4
Eaunes (31)....................185 F1
Eaux-Bonnes (64)...........182 B5
Eaux-Puiseaux (10)...........65 H5
Eauze (32)......................167 E3
Ébaty (21)......................101 G4
Ebblinghem (59)................2 C4
Eberbach-Seltz (67).........51 G2
Ebersheim (67)................71 G2
Ebersmunster (67)...........71 G2
Éblange (57)....................26 D4
Ébouleau (02)..................22 D2
Ébréon (16)....................122 B1
Ébreuil (03)...................113 G6
l'Écaille (08)....................23 F4
Écaillon (59).....................8 D2
Écalles-Alix (76)..............17 F4
Écardenville-la-
   Campagne (27)............40 C1
Écausseville (50).............12 D3
Écauville (27)..................40 C1
Eccica-Suarella (2A).......204 D6
Eccles (59)......................10 B3
Échalas (69)...................129 H5
Échallat (16)..................122 A3
Échallon (01)..................117 H4
Échalot (21).....................85 F3
Échalou (61)....................38 B4
Échandelys (63)..............127 H5
Échannay (21)................101 F1
Écharcon (91)..................42 D6
Échassières (03).............113 F5
Échauffour (61)................39 G5
Échavanne (70)................88 C3
Échay (21).......................103 F3
Échebrune (17)...............121 F4
l'Échelle (08)...................23 H1
l'Échelle-Saint-Aurin (80)...21 E2
les Échelles (73)............131 G6
Échemines (10)................65 H2
Échenans (25)..................88 B4
Échenans-sous-Mont-
   Vaudois (70)................88 C3
Échenay (52)...................68 A1
Échenevex (01)..............118 B3
Échenon (21)..................102 B2
Échenoz-la-Méline (70).....87 G3
Échenoz-le-Sec (70).........87 G4
Échevannes (21)..............86 A4
Échevannes (25).............103 H2
Échevis (26)...................145 E4
Échevronne (21)..............101 G2
Échigey (21)...................102 A2
Échillais (17)..................120 C1
Échilleuses (45)...............63 G4
Échinghen (62)...................1 F4
Échiré (79).....................107 H3
Échirolles (38)................145 G3
Échouboulains (77)..........64 C2
Échourgnac (24)..............136 C3
Eckartswiller (67).............50 C4
Eckbolsheim (67).............51 E5
Eckwersheim (67)............51 E5
Éclaibes (59)...................10 A3
Éclaires (51)....................46 D2
Éclance (10).....................67 E3
Éclans-Nenon (39)..........102 D2
Éclaron-Braucourt-Sainte-
   Livière (52)...................46 C6
Eclassan (07).................144 A3
Écleux (39).....................103 E3
Éclimeux (62)....................7 F1
Éclose-Badinières (38)....130 D5
Éclusier-Vaux (80)............8 B5
Écluzelles (28).................41 F5
Écly (08).........................23 G3
Écoche (42)....................115 F5
Écoivres (62).....................7 G2
École (73).......................132 B4
École-Valentin (25)..........87 F6
Écollemont (51)...............46 C6
Écommoy (72)..................78 B1
Écorcei (61).....................40 A5
les Écorces (25).............104 D1
Écorches (61)...................39 F3
Écordal (08).....................24 A3
Écorpain (72)....................60 D6
Écot (25)..........................88 C5
Écot-la-Combe (52)..........68 B4
Écotay-l'Olme (42).........128 D5
Écouché-les-Vallées (61)...38 D5
Écouen (95).....................42 D2
Écouflant (49)..................77 E4
Écoust-Saint-Mein (62)......8 C3
Écouves (61)....................60 A1
Écouviez (55)...................25 F3
l'Écouvotte (25)...............87 G6
Écoyeux (17)..................121 F2
Ecquedecques (62)............2 C6
Ecques (62)......................2 B5

Ecquetot (27)..................40 D1
Ecquevilly (78)................42 A3
Écrainville (76)................16 C4
les Écrennes (77)............64 B1
Écretteville-lès-Baons (76)...17 E4
Écretteville-sur-Mer (76)...16 D3
Écriennes (51).................46 B5
Écrille (39).....................117 G2
Écromagny (70)...............88 A1
Écrosnes (28)..................62 C1
Écrouves (54)..................48 A5
Ectot-l'Auber (76)............17 F4
Ectot-lès-Baons (76).........17 E4
Écueil (51).......................45 E1
Écueillé (36)....................96 A2
Écuélin (59).....................10 A3
Écuelle (70).....................86 C4
Écuelles (71)..................102 A4
Écuillé (49).......................76 D3
Écuires (62)......................6 D1
Écuisses (71)..................101 E5
Écully (69)......................130 A3
Écuras (16)....................123 E4
Écurat (17).....................121 E2
Écurcey (25).....................88 C5
Écurey-en-Verdunois (55)...25 E5
Écurie (62)........................8 B2
Écury-le-Repos (51).........45 F4
Écury-sur-Coole (51)........45 H3
Écutigny (21)..................101 F2
Écuvilly (60)....................21 F2
Edern (29).......................53 G2
Édon (16).......................122 D5
les Éduts (17)................108 A6
Eecke (59).........................2 D4
Effiat (63).......................113 H6
Effincourt (52).................68 A1
Effry (02).........................10 A6
Égat (66).......................199 H4
Égleny (89)......................83 E2
Égletons (19).................108 A5
Égligny (77).....................64 D2
Eglingen (68)...................89 E2
l'Église-aux-Bois (19)......125 E4
Église-Neuve-de-Vergt (24)...137 F3
Église-Neuve-d'Issac (24)...136 D4
Égliseneuve-
   d'Entraigues (63).......126 D6
Égliseneuve-des-
   Liards (63)..................127 H5
Égliseneuve-près-
   Billom (63)..................127 G3
les Églises-
   d'Argenteuil (17).........121 G1
Églisolles (63)................128 C6
les Églisottes-et-
   Chalaures (33).............136 A3
Égly (91)..........................42 C6
Égreville (77)...................64 B4
Égriselles-le-Bocage (89)...64 D5
Égry (45)..........................63 G5
Éguelshardt (57)..............50 C2
Eguenigue (90)................88 D2
l'Éguille (17)...................120 C2
Éguilles (13)...................175 H5
Éguilly (21)......................84 D6
Éguilly-sous-Bois (10)......67 E4
Eguisheim (68).................71 F5
Éguzon-Chantôme (36)....111 E3
Éhuns (70).......................87 H2
Eichhoffen (67)................71 F2
Eincheville (57)................49 F2
Einvaux (54)....................69 H1
Einville-au-Jard (54)........49 E5
Eix (55)...........................25 F6
Élan (08).........................24 B2
Élancourt (78)..................42 A4
Elbach (68)......................89 E3
Elbeuf (76).......................18 C5
Elbeuf-en-Bray (76).........19 G4
Elbeuf-sur-Andelle (76)....19 E4
Élencourt (60)..................19 H6
Élesmes (59)....................10 A2
Életot (76).......................16 C3
Éleu-dit-Leauwette (62)......8 B1
Élincourt (59)....................9 E4
Élincourt-Sainte-
   Marguerite (60)............21 F3
Élise-Daucourt (51)..........46 C2
Ellecourt (76)..................19 G1
Elliant (29)......................53 H3
Ellon (14)........................13 H6
Elne (66)........................201 F3
Éloie (90).........................88 C2
Éloise (74).....................118 A6
Éloyes (88)......................70 B4
Elsenheim (67)................71 G4
Elvange (57)....................49 E1
Elven (56)........................55 H6
Elzange (57)....................26 C3
Émagny (25)....................87 E6
Émalleville (27)...............40 D1
Émancé (78).....................41 H6
Émanville (27)..................17 F4
Émanville (76)..................17 F4
Émberménil (54)..............49 F5
Embres-et-
   Castelmaure (11).......187 H6
Embreville (80)..................6 B5
Embrun (05)...................161 E2
Embry (62).........................1 H6
Émerainville (77).............43 E4
Émerchicourt (59)..............9 E2
Émeringes (69)...............116 A5
Émerville (60)..................21 G6
Émeringes (69)...............116 A5
Éméville (14)....................14 C5
Émiéville (14)..................14 C5
Emlingen (68)..................89 F3

Emmerin (59).....................3 F5
Émondeville (50)..............13 E3
Empeaux (31).................168 C6
Empurany (07)................143 H5
Empuré (16)...................108 C6
Empury (58).....................83 H6
Encausse (32).................168 C4
Encausse-les-Thermes (31)...184 B4
Enchastrayes (04)...........161 E4
Enchenberg (57)...............50 B2
Encourtiech (09)..............185 E5
Endoufielle (32)..............168 C6
Énencourt-le-Sec (60)......19 H5
Énencourt-Léage (60).......19 H5
Enfonvelle (52)................69 E6
Engayrac (47).................151 G5
Engente (10).....................67 F3
Engenville (45).................63 F4
Enghien-les-Bains (95)....42 C3
Engins (38)....................145 F2
Englancourt (02)................9 H6
Englebelmer (80)...............8 A4
Englefontaine (59).............9 G3
Englesqueville-en-
   Auge (14)....................15 E3
Englesqueville-la-
   Percée (14).................13 G4
Englos (59)........................3 F6
Engomer (09)..................184 D5
Engwiller (67)..................50 D3
Ennemain (80)..................8 C6
Ennery (57)......................26 C4
Ennery (95)......................42 B2
Ennetières-en-Weppes (59)...3 F5
Ennevelin (59)...................3 G6
Ennezat (63)..................127 F2
Ennordres (18).................81 G5
Enquin-lez-Guinegatte (62)...2 B5
Enquin-sur-Baillons (62)....1 G5
Ens (65).........................196 D1
Ensigné (79)...................108 A5
Ensisheim (68).................71 F6
Ensuès-la-Redonne (13)...191 H5
Entrages (38).................146 A5
Entraigues (38)...............146 A5
Entraigues (63)...............127 G2
Entraigues-sur-la-
   Sorgue (84).................175 E2
Entrains-sur-Nohain (58)...83 E5
Entrammes (53)...............58 D5
Entrange (57)..................26 B3
Entraunes (06)...............161 G5
Entraygues-sur-
   Truyère (12)................154 C2
Eraines (14).....................38 D3
Erbajolo (2B)..................205 F2
Erbéviller-sur-Amezule (54)...49 E4
Erbray (44).......................75 E1
Erbrée (35)......................58 A4
Ercé (09)........................185 E6
Ercé-en-Lamée (35).........57 H5
Ercé-près-Liffré (35)........57 G1
Erceville (45)...................63 E4
Erches (80)......................21 E2
Ercheu (80)......................21 G2
Erchin (59)........................8 D2
Erching (57)....................28 A5
Erckartswiller (67)............50 C3
Ercourt (80)......................6 C4
Ercuis (60).......................20 C6
Erdeven (56)....................54 D6
Erdre-en-Anjou (49)..........76 C3
Éréac (22)........................56 B1
Ergersheim (67)...............50 D6
Ergnies (80).......................7 E4
Ergny (62).........................1 H5
Ergué-Gabéric (29).........53 G3
Érin (62)............................7 F1
Éringes (21).....................84 D4
Eringhem (59)....................2 B2
Érize-la-Brûlée (55)..........47 E3
Érize-la-Petite (55)...........47 E3
Érize-Saint-Dizier (55).....47 F4
Erlon (02).........................22 C2
Erloy (02)..........................9 H6
Ermenonville (60).............43 F1
Ermenonville-la-
   Grande (28).................62 A3
Ermenonville-la-Petite (28)...62 A3
Ermenouville (76)............17 E3
Ermont (95).....................42 C3
Ernée (53)........................58 C2
Ernemont-Boutavent (60)...19 H3
Ernemont-la-Villette (76)...19 G4
Ernemont-sur-Buchy (76)...19 E3
Ernes (14)........................39 E2
Ernestviller (57)..............27 G5
Erneville-aux-Bois (55).....47 G5
Ernolsheim-Bruche (67)....50 D6
Ernolsheim-lès-
   Saverne (67)................50 C4
Erny-Saint-Julien (62)........2 B5
Érôme (26).....................144 A3
Érondelle (80)....................6 D4
Érone (2B)......................205 F1
Éroudeville (50)...............12 D3
Erp (09).........................185 E5
Erquery (60).....................20 D4
Erquinghem-le-Sec (59).....3 F5
Erquinghem-Lys (59)..........3 F5
Erquinvillers (60).............20 D4
Erquy (22)........................34 A3
Err (66).........................199 H4
Erre (59)...........................9 E2
Errevet (70)......................88 D2
Errouville (54)..................26 A3
Ersa (2B)........................203 F1
Erstein (67)......................71 H1
Erstroff (57).....................49 G2

Ervauville (45) 64 C5
Ervillers (62) 8 B3
Ervy-le-Châtel (10) 66 A5
Esbareich (65) 183 H5
Esbarres (21) 102 B2
Esbly (77) 43 F3
Esboz-Brest (70) 88 A1
Escala (65) 183 G4
Escalans (40) 166 D1
l'Escale (04) 160 B6
Escales (11) 187 G3
Escalles (62) 1 F2
Escalquens (31) 169 G6
Escames (60) 19 H3
Escamps (46) 153 E4
Escamps (89) 83 F2
Escandolières (12) 154 A3
Escanecrabe (31) 184 B2
Escardes (51) 44 C5
l'Escarène (06) 179 F2
Escarmain (59) 9 F3
Escaro (66) 200 B4
Escassefort (47) 150 C2
Escatalens (82) 168 D2
Escaudain (59) 9 E2
Escaudes (33) 149 H4
Escaudœuvres (59) 9 E3
Escaunets (65) 182 D2
Escautpont (59) 9 F1
Escazeaux (82) 168 C3
Eschau (67) 51 E6
Eschbach (67) 51 E3
Eschbach-au-Val (68) 71 E5
Eschbourg (67) 50 B3
Eschentzwiller (68) 89 G2
Escherange (57) 26 B3
Esches (60) 20 B6
Eschwiller (67) 50 A3
Esclagne (09) 186 A5
Esclainvillers (80) 20 C2
Esclanèdes (48) 155 H3
Esclassan-Labastide (32) 184 A1
Esclauzels (46) 152 D4
Esclavelles (76) 19 E2
Esclavolles-Lurey (51) 65 G1
Escles (88) 69 G4
Escles-Saint-Pierre (60) 19 H1
Esclottes (47) 150 C1
Escobecques (59) 3 E5
Escœuilles (62) 1 G4
Escoire (24) 137 G2
Escolives-Sainte-Camille (89) 83 G3
Escombres-et-le-Chesnois (08) 24 D2
Escondeaux (65) 183 F2
Esconnets (65) 183 F4
Escorailles (15) 140 A3
Escornebœuf (32) 168 B5
Escorpain (28) 41 E5
Escos (64) 165 E6
Escosse (09) 185 G4
Escot (64) 182 A4
Escots (65) 183 F4
Escou (64) 182 A3
Escoubès (64) 182 C1
Escoubès-Pouts (65) 183 E4
Escoulis (31) 184 D4
Escouloubre (11) 200 A2
Escource (40) 148 C5
Escoussans (33) 149 H1
Escoussens (81) 170 C6
Escout (64) 182 A3
Escoutoux (63) 128 A3
Escoville (14) 14 C4
Escragnolles (06) 178 B4
Escrennes (45) 63 F5
Escrignelles (45) 82 B3
Escroux (81) 171 F4
Escueillens-et-Saint-Just-de-Bélengard (11) 186 C4
Escurès (64) 166 C6
Escurolles (03) 113 H5
Eslettes (76) 18 C3
Esley (88) 69 F4
Eslourenties-Daban (64) 182 D2
Esmans (77) 64 C3
Esmery-Hallon (80) 21 G2
Esmoulières (70) 88 B1
Esmoulins (70) 86 C5
Esnandes (17) 106 D4
Esnans (25) 87 H6
Esnes (59) 9 E4
Esnes-en-Argonne (55) 24 D6
Esnon (89) 65 F6
Esnouveaux (52) 68 B4
Espagnac (19) 139 F2
Espagnac-Sainte-Eulalie (46) 153 F2
Espalais (82) 168 B1
Espalem (43) 141 F1
Espalion (12) 154 D3
Espaly-Saint-Marcel (43) 142 C4
Espanès (31) 185 G1
Espaon (32) 184 C1
Esparron (05) 160 A3
Esparron (31) 184 B2
Esparron (83) 176 D5
Esparron-de-Verdon (04) 176 D4
Esparros (65) 183 G4
Esparsac (82) 168 C2
Espartignac (19) 124 D6
Espas (32) 167 E3
Espaubourg (60) 19 H4
Espèche (65) 183 G4
Espéchède (64) 182 D2
Espédaillac (46) 153 E2
Espelette (64) 180 C1
Espeluche (26) 158 B3
Espenel (26) 159 E1
Espérausses (81) 171 E5
Espéraza (11) 186 D6
Esperce (31) 185 F2
Espère (46) 152 C3
Espès-Undurein (64) 181 G2
Espeyrac (12) 154 C2
Espeyroux (46) 139 F6
Espezel (11) 199 H1
Espieilh (65) 183 F4
Espiens (47) 150 D6
Espiet (33) 135 G6
Espinas (82) 153 F6
Espinasse (15) 141 E5
Espinasse (63) 112 D6
Espinasse-Vozelle (03) 113 H5
Espinasses (05) 160 C3
Espinchal (63) 140 D1
Espins (14) 38 C2
Espira-de-Conflent (66) 200 C3
Espira-de-l'Agly (66) 201 F1
Espirat (63) 127 G3
Espiute (64) 181 F1
Esplantas-Vazeilles (43) 142 A5
Esplas (09) 185 G3
Esplas-de-Sérou (09) 185 F5
Espoey (64) 182 D2
Espondeilhan (34) 188 C1
Esprels (70) 87 H4
Esquay-Notre-Dame (14) 14 B5
Esquay-sur-Seulles (14) 14 A4
Esquéhéries (02) 9 G5
Esquelbecq (59) 2 C3
Esquennoy (60) 20 C2
Esquerchin (59) 8 C1
Esquerdes (62) 2 A4
Esquièze-Sère (65) 183 E6
Esquiule (64) 181 H3
les Essards (16) 136 B2
les Essards (17) 120 D2
les Essards-Taignevaux (39) 102 C4
Essarois (21) 85 F2
Essars (62) 2 D6
les Essarts (41) 79 E2
les Essarts-le-Roi (78) 42 A5
les Essarts-le-Vicomte (51) 44 C6
les Essarts-lès-Sézanne (51) 44 D5
Essarts en Bocage (85) 91 H3
Essay (61) 39 G6
Esse (16) 109 G6
Essé (35) 57 G4
Essegney (88) 69 G2
les Esseintes (33) 150 A2
Essert (90) 88 C3
Essert-Romand (74) 119 F4
Essertaux (80) 20 B1
Essertenne (71) 101 E5
Essertenne-et-Cecey (70) 86 C5
Essertines-en-Châtelneuf (42) 128 D4
Essertines-en-Donzy (42) 129 F3
Esserts-Blay (73) 132 D4
Esserval-Tartre (39) 103 G5
Essey (21) 101 E1
Essey-et-Maizerais (54) 48 A3
Essey-la-Côte (54) 69 H1
Essey-lès-Nancy (54) 48 D5
Essigny-le-Grand (02) 22 A1
Essigny-le-Petit (02) 9 E6
Essises (02) 44 B3
Essômes-sur-Marne (02) 44 B2
Esson (14) 38 C2
Essouvert (17) 107 G6
Essoyes (10) 67 E5
Essuiles (60) 20 C4
les Estables (43) 143 E5
Estables (48) 156 A1
Establet (26) 159 F3
Estadens (31) 184 C5
Estagel (66) 201 E1
Estaing (12) 154 D2
Estaing (65) 182 C5
Estaires (59) 2 D5
Estal (46) 139 F5
Estampes (32) 183 G1
Estampures (65) 183 G1
Estancarbon (31) 184 B4
Estandeuil (63) 127 H4
Estang (32) 166 C3
Estarvielle (65) 197 E1
Estavar (66) 199 H4
Esteil (63) 127 G6
Esténos (31) 184 A5
Estensan (65) 196 D1
Estérençuby (64) 181 E3
Esternay (51) 44 C5
Esterre (65) 183 E6
Estevelles (62) 3 E6
Esteville (76) 18 D3
Estézargues (30) 174 C2
Estialescq (64) 182 A3
Estibeaux (40) 165 F5
Estigarde (40) 166 C1
Estillac (47) 151 E6
Estipouy (32) 167 G6
Estirac (65) 166 D6
Estissac (10) 65 H3
Estivals (19) 138 C4
Estivareilles (03) 112 D3
Estivareilles (42) 128 D6
Estivaux (19) 138 C1
Estoher (66) 200 C3
Estos (64) 182 A3
Estoublon (04) 177 F2
Estouches (91) 63 F3
Estourmel (59) 9 E4
Estouy (45) 63 G4
Estrablin (38) 130 B5
Estramiac (32) 168 B3
Estrebay (08) 10 C6
Estrébœuf (80) 6 C3
l'Estréchure (30) 173 F1
Estrée (62) 1 G6
Estrée-Blanche (62) 2 B5
Estrée-Cauchy (62) 8 A1
Estrée-Wamin (62) 7 G2
Estréelles (62) 1 G6
Estrées (02) 9 E5
Estrées (59) 8 D2
Estrées-Deniécourt (80) 8 B6
Estrées-la-Campagne (14) 38 D2
Estrées-lès-Crécy (80) 7 E3
Estrées-Mons (80) 8 C6
Estrées-Saint-Denis (60) 21 E4
Estrées-sur-Noye (80) 20 C1
Estrennes (88) 69 F3
Estreux (59) 9 G2
Estrun (59) 9 E3
Esves-le-Moutier (37) 95 F3
Esvres (37) 79 E6
Eswars (59) 9 E3
Étable (73) 132 B5
Étables (07) 143 H3
Étagnac (16) 123 F2
Étaimpuis (76) 17 H4
Étain (55) 25 G6
Étaing (62) 8 C2
Étainhus (76) 15 G1
Étais (21) 84 D3
Étais-la-Sauvin (89) 83 E5
Étalans (25) 103 H2
Étalante (21) 85 F3
Étalle (08) 10 D6
Étalleville (76) 17 F3
Étalon (80) 21 F1
Étalondes (76) 6 B5
Étampes (91) 63 F2
Étampes-sur-Marne (02) 44 B2
l'Étang-Bertrand (50) 12 C3
l'Étang-la-Ville (78) 42 B4
Étang-sur-Arroux (71) 100 C4
l'Étang-Vergy (21) 101 G2
les Étangs (57) 26 D5
Étaples (62) 1 F6
Étaule (89) 84 A4
Étaules (17) 120 B3
Étaules (21) 85 G5
Étauliers (33) 135 E2
Etaux (74) 118 D6
Étaves-et-Bocquiaux (02) 9 F5
Étavigny (60) 43 G1
Etcharry (64) 181 F2
Etchebar (64) 181 G4
Éteignières (08) 10 D6
Eteimbes (68) 88 D2
Étel (56) 54 D6
Ételfay (80) 21 E2
Étercy (74) 132 A2
Éternoz (25) 103 G3
Éterpigny (62) 8 C3
Éterpigny (80) 8 C6
Éterville (14) 14 B5
Étevaux (21) 86 B6
Eth (59) 9 G2
Étienville (50) 12 D4
Étigny (89) 65 E5
les Étilleux (28) 61 E3
Étinehem-Méricourt (80) 8 A6
Étiolles (91) 42 D6
Étival (39) 117 H2
Étival-Clairefontaine (88) 70 C2
Étival-lès-le-Mans (72) 60 A6
Étivey (89) 84 B3
Étobon (70) 88 B3
Étoges (51) 45 E4
l'Étoile (39) 102 D6
l'Étoile (80) 7 E5
Étoile-Saint-Cyrice (05) 159 G4
Étoile-sur-Rhône (26) 144 B6
Éton (55) 25 G5
Étormay (21) 85 E4
Étouars (24) 123 E4
Étourvy (10) 66 B6
Étoutteville (76) 17 E4
Étouvans (25) 88 C4
Étouvelles (02) 22 C3
Étouy (60) 20 C4
Étrabonne (25) 103 E1
Étrappe (25) 88 B4
l'Étrat (42) 129 F5
Étray (25) 104 A2
Étraye (55) 25 E5
Étréaupont (02) 10 A6
Étrechet (36) 96 D5
Étréchy (18) 98 B2
Étréchy (51) 45 E3
Étréchy (91) 63 F1
Étréham (14) 13 H5
Étreillers (02) 21 H1
Étréjust (80) 6 D6
Étrelles (35) 58 A5
Étrelles-et-la-Montbleuse (70) 87 E5
Étrelles-sur-Aube (10) 65 H1
Étrembières (74) 118 C5
Étrépagny (27) 19 F5
Étrepigney (39) 102 D2
Étrépigny (08) 24 B2
Étrépilly (02) 44 B2
Étrépilly (77) 43 G2
Étrepy (51) 46 C4
Étretat (76) 16 B3
Étreux (02) 9 G5
Étreval (54) 69 F1
Étréville (27) 18 A5
Étrez (01) 116 D3
Étriac (16) 122 A5
Étriché (49) 77 E3
Étricourt-Manancourt (80) 8 C5
Étrigny (71) 116 B1
Étrochey (21) 85 E1
Étrœungt (59) 10 A4
Étroussat (03) 113 G5
Étrun (62) 8 A2
Etsaut (64) 182 A5
Ettendorf (67) 50 D3
Etting (57) 50 A2
Étueffont (90) 88 D2
Étupes (25) 88 C4
Éturqueraye (27) 18 A5
Étuz (70) 87 F6
Etzling (57) 27 G4
Eu (76) 6 B4
Euffigneix (52) 67 H4
Eugénie-les-Bains (40) 166 B4
Euilly-et-Lombut (08) 24 D2
Eulmont (54) 48 D4
Eup (31) 184 A5
Eurre (26) 144 B6
Eurville-Bienville (52) 46 D6
Eus (66) 200 C3
Euvezin (54) 48 A3
Euville (55) 47 H4
Euvy (51) 45 F5
Euzet (30) 174 A1
Évaillé (72) 78 D1
Évans (39) 103 E1
Évaux-et-Ménil (88) 69 G2
Évaux-les-Bains (23) 112 C5
Ève (60) 43 F2
Évecquemont (78) 42 A2
Évellys (56) 55 F3
Évenos (83) 193 E5
Évergnicourt (02) 23 E4
Everly (77) 64 D2
Évette-Salbert (90) 88 C2
Éveux (69) 129 G2
Évian-les-Bains (74) 119 E3
Évigny (08) 24 A1
Évillers (25) 103 H3
Évin-Malmaison (62) 8 C1
Évisa (2A) 204 C3
Évosges (01) 131 E1
Évran (22) 34 D6
Évrange (57) 26 B2
Évrecy (14) 14 B5
Èvres (55) 47 E2
Évreux (27) 40 D2
Évricourt (60) 21 F3
Évriguet (56) 56 A3
Évron (53) 59 F4
Évry (89) 65 E3
Évry (91) 42 D6
Évry-Grégy-sur-Yerre (77) 43 E6
Excenevex (74) 118 D3
Excideuil (24) 137 H1
Exermont (08) 24 C5
Exideuil (16) 123 F2
Exincourt (25) 88 C4
Exireuil (79) 108 B2
Exoudun (79) 108 B3
Expiremont (17) 135 G1
Eybens (38) 145 G3
Eybouleuf (87) 124 C3
Eyburie (19) 124 D6
Eycheil (09) 185 E5
Eydoche (38) 130 D6
Eygalayes (26) 159 G5
Eygalières (13) 175 F4
Eygaliers (26) 159 E5
Eygliers (05) 161 F1
Eygluy-Escoulin (26) 144 D6
Eyguières (13) 175 F4
Eygurande (19) 126 B4
Eygurande-et-Gardedeuil (24) 136 B3
Eyjeaux (87) 124 C3
Eymet (24) 150 D1
Eymeux (26) 144 C3
Eymouthiers (16) 123 E4
Eymoutiers (87) 125 E3
Eyne (66) 199 H4
Eynesse (33) 136 B5
Eyragues (13) 175 E3
Eyrans (33) 135 E2
Eyrein (19) 139 F1
Eyres-Moncube (40) 165 H4
Eyroles (26) 159 E4
Eysines (33) 135 E5
Eysson (25) 104 A1
Eysus (64) 182 A3
Eyvirat (24) 137 F1
Eywiller (67) 50 A3
Eyzahut (26) 158 C2
Eyzerac (24) 123 G6
les Eyzies-de-Tayac-Sireuil (24) 137 H5
Eyzin-Pinet (38) 130 B5
Ézanville (95) 42 D2
Èze (06) 179 F3
Ézy-sur-Eure (27) 41 F4

F

Fa (11) 186 D6
Fabas (09) 184 D4
Fabas (31) 184 C2
Fabas (82) 169 E3
Fabras (07) 157 F2
Fabrègues (34) 173 F6
Fabrezan (11) 187 G4
Faches-Thumesnil (59) 3 F5
Fâchin (58) 100 B3
la Fage-Montivernoux (48) 155 G1
la Fage-Saint-Julien (48) 141 F6
le Faget (31) 169 H6
Faget-Abbatial (32) 168 A6
Fagnières (51) 45 H3
Fagnon (08) 24 A1
Fahy-lès-Autrey (70) 86 C4
Failly (57) 26 C5
Faimbe (25) 88 B4
Fain-lès-Montbard (21) 84 D4
Fain-lès-Moutiers (21) 84 C4
Fains (27) 41 F2
Fains-Véel (55) 47 E4
Faissault (08) 23 H3
Fajac-en-Val (11) 187 E4
Fajac-la-Relenque (11) 186 A2
Fajoles (46) 138 B6
la Fajolle (11) 199 G1
Fajolles (82) 168 C2
Falaise (08) 24 B5
Falaise (14) 38 D3
la Falaise (78) 42 A3
Falck (57) 27 E4
Faleyras (33) 135 G6
Falga (31) 186 B1
le Falgoux (15) 140 C3
Falicon (06) 179 E3
Falkwiller (68) 89 E2
Fallencourt (76) 6 C6
Fallerans (25) 103 H2
Falleron (85) 91 E2
Falletans (39) 102 D2
Fallon (70) 88 A4
la Faloise (80) 20 C2
Fals (47) 168 A1
Falvy (80) 21 G1
Famars (59) 9 F2
Famechon (62) 7 H4
Famechon (80) 20 A1
Fameck (57) 26 B4
Fampoux (62) 8 B2
Fanjeaux (11) 186 C3
Fanlac (24) 137 H3
le Faou (29) 31 F6
le Faouët (22) 33 E3
le Faouët (56) 54 B3
Faramans (01) 130 C2
Faramans (38) 130 C6
Farbus (62) 8 B2
Farceaux (27) 19 F5
la Fare-en-Champsaur (05) 160 B1
la Fare-les-Oliviers (13) 175 G6
Farébersviller (57) 27 G5
Fareins (01) 116 B6
Faremoutiers (77) 43 H4
Farges (01) 118 A5
les Farges (24) 138 A3
Farges-Allichamps (18) 97 G5
Farges-en-Septaine (18) 98 A3
Farges-lès-Chalon (71) 101 G5
Farges-lès-Mâcon (71) 116 B2
Fargues (33) 149 H2
Fargues (40) 166 A4
Fargues (46) 152 B4
Fargues-Saint-Hilaire (33) 135 F5
Fargues-sur-Ourbise (47) 150 C5
Farincourt (52) 86 D2
Farinole (2B) 203 F3
la Farlède (83) 193 F5
Farnay (42) 129 G5
Farschviller (57) 27 G5
Fatines (72) 60 B5
Fatouville-Grestain (27) 15 G3
le Fau (15) 140 B3
Fauch (81) 170 C3
Faucigny (74) 118 D5
Faucogney-et-la-Mer (70) 88 A1
Faucompierre (88) 70 B4
Faucon (84) 158 D5
Faucon-de-Barcelonnette (04) 161 F3
Faucon-du-Caire (04) 160 B4
Fauconcourt (88) 70 A2
Faucoucourt (02) 22 B3
Faudoas (82) 168 C3
le Fauga (31) 185 F1
Faugères (07) 157 E3
Faugères (34) 172 B6
Fauguernon (14) 15 F4
Fauguerolles (47) 150 C3
Fauillet (47) 150 D3
le Faulq (14) 15 F4
Faulquemont (57) 49 F2
Faulx (54) 48 C4
Faumont (59) 8 D1
Fauquembergues (62) 2 A5
la Faurie (05) 159 H2
Faurilles (24) 151 F1
Fauroux (82) 151 H5
Faussergues (81) 171 E1
la Faute-sur-Mer (85) 106 B3
Fauverney (21) 102 A1
Fauville (27) 41 E2
Faux (08) 23 H3
Faux (24) 137 E6
Faux-Fresnay (51) 45 E6
Faux-la-Montagne (23) 125 F3
Faux-Mazuras (23) 125 E2
Faux-Vésigneul (51) 45 H4
Faux-Villecerf (10) 65 G3
Favalello (2B) 205 F2
Favars (19) 138 D2
Faverdines (18) 112 C1
Faverelles (45) 82 C4
Faverges-de-la-Tour (38) 131 E4
Faverges-Seythenex (74) 132 C3
Faverney (70) 87 F2
Faverois (90) 88 D4
Faverolles (02) 21 H6
Faverolles (15) 141 G5
Faverolles (52) 68 A6
Faverolles (61) 38 C5
Faverolles (80) 21 E2
Faverolles-en-Berry (36) 96 A2
Faverolles-et-Coëmy (51) 22 D6
Faverolles-la-Campagne (27) 40 C2
Faverolles-lès-Lucey (21) 85 G1
Faverolles-sur-Cher (41) 79 G6
la Favière (39) 103 G5
Favières (28) 61 H1
Favières (54) 69 E1
Favières (77) 43 F5
Favières (80) 6 C3
Favresse (51) 46 B5
Favreuil (62) 8 B4
Favrieux (78) 41 G3
le Favril (27) 15 H5
le Favril (28) 61 G1
le Favril (59) 9 G4
Fay (61) 39 H5
Fay (71) 102 B6
Fay (72) 60 A5
Fay (80) 8 B6
Fay-aux-Loges (45) 81 E1
Fay-de-Bretagne (44) 74 B3
Fay-en-Montagne (39) 103 E5
Fay-le-Clos (26) 144 B2
Fay-les-Étangs (60) 19 H6
Fay-lès-Marcilly (10) 65 G2
Faÿ-lès-Nemours (77) 64 A4
le Fay-Saint-Quentin (60) 20 B4
Fay-sur-Lignon (43) 143 E4
Faycelles (46) 153 G2
la Faye (16) 108 D6
Faye (41) 79 G2
Faye-la-Vineuse (37) 94 B3
Faye-l'Abbesse (79) 93 F4
Faye-sur-Ardin (79) 107 G2
le Fayel (60) 21 E5
Fayence (83) 178 B5
Fayet (02) 9 E6
Fayet (12) 171 H4
Fayet-le-Château (63) 127 H4
Fayet-Ronaye (63) 128 A6
Fayl-Billot (52) 86 C2
Faymont (70) 88 B3
Faymoreau (85) 107 G1
Fays (52) 67 G1
Fays (88) 70 B3
Fays-la-Chapelle (10) 66 A5
Fayssac (81) 170 B2
Febvin-Palfart (62) 2 B6
Fécamp (76) 16 C3
Féchain (59) 8 D2
Fêche-l'Église (90) 88 D4
Fécocourt (54) 69 F2
Fédry (70) 87 E3
Fegersheim (67) 51 E6
Fégréac (44) 74 A1
Feigères (74) 118 B5
Feigneux (60) 21 F6
Feignies (59) 10 A2
Feillens (01) 116 B3
Feings (41) 80 A5
Feings (61) 40 A6
Feins (35) 57 F1
Feins-en-Gâtinais (45) 82 B2
Feissons-sur-Isère (73) 132 D4
Feissons-sur-Salins (73) 132 D5
le Fel (12) 154 B2
Felce (2B) 205 G2
Feldbach (68) 89 F4
Feldkirch (68) 71 F6
Feliceto (2B) 202 D5
Félines (07) 143 H1
Félines (43) 142 B2
Félines-Minervois (34) 187 F2
Félines-sur-Rimandoule (26) 158 C2
Félines-Termenès (11) 187 F5
Felleries (59) 10 A4
Fellering (68) 70 D6
Felletin (23) 125 H2
Felluns (66) 200 C1
Felon (90) 88 D2
Felzins (46) 153 H2
Fenain (59) 9 E2
Fénay (21) 101 H1
Fendeille (11) 186 B3
Fénery (79) 93 F6
Fénétrange (57) 50 A3
Feneu (49) 76 D3
Féneyrols (82) 153 F6
Féniers (23) 125 G3
Fenioux (17) 121 F1
Fenioux (79) 107 H1
Fenneviller (54) 70 C1
Fénols (81) 170 B3
le Fenouiller (85) 90 D4
Fenouillet (31) 169 E5
Fenouillet (66) 200 B1
Fenouillet-du-Razès (11) 186 C4
Fépin (08) 11 E5
Fercé (44) 57 G6
Fercé-sur-Sarthe (72) 59 H6
Ferdrupt (88) 70 B6
la Fère (02) 22 A2
Fère-Champenoise (51) 45 F5
Fère-en-Tardenois (02) 44 C1
Fèrebrianges (51) 45 E4
la Férée (08) 23 G1
Férel (56) 73 G2
Ferfay (62) 2 C6

Féricy (77)............... 64 B2
Férin (59)............... 8 D2
Fermanville (50)............... 12 D1
la Fermeté (58)............... 99 E4
Ferney-Voltaire (01)............... 118 B4
Fernoël (63)............... 126 A3
Férolles (45)............... 81 E2
Férolles-Attilly (77)............... 43 E5
Féron (59)............... 10 A4
Ferques (59)............... 1 G3
Ferrals-les-Corbières (11)............... 187 G4
Ferrals-les-Montagnes (34).. 187 G1
Ferran (11)............... 186 C4
Ferrassières (26)............... 159 F6
le Ferré (35)............... 35 H5
Ferrensac (47)............... 151 F1
Ferrère (65)............... 183 H5
les Ferres (06)............... 178 D2
Ferrette (68)............... 89 F4
Ferreux-Quincey (10)............... 65 G2
la Ferrière (37)............... 79 E3
la Ferrière (38)............... 146 A1
la Ferrière (85)............... 91 H4
la Ferrière-Airoux (86)............... 109 E3
la Ferrière-au-Doyen (61)...... 39 H5
la Ferrière-aux-Étangs (61).... 38 B5
la Ferrière-Béchet (61)............... 39 F6
la Ferrière-Bochard (61)...... 59 H2
la Ferrière-en-
  Parthenay (79)............... 93 G6
Ferrière-et-Lafolie (52)...... 67 F2
Ferrière-la-Grande (59)...... 10 A3
Ferrière-la-Petite (59)............... 10 A3
Ferrière-Larçon (37)............... 95 F3
Ferrière-sur-Beaulieu (37)... 95 G2
la Ferrière-sur-Risle (27)...... 40 B2
Ferrières (17)............... 107 E4
Ferrières (54)............... 48 D6
Ferrières (60)............... 20 D3
Ferrières (65)............... 182 C5
Ferrières (80)............... 7 F6
Ferrières-en-Bray (76)............... 19 G4
Ferrières-en-Brie (77)............... 43 F4
Ferrières-en-Gâtinais (45)... 64 B5
Ferrières-Haut-Clocher (27)... 40 C2
Ferrières-la-Verrerie (61).... 39 G5
Ferrières-le-Lac (25)............... 88 D6
Ferrières-les-Bois (25)............... 103 E1
Ferrières-lès-Ray (70)............... 87 E4
Ferrières-lès-Scey (70)............... 87 F3
Ferrières-les-Verreries (34).. 173 F3
Ferrières-Poussarou (34)...... 188 A1
Ferrières-Saint-Hilaire (27).... 40 A2
Ferrières-Saint-Mary (15)... 141 E3
Ferrières-sur-Ariège (09)... 185 H6
Ferrières-sur-Sichon (03)... 128 A1
Ferrussac (43)............... 141 H3
Fertans (25)............... 103 G3
la Ferté (39)............... 102 D4
la Ferté-Alais (91)............... 63 G1
la Ferté-Beauharnais (41)... 80 D4
la Ferté-Bernard (72)............... 60 D4
la Ferté-Chevresis (02)............... 22 B2
la Ferté-en-Ouche (61)............... 39 H4
la Ferté-Gaucher (77)............... 44 B4
la Ferté-Hauterive (03)............... 113 H3
la Ferté-Imbault (41)............... 80 D6
la Ferté-Loupière (89)............... 82 D1
la Ferté Macé (61)............... 38 C6
la Ferté-Milon (02)............... 43 H1
la Ferté-Saint-Aubin (45)...... 80 D3
la Ferté-Saint-Cyr (41)............... 80 C3
la Ferté-Saint-Samson (76)... 19 F3
la Ferté-sous-Jouarre (77)... 44 A3
la Ferté-sur-Chiers (08)............... 25 E3
la Ferté-Vidame (28)............... 40 C6
Fertrève (58)............... 99 G4
Fescamps (80)............... 21 E2
Fesches-le-Châtel (25)............... 88 D4
Fesmy-le-Sart (02)............... 9 G4
Fesques (76)............... 19 F1
Fessanvilliers-
  Mattanvilliers (28)............... 40 D5
Fessenheim (68)............... 71 G6
Fessenheim-le-Bas (67)...... 50 D5
Fessevillers (25)............... 88 D6
les Fessey (70)............... 88 A1
Fessy (74)............... 118 D4
Festes-et-Saint-André (11).. 186 C5
Festieux (02)............... 22 D3
Festigny (51)............... 44 D2
Festigny (89)............... 83 F4
Festubert (62)............... 2 D6
le Fête (21)............... 101 E2
Féternes (74)............... 119 E3
Feucherolles (78)............... 42 A4
Feuchy (62)............... 8 B2
Feugarolles (47)............... 150 D5
Feugères (50)............... 12 D6
Feuges (10)............... 66 B2
Feuguerolles (27)............... 40 D1
Feuguerolles-Bully (14)...... 16 B5
Feuilla (11)............... 188 A6
Feuillade (16)............... 122 D4
la Feuillade (24)............... 138 C3
la Feuillée (29)............... 31 H6
Feuillères (80)............... 8 B5
la Feuillie (50)............... 12 D6
la Feuillie (76)............... 19 F4
Feule (25)............... 88 C5
Feuquières (60)............... 19 H2
Feuquières-en-Vimeu (80)..... 6 C4
Feurs (42)............... 129 E3
Feusines (36)............... 111 H2
Feux (18)............... 98 C1
Fèves (57)............... 26 B5
Féy (57)............... 26 B6
Fey-en-Haye (54)............... 48 B3

Feyt (19)............... 126 B4
Feytiat (87)............... 124 B3
Feyzin (69)............... 130 A4
Fiac (81)............... 170 A4
Ficaja (2B)............... 205 G1
Ficheux (62)............... 8 B3
Fichous-Riumayou (64)... 166 A6
le Fidelaire (27)............... 40 B3
le Fied (39)............... 103 E5
Fieffes-Montrelet (80)............... 7 F4
Fiefs (62)............... 2 B6
Fiennes (62)............... 1 G3
Fienvillers (80)............... 7 F4
Fierville-les-Mines (50)............... 12 C4
Fierville-les-Parcs (14)...... 15 F4
le Fieu (33)............... 136 A3
Fieulaine (02)............... 9 F6
Fieux (47)............... 167 G1
Figanières (83)............... 177 H5
Figari (2A)............... 207 F4
Figarol (31)............... 184 C4
Figeac (46)............... 153 G2
Fignévelle (88)............... 69 E6
Fignières (80)............... 20 D2
Filain (02)............... 22 B4
Filain (70)............... 87 G4
Fillé (72)............... 78 A1
Fillière (74)............... 118 C6
Fillières (54)............... 25 H4
Fillièvres (62)............... 7 F2
Fillinges (74)............... 118 D5
Fillols (66)............... 200 C3
Filstroff (57)............... 27 E3
Fiménil (88)............... 70 B4
Finestret (66)............... 200 C3
Finhan (82)............... 168 D2
les Fins (25)............... 104 C2
Fins (80)............... 8 C5
Fiquefleur-Équainville (27)... 15 F3
Firbeix (24)............... 123 H4
Firfol (14)............... 15 F5
Firmi (12)............... 154 A3
Firminy (42)............... 129 E6
Fislis (68)............... 89 G4
Fismes (51)............... 22 C5
Fitou (11)............... 188 A6
Fitz-James (60)............... 20 D5
Fixem (57)............... 26 C2
Fixin (21)............... 101 H1
Flacey (21)............... 86 A5
Flacey (28)............... 62 A4
Flacey-en-Bresse (71)............... 117 E1
la Flachère (38)............... 131 H6
Flachères (38)............... 130 D5
Flacourt (78)............... 41 G3
Flacy (89)............... 65 G4
Flagey (25)............... 103 G3
Flagey (52)............... 86 A2
Flagey-Echézeaux (21)............... 101 H2
Flagey-lès-Auxonne (21)...... 102 C2
Flagey-Rigney (25)............... 87 G5
Flagnac (12)............... 154 A2
Flagy (70)............... 87 G2
Flagy (71)............... 116 A2
Flagy (77)............... 64 C3
Flaignes-Havys (08)............... 23 G1
Flainval (54)............... 49 E5
Flamanville (50)............... 12 A3
Flamanville (76)............... 17 F4
Flamarens (32)............... 168 B1
la Flamengrie (02)............... 10 A5
la Flamengrie (59)............... 9 G2
Flamets-Frétils (76)............... 19 F2
Flammerans (21)............... 102 C1
Flammerécourt (52)............... 67 H2
Flancourt-Crescy-en-
  Roumois (27)............... 18 B5
Flangebouche (25)............... 104 B2
Flassan (84)............... 175 G1
Flassans-sur-Issole (83)... 193 G3
Flassigny (55)............... 25 F4
Flastroff (57)............... 27 E3
Flaucourt (80)............... 8 B6
Flaugeac (24)............... 136 D6
Flaujac-Gare (46)............... 153 F1
Flaujac-Poujols (46)............... 152 D4
Flaujagues (33)............... 136 A5
Flaumont-
  Waudrechies (59)............... 10 A4
Flaux (30)............... 174 C2
Flavacourt (60)............... 19 H5
Flaviac (07)............... 143 H6
Flavignac (87)............... 124 A3
Flavignerot (21)............... 101 G1
Flavigny (18)............... 98 B4
Flavigny (51)............... 45 F3
Flavigny-le-Grand-et-
  Beaurain (02)............... 9 G6
Flavigny-sur-Moselle (54)... 48 C6
Flavigny-sur-Ozerain (21)... 85 E4
Flavin (12)............... 154 C5
Flavy-le-Martel (02)............... 21 H2
Flavy-le-Meldeux (60)............... 21 G2
Flaxieu (01)............... 131 G2
Flaxlanden (68)............... 89 F2
Flayat (23)............... 126 A3
Flayosc (83)............... 177 G5
Fléac (16)............... 122 B4
Fléac-sur-Seugne (17)............... 121 F5
la Flèche (72)............... 77 G2
Fléchin (62)............... 2 B6
Fléchy (60)............... 20 B2
Flée (21)............... 84 C5
Flée (72)............... 78 C2
Fleigneux (08)............... 24 C1
Fleisheim (57)............... 50 A4
le Fleix (24)............... 136 C5

Fleix (86)............... 109 H4
Fléré-la-Rivière (36)............... 95 G3
Flers (61)............... 38 B4
Flers (62)............... 7 G2
Flers (80)............... 8 B4
Flers-en-Escrebieux (59)...... 8 D1
Flers-sur-Noye (80)............... 20 C2
Flesquières (59)............... 8 D4
Flesselles (80)............... 7 G5
Flétrange (57)............... 49 F1
Flêtre (59)............... 2 D4
Fléty (58)............... 100 A5
Fleurac (16)............... 122 A3
Fleurac (24)............... 137 H4
Fleurance (32)............... 167 H3
Fleurat (23)............... 111 F4
Fleurbaix (62)............... 3 E5
Fleuré (61)............... 39 E5
Fleuré (86)............... 109 F2
Fleurey (25)............... 88 C6
Fleurey-lès-Faverney (70)... 87 F2
Fleurey-lès-
  Lavoncourt (70)............... 86 D3
Fleurey-lès-Saint-Loup (70)... 69 G6
Fleurey-sur-Ouche (21)...... 85 G6
Fleurie (69)............... 116 A5
Fleuriel (03)............... 113 G4
Fleurieu-sur-Saône (69)... 130 A2
Fleurieux-sur-
  l'Arbresle (69)............... 129 H2
Fleurigné (35)............... 58 A2
Fleurines (60)............... 20 D6
Fleurville (71)............... 116 B2
Fleury (02)............... 21 H6
Fleury (11)............... 188 B3
Fleury (50)............... 37 E3
Fleury (57)............... 48 C2
Fleury (60)............... 20 A6
Fleury (62)............... 7 G1
Fleury (80)............... 20 B1
Fleury-devant-
  Douaumont (55)............... 25 F6
Fleury-en-Bière (77)............... 63 H2
Fleury-la-Forêt (27)............... 19 F4
Fleury-la-Montagne (71)... 115 E5
Fleury-la-Rivière (51)............... 45 E2
Fleury-la-Vallée (89)............... 83 F1
Fleury-les-Aubrais (45)...... 62 D6
Fleury-Mérogis (91)............... 42 D6
Fleury-sur-Andelle (27)...... 19 E5
Fleury-sur-Loire (58)............... 99 E5
Fleury-sur-Orne (14)............... 14 B5
Fléville (08)............... 24 C5
Fléville-devant-Nancy (54)... 48 D5
Fléville-Lixières (54)............... 25 H6
Flévy (57)............... 26 C4
Flexanville (78)............... 41 H4
Flexbourg (67)............... 50 C6
Fleys (89)............... 83 H2
Flez-Cuzy (58)............... 83 H4
Fligny (08)............... 10 C6
Flin (54)............... 70 B1
Flines-lès-Mortagne (59)...... 4 B6
Flines-lez-Raches (59)............... 8 D1
Flins-Neuve-Église (78)...... 41 G3
Flins-sur-Seine (78)............... 42 A3
Flipou (17)............... 18 D5
Flirey (54)............... 48 A3
Flixecourt (80)............... 7 F5
Flize (08)............... 24 B2
Flocourt (57)............... 49 E2
Flocques (76)............... 6 A4
Flogny-la-Chapelle (89)...... 65 H6
Floing (08)............... 24 C2
Floirac (17)............... 120 D5
Floirac (33)............... 135 F5
Floirac (46)............... 138 D5
FloracTrois Rivières (48).. 156 B5
Florange (57)............... 26 B3
Florémont (88)............... 69 G2
Florensac (34)............... 188 D2
Florent-en-Argonne (51)...... 46 D1
Florentin (81)............... 170 B3
Florentin-la-Capelle (12)... 154 C2
Floressas (46)............... 152 A3
Florimont (90)............... 89 E4
Florimont-Gaumier (24)... 152 B1
Floringhem (62)............... 2 C6
la Flotte (17)............... 106 B4
Flottemanville (50)............... 12 D3
Floudès (33)............... 150 A2
Floure (11)............... 187 F3
Flourens (31)............... 169 G5
Floursies (59)............... 10 A3
Floyon (59)............... 9 H4
Flumet (73)............... 132 D2
Fluquières (02)............... 21 H1
Fluy (80)............... 7 F6
Foameix-Ornel (55)............... 25 G6
Foce (2A)............... 207 E3
Focicchia (2B)............... 205 F3
Foëcy (18)............... 97 F2
le Fœil (22)............... 33 F5
Foisches (08)............... 11 H4
Foissac (12)............... 153 G3
Foissac (30)............... 174 A1
Foissiat (01)............... 116 D3
Foissy (21)............... 101 E2
Foissy-lès-Vézelay (89)... 83 H5
Foissy-sur-Vanne (89)............... 65 F4
Foix (09)............... 185 H5
Folcarde (31)............... 186 A1
Folembray (02)............... 22 A3
Folgensbourg (68)............... 89 G3
le Folgoët (29)............... 31 F3
la Folie (14)............... 13 G5
Folies (80)............... 21 E1

Folkling (57)............... 27 G5
Follainville-
  Dennemont (78)............... 41 H2
Folles (87)............... 110 D5
la Folletière-Abenon (14)... 39 H2
Folleville (27)............... 15 H5
Folleville (80)............... 20 C2
Folligny (50)............... 37 E3
Folschviller (57)............... 27 F6
Fomerey (88)............... 69 H3
Fomperron (79)............... 108 B2
Fonbeauzard (31)............... 169 F5
Foncegrive (21)............... 86 A3
Fonches-Fonchette (80)...... 21 F1
Foncine-le-Bas (39)............... 103 G6
Foncine-le-Haut (39)............... 103 G6
Foncquevillers (62)............... 8 A4
Fondamente (12)............... 172 A3
Fondettes (37)............... 78 D5
Fondremand (70)............... 87 F4
Fongrave (47)............... 151 E4
Fongueusemare (76)............... 16 C4
Fonroque (24)............... 151 E1
Fons (07)............... 157 G2
Fons (30)............... 173 H3
Fons (46)............... 153 G1
Fons-sur-Lussan (30)............... 157 G6
Fonsomme (02)............... 9 E6
Fonsorbes (31)............... 168 D6
Font-Romeu-Odeillo-
  Via (66)............... 199 H4
Fontain (25)............... 103 G1
Fontaine (10)............... 67 F4
Fontaine (90)............... 88 D3
Fontaine-au-Bois (59)............... 9 G4
Fontaine-au-Pire (59)............... 9 E4
Fontaine-Bellenger (27)...... 41 E1
Fontaine-Bonneleau (60)...... 20 B2
Fontaine-Chaalis (60)............... 43 F1
Fontaine-Chalendray (17)... 121 H1
Fontaine-Couverte (53)...... 58 A6
Fontaine-de-Vaucluse (84)... 175 G2
Fontaine-Denis-Nuisy (51)... 44 D6
Fontaine-en-Bray (76)............... 19 E2
Fontaine-en-Dormois (51)... 24 B6
Fontaine-Étoupefour (14)... 14 B5
Fontaine-Fourches (77)...... 65 E2
Fontaine-Française (21)...... 86 B4
Fontaine-Henry (14)............... 14 B4
Fontaine-la-Gaillarde (89)... 65 E4
Fontaine-la-Guyon (28)...... 61 H1
Fontaine-la-Louvet (27)...... 15 G5
Fontaine-la-Mallet (76)............... 15 F1
Fontaine-la-Rivière (91)...... 63 F3
Fontaine-l'Abbé (27)............... 40 B1
Fontaine-Lavaganne (60)...... 20 A3
Fontaine-le-Bourg (76)............... 18 D3
Fontaine-le-Comte (86)...... 109 E2
Fontaine-le-Dun (76)............... 17 F3
Fontaine-le-Pin (14)............... 38 D2
Fontaine-le-Port (77)............... 64 B1
Fontaine-le-Sec (80)............... 6 D5
Fontaine-les-Bassets (61)... 39 E3
Fontaine-lès-Boulans (62)... 2 B6
Fontaine-lès-Cappy (80)...... 8 B6
Fontaine-lès-Clercs (02)...... 21 H1
Fontaine-lès-Clerval (25)... 88 A5
Fontaine-les-Coteaux (41)... 79 E2
Fontaine-lès-Croisilles (62)... 8 C3
Fontaine-lès-Dijon (21)...... 85 H6
Fontaine-les-Grès (10)............... 66 A2
Fontaine-lès-Hermans (62)... 2 B6
Fontaine-lès-Luxeuil (70)... 87 H1
Fontaine-les-Ribouts (28)... 41 E5
Fontaine-lès-Vervins (02)... 9 H6
Fontaine-l'Étalon (62)............... 7 E2
Fontaine-Mâcon (10)............... 65 F2
Fontaine-Notre-Dame (02)... 9 F6
Fontaine-Notre-Dame (59)... 8 D3
Fontaine-Raoul (41)............... 61 G6
Fontaine-Saint-Lucien (60)... 20 B4
la Fontaine-Saint-
  Martin (72)............... 77 H2
Fontaine-Simon (28)............... 61 G1
Fontaine-sous-Jouy (27)...... 41 E2
Fontaine-sous-
  Montdidier (80)............... 20 D2
Fontaine-sous-Préaux (76)... 18 D4
Fontaine-sur-Ay (51)............... 45 F2
Fontaine-sur-Maye (80)............... 7 E3
Fontaine-sur-Somme (80)...... 7 E5
Fontaine-Uterte (02)............... 9 E6
Fontainebleau (77)............... 64 A2
Fontainebrux (39)............... 102 C6
Fontaines (71)............... 101 G5
Fontaines (85)............... 83 E3
Fontaines-d'Ozillac (17)... 121 G6
Fontaines-en-
  Duesmois (21)............... 85 E3
Fontaines-en-Sologne (41)... 80 B4
Fontaines-les-Sèches (21)... 84 C2
Fontaines-Saint-Clair (55)... 25 E5
Fontaines-Saint-
  Martin (69)............... 130 A2
Fontaines-sur-Marne (52)... 67 H1
Fontaines-sur-Saône (69)... 130 A2
Fontains (77)............... 64 C1
Fontan (06)............... 179 G1
Fontanès (30)............... 173 H3
Fontanès (34)............... 173 F4
Fontanès (42)............... 129 F5
Fontanes (46)............... 152 D5
Fontanès-de-Sault (11)...... 199 H1
Fontanges (15)............... 140 B3
Fontangy (21)............... 84 D6
Fontanières (23)............... 112 C6
Fontanil-Cornillon (38)...... 145 F2

Fontannes (43)............... 141 H2
Fontans (48)............... 155 H1
Fontarèches (30)............... 174 B1
Fontclaireau (16)............... 122 C2
Fontcouverte (11)............... 187 G4
Fontcouverte (17)............... 121 F2
Fontcouverte-la-
  Toussuire (73)............... 146 C2
la Fontelaye (76)............... 17 F4
Fontenai-les-Louvets (61)... 39 E6
Fontenai-sur-Orne (61)...... 39 E5
Fontenailles (77)............... 64 C1
Fontenay (36)............... 96 C3
Fontenay (71)............... 115 F2
Fontenay (76)............... 15 F1
Fontenay (88)............... 70 A3
Fontenay-aux-Roses (92)... 42 C4
Fontenay-de-Bossery (10)... 65 F2
Fontenay-en-Parisis (95)...... 42 D2
Fontenay-le-Comte (85)... 107 F2
Fontenay-le-Fleury (78)...... 42 B4
Fontenay-le-Marmion (14)... 14 B5
Fontenay-le-Pesnel (14)...... 14 A4
Fontenay-le-Vicomte (91)... 63 G1
Fontenay-lès-Briis (91)...... 42 C6
Fontenay-Mauvoisin (78)...... 41 G3
Fontenay-près-Chablis (89)... 83 H1
Fontenay-près-Vézelay (89)... 83 H5
Fontenay-Saint-Père (78)... 41 H2
Fontenay-sous-Bois (94)...... 42 D4
Fontenay-sous-
  Fouronnes (89)............... 83 G3
Fontenay-sur-Conie (28)...... 62 C4
Fontenay-sur-Eure (28)...... 62 A2
Fontenay-sur-Loing (45)...... 64 B5
Fontenay-sur-Mer (50)............... 13 E3
Fontenay-sur-Vègre (72)... 59 G6
Fontenay-Torcy (60)............... 19 G3
Fontenay-Trésigny (77)...... 43 G5
Fontenelle (02)............... 9 H5
Fontenelle (21)............... 86 B4
la Fontenelle (35)............... 35 G5
la Fontenelle (41)............... 61 F5
Fontenelle-Montby (25)...... 88 A5
les Fontenelles (25)............... 104 C1
Fontenet (17)............... 121 F1
Fontenille (16)............... 122 C1
Fontenille-Saint-Martin-
  d'Entraigues (79)............... 108 B5
Fontenilles (31)............... 168 D6
Fontenois-la-Ville (70)...... 69 G6
Fontenois-lès-
  Montbozon (70)............... 87 G4
Fontenotte (25)............... 87 H5
Fontenoy (02)............... 21 H5
Fontenoy (89)............... 83 E3
Fontenoy-la-Joûte (54)...... 70 B1
Fontenoy-le-Château (88)... 69 G6
Fontenoy-sur-Moselle (54)... 48 B5
Fontenu (39)............... 103 E6
Fonteny (57)............... 49 E3
Fonters-du-Razès (11)...... 186 B3
Fontès (34)............... 172 C6
Fontet (33)............... 150 B2
Fontette (10)............... 67 E5
Fontevraud-l'Abbaye (49)... 93 H1
Fontgombault (36)............... 95 H6
Fontguenand (36)............... 96 B1
Fontienne (04)............... 176 C1
Fontiers-Cabardès (11)...... 186 D2
Fontiès-d'Aude (11)............... 187 E3
Fontjoncouse (11)............... 187 H5
Fontoy (57)............... 26 A3
Fontpédrouse (66)............... 200 A4
Fontrabiouse (66)............... 199 H3
Fontrailles (65)............... 183 G2
Fontrieu (81)............... 171 E5
Fontvannes (10)............... 65 H3
Fontvieille (13)............... 174 D4
Forbach (57)............... 27 G4
Forcalqueiret (83)............... 193 F3
Forcalquier (04)............... 176 C2
la Force (11)............... 186 C3
la Force (24)............... 136 D5
Forcé (53)............... 58 D5
Forcelles-Saint-
  Gorgon (54)............... 69 F1
Forcelles-sous-
  Gugney (54)............... 69 F2
Forceville (80)............... 7 H4
Forceville-en-Vimeu (80)...... 6 D5
Forcey (52)............... 68 B4
Forciolo (2A)............... 207 E1
la Forclaz (74)............... 119 E3

Forges-la-Forêt (35)............... 57 H5
Forges-les-Bains (91)............... 42 B6
Forges-les-Eaux (76)............... 19 F3
Forges-sur-Meuse (55)...... 25 E6
Forges (31)............... 184 D1
la Forie (63)............... 128 B5
Forléans (21)............... 84 C5
Formentin (14)............... 15 E4
Formerie (60)............... 19 G2
Formigny La Bataille (14)... 13 G5
Formiguères (66)............... 199 H3
Fornex (09)............... 185 G3
Fors (79)............... 107 H4
Forstfeld (67)............... 51 G3
Forstheim (67)............... 51 E3
Fort-du-Plasne (39)............... 118 A1
Fort-Louis (67)............... 51 G3
Fort-Mahon-Plage (80)...... 6 C2
Fort-Moville (27)............... 15 G3
Fortan (41)............... 79 F1
Fortel-en-Artois (62)............... 7 F3
la Forteresse (38)............... 145 E1
Fortschwihr (68)............... 71 G4
Fos (31)............... 184 B6
Fos (34)............... 172 B6
Fos-sur-Mer (13)............... 191 H4
le Fossat (09)............... 185 F3
Fossé (08)............... 24 C4
Fossé (41)............... 79 H3
Fossé (66)............... 200 C1
la Fosse-Corduan (10)............... 65 G2
Fossemagne (24)............... 137 H3
Fossemanant (80)............... 20 B1
les Fosses (79)............... 107 H5
Fosses (95)............... 43 E2
Fossés-et-Baleyssac (33)... 150 B2
Fosseux (62)............... 7 H3
Fossieux (57)............... 48 D3
Fossoy (02)............... 44 C2
Foucarmont (76)............... 6 C6
Foucart (76)............... 16 D4
Foucaucourt-en-
  Santerre (80)............... 8 B6
Foucaucourt-Hors-
  Nesle (80)............... 6 C6
Foucaucourt-sur-
  Thabas (55)............... 47 E2
Fouchécourt (70)............... 87 F2
Fouchécourt (88)............... 69 E5
Foucherans (25)............... 103 G2
Foucherans (39)............... 102 C2
Fouchères (10)............... 66 C4
Fouchères (89)............... 64 D4
Fouchères-aux-Bois (55)...... 47 F6
Foucherolles (45)............... 64 C5
Fouchy (67)............... 71 E2
Foucrainville (27)............... 41 E3
Fouday (67)............... 71 E1
Fouencamps (80)............... 20 C1
Fouesnant (29)............... 53 G4
Foufflin-Ricametz (62)............... 7 G2
Foug (54)............... 48 A5
Fougaron (31)............... 184 C5
Fougax-et-Barrineuf (09)... 186 B6
Fougeré (85)............... 91 H4
Fougères (35)............... 58 A2
Fougères-sur-Bièvre (41)... 79 H5
les Fougerêts (56)............... 56 B6
Fougerolles (36)............... 111 G2
Fougerolles (70)............... 69 H6
Fougerolles-du-Plessis (53)... 58 B1
Fougueyrolles (24)............... 136 B5
la Fouillade (12)............... 153 G5
Fouilleuse (60)............... 20 D4
la Fouillouse (05)............... 160 B3
la Fouillouse (42)............... 129 F5
le Fouilloux (17)............... 135 H2
Fouilloy (60)............... 19 H2
Fouilloy (80)............... 7 H6
Fouju (77)............... 43 F6
Foulain (52)............... 68 A5
Foulangues (60)............... 20 C6
Foulayronnes (47)............... 151 F5
Foulbec (27)............... 15 G3
Foulcrey (57)............... 49 G5
Fouleix (24)............... 137 F4
Foulenay (39)............... 102 C4
Fouligny (57)............... 26 D5
Foulognes (14)............... 13 G6
Fouquebrune (16)............... 122 C5
Fouquenies (60)............... 20 A4
Fouquereuil (62)............... 2 D6
Fouquerolles (60)............... 20 B4
Fouquescourt (80)............... 21 E1
Fouqueure (16)............... 122 B2
Fouqueville (27)............... 18 B6
Fouquières-lès-
  Béthune (62)............... 2 D6
Fouquières-lès-Lens (62)...... 8 C1
Four (38)............... 130 C4
Fouras (17)............... 106 D6
Fourbanne (25)............... 87 H5
Fourcatier-et-Maison-
  Neuve (25)............... 104 A5
Fourcès (32)............... 167 F2
Fourchambault (58)............... 98 D3
Fourches (14)............... 39 E3
Fourcigny (80)............... 19 H1
Fourdrain (02)............... 22 B3
Fourdrinoy (80)............... 7 F6
Fourg (25)............... 103 E2
les Fourgs (25)............... 104 A4
Fourilles (03)............... 113 G4
Fourmagnac (46)............... 153 G1
Fourmetot (27)............... 15 H3
Fourmies (59)............... 10 B5
Fournaudin (89)............... 65 G4
Fourneaux (42)............... 129 E1

Fourneaux (50) 37 G2
Fourneaux (73) 147 E2
Fourneaux-le-Val (14) 38 D3
Fournels (48) 141 F6
Fournès (30) 174 C2
Fournes-Cabardès (11) 187 E2
Fournes-en-Weppes (59) 3 E5
le Fournet (14) 15 E4
Fournet-Blancheroche (25) 104 D1
Fournets-Luisans (25) 104 B2
Fourneville (14) 15 F3
Fournival (60) 20 C4
Fournols (63) 128 A5
Fouronnes (89) 83 F4
Fourques (30) 174 C4
Fourques (66) 201 E3
Fourques-sur-Garonne (47) 150 C3
Fourqueux (78) 42 B3
Fourquevaux (31) 169 G6
Fours (33) 135 E2
Fours (58) 99 H5
Fourtou (11) 187 E6
Foussais-Payré (85) 107 F1
Foussemagne (90) 88 D3
le Fousseret (31) 184 D2
Foussignac (16) 122 A3
Fouvent-Saint-Andoche (70) 86 D3
Fouzilhon (34) 172 B6
Foville (57) 48 D3
Fox-Amphoux (83) 177 E5
la Foye-Monjault (79) 107 G4
Fozières (34) 172 C4
Fozzano (2A) 207 E2
Fragnes-La Loyère (71) 101 G5
Frahier-et-Chatebier (70) 88 C3
Fraignot-et-Vesvrotte (21) 85 G3
Fraillicourt (08) 23 F2
Fraimbois (54) 49 F6
Frain (88) 69 E5
Frais (90) 88 D3
Fraisans (39) 103 E2
Fraisnes-en-Saintois (54) 69 F2
Fraisse (24) 136 C5
Fraisse-Cabardès (11) 186 D2
Fraissé-des-Corbières (11) 187 H5
Fraisse-sur-Agout (34) 171 G5
Fraisses (42) 129 E6
Fraissines (81) 171 E2
Fraissinet-de-Fourques (48) 156 A6
Fraize (88) 70 D3
Fralignes (10) 66 D4
la Framboisière (28) 40 C6
Frambouhans (25) 104 C1
Framecourt (62) 7 G2
Framerville-Rainecourt (80) 8 A6
Framicourt (80) 6 C5
Framont (70) 86 C4
Frampas (52) 67 F1
Francalmont (70) 87 G1
Francaltroff (57) 49 G2
Francarville (31) 169 H5
Francastel (60) 20 B3
Françay (41) 79 G3
Francazal (31) 184 D5
Francescas (47) 167 G1
Francheleins (01) 116 B6
Franchesse (03) 113 F1
Francheval (08) 24 C2
Franchevelle (70) 88 A2
la Francheville (08) 24 A1
Francheville (21) 85 G5
Francheville (39) 102 C5
Francheville (51) 46 A3
Francheville (54) 48 B4
Francheville (61) 39 E5
Francheville (69) 130 A3
Francières (60) 21 E4
Francières (80) 7 E4
Francillon (36) 96 B4
Francillon-sur-Roubion (26) 158 D2
Francilly-Selency (02) 8 D6
Francin (73) 132 A5
Franclens (74) 118 A6
François (79) 108 A3
Francon (31) 184 C3
Franconville (54) 69 H1
Franconville (95) 42 C3
Francoulès (46) 152 D3
Francourt (70) 86 D3
Francourville (28) 62 C2
Francs (33) 136 A4
Francueil (37) 79 G6
Franey (25) 103 E1
Frangy (74) 118 A6
Frangy-en-Bresse (71) 102 B6
Franken (68) 89 F3
Franleu (80) 6 C4
Franois (25) 103 F1
Franquevielle (31) 183 H4
Franqueville (02) 22 D1
Franqueville (27) 40 B1
Franqueville (80) 7 F4
Franqueville-Saint-Pierre (76) 18 D4
Frans (01) 130 A1
Fransart (80) 21 F1
Fransèches (23) 125 G1
Fransu (80) 7 F4
Fransures (80) 20 B2
Franvillers (80) 7 H5
Franxault (21) 102 B3
Frapelle (88) 70 D2
Fraquelfing (57) 49 H5
Fraroz (39) 103 G5
Frasnay-Reugny (58) 99 G3
Frasne (25) 103 G4
Frasne-le-Château (70) 87 E5
Frasne-les-Meulières (39) 102 C1
la Frasnée (39) 117 H1
le Frasnois (39) 103 F6
Frasnoy (59) 9 G2
Frasseto (2A) 205 E6
Frauenberg (57) 27 H5
Frausseilles (81) 170 A1
Fravaux (10) 67 E4
le Fraysse (81) 170 D3
Frayssinet (46) 152 D1
Frayssinet-le-Gélat (46) 152 B2
Frayssinhes (46) 139 F5
Frazé (28) 61 G3
Fréauville (76) 19 E1
Frebécourt (88) 68 D2
Frébuans (39) 102 C6
le Frêche (40) 166 C2
Fréchède (65) 183 F1
Fréchencourt (80) 7 H5
Fréchendets (65) 183 F4
le Fréchet (31) 184 C3
Fréchet-Aure (65) 183 G5
Fréchou (47) 167 F1
Fréchou-Fréchet (65) 183 F3
Frécourt (52) 68 B6
Frédéric-Fontaine (70) 88 B3
la Frédière (17) 121 F2
Frédille (36) 96 B3
Frégimont (47) 151 E5
Frégouville (32) 168 C5
Fréhel (22) 34 B3
Freigné (49) 75 F2
Freissinières (05) 147 E6
la Freissinouse (05) 160 B2
Freistroff (57) 26 D4
Freix-Anglards (15) 140 A4
Fréjairolles (81) 170 C3
Fréjeville (81) 170 C5
Fréjus (83) 194 C2
Fréland (68) 71 E4
Frelinghien (59) 3 F4
Frémainville (95) 42 A2
Frémécourt (95) 42 B1
Fréménil (54) 49 G6
Frémeréville-sous-les-Côtes (55) 47 H4
Frémery (57) 49 E3
Frémestroff (57) 49 G2
Frémicourt (62) 8 C4
Fremifontaine (88) 70 B3
Frémontiers (80) 20 A1
Frémonville (54) 49 H6
la Frénaye (76) 15 H2
Frencq (62) 1 F5
Frenelle-la-Grande (88) 69 F2
Frenelle-la-Petite (88) 69 F2
Freneuse (76) 18 C5
Freneuse (78) 41 G2
Freneuse-sur-Risle (27) 18 A6
Freney (73) 147 E2
le Freney-d'Oisans (38) 146 B3
Fréniches (60) 21 G2
Frénois (21) 85 G4
Frénois (88) 69 F4
Frénouville (14) 14 C5
Frépillon (95) 42 C2
Fresles (76) 19 E1
la Fresnaie-Fayel (61) 39 G4
la Fresnais (35) 35 E4
Fresnay (10) 67 F3
Fresnay-le-Comte (28) 62 B3
Fresnay-le-Gilmert (28) 62 A1
Fresnay-le-Long (76) 17 G4
Fresnay-le-Samson (61) 39 F3
Fresnay-l'Évêque (28) 62 D3
Fresnay-sur-Sarthe (72) 59 H3
le Fresne (27) 40 C3
le Fresne (51) 46 B3
le Fresne-Camilly (14) 14 B4
Fresne-Cauverville (27) 15 G4
Fresné-la-Mère (14) 38 D3
Fresne-l'Archevêque (27) 19 E5
Fresne-le-Plan (76) 19 E4
Fresne-Léguillon (60) 20 A6
le Fresne-Poret (50) 37 H5
Fresne-Saint-Mamès (70) 87 E4
Fresneaux-Montchevreuil (60) 20 A6
Fresnes (02) 22 A3
Fresnes (21) 84 D3
Fresnes (41) 80 A5
Fresnes (89) 84 A2
Fresnes (94) 42 D5
Fresnes-au-Mont (55) 47 G3
Fresnes-en-Saulnois (57) 49 E3
Fresnes-en-Tardenois (02) 44 C1
Fresnes-en-Woëvre (55) 47 H1
Fresnes-lès-Montauban (62) 8 C2
Fresnes-Mazancourt (80) 8 B6
Fresnes-sur-Apance (52) 69 E6
Fresnes-sur-Escaut (59) 9 F1
Fresnes-sur-Marne (77) 43 F3
Fresnes-Tilloloy (80) 6 D5
Fresneville (80) 6 D6
Fresney (27) 41 E3
Fresney-le-Puceux (14) 14 B5
Fresney-le-Vieux (14) 38 C2
Fresnicourt-le-Dolmen (62) 8 A1
Fresnières (60) 21 F3
Fresnois-la-Montagne (54) 25 G3
Fresnoy (62) 7 F2
Fresnoy-Andainville (80) 6 D6
Fresnoy-au-Val (80) 7 E6
Fresnoy-en-Chaussée (80) 20 D1
Fresnoy-en-Gohelle (62) 8 C2
Fresnoy-en-Thelle (60) 20 C6
Fresnoy-Folny (76) 6 B6
Fresnoy-la-Rivière (60) 21 F6
Fresnoy-le-Château (10) 66 C4
Fresnoy-le-Grand (02) 9 F5
Fresnoy-le-Luat (60) 21 E6
Fresnoy-lès-Roye (80) 21 F2
Frespech (47) 151 G4
Fresquiennes (76) 18 C3
Fressac (30) 173 G2
Fressain (59) 8 D2
Fressancourt (02) 22 B2
Fresse (70) 88 B2
Fresse-sur-Moselle (88) 70 C6
Fresselines (23) 111 F3
Fressenneville (80) 6 C4
Fressies (59) 8 D3
Fressin (62) 7 E1
Fressines (79) 108 A3
le Frestoy-Vaux (60) 21 E3
Fresville (50) 12 D4
Fréterive (73) 132 B4
Fréteval (41) 79 H1
Fréthun (62) 1 G2
Fretigney-et-Velloreille (70) 87 F4
Frétigny (28) 61 F2
Fretin (59) 3 G6
Frétoy (77) 44 A5
Frétoy-le-Château (60) 21 G2
la Frette (38) 131 E6
la Frette (71) 116 C1
la Frette-sur-Seine (95) 42 C3
Frettecuisse (80) 6 D6
Frettemeule (80) 6 C5
Fretterans (71) 102 B4
le Fréty (08) 23 G1
Freulleville (76) 17 H3
Frévent (62) 7 G2
Fréville (88) 68 C3
Fréville-du-Gâtinais (45) 63 G6
Frévillers (62) 7 H1
Frévin-Capelle (62) 8 A2
Freybouse (57) 49 G2
Freycenet-la-Cuche (43) 142 D5
Freycenet-la-Tour (43) 142 D5
Freychenet (09) 185 H6
Freyming-Merlebach (57) 27 F5
Freyssenet (07) 157 H1
Friaize (28) 61 G2
Friaucourt (80) 6 B4
Friauville (54) 48 A1
Fribourg (57) 49 G4
Fricamps (80) 7 E6
Frichemesnil (76) 17 G4
Fricourt (80) 8 B5
Fridefont (15) 141 F5
Friedolsheim (67) 50 C4
Frières-Faillouël (02) 21 H2
Friesen (68) 89 E3
Friesenheim (67) 71 H2
Frignicourt (51) 46 B5
Frise (80) 8 B5
Friville-Escarbotin (80) 6 B4
Frizon (88) 69 H3
Froberville (76) 16 C3
Frocourt (60) 20 A5
Frœningen (68) 89 F2
Frœschwiller (67) 51 E2
Froges (38) 145 H1
Frohen-sur-Authie (80) 7 F3
Frohmuhl (67) 50 B3
Froideconche (70) 87 H1
Froidefontaine (90) 88 D3
Froidestrées (02) 10 A5
Froideterre (70) 88 A2
Froidevaux (25) 88 B6
Froidfond (85) 91 E2
Froidmont-Cohartille (02) 22 C2
Froidos (55) 47 E2
Froissy (60) 20 B3
Frôlois (21) 85 E4
Frolois (54) 48 C6
Fromelennes (08) 11 F4
Fromelles (59) 3 E5
Fromental (87) 110 D5
Fromentières (51) 44 D3
Fromentières (53) 76 D1
Fromeréville-les-Vallons (55) 47 F1
Fromezey (55) 25 G6
Fromont (77) 63 H3
Fromy (08) 25 E3
Froncles (52) 67 H3
Fronsac (31) 184 A5
Fronsac (33) 135 G4
Frontenac (33) 135 H6
Frontenac (46) 153 G3
Frontenard (71) 102 A4
Frontenas (69) 129 G1
Frontenaud (71) 117 E1
Frontenay (39) 102 D5
Frontenay-Rohan-Rohan (79) 107 G4
Frontenex (73) 132 C4
Frontignan (34) 189 F1
Frontignan-de-Comminges (31) 184 A5
Frontignan-Savès (31) 184 C1
Fronton (31) 169 E3
Frontonas (38) 130 C4
Fronville (52) 67 H2
Frossay (44) 74 A5
Frotey-lès-Lure (70) 88 A3
Frotey-lès-Vesoul (70) 87 G3
Frouard (54) 48 C4
Frouville (95) 42 C1
Frouzins (31) 169 E6
Froville (54) 69 H1
Froyelles (80) 7 E3
Frozes (86) 94 A6
Frucourt (80) 6 D5
Frugerès-les-Mines (43) 141 G1
Fruges (62) 2 A6
Frugières-le-Pin (43) 141 H2
Fruncé (28) 61 H2
Fry (76) 19 F3
Fuans (25) 104 B2
Fublaines (77) 43 G3
le Fugeret (04) 178 A1
Fuilla (66) 200 B3
Fuissé (71) 116 B4
Fuligny (10) 67 F3
Fulleren (68) 89 E3
Fultot (76) 17 E3
Fulvy (89) 84 B2
Fumay (08) 11 E5
Fumel (47) 151 H3
Fumichon (14) 15 G5
Furchhausen (67) 50 C4
Furdenheim (67) 50 D5
Furiani (2B) 203 G4
Furmeyer (05) 160 A2
Fursac (23) 111 E5
Fussey (21) 101 G2
Fussy (18) 97 H2
Fustérouau (32) 166 D4
Fustignac (31) 184 C2
Futeau (55) 46 D2
Fuveau (13) 192 C2
Fyé (72) 60 A3

G

Gaas (40) 165 E5
Gabarnac (33) 149 H2
Gabarret (40) 166 D2
Gabaston (64) 182 C1
Gabat (64) 181 F1
Gabian (34) 172 B6
Gabillou (24) 137 H2
Gabre (09) 185 F4
Gabriac (12) 154 D3
Gabriac (48) 156 C6
Gabrias (48) 155 H3
Gacé (61) 39 G4
la Gacilly (56) 56 C6
Gâcogne (58) 100 A1
Gadancourt (95) 42 A2
Gadencourt (27) 41 F3
Gaël (35) 56 B2
Gageac-et-Rouillac (24) 136 C6
Gagnac-sur-Cère (46) 139 F5
Gagnac-sur-Garonne (31) 169 E4
Gagnières (30) 157 E5
Gagny (93) 43 E4
Gahard (35) 57 G1
Gailhan (30) 173 G3
Gaillac (81) 170 A3
Gaillac-d'Aveyron (12) 155 E4
Gaillac-Toulza (31) 185 G3
Gaillagos (65) 182 C5
Gaillan-en-Médoc (33) 120 C6
Gaillard (74) 118 C5
la Gaillarde (76) 17 F2
Gaillefontaine (76) 19 F2
Gaillères (40) 166 B2
Gaillon (27) 41 E1
Gaillon-sur-Montcient (78) 42 A2
Gainneville (76) 15 F2
Gaja-et-Villedieu (11) 186 D4
Gaja-la-Selve (11) 186 B3
Gajac (33) 150 A3
Gajan (09) 184 D5
Gajan (30) 174 A3
Gajoubert (87) 109 H5
Galametz (62) 7 F2
Galan (65) 183 G3
Galapian (47) 150 D5
Galargues (34) 173 G4
Galéria (2B) 204 B1
Galey (09) 184 C5
Galez (65) 183 G3
Galfingue (68) 89 E2
Galgan (12) 153 H3
Galgon (33) 135 G4
Galiax (32) 166 D5
Galié (31) 184 A5
Galinagues (11) 199 H1
Gallardon (28) 62 C1
Gallargues-le-Montueux (30) 173 H4
le Gallet (60) 20 B3
Galluis (78) 41 H4
Gamaches (80) 6 B5
Gamaches-en-Vexin (27) 19 F6
Gamarde-les-Bains (40) 165 F4
Gamarthe (64) 181 E3
Gambais (78) 41 G4
Gambaiseuil (78) 41 H5
Gambsheim (67) 51 F4
Gan (64) 182 B3
Ganac (09) 185 G5
Ganagobie (04) 176 D1
Gancourt-Saint-Étienne (76) 19 G3
Gandelain (61) 59 H1
Gandelu (02) 44 A2
Gandrange (57) 26 B4
Ganges (34) 173 E2
Gannat (03) 113 G6
Gannay-sur-Loire (03) 99 G6
Gannes (60) 20 C3
Gans (33) 150 A3
Ganties (31) 184 B4
Ganzeville (76) 16 C3
Gap (05) 160 B2
Gapennes (80) 7 E3
Gâprée (61) 39 G6
Garac (31) 168 C4
Garancières (78) 41 H4
Garancières-en-Beauce (28) 62 D2
Garancières-en-Drouais (28) 41 E5
Garanou (09) 199 F1
Garat (16) 122 C4
Garcelles-Secqueville (14) 14 C5
Garches (92) 42 C4
Garchizy (58) 98 D3
Garchy (58) 98 D1
Gardanne (13) 192 B2
la Garde (04) 177 H3
la Garde (38) 146 A3
la Garde (83) 193 F5
la Garde-Adhémar (26) 158 B4
Garde-Colombe (05) 159 H4
la Garde-Freinet (83) 194 A3
Gardefort (18) 98 B1
Gardegan-et-Tourtirac (33) 136 A5
Gardères (65) 182 D2
Gardes-le-Pontaroux (16) 122 C5
Gardie (11) 186 D4
Gardonne (24) 136 C5
Gardouch (31) 185 H1
Garein (40) 165 H1
la Garenne-Colombes (92) 42 C3
Garennes-sur-Eure (27) 41 F3
Les Garennes sur Loire (49) 77 E5
Garentreville (77) 63 H4
Garéoult (83) 193 F3
Garganvillar (82) 168 C2
Gargas (31) 169 F4
Gargas (84) 175 H2
Gargenville (78) 41 H2
Garges-lès-Gonesse (95) 42 D3
Gargilesse-Dampierre (36) 111 E2
Garidech (31) 169 G4
Gariès (82) 168 C3
Garigny (18) 98 C3
Garin (31) 197 F1
Garindein (64) 181 F3
Garlan (29) 32 A3
Garlède-Mondebat (64) 166 B6
Garlin (64) 166 B5
le Garn (30) 157 G5
la Garnache (85) 90 D2
Garnat-sur-Engièvre (03) 114 B1
Garnay (28) 41 E5
Garnerans (01) 116 B5
Garons (30) 174 B4
Garos (64) 166 A6
Garravet (32) 184 C1
Garrebourg (57) 50 B4
Garrevaques (81) 170 B6
Garrey (40) 165 F4
le Garric (81) 170 C2
Garrigues (34) 173 G4
Garrigues (81) 169 H4
Garrigues-Sainte-Eulalie (30) 174 A2
Garris (64) 181 F1
Garrosse (40) 165 F1
Gars (06) 178 B2
Gartempe (23) 111 F5
Gas (28) 41 G6
Gasny (27) 41 G2
Gasques (82) 151 H6
Gassin (83) 194 B4
Gastes (40) 148 B4
Gastines (53) 58 A6
Gastins (77) 43 H6
Gasville-Oisème (28) 62 B1
Gatey (39) 102 C4
Gathemo (50) 37 G4
Gatteville-le-Phare (50) 13 E1
Gattières (06) 179 E3
Gatuzières (48) 156 A6
Gaubertin (45) 63 G5
la Gaubretière (85) 92 B3
Gauchin-Légal (62) 8 A1
Gauchin-Verloingt (62) 7 G1
Gauchy (02) 9 E6
Gauciel (27) 41 E2
la Gaudaine (28) 61 F3
la Gaude (06) 178 D4
Gaudechart (60) 20 A3
Gaudent (65) 184 A5
Gaudiempré (62) 7 H3
Gaudiès (09) 186 A3
Gaudonville (32) 168 B3
Gaudreville-la-Rivière (27) 40 D3
Gaugeac (24) 151 G1
Gaujac (30) 174 C1
Gaujac (32) 168 B6
Gaujac (47) 150 B3
Gaujacq (40) 165 G4
Gaujan (32) 184 B1
le Gault-du-Perche (41) 61 F5
le Gault-Saint-Denis (28) 62 B3
le Gault-Soigny (51) 44 C4
Gauré (31) 169 G5
Gauriac (33) 135 E3
Gauriaguet (33) 135 G3
Gaussan (65) 183 H3
Gausson (22) 33 G6
Gauville (80) 19 H1
Gauville-la-Campagne (27) 40 D2
Gavarnie-Gèdre (65) 196 B1
Gavarret-sur-Aulouste (32) 167 H4
Gavaudun (47) 151 G2
Gavignano (2B) 205 F1
Gavisse (57) 26 C2
Gavray (50) 37 E3
le Gâvre (44) 74 C2
Gavrelle (62) 8 C2
Gâvres (56) 54 C6
Gavrus (14) 14 B5
Gayan (65) 183 E2
Gaye (51) 45 E5
Gayon (64) 166 C6
Gazaupouy (32) 167 G1
Gazave (65) 183 G4
Gazax-et-Baccarisse (32) 167 E5
Gazeran (78) 41 H6
Gazost (65) 183 E4
Geaune (40) 166 B5
Geay (17) 120 D2
Geay (79) 93 F4
Gée-Rivière (32) 166 C4
Geffosses (50) 12 C6
Géfosse-Fontenay (14) 13 F4
Gehée (36) 96 B3
Geishouse (68) 70 D6
Geispitzen (68) 89 G2
Geispolsheim (67) 51 E6
Geiswasser (68) 71 H5
Geiswiller (67) 50 D4
Gélacourt (54) 70 B1
Gélannes (10) 65 G1
Gélaucourt (54) 69 E1
Gellainville (28) 62 B2
Gellenoncourt (54) 49 E5
Gelles (63) 126 D3
Gellin (25) 103 H5
Gelos (64) 182 B2
Geloux (40) 165 H1
Gelucourt (57) 49 G4
Gelvécourt-et-Adompt (88) 69 G4
Gemaingoutte (88) 70 D3
Gembrie (65) 184 A5
Gemeaux (21) 85 H5
Gémenos (13) 192 C4
Gémigny (45) 62 C6
Gémil (31) 169 G4
Gemmelaincourt (88) 69 E3
Gémonval (25) 88 B4
Gémonville (54) 69 E2
Gémozac (17) 121 E4
Genac-Bignac (16) 122 B2
Genainville (95) 41 H1
Genas (69) 130 B3
Génat (09) 199 E1
Genay (21) 84 C4
Genay (69) 130 A2
Gençay (86) 109 E3
Gendreville (88) 68 D3
Gendrey (39) 102 D1
Génébrières (82) 169 F2
Genech (59) 3 G6
Génelard (71) 115 F1
Générac (30) 174 B4
Générac (33) 135 F2
Générargues (30) 173 G1
Générest (65) 183 H5
Generville (11) 186 B3
le Genest-Saint-Isle (53) 58 C4
Genestelle (07) 157 G1
Geneston (44) 91 G1
la Genête (71) 116 C2
la Genétouze (17) 136 A2
La Genétouze (85) 91 F4
Genêts (50) 35 G3
les Genettes (61) 40 A5
Geneuille (25) 87 F6
la Genevraie (61) 39 G5
la Genevraye (77) 64 A3
Genevreuille (70) 87 H3
Genevrey (70) 87 H2
Genevrières (52) 86 C2
la Genevroye (52) 67 H3
Geney (25) 88 B4
la Geneytouse (87) 124 C3
Génicourt (95) 42 B2
Génicourt-sur-Meuse (55) 47 G2
Genilac (42) 129 G5
Genillé (37) 95 G2
Génis (24) 138 A1
Génissac (33) 135 G5
Génissieux (26) 144 C3
Genlis (21) 102 B1
Gennes (25) 103 G1
Gennes-Ivergny (62) 7 E2
Gennes-sur-Glaize (53) 76 D1
Gennes-sur-Seiche (35) 58 A5
Gennes-Val de Loire (49) 77 F6
Gennetines (03) 114 A1
Genneton (79) 93 E2
Genneville (14) 15 F3
Gennevilliers (92) 42 C3
Genod (39) 117 F3
Génolhac (30) 156 D4
Génos (31) 184 A5
Génos (65) 197 E1
Genouillac (16) 123 E2
Genouillac (23) 111 H3
Genouillé (17) 107 F6
Genouillé (86) 109 E5
Genouilleux (01) 116 B5
Genouilly (18) 96 D2
Genouilly (71) 115 H1
Gensac (33) 136 B6
Gensac (65) 183 E1
Gensac (82) 168 C2
Gensac-de-Boulogne (31) 184 A3
Gensac-la-Pallue (16) 121 H4
Gensac-sur-Garonne (31) 184 D3
Genté (16) 121 G4
Gentelles (80) 7 H6
Gentilly (94) 42 D4

Gentioux-Pigerolles (23)........ 125 F3
Genvry (60)........................... 21 G3
Georfans (70)......................... 88 A4
Géovreisset (01)................... 117 G4
Ger (50).................................. 37 H5
Ger (64)................................ 182 D2
Ger (65)................................ 182 A4
Geraise (39).......................... 103 F3
Gérardmer (88)....................... 70 C5
Géraudot (10)......................... 66 C3
Gerbaix (73)......................... 131 G4
Gerbamont (88)....................... 70 C5
Gerbécourt (57)...................... 49 E3
Gerbécourt-et-
  Haplemont (54)..................... 69 F1
Gerbépal (88)......................... 70 C4
Gerberoy (60)......................... 19 H3
Gerbéviller (54)...................... 70 A1
Gercourt-et-
  Drillancourt (55)................... 25 E5
Gercy (02).............................. 22 D1
Gerde (65)............................ 183 F4
Gerderest (64)...................... 182 D1
Gère-Bélesten (64)................ 182 B4
Gergny (02)............................ 10 A6
Gergueil (21)......................... 101 G1
Gergy (71)............................ 101 H4
Gerland (21)......................... 101 H2
Germ (65)............................. 197 E1
Germagny (71)...................... 101 F6
Germaine (02)........................ 21 H1
Germaine (51)........................ 45 F1
Germaines (52)....................... 85 H2
Germainville (28).................... 41 F5
Germainvilliers (52)............... 68 D4
Germay (52)........................... 68 B2
Germéfontaine (25)................ 104 B1
Germenay (58)........................ 99 G1
Germignac (17)..................... 121 G4
Germigney (39)...................... 103 E3
Germigney (70)....................... 86 C5
Germigny (51)......................... 22 D6
Germigny (89)........................ 65 H6
Germigny-des-Prés (45)........... 81 F1
Germigny-l'Évêque (77).......... 43 G3
Germigny-l'Exempt (18)........... 98 C4
Germigny-sous-
  Coulombs (77)...................... 44 A2
Germigny-sur-Loire (58).......... 98 D3
Germinon (51)........................ 45 G4
Germiny (54).......................... 48 B6
Germisay (52)........................ 68 B2
Germolles-sur-Grosne (71)..... 116 A4
Germond-Rouvre (79)............. 107 H2
Germondans (25).................... 87 G5
Germont (08)......................... 24 B4
Germonville (54)..................... 69 G2
Germs-sur-l'Oussouet (65)..... 183 E4
Gernelle (08).......................... 24 B1
Géronce (64)........................ 181 H2
Gerponville (76)..................... 16 D3
Gerrots (14)........................... 15 E4
Gerstheim (67)....................... 71 H1
Gertwiller (67)....................... 71 G1
Geruge (39).......................... 117 F1
Gervans (26)......................... 144 A3
Gerville (76).......................... 16 C4
Géry (55)............................... 47 F4
Gerzat (63).......................... 127 F2
Gesnes (53)........................... 59 E4
Gesnes-en-Argonne (55)......... 24 D5
Gesnes-le-Gandelin (72)......... 59 H2
Gespunsart (08)..................... 24 B1
Gestas (64).......................... 181 G1
Gestel (56)............................ 54 C5
Gestiès (09)......................... 199 E1
Gesvres (53).......................... 59 G2
Gesvres-le-Chapitre (77)........ 43 G2
Gétigné (44)........................... 75 E6
les Gets (74)........................ 119 F5
Geu (65)............................... 182 D4
Geudertheim (67).................... 51 E4
Géus-d'Arzacq (64)............... 165 H6
Geüs-d'Oloron (64)............... 181 H2
Gévezé (35)........................... 57 E2
Gevigney-et-Mercey (70)........ 87 E2
Geville (54)............................ 47 H4
Gevingey (39)....................... 117 F1
Gevresin (25)........................ 103 G3
Gevrey-Chambertin (21)......... 101 H1
Gevrolles (21)......................... 67 F6
Gevry (39)............................ 102 C3
Gex (01)............................... 118 B3
Geyssans (26)....................... 144 C3
Gez (65)............................... 182 D5
Gez-Ez-Angles (65).............. 183 E4
Gézaincourt (80)...................... 7 G4
Gézier-et-Fontenelay (70)....... 87 E6
Gézoncourt (54)..................... 48 B4
Ghisonaccia (2B).................. 205 G5
Ghisoni (2B)......................... 205 F4
Ghissignies (59)....................... 9 G3
Ghyvelde (59).......................... 2 C1
Giat (63)............................... 126 A3
Gibeaumeix (54)..................... 48 A6
Gibel (31)............................. 185 H2
Gibourne (17)....................... 121 G1
Gibret (40)........................... 165 F4
le Gicq (17).......................... 121 H1
Gidy (45)................................ 62 D6
Giel-Courteilles (61)............... 38 D4
Gien (45).............................. 82 A3
Gien-sur-Cure (58)................ 100 B2
Gières (38)........................... 145 G2
la Giettaz (73)...................... 132 D2

Gièvres (41)........................... 96 C1
Giey-sur-Aujon (52)................ 85 H1
Giez (74).............................. 132 B3
Gif-sur-Yvette (91)................. 42 B5
Giffaumont-
  Champaubert (51)................. 67 F1
Gigean (34).......................... 173 E6
Gignac (34).......................... 172 D5
Gignac (46).......................... 138 C4
Gignac (84).......................... 176 B2
Gignac-la-Nerthe (13)........... 191 H5
Gignat (63).......................... 127 F6
Gignéville (88)....................... 69 E4
Gigney (88)........................... 69 H3
Gigny (39)............................ 117 F2
Gigny (89)............................. 84 C2
Gigny-Bussy (51).................... 46 B6
Gigny-sur-Saône (71)............ 101 H6
Gigondas (84)....................... 158 C6
Gigors (04)........................... 160 C3
Gigors-et-Lozeron (26).......... 144 C6
Gigouzac (46)....................... 152 C2
Gijounet (81)........................ 171 F4
Gildwiller (68)........................ 89 E2
Gilette (06).......................... 178 D2
Gilhac-et-Bruzac (07)........... 144 A5
Gilhoc-sur-Ormèze (07)........ 143 H4
Gillancourt (52)..................... 67 G4
Gillaumé (52)......................... 68 B1
Gilles (28)............................. 41 F3
Gilley (25).......................... 104 B2
Gilley (52)............................. 86 D3
Gillois (39).......................... 103 G5
Gillonnay (38)...................... 130 D6
Gilly-lès-Cîteaux (21).......... 101 H2
Gilly-sur-Isère (73).............. 132 C4
Gilly-sur-Loire (71).............. 114 C2
Gilocourt (60)........................ 21 F6
Gimat (82)........................... 168 C3
Gimbrède (32)...................... 168 A1
Gimeaux (63)........................ 127 F1
Gimécourt (55)....................... 47 F4
Gimel-les-Cascades (19)....... 139 F3
Gimeux (16).......................... 121 G4
la Gimond (42)..................... 129 F5
Gimont (32).......................... 168 B5
Gimouille (58)........................ 98 D4
Ginai (61).............................. 39 F4
Ginals (82).......................... 153 F6
Ginasservis (83)................... 176 B4
Ginchy (80)............................. 8 B5
Gincla (11)........................... 200 B1
Gincrey (55).......................... 25 G6
Gindou (46).......................... 152 B2
Ginestas (11)....................... 187 H3
Ginestet (24)....................... 136 D5
Ginoles (11)......................... 186 C6
Ginouillac (46)..................... 152 D1
la Gohannière (50)................. 37 E4
Gintrac (46)......................... 139 E5
Giocatojo (2B)..................... 203 F6
Gionges (51).......................... 45 F3
Giou-de-Mamou (15)............ 140 B5
Gioux (23)........................... 125 G3
Gipcy (03)........................... 113 F2
Girac (46)........................... 139 E5
Girancourt (88)...................... 69 G4
Giraumont (54)...................... 26 A5
Giraumont (60)...................... 21 F4
Girauvoisin (55)..................... 47 G4
Gircourt-lès-Viéville (88)....... 69 G2
Girecourt-sur-Durbion (88)..... 70 A3
Girefontaine (70)................... 69 G6
Giremoutiers (77).................. 43 H4
Girgols (15)......................... 140 B4
Giriviller (54)........................ 70 A1
Girmont-Val-d'Ajol (88)......... 70 A6
Girolles (45).......................... 64 A5
Girolles (89).......................... 83 H4
Giromagny (90)...................... 88 C2
Giron (01)........................... 117 H4
Gironcourt-sur-Vraine (88)..... 69 E3
Gironde-sur-Dropt (33)......... 150 A2
Girondelle (08)...................... 10 D6
Gironville (77)........................ 63 H4
Gironville-sur-Essonne (91).... 63 G2
le Girouard (85)..................... 91 F5
Giroussens (81)..................... 169 H4
Giroux (36)........................... 96 D3
Giry (58).............................. 99 F1
Giscaro (32)........................ 168 B5
Giscos (33).......................... 149 H5
Gisors (27)............................ 19 G6
Gissac (12).......................... 171 H3
Gissey-le-Vieil (21)................ 85 E4
Gissey-sous-Flavigny (21)...... 85 E4
Gissey-sur-Ouche (21).......... 101 G1
Gisy-les-Nobles (89).............. 64 D3
Giuncaggio (2B)................... 205 G3
Giuncheto (2A)..................... 206 D3
Givardon (18)........................ 98 B5
Givenchy-en-Gohelle (62)........ 8 B1
Givenchy-le-Noble (62)............ 7 H2
Givenchy-lès-la-
  Bassée (62)........................... 2 D6
Giverny (27)........................... 41 G2
Giverville (27)........................ 15 H4
Givet (08).............................. 11 H4
Givonne (08).......................... 24 C2
Givors (69).......................... 130 A4
Givraines (45)........................ 63 G4
Givrand (85).......................... 90 D4
Givraval (55).......................... 47 F5
le Givre (85).......................... 91 G6
Givrezac (17)....................... 121 E4
Givron (08)............................ 23 G2
Givry (08).............................. 23 H4
Givry (71)............................ 101 F5
Givry (89).............................. 83 H4

Givry-en-Argonne (51)............ 46 C3
Givry-lès-Loisy (51)................ 45 E3
Givrycourt (57)....................... 49 H3
Gizaucourt (51)...................... 46 C2
Gizay (86)........................... 109 F2
Gizeux (37)............................ 78 A5
Gizia (39)............................ 117 F2
Gizy (02)............................... 22 D3
Glageon (59)......................... 10 B4
Glaignes (60)......................... 21 F6
Glaine-Montaigut (63).......... 127 G3
Glaire (08)............................. 24 C2
le Glaizil (05)....................... 146 A6
Glamondans (25).................... 87 H6
Gland (02)............................. 44 C2
Gland (89)............................. 84 C2
Glandage (26)...................... 159 G1
Glandon (87)........................ 124 B5
Glanes (46).......................... 139 F5
Glanges (87)........................ 124 B4
Glannes (51).......................... 46 A5
Glanon (21)......................... 102 A3
Glanville (14)......................... 15 E4
Glatens (82)......................... 168 B3
Glatigny (57)......................... 26 C5
Glatigny (60)......................... 19 H4
Glay (25).............................. 88 D5
Gleizé (69).......................... 129 H1
Glénay (79)............................ 93 F4
Glénic (23).......................... 111 G5
Glénouze (86)........................ 93 H3
Glère (25)............................. 88 D5
Glisolles (27)......................... 40 D2
Glisy (80)............................... 7 G6
Glomel (22)........................... 54 C1
Glonville (54)......................... 70 B1
Glorianes (66)...................... 200 D3
Glos (14).............................. 15 F5
Glos-sur-Risle (27)................ 18 A6
Gluiras (07)......................... 143 G5
Glun (07)............................. 144 A4
Glux-en-Glenne (58)............ 100 B4
Goas (82)............................ 168 C3
la Godefroy (50).................... 35 H3
Godenvillers (60)................... 20 D3
Goderville (76)....................... 16 C4
Godewaersvelde (59)............... 2 D3
Godisson (61)........................ 39 G5
la Godivelle (63).................. 141 E1
Godoncourt (88).................... 69 E5
Gœrlingen (67)...................... 50 A4
Gœrsdorf (67)........................ 51 E2
Gœs (64)............................. 182 A3
Goetzenbruck (57).................. 50 C2
Gœulzin (59).......................... 8 D2
Gogney (54)........................... 49 G5
Gognies-Chaussée (59)........... 10 A2
Gohory (28)........................... 61 H4
Goin (57).............................. 48 C2
Goincourt (60)........................ 20 A4
Golancourt (60)...................... 21 G2
Golbey (88)........................... 69 H4
Goldbach-Altenbach (68)........ 71 E6
Golfech (82)......................... 151 G6
Golinhac (12)....................... 154 C2
Golleville (50)........................ 12 C3
Gombergean (41)................... 79 G3
Gomelange (57)..................... 26 D4
Gomené (22).......................... 56 A2
Gomer (64).......................... 182 C2
Gometz-la-Ville (91)............... 42 B5
Gometz-le-Châtel (91)............ 42 B5
Gomiécourt (62)...................... 8 B4
Gommecourt (62)..................... 8 A4
Gommecourt (78)................... 41 G2
Gommegnies (59)..................... 9 G2
Gommenec'h (22)................... 33 F3
Gommersdorf (68).................. 89 E3
Gommerville (28).................... 62 D3
Gommerville (76).................... 15 G1
Gomméville (21)..................... 66 D6
Gomont (08).......................... 23 F4
Goncelin (38)....................... 146 A1
Goncourt (52)........................ 68 C3
Gond-Pontouvre (16)............ 122 C4
Gondecourt (59)...................... 3 F6
Gondenans-les-
  Moulins (25)........................ 87 H4
Gondenans-Montby (25)......... 88 A5
Gondeville (16).................... 121 H3
Gondrecourt-Aix (54)............. 25 H6
Gondrecourt-le-
  Château (55)........................ 68 C1
Gondreville (45)..................... 64 A5
Gondreville (54)..................... 48 B5
Gondreville (60)..................... 21 G6
Gondrexange (57)................... 49 H5
Gondrexon (54)...................... 49 G5
Gondrin (32)........................ 167 F2
les Gonds (17)..................... 121 E3
Gonesse (95)......................... 42 D3
Gonez (65)........................... 183 F3
Gonfaron (83)...................... 193 H3
Gonfreville (50)...................... 12 D5
Gonfreville-Caillot (76)........... 16 C4
Gonfreville-l'Orcher (76)......... 15 F2
la Gonfrière (61).................... 39 H4
Gonnehem (62)........................ 2 C6
Gonnelieu (59)........................ 8 D4
Gonnetot (76)........................ 17 F3
Gonneville-en-Auge (14)......... 14 C4
Gonneville-la-Mallet (76)........ 16 B4
Gonneville-Le Theil (50)......... 12 D2
Gonneville-sur-
  Honfleur (14)....................... 15 F3
Gonneville-sur-Mer (14).......... 14 D4

Gonneville-sur-Scie (76)......... 17 G3
Gonsans (25)........................ 103 H1
Gontaud-de-Nogaret (47)...... 150 D3
la Gonterie-
  Boulouneix (24).................. 123 E6
Gonzeville (76)....................... 17 E3
Goos (40)............................ 165 F4
Gorbio (06).......................... 179 F3
Gorcy (54)............................. 25 G3
Gordes (84).......................... 175 G2
Gorenflos (80)......................... 7 F4
Gorges (44)........................... 75 E6
Gorges (50)........................... 12 D5
Gorges (80)............................ 7 F4
Gorges du Tarn
  Causses (48)...................... 155 H4
la Gorgue (59)......................... 2 D5
Gorhey (88)........................... 69 G4
Gornac (33)......................... 150 A1
Gorniès (34)........................ 173 E3
Gorre (87)........................... 123 H3
Gorrevod (01)...................... 116 C3
Gorron (53)........................... 58 C2
Gorses (46)......................... 139 F6
Gorze (57)............................ 48 B2
Gosnay (62)............................ 2 D6
Gosné (35)............................ 57 F1
Gosselming (57)..................... 49 H4
Gotein-Libarrenx (64)........... 181 F3
Gottenhouse (67)................... 50 C4
Gottesheim (67)..................... 50 C4
Gouaix (77)........................... 65 E1
Goualade (33)...................... 150 A4
Gouarec (22)......................... 54 D1
Gouaux (65)......................... 183 G6
Gouaux-de-Larboust (31)...... 197 E1
Gouaux-de-Luchon (31)........ 184 A6
Goudargues (30)................... 157 G5
Goudelancourt-lès-
  Berrieux (02)........................ 22 D4
Goudelancourt-lès-
  Pierrepont (02)..................... 22 D2
Goudelin (22)......................... 33 F3
Goudet (43)......................... 142 C5
Goudex (31)......................... 184 C2
Goudon (65)......................... 183 F3
Goudourville (82).................. 151 H6
Gouesnach (29)..................... 53 F3
la Gouesnière (35)................. 35 E4
Gouesnou (29)....................... 31 E4
Gouex (86).......................... 109 G3
Gouézec (29)......................... 53 G1
Gouffern en Auge (61)............ 39 F4
Gougenheim (67).................... 50 D4
Gouhelans (25)...................... 87 H5
Gouhenans (70)..................... 88 A3
Gouillons (28)........................ 62 D3
Gouise (03).......................... 114 A3
Goujounac (46)..................... 152 B2
la Goulafrière (27)................. 39 H3
Goulet (61)............................ 39 E5
Goulien (29).......................... 52 D2
Goulier (09)......................... 198 D1
Goulles (19)......................... 139 G4
les Goulles (21)..................... 85 G1
Gouloux (58)........................ 100 B1
Goult (84)............................ 175 G3
Goulven (29).......................... 31 F2
Goumois (25)......................... 88 D6
Goupillières (14).................... 38 B2
Goupillières (27).................... 40 B1
Goupillières (76).................... 18 C3
Goupillières (78).................... 41 H3
Gouraincourt (55).................. 25 G5
Gourbera (40)...................... 165 E3
Gourbit (09)......................... 199 E1
Gourchelles (60).................... 19 G2
Gourdan-Polignan (31).......... 184 A4
Gourdièges (15).................... 140 D5
Gourdon (06)....................... 178 C4
Gourdon (07)....................... 157 G1
Gourdon (46)....................... 152 C1
Gourdon (71)....................... 115 G1
Gourdon-Murat (19)............. 125 F5
Gourgançon (51).................... 45 F5
Gourgé (79)........................... 93 G5
Gourgeon (70)....................... 87 E2
Gourgue (65)....................... 183 F4
Gourhel (56)......................... 56 A4
Gourin (56)........................... 54 B2
Gourlizon (29)....................... 53 E2
Gournay (36)....................... 111 F1
Gournay-en-Bray (76)............ 19 G4
Gournay-le-Guérin (27).......... 40 B5
Gournay-sur-Aronde (60)....... 21 E4
Gournay-sur-Marne (93)......... 43 E4
les Gours (16)...................... 122 A1
Gours (33).......................... 136 A4
Gourvieille (11).................... 186 A2
Gourville (16)....................... 122 A2
Gourvillette (17)................... 121 H1
Goussainville (28).................. 41 G4
Goussainville (95).................. 42 D2
Goussancourt (02).................. 44 D1
Gousse (40)......................... 165 F3
Goussonville (78)................... 41 H3
Goustranville (14).................. 14 D4
Gout-Rossignol (24)............. 122 D6
la Goutelle (63)..................... 126 C2
Goutevernisse (31)............... 185 E3
Goutrens (12)....................... 154 B3
Gouts (40)........................... 165 G3
Gouttières (63)..................... 113 E6
Goutz (32)........................... 168 A3
Gouvernes (77)...................... 43 F4
Gouves (62)............................ 8 A2
Gouvets (50).......................... 37 F2

Gouvieux (60)....................... 42 D1
Gouville sur Mer (50)............. 36 D1
Gouvix (14)........................... 38 C2
Goux (32)............................ 166 D5
Goux-lès-Dambelin (25).......... 88 B5
Goux-les-Usiers (25)............ 103 H3
Goux-sous-Landet (25).......... 103 F2
Gouy (02)............................... 9 E5
Gouy (76).............................. 18 D5
Gouy-en-Artois (62)................. 8 A3
Gouy-en-Ternois (62)............... 7 G2
Gouy-les-Groseillers (60)........ 20 B2
Gouy-Saint-André (62).............. 7 E1
Gouy-Servins (62)................... 8 A1
Gouy-sous-Bellonne (62).......... 8 C2
Gouzangrez (95)..................... 42 A1
Gouzeaucourt (59).................... 8 D4
Gouzens (31)........................ 185 E3
Gouzon (23)......................... 112 A5
Goven (35)............................ 57 E3
Goviller (54).......................... 69 F1
Goxwiller (67)........................ 71 G1
Goyencourt (80)..................... 21 E2
Goyrans (31)........................ 169 F6
Grabels (34)......................... 173 F5
Graçay (18)............................ 96 D2
Grâce-Uzel (22)...................... 55 G1
Grâces (22)........................... 33 E4
Gradignan (33)..................... 135 E6
Graffigny-Chemin (52)............ 68 C4
Gragnague (31).................... 169 G5
Graignes-Mesnil-
  Angot (50)........................... 13 E5
Grailhen (65)....................... 183 G6
Graimbouville (76).................. 15 G1
Graincourt-lès-
  Havrincourt (62).................... 8 D4
Grainville-la-
  Teinturière (76).................... 17 E3
Grainville-Langannerie (14)..... 38 D2
Grainville-sur-Odon (14)......... 14 A5
Grainville-sur-Ry (76)............. 19 E4
Grainville-Ymauville (76)......... 16 C4
le Grais (61).......................... 38 C5
Graissessac (34).................. 172 A5
Graix (42)............................ 143 G1
Gramat (46)......................... 139 E6
la Gouesnière (35)................. 36 E4 [duplicate?]
Gramazie (11)...................... 186 C4
Grambois (84)...................... 176 B4
Grammond (42)..................... 129 F5
Grammont (70)....................... 88 A4
Gramond (12)....................... 154 B5
Gramont (82)....................... 168 A2
Granace (2A)........................ 207 E3
Grancey-le-Château-
  Neuvelle (21)....................... 85 H1
Grancey-sur-Ource (21).......... 67 E6
Grand (88)............................. 68 B2
Grand-Auverné (44)................ 75 E2
le Grand-Bornand (74).......... 132 C1
le Grand-Bourg (23)............. 111 E5
Grand-Brassac (24).............. 136 D1
Grand-Camp (27).................... 40 A2
Grand-Camp (76).................... 15 H1
le Grand-Celland (50)............. 37 F5
Grand-Champ (56).................. 55 F5
Grand-Charmont (25)............. 88 C4
le Grand-Combe (30)............ 157 E6
Grand-Corent (01)................ 117 F5
Grand-Couronne (76).............. 18 C5
la Grand-Croix (42).............. 129 G5
Grand-Failly (54).................... 25 F4
Grand-Fayt (59)....................... 9 H4
Grand-Fort-Philippe (59).......... 2 A2
Grand-Fougeray (35).............. 57 E6
Grand-Laviers (80)................... 6 D4
le Grand-Lemps (38)............. 131 E6
le Grand-Lucé (72)................. 78 C1
le Grand-Madieu (16)........... 122 D1
le Grand-Pressigny (37)......... 95 E4
Le Grand-Quevilly (76)............ 18 C4
Grand-Rozoy (02)................... 22 A6
Grand-Rullecourt (62).............. 7 H3
le Grand-Serre (26).............. 144 C2
Grand-Verly (02)...................... 9 G5
le Grand-Village-Plage (17)... 120 B1
Grand Bourgtheroulde (27)...... 18 B5
Grandcamp-Maisy (14)........... 13 F4
Grandchamp (08)................... 23 G2
Grandchamp (52).................... 86 B2
Grandchamp (72).................... 60 B3
Grandchamp (78).................... 41 G5
Grandchamps-des-
  Fontaines (44)...................... 74 C2
Grand'Combe-
  Châteleu (25)..................... 104 B3
Grand'Combe-des-
  Bois (25)............................. 104 D2
Grandcourt (76)....................... 6 B6
Grandcourt (80)....................... 8 A4
la Grande-Fosse (88).............. 70 D2
la Grande-Motte (34)............ 173 H6
la Grande-Paroisse (77).......... 64 B2
la Grande-Résie (70).............. 86 C6
Grande-Rivière (39)............. 118 A1
Grande-Synthe (59)................. 2 B1
la Grande-Verrière (71)......... 100 C4
Grandecourt (70).................... 87 E3
les Grandes-Armoises (08)..... 24 C3
les Grandes-Chapelles (10)..... 66 A2
les Grandes-Loges (51).......... 45 H2
les Grandes-Ventes (76)......... 17 H4
Grandeyrolles (63)............... 127 E5
Grandfontaine (25)............... 103 F1
Grandfontaine (67).................. 71 E1
Grandfontaine-sur-
  Creuse (25)........................ 104 A1

Grandfresnoy (60).................. 21 E5
Grandham (08)....................... 24 B5
Grandjean (17)..................... 121 E2
Grand'Landes (85).................. 91 F3
Grandlup-et-Fay (02).............. 22 C2
Grandparigny (50).................. 37 F5
Grandpré (08)........................ 24 B5
Grandpuits-Bailly-
  Carrois (77)........................ 43 G6
Grandrieu (48)..................... 142 A6
Grandrieux (02)...................... 23 F2
Grandrif (63)....................... 128 B5
Grandris (69)....................... 115 H6
Grandrû (60).......................... 21 G3
Grandrupt (88)....................... 70 D2
Grandrupt-de-Bains (88)......... 69 G5
les Grands-Chézeaux (87)..... 110 D3
Grandsaigne (19)................. 125 F5
Grandval (63)....................... 128 A5
Grandvals (48)..................... 155 F1
Grandvaux (71).................... 115 G3
Grandvelle-et-le-
  Perrenot (70)....................... 87 F4
Grandvillars (90).................... 88 D4
la Grandville (08)................... 24 B1
Grandville (10)....................... 45 G6
Grandvillers (88).................... 70 B3
Grandvillers-aux-Bois (60)...... 21 E4
Grandvilliers (27)................... 40 D4
Grandvilliers (60)................... 20 A2
Grane (26)........................... 158 C1
Granès (11).......................... 186 D6
la Grange (25)........................ 88 B6
Grange-de-Vaivre (39).......... 103 E3
Grangermont (45)................... 63 G4
les Granges (10)..................... 66 B5
Granges (71)........................ 101 F6
Granges-Aumontzey (88)........ 70 C4
Granges-d'Ans (24).............. 138 C2
les Granges-
  Gontardes (26)................... 158 B4
Granges-la-Ville (70).............. 88 B3
Granges-le-Bourg (70)............ 88 B3
les Granges-le-Roi (91).......... 63 E1
Granges-les-
  Beaumont (26).................... 144 B4
Granges-Narboz (25)............ 104 A4
Granges-sur-Aube (51)........... 45 E6
Granges-sur-Lot (47)............ 151 E4
les Grangettes (25).............. 103 H4
Grangues (14)........................ 14 D4
Granieu (38)........................ 131 F4
Grans (13)........................... 175 F5
Granville (50)......................... 36 C3
Granzay-Gript (79)............... 107 H4
Gras (07)............................. 157 H3
les Gras (25)....................... 104 B3
Grassac (16)........................ 122 D4
Grasse (06).......................... 178 C4
Grassendorf (67).................... 50 D3
Grateloup-Saint-
  Gayrand (47)...................... 150 D3
Gratens (31)........................ 184 D2
Gratentour (31).................... 169 F4
Gratibus (80)......................... 20 D2
Gratot (50)............................ 36 D1
Gratreuil (51)......................... 24 A6
Grattepanche (80).................. 20 C1
le Gratteris (25)................... 103 G1
Grattery (70).......................... 87 F3
le Grau-du-Roi (30).............. 173 H6
Graulhet (81)....................... 170 B4
Grauves (51).......................... 45 F3
Graval (76)............................ 19 F2
la Grave (05)....................... 146 C3
Gravelines (59)........................ 2 A2
la Gravelle (53)...................... 58 B4
Gravelotte (57)...................... 26 B5
Graveron-Sémerville (27)....... 40 C1
Graves-Saint-Amant (16)...... 122 A4
Graveson (13)...................... 174 D3
Gravières (07)...................... 157 E4
Gravigny (27)........................ 40 D2
Gravon (77)........................... 64 D2
Gray (70)............................... 86 C5
Gray-la-Ville (70)................... 86 C5
Grayan-et-l'Hôpital (33)........ 120 B5
Graye-et-Charnay (39).......... 117 F2
Graye-sur-Mer (14)................ 14 B3
Grayssas (47)...................... 151 G6
Grazac (31).......................... 185 G2
Grazac (43).......................... 143 E2
Grazac (81).......................... 169 G3
Grazay (53)........................... 59 E3
Gréalou (46)........................ 153 F3
Gréasque (13)...................... 192 C2
Grébault-Mesnil (80)................ 6 C5
Grécourt (80)......................... 21 G2
Gredisans (39)..................... 102 C2
la Grée-Saint-Laurent (56)...... 56 A3
Gréez-sur-Roc (72)................ 61 E4
Greffeil (11)......................... 187 E4
Grèges (76)............................ 17 G2
Grémecey (57)....................... 49 E4
Grémévillers (60).................... 19 H3
Gremilly (55)......................... 25 F5
Grémonville (76).................... 17 E3
Grenade (31)........................ 169 E4
Grenade-sur-l'Adour (40)...... 166 A3
Grenant (52).......................... 86 C2
Grenant-lès-
  Sombernon (21)................. 101 F1
Grenay (38).......................... 130 C4
Grenay (62)............................ 8 B1
Grendelbruch (67).................. 71 F1
Greneville-en-Beauce (45)...... 63 E4
Grenier-Montgon (43)........... 141 F2
Gréning (57)........................... 49 G3

Grenoble (38) 145 G2
Grenois (58) 83 F6
Grentheville (14) 14 C5
Gréolières (06) 178 C3
Gréoux-les-Bains (04) 176 D4
Grépiac (31) 185 G1
le Grès (31) 168 D4
Grésigny-Sainte-Reine (21) .. 84 D4
Gresin (73) 131 F4
la Gresle (42) 115 F6
Gresse-en-Vercors (38) 145 F5
Gressey (78) 41 G4
Gresswiller (67) 50 C6
Gressy (77) 43 F3
Grésy-sur-Aix (73) 131 H3
Grésy-sur-Isère (73) 132 B4
Gretz-Armainvilliers (77) 43 F5
Greuville (76) 17 F3
Greux (88) 68 D1
la Grève-sur-Mignon (17) ... 107 F4
Grévillers (62) 8 B4
Grevilly (71) 116 B2
Grez (60) 20 A2
le Grez (72) 59 G4
Grez-en-Bouère (53) 77 E1
Grez-Neuville (49) 76 D3
Grez-sur-Loing (77) 64 A3
Grézac (17) 120 D4
Grézels (46) 152 A3
Grèzes (43) 141 H5
Grèzes (46) 153 F2
Grèzes (48) 155 H3
Grézet-Cavagnan (47) 150 C4
Grézian (65) 183 G6
Grézieu-la-Varenne (69) 129 H3
Grézieu-le-Marché (69) 129 F4
Grézieux-le-Fromental (42) .. 129 E4
Grézillac (33) 135 H5
Grézolles (42) 128 C2
Gricourt (02) 9 E6
Grièges (01) 116 B4
Gries (67) 51 E4
Griesbach-au-Val (68) 71 E5
Griesheim-près-
Molsheim (67) 50 D6
Griesheim-sur-Souffel (67) .. 51 E5
Grignan (26) 158 C4
Grigneuseville (76) 17 H4
Grignols (24) 137 E3
Grignols (33) 150 A4
Grignon (21) 84 D4
Grignon (73) 132 C4
Grignoncourt (88) 69 E6
Grigny (62) 7 E1
Grigny (69) 130 A4
Grigny (91) 42 D6
la Grigonnais (44) 74 C2
Grillon (84) 158 C4
Grilly (01) 118 B3
Grimaucourt-en-
Woëvre (55) 47 G1
Grimaucourt-près-
Sampigny (55) 47 G4
Grimaud (83) 194 A4
la Grimaudière (86) 93 H5
Grimault (89) 84 A3
Grimbosq (14) 38 C2
Grimesnil (50) 37 E2
Grimonviller (54) 69 F2
Grincourt-lès-Pas (62) 7 H3
Grindorff-Bizing (57) 26 D3
la Gripperie-Saint-
Symphorien (17) 120 C2
Le Grippon (50) 37 E4
Gripport (54) 69 G2
Griscourt (54) 48 B4
Griselles (21) 84 C1
Griselles (45) 64 B5
Grisolles (02) 44 B1
Grisolles (82) 169 E3
Grisy-les-Plâtres (95) 42 B1
Grisy-Suisnes (77) 43 F5
Grisy-sur-Seine (77) 65 E2
Grives (24) 137 H6
Grivesnes (80) 20 D2
Grivillers (80) 21 E2
Grivy-Loisy (08) 24 A4
la Groise (59) 9 G4
Groises (18) 98 B1
Groissiat (01) 117 G4
Groisy (74) 118 C6
Groix (56) 54 B6
Groléjac (24) 138 B6
Gron (18) 98 B2
Gron (89) 65 E4
Gronard (02) 22 D1
Gros-Chastang (19) 139 F2
Gros-Réderching (57) 28 A5
Grosbliederstroff (57) 27 G5
Grosbois (25) 87 H6
Grosbois-en-
Montagne (21) 85 E6
Grosbois-lès-Tichey (21) 102 B3
Grosbreuil (85) 91 F5
les Groseillers (79) 107 H1
Groslay (95) 42 D3
Groslée-Saint-Benoit (01) .. 131 F3
Grosley-sur-Risle (27) 40 B2
Grosmagny (90) 88 C2
Grosne (90) 88 D3
Grospierres (07) 157 F4
Grosrouvre (78) 41 H4
Grosrouvres (54) 48 A4
Grossa (2A) 206 D4
Grosseto-Prugna (2A) 206 D1
Grossœuvre (27) 41 E4
Grossouvre (18) 98 C4

Grostenquin (57) 49 G2
Grosville (50) 12 B3
Grouches-Luchuel (80) 7 G3
Grougis (02) 9 F5
la Groutte (18) 97 H6
Grozon (39) 103 E4
Gruchet-le-Valasse (76) 15 H1
Gruchet-Saint-Siméon (76) .. 17 F3
Grues (85) 106 B2
Gruey-lès-Surance (88) 69 G5
Gruffy (74) 132 A2
Grugé-l'Hôpital (49) 76 B2
Grugies (02) 22 A1
Grugny (76) 17 G4
Gruissan (11) 188 B4
Grumesnil (76) 19 G3
Grun-Bordas (24) 137 E4
Grundviller (57) 49 H1
Gruny (80) 21 F2
Grury (71) 100 A6
Gruson (59) 3 G5
Grussenheim (68) 71 G4
Grust (65) 182 D6
Gruyères (08) 24 A2
le Gua (17) 120 C3
le Gua (38) 145 F4
Guagno (2A) 204 D3
Guainville (28) 41 F3
Guarbecque (62) 2 C5
Guargualé (2A) 206 D1
Guchan (65) 183 G6
Guchen (65) 183 G6
Gudas (09) 185 H5
Gudmont-Villiers (52) 67 H2
le Gué-d'Alléré (17) 107 E4
le Gué-de-Longroi (28) 62 C1
Le Gué-de-Velluire (85) 107 E3
Gué-d'Hossus (08) 10 D5
Guebenhouse (57) 27 G5
Gueberschwihr (68) 71 F5
Guébestroff (57) 49 G3
Guéblange-lès-Dieuze (57) .. 49 F4
Guébling (57) 49 G3
Guebwiller (68) 71 E6
Guécélard (72) 78 A1
Guégon (56) 55 H4
Guéhébert (50) 37 E2
Guéhenno (56) 55 G4
Gueltas (56) 55 G2
Guémappe (62) 8 C3
Guémar (68) 71 F3
Guémené-Penfao (44) 74 B1
Guémené-sur-Scorff (56) 54 D2
Guemps (62) 1 H2
Guénange (57) 26 C4
Guengat (29) 53 F2
Guénin (56) 55 E4
Guenroc (22) 34 C6
Guenrouet (44) 74 A2
Guenviller (57) 27 F5
Guêprei (61) 39 E4
Guer (56) 56 C4
Guérande (44) 73 F4
Guérard (77) 43 G4
Guerbigny (80) 21 E2
la Guerche (37) 95 E4
la Guerche-de-
Bretagne (35) 58 A6
la Guerche-sur-
l'Aubois (18) 98 C4
Guercheville (77) 63 H3
Guéreins (01) 116 B6
Guéret (23) 111 G5
Guerfand (71) 101 H5
Guérigny (58) 99 E3
Guérin (47) 150 B3
la Guérinière (85) 90 B1
Guerlédan (22) 55 F1
Guerlesquin (29) 32 B4
Guermange (57) 49 G4
Guermantes (77) 43 F4
Guern (56) 55 E3
le Guerno (56) 73 F1
Guerny (27) 19 G6
Guéron (14) 13 H5
Guerpont (55) 47 F5
Guerquesalles (61) 39 F3
les Guerreaux (71) 114 D2
Guerstling (57) 27 E3
Guerting (57) 27 E4
Guerville (76) 6 B5
Guerville (78) 41 H3
Gueschart (80) 7 E3
Guesnain (59) 8 D2
Guesnes (86) 94 A4
Guessling-Hémering (57) 49 F2
Guéthary (64) 164 A6
Gueudecourt (80) 8 A4
Gueugnon (71) 115 E1
Gueures (76) 17 F2
Gueutteville (76) 17 G4
Gueutteville-les-Grès (76) ... 17 E2
Gueux (51) 23 E6
Guevenatten (68) 89 E2
Guewenheim (68) 89 E2
Gugnécourt (88) 70 B3
Gugney (54) 69 F2
Gugney-aux-Aulx (88) 69 G3
Guibeville (91) 42 C6
Guichainville (27) 41 E3
Guiche (64) 164 D5
la Guiche (71) 115 G2
Guichen (35) 57 E4
Guiclan (29) 31 H3
Guidel (56) 54 B5
la Guierche (72) 60 B4
Guignecourt (60) 20 B4
Guignemicourt (80) 7 F6

Guignen (35) 56 D4
Guignes (77) 43 F6
Guigneville (45) 63 F4
Guigneville-sur-
Essonne (91) 63 G2
Guignicourt (02) 23 E4
Guignicourt-sur-Vence (08) .. 24 A2
Guigny (62) 7 F2
Guiler-sur-Goyen (29) 53 E2
Guilers (29) 30 D4
Guilherand-Granges (07) ... 144 B5
Guillac (33) 135 H6
Guillac (56) 56 A4
Guillaucourt (80) 8 A6
Guillaumes (06) 161 G6
Guillemont (80) 8 B5
la Guillermie (03) 128 A1
Guillerval (91) 63 E2
Guillestre (05) 161 F1
Guilleville (28) 62 D4
Guilliers (56) 56 A3
Guilligomarc'h (29) 54 C3
Guillon (89) 84 B4
Guillon-les-Bains (25) 87 H6
Guillonville (28) 62 C5
Guillos (33) 149 F2
Guilly (36) 96 C3
Guilly (45) 81 F2
Guilvinec (29) 53 E4
Guimaëc (29) 32 B2
Guimiliau (29) 31 G4
Guimps (16) 121 H5
Guinarthe-Parenties (64) 181 F1
Guincourt (08) 24 A3
Guindrecourt-aux-
Ormes (52) 67 G1
Guindrecourt-sur-
Blaise (52) 67 G3
Guinecourt (62) 7 F2
Guînes (62) 1 G3
Guingamp (22) 33 E4
Guinglange (57) 27 E6
Guinkirchen (57) 26 D4
Guinzeling (57) 49 G3
Guipavas (29) 31 E4
Guipel (35) 57 F1
Guipry-Messac (35) 57 E5
Guipy (58) 99 G1
Guiry-en-Vexin (95) 42 A1
Guiscard (60) 21 G2
Guiscriff (56) 54 B2
Guise (02) 9 G6
Guiseniers (27) 19 F6
le Guislain (50) 37 F2
Guissény (29) 31 E2
Guisy (62) 7 E2
Guitalens-L'Albarède (81) .. 170 B5
Guitera-les-Bains (2A) 205 E6
Guitinières (17) 121 F5
Guitrancourt (78) 41 H2
Guîtres (33) 135 H3
Guitté (22) 56 C1
Guitry (27) 19 F6
Guivry (02) 21 H2
Guizancourt (80) 20 A2
Guizengeard (16) 135 H1
Guizerix (65) 183 H2
Gujan-Mestras (33) 148 C1
Gumbrechtshoffen (67) 50 D3
Gumery (10) 65 F2
Gumiane (26) 159 E3
Gumières (42) 128 D5
Gumond (19) 139 F2
Gundershoffen (67) 50 D3
Gundolsheim (68) 71 F6
Gungwiller (67) 50 A3
Gunsbach (68) 71 E5
Gunstett (67) 51 E2
Guntzviller (57) 50 B4
Guny (02) 22 A3
Guran (31) 184 A6
Gurat (16) 122 C6
Gurcy-le-Châtel (77) 64 D2
Gurgy (89) 83 F1
Gurgy-la-Ville (21) 85 G1
Gurgy-le-Château (21) 85 G1
Gurmençon (64) 182 A3
Gurs (64) 181 H2
Gurunhuel (22) 32 D4
Gury (60) 21 F3
Gussainville (55) 47 H1
Gussignies (59) 9 G2
Guyancourt (78) 42 B5
Guyans-Durnes (25) 103 H2
Guyans-Vennes (25) 104 B1
Guyencourt (02) 22 D5
Guyencourt-Saulcourt (80) 8 D5
Guyencourt-sur-Noye (80) ... 20 C1
la Guyonnière (85) 91 H2
Guyonvelle (52) 86 D1
Guzargues (34) 173 G5
Gy (70) 87 E5
Gy-en-Sologne (41) 80 B5
Gy-les-Nonains (45) 64 B6
Gy-l'Évêque (89) 83 F3
Gye (54) 48 B6
Gyé-sur-Seine (10) 66 D5

H

Habarcq (62) 8 A2
Habas (40) 165 F5
Habère-Lullin (74) 118 D4
Habère-Poche (74) 119 E4
l'Habit (27) 41 F4
Hablainville (54) 49 G6
Habloville (61) 38 D4
Haboudange (57) 49 F3

Habsheim (68) 89 G2
Hachan (65) 183 H2
Hâcourt (52) 68 C4
Hacqueville (27) 19 F6
Hadancourt-le-Haut-
Clocher (60) 42 A1
Hadigny-les-Verrières (88) ... 70 A2
Hadol (88) 70 A4
Haegen (67) 50 C4
Hagécourt (88) 69 G3
Hagedet (65) 166 D6
Hagen (57) 26 B2
Hagenbach (68) 89 E3
Hagenthal-le-Bas (68) 89 G4
Hagenthal-le-Haut (68) 89 G4
Haget (32) 183 F1
Hagetaubin (64) 165 H6
Hagetmau (40) 165 H4
Hagéville (54) 48 A2
Hagnéville-et-
Roncourt (88) 68 D3
Hagnicourt (08) 24 A3
Hagondange (57) 26 B4
la Hague (50) 12 B1
la Haie-Fouassière (44) 74 D6
la Haie-Traversaine (53) 59 E2
les Haies (69) 129 H5
Haigneville (54) 69 H1
Haillainville (88) 70 A2
le Haillan (33) 135 E5
Hailles (80) 20 D1
Haillicourt (62) 2 C6
Haimps (17) 121 H2
Haims (86) 110 A2
Hainvillers (60) 21 E3
Haironville (55) 47 E5
Haisnes (62) 3 E6
Halinghen (62) 1 F5
Hallencourt (80) 6 D5
Hallennes-lez-
Haubourdin (59) 3 F5
Hallering (57) 27 E5
les Halles (69) 129 F3
Halles-sous-les-Côtes (55) .. 24 D4
Hallignicourt (52) 46 C6
Hallines (62) 2 A4
Hallivillers (80) 20 C2
Halloville (54) 49 H6
Halloy (60) 20 A2
Halloy (62) 7 H3
Halloy-lès-Pernois (80) 7 F4
Hallu (80) 21 F1
Halluin (59) 3 G4
Halsou (64) 180 C1
Halstroff (57) 26 D3
le Ham (50) 12 D4
le Ham (53) 59 F2
Ham (80) 21 G1
Ham-en-Artois (62) 2 C5
Ham-les-Moines (08) 11 H6
Ham-sous-Varsberg (57) 27 E5
Ham-sur-Meuse (08) 11 F4
Hamars (14) 27 H6
Hambach (57) 49 H2
Hambers (53) 59 F3
Hamblain-les-Prés (62) 8 C2
Hambye (50) 37 E2
Hamel (59) 8 A2
le Hamel (60) 20 A2
le Hamel (80) 8 A6
Hamelet (80) 7 H6
Hamelin (50) 37 F6
Hamelincourt (62) 8 B3
Hames-Boucres (62) 1 G3
Hammeville (54) 69 F1
Hamonville (54) 48 A3
Hampigny (10) 67 E2
Hampont (57) 49 F3
Han-devant-
Pierrepont (54) 25 G4
Han-lès-Juvigny (55) 25 E4
Han-sur-Meuse (55) 47 G3
Han-sur-Nied (57) 49 F2
Hanc (79) 108 C6
Hanches (28) 41 G6
Hancourt (80) 8 D5
Handschuheim (67) 50 D5
Hangard (80) 20 D1
Hangenbieten (67) 50 D6
Hangest-en-Santerre (80) 21 E1
Hangest-sur-Somme (80) 7 E4
Hangviller (57) 50 B4
Hannaches (60) 19 H4
Hannapes (02) 9 G5
Hannappes (08) 23 F1
Hannescamps (62) 8 A3
Hannocourt (57) 49 E3
Hannogne-Saint-
Martin (08) 24 B2
Hannogne-Saint-
Rémy (08) 23 G3
Hannonville-sous-les-
Côtes (55) 47 H2
Hannonville-Suzémont (54) .. 48 A1
le Hanouard (76) 17 E3
Hans (51) 46 C1
Hantay (59) 3 E6
Hanvec (29) 31 F5
Hanviller (57) 28 B5
Hanvoile (60) 19 H4
Haplincourt (62) 8 B4
Happencourt (02) 21 H1
Happonvilliers (28) 61 G3
Haramont (02) 21 H4
Haraucourt (08) 24 C2
Haraucourt (54) 49 E5
Haraucourt-sur-Seille (57) ... 49 F4

Haravesnes (62) 7 F2
Haravilliers (95) 42 B1
Harbonnières (80) 8 A6
Harbouey (54) 49 H6
Harcanville (76) 17 E3
Harchéchamp (88) 68 D2
Harcigny (02) 23 E1
Harcourt (27) 40 B1
Harcy (08) 11 E6
Hardancourt (88) 70 A2
Hardanges (53) 59 F2
Hardecourt-aux-Bois (80) 8 B5
Hardencourt-Cocherel (27) .. 41 E2
Hardifort (59) 2 C3
Hardinghen (62) 1 G3
Hardinvast (50) 12 C2
la Harengère (27) 18 C6
Harfleur (76) 15 F2
Hargarten-aux-Mines (57) ... 27 E4
Hargeville (78) 41 H3
Hargicourt (02) 8 D5
Hargicourt (80) 20 D2
Hargnies (08) 11 F5
Hargnies (59) 9 H3
Harly (02) 9 E6
Harmonville (88) 69 E1
la Harmoye (22) 33 F6
Harnes (62) 8 C1
Harol (88) 69 G4
Haroué (54) 69 G1
Harponville (80) 7 H5
Harprich (57) 49 F2
Harquency (27) 19 F6
Harreberg (57) 50 B5
Harréville-les-
Chanteurs (52) 68 C3
Harricourt (08) 24 C4
Harskirchen (67) 50 A2
Hartennes-et-Taux (02) 22 A6
Hartmannswiller (68) 71 E6
Hartzviller (57) 50 A5
Harville (55) 47 H1
Hary (02) 23 E1
Haselbourg (57) 50 B5
Hasnon (59) 9 E1
Hasparren (64) 180 D1
Haspelschiedt (57) 28 C5
Haspres (59) 9 F3
Hastingues (40) 164 D5
Hatrize (54) 26 A5
Hatten (67) 51 F2
Hattencourt (80) 21 F1
Hattenville (76) 16 D4
Hattigny (57) 49 H5
Hattmatt (67) 50 C4
Hattstatt (68) 71 F5
Hauban (65) 183 F4
Haubourdin (59) 3 F5
Hauconcourt (57) 26 C4
Haucourt (60) 19 H4
Haucourt (62) 8 C3
Haucourt (76) 19 G2
Haucourt-en-
Cambrésis (59) 9 E4
Haucourt-Moulaine (54) 25 H3
Haudainville (55) 47 F1
Haudiomont (55) 47 G1
Haudivillers (60) 20 B4
Haudonville (54) 70 A1
Haudrecy (08) 11 G6
Haudricourt (76) 19 G2
Haulchin (59) 9 F2
Haulies (32) 168 A6
Haulmé (08) 11 F6
Haumont-près-
Samogneux (55) 25 E6
Hauriet (40) 165 G4
Hausgauen (68) 89 F3
Haussez (76) 19 G3
Haussignémont (51) 46 C5
Haussimont (51) 45 G5
Haussonville (54) 48 D6
Haussy (59) 9 F3
Haut-Bocage (03) 112 D2
Haut-Clocher (57) 49 H4
le Haut-Corlay (22) 33 E6
Haut-de-Bosdarros (64) 182 C3
Haut-du-Them-Château-
Lambert (70) 88 B1
Haut-Lieu (59) 10 A4
Haut-Loquin (62) 1 H4
Haut-Mauco (40) 165 H3
Le Haut Soultzbach (68) 88 D2
Haut Valromey (01) 117 H6
Hautage (65) 183 H4
Hautbos (60) 19 H2
Haute-Amance (52) 86 C1
Haute-Avesnes (62) 8 A2
la Haute-Beaume (05) 159 G2
Haute-Épine (60) 20 A3
Haute-Goulaine (44) 74 D5
Haute-Isle (95) 41 G2
Haute-Kontz (57) 26 C2
la Haute-Maison (77) 43 H4
Haute-Rivoire (69) 129 F3
Haute-Vigneulles (57) 27 E5
Hautecloque (62) 7 G2
Hautecour (39) 117 H1
Hautecour (73) 132 D5
Hautecourt-
Romanèche (01) 117 F5
Hautefage (19) 139 F3
Hautefage-la-Tour (47) 151 G4
Hautefaye (24) 123 E5

Hautefeuille (77) 43 G5
Hautefond (71) 115 F3
Hautefontaine (60) 21 G5
Hautefort (24) 138 A2
Hauteluce (73) 132 D3
Hauterive (03) 114 A6
Hauterive (61) 60 B1
Hauterive (89) 83 G1
Hauterive-la-Fresse (25) 104 A3
Hauterives (26) 144 B2
Hauteroche (21) 85 E4
Hauteroche (39) 102 D6
les Hautes-Rivières (08) 11 F6
Hautesvignes (47) 150 D3
Hautevelle (70) 87 G1
Hautevesnes (02) 44 A1
Hauteville (02) 9 F6
Hauteville (08) 23 G3
Hauteville (51) 46 C6
Hauteville (62) 8 A2
Hauteville (73) 132 B5
la Hauteville (78) 41 G5
Hauteville-la-Guichard (50) .. 13 E6
Hauteville-lès-Dijon (21) 85 G6
Hauteville-Lompnes (01) 131 F1
Hauteville-sur-Fier (74) 131 H1
Hauteville-sur-Mer (50) 36 D2
Haution (02) 9 H6
Hautmont (59) 10 A3
Hautot-l'Auvray (76) 17 E4
Hautot-le-Vatois (76) 17 E4
Hautot-Saint-Sulpice (76) 17 E4
Hautot-sur-Mer (76) 17 G2
Hautot-sur-Seine (76) 18 C5
Les Hauts d'Anjou (49) 76 D3
Hauts de Bienne (39) 118 B2
les Hauts-de-Chée (55) 47 E3
les Hauts de Forterre (89) ... 83 E3
Hautteville-Bocage (50) 12 D4
Hautvillers (51) 45 E2
Hautvillers-Ouville (80) 6 D3
Hauville (27) 18 A4
Hauviné (08) 23 G5
Haux (33) 135 G6
Haux (64) 181 G4
Havange (57) 26 A3
Havelu (28) 41 G4
Haveluy (59) 9 E2
Havernas (80) 7 F5
Haverskerque (59) 2 C5
Le Havre (76) 15 E2
Havrincourt (62) 8 D4
l'Haÿ-les-Roses (94) 42 D4
Hayange (57) 26 B3
Haybes (08) 11 E5
La Haye (50) 12 C5
la Haye (76) 19 E4
la Haye (88) 69 G5
la Haye-Aubrée (27) 18 A4
la Haye-Bellefond (50) 37 F2
la Haye-de-Calleville (27) 18 B6
la Haye-de-Routot (27) 18 A4
la Haye-d'Ectot (50) 12 B4
la Haye-du-Theil (27) 18 B6
la Haye-le-Comte (27) 18 D6
la Haye-Malherbe (27) 18 C6
la Haye-Pesnel (50) 37 E4
la Haye-Saint-
Sylvestre (27) 40 A3
les Hayes (41) 79 E2
Hayes (57) 26 D5
Haynecourt (59) 8 D3
les Hays (39) 102 C4
Hazebrouck (59) 2 C4
Hazembourg (57) 49 H2
le Heaulme (95) 42 B1
Héauville (50) 12 B2
Hébécourt (27) 19 G5
Hébécourt (80) 20 C1
Héberville (76) 17 E3
Hébuterne (62) 8 A3
Hèches (65) 183 G5
Hecken (68) 89 E2
Hecmanville (27) 40 A1
Hécourt (27) 41 F3
Hécourt (60) 19 G3
Hecq (59) 9 G3
Hectomare (27) 18 B6
Hédauville (80) 8 A4
Hédé-Bazouges (35) 57 E1
Hédouville (95) 42 C1
Hegeney (67) 51 E3
Hégenheim (68) 89 G3
Heidolsheim (67) 71 G3
Heidwiller (68) 89 F2
Heiligenberg (67) 50 C6
Heiligenstein (67) 71 F1
Heillecourt (54) 48 C5
Heilles (60) 20 C5
Heilly (80) 7 H5
Heiltz-le-Hutier (51) 46 C5
Heiltz-le-Maurupt (51) 46 C4
Heiltz-l'Évêque (51) 46 C4
Heimersdorf (68) 89 F3
Heimsbrunn (68) 89 E2
Heining-lès-
Bouzonville (57) 27 E3
Heippes (55) 47 F2
Heiteren (68) 71 G5
Heiwiller (68) 89 F3
Hélesmes (59) 9 E2
Hélette (64) 180 D2
Helfaut (62) 2 B4
Helfrantzkirch (68) 89 G3
Helléan (56) 56 A4
Hellering-lès-
Fénétrange (57) 50 A4

Helleville (50) 12 B2
Hellimer (57) 49 G2
Héloup (61) 59 H2
Helstroff (57) 26 D5
Hem (59) 3 G5
Hem-Hardinval (80) 7 G3
Hem-Lenglet (59) 8 D3
Hem-Monacu (80) 8 B5
Hémevez (50) 12 D3
Hémévillers (60) 21 E4
Hémilly (57) 49 E1
Héming (57) 49 H5
Hémonstoir (22) 55 F2
Hénaménil (54) 49 F5
Hénanbihen (22) 34 B4
Hénansal (22) 34 A4
Hendaye (64) 180 A1
Hendecourt-lès-
Cagnicourt (62) 8 C3
Hendecourt-lès-
Ransart (62) 8 B3
Hénencourt (80) 7 H5
Hengoat (22) 33 E2
Hengwiller (67) 50 C5
Hénin-Beaumont (62) 8 C1
Hénin-sur-Cojeul (62) 8 B3
Héninel (62) 8 B3
Hennebont (56) 54 D5
Hennecourt (88) 69 G3
Hennemont (55) 47 H1
Henneveux (62) 1 G4
Hennezel (88) 69 F5
Hennezis (27) 19 F6
Hénon (22) 33 H5
Hénonville (60) 20 A6
Hénouville (76) 18 C4
Henrichemont (18) 81 H6
Henridorff (57) 50 B4
Henriville (57) 27 F5
Hénu (62) 7 H3
Henvic (29) 31 H3
Hérange (57) 50 B4
Herbault (41) 79 G3
l'Herbergement (85) 91 G2
Herbeuval (08) 25 E3
Herbeuville (55) 47 H2
Herbeville (78) 42 A3
Herbéviller (54) 49 G6
Herbeys (38) 145 G3
les Herbiers (85) 92 B4
Herbignac (44) 73 G3
Herbinghen (62) 1 G4
Herbisse (10) 45 G6
Herbitzheim (67) 50 A2
Herblay (95) 42 C3
Herbsheim (67) 71 H2
Hercé (53) 58 C1
Herchies (60) 20 A4
la Hérelle (60) 20 C3
Hérenguerville (50) 36 D2
Hérépian (34) 172 A5
Hères (65) 166 D5
Hergnies (59) 4 B6
Hergugney (88) 69 G2
Héric (44) 74 C3
Héricourt (62) 7 G2
Héricourt (70) 88 C3
Héricourt-en-Caux (76) 17 E4
Héricourt-sur-Thérain (60) 19 G3
Héricy (77) 64 B2
la Hérie (02) 10 B6
le Hérie-la-Viéville (02) 22 C1
Hériménil (54) 49 E6
Hérimoncourt (25) 88 D5
Hérin (59) 9 F2
Hérissart (80) 7 G5
Hérisson (03) 112 D2
Herleville (80) 8 B6
la Herlière (62) 7 H3
Herlies (59) 3 E5
Herlin-le-Sec (62) 7 G2
Herlincourt (62) 7 G2
Herly (62) 1 H6
Herly (80) 21 F1
L'Herm (09) 185 H5
Herm (40) 164 D3
Hermanville (76) 17 G3
Hermanville-sur-Mer (14) 14 C4
les Hermaux (48) 155 F3
Hermaville (62) 8 A2
Hermé (77) 65 E1
Hermelange (57) 50 A5
Hermelinghen (62) 1 G3
l'Hermenault (85) 107 E1
Herment (63) 126 B3
Hermeray (78) 41 G6
Hermes (60) 20 B5
Herméville (57) 16 B4
Herméville-en-Woëvre (55) 25 G6
Hermies (62) 8 C4
Hermillon (73) 146 C1
Hermin (62) 7 H1
l'Hermitage (57) 57 E2
les Hermites (37) 79 E3
Hermival-les-Vaux (14) 15 F5
Hermonville (51) 22 D5
Hernicourt (62) 7 G1
Herny (57) 49 E2
le Héron (76) 19 E4
Héronchelles (76) 19 E3
Hérouville (95) 42 C3
Hérouville-Saint-Clair (14) 14 C4
Hérouvillette (14) 14 C4
Herpelmont (88) 70 B4
Herpont (51) 46 B2
Herpy-l'Arlésienne (08) 23 F3
Herqueville (27) 18 D6

Herran (31) 184 C5
Herré (40) 166 D1
Herrère (64) 182 A3
Herrin (59) 3 F6
Herrlisheim (67) 51 F4
Herrlisheim-près-
Colmar (68) 71 F5
Herry (18) 98 C1
Herserange (54) 25 H3
Hersin-Coupigny (62) 8 A1
Hertzing (57) 49 H5
Hervelinghen (62) 1 F3
Hervilly (80) 8 D5
Héry (58) 99 G1
Héry (89) 83 G1
Héry-sur-Alby (74) 132 A2
Herzeele (59) 2 C3
Hesbécourt (80) 8 D5
Hescamps (80) 19 H2
Hesdigneul-lès-
Béthune (62) 2 D6
Hesdigneul-lès-
Boulogne (62) 1 F5
Hesdin (62) 7 E1
Hesdin-l'Abbé (62) 1 F4
Hésingue (68) 89 G3
Hesmond (62) 7 E1
Hesse (57) 50 A5
Hessenheim (67) 71 G3
Hestroff (57) 26 D4
Hestrud (59) 10 B3
Hestrus (62) 7 G1
Hétomesnil (60) 20 A3
Hettange-Grande (57) 26 B3
Hettenschlag (68) 71 G5
Heubécourt-Haricourt (27) 41 G1
Heuchin (62) 2 B6
Heucourt-Croquoison (80) 6 D5
Heudebouville (27) 18 D6
Heudicourt (27) 19 G5
Heudicourt (80) 8 D5
Heudicourt-sous-les-
Côtes (55) 47 H3
Heudreville-en-
Lieuvin (27) 15 H4
Heudreville-sur-Eure (27) 41 E1
Heugas (40) 165 E4
Heugleville-sur-Scie (76) 17 G3
Heugnes (36) 96 A3
Heugueville-sur-
Sienne (50) 36 D1
Heuilley-le-Grand (52) 86 B2
Heuilley-sur-Saône (21) 86 C6
Heuland (14) 15 E4
Heume-l'Église (63) 126 C3
la Heunière (27) 41 F2
Heuqueville (27) 19 E5
Heuqueville (76) 16 B4
Heuringhem (62) 2 B4
Heurteauville (76) 18 B4
Heutrégiville (51) 23 G5
Heuzecourt (80) 7 F3
Hévilliers (55) 47 F6
Heyrieux (38) 130 C4
Hézecques (62) 2 A6
le Hézo (56) 73 E1
Hibarette (65) 183 E3
Hières-sur-Amby (38) 130 D3
Hiergues (08) 11 F4
Hiermont (80) 7 F3
Hiers-Brouage (17) 120 C2
Hiersac (16) 122 B4
Hiesse (16) 109 F6
Hiéville (50) 13 E4
Higuères-Souye (64) 182 C1
Hilbesheim (57) 50 A4
Hillion (22) 33 H4
Hinacourt (02) 22 A1
Hinckange (57) 26 D5
Hindisheim (67) 71 H1
Hindlingen (68) 89 E3
Hinges (62) 2 D5
le Hinglé (22) 34 C6
Hinsbourg (67) 50 B3
Hinsingen (67) 49 H2
Hinx (40) 165 F4
Hipsheim (67) 71 H1
Hirel (35) 35 E4
Hirschland (67) 50 A3
Hirsingue (68) 89 F3
Hirson (02) 10 B6
Hirtzbach (68) 89 F3
Hirtzfelden (68) 71 G6
His (31) 184 C4
Hitte (65) 183 F3
Hochfelden (67) 50 D4
Hochstatt (68) 89 F2
Hochstett (67) 51 E4
Hocquigny (50) 37 E3
Hocquinghen (62) 1 H4
Hodenc-en-Bray (60) 19 H4
Hodenc-l'Évêque (60) 20 B5
Hodeng-au-Bosc (76) 6 C6
Hodeng-Hodenger (76) 19 F3
Hodent (95) 41 H1
Hœdic (56) 72 C4
Hœnheim (67) 51 E5
Hœrdt (67) 51 E4
Hoffen (67) 51 F2
les Hogues (27) 19 E4
la Hoguette (14) 38 D3
Hohengœft (67) 50 C5
Hohfrankenheim (67) 50 D4
Hohrod (68) 71 E5

le Hohwald (67) 71 F1
Holacourt (57) 49 E2
Holling (57) 26 D4
Holnon (02) 8 D6
Holque (59) 2 B3
Holtzheim (67) 50 D6
Holving (57) 49 H2
le Hom (14) 38 B2
Hombleux (80) 21 G2
Homblières (02) 9 E6
Hombourg (68) 89 G1
Hombourg-Budange (57) 26 C4
Hombourg-Haut (57) 27 F5
l'Hôme-Chamondot (61) 40 B6
Homécourt (54) 26 A4
Hommarting (57) 50 A4
Hommert (57) 50 B5
Hommes (37) 78 B5
le Hommet-
d'Arthenay (50) 13 E6
Homps (11) 187 G3
Homps (32) 168 B3
Hon-Hergies (59) 9 H2
Hondainville (60) 20 C5
Hondeghem (59) 2 C4
Hondevilliers (77) 44 B3
Hondouville (27) 40 D1
Hondschoote (59) 2 D2
Honfleur (14) 15 F2
Honguemare-
Guenouville (27) 18 B5
Honnechy (59) 9 F4
Honnecourt-sur-
Escaut (59) 8 D5
L'Honor-de-Cos (82) 152 C6
Honskirch (57) 49 H2
Hontanx (40) 166 B3
Hôpital-Camfrout (29) 31 F5
l'Hôpital-d'Orion (64) 165 F6
l'Hôpital-du-Grosbois (25) 103 H1
l'Hôpital-le-Grand (42) 129 E5
l'Hôpital-le-Mercier (71) 115 E3
l'Hôpital-Saint-Blaise (64) 181 G2
l'Hôpital-Saint-Lieffroy (25) 88 A5
l'Hôpital-sous-
Rochefort (42) 128 C3
les Hôpitaux-Neufs (25) 104 A5
les Hôpitaux-Vieux (25) 104 A5
Horbourg-Wihr (68) 71 F4
Hordain (59) 9 E3
la Horgne (08) 24 A2
Horgues (65) 183 E3
l'Horme (42) 129 G5
Hornoy-le-Bourg (80) 6 D6
le Horps (53) 59 E2
Horsarrieu (40) 165 H4
Horville-en-Ornois (55) 68 B1
l'Hosmes (27) 40 D4
l'Hospitalet (04) 176 C1
l'Hospitalet-du-Larzac (12) 172 B2
l'Hospitalet-près-
l'Andorre (09) 199 F3
Hosta (64) 181 E3
Hoste (57) 27 G5
Hostens (33) 149 E3
Hostiaz (01) 131 E2
Hostun (26) 144 D4
l'Hôtellerie (14) 15 G5
Hotot-en-Auge (14) 14 D5
Hottot-les-Bagues (14) 14 A5
Hottviller (57) 28 B5
la Houblonnière (14) 15 E5
les Houches (74) 133 F1
Houchin (62) 2 D6
Houdain (62) 7 H1
Houdain-lez-Bavay (59) 9 H2
Houdan (78) 41 G5
Houdancourt (60) 21 E5
Houdelaincourt (55) 47 G6
Houdemont (54) 48 C6
Houdetot (76) 17 E3
Houdilcourt (08) 23 F4
Houdreville (54) 69 F1
Houécourt (88) 69 E3
Houeillès (47) 150 B5
Houetteville (27) 40 D1
Houéville (88) 68 D2
Houeydets (65) 183 G3
le Houga (32) 166 C3
Houilles (78) 42 C3
Houlbec-Cocherel (27) 41 F2
Houldizy (08) 24 A1
Houlette (16) 121 H3
Houlgate (14) 14 D4
Houlle (62) 2 A3
le Houlme (76) 18 C4
l'Houmeau (17) 106 C4
Hounoux (11) 186 B4
Houplin-Ancoisne (59) 3 F5
Houplines (59) 3 F4
Houppeville (76) 18 C3
Houquetot (76) 16 C4
Hourc (65) 183 F2
Hourges (51) 22 D6
Hours (64) 182 D3
Hourtin (33) 134 B2
Houry (02) 22 D1
Houssay (41) 79 F2
Houssay (53) 58 D6
la Houssaye (27) 40 B2
la Houssaye-Béranger (76) 17 G4
la Houssaye-en-Brie (77) 43 G5
le Housseau-
Brétignolles (53) 59 E1
Houssen (68) 71 F4

Housseras (88) 70 B2
Housset (02) 22 C1
Housséville (54) 69 F2
la Houssière (88) 70 C3
la Houssoye (60) 19 H5
Houtaud (25) 104 A4
Houtkerque (59) 2 D3
Houville-en-Vexin (27) 19 E5
Houville-la-Branche (28) 62 C2
Houvin-Houvigneul (62) 7 G2
Houx (28) 41 G6
Hoymille (59) 2 C2
Huanne-Montmartin (25) 87 H5
Hubersent (62) 1 F5
Hubert-Folie (14) 14 C5
Huberville (50) 12 D3
Huby-Saint-Leu (62) 7 E1
Huchenneville (80) 6 D4
Huclier (62) 7 G1
Hucqueliers (62) 1 G5
Hudimesnil (50) 36 D3
Hudiviller (54) 49 E6
Huelgoat (29) 32 A5
Huest (27) 41 E2
Huêtre (45) 62 C6
Huez (38) 146 A3
Hugier (70) 86 D6
Hugleville-en-Caux (76) 17 F4
Huillé (49) 77 F3
Huilliécourt (52) 68 C4
Huilly-sur-Seille (71) 116 C1
Huiron (51) 46 A5
Huismes (37) 94 B1
Huisnes-sur-Mer (50) 35 G4
Huisseau-en-Beauce (41) 79 F2
Huisseau-sur-Cosson (41) 80 A4
Huisseau-sur-Mauves (45) 80 C1
l'Huisserie (53) 58 C5
Hulluch (62) 3 E6
Hultehouse (57) 50 B4
Humbauville (51) 46 A5
Humbécourt (52) 46 D6
Humbercamps (62) 7 H3
Humbercourt (80) 7 H3
Humbert (62) 1 G6
Humberville (52) 68 B3
Humbligny (18) 98 A1
Humerœuille (62) 7 F1
Humes-Jorquenay (52) 86 A1
Humières (62) 7 F1
Hunawihr (68) 71 F3
Hundling (57) 27 G5
Hundsbach (68) 89 F3
Huningue (68) 89 H3
Hunspach (67) 51 F2
Hunting (57) 26 C3
Huos (31) 184 A4
Huparlac (12) 154 D1
Huppy (80) 6 D5
Hurbache (88) 70 C2
Hure (33) 150 B2
Hurecourt (70) 69 F6
Hures-la-Parade (48) 155 H5
Huriel (03) 112 C3
Hurigny (71) 116 B3
Hurtières (38) 146 A1
Hurtigheim (67) 50 D5
Husseren-les-
Châteaux (68) 71 F5
Husseren-Wesserling (68) 70 D6
Hussigny-Godbrange (54) 25 H3
Huttendorf (67) 50 D3
Huttenheim (67) 71 G2
Hyds (03) 113 E4
Hyémondans (25) 88 B5
Hyères (83) 193 G5
Hyet (70) 87 F4
Hyèvre-Magny (25) 88 A5
Hyèvre-Paroisse (25) 88 A5
Hymont (88) 69 F3
Hypercourt (80) 21 F1

I

Ibarrolle (64) 181 E3
Ibigny (57) 49 H5
Ibos (65) 183 E3
Ichtratzheim (67) 51 E6
Ichy (77) 63 H4
Idaux-Mendy (64) 181 F3
Idrac-Respaillès (32) 167 G6
Idron (64) 182 C2
Ids-Saint-Roch (18) 97 F6
Iffendic (35) 56 D2
les Iffs (35) 57 E1
Ifs (14) 14 B5
les Ifs (76) 6 B6
Igé (61) 60 D3
Igé (71) 116 B3
Ignaucourt (80) 20 D1
Ignaux (09) 199 G2
Igney (54) 49 G5
Igney (88) 69 H3
Ignol (18) 98 B4
Igny (70) 86 D4
Igny (91) 42 C5
Igny-Comblizy (51) 44 D2
Igon (64) 182 C3
Igornay (71) 100 D3
Igoville (27) 18 D5
Iguerande (71) 115 E2
Iholdy (64) 181 E2

Île-de-Bréhat (22) 33 F1
Île-de-Sein (29) 52 B2
l'Île-d'Elle (85) 107 E3
Île-d'Houat (56) 72 C3
l'Île-d'Olonne (85) 91 E5
l'Île-d'Yeu (85) 90 A3
l'Île-Molène (29) 30 B4
l'Île-Rousse (2B) 202 D5
l'Île-Saint-Denis (93) 42 D3
l'Île-Tudy (29) 53 F4
Ilharre (64) 181 F1
Ilhat (09) 186 A5
les Ilhes (11) 187 E2
Ilhet (65) 183 G5
Ilheu (65) 184 A5
Illange (57) 26 B3
Illartein (09) 184 C5
Illats (33) 149 G2
Ille-sur-Têt (66) 200 D2
Illeville-sur-Montfort (27) 18 A5
Illfurth (68) 89 F2
Illhaeusern (68) 71 G3
Illiat (01) 116 B5
Illier-et-Laramade (09) 199 E1
Illiers-Combray (28) 61 H3
Illiers-l'Évêque (27) 41 E4
Illies (59) 3 E6
Illifaut (22) 56 B2
Illkirch-Graffenstaden (67) 51 E6
Illois (76) 19 G1
Illoud (52) 68 C4
Illy (08) 24 C1
Ilonse (06) 178 D1
Imbleville (76) 17 F4
Imécourt (08) 24 C5
Imling (57) 50 A4
Imphy (58) 99 E4
Inaumont (08) 23 G3
Incarville (27) 18 D6
Incheville (76) 6 B5
Inchy (59) 9 F4
Inchy-en-Artois (62) 8 D3
Incourt (62) 7 F1
Indevillers (25) 88 D6
Indre (44) 74 C5
Ineuil (18) 97 G5
Ingenheim (67) 50 D4
Ingersheim (68) 71 F4
Inglange (57) 26 C3
Ingolsheim (67) 51 F2
Ingouville (76) 17 E2
Ingrandes (36) 110 A1
Ingrandes (86) 94 D4
Ingrandes-Le Fresne sur
Loire (49) 76 B5
Ingrannes (45) 63 F6
Ingré (45) 80 D1
Inguiniel (56) 54 D3
Ingwiller (67) 50 C3
Injoux-Génissiat (01) 117 H6
Innenheim (67) 50 D6
Innimond (01) 131 F3
Inor (55) 24 D3
Insming (57) 49 G2
Insviller (57) 49 H3
Intres (07) 143 F4
Intréville (28) 62 D3
Intville-la-Guétard (45) 63 F3
Inval-Boiron (80) 6 D6
Inxent (62) 1 G6
Inzinzac-Lochrist (56) 54 D4
Ippécourt (55) 47 E2
Ippling (57) 27 G5
Irai (61) 40 B5
Irais (79) 93 G4
Irancy (89) 83 G3
Iré-le-Sec (55) 25 E4
Irigny (69) 130 A4
Irissarry (64) 180 D2
Irles (80) 8 A4
Irodouër (35) 56 D1
Iron (02) 9 G5
Irouléguy (64) 180 D3
Irreville (27) 41 E1
Irvillac (29) 31 F5
Is-en-Bassigny (52) 68 B5
Is-sur-Tille (21) 85 H4
Isbergues (62) 2 C5
Isches (88) 69 E5
Isdes (45) 81 F3
Isenay (58) 99 H4
Isigny-le-Buat (50) 37 F5
Isigny-sur-Mer (14) 13 F5
Island (89) 83 H5
Isle (87) 124 B3
l'Isle-Adam (95) 42 C1
l'Isle-Arné (32) 168 A5
Isle-Aubigny (10) 66 C1
Isle-Aumont (10) 66 B4
l'Isle-Bouzon (32) 168 A2
l'Isle-d'Abeau (38) 130 D4
l'Isle-de-Noé (32) 167 G5
l'Isle-d'Espagnac (16) 122 C4
l'Isle-en-Dodon (31) 184 C1
Isle-et-Bardais (03) 98 B6
l'Isle-Jourdain (32) 168 C3
l'Isle-Jourdain (86) 109 G4
Isle-Saint-Georges (33) 135 F6
l'Isle-sur-la-Sorgue (84) 175 F2
l'Isle-sur-le-Doubs (25) 88 B5
l'Isle-sur-Marne (51) 46 B6
l'Isle-sur-Serein (89) 84 A4
Isles-les-Bardel (14) 38 C3
Isles-les-Meldeuses (77) 43 H2
Isles-lès-Villenoy (77) 43 G3
Isles-sur-Suippe (51) 23 F5

les Islettes (55) 46 D1
Isneauville (76) 18 D4
Isola (06) 162 B5
Isolaccio-di-Fiumorbo (2B) 205 F5
Isômes (52) 86 B3
Ispagnac (48) 156 A4
Ispoure (64) 180 D3
Isques (62) 1 F4
Issac (24) 136 D4
Issamoulenc (07) 143 G6
Issancourt-et-Rumel (08) 24 B1
Issanlas (07) 142 D6
Issans (25) 88 C4
Issé (44) 74 D1
Isse (51) 45 G2
Issel (11) 186 B2
Issendolus (46) 153 F1
Issenhausen (67) 50 D3
Issenheim (68) 71 F6
Issepts (46) 153 F1
Isserpent (03) 114 B5
Isserteaux (63) 127 G4
Issigeac (24) 151 F1
Issirac (30) 157 G5
Issoire (63) 127 G5
Issor (64) 181 H4
Issou (78) 41 H3
Issoudun (36) 97 E4
Issoudun-Létrieix (23) 112 A6
Issus (31) 185 G1
Issy-les-Moulineaux (92) 42 C4
Issy-l'Évêque (71) 100 B6
Istres (13) 191 G4
les Istres-et-Bury (51) 45 F3
Isturits (64) 181 E1
Itancourt (02) 22 A1
Iteuil (86) 109 E2
Ittenheim (67) 50 D5
Itterswiller (67) 71 F2
Itteville (91) 63 G1
Itxassou (64) 180 C1
Itzac (81) 170 A1
Ivergny (62) 7 G3
Iverny (77) 43 F2
Iviers (02) 23 F1
Iville (27) 40 C1
Ivors (60) 43 H1
Ivory (39) 103 F4
Ivoy-le-Pré (18) 81 H6
Ivrey (39) 103 F3
Ivry-la-Bataille (27) 41 F3
Ivry-le-Temple (60) 20 A6
Ivry-sur-Seine (94) 42 D4
Iwuy (59) 9 E3
Izaourt (65) 184 A5
Izaut-de-l'Hôtel (31) 184 B5
Izaux (65) 183 G4
Izé (53) 59 F3
Izeaux (38) 145 E1
Izel-lès-Équerchin (62) 8 C2
Izel-lès-Hameau (62) 7 H2
Izenave (01) 117 F6
Izernore (01) 117 G4
Izeron (38) 145 E3
Izeste (64) 182 B4
Izeure (21) 102 A2
Izier (21) 86 A6
Izieu (01) 131 F4
Izon (33) 135 G4
Izon-la-Bruisse (26) 159 G5
Izotges (32) 166 D5

J

Jablines (77) 43 F3
Jabreilles-les-Bordes (87) 124 C1
Jabrun (15) 141 E6
Jacob-Bellecombette (73) 131 H5
Jacou (34) 173 F5
Jacque (65) 183 F2
Jagny-sous-Bois (95) 42 D2
Jaignes (77) 43 H3
Jaillans (26) 144 C4
la Jaille-Yvon (49) 76 D2
Jaillon (54) 48 B4
Jailly (58) 99 F2
Jailly-les-Moulins (21) 85 E5
Jainvillotte (88) 68 D3
Jalesches (23) 111 H4
Jaleyrac (15) 140 A2
Jaligny-sur-Besbre (03) 114 B3
Jallanges (21) 102 A3
Jallans (28) 62 A5
Jallaucourt (57) 49 E3
Jallerange (25) 103 E1
Jalognes (18) 98 B1
Jalogny (71) 116 A3
Jâlons (51) 45 G2
Jambles (71) 101 F5
Jambville (78) 42 A2
Jaméricourt (60) 19 H5
Jametz (55) 25 E4
Janailhac (87) 124 B4
Janaillat (23) 111 F6
Jancigny (21) 86 B5
Jandun (08) 23 H2
Janneyrias (38) 130 C3
Jans (44) 74 C1
Janville (14) 14 D5
Janville (28) 62 D4
Janville (60) 21 F4
Janville-sur-Juine (91) 63 F1
Janvilliers (51) 44 D3
Janvry (51) 22 D6
Janvry (91) 42 C6

Janzé (35) 57 G4
Jarcieu (38) 144 B1
la Jard (17) 121 F4
Jard-sur-Mer (85) 91 F6
le Jardin (19) 139 G1
Jardin (38) 130 B5
Jardres (86) 109 F1
Jargeau (45) 81 E1
Jarjayes (05) 160 C3
Jarménil (88) 70 A4
Jarnac (16) 121 H3
Jarnac-Champagne (17) 121 G4
Jarnages (23) 111 H5
la Jarne (17) 106 D5
Jarnieux (69) 129 G1
Jarnosse (42) 115 F6
Jarny (54) 26 A5
Jarret (65) 183 E4
la Jarrie (17) 106 D5
Jarrie (38) 145 G3
la Jarrie-Audouin (17) 107 G6
Jarrier (73) 146 C1
Jars (18) 82 A5
Jarsy (73) 132 B4
Jarville-la-Malgrange (54) 48 D5
Jarzé Villages (49) 77 F4
Jas (42) 129 F3
Jasney (70) 87 G1
Jassans-Riottier (01) 130 A1
Jasseines (10) 66 D1
Jasseron (01) 117 E4
Jasses (64) 181 H2
Jatxou (64) 180 C1
Jau-Dignac-et-Loirac (33) 120 C6
Jaucourt (52) 67 E3
la Jaudonnière (85) 92 B6
Jaudrais (28) 40 D6
Jaujac (07) 157 F2
Jauldes (16) 122 C3
Jaulges (89) 65 H6
Jaulgonne (02) 44 C2
Jaulnay (37) 94 C4
Jaulnes (77) 65 E2
Jaulny (54) 48 B2
Jaulzy (60) 21 G5
Jaunac (07) 143 F5
Jaunay-Marigny (86) 94 C6
Jaure (24) 137 E3
Jausiers (04) 161 G3
Jaux (60) 21 F5
Jauzé (72) 60 C4
Javaugues (43) 141 H2
Javené (35) 58 A2
Javerdat (87) 123 H1
Javerlhac-et-la-Chapelle-Saint-Robert (24) 123 E5
Javernant (10) 66 A4
la Javie (04) 160 D5
Javrezac (16) 121 G3
Javron-les-Chapelles (53) 59 F2
Jax (43) 142 A3
Jaxu (64) 181 E3
Jayac (24) 138 B4
Jayat (01) 116 D3
Jazeneuil (86) 108 C2
Jazennes (17) 121 E4
Jeancourt (02) 8 D6
Jeandelaincourt (54) 48 D3
Jeandelize (54) 48 A1
Jeanménil (88) 70 B2
Jeantes (02) 23 E1
Jebsheim (68) 71 G4
Jegun (32) 167 G4
la Jemaye-Ponteyraud (24) .. 136 C2
Jenlain (59) 9 G2
Jenzat (03) 113 G5
Jésonville (88) 69 F4
Jessains (10) 67 E3
Jetterswiller (67) 50 C5
Jettingen (68) 89 F3
Jeu-les-Bois (36) 96 D6
Jeu-Maloches (36) 96 B3
Jeufosse (78) 41 G2
Jeugny (10) 66 B5
Jeumont (59) 10 B2
Jeurre (39) 117 H3
Jeux-lès-Bard (21) 84 C4
Jeuxey (88) 70 A4
Jevoncourt (54) 69 G2
Jezainville (54) 48 C3
Jézeau (65) 183 G6
Joannas (07) 157 F2
Job (63) 128 B4
Joch (66) 200 D3
Jœuf (54) 26 A4
Joganville (50) 12 D3
Joigny (89) 65 E6
Joigny-sur-Meuse (08) 11 F6
Joinville (52) 67 H2
Joinville-le-Pont (94) 42 D4
Joiselle (51) 44 C5
Jolimetz (59) 9 G3
Jolivet (54) 49 E6
Jonage (69) 130 B3
Joncels (34) 172 B4
la Jonchère (85) 91 G6
la Jonchère-Saint-Maurice (87) 124 C1
Jonchères (26) 159 F2
Joncherey (90) 88 D4
Jonchery (52) 67 H4
Jonchery-sur-Suippe (51) 46 A1
Jonchery-sur-Vesle (51) 22 D6
Joncourt (02) 9 E5
Joncreuil (10) 67 E1
Joncy (71) 115 H1
Jongieux (73) 131 G2
Jonquerettes (84) 175 E2

Jonquery (51) 45 E1
Jonquières (11) 187 G5
Jonquières (34) 172 D5
Jonquières (60) 21 E5
Jonquières (81) 170 C5
Jonquières (84) 158 C6
Jonquières-Saint-Vincent (30) 174 C3
Jons (69) 130 C3
Jonval (08) 24 A3
Jonvelle (70) 69 E6
Jonville-en-Woëvre (55) 48 A2
Jonzac (17) 121 F5
Jonzier-Épagny (74) 118 B6
Jonzieux (42) 143 F1
Joppécourt (54) 25 H4
Jort (14) 39 E2
Jorxey (88) 69 G3
Josat (43) 142 A2
Josnes (41) 80 B2
Josse (40) 164 D4
Josselin (56) 55 H4
Jossigny (77) 43 F4
Jou-sous-Monjou (15) 140 C5
Jouac (87) 110 C3
Jouaignes (02) 22 B5
Jouancy (89) 84 B3
Jouarre (77) 44 A3
Jouars-Pontchartrain (78) 42 A4
Jouaville (54) 26 A5
Joucas (84) 175 G2
Joucou (11) 199 H1
Joudes (71) 117 E2
Joudreville (54) 25 H5
Joué-du-Bois (61) 38 D6
Joué-du-Plain (61) 38 D5
Joué-en-Charnie (72) 59 G5
Joué-l'Abbé (72) 60 B4
Joué-lès-Tours (37) 78 D6
Joué-sur-Erdre (44) 75 E3
Jouet-sur-l'Aubois (18) 98 C3
Jouey (21) 101 E2
Jougne (25) 104 A5
Jouhe (39) 102 C2
Jouhet (86) 109 H2
Jouillat (23) 111 G4
Jouques (13) 176 B5
Jouqueviel (81) 153 H6
Jourgnac (87) 124 A3
Journans (01) 117 E5
Journet (86) 110 A2
Journiac (24) 137 G4
Journy (62) 1 H4
Jours-lès-Baigneux (21) 85 E3
Joursac (15) 141 E3
Joussé (86) 109 F4
Jouvençon (71) 116 C1
Joux (69) 129 F2
Joux-la-Ville (89) 83 H3
Jouy (28) 62 B1
Jouy (89) 64 C4
Jouy-aux-Arches (57) 48 C2
Jouy-en-Argonne (55) 47 E1
Jouy-en-Josas (78) 42 C4
Jouy-en-Pithiverais (45) 63 E4
Jouy-le-Châtel (77) 43 H5
Jouy-le-Moutier (95) 42 B2
Jouy-le-Potier (45) 80 C2
Jouy-lès-Reims (51) 23 E6
Jouy-Mauvoisin (78) 41 G3
Jouy-sous-Thelle (60) 20 A5
Jouy-sur-Eure (27) 41 E2
Jouy-sur-Morin (77) 44 B4
Joyeuse (07) 157 F3
Joyeux (01) 130 C1
Joze (63) 127 G2
Jozerand (63) 127 F1
Jû-Belloc (32) 166 D5
Juaye-Mondaye (14) 13 H6
Jubainville (88) 68 D1
Jublains (53) 59 E3
le Juch (29) 53 F2
Jugazan (33) 135 H6
Jugeals-Nazareth (19) 138 D3
Jugon-les-Lacs - Commune nouvelle (22) 34 B5
Jugy (71) 116 B1
Juicq (17) 121 F2
Juif (71) 102 A6
Juignac (16) 122 B6
Juigné-des-Moutiers (44) 75 F1
Juigné-sur-Sarthe (72) 77 F1
Juignettes (27) 40 A4
Juillac (19) 138 B1
Juillac (32) 167 E6
Juillac (33) 136 A6
Juillac-le-Coq (16) 121 H4
Juillan (65) 183 E3
Juillé (16) 122 C1
Juillé (72) 60 A3
Juillé (79) 108 A5
Juillenay (21) 84 C6
Juilles (32) 168 B5
Juilly (21) 85 F4
Juilly (77) 43 F2
Jujols (66) 200 B3
Jujurieux (01) 117 F6
Julianges (48) 141 G5
Juliénas (69) 116 A4
Julienne (16) 121 H3
Julianges (43) 142 B1
Jullié (69) 116 A4
Jullouville (50) 36 D4
Jully (89) 84 C2
Jully-lès-Buxy (71) 101 F6
Jully-sur-Sarce (10) 66 C5
Julos (65) 183 E4

Julvécourt (55) 47 E2
Jumeauville (78) 41 H3
Jumeaux (63) 127 G6
Jumel (80) 20 C1
Jumelles (27) 41 E3
Jumencourt (02) 22 A4
Jumièges (76) 18 B4
Jumigny (02) 22 C4
Jumilhac-le-Grand (24) 123 H5
Junas (30) 173 H4
Junay (89) 84 A1
Juncalas (65) 183 E4
les Junies (46) 152 B3
Juniville (08) 23 G5
Jupilles (72) 78 C2
Jurançon (64) 182 B2
Juranville (45) 63 H5
Juré (42) 128 C2
Jurignac (16) 122 A5
Jurvielle (31) 197 E1
Jury (57) 48 D1
Juscorps (79) 107 H4
Jusix (47) 150 B2
Jussac (15) 140 A4
Jussarupt (88) 70 B4
Jussas (17) 135 G1
Jussecourt-Minecourt (51) 46 C4
Jussey (70) 87 E1
Jussy (02) 21 H2
Jussy (57) 26 B5
Jussy (89) 83 G3
Jussy-Champagne (18) 98 A3
Jussy-le-Chaudrier (18) 98 C2
Justian (32) 167 F3
Justine-Herbigny (08) 23 G3
Justiniac (09) 185 G3
Jutigny (77) 64 D1
Juvaincourt (88) 69 F2
Juvancourt (10) 67 E3
Juvanzé (10) 67 E3
Juvardeil (49) 77 E3
Juvelize (57) 49 F4
Juvignac (34) 173 F5
Juvigné (53) 58 B3
Juvignies (60) 20 B3
Juvigny (02) 22 A4
Juvigny (51) 45 G2
Juvigny (74) 118 C4
Juvigny-en-Perthois (55) 47 E6
Juvigny les Vallées (50) 37 G5
Juvigny-sur-Loison (55) 25 E4
Juvigny-sur-Orne (61) 39 E5
Juvigny-sur-Seulles (14) 14 A5
Juvigny Val d'Andaine (61) 38 B6
Juville (57) 48 D3
Juvinas (07) 157 F1
Juvincourt-et-Damary (02) 22 D4
Juvisy-sur-Orge (91) 42 D5
Juvrecourt (54) 49 F4
Juxue (64) 181 F2
Juzanvigny (10) 67 E2
Juzennecourt (52) 67 G4
Juzes (31) 186 A1
Juzet-de-Luchon (31) 197 F1
Juzet-d'Izaut (31) 184 B5
Juziers (78) 42 A2

Kalhausen (57) 50 A2
Kaltenhouse (67) 51 E3
Kanfen (57) 26 B2
Kappelen (68) 89 G3
Kappelkinger (57) 49 H2
Katzenthal (68) 71 F4
Kauffenheim (67) 51 G3
Kaysersberg Vignoble (68) 71 F4
Kédange-sur-Canner (57) 26 C3
Keffenach (67) 51 F2
Kembs (68) 89 G2
Kemplich (57) 26 D3
Kerbach (57) 27 G5
Kerbors (22) 33 E1
Kerfot (22) 33 F2
Kerfourn (56) 55 F3
Kergloff (29) 32 B6
Kergrist (56) 55 F2
Kergrist-Moëlou (22) 32 D6
Kerien (22) 32 D5
Kerlaz (29) 53 E2
Kerling-lès-Sierck (57) 26 C3
Kerlouan (29) 31 E2
Kermaria-Sulard (22) 32 D2
Kermoroc'h (22) 33 E3
Kernascléden (56) 54 C3
Kernilis (29) 31 E3
Kernouës (29) 31 E3
Kerpert (22) 33 E5
Kerprich-aux-Bois (57) 49 H4
Kersaint-Plabennec (29) 31 E4
Kertzfeld (67) 71 G2
Kervignac (56) 54 D5
Keskastel (67) 50 A2
Kesseldorf (67) 51 G3
Kienheim (67) 50 D5
Kiffis (68) 89 F4
Killem (59) 2 C1
Kilstett (67) 51 F4
Kindwiller (67) 50 D3
Kingersheim (68) 89 F1
Kintzheim (67) 71 F3
Kirchberg (68) 88 D1
Kirchheim (67) 50 D5
Kirrberg (67) 50 A3
Kirrwiller (67) 50 D3
Kirsch-lès-Sierck (57) 26 D1

Kirschnaumen (57) 26 D3
Kirviller (57) 49 H2
Klang (57) 26 D3
Kleingœft (67) 50 C5
Knœringue (68) 89 G3
Knœrsheim (67) 50 C5
Knutange (57) 26 A3
Kœnigsmacker (57) 26 C3
Kœstlach (68) 89 F4
Kœtzingue (68) 89 G2
Kœur-la-Grande (55) 47 G4
Kœur-la-Petite (55) 47 G4
Kogenheim (67) 71 G2
Kolbsheim (67) 50 D6
Krautergersheim (67) 71 G1
Krautwiller (67) 51 E4
le Kremlin-Bicêtre (94) 42 D4
Kriegsheim (67) 51 E4
Kruth (68) 70 D6
Kunheim (68) 71 G4
Kuntzig (57) 26 C3
Kurtzenhouse (67) 51 E4
Kuttolsheim (67) 50 D5
Kutzenhausen (67) 51 F2

Laà-Mondrans (64) 165 G6
Laas (32) 167 F6
Laas (45) 63 F5
Laàs (64) 181 G1
Labalme (01) 117 F6
Labarde (33) 135 E3
Labaroche (68) 71 E4
Labarthe (32) 167 H6
Labarthe (82) 152 B5
Labarthe-Bleys (81) 170 A1
Labarthe-Inard (31) 184 C4
Labarthe-Rivière (31) 184 A4
Labarthe-sur-Lèze (31) 185 F1
Labarthète (32) 166 C5
Labassère (65) 183 E4
Labastide (65) 183 G4
Labastide-Beauvoir (31) 185 H1
Labastide-Castel-Amouroux (47) 150 C4
Labastide-Cézéracq (64) 182 A1
Labastide-Chalosse (40) 165 H5
Labastide-Clermont (31) 184 D2
Labastide-d'Anjou (11) 186 B2
Labastide-d'Armagnac (40) 166 C2
Labastide-de-Lévis (81) 170 B2
Labastide-de-Penne (82) 152 D5
Labastide-de-Virac (07) 157 G4
Labastide-du-Haut-Mont (46) 139 G6
Labastide-du-Temple (82) 169 E1
Labastide-du-Vert (46) 152 B3
Labastide-en-Val (11) 187 F4
Labastide-Esparbairenque (11) 187 E2
Labastide-Gabausse (81) 170 B1
Labastide-Villefranche (64) 165 E6
Labastidette (31) 185 E1
Labathude (46) 153 G1
Labatie-d'Andaure (07) 143 G4
Labatmale (64) 182 D3
Labatut (09) 185 G3
Labatut (40) 165 E5
Labatut (64) 183 E1
Labatut-Rivière (65) 166 D6
Labbeville (95) 42 C1
Labeaume (07) 157 F3
Labécède-Lauragais (11) 186 C2
Labège (31) 169 F6
Labégude (07) 157 G2
Labéjan (32) 167 G6
Labenne (40) 164 B5
Labergement-Foigney (21) 102 B1
Labergement-lès-Auxonne (21) 102 C2
Labergement-lès-Seurre (21) 102 A3
Labergement-Sainte-Marie (25) 103 H5
Laberlière (60) 21 E3
Labescau (33) 150 A3
Labesserette (15) 154 B1
Labessette (63) 126 B5
Labessière-Candeil (81) 170 B4
Labets-Biscay (64) 181 F1
Labeuville (55) 48 A1
Labeuvrière (62) 2 C6
Labeyrie (64) 165 H5
Lablachère (07) 157 F3
Laboissière-en-Santerre (80) 21 E2
Laboissière-en-Thelle (60) 20 B6
Laborde (65) 183 G4
Laborel (26) 159 G5
Labosse (60) 19 H5
Labouheyre (40) 148 C6
Laboulbène (81) 170 C5
Laboule (07) 157 E2
Labourgade (82) 168 D2

Labourse (62) 2 D6
Laboutarie (81) 170 B4
Labretonie (47) 150 D3
Labrihe (32) 168 B4
Labrit (40) 149 F6
Labroquère (31) 184 A4
Labrousse (15) 140 B5
Labroye (62) 7 E2
Labruguière (81) 170 C6
Labruyère (21) 102 A3
Labruyère (60) 20 D5
Labruyère-Dorsa (31) 185 G1
Labry (54) 26 A5
Laburgade (46) 152 D4
Lac-des-Rouges-Truites (39) 118 B1
le Lac-d'Issarlès (07) 142 D6
Lacabarède (81) 187 F1
Lacadée (64) 165 G5
Lacajunte (40) 166 A5
Lacanau (33) 134 B4
Lacanche (21) 101 E3
Lacapelle-Barrès (15) 140 C5
Lacapelle-Biron (47) 151 H2
Lacapelle-Cabanac (46) 152 A3
Lacapelle-del-Fraisse (15) 140 A6
Lacapelle-Livron (82) 153 E5
Lacapelle-Marival (46) 153 F1
Lacapelle-Pinet (81) 170 D1
Lacapelle-Ségalar (81) 170 B1
Lacapelle-Viescamp (15) 139 H5
Lacarre (64) 181 E3
Lacarry-Arhan-Charritte-de-Haut (64) 181 F4
Lacassagne (65) 183 F2
Lacaugne (31) 185 E2
Lacaune (81) 171 F4
Lacaussade (47) 151 G3
Lacave (09) 184 D5
Lacave (46) 138 C6
Lacaze (81) 171 E4
Lacelle (19) 125 E4
Lacenas (69) 129 H1
Lacépède (47) 151 E4
Lachaise (16) 121 H5
Lachalade (55) 46 D1
Lachambre (57) 27 F5
Lachamp (48) 155 H2
Lachamp-Raphaël (07) 143 F6
Lachapelle (47) 150 C2
Lachapelle (80) 20 A1
Lachapelle (82) 168 B2
Lachapelle (54) 70 C1
Lachapelle-aux-Pots (60) 19 H4
Lachapelle-Auzac (46) 138 C5
Lachapelle-en-Blaisy (52) 67 G4
Lachapelle-Graillouse (07) 142 D6
Lachapelle-Saint-Pierre (60) 20 B6
Lachapelle-sous-Aubenas (07) 157 G2
Lachapelle-sous-Chanéac (07) 143 F5
Lachapelle-sous-Chaux (90) 88 C2
Lachapelle-sous-Gerberoy (60) 19 H3
Lachapelle-sous-Rougemont (90) 88 D2
Lachassagne (69) 129 H1
Lachau (26) 159 G5
Lachaussée (55) 48 A2
Lachaussée-du-Bois-d'Écu (60) 20 B3
Lachelle (60) 21 E4
Lachy (51) 44 D5
Lacollonge (90) 88 D2
Lacombe (11) 186 D1
Lacommande (64) 182 A2
Lacoste (34) 172 C5
Lacoste (84) 175 H3
Lacougotte-Cadoul (81) 169 H5
Lacour (82) 151 H5
Lacour-d'Arcenay (21) 84 C6
Lacourt (09) 185 E5
Lacourt-Saint-Pierre (82) 169 E2
Lacq (64) 182 A1
Lacquy (40) 166 B2
Lacrabe (40) 165 H5
Lacres (62) 1 F5
Lacroisille (81) 170 A5
Lacroix-Barrez (12) 140 C6
Lacroix-Falgarde (31) 169 F6
Lacroix-Saint-Ouen (60) 21 F5
Lacroix-sur-Meuse (55) 47 G2
Lacropte (24) 137 G4
Lacrost (71) 116 C1
Lacrouzette (81) 170 D5
Lacs (36) 111 H1
Ladapeyre (23) 111 H4
Ladaux (33) 135 H6
Ladern-sur-Lauquet (11) 187 E4
Ladevèze-Rivière (32) 167 E5
Ladevèze-Ville (32) 166 D6
Ladignac-le-Long (87) 124 A5
Ladignac-sur-Rondelles (19) 139 E2
Ladinhac (15) 154 B1
Ladirat (46) 139 F6
Ladiville (16) 122 A5
Ladoix-Serrigny (21) 101 G3
Ladon (45) 63 H6
Lados (33) 150 A3
Ladoye-sur-Seille (39) 103 E5
Lafage (11) 186 B3
Lafage-sur-Sombre (19) 139 G2
Lafare (84) 158 D6

Lafarre (07) 143 G3
Lafarre (43) 142 D6
Lafat (23) 111 E4
Lafauche (52) 68 C3
Laféline (03) 113 G3
Laferté-sur-Amance (52) 86 D1
Laferté-sur-Aube (52) 67 F5
Lafeuillade-en-Vézie (15) 140 B6
Laffaux (02) 22 B4
Laffite-Toupière (31) 184 C3
Laffrey (38) 145 G4
Lafitole (65) 183 E1
Lafitte (82) 168 D2
Lafitte-sur-Lot (47) 150 D4
Lafitte-Vigordane (31) 185 E2
Lafox (47) 151 F6
Lafrançaise (82) 152 B6
Lafraye (60) 20 B4
Lafresguimont-Saint-Martin (80) 19 H1
Lafrimbolle (57) 50 A6
Lagamas (34) 172 D5
Lagarde (09) 186 B5
Lagarde (31) 185 H2
Lagarde (32) 167 H2
Lagarde (57) 49 G5
Lagarde (65) 183 E2
Lagarde-d'Apt (84) 176 A2
Lagarde-Enval (19) 139 E2
Lagarde-Hachan (32) 183 H1
Lagarde-Paréol (84) 158 B5
Lagardelle (46) 152 B3
Lagardelle-sur-Lèze (31) 185 F1
Lagardère (32) 167 F3
Lagardiolle (81) 170 B6
Lagarrigue (47) 150 D5
Lagarrigue (81) 170 D6
Lageon (79) 93 G5
Lagery (51) 22 D6
Lagesse (10) 66 B6
Lagleygeolle (19) 138 D3
Laglorieuse (40) 166 B2
Lagnes (84) 175 G3
Lagney (54) 48 A5
Lagnicourt-Marcel (62) 8 C3
Lagnieu (01) 130 D2
Lagny (60) 21 F3
Lagny-le-Sec (60) 43 F2
Lagny-sur-Marne (77) 43 F4
Lagor (64) 181 H1
Lagorce (07) 157 G3
Lagorce (33) 135 H3
Lagord (17) 106 C4
Lagos (64) 182 C3
Lagrâce-Dieu (31) 185 F2
Lagrange (40) 166 D2
Lagrange (65) 183 G4
Lagrange (90) 88 D2
Lagrasse (11) 187 G4
Lagraulet-du-Gers (32) 167 F2
Lagraulet-Saint-Nicolas (31) 168 C3
Lagraulière (19) 138 D1
Lagrave (81) 170 B3
Lagruère (47) 150 C4
Laguenne (19) 139 E2
Laguépie (82) 153 G6
Laguian-Mazous (32) 183 F1
Laguinge-Restoue (64) 181 G4
Laguiole (12) 155 E1
Lagupie (47) 150 C2
Lahage (31) 184 D1
Lahas (32) 168 B6
Lahaymeix (55) 47 F3
Lahayville (55) 48 A3
Laheycourt (55) 46 D3
Lahitère (31) 185 E4
Lahitte (32) 168 A5
Lahitte-Toupière (65) 166 D6
Lahonce (64) 164 C6
Lahontan (64) 165 G5
Lahosse (40) 165 G4
Lahourcade (64) 182 A1
Lahoussoye (80) 7 H5
Laifour (08) 11 E6
la Laigne (17) 107 F4
Laigné (53) 76 C1
Laigné-en-Belin (72) 78 B1
Laignelet (35) 58 A2
Laignes (21) 84 D1
Laigneville (60) 20 D5
Laigny (02) 9 H6
Laillé (35) 57 E4
Lailly (89) 65 F4
Lailly-en-Val (45) 80 C2
Laimont (55) 46 D4
Lain (89) 83 E3
Laines-aux-Bois (10) 66 A4
Lainsecq (89) 83 E4
Lainville-en-Vexin (78) 41 H2
Laire (25) 88 C4
Laires (62) 2 B6
Lairière (11) 187 F5
Lairoux (85) 91 H6
Laissac-Sévérac l'Église (12) 155 E4
Laissaud (73) 132 A6
Laissey (25) 87 G6
Laître-sous-Amance (54) 48 D4
Laives (71) 116 B1
Laix (54) 25 H4
Laiz (01) 116 B4
Laizé (71) 116 B3
Laize-Clinchamps (14) 14 B5
Laizy (71) 100 C4
Lajo (48) 141 H6
Lajoux (39) 118 A3

Lalacelle (61) 59 G1
Lalande (89) 83 E3
Lalande-de-Pomerol (33) 135 H4
Lalande-en-Son (60) 19 G5
Lalandelle (60) 19 H5
Lalandusse (47) 151 E1
Lalanne (32) 168 A3
Lalanne (65) 184 A2
Lalanne-Arqué (32) 184 A2
Lalanne-Trie (65) 183 G2
Lalaye (67) 71 E2
Lalbenque (46) 152 D4
Laleu (61) 39 G6
Laleu (80) 7 E5
Lalevade-d'Ardèche (07) 157 F2
Lalheue (71) 116 B1
Lalinde (24) 137 F5
Lalizolle (03) 113 F5
Lallaing (59) 8 D1
Lalleu (35) 57 G5
Lalley (38) 145 G6
Lalobbe (08) 23 G2
Lalœuf (54) 69 F1
Lalongue (64) 166 C6
Lalonquette (64) 166 B6
Laloubère (65) 183 E3
Lalouret-Laffiteau (31) 184 B3
Lalouvesc (07) 143 G3
Laluque (40) 165 E2
Lama (2B) 203 E5
Lamadeleine-Val-des-
   Anges (90) 88 D2
Lamagdelaine (46) 152 D3
Lamagistère (82) 151 G6
Lamaguère (32) 168 A6
Lamaids (03) 112 C4
Lamalou-les-Bains (34) 172 A5
Lamancine (52) 67 H4
Lamanère (66) 200 D5
Lamanon (13) 175 F4
Lamarche (88) 68 D5
Lamarche-sur-Saône (21) .. 102 C1
Lamargelle (21) 85 F4
Lamaronde (80) 19 H1
Lamarque (33) 134 D3
Lamarque-Pontacq (65) 182 D3
Lamarque-Rustaing (65) 183 G2
Lamasquère (31) 168 D6
Lamastre (07) 143 G4
Lamath (54) 49 E6
Lamayou (64) 183 E1
Lamazère (32) 167 G5
Lamazière-Basse (19) 139 G1
Lamazière-Haute (19) 126 A4
Lambach (57) 50 C1
Lamballe (22) 34 A5
Lambersart (59) 3 F5
Lamberville (50) 37 H1
Lamberville (76) 17 G3
Lambesc (13) 175 H5
Lamblore (28) 40 C6
Lambres (62) 2 B5
Lambres-lez-Douai (59) 8 D2
Lambrey (70) 87 E2
Lambruisse (04) 177 G1
Laméac (65) 183 F2
Lamécourt (60) 20 D4
Lamelouze (30) 156 D6
Lamenay-sur-Loire (58) 99 G3
Lametz (08) 24 A3
Lamillarié (81) 170 C3
Lammerville (76) 17 F3
Lamnay (72) 61 E5
Lamongerie (19) 124 D5
Lamontélarié (81) 171 F3
Lamontgie (63) 127 G6
Lamontjoie (47) 167 H1
Lamonzie-Montastruc (24) . 137 E5
Lamonzie-Saint-
   Martin (24) 136 D5
Lamorlaye (60) 42 D1
Lamorville (55) 47 G3
Lamothe (40) 165 H3
Lamothe (43) 141 H1
Lamothe-Capdeville (82) ... 169 E1
Lamothe-Cassel (46) 152 D2
Lamothe-Cumont (82) 168 B3
Lamothe-Fénelon (46) 138 C6
Lamothe-Goas (32) 167 H3
Lamothe-Landerron (33) ... 150 B2
Lamothe-Montravel (24) 136 A5
Lamotte-Beuvron (41) 81 E4
Lamotte-Brebière (80) 7 G6
Lamotte-Buleux (80) 6 D3
Lamotte-du-Rhône (84) 158 A6
Lamotte-Warfusée (80) 8 A6
Lamouilly (55) 25 E3
Lamoura (39) 118 A3
Lampaul-Guimiliau (29) 31 G4
Lampaul-Plouarzel (29) 30 C4
Lampaul-
   Ploudalmézeau (29) 30 D3
Lampertheim (67) 51 E5
Lampertsloch (67) 51 E2
Lamure-sur-Azergues (69) . 115 H6
Lanans (25) 88 A6
Lanarce (07) 156 D1
Lanarvily (29) 31 E3
Lanas (07) 157 G3
Lancé (41) 79 G3
Lanchères (80) 6 B3
Lanches-Saint-Hilaire (80) ... 7 F4
Lanchy (02) 21 G1
Lancié (69) 116 A5
Lancieux (22) 34 C4
Lançon (08) 24 B6
Lançon (65) 183 G6

Lançon-Provence (13) 175 G5
Lancrans (01) 118 A5
Landange (57) 49 H5
Landas (59) 3 H6
Landau (56) 55 E5
Landaville (88) 68 D3
Landavran (35) 57 H2
la Lande-Chasles (49) 77 G4
la Lande-d'Airou (50) 37 E3
la Lande-de-Fronsac (33) .. 135 G4
la Lande-de-Goult (61) 39 E6
la Lande-de-Lougé (61) 38 D5
la Lande-Patry (61) 38 B4
la Lande-Saint-Léger (27) ... 15 G4
la Lande-Saint-
   Siméon (61) 38 C4
Landéan (35) 58 A1
Landebaëron (22) 33 E3
la Landec (22) 34 C5
Landécourt (54) 69 H1
Landéda (29) 30 D3
Landéhen (22) 34 A5
Landeleau (29) 54 A1
Landelles (28) 61 H1
Landelles-et-Coupigny (14) . 37 G3
Landeronde (85) 91 F4
Landerrouat (33) 136 B6
Landerrouet-sur-Ségur (33) 150 B1
Landersheim (67) 50 D4
Landes (17) 107 G6
les Landes-Genusson (85) .. 92 A3
Landes-le-Gaulois (41) 79 G3
Landes-sur-Ajon (14) 14 A5
Landes-Vieilles-et-
   Neuves (76) 19 G1
Landévant (56) 54 D5
Landévennec (29) 31 F5
Landevieille (85) 90 D4
Landeyrat (15) 140 D2
Landifay-et-
   Bertaignemont (02) 22 C1
Landigou (61) 38 B4
le Landin (27) 18 B4
Landiras (33) 149 G2
Landisacq (61) 38 A4
Landivisiau (29) 31 G4
Landivy (53) 58 B1
Landogne (63) 126 C2
Landorthe (31) 184 B4
Landos (43) 142 C6
Landouzy-la-Cour (02) 10 A6
Landouzy-la-Ville (02) 10 B6
Landrais (17) 107 E5
le Landreau (44) 75 E5
Landrecies (59) 9 G4
Landrecourt-Lempire (55) ... 47 F1
Landremont (54) 48 C3
Landres (54) 25 H5
Landres-et-Saint-
   Georges (08) 24 C5
Landresse (25) 88 A6
Landrethun-le-Nord (62) 1 G3
Landrethun-lès-Ardres (62) .. 1 H3
Landrévarzec (29) 53 G2
Landreville (10) 66 D5
Landrichamps (08) 11 F4
Landricourt (02) 22 A4
Landricourt (51) 46 C6
Landroff (57) 49 F2
Landry (73) 133 E4
Landser (68) 89 G2
Landudal (29) 53 G2
Landudec (29) 53 E2
Landujan (35) 56 D1
Landunvez (29) 30 C3
Lanespède (65) 183 F3
Lanester (56) 54 C5
Lanet (11) 187 F5
Laneuville (52) 68 D6
Laneuvelotte (54) 48 D4
Laneuveville-aux-Bois (54) . 49 F5
Laneuveville-derrière-
   Foug (54) 48 A5
Laneuveville-devant-
   Bayon (54) 69 G1
Laneuveville-devant-
   Nancy (54) 48 D5
Laneuveville-en-
   Saulnois (57) 49 E3
Laneuveville-lès-
   Lorquin (57) 49 H5
Laneuville-à-Rémy (52) 67 G1
Laneuville-au-Pont (51) 46 C6
Laneuville-au-Rupt (55) 47 H5
Laneuville-sur-Meuse (55) . 24 D4
Lanfains (22) 33 F6
Lanfroicourt (54) 48 D3
Langan (35) 57 E1
Langast (22) 55 H1
Langatte (57) 49 H5
Langé (36) 96 B3
Langeac (43) 141 H3
Langeais (37) 78 C6
Langensoultzbach (67) 51 E2
Langeron (58) 98 D5
Langesse (45) 82 A2
Langey (28) 61 F6
Langlade (30) 174 A3
Langley (88) 69 G2
Langoat (22) 32 D2
Langoëlan (56) 54 D2
Langogne (48) 156 C1
Langoiran (33) 149 G1
Langolen (29) 53 G2
Langon (33) 149 H2
Langon (35) 56 D6
Langon (41) 96 D1

le Langon (85) 107 E2
Langonnet (56) 54 B2
Langouet (35) 57 E1
Langres (52) 86 B1
Langrolay-sur-Rance (22) ... 34 D4
Langrune-sur-Mer (14) 14 B3
Languédias (22) 34 C6
Languenan (22) 34 C5
Langueux (22) 33 G4
Languevoisin-
   Quiquery (80) 21 F1
Languidic (56) 54 D4
Languimberg (57) 49 G4
Langy (03) 114 A4
Lanhélin (35) 35 E5
Lanhères (55) 25 G6
Lanhouarneau (29) 31 F3
Laniidut (29) 30 C4
Laning (57) 49 G2
Laniscourt (02) 22 B3
Lanleff (22) 33 F3
Lanloup (22) 33 F2
Lanmérin (22) 32 D2
Lanmeur (29) 32 B3
Lanmodez (22) 33 E1
Lanne (65) 183 E3
Lanne-en-Barétous (64) 181 G3
Lanne-Soubiran (32) 166 C4
Lannéanou (29) 32 A4
Lannebert (22) 33 F3
Lannecaube (64) 166 C6
Lannédern (29) 31 H6
Lannemaignan (32) 166 C2
Lannemezan (65) 183 G4
Lannepax (32) 167 F3
Lanneplaà (64) 165 F6
Lanneray (28) 61 H5
Lannes (47) 167 F1
Lanneuffret (29) 31 F4
Lannilis (29) 30 D3
Lannion (22) 32 C2
Lannoy (59) 3 G5
Lannoy-Cuillère (60) 19 G2
Lannux (32) 166 C5
Lano (2B) 205 F1
Lanobre (15) 126 B6
Lanouaille (24) 124 A6
Lanouée (56) 55 H3
Lanoux (09) 185 F4
Lanquais (24) 137 F6
Lanques-sur-Rognon (52) ... 68 B5
Lanquetot (76) 15 H1
Lanrelas (22) 56 B1
Lanrigan (35) 35 F6
Lanrivain (22) 32 D6
Lanrivoaré (29) 30 D4
Lanrodec (22) 33 F4
Lans (71) 101 H5
Lans-en-Vercors (38) 145 F3
Lansac (33) 135 F3
Lansac (65) 183 F3
Lansac (66) 200 D1
Lansargues (34) 173 H5
Lanta (31) 169 G6
Lantabat (64) 181 E2
Lantages (10) 66 C5
Lantan (18) 98 A4
Lantéfontaine (54) 26 A4
Lantenay (01) 117 G6
Lantenay (21) 85 G6
Lantenne-Vertière (25) 103 E1
Lantenot (70) 88 A2
la Lanterne-et-les-
   Armonts (70) 88 A1
Lanteuil (19) 138 D3
Lanthenans (25) 88 B5
Lanthes (21) 102 B3
Lantic (22) 33 F3
Lantignié (69) 116 A5
Lantillac (56) 55 G4
Lantilly (21) 84 D4
Lanton (33) 134 B6
Lantosque (06) 179 E1
Lantriac (43) 142 D4
Lanty (58) 100 A5
Lanty-sur-Aube (52) 67 F5
Lanuéjols (30) 155 H6
Lanuéjols (48) 156 B3
Lanuéjouls (12) 153 H4
Lanvallay (22) 34 D5
Lanvaudan (56) 54 D4
Lanvellec (22) 32 C3
Lanvénégen (56) 54 B3
Lanvéoc (29) 31 E5
Lanvollon (22) 33 F3
Lanzac (46) 138 C5
Laon (02) 22 C3
Laons (28) 40 D5
Lapalisse (03) 114 A4
Lapalud (84) 158 A5
Lapan (18) 97 G4
Lapanouse-de-Cernon (12) 172 A2
Laparade (47) 151 E4
Laparrouquial (81) 170 B3
Lapège (09) 199 E1
Lapenche (82) 152 D5
Lapenne (09) 186 A4
Lapenty (50) 37 G6
Laperche (47) 151 E3
Laperrière-sur-Saône (21) 102 B2
Lapeyre (65) 183 G2
Lapeyrère (31) 185 F3
Lapeyrouse (01) 130 B1
Lapeyrouse (63) 113 G5
Lapeyrouse-Fossat (31) 169 F4
Lapeyrouse-Mornay (26) ... 144 B1
Lapeyrugue (15) 154 C1
Lapleau (19) 139 G2

Laplume (47) 151 E6
Lapoutroie (68) 71 E4
Lapouyade (33) 135 G3
Lappion (02) 23 E3
Laprade (11) 186 D1
Laprade (16) 136 C1
Laprugne (03) 128 B3
Laps (63) 127 G4
Lapte (43) 143 E2
Lapugnoy (62) 2 C6
Laquenexy (57) 26 C6
Laqueuille (63) 126 C4
Laragne-Montéglin (05) 160 A4
Larajasse (69) 129 G4
Laramière (46) 153 F4
Laran (65) 183 H3
Larbey (40) 165 G4
Larbont (09) 185 F5
Larbroye (60) 21 G3
Larcan (31) 184 B3
Larcat (09) 199 E1
Larçay (37) 79 E6
Larceveau-Arros-
   Cibits (64) 181 E2
Larchamp (53) 58 B2
Larchant (77) 63 H3
Larche (19) 138 C3
le Larderet (39) 103 F5
Lardier-et-Valença (05) 160 B3
le Lardin-Saint-Lazare (24) 138 A3
Lardy (91) 63 F1
Larée (32) 166 D2
Laréole (31) 168 C4
Largeasse (79) 93 E6
Largentière (07) 157 F3
Largillay-Marsonnay (39) .. 117 G1
Largitzen (68) 89 E3
Largny-sur-Automne (02) ... 21 G6
Larians-et-Munans (70) 87 G5
Larivière (90) 88 D2
Larivière-Arnoncourt (52) ... 68 D5
Larmor-Baden (56) 72 C1
Larmor-Plage (56) 54 C5
Larnage (26) 144 A3
Larnagol (46) 153 E3
Larnas (07) 157 H3
Larnat (09) 199 E1
Larnaud (39) 102 C6
Larnod (25) 103 F1
Laroche-près-Feyt (19) 126 B4
Laroche-Saint-
   Cydroine (89) 65 F6
Larochemillay (58) 100 B4
Larodde (63) 126 B5
Laroin (64) 182 B2
Laronxe (54) 49 F6
Laroque (33) 149 H1
Laroque (34) 173 E2
Laroque-des-Albères (66) . 201 F4
Laroque-d'Olmes (09) 186 B5
Laroque-Timbaut (47) 151 G5
Laroquebrou (15) 139 H4
Laroquevieille (15) 140 B4
Larouillies (59) 10 A5
Larra (31) 168 D4
Larrau (64) 181 F4
Larrazet (82) 168 C2
Larré (56) 55 H6
Larré (61) 60 A1
Larressingle (32) 167 F2
Larressore (64) 180 C1
Larret (70) 86 D3
Larreule (64) 166 A6
Larreule (65) 183 E1
Larrey (21) 84 D1
Larribar-Sorhapuru (64) 181 F2
Larringes (74) 119 E3
Larrivière-Saint-Savin (40) 166 A3
Larrivoire (39) 117 H3
Larroque (31) 184 A3
Larroque (65) 183 H1
Larroque-Engalin (32) 167 H2
Larroque-Saint-Sernin (32) 167 G3
Larroque-sur-l'Osse (32) .. 167 F2
Larroque-Toirac (46) 153 F3
Lartigue (32) 168 A5
Lartigue (33) 150 A5
Laruns (64) 182 B5
Laruscade (33) 135 G3
Larzac (24) 137 H6
Larzicourt (51) 46 B5
Lasalle (30) 173 F1
Lasbordes (11) 186 C2
Lascabanes (46) 152 B4
Lascaux (19) 138 B1
Lascazères (65) 166 D6
Lascelle (15) 140 B4
Lasclaveries (64) 182 C1
Lasfaillades (81) 171 E6
Lasgraisses (81) 170 B3
Laslades (65) 183 G2
Lassales (65) 183 H3
Lassay-les-Châteaux (53) .. 59 E1
Lassay-sur-Croisne (41) 80 B4
Lasse (64) 180 D3
Lasserade (32) 166 D5
Lasséran (32) 167 H5
Lasserre (09) 185 H4
Lasserre (31) 168 D5
Lasserre (47) 167 G1
Lasserre (64) 166 C6
Lasserre-de-Prouille (11) .. 186 A3
Lasseube (64) 182 B3
Lasseube-Propre (32) 167 H5
Lasseubetat (64) 182 B3

Lassicourt (10) 66 D2
Lassigny (60) 21 F3
Lasson (89) 65 H5
Lassouts (12) 155 E3
Lassur (09) 199 F1
Lassy (35) 56 D4
Lassy (95) 42 D2
Lastic (15) 141 F3
Lastic (63) 126 B4
Lastours (31) 187 E2
Lataule (60) 21 E3
le Latet (39) 103 F5
la Latette (39) 103 G5
Lathuile (74) 132 B2
Lathus-Saint-Rémy (86) 110 A3
Latillé (86) 108 C1
Latilly (02) 44 B1
Latoue (31) 184 B3
Latouille-Lentillac (46) 139 F5
Latour (31) 185 E3
Latour-Bas-Elne (66) 201 G3
Latour-de-Carol (66) 199 G4
Latour-de-France (66) 200 D1
Latour-en-Woëvre (55) 48 A1
Latrape (31) 185 E3
Latrecey-Ormoy-sur-
   Aube (52) 67 F6
Latresne (33) 135 F6
Latrille (40) 166 B5
Latronche (19) 139 H2
Latronquière (46) 139 G6
Lattainville (60) 19 H6
Lattes (34) 173 H6
Lattre-Saint-Quentin (62) 8 A2
Lau-Balagnas (65) 182 D5
Laubach (67) 51 E3
Laubert (48) 156 B2
les Laubies (48) 156 A1
Laubressel (10) 66 C3
Laubrières (53) 58 A6
Laucourt (80) 21 E2
Laudrefang (57) 27 E5
Laudun-l'Ardoise (30) 174 D1
Laugnac (47) 151 F4
Laujuzan (32) 166 C3
Laulne (50) 12 D5
Laumesfeld (57) 26 D3
Launac (31) 168 D4
Launaguet (31) 169 F5
Launay (27) 40 B1
Launay-Villiers (53) 58 B4
Launois-sur-Vence (08) 23 H2
Launoy (02) 22 B6
Launstroff (57) 26 D2
la Laupie (26) 158 B2
Laurabuc (11) 186 B3
Laurac (11) 186 B3
Laurac-en-Vivarais (07) 157 F3
Lauraët (32) 167 F2
Lauraguel (11) 186 B4
Laure-Minervois (11) 187 F3
Laurède (40) 165 G3
Laurenan (22) 55 H1
Laurens (34) 172 B6
Lauresses (46) 139 G6
Lauret (34) 173 F3
Lauret (40) 166 B5
Laurie (15) 141 F2
Laurière (87) 110 D6
Lauris (84) 175 H4
Lauroux (34) 172 B4
Laussonne (43) 142 D4
Laussou (47) 151 G2
Lautenbach (68) 71 E6
Lautenbachzell (68) 71 E6
Lauterbourg (67) 51 G2
Lauthiers (86) 109 G1
Lautignac (31) 184 D1
Lautrec (81) 170 C4
Lauw (68) 88 D2
Lauwin-Planque (59) 8 C1
Lauzach (56) 73 E1
Lauzerte (82) 152 A5
Lauzerville (31) 169 G6
Lauzès (46) 152 D2
le Lauzet-Ubaye (04) 161 E3
Lauzun (47) 151 E2
Lavacquerie (60) 20 B2
Laval (30) 145 H2
Laval (53) 58 C5
Laval-d'Aix (26) 159 F1
Laval-d'Aurelle (07) 156 D2
Laval-de-Cère (46) 139 F5
Laval-du-Tarn (48) 155 H4
Laval-en-Brie (77) 64 C2
Laval-en-Laonnois (02) 22 C4
Laval-le-Prieuré (25) 104 B1
Laval-Morency (08) 10 D6
Laval-Pradel (30) 157 E5
Laval-Roquecezière (12) .. 171 H4
Laval-Saint-Roman (30) ... 157 H5
Laval-sur-Doulon (43) 142 A1
Laval-sur-Luzège (19) 139 G2
Laval-sur-Tourbe (51) 46 B1
Laval-sur-Vologne (88) 70 B3
Lavalade (24) 151 G1
Lavaldens (38) 145 H4
Lavalette (11) 186 D3
Lavalette (31) 169 G5
Lavalette (34) 172 B5
Lavallée (55) 47 F4
Lavancia-Epercy (39) 117 G3
le Lavandou (83) 193 H5
Lavangeot (39) 102 D2
Lavannes (51) 23 F5
Lavans-lès-Dole (39) 102 D2
Lavans-lès-Saint-
   Claude (39) 117 H3

Lavans-Quingey (25) 103 F2
Lavans-sur-Valouse (39) ... 117 G3
Lavans-Vuillafans (25) 103 H2
Lavaqueresse (02) 9 G5
Lavardac (47) 150 D6
Lavardens (32) 167 G4
Lavardin (41) 79 F2
Lavardin (72) 60 A5
Lavaré (72) 60 D5
Lavars (38) 145 G5
Lavatoggio (2B) 202 C5
Lavau (10) 66 B3
Lavau (89) 82 C4
Lavau-sur-Loire (44) 74 A4
Lavaudieu (43) 141 H2
Lavaufranche (23) 112 B4
Lavault-de-Frétoy (58) 100 B2
Lavault-Sainte-Anne (03) .. 112 D4
Lavaur (24) 152 A2
Lavaur (81) 169 H4
Lavaurette (82) 153 E6
Lavausseau (86) 108 C1
Lavaveix-les-Mines (23) ... 111 H6
Lavazan (33) 150 A4
Laveissenet (15) 140 D3
Laveissière (15) 140 D3
Lavelanet (09) 186 A6
Lavelanet-de-
   Comminges (31) 184 D3
Laveline-devant-
   Bruyères (88) 70 B4
Laveline-du-Houx (88) 70 B4
Laventie (62) 3 E5
Laveraët (32) 167 E6
Lavercantière (46) 152 C2
Laverdines (18) 98 B3
Lavergne (46) 139 E6
Lavergne (47) 150 D2
Lavernat (72) 78 B2
Lavernay (25) 103 E1
Lavernhe (12) 155 E6
Lavernose-Lacasse (31) ... 185 E1
Lavernoy (52) 68 C6
Laverrière (60) 20 A2
Laversine (02) 21 H5
Laversines (60) 20 B4
Lavérune (34) 173 F5
Laveyron (26) 144 A2
Laveyrune (07) 156 D2
Laveyssière (24) 136 D4
Lavieu (42) 128 D5
Laviéville (80) 8 A5
Lavigerie (15) 140 C3
Lavignac (87) 124 A3
Lavigney (70) 87 E2
Lavigny (39) 102 D6
Lavillatte (07) 156 D1
Laville-aux-Bois (52) 68 A5
Lavilledieu (07) 157 G2
Lavilleneuve (52) 68 C5
Lavilleneuve-au-Roi (52) 67 G4
Lavilletertre (60) 42 A1
Lavincourt (55) 47 E5
Laviolle (07) 143 F6
Laviron (07) 88 B6
Lavit (82) 168 B2
Lavoine (03) 128 B1
Lavoncourt (70) 87 E3
Lavours (01) 131 G2
Lavoûte-Chilhac (43) 141 H3
Lavoûte-sur-Loire (43) 142 C3
Lavoux (86) 109 F1
Lavoye (55) 47 E2
Lawarde-Mauger-
   l'Hortoy (80) 20 C2
Laxou (54) 48 C5
Lay (42) 129 E1
Lay-Lamidou (64) 181 H2
Lay-Saint-Christophe (54) .. 48 D4
Lay-Saint-Remy (54) 48 A5
Laye (05) 160 B1
Laymont (32) 184 D1
Layrac (47) 151 F6
Layrac-sur-Tarn (31) 169 G3
Layrisse (65) 183 E3
Lays-sur-le-Doubs (71) 102 B4
Laz (29) 53 H1
Lazenay (18) 97 E3
Lazer (05) 160 A4
Léalvillers (80) 7 H4
Léaupartie (14) 15 E4
Léaz (01) 118 A5
Lebetain (90) 88 D4
Lebeuville (54) 69 G1
Lebiez (62) 1 H6
Leboulin (32) 168 A5
Lebucquière (62) 8 C4
Lecci (2A) 207 G2
Lecelles (59) 4 A6
Lecey (52) 86 B1
Lechâtelet (21) 102 A3
Léchelle (62) 8 C4
Léchelle (77) 44 B6
la Léchère (73) 132 D5
les Lèches (24) 136 D4
Lécluse (59) 8 C2
Lécourt (52) 68 B5
Lécousse (35) 58 A2
Lecques (30) 173 G3
Lect (39) 117 G3
Lectoure (32) 167 H2
Lecumberry (64) 181 E3
Lécussan (31) 183 H3
Lédas-et-Penthiès (81) 170 D1
Lédat (47) 151 F3
Lédenon (30) 174 C2
Lédergues (12) 171 E1
Lederzeele (59) 2 B3
Ledeuix (64) 181 H3
Lédignan (30) 173 H2

Ledinghem (62) 1 H5
Ledringhem (59) 2 C3
Lée (64) 182 C2
Leers (59) 3 G4
Lées-Athas (64) 181 H5
Lefaux (62) 1 F6
Leffard (14) 38 C3
Leffincourt (08) 23 H5
Leffonds (52) 67 H6
Leffrinckoucke (59) 2 C1
Leforest (62) 8 D1
Lège (31) 184 A6
Legé (91) 91 F2
Lège-Cap-Ferret (33) 134 B5
Légéville-et-Bonfays (88) 69 G4
Léglantiers (60) 20 D4
Légny (69) 129 G2
Léguevin (31) 168 D5
Léguillac-de-l'Auche (24) 137 E2
Lehaucourt (02) 9 E6
Léhon (22) 34 D5
Leigné-les-Bois (86) 95 E5
Leigné-sur-Usseau (86) 94 C4
Leignes-sur-Fontaine (86) ...109 H2
Leigneux (42) 128 C3
Leimbach (68) 89 E1
Leintrey (54) 49 G5
Lélex (01) 118 A4
Lélin-Lapujolle (32) 166 C4
Lelling (57) 49 F2
Lemainville (54) 69 G1
Lembach (67) 51 E2
Lemberg (57) 50 C2
Lembeye (64) 166 C6
Lembras (24) 137 E5
Lemé (02) 9 H6
Lème (64) 166 B6
Leménil-Mitry (54) 69 G1
Lémeré (37) 94 B2
Lemmecourt (88) 68 D3
Lemmes (55) 47 F2
Lemoncourt (57) 49 E3
Lempaut (81) 170 B6
Lempdes (63) 127 F3
Lempdes-sur-Allagnon (43) ..141 G1
Lempire (02) 8 D5
Lemps (07) 144 A3
Lemps (26) 159 F4
Lempty (63) 127 G2
Lempzours (24) 137 G1
Lemud (57) 48 D2
Lemuy (39) 103 F4
Lénax (03) 114 C4
Lencloître (86) 94 B5
Lencouacq (40) 149 G6
Lengelsheim (57) 28 B5
Lengronne (50) 37 E2
Lenharrée (51) 45 G4
Léning (57) 49 G2
Lennon (29) 53 H1
Lenoncourt (54) 48 D5
Lens (62) 8 B1
Lens-Lestang (26) 144 C1
Lent (01) 116 D5
Lent (39) 103 F5
Lentigny (42) 128 C1
Lentillac-du-Causse (46) 153 E2
Lentillac-Saint-Blaise (46) ...153 H2
Lentillères (07) 157 F2
Lentilles (10) 67 F1
Lentilly (69) 129 H2
Lentiol (38) 144 C1
Lento (2B) 203 F5
Léobard (46) 152 C1
Léogeats (33) 149 G2
Léognan (33) 135 G6
Léojac (82) 169 F2
Léon (40) 164 C2
Léoncel (26) 144 D5
Léotoing (43) 141 F1
Léouville (45) 63 F4
Léoville (17) 121 G6
Lépanges-sur-Vologne (88) 70 B4
Lépaud (23) 112 B4
Lépin-le-Lac (73) 131 G5
Lépinas (23) 111 G6
Lépine (62) 6 D1
Lépron-les-Vallées (08) 23 H1
Lepuix (90) 88 C2
Lepuix-Neuf (90) 89 E1
Léran (09) 186 B5
Lercoul (09) 199 E1
Léré (18) 82 B5
Léren (64) 165 E6
Lérigneux (42) 128 C3
Lerm-et-Musset (33) 150 A4
Lerné (37) 94 A2
Lérouville (55) 47 G4
Lerrain (88) 69 G4
Léry (21) 85 F4
Léry (27) 18 D5
Lerzy (02) 9 H5
Lesbœufs (80) 8 B4
Lesbois (53) 58 C1
Lescar (64) 182 B2
Leschaux (74) 132 B3
Leschelle (02) 9 H5
Lescheraines (73) 132 A3
Leschères (39) 117 H2
Leschères-sur-le-
  Blaiseron (52) 67 H4
Lescherolles (77) 44 B5
Lescheroux (01) 116 D3
Lesches (77) 43 F3
Lesches-en-Diois (26) 159 F2
Lescouët-Gouarec (22) 54 C2
Lescousse (09) 185 G4
Lescout (81) 170 B6

Lescun (64) 181 H5
Lescuns (31) 184 D3
Lescure (09) 185 E5
Lescure-d'Albigeois (81) 170 C2
Lescure-Jaoul (12) 153 H5
Lescurry (65) 183 F2
Lesdain (59) 9 E4
Lesdins (02) 9 E6
Lesges (02) 22 B5
Lésignac-Durand (16) 123 F2
Lésigny (77) 43 E5
Lésigny (86) 95 E5
le Leslay (22) 33 F5
Lesme (71) 114 C1
Lesménils (54) 48 C3
Lesmont (10) 66 D2
Lesneven (29) 31 F3
Lesparre-Médoc (33) 134 C1
Lesparrou (09) 186 B6
Lespéron (07) 156 D1
Lesperon (40) 165 E1
Lespesses (62) 2 C5
Lespielle (64) 166 C6
Lespignan (34) 188 B3
Lespinasse (31) 169 E4
Lespinassière (11) 187 F1
Lespinoy (62) 6 D1
Lespiteau (31) 184 B4
Lespouey (65) 183 F3
Lespourcy (64) 182 D1
Lespugue (31) 184 A3
Lesquerde (66) 200 C1
Lesquielles-Saint-
  Germain (02) 9 G5
Lesquin (59) 3 G5
Lessac (16) 109 G6
Lessard-en-Bresse (71) 102 A5
Lessard-et-le-Chêne (14) 15 E5
Lessard-le-National (71) 101 G4
Lessay (50) 12 C5
Lesse (57) 49 E2
Lesseux (88) 70 D3
Lessy (57) 26 B5
Lestanville (76) 17 F3
Lestards (19) 125 F5
Lestelle-Bétharram (64) 182 C3
Lestelle-de-Saint-
  Martory (31) 184 C4
Lesterps (16) 109 H6
Lestiac-sur-Garonne (33) 149 G1
Lestiou (41) 80 D2
Lestrade-et-Thouels (12) 171 F1
Lestre (50) 13 E3
Lestrem (62) 2 D5
Létanne (08) 24 D3
Lételon (03) 112 D1
Letia (2A) 204 C3
Létricourt (54) 48 D3
Letteguives (27) 19 E4
Lettret (05) 160 B3
Leubringhen (62) 1 F3
Leuc (11) 187 E4
Leucamp (15) 140 B6
Leucate (11) 188 B6
Leuchey (52) 86 A2
Leudeville (91) 63 G1
Leudon-en-Brie (77) 44 A5
Leuglay (21) 85 F2
Leugny (86) 95 E4
Leugny (89) 83 E3
Leuhan (29) 54 A2
Leuilly-sous-Coucy (02) 22 A4
Leulinghem (62) 2 A4
Leulinghen-Bernes (62) 1 F3
Leurville (52) 68 B3
Leury (02) 22 A4
Leutenheim (67) 51 G3
Leuville-sur-Orge (91) 42 C6
Leuvrigny (51) 44 D2
le Leuy (40) 165 H3
Leuze (02) 10 B6
Levainville (28) 62 C1
Leval (59) 9 H3
Leval (90) 88 D2
Levallois-Perret (92) 42 C3
Levaré (53) 58 C1
Levécourt (52) 68 C4
Levens (06) 179 E2
Levergies (02) 9 E6
Levernois (21) 101 G3
Lèves (28) 62 B1
les Lèves-et-
  Thoumeyragues (33) 136 B6
Levesville-la-Chenard (28) 62 D3
Levet (18) 97 G4
Levie (2A) 207 E2
Levier (25) 103 G3
Lévignac (31) 168 D5
Lévignac-de-Guyenne (47) ...150 C2
Lévignacq (40) 164 D1
Lévignen (60) 43 G1
Lévigny (10) 67 F3
Levis (89) 83 E3
Lévis-Saint-Nom (78) 42 A5
Levoncourt (55) 47 F4
Levoncourt (68) 89 E4
Levroux (36) 96 C3
Lewarde (59) 8 D2
Lexy (54) 25 G3
Ley (57) 49 F4
Leychert (09) 185 H5
Leyme (46) 139 F6
Leymen (68) 89 G4
Leyment (01) 130 D1

Leynes (71) 116 A4
Leynhac (15) 154 A1
Leyr (54) 48 D4
Leyrat (23) 112 B3
Leyrieu (38) 130 D3
Leyritz-Moncassin (47) 150 C4
Leyssard (01) 117 F5
Leyvaux (15) 141 E1
Lez (31) 184 B6
lez-Fontaine (59) 10 B3
Lézan (30) 173 G2
Lézardrieux (22) 33 E2
Lézat-sur-Lèze (09) 185 F2
Lezay (79) 108 C4
Lezennes (59) 3 G5
Lezey (57) 49 F4
Lézignan (65) 183 E4
Lézignan-Corbières (11) 187 G3
Lézignan-la-Cèbe (34) 172 C6
Lézigné (49) 77 F3
Lézigneux (42) 128 D5
Lézinnes (89) 84 B2
Lezoux (63) 127 G2
Lhéraule (60) 19 H4
Lherm (31) 185 E1
Lherm (46) 152 B2
Lhéry (51) 22 D6
Lhez (65) 183 F3
Lhommaizé (86) 109 G2
Lhomme (72) 78 D2
L'Hôpital (01) 117 H6
Lhor (57) 49 G3
Lhospitalet (46) 152 C4
Lhoumois (79) 93 G6
Lhuis (01) 131 F3
Lhuître (10) 45 G6
Lhuys (02) 22 B6
Liac (65) 183 E1
Liancourt (60) 20 D5
Liancourt-Fosse (80) 21 F1
Liancourt-Saint-Pierre (60) 19 H6
Liart (08) 23 G1
Lias (32) 168 D6
Lias-d'Armagnac (32) 166 D3
Liausson (34) 172 C5
Libaros (65) 183 G3
Libercourt (62) 3 F6
Libermont (60) 21 G2
Libourne (33) 135 G5
Licey-sur-Vingeanne (21) 86 B4
Lichans-Sunhar (64) 181 G4
Lichères (16) 122 C2
Lichères-près-
  Aigremont (89) 83 H2
Lichères-sur-Yonne (89) 83 G4
Lichos (64) 181 G2
Lichtenberg (67) 50 C2
Licourt (80) 21 F1
Licq-Athérey (64) 181 G4
Licques (62) 1 H3
Licy-Clignon (02) 44 B2
Lidrezing (57) 49 F3
Liebenswiller (68) 89 G4
Liebsdorf (68) 89 F4
Liebvillers (25) 88 C5
Liederschiedt (57) 28 C5
Lieffrans (70) 87 F4
le Liège (37) 95 G1
Liéhon (57) 48 D2
Liencourt (62) 7 H2
Lieoux (31) 184 B3
Liepvre (68) 71 F3
Liéramont (80) 8 C5
Liercourt (80) 6 D4
Lières (62) 2 C6
Liergues (69) 129 G1
Liernais (21) 100 D1
Liernolles (03) 114 C3
Lierval (02) 22 C4
Lierville (60) 42 A1
Lies (65) 183 F4
Liesle (25) 103 E3
Liesse-Notre-Dame (02) 22 D3
Liessies (59) 10 B4
Liesville-sur-Douve (50) 13 E4
Liettres (62) 2 B5
Lieu-Saint-Amand (59) 9 E2
Lieuche (06) 178 C1
Lieucourt (70) 86 D6
Lieudieu (38) 130 C6
Lieurac (09) 186 A5
Lieuran-Cabrières (34) 172 C5
Lieuran-lès-Béziers (34) 188 C1
Lieurey (27) 15 H4
Lieuron (35) 56 D5
Lieusaint (50) 12 D3
Lieusaint (77) 43 E6
Lieutadès (15) 140 D6
Lieuvillers (60) 20 D4
Liévans (70) 87 H3
Liévin (62) 8 B1
Liez (02) 22 A2
Liez (85) 107 F3
Liézey (88) 70 C4
Liffol-le-Grand (88) 68 C3
Liffol-le-Petit (52) 68 B3
Liffré (35) 57 G2
Ligardes (32) 167 G1
Ligescourt (80) 6 D2
Liginiac (19) 126 A6
Liglet (86) 110 B2
Lignac (36) 110 C2
Lignairolles (11) 186 B4
Lignan-de-Bazas (33) 149 H3
Lignan-de-Bordeaux (33) 135 F6
Lignan-sur-Orb (34) 188 B2
Lignareix (19) 125 H4

Ligné (16) 122 B1
Ligné (44) 75 E3
Lignères (61) 39 G5
Lignereuil (62) 7 H2
Lignerolles (03) 112 C4
Lignerolles (21) 85 G1
Lignerolles (27) 41 E4
Lignerolles (36) 112 A2
Ligneyrac (19) 138 D4
Lignières (10) 66 A6
Lignières (18) 97 F6
Lignières (41) 79 G1
Lignières (80) 21 E2
Lignières-Châtelain (80) 19 H1
Lignières-de-Touraine (37) 78 C6
Lignières-en-Vimeu (80) 6 D6
Lignières-Orgères (53) 38 D6
Lignières-Sonneville (16) 121 H4
Lignières-sur-Aire (55) 47 F4
Lignol (56) 54 D3
Lignol-le-Château (10) 67 F4
Lignon (51) 46 A6
Lignorelles (89) 83 G1
Lignou (61) 38 C5
Ligny-en-Barrois (55) 47 F5
Ligny-en-Brionnais (71) 115 F4
Ligny-en-Cambrésis (59) 9 E4
Ligny-le-Châtel (89) 83 H1
Ligny-le-Ribault (45) 80 C3
Ligny-lès-Aire (62) 2 B6
Ligny-Saint-Flochel (62) 7 H2
Ligny-sur-Canche (62) 7 G2
Ligny-Thilloy (62) 8 B4
Ligré (37) 94 B2
Ligron (72) 77 H2
Ligsdorf (68) 89 F4
Ligueil (37) 95 E3
Ligueux (33) 136 C6
Ligueux (24) 137 F2
Ligugé (86) 109 E2
Lihons (80) 21 E1
Lihus (60) 20 A3
les Lilas (93) 42 D4
Lilhac (31) 184 B2
Lille (59) 3 F5
Lillebonne (76) 15 H1
Lillemer (35) 35 E4
Lillers (62) 2 C5
Lilly (27) 19 F4
Limalonges (79) 108 D5
Limans (04) 176 C2
Limanton (58) 99 H3
Limas (69) 129 H1
Limay (78) 41 H2
Limbrassac (09) 186 A5
Limé (02) 22 B5
Limeil-Brévannes (94) 43 E5
Limendous (64) 182 D2
Limeray (37) 79 F5
Limersheim (67) 71 H1
Limerzel (56) 73 G1
Limésy (76) 17 F4
Limeuil (24) 137 G5
Limeux (18) 97 F3
Limeux (80) 6 D5
Limey-Remenauville (54) 48 B3
Limeyrat (24) 137 H3
Limoges (87) 124 B2
Limoges-Fourches (77) 43 F6
Limogne-en-Quercy (46) 153 E4
Limoise (03) 98 D6
Limon (58) 99 F4
Limonest (69) 130 A2
Limons (63) 127 H1
Limont-Fontaine (59) 10 A3
Limony (07) 144 A1
Limours (91) 42 B6
Limousis (11) 187 E2
Limoux (11) 186 D5
la Limouzinière (44) 91 F1
Limpiville (76) 16 D4
Linac (46) 153 H1
Linard (23) 111 G3
Linards (87) 124 C4
Linars (16) 122 B4
Linas (91) 42 C6
Linay (08) 24 D2
Linazay (86) 108 D5
Lindebeuf (76) 17 F4
le Lindois (16) 123 E3
Lindre-Basse (57) 49 G4
Lindre-Haute (57) 49 G4
Lindry (89) 83 F2
Linexert (70) 88 A2
Lingé (36) 95 G5
Lingeard (50) 37 G4
Lingèvres (14) 13 H6
Linghem (62) 2 B5
Lingolsheim (67) 51 E6
Lingreville (50) 36 D2
Linguizzetta (2B) 205 G2
Liniers (86) 109 F1
Liniez (36) 96 C3
Linsdorf (68) 89 G4
Linselles (59) 3 F4
Linthal (68) 71 E6
Linthelles (51) 45 E5
Linthes (51) 45 E5
Lintot (76) 16 A4
Lintot-les-Bois (76) 17 G3
Linxe (40) 164 D2
Liny-devant-Dun (55) 24 D5
Linzeux (62) 7 F2
Liocourt (57) 48 D3
Liomer (80) 6 D6
Le Lion-d'Angers (49) 76 D3
Lion-devant-Dun (55) 25 E4

Lion-en-Beauce (45) 62 D5
Lion-en-Sullias (45) 81 H3
Lion-sur-Mer (14) 14 C3
Liorac-sur-Louyre (24) 137 E5
Liouc (30) 173 G3
Liourdres (19) 139 E5
Lioux (84) 175 H2
Lioux-les-Monges (23) 126 B1
Liposthey (40) 148 D5
Lipsheim (67) 51 E6
Lirac (30) 174 D1
Lirey (10) 66 B4
Lironcourt (88) 69 E6
Lironville (54) 48 B3
Liry (08) 24 A5
Lisbourg (62) 2 A6
Lisieux (14) 15 F5
Lisle (24) 137 E1
Lisle (41) 79 G1
Lisle-en-Barrois (55) 47 E3
Lisle-en-Rigault (55) 46 D5
Lisle-sur-Tarn (81) 169 H3
Lislet (02) 23 E2
Lison (14) 13 F5
Lisores (14) 39 F3
Lisors (27) 19 F5
Lissac (09) 185 G3
Lissac (43) 142 B3
Lissac-et-Mouret (46) 153 G2
Lissac-sur-Couze (19) 138 C3
Lissay-Lochy (18) 97 G4
Lisse-en-Champagne (51) 46 B4
Lisses (91) 42 D6
Lisseuil (63) 113 F6
Lissey (55) 25 E5
Lissieu (69) 129 H2
Lissy (77) 43 F6
Listrac-de-Durèze (33) 136 A6
Listrac-Médoc (33) 134 D3
Lit-et-Mixe (40) 164 D1
Litteau (14) 13 F6
Littenheim (67) 50 C4
Litz (60) 20 C4
Livaie (61) 59 H1
Livarot-Pays-d'Auge (14) 39 F2
Liverdun (54) 48 C4
Liverdy-en-Brie (77) 43 F5
Livernon (46) 153 F2
Livers-Cazelles (81) 170 B1
Livet (53) 59 E4
Livet-en-Saosnois (72) 60 B2
Livet-et-Gavet (38) 145 H3
Livet-sur-Authou (27) 18 A6
Livilliers (95) 42 B2
Livinhac-le-Haut (12) 154 A2
la Livinière (34) 187 G2
Livré-la-Touche (53) 58 B6
Livré-sur-Changeon (35) 57 H2
Livron (64) 182 D3
Livron-sur-Drôme (26) 144 A6
Livry (58) 98 D5
Livry-Gargan (93) 43 E3
Livry-Louvercy (51) 45 H1
Livry-sur-Seine (77) 64 A1
Lixhausen (67) 50 D4
Lixheim (57) 50 A4
Lixing-lès-Rouhling (57) 27 G5
Lixing-lès-Saint-Avold (57) 49 G2
Lixy (89) 64 D4
Lizac (82) 168 D1
Lizant (86) 109 E6
Lizeray (36) 96 D3
Lizières (23) 111 E3
Lizine (25) 103 F2
Lizines (77) 64 D1
Lizio (56) 55 H4
Lizos (65) 183 F2
Lizy (02) 22 B4
Lizy-sur-Ourcq (77) 43 H2
la Llagonne (66) 200 C4
Llauro (66) 201 E3
Llo (66) 199 H4
Llupia (66) 201 E3
Lobsann (67) 51 E2
Loc-Brévalaire (29) 31 E3
Loc-Eguiner (29) 31 G4
Loc-Envel (22) 32 C4
Locarn (22) 32 C6
Loché-sur-Indrois (37) 95 H2
Loches (37) 95 G2
Loches-sur-Ource (10) 66 D5
Lochieu (01) 131 G1
Lochwiller (67) 50 D4
Locmalo (56) 54 D2
Locmaria (56) 72 B4
Locmaria-Berrien (29) 32 A5
Locmaria-Grand-
  Champ (56) 55 F5
Locmaria-Plouzané (29) 30 D5
Locmariaquer (56) 72 C1
Locmélar (29) 31 G4
Locminé (56) 55 F4
Locmiquélic (56) 54 C5
Locoal-Mendon (56) 55 E6
Locon (62) 2 C5
Loconville (60) 19 H6
Locqueltas (56) 55 G4
Locquénolé (29) 31 H3
Locquignol (59) 9 G3
Locquirec (29) 32 B2
Locronan (29) 53 F2
Loctudy (29) 53 F4
Locunolé (29) 54 B3
Loddes (03) 114 C4
Lodes (31) 184 A3
Lodève (34) 172 C4
Lods (25) 103 H3
Lœuilley (70) 86 B5

Lœuilly (80) 20 B1
Loffre (59) 8 D2
la Loge (62) 7 E1
la Loge-aux-Chèvres (10) 66 D3
Loge-Fougereuse (85) 92 D6
la Loge-Pomblin (10) 66 B5
les Loges (14) 37 H2
les Loges (52) 86 C2
les Loges (76) 16 B4
les Loges-en-Josas (78) 42 B5
les Loges-Marchis (50) 37 H5
les Loges-Marguron (10) 66 B5
les Loges-Saulces (14) 38 C3
les Loges-sur-Brécey (50) 37 F4
Lognes (77) 43 E4
Logny-Bogny (08) 23 G1
Logny-lès-Aubenton (02) 23 F1
Logonna-Daoulas (29) 31 F5
Logrian-Florian (30) 173 G2
Logron (28) 61 H4
Loguivy-Plougras (22) 32 C4
Lohéac (35) 56 D5
Lohitzun-Oyhercq (64) 181 F2
Lohr (67) 50 B3
Lohuec (22) 32 C4
Loigné-sur-Mayenne (53) 76 C1
Loigny-la-Bataille (28) 62 C5
Loir en Vallée (72) 78 D2
Loiré (49) 76 B3
Loire-Authion (49) 77 F5
Loire-les-Marais (17) 107 E6
Loiré-sur-Nie (17) 121 H1
Loire-sur-Rhône (69) 130 A5
Loireauxence (44) 75 G4
Loiron-Ruillé (53) 58 B5
Loisail (61) 60 D1
Loisey (55) 47 F4
Loisia (39) 117 F2
Loisieux (73) 131 G4
Loisin (74) 118 D4
Loison (55) 25 G5
Loison-sous-Lens (62) 8 B1
Loison-sur-Créquoise (62) 7 E1
Loisy (54) 48 C3
Loisy (71) 116 C1
Loisy-en-Brie (51) 45 E3
Loisy-sur-Marne (51) 46 A5
Loivre (51) 23 E5
Loix (17) 106 B4
Lolif (50) 37 E4
Lolme (24) 151 E1
Lombard (25) 103 E2
Lombard (39) 102 C5
Lombers (81) 170 C4
Lombez (32) 168 B6
Lombia (64) 182 D2
Lombrès (65) 183 H4
Lombreuil (45) 64 A6
Lombron (72) 60 C5
Lommerange (57) 26 A3
Lommoye (78) 41 F2
Lomné (65) 183 G4
Lomont (70) 88 B3
Lomont-sur-Crête (25) 88 A6
Lompnas (01) 131 E2
Lompnieu (01) 131 F1
Lompret (59) 3 F5
Lonçon (64) 166 A6
la Londe (76) 18 C5
la Londe-les-Maures (83) 193 G5
Londigny (16) 108 D6
Londinières (76) 6 B6
Long (80) 7 E2
Longages (31) 185 E2
Longaulnay (35) 56 D1
Longavesnes (80) 8 D5
Longchamp (21) 102 B1
Longchamp (52) 68 B4
Longchamp (88) 70 A3
Longchamp-sous-
  Châtenois (88) 69 E3
Longchamps (27) 19 F5
Longchamps-sur-Aire (55) 47 F3
Longchaumois (39) 118 A2
Longcochon (39) 103 G5
Longeau-Percey (52) 86 B2
Longeault (21) 102 B1
Longeaux (55) 47 F5
Longechaux (25) 104 A1
Longechenal (38) 130 D6
Longecourt-en-Plaine (21) 102 A1
Longecourt-lès-
  Culêtre (21) 101 E2
Longemaison (25) 104 B2
Longepierre (71) 102 B4
Longes (69) 129 H5
Longessaigne (69) 129 F3
Longeve (17) 106 C3
Longèves (17) 107 E2
Longèves (85) 107 E2
Longeville (25) 103 H3
la Longeville (25) 104 B3
Longeville-en-Barrois (55) 47 E5
Longeville-lès-Metz (57) 26 B5
Longeville-lès-Saint-
  Avold (57) 27 E5
Longeville-sur-Mer (85) 91 H4
Longeville-sur-Mogne (10) 66 B4
Longevilles-Mont-d'Or (25) ..104 A5
Longfossé (62) 1 G5
la Longine (70) 70 B6
Longjumeau (91) 42 C5
Longlaville (54) 25 H3
Longmesnil (76) 19 F3

Longnes (72).............................59 H5
Longnes (78).............................41 G3
Longny les Villages (61).......61 E1
Longperrier (77)......................43 F2
Longpont (02)..........................21 H6
Longpont-sur-Orge (91).......42 C6
Longpré-le-Sec (10)..............66 D4
Longpré-les-Corps-
   Saints (80)...........................7 E5
Longré (16).............................108 C6
Longroy (76)...............................6 B5
Longsols (10)...........................66 C2
Longué-Jumelles (49)............77 G5
Longueau (80)............................7 G6
Longuefuye (53)......................76 D1
Longueil (76)............................17 F2
Longueil-Annel (60)...............21 F4
Longueil-Sainte-Marie (60)...21 E5
Longuenée-en-Anjou (49)......76 D3
Longuenesse (62)......................2 B4
Longuenoë (61)........................59 H1
Longuerue (76)........................19 E3
Longues-sur-Mer (14)............13 H5
Longuesse (95)........................42 A2
Longueval (80)...........................8 B5
Longueville (14).......................13 G5
Longueville (47)....................150 C3
Longueville (50)......................36 D3
la Longueville (59)....................9 H2
Longueville (62)........................1 G4
Longueville (77)......................64 D1
Longueville-sur-Aube (10).....66 A1
Longueville-sur-Scie (76)......17 G3
Longuevillette (80)....................7 G4
Longuyon (54)..........................25 G4
Longvic (21)............................85 H6
Longvillers (14)........................38 B2
Longvilliers (62)........................1 F6
Longvilliers (78).......................42 B6
Longwé (08)..............................24 B5
Longwy (54)..............................25 H3
Longwy-sur-le-Doubs (39)...102 C3
Lonlay-l'Abbaye (61)..............38 A5
Lonlay-le-Tesson (61)............38 C5
Lonnes (16)............................122 C1
Lonny (08)................................24 A1
Lonrai (61)...............................60 A1
Lons (64)................................182 B2
Lons-le-Saunier (39)............102 D6
Lonzac (17)............................121 G4
le Lonzac (19)........................125 E6
Looberghe (59)...........................2 B2
Loon-Plage (59)..........................2 A2
Loos (59)....................................3 F5
Loos-en-Gohelle (62)...............8 B1
Looze (89)................................65 F6
Lopérec (29)............................31 G6
Loperhet (29)...........................31 F5
Lopigna (2A)..........................204 C4
Loqueffret (29)........................31 H5
Lor (02)....................................23 E3
Loray (25)..............................104 D1
Lorcières (15)........................141 G5
Lorcy (45)................................63 H5
Lordat (09).............................199 F1
Lorentzen (67)..........................50 A2
Loreto-di-Casinca (2B)........203 G6
Loreto-di-Tallano (2A).........207 E2
Lorette (64)............................129 G5
le Loreur (50)..........................36 D3
Loreux (41)...............................80 D5
le Lorey (50)............................37 E1
Lorey (54).................................69 G1
Lorges (41)...............................80 B2
Lorgies (62)................................3 E5
Lorgues (83)..........................193 H2
Lorient (56)..............................54 C5
Loriges (03)............................113 H4
Lorignac (17)..........................121 E5
Lorigné (79)...........................108 C5
Loriol-du-Comtat (84)..........175 F1
Loriol-sur-Drôme (26)..........144 A6
Lorlanges (43)........................141 G1
Lorleau (27)..............................19 F4
Lormaison (60).........................20 B6
Lormaye (28)............................41 G6
Lormes (58)...............................83 H6
Lormont (33)..........................135 F5
Lornay (74).............................131 H1
Loromontzey (54)...................69 H1
le Loroux (35)..........................58 B2
le Loroux-Bottereau (44)......75 E5
Lorp-Sentaraille (09)............184 D5
Lorquin (57).............................49 H5
Lorrez-le-Bocage-
   Préaux (77)........................64 B4
Lorris (45)................................81 H1
Lorry-lès-Metz (57)................26 B5
Lorry-Mardigny (57)..............48 C2
Lortet (65)..............................183 G4
Los Masos (66)......................200 C3
Loscouët-sur-Meu (22)...........56 A2
Losne (21)..............................102 B2
Losse (40)...............................150 A6
Lostanges (19).......................139 E4
Lostroff (57)............................49 G3
Lothey (29)..............................53 G1
Lottinghen (62)..........................1 G4
Louailles (72)...........................77 F2
Louan-Villegruis-
   Fontaine (77)....................44 C6
Louannec (22)..........................32 C1
Louans (37)..............................95 E1
Louargat (22)...........................32 D4
Louâtre (02)..............................21 H6
Loubajac (65).........................182 D3
Loubaresse (07)......................157 E2
Loubaut (09)...........................185 E4

Loubédat (32).........................166 D4
Loubejac (24).........................152 A2
Loubens (09)...........................185 G5
Loubens (33)...........................150 B1
Loubens-Lauragais (31)........169 H6
Loubers (81)...........................170 A1
Loubersan (32)........................167 G6
Loubès-Bernac (47)...............136 C6
Loubeyrat (63)........................127 E1
Loubieng (64).........................165 G6
la Loubière (12)......................154 C4
Loubières (09)........................185 H5
Loubigné (79).........................108 B6
Loubillé (79)...........................108 B6
Loubressac (46).....................139 E5
Lozay (17)...............................107 G6
Loze (82).................................153 F5
Lozinghen (62)...........................2 C6
Lozzi (2B)................................204 D2
Luant (36).................................96 B6
le Luart (72).............................60 D5
Lubbon (40)............................150 B6
Lubécourt (57).........................49 E3
Lubersac (19).........................124 C6
Lubey (54).................................25 H6
Lubilhac (43)..........................141 G2
Lubine (88)...............................71 E2
Lublé (37)..................................78 B4
Lubret-Saint-Luc (65)...........183 G2
Luby-Betmont (65).................183 G2
Luc (48)..................................156 D2
Luc (65)..................................183 F3
le Luc (83)..............................193 H2
Luc-Armau (64).....................182 D1
Luc-en-Diois (26)..................159 F2
Luc-la-Primaube (12)............154 C5
Luc-sur-Aude (11).................186 D5
Luc-sur-Mer (14)......................14 C3
Luc-sur-Orbieu (11)..............187 H3
Lucarré (64)...........................182 D1
Luçay-le-Libre (36)..................96 D3
Luçay-le-Mâle (36)..................96 B2
Lucbardez-et-Bargues (40)...166 B2
Lucciana (2B).........................203 G5
Lucé (28)...................................62 B2
Lucé-sous-Ballon (72).............60 B4
Luceau (72)...............................78 C2
Lucelle (68)...............................89 F5
Lucenay (69)...........................129 H2
Lucenay-le-Duc (21)................85 E3
Lucenay-lès-Aix (58)................99 F6
Lucenay-l'Évêque (71)...........100 C3
Lucéram (06)..........................179 F2
la Lucerne-
   d'Outremer (50)...............36 D4
Lucey (21)................................85 G1
Lucey (54).................................48 A5
Lucey (73)...............................131 G3
Lucgarier (64).........................182 C3
Luchapt (86)...........................109 H5
Luchat (17).............................120 D3
Luché-Pringé (72).....................78 A2
Luché-sur-Brioux (79)...........108 B5
Luché-Thouarsais (79).............93 H4
Lucheux (80)..............................7 G3
Luchy (60).................................20 B3
Lucinges (74).........................118 D4
Lucmau (33)...........................149 G4
Luçon (85)..............................106 C2
Lucq-de-Béarn (64)...............181 H2
Lucquy (08)...............................23 H3
les Lucs-sur-
   Boulogne (85)..................91 G3
Lucy (57)...................................49 E3
Lucy (76)...................................19 F1
Lucy-le-Bocage (02)................44 B2
Lucy-le-Bois (89).....................84 A4
Lucy-sur-Cure (89)..................83 H3
Lucy-sur-Yonne (89)................83 G4
le Lude (72)...............................78 A3
Ludes (51).................................45 F1
Ludesse (63)..........................127 F4
Ludiès (09).............................185 H4
Ludon-Médoc (33).................135 E4
Ludres (54)...............................48 C5
Lüe (40)..................................148 C5
Luemschwiller (68)..................89 F2
Lugagnan (65)........................153 E4
Lugagnac (46)........................152 D3
Lugaignac (33).......................135 H5
Lugan (12)..............................154 A3
Lugan (81)..............................169 H6
Lugarde (15)...........................140 C2
Lugasson (33).........................135 H6
Luglon (40)............................149 E6
Lugny (02)................................22 D1
Lugny (71)...............................116 B2
Lugny-Bourbonnais (18)..........98 B4
Lugny-Champagne (18)...........98 B3
Lugny-lès-Charolles (71).......115 F3
Lugo-di-Nazza (2B)...............205 F4
Lugon-et-l'Île-du-
   Carnay (33)......................135 G4
Lugos (33)..............................148 D3
Lugrin (74)..............................119 F2
Lugy (62)....................................2 A6
le Luhier (25).........................104 C1
Luigny (28)...............................61 G1
Luisant (28)..............................62 B2
Luisetaines (77).......................64 D2
Luitré (35).................................58 A3
Lullin (74)...............................119 E4
Lully (74)................................118 D4
Lumbin (38)............................145 H1
Lumbres (62)..............................2 A4
Lumeau (28)..............................62 C5
Lumes (08)...............................24 B1
Lumigny-Nesles-
   Ormeaux (77)..................43 G5

Louvres (95).............................43 E2
Louvroil (59)..............................10 A2
Louye (27)................................41 E4
Louzac-Saint-André (16).......121 G3
Louzes (72)...............................60 B2
Louzignac (17)........................121 H2
Louzouer (45)...........................64 B5
Louzy (79)................................93 G3
Lovagny (74)............................132 A1
Loyat (56).................................56 A3
la Loye (39)............................102 D3
Loye-sur-Arnon (18)..............112 B1
Loyettes (01)...........................130 C3
Lozanne (69)...........................129 H2
Lozay (17)...............................107 G6
Loze (82).................................153 F5
Lozinghen (62)...........................2 C6
Lozzi (2B)................................204 D2
Luant (36).................................96 B6
le Luart (72).............................60 D5

Lumio (2B)..............................202 C5
Lunac (12)...............................153 H5
Lunan (46)..............................153 G2
Lunas (24)..............................136 D5
Lunas (34)..............................172 B4
Lunay (41).................................79 F2
Luneau (03)............................114 D3
Lunegarde (46).......................153 E1
Lunel (34)...............................173 H5
Lunel-Viel (34).......................173 H5
Luneray (76).............................17 F2
Lunery (18)...............................97 G4
Lunéville (54)............................49 E6
le Luot (50)...............................37 E4
Lupcourt (54)............................48 D6
Lupé (42)................................129 H6
Lupersat (23)..........................126 A1
Lupiac (32).............................167 E4
Luplanté (28)............................62 A3
Luppé-Violles (32).................166 C4
Luppy (57).................................48 D2
Lupsault (16)..........................122 A1
Lupstein (67)............................50 C4
Luquet (65).............................182 D2
Lurais (36)................................95 F6
Luray (28)................................41 F5
Lurbe-Saint-Christau (64).....182 A3
Lurcy (01)...............................116 B6
Lurcy-le-Bourg (58).................99 F2
Lurcy-Lévis (03)......................98 C6
Luré (42).................................128 C2
Lure (70)...................................88 A2
Lureuil (36)...............................95 G5
Luri (2B)..................................203 F2
Luriecq (42)............................128 D6
Lurs (04).................................176 D2
Lury-sur-Arnon (18)................97 E2
Lus-la-Croix-Haute (26)........159 H1
Lusanger (44)...........................74 D1
Luscan (31)............................184 A5
Lusignac (24)..........................136 C1
Lusignan (86).........................108 D2
Lusignan-Petit (47)................151 E5
Lusigny (03)...........................114 A1
Lusigny-sur-Barse (10)...........66 C3
Lusigny-sur-Ouche (21)........101 F2
Lussac (16).............................122 D2
Lussac (17).............................121 F5
Lussac (33).............................136 A4
Lussac-les-Châteaux (86).....109 G3
Lussac-les-Églises (87).........110 B3
Lussagnet (40)........................166 C3
Lussagnet-Lusson (64)..........182 C1
Lussan (30).............................157 G6
Lussan (32).............................168 A5
Lussan-Adeilhac (31)............184 C2
Lussant (17)...........................120 D1
Lussas (07).............................157 G2
Lussas-et-
   Nontronneau (24)..........123 E5
Lussat (23).............................112 B5
Lussat (63).............................127 F2
Lussault-sur-Loire (37)...........79 F5
Lusse (88)................................70 D2
Lusseray (79).........................108 B5
Lustar (65).............................183 G2
Luthenay-Uxeloup (58)...........99 E5
Lutilhous (65).........................183 G4
Luttange (57)............................26 C4
Luttenbach-près-
   Munster (68)....................71 E5
Lutter (68)................................89 G4
Lutterbach (68)........................89 F2
Lutzelbourg (57)......................50 B4
Lutzelhouse (67)......................50 B6
Luvigny (88).............................50 A6
Lux (21).....................................86 A4
Lux (31)..................................186 A1
Lux (71)..................................101 G5
Luxé (16).................................122 B2
Luxe-Sumberraute (64).........181 E1
Luxémont-et-
   Villotte (51)......................46 B5
Luxeuil-les-Bains (70)............87 H1
Luxey (40)..............................149 F5
Luxiol (25)................................87 H5
Luyères (10).............................66 B2
Luynes (37)..............................78 C5
Luz-Saint-Sauveur (65).........183 E6
Luzancy (77).............................44 A3
Luzarches (95).........................42 D1
Luzay (79).................................93 G4
Luzé (37)..................................94 C3
Luze (70)...................................88 A3
Luzech (46)............................152 B3
Luzenac (09)..........................199 F1
Luzeret (36)...........................110 D2
la Luzerne (50)........................13 F6
Luzillat (63)...........................127 G1
Luzillé (37)...............................95 G1
Luzinay (38)...........................130 B4
Luzoir (02)................................10 A6
Luzy (58).................................100 B5
Luzy-Saint-Martin (55)...........24 D3
Luzy-sur-Marne (52)...............68 A5
Ly-Fontaine (02)......................22 A2
Lyas (07).................................157 H1
Lyaud (74)..............................119 E3
Lye (36).....................................96 B1
Lynde (59)...................................2 C4
Lyoffans (70)............................88 B3
Lyon (69).................................130 A3
Lyons-la-Forêt (27)..................19 F4
Lys (58)...................................83 G6
Lys (64)..................................182 B3
Lys-Haut-Layon (49)...............93 E2
Lys-lez-Lannoy (59)..................3 G5
Lys-Saint-Georges (36)........111 G1

M

Maast-et-Violaine (02)............22 B6
Maâtz (52)................................86 B3
Mably (42)..............................115 E6
Macau (33).............................135 E4
Macaye (64)............................180 D1
Macé (61)..................................39 F5
Macey (10)................................66 A3
Machault (08)...........................23 H5
Machault (77)...........................64 B2
Maché (85)...............................91 E2
Machecoul-Saint-
   Même (44).........................91 E1
Mâchecourt (02)......................22 D2
Machemont (60).......................21 F4
Macheren (57)..........................27 F5
Machézal (42)........................129 E2
Machiel (80)................................6 D2
Machilly (74)...........................118 D4
la Machine (58)........................99 F4
Machy (10)................................66 B4
Machy (80)..................................6 D2
Mackenheim (67)......................71 G3
Mackwiller (67).........................50 B2
Maclas (42).............................143 H1
Macogny (02)...........................44 A1
Mâcon (71)..............................116 B4
Maconcourt (88).......................69 E2
Maconge (21)..........................101 E3
Macornay (39)........................102 D6
Macqueville (17).....................121 H2
Macquigny (02)..........................9 F6
Madaillan (47)........................151 E5
Madecourt (88).........................69 F3
Madegney (88).........................69 G3
la Madelaine-sous-
   Montreuil (62)....................1 G1
la Madeleine (59).......................3 F5
la Madeleine-Bouvet (61).......61 E1
la Madeleine-de-
   Nonancourt (27)..............41 E4
la Madeleine-sur-
   Loing (77)..........................64 A4
la Madeleine-
   Villefrouin (41).................80 A2
Madic (15)..............................140 B1
Madière (09)...........................185 G4
Madirac (33)...........................135 G6
Madiran (65)...........................166 D5
Madonne-et-Lamerey (88).......69 G3
Madranges (19)......................125 E6
Madré (53)................................59 F1
Madriat (63)............................127 F6
Maël-Carhaix (22)....................32 C6
Maël-Pestivien (22)................32 D5
Maen Roch (35)........................35 H6
Maennolsheim (67)..................50 C4
Maffliers (95)...........................42 C2
Maffrécourt (51).......................46 C1
Magalas (34)..........................188 C1
la Magdelaine-sur-
   Tarn (31)..........................169 F3
la Magdeleine (16).................108 C6
le Mage (61)............................61 E1
Magenta (51)...........................45 F2
Magescq (40)..........................164 D3
Magland (74)..........................119 F6
Magnac-Bourg (87)...............124 C4
Magnac-Lavalette-
   Villars (16)......................122 C5
Magnac-sur-Touvre (16).......122 C4
Magnan (32)...........................166 C3
Magnant (10)............................66 D4
Magnanville (78)......................41 G3
Magnas (32)...........................168 A3
Magnat-l'Étrange (23)...........125 F3
Magné (79)..............................107 G3
Magné (86).............................109 E3
Magnet (03)............................114 B5
Magneux (51)...........................22 C5
Magneux (52)...........................67 G1
Magneux-Haute-Rive (42).....129 E4
Magneville (50)........................12 C3
Magnicourt (10).......................66 D2
Magnicourt-en-Comte (62)......7 H1
Magnien (21)..........................101 E2
Magnières (54).........................70 A1
Magnieu (01)..........................131 G3
les Magnils-Reigniers (85)......91 H6
Magnivray (70).........................88 A2
Magnoncourt (70)....................69 G6
le Magnoray (70).....................87 H4
Magny (28)................................61 H3
le Magny (36).........................111 G1
Magny (68)...............................89 E3
les Magny (70).........................88 A4
Magny (89)...............................84 A5
Magny-Châtelard (25)...........103 H1
Magny-Cours (58)...................98 D4
Magny-Danigon (70)...............88 B2
Magny-en-Bessin (14)............14 A3
Magny-en-Vexin (95)..............41 H1
Magny-Fouchard (10).............67 E3
Magny-Jobert (70)...................88 B3
Magny-la-Ville (21)..................84 D5
Magny-Lambert (21)................85 E3
Magny-le-Désert (61)..............38 C6
Magny-le-Hongre (77).............43 F4
Magny-lès-Aubigny (21)........102 A3
Magny-les-Hameaux (78).......42 B5
Magny-lès-Jussey (70)............87 F1

Magny-lès-Villers (21)...........101 G2
Magny-Lormes (58).................83 H6
Magny-Montarlot (21)............102 B1
Magny-Saint-Médard (21)......86 A5
Magny-Saint-Tille (21)..........102 A1
Magny-Vernois (70).................88 A3
Magoar (22)..............................33 E5
Magrie (11).............................186 D5
Magrin (81).............................170 A6
Magstatt-le-Bas (68)...............89 G3
Magstatt-le-Haut (68).............89 G3
Mahalon (29)............................52 D2
Maheru (61)..............................39 H5
Maîche (25)...............................88 C5
Maidières (54)..........................48 B3
Maignaut-Tauzia (32)............167 G3
Maigné (72)...............................59 H6
Maignelay-Montigny (60).......20 D3
Mailhac (11)...........................187 H2
Mailhac-sur-Benaize (87)......110 C4
Mailhoc (81)...........................170 B2
Mailholas (31)........................185 E3
Maillane (13)..........................174 D3
Maillas (40)............................149 H5
Maillat (01).............................117 G5
Maillé (37)................................94 D3
Maillé (85)..............................107 F3
Maillé (86)................................94 A6
Maillebois (28).........................40 D6
Mailleroncourt-
   Charette (70)...................87 G2
Mailleroncourt-Saint-
   Pancras (70)....................69 G6
Maillet (36).............................111 F1
Mailley-et-Chazelot (70).........87 F4
Maillezais (85).......................107 F3
Maillot (89)...............................65 E4
Mailly (71)..............................115 E5
Mailly-Champagne (51)..........45 F1
Mailly-la-Ville (89)...................83 G4
Mailly-le-Camp (10)................45 G5
Mailly-le-Château (89)............83 G4
Mailly-Maillet (80).....................8 A4
Mailly-Raineval (80)................20 D1
Mailly-sur-Seille (54)..............48 D3
les Maillys (21)......................102 B2
Maimbeville (60)......................20 D4
Maincy (77)..............................64 A1
Maine-de-Boixe (16)..............122 C2
Maing (59)..................................9 F2
Mainneville (27).......................19 G5
Mainsat (23)...........................112 B6
Maintenay (62)...........................6 D2
Maintenon (28).........................41 G6
Mainvillers (57)........................49 E2
Mainvilliers (28).......................62 B2
Mainxe (16).............................121 H4
Mainzac (16)...........................123 E5
Mairé (86).................................95 E4
Mairé-Levescault (79)...........108 C5
Mairieux (59)............................10 A2
Mairy-Mainville (54)................25 H5
Mairy-sur-Marne (51)..............45 H3
Maisdon-sur-Sèvre (44)..........75 E6
Maisey-le-Duc (21)..................85 E1
Maisnières (80)..........................6 C5
Maisnil (62)...............................7 G2
Maisnil-lès-Ruitz (62)...............8 A1
Maisod (39).............................117 G2
Maison-des-Champs (10)........67 E3
la Maison-Dieu (58)................83 G5
Maison-Feyne (23).................111 F3
Maison-Ponthieu (80)...............7 E3
Maison-Roland (80)...................7 E4
Maison-Rouge (77)..................64 D1
Maisoncelle (62)........................7 F1
Maisoncelle-et-Villers (08).....24 C3
Maisoncelle-Saint-
   Pierre (60)........................20 B4
Maisoncelle-Tuilerie (60)........20 B3
Maisoncelles (52)....................68 C4
Maisoncelles (72)....................60 D4
Maisoncelles-du-
   Maine (53)........................58 D6
Maisoncelles-en-Brie (77)......43 H4
Maisoncelles-en-
   Gâtinais (77)....................64 A4
Maisoncelles-Pelvey (14).......38 A1
Maisoncelles-sur-Ajon (14)....38 B2
Maisonnais (18)......................112 A1
Maisonnais-sur-
   Tardoire (87)..................123 F2
Maisonnay (79)......................108 B5
Maisonneuve (86)....................94 A5
Maisonnisses (23)..................111 G6
Maisons (11)...........................187 G6
Maisons (14).............................13 H5
Maisons (28).............................62 D2
Maisons-Alfort (94).................42 D4
Maisons-du-Bois-
   Lièvremont (89)..............104 A3
Maisons-en-
   Champagne (51)..............46 A5
Maisons-Laffitte (78)..............42 C3
Maisons-lès-Chaource (10).....66 B6
Maisons-lès-Soulaines (10).....67 E3
Maisonsgoutte (67).................71 E2
Maisontiers (79).......................93 H6
Maisse (91)...............................63 G2
Maissemy (02)...........................8 D6
Maixe (54).................................49 E5
Maizeray (55)...........................47 H1
Maizeroy (57)...........................26 D5
Maizet (14)................................14 B5
Maizey (55)...............................47 G3
Maizicourt (80)..........................7 F3

Maizières (14) 38 D2
Maizières (52) 67 H1
Maizières (54) 48 C6
Maizières (62) 7 H2
Maizières (70) 87 F4
Maizières-la-Grande-
 Paroisse (10) 65 H1
Maizières-lès-Brienne (10) .. 67 E2
Maizières-lès-Metz (57) .. 26 B4
Maizières-lès-Vic (57) 49 G4
Maizières-sur-Amance (52) .. 86 C1
Maizilly (42) 115 F5
Maizy (02) 22 C5
Majastres (04) 177 F2
Malabat (32) 183 F1
la Malachère (70) 87 F5
Malafretaz (01) 116 D4
Mâlain (21) 85 F6
Malaincourt (88) 68 D3
Malaincourt-sur-
 Meuse (52) 68 C4
Malakoff (92) 42 C4
Malancourt (55) 24 D6
Malandry (08) 24 D3
Malange (39) 102 D1
Malans (25) 103 G3
Malans (70) 102 D1
Malansac (56) 56 B6
Malarce-sur-la-Thines (07) .. 157 E3
Malataverne (26) 158 A3
Malaucène (84) 158 D6
Malaucourt-sur-Seille (57) .. 48 D3
Malaunay (76) 18 C3
Malause (82) 168 C1
Malaussanne (64) 166 A5
Malaussène (06) 178 D2
Malauzat (63) 127 E2
Malavillers (54) 26 A3
Malay (71) 116 A1
Malay-le-Grand (89) 65 E4
Malay-le-Petit (89) 65 E4
Malbo (15) 140 C4
Malbosc (07) 157 E4
Malbouhans (70) 88 B2
Malbrans (25) 103 G2
Malbuisson (25) 104 A5
Malegoude (09) 186 B4
Malemort (19) 138 D3
Malemort-du-Comtat (84) .. 175 G1
la Malène (48) 155 H5
Le Malesherbois (45) 63 G3
Malestroit (56) 56 A5
Maleville (12) 153 H4
Malguénac (56) 55 E2
Malherbe-sur-Ajon (14) ... 14 A5
la Malhoure (22) 34 A5
Malicornay (36) 111 E1
Malicorne (03) 113 E4
Malicorne-sur-Sarthe (72) .. 77 G1
Maligny (21) 101 E2
Maligny (89) 83 H1
Malijai (04) 177 E1
Malincourt (59) 9 E4
Malintrat (63) 127 F3
Malissard (26) 144 B5
Mallefougasse-Augès (04) .. 176 D1
Malleloy (54) 48 C4
Mallemoisson (04) 177 E1
Mallemort (13) 175 G4
Malléon (09) 185 H5
Malleret (23) 126 A3
Malleret-Boussac (23) 112 A4
Malleval (42) 129 H6
Malleval-en-Vercors (38) .. 145 E3
Malleville-les-Grès (76) ... 16 D2
Malleville-sur-le-Bec (27) .. 18 A6
Mallièvre (85) 92 C4
Malling (57) 26 C2
la Malmaison (02) 23 E3
Malmerspach (68) 88 D1
Malmy (51) 46 C1
Malons-et-Elze (30) 157 E4
Malouy (27) 15 H5
Malpart (80) 20 D2
Malpas (25) 103 H4
Malras (11) 186 D4
Malrevers (43) 142 C3
Malroy (57) 26 C5
Maltat (71) 100 A6
Maltot (14) 14 B5
Malval (23) 111 G3
Malvalette (43) 143 E1
Malves-en-Minervois (11) .. 187 E3
Malvezie (31) 184 A5
Malvières (43) 142 B1
Malviès (11) 186 D4
Malville (44) 74 B4
Malvillers (70) 86 D2
Malzéville (54) 48 C5
le Malzieu-Forain (48) ... 141 G5
le Malzieu-Ville (48) 141 G5
Malzy (02) 9 G6
Mamers (72) 60 C2
Mametz (62) 2 B5
Mametz (80) 8 B5
Mamey (54) 48 B3
Mamirolle (25) 103 G1
Manas (26) 158 C2
Manas-Bastanous (32) ... 183 G1
Manaurie (24) 137 H4
la Mancelière (28) 40 C5
Mancenans (25) 88 A4
Mancenans-Lizerne (25) .. 88 C6
Mancey (71) 116 B1
Manciet (32) 166 D3
Mancioux (31) 184 C3
Mancy (51) 45 E3
Mandagout (30) 173 G2

Mandailles-Saint-
 Julien (15) 140 C4
Mandelieu-la-Napoule (06) .. 178 C5
Manderen (57) 26 D2
Mandeure (25) 88 C4
Mandeville (27) 18 C6
Mandeville-en-Bessin (14) .. 13 G5
Mandray (88) 70 D3
Mandres (27) 40 C5
Mandres-aux-Quatre-
 Tours (54) 48 A4
Mandres-en-Barrois (55) .. 68 B1
Mandres-la-Côte (52) 68 B5
Mandres-les-Roses (94) ... 43 E5
Mandres-sur-Vair (88) 69 E3
Mandrevillars (70) 88 C3
Manduel (30) 174 B3
Mane (04) 176 C2
Mane (31) 184 C4
Manéglise (76) 15 F1
Manéhouville (76) 17 G2
Manent-Montané (32) 184 A2
Manerbe (14) 15 F5
Mangiennes (55) 25 F5
Manglieu (63) 127 G4
Mangonville (54) 69 G1
Manhac (12) 154 B5
Manheulles (55) 47 H1
Manhoué (57) 48 D4
Manicamp (02) 21 H3
Manigod (74) 132 C2
Manin (62) 7 H2
Maninghem (62) 1 G6
Maninghen-Henne (62) 1 F4
Maniquerville (76) 16 C4
Manlay (21) 100 D2
Manneville-ès-Plains (76) .. 17 E2
Manneville-la-Goupil (76) .. 16 C1
Manneville-la-Pipard (14) .. 15 F4
Manneville-la-Raoult (27) .. 15 F3
Manneville-sur-Risle (27) .. 15 H3
Mannevillette (76) 16 B4
Mano (40) 149 E3
le Manoir (14) 14 A3
le Manoir (27) 18 D5
Manois (52) 68 B3
Manom (57) 26 B3
Manoncourt-en-
 Vermois (54) 48 D6
Manoncourt-en-
 Woëvre (54) 48 B4
Manonville (54) 48 B4
Manonviller (54) 49 F6
Manosque (04) 176 C3
Manot (16) 123 F1
Manou (28) 61 F1
Manre (08) 24 A6
Le Mans (72) 60 B5
Mansac (19) 138 B3
Mansan (65) 183 F2
Mansat-la-Courrière (23) .. 125 E1
Mansempuy (32) 168 B4
Mansencôme (32) 167 F3
Manses (09) 186 A4
Mansigné (72) 78 A2
Mansle (16) 122 C2
Manso (2B) 204 C2
Mansonville (82) 168 B1
Manspach (68) 89 E3
Mant (40) 166 A5
Mantallot (22) 32 D2
Mantenay-Montlin (01) .. 116 D3
Mantes-la-Jolie (78) 41 H2
Mantes-la-Ville (78) 41 H3
Mantet (66) 200 B4
Manteyer (05) 160 B2
Manthelan (37) 95 E2
Manthes (26) 144 B1
Mantilly (61) 37 H6
Mantoche (70) 86 C5
Mantry (39) 102 D5
Manvieux (14) 14 A3
Many (57) 49 E2
Manzac-sur-Vern (24) ... 137 E3
Manzat (63) 127 E1
Manziat (01) 116 C3
Marac (52) 68 A6
Marainville-sur-Madon (88) .. 69 G2
Marainviller (54) 49 F6
le Marais-la-Chapelle (14) .. 39 E3
Marais-Vernier (27) 15 G2
Marambat (32) 167 F3
Marandeuil (21) 86 B6
Marange-Silvange (57) ... 26 B5
Marange-Zondrange (57) .. 27 E5
Marans (17) 106 D3
Maransin (33) 135 G3
Marant (62) 1 G6
Maranville (52) 67 G4
Maranwez (08) 23 G2
Marast (70) 87 H4
Marat (63) 128 B4
Maraussan (34) 188 B2
Maravat (32) 168 A4
Maray (41) 96 D1
Maraye-en-Othe (10) 65 H4
Marbache (54) 48 C4
Marbaix (59) 9 H4
Marbeuf (27) 40 C1
Marbéville (52) 67 G3
Marboué (28) 61 H5
Marbois (27) 40 C3
Marboz (01) 117 E3
Marby (08) 23 G1
Marc-la-Tour (19) 139 E2
Marçais (18) 97 G6
Marçay (37) 94 B2
Marçay (86) 108 D2

Marcé (49) 77 F3
Marcé-sur-Esves (37) 94 D3
Marcelcave (80) 8 A6
Marcellaz (74) 118 C5
Marcellaz-Albanais (74) .. 131 H2
Marcellois (21) 85 E6
Marcellus (47) 150 B3
Marcenais (33) 135 G3
Marcenat (03) 114 A5
Marcenat (15) 140 D1
Marcenay (21) 84 D1
Marcenod (42) 129 G5
Marcey-les-Grèves (50) .. 35 H3
Marchais (02) 22 D3
Marchamp (01) 131 F3
Marchampt (69) 115 H6
Marchastel (15) 140 C2
Marchastel (48) 155 F7
Marchaux (25) 87 G6
la Marche (58) 98 D2
Marché-Allouarde (80) ... 21 F2
Marchélepot (80) 21 F1
Marchemaisons (61) 60 B1
Marchémoret (77) 43 F2
Marchenoir (41) 80 A2
Marcheprime (33) 148 D1
les Marches (73) 132 A5
Marcheseuil (21) 100 D2
Marchésieux (50) 13 E6
Marchéville (28) 61 H2
Marchéville-en-
 Woëvre (55) 47 H1
Marchezais (28) 41 F4
Marchiennes (59) 9 E1
Marciac (32) 167 E6
Marcieu (38) 145 G5
Marcieux (73) 131 G4
Marcigny (71) 115 E4
Marcigny-sous-Thil (21) .. 84 D5
Marcilhac-sur-Célé (46) .. 153 E2
Marcillac (33) 135 F1
Marcillac-la-Croisille (19) .. 139 G2
Marcillac-la-Croze (19) .. 139 E4
Marcillac-Lanville (16) ... 122 B2
Marcillac-Saint-
 Quentin (24) 138 A5
Marcillac-Vallon (12) ... 154 B3
Marcillat (63) 113 F6
Marcillat-en-
 Combraille (03) 112 D5
Marcillé-la-Ville (53) 59 E3
Marcillé-Raoul (35) 35 F6
Marcillé-Robert (35) 57 G4
Marcilloles (38) 144 C1
Marcilly (50) 37 E5
Marcilly (77) 43 G2
Marcilly-d'Azergues (69) .. 129 H2
Marcilly-en-Bassigny (52) .. 86 C1
Marcilly-en-Beauce (41) .. 79 F2
Marcilly-en-Gault (41) ... 80 D5
Marcilly-en-Villette (45) .. 81 E2
Marcilly-et-Dracy (21) ... 84 D5
Marcilly-la-Campagne (27) .. 41 E4
Marcilly-la-Gueurce (71) .. 115 F3
Marcilly-le-Châtel (42) ... 128 D4
Marcilly-le-Hayer (10) ... 65 G3
Marcilly-lès-Buxy (71) ... 101 E6
Marcilly-Ogny (21) 100 D1
Marcilly-sur-Eure (27) ... 41 E4
Marcilly-sur-Maulne (37) .. 78 B4
Marcilly-sur-Seine (51) ... 65 G1
Marcilly-sur-Tille (21) 85 H4
Marcilly-sur-Vienne (37) .. 94 D3
Marck (62) 1 H2
Marckolsheim (67) 71 G3
Marclopt (42) 129 E4
Marcoing (59) 8 D4
Marcolès (15) 140 A6
Marcollin (38) 144 C1
Marcols-les-Eaux (07) ... 143 F6
Marçon (72) 78 C2
Marcorignan (11) 188 A3
Marcoussis (91) 42 C6
Marcoux (04) 160 D6
Marcoux (42) 128 D3
Marcq (08) 24 C5
Marcq (78) 41 H4
Marcq-en-Barœul (59) 3 F5
Marcq-en-Ostrevent (59) .. 9 E1
Marcy (02) 9 F6
Marcy (58) 83 E6
Marcy (69) 129 H2
Marcy-l'Étoile (69) 129 H3
Marcy-sous-Marle (02) ... 22 C2
Mardeuil (51) 45 E2
Mardié (45) 81 E1
Mardilly (61) 39 G4
Mardor (52) 86 A1
Mareau-aux-Bois (45) 63 F1
Mareau-aux-Prés (45) 80 C1
Mareil-en-Champagne (72) .. 59 G6
Mareil-le-Guyon (78) 42 A4
Mareil-Marly (78) 42 B3
Mareil-sur-Loir (72) 77 H2
Mareil-sur-Mauldre (78) .. 42 A4
Mareilles (52) 68 A4
Marenla (62) 6 D1
Marennes (17) 120 B2
Marennes (69) 130 B4
Maresché (72) 60 A4
Maresches (59) 9 F2
Maresquel-
 Ecquemicourt (62) 7 E1
Marest (62) 7 G1

Marest-Dampcourt (02) ... 21 H3
Marest-sur-Matz (60) 21 F4
Marestaing (32) 168 C5
Marestmontiers (80) 20 D2
Maresville (62) 1 F6
les Marêts (77) 44 B5
Maretz (59) 9 F4
Mareugheol (63) 127 F6
Mareuil (16) 122 A3
Mareuil-Caubert (80) 6 D4
Mareuil-en-Brie (51) 44 D3
Mareuil-en-Dôle (02) 22 B6
Mareuil en Périgord (24) .. 122 D6
Mareuil-la-Motte (60) 21 F3
Mareuil-le-Port (51) 44 D2
Mareuil-sur-Arnon (18) ... 97 F4
Mareuil-sur-Cher (41) 79 H6
Mareuil-sur-Lay-
 Dissais (85) 91 H5
Mareuil-sur-Ourcq (60) ... 43 H1
Marey (88) 69 E5
Marey-lès-Fussey (21) ... 101 G2
Marey-sur-Tille (21) 85 H3
Marfaux (51) 45 E1
Marfontaine (02) 22 D1
Margaux-Cantenac (33) .. 135 E3
Margencel (74) 118 D3
Margency (95) 42 C2
Margerides (19) 126 A6
Margerie-Chantagret (42) .. 128 D5
Margerie-Hancourt (51) ... 66 D1
Margès (26) 144 C3
Margival (02) 22 B4
Margny (08) 25 E2
Margny (51) 44 D3
Margny-aux-Cerises (60) .. 21 F2
Margny-lès-
 Compiègne (60) 21 F4
Margny-sur-Matz (60) 21 F3
Margon (28) 61 E3
Margon (34) 188 C1
Margouët-Meymes (32) .. 167 E4
Margueray (50) 37 F3
Marguerittes (30) 174 B3
Margueron (33) 136 C6
Marguestau (32) 166 D2
Margut (08) 25 E3
Mariac (07) 143 F5
Maricourt (80) 8 B5
Marie (06) 178 D1
Marieulles (57) 48 C2
Marieux (80) 7 H4
Marigna-sur-Valouse (39) .. 117 F2
Marignac (17) 121 F5
Marignac (31) 184 A6
Marignac (82) 168 B3
Marignac-en-Diois (26) .. 145 E6
Marignac-Lasclares (31) .. 184 D2
Marignac-Laspeyres (31) .. 184 C3
Marignana (2A) 204 C3
Marignane (13) 191 H4
Marigné-Laillé (72) 78 B1
Marigné-Peuton (53) 76 C1
Marignier (74) 119 E5
Marignieu (01) 131 G2
Marigny (03) 113 G1
Marigny (39) 103 E6
Marigny (51) 45 E5
Marigny (71) 101 E6
Marigny (79) 107 H4
Marigny-Chemereau (86) .. 108 D2
Marigny-en-Orxois (02) ... 44 A2
Marigny-le-Cahouët (21) .. 84 D5
Marigny-le-Châtel (10) ... 65 G2
Marigny-Le-Lozon (50) ... 37 F1
Marigny-l'Église (58) 84 B4
Marigny-lès-Reullée (21) .. 101 H3
Marigny-les-Usages (45) .. 63 E6
Marigny-Marmande (37) .. 94 C3
Marigny-Saint-Marcel (74) .. 131 H2
Marigny-sur-Yonne (58) .. 99 G1
Marillac-le-Franc (16) ... 122 D3
Marillet (85) 107 G1
Marimbault (33) 149 H3
Marimont-lès-
 Bénestroff (57) 49 G3
Marin (74) 119 E3
Marines (95) 42 B1
Maringes (42) 129 F4
Maringues (63) 127 G2
Mariol (03) 114 A6
Marions (33) 150 A4
Marizy-Saint-Mard (02) ... 44 A1
Marizy-Sainte-
 Geneviève (02) 44 A1
Marle (02) 22 D1
Marlemont (08) 23 G1
Marlenheim (67) 50 D5
Marlers (80) 19 H1
Marles-en-Brie (77) 43 G5
Marles-les-Mines (62) 2 D6
Marles-sur-Canche (62) 6 D1
Marlhes (42) 143 F2
Marliac (31) 185 G3
Marliens (21) 102 A1
Marlieux (01) 116 D6
Marly (57) 48 C2
Marly (59) 9 F2
Marly-Gomont (02) 9 H6
Marly-la-Ville (95) 43 E2
Marly-le-Roi (78) 42 B4
Marly-sous-Issy (71) 100 A6
Marly-sur-Arroux (71) ... 115 F1
Marmagne (18) 97 G2
Marmagne (21) 84 D3
Marmagne (71) 100 D5

Marmande (47) 150 C3
Marmanhac (15) 140 B4
Marminiac (46) 152 B1
Marmont-Pachas (47) ... 167 H1
Marnac (24) 137 H6
Marnans (38) 144 D1
Marnaves (81) 170 A1
Marnay (70) 87 E6
Marnay (71) 101 H6
Marnay (86) 109 E3
Marnay-sur-Marne (52) .. 68 A5
Marnay-sur-Seine (10) ... 65 F1
Marnaz (74) 119 E6
la Marne (44) 91 E1
Marnes (79) 93 H4
Marnes-la-Coquette (92) .. 42 C4
Marnézia (39) 117 G1
Marnhagues-et-Latour (12) .. 172 A3
Marnoz (39) 103 E3
Marœuil (62) 8 A2
Maroilles (59) 9 H4
la Marolle-en-Sologne (41) .. 80 C4
Marolles (14) 15 G5
Marolles (41) 79 H3
Marolles (51) 46 B5
Marolles (60) 43 H1
Marolles-en-Beauce (91) .. 63 F2
Marolles-en-Brie (77) 44 A4
Marolles-en-Brie (94) 43 E5
Marolles-en-Hurepoix (91) .. 63 G1
Marolles-lès-Bailly (10) .. 66 C4
Marolles-les-Braults (72) .. 60 B3
Marolles-les-Buis (28) 61 F2
Marolles-lès-Saint-
 Calais (72) 61 E6
Marolles-sous-
 Lignières (10) 66 A6
Marolles-sur-Seine (77) .. 64 C2
Marollette (72) 60 C2
Marols (42) 128 D6
Maromme (76) 18 C4
Mâron (36) 96 B5
Maron (54) 48 C5
Maroncourt (88) 69 G3
Marpaps (40) 165 G5
Marpent (59) 9 E2
Marpiré (35) 57 H2
Marquaix (80) 8 D5
Marquay (24) 138 A5
Marquay (62) 7 H1
Marquefave (31) 185 E2
Marquéglise (60) 21 E4
Marquein (11) 186 A2
Marquerie (65) 183 F2
Marques (76) 19 G1
Marquette-en-
 Ostrevant (59) 9 E2
Marquette-lez-Lille (59) 3 F4
Marquillies (59) 3 E6
Marquion (62) 8 D3
Marquise (62) 1 F3
Marquivillers (80) 21 E2
Marquixanes (66) 200 C3
Marray (37) 78 D3
la Marre (39) 103 E5
Marre (55) 25 E6
Mars (07) 143 F4
les Mars (23) 126 B1
Mars (30) 172 D2
Mars (42) 115 F5
Mars-la-Tour (54) 26 A5
Mars-sous-Bourcq (08) ... 24 A4
Mars-sur-Allier (58) 98 D5
Marsa (11) 200 A1
Marsac (16) 122 B3
Marsac (23) 111 E6
Marsac (65) 183 E2
Marsac (82) 168 B2
Marsac-en-Livradois (63) .. 128 B6
Marsac-sur-Don (44) 74 C2
Marsac-sur-l'Isle (24) ... 137 F2
Marsainvilliers (45) 63 F4
Marsais (17) 107 G5
Marsais-Sainte-
 Radégonde (85) 107 E1
Marsal (57) 49 F4
Marsalès (24) 151 G1
Marsan (32) 168 A5
Marsangis (51) 45 E4
Marsangy (89) 65 E3
Marsannay-la-Côte (21) .. 101 H1
Marsannay-le-Bois (21) ... 85 H6
Marsanne (26) 158 B2
Marsas (33) 135 G2
Marsas (65) 183 F4
Marsat (63) 127 F2
Marsaz (26) 144 B3
Marseillan (32) 167 F6
Marseillan (34) 189 E2
Marseillan (65) 183 F2
Marseille (13) 192 B4
Marseille-en-
 Beauvaisis (60) 20 A3
Marseilles-lès-
 Aubigny (18) 98 C3
Marseillette (11) 187 F3
Marsillargues (34) 173 H5
Marsilly (17) 106 C3
Marsilly (57) 26 C5
Marsolan (32) 167 H2
Marson (51) 46 A3
Marson-sur-Barboure (55) .. 47 G5
Marsonnas (01) 116 D3
Marsoulas (31) 184 D4
Marssac-sur-Tarn (81) ... 170 B2

Martagny (27) 19 G5
Martailly-lès-Brancion (71) .. 116 B2
Martainneville (80) 6 C5
Martainville (14) 38 C2
Martainville (27) 15 G3
Martainville-Épreville (76) .. 19 E4
Martaizé (86) 94 A4
Martel (46) 138 D5
Marthemont (54) 48 C6
Marthille (57) 49 F3
Marthod (73) 132 C3
Marthon (16) 122 D4
Martiel (12) 153 F4
Martigna (39) 117 G3
Martignargues (30) 173 H1
Martignas-sur-Jalle (33) .. 134 D5
Martignat (01) 117 G4
Martigné-Ferchaud (35) .. 57 H5
Martigné-sur-
 Mayenne (53) 58 D3
Martigny (02) 10 B6
Martigny (76) 17 H2
Martigny-Courpierre (02) .. 22 C4
Martigny-le-Comte (71) .. 115 G2
Martigny-les-Bains (88) .. 69 E4
Martigny-les-
 Gerbonvaux (88) 68 D1
Martigny-sur-l'Ante (14) .. 38 D3
Martigues (13) 191 G5
Martillac (33) 135 E6
Martin-Église (76) 17 G2
Martincourt (54) 48 B4
Martincourt (60) 19 H3
Martincourt-sur-
 Meuse (55) 24 D3
le Martinet (30) 157 E5
Martinet (85) 91 E4
Martinpuich (62) 8 B4
Martinvast (50) 12 C2
Martinvelle (88) 69 F6
Martisserre (31) 184 C1
Martizay (36) 95 G5
Martot (27) 18 C5
la Martre (83) 178 A3
Martres (33) 150 A1
les Martres-d'Artière (63) .. 127 G2
Martres-de-Rivière (31) .. 184 A4
Martres-sur-Morge (63) .. 127 F1
Martres-Tolosane (31) .. 184 D3
Martrin (12) 171 F2
Martrois (21) 85 E6
la Martyre (29) 31 F4
les Martys (11) 186 D1
Maruéjols-lès-Gardon (30) .. 173 H2
Marval (87) 123 G4
Marvaux-Vieux (08) 24 A5
Marvejols (48) 155 H3
Marvelise (25) 88 B4
Marville (55) 25 F4
Marville-Moutiers-
 Brûlé (28) 41 F5
Mary (71) 115 H1
Mary-sur-Marne (77) 43 H2
Marzan (56) 73 G2
Marzens (81) 170 A5
Marzy (58) 98 D4
le Mas (06) 178 C3
Mas-Blanc-des-
 Alpilles (13) 174 D4
Mas-Cabardès (11) 187 E2
Mas-d'Agenais (47) 150 C3
Mas-d'Artige (23) 125 H3
Mas-d'Auvignon (32) ... 167 G3
le Mas-d'Azil (09) 185 F4
le Mas-de-Londres (34) .. 173 E4
le Mas-de-Tence (43) ... 143 F3
Mas-des-Cours (11) 187 E4
Mas-Grenier (82) 168 D3
Mas-Saint-Chély (48) ... 155 H5
Mas-Saintes-Puelles (11) .. 186 B2
Masbaraud-Mérignat (23) .. 125 E1
Mascaraàs-Haron (64) ... 166 C5
Mascaras (32) 167 F6
Mascaras (65) 183 F3
Mascarville (31) 169 H6
Masclat (46) 138 B6
Masevaux-
 Niederbruck (68) 88 D1
Maslacq (64) 165 G6
Masléon (87) 124 D3
Maslives (41) 80 A3
le Masnau-
 Massuguiès (81) 171 E4
Masnières (59) 8 D4
Masny (59) 8 D2
Masparraute (64) 181 E1
Maspie-Lalonquère-
 Juillacq (64) 182 D1
Masquières (47) 152 A4
Massabrac (31) 185 F3
Massac (11) 187 F6
Massac (17) 121 H2
Massac-Séran (81) 170 A5
Massaguel (81) 170 C6
Massals (81) 171 E3
Massanes (30) 173 H2
Massangis (89) 84 A3
Massat (09) 185 F6
Massay (18) 97 E2
Massegros Causses
 Gorges (48) 155 G5
Masseilles (33) 150 A3
Massels (47) 151 G4
Massérac (44) 74 B1
Masseret (19) 124 C5
Masseube (32) 184 A1
Massiac (15) 141 F2

Massieu (38) 131 F6
Massieux (01) 130 A2
Massiges (51) 46 B1
Massignac (16) 123 F3
Massignieu-de-Rives (01) .. 131 G3
Massillargues-Attuech (30) .. 173 G2
Massilly (71) 116 A2
Massingy (21) 85 E1
Massingy (74) 131 H2
Massingy-lès-Semur (21) .. 84 D4
Massingy-lès-Vitteaux (21) .. 85 E5
Massognes (86) 94 A5
Massoins (06) 178 D2
Massongy (74) 118 D3
Massoulès (47) 151 G4
Massugas (33) 136 B6
Massy (76) 19 E2
Massy (91) 42 C5
Mastaing (59) 9 E2
Matafelon-Granges (01) .. 117 G4
les Matelles (34) 173 F4
Matemale (66) 200 A3
Matha (17) 121 G2
Mathaux (10) 66 D2
Mathay (25) 88 C5
Mathenay (39) 102 D4
les Mathes (17) 120 B3
Mathieu (14) 14 B4
Mathons (52) 67 H2
Mathonville (76) 19 E2
Matignicourt-
Goncourt (51) 46 B5
Matignon (22) 34 B4
Matigny (80) 21 G1
Matougues (51) 45 G2
Matour (71) 115 H4
Matra (2B) 205 G2
Matringhem (62) 2 A6
Mattaincourt (88) 69 F3
Mattexey (54) 70 A1
Matton-et-Clémency (08) .. 24 C2
Matzenheim (67) 71 H1
Maubec (38) 130 D5
Maubec (82) 168 B3
Maubec (84) 175 G3
Maubert-Fontaine (08) .. 10 D6
Maubeuge (59) 10 A2
Maubourguet (65) 166 D6
Mauchamps (91) 63 F1
Maucomble (76) 19 E2
Maucor (64) 182 C1
Maucourt (60) 21 G2
Maucourt (80) 21 E1
Maucourt-sur-Orne (55) .. 25 F6
Maudétour-en-Vexin (95) .. 41 H2
Mauges-sur-Loire (49) .. 76 C5
Mauguio (34) 173 G5
Maulan (55) 47 F5
Maulay (86) 94 B3
Maulde (59) 4 A6
Maule (78) 42 A3
Mauléon (79) 92 C3
Mauléon-Barousse (65) .. 184 A5
Mauléon-d'Armagnac (32) .. 166 C2
Mauléon-Licharre (64) .. 181 G2
Maulers (60) 20 B3
Maulette (78) 41 G4
Maulévrier (49) 92 D3
Maulévrier-Sainte-
Gertrude (76) 18 A3
Maulichères (32) 166 C4
Maumusson (44) 75 F3
Maumusson (82) 168 B2
Maumusson-Laguian (32) .. 166 C5
Mauny (76) 18 B5
Maupas (10) 66 B4
Maupas (32) 166 C3
Mauperthuis (77) 43 H5
Maupertuis (50) 37 F2
Maupertus-sur-Mer (50) .. 12 D2
Mauprévoir (86) 109 F5
Mauquenchy (76) 19 F3
Mauran (31) 184 D3
Maure (64) 182 D1
Maurecourt (78) 42 B2
Mauregard (77) 43 E2
Mauregny-en-Haye (02) .. 22 D3
Maureilhan (34) 188 B2
Maureillas-las-Illas (66) .. 201 E4
Mauremont (31) 185 H1
Maurens (24) 136 D5
Maurens (31) 186 A1
Maurens (32) 168 B5
Maurens-Scopont (81) .. 169 H5
Maurepas (78) 42 A5
Maurepas (80) 8 B5
Mauressac (31) 185 F2
Mauressargues (30) .. 173 H2
Maureville (31) 169 G6
Mauriac (15) 140 A2
Mauriac (33) 136 A6
Mauries (40) 166 B5
Maurines (15) 141 F5
Maurois (59) 9 F4
Mauron (56) 56 B3
Mauroux (32) 168 B2
Mauroux (46) 152 A3
Maurrin (40) 166 B3
Maurs (15) 153 H1
Maurupt-le-Montois (51) .. 46 C5
Maury (66) 200 D1
Mausoléo (2B) 202 D6
Maussac (19) 125 G4
Maussane-les-Alpilles (13) .. 175 E4
Maussans (70) 87 G5
Mautes (23) 126 A1
Mauvages (55) 47 G6
Mauvaisin (31) 185 G2

Mauves (07) 144 A4
Mauves-sur-Huisne (61) .. 60 D2
Mauves-sur-Loire (44) .. 75 E4
Mauvezin (31) 184 C1
Mauvezin (32) 168 B4
Mauvezin (65) 183 G4
Mauvezin-d'Armagnac (40) .. 166 C2
Mauvezin-de-Prat (09) .. 184 D5
Mauvezin-de-Sainte-
Croix (09) 185 E4
Mauvezin-sur-Gupie (47) .. 150 C2
Mauvières (36) 110 B1
Mauvilly (21) 85 F3
Maux (58) 99 H3
Mauzac (31) 185 F2
Mauzac-et-Grand-
Castang (24) 137 F5
Mauzé-sur-le-Mignon (79) .. 107 F4
Mauzé-Thouarsais (79) .. 93 F3
Mauzens-et-Miremont (24) .. 137 G4
Mauzun (63) 127 H4
Mavaleix-et-Miremont (24) .. A1
Maves (41) 80 A2
Mavilly-Mandelot (21) .. 101 F3
la Maxe (57) 26 C5
Maxent (35) 56 C4
Maxéville (54) 48 C5
Maxey-sur-Meuse (88) .. 68 D1
Maxey-sur-Vaise (55) .. 68 D1
Maxilly-sur-Léman (74) .. 119 F3
Maxilly-sur-Saône (21) .. 86 B6
Maxou (46) 152 C3
Maxstadt (57) 49 G2
May-en-Multien (77) .. 43 H2
le May-sur-Èvre (49) .. 92 C2
May-sur-Orne (14) .. 14 B5
Mayac (24) 137 G2
Mayenne (53) 58 D3
Mayet (72) 78 B2
le Mayet-de-
Montagne (03) 114 C6
le Mayet-d'École (03) 113 H5
Maynal (39) 117 F1
les Mayons (83) 193 H3
Mayot (02) 22 A2
Mayrac (46) 138 C5
Mayran (12) 154 B4
Mayrègue (31) 183 H6
Mayres (07) 157 E1
Mayres (63) 142 B1
Mayres-Savel (38) 145 G5
Mayreville (11) 186 A3
Mayrinhac-Lentour (46) .. 139 E6
Mayronnes (11) 187 F5
Maysel (60) 20 C6
Mazamet (81) 170 D6
Mazan (84) 175 G1
Mazan-l'Abbaye (07) .. 157 E1
Mazangé (41) 79 F1
Mazaugues (83) 193 E3
Mazaye (63) 126 D3
Mazé-Milon (49) 77 F5
le Mazeau (85) 107 F3
Mazeirat (23) 111 G5
Mazeley (88) 69 H3
Mazerat-Aurouze (43) .. 142 A3
Mazeray (17) 121 F1
Mazères (09) 185 H3
Mazères (33) 149 H3
Mazères-de-Neste (65) .. 183 H4
Mazères-Lezons (64) .. 182 B2
Mazères-sur-Salat (31) .. 184 C4
Mazerny (08) 24 A3
Mazerolles (16) 123 E3
Mazerolles (17) 121 E4
Mazerolles (40) 166 A4
Mazerolles (64) 166 A6
Mazerolles (65) 183 G2
Mazerolles (86) 109 G3
Mazerolles-du-Razès (11) .. 186 C4
Mazerolles-le-Salin (25) .. 103 F1
Mazerulles (54) 49 E4
Mazet-Saint-Voy (43) .. 143 E4
Mazeuil (86) 94 A5
Mazeyrat-d'Allier (43) .. 142 A3
Mazeyrolles (24) 152 A1
la Mazière-aux-Bons-
Hommes (23) 126 A2
Mazières (16) 123 E2
Mazières-de-Touraine (37) .. 78 C5
Mazières-en-Gâtine (79) .. 108 A1
Mazières-en-Mauges (49) .. 92 C2
Mazières-Naresse (47) .. 151 F1
Mazières-sur-Béronne (79) .. 108 B5
Mazille (71) 115 H3
Mazingarbe (62) 2 D6
Mazinghem (62) 2 B5
Mazinghien (59) 9 G4
Mazion (33) 135 E2
Mazirat (03) 112 C5
Mazirot (88) 69 F2
le Mazis (80) 6 D6
Mazouau (65) 183 G4
Mazuby (11) 199 H1
les Mazures (08) 11 E6
Mazzola (2B) 205 F2
Méailles (04) 178 A1
Méallet (15) 140 A2
Méasnes (23) 111 F3
Meaucé (28) 61 F1
la Meauffe (50) 13 F6
la Méaugon (22) 33 G4
Meaulne-Vitray (03) .. 112 D1
Méaulte (80) 8 A5
Méautis (50) 13 E5
Meaux (77) 43 G3

Meaux-la-Montagne (69) .. 115 G6
Meauzac (82) 169 E1
Mecé (35) 57 H2
Mechmont (46) 152 C2
Mécleuves (57) 48 D2
Mecquignies (59) 9 H2
Mécrin (55) 47 G4
Mécringes (51) 44 C4
Médan (78) 42 B3
Médavy (61) 39 F5
Medeyrolles (63) 128 B6
Médière (25) 88 B4
Médillac (16) 136 B2
Médis (17) 120 C3
Médonville (88) 68 D4
Médréac (35) 56 C1
Mées (40) 165 E3
le Mée-sur-Seine (77) .. 64 A1
les Mées (04) 176 D1
Mées (40) 165 E4
les Mées (72) 60 B3
Mégange (57) 26 D4
Mégève (74) 133 E2
Mégevette (74) 119 E4
Mégrit (22) 34 B6
Méharicourt (80) 21 E1
Méharin (64) 181 E1
Méhers (41) 80 A6
Méhoncourt (54) 69 H1
Méhoudin (61) 59 F1
Mehun-sur-Yèvre (18) .. 97 F2
Meigneux (77) 64 D1
Meigneux (80) 19 H1
Meilhac (87) 124 A3
Meilhan (32) 184 B1
Meilhan (40) 165 G2
Meilhan-sur-Garonne (47) .. 150 B2
Meilhards (19) 124 D5
Meilhaud (63) 127 F5
Meillac (35) 35 E6
Meillant (18) 97 H5
Meillard (03) 113 H3
le Meillard (80) 7 F3
la Meilleraie-Tillay (85) .. 92 C5
Meilleray (77) 44 B4
la Meilleraye-de-
Bretagne (44) 75 E2
Meillerie (74) 119 F2
Meillers (03) 113 G2
Meillon (64) 182 C2
Meillonnas (01) 117 E4
Meilly-sur-Rouvres (21) .. 101 E1
Meisenthal (57) 50 C2
Meistratzheim (67) 71 G1
le Meix (21) 85 G3
le Meix-Saint-Epoing (51) .. 44 D5
le Meix-Tiercelin (51) .. 46 A6
Méjannes-le-Clap (30) .. 157 G5
Méjannes-lès-Alès (30) .. 173 H1
Mela (2A) 207 E2
Mélagues (12) 171 H4
Mélamare (76) 15 G1
Melay (52) 87 E1
Melay (71) 115 E5
le Mêle-sur-Sarthe (61) .. 60 C1
Mélecey (70) 88 A4
Melesse (35) 57 F2
Melgven (29) 53 H3
Mélicocq (60) 21 F4
Mélicourt (27) 39 H3
Méligny-le-Grand (55) .. 47 G5
Méligny-le-Petit (55) .. 47 G5
Melin (70) 87 E2
Melincourt (70) 87 F1
Mélisey (70) 88 B2
Mélisey (89) 84 B1
Meljac (12) 154 B6
Mellac (29) 54 B4
Mellé (35) 58 A1
Melle (79) 108 B4
Mellecey (71) 101 F5
Melleran (79) 108 C5
Melleray (72) 61 E5
Melleroy (45) 82 C1
Melles (31) 184 B6
Melleville (76) 6 B4
Mellionnec (22) 54 D1
Mello (60) 20 C6
Meloisey (21) 101 F3
Melrand (56) 55 E3
Melsheim (67) 50 D4
Melun (77) 64 A1
Melve (04) 160 B4
Melz-sur-Seine (77) .. 65 E1
Membrey (70) 86 D3
la Membrolle-sur-
Choisille (37) 78 D5
Méménil (88) 70 B3
Memmelshoffen (67) .. 51 F2
le Mémont (25) 104 C1
Menades (89) 83 H5
Ménarmont (88) 70 B1
Menars (41) 80 A3
Menat (63) 113 E6
Menaucourt (55) 47 F5
Mencas (62) 2 A6
Menchhoffen (67) 50 C3
Mende (48) 156 A3
Mendionde (64) 180 D1
Menditte (64) 181 F3
Mendive (64) 181 E3
le Mené (22) 34 A6
Ménéac (56) 56 A2
Ménerbes (84) 175 G3
Ménerval (76) 19 G3
Ménerville (78) 41 G3
Menesble (21) 85 G2
Méneslies (80) 6 B4

Ménesplet (24) 136 B4
Ménesqueville (27) .. 19 E5
Ménessaire (21) 100 C2
Menestreau (58) 83 E5
Menestreau-en-Villette (45) .. 81 E3
Menet (15) 140 B2
Menetou-Couture (18) .. 98 C3
Menetou-Râtel (18) .. 82 B6
Menetou-Salon (18) .. 97 H1
Menetou-sur-Nahon (36) .. 96 C1
Ménétréol-sous-
Sancerre (18) 82 B6
Ménétréol-sur-Sauldre (18) .. 81 F5
Ménétréols-sous-
Vatan (36) 96 D3
Ménetreuil (71) 116 D1
Ménétreux-le-Pitois (21) .. 84 D4
Ménétrol (63) 127 F2
Menétru-le-Vignoble (39) .. 102 D5
Menétrux-en-Joux (39) .. 103 E6
Ménévillers (60) 21 E3
Menglon (26) 159 F1
Ménigoute (79) 108 C2
Ménil (53) 76 D2
le Ménil (88) 70 C6
Ménil-Annelles (08) .. 23 H4
Ménil-aux-Bois (55) .. 47 G4
le Ménil-Bérard (61) .. 39 H5
le Ménil-Broût (61) .. 60 B1
le Ménil-Ciboult (61) .. 37 H4
le Ménil-de-Briouze (61) .. 38 C5
Ménil-de-Senones (88) .. 70 D2
Ménil-en-Xaintois (88) .. 69 E3
Ménil-Erreux (61) 60 B1
Ménil-Froger (61) 39 G5
Ménil-Gondouin (61) .. 38 C4
le Ménil-Guyon (61) .. 39 G6
Ménil-Hermei (61) .. 38 C4
Ménil-Hubert-en-
Exmes (61) 39 G4
Ménil-Hubert-sur-Orne (61) .. 38 C3
Ménil-la-Horgne (55) .. 47 G5
Ménil-la-Tour (54) .. 48 A4
Ménil-Lépinois (08) .. 23 G5
le Ménil-Scelleur (61) .. 38 D6
Ménil-sur-Belvitte (88) .. 70 B2
Ménil-sur-Saulx (55) .. 47 E6
le Ménil-Vicomte (61) .. 39 G4
Ménil-Vin (61) 38 C3
la Ménitré (49) 77 F5
Mennecy (91) 63 G1
Mennessis (02) 22 A2
Mennetou-sur-Cher (41) .. 96 D1
Menneval (27) 15 H5
Menneville (02) 23 E4
Menneville (62) 1 G4
Mennevret (02) 9 F5
Mennouveaux (52) .. 68 B5
Ménoire (19) 139 E3
Menomblet (85) 92 D5
Menoncourt (90) 88 D2
Ménonval (76) 19 F1
Menotey (39) 102 C2
Menou (58) 83 E6
Menouville (95) 42 B1
le Menoux (36) 111 E2
Menoux (70) 87 F1
Mens (38) 145 G6
Mensignac (24) 137 E2
Menskirch (57) 26 D3
Mentheville (76) 16 C4
Menthon-Saint-
Bernard (74) 132 B2
Menthonnex-en-
Bornes (74) 118 C6
Menthonnex-sous-
Clermont (74) 131 H1
Mentières (15) 141 H4
Menton (06) 179 G3
Mentque-Nortbécourt (62) .. 2 A4
Menucourt (95) 42 B2
les Menus (61) 61 F1
Menville (31) 168 D5
Méobecq (36) 96 A6
Méolans-Revel (04) .. 161 E3
Méounes-lès-
Montrieux (83) 193 E4
Mer (41) 80 B3
Méracq (64) 166 A6
Méral (53) 58 B6
Méras (09) 185 F3
Mercatel (62) 8 B3
Mercenac (09) 184 D5
Merceuil (21) 101 G4
Mercey (27) 41 F2
Mercey-le-Grand (25) .. 103 E1
Mercey-sur-Saône (70) .. 86 D4
Merck-Saint-Liévin (62) .. 2 A5
Merckeghem (59) 2 B3
Mercœur (19) 139 F4
Mercœur (43) 141 G2
Mercuer (07) 157 G2
Mercuès (46) 152 C3
Mercurey (71) 101 F5
Mercurol-Veaunes (26) .. 144 B3
Mercury (73) 132 C3
Mercus-Garrabet (09) .. 185 H6
Mercy (03) 114 B2
Mercy (89) 65 G5
Mercy-le-Bas (54) .. 25 H4
Mercy-le-Haut (54) .. 25 H5
Merdrignac (22) 56 A2
Méré (78) 41 H4
Méré (89) 83 H1
Méreau (18) 97 E2
Méréaucourt (80) 19 H2

Méréglise (28) 61 H3
Mérélessart (80) 6 D5
Mérens (32) 167 H4
Mérens-les-Vals (09) .. 199 G2
Mérenvielle (31) 168 D5
Méreuil (05) 159 H4
Méréville (54) 48 C6
Méréville (91) 63 E3
Merey (27) 41 F3
Mérey-sous-Montrond (25) .. 103 G2
Mérey-Vieilley (25) .. 87 F6
Mergey (10) 66 A2
Meria (2B) 203 G2
Mérial (11) 199 H1
Méricourt (62) 8 B1
Méricourt (80) 21 G2
Méricourt-en-Vimeu (80) .. 7 E6
Méricourt-l'Abbé (80) .. 8 A5
Mériel (95) 42 C2
Mérifons (34) 172 B5
Mérignac (16) 122 A3
Mérignac (17) 135 G1
Mérignac (33) 135 E5
Mérignas (33) 136 A6
Mérignat (01) 117 F6
Mérignies (59) 3 G6
Mérigny (36) 110 A1
Mérigon (09) 185 E4
Mérilheu (65) 183 F4
Mérillac (22) 56 A1
Mérinchal (23) 126 B2
Mérindol (84) 175 G4
Mérindol-les-Oliviers (26) .. 158 D5
Mérinville (45) 64 C5
le Mériot (10) 65 F1
Mériten (64) 181 G1
Merkwiller-
Pechelbronn (67) .. 51 E2
Merlas (38) 131 F6
la Merlatière (85) 91 H3
Merlaut (51) 46 B5
Merle-Leignec (42) .. 142 D1
Merléac (22) 33 F6
le Merlerault (61) 39 G5
Merles (82) 168 C1
Merles-sur-Loison (55) .. 25 F5
Merlevenez (56) 54 D5
Merlieux-et-
Fouquerolles (02) .. 22 B4
Merlimont (62) 6 C1
Merlines (19) 126 B4
Mernel (35) 56 D4
Mérobert (91) 63 E2
Mérona (39) 117 G1
Mérouville (28) 62 D3
Meroux (90) 88 D3
Merpins (16) 121 G3
Merrey (52) 68 C5
Merrey-sur-Arce (10) .. 66 D5
Merri (61) 39 E3
Merris (59) 2 D4
Merry-la-Vallée (89) .. 83 E2
Merry-Sec (89) 83 F3
Merry-sur-Yonne (89) .. 83 G4
Mers-les-Bains (80) .. 6 B4
Mers-sur-Indre (36) .. 111 G1
Merschweiller (57) .. 26 D2
Mersuay (70) 87 G2
Merten (57) 27 E4
Mertrud (52) 67 G2
Mertzen (68) 89 E1
Mertzwiller (67) 51 E3
Méru (60) 20 B6
Mervans (71) 102 A5
Mervent (85) 107 F1
Mervilla (31) 169 F6
Merville (31) 169 E4
Merville (59) 2 D5
Merville-Franceville-
Plage (14) 14 C4
Merviller (54) 70 B1
Merxheim (68) 71 F6
Méry (73) 131 H4
Méry-Bissières-en-
Auge (14) 14 D5
Méry-ès-Bois (18) .. 81 G6
Méry-la-Bataille (60) .. 21 E3
Méry-Prémecy (51) .. 22 D6
Méry-sur-Cher (18) .. 97 E1
Méry-sur-Marne (77) .. 44 A3
Méry-sur-Oise (95) .. 42 C2
Méry-sur-Seine (10) .. 66 A1
le Mesge (80) 7 E5
Mesgrigny (10) 65 H1
Mésigny (74) 132 A1
Meslan (56) 54 C3
Mesland (41) 79 G4
Meslay (14) 38 C2
Meslay (41) 79 G2
Meslay-du-Maine (53) .. 59 E6
Meslay-le-Grenet (28) .. 62 A2
Meslay-le-Vidame (28) .. 62 A3
Meslières (25) 88 D5
Mesmay (25) 103 E2
Mesmont (08) 23 G3
Mesmont (21) 85 F6
Mesnac (16) 121 G2
Mesnard-la-Barotière (85) .. 92 A4
Mesnay (39) 103 E4

les Mesneux (51) 23 E6
la Mesnière (61) 60 C1
Mesnières-en-Bray (76) .. 19 E3
le Mesnil (50) 12 B4
le Mesnil-Adelée (50) .. 37 F5
le Mesnil-Amand (50) .. 37 E3
le Mesnil-Amelot (77) .. 43 E2
le Mesnil-Amey (50) .. 37 F1
le Mesnil-au-Grain (14) .. 38 B2
le Mesnil-au-Val (50) .. 12 D2
le Mesnil-Aubert (50) .. 37 E2
le Mesnil-Aubry (95) .. 42 D2
Mesnil-Bruntel (80) .. 8 C6
Mesnil-Conteville (60) .. 20 A2
Mesnil-Domqueur (80) .. 7 E4
le Mesnil-Durdent (76) .. 17 E3
Mesnil-en-Arrouaise (80) .. 8 C5
le Mesnil-en-Ouche (27) .. 40 B2
le Mesnil-en-Thelle (60) .. 42 C1
le Mesnil-Esnard (76) .. 18 D4
le Mesnil-Eudes (14) .. 15 F5
le Mesnil-Eury (50) .. 13 E6
Mesnil-Follemprise (76) .. 19 E1
le Mesnil-Fuguet (27) .. 40 D2
le Mesnil-Garnier (50) .. 37 E3
le Mesnil-Gilbert (50) .. 37 G4
le Mesnil-Guillaume (14) .. 15 F5
le Mesnil-Hardray (27) .. 40 C3
le Mesnil-Herman (50) .. 37 F2
le Mesnil-Jourdain (27) .. 40 D1
Mesnil-la-Comtesse (10) .. 66 B1
le Mesnil-le-Roi (78) .. 42 B3
Mesnil-Lettre (10) 66 C2
Mesnil-Lieubray (76) .. 19 F3
le Mesnil-Martinsart (80) .. 8 A4
Mesnil-Mauger (76) .. 19 F2
le Mesnil-Ozenne (50) .. 37 F5
Mesnil-Panneville (76) .. 18 B3
le Mesnil-Raoul (76) .. 18 D4
le Mesnil-Réaume (76) .. 6 B5
le Mesnil-Robert (14) .. 37 G3
le Mesnil-Rogues (50) .. 37 E3
Mesnil-Rousset (27) .. 40 A3
le Mesnil-Rouxelin (50) .. 13 F6
le Mesnil-Saint-Denis (78) .. 42 B4
le Mesnil-Saint-Firmin (60) .. 20 C3
Mesnil-Saint-Georges (80) .. 20 D2
Mesnil-Saint-Laurent (02) .. 22 A1
Mesnil-Saint-Loup (10) .. 65 H3
Mesnil-Saint-Nicaise (80) .. 21 F1
le Mesnil-Saint-Père (10) .. 66 C3
Mesnil-Sellières (10) .. 66 C3
le Mesnil-Simon (14) .. 15 E5
le Mesnil-Simon (28) .. 41 G3
le Mesnil-sous-
Jumièges (76) 18 B4
Mesnil-sous-Vienne (27) .. 19 G5
le Mesnil-sur-Blangy (14) .. 15 F4
le Mesnil-sur-Bulles (60) .. 20 C4
le Mesnil-sur-l'Estrée (27) .. 41 E4
le Mesnil-sur-Oger (51) .. 45 F3
le Mesnil-Thébrius (60) .. 20 A5
le Mesnil-Thomas (28) .. 40 D6
le Mesnil-Véneron (50) .. 13 E6
Mesnil-Verclives (27) .. 19 F5
le Mesnil-Villeman (50) .. 37 E3
le Mesnil-Villement (14) .. 38 C3
les Mesnilbus (50) .. 12 D6
le Mesnillard (50) .. 37 F5
Mesnils-sur-Iton (27) .. 40 D4
Mesnois (39) 117 G1
les Mesnuls (78) 42 A5
Mespaul (29) 31 G3
Mesplède (64) 165 G6
Mesples (03) 112 B3
Mespuits (91) 63 F3
Mesquer (44) 73 F3
Messac (17) 121 G6
Messanges (21) 101 G2
Messanges (40) 164 C3
Messas (45) 80 B2
Messé (79) 108 D4
Messei (61) 38 B5
Messein (54) 48 C6
Messeix (63) 126 B4
Messemé (86) 94 A3
Messery (74) 118 C3
Messey-sur-Grosne (71) .. 116 A1
Messia-sur-Sorne (39) .. 102 D6
Messigny-et-Vantoux (21) .. 85 H5
Messimy (69) 129 H4
Messimy-sur-Saône (01) .. 116 B6
Messincourt (08) 24 D2
Messon (10) 66 A3
Messy (77) 43 F3
Mesterrieux (33) 150 B1
Mestes (19) 125 H5
Mesves-sur-Loire (58) .. 98 C1
Mesvres (71) 100 C5
Métabief (25) 104 A5
les Métairies (16) 121 H3
Métairies-Saint-Quirin (57) .. 50 A5
Méteren (59) 2 D4
Méthamis (84) 175 G1
Métigny (80) 7 E5
Metting (57) 50 B3
Mettray (37) 78 D5
Metz (57) 26 C5
Metz-en-Couture (62) .. 8 C4
Metz-le-Comte (58) .. 83 G6
Metz-Robert (10) 66 B5
Metzeral (68) 70 D5
Metzeresche (57) .. 26 C4
Metzervisse (57) .. 26 C3
Metzing (57) 27 G5
Meucon (56) 55 G6
Meudon (92) 42 C4
Meuilley (21) 101 G2

Meulan-en-Yvelines (78) 42 A2
Meulers (76) 17 H2
Meulson (21) 85 F3
Meunet-Planches (36) 97 E5
Meunet-sur-Vatan (36) 96 D3
Meung-sur-Loire (45) 80 C2
Meurcé (72) 60 B3
Meurchin (62) 3 E6
Meurcourt (70) 87 G2
la Meurdraquière (50) 37 E3
Meures (52) 67 H4
Meurival (02) 22 D5
Meursac (17) 120 D3
Meursanges (21) 101 H3
Meursault (21) 101 G3
Meurville (10) 67 E4
Meusnes (41) 96 B1
Meussia (39) 117 H2
Meuvaines (14) 14 A3
Meux (17) 121 G5
le Meux (60) 21 E5
Meuzac (87) 124 C5
Mévoisins (28) 62 B1
Mévouillon (26) 159 F5
Meximieux (01) 130 C2
Mexy (54) 25 H3
Mey (57) 26 C5
Meyenheim (68) 71 F6
Meylan (38) 145 G2
Meymac (19) 125 G5
Meynes (30) 174 C3
Meyrals (24) 137 H5
Meyrannes (30) 157 E5
Meyrargues (13) 176 B5
Meyras (07) 157 F1
Meyreuil (13) 192 B2
Meyrié (38) 130 D5
Meyrieu-les-Étangs (38) 130 C5
Meyrieux-Trouet (73) 131 G4
Meyrignac-l'Église (19) 125 E6
Meyronne (24) 138 D5
Meyrueis (48) 156 A6
Meys (69) 129 F4
Meyssac (19) 138 D4
Meysse (07) 158 A2
Meyssiez (38) 130 C6
la Meyze (87) 124 A4
Meyzieu (69) 130 B3
Mézangers (53) 59 E4
Mèze (34) 189 E1
Mézel (04) 177 F1
Mezel (63) 127 G3
Mézens (81) 169 G4
Mézeray (72) 77 H1
Mézères (43) 142 D3
Mézériat (01) 116 C4
Mézerolles (80) 7 F3
Mézerville (11) 186 A3
Mézidon Vallée
   d'Auge (14) 14 D5
la Mézière (35) 57 E2
Mézière-au-Perche (28) 61 H3
Mézières-en-Brenne (36) 95 H5
Mézières-en-Drouais (28) 41 F5
Mézières-en-Gâtinais (45) 63 H5
Mézières-en-Santerre (80) 20 D1
Mézières-en-Vexin (27) 41 F1
Mézières-lez-Cléry (45) 80 C2
Mézières-sous-
   Lavardin (72) 59 H4
Mézières-sur-
   Couesnon (35) 57 G1
Mézières-sur-Oise (02) 22 A1
Mézières-sur-
   Ponthouin (72) 60 B4
Mézières-sur-Seine (78) 41 H3
Mézilhac (07) 143 F6
Mézilles (89) 82 D3
Mézin (47) 167 F1
Méziré (90) 88 D4
Mézos (40) 148 B6
Mézy-Moulins (02) 44 C2
Mézy-sur-Seine (78) 42 A2
Mhère (58) 100 A1
Mialet (24) 123 G5
Mialet (30) 173 G1
Mialos (64) 166 A6
Miannay (80) 6 C4
Michelbach-le-Bas (68) 89 G3
Michelbach-le-Haut (68) 89 G3
Michery (89) 64 D3
Midrevaux (88) 68 C2
Mièges (39) 103 G5
Miélan (32) 183 G1
Miermaigne (28) 61 F3
Miers (46) 138 D5
Miéry (39) 102 D5
Mietesheim (67) 50 D3
Mieussy (74) 119 E5
Mieuxcé (61) 59 H2
Migé (89) 83 F3
Migennes (89) 65 F6
Miglos (09) 199 E1
Mignaloux-Beauvoir (86) 109 E1
Mignavillers (70) 88 A3
Migné (36) 96 A6
Migné-Auxances (86) 109 E1
Mignères (45) 64 A5
Mignerette (45) 63 H5
Mignéville (54) 49 G6
Mignières (28) 62 A2
Mignovillard (39) 103 G5
Migny (36) 97 E3
Migron (17) 121 G2
Mijanès (09) 199 H2
Mijoux (01) 118 B3
la Milesse (72) 60 A5

Milhac (46) 138 B6
Milhac-de-Nontron (24) 123 F6
Milhars (81) 153 F6
Milhas (31) 184 B5
Milhaud (30) 174 A4
Milhavet (81) 170 B1
Milizac-Guipronvel (29) 30 C4
Millac (86) 109 G5
Millam (59) 2 B3
Millançay (41) 80 C5
Millas (66) 201 E2
Millau (12) 172 A1
Millay (58) 100 B5
Millebosc (76) 6 B5
Millemont (78) 41 H4
Millencourt (80) 8 A5
Millencourt-en-
   Ponthieu (80) 7 E3
Millery (21) 84 C4
Millery (54) 48 C4
Millery (69) 130 A4
Millevaches (19) 125 G4
Millières (50) 12 D6
Millières (52) 68 B4
Millonfosse (59) 9 E1
Milly-la-Forêt (91) 63 H2
Milly-Lamartine (71) 116 A3
Milly-sur-Bradon (55) 24 D4
Milly-sur-Thérain (60) 20 A4
Milon-la-Chapelle (78) 42 B5
Mimbaste (40) 165 E4
Mimet (13) 192 B3
Mimeure (21) 101 E2
Mimizan (40) 148 A5
Minaucourt-le-Mesnil-lès-
   Hurlus (51) 46 B1
Minerve (34) 187 G2
Mingot (65) 183 F1
Mingoval (62) 8 A1
Miniac-Morvan (35) 35 E5
Miniac-sous-Bécherel (35) 56 D1
le Minihic-sur-Rance (35) 34 D4
Minihy-Tréguier (22) 33 E2
Minorville (54) 48 B4
Minot (21) 85 G3
Minversheim (67) 50 D4
Minzac (24) 136 B4
Minzier (74) 118 B6
Miolles (81) 171 E3
Mionnay (01) 130 B2
Mions (69) 130 B4
Mios (33) 148 C1
Miossens-Lanusse (64) 166 B6
Mirabeau (04) 177 E1
Mirabeau (84) 176 B4
Mirabel (07) 157 H2
Mirabel (82) 152 C6
Mirabel-aux-
   Baronnies (26) 158 D5
Mirabel-et-Blacons (26) 158 D1
Miramas (13) 175 F5
Mirambeau (17) 121 F6
Mirambeau (31) 184 C1
Miramont-d'Astarac (32) 167 G6
Miramont-de-
   Comminges (31) 184 B4
Miramont-de-
   Guyenne (47) 150 D2
Miramont-de-Quercy (82) 152 A5
Miramont-Latour (32) 168 A4
Miramont-Sensacq (40) 166 B5
Mirande (32) 167 G6
Mirandol-
   Bourgnounac (81) 153 H6
Miré-manes (32) 167 G5
Miraumont (80) 8 B4
Miraval-Cabardès (11) 187 E2
Mirbel (52) 67 H3
Miré (49) 77 E2
Mirebeau (86) 94 A5
Mirebeau-sur-Bèze (21) 86 B5
Mirecourt (88) 69 F3
Mirefleurs (63) 127 F4
Miremont (31) 185 F2
Miremont (63) 126 C2
Mirepeisset (11) 188 A3
Mirepeix (64) 182 C3
Mirepoix (09) 186 B4
Mirepoix (32) 168 A4
Mirepoix-sur-Tarn (31) 169 G3
Mireval (34) 173 F6
Mireval-Lauragais (11) 186 B3
Miribel (01) 130 B2
Miribel (26) 144 C2
Miribel-Lanchâtre (38) 145 F4
Miribel-les-Échelles (38) 131 G6
Mirmande (26) 158 B1
le Miroir (71) 117 E2
Mirvaux (80) 7 G5
Mirville (76) 16 C4
Miscon (26) 159 F2
Miserey (27) 41 E2
Miserey-Salines (25) 87 F6
Misérieux (01) 130 A1
Misery (80) 8 B6
Missé (79) 93 G3
Missècle (81) 170 B4
Missègre (11) 187 E5
Missery (21) 84 D6
Missillac (44) 73 H2
Missiriac (56) 56 A5
Misson (40) 165 E5
Missy (14) 13 H6
Missy-aux-Bois (02) 21 H5
Missy-lès-Pierrepont (02) 22 D2
Missy-sur-Aisne (02) 22 B5
Misy-sur-Yonne (77) 64 D3

Mitry-Mory (77) 43 E3
Mittainville (78) 41 G5
Mittainvilliers-Vérigny (28) 61 H1
Mittelbergheim (67) 71 F1
Mittelbronn (57) 50 B4
Mittelhausbergen (67) 51 E5
Mittelschaeffolsheim (67) 50 D4
Mittelwihr (68) 71 F4
Mittersheim (57) 49 H3
Mittlach (68) 70 D5
Mitzach (68) 70 D6
Mizérieux (42) 129 E3
Mizoën (38) 146 B3
Moca-Croce (2A) 207 E1
Modane (73) 147 E2
Modène (84) 175 G1
Moëlan-sur-Mer (29) 54 A4
Mœrnach (68) 89 F4
Moëslains (52) 46 C6
Mœurs-Verdey (51) 44 D5
Mœuvres (62) 8 D3
Mœze (17) 120 C1
Moffans-et-
   Vacheresse (70) 88 A3
Mogeville (55) 25 F6
Mognéneins (01) 116 B5
Mognéville (55) 46 D4
Mogneville (60) 20 D5
Mogues (08) 25 E2
Mohon (56) 55 H3
Moidieu-Détourbe (38) 130 B5
Moigny-sur-École (91) 63 G2
Moigné (70) 87 H4
Moineville (54) 26 A4
Moinville-la-Jeulin (28) 62 C2
Moirans (38) 145 F1
Moirans-en-Montagne (39) .. 117 H2
Moirax (47) 151 F6
Moiré (69) 129 G1
Moiremont (51) 46 C1
Moirey-Flabas-
   Crépion (55) 25 F5
Moiron (39) 102 D6
Moiry (08) 25 E3
Moisdon-la-Rivière (44) 75 E1
Moisenay (77) 64 A1
Moislains (80) 8 C5
Moissac (82) 168 D1
Moissac-Bellevue (83) 177 F4
Moissac-Vallée-
   Française (48) 156 C6
Moissannes (87) 124 D2
Moissat (63) 127 G3
Moisselles (95) 42 D2
Moissey (39) 102 C1
Moissieu-sur-Dolon (38) 130 B6
Moisson (78) 41 G2
Moissy-Cramayel (77) 43 E6
Moissy-Moulinot (58) 83 G6
Moisville (27) 40 D4
Moisy (41) 79 H1
Moïta (2B) 205 G2
les Moitiers-d'Allonne (50) .. 12 B4
Moitron (21) 85 F3
Moitron-sur-Sarthe (72) 59 H3
Moivre (51) 46 B3
Moivrons (54) 48 D4
Molac (56) 56 A6
Molagnies (76) 19 G3
Molain (02) 9 F5
Molain (39) 103 E5
Molamboz (39) 103 E4
Molandier (11) 185 H3
Molas (31) 184 B1
Molay (39) 102 C3
Molay (70) 86 D2
Môlay (89) 84 A2
le Molay-Littry (14) 13 G5
la Môle (83) 194 A4
Moléans (28) 62 A5
Molèdes (15) 141 E2
Molesme (21) 66 C6
Molezon (48) 156 B6
Moliens (60) 19 H4
Molières (24) 137 F6
Molières (46) 139 G2
Molières (82) 152 C6
les Molières (91) 42 B5
Molières-Cavaillac (30) 172 D2
Molières-sur-Cèze (30) 157 E5
Moliets-et-Maa (40) 164 C2
Molinchart (02) 22 B3
Molines-en-Queyras (05) 147 F6
Molinet (03) 114 D2
Molinges (39) 117 H3
Molinons (89) 65 F4
Molinot (21) 101 E3
Molins-sur-Aube (10) 66 D2
Molitg-les-Bains (66) 200 C2
Mollans (70) 87 H3
Mollans-sur-Ouvèze (26) 158 D5
Mollau (68) 70 D6
Mollégès (13) 175 F3
Mollkirch (67) 50 D6
les Mollettes (73) 132 A5
Molleville (11) 186 A2
Molliens-au-Bois (80) 7 G5
Molliens-Dreuil (80) 7 E6
Mollkirch (67) 50 D6
Molompize (15) 141 F2
Molosmes (89) 84 B1
Moloy (21) 85 G4
Molphey (21) 84 C6
Molring (57) 49 G3
Molsheim (67) 50 D6
Moltifao (2B) 203 E4
Momas (64) 166 A6
Mombrier (33) 135 G2

Momères (65) 183 E3
Momerstroff (57) 27 E5
Mommenheim (67) 50 D4
Momuy (40) 165 H5
Momy (64) 182 D1
Monacia-d'Aullène (2A) 207 E4
Monacia-d'Orezza (2B) 205 G1
Monampteuil (02) 22 C4
Monassut-Audiracq (64) 182 C1
le Monastère (12) 154 C4
le Monastier-sur-
   Gazeille (43) 142 D5
Monay (39) 102 D5
Monbahus (47) 151 E2
Monbalen (47) 151 F4
Monbardon (32) 184 B1
Monbazillac (24) 136 D6
Monbéqui (82) 168 D3
Monblanc (32) 184 D1
Monbrun (32) 168 C5
Moncale (2B) 202 C6
Moncassin (32) 183 H1
Moncaup (31) 184 B5
Moncaup (64) 166 D6
Moncaut (47) 151 E6
Moncayolle-Larrory-
   Mendibieu (64) 181 G2
Moncé-en-Belin (72) 78 A1
Moncé-en-Saosnois (72) 60 C3
Monceau-le-Neuf-et-
   Faucouzy (02) 22 C1
Monceau-le-Waast (02) 22 C3
Monceau-lès-Leups (02) 22 B2
Monceau-Saint-Waast (59) 9 H3
Monceau-sur-Oise (02) 9 G6
les Monceaux (14) 15 E5
Monceaux (60) 20 D5
Monceaux-en-Bessin (14) 13 H5
Monceaux-l'Abbaye (60) 19 G2
Monceaux-le-Comte (58) 83 G6
Monceaux-sur-
   Dordogne (19) 139 F3
Moncel-lès-Lunéville (54) 49 F6
Moncel-sur-Seille (54) 49 E4
Moncel-sur-Vair (88) 68 D2
la Moncelle (08) 24 C2
Moncetz-l'Abbaye (51) 46 B6
Moncetz-Longevas (51) 45 H3
Moncey (25) 87 G5
Monchaux-Soreng (76) 6 C5
Monchaux-sur-Écaillon (59) ... 9 F2
Moncheaux (59) 8 D1
Moncheaux-lès-
   Frévent (62) 7 G2
Monchecourt (59) 8 D2
Monchel-sur-Canche (62) 7 F2
Moncheux (57) 48 D3
Monchiet (62) 8 A3
Monchy-au-Bois (62) 8 A3
Monchy-Breton (62) 7 H1
Monchy-Cayeux (62) 7 G1
Monchy-Humières (60) 21 E4
Monchy-Lagache (80) 8 C6
Monchy-le-Preux (62) 8 C2
Monchy-Saint-Éloi (60) 20 D6
Monchy-sur-Eu (76) 6 B5
Moncla (64) 166 C5
Monclar (32) 167 F2
Monclar (47) 151 E3
Monclar-de-Quercy (82) 169 G2
Monclar-sur-Losse (32) 167 F6
Moncley (25) 87 E6
Moncontour (22) 33 H6
Moncontour (86) 93 H4
Moncorneil-Grazan (32) 184 A1
Moncourt (57) 49 F5
Moncoutant (79) 92 D5
Moncrabeau (47) 167 G1
Moncy (61) 38 A4
Mondavezan (31) 184 D3
Mondelange (57) 26 B4
Mondement-
   Montgivroux (51) 45 E4
Mondescourt (60) 21 H3
Mondevert (35) 58 A4
Mondeville (14) 14 C4
Mondeville (91) 63 G1
Mondicourt (62) 7 H3
Mondigny (08) 24 A2
Mondilhan (31) 184 B2
Mondion (86) 94 C4
Mondon (25) 87 H5
Mondonville (31) 169 E5
Mondonville-Saint-
   Jean (28) 62 D2
Mondorff (57) 26 C2
Mondoubleau (41) 61 F6
Mondouzil (31) 169 G5
Mondragon (84) 158 A5
Mondrainville (14) 14 B5
Mondrepuis (02) 10 B5
Mondreville (78) 41 G3
Mondreville (77) 63 H4
Monein (64) 200 A4
Monès (31) 184 D1
Monesple (09) 185 G4
Monestier (03) 113 G2
Monestier (07) 143 G2
Monestier (24) 136 C6
le Monestier (63) 128 A5
Monestier-d'Ambel (38) 145 H6
Monestier-de-
   Clermont (38) 145 F5
le Monestier-
   du-Percy (38) 145 H6
Monestier-Merlines (19) 126 B4
Monestier-Port-Dieu (19) .. 126 B5
Monestiés (81) 170 B1

Monestrol (31) 185 H2
Monétay-sur-Allier (03) 113 H3
Monétay-sur-Loire (03) 114 C3
Monéteau (89) 83 F1
Monêtier-Allemont (05) 160 A4
le Monêtier-les-Bains (05) .. 146 D4
Monfaucon (24) 136 C5
Monfaucon (65) 183 F1
Monferran-Plavès (32) 167 H6
Monferran-Savès (32) 168 C5
Monflanquin (47) 151 G2
Monfort (32) 168 B3
Monfréville (14) 13 F5
Mongaillard (47) 150 D5
Mongausy (32) 168 B6
Mongauzy (33) 150 B2
Monget (40) 165 H5
Monguilhem (32) 166 C3
Monheurt (47) 150 D4
Monhoudou (72) 60 B3
Monieux (84) 175 H1
Monistrol-d'Allier (43) 142 A4
Monistrol-sur-Loire (43) 143 E2
Monlaur-Bernet (32) 183 H2
Monléon-Magnoac (65) 183 H3
Monlet (43) 142 B2
Monlezun (32) 167 E6
Monlezun-
   d'Armagnac (32) 166 C3
Monlong (65) 183 H3
Monmadalès (24) 137 E6
Monmarvès (24) 151 F1
Monnaie (37) 79 E4
Monneren (57) 26 D3
la Monnerie-le-Montel (63) .. 128 A2
Monnerville (91) 63 E3
Monnes (02) 44 A1
Monnet-la-Ville (39) 103 E6
Monnetay (39) 117 F2
Monnetier-Mornex (74) 118 C5
Monneville (60) 20 A6
Monnières (39) 102 C2
Monnières (44) 75 E6
Monoblet (30) 173 F2
Monpardiac (32) 167 F6
Monpazier (24) 151 H1
Monpezat (64) 166 D6
Monplaisant (24) 137 H6
Monprimblanc (33) 149 H1
Mons (16) 122 A2
Mons (17) 121 G2
Mons (30) 173 H1
Mons (31) 169 G5
Mons (34) 171 H6
Mons (63) 127 H1
Mons (83) 178 B4
Mons-Boubert (80) 6 C4
Mons-en-Barœul (59) 3 G5
Mons-en-Laonnois (02) 22 B3
Mons-en-Montois (77) 64 D1
Mons-en-Pévèle (59) 3 F2
Monsac (24) 137 F6
Monsaguel (24) 137 E6
Monségur (33) 150 B1
Monségur (40) 165 H5
Monségur (47) 151 G3
Monségur (64) 183 E1
la Monselie (15) 140 B1
Monsempron-Libos (47) 151 H3
Monsireigne (85) 92 B5
Monsols (69) 115 H5
Monsteroux-Milieu (38) 130 B6
Monsures (80) 20 B2
Monswiller (67) 50 C4
Mont (64) 165 G6
Mont (65) 197 E1
Mont (71) 114 D1
le Mont (88) 70 D1
Mont-Bernanchon (62) 2 D5
Mont-Bonvillers (54) 25 H5
Mont-Cauvaire (76) 18 C3
Mont-d'Astarac (32) 184 A1
Mont-Dauphin (05) 161 F1
Mont-de-Galié (31) 184 A5
Mont-de-Laval (25) 104 C1
Mont-de-Marrast (32) 183 G1
Mont-de-Marsan (40) 166 A2
Mont-de-Vougney (25) 88 C6
Mont-devant-Sassey (55) 24 D4
Mondigny (08) ...... le Mont-Dieu (08) 24 B3
le Mont-Dieu (08) 24 B3
Mont-Disse (64) 166 C5
Mont-Dol (35) 35 E4
Mont-Dore (63) 126 D5
Mont-d'Origny (02) 9 F6
Mont-et-Marré (58) 99 G3
Mont-l'Étroit (54) 68 D1
Mont-l'Évêque (60) 43 E1
Mont-le-Vernois (70) 87 F3
Mont-le-Vignoble (54) 48 A6
Mont-lès-Lamarche (88) 69 E5
Mont-lès-Neufchâteau (88) .. 68 C2
Mont-lès-Seurre (71) 102 A4
Mont-Louis (66) 200 A4
Mont Lozère et Goulet (48) .. 156 C3
Mont-Notre-Dame (02) 22 C6
Mont-Ormel (61) 39 F4
Mont-près-Chambord (41) .. 80 A4
Mont-Roc (81) 170 D4
le Mont-Saint-Adrien (60) .. 20 A4
Mont-Saint-Aignan (76) 18 C4
Mont-Saint-Éloi (62) 8 A2
Mont-Saint-Jean (02) 23 F1
Mont-Saint-Jean (21) 84 D6
Mont-Saint-Jean (72) 59 G3
Mont-Saint-Léger (70) 87 E3
Mont-Saint-Martin (02) 22 C6
Mont-Saint-Martin (08) 24 A5

Mont-Saint-Martin (38) 145 G1
Mont-Saint-Martin (54) 25 H3
le Mont-Saint-Michel (50) 35 G4
Mont-Saint-Père (02) 44 C2
Mont-Saint-Remy (08) 23 H5
Mont-Saint-Sulpice (89) 65 G6
Mont-Saint-Vincent (71) 115 H1
Mont-Saxonnex (74) 119 E6
Mont-sous-Vaudrey (39) .. 102 D3
Mont-sur-Courville (51) 22 C6
Mont-sur-Meurthe (54) 49 E6
Mont-sur-Monnet (39) 103 F6
Montabard (61) 39 E4
Montabot (50) 37 F2
Montacher-Villegardin (89) .. 64 C4
Montadet (32) 184 C1
Montady (34) 188 B2
Montagagne (09) 185 F5
Montagna-le-
   Reconduit (39) 117 E2
Montagnac (30) 173 H2
Montagnac (34) 188 D1
Montagnac-
   d'Auberoche (24) 137 G2
Montagnac-la-
   Crempse (24) 137 E4
Montagnac-Montpezat (04) .. 177 G3
Montagnac-sur-
   Auvignon (47) 151 E6
Montagnac-sur-Lède (47) .. 151 G2
Montagnat (01) 117 E5
Montagne (33) 135 H4
Montagne (38) 144 D3
la Montagne (44) 74 C5
la Montagne (70) 70 B6
Montagne-Fayel (80) 7 E6
Montagney (70) 86 D6
Montagney-Servigney (25) .. 87 H4
Montagnieu (01) 131 E3
Montagnieu (38) 131 E5
Montagnol (12) 171 H3
Montagnole (73) 131 H5
Montagny (42) 115 F6
Montagny (69) 129 H4
Montagny (73) 133 E5
Montagny-en-Vexin (60) 41 H1
Montagny-lès-Beaune (21) .. 101 G3
Montagny-lès-Buxy (71) 101 F6
Montagny-les-Lanches (74) .. 132 A2
Montagny-lès-Seurre (21) .. 102 A3
Montagny-près-
   Louhans (71) 102 B3
Montagny-Sainte-
   Félicité (60) 43 F1
Montagny-sur-Grosne (71) .. 115 H3
Montagoudin (33) 150 B2
Montagrier (24) 136 D2
Montagudet (82) 152 A5
Montagut (64) 166 A5
Montaignac-Saint-
   Hippolyte (19) 139 F1
Montaigu (02) 22 D3
Montaigu (39) 102 D6
Montaigu (85) 91 H2
Montaigu-de-Quercy (82) .. 151 H4
Montaigu-la-Brisette (50) 12 D2
Montaigu-le-Blin (03) 114 B4
Montaigu-les-Bois (50) 37 E3
Montaiguët-en-Forez (03) .. 114 C4
Montaigut (63) 113 G6
Montaigut-le-Blanc (23) 111 F5
Montaigut-le-Blanc (63) 127 F5
Montaigut-sur-Save (31) 168 D4
Montaillé (72) 61 E4
Montailleur (73) 132 C4
Montaillou (09) 199 G1
Montain (39) 102 D6
Montainville (78) 42 A3
Montalba-le-Château (66) .. 200 D2
Montalembert (79) 108 D5
Montalet-le-Bois (78) 41 H2
Montalieu-Vercieu (38) 131 E2
Montalzat (82) 152 D6
Montambert (58) 99 H5
Montamel (46) 152 C2
Montamisé (86) 109 F1
Montanay (69) 130 A2
Montancy (25) 89 E5
Montandon (25) 88 C6
Montaner (64) 183 E2
Montanges (01) 117 H5
Montans (81) 170 A3
Montapas (58) 99 G3
Montarcher (42) 128 D6
Montardit (09) 185 E4
Montardon (64) 182 C1
Montaren-et-Saint-
   Médiers (30) 174 B1
Montargis (45) 64 A6
Montarlot-lès-Rioz (70) 87 F3
Montarnaud (34) 173 E4
Montastruc (47) 151 E1
Montastruc (65) 183 G3
Montastruc (82) 169 E1
Montastruc-de-Salies (31) .. 184 C5
Montastruc-la-
   Conseillère (31) 169 G4
Montastruc-Savès (31) 184 D2
le Montat (46) 152 C4
Montataire (60) 20 D6
Montauban (82) 169 E2
Montauban-de-
   Bretagne (35) 56 C2
Montauban-de-
   Luchon (31) 197 F1

Montauban-de-
Picardie (80) 8 B5
Montauban-sur-
l'Ouvèze (26) 159 F5
Montaud (34) 173 G4
Montaud (38) 145 F2
Montaudin (53) 58 B2
Montaulieu (26) 159 E4
Montaulin (10) 66 B3
Montauriol (11) 186 A3
Montauriol (47) 151 F2
Montauriol (66) 201 E3
Montauriol (81) 170 D1
Montauroux (83) 178 B5
Montaut (09) 185 H3
Montaut (24) 137 E6
Montaut (31) 185 F2
Montaut (32) 183 H1
Montaut (40) 165 H4
Montaut (47) 151 F2
Montaut (64) 182 C3
Montaut-les-Créneaux (32) .. 168 A4
Montautour (35) 58 A3
Montauville (54) 48 B3
Montay (59) 9 F4
Montayral (47) 151 H3
Montazeau (24) 136 B5
Montazels (11) 186 D6
Montbard (21) 84 C3
Montbarla (82) 152 A5
Montbarrey (39) 102 D3
Montbarrois (45) 63 G5
Montbartier (82) 169 E2
Montbavin (02) 22 B3
Montbazens (12) 154 A3
Montbazin (34) 173 E6
Montbazon (37) 78 D6
Montbel (09) 186 B5
Montbel (48) 156 C2
Montbéliard (25) 88 C4
Montbéliardot (25) 104 C1
Montbellet (71) 116 B2
Montbenoît (25) 104 B4
Montberaud (31) 185 E4
Montbernard (31) 184 B2
Montberon (31) 169 F4
Montbert (44) 91 G1
Montberthault (21) 84 B5
Montbeton (82) 169 E2
Montbeugny (03) 114 A2
Montbizot (72) 60 A4
Montblainville (55) 24 C6
Montblanc (34) 188 D1
Montboillon (70) 87 E5
Montboissier (28) 62 A4
Montbolo (66) 200 D4
Montbonnot-Saint-
Martin (38) 145 G2
Montboucher (23) 124 D1
Montboucher-sur-
Jabron (26) 158 B2
Montboudif (15) 140 C1
Montbouton (90) 88 D4
Montbouy (45) 82 B1
Montboyer (16) 136 B1
Montbozon (70) 87 G4
Montbrand (05) 159 G2
Montbras (55) 68 D1
Montbray (50) 37 F3
Montbré (51) 45 F1
Montbrehain (02) 9 E5
Montbrison (42) 128 D4
Montbrison-sur-Lez (26) ... 158 C3
Montbron (16) 123 E4
Montbronn (57) 50 B2
Montbrun (46) 153 F3
Montbrun-Bocage (31) 185 E4
Montbrun-des-
Corbières (11) 187 G3
Montbrun-Lauragais (31) . 185 G1
Montbrun-les-Bains (26).. 159 F6
Montcabrier (46) 152 A2
Montcabrier (81) 169 H5
Montcaret (24) 136 B5
Montcarra (38) 131 E4
Montcavrel (62) 1 G6
Montceau-et-
Écharnant (21) 101 F3
Montceau-les-Mines (71).. 100 D6
Montceaux (01) 116 B6
Montceaux-lès-Meaux (77).. 43 H3
Montceaux-lès-
Provins (77) 44 B5
Montceaux-lès-Vaudes (10).. 66 B4
Montceaux-l'Étoile (71)..... 115 E3
Montceaux-Ragny (71)...... 116 B1
Montcel (63) 127 E1
Montcel (73) 131 H3
Montcenis (71) 100 D5
Montcet (01) 116 D5
Montcey (70) 87 G3
Montchaboud (38) 145 G3
Montchal (42) 129 F2
Montchâlons (02) 22 C4
Montchamp (15) 141 F4
Montchanin (71) 101 E6
Montcharvot (52) 86 D1
Montchauvet (78) 41 F4
Montchenu (26) 144 B2
Montcheutin (08) 24 B5
Montchevrel (61) 39 G6
Montchevrier (36) 111 F2
Montclar (04) 160 D3
Montclar (11) 186 D4
Montclar (12) 171 F2
Montclar-de-
Comminges (31) 184 D1
Montclar-Lauragais (31).... 185 H2

Montclar-sur-
Gervanne (26) 144 C6
Montclard (43) 142 A2
Montcléra (46) 152 B2
Montclus (05) 159 H3
Montclus (30) 157 G5
Montcombroux-les-
Mines (03) 114 C3
Montcony (71) 102 B6
Montcornet (02) 23 E2
Montcornet (08) 11 E6
Montcourt (70) 69 E6
Montcourt-
Fromonville (77)............... 64 A3
Montcoy (71) 101 H5
Montcresson (45) 82 B1
Montcuit (50) 37 E1
Montcuq-en-Quercy-
Blanc (46) 152 B4
Montcusel (39) 117 G3
Montcy-Notre-Dame (08) .. 24 B1
Montdardier (30) 172 D2
Montdauphin (77) 44 B4
Montdidier (57) 49 G3
Montdidier (80) 20 D2
Montdoré (70) 69 F6
Montdoumerc (46) 152 D5
Montdragon (81) 170 B4
Montdurausse (81) 169 G2
Monte (2B) 203 G6
Monteaux (41) 79 G5
Montebourg (50) 12 D3
Montech (82) 168 D2
Montécheroux (25) 88 C5
Montegrosso (2B) 202 C5
Montégut (32) 167 H5
Montégut (40) 166 C2
Montégut (65) 183 H4
Montégut-Arros (32) 183 F1
Montégut-Bourjac (31) 184 D2
Montégut-en-
Couserans (09) 184 D4
Montégut-Lauragais (31)... 186 B1
Montégut-Plantaurel (09).. 185 G4
Montégut-Savès (32) 184 C1
Monteignet-sur-
l'Andelot (03) 113 H6
le Monteil (15) 140 B2
le Monteil (43) 142 C4
le Monteil-au-Vicomte (23).. 125 F1
Monteils (12) 153 G5
Monteils (30) 173 H1
Monteils (82) 152 D6
Montel-de-Gelat (63) 126 B1
Montéléger (26) 144 B5
Montélier (26) 144 C5
Montélimar (26) 158 A2
le Montellier (01) 130 C1
Montels (09) 185 G5
Montels (34) 188 B2
Montels (81) 170 A2
Montembœuf (16) 123 E3
Montenach (57) 26 D2
Montenay (53) 58 C3
Montendre (17) 135 G1
Montendry (73) 132 B5
Montenescourt (62) 8 A2
Monteneuf (56) 56 B5
Montenils (77) 44 C4
Montenois (25) 88 B4
Montenoison (58) 99 F1
Montenoy (54) 48 D4
Montépilloy (60) 21 E6
Monteplain (39) 103 E2
Montépreux (51) 45 G5
Monterblanc (56) 55 G5
Montereau (45) 81 H1
Montereau-Fault-
Yonne (77) 64 C2
Montereau-sur-le-Jard (77).. 43 F6
Monterfil (35) 56 D3
Montérolier (76) 19 E2
Montertelot (56) 56 A4
Montescot (66) 201 F3
Montescourt-
Lizerolles (02) 21 H2
Montespan (31) 184 C4
Montesquieu (34) 172 B6
Montesquieu (47) 150 D5
Montesquieu (82) 169 F2
Montesquieu-Avantès (09).. 185 E5
Montesquieu-des-
Albères (66) 201 F4
Montesquieu-Guittaut (31).. 184 B2
Montesquieu-
Lauragais (31) 185 H1
Montesquieu-
Volvestre (31) 185 E3
Montesquiou (32) 167 F5
Montessaux (70) 88 A2
Montesson (78) 42 C3
Montestruc-sur-Gers (32).. 167 H3
le Montet (03) 113 H3
Montet-et-Bouxal (46) 153 G1
Monteton (47) 150 C2
Monteux (84) 175 F1
Montévrain (77) 43 F4
Monteynard (38) 145 G4
Montézic (12) 154 C1
Montfa (09) 185 E4
Montfa (81) 170 C4
Montfalcon (38) 144 C2
Montfarville (50) 13 E2
Montfaucon (02) 44 B3
Montfaucon (25) 103 D1
Montfaucon (30) 174 D1
Montfaucon (46) 152 D1

Montfaucon-
d'Argonne (55) 24 D6
Montfaucon-en-Velay (43).. 143 F2
Montfermeil (93) 43 E3
Montfermier (82) 152 C5
Montfermy (63) 126 D2
Montferrand (11) 186 A2
Montferrand-du-
Périgord (24) 137 G6
Montferrand-la-Fare (26).. 159 F4
Montferrand-le-
Château (25) 103 F1
Montferrat (38) 131 F5
Montferrat (83) 177 H5
Montferrer (66) 200 D4
Montferrier (09) 186 A6
Montferrier-sur-Lez (34) ... 173 F5
Montfey (10) 65 H5
Montfiquet (14) 13 G6
Montfleur (39) 117 F3
Montflours (53) 58 D4
Montflovin (25) 104 A3
Montfort (04) 176 D1
Montfort (64) 181 G1
Montfort-en-Chalosse (40).. 165 F4
Montfort-l'Amaury (78) 41 H4
Montfort-le-Gesnois (72) ... 60 C5
Montfort-sur-Argens (83).. 193 F2
Montfort-sur-Boulzane (11).. 200 B2
Montfort-sur-Meu (35) 56 D2
Montfort-sur-Risle (27) 18 A5
Montfranc (12) 171 E3
Montfrin (30) 174 C3
Montfroc (26) 159 G6
Montfuron (04) 176 C3
Montgaillard (09) 185 H6
Montgaillard (11) 187 G6
Montgaillard (40) 166 A4
Montgaillard (65) 183 E4
Montgaillard (81) 169 G3
Montgaillard (82) 168 B2
Montgaillard-de-
Salies (31) 184 C4
Montgaillard-
Lauragais (31) 185 H1
Montgaillard-sur-Save (31).. 184 B3
Montgardin (05) 160 C2
Montgaroult (61) 38 D4
Montgauch (09) 184 D5
Montgaudry (61) 60 C2
Montgazin (31) 185 F2
Montgé-en-Goële (77) 43 F2
Montgeard (31) 185 H2
Montgenèvre (05) 147 F4
Montgenost (51) 44 C6
Montgérain (60) 20 D3
Montgeron (91) 42 D5
Montgeroult (95) 42 B2
Montgesoye (25) 103 H2
Montgesty (46) 152 B2
Montgey (81) 170 A6
Montgibaud (19) 124 C5
Montgilbert (73) 132 C5
Montgiscard (31) 185 G1
Montgivray (36) 111 H1
Montgobert (02) 21 H5
Montgon (08) 24 A4
Montgradail (11) 186 C4
Montgras (31) 184 D1
Montgreleix (63) 141 F1
Montgru-Saint-Hilaire (02).. 44 B1
Montguers (26) 159 F5
Montgueux (10) 66 A3
Montguyon (17) 135 H2
les Monthairons (55) 47 F2
Montharville (28) 62 A4
Monthault (35) 37 F6
Monthaut (11) 186 C4
Monthelie (21) 101 G3
Monthelon (51) 45 E2
Monthelon (71) 100 C4
Monthenault (02) 22 C4
Montheries (52) 67 G4
Monthermé (08) 11 F6
Monthiers (02) 44 B2
Monthieux (01) 130 B1
Monthion (73) 132 C4
Monthodon (37) 79 E3
Monthoiron (86) 94 D6
Monthois (08) 24 B5
Montholier (39) 102 D4
Montholon (89) 83 E1
Monthou-sur-Bièvre (41) 79 H5
Monthou-sur-Cher (41) 79 H6
Monthuchon (50) 37 E1
Monthurel (02) 44 C2
Monthureux-le-Sec (88) 69 F4
Monthureux-sur-
Saône (88) 69 E5
Monthyon (77) 43 G2
Monticello (2B) 202 D5
Montier-en-l'Isle (10) 67 E3
Montiéramey (10) 66 C4
Montierchaume (36) 96 D5
Montiers (60) 20 D4
Montiers-sur-Saulx (55) 68 A1
Monties (32) 184 B1
Montignac (24) 138 A3
Montignac (33) 149 H1
Montignac (65) 183 F3
Montignac-Charente (16) .. 122 A2
Montignac-de-Lauzun (47).. 151 E2
Montignac-le-Coq (16) 136 C1
Montignac-Toupinerie (47).. 150 D2
Montignargues (30) 173 H2
Montigné (16) 122 A2
Montigné-le-Brillant (53).... 58 C5

Montigné-lès-Rairies (49)... 77 G3
Montigny (14) 38 B2
Montigny (18) 98 A1
Montigny (45) 63 E5
Montigny (54) 49 G6
Montigny (76) 18 C4
Montigny-aux-
Amognes (58) 99 E3
Montigny-devant-
Sassey (55) 24 D4
Montigny-en-
Arrouaise (02) 9 F6
Montigny-en-
Cambrésis (59) 9 F4
Montigny-en-
Gohelle (62) 8 C1
Montigny-en-Morvan (58).. 100 A2
Montigny-en-
Ostrevent (59) 8 D2
Montigny-la-Resle (89) 83 G1
Montigny-l'Allier (02) 43 H1
Montigny-le-
Bretonneux (78) 42 B4
Montigny-le-Chartif (28) 61 G3
Montigny-le-Franc (02) 22 D2
Montigny-le-Guesdier (77).. 65 E2
Montigny-Lencoup (77) 64 C2
Montigny-Lengrain (02) 21 G5
Montigny-lès-Arsures (39).. 103 E4
Montigny-lès-Cherlieu (70).. 87 E2
Montigny-lès-Condé (02) 44 C3
Montigny-lès-
Cormeilles (95) 42 C3
Montigny-lès-
Jongleurs (80) 7 F3
Montigny-lès-Metz (57) 26 B5
Montigny-lès-Monts (10) 66 A5
Montigny-lès-
Vaucouleurs (55) 47 H6
Montigny-lès-Vesoul (70) ... 87 F3
Montigny-Montfort (21) 84 C4
Montigny-Mornay-
Villeneuve-sur-
Vingeanne (21) 86 B4
Montigny-Saint-
Barthélemy (21) 84 C5
Montigny-sous-Marle (02) .. 22 D1
Montigny-sur-
Armançon (21) 84 D5
Montigny-sur-Aube (21) 67 E4
Montigny-sur-Avre (28) 40 D5
Montigny-sur-Canne (58).... 99 G4
Montigny-sur-Chiers (54).... 25 G4
Montigny-sur-Crécy (02) 22 C2
Montigny-sur-l'Ain (39) 103 E6
Montigny-sur-l'Hallue (80)... 7 H5
Montigny-sur-Loing (77) 64 A3
Montigny-sur-Meuse (08) ... 11 E4
Montigny-sur-Vence (08) 24 A2
Montigny-sur-Vesle (51) 22 D5
Montillières (49) 93 E1
Montillot (89) 83 G4
Montilly (03) 113 H1
Montilly-sur-Noireau (61) 38 B4
Montils (17) 121 F4
les Montils (41) 79 H4
Montipouret (36) 111 G1
Montirat (11) 187 E3
Montirat (81) 153 H6
Montireau (28) 61 G2
Montiron (32) 168 B5
Montivernage (25) 88 A6
Montivilliers (76) 15 F1
Montjardin (11) 186 C5
Montjaux (12) 171 H1
Montjavoult (60) 19 G6
Montjay (05) 159 G4
Montjay (71) 102 B5
Montjean (16) 108 C6
Montjean (53) 58 B5
Montjoi (11) 187 F5
Montjoi (82) 151 H6
Montjoie-en-
Couserans (09) 185 E5
Montjoie-le-Château (25).... 88 D5
Montjoie-Saint-Martin (50).. 35 H5
Montjoire (31) 169 F4
Montjoux (26) 158 B3
Montjoyer (26) 158 B3
Montjustin (04) 176 B3
Montjustin-et-Velotte (70)... 87 H3
Montlainsia (39) 117 F3
Montlandon (28) 61 G2
Montlaur (11) 187 F4
Montlaur (12) 171 H3
Montlaur (31) 169 G6
Montlaur-en-Diois (26) 159 E1
Montlaux (04) 176 D1
Montlauzun (46) 152 B5
Montlay-en-Auxois (21) 84 C6
Montlebon (25) 104 B2
Montlevicq (36) 111 H1
Montlevon (02) 44 C2
Montlhéry (91) 42 C6
Montliard (45) 63 G6
Montlieu-la-Garde (17) 135 G2
Montlignon (95) 42 C2
Montliot-et-Courcelles (21).. 85 E1
Montlivault (41) 80 A3
Montloué (02) 23 E2
Montlouis (18) 97 F5
Montlouis-sur-Loire (37) 78 D5
Montluçon (03) 112 D4
Montluel (01) 130 B2
Montmachoux (77) 64 C3
Montmacq (60) 21 F4
Montmagny (95) 42 D3
Montmahoux (25) 103 G3

Montmain (21) 102 A3
Montmain (76) 18 D4
Montmançon (21) 86 B6
Montmarault (03) 113 H4
Montmarlon (39) 103 F4
Montmartin (60) 21 E4
Montmartin-en-
Graignes (50) 13 F5
Montmartin-le-Haut (10) 67 E4
Montmartin-sur-Mer (50).... 36 D2
Montmaur (05) 160 A2
Montmaur (11) 186 A1
Montmaurin (31) 184 A3
Montmédy (55) 25 E3
Montmeillant (08) 23 G2
Montmélard (71) 115 G4
Montmelas-Saint-
Sorlin (69) 129 G1
Montmélian (73) 132 A5
Montmérac (16) 121 H5
Montmerle-sur-Saône (01).. 116 B6
Montmerrei (61) 39 E5
Montmeyan (83) 177 E5
Montmeyran (26) 144 B6
Montmirail (51) 44 C4
Montmirail (72) 61 E5
Montmiral (26) 144 C3
Montmirat (30) 173 H3
Montmirey-la-Ville (39) 102 C1
Montmirey-le-Château (39).. 102 D1
Montmoreau (16) 122 B6
Montmorency (95) 42 D3
Montmorency-
Beaufort (10) 67 E1
Montmorillon (86) 110 A3
Montmorin (05) 159 G3
Montmorin (63) 127 G4
Montmorot (39) 102 D6
Montmort (71) 100 B6
Montmort-Lucy (51) 45 E3
Montmotier (88) 69 G6
Montmoyen (21) 85 F2
Montmurat (15) 153 H2
Montner (66) 200 D2
Montoillot (21) 101 F1
Montoir-de-Bretagne (44)... 73 H4
Montoire-sur-le-Loir (41) 79 E2
Montois-la-Montagne (57)... 26 B4
Montoison (26) 144 B6
Montoldre (03) 114 A4
Montolieu (11) 186 D2
Montolivet (77) 44 B4
Montonvillers (80) 7 G5
Montord (03) 113 H4
Montory (64) 181 G4
Montot (21) 102 B2
Montot (70) 86 D4
Montot-sur-Rognon (52) 68 A3
Montouliers (34) 188 A2
Montoulieu (09) 185 H6
Montoulieu (34) 173 F2
Montoulieu-Saint-
Bernard (31) 184 C3
Montournais (85) 92 C4
Montourtier (53) 59 E3
Montoussé (65) 183 G4
Montoussin (31) 184 D2
Montpellier (34) 173 F5
Montpellier-de-
Médillan (17) 121 E4
Montpensier (63) 113 G6
Montperreux (25) 104 A4
Montpeyroux (12) 154 C2
Montpeyroux (24) 136 B5
Montpeyroux (34) 172 D5
Montpeyroux (63) 127 F4
Montpezat (30) 173 H3
Montpezat (32) 184 C1
Montpezat (47) 151 E3
Montpezat-de-Quercy (82).. 152 D5
Montpezat-sous-
Bauzon (07) 157 F1
Montpinchon (50) 37 E2
Montpinier (81) 170 C5
Montpitol (31) 169 G4
Montplonne (55) 47 E5
Montpon-Ménestérol (24).. 136 B4
Montpont-en-Bresse (71)... 116 D1
Montpothier (10) 44 C6
Montpouillan (47) 150 B3
Montrabé (31) 169 F5
Montrabot (50) 37 H1
Montracol (01) 116 D5
Montravers (79) 92 D4
Montréal (07) 157 F3
Montréal (11) 186 C3
Montréal (32) 167 E2
Montréal (89) 84 B4
Montréal-la-Cluse (01) 117 G6
Montréal-les-Sources (26).. 159 E4
Montrécourt (59) 9 F3
Montredon (46) 153 H2
Montredon-des-
Corbières (11) 188 A3
Montredon-
Labessonnié (81) 170 D4
Montregard (43) 143 F3
Montrelais (44) 76 B5
Montrem (24) 137 E3
Montrésor (37) 95 H2
Montret (71) 102 B6
Montreuil (28) 41 F4
Montreuil (62) 1 F6
Montreuil (85) 107 G2
Montreuil (93) 42 D4
Montreuil-au-Houlme (61)... 38 D5

Montreuil-aux-Lions (02) 44 A2
Montreuil-Bellay (49) 93 G2
Montreuil-Bonnin (86) 108 D1
Montreuil-des-Landes (35).. 58 A3
Montreuil-en-Auge (14) 15 E5
Montreuil-en-Caux (76) 17 G4
Montreuil-en-Touraine (37).. 79 F5
Montreuil-Juigné (49) 76 D3
Montreuil-la-Cambe (61) 39 E3
Montreuil-l'Argillé (27) 39 H3
Montreuil-le-Chétif (72) 59 H3
Montreuil-le-Henri (72) 78 D1
Montreuil-Poulay (53) 59 E2
Montreuil-sous-
Pérouse (35) 58 A4
Montreuil-sur-Barse (10)..... 66 C4
Montreuil-sur-Blaise (52) 67 G1
Montreuil-sur-Brêche (60)... 20 C4
Montreuil-sur-Epte (95) 41 G1
Montreuil-sur-Ille (35) 57 F1
Montreuil-sur-Loir (49) 77 E3
Montreuil-sur-Lozon (50) 13 E6
Montreuil-sur-Maine (49) 76 D3
Montreuil-sur-Thérain (60)... 20 B5
Montreuil-sur-
Thonnance (52) 68 A1
Montreuillon (58) 99 H2
Montreux (54) 49 H6
Montreux-Château (90) 88 D3
Montreux-Jeune (68) 88 D3
Montreux-Vieux (68) 88 D3
Montrevault-sur-Èvre (49) .. 75 G5
Montrevel (38) 131 E5
Montrevel (39) 117 F3
Montrevel-en-Bresse (01).. 116 D3
Montréverd (85) 91 G2
Montrichard Val de
Cher (41) 79 G6
Montricher-Albanne (73) ... 146 C2
Montricoux (82) 169 G1
Montrieux-en-Sologne (41).. 80 C4
Montrigaud (26) 144 C2
Montriond (74) 119 F4
Montrodat (48) 155 H3
Montrol-Sénard (87) 110 A6
Montrollet (16) 123 G1
Montromant (69) 129 G3
Montrond (05) 159 H4
Montrond (39) 103 E5
Montrond-le-Château (25).. 103 G2
Montrond-les-Bains (42)... 129 E4
Montrosier (81) 153 F6
Montrottier (69) 129 G3
Montroty (76) 19 G4
Montrouge (92) 42 D4
Montrouveau (41) 79 E2
Montroy (17) 106 D5
Montrozier (12) 154 D4
Montry (77) 43 G3
Monts (37) 78 D6
Monts (60) 20 A6
Les Monts d'Andaine (61)... 38 C5
Les Monts d'Aunay (14) 38 A4
Les Monts du
Roumois (27) 18 B5
Monts-en-Bessin (14) 14 A5
Monts-en-Ternois (62) 7 G2
Monts-sur-Guesnes (86) 94 B4
les Monts-Verts (48) 141 F5
Montsalès (12) 153 G3
Montsalier (04) 176 B1
Montsalvy (15) 154 B1
Montsapey (73) 132 C5
Montsauche-les-
Settons (58) 100 B1
Le Montsaugeonnais (52)... 86 B3
Montsaunès (31) 184 C4
Montsec (55) 47 H3
Montsecret-
Clairefougère (61) 38 A4
Montségur (09) 186 A6
Montségur-sur-Lauzon (26).. 158 B4
Montselgues (07) 156 D3
Montsenelle (50) 12 D5
Montséret (11) 187 H4
Montsérié (65) 183 H4
Montseron (09) 185 F5
Montseveroux (38) 130 B6
Montsoreau (49) 94 A1
Montsoué (40) 166 A4
Montsoult (95) 42 D2
Montsûrs-Saint-
Céneré (53) 59 E4
Montsurvent (50) 36 D1
Montsuzain (10) 66 B2
Monturenx-et-
Prantigny (70) 86 D4
Montureux-lès-Baulay (70).. 87 F1
Montusclat (43) 142 D4
Montussaint (25) 87 H5
Montussan (33) 135 F5
Montval-sur-Loir (72) 78 C3
Montvalen (81) 169 G3
Montvalent (46) 138 D5
Montvalezan (73) 133 F4
Montvendre (26) 144 C5
Montverdun (42) 128 D3
Montvernier (73) 146 C1
Montvert (15) 139 G4
Montvicq (03) 113 G4
Montville (76) 18 C3
Montzéville (55) 25 E6
Monviel (47) 151 E2
Monze (11) 187 E4
Moon-sur-Elle (50) 13 F6
Moosch (68) 88 D1
Mooslargue (68) 89 F4

Moraches (58)................99 G1
Moragne (17)................107 E6
Morainville (28)................62 D2
Morainville-Jouveaux (27).....15 G4
Morainvilliers (78)................42 A3
Morancé (69)................129 H2
Morancez (28)................62 B2
Morancourt (52)................67 G2
Morand (37)................79 F4
Morangis (51)................45 E3
Morangis (91)................42 D5
Morangles (60)................42 C1
Morannes sur Sarthe-
  Daumeray (49)................77 E2
Moranville (55)................47 G1
Moras (38)................130 D4
Moras-en-Valloire (26)...144 B1
Morbecque (59)................2 C4
Morbier (39)................118 B1
Morcenx (40)................165 F1
Morchain (80)................21 F1
Morchies (62)................8 C4
Morcourt (02)................9 E6
Morcourt (80)................8 A6
Mordelles (35)................57 E3
Moréac (56)................55 H4
Morée (41)................79 H1
Moreilles (85)................106 D2
Morelmaison (88)................69 E3
Morembert (10)................66 C1
Morestel (38)................131 E4
Moret-Loing-et-
  Orvanne (77)................64 B2
Morette (38)................145 E1
Moreuil (80)................20 D1
Morey (71)................101 F5
Morey-Saint-Denis (21).......101 H1
Morfontaine (54)................25 H4
Morganx (40)................165 H5
Morgemoulin (55)................25 G6
Morgny (27)................19 F5
Morgny-en-Thiérache (02)...23 E1
Morgny-la-
  Pommeraye (76)................18 D3
Morhange (57)................49 F3
Moriat (63)................127 G6
Morienne (76)................19 G1
Morienval (60)................21 F5
Morières-lès-Avignon (84)...175 E2
Moriers (28)................62 A4
Morieux (22)................33 H4
Moriez (04)................177 H2
Morigny (50)................37 G3
Morigny-Champigny (91)...63 F2
Morillon (74)................119 F5
Moringhem (62)................2 A4
Morionvilliers (52)................68 B2
Morisel (80)................20 D1
Moriville (88)................69 H2
Moriviller (54)................69 H1
Morizécourt (88)................69 E5
Morizès (33)................150 A2
Morlaàs (64)................182 C2
Morlac (18)................97 G6
Morlaix (29)................32 A3
Morlancourt (80)................8 A5
Morlanne (64)................165 H6
Morlet (71)................101 E4
Morley (55)................47 F6
Morlhon-le-Haut (12).......153 G5
Morlincourt (60)................21 G3
Mormant (77)................43 G6
Mormant-sur-
  Vernisson (45)................64 A6
Mormès (32)................166 C3
Mormoiron (84)................175 G1
Mornac (16)................122 C3
Mornac-sur-Seudre (17)...120 C3
Mornand-en-Forez (42)...128 D4
Mornans (26)................158 D2
Mornant (69)................129 H4
Mornas (84)................158 A6
Mornay (71)................115 G2
Mornay-Berry (18)................98 C3
Mornay-sur-Allier (18)...98 D5
Moroges (71)................101 F5
Morogues (18)................98 A1
Morosaglia (2B)................205 F1
Morre (25)................103 G1
Morsain (02)................21 H4
Morsains (51)................44 C4
Morsalines (50)................13 E2
Morsan (27)................15 H5
Morsang-sur-Orge (91).....42 D5
Morsang-sur-Seine (91)...43 E6
Morsbach (57)................27 G5
Morsbronn-les-Bains (67)...51 E3
Morschwiller (67)................50 D3
Morschwiller-le-Bas (68).....89 F2
Morsiglia (2B)................203 F2
Mortagne (88)................70 B3
Mortagne-au-Perche (61)...60 D1
Mortagne-du-Nord (59)......4 A6
Mortagne-sur-Gironde (17)..120 D5
Mortagne-sur-Sèvre (85)...92 B3
Mortain-Bocage (50)........37 G5
Mortcerf (77)................43 G4
la Morte (38)................145 H4
Morteau (25)................104 B3
Morteaux-Coulibœuf (14)...39 E3
Mortefontaine (02)................21 G5
Mortefontaine (60)................43 E1
Mortefontaine-en-
  Thelle (60)................20 B6
Mortemart (87)................110 A6
Mortemer (60)................21 E3
Mortemer (76)................19 F1
Mortery (77)................44 A6

Morthomiers (18)................97 G3
Mortiers (02)................22 C2
Mortiers (17)................121 G6
Morton (86)................93 H2
Mortrée (61)................39 F5
Mortroux (23)................111 G3
Morval (62)................8 B5
Morvillars (90)................88 D4
Morville (50)................12 D3
Morville (88)................68 D3
Morville-en-Beauce (45)...63 F3
Morville-lès-Vic (57)................49 F4
Morville-sur-Andelle (76)...19 E4
Morville-sur-Nied (57)................49 E2
Morville-sur-Seille (54)...48 C3
Morvillers (60)................19 H3
Morvillers-Saint-
  Saturnin (80)................19 H1
Morvilliers (10)................67 E2
Morvilliers (28)................40 C6
Mory (62)................8 B3
Mory-Montcrux (60)................20 C3
Morzine (74)................119 F4
Mosles (14)................13 H5
Moslins (51)................45 E3
Mosnac (16)................122 A4
Mosnac (17)................121 F5
Mosnay (36)................111 E1
Mosnes (37)................79 G5
Mosset (66)................200 B2
Mosson (21)................85 E1
Mostuéjouls (12)................155 G6
Motey-Besuche (70)................86 D6
Motey-sur-Saône (70)................86 D4
la Mothe-Saint-Héray (79)...108 B3
Mothern (67)................51 G2
Motreff (29)................54 B1
la Motte (22)................55 G1
la Motte (83)................194 A2
la Motte-Chalancon (26)...159 F3
la Motte-d'Aigues (84)...176 B4
la Motte-d'Aveillans (38)...145 G4
la Motte-de-Galaure (26)...144 B2
la Motte-du-Caire (04)...160 B4
la Motte-en-Bauges (73)...132 B3
la Motte-en-
  Champsaur (05)................146 B6
la Motte-Fanjas (26)................144 D4
la Motte-Feuilly (36)................111 H2
la Motte-Fouquet (61)................38 C6
la Motte-Saint-Jean (71)...114 D2
la Motte-Saint-Martin (38)...145 G4
la Motte-Servolex (73)...131 H4
la Motte-Ternant (21)...84 C6
la Motte-Tilly (10)................65 F1
Mottereau (28)................61 G3
Motteville (76)................17 F4
Mottier (38)................130 D6
Motz (73)................131 G1
Mouacourt (54)................49 F5
Mouais (44)................57 H6
Mouans-Sartoux (06)...178 C5
Mouaville (54)................25 H6
Mouazé (35)................57 F2
Mouchamps (85)................92 A5
Mouchan (32)................167 F2
Mouchard (39)................103 E3
la Mouche (50)................37 E4
Mouchès (32)................167 G5
Mouchin (59)................3 H6
Mouchy-le-Châtel (60)...20 B5
Moudeyres (43)................142 D5
Mouen (14)................14 B5
Mouettes (27)................41 F3
Mouffy (89)................83 F3
Mouflaines (27)................19 F6
Mouflers (80)................7 E4
Mouflières (80)................6 D6
Mougins (06)................178 D5
Mougon-Thorigné (79)...108 A4
Mouguerre (64)................164 B6
Mouhers (36)................111 F1
Mouhet (36)................110 D3
Mouhous (64)................166 B6
Mouillac (33)................135 G4
Mouillac (82)................153 E5
Mouilleron (52)................85 H3
Mouilleron-le-Captif (85)...91 G4
Mouilleron-Saint-
  Germain (85)................92 C6
Mouilly (55)................47 G2
Moulainville (55)................47 G1
Moularès (81)................170 D1
Moulay (53)................58 D3
Moulayrès (81)................170 B4
Moulédous (65)................183 F3
Moulès-et-Baucels (34)...173 E2
Mouleydier (24)................137 E5
Moulézan (30)................173 H2
Moulhard (28)................61 G4
Mouliets-et-
  Villemartin (33)................136 A5
Moulihervé (49)................77 H5
Moulin-Mage (81)................171 G4
Moulin-Neuf (09)................186 B4
Moulin-Neuf (24)................136 B4
Moulin-sous-Touvent (60)...21 G4
Moulineaux (76)................18 C5
Moulines (14)................38 C2
Moulines (50)................37 G6
Moulinet (06)................179 F2
Moulinet (47)................151 F2
le Moulinet-sur-Solin (45)...82 A2
Moulins (02)................22 C4
Moulins (03)................113 H2
Moulins (35)................57 G4

Moulins en Bessin (14)...14 A4
Moulins-en-
  Tonnerrois (89)................84 B2
Moulins-Englibert (58)...100 A3
Moulins-la-Marche (61)...39 H5
Moulins-le-Carbonnel (72)...59 H2
Moulins-lès-Metz (57)...26 B5
Moulins-Saint-Hubert (55)...24 D3
Moulins-sur-Céphons (36)...96 B3
Moulins-sur-Orne (61)...39 E4
Moulins-sur-Ouanne (89)...83 E3
Moulins-sur-Yèvre (18)...97 H3
Moulis (09)................184 D5
Moulis-en-Médoc (33)...134 D3
Moulismes (86)................109 H3
Moulle (62)................2 A3
Moulon (33)................135 H5
Moulon (45)................63 H6
Moulotte (55)................48 A1
Moult-Chicheboville (14)...14 D5
Moumoulous (65)................183 F2
Moumour (64)................181 H3
Mounes-Prohencoux (12)...171 G4
Mourède (32)................167 F3
Mourens (33)................149 H1
Mourenx (64)................182 A1
Mouret (12)................154 C3
Moureuille (63)................113 E6
Mouriès (13)................175 E4
Mouriez (62)................7 E2
Mourioux-Vieilleville (23)...111 E6
Mourjou (15)................154 A1
Mourmelon-le-Grand (51)...45 H1
Mourmelon-le-Petit (51)...45 H1
Mournans-Charbonny (39)...103 G5
Mouron (08)................24 B5
Mouron-sur-Yonne (58)...99 H2
Mouroux (77)................43 H4
Mours (95)................18 D6
Mours-Saint-Eusèbe (26)...144 C3
Mourvilles-Basses (31)...169 G6
Mourvilles-Hautes (31)...186 A1
Mouscardès (40)................165 F5
Moussac (30)................174 A2
Moussac (86)................109 G4
Moussages (15)................140 B2
Moussan (11)................188 A3
Moussé (35)................57 H4
Mousseaux-lès-Bray (77)...64 D2
Mousseaux-Neuville (27)...41 E3
Mousseaux-sur-Seine (78)...41 G2
Moussey (10)................66 B4
Moussey (57)................49 G5
Moussey (88)................70 D1
les Moussières (39)................118 A3
Mousson (54)................48 C3
Moussonvilliers (61)................40 B6
Moussoulens (11)................186 B3
Moussy (51)................45 E2
Moussy (58)................99 F2
Moussy (95)................42 A1
Moussy-le-Neuf (77)................43 E2
Moussy-le-Vieux (77)................43 E2
Moussy-Verneuil (02)...22 C4
Moustajon (31)................197 F1
Moustéru (22)................32 D4
Moustey (40)................149 E4
Moustier (47)................150 D1
Moustier-en-Fagne (59)...10 B4
Moustier-Ventadour (19)...125 G6
Moustiers-Sainte-
  Marie (04)................177 F3
le Moustoir (22)................32 C6
Moustoir-Ac (56)................55 F4
le Moutaret (38)................132 A6
Mouterhouse (57)................50 C2
Mouterre-Silly (86)................94 A3
Mouterre-sur-Blourde (86)...109 G5
Mouthe (25)................103 H6
le Moutherot (25)................103 E1
Mouthier-en-Bresse (71)...102 C4
Mouthier-Haute-Pierre (25)...103 H3
Mouthiers-sur-Boëme (16)...122 B5
Mouthoumet (11)................187 F5
Moutier-d'Ahun (23)................111 H6
Moutier-Malcard (23)................111 F3
Moutier-Rozeille (23)................125 H2
Moutiers (28)................62 C3
Moutiers (35)................58 A5
Moutiers (54)................26 A4
Moûtiers (73)................132 D5
Moutiers-au-Perche (61)...61 F1
les Moutiers-en-Auge (14)...39 E3
les Moutiers-en-
  Cinglais (14)................38 C2
Moutiers-en-Puisaye (89)...82 D4
les Moutiers-en-Retz (44)...74 A6
Moutiers-Saint-Jean (21)...84 C4
Moutiers-sous-
  Chantemerle (79)................92 D6
Moutiers-sur-le-Lay (85)...106 C1
Mouton (16)................122 C2
Moutonne (39)................117 G2
Moutonneau (16)................122 C1
Moutoux (39)................103 F5
Moutrot (54)................48 B6
Mouvaux (59)................3 G4
Moux (11)................187 G3
Moux-en-Morvan (58)...100 C2
Mouxy (73)................131 H3
Mouy (60)................20 C5
Mouy-sur-Seine (77)................64 D2
Mouzay (37)................95 F2
Mouzay (55)................24 D4
Mouzeil (44)................75 E3

Mouzens (81)................170 A6
Mouzeil-Saint-Martin (85)..106 D2
Mouzieys-Panens (81)...170 A1
Mouzieys-Teulet (81)...170 D3
Mouzillon (44)................75 E6
Mouzon (08)................24 D3
Mouzon (16)................123 E2
Moval (90)................88 D3
Moÿ-de-l'Aisne (02)................22 A1
Moyaux (14)................15 G4
Moydans (05)................159 F4
Moye (74)................131 H2
Moyemont (88)................70 A2
Moyen (54)................70 A1
Moyencourt (80)................21 G2
Moyencourt-lès-Poix (80)...20 A1
Moyenmoutier (88)................70 C2
Moyenneville (60)................21 E4
Moyenneville (62)................8 B3
Moyenneville (80)................6 D4
Moyenvic (57)................49 F4
Moyeuvre-Grande (57)...26 B4
Moyeuvre-Petite (57)...26 B4
Moyon Villages (50)................37 F2
Moyrazès (12)................154 B4
Moyvillers (60)................21 E4
Mozac (63)................127 F2
Mozé-sur-Louet (49)................76 D5
Muchedent (76)................17 H3
Mudaison (34)................173 G5
Muel (35)................56 C2
Muespach (68)................89 G3
Muespach-le-Haut (68)...89 G3
Mugron (40)................165 G3
Muhlbach-sur-Bruche (67)...50 B6
Muhlbach-sur-
  Munster (68)................70 D5
Muides-sur-Loire (41)...80 B3
Muidorge (60)................20 B3
Muids (27)................19 E5
Muille-Villette (80)................21 G2
Muirancourt (60)................21 G2
Muizon (51)................22 D5
les Mujouls (06)................178 C2
la Mulatière (69)................130 A3
Mulcent (78)................41 G3
Mulcey (57)................49 F4
Mulhausen (67)................50 D3
Mulhouse (68)................89 F2
Mulsanne (72)................60 B6
Mulsans (41)................80 A3
Mun (65)................183 G2
Munchausen (67)................51 G2
Munchhouse (68)................71 G6
Muncq-Nieurlet (62)................2 A3
Mundolsheim (67)................51 E5
Muneville-le-Bingard (50)...12 D6
Muneville-sur-Mer (50)...36 D2
le Mung (17)................121 E1
Munster (57)................49 H3
Munster (68)................71 E5
Muntzenheim (68)................71 G4
Munwiller (68)................71 F6
Mur-de-Barrez (12)................140 C6
Mur-de-Sologne (41)...80 B5
Muracciole (2B)................205 F3
Murasson (12)................171 G4
Murat (03)................113 F3
Murat (15)................140 D3
Murat-le-Quaire (63)...126 C5
Murat-sur-Vèbre (81)...171 G5
Murato (2B)................203 F5
la Muraz (74)................118 C5
Murbach (68)................71 E6
la Mure (38)................145 G5
la Mure-Argens (04)...177 H1
Mureaumont (60)................19 G2
Les Mureaux (78)................42 A2
Mureils (26)................144 B2
Mûres (74)................132 A2
Muret (31)................185 F1
Muret-et-Crouttes (02)...22 B6
Muret-le-Château (12)...154 C3
la Murette (38)................131 F6
Murianette (38)................145 G2
Murinais (38)................144 D2
Murles (34)................173 E5
Murlin (58)................99 E2
Muro (2B)................202 C5
Murol (63)................127 E5
Murols (12)................154 C1
Muron (17)................107 E6
Murs (36)................95 G4
Murs (84)................175 G2
Mûrs-Erigné (49)................76 D5
Murtin-et-Bogny (08)...23 H1
Murvaux (55)................25 E4
Murviel-lès-Béziers (34)...188 B1
Murviel-lès-
  Montpellier (34)................173 E5
Murville (54)................25 H5
Murzo (2A)................204 C4
Mus (30)................174 A4
Muscourt (02)................22 D5
Musculdy (64)................181 F3
Musièges (74)................118 A6
Musigny (21)................101 E2
Mussey-sur-Marne (52)...67 H2
Mussidan (24)................136 D4
Mussig (67)................71 G3
Mussy-la-Fosse (21)...84 D4
Mussy-sous-Dun (71)...115 G4
Mussy-sur-Seine (10)...66 D6
Mutigney (39)................86 D2
Mutigny (51)................45 F2
Mutrécy (14)................14 B5
Muttersholtz (67)................71 G3

Mutzenhouse (67)................50 D4
Mutzig (67)................50 D6
le Muy (83)................194 B2
Muzeray (55)................25 G5
Muzillac (56)................73 F2
Muzy (27)................41 E4
Myans (73)................132 A5
Myennes (58)................82 C5
Myon (25)................103 F3

N

Nabas (64)................181 G1
Nabinaud (16)................136 C1
Nabirat (24)................138 B6
Nabringhen (62)................1 G4
Nachamps (17)................107 G6
Nadaillac (24)................138 B4
Nadaillac-de-Rouge (46)...138 C5
Nades (03)................113 F5
Nadillac (46)................152 D2
Nagel-Séez-Mesnil (27)...40 C3
Nages (81)................171 G5
Nages-et-Solorgues (30)...174 A4
Nahuja (66)................199 H4
Nailhac (24)................138 A2
Naillat (23)................111 E4
Nailloux (31)................185 H2
Nailly (89)................64 D4
Naintré (86)................94 C5
Nainville-les-Roches (91)...63 H1
Naisey-les-Granges (25)...103 H1
Naives-en-Blois (55)...47 G5
Naives-Rosières (55)...47 F4
Naix-aux-Forges (55)...47 F6
Najac (12)................153 G5
Nalliers (85)................106 D2
Nalliers (86)................109 H1
Nalzen (09)................186 A6
Nambsheim (68)................71 G6
Nampcel (60)................21 G4
Nampcelles-la-Cour (02)...23 E1
Nampont (80)................6 D2
Namps-Maisnil (80)................20 B1
Nampteuil-sous-Muret (02)...22 B5
Nampty (80)................20 B1
Nan-sous-Thil (21)................84 D6
Nançay (18)................81 E6
Nance (39)................102 C5
Nances (73)................131 G4
Nanchez (39)................118 A2
Nanclars (16)................122 C2
Nançois-le-Grand (55)...47 F5
Nançois-sur-Ornain (55)...47 F5
Nancras (17)................120 D3
Nancray (25)................103 G1
Nancray-sur-Rimarde (45)...63 G5
Nancuise (39)................117 F2
Nancy (54)................48 C5
Nancy-sur-Cluses (74)...119 E6
Nandax (42)................115 F6
Nandy (77)................43 E6
Nangis (77)................64 C1
Nangy (74)................118 D5
Nannay (58)................99 E1
Nans (25)................88 A4
les Nans (39)................103 F5
Nans-les-Pins (83)................192 D3
Nans-sous-Sainte-
  Anne (25)................103 F3
Nant (12)................172 B2
Nant-le-Grand (55)................47 E5
Nant-le-Petit (55)................47 E5
Nanteau-sur-Essonne (77)...63 G3
Nanteau-sur-Lunain (77)...64 B3
Nanterre (92)................42 C3
Nantes (44)................74 D5
Nantes-en-Ratier (38)...145 H4
Nanteuil (79)................108 B3
Nanteuil-Auriac-de-
  Bourzac (24)................122 C2
Nanteuil-en-Vallée (16)...109 E6
Nanteuil-la-Forêt (51)...45 E1
Nanteuil-la-Fosse (02)...22 B4
Nanteuil-la-Haudouin (60)...43 F1
Nanteuil-lès-Meaux (77)...43 G3
Nanteuil-Notre-Dame (02)...44 B1
Nanteuil-sur-Aisne (08)...23 G3
Nanteuil-sur-Marne (77)...44 A3
Nantheuil (24)................123 G6
Nanthiat (24)................123 H6
Nantiat (87)................124 A1
Nantillé (17)................121 F2
Nantillois (55)................24 D5
Nantilly (70)................86 C5
Nantoin (38)................130 D6
Nantois (55)................47 F6
Nanton (71)................116 B1
Nantouillet (77)................43 F2
Nantoux (21)................101 G3
Nantua (01)................117 G5
Naours (80)................7 G5
Narbéfontaine (57)................27 E5
Narbief (25)................104 C2
Narbonne (11)................188 A3
Narcastet (64)................182 C2
Narcy (52)................47 E6
Narcy (58)................98 D1
Nargis (45)................64 B5
Narnhac (15)................140 D5
Narp (64)................181 G1
Narrosse (40)................165 E4
Nasbinals (48)................155 F2
Nassandres sur Risle (27)...40 B1
Nassiet (40)................165 G5
Nassigny (03)................112 D2
Nastringues (24)................136 B5

Natzwiller (67)................71 E1
Naucelle (12)................154 A6
Naucelles (15)................140 A5
Naujac-sur-Mer (33)...134 C1
Naujan-et-Postiac (33)...135 H6
Nauroy (02)................9 E5
Naussac (12)................153 H3
Naussac-Fontanes (48)...156 C1
Naussannes (24)................137 F6
Nauvay (72)................60 C2
Nauviale (12)................154 B3
Navacelles (30)................157 F6
Navailles-Angos (64)...182 C1
Navarrenx (64)................181 G2
Naveil (41)................79 F2
Navenne (70)................87 G3
Naves (03)................113 G5
Naves (19)................139 E1
Naves (59)................9 E3
Naves (81)................170 C6
Nâves-Parmelan (74)...132 B1
Navilly (71)................102 A4
Nay (50)................12 D5
Nay (64)................182 C3
Nayemont-les-Fosses (88)...70 D2
le Nayrac (12)................154 C2
Nazelles-Négron (37)...79 F5
Néac (33)................135 H4
Néant-sur-Yvel (56)................56 B3
Neau (53)................59 E4
Neaufles-Auvergny (27)...40 B3
Neaufles-Saint-Martin (27)...19 G6
Neauphe-sous-Essai (61)...39 F6
Neauphe-sur-Dive (61)...39 F4
Neauphle-le-Château (78)...42 A4
Neauphle-le-Vieux (78)...42 A4
Neauphlette (78)................41 G3
Neaux (42)................129 E1
Nébian (34)................172 C5
Nébias (11)................186 C6
Nébing (57)................49 G3
Nébouzat (63)................126 D3
Nécy (61)................39 E4
Nedde (87)................125 E3
Nédon (62)................2 B6
Nédonchel (62)................2 B6
Neewiller-près-
  Lauterbourg (67)................51 G2
Neffes (05)................160 B3
Neffiès (34)................172 C6
Néfiach (66)................200 D2
Nègrepelisse (82)................169 F1
Négreville (50)................12 C3
Négrondes (24)................137 G1
Néhou (50)................12 C4
Nelling (57)................49 G2
Nemours (77)................64 A3
Nempont-Saint-Firmin (62)...6 D2
Nénigan (31)................184 B2
Néons-sur-Creuse (36)...95 F5
Néoules (83)................193 F3
Néoux (23)................125 H2
Nepvant (55)................24 D3
Nérac (47)................150 D6
Nerbis (40)................165 G3
Nercillac (16)................121 H3
Néré (17)................121 H1
Néret (36)................112 A1
Nérigean (33)................135 G5
Nérignac (86)................109 G4
Néris-les-Bains (03)...112 D4
Nernier (74)................118 D3
Néron (28)................41 F6
Néronde (42)................129 E2
Néronde-sur-Dore (63)...127 H3
Nérondes (18)................98 B3
Ners (30)................173 H1
Nersac (16)................122 B4
Nervieux (42)................129 E3
Nerville-la-Forêt (95)...42 C2
Néry (60)................21 F6
Neschers (63)................127 F5
Nescus (09)................185 F5
Nesle (80)................21 F1
Nesle-et-Massoult (21)...84 D2
Nesle-Hodeng (76)................19 F2
Nesle-la-Reposte (51)...44 C6
Nesle-le-Repons (51)...44 C6
Nesle-l'Hôpital (80)................6 C6
Nesle-Normandeuse (76)...6 C6
Neslette (80)................6 C6
Nesles (62)................1 F5
Nesles-la-Montagne (02)...44 B2
Nesles-la-Vallée (95)...42 C1
Nesmy (85)................91 G5
Nesploy (45)................63 G6
Nespouls (19)................138 C4
Nessa (2B)................202 D5
Nestier (65)................183 H4
Nettancourt (55)................46 D3
Neublans-
  Abergement (39)................102 B4
Neubois (67)................71 F2
le Neubourg (27)................40 C1
Neuchâtel-Urtière (25)...88 C5
Neuf-Berquin (59)................2 D5
Neuf-Brisach (68)................71 G5
Neuf-Église (63)................113 E6
Neuf-Marché (76)................19 G4
Neuf-Mesnil (59)................10 A2
Neufbosc (76)................19 E2
le Neufbourg (50)................37 G5
Neufchâteau (88)................68 D2
Neufchâtel-en-Bray (76)...19 E1
Neufchâtel-en-
  Saosnois (72)................60 B2
Neufchâtel-Hardelot (62)...1 F5
Neufchâtel-sur-Aisne (02)...23 E4

Neufchef (57) 26 B3
Neufchelles (60) 43 H1
Neuffons (33) 150 B1
Neuffontaines (58) 83 G6
Neufgrange (57) 27 H5
Neuflieux (02) 21 H3
Neuflize (08) 23 G4
Neufmaison (08) 23 H1
Neufmaisons (54) 70 C1
Neufmanil (08) 24 B1
Neufmesnil (50) 12 C5
Neufmoulin (80) 7 E4
Neufmoulins (57) 49 H5
Neufmoutiers-en-Brie (77) 43 G5
le Neufour (55) 46 D1
Neufvillage (57) 49 G2
Neufvy-sur-Aronde (60) 21 E4
Neugartheim-Ittlenheim (67) 50 D5
Neuhaeusel (67) 51 G3
Neuil (37) 94 D2
Neuilh (65) 183 E4
Neuillac (17) 121 G5
Neuillay-les-Bois (36) 96 B5
Neuillé (49) 77 H6
Neuillé-le-Lierre (37) 79 F4
Neuillé-Pont-Pierre (37) 78 C4
Neuilly (27) 41 F3
Neuilly (58) 99 F1
Neuilly-en-Donjon (03) 114 D3
Neuilly-en-Dun (18) 98 B5
Neuilly-en-Sancerre (18) 82 A6
Neuilly-en-Thelle (60) 20 C6
Neuilly-en-Vexin (95) 42 B1
Neuilly-le-Bisson (61) 60 B1
Neuilly-le-Brignon (37) 95 E3
Neuilly-le-Dien (80) 7 E3
Neuilly-le-Réal (03) 114 A2
Neuilly-le-Vendin (53) 59 F1
Neuilly-lès-Dijon (21) 85 H6
Neuilly-l'Évêque (52) 68 B6
Neuilly-l'Hôpital (80) 6 D3
Neuilly-Plaisance (93) 43 E4
Neuilly-Saint-Front (02) 44 A1
Neuilly-sous-Clermont (60) 20 C5
Neuilly-sur-Marne (93) 43 E4
Neuilly-sur-Seine (92) 42 C3
Neuilly-sur-Suize (52) 67 H5
Neulette (62) 7 F1
Neulise (42) 129 E2
Neulles (17) 121 G5
Neulliac (56) 55 F2
Neung-sur-Beuvron (41) 80 C4
Neunkirchen-lès-Bouzonville (57) 27 E3
Neure (03) 98 C6
Neurey-en-Vaux (70) 87 G2
Neurey-lès-la-Demie (70) 87 G3
Neussargues en Pinatelle (15) 141 E3
Neuve-Chapelle (62) 3 E5
Neuve-Église (67) 71 F2
la Neuve-Grange (27) 19 F5
la Neuve-Lyre (27) 40 B3
Neuve-Maison (02) 10 A5
Neuvecelle (74) 119 E3
Neuvéglise-sur-Truyère (15) 141 E5
Neuvelle-lès-Cromary (70) 87 F5
Neuvelle-lès-la-Charité (70) 87 F4
la Neuvelle-lès-Lure (70) 88 A2
la Neuvelle-lès-Scey (70) 87 E2
Neuvelle-lès-Voisey (52) 86 D1
Neuves-Maisons (54) 48 C6
la Neuveville-devant-Lépanges (88) 70 B4
la Neuveville-sous-Châtenois (88) 69 E3
la Neuveville-sous-Montfort (88) 69 F3
Neuvic (19) 139 H1
Neuvic (24) 136 D3
Neuvic-Entier (87) 124 D3
Neuvicq (17) 135 G2
Neuvicq-le-Château (17) 121 H2
Neuvillalais (72) 59 H4
Neuville (19) 139 E3
la Neuville (59) 3 F6
Neuville (63) 127 H3
la Neuville-à-Maire (08) 24 B3
la Neuville-au-Bois (80) 6 D5
Neuville-au-Cornet (62) 7 G2
la Neuville-au-Plain (50) 13 E4
la Neuville-au-Pont (51) 46 C1
la Neuville-aux-Bois (45) 63 E5
la Neuville-aux-Bois (51) 46 C3
la Neuville-aux-Joûtes (08) 10 C6
la Neuville-aux-Larris (51) 45 E1
Neuville-Bosc (60) 20 A6
la Neuville-Bosmont (02) 22 D2
Neuville-Bourjonval (62) 8 C4
la Neuville-Chant-d'Oisel (76) 18 D5
Neuville-Coppegueule (80) 6 D6
Neuville-Day (08) 24 A4
Neuville-de-Poitou (86) 94 B6
la Neuville-du-Bosc (27) 18 B6
Neuville-en-Avesnois (59) 9 G3
Neuville-en-Beaumont (50) 12 C4
la Neuville-en-Beine (02) 21 H2
Neuville-en-Ferrain (59) 3 G4
la Neuville-en-Hez (60) 20 C5
la Neuville-en-Tourne-à-Fuy (08) 23 G5
Neuville-en-Verdunois (55) 47 F3
la Neuville-Ferrières (76) 19 F2
la Neuville-Garnier (60) 20 A5

la Neuville-Housset (02) 22 C1
la Neuville-lès-Bray (80) 8 B5
Neuville-les-Dames (01) 116 C5
la Neuville-lès-Decize (58) 99 E5
la Neuville-lès-Dorengt (02) 9 G5
Neuville-lès-Lœuilly (80) 20 B1
Neuville-lès-This (08) 24 A1
la Neuville-lès-Vaucouleurs (55) 47 H6
la Neuville-lès-Wasigny (08) 23 G2
Neuville-lez-Beaulieu (08) 10 C6
La Neuville-Roy (60) 20 D4
Neuville-Saint-Amand (02) 22 A1
la Neuville-Saint-Pierre (60) 20 B3
Neuville-Saint-Rémy (59) 8 D3
Neuville-Saint-Vaast (62) 8 B2
la Neuville-Sire-Bernard (80) 20 D1
Neuville-sous-Montreuil (62) 1 G6
Neuville-sur-Ailette (02) 22 C4
Neuville-sur-Ain (01) 117 F6
Neuville-sur-Authou (27) 15 H4
Neuville-sur-Brenne (37) 79 F3
Neuville-sur-Escaut (59) 9 E2
Neuville-sur-Essonne (45) 63 G4
Neuville-sur-Margival (02) 22 B4
Neuville-sur-Oise (95) 42 B2
Neuville-sur-Ornain (55) 46 D4
la Neuville-sur-Oudeuil (60) 20 A3
la Neuville-sur-Ressons (60) 21 E3
Neuville-sur-Saône (69) 130 A2
Neuville-sur-Sarthe (72) 60 A5
Neuville-sur-Seine (10) 66 D3
Neuville-sur-Touques (61) 39 G3
Neuville-sur-Vanne (10) 65 H3
la Neuville-Vault (60) 20 A4
Neuville-Vitasse (62) 8 B3
Neuviller-lès-Badonviller (54) 49 H6
Neuviller-sur-Moselle (54) 69 G1
Neuvillers-sur-Fave (88) 70 D3
Neuvillette (02) 9 F6
Neuvillette (80) 7 G3
Neuvillette-en-Charnie (72) 59 G5
Neuvilley (39) 102 D4
Neuvilly (59) 9 F4
Neuvilly-en-Argonne (55) 46 D1
Neuvireuil (62) 8 C2
Neuvizy (08) 23 H2
Neuvy (03) 113 H2
Neuvy (41) 80 B4
Neuvy (51) 44 C5
Neuvy-au-Houlme (61) 38 D4
Neuvy-Bouin (79) 93 E6
Neuvy-Deux-Clochers (18) 98 B1
Neuvy-en-Beauce (28) 62 D3
Neuvy-en-Champagne (72) 59 H5
Neuvy-en-Dunois (28) 62 B4
Neuvy-en-Sullias (45) 81 F2
Neuvy-Grandchamp (71) 114 B1
Neuvy-le-Barrois (18) 98 D5
Neuvy-le-Roi (37) 78 D3
Neuvy-Pailloux (36) 96 D4
Neuvy-Saint-Sépulchre (36) 111 F1
Neuvy-Sautour (89) 65 H5
Neuvy-sur-Barangeon (18) 81 F6
Neuvy-sur-Loire (58) 82 B4
Neuwiller (68) 89 G4
Neuwiller-lès-Saverne (67) 50 C3
Névache (05) 147 E4
Nevers (58) 98 D3
Névez (29) 53 H4
Névian (11) 188 A3
Néville (76) 17 E3
Nevoy (45) 81 H3
Nevy-lès-Dole (39) 102 C3
Nevy-sur-Seille (39) 102 D5
Nexon (87) 124 A4
Ney (39) 103 F5
Neydens (74) 118 B5
les Neyrolles (01) 117 G5
Neyron (01) 130 B2
Nézel (78) 42 A3
Nézignan-l'Évêque (34) 188 D1
Niafles (53) 76 B1
Niaux (09) 199 E1
Nibas (80) 6 C4
Nibelle (45) 63 G6
Nibles (04) 160 B5
Nice (06) 179 E4
Nicey (21) 84 C1
Nicey-sur-Aire (55) 47 F3
Nicole (47) 150 D4
Nicorps (50) 37 E1
Niderhoff (57) 50 A5
Niderviller (57) 50 A4
Niederbronn-les-Bains (67) 50 D2
Niederentzen (68) 71 F5
Niederhaslach (67) 50 C6
Niederhausbergen (67) 51 E5
Niederhergheim (68) 71 F5
Niederlauterbach (67) 51 G2
Niedermodern (67) 50 D3
Niedermorschwihr (68) 71 F4
Niedernai (67) 71 G1
Niederrœdern (67) 51 G2
Niederschaeffolsheim (67) 51 E4
Niedersoultzbach (67) 50 C3
Niedersteinbach (67) 28 D6

Niederstinzel (57) 50 A3
Niedervisse (57) 27 E5
Nielles-lès-Ardres (62) 1 H3
Nielles-lès-Bléquin (62) 1 H4
Nielles-lès-Calais (62) 1 G2
Nieppe (59) 3 E4
Niergnies (59) 9 E4
Nieudan (15) 139 H4
Nieuil (16) 123 E2
Nieuil-l'Espoir (86) 109 F2
Nieul (87) 124 A1
Nieul-le-Dolent (85) 91 F5
Nieul-le-Virouil (17) 121 F6
Nieul-lès-Saintes (17) 121 E3
Nieul-sur-l'Autise (85) 107 F2
Nieul-sur-Mer (17) 106 C4
Nieul-sur-Seudre (17) 120 C2
Nieurlet (59) 2 B3
Niévroz (01) 130 C2
Niffer (68) 89 G2
Niherne (36) 96 B5
Nilvange (57) 26 B3
Nîmes (30) 174 B3
Ninville (52) 68 B5
Niort (79) 107 H3
Niort-de-Sault (11) 199 H1
Niozelles (04) 176 D2
Nissan-lez-Enserune (34) 188 B2
Nistos (65) 183 H5
Nitry (89) 83 H3
Nitting (57) 50 A5
Nivelle (59) 4 B6
Nivigne et Suran (01) 117 F4
Nivillac (56) 73 G2
Nivillers (60) 20 B4
Nizas (32) 166 D4
Nizas (34) 172 C6
Nizerolles (03) 114 B6
Nizy-le-Comte (02) 23 E3
la Nocle-Maulaix (58) 99 H5
Nocario (2B) 205 G1
Noceta (2B) 205 F3
Nochize (71) 115 F3
Noé (31) 185 E2
Noé (89) 65 E4
Noé-les-Mallets (10) 67 E5
la Noë-Poulain (27) 15 H4
Noël-Cerneux (25) 104 C2
les Noës (42) 114 D6
les Noës-près-Troyes (10) 66 B3
Nœux-lès-Auxi (62) 7 F3
Nœux-les-Mines (62) 2 D6
Nogaret (31) 170 A6
Nogaro (32) 166 D4
Nogent (52) 68 B5
Nogent-en-Othe (10) 65 H4
Nogent-l'Abbesse (51) 23 F6
Nogent-l'Artaud (02) 44 B3
Nogent-le-Bernard (72) 60 C3
Nogent-le-Phaye (28) 62 B2
Nogent-le-Roi (28) 41 G6
Nogent-le-Rotrou (28) 61 E3
Nogent-le-Sec (27) 40 C3
Nogent-lès-Montbard (21) 84 D4
Nogent-sur-Aube (10) 66 C1
Nogent-sur-Eure (28) 62 A2
Nogent-sur-Loir (72) 78 C3
Nogent-sur-Marne (94) 43 E4
Nogent-sur-Oise (60) 20 D6
Nogent-sur-Seine (10) 65 F1
Nogent-sur-Vernisson (45) 82 A1
Nogentel (02) 44 B2
Nogna (39) 117 G1
Noguères (64) 182 A1
Nohanent (63) 127 E3
Nohant-en-Goût (18) 98 A2
Nohant-en-Graçay (18) 96 D2
Nohant-Vic (36) 111 G1
Nohèdes (66) 200 B3
Nohic (82) 169 F3
Noidan (21) 84 D6
Noidans-le-Ferroux (70) 87 F4
Noidans-lès-Vesoul (70) 87 G4
Noidant-Chatenoy (52) 86 B2
Noidant-le-Rocheux (52) 86 A1
Noilhan (32) 168 B6
Nointel (60) 20 D5
Nointel (95) 42 C1
Nointot (76) 15 H1
Noircourt (02) 23 F2
Noirefontaine (25) 88 C5
Noirémont (60) 20 B3
Noirétable (42) 128 B3
Noirlieu (51) 46 C3
Noirmoutier-en-l'Île (85) 90 B1
Noiron (70) 86 D5
Noiron-sous-Gevrey (21) 102 A1
Noiron-sur-Bèze (21) 86 B5
Noiron-sur-Seine (21) 66 D6
Noironte (25) 87 E6

Noirval (08) 24 B4
Noiseau (94) 43 E4
Noisiel (77) 43 E4
Noisseville (57) 26 C5
Noisy-le-Grand (93) 43 E4
Noisy-le-Roi (78) 42 B4
Noisy-le-Sec (93) 43 E4
Noisy-Rudignon (77) 64 C3
Noisy-sur-École (77) 63 H2
Noisy-sur-Oise (95) 42 D1
Noizay (37) 79 F5
Nojeon-en-Vexin (27) 19 F5
Nolay (21) 101 F4
Nolay (58) 99 E2
Nolléval (76) 19 F4
Nollieux (42) 128 D3
Nomain (59) 9 E2
Nomdieu (47) 167 G1
Nomécourt (52) 67 H2
Nomeny (54) 48 D3
Nomexy (88) 69 H3
Nommay (25) 88 C4
Nompatelize (88) 70 C2
Nonac (16) 122 B6
Nonancourt (27) 41 E4
Nonant (14) 14 A4
Nonant-le-Pin (61) 39 F5
Nonards (19) 139 E4
Noncourt-sur-le-Rongeant (52) 68 A2
Nonette-Orsonnette (63) 127 G6
Nonglard (74) 132 A1
Nonhigny (54) 49 H6
Nonières (07) 143 G5
Nonsard-Lamarche (55) 48 A3
Nontron (24) 123 F5
Nonville (77) 64 B3
Nonville (88) 69 F5
Nonvilliers-Grandhoux (28) 61 G3
Nonza (2B) 203 F3
Nonzeville (88) 70 B3
Noordpeene (59) 2 B3
Nordausques (62) 2 A3
Nordheim (67) 50 D5
Nordhouse (67) 71 H1
Noreuil (62) 8 C3
Norges-la-Ville (21) 85 H5
Normandel (61) 40 B5
Normanville (27) 40 D2
Normanville (76) 16 D4
Normier (21) 84 D6
Norolles (14) 15 F4
Noron-la-Poterie (14) 13 H6
Noron-l'Abbaye (14) 38 D3
Noroy (60) 20 D4
Noroy-le-Bourg (70) 87 H3
Noroy-le-Veneur (57) 26 B5
Noroy-sur-Ourcq (02) 21 H6
Norrent-Fontes (62) 2 B5
Norrey-en-Auge (14) 39 E3
Norrois (51) 46 B5
Norroy (88) 69 E3
Norroy-le-Sec (54) 25 H5
Norroy-le-Veneur (57) 26 B5
Norroy-lès-Pont-à-Mousson (54) 48 B3
Nort-Leulinghem (62) 2 A3
Nort-sur-Erdre (44) 74 D3
Nortkerque (62) 1 H3
Norville (76) 18 A4
la Norville (91) 42 C6
Nossage-et-Bénévent (05) 159 H4
Nossoncourt (88) 70 B2
Nostang (56) 54 D5
Noth (23) 111 E4
Nothalten (67) 71 F2
Notre-Dame-d'Aliermont (76) 6 A6
Notre-Dame-de-Bellecombe (73) 132 D2
Notre-Dame-de-Bliquetuit (76) 18 A4
Notre-Dame-de-Boisset (42) 128 D1
Notre-Dame-de-Bondeville (76) 18 C4
Notre-Dame-de-Cenilly (50) 37 F2
Notre-Dame-de-Commiers (38) 145 G4
Notre-Dame-de-la-Rouvière (30) 173 E1
Notre-Dame-de-Livaye (14) 15 E5
Notre-Dame-de-Livoye (50) 37 F4
Notre-Dame-de-Londres (34) 173 F3
Notre-Dame-de-l'Isle (27) 41 F1
Notre-Dame-de-l'Osier (38) 145 E2
Notre-Dame-de-Mésage (38) 145 G3
Notre-Dame-de-Monts (85) 90 C2
Notre-Dame-de-Riez (85) 90 D3
Notre-Dame-d'Épine (27) 15 H4
Notre-Dame-des-Landes (44) 74 C3
Notre-Dame-des-Millières (73) 132 C4
Notre-Dame-d'Estrées-Corbon (14) 15 E5
Notre-Dame-d'Oé (37) 78 D5
Notre-Dame-du-Bec (76) 15 F1
Notre-Dame-du-Cruet (73) 132 C6
Notre-Dame-du-Hamel (27) 39 H3
Notre-Dame-du-Parc (76) 17 G3
Notre-Dame-du-Pé (72) 77 F2

Notre-Dame-du-Pré (73) 133 E5
Nottonville (28) 62 B5
la Nouaille (23) 125 G2
Nouaillé-Maupertuis (86) 109 E2
Nouainville (50) 12 C2
Nouan-le-Fuzelier (41) 81 E4
Nouans (72) 60 B3
Nouans-les-Fontaines (37) 96 A2
Nouart (08) 24 C4
Nouâtre (37) 94 D3
la Nouaye (35) 56 D2
la Noue (51) 44 D5
Noueilles (31) 185 G1
Noues de Sienne (14) 37 G3
Nougaroulet (32) 168 A4
Nouhant (23) 112 B4
Nouic (87) 110 A6
Nouilhan (65) 183 F1
les Nouillers (17) 121 E1
Nouillonpont (55) 25 G5
Nouilly (57) 26 C5
Noulens (32) 167 E3
Nourard-le-Franc (60) 20 C4
Nourray (41) 79 G2
Nousse (40) 165 F4
Nousseviller-lès-Bitche (57) 28 B5
Nousseviller-Saint-Nabor (57) 27 G5
Nousty (64) 182 C2
Nouvelle-Église (62) 1 H2
Nouvion (80) 6 D3
le Nouvion-en-Thiérache (02) 9 H5
Nouvion-et-Catillon (02) 22 B2
Nouvion-le-Comte (02) 22 B2
Nouvion-le-Vineux (02) 22 C4
Nouvion-sur-Meuse (08) 24 B2
Nouvoitou (35) 57 F3
Nouvron-Vingré (02) 21 H4
Nouzerines (23) 111 H3
Nouzerolles (23) 111 F3
Nouziers (23) 111 G3
Nouzilly (37) 79 E4
Nouzonville (08) 24 B1
Novacelles (63) 128 A6
Novalaise (73) 131 G4
Novale (2B) 205 G2
Novéant-sur-Moselle (57) 48 B2
Novel (74) 119 G3
Novella (2B) 203 E5
Noves (13) 175 E3
Noviant-aux-Prés (54) 48 B4
Novillard (90) 88 D3
Novillars (25) 87 G6
Novillers (60) 20 B6
Novion-Porcien (08) 23 G3
Novy-Chevrières (08) 23 H3
Noyal (22) 34 A5
Noyal-Châtillon-sur-Seiche (35) 57 F3
Noyal-Muzillac (56) 73 F1
Noyal-Pontivy (56) 55 F3
Noyal-sous-Bazouges (35) 35 F6
Noyal-sur-Brutz (44) 57 G6
Noyal-sur-Vilaine (35) 57 G3
Noyales (02) 9 F6
Noyant-d'Allier (03) 113 G2
Noyant-de-Touraine (37) 94 D2
Noyant-et-Aconin (02) 22 A5
Noyant-Villages (49) 78 A3
Noyarey (38) 145 F2
Noyelle-Vion (62) 7 H2
Noyelles-en-Chaussée (80) 7 E3
Noyelles-Godault (62) 8 C1
Noyelles-lès-Humières (62) 7 F1
Noyelles-lès-Seclin (59) 3 F5
Noyelles-lès-Vermelles (62) 2 D6
Noyelles-sous-Bellonne (62) 8 C2
Noyelles-sous-Lens (62) 8 B1
Noyelles-sur-Escaut (59) 8 D4
Noyelles-sur-Mer (80) 6 C3
Noyelles-sur-Sambre (59) 9 H3
Noyelles-sur-Selle (59) 9 E2
Noyellette (62) 8 A2
Noyen-sur-Sarthe (72) 77 G1
Noyen-sur-Seine (77) 65 E1
le Noyer (05) 160 B1
le Noyer (18) 82 A6
le Noyer (73) 132 A3
le Noyer-en-Ouche (27) 40 B2
Noyers (27) 19 G6
Noyers (45) 81 H1
Noyers (52) 68 C5
Noyers (89) 84 A3
Noyers-Auzécourt (55) 46 D3
Noyers-Pont-Maugis (08) 24 C2
Noyers-Saint-Martin (60) 20 C3
Noyers-sur-Cher (41) 96 A1
Noyers-sur-Jabron (04) 160 A6
Noyon (60) 21 G3
Nozay (10) 66 B1
Nozay (44) 74 C2
Nozay (91) 42 C5
Nozeroy (39) 103 G6
Nozières (07) 143 G4
Nozières (18) 97 H6
Nuaillé (49) 75 H2
Nuaillé-d'Aunis (17) 107 E4
Nuaillé-sur-Boutonne (17) 107 H6
Nuars (58) 83 G6
Nubécourt (55) 47 E2
Nucourt (95) 42 A1
Nueil-les-Aubiers (79) 92 D3
Nueil-sous-Faye (86) 94 B3
Nuillé-le-Jalais (72) 60 C5

Nuillé-sur-Vicoin (53) 58 C5
Nuisement-sur-Coole (51) 45 H4
Nuits (89) 84 C2
Nuits-Saint-Georges (21) 101 H2
Nullemont (76) 19 G1
Nully (52) 67 F2
Nuncq-Hautecôte (62) 7 G2
Nuret-le-Ferron (36) 96 A6
Nurieux-Volognat (01) 117 F5
Nurlu (80) 8 C5
Nuzéjouls (46) 152 C3
Nyer (66) 200 B4
Nyons (26) 158 D4

O

Obenheim (67) 71 H2
Oberbronn (67) 50 D2
Oberbruck (68) 88 D1
Oberdorf-Spachbach (67) 51 E2
Oberdorff (57) 27 E4
Oberentzen (68) 71 F6
Obergailbach (57) 28 A5
Oberhaslach (67) 50 C6
Oberhausbergen (67) 51 E5
Oberhergheim (68) 71 F5
Oberhoffen-lès-Wissembourg (67) 51 F1
Oberhoffen-sur-Moder (67) 51 F4
Oberlarg (68) 89 F4
Oberlauterbach (67) 51 G2
Obermodern-Zutzendorf (67) 50 D3
Obermorschwihr (68) 71 F5
Obermorschwiller (68) 89 F3
Obernai (67) 71 G1
Oberrœdern (67) 51 F2
Obersaasheim (68) 71 G5
Oberschaeffolsheim (67) 50 D5
Obersoultzbach (67) 50 C3
Obersteinbach (67) 28 D6
Oberstinzel (57) 50 A4
Obervisse (57) 27 E5
Obies (59) 9 H2
Objat (19) 138 C2
Oblinghem (62) 2 D6
Obrechies (59) 10 A3
Obreck (57) 49 F3
Obsonville (77) 63 H4
Obterre (36) 95 G4
Obtrée (21) 85 E1
Ocana (2A) 204 D5
Occagnes (61) 39 E4
Occey (52) 86 A3
Occhiatana (2B) 202 D5
Occoches (80) 7 G3
Ochancourt (80) 6 C4
Oches (08) 24 C3
Ochey (54) 48 B6
Ochtezeele (59) 2 B3
Ocquerre (77) 43 H2
Ocqueville (76) 17 E3
Octeville-l'Avenel (50) 12 D3
Octeville-sur-Mer (76) 15 E1
Octon (34) 172 C5
Odars (31) 169 G6
Odenas (69) 116 A6
Oderen (68) 70 D6
Odomez (59) 9 F1
Odos (65) 183 E3
Odratzheim (67) 50 D5
Œlleville (88) 69 F2
Oermingen (67) 50 A2
Œting (57) 27 G5
Œuf-en-Ternois (62) 7 F2
Œuilly (02) 22 C5
Œuilly (51) 45 E2
Oeyregave (40) 165 E5
Oeyreluy (40) 165 E4
Offekerque (62) 1 H2
Offemont (90) 88 C3
Offendorf (67) 51 F4
Offignies (80) 19 H1
Offin (62) 7 E1
Offlanges (39) 102 D1
Offoy (60) 20 A2
Offoy (80) 21 G1
Offranville (76) 17 G2
Offrethun (62) 1 F3
Offroicourt (88) 69 F3
Offwiller (67) 50 D3
Ogenne-Camptort (64) 181 H2
Oger (51) 45 F3
Ogeu-les-Bains (64) 182 A3
Ogéviller (54) 49 G6
Ogliastro (2B) 203 F3
Ognes (02) 21 H3
Ognes (51) 45 E5
Ognes (60) 43 G2
Ognéville (54) 69 F1
Ognolles (60) 21 G2
Ognon (60) 21 E6
Ogy-Montoy-Flanville (57) 26 C5
Ohain (59) 10 B4
Oherville (76) 17 E3
Ohis (02) 10 A5
Ohlungen (67) 51 E3
Ohnenheim (67) 71 G3
Oigney (70) 87 E2
Oignies (62) 3 F6
Oigny (21) 85 F4
Oigny (41) 61 F5
Oigny-en-Valois (02) 21 H6
Oinville-Saint-Liphard (28) 62 D4
Oinville-sous-Auneau (28) 62 C2
Oinville-sur-Montcient (78) 42 A2
Oiron (79) 93 H3

Oiry (51) ... 45 F2
Oiselay-et-Grachaux (70) ... 87 E5
Oisemont (80) ... 6 D5
Oisilly (21) ... 86 B5
Oisly (41) ... 80 A5
Oison (45) ... 62 D4
Oisseau (53) ... 58 D2
Oisseau-le-Petit (72) ... 60 A2
Oissel (76) ... 18 C5
Oissery (77) ... 43 F2
Oissy (80) ... 7 E6
Oisy (02) ... 9 G5
Oisy (58) ... 83 F5
Oisy (59) ... 9 F2
Oisy-le-Verger (62) ... 8 D3
Oizé (72) ... 78 A1
Oizon (18) ... 81 H5
Olargues (34) ... 171 H6
Olby (63) ... 126 D3
Olcani (2B) ... 203 F3
Oléac-Debat (65) ... 183 F2
Oléac-Dessus (65) ... 183 F3
Olemps (12) ... 154 C4
Olendon (14) ... 38 D2
Oletta (2B) ... 203 F4
Olette (66) ... 200 B3
Olivese (2A) ... 207 E1
Olivet (45) ... 80 D1
Olivet (53) ... 58 C4
Olizy (51) ... 44 D1
Olizy-Primat (08) ... 24 B5
Olizy-sur-Chiers (55) ... 24 D3
Ollainville (88) ... 68 D3
Ollainville (91) ... 42 C6
Ollans (25) ... 87 G5
Ollé (28) ... 61 H2
Olley (54) ... 48 A1
Ollezy (02) ... 21 H2
Ollières (83) ... 192 D2
les Ollières-sur-
  Eyrieux (07) ... 143 H6
Olliergues (63) ... 128 A4
Ollioules (83) ... 193 E5
Olloix (63) ... 127 E4
les Olmes (69) ... 129 G2
Olmet (63) ... 128 A4
Olmet-et-Villecun (34) ... 172 B4
Olmeta-di-Capocorso (2B) ... 203 F3
Olmeta-di-Tuda (2B) ... 203 F5
Olmeto (2A) ... 206 D2
Olmi-Cappella (2B) ... 202 D5
Olmiccia (2A) ... 207 E2
Olmo (2B) ... 203 G6
Olonne-sur-Mer (85) ... 91 E5
Olonzac (34) ... 187 G3
Oloron-Sainte-Marie (64) ... 182 A3
Ols-et-Rinhodes (12) ... 153 G3
Oltingue (68) ... 89 G4
Olwisheim (67) ... 51 E4
Omblèze (26) ... 144 D5
Ombrée d'Anjou (49) ... 76 A2
Omécourt (60) ... 19 H3
Omelmont (54) ... 69 F1
les Omergues (04) ... 159 G6
Omerville (95) ... 41 H1
Omessa (2B) ... 205 E2
Omet (33) ... 149 H1
Omex (65) ... 182 D4
Omey (51) ... 46 A4
Omicourt (08) ... 24 B2
Omissy (02) ... 9 E6
Omméray (57) ... 49 F4
Ommoy (61) ... 39 E3
Omont (08) ... 24 B3
Omonville (76) ... 17 G3
Omps (15) ... 139 H5
Oms (66) ... 201 E3
Onans (25) ... 88 B4
Onard (40) ... 165 F3
Onay (70) ... 86 D5
Oncieu (01) ... 131 E1
Oncy-sur-École (91) ... 63 H2
Ondes (31) ... 169 E4
Ondres (40) ... 164 B5
Ondreville-sur-
  Essonne (45) ... 63 G4
Onesse-Laharie (40) ... 148 B6
Onet-le-Château (12) ... 154 C4
Oneux (80) ... 7 E4
Ongles (04) ... 176 C1
Onglières (39) ... 103 G5
Onjon (10) ... 66 C2
Onlay (58) ... 100 A4
Onnaing (59) ... 9 G1
Onnion (74) ... 119 E5
Onoz (39) ... 117 G2
Ons-en-Bray (60) ... 19 H4
Ontex (73) ... 131 G3
Onville (54) ... 48 B2
Oô (31) ... 197 E1
Oost-Cappel (59) ... 2 D1
Opio (06) ... 178 C4
Opoul-Périllos (66) ... 187 H6
Oppède (84) ... 175 G3
Oppedette (04) ... 176 B2
Oppenans (70) ... 87 H3
Oppy (62) ... 8 C2
Optevoz (38) ... 130 D3
Oraàs (64) ... 165 E6
Oradour (16) ... 122 A1
Oradour-Fanais (16) ... 109 H5
Oradour-Saint-Genest (87) ... 110 B4
Oradour-sur-Glane (87) ... 123 H1
Oradour-sur-Vayres (87) ... 123 G3
Orain (21) ... 86 B3
Orainville (02) ... 23 E5
Oraison (04) ... 176 D2
Orange (84) ... 158 A6

Orbagna (39) ... 117 F1
Orbais-l'Abbaye (51) ... 44 D3
Orban (81) ... 170 B3
Orbec (14) ... 39 H2
Orbeil (63) ... 127 G5
Orbessan (32) ... 167 H6
Orbey (68) ... 71 E4
Orbigny (37) ... 95 H1
Orbigny-au-Mont (52) ... 86 B1
Orbigny-au-Val (52) ... 86 B1
l'Orbrie (85) ... 107 F2
Orçay (41) ... 97 F1
Orcemont (78) ... 41 H6
Orcenais (18) ... 97 H6
Orcet (63) ... 127 F4
Orcevaux (52) ... 86 A2
Orchamps (39) ... 102 D2
Orchamps-Vennes (25) ... 104 B2
Orches (86) ... 94 B4
Orchies (59) ... 3 G6
Orcier (74) ... 119 E3
Orcières (05) ... 160 D1
Orcinas (26) ... 158 D2
Orcines (63) ... 127 E3
Orcival (63) ... 126 D4
Orconte (51) ... 46 C5
Ordan-Larroque (32) ... 167 G4
Ordiarp (64) ... 181 F3
Ordizan (65) ... 183 F4
Ordonnac (33) ... 134 D1
Ordonnaz (01) ... 131 F2
Ore (31) ... 184 A5
Orée d'Anjou (49) ... 75 E4
Orègue (64) ... 181 E1
Oreilla (66) ... 200 B3
Orelle (73) ... 146 D2
Oresmaux (80) ... 20 C1
Organ (65) ... 183 H2
Orgeans-
  Blanchefontaine (25) ... 88 C6
Orgedeuil (16) ... 123 E3
Orgeix (09) ... 199 G2
Orgelet (39) ... 117 G2
Orgères (35) ... 57 F4
Orgères (61) ... 39 G4
Orgères-en-Beauce (28) ... 62 C4
Orgerus (78) ... 41 H4
Orges (52) ... 67 G5
Orgeux (21) ... 86 A6
Orgeval (02) ... 22 C4
Orgeval (78) ... 42 B3
Orgibet (09) ... 184 C5
Orglandes (50) ... 12 D4
Orgnac-l'Aven (07) ... 157 G5
Orgnac-sur-Vézère (19) ... 138 C1
Orgon (13) ... 175 F3
Orgueil (82) ... 169 F3
Oricourt (70) ... 87 H3
Orieux (65) ... 183 G3
Orignac (65) ... 183 F4
Origne (33) ... 149 F3
Origné (53) ... 58 D6
Orignolles (17) ... 135 H2
Origny (21) ... 85 E3
Origny-en-Thiérache (02) ... 10 A6
Origny-le-Roux (61) ... 60 C2
Origny-le-Sec (10) ... 65 H2
Origny-Sainte-Benoite (02) ... 9 F6
Orin (64) ... 181 H2
Orincles (65) ... 183 E4
Oriocourt (57) ... 49 E3
Oriol-en-Royans (26) ... 144 D4
Oriolles (16) ... 121 H6
Orion (64) ... 181 G1
Oris-en-Rattier (38) ... 145 H5
Orist (40) ... 164 D4
Orival (16) ... 136 B1
Orival (76) ... 18 C5
Orléans (45) ... 80 D1
Orleix (65) ... 183 F2
Orliac (24) ... 152 A1
Orliac-de-Bar (19) ... 139 E1
Orliaguet (24) ... 138 B5
Orliénas (69) ... 129 H4
Orlu (09) ... 199 G2
Orly (94) ... 42 D5
Orly-sur-Morin (77) ... 44 A3
Ormancey (52) ... 86 A1
Ormenans (70) ... 87 G5
Ormersviller (57) ... 28 B5
Ormes (10) ... 66 B1
Ormes (27) ... 40 C2
Ormes (45) ... 62 D6
Ormes (51) ... 23 E6
Ormes (71) ... 116 C1
les Ormes (86) ... 94 D3
les Ormes (89) ... 83 E1
les Ormes-sur-Voulzie (77) ... 64 D2
Ormesson (77) ... 64 A4
Ormesson-sur-Marne (94) ... 43 E4
Ormoiche (70) ... 87 H1
Ormoy (28) ... 41 F6
Ormoy (70) ... 87 F1
Ormoy (89) ... 65 F6
Ormoy (91) ... 42 D6
Ormoy-la-Rivière (91) ... 63 F2
Ormoy-le-Davien (60) ... 43 G1
Ormoy-lès-
  Sexfontaines (52) ... 67 H4
Ormoy-Villers (60) ... 43 G1
Ornacieux (38) ... 130 D6
Ornaisons (11) ... 187 H3
Ornans (25) ... 103 G2
Ornes (55) ... 25 F6
Ornex (01) ... 118 B4
Ornézan (32) ... 167 H6

Orniac (46) ... 153 E3
Ornolac-Ussat-les-
  Bains (09) ... 199 E1
Ornon (38) ... 146 A3
Orny (57) ... 48 D2
Oroër (60) ... 20 B4
Oroix (65) ... 183 E2
Oron (57) ... 49 E3
Oroux (79) ... 93 G6
Orphin (78) ... 41 H6
Orpierre (05) ... 159 H4
Orquevaux (52) ... 68 B3
les Orres (05) ... 161 E2
Orret (21) ... 85 F4
Orriule (64) ... 181 G1
Orrouer (28) ... 61 H2
Orrouy (60) ... 21 F6
Orry-la-Ville (60) ... 43 E1
Ors (59) ... 9 G4
Orsan (30) ... 158 A6
Orsanco (64) ... 181 E2
Orsans (11) ... 186 B4
Orsans (25) ... 104 A1
Orsay (91) ... 42 C5
Orschwihr (68) ... 71 E6
Orschwiller (67) ... 71 F3
Orsennes (36) ... 111 F2
Orsinval (59) ... 9 G2
Ortaffa (66) ... 201 F3
Ortale (2B) ... 205 G2
Orthevielle (40) ... 164 D5
Orthez (64) ... 165 G6
Orthoux-Sérignac-
  Quilhan (30) ... 173 G3
Ortillon (10) ... 66 C1
Ortiporio (2B) ... 203 F6
Orto (2A) ... 204 D3
Ortoncourt (88) ... 70 A2
Orus (09) ... 198 D1
Orval (18) ... 97 H6
Orval sur Sienne (50) ... 36 D2
Orvault (44) ... 74 C4
Orvaux (27) ... 40 D3
Orve (25) ... 88 B6
Orveau (91) ... 63 F2
Orville (21) ... 86 A4
Orville (36) ... 96 D2
Orville (45) ... 63 G4
Orville (62) ... 7 G4
Orvillers-Sorel (60) ... 21 E3
Orvilliers (78) ... 41 G4
Orvilliers-Saint-Julien (10) ... 65 H2
Orx (40) ... 164 C5
Os-Marsillon (64) ... 182 A1
Osani (2A) ... 204 B2
Osches (55) ... 47 E2
Osenbach (68) ... 71 E5
Oslon (71) ... 101 H5
Osly-Courtil (02) ... 21 H5
Osmanville (14) ... 13 F5
Osmery (18) ... 98 A4
Osmets (65) ... 183 F2
Osmoy (18) ... 97 H3
Osmoy (78) ... 41 H4
Osmoy-Saint-Valery (76) ... 19 E1
Osne-le-Val (52) ... 68 A1
Osnes (08) ... 24 D2
Osny (95) ... 42 B2
Ossages (40) ... 165 F5
Ossas-Suhare (64) ... 181 G3
Osse (25) ... 87 G6
Osse-en-Aspe (64) ... 181 H5
Osséja (66) ... 199 H5
Osselle-Routelle (25) ... 103 E2
Ossen (65) ... 182 D4
Ossenx (64) ... 181 G1
Osserain-Rivareyte (64) ... 181 F1
Ossès (64) ... 180 D2
Ossey-les-Trois-
  Maisons (10) ... 65 G2
Ossun (65) ... 183 E3
Ossun-Ez-Angles (65) ... 183 E4
Ostabat-Asme (64) ... 181 E2
Ostel (02) ... 22 B4
Ostheim (68) ... 71 F4
Osthoffen (67) ... 50 D5
Osthouse (67) ... 71 H1
Ostreville (62) ... 7 G1
Ostricourt (59) ... 8 C1
Ostwald (67) ... 51 E6
Ota (2A) ... 204 C3
Othe (54) ... 25 F3
Othis (77) ... 43 F2
Ottange (57) ... 26 A2
Ottersthal (67) ... 50 C4
Otterswiller (67) ... 50 C4
Ottmarsheim (68) ... 89 G1
Ottonville (57) ... 26 D4
Ottrott (67) ... 71 F1
Ottwiller (67) ... 50 B3
Ouagne (58) ... 83 F5
Ouainville (76) ... 16 D3
Ouanne (89) ... 83 F3
Ouarville (28) ... 62 C3
Ouchamps (41) ... 79 H5
Ouches (42) ... 128 C1
Oucques La Nouvelle (41) ... 79 H2
Oudalle (76) ... 15 F2
Oudan (58) ... 83 E6
Oudeuil (60) ... 20 A3
Oudezeele (59) ... 2 C3
Oudincourt (52) ... 67 H4
Oudon (44) ... 75 E4
Oudrenne (57) ... 26 C3
Oudry (71) ... 115 F1
Oueilloux (65) ... 183 F3
Ouerre (28) ... 41 F5

Ouessant (29) ... 30 A4
Ouézy (14) ... 14 D5
Ouffières (14) ... 38 B2
Ouge (70) ... 86 D2
Ouges (21) ... 102 A1
Ougney (39) ... 102 D1
Ougney-Douvot (25) ... 87 G6
Ougny (58) ... 99 H3
Ouhans (25) ... 103 H3
Ouides (43) ... 142 B5
Ouillon (64) ... 182 C2
Ouilly-du-Houley (14) ... 15 G5
Ouilly-le-Tesson (14) ... 38 D2
Ouilly-le-Vicomte (14) ... 15 F5
Ouistreham (14) ... 14 C4
Oulches (36) ... 110 C1
Oulches-la-Vallée-
  Foulon (02) ... 22 D4
Oulchy-la-Ville (02) ... 22 A6
Oulchy-le-Château (02) ... 22 A6
Oulins (28) ... 41 F4
Oulles (38) ... 146 A3
Oullins (69) ... 130 A3
Oulmes (85) ... 107 F2
Oulon (58) ... 99 F2
Ounans (39) ... 102 D3
Oupia (34) ... 187 H2
Our (39) ... 102 D2
Ourches (26) ... 144 C6
Ourches-sur-Meuse (55) ... 47 H5
Ourde (65) ... 183 H5
Ourdis-Cotdoussan (65) ... 183 E4
Ourdon (65) ... 183 E4
Ourouer-les-
  Bourdelins (18) ... 98 B4
Ouroux (69) ... 115 H4
Ouroux-en-Morvan (58) ... 100 A2
Ouroux-sous-le-Bois-
  Sainte-Marie (71) ... 115 G3
Ouroux-sur-Saône (71) ... 101 H6
Oursbelille (65) ... 183 E2
Oursel-Maison (60) ... 20 B3
Ourton (62) ... 7 H1
Ourville-en-Caux (76) ... 16 D3
Ousse (64) ... 182 C2
Ousse-Suzan (40) ... 165 G2
Oussières (39) ... 102 D4
Ousson-sur-Loire (45) ... 82 B4
Oussoy-en-Gâtinais (45) ... 82 A1
Oust (09) ... 185 G6
Oust-Marest (80) ... 6 B4
Ousté (65) ... 183 E4
Outarville (45) ... 63 E4
Outines (51) ... 67 E1
Outreau (62) ... 1 F4
Outrebois (80) ... 7 G3
Outremécourt (52) ... 68 D3
Outrepont (51) ... 46 B4
Outriaz (01) ... 117 G6
Ouvans (25) ... 88 A6
Ouve-Wirquin (62) ... 2 A5
Ouveillan (11) ... 188 A2
Ouville (50) ... 37 E2
Ouville-la-Rivière (76) ... 17 F2
Ouville-l'Abbaye (76) ... 17 F4
Ouvrouer-les-Champs (45) ... 81 F2
Ouzilly (86) ... 94 C5
Ouzouer-des-Champs (45) ... 82 A1
Ouzouer-le-Doyen (41) ... 62 A6
Ouzouer-sous-
  Bellegarde (45) ... 63 G6
Ouzouer-sur-Loire (45) ... 81 H2
Ouzouer-sur-Trézée (45) ... 82 B3
Ouzous (65) ... 182 D4
Ovanches (70) ... 87 F3
Ovillers-la-Boisselle (80) ... 8 A5
Oxelaëre (59) ... 2 C3
Oyé (71) ... 115 F4
Oye-et-Pallet (25) ... 104 A4
Oye-Plage (62) ... 1 H2
Oyes (51) ... 45 E4
Oyeu (38) ... 131 E6
Oyonnax (01) ... 117 G4
Oyré (86) ... 94 D4
Oyrières (70) ... 86 C4
Oysonville (28) ... 62 D2
Oytier-Saint-Oblas (38) ... 130 B5
Oz (38) ... 146 A3
Ozan (01) ... 116 C3
Oze (05) ... 159 H3
Ozenay (71) ... 116 B2
Ozenx-Montestrucq (64) ... 165 G6
Ozerailles (54) ... 25 H6
Ozeville (50) ... 13 E3
Ozières (52) ... 68 B4
Ozillac (17) ... 121 G6
Ozoir-la-Ferrière (77) ... 43 F5
Ozolles (71) ... 115 G3
Ozon (07) ... 144 A3
Ozon (65) ... 183 F3
Ozouer-le-Voulgis (77) ... 43 F6
Ozourt (40) ... 165 F4

P

Paars (02) ... 22 C5
Pabu (22) ... 33 E3
la Pacaudière (42) ... 114 D6
Pacé (35) ... 57 E2
Pacé (61) ... 59 H1
Pact (38) ... 144 B1
Pacy-sur-Armançon (89) ... 84 B2
Pacy-sur-Eure (27) ... 41 E2
Padern (11) ... 187 G6
Padiès (81) ... 170 D1
Padirac (46) ... 139 E6
Padoux (88) ... 70 A3

Pageas (87) ... 123 H4
Pagney (39) ... 103 E1
Pagney-derrière-
  Barine (54) ... 48 A5
Pagnoz (39) ... 103 E3
Pagny-la-Blanche-Côte (55) ... 48 A6
Pagny-la-Ville (21) ... 102 A3
Pagny-le-Château (21) ... 102 A3
Pagny-lès-Goin (57) ... 48 D2
Pagny-sur-Meuse (55) ... 48 A5
Pagny-sur-Moselle (54) ... 48 B2
Pagolle (64) ... 181 F2
Pailhac (65) ... 183 G6
Pailharès (07) ... 143 G3
Pailherols (15) ... 140 C5
Pailhès (09) ... 185 F4
Pailhès (34) ... 188 C1
Paillart (60) ... 20 C2
Paillé (17) ... 107 H6
Paillencourt (59) ... 9 E3
Paillet (33) ... 149 G1
Pailloles (47) ... 151 F3
le Pailly (52) ... 86 B2
Pailly (89) ... 65 E3
Paimbœuf (44) ... 73 H4
Paimpol (22) ... 33 F2
Paimpont (35) ... 56 C3
Painblanc (21) ... 101 F2
Pair-et-Grandrupt (88) ... 70 D3
Paissy (02) ... 22 C4
Paisy-Cosdon (10) ... 65 G4
Paizay-le-Chapt (79) ... 108 B5
Paizay-le-Sec (86) ... 109 H1
Paizay-le-Tort (79) ... 108 B5
Paizay-Naudouin-
  Embourie (16) ... 108 C6
Pajay (38) ... 144 C1
Palairac (11) ... 187 G5
le Palais (56) ... 72 B3
le Palais-sur-Vienne (87) ... 124 B2
Palaiseau (91) ... 42 C5
Palaiseul (52) ... 86 B2
Palaja (11) ... 187 E3
Palaminy (31) ... 184 D3
Palante (70) ... 88 B3
Palantine (25) ... 103 F2
Palasca (2B) ... 202 D5
Palau-de-Cerdagne (66) ... 199 G5
Palau-del-Vidre (66) ... 201 F3
Palavas-les-Flots (34) ... 173 G6
Palazinges (19) ... 138 D3
Paley (77) ... 64 B4
Palhers (48) ... 155 H3
Palinges (71) ... 115 F2
Palise (25) ... 87 F5
Palisse (19) ... 125 H6
Palladuc (63) ... 128 A2
Pallanne (32) ... 167 F6
Palleau (71) ... 101 H4
Pallegney (88) ... 69 H3
le Pallet (44) ... 75 E6
Palleville (81) ... 170 B6
la Pallu (53) ... 59 F1
Palluau (85) ... 91 F3
Palluau-sur-Indre (36) ... 96 A4
Palluaud (16) ... 136 C1
Pallud (73) ... 132 C3
Palluel (62) ... 8 D2
Palmas d'Aveyron (12) ... 155 E4
la Palme (11) ... 188 A5
Palneca (2B) ... 205 F5
Palogneux (42) ... 128 C3
la Palud-sur-Verdon (04) ... 177 G3
Paluel (76) ... 16 D2
Pamfou (77) ... 64 B2
Pamiers (09) ... 185 H4
Pampelonne (81) ... 154 A6
Pamplie (79) ... 107 H1
Pamproux (79) ... 108 C3
Panassac (32) ... 184 A1
Panazol (87) ... 124 B2
Pancé (35) ... 57 F5
Pancheraccia (2B) ... 205 G3
Pancy-Courtecon (02) ... 22 C4
Pandrignes (19) ... 139 E2
Pange (57) ... 26 D5
Panges (21) ... 85 F6
Panilleuse (27) ... 41 G2
Panissage (38) ... 131 E5
Panissières (42) ... 129 F3
Panjas (32) ... 166 D3
Pannecé (44) ... 75 F3
Pannecières (45) ... 63 F3
Pannes (45) ... 64 A6
Pannes (54) ... 48 A3
Pannessières (39) ... 102 D6
Panon (72) ... 60 B2
Panossas (38) ... 130 C4
la Panouse (48) ... 156 B1
Pansey (52) ... 68 A1
Pantin (93) ... 42 D3
Panzoult (37) ... 94 C2
Papleux (02) ... 9 H5
Paradou (13) ... 174 D4
Parassy (18) ... 97 H1
Parata (2B) ... 205 G1
Paray-Douaville (78) ... 62 D2
Paray-le-Frésil (03) ... 114 B1
Paray-le-Monial (71) ... 115 E3
Paray-sous-Brailles (03) ... 114 A4
Paray-Vieille-Poste (91) ... 42 D5
Paraza (11) ... 187 H3
Parbayse (64) ... 182 A2
le Parc (50) ... 37 E4
Parc-d'Anxtot (76) ... 15 G1
Parçay-Meslay (37) ... 79 E5
Parçay-sur-Vienne (37) ... 94 C2
Parcé (35) ... 58 A3
Parcé-sur-Sarthe (72) ... 77 G1

Parcey (39) ... 102 C3
Parcieux (01) ... 130 A2
Parcoul-Chenaud (24) ... 136 B2
le Parcq (62) ... 7 F1
Parcy-et-Tigny (02) ... 22 A6
Pardailhan (34) ... 187 H1
Pardaillan (47) ... 150 D1
Pardies (64) ... 182 A1
Pardies-Piétat (64) ... 182 C3
Pardines (63) ... 127 F5
Paréac (65) ... 183 E4
Pareid (55) ... 47 H1
Parempuyre (33) ... 135 E4
Parennes (72) ... 59 G4
Parent (63) ... 127 F4
Parentignat (63) ... 127 G5
Parentis-en-Born (40) ... 148 B4
Parenty (62) ... 1 G5
Parey-Saint-Césaire (54) ... 48 C6
Parey-sous-Montfort (88) ... 69 E3
Parfondeval (02) ... 23 F1
Parfondeval (61) ... 60 D1
Parfondru (02) ... 22 C3
Parfondrupt (55) ... 47 H1
Parfouru-sur-Odon (14) ... 14 A5
Pargnan (02) ... 22 C5
Pargny (80) ... 21 G1
Pargny-Filain (02) ... 22 B4
Pargny-la-Dhuys (02) ... 44 C3
Pargny-les-Bois (02) ... 22 C2
Pargny-lès-Reims (51) ... 23 E6
Pargny-sous-Mureau (88) ... 68 C2
Pargny-sur-Saulx (51) ... 46 C4
Pargues (10) ... 66 C5
Parignargues (30) ... 174 A3
Parigné (35) ... 58 A1
Parigné-le-Pôlin (72) ... 78 A1
Parigné-l'Évêque (72) ... 60 B6
Parigné-sur-Braye (53) ... 58 D2
Parigny (42) ... 128 D1
Parigny-la-Rose (58) ... 83 F6
Parigny-les-Vaux (58) ... 98 D3
Paris (75) ... 42 D4
Paris-l'Hôpital (71) ... 101 F4
Parisot (81) ... 169 H4
Parisot (82) ... 153 F5
Parlan (15) ... 139 G6
Parleboscq (40) ... 166 D2
Parly (89) ... 83 E2
Parmain (95) ... 42 C1
Parmilieu (38) ... 130 D2
Parnac (36) ... 110 C2
Parnac (46) ... 152 C3
Parnans (26) ... 144 C3
Parnay (18) ... 98 A5
Parnay (49) ... 93 H1
Parné-sur-Roc (53) ... 58 D5
Parnes (60) ... 19 G6
Parnoy-en-Bassigny (52) ... 68 D3
les Paroches (55) ... 47 G3
Paron (89) ... 65 E4
Paroy (25) ... 103 F3
Paroy (77) ... 64 D1
Paroy-en-Othe (89) ... 65 F5
Paroy-sur-Saulx (52) ... 68 A1
Paroy-sur-Tholon (89) ... 65 E6
Parpeville (02) ... 22 B1
Parranquet (47) ... 151 G1
Parroy (54) ... 49 F5
Pars-lès-Chavanges (10) ... 66 D1
Pars-lès-Romilly (10) ... 65 G1
Parsac-Rimondeix (23) ... 112 A5
Parthenay (79) ... 93 F6
Parthenay-de-
  Bretagne (35) ... 57 E2
Partinello (2A) ... 204 B2
Parux (54) ... 49 H6
Parves et Nattages (01) ... 131 G3
Parville (27) ... 40 D2
Parvillers-le-Quesnoy (80) ... 21 E1
Parzac (16) ... 122 D1
le Pas (53) ... 58 D1
Pas-de-Jeu (79) ... 93 H3
Pas-en-Artois (62) ... 7 H3
le Pas-Saint-l'Homer (61) ... 61 F1
Pasilly (89) ... 84 B3
Paslières (63) ... 127 H2
Pasly (02) ... 22 A5
Pasques (21) ... 85 G6
le Pasquier (39) ... 103 F5
Passa (66) ... 201 E3
le Passage (38) ... 131 E5
le Passage (47) ... 151 F5
Passais Villages (61) ... 37 H6
le Passage (47) ... 151 F5
Passavant (25) ... 87 H6
Passavant-en-
  Argonne (51) ... 46 D2
Passavant-la-Rochère (70) ... 69 F6
Passavant-sur-Layon (49) ... 93 F2
Passel (60) ... 21 G3
Passenans (39) ... 102 D5
Passins (38) ... 131 E3
Passirac (16) ... 122 A6
Passonfontaine (25) ... 104 A2
Passy (71) ... 115 H2
Passy (74) ... 133 E1
Passy (89) ... 65 E5
Passy-en-Valois (02) ... 44 A1
Passy-Grigny (51) ... 44 D1
Passy-sur-Marne (02) ... 44 C2
Passy-sur-Seine (77) ... 65 E2
Pastricciola (2A) ... 204 D4
Patay (45) ... 62 C5
Patornay (39) ... 117 G1
Patrimonio (2B) ... 203 F4
Pau (64) ... 182 B2
Paucourt (45) ... 64 B5
Paudy (36) ... 96 D3
Pauilhac (32) ... 167 H3

Pauillac (33) ... 134 D2
Paule (22) ... 54 C1
Paulhac (15) ... 140 D4
Paulhac (31) ... 169 G4
Paulhac (43) ... 141 G1
Paulhac-en-Margeride (48)... 141 G5
Paulhaguet (43) ... 141 H2
Paulhan (34) ... 172 D6
Paulhe (12) ... 155 F6
Paulhenc (15) ... 140 D5
Pauligne (11) ... 186 D4
Paulin (24) ... 138 B4
Paulinet (81) ... 171 E3
Paulmy (37) ... 95 F3
Paulnay (36) ... 95 G5
Paulx (44) ... 91 E1
Paunat (24) ... 137 G5
Paussac-et-Saint-
   Vivien (24) ... 137 E1
Pauvres (08) ... 23 H4
Pavant (02) ... 44 B3
Pavezin (42) ... 129 H6
Pavie (2B) ... 167 H5
le Pavillon-Sainte-
   Julie (10) ... 66 A2
les Pavillons-sous-
   Bois (93) ... 43 E3
Pavilly (76) ... 18 C3
Payns (10) ... 66 A2
Payra-sur-l'Hers (11) ... 186 B3
Payrac (46) ... 138 C6
Payré (86) ... 108 D3
Payrignac (46) ... 138 B6
Payrin-Augmontel (81) ... 170 D6
Payros-Cazautets (40) ... 166 B5
Payroux (86) ... 109 F4
Pays de Belvès (24) ... 137 H6
Pays de Clerval (25) ... 88 A5
Payssous (31) ... 184 B5
Payzac (07) ... 157 E3
Payzac (24) ... 124 A6
Pazayac (24) ... 138 B3
Paziols (11) ... 187 G6
Pazy (58) ... 99 G1
le Péage-de-
   Roussillon (38) ... 144 A1
Péas (51) ... 45 E5
Peaugres (07) ... 143 H2
Péaule (56) ... 73 G1
Péault (85) ... 91 H6
Pébées (32) ... 184 D1
Pébrac (43) ... 141 H4
Pech (09) ... 199 F1
Pech-Luna (11) ... 186 A3
Péchabou (31) ... 169 F6
Pécharic-et-le-Py (11) ... 186 A3
Péchaudier (81) ... 170 A6
Pechbonnieu (31) ... 169 F4
Pechbusque (31) ... 169 F6
le Pêchereau (36) ... 111 E1
Les Pechs du Vers (46) ... 152 D2
Pécorade (40) ... 166 B4
le Pecq (78) ... 42 B3
Pecquencourt (59) ... 8 D1
Pecqueuse (91) ... 42 B6
Pécy (77) ... 43 H6
Pédernec (22) ... 32 D3
Pégairolles-de-Buèges (34) .. 172 D1
Pégairolles-de-
   l'Escalette (34) ... 172 C4
Pégomas (06) ... 178 C5
le Pègue (26) ... 158 C3
Péguilhan (31) ... 184 B2
Peigney (52) ... 86 B1
Peillac (56) ... 56 B6
Peille (06) ... 179 F3
Peillon (06) ... 179 F3
Peillonnex (74) ... 118 C3
Peintre (39) ... 102 C1
les Peintures (33) ... 136 A3
Peipin (04) ... 160 B6
Peisey-Nancroix (73) ... 133 F4
Pel-et-Der (10) ... 66 D2
Pélissanne (13) ... 175 G5
Pellafol (38) ... 145 H6
Pelleautier (05) ... 160 B2
Pellefigue (32) ... 168 A6
Pellegrue (33) ... 136 B6
Pelleport (31) ... 168 D4
Pellerey (21) ... 85 F4
le Pellerin (44) ... 74 B5
la Pellerine (49) ... 78 A5
la Pellerine (53) ... 58 B2
Pellevoisin (36) ... 96 A3
Pelonne (26) ... 159 F4
Pelouse (48) ... 156 B2
Pelousey (25) ... 87 E6
Peltre (57) ... 48 D1
Pélussin (42) ... 129 H6
Pelves (62) ... 8 C2
Penchard (77) ... 43 G3
Pencran (29) ... 31 F4
Pendé (80) ... 6 C3
Pénestin (56) ... 73 F2
Penguily (22) ... 34 A6
Penin (62) ... 7 H2
Penmarch (29) ... 53 E4
Pennautier (11) ... 187 E3
la Penne (06) ... 178 C2
Penne (81) ... 169 H1
Penne-d'Agenais (47) ... 151 G4
la Penne-sur-
   Huveaune (13) ... 192 B4
la Penne-sur-l'Ouvèze (26)... 159 E5
Pennedepie (14) ... 15 F3
Pennes-le-Sec (26) ... 159 E2
les Pennes-Mirabeau (13)... 192 A3

Pennesières (70) ... 87 F4
Penol (38) ... 130 C6
Pensol (87) ... 123 G4
Penta-Acquatella (2B)... 203 G6
Penta-di-Casinca (2B)... 203 G6
Penvénan (22) ... 32 D1
Péone (06) ... 162 A6
Pépieux (11) ... 187 G2
Pérassay (36) ... 112 A2
Peray (72) ... 60 C3
Perceneige (89) ... 65 E3
Percey (89) ... 65 H6
Percey-le-Grand (70) ... 86 B3
le Perchay (95) ... 42 A1
la Perche (18) ... 112 C1
Perche en Nocé (61) ... 61 E2
Perchède (32) ... 166 C3
Percy (38) ... 145 G6
Percy-en-Normandie (50) ... 37 F3
Perdreauville (78) ... 41 G3
Péré (17) ... 107 E5
Péré (65) ... 183 G4
Péreille (09) ... 186 A6
Perelli (2B) ... 205 G2
Pérenchies (59) ... 3 F5
Péret (34) ... 172 C6
Péret-Bel-Air (19) ... 125 G6
Péreyres (07) ... 143 E6
Pergain-Taillac (32) ... 167 H1
Peri (2A) ... 204 D5
le Périer (38) ... 146 A4
Périers (50) ... 12 D6
Périers-en-Auge (14) ... 14 C4
Périers-sur-le-Dan (14) ... 14 C4
Pérignac (16) ... 122 B5
Pérignac (17) ... 121 F4
Pérignat-lès-Sarliève (63)... 127 F3
Pérignat-sur-Allier (63)... 127 F3
Périgné (79) ... 108 A5
Périgneux (42) ... 129 E6
Périgny (03) ... 114 B4
Périgny (14) ... 38 B3
Périgny (17) ... 106 D5
Périgny (41) ... 79 G2
Périgny (94) ... 43 E5
Périgny-la-Rose (10) ... 65 G1
Périgueux (24) ... 137 F2
Périssac (33) ... 135 G4
Perles-et-Castelet (09) ... 199 F2
Pern (46) ... 152 C3
Pernand-Vergelesses (21)...101 G2
Pernant (02) ... 21 H5
Pernay (37) ... 78 C5
la Pernelle (50) ... 13 E2
Pernes (62) ... 2 B6
Pernes-lès-Boulogne (62) ... 1 F4
Pernes-les-Fontaines (84) ... 175 F2
Pernois (80) ... 7 H4
Pero-Casevecchie (2B)... 205 G1
Pérols (34) ... 173 G6
Pérols-sur-Vézère (19) ... 125 F5
Péron (01) ... 118 A5
Péronnas (01) ... 116 D5
Péronne (71) ... 116 B3
Péronne (80) ... 8 C5
Péronne-en-Mélantois (59)... 3 G5
Péronville (28) ... 62 B5
Pérouges (01) ... 130 C2
la Pérouille (36) ... 96 B6
Pérouse (90) ... 88 D3
Péroy-les-Gombries (60) ... 43 G1
Perpezac-le-Blanc (19) ... 138 B2
Perpezac-le-Noir (19) ... 138 D1
Perpezat (63) ... 126 D4
Perpignan (66) ... 201 F2
Perquie (40) ... 166 B2
Perrancey-les-Vieux-
   Moulins (52) ... 86 A1
le Perray-en-Yvelines (78) ... 42 A4
Perrecy-les-Forges (71) ... 115 F1
le Perréon (69) ... 116 A6
Perreuil (71) ... 101 E5
Perreux (42) ... 115 E6
le Perreux-sur-Marne (94) ... 43 E4
Perrex (01) ... 116 C4
Perrier (63) ... 127 F5
le Perrier (85) ... 90 C3
Perrières (14) ... 38 D2
Perriers-en-Beauficel (50)... 37 G4
Perriers-sur-Andelle (27) ... 19 E4
Perrignier (74) ... 118 D3
Perrigny (39) ... 102 D6
Perrigny (89) ... 83 F2
Perrigny-lès-Dijon (21)...101 H1
Perrigny-sur-
   Armançon (89) ... 84 C3
Perrigny-sur-l'Ognon (21)... 86 C6
Perrigny-sur-Loire (71) ... 114 D2
Perrogney-les-
   Fontaines (52) ... 86 A2
le Perron (50) ... 37 H1
Perros-Guirec (22) ... 32 C1
Perrou (61) ... 38 B6
Perrouse (70) ... 87 F5
Perroy (58) ... 82 D5
Perruel (27) ... 19 E4
Perrusse (52) ... 68 C5
Perrusson (37) ... 95 G2
Pers (79) ... 108 C4
Pers-en-Gâtinais (45) ... 64 B5
Pers-Jussy (74) ... 118 C5
Persac (86) ... 109 G3
Persan (95) ... 42 C1
Persquen (56) ... 54 D3
Perthes (52) ... 46 C5
Perthes (77) ... 63 H1
Perthes-lès-Brienne (10) ... 67 E2

Pertheville-Ners (14) ... 39 E3
le Perthus (66) ... 201 E6
le Pertre (35) ... 58 B5
le Pertuis (43) ... 142 D3
Pertuis (84) ... 176 A4
la Péruse (16) ... 123 E2
Pervenchères (61) ... 60 C2
Perville (82) ... 151 G6
Pescadoires (46) ... 152 B3
Peschadoires (63) ... 127 H2
le Pescher (19) ... 139 E4
Péseux (25) ... 88 B6
Peseux (39) ... 102 C3
Peslières (63) ... 127 H6
Pesmes (70) ... 86 C6
Pessac (33) ... 135 E5
Pessac-sur-Dordogne (33)... 136 B5
Pessan (32) ... 167 H5
Pessans (25) ... 103 F2
Pessat-Villeneuve (63) ... 127 F2
la Pesse (39) ... 118 A4
Pessines (17) ... 121 E3
Pessoulens (32) ... 168 B3
Petersbach (67) ... 50 B3
Petit-Auverné (44) ... 75 E2
Petit-Bersac (24) ... 136 C1
le Petit-Bornand-les-
   Glières (74) ... 118 D6
Petit-Caux (76) ... 17 H1
le Petit-Celland (50) ... 37 F5
Petit-Couronne (76) ... 18 C5
Petit-Croix (90) ... 88 D3
Petit-Failly (54) ... 25 F4
Petit-Fayt (59) ... 9 H4
le Petit-Fougeray (35)... 57 F4
Petit-Landau (68) ... 89 G2
Petit-Mars (44) ... 74 D3
le Petit-Mercey (39) ... 103 E1
Petit-Mesnil (10) ... 67 E3
Petit-Noir (39) ... 102 B4
Petit-Palais-et-
   Cornemps (33) ... 136 A4
le Petit-Pressigny (37) ... 95 F4
le Petit-Quevilly (76) ... 18 C4
Petit-Réderching (57) ... 28 A5
Petit-Tenquin (57) ... 49 G2
Petit-Verly (02) ... 9 F5
la Petite-Boissière (79) ... 92 C4
Petite-Chaux (25) ... 103 H6
Petite-Forêt (59) ... 9 F2
la Petite-Fosse (88) ... 70 D2
la Petite-Marche (03) ... 112 C5
la Petite-Pierre (67)... 50 B3
la Petite-Raon (88) ... 70 D1
Petite-Rosselle (57) ... 27 F4
la Petite-Verrière (71) ... 100 C3
Petitefontaine (90) ... 88 D2
les Petites-Armoises (08)... 24 B4
les Petites-Loges (51) ... 45 G1
Petitmagny (90) ... 88 D2
Petitmont (54) ... 49 H6
Petiville (14) ... 14 D4
Petiville (76) ... 15 H2
Petosse (85) ... 107 E2
Petreto-Bicchisano (2A)... 206 D2
Pettoncourt (57) ... 49 E4
Pettonville (54) ... 49 G6
Peujard (33) ... 135 F3
Peumerit (29) ... 53 E3
Peumerit-Quintin (22) ... 32 D5
Peuplingues (62) ... 1 G2
Peuton (53) ... 58 C6
Peuvillers (55) ... 25 E4
Peux-et-Couffouleux (12)... 171 G4
Pévange (57) ... 49 F3
Pévy (51) ... 22 D5
Pexiora (11) ... 186 C3
Pexonne (54) ... 70 C1
Pey (40) ... 164 D4
Peymeinade (06) ... 178 C4
Peynier (13) ... 192 C2
Peypin (13) ... 192 C3
Peypin-d'Aigues (84) ... 176 B3
Peyrabout (23) ... 111 G6
le Peyrat (09) ... 186 B5
Peyrat-de-Bellac (87) ... 110 B5
Peyrat-la-Nonière (23) ... 112 A6
Peyrat-le-Château (87) ... 125 E3
la Peyratte (79) ... 93 G6
Peyraube (65) ... 183 F3
Peyraud (07) ... 144 A1
Peyre (40) ... 165 H5
Peyre en Aubrac (48) ... 155 G1
Peyrecave (32) ... 168 B2
Peyrefitte-du-Razès (11) ... 186 C4
Peyrefitte-sur-l'Hers (11) ... 186 A3
Peyregoux (81) ... 170 C4
Peyrehorade (40) ... 165 E5
Peyreleau (12) ... 155 G6
Peyrelevade (19) ... 125 G4
Peyrelongue-Abos (64) ... 182 D1
Peyremale (30) ... 157 E6
Peyrens (11) ... 186 B2
Peyrestortes (66) ... 201 F2
Peyret-Saint-André (65) ... 183 H2
Peyriac-de-Mer (11) ... 188 A4
Peyriac-Minervois (11) ... 187 F2
Peyrière (47) ... 150 D2
Peyrieu (01) ... 131 F4
Peyrignac (24) ... 138 A3
Peyriguère (65) ... 183 F2
Peyrilhac (87) ... 124 A1
Peyrillac-et-Millac (24) ... 138 C5
Peyrilles (46) ... 152 C2
Peyrins (26) ... 144 C3
Peyrissac (19) ... 125 E5
Peyrissas (31) ... 184 C2

Peyrole (81) ... 170 A3
Peyrolles (11) ... 187 E5
Peyrolles (30) ... 173 F1
Peyrolles-en-Provence (13) .. 176 B5
Peyroules (04) ... 178 A3
Peyrouse (65) ... 182 D4
Peyrouzet (31) ... 184 B3
Peyruis (04) ... 176 D1
Peyrun (65) ... 183 F2
Peyrus (26) ... 144 C5
Peyrusse (15) ... 141 E2
Peyrusse-Grande (32) ... 167 E5
Peyrusse-le-Roc (12) ... 153 H3
Peyrusse-Massas (32) ... 167 H4
Peyrusse-Vieille (32) ... 167 E5
Peyssies (31) ... 185 E2
Peyzac-le-Moustier (24) ... 137 H4
Peyzieux-sur-Saône (01) ... 116 B5
Pézarches (77) ... 43 H5
Pezé-le-Robert (72) ... 59 H4
Pézenas (34) ... 188 D1
Pézènes-les-Mines (34) ... 172 B5
Pezens (11) ... 186 D3
Pézilla-de-Conflent (66) ... 200 C2
Pézilla-la-Rivière (66) ... 201 E2
Pezou (41) ... 79 G1
Pezuls (24) ... 137 F5
Pfaffenheim (68) ... 71 F5
Pfalzweyer (67) ... 50 B4
Pfastatt (68) ... 89 F1
Pfetterhouse (68) ... 89 E4
Pfulgriesheim (67) ... 51 E5
Phaffans (67) ... 88 D3
Phalempin (59) ... 3 F6
Phalsbourg (57) ... 50 B4
Philippsbourg (57) ... 50 D2
Philondenx (40) ... 166 A5
Phlin (54) ... 48 D3
Pia (66) ... 201 F2
Piacé (72) ... 60 A3
le Pian-Médoc (33) ... 135 E4
le Pian-sur-Garonne (33)... 149 H2
Piana (2A) ... 204 B3
Pianello (2B) ... 205 G2
Pianottoli-Caldarello (2A) ... 207 E4
les Piards (39) ... 117 H2
la Piarre (05) ... 159 G3
Piazzali (2B) ... 205 G2
Piazzole (2B) ... 205 G1
Piblange (57) ... 26 D4
Pibrac (31) ... 169 E5
Picarreau (39) ... 103 E5
Picauville (50) ... 12 D4
Pichanges (21) ... 86 A5
Picherande (63) ... 126 D6
Picquigny (80) ... 7 F5
Pie-d'Orezza (2B) ... 205 G1
Pied-de-Borne (48) ... 156 D3
Piedicorte-di-Gaggio (2B) .. 205 F3
Piedicroce (2B) ... 205 G1
Piedigriggio (2B) ... 203 E6
Piedipartino (2B) ... 205 G1
Piégon (26) ... 158 D5
Piégros-la-Clastre (26) ... 158 D1
Piégut (04) ... 160 C3
Piégut-Pluviers (24) ... 123 F4
Piencourt (27) ... 15 G5
Piennes (54) ... 25 H5
Piennes-Onvillers (80) ... 21 E3
Pierlas (06) ... 178 D1
la Pierre (38) ... 145 H1
Pierre-Bénite (69) ... 130 A3
Pierre-Buffière (87) ... 124 B4
Pierre-Châtel (38) ... 145 G4
Pierre-de-Bresse (71) ... 102 B4
Pierre-la-Treiche (54) ... 48 B5
Pierre-Levée (77) ... 43 H3
Pierre-Morains (51) ... 45 F4
Pierre-Percée (54) ... 70 C1
Pierre-Perthuis (89) ... 83 H5
Pierreclos (71) ... 116 A4
Pierrecourt (70) ... 86 C3
Pierrecourt (76) ... 6 C6
Pierrefeu (06) ... 178 D2
Pierrefeu-du-Var (83) ... 193 G4
Pierrefiche (12) ... 155 E3
Pierrefiche (48) ... 156 C1
Pierrefiques (76) ... 16 A3
Pierrefitte (19) ... 124 D6
Pierrefitte (23) ... 112 A5
Pierrefitte (79) ... 93 F4
Pierrefitte (88) ... 69 G4
Pierrefitte-en-Auge (14) ... 15 F4
Pierrefitte-en-
   Beauvaisis (60) ... 20 A4
Pierrefitte-en-Cinglais (14)... 38 C3
Pierrefitte-ès-Bois (45) ... 82 A4
Pierrefitte-Nestalas (65) ... 182 D5
Pierrefitte-sur-Aire (55) ... 47 F3
Pierrefitte-sur-Loire (03) ... 114 C2
Pierrefitte-sur-Sauldre (41) .. 81 F4
Pierrefitte-sur-Seine (93) ... 42 D3
Pierrefonds (60) ... 21 G5
Pierrefontaine-lès-
   Blamont (25) ... 88 C5
Pierrefontaine-les-
   Varans (25) ... 104 B1
Pierrefort (15) ... 140 D5
Pierregot (80) ... 7 G5
Pierrelatte (26) ... 158 A4
Pierrelaye (95) ... 42 C2
Pierrelongue (26) ... 159 E5
Pierremande (02) ... 21 H3
Pierremont (02) ... 7 G1
Pierremont-sur-
   Amance (52) ... 86 D2
Pierrepont (02) ... 22 D2

Pierrepont (14) ... 38 C3
Pierrepont (54) ... 25 G4
Pierrepont-sur-Avre (80) ... 20 D2
Pierrepont-sur-
   l'Arentèle (88) ... 70 B3
Pierrerue (04) ... 176 D2
Pierrerue (34) ... 188 A1
Pierres (28) ... 41 G6
Pierreval (76) ... 18 D3
Pierrevert (04) ... 176 C3
Pierreville (50) ... 12 B3
Pierreville (54) ... 48 C6
Pierrevillers (57) ... 26 B4
Pierric (44) ... 74 C1
Pierry (51) ... 45 E2
Pietra-di-Verde (2B) ... 205 G2
Pietracorbara (2B) ... 203 G2
Pietralba (2B) ... 203 E5
Pietraserena (2B) ... 205 G3
Pietricaggio (2B) ... 205 G2
Pietrosella (2A) ... 206 C1
Pietroso (2B) ... 205 F3
Piets-Plasence-
   Moustrou (64) ... 166 A6
Pieusse (11) ... 186 D4
les Pieux (50) ... 12 B3
Pièvre (28) ... 203 F5
Piffonds (89) ... 64 D5
Pigna (2B) ... 202 C5
Pignan (34) ... 173 F5
Pignans (83) ... 193 G3
Pignicourt (02) ... 23 E4
Pignols (63) ... 127 G4
Pigny (18) ... 97 H2
Pihem (62) ... 2 A4
Pihen-lès-Guînes (62) ... 1 G3
Pila-Canale (2A) ... 206 D1
Pillac (16) ... 136 C1
Pillemoine (39) ... 103 F6
les Pilles (26) ... 158 D4
Pillon (55) ... 25 G5
Pimbo (40) ... 166 B5
Pimelles (89) ... 84 B1
Pimorin (39) ... 117 F2
Pimprez (60) ... 21 G4
le Pin (03) ... 114 D3
le Pin (14) ... 15 G4
le Pin (17) ... 135 G1
le Pin (30) ... 174 C1
le Pin (38) ... 129 H6
le Pin (39) ... 102 D6
le Pin (44) ... 75 F2
le Pin (70) ... 87 E6
le Pin (77) ... 43 E3
le Pin (79) ... 92 D4
le Pin (82) ... 168 C1
le Pin-au-Haras (61) ... 39 F4
le Pin-en-Mauges (49) ... 75 H4
le Pin-la-Garenne (61) ... 60 D2
le Pin-Murelet (31) ... 184 D1
Pinas (65) ... 183 H4
Pinay (42) ... 128 D2
Pincé (72) ... 77 F1
Pindères (47) ... 150 B5
Pindray (86) ... 109 H2
les Pineaux (85) ... 91 H5
Pinel-Hauterive (47) ... 151 E3
Pinet (34) ... 189 E1
Pineuilh (33) ... 136 C5
Piney (10) ... 66 C2
Pino (2B) ... 203 F2
Pinols (43) ... 141 H4
Pinon (02) ... 22 B4
les Pins (16) ... 122 D2
Pins-Justaret (31) ... 169 E6
Pinsac (46) ... 138 C5
Pinsaguel (31) ... 169 E6
Pinsot (38) ... 132 B6
Pintac (65) ... 183 E2
Pinterville (27) ... 18 D6
Pintheville (55) ... 47 H1
les Pinthières (28) ... 41 G5
Piobetta (2B) ... 205 G2
Pioggiola (2B) ... 202 D5
Piolenc (84) ... 158 B6
Pionnat (23) ... 111 H5
Pionsat (63) ... 112 D6
Pioussay (79) ... 108 C6
Pipriac (35) ... 56 D5
Piquecos (82) ... 169 E1
Pirajoux (01) ... 117 E3
Piré-sur-Seiche (35) ... 57 G4
Pirey (25) ... 87 F6
Piriac-sur-Mer (44) ... 73 E3
Pirmil (72) ... 59 G6
Pirou (50) ... 12 C6
Pis (32) ... 168 A3
Pisany (17) ... 120 D3
Piscop (95) ... 42 D2
Piseux (27) ... 40 C4
Pisieu (38) ... 130 C6
Pisseleu (60) ... 20 A3
Pisseleux (02) ... 21 G6
Pisseloup (52) ... 86 D1
Pissos (40) ... 148 D4
Pissotte (85) ... 107 F2
Pissy (80) ... 7 F6
Pissy-Pôville (76) ... 18 B4
Pitgam (59) ... 2 B2
Pithiviers (45) ... 63 F4
Pithiviers-le-Vieil (45) ... 63 F4
Pithon (02) ... 21 G1
Pîtres (27) ... 18 D5
Pittefaux (62) ... 1 F4
Pizay (01) ... 130 C2
Pizieux (72) ... 60 B3
le Pizou (24) ... 136 B4
le Pla (09) ... 199 H2

Plabennec (29) ... 31 E4
Placé (53) ... 58 C3
les Places (27) ... 15 G5
Placey (25) ... 103 E1
Plachy-Buyon (80) ... 20 B1
Placy (14) ... 38 C2
le Plagnal (07) ... 156 D1
Plagne (01) ... 117 H5
Plagne (31) ... 184 D3
La Plagne Tarentaise (73)... 133 E4
Plagnole (31) ... 184 D1
Plaigne (11) ... 186 A3
Plailly (60) ... 43 E2
Plaimbois-du-Miroir (25) ... 104 C1
Plaimbois-Vennes (25) ... 104 B1
Plaimpied-Givaudins (18)... 97 H3
la Plaine (49) ... 92 D2
Plaine (67) ... 71 E1
Plaine-de-Walsch (57) ... 50 A5
Plaine-Haute (22) ... 33 G5
la Plaine-sur-Mer (44) ... 73 G5
Plainemont (70) ... 87 G1
Plaines-Saint-Lange (10)... 66 D6
Plainfaing (88) ... 70 D4
Plainoiseau (39) ... 102 D6
les Plains-et-Grands-
   Essarts (25) ... 88 D6
Plaintel (22) ... 33 G5
Plainval (60) ... 20 D3
Plainville (27) ... 15 G5
Plainville (60) ... 20 D3
Plaisance (12) ... 171 E2
Plaisance (24) ... 151 E1
Plaisance (32) ... 166 D5
Plaisance (86) ... 109 H3
Plaisance-du-Touch (31) ... 169 E6
Plaisia (39) ... 117 G2
Plaisians (26) ... 159 E5
Plaisir (78) ... 42 A4
Plaissan (34) ... 172 D6
le Plan (31) ... 184 D3
Plan (38) ... 145 E1
Plan-d'Aups-Sainte-
   Baume (83) ... 192 D3
Plan-de-Baix (26) ... 144 C6
Plan-de-Cuques (13) ... 192 B3
le Plan-de-la-Tour (83) ... 194 A3
Plan-d'Orgon (13) ... 175 F3
Planaise (73) ... 132 A5
Planay (21) ... 84 D2
Planay (73) ... 133 E6
la Planche (44) ... 91 G1
Plancher-Bas (70) ... 88 C2
Plancher-les-Mines (70) ... 88 C2
Plancherine (73) ... 132 C3
les Planches-en-
   Montagne (39) ... 103 G6
les Planches-près-
   Arbois (39) ... 103 E4
Planchez (58) ... 100 B2
Plancoët (22) ... 34 C4
Plancy-l'Abbaye (10) ... 45 F6
la Planée (25) ... 103 H4
Planès (66) ... 200 A4
Planèzes (66) ... 200 D1
Planfoy (42) ... 143 F1
Planguenoual (22) ... 33 H4
Planioles (46) ... 153 G2
le Planois (71) ... 102 B5
le Planquay (27) ... 15 G5
Planquery (14) ... 13 G6
Planques (62) ... 7 F1
Planrupt (52) ... 67 F1
les Plans (30) ... 157 F6
les Plans (34) ... 172 B4
le Plantay (01) ... 116 D6
les Plantiers (30) ... 173 E1
la Plantis (61) ... 39 G6
Planty (10) ... 65 G3
Planzolles (07) ... 157 E3
Plappeville (57) ... 26 B5
Plasne (39) ... 103 E5
Plasnes (27) ... 15 H5
Plassac (17) ... 121 F5
Plassac (33) ... 135 E3
Plassac-Rouffiac (16) ... 122 B5
Plassay (17) ... 121 E2
Plats (07) ... 144 A4
Plaudren (56) ... 55 G5
Plauzat (63) ... 127 F4
Plavilla (11) ... 186 B4
Plazac (24) ... 137 H4
Pleaux (15) ... 139 H3
Plébouille (22) ... 34 B4
Pléchâtel (35) ... 57 E5
Plédéliac (22) ... 34 B5
Plédran (22) ... 33 G5
Pléguien (22) ... 33 F3
Pléhédel (22) ... 33 F3
Pleine-Fougères (35) ... 35 G4
Pleine-Selve (02) ... 22 D1
Pleine-Selve (33) ... 135 E1
Pleine-Sève (76) ... 17 E3
Plélan-le-Grand (35) ... 56 C3
Plélan-le-Petit (22) ... 34 C5
Plélauff (22) ... 54 D1
Plémet (22) ... 33 F4
Plémy (22) ... 33 G6
Plénée-Jugon (22) ... 34 B5
Pléneuf-Val-André (22) ... 34 A4
Plénise (39) ... 103 G5
Plénisette (39) ... 103 G5
Plerguer (35) ... 35 F4
Plérin (22) ... 33 G4
Plerneuf (22) ... 33 F4
Plescop (56) ... 55 F6
Plesder (35) ... 34 D5

Plésidy (22)..............33 E5
Pleslin-Trigavou (22)......34 D4
Plesnois (57)............26 B5
Plesnoy (52)............86 C1
Plessé (44)..............74 B2
le Plessier-Huleu (02)....22 A6
le Plessier-
Rozainvillers (80).....20 D1
le Plessier-sur-Bulles (60)......20 C4
le Plessier-sur-Saint-
Just (60)..............20 D4
le Plessis-aux-Bois (77)....43 F2
Plessis-Barbuise (10)......44 C6
le Plessis-Belleville (60)....43 F2
le Plessis-Bouchard (95)....42 C2
le Plessis-Brion (60)......21 F4
Plessis-de-Roye (60)......21 F3
le Plessis-Dorin (41)......61 F5
le Plessis-Feu-
Aussoux (77)..........43 H5
le Plessis-Gassot (95)......42 D2
le Plessis-Grammoire (49)....77 E4
le Plessis-Grohan (27)......40 D3
le Plessis-Hébert (27)......41 F2
le Plessis-Lastelle (50)......12 D5
le Plessis-l'Échelle (41)......80 A2
le Plessis-l'Évêque (77)......43 F2
le Plessis-Luzarches (95)....42 D2
le Plessis-Pâté (91)......42 D6
le Plessis-Patte-d'Oie (60)....21 G2
le Plessis-Placy (77)......43 H2
le Plessis-Robinson (92)....42 C4
Plessis-Saint-Benoist (91)...63 E2
le Plessis-Saint-Jean (89)....65 E3
le Plessis-Sainte-
Opportune (27)........40 C2
le Plessis-Trévise (94)......43 E4
Plestan (22)..............34 A5
Plestin-les-Grèves (22)....32 B3
Pleubian (22)..............33 E1
Pleucadeuc (56)..........56 A5
Pleudaniel (22)..........33 E2
Pleudihen-sur-Rance (22)....34 D5
Pleugriffet (56)..........55 G3
Pleugueneuc (35)..........34 D6
Pleumartin (86)..........95 E5
Pleumeleuc (35)..........56 D2
Pleumeur-Bodou (22)......32 C2
Pleumeur-Gautier (22)....33 E1
Pleure (39)..............102 C4
Pleurs (51)..............45 E5
Pleurtuit (35)..........34 D4
Pleuven (29)..............53 G3
Pleuvezain (88)..........69 E2
Pleuville (16)..........109 F6
Pléven (22)..............34 B5
Plévenon (22)..........34 B3
Plévin (22)..............54 B1
Pleyben (22)..............31 G6
Pleyber-Christ (29)......31 H4
Pliboux (79)............108 D5
Plichancourt (51)........46 B5
Plieux (32)..............168 A2
Plivot (51)..............45 F2
Plobannalec-Lesconil (29)....53 F4
Plobsheim (67)..........51 E6
Ploemel (56)..........55 E6
Ploemeur (56)..........54 C5
Ploërdut (56)..........54 D2
Ploeren (56)..........55 F6
Ploërmel (56)..........56 A4
Plœuc-l'Hermitage (22)....33 G6
Ploëven (29)..........53 F1
Ploëzal (22)............33 E2
Plogastel-Saint-
Germain (29)..........53 E3
Plogoff (29)............52 C2
Plogonnec (29)..........53 F2
Ploisy (02)..............23 E1
Plombières-les-Bains (88)...70 A6
Plombières-lès-Dijon (21)...85 G6
Plomelin (29)..........53 F3
Plomeur (29)..........53 E4
Plomion (02)..............23 E1
Plomodiern (29)..........53 F1
Plonéis (29)..............53 F2
Plonéour-Lanvern (29)....53 E3
Plonévez-du-Faou (29)....32 A6
Plonévez-Porzay (29)....53 F1
Plorec-sur-Arguenon (22)....34 B5
Plottes (71)............116 B2
Plou (18)..............97 F3
Plouagat (22)..........33 F4
Plouaret (22)..........32 C3
Plouarzel (29)..........30 C4
Plouasne (22)..........56 D1
Plouay (56)..........54 C4
Ploubalanec (22)........33 F2
Ploubezre (22)..........32 C2
Ploudalmézeau (29)......30 D3
Ploudaniel (29)..........31 F3
Ploudiry (29)............31 G4
Plouëc-du-Trieux (22)....33 E3
Plouédern (29)..........31 F4
Plouégat-Guérand (29)....32 A3
Plouégat-Moysan (29)....32 B3
Plouénan (29)..........31 H3
Plouër-sur-Rance (22)....34 D4
Plouescat (29)..........31 G2
Plouézec (22)..........33 F2
Plouezoc'h (29)..........32 A3
Ploufragan (22)..........33 G4
Plougar (29)............31 G3
Plougasnou (29)..........32 A2
Plougastel-Daoulas (29)....31 E5
Plougonvelin (29)........30 C5
Plougonven (29)..........32 A4
Plougonver (22)..........32 C4

Plougoulm (29)..........31 G2
Plougoumelen (56)......55 F6
Plougourvest (29)......31 G3
Plougras (22)..........32 B4
Plougrescant (22)......33 E1
Plouguenast (22)......55 G1
Plouguerneau (29)......31 E3
Plouguernével (22)......54 D1
Plouguiel (22)..........32 D1
Plouguin (29)..........30 D3
Plouha (22)..............33 F3
Plouharnel (56)..........72 B1
Plouhinec (29)..........52 D2
Plouhinec (56)..........54 D6
Plouider (29)..........31 F3
Plouigneau (29)..........32 B3
Plouisy (22)..............33 E3
Ploulec'h (22)..........32 C2
Ploumagoar (22)........33 E4
Ploumilliau (22)........32 C2
Ploumoguer (29)........30 C4
Plounéour-Brignogan-
Plages (29)..........31 F2
Plounéour-Ménez (29)....31 H4
Plounérin (22)..........32 C3
Plounéventer (29)......31 F4
Plounévez-Lochrist (29)....31 F3
Plounévez-Moëdec (22)....32 C4
Plounévez-Quintin (22)....32 D6
Plounévézel (29)........32 B6
Plourac'h (22)..........32 B5
Plouray (56)..........54 C2
Plourhan (22)..........33 G3
Plourin (29)..........30 C3
Plourin-lès-Morlaix (29)....32 A4
Plourivo (22)..........33 E2
Plouvain (62)..........8 C2
Plouvara (22)..........33 F4
Plouvien (29)..........31 E3
Plouvorn (29)..........31 G3
Plouyé (29)..........32 A6
Plouzané (29)..........30 D4
Plouzélambre (22)......32 C3
Plouzévédé (29)........31 G3
Plovan (29)..........53 E3
Ployart-et-Vaurseine (02)....22 D4
le Ployron (60)..........20 D3
Plozévet (29)..........52 D2
Pludual (22)..........33 F3
Pluduno (22)..........34 B4
Plufur (22)..........32 B3
Pluguffan (29)..........53 F3
Pluherlin (56)..........56 A6
Plumaudan (22)..........34 C6
Plumaugat (22)..........56 B1
Plumelec (56)..........55 G5
Pluméliau (56)..........55 F3
Plumelin (56)..........55 F5
Plumergat (56)..........55 F5
Plumetot (14)..........14 C4
Plumieux (22)..........55 H2
Plumont (39)..........103 E3
Pluneret (56)..........55 E6
Plurien (22)..........34 B3
Plusquellec (22)........32 C5
Plussulien (22)........33 E6
Pluvault (21)..........102 B1
Pluvet (21)..........102 B1
Pluvigner (56)..........55 F5
Pluzunet (22)..........32 D3
Pocancy (51)..........45 G3
Pocé-les-Bois (35)......57 H3
Pocé-sur-Cisse (37)....79 F5
Podensac (33)..........149 G1
le Poët (05)..........160 A5
le Poët-Célard (26)....158 D2
le Poët-en-Percip (26)....159 F5
le Poët-Laval (26)......158 C3
le Poët-Sigillat (26)....159 E4
Pœuilly (80)..........8 D6
Poey-de-Lescar (64)....182 B1
Poey-d'Oloron (64)......181 H2
Poëzat (03)..........113 G6
Poggio-di-Nazza (2B)....205 F4
Poggio-di-Venaco (2B)....205 E3
Poggio-d'Oletta (2B)....203 F4
Poggio-Marinaccio (2B)....203 F6
Poggio-Mezzana (2B)....205 G1
Poggiolo (2A)..........204 D3
Pogny (51)..........46 A4
Poids-de-Fiole (39)....117 G1
Poigny (78)..........65 E1
Poigny-la-Forêt (78)....41 H5
Poil (58)..............100 B4
Poilcourt-Sydney (08)....23 F4
Poilhes (34)..........188 B2
Poillé-sur-Vègre (72)....59 F6
Poilley (35)..........35 H5
Poilley (50)..........35 H5
Poilly (51)..........22 D6
Poilly-lez-Gien (45)....81 H3
Poilly-sur-Serein (89)....84 A2
Poilly-sur-Tholon (89)....83 E1
Poinçon-lès-Larrey (21)....84 D1
le Poinçonnet (36)......96 C5
Poincy (77)..........43 G3
Poinsenot (52)..........86 C2
Poinson-lès-Fayl (52)....86 C2
Poinson-lès-Grancey (52)...85 G3
Poinsons-lès-Nogent (52)...68 B6
Pointel (61)..........38 C5
Pointis-de-Rivière (31)....184 A4
Pointis-Inard (31)......184 B4
Pointre (39)..........102 C1
le Poiré-sur-Velluire (85)....107 E2
Le Poiré-sur-Vie (85)....91 F3
Poiroux (85)..........91 F6

Poisat (38)..........145 G2
Poiseul (21)..........68 C6
Poiseul-la-Grange (21)....85 F4
Poiseul-la-Ville-et-
Laperrière (21)........85 E4
Poiseux (58)..........99 E2
Poisieux (18)..........97 F3
le Poislay (41)..........61 G5
Poisson (71)..........115 E3
Poissons (52)..........68 A2
Poissy (78)..........42 B3
Poisvilliers (28)......62 B1
Poisy (74)..........132 A1
Poitiers (86)..........109 E1
Poivres (10)..........45 G5
Poix (51)..........46 B3
Poix-de-Picardie (80)....20 A1
Poix-du-Nord (59)......9 G3
Poix-Terron (08)......24 A2
Le Poizat-Lalleyriat (01)....117 H5
Polaincourt-et-
Clairefontaine (70)....87 F1
Polastron (31)........184 C2
Polastron (32)........168 B6
Poleymieux-au-Mont-
d'Or (69)............130 A2
Poliénas (38)..........145 E2
Polignac (17)..........135 G1
Polignac (43)..........142 C4
Poligné (35)..........57 E5
Poligny (05)..........160 B1
Poligny (10)..........66 C4
Poligny (39)..........103 E5
Poligny (77)..........64 A4
Polincove (62)..........2 A3
Polisot (10)..........66 D5
Polisy (10)..........66 D5
Pollestres (66)......201 F3
Polliat (01)..........116 D4
Pollieu (01)..........131 G2
Pollionnay (69)......129 H3
Polminhac (15)........140 B5
Polveroso (2B)........205 G1
Pomacle (51)..........23 F5
la Pomarède (11)......186 B1
Pomarède (46)........152 B2
Pomarez (40)..........165 F4
Pomas (11)..........186 D4
Pomayrols (12)........155 F3
Pomerol (33)..........135 H4
Pomérols (34)........189 E2
Pomeys (69)..........129 F4
Pommard (21)..........101 G3
Pommera (62)..........7 H3
la Pommeraye (14)....38 C3
Pommeret (22)..........33 H5
Pommereuil (59)......9 G4
Pommereux (76)......19 G3
Pommeréval (76)......19 E1
Pommerieux (53)......76 C1
Pommérieux (57)......48 C2
Pommerit-Jaudy (22)....32 D2
Pommerit-le-Vicomte (22)...33 E3
Pommerol (26)........159 F3
Pommeuse (77)......43 H4
Pommevic (82)........168 C1
Pommier (62)..........8 A3
Pommier-de-
Beaurepaire (38)....130 C6
Pommiers (02)..........22 A5
Pommiers (30)........172 D2
Pommiers (36)........111 E2
Pommiers (42)........129 E2
Pommiers (69)........129 H1
Pommiers-Moulons (17)...135 G1
Pomoy (70)..........87 H3
Pompaire (79)........108 A1
Pompéjac (33)........149 H3
Pompertuzat (31)......169 F6
Pompey (54)..........48 C4
Pompiac (32)........168 C6
le Pompidou (48)......156 B6
Pompierre (88)........68 D3
Pompierre-sur-Doubs (25)...88 A5
Pompiey (47)..........150 C5
Pompignac (33)......135 F5
Pompignan (30)......173 F3
Pompignan (82)......168 D4
Pompogne (47)........150 B5
Pomponne (77)......43 F4
Pomport (24)..........136 D6
Pomps (64)..........165 H6
Pomy (11)..........186 C4
Poncey-lès-Athée (21)....102 C1
Poncey-sur-l'Ignon (21)....85 F4
le Ponchel (62)..........7 F3
Ponches-Estruval (80)....6 D2
Ponchon (60)..........20 B5
Poncin (01)..........117 F6
Poncins (42)..........129 E3
Pondaurat (33)......150 A2
le Pondy (18)..........98 A5
Ponet-et-Saint-Auban (26)...144 D6
Ponlat-Taillebourg (31)....184 A4
Pons (17)..........121 F4
Ponsampère (32)......183 G1
Ponsan-Soubiran (32)....183 H1
Ponsas (26)..........144 A3
Ponson-Debat-Pouts (64)...182 D2
Ponson-Dessus (64)....182 D2
Ponsonnas (38)......145 G5
Pont (21)..........102 B2
Pont-à-Marcq (59)......3 G6
Pont-à-Mousson (54)....48 C3
Pont-à-Vendin (62)......3 E6
Pont-Arcy (02)..........22 C5
Pont-Audemer (27)......15 H3

Pont-Authou (27)......18 A6
Pont-Aven (29)........54 A4
Pont-Bellanger (14)....37 G2
Le Pont-Chrétien-
Chabenet (36)........110 D1
Pont-Croix (29)......52 D2
Pont-d'Ain (01)......117 E6
le Pont-de-Barret (26)....158 C2
le Pont-de-Beauvoisin (38)...131 F5
le Pont-de-Beauvoisin (73)...131 F5
Pont-de-Buis-lès-
Quimerch (29)........31 G6
le Pont-de-Chéruy (38)....130 C3
le Pont-de-Claix (38)....145 G3
le Pont-de-Labeaume (07)...157 F1
Pont-de-Larn (81)......170 D6
Pont-de-l'Arche (27)....18 D5
Pont-de-l'Isère (26)....144 A4
Pont-de-Metz (80)......7 F6
Pont de Montvert - Sud
Mont Lozère (48)....156 C4
le Pont-de-Poitte (39)....117 G1
le Pont-de-Roide-
Vermondans (25)......88 C5
Pont-de-Ruan (37)......94 D1
le Pont-de-Salars (12)....154 D5
Pont-de-Vaux (01)......116 C3
Pont-de-Veyle (01)......116 B4
Pont-d'Héry (39)......103 F4
Pont-d'Ouilly (14)......38 C3
Pont-du-Bois (70)......69 F6
Pont-du-Casse (47)....151 F5
Pont-du-Château (63)....127 G3
Pont-du-Navoy (39)....103 E6
Pont-en-Royans (38)....144 D3
Pont-et-Massène (21)....84 D5
Pont-Évêque (38)......130 B5
Pont-Farcy (14)........37 G2
Pont-Hébert (50)......13 F6
Pont-la-Ville (52)......67 G5
Pont-l'Abbé (29)......53 F4
Pont-l'Abbé-d'Arnoult (17)...120 D2
Pont-les-Bonfays (88)....69 F4
Pont-les-Moulins (25)....87 H6
Pont-l'Évêque (14)......15 F4
Pont-l'Évêque (60)......21 G3
Pont-Melvez (22)......32 D4
Pont-Noyelles (80)......7 H5
le Pont-Péan (35)......57 E3
Pont-Remy (80)........6 D4
Pont-Saint-Esprit (30)....158 A5
Pont-Saint-Mard (02)....22 A4
Pont-Saint-Martin (44)....74 C6
Pont-Saint-Pierre (27)....18 D5
Pont-Saint-Vincent (54)...48 C6
Pont-Sainte-Marie (10)....66 B3
Pont-Sainte-Maxence (60)...21 E5
Pont-Salomon (43)......143 E1
Pont-Scorff (56)......54 C4
Pont-sur-l'Ognon (70)....87 H4
Pont-sur-Madon (88)....69 F2
Pont-sur-Meuse (55)....47 G4
Pont-sur-Sambre (59)....9 H3
Pont-sur-Seine (10)....65 G1
Pont-sur-Vanne (89)....65 F4
Pont-sur-Yonne (89)....64 D3
Pontacq (64)..........182 D2
Pontailler-sur-Saône (21)...86 B6
Pontaix (26)..........144 D6
Pontamafrey-
Montpascal (73)......146 C1
Pontarion (23)........125 E2
Pontarlier (25)........104 A4
Pontarmé (60)..........43 E1
Pontaubault (50)......35 H4
Pontaubert (89)......83 H5
Pontault-Combault (77)...43 E4
Pontaumur (63)........126 C2
Pontavert (02)..........22 D4
Pontcarré (77)........43 F4
Pontcey (70)..........87 F3
Pontchardon (61)......39 G3
Pontcharra (38)......132 A6
Pontcharra-sur-
Turdine (69)........129 G2
Pontcharraud (23)....125 H2
Pontchâteau (44)......73 H3
Pontcirq (46)........152 B2
Pontécoulant (14)......38 B3
Ponteilla (66)........201 E3
Ponteils-et-Brésis (30)....156 D4
Pontenx-les-Forges (40)...148 B5
le Pontet (73)........132 B5
le Pontet (84)........175 E2
les Pontets (25)......103 H5
Pontevès (83)........177 E5
Pontfaverger-
Moronvilliers (51)....23 G5
Pontgibaud (63)......126 D2
Pontgouin (28)........61 G1
Ponthévrard (78)......62 D1
Ponthion (51)..........46 B5
Ponthoile (80)..........6 C3
Pontiacq-Viellepinte (64)...182 D1
Pontigny (89)..........83 G1
Pontis (04)..........160 D2
Pontivy (56)..........55 F2
Pontlevoy (41)........79 H5
Pontmain (53)..........58 B1
Pontoise (95)..........42 B2
Pontoise-lès-Noyon (60)...21 G3
Pontonx-sur-l'Adour (40)...165 F3
Pontorson (50)........35 G4
Pontours (24)........137 F5
Pontoux (71)..........102 A4
Pontoy (57)..........48 D2
Pontpierre (57)......49 F2

Pontpoint (60)..........21 E5
Pontrieux (22)........33 E2
Pontru (02)..........8 D6
Pontruet (02)..........8 D6
Ponts (50)..........35 H3
les Ponts-de-Cé (49)....77 E5
Ponts-et-Marais (76)....6 B4
Ponts sur Seulles (14)....14 B4
Pontvallain (72)......78 A2
Popian (34)..........172 D5
Popolasca (2B)........203 E1
Porcaro (56)..........56 B4
Porcelette (57)......27 E5
Porchères (33)........136 A4
la Porcherie (87)......124 D5
Porcheux (60)..........19 H5
Porcheville (78)......41 H3
Porcieu-Amblagnieu (38)...131 E2
Pordic (22)..........33 G4
le Porge (33)........134 B5
Pornic (44)..........73 H4
Pornichet (44)........73 G4
Porquéricourt (60)....21 G3
Porri (2B)..........203 G6
Porspoder (29)........30 C3
Port (01)..........117 G5
le Port (09)..........185 F6
Port-Brillet (53)......58 B4
Port-de-Bouc (13)......191 G5
Port-de-Lanne (40)....164 D5
Port-de-Piles (86)......94 D3
Port-d'Envaux (17)....121 E2
Port-en-Bessin-
Huppain (14)........13 H5
Port-Jérôme-sur-Seine (76)...15 H2
Port-la-Nouvelle (11)....188 B5
Port-Launay (29)......31 G6
Port-le-Grand (80)......6 D3
Port-Lesney (39)......103 E3
Port-Louis (56)........54 C6
le Port-Marly (78)......42 B4
Port-Mort (27)........41 F1
Port-Saint-Louis-du-
Rhône (13)..........191 E5
Port-Saint-Père (44)....74 B6
Port-Sainte-Foy-et-
Ponchapt (24)........136 C5
Port-Sainte-Marie (47)...150 D5
Port-sur-Saône (70)....87 F3
Port-sur-Seille (54)....48 C3
Port-Vendres (66)......201 G4
Port-Villez (78)......41 G2
la Porta (2B)..........205 F1
Porta (66)..........199 F4
Portbail (50)..........12 B4
Porte des Pierres
Dorées (69)........129 H1
La Porte de la Der (52)....67 F1
Porte du Ried (68)......71 F4
Porte-Joie (27)........18 D6
Porté-Puymorens (66)...199 G3
le Portel (62)..........1 E4
Portel-des-Corbières (11)...188 A5
Portes (27)..........40 C2
Portes (30)..........157 E5
Les Portes du Coglais (35)...35 H5
les Portes-en-Ré (17)....106 A4
Portes-en-Valdaine (26)...158 C3
Portes-lès-Valence (26)...144 B5
Portet (64)..........166 C5
Portet-d'Aspet (31)....184 C6
Portet-de-Luchon (31)....197 E1
Portet-sur-Garonne (31)...169 F6
Portets (33)..........149 G1
Portieux (88)..........69 F2
Portiragnes (34)......188 D2
Porto-Vecchio (2A)....207 H3
Ports (37)..........94 D3
Posanges (21)........85 E5
Poses (27)..........18 D5
Possesse (51)..........46 C3
la Possonnière (49)....76 D5
la Postolle (89)......65 F3
Postroff (57)........50 A2
Potangis (51)........44 D6
Potelières (30)......157 F5
Potelle (59)..........9 G3
la Poterie-Cap-
d'Antifer (76)........16 B4
la Poterie-Mathieu (27)...15 H4
Pothières (21)........84 D1
Potigny (14)..........38 D2
Potte (80)..........21 F1
Pouan-les-Vallées (10)...66 B1
Pouançay (86)........93 H2
Pouant (86)..........94 B3
Poubeau (31)........197 E1
Poucharramet (31)....185 E1
Poudenas (47)......167 F1
Poudenx (40)........165 H5
Poudis (81)..........170 B6
Poueyferré (65)......182 D4
Pouffonds (79)......108 B4
la Pouge (23)........125 F1
le Pouget (34)........172 D5
Pougnadoresse (30)....174 C1
Pougne-Hérisson (79)....93 E6
Pougny (01)..........118 A5
Pougny (58)..........82 C6
Pougues-les-Eaux (58)...98 D3
Pougy (10)..........66 C2
Pouillac (17)..........135 G1
Pouillat (01)..........117 F3
Pouillé (41)..........79 H6
Pouillé (85)..........107 E1
Pouillé (86)..........109 F2
Pouillé-les-Côteaux (44)...75 F2

Pouillenay (21)........84 D4
Pouilley-Français (25)....103 E1
Pouilley-les-Vignes (25)...103 F1
Pouillon (40)..........165 E5
Pouillon (51)..........23 E5
Pouilloux (71)......115 G1
Pouilly (57)..........48 C2
Pouilly (60)..........20 A6
Pouilly-en-Auxois (21)...101 E1
Pouilly-les-Feurs (42)...115 E6
Pouilly-les-Nonains (42)...115 E6
Pouilly-sous-Charlieu (42)...115 E5
Pouilly-sur-Loire (58)....98 C1
Pouilly-sur-Meuse (55)....24 D3
Pouilly-sur-Saône (21)...102 A3
Pouilly-sur-Serre (02)....22 C2
Pouilly-sur-Vingeanne (21)...86 B4
le Poujol-sur-Orb (34)....172 A6
Poujols (34)..........172 C4
Poulaines (36)........96 C2
Poulainville (80)......7 G5
Poulan-Pouzols (81)....170 B3
Poulangy (52)........68 A5
Pouldergat (29)......53 E2
Pouldouran (22)......33 E2
Pouldreuzic (29)......53 E2
Poule-les-Écharmeaux (69)...115 G5
Pouliacq (64)........166 B6
les Poulières (88)......70 C3
Pouligney-Lusans (25)...87 G6
Pouligny-Notre-Dame (36)...111 H2
Pouligny-Saint-Martin (36)...111 H2
Pouligny-Saint-Pierre (36)...95 G6
le Pouliguen (44)......73 F4
Poullan-sur-Mer (29)....53 E2
Poullaouen (29)......32 B5
Poullignac (16)......122 A6
Poulx (30)..........174 B2
Poumarous (65)......183 F3
Poupas (82)..........168 B2
Poupry (28)..........62 D5
Pouques-Lormes (58)....83 H6
Pourcharesses (48)....156 D3
Pourchères (07)......157 H1
Pourcieux (83)......192 D2
Pourcy (51)..........45 E1
Pourlans (71)........102 B4
Pournoy-la-Chétive (57)...48 C2
Pournoy-la-Grasse (57)...48 D2
Pourrain (89)........83 E2
Pourrières (83)......192 D2
Poursac (16)........122 C1
Poursay-Garnaud (17)...121 F2
Poursiugues-Boucoue (64)...166 B5
Pouru-aux-Bois (08)....24 D2
Pouru-Saint-Remy (08)...24 D2
Poussan (34)..........189 F1
Poussanges (23)......125 H2
Poussay (88)..........69 F3
Pousseaux (58)......83 F4
Poussignac (47)......150 B4
Pousthomy (12)......171 F3
le Pout (33)........135 G6
Pouvrai (61)..........60 D3
Pouxeux (88)..........70 A4
Pouy (65)..........184 A2
Pouy-de-Touges (31)....184 D2
Pouy-Loubrin (32)......167 H6
Pouy-Roquelaure (32)...167 H1
Pouy-sur-Vannes (10)....65 G3
Pouyastruc (65)......183 F2
Pouydesseaux (40)....166 B2
Pouydraguin (32)......166 D4
Pouylebon (32)......167 F6
Pouzac (65)..........183 F4
Pouzauges (85)......92 C5
Pouzay (37)..........94 D2
Pouze (31)..........185 G1
Pouzilhac (30)......174 C1
le Pouzin (07)........144 A6
Pouzol (63)..........113 F6
Pouzolles (34)......188 C1
Pouzols (34)..........172 D5
Pouzols-Minervois (11)...187 H2
Pouzy-Mésangy (03)....98 C6
Poyanne (40)..........165 F3
Poyans (70)..........86 C5
Poyartin (40)........165 F4
Poyols (26)..........159 F2
Pozières (80)..........8 B5
le Pradal (34)........172 A5
les Pradeaux (63)......127 G5
Pradelle (26)........159 E2
Pradelles (43)......142 C6
Pradelles (59)..........2 D4
Pradelles-Cabardès (11)...187 E1
Pradelles-en-Val (11)....187 H4
Pradère-les-Bourguets (31)...168 D5
Prades (07)..........157 F2
Prades (09)..........199 G1
Prades (43)..........142 A4
Prades (66)..........200 C3
Prades (81)..........170 B5
Prades-d'Aubrac (12)....155 E3
Prades-le-Lez (34)....173 F4
Prades-Salars (12)....154 D5
Prades-sur-Vernazobre (34)...188 A1
le Pradet (83)........193 F5
Pradières (09)......185 H5
Pradiers (15)........141 E2
Pradinas (12)........154 A5
Pradines (19)........125 F5
Pradines (42)......129 E1
Pradines (46)......152 C3
Pradons (07)........157 G3
Prads-Haute-Bléone (04)...161 E5
Prahecq (79)..........108 A4

Prailles (79).........................108 A3
Pralognan-la-Vanoise (73) ...133 E6
Prâlon (21) 85 F6
Pralong (42) 128 D4
Pranles (07) 143 G6
Pranzac (16) 122 D4
Praslay (52) 85 H2
Praslin (10) 66 C5
Prasville (28) 62 C3
Prat (22) 32 D3
Prat-Bonrepaux (09) 184 D5
Prato-di-Giovellina (2B) 205 E1
Prats-de-Carlux (24) 138 B5
Prats-de-Mollo-la-
   Preste (66) 200 C5
Prats-de-Sournia (66) 200 C2
Prats-du-Périgord (24) 152 A1
Pratviel (81) 170 A5
Pratz (39) 117 H3
Pray (41) 79 G3
Praye (54) 69 F1
Prayols (09) 185 H6
Prayssac (46) 152 B3
Prayssas (47) 151 E5
Praz-sur-Arly (74) 132 D2
le Pré-d'Auge (14) 15 E3
Pré-en-Pail-Saint-
   Samson (53) 59 G1
Pré-Saint-Évroult (28) 62 A4
le Pré-Saint-Gervais (93) 42 D3
Pré-Saint-Martin (28) 62 B4
Préaux (07) 143 H3
les Préaux (27) 15 G3
Préaux (36) 95 H3
Préaux (53) 59 E6
Préaux (76) 18 D4
Préaux-Bocage (14) 38 B2
Prébois (38) 145 G6
Précey (50) 35 H4
Préchac (32) 167 H3
Préchac (33) 149 G3
Préchac (65) 182 D5
Préchac-sur-Adour (32) 166 D5
Préchacq-Josbaig (64) 181 F2
Préchacq-les-Bains (40) 165 F3
Préchacq-Navarrenx (64) 181 F2
Précieux (42) 129 E5
Précigné (72) 77 F2
Précilhon (64) 182 A3
Précy (18) 98 C2
Précy-le-Sec (89) 83 H4
Précy-Notre-Dame (10) 66 D2
Précy-Saint-Martin (10) 66 D2
Précy-sous-Thil (21) 84 C5
Précy-sur-Marne (77) 43 F3
Précy-sur-Oise (60) 20 C6
Précy-sur-Vrin (89) 64 D2
Prédefin (62) 2 B6
Préfailles (44) 73 G5
Prégilbert (89) 83 G3
Préguillac (17) 121 E3
Préhy (89) 83 H2
Preignac (33) 149 H2
Preignan (32) 167 H4
Preigney (70) 86 D2
Preixan (11) 186 D4
Prémanon (39) 118 B2
Premeaux-Prissey (21) 101 H2
Prémery (58) 99 E2
Prémesques (59) 3 F5
Prémeyzel (01) 131 F3
Prémian (34) 171 G6
Premières (21) 102 B1
Prémierfait (10) 66 A1
les Premiers Sapins (25) 104 A2
Prémilhat (03) 112 C4
Prémillieu (01) 131 F2
Prémont (02) 9 E5
Prémontré (02) 22 B3
Prendeignes (46) 153 H1
Préneron (32) 167 F4
la Prénessaye (22) 55 H2
Prenois (21) 85 G6
Prény (54) 48 B2
Préporché (58) 100 A4
les Prés (26) 159 G2
Présailles (43) 142 D5
Préseau (59) 9 F2
Présentevillers (25) 88 C4
Préserville (31) 169 G6
Présilly (39) 117 G3
Présilly (74) 118 B5
Presle (73) 132 B5
Presles (14) 145 E3
Presles (38) 145 E3
Presles (95) 42 C1
Presles-en-Brie (77) 43 F5
Presles-et-Boves (02) 22 B5
Presles-et-Thierny (02) 22 C4
Presly (18) 81 G6
Presnoy (45) 63 H6
Pressac (86) 109 F5
Pressagny-
   l'Orgueilleux (27) 41 F1
Pressignac (16) 123 F2
Pressignac-Vicq (24) 137 F5
Pressigny (52) 86 D2
Pressigny (79) 93 G5
Pressigny-les-Pins (45) 82 A1
Pressins (38) 131 F5
Pressy (62) 2 B6
Pressy-sous-Dondin (71) 115 H2
la Prétière (25) 88 B5
Pretin (39) 103 E4
Prétot-Vicquemare (76) 17 F3
Prêtreville (14) 39 G2
Préty (71) 116 C2
Pretz-en-Argonne (55) 47 E3

Preuilly (18) 97 F2
Preuilly-la-Ville (36) 95 F6
Preuilly-sur-Claise (37) 95 F4
Preures (62) 1 G5
Preuschdorf (67) 51 E2
Preuseville (76) 6 B6
Preutin-Higny (54) 25 H5
le Puech (34) 172 C5
Puéchabon (34) 173 E4
Puéchoursi (81) 170 A6
Puechredon (30) 173 G2
Puessans (25) 87 H5
Puget (84) 175 H4
Puget-Rostang (06) 178 C1
Puget-sur-Argens (83) 194 B2
Puget-Théniers (06) 178 C2
Puget-Ville (83) 193 G3
Pugey (25) 103 F1
Puginier (11) 186 B2
Pugnac (33) 135 F3
Pugny (79) 93 E5
Pugny-Chatenod (73) 131 H3
Puichéric (11) 187 G3
le Puid (88) 70 D2
Puihardy (79) 107 G1
Puilacher (34) 172 D6
Puilaurens (11) 200 B1
Puilboreau (17) 106 D4
Puilly-et-Charbeaux (08) 25 E2
Puimichel (04) 177 E2
Puimisson (34) 188 C1
Puimoisson (04) 177 E3
la Puisaye (28) 40 C6
Puiseaux (45) 63 H4
Puiselet-le-Marais (91) 63 F2
Puisenval (76) 6 B6
le Puiset (28) 62 D4
Puiseux (08) 23 H3
Puiseux (28) 41 F6
Puiseux-en-Bray (60) 19 G4
Puiseux-en-France (95) 43 E2
Puiseux-en-Retz (02) 21 H5
Puiseux-le-Hauberger (60) 20 B6
Puiseux-Pontoise (95) 42 B2
Puisieulx (51) 45 F1
Puisieux (62) 8 A4
Puisieux (77) 43 G2
Puisieux-et-Clanlieu (02).........9 G6
Puissalicon (34) 188 C1
Puisseguin (33) 136 A4
Puisserguier (34) 188 B2
Puits (21) 84 D2
Puits-et-Nuisement (10) 66 D4
Puits-la-Vallée (60) 20 B3
Puivert (11) 186 C6
Pujaudran (32) 168 D5
Pujaut (30) 174 D2
Pujo (65) 183 E2
Pujo-le-Plan (40) 166 B3
les Pujols (09) 185 H4
Pujols (33) 136 A6
Pujols (47) 151 F4
Pujols-sur-Ciron (33) 149 G2
le Puley (71) 101 E6
Puligny-Montrachet (21) 101 F4
Pullay (27) 40 C5
Pulligny (54) 48 C6
Pulnay (54) 69 F2
Pulnoy (54) 48 D5
Pulvérières (63) 126 D2
Pulversheim (68) 89 F1
Punchy (80) 21 F1
Punerot (88) 68 D1
Puntous (65) 183 H2
Pupillin (39) 103 E4
Pure (08) 24 D2
Purgerot (70) 87 F2
Pusey (70) 87 G3
Pusignan (69) 130 C3
Pussay (91) 63 E3
Pussigny (37) 94 D3
Pusy-et-Épenoux (70) 87 G3
Putanges-le-Lac (61) 38 D4
Puteaux (92) 42 C3
Putot-en-Auge (14) 14 D4
Puttelange-aux-Lacs (57) 49 H1
Puttelange-lès-
   Thionville (57) 26 C2
Puttigny (57) 49 F3
Puxe (54) 48 A1
Puxieux (54) 48 B1
le Puy (33) 150 B1
le Puy (33) 87 G6
Puy-d'Arnac (19) 139 E4
Puy-de-Serre (85) 107 F1
Puy-du-Lac (17) 121 E1
Le Puy-en-Velay (43) 142 C4
Puy-Guillaume (63) 127 H1
Puy-l'Évêque (46) 152 A3
Puy-Malsignat (23) 112 A6
le Puy-Notre-Dame (49) 93 G2
Puy-Saint-André (05) 147 E5
Puy-Saint-Eusèbe (05) 160 D2
Puy-Saint-Gulmier (63) 126 C3
Puy-Saint-Martin (26) 158 C2
Puy-Saint-Pierre (05) 147 E5
Puy-Saint-Vincent (05) 146 D5
le Puy-Sainte-
   Réparade (13) 176 A5
Puy-Sanières (05) 161 A5
Puybarban (33) 150 A2
Puybegon (81) 170 A4
Puybrun (46) 139 E5
Puycalvel (81) 170 B5
Puycasquier (32) 168 A4
Puycelsi (81) 169 H2
Puycornet (82) 152 B6
Puydaniel (31) 185 F2
Puydarrieux (65) 183 G2
la Puye (86) 109 H1

Puceul (44) 74 C2
le Puch (09) 199 H2
Puch-d'Agenais (47) 150 C4
Puchay (27) 19 F5
Puchevillers (80) 7 G4
le Puech (34) 172 C5
Puéchabon (34) 173 E4
Puéchoursi (81) 170 A6
Puechredon (30) 173 G2
Puessans (25) 87 H5
Puget (84) 175 H4
Puget-Rostang (06) 178 C1
Puget-sur-Argens (83) 194 B2
Puget-Théniers (06) 178 C2
Puget-Ville (83) 193 G3
Pugey (25) 103 F1
Puginier (11) 186 B2
Pugnac (33) 135 F3
Pugny (79) 93 E5
Pugny-Chatenod (73) 131 H3
Puichéric (11) 187 G3
le Puid (88) 70 D2
Puihardy (79) 107 G1
Puilacher (34) 172 D6
Puilaurens (11) 200 B1
Puilboreau (17) 106 D4
Puilly-et-Charbeaux (08) 25 E2

Puygaillard-de-
   Lomagne (82) 168 B2
Puygaillard-de-Quercy (82) ..169 G1
Puygiron (26) 158 B2
Puygouzon (81) 170 C3
Puygros (73) 132 A4
Puyjourdes (46) 153 F4
Puylagarde (82) 153 F5
Puylaroque (82) 152 D5
Puylaurens (81) 170 B6
Puylausic (32) 184 C1
Puyloubier (13) 192 C1
Puymaurin (31) 184 B2
Puyméras (84) 158 D5
Puymiclan (47) 150 D3
Puymirol (47) 151 G6
Puymoyen (16) 122 C4
Puynormand (33) 136 A4
Puyol-Cazalet (40) 166 A5
Puyoô (64) 165 F5
Puyravault (17) 107 E5
Puyravault (85) 106 D3
Puyréaux (16) 122 C2
Puyrolland (17) 107 G6
Puységur (32) 167 H4
Puysségur (31) 168 C4
Puysserampion (47) 150 D2
Puyvalador (66) 200 A3
Puyvert (84) 175 H4
Puzeaux (80) 21 F1
Puzieux (57) 48 D3
Puzieux (88) 69 F2
Py (66) 200 B4
la Pyle (27) 18 B6
Pys (80) 8 B4

Q

Quaëdypre (59) 2 C2
Quaix-en-Chartreuse (38) 145 G2
Quantilly (18) 97 H1
Quarante (34) 188 A2
Quarouble (59) 9 G1
Quarré-les-Tombes (89) 84 A6
la Quarte (70) 86 D2
le Quartier (63) 113 E6
Quasquara (2A) 205 E6
Quatre-Champs (08) 24 B4
les Quatre-Routes-du-
   Lot (46) 138 D4
Quatremare (27) 40 D1
Quatzenheim (67) 50 D5
Quéant (62) 8 C3
Queaux (86) 109 G3
Québriac (35) 35 E6
Quédillac (35) 56 C1
Queige (73) 132 D3
Quelaines-Saint-Gault (53) 58 C6
Quelmes (62) 2 A4
Quéménéven (29) 53 F1
Quemigny-Poisot (21) 101 G1
Quemigny-sur-Seine (21) 85 E3
Quemper-Guézennec (22) 33 E2
Quemperven (22) 32 D2
Quend (80) 6 C2
Quenne (89) 83 G2
Quenoche (70) 87 F4
Quenza (2A) 207 E2
Quercamps (62) 1 H4
Quercitello (2B) 205 F1
Quérénaing (59) 9 F2
Quérigut (09) 199 H2
Quernes (62) 2 B5
Querrien (29) 54 B3
Querrieu (80) 7 H5
Quers (70) 87 H2
Quesmy (60) 21 G2
le Quesne (80) 6 D6
le Quesnel (80) 21 E1
le Quesnel-Aubry (60) 20 C4
le Quesnoy (59) 9 G3
le Quesnoy-en-Artois (62) 7 E2
Quesnoy-le-Montant (80) 6 C4
Quesnoy-sur-Airaines (80) 7 E5
Quesnoy-sur-Deûle (59) 3 F4
Quesques (62) 1 G4
Quessigny (27) 41 F4
Quessoy (22) 33 H5
Questembert (56) 55 H6
Questrecques (62) 1 F5
Quet-en-Beaumont (38) 145 H5
Quetigny (21) 101 H1
Quettehou (50) 13 E2
Quettreville-sur-
   Sienne (50) 36 D2
Queudes (51) 44 D6
la Queue-en-Brie (94) 43 E4
la Queue-les-Yvelines (78) 41 H4
Queuille (63) 126 D1
Quevauvillers (80) 20 B1
Quéven (56) 54 C5
Quévert (22) 34 C5
Quevillon (76) 18 B5
Quevilloncourt (54) 69 F1
Quévreville-la-Poterie (76) 18 D5
Quévy (33) 120 C6
Queyrières (43) 142 D3
Queyssac (24) 137 E5
Queyssac-les-Vignes (19) 139 E4
Quézac (15) 153 H1
Quiberon (56) 72 B2
Quiberville (76) 17 F2
Quibou (50) 37 F1
Quié (09) 199 E1
Quiers (77) 43 G6
Quiers-sur-Bézonde (45) 63 G6
Quiéry-la-Motte (62) 8 C2

Quierzy (02) 21 H3
Quiestède (62) 2 B4
Quiévelon (59) 10 B3
Quiévrechain (59) 9 G1
Quièvrecourt (76) 19 E1
Quiévy (59) 9 F3
Quilen (62) 1 G6
Quillan (11) 186 D6
Quillebeuf-sur-Seine (27) 15 H2
le Quillio (22) 55 F1
Quilly (08) 24 A4
Quilly (44) 74 A3
Quimper (29) 53 F3
Quimperlé (29) 54 B4
Quincampoix (76) 18 D3
Quincampoix-Fleuzy (60) 19 G1
Quinçay (86) 108 D1
Quincerot (21) 84 C3
Quincerot (89) 66 B6
Quincey (21) 101 H2
Quincey (70) 87 G3
Quincié-en-Beaujolais (69) ...116 A5
Quincieu (38) 145 E1
Quincieux (69) 130 A2
Quincy (18) 97 F2
Quincy-Basse (02) 22 A4
Quincy-Landzécourt (55) 25 E4
Quincy-le-Vicomte (21) 84 C4
Quincy-sous-le-Mont (02) 22 B5
Quincy-sous-Sénart (91) 43 E5
Quincy-Voisins (77) 43 G3
Quinéville (50) 13 E3
Quingey (25) 103 F2
Quinquempoix (60) 20 C3
Quins (12) 154 B5
Quinsac (24) 123 F6
Quinsac (33) 135 F6
Quinson (04) 177 E4
Quinssaines (03) 112 C4
Quint-Fonsegrives (31) 169 F5
Quintal (74) 132 A2
la Quinte (72) 59 H5
Quintenas (07) 143 H2
Quintenic (22) 34 A4
Quintigny (39) 102 D5
Quintillan (11) 187 G5
Quintin (22) 33 F5
le Quiou (22) 34 D6
Quirbajou (11) 200 A1
Quiry-le-Sec (80) 20 C2
Quissac (30) 173 G3
Quissac (46) 153 E2
Quistinic (56) 54 D4
Quittebeuf (27) 40 D1
Quivières (80) 21 G1
Quœux-Haut-Maînil (62) 7 F2

R

Rabastens (81) 169 H3
Rabastens-de-Bigorre (65) 183 F1
Rabat-les-Trois-
   Seigneurs (09) 185 G6
la Rabatelière (85) 91 H3
Rabou (05) 160 B2
Rabouillet (66) 200 C2
Racécourt (88) 69 G3
Rachecourt-sur-Marne (52) 67 H1
Rachecourt-Suzémont (52) 67 G2
Râches (59) 8 D1
Racines (10) 65 H5
la Racineuse (71) 102 A5
Racquinghem (62) 2 B4
Racrange (57) 49 F3
Raddon-et-Chapendu (70) 88 A1
Radenac (56) 55 G4
Radepont (27) 19 E5
Radinghem (62) 2 A6
Radinghem-en-
   Weppes (59) 3 E5
Radonvilliers (10) 66 D2
Raedersdorf (68) 89 F4
Raedersheim (68) 71 F6
Raffetot (76) 15 H1
Rageade (15) 141 G3
Rahart (41) 79 G1
Rahay (72) 61 E6
Rahling (57) 50 B2
Rahon (25) 88 B6
Rahon (39) 102 C3
Rai (61) 40 A4
Raids (50) 12 D5
Raillencourt-Sainte-
   Olle (59) 8 D3
Railleu (66) 200 A3
Raillicourt (08) 24 A2
Raillimont (02) 23 F2
Raimbeaucourt (59) 8 D1
Rainans (39) 102 C2
Raincheval (80) 7 H4
Raincourt (70) 87 E1
Rainfreville (76) 17 F3
Rainneville (80) 7 H4
Rainsars (59) 10 A4
Rainville (88) 69 E2
Rainvillers (60) 20 A4
les Rairies (49) 77 G3
Raismes (59) 9 F1
Raissac (09) 186 A6
Raissac-d'Aude (11) 187 H3
Raissac-sur-Lampy (11) 186 D3
Raival (55) 47 F3
Raix (16) 108 C6
Raizeux (78) 41 G6
Ramasse (01) 117 E5
Ramatuelle (83) 194 B4

Rambaud (05) 160 C2
Rambervillers (88) 70 B2
Rambluzin-et-Benoîte-
   Vaux (55) 47 F2
Rambouillet (78) 42 A6
Rambucourt (55) 48 A4
Ramburelles (80) 6 C5
Rambures (80) 6 C5
Ramecourt (62) 7 G2
Ramecourt (88) 69 F3
Ramerupt (10) 66 C1
Ramicourt (02) 9 E5
Ramillies (59) 9 E3
Ramonchamp (88) 70 B6
Ramonville-Saint-
   Agne (31) 169 F6
Ramoulu (45) 63 F4
Ramous (64) 165 F5
Ramousies (59) 10 A4
Ramouzens (32) 167 E3
Rampan (50) 13 F6
Rampieux (24) 151 G1
Rampillon (77) 64 C1
Rampoux (46) 152 C2
Rancé (01) 130 A1
Rancenay (25) 103 F1
Rancennes (08) 11 F4
Rances (10) 67 E1
Ranchal (69) 115 G5
Ranchot (39) 103 E2
Ranchy (14) 13 H5
Rancogne (16) 122 D3
Rançon (87) 110 B5
Rançonnières (52) 68 C6
Rancourt (80) 8 C5
Rancourt (88) 69 F3
Rancourt-sur-Ornain (55) 46 D4
Rancy (71) 116 D1
Randan (63) 127 G1
Randens (73) 132 C5
Randevillers (25) 88 A6
Rânes (61) 38 D5
Rang (25) 88 B5
Rang-du-Fliers (62) 6 C1
Rangecourt (52) 68 C5
Rangen (67) 50 C5
Ranguevaux (57) 26 B4
Rannée (35) 57 H4
Ranrupt (67) 71 E2
Rans (39) 103 E2
Ransart (62) 8 A3
Ranspach (68) 70 D6
Ranspach-le-Bas (68) 89 G3
Ranspach-le-Haut (68) 89 G3
Rantigny (60) 20 D5
Ranton (86) 93 H3
Rantzwiller (68) 89 F2
Ranville (14) 14 C4
Ranville-Breuillaud (16) 122 A1
Ranzevelle (70) 69 F6
Ranzières (55) 47 G2
Raon-aux-Bois (88) 70 A5
Raon-lès-Leau (54) 50 A6
Raon-l'Étape (88) 70 C2
Raon-sur-Plaine (88) 50 A6
Rapaggio (2B) 205 G1
Rapale (2B) 203 F5
Rapey (88) 69 G3
Rapilly (14) 38 C3
Rapsécourt (51) 46 C2
Raray (60) 21 E6
Rarécourt (55) 47 E2
Rasiguères (66) 200 D1
Raslay (86) 93 H2
Rasteau (84) 158 C5
Ratenelle (71) 116 C2
Ratières (26) 144 B2
Ratte (71) 102 B6
Ratzwiller (67) 50 B2
Raucoules (43) 143 F2
Raucourt (54) 48 D3
Raucourt-au-Bois (59) 9 G3
Raucourt-et-Flaba (08) 24 C3
Raulhac (15) 140 C5
Rauret (43) 142 B6
Rauville-la-Bigot (50) 12 C3
Rauville-la-Place (50) 12 D4
Rauwiller (67) 50 A4
Rauzan (33) 135 H6
Raveau (58) 98 D2
Ravel (63) 127 G3
Ravenel (60) 20 D4
Ravenoville (50) 13 E3
Raves (88) 70 D3
Ravières (89) 84 C2
Ravigny (53) 59 H1
Raville (57) 26 D5
Raville-sur-Sânon (54) 49 E5
Ravilloles (39) 117 H2
la Ravoire (73) 131 H5
Ray-sur-Saône (70) 87 E3
Raye-sur-Authie (62) 7 E2
Rayet (47) 151 G1
Raymond (18) 98 A4
Raynans (25) 88 C4
Rayol-Canadel-sur-
   Mer (83) 194 A5
Rayssac (81) 170 D3
Razac-de-Saussignac (24) 136 C6
Razac-d'Eymet (24) 151 E1
Razac-sur-l'Isle (24) 137 E2
Raze (70) 87 F3
Razecueillé (31) 184 B5
Razengues (32) 168 C5
Razès (87) 110 C6
Razimet (47) 150 C4
Razines (37) 94 C3

Réal (66)..................200 A3
Réalcamp (76)..............6 C6
Réallon (05)..............160 D2
Réalmont (81)............170 C4
Réalville (82)...........169 F1
Réans (32)...............166 D3
Réau (77).................43 E6
Réaumont (38)...........131 F6
Réaumur (85)............92 C5
Réaup-Lisse (47)........150 C6
Réauville (26)..........158 B3
Réaux sur Trèfle (17)...121 G5
Rebais (77)..............44 A4
Rébénacq (64)..........182 B3
Rebergues (62)...........1 H4
Rebets (76).............19 E3
Rebeuville (88).........68 D2
Rebigue (31)...........169 F6
Rebourguil (12)........171 G3
Reboursin (36)..........96 D2
Rebréchien (45).........63 E6
Rebreuve-Ranchicourt (62)...7 H1
Rebreuve-sur-Canche (62)....7 G2
Rebreuviette (62)........7 G2
Recanoz (39)...........102 C5
Recey-sur-Ource (21)....85 G2
Réchésy (90)............89 E4
Réchicourt-la-Petite (54)...49 F5
Réchicourt-le-Château (57)...49 G5
Récicourt (55)..........47 E1
Réclainville (28).......62 C3
Reclesne (71)..........100 C3
Reclinghem (62)..........2 A5
Réclonville (54)........49 G6
Recloses (77)...........64 A3
Recologne (25)..........87 E6
Recologne (70)..........86 D4
Recologne-lès-Rioz (70)....87 F4
Recoubeau-Jansac (26)...159 F1
Recoules-d'Aubrac (48)...155 F1
Recoules-de-Fumas (48)...155 H2
Récourt (62).............8 C3
Récourt-le-Creux (55)....47 F2
Recouvrance (90)........88 D3
Recques-sur-Course (62)..1 G6
Recques-sur-Hem (62).....2 A3
Recquignies (59)........10 A2
Reculfoz (25)..........103 G6
Recurt (65)............183 H3
Recy (51)...............45 H3
Rédange (57)............26 A2
Rédené (29).............54 B4
Redessan (30)..........174 C3
Réding (57).............50 A4
Redon (35)..............74 A1
la Redorte (11)........187 G3
Redortiers (04)........159 G6
Réez-Fosse-Martin (60)...43 G1
Reffannes (79).........108 B1
Reffroy (55)............47 G6
Reffuveille (50)........37 F5
Régades (31)...........184 B4
Régat (09).............186 B5
Regnauville (62).........7 E2
Regnévelle (88).........69 F6
Regnéville-sur-Mer (50)...36 D2
Regnéville-sur-Meuse (55)...25 E6
Regney (88)............69 G3
Régnié-Durette (69)....116 A5
Regnière-Écluse (80).....6 D2
Regniowez (08).........10 D5
Regny (02)..............22 B1
Régny (42).............129 E1
la Regrippière (44).....75 F5
Réguiny (56)............55 G3
Réguisheim (68).........71 F6
Régusse (83)...........177 F4
Rehaincourt (88)........70 A2
Rehainviller (54).......49 E6
Rehaupal (88)...........70 B4
Reherrey (54)...........49 G6
Réhon (54)..............25 H3
Reichsfeld (67).........71 F2
Reichshoffen (67).......50 D2
Reichstett (67).........51 E5
Reignac (16)...........121 H6
Reignac (33)...........135 F2
Reignac-sur-Indre (37)...95 F1
Reignat (63)...........127 G3
Reigneville-Bocage (50)...12 D4
Reignier-Ésery (74)....118 C5
Reigny (18)............112 B1
Reilhac (15)...........140 A4
Reilhac (46)...........153 E1
Reilhaguet (46)........138 C6
Reilhanette (26).......159 F6
Reillanne (04).........176 B3
Reillon (54)............49 G6
Reilly (60).............19 H6
Reims (51)..............23 E6
Reims-la-Brûlée (51)....46 B5
Reinhardsmunster (67)...50 B5
Reiningue (68)..........89 F2
Reipertswiller (67).....50 C2
Reithouse (39)........117 G1
Réjaumont (32).........167 H3
Réjaumont (65).........183 H3
Rejet-de-Beaulieu (59)...9 G4
Relanges (88)...........69 F4
Relans (39)............102 C5
le Relecq-Kerhuon (29)...31 E4
Relevant (01)..........116 C6
Rely (62)................2 B5
Remaisnil (80)...........7 F3
Rémalard en Perche (61)...61 E2
Remaucourt (02).........9 E6
Remaucourt (08).........23 F3
la Remaudière (44).......75 E5

Remaugies (80)..........21 E3
Remauville (77).........64 B4
Rembercourt-
  Sommaisne (55)........47 E3
Rembercourt-sur-Mad (54)...48 B2
Rémécourt (60)..........20 D4
Rémelfang (57)..........26 D4
Rémelfing (57)..........27 H5
Rémeling (57)...........26 D3
Remennecourt (55).......46 D4
Remenoville (54)........69 H1
Rémérangles (60)........20 C4
Réméréville (54)........49 E5
Rémering (57)...........27 E4
Rémering-lès-
  Puttelange (57).......49 H2
Remicourt (51)..........46 C3
Remicourt (88)..........69 F3
Remiencourt (80)........20 C1
Remies (02).............22 B2
Remigny (02)............22 A2
Remigny (71)...........101 F4
Rémilly (57)............49 E2
Rémilly (58)...........100 A5
Remilly-Aillicourt (08)...24 C2
Remilly-en-Montagne (21)...85 F6
Remilly Les Marais (50)...13 E6
Remilly-les-Pothées (08)...23 H1
Remilly-sur-Tille (21)....86 A6
Remilly-Wirquin (62).....2 A5
Réminiac (56)...........56 B5
Remiremont (88).........70 B5
Remoiville (55).........25 E4
Remollon (05)..........160 C3
Remomeix (88)...........70 D3
Remoncourt (54)........49 G5
Remoncourt (88).........69 F3
Rémondans-Vaivre (25)...88 C5
Remoray-Boujeons (25)...103 H5
Remouillé (44).........91 G1
Remoulins (30).........174 C2
Removille (88)..........69 E2
Rempnat (87)...........125 F4
la Remuée (76).........15 G1
Rémuzat (26)...........159 E4
Remy (60)...............21 E4
Rémy (62)................8 C3
Renac (35)..............56 D6
Renage (38)............145 E1
Renaison (42)..........114 D6
Renansart (02)..........22 B2
Renaucourt (70)........86 D3
la Renaudie (63).......128 B3
Renauvoid (88)..........69 H4
Renay (41)..............79 G1
Renazé (53).............76 B1
Rencurel (38)..........145 E3
René (72)...............60 B3
Renédale (25)..........103 H3
Renescure (59)...........2 B4
Renève (21).............86 B5
Renneville (08).........23 F2
Renneville (27).........19 E4
Renneville (31)........186 A2
Renno (2A).............204 C3
le Renouard (61)........39 F3
Rennepont (52)..........67 F4
Rennes (35).............57 F3
Rennes-en-
  Grenouilles (53)......59 E1
Rennes-le-Château (11)...186 D6
Rennes-les-Bains (11)...187 E6
Rennes-sur-Loue (25)....103 F3
Renneval (02)...........23 E1
Renneville (08).........23 F2
Renneville (27).........19 E4
Renneville (31)........186 A2
Renno (2A).............204 C3
le Renouard (61)........39 F3
Rentières (63).........127 F6
Renty (62)..............1 H5
Renung (40)............166 B4
Renwez (08).............11 E6
la Réole (33)..........150 B2
la Réorthe (85).........92 A6
Réotier (05)...........161 F1
Repaix (54).............49 G5
la Répara-Auriples (26)...158 C1
Réparsac (16)..........121 H3
Repel (88)..............69 E2
Replonges (01).........116 B4
Reppe (90).............88 D2
Requeil (72)............78 A2
Réquista (12)..........171 E1
Résenlieu (61)..........39 G4
la Résie-Saint-Martin (70)...86 D6
Résigny (02)............23 F1
Resson (55).............47 E4
Ressons-le-Long (02)....21 H5
Ressons-sur-Matz (60)...21 E3
les Ressuintes (28).....40 C6
Restigné (37)...........78 A6
Restinclières (34).....173 G4
le Retail (79).........107 H1
Rétaud (17)...........121 E3
Reterre (23)...........112 C6
Rethel (08)............23 G4
Retheuil (02)...........21 G5
Rethondes (60).........21 F4
Rethonvillers (80)......21 F2
Retiers (35)............57 G4
Retjons (40)...........149 G6
Retonfey (57)...........26 C5
Rétonval (76)..........19 F1
Retournac (43).........142 D2
Retschwiller (67).......51 F2
Rettel (57)............26 C2
Rety (62)................1 G3

Retzwiller (68).........89 E3
Reugney (25)...........103 G3
Reugny (03)............112 D2
Reugny (37).............79 F5
Reuil (51)..............45 E2
Reuil-en-Brie (77)......44 A3
Reuil-sur-Brêche (60)....20 B3
Reuilly (27)............41 E2
Reuilly (36)............97 E3
Reuilly-Sauvigny (02)....44 C2
Reulle-Vergy (21).......101 G2
Reumont (59)............9 F4
la Réunion (47).........150 B4
Reutenbourg (67)........50 C5
Reuville (76)...........17 F3
Reux (14)...............15 E4
Réville (50)............44 C5
Réveillon (51).........44 C5
Réveillon (61)..........60 D1
Revel (31).............186 C1
Revel (38)............145 H2
Revel-Tourdan (38).....130 B6
Revelles (80)...........7 F6
Revens (30)...........172 B1
Reventin-Vaugris (38)...130 A6
Revercourt (28).........40 D5
Revest-des-Brousses (04)...176 B2
Revest-du-Bion (04)....176 B1
le Revest-les-Eaux (83)...193 E5
Revest-les-Roches (06)...178 D2
Revest-Saint-Martin (04)...176 C1
Reviers (14)............14 B3
Revigny (39)...........102 D6
Revigny-sur-Ornain (55)...46 D4
Réville (50)............13 E2
Réville-aux-Bois (55)...25 E5
Revin (08).............11 E5
Revonnas (01)..........117 E5
Rexingen (67)..........50 B3
Rexpoëde (59)...........3 F3
Reyersviller (57).......28 B6
Reygade (19)..........139 F4
Reynel (52).............68 B3
Reyniès (82)..........169 F2
Reyrevignes (46).......153 F2
Reyrieux (01)..........130 A1
Reyssouze (01).........116 C3
Reyvroz (74)..........119 E3
Rezay (18)..............97 F6
Rezé (44)...............74 C5
Rézentières (15).......141 F3
Rezonville (57).........26 A5
Rezza (2A)............204 D4
Rhèges (10).............66 A1
le Rheu (35)............57 E3
Rhinau (67).............71 H2
Rhodes (57).............49 H4
Rhodon (41).............79 H2
Rhuis (60)..............21 E5
Ri (61).................38 D4
Ria-Sirach (66).........200 C3
Riaillé (44)............75 E2
le Rialet (81).........171 E6
Rians (18)..............98 A2
Rians (83).............176 C5
Riantec (56)............54 C5
Riaucourt (52).........67 H4
Riaville (55)...........47 H1
Ribagnac (24).........136 D6
Ribarrouy (64).........166 B6
Ribaute (11)..........187 G4
Ribaute-les-Tavernes (30)...173 H1
le Ribay (53)..........59 F2
Ribeaucourt (55)........68 B1
Ribeaucourt (80).........7 F4
Ribeauville (02)........9 G4
Ribeauvillé (68)........71 F3
Ribécourt-Dreslincourt (60)...21 F4
Ribécourt-la-Tour (59)....8 D4
Ribemont (02)...........22 B1
Ribemont-sur-Ancre (80)...7 H5
Ribennes (48).........155 H2
Ribérac (24)..........136 D2
Ribes (07).............157 F4
Ribeyret (05)..........159 G3
Ribouisse (11).........186 B3
Riboux (83)............192 D3
la Ricamarie (42)......129 F6
Ricarville-du-Val (76)...19 E1
Ricaud (11)...........186 D2
Ricaud (65)...........183 F3
les Riceys (10).........66 D6
la Richardais (35)......34 D4
Richardménil (54)......48 C6
Richarville (91)........63 E1
la Riche (37)...........78 D5
Riche (57)..............49 F3
Richebourg (52).........67 H5
Richebourg (62).........2 D5
Richebourg (78)........41 G4
Richecourt (55).........48 A3
Richelieu (37).........94 B3
Richeling (57).........49 H2
Richemont (57).........26 B4
Richemont (76).........19 G1
Richerenches (84)......158 C4
Richeval (57)..........49 H5
Richeville (27).........19 F6
Richtolsheim (67).......71 G3
Richwiller (68).........89 F1
Ricourt (32)..........167 E6
Ricquebourg (60).......21 E3
Riec-sur-Bélon (29).....54 A4
Riedisheim (68)........89 F2
Riedseltz (67).........51 F2
Riel-les-Eaux (21).....67 E6
Riencourt (80)..........7 E6

Riencourt-lès-
  Bapaume (62)..........8 B4
Riencourt-lès-
  Cagnicourt (62)........8 C3
Riervescemont (90)......88 C2
Riespach (68)...........89 F3
Rieucazé (31)..........184 B4
Rieucros (09)..........186 A4
Rieulay (59)............9 E3
Rieumajou (31).........186 A1
Rieumes (31)..........184 D1
Rieupeyroux (12).......153 H5
Rieussec (34).........187 G1
Rieutort-de-Randon (48)...156 A2
Rieux (51)..............44 C4
Rieux (56)..............73 H1
Rieux (60)..............20 D5
Rieux (76)..............6 C5
Rieux-de-Pelleport (09)...185 H4
Rieux-en-Cambrésis (59)...9 E3
Rieux-en-Val (11)......187 F4
Rieux-Minervois (11)...187 F3
Rieux-Volvestre (31)...185 E3
Riez (04).............177 E3
Rigarda (66)..........200 C3
Rigaud (06)...........178 C1
Rignac (12)...........154 A4
Rignac (46)...........138 D6
Rigney (25)............87 G5
Rignieux-le-Franc (01)...130 C1
Rignosot (25)...........87 G5
Rignovelle (70).........88 A2
Rigny (70)..............86 D5
Rigny-la-Nonneuse (10)...65 G2
Rigny-la-Salle (55).....48 A6
Rigny-le-Ferron (10)....65 G4
Rigny-Saint-Martin (55)...48 A6
Rigny-sur-Arroux (71)...115 E2
Rigny-Ussé (37).........94 B1
Riguepeu (32).........167 F5
Rilhac-Lastours (87)...124 A4
Rilhac-Rancon (87).....124 B2
Rilhac-Treignac (19)...124 D5
Rilhac-Xaintrie (19)...139 H3
Rillans (25)............87 H5
Rillé (37)..............78 B5
Rilleux-la-Pape (69)...130 B2
Rilly-la-Montagne (51)...45 F1
Rilly-Sainte-Syre (10)...66 A2
Rilly-sur-Aisne (08)....24 A4
Rilly-sur-Loire (41)....79 G5
Rilly-sur-Vienne (37)...94 C3
Rimaucourt (52).........68 B3
Rimbach-près-
  Guebwiller (68).......71 E6
Rimbach-près-
  Masevaux (68).........88 D1
Rimbachzell (68)........71 E6
Rimbez-et-Baudiets (40)...167 E1
Rimboval (62)...........1 H6
Rimeize (48)...........141 G6
Rimling (57)............28 A5
Rimogne (08)............10 D6
Rimon-et-Savel (26)....159 E1
Rimons (33)............150 B1
Rimont (09)............185 E5
Rimou (35)..............35 G6
Rimplas (06)...........162 C6
Rimsdorf (67)...........50 A2
Rinxent (62).............1 F3
Riocaud (33)...........136 C6
Riolas (31)............184 C2
Riols (34).............171 G6
le Riols (81)..........153 F6
Riom (63)..............127 F2
Riom-ès-Montagnes (15)...140 C2
Rioms (63).............159 F5
Rion-des-Landes (40)...165 F2
Rions (33).............149 G1
Riorges (42)...........115 E6
Riotord (43)...........143 F2
Rioux (17)............121 E4
Rioux-Martin (16)......136 A2
Rioz (70)...............87 F5
Riquewihr (68)..........71 F4
Ris (63)...............127 H1
Ris (65)...............183 G6
Ris-Orangis (91).......42 D6
Riscle (32)............166 C4
Risoul (05)...........161 F1
Ristolas (05).........147 G6
Rittershoffen (67).....51 F2
Ritzing (57)...........26 D2
Riupeyrous (64)........182 C1
Rivarennes (36)........110 D1
Rivarennes (37)........94 C1
Rivas (42).............129 G5
Rive-de-Gier (42)......129 G5
Rivedoux-Plage (17)....106 C4
Rivehaute (64).........181 G1
Rivel (11)............186 B6
Rivemont (09)..........185 E5
Riverie (69)...........129 G4
Rivery (80).............7 G6
les Rives (34).........172 B3
Rives (47).............151 G1
Rives d'Andaine (61)....38 D4
Rives de l'Yon (85).....91 H5
Rives Dervoises (52)....67 E1
Rives-en-Seine (76)....18 A3
la Rivière (33).......135 G4
la Rivière (38).......131 F6

la Rivière (38).........145 F2
Rivière (62)............8 A3
la Rivière-de-Corps (10)...66 A3
la Rivière-Drugeon (25)...103 H4
la Rivière-Enverse (74)...119 F5
la Rivière-les-Fosses (52)...86 A3
Rivière-Saas-et-
  Gourby (40)..........164 D4
la Rivière-Saint-
  Sauveur (14)..........15 F3
Rivière-sur-Tarn (12)...155 F6
Rivières (16)...........122 B3
Rivières (30)..........157 F5
Rivières (81)..........170 A3
les Rivières-Henruel (51)...46 A5
Rivières-le-Bois (52)...86 B2
Riville (76)............16 D3
Rivolet (69)..........129 G1
la Rixe (39)...........103 G5
la Rixe (58)............83 F5
Rixheim (68)...........89 G2
la Rixouse (39)........118 A2
Rizaucourt-Buchey (52)...67 F3
Roaillan (33)..........149 H3
Roaix (84).............158 C5
Roanne (42)...........115 E6
Roannes-Saint-Mary (15)...140 A5
Robécourt (88).........68 D4
Robecq (62).............2 C5
Robersart (59)..........9 G3
Robert-Espagne (55)....46 D5
Robertot (76)..........17 E3
Roberval (60)..........21 E6
Robiac-Rochessadoule (30)...157 E5
la Robine-sur-Galabre (04)...160 C6
Robion (84)...........175 G3
le Roc (46)...........138 C5
Rocamadour (46).......138 D6
Rocbaron (83).........193 F3
Rocé (41)..............79 G2
Roche (38)............130 C4
Roche (42)............128 C4
la Roche-Bernard (56)...73 G2
la Roche-Blanche (44)...75 F3
la Roche-Blanche (63)...127 F4
la Roche-Canillac (19)...139 F2
la Roche-Chalais (24)...136 A2
Roche-Charles-la-
  Mayrand (63)........127 E6
la Roche-Clermault (37)...94 B2
la Roche-d'Agoux (63)...112 D6
la Roche-de-Glun (26)...144 A4
la Roche-de-Rame (05)...147 E6
la Roche-Derrien (22)...32 D2
la Roche-des-Arnauds (05)...160 B2
la Roche-en-Brenil (21)...84 B6
Roche-en-Régnier (43)...142 C2
la Roche-et-Raucourt (70)...86 D3
la Roche-Guyon (95)....41 G2
Roche-la-Molière (42)...129 F6
la Roche-l'Abeille (87)...124 B4
la Roche-Peyroux (19)...126 A6
Roche-lès-Clerval (25)...88 A5
Roche-lez-Beaupré (25)...87 G6
la Roche-Mabile (61)....59 H1
la Roche-Maurice (29)....31 F4
la Roche-Morey (70).....86 D2
la Roche-Noire (63)....127 F4
la Roche-Posay (86)....95 E5
la Roche-Rigault (86)...94 A3
Roche-Saint-Secret-
  Béconne (26).........158 C3
la Roche-sur-Foron (74)...118 D6
la Roche-sur-Grane (26)...158 C1
la Roche-sur-le-Buis (26)...159 E5
Roche-sur-Linotte-et-
  Sorans-les-Cordiers (70)...87 G4
La Roche-sur-Yon (85)...91 G4
la Roche-Vanneau (21)...85 E5
la Roche-Vineuse (71)...116 A3
Rochebaudin (26).......158 C2
la Rochebeaucourt-et-
  Argentine (24).......122 D5
Rochebrune (05)........160 C3
Rochebrune (26)........159 E4
Rochechinard (26)......144 D4
Rochechouart (87).....123 G2
Rochecolombe (07)......157 G3
Rochecorbon (37).......79 E5
Rochefort (17).........120 C1
Rochefort (73)........131 G4
Rochefort-du-Gard (30)...174 D2
Rochefort-en-Terre (56)...56 A6
Rochefort-en-Valdaine (26)...158 B3
Rochefort-en-
  Yvelines (78)........42 B6
Rochefort-Montagne (63)...126 D4
Rochefort-Samson (26)...144 C4
Rochefort-sur-Brévon (21)...85 F2
Rochefort-sur-la-Côte (52)...68 A4
Rochefort-sur-Loire (49)...76 D5
Rochefort-sur-Nenon (39)...102 D2
la Rochefoucauld (16)...122 D3
Rochefourchat (26).....159 E2
la Rochegiron (04).....176 B1
Rochegude (26).........158 B5
Rochegude (30).........157 F5
Rochejean (25)........103 H5
la Rochelle (17).......106 C5
la Rochelle (70).......86 D2
Rochemaure (07).......158 A2
la Rochénard (79).....107 G4
Rochepaule (07).......143 G5
la Rochepot (21)......101 F4
Rocher (07)...........157 F2
Roches (23)...........111 H4
Roches (41)............80 A2
Roches-Bettancourt (52)...68 A3

les Roches-de-
  Condrieu (38)........130 A6
Roches-lès-Blamont (25)...88 C5
les Roches-l'Évêque (41)...79 F2
Roches-Prémarie-
  Andillé (86).........109 E2
Rocheservière (85)......91 F2
Rochessauve (07)......158 A1
Rochesson (88).........70 C5
Rochetaillée (52).......85 H1
Rochetaillée-sur-
  Saône (69)...........130 A2
Rochetoirin (38).......131 E4
Rochetrejoux (85)......92 B5
la Rochette (04).......178 C2
la Rochette (05).......160 C2
la Rochette (07).......143 E5
la Rochette (16).......122 D2
la Rochette (73).......132 B5
la Rochette (77).......64 A1
la Rochette-du-Buis (26)...159 F5
Rocheville (50).........12 C3
Rochonvillers (57)......26 B3
Rochy-Condé (60).......20 B5
Rocles (03)...........113 F3
Rocles (07)...........157 F2
Rocles (48)...........156 C1
Roclincourt (62).........8 B2
Rocourt-Saint-Martin (02)...44 B1
Rocquancourt (14)......14 C5
Rocquefort (76)........17 E4
Rocquemont (60)........21 F6
Rocquemont (76)........19 E3
Rocquencourt (60)......20 C2
Rocquencourt (78)......42 B4
Rocques (14)...........15 F5
Rocquigny (02).........10 A5
Rocquigny (08).........23 F2
Rocquigny (62)..........8 C4
Rocroi (08)............10 D5
Rodalbe (57)...........49 F3
Rodelinghem (62)........1 G3
Rodelle (12)..........154 C3
Rodemack (57)..........26 C2
Roderen (68)...........89 E1
Rodern (68)............71 F3
Rodès (66)............200 D2
Rodez (12)............154 C4
Rodilhan (30).........174 B3
Rodome (11)...........199 H1
la Roë (53)............58 A6
Rœllecourt (62).........7 G2
Rœschwoog (67).........51 G3
Rœulx (59).............9 E2
Rœux (62)..............8 C2
Roézé-sur-Sarthe (72)...60 A6
Roffey (89)............84 A1
Roffiac (15)..........141 E4
Rogécourt (02).........22 B2
Rogerville (76)........15 F2
Rogéville (54).........48 B4
Roggenhouse (68).......71 G6
Rogliano (2B).........203 F1
Rogna (39)............117 H3
Rognac (13)...........191 H4
Rognaix (73)..........132 D4
Rognes (13)...........175 H5
Rognon (25)............87 H5
Rognonas (13).........175 E3
Rogny (02).............22 D1
Rogny-les-Sept-
  Écluses (89).........82 B2
Rogy (80)..............20 B2
Rohaire (28)...........40 B5
Rohan (56).............55 G3
Rohr (67)..............50 D4
Rohrbach-lès-Bitche (57)...28 A6
Rohrwiller (67)........51 F4
Roiffé (86)............94 A2
Roiffieux (07)........143 H2
Roiglise (80)..........21 F2
Roilly (21)............84 C5
Roinville (28).........62 C2
Roinville (91).........63 E1
Roinvilliers (91)......63 F3
Roisel (80).............8 D5
les Roises (55)........68 C1
Roisey (42)...........129 H6
Roissard (38).........145 F5
Roissy-en-Brie (77)....43 F4
Roissy-en-France (95)...43 E2
Roiville (61)..........39 G3
Roizy (08).............23 F4
Rolampont (52).........68 A6
Rolbing (57)...........28 A4
Rollainville (88)......68 D2
Rollancourt (62)........7 F1
Rolleboise (78)........41 G2
Rolleville (76)........15 F1
Rollot (80)............21 E3
Rom (79)..............108 D4
Romagnat (63).........127 F3
la Romagne (08)........23 G2
la Romagne (35)........135 H6
Romagné (35)...........35 H6
la Romagne (49)........92 B2
Romagne (86)..........109 E4
Romagne-sous-les-
  Côtes (55)...........25 E6
Romagne-sous-
  Montfaucon (55)......24 D5
Romagnieu (38)........131 F4
Romagny (68)..........89 E3
Romagny Fontenay (50)...37 G5
Romagny-sous-
  Rougemont (90).......88 D2

Romain (25) 87 H5
Romain (39) 103 E1
Romain (51) 22 D5
Romain (54) 69 H1
Romain-aux-Bois (88) 68 D5
Romain-sur-Meuse (52) ... 68 C4
la Romaine (70) 87 E4
Romainville (93) 42 H4
Roman (27) 40 D4
Romanèche-Thorins (71) . 116 B5
Romange (39) 102 D2
Romans (01) 116 C5
Romans (79) 108 A3
Romans-sur-Isère (26) ... 144 C4
Romanswiller (67) 50 C5
Romazières (17) 108 B6
Romazy (35) 35 G6
Rombach-le-Franc (68) ... 71 E3
Rombas (57) 26 B4
Rombies-et-
    Marchipont (59) 9 G2
Rombly (62) 2 B5
Romegoux (17) 120 D1
Romelfing (57) 49 H3
Romenay (71) 116 D2
Romeny-sur-Marne (02) ... 44 B3
Romeries (59) 9 F3
Romery (02) 9 G6
Romery (51) 45 E2
Romescamps (60) 19 H2
Romestaing (47) 150 B3
Romeyer (26) 145 E6
la Romieu (32) 167 G2
Romigny (51) 44 D1
Romiguières (34) 172 B3
Romillé (35) 56 D2
Romilly (41) 61 G6
Romilly-la-Puthenaye (27) 40 C2
Romilly-sur-Andelle (27) . 18 D5
Romilly-sur-Seine (10) ... 65 G1
Romont (88) 70 A2
Romorantin-Lanthenay (41) 80 C6
Rompon (07) 143 H6
Rônai (61) 38 D4
Roncenay (10) 66 B4
Roncey (50) 37 E2
Ronchamp (70) 88 B2
Ronchaux (25) 103 F3
Ronchères (02) 44 C1
Ronchères (89) 82 D3
Roncherolles-en-Bray (76) 19 F3
Roncherolles-sur-le-
    Vivier (76) 18 D4
Ronchin (59) 3 F5
Ronchois (76) 19 G2
Roncourt (57) 26 B5
Roncq (59) 3 G4
la Ronde (17) 107 F3
la Ronde-Haye (50) 12 D6
Rondefontaine (25) 103 H5
Ronel (81) 170 C3
Rongères (03) 114 A4
Ronnet (03) 112 D5
Ronno (69) 129 F1
Ronquerolles (95) 42 C1
Ronsenac (16) 122 C5
Ronssoy (80) 8 D5
Rontalon (69) 129 H4
Rontignon (64) 182 C2
Ronvaux (55) 47 G1
Roost-Warendin (59) 8 D1
Roppe (90) 88 D2
Roppenheim (67) 51 G3
Roppentzwiller (68) 89 F3
Roppeviller (57) 28 C5
la Roque-Alric (84) 158 D6
la Roque-Baignard (14) ... 15 E5
la Roque-d'Anthéron (13) 175 H4
la Roque-en-Provence (06) 178 C2
la Roque-Esclapon (83) . 178 A4
la Roque-Gageac (24) .. 138 A6
la Roque-Sainte-
    Marguerite (12) 172 B1
la Roque-sur-Cèze (30) . 157 H6
la Roque-sur-Pernes (84) 175 G2
Roquebillière (06) 179 E1
Roquebrun (34) 172 A4
Roquebrune (32) 167 F4
Roquebrune (33) 150 B1
Roquebrune-Cap-
    Martin (06) 179 G3
Roquebrune-sur-
    Argens (83) 194 B2
la Roquebrussanne (83) . 193 E3
Roquecor (82) 151 H4
Roquecourbe (81) 170 D5
Roquecourbe-
    Minervois (11) 187 G3
Roquedur (30) 173 E2
Roquefère (11) 187 E2
Roquefeuil (11) 199 H1
Roquefixade (09) 186 A6
Roquefort (32) 167 H4
Roquefort (40) 166 B1
Roquefort (47) 151 E6
Roquefort-de-Sault (11) . 200 A2
Roquefort-des-
    Corbières (11) 188 A5
Roquefort-la-Bédoule (13) 192 C4
Roquefort-les-
    Cascades (09) 186 A5
Roquefort-les-Pins (06) . 178 D4
Roquefort-sur-
    Garonne (31) 184 C3
Roquefort-sur-Soulzon (12) 171 H2
Roquelaure (32) 167 H4
Roquelaure-Saint-
    Aubin (32) 168 C5

Roquemaure (30) 174 D1
Roquemaure (81) 169 G3
Roquepine (32) 167 G2
Roqueredonde (34) 172 B4
Roques (31) 169 E6
Roques (32) 167 F3
Roquesérière (31) 169 G4
Roquessels (34) 172 B6
Roquestéron (06) 178 C2
Roquetaillade (11) 186 D5
la Roquette (27) 19 E6
la Roquette-sur-
    Siagne (06) 178 C5
la Roquette-sur-Var (06) 179 E3
Roquettes (31) 169 E6
Roquevaire (13) 192 C3
Roquevidal (81) 170 A5
Roquiague (64) 181 G3
la Roquille (33) 136 C6
Rorbach-lès-Dieuze (57) . 49 G3
Rorschwihr (68) 71 F3
Rosans (05) 159 F4
Rosay (39) 117 F2
Rosay (76) 17 H4
Rosay (78) 41 G3
Rosay-sur-Lieure (27) ... 19 E5
Rosazia (2A) 204 C4
Rosbruck (57) 27 F5
Roscanvel (29) 30 D5
Roscoff (29) 31 H2
Rosel (14) 14 B4
Rosenau (68) 89 G3
Rosenwiller (67) 50 C6
Roset-Fluans (25) 103 E2
Rosey (70) 87 F4
Rosey (71) 101 F6
Rosheim (67) 50 C6
la Rosière (70) 70 B6
Rosières (43) 142 D3
Rosières (60) 43 F1
Rosières (81) 170 C1
Rosières-aux-Salines (54) 48 D6
Rosières-en-Haye (54) ... 48 B4
Rosières-en-Santerre (80) 21 E1
Rosières-près-Troyes (10) 66 B3
Rosières-sur-Barbèche (25) 88 B6
Rosières-sur-Mance (70) . 87 E1
Rosiers-de-Juillac (19) . 138 B1
Rosiers-d'Égletons (19) 139 F1
les Rosiers-sur-Loire (49) 77 F5
Rosis (34) 171 H5
Rosnay (36) 95 H6
Rosnay (51) 22 D6
Rosnay (85) 91 H5
Rosnay-l'Hôpital (10) ... 66 D2
Rosnoën (29) 31 F6
Rosny-sous-Bois (93) ... 43 E4
Rosny-sur-Seine (78) 41 G2
Rosoy (60) 20 D5
Rosoy (89) 65 E4
Rosoy-en-Multien (60) ... 43 H2
Rospez (22) 32 D2
Rospigliani (2B) 205 F3
Rosporden (29) 53 H3
Rosselange (57) 26 B4
Rossfeld (67) 71 H2
Rossillon (01) 131 F2
Rosteig (67) 50 B2
Rostrenen (22) 54 D1
Rosult (59) 9 E1
Rosureux (25) 104 C1
Rotalier (39) 117 F1
Rotangy (60) 20 A3
Rothau (67) 71 E1
Rothbach (67) 50 D3
Rotherens (73) 132 B5
la Rothière (10) 67 E3
Rothois (60) 20 A3
Rothonay (39) 117 F2
Rots (14) 14 B4
Rott (67) 29 E6
Rottelsheim (67) 51 E4
Rottier (26) 159 F3
Rou-Marson (49) 93 G1
Rouairoux (81) 171 E6
Rouans (44) 74 B5
la Rouaudière (53) 76 A1
Roubaix (59) 3 G4
Roubia (11) 187 H3
Roubion (06) 162 B6
Roucourt (59) 8 D2
Roucy (02) 22 D5
Roudouallec (56) 54 A2
Rouécourt (52) 67 H3
Rouède (31) 184 C4
Rouelles (52) 85 H2
Rouen (76) 18 C4
Rouessé-Fontaine (72) ... 60 A3
Rouessé-Vassé (72) 59 G4
Rouet (34) 173 F3
Rouez (72) 59 G4
Rouffach (68) 71 F5
Rouffange (39) 103 E1
Rouffiac (15) 139 G4
Rouffiac (16) 136 B1
Rouffiac (17) 121 F3
Rouffiac (81) 170 B3
Rouffiac-d'Aude (11) .. 186 D4
Rouffiac-des-Corbières (11) 187 F6
Rouffiac-Tolosan (31) .. 169 F5
Rouffignac (17) 135 F1
Rouffignac-de-
    Sigoulès (24) 136 D6
Rouffignac-Saint-Cernin-
    de-Reilhac (24) 137 H4
Rouffilhac (46) 138 C6

Rouffy (51) 45 F3
Rougé (44) 57 G6
Rouge-Perriers (27) 40 C1
Rougefay (62) 7 F2
Rougegoutte (90) 88 C2
Rougemont (21) 84 C3
Rougemont (25) 87 H4
Rougemont-le-
    Château (90) 88 D2
Rougemontiers (27) 18 A5
Rougemontot (25) 87 G5
Rougeou (41) 80 B6
Rougeries (02) 22 D1
les Rouges-Eaux (88) ... 70 C3
Le Rouget-Pers (15) ... 139 H5
Rougeux (52) 86 C2
Rougiers (83) 193 E3
Rougnac (16) 122 D5
Rougnat (23) 112 C6
Rougon (04) 177 G3
Rouhe (25) 103 F2
Rouhling (57) 27 G5
Rouillac (16) 122 A3
Rouillac (22) 34 B6
Rouillé (86) 108 C2
Rouillon (72) 60 A5
Rouilly (77) 44 B6
Rouilly-Sacey (10) 66 C3
Rouilly-Saint-Loup (10) . 66 B3
Roujan (34) 172 C6
Roulans (25) 87 G6
le Roulier (88) 70 B4
Roullens (11) 186 D4
Roullet-Saint-Estèphe (16) 122 B4
Roumagne (47) 150 D2
Roumare (76) 18 C3
Roumazières-Loubert (16) 123 E2
Roumégoux (15) 139 H5
Roumégoux (81) 170 C4
Roumengoux (09) 186 B4
Roumens (31) 186 B1
Roumoules (04) 177 E3
Rountzenheim (67) 51 F3
Roupeldange (57) 26 D4
Rouperroux (61) 39 E6
Rouperroux-le-Coquet (72) 60 C3
Roupy (02) 21 H1
la Rouquette (12) 153 G5
Roure (06) 162 C6
le Rouret (06) 178 D4
Rousies (59) 10 A2
Roussac (87) 110 C6
Roussas (26) 158 B3
Roussayrolles (81) 170 A1
Rousseloy (60) 20 C5
Roussennac (12) 154 A3
Roussent (62) 6 D2
les Rousses (39) 118 B2
Rousset (05) 160 C3
Rousset (13) 192 C2
Rousset-les-Vignes (26) 158 D4
Le Rousset-Marizy (71) 115 G1
Roussieux (26) 159 F4
Roussillon (38) 144 A1
Roussillon (84) 176 A2
Roussillon-en-Morvan (71) 100 C3
Roussines (16) 123 E3
Roussines (36) 110 D2
Rousson (30) 157 E6
Rousson (89) 65 E5
Roussy-le-Village (57) ... 26 B2
Routes (76) 17 E3
Routier (11) 186 C4
Routot (27) 18 A5
Rouvenac (11) 186 C6
Rouves (54) 48 C3
la Rouvière (30) 174 A2
Rouvignies (59) 9 F2
Rouville (60) 21 F6
Rouville (76) 16 D4
Rouvillers (60) 21 E4
Rouvray (21) 84 B5
Rouvray (27) 41 E2
Rouvray (89) 83 G1
Rouvray-Catillon (76) ... 19 F3
Rouvray-Saint-Denis (28) 62 D3
Rouvray-Sainte-Croix (45) 62 C5
Rouvrel (80) 20 C1
Rouvres (14) 38 D2
Rouvres (28) 41 F4
Rouvres (77) 43 F2
Rouvres-en-Multien (60) 43 H1
Rouvres-en-Plaine (21) 102 A1
Rouvres-en-Woëvre (55) 25 G6
Rouvres-en-Xaintois (88) 69 F3
Rouvres-la-Chétive (88) 68 D3
Rouvres-les-Bois (36) .. 96 C3
Rouvres-les-Vignes (10) 67 E2
Rouvres-Saint-Jean (45) 63 F3
Rouvres-sous-Meilly (21) 101 E1
Rouvrois-sur-Meuse (55) 47 G3
Rouvrois-sur-Othain (55) 25 G5
Rouvroy (02) 9 E6
Rouvroy (62) 8 C1
Rouvroy-en-Santerre (80) 21 E1
Rouvroy-les-Merles (60) 20 C2
Rouvroy-sur-Audry (08) 23 H1
Rouvroy-sur-Marne (52) 67 H2
Rouvroy-sur-Serre (02) 23 E3
le Roux (07) 157 E1
Rouxmesnil-Bouteilles (76) 17 G2
Rouy (58) 99 G3
Rouy-le-Grand (80) 21 G1
Rouy-le-Petit (80) 21 G1
Rouze (09) 199 H2

Rouzède (16) 123 E3
Rouziers (15) 139 H6
Rouziers-de-Touraine (37) 78 D4
le Rove (13) 192 A3
Roville-aux-Chênes (88) 70 A2
Roville-devant-Bayon (54) 69 G1
Rovon (38) 145 E2
Roy-Boissy (60) 19 H3
Royan (17) 120 C4
Royas (38) 130 C5
Royat (63) 127 E3
Royaucourt (60) 20 D3
Royaucourt-et-
    Chailvet (02) 22 B4
Royaumeix (54) 48 B4
Roybon (38) 144 D2
Roye (70) 88 A3
Roye (80) 21 F2
Roye-sur-Matz (60) 21 F3
Royer (71) 116 B1
Royère-de-Vassivière (23) 125 F2
Royères (87) 124 C2
Roynac (26) 158 C2
Royon (62) 1 H6
Royville (76) 17 F3
Roz-Landrieux (35) 35 E4
Roz-sur-Couesnon (35) . 35 F4
Rozay-en-Brie (77) 43 G5
le Rozel (50) 12 B3
Rozelieures (54) 69 H1
Rozérieulles (57) 26 B5
Rozerotte (88) 69 F3
Rozès (32) 167 G3
Rozet-Saint-Albin (02) . 44 B1
Rozier-Côtes-d'Aurec (42) 142 D1
Rozier-en-Donzy (42) .. 129 E3
Rozières-en-Beauce (45) 62 C6
Rozières-sur-Crise (02) . 22 A5
Rozières-sur-Mouzon (88) 68 D4
Roziers-Saint-Georges (87) 124 D3
Rozoy-Bellevalle (02) ... 44 C3
Rozoy-le-Vieil (45) 64 C5
Rozoy-sur-Serre (02) ... 23 F2
Ruages (58) 83 G6
Ruan (45) 62 D5
Ruan-sur-Egvonne (41) . 61 G6
Ruaudin (72) 60 B6
Rubelles (77) 64 A1
Rubempré (80) 7 G5
Rubercy (14) 13 G5
Rubescourt (80) 20 D3
Rubigny (08) 23 F2
Rubrouck (59) 2 B3
Ruca (22) 34 B4
Ruch (33) 136 A6
Rudeau-Ladosse (24) .. 123 E5
Rudelle (46) 153 F1
Rue (80) 6 C2
la Rue-Saint-Pierre (60) 20 C4
la Rue-Saint-Pierre (76) 18 D3
Ruederbach (68) 89 F3
Rueil-la-Gadelière (28) . 40 C5
Rueil-Malmaison (92) .. 42 C4
Ruelisheim (68) 89 F1
Ruelle-sur-Touvre (16) 122 C4
les Rues-des-Vignes (59) 9 E4
Ruesnes (59) 9 G3
Rueyres (46) 153 F1
Ruffec (16) 108 D6
Ruffec (36) 110 B1
Ruffey-le-Château (25) . 87 E6
Ruffey-lès-Beaune (21) 101 G3
Ruffey-lès-Echirey (21) 85 H6
Ruffey-sur-Seille (39) . 102 C5
Ruffiac (47) 150 B4
Ruffiac (56) 56 B5
Ruffieu (01) 131 F1
Ruffieux (73) 131 G2
Ruffigné (44) 57 G6
Rugles (27) 40 B4
Rugney (88) 69 G2
Rugny (89) 84 B1
Ruhans (70) 87 G5
Ruillé-en-Champagne (72) 59 H5
Ruillé-Froid-Fonds (53) . 58 D6
Ruisseauville (62) 2 A6
Ruitz (62) 8 A1
Rullac-Saint-Cirq (12) . 154 B6
Rully (14) 38 B6
Rully (60) 21 E6
Rully (71) 101 F4
Rumaucourt (62) 8 C3
Rumegies (59) 3 H6
Rumersheim-le-Haut (68) 71 G6
Rumesnil (14) 15 E4
Rumigny (08) 23 G1
Rumigny (80) 20 C1
Rumilly (62) 1 H5
Rumilly-en-Cambrésis (59) 8 D4
Rumilly-lès-Vaudes (10) 66 C4
Ruminghem (62) 2 A3
Rumont (55) 47 F4
Rumont (77) 63 H3
Runan (22) 33 E2
Rungis (94) 42 D5
Ruoms (07) 157 G3
Rupéreux (77) 44 B6
Ruppes (88) 68 D2
Rupt (52) 67 H2
Rupt-aux-Nonains (55) . 47 E5
Rupt-devant-Saint-
    Mihiel (55) 47 F3
Rupt-en-Woëvre (55) ... 47 G2
Rupt-sur-Moselle (88) .. 70 B6
Rupt-sur-Othain (55) ... 25 F4
Rupt-sur-Saône (70) ... 87 E3
Rurange-lès-Thionville (57) 26 C4

Rurey (25) 103 F2
Rusio (2B) 205 F2
Russ (67) 50 B6
Russange (57) 26 A2
le Russey (25) 104 C1
Russy-Bémont (60) 21 G6
Rustenhart (68) 71 G6
Rustiques (11) 187 F3
Rustrel (84) 176 A2
Rustroff (57) 26 D2
Rutali (2B) 203 F5
Ruvigny (10) 66 B3
Ruy-Montceau (38) 130 D4
Ruyaulcourt (62) 8 C4
Ruynes-en-Margeride (15) 141 F4
Ry (76) 19 E4
Rye (39) 102 C4
Ryes (14) 14 A3

S

Saâcy-sur-Marne (77) ... 44 A3
Saales (67) 70 D2
Saâne-Saint-Just (76) .. 17 F3
Saasenheim (67) 71 H3
Sabadel-Latronquière (46) 153 G1
Sabadel-Lauzès (46) ... 152 D2
Sabaillan (32) 184 B1
Sabalos (65) 183 F2
Sabarat (09) 185 F4
Sabarros (65) 183 H3
Sabazan (32) 166 D4
Sablé-sur-Sarthe (72) ... 77 F1
les Sables-d'Olonne (85) 91 E6
Sablet (84) 158 C6
Sablières (07) 157 E3
Sablonceaux (17) 120 D3
Sablonnières (77) 44 B4
Sablons (33) 135 H4
Sablons (38) 144 A1
Sablons sur Huisne (61) 61 F2
Sabonnères (31) 184 D1
la Sabotterie (08) 24 A3
Sabran (30) 157 H6
Sabres (40) 149 E6
Saccourvielle (31) 197 F1
Sacé (53) 58 D4
Sacey (50) 35 G5
Saché (37) 94 D1
Sachin (62) 2 B6
Sachy (08) 24 D2
Sacierges-Saint-
    Martin (36) 110 D2
Saclas (91) 63 E2
Saclay (91) 42 C5
Saconin-et-Breuil (02) . 21 H5
Sacoué (65) 184 A5
Sacquenay (21) 86 B4
Sacquenville (27) 40 D2
Sacy (51) 45 E1
Sacy-le-Grand (60) 20 D5
Sacy-le-Petit (60) 21 E5
Sadeillan (32) 183 G1
Sadillac (24) 136 D6
Sadirac (33) 135 F6
Sadournin (65) 183 G2
Sadroc (19) 138 D2
Saessolsheim (67) 50 D4
Saffais (54) 48 D6
Saffloz (39) 103 F6
Saffré (44) 74 D2
Saffres (21) 85 E6
Sagelat (24) 137 H6
Sagnat (23) 111 E4
Sagnes-et-Goudoulet (07) 143 E6
Sagonne (18) 98 B5
Sagy (71) 117 E1
Sagy (95) 42 A2
Sahorre (66) 200 B4
Sahune (26) 159 E4
Sahurs (76) 18 B5
Sai (61) 39 E4
Saignes (15) 140 B1
Saignes (46) 153 F1
Saigneville (80) 6 C4
Saignon (84) 176 A3
Saiguède (31) 168 D6
Sail-les-Bains (42) 114 D4
Sail-sous-Couzan (42) 128 C3
Sailhan (65) 196 D1
Saillac (19) 138 D4
Saillac (46) 153 E4
Saillagouse (66) 199 H4
Saillans (26) 158 D1
Saillans (33) 135 G4
Saillant (63) 142 D1
Saillat-sur-Vienne (87) 123 G2
Saillenard (71) 102 C6
Sailly (08) 24 D2
Sailly (52) 68 A2
Sailly (71) 115 H2
Sailly (78) 41 H2
Sailly-Achâtel (57) 48 D3
Sailly-au-Bois (62) 8 A4
Sailly-en-Ostrevent (62) 8 C2
Sailly-Flibeaucourt (80) . 6 D3
Sailly-Laurette (80) 8 A6
Sailly-le-Sec (80) 8 A6
Sailly-lez-Cambrai (59) .. 8 D3
Sailly-lez-Lannoy (59) ... 3 G5
Sailly-Saillisel (80) 8 C5
Sailly-sur-la-Lys (62) 3 E5
Sain-Bel (69) 129 G3
Saincaize-Meauce (58) .. 98 D4
Sainghin-en-
    Mélantois (59) 3 G5

Sainghin-en-Weppes (59) 3 E6
Sainneville (76) 15 F1
Sainpuits (89) 83 E4
Sains (35) 35 F4
Sains-du-Nord (59) 10 A4
Sains-en-Amiénois (80) 20 C1
Sains-en-Gohelle (62) ... 8 A1
Sains-lès-Fressin (62) ... 1 H6
Sains-lès-Marquion (62) . 8 D3
Sains-lès-Pernes (62) 2 B6
Sains-Morainvillers (60) 20 D3
Sains-Richaumont (02) . 22 C1
le Saint (56) 54 B2
Saint-Abit (64) 182 C3
Saint-Abraham (56) 56 A5
Saint-Acheul (80) 7 F3
Saint-Adjutory (16) ... 123 E3
Saint-Adrien (22) 33 E4
Saint-Affrique (12) ... 171 G2
Saint-Affrique-les-
    Montagnes (81) 170 C6
Saint-Agathon (22) 33 E4
Saint-Agil (41) 61 F5
Saint-Agnan (58) 84 B6
Saint-Agnan (71) 114 D2
Saint-Agnan (81) 169 H4
Saint-Agnan (89) 64 C3
Saint-Agnan-de-
    Cernières (27) 39 H3
Saint-Agnan-en-
    Vercors (26) 145 E5
Saint-Agnan-sur-
    Sarthe (61) 39 H6
Saint-Agnant (17) 120 C1
Saint-Agnant-de-
    Versillat (87) 111 E4
Saint-Agnant-près-
    Crocq (23) 126 A3
Saint-Agne (24) 137 E5
Saint-Agnet (40) 166 B5
Saint-Agnin-sur-Bion (38) 130 D5
Saint-Agoulin (63) 113 G6
Saint-Agrève (07) 143 F4
Saint-Aignan (08) 24 B2
Saint-Aignan (33) 135 G4
Saint-Aignan (41) 96 A1
Saint-Aignan (56) 55 E1
Saint-Aignan (72) 60 B4
Saint-Aignan (82) 168 C1
Saint-Aignan-de-
    Couptrain (53) 59 F1
Saint-Aignan-de-
    Cramesnil (14) 14 C5
Saint-Aignan-des-
    Noyers (18) 98 B5
Saint-Aignan-
    Grandlieu (44) 74 C6
Saint-Aignan-le-
    Jaillard (45) 81 G2
Saint-Aignan-sur-Roë (53) 76 A1
Saint-Aignan-sur-Ry (76) 19 E4
Saint-Aigny (36) 110 B1
Saint-Aigulin (17) 136 A2
Saint-Ail (54) 26 A5
Saint-Albain (71) 116 B3
Saint-Alban (01) 117 F6
Saint-Alban (22) 34 A4
Saint-Alban (31) 169 F4
Saint-Alban-Auriolles (07) 157 F4
Saint-Alban-d'Ay (07) . 143 H2
Saint-Alban-de-
    Montbel (73) 131 G5
Saint-Alban-de-Roche (38) 130 D4
Saint-Alban-des-
    Villards (73) 146 B1
Saint-Alban-
    d'Hurtières (73) 132 C5
Saint-Alban-du-Rhône (38) 130 A6
Saint-Alban-en-
    Montagne (07) 156 D1
Saint-Alban-les-Eaux (42) 128 C1
Saint-Alban-Leysse (73) 131 H4
Saint-Alban-sur-
    Limagnole (48) 141 G6
Saint-Albin-de-
    Vaulserre (38) 131 G5
Saint-Alexandre (30) . 158 A5
Saint-Algis (02) 9 H6
Saint-Allouestre (56) ... 55 G4
Saint-Alpinien (23) ... 125 H1
Saint-Alyre-d'Arlanc (63) 142 A1
Saint-Alyre-ès-
    Montagne (63) 141 E1
Saint-Amadou (09) ... 186 A4
Saint-Amancet (81) ... 186 C1
Saint-Amand (23) 125 H1
Saint-Amand (50) 7 H3
Saint-Amand-de-Coly (24) 138 B4
Saint-Amand-de-Vergt (24) 137 F4
Saint-Amand-en-
    Puisaye (58) 82 D4
Saint-Amand-
    Jartoudeix (23) 124 D2
Saint-Amand-le-Petit (87) 125 E3
Saint-Amand-les-Eaux (59) 9 F1
Saint-Amand-Longpré (41) 79 F3
Saint-Amand-
    Magnazeix (87) 110 D5
Saint-Amand-
    Montrond (18) 97 H6
Saint-Amand-sur-Fion (51) 46 B4
Saint-Amand-sur-
    Ornain (55) .... 47 Fô
Saint-Amand-sur-
    Sèvre (79) 92 C4
Saint-Amand-Villages (50) 37 G1
Saint-Amandin (15) ... 140 C1
Saint-Amans (09) 185 G4

Saint-Amans (11)................... 186 B3
Saint-Amans (48) 156 A2
Saint-Amans-de-
Pellagal (82)................... 152 A5
Saint-Amans-des-Cots (12) ... 154 C1
Saint-Amans-du-Pech (82)... 151 G4
Saint-Amans-Soult (81) 187 F1
Saint-Amans-Valtoret (81) ... 187 F1
Saint-Amant-de-Boixe (16) ... 122 B2
Saint-Amant-de-
Bonnieure (16) 122 C2
Saint-Amant-de-
Nouère (16) 122 B3
Saint-Amant-Roche-
Savine (63) 128 A5
Saint-Amant-Tallende (63) ... 127 F4
Saint-Amarin (68)................... 70 D6
Saint-Ambreuil (71) 101 G6
Saint-Ambroix (18)................. 97 F4
Saint-Ambroix (30) 157 F5
Saint-Amé (88) 70 B5
Saint-Amour (39) 117 E2
Saint-Amour-Bellevue (71) ... 116 B4
Saint-Andelain (58) 82 C6
Saint-Andéol (26) 144 D6
Saint-Andéol (38) 145 F4
Saint-Andéol-de-Berg (07) ... 157 H3
Saint-Andéol-de-
Fourchades (07) 143 F5
Saint-Andéol-de-Vals (07)... 157 G1
Saint-Andéol-le-
Château (69) 129 H5
Saint-Andeux (21) 84 B5
Saint-Andiol (13) 175 E3
Saint-André (31) 184 C2
Saint-André (32) 168 B6
Saint-André (66) 201 F3
Saint-André (73) 147 E2
Saint-André (81) 171 E2
Saint-André-Capcèze (48)... 156 D4
Saint-André-d'Allas (24) 138 A5
Saint-André-d'Apchon (42) ... 114 D6
Saint-André-de-Bâgé (01)... 116 C4
Saint-André-de-Boëge (74)... 118 D4
Saint-André-de-Bohon (50) ... 13 E5
Saint-André-de-
Briouze (61) 38 C4
Saint-André-de-
Buèges (34) 173 E3
Saint-André-de-
Chalencon (43) 142 C2
Saint-André-de-Corcy (01)... 130 B1
Saint-André-de-
Cruzières (07) 157 F5
Saint-André-de-
Cubzac (33) 135 F4
Saint-André-de-
Double (24)................... 136 C3
Saint-André-de-la-
Roche (06) 179 E3
Saint-André-de-
Lancize (48) 156 C5
Saint-André-de-
l'Épine (50) 13 F6
Saint-André-de-l'Eure (27) ... 41 E3
Saint-André-de-Lidon (17)... 120 D4
Saint-André-de-
Majencoules (30) 173 E2
Saint-André-de-
Messei (61)...................... 38 B5
Saint-André-de-Najac (12)... 153 G6
Saint-André-de-
Roquelongue (11) 187 H4
Saint-André-de-
Roquepertuis (30) 157 G5
Saint-André-de-
Rosans (05) 159 F4
Saint-André-de-
Sangonis (34) 172 D5
Saint-André-de-
Seignanx (40) 164 C5
Saint-André-de-
Valborgne (30)............... 156 B6
Saint-André-de-
Vézines (12) 155 G6
Saint-André-d'Embrun (05)... 161 E2
Saint-André-des-Eaux (22) ... 34 D6
Saint-André-des-Eaux (44)... 73 G4
Saint-André-
d'Hébertot (14).................. 15 F3
Saint-André-d'Huiriat (01) ... 116 C5
Saint-André-
d'Oléargues (30) 157 H6
Saint-André-du-Bois (33)... 150 A2
Saint-André-en-
Barrois (55).................... 47 E2
Saint-André-en-Bresse (71) .. 102 A4
Saint-André-en-
Morvan (58) 83 H5
Saint-André-en-
Royans (38) 144 D3
Saint-André-en-Terre-
Plaine (89) 84 B5
Saint-André-en-
Vivarais (07) 143 F3
Saint-André-et-
Appelles (33)................. 136 B6
Saint-André-Farivillers (60)... 20 C3
Saint-André-Goule-
d'Oie (85).......................... 92 A4
Saint-André-la-Côte (69)... 129 G4
Saint-André-Lachamp (07) ... 157 F3
Saint-André-le-
Bouchoux (01)............... 116 D5
Saint-André-le-Coq (63)....... 127 E1
Saint-André-le-Désert (71)... 115 H2
Saint-André-le-Gaz (38) 131 F5
Saint-André-le-Puy (42) ... 129 E4

Saint-André-les-Alpes (04) ... 177 H2
Saint-André-les-
Vergers (10)...................... 66 B3
Saint-André-lez-Lille (59)......... 3 F5
Saint-André-sur-Cailly (76) ... 18 D3
Saint-André-sur-Orne (14) ... 14 B5
Saint-André-sur-Sèvre (79)... 92 D5
Saint-André-sur-Vieux-
Jonc (01)........................116 D5
Saint-Androny (33)............. 135 E2
Saint-Ange-et-Torçay (28) ... 41 E6
Saint-Ange-le-Viel (77).......... 64 B3
Saint-Angeau (16) 122 C2
Saint-Angel (03) 112 D3
Saint-Angel (19) 125 H5
Saint-Angel (63) 127 E1
Saint-Anthème (63) 128 C5
Saint-Anthot (21)................... 85 E6
Saint-Antoine (15) 154 A1
Saint-Antoine (25) 104 A5
Saint-Antoine (32) 168 B1
Saint-Antoine-de-
Breuilh (24) 136 B5
Saint-Antoine-de-
Ficalba (47) 151 F4
Saint-Antoine-du-
Queyret (33) 136 A6
Saint-Antoine-du-
Rocher (37).................... 78 D4
Saint Antoine l'Abbaye (38).. 144 D2
Saint-Antoine-la-Forêt (76) ... 15 G1
Saint-Antoine-sur-
l'Isle (33) 136 B4
Saint-Antonin (06) 178 C2
Saint-Antonin (32) 168 B4
Saint-Antonin-de-
Lacalm (81).................... 170 D4
Saint-Antonin-de-
Sommaire (27) 40 A2
Saint-Antonin-du-Var (83) ... 193 G1
Saint-Antonin-Noble-
Val (82)........................... 153 E6
Saint-Antonin-sur-
Bayon (13) 192 C2
Saint-Aoustrille (36)............. 96 D4
Saint-Août (36) 97 E6
Saint-Apollinaire (05) 160 D2
Saint-Apollinaire (21).......... 85 H6
Saint-Apollinaire-de-
Rias (07)........................ 143 G5
Saint-Appolinaire (69) 129 F1
Saint-Appolinard (38) 144 D2
Saint-Appolinard (42) 143 H1
Saint-Aquilin (24) 136 D2
Saint-Aquilin-de-
Corbion (61)...................... 39 H6
Saint-Araille (31) 184 D4
Saint-Arailles (32) 167 F5
Saint-Arcons-d'Allier (43) ... 142 A4
Saint-Arcons-de-
Barges (43) 142 C6
Saint-Arey (38) 145 G5
Saint-Armel (35) 57 F4
Saint-Armel (56) 72 D1
Saint-Armou (64) 182 C1
Saint-Arnac (66) 200 C1
Saint-Arnoult (14)................... 15 E3
Saint-Arnoult (41) 79 F3
Saint-Arnoult (60) 19 H2
Saint-Arnoult (76)................... 18 A3
Saint-Arnoult-des-
Bois (28) 61 H1
Saint-Arnoult-en-
Yvelines (78) 42 A6
Saint-Arroman (32) 183 H1
Saint-Arroman (65) 183 G4
Saint-Arroumex (82) 168 C2
Saint-Astier (24) 137 E3
Saint-Astier (47) 136 C6
Saint-Auban (06) 178 B3
Saint-Auban-d'Oze (05) 160 A3
Saint-Auban-sur-
l'Ouvèze (26) 159 F5
Saint-Aubert (59) 9 F3
Saint-Aubin (02) 21 H4
Saint-Aubin (10) 65 F1
Saint-Aubin (21) 101 F4
Saint-Aubin (36) 97 E5
Saint-Aubin (39) 102 B3
Saint-Aubin (40) 165 G4
Saint-Aubin (47) 151 G3
Saint-Aubin (59) 10 A3
Saint-Aubin (62) 6 C1
Saint-Aubin (91) 42 B5
Saint-Aubin-Celloville (76)... 18 D5
Saint-Aubin-
d'Appenai (61) 60 C1
Saint-Aubin-
d'Arquenay (14) 14 C4
Saint-Aubin-
d'Aubigné (35) 57 F1
Saint-Aubin-de-Blaye (33) ... 135 F1
Saint-Aubin-de-
Bonneval (61)................... 39 G3
Saint-Aubin-
de-Branne (33) 135 H6
Saint-Aubin-de-
Cadelech (24) 151 E1
Saint-Aubin-de-
Courteraie (61)................ 39 H6
Saint-Aubin-de-Crétot (76)... 18 A3
Saint-Aubin-de-
Languais (24) 137 E6
Saint-Aubin-de-
Locquenay (72) 59 H3
Saint-Aubin-de-Médoc (33)... 134 D4
Saint-Aubin-de-
Nabirat (24) 152 B1

Saint-Aubin-de-
Scellon (27) 15 G5
Saint-Aubin-de-
Terregatte (50) 35 H4
Saint-Aubin-
d'Écrosville (27) 40 C1
Saint-Aubin-des-Bois (14) ... 37 F3
Saint-Aubin-des-Bois (28) ... 62 A1
Saint-Aubin-des-
Châteaux (44)................. 57 G6
Saint-Aubin-des-
Chaumes (58) 83 H5
Saint-Aubin-des-
Coudrais (72) 60 D4
Saint-Aubin-des-
Landes (35)..................... 57 H3
Saint-Aubin-des-
Ormeaux (85).................. 92 B3
Saint-Aubin-des-
Préaux (50) 36 D3
Saint-Aubin-du-
Cormier (35) 57 G1
Saint-Aubin-du-Désert (53) ... 59 G3
Saint-Aubin-du-Perron (50) ... 12 D6
Saint-Aubin-du-Plain (79) ... 93 E4
Saint-Aubin-du-
Thenney (27) 39 H2
Saint-Aubin-en-Bray (60)...... 19 H4
Saint-Aubin-en-
Charollais (71) 115 F2
Saint-Aubin-Épinay (76) 18 D4
Saint-Aubin-Fosse-
Louvain (53) 58 C1
Saint-Aubin-la-Plaine (85) ... 106 D1
Saint-Aubin-le-Cauf (76) 17 H2
Saint-Aubin-le-Cloud (79)... 93 F6
Saint-Aubin-le-
Dépeint (37).................... 78 C3
Saint-Aubin-le-Monial (03) ... 113 F2
Saint-Aubin-le-
Vertueux (27) 40 A2
Saint-Aubin-lès-Elbeuf (76) ... 18 C5
Saint-Aubin-les-
Forges (58) 99 E2
Saint-Aubin-Montenoy (80)...... 7 E6
Saint-Aubin-Rivière (80)......... 6 D6
Saint-Aubin-Routot (76)......... 15 G2
Saint-Aubin-sous-
Erquery (60) 20 D4
Saint-Aubin-sur-
Gaillon (27) 41 E1
Saint-Aubin-sur-Loire (71) ... 114 C1
Saint-Aubin-sur-Mer (14) ... 14 B3
Saint-Aubin-sur-Mer (76) 17 F2
Saint-Aubin-sur-
Quilleboeuf (27) 15 H2
Saint-Aubin-sur-Scie (76)... 17 G2
Saint-Aubin-sur-Yonne (89) ... 65 E6
Saint-Augustin (17) 120 B3
Saint-Augustin (19) 125 E6
Saint-Augustin (62) 2 B5
Saint-Augustin (77) 43 H4
Saint-Augustin-des-
Bois (49) 76 C4
Saint-Aulaire (19) 138 B2
Saint-Aulais-la-
Chapelle (16) 122 A6
Saint-Aulaye-
Puymangou (24) 136 B2
Saint-Aunès (34) 173 G5
Saint-Aunix-Lengros (32) ... 166 D5
Saint-Aupre (38) 131 F6
Saint-Austremoine (43) 141 G3
Saint-Auvent (87) 123 G2
Saint-Avaugourd-des-
Landes (85)...................... 91 F6
Saint-Avé (56) 55 G6
Saint-Aventin (31) 197 F1
Saint-Avertin (37) 79 E6
Saint-Avit (16) 136 B2
Saint-Avit (26) 144 B2
Saint-Avit (40) 166 A2
Saint-Avit (41) 61 F5
Saint-Avit (47) 150 C2
Saint-Avit (63) 126 B2
Saint-Avit-de-Soulège (33) ... 136 B6
Saint-Avit-de-Tardes (23)... 125 H2
Saint-Avit-de-Vialard (24) ... 137 G5
Saint-Avit-Frandat (32) 168 A2
Saint-Avit-le-Pauvre (23)... 125 G1
Saint-Avit-Rivière (24)........ 137 G6
Saint-Avit-les-
Guespières (28) 61 H3
Saint-Avit-Saint-
Nazaire (33) 136 C5
Saint-Avit-Sénieur (24) 137 F6
Saint-Avold (57) 27 F5
Saint-Avre (73) 132 C6
Saint-Ay (45)........................... 80 C1
Saint-Aybert (59) 9 G1
Saint-Babel (63) 127 G5
Saint-Baldoph (73) 131 H5
Saint-Bandry (02) 21 H5
Saint-Baraing (39) 102 C3
Saint-Barbant (87) 109 H5
Saint-Bard (23) 126 A2
Saint-Bardoux (26) 144 B3
Saint-Barnabé (22) 55 G2
Saint-Barthélemy (38) 144 C1
Saint-Barthélemy (40) 164 C5
Saint-Barthélemy (50)........... 37 G5
Saint-Barthélemy (56) 55 E4
Saint-Barthélemy (70)........... 88 B2
Saint-Barthélemy (77)........... 44 B4
Saint-Barthélemy-
d'Agenais (47).............. 150 D3

Saint-Barthélemy-
d'Anjou (49) 77 E4
Saint-Barthélemy-de-
Bellegarde (24)............. 136 C3
Saint-Barthélemy-de-
Bussière (24) 123 F4
Saint-Barthélemy-de-
Séchilienne (38) 145 H3
Saint-Barthélemy-de-
Vals (26)......................... 144 A3
Saint-Barthélemy-
Grozon (07).................... 143 H4
Saint-Barthélemy-le-
Meil (07) 143 G5
Saint-Barthélemy-le-
Plain (07)........................ 144 A4
Saint-Barthélemy-
Lestra (42) 129 F3
Saint-Basile (07) 143 G4
Saint-Baslemont (88) 69 F4
Saint-Baudel (18) 97 F5
Saint-Baudelle (53) 58 D3
Saint-Baudille-de-la-
Tour (38) 130 D3
Saint-Baudille-et-Pipet (38) ... 145 G6
Saint-Bauld (37) 95 F2
Saint-Baussant (54) 48 A3
Saint-Bauzeil (09) 185 G4
Saint-Bauzély (30) 174 A2
Saint-Bauzile (07) 158 A1
Saint-Bauzile (48) 156 A3
Saint-Bauzille-de-
Montmel (34) 173 G4
Saint-Bauzille-de-
Putois (34) 173 E3
Saint-Bazile (87) 123 G3
Saint-Bazile-de-
Meyssac (19) 139 E4
Saint-Béat (31) 184 A6
Saint-Beaulize (12) 172 A3
Saint-Beauzeil (82).............. 151 H4
Saint-Beauzély (12) 155 E6
Saint-Beauzire (43) 141 G2
Saint-Beauzire (63) 127 F2
Saint-Bénézet (30) 173 H2
Saint-Bénigne (01) 116 C2
Saint-Benin (59) 9 F4
Saint-Benin-d'Azy (58)........... 99 F3
Saint-Benin-des-Bois (58)..... 99 F2
Saint-Benoist-sur-Mer (85) ... 91 G6
Saint-Benoist-sur-
Vanne (10) 65 G4
Saint-Benoît (04) 178 B2
Saint-Benoît (11) 186 C5
Saint-Benoît (86) 109 E1
Saint-Benoît-de-
Carmaux (81) 170 C1
Saint-Benoît-des-
Ombres (27) 15 H4
Saint-Benoît-des-
Ondes (35) 35 E4
Saint-Benoît-
d'Hébertot (14)................ 15 F3
Saint-Benoît-du-Sault (36)... 110 D3
Saint-Benoit-en-Diois (26) ... 159 E1
Saint-Benoît-la-
Chipotte (88)................... 70 B2
Saint-Benoît-la-Forêt (37) ... 94 B1
Saint-Benoît-sur-Loire (45) ... 81 F2
Saint-Benoît-sur-Seine (10) ... 66 A2
Saint-Bérain (43) 142 A4
Saint-Bérain-sous-
Sanvignes (71) 100 D6
Saint-Bérain-sur-
Dheune (71) 101 F5
Saint-Bernard (01) 129 H1
Saint-Bernard (21) 101 H2
Saint-Bernard (38) 145 H1
Saint-Bernard (68) 89 E2
Saint-Béron (73) 131 G5
Saint-Berthevin (53) 58 C5
Saint-Berthevin-la-
Tannière (53) 58 B2
Saint-Bertrand-de-
Comminges (31) 184 A5
Saint-Biez-en-Belin (72)........ 78 B1
Saint-Bihy (22)........................ 33 F5
Saint-Blaise (06) 179 E3
Saint-Blaise (74) 118 B6
Saint-Blaise-du-Buis (38) ... 131 F6
Saint-Blaise-la-Roche (67) ... 71 E1
Saint-Blancard (32) 184 A2
Saint-Blimont (80).................... 6 C4
Saint-Blin (52) 68 B3
Saint-Boès (64) 165 F5
Saint-Bohaire (41) 79 H3
Saint-Boil (71)...................... 101 F6
Saint-Boingt (54) 69 H1
Saint-Bomer (28) 61 E4
Saint-Bômer-les-
Forges (61) 38 A5
Saint-Bon (51) 44 C5
Saint-Bonnet (16) 122 A5
Saint-Bonnet-
Avalouze (19) 139 E2
Saint-Bonnet-Briance (87)... 124 C3
Saint-Bonnet-de-Bellac (87) ... 110 A5
Saint-Bonnet-de-
Chavagne (38) 144 D3
Saint-Bonnet-de-
Chirac (48) 155 G3
Saint-Bonnet-de-
Condat (15).................... 140 D2
Saint-Bonnet-de-Cray (71)... 115 E5
Saint-Bonnet-de-Four (03)... 113 F4

Saint-Bonnet-de-Joux (71) ... 115 G2
Saint-Bonnet-de-Mure (69) ... 130 B4
Saint-Bonnet-de-
Rochefort (03) 113 G5
Saint-Bonnet-de-
Salendrinque (30) 173 F1
Saint-Bonnet-de-
Salers (15) 140 B3
Saint-Bonnet-de-
Valclérieux (26) 144 C2
Saint-Bonnet-de-Vieille-
Vigne (71) 115 F2
Saint-Bonnet-des-
Bruyères (69) 115 H4
Saint-Bonnet-des-
Quarts (42) 114 D5
Saint-Bonnet-du-Gard (30) ... 174 C2
Saint-Bonnet-Elvert (19) ... 139 F3
Saint-Bonnet-en-
Bresse (71) 102 A4
Saint-Bonnet-en-
Champsaur (05) 160 B1
Saint-Bonnet-la-
Rivière (19) 138 B1
Saint Bonnet-Laval (48) 142 B6
Saint-Bonnet-le-Bourg (63) ... 128 A6
Saint-Bonnet-le-
Chastel (63) 128 A6
Saint-Bonnet-le-
Château (42) 128 D6
Saint-Bonnet-le-
Courreau (42) 128 C4
Saint-Bonnet-le-Froid (43) ... 143 F3
Saint-Bonnet-
l'Enfantier (19) 138 C1
Saint-Bonnet-lès-Allier (63) ... 127 G3
Saint-Bonnet-les-
Oules (42) 129 F5
Saint-Bonnet-les-Tours-de-
Merle (19) 139 G4
Saint-Bonnet-près-
Bort (19) 126 A5
Saint-Bonnet-près-
Orcival (63) 126 D4
Saint-Bonnet-près-
Riom (63) 127 F2
Saint-Bonnet-sur-
Gironde (17) 121 E6
Saint-Benin-Tronçais (03)... 112 D1
Saint-Bonnot (58) 99 E1
Saint-Bouize (18) 98 C1
Saint-Brancher (89).............. 84 A5
Saint-Branchs (37)................ 95 E1
Saint-Brandan (22) 33 F5
Saint-Brès (30) 157 F5
Saint-Brès (32) 168 A4
Saint-Brès (34) 173 G5
Saint-Bresson (30) 173 E2
Saint-Bresson (70) 88 A1
Saint-Bressou (46) 153 G1
Saint-Brevin-les-Pins (44) ... 73 H4
Saint-Briac-sur-Mer (35) 34 C4
Saint-Brice (16) 121 G3
Saint-Brice (33) 150 A1
Saint-Brice (50) 35 H3
Saint-Brice (53) 77 E1
Saint-Brice (61) 38 A6
Saint-Brice (77) 65 E1
Saint-Brice-Courcelles (51) ... 23 E6
Saint-Brice-de-
Landelles (50) 37 F6
Saint-Brice-sous-Forêt (95) ... 42 D2
Saint-Brice-sous-
Rânes (61) 38 D5
Saint-Brice-sur-Vienne (87) ... 123 H2
Saint-Brieuc (22) 33 G4
Saint-Brieuc-de-
Mauron (56) 56 B3
Saint-Brieuc-des-Iffs (35)....... 57 E1
Saint-Bris-des-Bois (17)....... 121 F3
Saint-Bris-le-Vineux (89)....... 83 G2
Saint-Brisson (58) 100 B1
Saint-Brisson-sur-
Loire (45) 82 A3
Saint-Broing (70) 86 D5
Saint-Broing-les-
Moines (21) 85 F3
Saint-Broingt-le-Bois (52)..... 86 B2
Saint-Broingt-les-
Fosses (52) 86 A2
Saint-Broladre (35) 35 F4
Saint-Bueil (38) 131 G5
Saint-Calais (72) 61 E6
Saint-Calais-du-Désert (53) ... 59 G1
Saint-Calez-en-
Saosnois (72) 60 B3
Saint-Cannat (13) 175 H5
Saint-Caprais (03) 112 C2
Saint-Caprais (18) 97 G4
Saint-Caprais (32) 168 A5
Saint-Caprais (46) 152 B2
Saint-Caprais-de-
Blaye (33) 135 F1
Saint-Caprais-de-
Bordeaux (33)............... 135 H6
Saint-Caprais-de-Lerm (47) ... 151 F5
Saint-Capraise-de-
Lalinde (24) 137 E5
Saint-Capraise-
d'Eymet (24)................. 151 E1
Saint-Caradec (22) 55 F1
Saint-Caradec-
Trégomel (56) 54 C3
Saint-Carné (22) 34 C5
Saint-Carreuc (22) 33 G5
Saint-Cassien (24) 151 G1

Saint-Cassien (38) 145 F1
Saint-Cassin (73) 131 H5
Saint-Cast-le-Guildo (22) 34 B3
Saint-Castin (64) 182 C1
Saint-Célerin (72) 60 C4
Saint-Céneri-le-Gérei (61) ... 59 H2
Saint-Céols (18) 98 A1
Saint-Céré (46) 139 F5
Saint-Cergues (74) 118 D4
Saint-Cernin (15) 140 A4
Saint-Cernin-de-
Labarde (24) 137 E6
Saint-Cernin-de-
Larche (19) 138 C3
Saint-Cernin-de-
l'Herm (24) 152 A2
Saint-Césaire (17) 121 F3
Saint-Césaire-de-
Gauzignan (30) 173 H1
Saint-Cézaire-sur-
Siagne (06) 178 B4
Saint-Cézert (31) 168 D4
Saint-Chabrais (23) 112 A5
Saint-Chaffrey (05) 147 F5
Saint-Chamant (15) 140 A3
Saint-Chamant (19) 139 F3
Saint-Chamarand (46) 152 C1
Saint-Chamas (13) 191 G3
Saint-Chamassy (24) 137 F5
Saint-Chamond (42) 129 G6
Saint-Champ (01) 131 G3
Saint-Chaptes (30) 174 A2
Saint-Charles-la-Forêt (53) ... 59 E6
Saint-Chartier (36)............... 111 G1
Saint-Chef (38) 130 D4
Saint-Chels (36) 153 F3
Saint-Chély-d'Apcher (48) ... 141 G6
Saint-Chély-d'Aubrac (12) ... 155 E2
Saint-Chéron (51) 46 A6
Saint-Chéron (91) 63 E1
Saint-Chinian (34) 188 A1
Saint-Christ-Briost (80) 8 C6
Saint-Christaud (31) 184 D3
Saint-Christaud (32) 167 F6
Saint-Christo-en-Jarez (42)... 129 G5
Saint-Christol (07) 143 F5
Saint-Christol (34) 173 H4
Saint-Christol (84) 176 A1
Saint-Christol-de-
Rodières (30) 157 H5
Saint-Christol-
lès-Alès (30) 173 H1
Saint-Christoly-de-
Blaye (33) 135 F3
Saint-Christoly-Médoc (33) ... 120 D6
Saint-Christophe (03)........... 114 B5
Saint-Christophe (16).......... 123 G1
Saint-Christophe (17).......... 107 E5
Saint-Christophe (23).......... 111 G6
Saint-Christophe (28).......... 62 A5
Saint-Christophe (69).......... 115 H4
Saint-Christophe (73).......... 131 G6
Saint-Christophe (81).......... 153 G6
Saint-Christophe (86)............ 94 C3
Saint-Christophe-à-
Berry (02)........................ 21 H4
Saint-Christophe-
d'Allier (43) 142 B5
Saint-Christophe-de-
Chaulieu (61) 37 H4
Saint-Christophe-de-
Double (33)................... 136 A3
Saint-Christophe-de-
Valains (35)..................... 35 G6
Saint-Christophe-des-
Bardes (33).................... 135 H5
Saint-Christophe-des-
Bois (35) 57 H2
Saint-Christophe-
Dodinicourt (10) 66 D2
Saint-Christophe-du-
Bois (49) 92 B2
Saint-Christophe-du-
Foc (50).......................... 12 B2
Saint-Christophe-du-
Jambet (72) 59 H3
Saint-Christophe-du-
Ligneron (85) 91 E3
Saint-Christophe-du-
Luat (53) 59 E4
Saint-Christophe-en-
Bazelle (36)................... 96 C2
Saint-Christophe-en-
Boucherie (36)................ 97 F6
Saint-Christophe-en-
Bresse (71) 101 H5
Saint-Christophe-en-
Brionnais (71) 115 F4
Saint-Christophe-en-
Champagne (72) 59 G6
Saint-Christophe-en-
Oisans (38) 146 B4
Saint-Christophe-et-le-
Laris (26) 144 C2
Saint-Christophe-le-
Chaudry (18).................. 112 B1
Saint-Christophe-sur-
Avre (27) 40 B5
Saint-Christophe-sur-
Condé (27) 15 H4
Saint-Christophe-sur-
Dolaison (43) 142 C4
Saint-Christophe-sur-
Guiers (38) 131 G6
Saint-Christophe-sur-le-
Nais (37) 78 C3
Saint-Christophe-sur-
Roc (79) 108 A2

Saint-Christophe-Vallon (12) 154 B3
Saint-Cibard (33) 136 A4
Saint-Cierge-la-Serre (07) 143 H6
Saint-Cierge-sous-le-Cheylard (07) 143 G5
Saint-Ciergues (52) 86 A1
Saint-Ciers-Champagne (17) 121 G5
Saint-Ciers-d'Abzac (33) 135 G3
Saint-Ciers-de-Canesse (33) 135 E3
Saint-Ciers-du-Taillon (17) 121 E6
Saint-Ciers-sur-Bonnieure (16) 122 C2
Saint-Ciers-sur-Gironde (33) 135 E1
Saint-Cirgue (81) 170 D2
Saint-Cirgues (43) 141 H3
Saint-Cirgues (46) 153 H1
Saint-Cirgues-de-Jordanne (15) 140 B4
Saint-Cirgues-de-Malbert (15) 140 A3
Saint-Cirgues-de-Prades (07) 157 F2
Saint-Cirgues-en-Montagne (07) 142 D6
Saint-Cirgues-la-Loutre (19) 139 G3
Saint-Cirgues-sur-Couze (63) 127 F5
Saint-Cirice (82) 168 B1
Saint-Cirq (24) 137 G5
Saint-Cirq (82) 152 D6
Saint-Cirq-Lapopie (46) 153 E3
Saint-Cirq-Madelon (46) 138 B6
Saint-Cirq-Souillaguet (46).. 152 C1
Saint-Civran (36) 110 D2
Saint-Clair (07) 143 H2
Saint-Clair (46) 152 C1
Saint-Clair (82) 151 H6
Saint-Clair (86) 94 A4
Saint-Clair-d'Arcey (27) 40 A2
Saint-Clair-de-Halouze (61).... 38 A5
Saint-Clair-de-la-Tour (38) 131 E4
Saint-Clair-du-Rhône (38) 130 A6
Saint-Clair-sur-Epte (95).... 19 G6
Saint-Clair-sur-Galaure (38).. 144 C2
Saint-Clair-sur-l'Elle (50) 13 F6
Saint-Clair-sur-les-Monts (76) 17 E4
Saint-Clar (32) 168 A3
Saint-Clar-de-Rivière (31) 185 E1
Saint-Claud (16) 123 E2
Saint-Claude (39) 118 A3
Saint-Claude-de-Diray (41).... 80 A3
Saint-Clément (02) 23 E1
Saint-Clément (03) 114 C6
Saint-Clément (07) 143 E5
Saint-Clément (15) 140 C4
Saint-Clément (19) 138 D1
Saint-Clément (30) 173 G3
Saint-Clément (54) 49 F6
Saint-Clément (89) 65 E4
Saint-Clément-à-Arnes (08) 23 H5
Saint-Clément-de-la-Place (49) 76 C4
Saint-Clément-de-Régnat (63) 127 G1
Saint-Clément-de-Rivière (34) 173 F5
Saint-Clément-de-Valorgue (63) 128 C5
Saint-Clément-de-Vers (69).. 115 G5
Saint-Clément-des-Baleines (17) 106 A4
Saint-Clément-des-Levées (49) 77 G6
Saint-Clément-les-Places (69) 129 F3
Saint-Clément-Rancoudray (50) 37 H5
Saint-Clément-sur-Durance (05) 161 E1
Saint-Clément-sur-Guye (71) 115 H1
Saint-Clément-sur-Valsonne (69) 129 F2
Saint-Clet (22) 33 E3
Saint-Cloud (92) 42 C4
Saint-Colomb-de-Lauzun (47) 151 E2
Saint-Colomban (44) 91 F1
Saint-Colomban-des-Villards (73) 146 B1
Saint-Côme (33) 149 H3
Saint-Côme-de-Fresné (14) 14 A3
Saint-Côme-d'Olt (12) 154 D3
Saint-Côme-et-Maruéjols (30) 173 H3
Saint-Congard (56) 56 B5
Saint-Connan (22) 33 E5
Saint-Connec (22) 55 F1
Saint-Constant-Fournoulès (15) 153 H1
Saint-Contest (14) 14 B4
Saint-Corneille (72) 60 B5
Saint-Cosme (68) 89 E2
Saint-Cosme-en-Vairais (72) 60 C3
Saint-Couat-d'Aude (11) 187 G3
Saint-Couat-du-Razès (11) 186 C5
Saint-Coulitz (29) 53 G1
Saint-Coulomb (35) 35 E3
Saint-Coutant (16) 123 E1
Saint-Coutant (79) 108 C4

Saint-Coutant-le-Grand (17) 121 E1
Saint-Créac (32) 168 B2
Saint-Créac (65) 183 E4
Saint-Crépin (05) 147 E6
Saint-Crépin (17) 107 F6
Saint-Crépin-aux-Bois (60) 21 G4
Saint-Crépin-d'Auberoche (24) 137 G3
Saint-Crépin-de-Richemont (24) 123 E6
Saint-Crépin-et-Carlucet (24) 138 B4
Saint-Crépin-Ibouvillers (60) 20 A6
Saint-Crespin (76) 17 G3
Saint-Cricq (32) 168 C4
Saint-Cricq-Chalosse (40) 165 G4
Saint-Cricq-du-Gave (40) 165 E5
Saint-Cricq-Villeneuve (40).. 166 B2
Saint-Cybardeaux (16) 122 A3
Saint-Cybranet (24) 138 A6
Saint-Cyprien (19) 138 B2
Saint-Cyprien (24) 137 H5
Saint-Cyprien (42) 129 E5
Saint-Cyprien (46) 152 B5
Saint-Cyprien (66) 201 G3
Saint-Cyr (07) 143 H2
Saint-Cyr (50) 12 D3
Saint-Cyr (71) 101 G6
Saint-Cyr (87) 123 H3
Saint-Cyr-au-Mont-d'Or (69) 130 A2
Saint-Cyr-de-Favières (42) 128 D1
Saint-Cyr-de-Salerne (27) 18 A6
Saint-Cyr-de-Valorges (42) 129 E2
Saint-Cyr-des-Gâts (85) 107 E1
Saint-Cyr-du-Bailleul (50) 37 H6
Saint-Cyr-du-Doret (17) 107 E4
Saint-Cyr-du-Gault (41) 79 F3
Saint-Cyr-en-Arthies (95) 41 H2
Saint-Cyr-en-Bourg (49) 93 H1
Saint-Cyr-en-Pail (53) 59 G1
Saint-Cyr-en-Talmondais (85) 91 G6
Saint-Cyr-en-Val (45) 80 D2
Saint-Cyr-la-Campagne (27) 18 C6
Saint-Cyr-la-Lande (79) 93 G2
Saint-Cyr-la-Rivière (91) 63 F3
Saint-Cyr-la-Roche (19) 138 C2
Saint-Cyr-la-Rosière (61) 60 D3
Saint-Cyr-le-Chatoux (69) 115 H6
Saint-Cyr-le-Gravelais (53) 58 B5
Saint-Cyr-l'École (78) 42 B4
Saint-Cyr-les-Champagnes (24) 138 B1
Saint-Cyr-les-Colons (89) 83 G2
Saint-Cyr-les-Vignes (42) 129 E4
Saint-Cyr-Montmalin (39) 103 E4
Saint-Cyr-sous-Dourdan (91) 42 B6
Saint-Cyr-sur-le-Rhône (69).. 130 A5
Saint-Cyr-sur-Loire (37) 78 D5
Saint-Cyr-sur-Menthon (01)..116 C4
Saint-Cyr-sur-Mer (83) 192 D5
Saint-Cyr-sur-Morin (77) 44 A3
Saint-Cyran-du-Jambot (36) 95 G3
Saint-Dalmas-le-Selvage (06) 161 G4
Saint-Daunès (46) 152 B4
Saint-Denis (11) 186 D2
Saint-Denis (30) 157 F5
Saint-Denis (93) 42 D3
Saint-Denis-Catus (46) 152 C2
Saint-Denis-Combarnazat (63) 127 G1
Saint-Denis-d'Aclon (76) 17 F2
Saint-Denis-d'Anjou (53) 77 E1
Saint-Denis-d'Augerons (27) 39 H3
Saint-Denis-d'Authou (28) 61 F3
Saint-Denis-de-Cabanne (42) 115 F5
Saint-Denis-de-Gastines (53) 58 C2
Saint-Denis-de-Jouhet (36) 111 G2
Saint-Denis-de-l'Hôtel (45) 81 E1
Saint-Denis-de-Mailloc (14) 15 F5
Saint-Denis-de-Méré (14) 38 B3
Saint-Denis-de-Palin (18) 97 H4
Saint-Denis-de-Pile (33) 135 H4
Saint-Denis-de-Vaux (71) 101 F5
Saint-Denis-des-Coudrais (72) 60 C4
Saint-Denis-des-Monts (27) 18 B6
Saint-Denis-des-Murs (87) 124 D3
Saint-Denis-des-Puits (28) 61 G2
Saint-Denis-d'Oléron (17) 106 B6
Saint-Denis-d'Orques (72) 59 E6
Saint-Denis-du-Maine (53) 59 E6
Saint-Denis-du-Payré (85) 106 C2
Saint-Denis-en-Bugey (01) 130 D1
Saint-Denis-en-Margeride (48) 156 A1
Saint-Denis-en-Val (45) 80 D1
Saint-Denis-la-Chevasse (85) 91 G3
Saint-Denis-le-Ferment (27) 19 G5
Saint-Denis-le-Gast (50) 37 E2
Saint-Denis-le-Thiboult (76) 19 E4
Saint-Denis-le-Vêtu (50) 37 E2
Saint-Denis-lès-Bourg (01) .. 116 D5
Saint-Denis-lès-Martel (46).. 138 D5

Saint-Denis-les-Ponts (28) 61 H5
Saint-Denis-lès-Rebais (77) 44 A4
Saint-Denis-lès-Sens (89) 65 E4
Saint-Denis-sur-Coise (42) .. 129 F4
Saint-Denis-sur-Huisne (61) 60 D1
Saint-Denis-sur-Loire (41) 80 A3
Saint-Denis-sur-Sarthon (61) 59 H1
Saint-Denis-sur-Scie (76) 17 G4
Saint-Deniscourt (60) 19 H3
Saint-Denœux (62) 1 G6
Saint-Denoual (22) 34 B4
Saint-Derrien (29) 31 F3
Saint-Désert (71) 101 F5
Saint-Désir (14) 15 F5
Saint-Désirat (07) 144 A2
Saint-Désiré (03) 112 C2
Saint-Dézéry (30) 174 A2
Saint-Didier (21) 84 C6
Saint-Didier (35) 57 G3
Saint-Didier (39) 102 C6
Saint-Didier (58) 83 G6
Saint-Didier (84) 175 G2
Saint-Didier-au-Mont-d'Or (69) 130 A2
Saint-Didier-d'Aussiat (01)...116 D4
Saint-Didier-de-Bizonnes (38) 130 D5
Saint-Didier-de-Formans (01) 130 A1
Saint-Didier-de-la-Tour (38).. 131 E5
Saint-Didier-des-Bois (27) 18 C6
Saint-Didier-en-Bresse (71) .. 102 A4
Saint-Didier-en-Brionnais (71) 115 E4
Saint-Didier-en-Donjon (03) 114 D3
Saint-Didier-en-Velay (43) .. 143 E1
Saint-Didier-la-Forêt (03) 113 H5
Saint-Didier-sous-Aubenas (07) 157 G2
Saint-Didier-sous-Écouves (61) 39 E6
Saint-Didier-sur-Arroux (71) 100 C5
Saint-Didier-sur-Beaujeu (69) 115 H5
Saint-Didier-sur-Chalaronne (01) 116 B5
Saint-Didier-sur-Doulon (43).. 142 A1
Saint-Didier-sur-Rochefort (42) 128 C3
Saint-Dié-des-Vosges (88) 70 D3
Saint-Dier-d'Auvergne (63)...127 H4
Saint-Diéry (63) 127 E5
Saint-Dionisy (30) 174 A3
Saint-Divy (29) 31 E4
Saint-Dizant-du-Bois (17) 121 F6
Saint-Dizant-du-Gua (17) 121 E5
Saint-Dizier (52) 46 D6
Saint-Dizier-en-Diois (26) .. 159 F3
Saint-Dizier-la-Tour (23) 112 A5
Saint-Dizier-les-Domaines (23) 111 H4
Saint-Dizier-l'Évêque (90) 88 D4
Saint-Dizier-Leyrenne (23) .. 111 F6
Saint-Dolay (56) 73 H2
Saint-Domet (23) 112 B6
Saint-Domineuc (35) 35 E6
Saint-Donan (22) 33 F5
Saint-Donat (63) 126 C6
Saint-Donat-sur-l'Herbasse (26) 144 B3
Saint-Dos (64) 165 E6
Saint-Doulchard (18) 97 G2
Saint-Drézéry (34) 173 G4
Saint-Dyé-sur-Loire (41) 80 B3
Saint-Edmond (71) 115 F5
Saint-Égrève (38) 145 G2
Saint-Élier (27) 40 C2
Saint-Éliph (28) 61 G2
Saint-Élix (32) 168 A6
Saint-Élix-le-Château (31).... 185 E2
Saint-Élix-Séglan (31) 184 C3
Saint-Élix-Theux (32) 183 H1
Saint-Ellier-du-Maine (53).... 58 B2
Saint-Ellier-les-Bois (61) 59 H1
Saint-Éloi (01) 130 C1
Saint-Éloi (23) 111 F6
Saint-Éloi (58) 99 E4
Saint-Éloi-de-Fourques (27) 18 B6
Saint-Éloy (29) 31 G5
Saint-Éloy-d'Allier (03) 112 B2
Saint-Éloy-de-Gy (18) 97 G2
Saint-Éloy-la-Glacière (63) 128 A5
Saint-Éloy-les-Mines (63) 113 E5
Saint-Éloy-les-Tuileries (19) 124 B6
Saint-Éman (28) 61 H3
Saint-Émiland (71) 101 E4
Saint-Émilion (33) 135 H5
Saint-Ennemond (03) 99 F6
Saint-Epvre (57) 49 E2
Saint-Erblon (35) 57 F3
Saint-Erblon (53) 76 A1
Saint-Erme-Outre-et-Ramecourt (02) 22 D4
Saint-Escobille (91) 63 E2
Saint-Esteben (64) 181 E1
Saint-Estèphe (24) 123 F4
Saint-Estèphe (33) 134 D1
Saint-Estève (66) 201 F3
Saint-Estève-Janson (13)...176 A4
Saint-Étienne (42) 129 F6
Saint-Étienne-à-Arnes (08) 23 H5

Saint-Étienne-au-Mont (62)...... 1 F4
Saint-Étienne-au-Temple (51) 45 H2
Saint-Étienne-aux-Clos (19).. 126 B5
Saint-Étienne-Cantalès (15) 139 H5
Saint-Étienne-d'Albagnan (34) 171 G6
Saint-Étienne-de-Baïgorry (64) 180 D3
Saint-Étienne-de-Boulogne (07) 157 G1
Saint-Étienne-de-Brillouet (85) 106 D1
Saint-Étienne-de-Carlat (15) 140 B5
Saint-Étienne-de-Chigny (37) 78 C5
Saint-Étienne-de-Chomeil (15) 140 B1
Saint-Étienne-de-Crossey (38) 131 F6
Saint-Étienne-de-Cuines (73) 146 C1
Saint-Étienne-de-Fontbellon (07) 157 G2
Saint-Étienne-de-Fougères (47) 151 E3
Saint-Étienne-de-Gourgas (34) 172 C4
Saint-Étienne-de-Lisse (33) ... 135 H5
Saint-Étienne-de-l'Olm (30) 173 H1
Saint-Étienne-de-Lugdarès (07) 156 D2
Saint-Étienne-de-Maurs (15) 153 H1
Saint-Étienne-de-Mer-Morte (44) 91 E4
Saint-Étienne-de-Montluc (44) 74 B4
Saint-Étienne-de-Puycorbier (24) 136 C3
Saint-Étienne-de-Saint-Geoirs (38) 144 D1
Saint-Étienne-de-Serre (07).. 143 G6
Saint-Étienne-de-Tinée (06) 162 A5
Saint-Étienne-de-Tulmont (82) 169 F1
Saint-Étienne-de-Valoux (07) 144 A2
Saint-Étienne-de-Vicq (03) .. 114 B5
Saint-Étienne-de-Villeréal (47) 151 G2
Saint-Étienne-des-Champs (63) 126 B2
Saint-Étienne-des-Guérets (41) 79 G4
Saint-Étienne-des-Oullières (69) 116 A6
Saint-Étienne-des-Sorts (30) 158 A6
Saint-Étienne-d'Orthe (40).. 164 D5
Saint-Étienne-du-Bois (01) .. 117 E4
Saint-Étienne-du-Bois (85) .. 91 F3
Saint-Étienne-du-Grès (13).. 174 D4
Saint-Étienne-du-Gué-de-l'Isle (22) 55 H2
Saint-Étienne-du-Rouvray (76) 18 C5
Saint-Étienne-du-Valdonnez (48) 156 B3
Saint-Étienne-du-Vauvray (27) 18 D6
Saint-Étienne-du-Vigan (43) 142 C6
Saint-Étienne-en-Bresse (71) 102 A6
Saint-Étienne-Estréchoux (34) 172 A5
Saint-Étienne-la-Cigogne (79) 107 G5
Saint-Étienne-la-Geneste (19) 126 A6
Saint-Étienne-la-Thillaye (14) 15 E4
Saint-Étienne-la-Varenne (69) 116 A6
Saint-Étienne-l'Allier (27) 15 H4
Saint-Étienne-Lardeyrol (43) 142 D4
Saint-Étienne-le-Laus (05) .. 160 C3
Saint-Étienne-le-Molard (42) 128 D3
Saint-Étienne-les-Orgues (04) 176 C1
Saint-Étienne-lès-Remiremont (88) 70 B5
Saint-Étienne-Roilaye (60) .. 21 G5
Saint-Étienne-sous-Bailleul (27) 41 F1
Saint-Étienne-sous-Barbuise (10) 66 B1
Saint-Étienne-sur-Blesle (43) 141 F1
Saint-Étienne-sur-Chalaronne (01) 116 B5
Saint-Étienne-sur-Reyssouze (01) 116 C3
Saint-Étienne-sur-Suippe (51) 23 F5
Saint-Étienne-sur-Usson (63) 127 H5
Saint-Étienne-Vallée-Française (48) 156 C6
Saint-Eugène (02) 44 C2
Saint-Eugène (17) 121 G5

Saint-Eugène (71) 100 C6
Saint-Eulien (51) 46 C5
Saint-Euphraise-et-Clairizet (51) 22 D6
Saint-Euphrône (21) 84 D5
Saint-Eusèbe (71) 101 E6
Saint-Eusèbe (74) 131 H1
Saint-Eusèbe-en-Champsaur (05) 146 A6
Saint-Eustache (74) 132 B2
Saint-Eustache-la-Forêt (76) .. 15 G1
Saint-Eutrope-de-Born (47) .. 151 F2
Saint-Évarzec (29) 53 G3
Saint-Evroult-de-Montfort (61) 39 G4
Saint-Evroult-Notre-Dame-du-Bois (61) 39 H4
Saint-Exupéry (33) 150 A1
Saint-Exupéry-les-Roches (19) 126 A5
Saint-Fargeau (89) 82 C3
Saint-Fargeau-Ponthierry (77) 63 H1
Saint-Fargeol (03) 112 D5
Saint-Faust (64) 182 B2
Saint-Félicien (07) 143 H3
Saint-Féliu-d'Amont (66) 201 E2
Saint-Féliu-d'Avall (66) 201 E2
Saint-Félix (03) 114 A5
Saint-Félix (16) 122 A6
Saint-Félix (17) 107 G5
Saint-Félix (46) 153 F2
Saint-Félix (74) 131 H2
Saint-Félix-de-Bourdeilles (24) 123 E6
Saint-Félix-de-Foncaude (33) 150 A1
Saint-Félix-de-l'Héras (34) .. 172 B3
Saint-Félix-de-Lodez (34) .. 172 D5
Saint-Félix-de-Lunel (12) 154 C2
Saint-Félix-de-Pallières (30) 173 G2
Saint-Félix-de-Reillac-et-Mortemart (24) 137 G4
Saint-Félix-de-Rieutord (09) 185 H5
Saint-Félix-de-Sorgues (12).. 171 H3
Saint-Félix-de-Tournegat (09) 186 A5
Saint-Félix-de-Villadeix (24) 137 F5
Saint-Félix-Lauragais (31) .. 186 B1
Saint-Fergeux (08) 23 F3
Saint-Ferjeux (70) 88 A4
Saint-Ferme (33) 150 B1
Saint-Ferréol (74) 132 C3
Saint-Ferréol-d'Auroure (43) 143 E1
Saint-Ferréol-de-Comminges (31) 184 B2
Saint-Ferréol-des-Côtes (63) 128 B5
Saint-Ferréol-Trente-Pas (26) 159 E3
Saint-Ferriol (11) 186 D6
Saint-Fiacre (22) 33 E5
Saint-Fiacre (77) 43 G3
Saint-Fiacre-sur-Maine (44).. 74 D6
Saint-Fiel (23) 111 G5
Saint-Firmin (05) 146 A6
Saint-Firmin (54) 69 F2
Saint-Firmin (58) 99 F3
Saint-Firmin (71) 101 E5
Saint-Firmin-des-Bois (45) 64 B6
Saint-Firmin-des-Prés (41).... 79 G1
Saint-Firmin-sur-Loire (45) 82 A3
Saint-Flavy (10) 65 H2
Saint-Florent (2B) 203 F4
Saint-Florent (45) 81 H3
Saint-Florent-sur-Auzonnet (30) 157 E5
Saint-Florent-sur-Cher (18) .. 97 G3
Saint-Florentin (36) 96 D3
Saint-Florentin (89) 65 G6
Saint-Floret (63) 127 F5
Saint-Floris (62) 2 C5
Saint-Flour (15) 141 F4
Saint-Flour (63) 127 H4
Saint-Flour-de-Mercoire (48) 156 C1
Saint-Floxel (50) 12 D3
Saint-Folquin (62) 2 A2
Saint-Fons (69) 130 A3
Saint-Forgeot (71) 100 D5
Saint-Forget (78) 42 B5
Saint-Forgeux (69) 129 G2
Saint-Forgeux-Lespinasse (42) 114 D5
Saint-Fort (53) 76 D1
Saint-Fort-sur-Gironde (17) .. 121 E5
Saint-Fort-sur-le-Né (16) 121 G4
Saint-Fortunat-sur-Eyrieux (07) 143 H6
Saint-Fraigne (16) 122 B1
Saint-Fraimbault (61) 58 D1
Saint-Fraimbault-de-Prières (53) 59 E2
Saint-Frajou (31) 184 C2
Saint-Franc (73) 131 G5
Saint-Franchy (58) 99 F2
Saint-François-de-Sales (73) 132 A3
Saint-François-Lacroix (57) .. 26 D3
Saint-François-Longchamp (73) 132 C6
Saint-Frégant (29) 31 E3

Saint-Fréjoux (19) 126 A5
Saint-Frézal-d'Albuges (48) .. 156 C2
Saint-Frichoux (11) 187 F3
Saint-Frion (23) 125 H2
Saint-Fromond (50) 13 F6
Saint-Front (16) 122 C2
Saint-Front (43) 143 E4
Saint-Front-d'Alemps (24) .. 137 F1
Saint-Front-de-Pradoux (24) 136 D3
Saint-Front-la-Rivière (24) .. 123 F5
Saint-Front-sur-Lémance (47) 151 H2
Saint-Front-sur-Nizonne (24) 123 E5
Saint-Froult (17) 120 C1
Saint-Fulgent (85) 92 A4
Saint-Fulgent-des-Ormes (61) 60 C3
Saint-Fuscien (80) 7 G6
Saint-Gal (48) 156 A1
Saint-Gal-sur-Sioule (63) 113 F6
Saint-Galmier (42) 129 F5
Saint-Gand (70) 87 E4
Saint-Ganton (35) 56 D6
Saint-Gatien-des-Bois (14) ... 15 F3
Saint-Gaudens (31) 184 B4
Saint-Gaudent (86) 109 E5
Saint-Gaudéric (11) 186 B4
Saint-Gaultier (36) 110 D1
Saint-Gauzens (81) 170 A4
Saint-Gein (40) 166 B3
Saint-Gelais (79) 107 H3
Saint-Gély-du-Fesc (34) 173 F5
Saint-Génard (79) 108 B5
Saint-Gence (87) 124 A1
Saint-Généroux (79) 93 G4
Saint-Genès-Champanelle (63) 127 E3
Saint-Genès-Champespe (63) 126 C6
Saint-Genès-de-Blaye (33) ... 135 E2
Saint-Genès-de-Castillon (33) 136 A5
Saint-Genès-de-Fronsac (33) 135 G4
Saint-Genès-de-Lombaud (33) 135 F6
Saint-Genès-du-Retz (63)...113 G6
Saint-Genès-la-Tourette (63) 127 H5
Saint-Genest (03) 112 D4
Saint-Genest (88) 70 A2
Saint-Genest-d'Ambière (86) 94 C5
Saint-Genest-de-Beauzon (07) 157 F3
Saint-Genest-de-Contest (81) 170 C4
Saint-Genest-Lachamp (07) 143 F5
Saint-Genest-Lerpt (42) 129 F6
Saint-Genest-Malifaux (42) .. 143 F1
Saint-Genest-sur-Roselle (87) 124 C3
Saint-Geneys-près-Saint-Paulien (43) 142 C3
Saint-Gengoulph (02) 44 A1
Saint-Gengoux-de-Scissé (71) 116 B2
Saint-Gengoux-le-National (71) 116 A1
Saint-Geniès (24) 138 B4
Saint-Geniès-Bellevue (31).. 169 F5
Saint-Geniès-de-Comolas (30) 174 D1
Saint-Geniès-de-Fontedit (34) 188 C1
Saint-Geniès-de-Malgoirès (30) 173 H2
Saint-Geniès-de-Varensal (34) 171 H5
Saint-Geniès-des-Mourgues (34) 173 G4
Saint-Geniez (04) 160 B5
Saint-Geniez d'Olt et d'Aubrac (12) 155 E3
Saint-Geniez-ô-Merle (19) .. 139 G3
Saint-Genis-de-Saintonge (17) 121 F5
Saint-Génis-des-Fontaines (66) 201 F3
Saint-Genis-d'Hiersac (16) .. 122 B3
Saint-Genis-du-Bois (33) 150 A1
Saint-Genis-l'Argentière (69) 129 G3
Saint-Genis-Laval (69) 130 A4
Saint-Genis-les-Ollières (69) 129 H3
Saint-Genis-Pouilly (01) 118 B4
Saint-Genis-sur-Menthon (01) 116 C4
Saint-Genix-sur-Guiers (73) 131 F4
Saint-Genou (36) 96 A4
Saint-Genouph (37) 78 D5
Saint-Geoire-en-Valdaine (38) 131 F6
Saint-Geoirs (38) 145 E1
Saint-Georges (15) 141 F4
Saint-Georges (16) 122 C1
Saint-Georges (32) 168 B4
Saint-Georges (47) 151 H3
Saint-Georges (57) 49 H5
Saint-Georges (62) 7 F2
Saint-Georges (82) 153 E5
Saint-Georges-Antignac (17) 121 F5

Saint-Georges-Armont (25) 88 B5
Saint-Georges-Blancaneix (24) 136 C5
Saint-Georges-Buttavent (53) 58 D2
Saint-Georges-d'Annebecq (61) 38 D5
Saint-Georges-d'Aurac (43) 142 A3
Saint-Georges-de-Baroille (42) 128 D2
Saint-Georges-de-Chesné (35) 57 H1
Saint-Georges-de-Commiers (38) 145 G4
Saint-Georges-de-Didonne (17) 120 C4
Saint-Georges-de-Gréhaigne (35) 35 G4
Saint-Georges-de-la-Couée (72) 78 D1
Saint-Georges-de-la-Rivière (50) 12 B4
Saint-Georges-de-Livoye (50) 37 F4
Saint-Georges-de-Longuepierre (17) .. 107 H6
Saint-Georges-de-Luzençon (12) 171 H1
Saint-Georges-de-Mons (63) 126 D1
Saint-Georges-de-Montaigu (85) 91 H2
Saint-Georges-de-Montclard (24) 137 E5
Saint-Georges-de-Noisné (79) 108 A2
Saint-Georges-de-Pointindoux (85) ... 91 H4
Saint-Georges-de-Poisieux (18) 97 H6
Saint-Georges-de-Reintembault (35) ... 37 E6
Saint-Georges-de-Reneins (69) 116 A6
Saint-Georges-de-Rex (79) ... 107 F4
Saint-Georges-de-Rouelley (50) 37 H5
Saint-Georges-d'Elle (50) 13 G6
Saint-Georges-des-Agoûts (17) 121 E6
Saint-Georges-des-Coteaux (17) 121 E2
Saint-Georges-des-Groseillers (61) 38 B4
Saint-Georges-d'Espéranche (38) 130 C5
Saint-Georges-d'Hurtières (73) 132 C4
Saint-Georges-d'Oléron (17) 106 B6
Saint-Georges-d'Orques (34) 173 F5
Saint-Georges-du-Bois (17) 107 F5
Saint-Georges-du-Bois (72) 60 A6
Saint-Georges-du-Mesnil (27) 15 H4
Saint-Georges-du-Rosay (72) 60 C4
Saint-Georges-du-Vièvre (27) 15 H4
Saint-Georges-en-Couzan (42) 128 C4
Saint-Georges-Haute-Ville (42) 128 D5
Saint-Georges-la-Pouge (23) 125 F1
Saint-Georges-Lagricol (43) 142 C1
Saint-Georges-le-Fléchard (53) 59 E5
Saint-Georges-le-Gaultier (72) 59 G3
Saint-Georges-lès-Baillargeaux (86) 94 C6
Saint-Georges-les-Bains (07) 144 A5
Saint-Georges-les-Landes (87) 110 C3
Saint-Georges-Montcocq (50) 37 G1
Saint-Georges-Motel (27) 41 F4
Saint-Georges-Nigremont (23) 125 H2
Saint-Georges-sur-Allier (63) 127 G4
Saint-Georges-sur-Arnon (36) 97 F3
Saint-Georges-sur-Baulche (89) 83 F2
Saint-Georges-sur-Cher (41) 79 G6
Saint-Georges-sur-Erve (53) 59 F4
Saint-Georges-sur-Eure (28) 62 A4
Saint-Georges-sur-Fontaine (76) 18 D3
Saint-Georges-sur-la-Prée (18) 97 E1
Saint-Georges-sur-l'Aa (59) 2 A2
Saint-Georges-sur-Loire (49) 76 C5
Saint-Georges-sur-Moulon (18) 97 H2

Saint-Georges-sur-Renon (01) 116 C6
Saint-Geours-d'Auribat (40) 165 F3
Saint-Geours-de-Maremne (40) 164 D4
Saint-Gérand (56) 55 F2
Saint-Gérand-de-Vaux (03) .. 114 A3
Saint-Gérand-le-Puy (03) .. 114 B4
Saint-Géraud (47) 150 C2
Saint-Géraud-de-Corps (24) 136 C4
Saint-Géréon (44) 75 F4
Saint-Germain (07) 157 G2
Saint-Germain (10) 66 A3
Saint-Germain (54) 69 H1
Saint-Germain (70) 88 A2
Saint-Germain (86) 110 A1
Saint-Germain-au-Mont-d'Or (69) 130 A2
Saint-Germain-Beaupré (23) 111 E4
Saint-Germain-Chassenay (58) 99 F5
Saint-Germain-d'Anxure (53) 58 D3
Saint-Germain-d'Arcé (72) 78 B3
Saint-Germain-d'Aunay (61) 39 G3
Saint-Germain-de-Belvès (24) 137 H6
Saint-Germain-de-Calberte (48) 156 C5
Saint-Germain-de-Clairefeuille (61) 39 G5
Saint-Germain-de-Coulamer (53) 59 G3
Saint-Germain-de-Fresney (27) 41 E3
Saint-Germain-de-Grave (33) 149 H1
Saint-Germain-de-Joux (01) 117 H5
Saint-Germain-de-la-Coudre (61) 60 D3
Saint-Germain-de-la-Grange (78) 42 A4
Saint-Germain-de-la-Rivière (33) 135 G4
Saint-Germain-de-Livet (14) 39 F2
Saint-Germain-de-Longue-Chaume (79) 93 F5
Saint-Germain-de-Lusignan (17) 121 F5
Saint-Germain-de-Marencennes (17) 107 F5
Saint-Germain-de-Martigny (61) 39 H6
Saint-Germain-de-Modéon (21) 84 B6
Saint-Germain-de-Montbron (16) 122 D4
Saint-Germain-de-Pasquier (27) 18 C6
Saint-Germain-de-Prinçay (85) 92 B5
Saint-Germain-de-Salles (03) 113 G5
Saint-Germain-de-Tournebut (50) 12 D3
Saint-Germain-de-Varreville (50) 13 E4
Saint-Germain-de-Vibrac (17) 121 G6
Saint-Germain-d'Elle (50) 37 H1
Saint-Germain-des-Angles (27) 40 D2
Saint-Germain-des-Bois (18) 97 H4
Saint-Germain-des-Bois (58) 83 F6
Saint-Germain-des-Champs (89) 84 A5
Saint-Germain-des-Essourts (76) 19 E3
Saint-Germain-des-Fossés (03) 114 A5
Saint-Germain-des-Grois (61) 61 E2
Saint-Germain-des-Prés (24) 137 H1
Saint-Germain-des-Prés (45) 64 B6
Saint-Germain-des-Prés (49) 76 C5
Saint-Germain-des-Prés (81) 170 B6
Saint-Germain-d'Esteuil (33) 134 D1
Saint-Germain-d'Étables (76) 17 H2
Saint-Germain-du-Bel-Air (46) 152 C2
Saint-Germain-du-Bois (71) 102 B5
Saint-Germain-du-Corbéis (61) 60 A2
Saint-Germain-du-Pert (14) 13 F5
Saint-Germain-du-Pinel (35) 58 A5
Saint-Germain-du-Plain (71) 101 H6
Saint-Germain-du-Puch (33) 135 G5
Saint-Germain-du-Puy (18) ... 97 H2
Saint-Germain-du-Salembre (24) 136 D3

Saint-Germain-du-Seudre (17) 121 E5
Saint-Germain-du-Teil (48) 155 G3
Saint-Germain-en-Brionnais (71) 115 F3
Saint-Germain-en-Coglès (35) 35 H6
Saint-Germain-en-Laye (78) 42 B3
Saint-Germain-en-Montagne (39) 103 F5
Saint-Germain-et-Mons (24) 137 E5
Saint-Germain-la-Blanche-Herbe (14) 14 B4
Saint-Germain-la-Campagne (27) 39 H2
Saint-Germain-la-Montagne (42) 115 G5
Saint-Germain-la-Poterie (60) 20 A4
Saint-Germain-la-Ville (51) .. 46 A3
Saint-Germain-Langot (14) .. 38 C3
Saint-Germain-Laprade (43) 142 C4
Saint-Germain-Laval (42) .. 128 D2
Saint-Germain-Laval (77) .. 64 C2
Saint-Germain-Lavolps (19) 125 H4
Saint-Germain-Laxis (77) ... 43 F6
Saint-Germain-le-Châtelet (90) 88 D2
Saint-Germain-le-Fouilloux (53) 58 C4
Saint-Germain-le-Gaillard (28) 61 H2
Saint-Germain-le-Gaillard (50) 12 B3
Saint-Germain-le-Guillaume (53) 58 C3
Saint-Germain-le-Rocheux (21) 85 E2
Saint-Germain-le-Vasson (14) 38 C2
Saint-Germain-le-Vieux (61) 39 G6
Saint-Germain-lès-Arpajon (91) 42 C6
Saint-Germain-les-Belles (87) 124 C4
Saint-Germain-lès-Buxy (71) 101 G6
Saint-Germain-lès-Corbeil (91) 43 E6
Saint-Germain-lès-Paroisses (01) 131 F3
Saint-Germain-lès-Senailly (21) 84 C4
Saint-Germain-les-Vergnes (19) 138 D2
Saint-Germain-Lespinasse (42) 114 D6
Saint-Germain-l'Herm (63) 128 A6
Saint-Germain-Nuelles (69) 129 G2
Saint-Germain-près-Herment (63) 126 B3
Saint-Germain-sous-Cailly (76) 18 D3
Saint-Germain-sous-Doue (77) 44 A4
Saint-Germain-sur-Avre (27) 41 E4
Saint-Germain-sur-Ay (50) .. 12 C5
Saint-Germain-sur-Bresle (80) 6 C6
Saint-Germain-sur-Eaulne (76) 19 F1
Saint-Germain-sur-École (77) 63 H1
Saint-Germain-sur-Ille (35) .. 57 F1
Saint-Germain-sur-Meuse (55) 47 H5
Saint-Germain-sur-Morin (77) 43 G4
Saint-Germain-sur-Renon (01) 116 D6
Saint-Germain-sur-Rhône (74) 117 H6
Saint-Germain-sur-Sarthe (72) 60 A3
Saint-Germain-sur-Sèves (50) 12 D5
Saint-Germain-sur-Vienne (37) 94 A1
Saint-Germain-Village (27) 15 H3
Saint-Germainmont (08) ... 23 F4
Saint-Germé (32) 166 C4
Saint-Germer-de-Fly (60) ... 19 G4
Saint-Germier (31) 186 A1
Saint-Germier (32) 168 C5
Saint-Germier (79) 108 C2
Saint-Germier (81) 170 C5
Saint-Géron (43) 141 G1
Saint-Gérons (15) 139 H5
Saint-Gervais (30) 157 H6
Saint-Gervais (33) 135 E3
Saint-Gervais (38) 145 E2
Saint-Gervais (85) 90 C2
Saint-Gervais (95) 41 H1
Saint-Gervais-d'Auvergne (63) 126 D1
Saint-Gervais-de-Vic (72) ... 79 E1
Saint-Gervais-des-Sablons (61) 39 F3

Saint-Gervais-du-Perron (61) 60 A1
Saint-Gervais-en-Belin (72) ... 78 B1
Saint-Gervais-en-Vallière (71) 101 H4
Saint-Gervais-la-Forêt (41) ... 80 A4
Saint-Gervais-les-Bains (74) 133 E1
Saint-Gervais-les-Trois-Clochers (86) 94 C4
Saint-Gervais-sous-Meymont (63) 128 A4
Saint-Gervais-sur-Couches (71) 101 E4
Saint-Gervais-sur-Mare (34) 172 A5
Saint-Gervais-sur-Roubion (26) 158 B2
Saint-Gervasy (30) 174 B3
Saint-Gervazy (63) 127 F6
Saint-Géry (24) 136 C4
Saint-Géry-Vers (46) 152 D3
Saint-Geyrac (24) 137 G3
Saint-Gibrien (51) 45 H3
Saint-Gildas (22) 33 F5
Saint-Gildas-de-Rhuys (56) ... 72 D2
Saint-Gildas-des-Bois (44) .. 74 A2
Saint-Gilles (30) 174 B5
Saint-Gilles (35) 57 E2
Saint-Gilles (36) 110 D2
Saint-Gilles (50) 37 F1
Saint-Gilles (51) 22 C6
Saint-Gilles (71) 101 F4
Saint-Gilles-Croix-de-Vie (85) 90 D4
Saint-Gilles-de-Crétot (76) .. 18 A3
Saint-Gilles-de-la-Neuville (76) 15 G1
Saint-Gilles-des-Marais (61) 38 A6
Saint-Gilles-les-Bois (22) ... 33 E3
Saint-Gilles-les-Forêts (87) .. 124 D4
Saint-Gilles-Pligeaux (22) .. 33 E5
Saint-Gilles-Vieux-Marché (22) 55 F1
Saint-Gineis-en-Coiron (07) 157 H2
Saint-Gingolph (74) 119 G3
Saint-Girons (09) 185 E5
Saint-Girons-d'Aiguevives (33) 135 F2
Saint-Girons-en-Béarn (64) .. 165 F5
Saint-Gladie-Arrive-Munein (64) 181 F1
Saint-Glen (22) 34 A6
Saint-Goazec (29) 54 A1
Saint-Gobain (02) 22 A3
Saint-Gobert (02) 22 D1
Saint-Goin (64) 181 H2
Saint-Gondon (45) 81 H3
Saint-Gondran (35) 57 E1
Saint-Gonlay (35) 56 C2
Saint-Gonnery (56) 55 G2
Saint-Gor (40) 166 C1
Saint-Gorgon (56) 73 G1
Saint-Gorgon (88) 70 B2
Saint-Gorgon-Main (25) .. 104 A3
Saint-Gourgon (41) 79 F3
Saint-Gourson (16) 122 D1
Saint-Goussaud (23) 111 E6
Saint-Gratien (80) 7 G5
Saint-Gratien (95) 42 C3
Saint-Gratien-Savigny (58) .. 99 H4
Saint-Gravé (56) 56 B6
Saint-Grégoire (35) 57 F2
Saint-Grégoire (81) 170 C2
Saint-Grégoire-d'Ardennes (17) 121 F5
Saint-Grégoire-du-Vièvre (27) 15 H4
Saint-Griède (32) 166 C4
Saint-Groux (16) 122 C2
Saint-Guilhem-le-Désert (34) 172 D4
Saint-Guillaume (38) 145 F4
Saint-Guinoux (35) 35 E4
Saint-Guiraud (34) 172 C5
Saint-Guyomard (56) 55 H5
Saint-Haon (43) 142 B6
Saint-Haon-le-Châtel (42) .. 114 D6
Saint-Haon-le-Vieux (42) .. 114 D6
Saint-Héand (42) 129 F5
Saint-Hélen (22) 34 D5
Saint-Hélier (21) 85 F5
Saint-Hellier (76) 17 H3
Saint-Herblain (44) 74 C5
Saint-Hérent (63) 127 F6
Saint-Hernin (29) 54 B1
Saint-Hervé (22) 33 G6
Saint-Hilaire (03) 113 F2
Saint-Hilaire (11) 186 D4
Saint-Hilaire (25) 87 G6
Saint-Hilaire (31) 185 E1
Saint-Hilaire (38) 145 H1
Saint-Hilaire (43) 141 H1
Saint-Hilaire (46) 139 G6
Saint-Hilaire (63) 112 D6
Saint-Hilaire (91) 63 E2
Saint-Hilaire-au-Temple (51) 45 H2
Saint-Hilaire-Bonneval (87) 124 B3
Saint-Hilaire-Cottes (62) 2 C5
Saint-Hilaire-Cusson-la-Valmitte (42) 142 D1
Saint-Hilaire-de-Beauvoir (34) 173 G4
Saint-Hilaire-de-Brens (38) .. 130 D4

Saint-Hilaire-de-Brethmas (30) 173 H1
Saint-Hilaire-de-Briouze (61) 38 C5
Saint-Hilaire-de-Chaléons (44) 74 B6
Saint-Hilaire-de-Clisson (44) 91 H1
Saint-Hilaire-de-Court (18) 97 E1
Saint-Hilaire-de-Gondilly (18) 98 C3
Saint-Hilaire-de-la-Côte (38) 130 D6
Saint-Hilaire-de-la-Noaille (33) 150 B2
Saint-Hilaire-de-Lavit (48) .. 156 D5
Saint-Hilaire-de-Loulay (85) 91 H1
Saint-Hilaire-de-Lusignan (47) 151 E5
Saint-Hilaire-de-Riez (85) ... 90 D4
Saint-Hilaire-de-Villefranche (17) 121 F2
Saint-Hilaire-de-Voust (85) .. 107 G1
Saint-Hilaire-des-Landes (35) 35 H6
Saint-Hilaire-des-Loges (85) 107 F2
Saint-Hilaire-d'Estissac (24) 137 E4
Saint-Hilaire-d'Ozilhan (30) .. 174 C2
Saint-Hilaire-du-Bois (17) ... 121 F6
Saint-Hilaire-du-Bois (33) .. 150 A1
Saint-Hilaire-du-Harcouët (50) 37 F6
Saint-Hilaire-du-Maine (53) .. 58 C4
Saint-Hilaire-du-Rosier (38) 144 D3
Saint-Hilaire-en-Lignières (18) 97 F6
Saint-Hilaire-en-Morvan (58) 100 A3
Saint-Hilaire-en-Woëvre (55) 47 H1
Saint-Hilaire-Foissac (19) .. 139 G1
Saint-Hilaire-Fontaine (58) 99 G5
Saint-Hilaire-la-Croix (63) .. 113 H6
Saint-Hilaire-la-Forêt (85) ... 91 F6
Saint-Hilaire-la-Gérard (61) .. 39 E6
Saint-Hilaire-la-Gravelle (41) 61 H6
Saint-Hilaire-la-Palud (79) .. 107 F4
Saint-Hilaire-la-Plaine (23) .. 111 G5
Saint-Hilaire-la-Treille (87) .. 110 C4
Saint-Hilaire-le-Château (23) 125 F1
Saint-Hilaire-le-Châtel (61) .. 39 H6
Saint-Hilaire-le-Grand (51) .. 46 A1
Saint-Hilaire-le-Petit (51) ... 23 G6
Saint-Hilaire-le-Vouhis (85) .. 92 A5
Saint-Hilaire-les-Andrésis (45) 64 C5
Saint-Hilaire-les-Courbes (19) 125 E4
Saint-Hilaire-les-Monges (63) 126 C3
Saint-Hilaire-les-Places (87) 124 A4
Saint-Hilaire-lez-Cambrai (59) 9 F3
Saint-Hilaire-Luc (19) 139 H1
Saint-Hilaire-Petitville (50) ... 13 E5
Saint-Hilaire-Peyroux (19) .. 138 D2
Saint-Hilaire-Saint-Mesmin (45) 80 D1
Saint-Hilaire-sous-Charlieu (42) 115 F5
Saint-Hilaire-sous-Romilly (10) 65 G1
Saint-Hilaire-sur-Benaize (36) 110 B1
Saint-Hilaire-sur-Erre (61) 61 E3
Saint-Hilaire-sur-Helpe (59) .. 10 A4
Saint-Hilaire-sur-Puiseaux (45) 82 A1
Saint-Hilaire-sur-Risle (61) 39 H5
Saint-Hilaire-Taurieux (19) .. 139 E3
Saint-Hilarion (78) 41 H6
Saint-Hilliers (77) 44 A6
Saint-Hippolyte (12) 154 C1
Saint-Hippolyte (15) 140 C2
Saint-Hippolyte (17) 120 D1
Saint-Hippolyte (25) 88 C6
Saint-Hippolyte (33) 135 H5
Saint-Hippolyte (37) 95 G3
Saint-Hippolyte (66) 201 F1
Saint-Hippolyte (68) 71 F3
Saint-Hippolyte-de-Caton (30) 173 H1
Saint-Hippolyte-de-Montaigu (30) 174 C1
Saint-Hippolyte-le-Graveyron (84) .. 158 D6
Saint-Honoré (38) 145 G4
Saint-Honoré (76) 17 H3
Saint-Honoré-les-Bains (58) 100 A4
Saint-Hostien (43) 142 D4
Saint-Hubert (57) 26 C4
Saint-Huruge (71) 115 H1
Saint-Hymer (14) 15 F4
Saint-Hymetière (39) 117 G3
Saint-Igeaux (22) 33 E6
Saint-Igest (12) 153 G4
Saint-Ignan (31) 184 B3
Saint-Ignat (63) 127 G2

Saint-Igny-de-Roche (71) 115 F5
Saint-Igny-de-Vers (69) 115 G4
Saint-Illide (15) 139 H4
Saint-Illiers-la-Ville (78) 41 G3
Saint-Illiers-le-Bois (78) 41 F3
Saint-Ilpize (43) 141 G2
Saint-Imoges (51) 45 F1
Saint-Inglevert (62) 1 F3
Saint-Ismier (38) 145 H2
Saint-Izaire (12) 171 F2
Saint-Jacques (04) 177 G2
Saint-Jacques-d'Aliermont (76) 17 H2
Saint-Jacques-d'Ambur (63) 126 D2
Saint-Jacques-d'Atticieux (07) 143 H1
Saint-Jacques-de-la-Lande (35) 57 F3
Saint-Jacques-de-Néhou (50) 12 C4
Saint-Jacques-de-Thouars (79) 93 G3
Saint-Jacques-des-Arrêts (69) 116 A4
Saint-Jacques-des-Blats (15) 140 C4
Saint-Jacques-des-Guérets (41) 79 E2
Saint-Jacques-en-Valgodemard (05) .. 146 A6
Saint-Jacques-sur-Darnétal (76) 18 D4
Saint-Jacut-de-la-Mer (22) .. 34 C4
Saint-Jacut-les-Pins (56) 56 B6
Saint-Jal (19) 124 D6
Saint-James (50) 35 H5
Saint-Jammes (64) 182 C1
Saint-Jans-Cappel (59) 2 D4
Saint-Jean (31) 169 F5
Saint-Jean-aux-Amognes (58) 99 E3
Saint-Jean-aux-Bois (08) ... 23 G2
Saint-Jean-aux-Bois (60) ... 21 F5
Saint-Jean-Bonnefonds (42) 129 F6
Saint-Jean-Brévelay (56) ... 55 G5
Saint-Jean-Cap-Ferrat (06) .. 179 F4
Saint-Jean-Chambre (07) ... 143 G5
Saint-Jean-d'Aigues-Vives (09) 186 B6
Saint-Jean-d'Alcapiès (12) .. 171 H2
Saint-Jean-d'Angély (17) ... 121 F4
Saint-Jean-d'Angle (17) ... 120 C2
Saint-Jean-d'Ardières (69) .. 116 B5
Saint-Jean-d'Arves (73) ... 146 C2
Saint-Jean-d'Arvey (73) ... 132 A4
Saint-Jean-d'Assé (72) ... 60 A4
Saint-Jean-d'Ataux (24) .. 136 D3
Saint-Jean-d'Aubrigoux (43) 142 B1
Saint-Jean-d'Aulps (74) ... 119 F4
Saint-Jean-d'Avelanne (38) .. 131 F5
Saint-Jean-de-Barrou (11) ... 187 H5
Saint-Jean-de-Bassel (57) ... 49 H4
Saint-Jean-de-Beauregard (91) 42 C5
Saint-Jean-de-Belleville (73) 132 D6
Saint-Jean-de-Beugné (85) 106 D1
Saint-Jean-de-Blaignac (33) 135 H5
Saint-Jean-de-Bœuf (21) ... 101 F1
Saint-Jean-de-Boiseau (44) ... 74 C5
Saint-Jean-de-Bonneval (10) 66 B4
Saint-Jean-de-Bournay (38) 130 C5
Saint-Jean-de-Braye (45) ... 80 D1
Saint-Jean-de-Buèges (34) 173 E3
Saint-Jean-de-Ceyrargues (30) 174 A1
Saint-Jean-de-Chevelu (73) 131 G3
Saint-Jean-de-Côle (24) ... 123 G6
Saint-Jean-de-Cornies (34) .. 173 G4
Saint-Jean-de-Couz (73) ... 131 G5
Saint-Jean-de-Crieulon (30) 173 G2
Saint-Jean-de-Cuculles (34) 173 F4
Saint-Jean-de-Daye (50) ... 13 F5
Saint-Jean-de-Duras (47) .. 150 D1
Saint-Jean-de-Folleville (76) 15 H2
Saint-Jean-de-Fos (34) 172 D4
Saint-Jean-de-Gonville (01) 118 A4
Saint-Jean-de-la-Blaquière (34) 172 C4
Saint-Jean-de-la-Croix (49) .. 76 D5
Saint-Jean-de-la-Haize (50) .. 35 H3
Saint-Jean-de-la-Léqueraye (27) 15 H4
Saint-Jean-de-la-Motte (72) 77 H2
Saint-Jean-de-la-Neuville (76) 15 G1
Saint-Jean-de-la-Porte (73) .. 132 B5
Saint-Jean-de-la-Rivière (50) 12 B4
Saint-Jean-de-la-Ruelle (45) 80 D1
Saint-Jean-de-Laur (46) ... 153 F4
Saint-Jean-de-Lier (40) ... 165 F3
Saint-Jean-de-Linières (49) 76 D4

Saint-Jean-de-
Liversay (17) 107 E6
Saint-Jean-de-Livet (14) 15 F5
Saint-Jean-de-Losne (21) 102 B2
Saint-Jean-de-Luz (64) 180 B1
Saint-Jean-de-Marcel (81) 170 C1
Saint-Jean-de-
Marsacq (40) 164 D4
Saint-Jean-de-Maruéjols-
et-Avéjan (30) 157 F5
Saint-Jean-de-
Maurienne (73) 146 C1
Saint-Jean-de-
Minervois (34) 187 H2
Saint-Jean-de-
Moirans (38) 145 F1
Saint-Jean-de-Monts (85)...... 90 C3
Saint-Jean-de-Muzols (07) 144 A3
Saint-Jean-de-Nay (43) 142 B4
Saint-Jean-de-Niost (01)....... 130 D2
Saint-Jean-de-Paracol (11) 186 C6
Saint-Jean-de-
Rebervilliers (28) 41 E6
Saint-Jean-de-Rives (81) 169 H4
Saint-Jean-de-Sauves (86) 94 A4
Saint-Jean-de-Savigny (50) 13 F6
Saint-Jean-de-Serres (30) 173 G2
Saint-Jean-de-Sixt (74) 132 C1
Saint-Jean-de-
Soudain (38) 131 E5
Saint-Jean-de-
Tholome (74) 118 D5
Saint-Jean-de-
Thouars (79) 93 G3
Saint-Jean-de-Thurac (47) 151 F6
Saint-Jean-de-
Thurigneux (01) 130 A1
Saint-Jean-de-Touslas (69) ... 129 H5
Saint-Jean-de-Trézy (71)...... 101 E5
Saint-Jean-de-
Valériscle (30) 157 E5
Saint-Jean-de-Vals (81) 170 C5
Saint-Jean-de-Vaulx (38) 145 G4
Saint-Jean-de-Vaux (71) 101 F5
Saint-Jean-de-Védas (34) 173 F6
Saint-Jean-de-Verges (09) 185 H5
Saint-Jean-d'Elle (50) 37 G1
Saint-Jean-Delnous (12) 171 E1
Saint-Jean-des-
Champs (50) 36 D3
Saint-Jean-des-
Échelles (72) 61 E4
Saint-Jean-des-
Ollières (63) 127 H4
Saint-Jean-des-Vignes (69) ... 129 H2
Saint-Jean-d'Estissac (24) 137 E4
Saint-Jean-d'Étreux (39)....... 117 E3
Saint-Jean-devant-
Possesse (51) 46 C4
Saint-Jean-d'Eyraud (24)...... 136 D4
Saint-Jean-d'Hérans (38)...... 145 G5
Saint-Jean-d'Heurs (63) 127 H3
Saint-Jean-d'Illac (33) 134 D5
Saint-Jean-d'Ormont (88)...... 70 D2
Saint-Jean-du-Bois (72) 77 H1
Saint-Jean-du-Bouzet (82) 168 B2
Saint-Jean-du-Bruel (12) 172 C2
Saint-Jean-du-
Cardonnay (76) 18 C3
Saint-Jean-du-
Castillonnais (09) 184 C5
Saint-Jean-du-Corail-des-
Bois (50) 37 F4
Saint-Jean-du-Doigt (29) 32 A2
Saint-Jean-du-Falga (09) 185 H4
Saint-Jean-du-Gard (30) 173 F1
Saint-Jean-du-Pin (30) 173 G1
Saint-Jean-du-
Thenney (27) 39 H2
Saint-Jean-en-Royans (26) ... 144 D4
Saint-Jean-en-Val (63) 127 G5
Saint-Jean-et-Saint-
Paul (12) 171 H2
Saint-Jean-
Froidmentel (41) 61 H6
Saint-Jean-Kerdaniel (22)...... 33 F4
Saint-Jean-
Kourtzerode (57) 50 B4
Saint-Jean-la-Bussière (69) .. 129 F1
Saint-Jean-la-
Fouillouse (48) 156 B1
Saint-Jean-la-Poterie (56)...... 73 H1
Saint-Jean-la-Vêtre (42) 128 B3
Saint-Jean-Lachalm (43)....... 142 B5
Saint-Jean-Laginesse (46) 139 E6
Saint-Jean-Lasseille (66) 201 F3
Saint-Jean-le-Blanc (45) 80 D1
Saint-Jean-le-
Centenier (07) 157 H2
Saint-Jean-le-Comtal (32).... 167 G5
Saint-Jean-le-Thomas (50).... 36 D4
Saint-Jean-le-Vieux (01)....... 117 F6
Saint-Jean-le-Vieux (38) 145 H2
Saint-Jean-le-Vieux (64) 181 E3
Saint-Jean-lès-Buzy (55)...... 47 H1
Saint-Jean-les-Deux-
Jumeaux (77) 43 H3
Saint-Jean-lès-
Longuyon (54).................. 25 F4
Saint-Jean-
Lespinasse (46) 139 E5
Saint-Jean-Lherm (31)........ 169 G4
Saint-Jean-Ligoure (87) 124 B4
Saint-Jean-Mirabel (46) 153 H2
Saint-Jean-Pied-de-
Port (64) 180 D3
Saint-Jean-Pierre-
Fixte (28) 61 E3

Saint-Jean-Pla-de-
Corts (66) 201 E4
Saint-Jean-Poudge (64)...... 166 C6
Saint-Jean-Poutge (32)........ 167 G4
Saint-Jean-Rohrbach (57)...... 49 G2
Saint-Jean-Roure (07) 143 F5
Saint-Jean-Saint-
Germain (37) 95 G2
Saint-Jean-Saint-
Gervais (63) 127 G6
Saint-Jean-Saint-Maurice-
sur-Loire (42) 128 D1
Saint-Jean-Saint-
Nicolas (05) 160 C1
Saint-Jean-Saverne (67) 50 C4
Saint-Jean-
Soleymieux (42) 128 D5
Saint-Jean-sur-
Couesnon (35) 57 H1
Saint-Jean-sur-
Mayenne (53) 58 D4
Saint-Jean-sur-Moivre (51) 46 B3
Saint-Jean-sur-
Reyssouze (01) 116 C3
Saint-Jean-sur-Tourbe (51)...... 46 B1
Saint-Jean-sur-Veyle (01)..... 116 C4
Saint-Jean-sur-Vilaine (35) 57 H3
Saint-Jean-Trolimon (29)...... 53 E4
Saint-Jeannet (04) 177 E2
Saint-Jeannet (06) 178 D3
Saint-Jeanvrin (18)........... 112 A1
Saint-Jeoire (74) 119 E5
Saint-Jeoire-Prieuré (73) 132 A5
Saint-Jeure-
d'Andaure (07) 143 G4
Saint-Jeure-d'Ay (07)......... 143 H3
Saint-Jeures (43) 143 E3
Saint-Joachim (44)............. 73 G3
Saint-Jodard (42) 128 D2
Saint-Joire (55) 47 G6
Saint-Jorioz (74) 132 B2
Saint-Jory (31) 169 E4
Saint-Jory-de-Chalais (24)..... 123 G5
Saint-Jory-las-Bloux (24) 137 H1
Saint-Joseph (42) 129 G5
Saint-Joseph-de-
Rivière (38) 131 G6
Saint-Joseph-des-
Bancs (07) 157 G1
Saint-Josse (62).................. 1 F6
Saint-Jouan-de-l'Isle (22) 56 C1
Saint-Jouan-des-
Guérets (35) 34 D4
Saint-Jouin (14) 14 D4
Saint-Jouin-Bruneval (76) 16 B4
Saint-Jouin-de-Blavou (61) 60 C1
Saint-Jouin-de-
Marnes (79) 93 H4
Saint-Jouin-de-Milly (79)...... 92 D5
Saint-Jouvent (87)............. 124 A1
Saint-Juan (25) 87 H6
Saint-Judoce (22) 34 D6
Saint-Juéry (12) 171 F3
Saint-Juéry (48) 141 F6
Saint-Juéry (81) 170 C2
Saint-Juire-
Champgillon (85) 106 D1
Saint-Julia (31) 170 A6
Saint-Julia-de-Bec (11)...... 186 D6
Saint-Julien (21)............... 86 A5
Saint-Julien (22)............... 33 G5
Saint-Julien (34) 171 H6
Saint-Julien (69)............. 116 A6
Saint-Julien (83) 176 D4
Saint-Julien (88) 69 E5
Saint-Julien-aux-Bois (19) ... 139 G3
Saint-Julien-
Beychevelle (33) 134 D2
Saint-Julien-Boutières (07).... 143 F4
Saint-Julien-Chapteuil (43)... 142 D4
Saint-Julien-d'Ance (43) 142 C1
Saint-Julien-
d'Armagnac (40) 166 C2
Saint-Julien-d'Asse (04) 177 E2
Saint-Julien-de-Briola (11)... 186 B4
Saint-Julien-de-
Cassagnas (30) 157 F6
Saint-Julien-de-
Chédon (41) 79 G6
Saint-Julien-de-Civry (71)... 115 F3
Saint-Julien-de-
Concelles (44) 75 E5
Saint-Julien-de-
Coppel (63) 127 G4
Saint-Julien-de-
Crempse (24) 137 E4
Saint-Julien-de-Gras-
Capou (09) 186 A5
Saint-Julien-de-Jonzy (71)... 115 F4
Saint-Julien-de-la-
Liègue (27) 41 E1
Saint-Julien-
de-la-Nef (30) 173 E2
Saint-Julien-de-
Lampon (24) 138 B5
Saint-Julien-de-
l'Escap (17) 121 F1
Saint-Julien-de-
l'Herms (38)................. 130 C6
Saint-Julien-de-
Peyrolas (30) 157 H5
Saint-Julien-de-
Toursac (15) 139 H6
Saint-Julien-des-
Vouvantes (44) 75 F1
Saint-Julien-des-
Chazes (43) 142 A2

Saint-Julien-des-
Landes (85) 91 E4
Saint-Julien-des-
Points (48) 156 D5
Saint-Julien-d'Eymet (24)..... 151 E1
Saint-Julien-d'Oddes (42) 128 D2
Saint-Julien-du-Gua (07) 143 G6
Saint-Julien-du-Pinet (43) 142 D3
Saint-Julien-du-Puy (81) 170 B4
Saint-Julien-du-Sault (89) 65 E5
Saint-Julien-du-Serre (07) ... 157 G1
Saint-Julien-du-
Terroux (53) 59 F1
Saint-Julien-du-
Verdon (04) 177 H2
Saint-Julien-en-
Beauchêne (05) 159 H2
Saint-Julien-en-Born (40) 148 A6
Saint-Julien-en-
Champsaur (05) 160 C1
Saint-Julien-en-
Genevois (74) 118 B5
Saint-Julien-en-Quint (26) ... 144 D5
Saint-Julien-en-Saint-
Alban (07) 143 H6
Saint-Julien-en-
Vercors (26) 145 E4
Saint-Julien-Gaulène (81)... 170 D2
Saint-Julien-la-
Geneste (63) 112 D6
Saint-Julien-la-Genête (23) .. 112 C5
Saint-Julien-la-Vêtre (42)... 128 B3
Saint-Julien-
Labrousse (07) 143 G5
Saint-Julien-l'Ars (86)....... 109 F1
Saint-Julien-le-Châtel (23).... 112 C5
Saint-Julien-le-Pèlerin (19) .. 139 G4
Saint-Julien-le-Petit (87) 125 E2
Saint-Julien-le-Roux (07) 143 H5
Saint-Julien-le-
Vendômois (19) 124 B6
Saint-Julien-lès-Gorze (54)... 48 B2
Saint-Julien-lès-Metz (57)...... 26 C5
Saint-Julien-lès-
Montbéliard (25) 88 B4
Saint-Julien-les-
Rosiers (30) 157 E6
Saint-Julien-lès-
Russey (25) 104 C1
Saint-Julien-les-Villas (10)... 66 B3
Saint-Julien-Maumont (19) .. 138 D4
Saint-Julien-
Molhesabate (43) 143 F2
Saint-Julien-Molin-
Molette (42) 143 H1
Saint-Julien-Mont-
Denis (73) 146 C1
Saint-Julien-Puy-
Lavèze (63) 126 C4
Saint-Julien-sous-les-
Côtes (55) 47 H4
Saint-Julien-sur-
Bibost (69) 129 G3
Saint-Julien-sur-
Calonne (14) 15 F4
Saint-Julien-sur-Cher (41) 96 D1
Saint-Julien-sur-
Dheune (71)................. 101 E5
Saint-Julien-sur-
Garonne (31) 185 E3
Saint-Julien-sur-
Reyssouze (01) 116 D3
Saint-Julien-sur-
Sarthe (61)................... 60 C1
Saint-Julien-sur-Veyle (01)... 116 C5
Saint-Julien-Vocance (07)... 143 G3
Saint-Junien (87) 123 G2
Saint-Junien-la-
Bregère (23) 125 E2
Saint-Junien-les-
Combes (87) 110 B6
Saint-Jure (54) 48 D3
Saint-Jurs (04) 177 F2
Saint-Just (01) 117 E5
Saint-Just (18) 97 H3
Saint-Just (24) 137 E1
Saint-Just (34) 173 H5
Saint-Just (35) 56 D6
Saint-Just (63) 127 G6
Saint-Just-Chaleyssin (38)... 130 B4
Saint-Just-d'Ardèche (07).... 157 H5
Saint-Just-d'Avray (69) 129 F1
Saint-Just-de-Claix (38) 144 D3
Saint-Just-en-Bas (42) 128 C3
Saint-Just-en-Brie (77)...... 43 H6
Saint-Just-en-
Chaussée (60) 20 D4
Saint-Just-en-
Chevalet (42) 128 C2
Saint-Just-et-le-Bézu (11).... 186 D6
Saint-Just-et-
Vacquières (30) 174 A1
Saint-Just-Ibarre (64) 181 E3
Saint-Just-la-Pendue (42)... 129 E2
Saint-Just-le-Martel (87).... 124 C2
Saint-Just-Luzac (17) 120 C2
Saint-Just-Malmont (43)..... 143 F1
Saint-Just-près-
Brioude (43) 141 G2
Saint-Just-Saint-
Rambert (42) 129 E5
Saint-Just-Sauvage (51)...... 65 H1
Saint-Just-sur-Dive (49) 93 H1
Saint-Just-sur-Viaur (12).... 154 B6
Saint-Justin (32) 167 E6
Saint-Justin (40) 166 C2
Saint-Juvat (22) 34 D6
Saint-Juvin (08) 24 C5

Saint-Lactencin (36) 96 B4
Saint-Lager (69).............. 116 A6
Saint-Lager-Bressac (07)..... 158 A1
Saint-Lamain (39) 102 D5
Saint-Lambert (14) 38 B3
Saint-Lambert (78) 42 B5
Saint-Lambert-et-Mont-de-
Jeux (08) 24 A4
Saint-Lambert-la-
Potherie (49)................. 76 D4
Saint-Lambert-sur-
Dive (61) 39 F4
Saint-Langis-lès-
Mortagne (61) 60 D1
Saint-Lanne (65) 166 D5
Saint-Laon (86) 93 H3
Saint-Lary (09) 184 C6
Saint-Lary (32) 167 G4
Saint-Lary-Boujean (31)..... 184 B3
Saint-Lary-Soulan (65) 196 D1
Saint-Lattier (38) 144 D3
Saint-Launeuc (22) 56 B1
Saint-Laure (63) 127 G2
Saint-Laurent (08) 24 B1
Saint-Laurent (18) 97 F1
Saint-Laurent (22) 32 D3
Saint-Laurent (23) 111 G5
Saint-Laurent (31) 184 B2
Saint-Laurent (47) 150 D5
Saint-Laurent (74) 118 D6
Saint-Laurent-Blangy (62) 8 B2
Saint-Laurent-
Bretagne (64) 182 C1
Saint-Laurent-
Chabreuges (43) 141 G2
Saint-Laurent-d'Agny (69)... 129 H4
Saint-Laurent-
d'Aigouze (30) 173 H5
Saint-Laurent-
d'Andenay (71) 101 E6
Saint-Laurent-d'Arce (33) ... 135 F3
Saint-Laurent-de-
Brèvedent (76) 15 F1
Saint-Laurent-de-
Carnols (30) 157 H5
Saint-Laurent-de-
Cerdans (66) 200 D5
Saint-Laurent-de-Céris (16) .. 123 E1
Saint-Laurent-de-
Chamousset (69) 129 F3
Saint-Laurent-de-
Cognac (16) 121 G3
Saint-Laurent-de-
Condel (14) 38 C2
Saint-Laurent-de-
Cuves (50) 37 F4
Saint-Laurent-de-
Gosse (40) 164 C5
Saint-Laurent-de-
Jourdes (86) 109 F3
Saint-Laurent-de-la-
Barrière (17) 107 F6
Saint-Laurent-de-la-
Cabrerisse (11) 187 G4
Saint-Laurent-de-la-
Prée (17) 106 D6
Saint-Laurent-de-la-
Salanque (66) 201 G1
Saint-Laurent-de-la-
Salle (85).................... 107 E1
Saint-Laurent-de-
Lévézou (12) 155 E6
Saint-Laurent-de-Lin (37) ... 78 B4
Saint-Laurent-de-
Mure (69) 130 B4
Saint-Laurent-de-
Muret (48) 155 G2
Saint-Laurent-de-
Neste (65) 183 H4
Saint-Laurent-de-
Terregatte (50) 37 E6
Saint-Laurent-de-
Veyrès (48).................. 141 F6
Saint-Laurent-des-
Arbres (30) 174 D1
Saint-Laurent-des-
Bois (27) 41 E4
Saint-Laurent-des-
Bois (41) 80 A1
Saint-Laurent-des-
Combes (16) 136 B1
Saint-Laurent-des-
Combes (33) 135 H5
Saint-Laurent-des-
Hommes (24) 136 C4
Saint-Laurent-des-
Mortiers (53)................. 77 E2
Saint-Laurent-des-
Vignes (24) 136 D6
Saint-Laurent-d'Olt (12) 155 F3
Saint-Laurent-d'Onay (26) .. 144 C2
Saint-Laurent-du-Bois (33) .. 150 A1
Saint-Laurent-du-Cros (05) .. 160 B1
Saint-Laurent-du-
Mont (14) 15 E5
Saint-Laurent-du-Pape (07) .. 144 A6
Saint-Laurent-du-Plan (33) .. 150 A1
Saint-Laurent-du-Pont (38) .. 131 G6
Saint-Laurent-du-
Tencement (27) 39 H3
Saint-Laurent-
du-Var (06) 179 E4
Saint-Laurent-du-
Verdon (04) 177 E4
Saint-Laurent-en-
Beaumont (38) 145 H4
Saint-Laurent-en-
Brionnais (71) 115 F4

Saint-Laurent-en-Caux (76) ... 17 F3
Saint-Laurent-en-
Gâtines (37) 79 E4
Saint-Laurent-en-
Grandvaux (39)............. 118 A1
Saint-Laurent-en-
Royans (26) 144 D4
Saint-Laurent-la-
Conche (42) 129 E4
Saint-Laurent-la-
Gâtine (28) 41 G5
Saint-Laurent-la-
Vallée (24) 137 H6
Saint-Laurent-la-
Vernède (30) 174 B1
Saint-Laurent-
l'Abbaye (58) 82 C6
Saint-Laurent-le-
Minier (30) 173 E2
Saint-Laurent-les-
Bains (07) 156 D2
Saint-Laurent-les-
Églises (87) 124 C1
Saint-Laurent-les-
Tours (46) 139 F5
Saint-Laurent-Lolmie (46)... 152 B5
Saint-Laurent-Médoc (33) ... 134 D2
Saint-Laurent-Nouan (41)..... 80 B3
Saint-Laurent-
Rochefort (42) 128 C3
Saint-Laurent-sous-
Coiron (07) 157 G2
Saint-Laurent-sur-
Gorre (87) 123 H3
Saint-Laurent-sur-Mer (14) ... 13 G4
Saint-Laurent-sur-
Othain (55) 25 F4
Saint-Laurent-sur-Oust (56)... 56 B5
Saint-Laurent-sur-
Saône (01) 116 B4
Saint-Laurent-sur-
Sèvre (85) 92 C3
Saint-Laurs (79) 107 G1
Saint-Léger (06) 178 B1
Saint-Léger (16) 122 B5
Saint-Léger (17) 121 F4
Saint-Léger (47) 150 D5
Saint-Léger (53) 59 E5
Saint-Léger (62) 8 B3
Saint-Léger (73) 132 C6
Saint-Léger (77) 44 A4
Saint-Léger-aux-Bois (60) ... 21 G4
Saint-Léger-aux-Bois (76) 6 C6
Saint-Léger-Bridereix (23) ... 111 E4
Saint-Léger-de-Balson (33) .. 149 F3
Saint-Léger-de-
Fougeret (58) 100 A3
Saint-Léger-de-la-
Martinière (79) 108 B4
Saint-Léger-de-
Montbrillais (86) 93 H2
Saint-Léger-de-
Montbrun (79) 93 G3
Saint-Léger-de-Peyre (48) ... 155 H2
Saint-Léger-de-Rôtes (27)..... 40 A1
Saint-Léger-des-
Aubées (28) 62 C2
Saint-Léger-des-Bois (49) 76 D4
Saint-Léger-des-Prés (35) 35 F6
Saint-Léger-des-
Vignes (58) 99 F5
Saint-Léger-du-Bois (71)..... 101 E3
Saint-Léger-du-Bourg-
Denis (76) 18 D4
Saint-Léger-du-
Gennetey (27) 18 A5
Saint-Léger-du-
Malzieu (48) 141 G5
Saint-Léger-du-
Ventoux (84) 159 E5
Saint-Léger-Dubosq (14) 14 D4
Saint-Léger-en-Bray (60)..... 20 A5
Saint-Léger-en-
Yvelines (78) 41 H5
Saint-Léger-la-
Montagne (87) 110 D6
Saint-Léger-le-
Guérétois (23) 111 F5
Saint-Léger-le-Petit (18) 98 C2
Saint-Léger-lès-Authie (80).... 7 F4
Saint-Léger-lès-
Domart (80) 7 F4
Saint-Léger-lès-
Mélèzes (05) 160 C1
Saint-Léger-lès-Paray (71) ... 115 E2
Saint-Léger-les-Vignes (44) ... 74 B6
Saint-Léger-
Magnazeix (87) 110 C4
Saint-Léger-près-
Troyes (10) 66 B4
Saint-Léger-sous-
Beuvray (71) 100 B4
Saint-Léger-sous-
Brienne (10) 66 D2
Saint-Léger-sous-
Cholet (49) 92 C2
Saint-Léger-sous-la-
Bussière (71) 115 H4
Saint-Léger-sous-
Margerie (10)................. 66 D1
Saint-Léger-sur-Bresle (80) 6 C6
Saint-Léger-sur-
Dheune (71)................. 101 F5
Saint-Léger-sur-
Roanne (42) 115 G6
Saint-Léger-sur-Sarthe (61).... 60 C1
Saint-Léger-sur-
Vouzance (03) 114 D3

Saint-Léger-Triey (21)........... 86 B6
Saint-Léger-Vauban (89)...... 84 B6
Saint-Léomer (86) 110 A3
Saint-Léon (03) 114 C3
Saint-Léon (31) 185 G1
Saint-Léon (33) 135 G6
Saint-Léon (47) 150 C5
Saint-Léon-d'Issigeac (24) ... 151 F1
Saint-Léon-sur-l'Isle (24) 137 E3
Saint-Léon-sur-Vézère (24) .. 137 H4
Saint-Léonard (32) 168 A3
Saint-Léonard (51) 23 F6
Saint-Léonard (62) 1 F1
Saint-Léonard (76) 16 C3
Saint-Léonard (88) 70 D3
Saint-Léonard-de-
Noblat (87) 124 C2
Saint-Léonard-des-
Bois (72) 59 H2
Saint-Léonard-des-
Parcs (61) 39 G5
Saint-Léonard-en-
Beauce (41) 80 A1
Saint-Léons (12) 155 F6
Saint-Léopardin-
d'Augy (03) 98 D6
Saint-Léry (56) 56 B3
Saint-Leu-d'Esserent (60) 20 C6
Saint-Leu-la-Forêt (95) 42 C2
Saint-Lézer (65) 183 E1
Saint-Lieux-Lafenasse (81) ... 170 C4
Saint-Lieux-lès-Lavaur (81) .. 169 H4
Saint-Lin (79) 108 A1
Saint-Lions (04) 177 G1
Saint-Lizier (09) 184 D5
Saint-Lizier-du-Planté (32) .. 184 C1
Saint-Lô (50) 37 G1
Saint-Lô-d'Ourville (50) 12 C4
Saint-Lon-les-Mines (40) 164 D5
Saint-Longis (72) 60 C2
Saint-Lormel (22) 34 C4
Saint-Lothain (39) 102 D5
Saint-Loube (32) 184 D1
Saint-Loubert (33) 150 A2
Saint-Loubès (33) 135 F4
Saint-Loubouer (40) 166 A4
Saint-Louet-sur-
Seulles (14) 38 A1
Saint-Louet-sur-Vire (50)...... 37 G2
Saint-Louis (57) 50 B4
Saint-Louis (68) 89 H3
Saint-Louis-de-
Montferrand (33) 135 F4
Saint-Louis-en-l'Isle (24) 136 D3
Saint-Louis-et-Parahou (11).. 200 B1
Saint-Louis-lès-Bitche (57) 50 C2
Saint-Loup (03) 114 A3
Saint-Loup (17) 107 G6
Saint-Loup (23) 112 B5
Saint-Loup (39) 102 B3
Saint-Loup (41) 96 D1
Saint-Loup (50) 35 H3
Saint-Loup (51) 45 E5
Saint-Loup (58) 82 C5
Saint-Loup (69) 129 G2
Saint-Loup (82) 168 B1
Saint-Loup-Cammas (31)..... 169 F4
Saint-Loup-de-
Buffigny (10) 65 G2
Saint-Loup-de-Gonois (45) ... 64 C5
Saint-Loup-de-Naud (77) 64 D1
Saint-Loup-de-
Varennes (71) 101 G6
Saint-Loup-des-
Chaumes (18) 97 G5
Saint-Loup-des-Vignes (45) .. 63 G5
Saint-Loup-d'Ordon (89)...... 64 D6
Saint-Loup-du-Dorat (53) 59 E6
Saint-Loup-du-Gast (53) 59 F2
Saint-Loup-en-
Champagne (08) 23 F4
Saint-Loup-en-
Comminges (31) 184 A3
Saint-Loup-Géanges (71)....101 H4
Saint-Loup-Hors (14)......... 13 H5
Saint-Loup-Lamairé (79)...... 93 G5
Saint-Loup-Nantouard (70) ... 86 D5
Saint-Loup-sur-Aujon (52).... 85 H1
Saint-Loup-sur-
Semouse (70) 87 G1
Saint-Loup-Terrier (08)........ 24 A3
Saint-Lubin-de-
Cravant (28) 40 D5
Saint-Lubin-de-la-
Haye (28) 41 G4
Saint-Lubin-des-
Joncherets (28) 41 E4
Saint-Lubin-en-
Vergonnois (41) 79 H3
Saint-Luc (27) 41 E3
Saint-Lucien (28) 41 G6
Saint-Lucien (76) 19 E3
Saint-Lumier-en-
Champagne (51) 46 B4
Saint-Lumier-la-
Populeuse (51) 46 C5
Saint-Lumine-de-
Clisson (44) 75 E6
Saint-Lumine-de-
Coutais (44) 74 B6
Saint-Lunaire (35) 34 C3
Saint-Luperce (28) 61 H2
Saint-Lupicin (10) 65 G3
Saint-Lyé (10) 66 A2
Saint-Lyé-la-Forêt (45) 63 E5
Saint-Lyphard (44)............ 73 G3
Saint-Lys (31) 168 D6
Saint-Macaire (33) 149 H2

Saint-Macaire-du-Bois (49) 93 F2
Saint-Maclou (27) 15 G3
Saint-Maclou-de-
  Folleville (76) 17 G4
Saint-Maclou-la-Brière (76) .. 16 C4
Saint-Macoux (86) 108 D5
Saint-Maden (22) 34 C6
Saint-Magne (33) 149 E2
Saint-Magne-de-
  Castillon (33) 136 A5
Saint-Maigner (63) 112 D6
Saint-Maigrin (17) 121 G6
Saint-Maime (04) 176 C2
Saint-Maime-de-
  Péreyrol (24) 137 E4
Saint-Maixant (23) 125 H1
Saint-Maixant (33) 149 H2
Saint-Maixant (72) 60 D5
Saint-Maixent-de-
  Beugné (79) 107 G2
Saint-Maixent-l'École (79) .. 108 B3
Saint-Maixent-sur-Vie (85) .. 90 D3
Saint-Maixme-
  Hauterive (28) 40 D6
Saint-Malo (35) 34 D3
Saint-Malo-de-
  Beignon (56) 56 C4
Saint-Malo-de-
  Guersac (44) 73 H4
Saint-Malo-de-la-
  Lande (50) 36 D1
Saint-Malo-de-Phily (35) 57 E5
Saint-Malo-des-Trois-
  Fontaines (56) 56 A3
Saint-Malô-du-Bois (85) 92 C3
Saint-Malo-en-
  Donziois (58) 83 E6
Saint-Malon-sur-Mel (35) 56 C3
Saint-Mamert (69) 115 H4
Saint-Mamert-du-Gard (30) .. 173 H3
Saint-Mamet (31) 197 F1
Saint-Mamet-la-
  Salvetat (15) 140 A5
Saint-Mammès (77) 64 B2
Saint-Mandé (94) 42 D4
Saint-Mandé-sur-
  Brédoire (17) 108 A6
Saint-Mandrier-sur-
  Mer (83) 193 E5
Saint-Manvieu-Norrey (14).... 14 B4
Saint-Marc-à-Frongier (23) .. 125 G2
Saint-Marc-à-Loubaud (23) .. 125 F2
Saint-Marc-du-Cor (41) 61 F6
Saint-Marc-
  Jaumegarde (13) 176 B6
Saint-Marc-la-Lande (79) 107 H2
Saint-Marc-le-Blanc (35) 35 G6
Saint-Marc-sur-
  Couesnon (35) 57 H1
Saint-Marc-sur-Seine (21) 85 E3
Saint-Marcan (35) 35 F4
Saint-Marceau (08) 24 A2
Saint-Marceau (72) 60 A4
Saint-Marcel (01) 130 D1
Saint-Marcel (08) 23 H1
Saint-Marcel (27) 41 F2
Saint-Marcel (36) 111 E1
Saint-Marcel (54) 26 A5
Saint-Marcel (56) 56 A5
Saint-Marcel (70) 87 E1
Saint-Marcel (71) 101 G5
Saint-Marcel (73) 132 D6
Saint-Marcel-Bel-
  Accueil (38) 130 D4
Saint-Marcel-Campes (81) .. 170 B1
Saint-Marcel-
  d'Ardèche (07) 157 H4
Saint-Marcel-de-
  Careiret (30) 157 H6
Saint-Marcel-de-
  Félines (42) 129 E2
Saint-Marcel-du-
  Périgord (24) 137 F5
Saint-Marcel-d'Urfé (42) 128 C2
Saint-Marcel-en-
  Marcillat (03) 112 D5
Saint-Marcel-en-Murat (03).. 113 F4
Saint-Marcel-l'Éclairé (69) .. 129 F2
Saint-Marcel-lès-
  Annonay (07) 143 H2
Saint-Marcel-lès-
  Sauzet (26) 158 B2
Saint-Marcel-lès-
  Valence (26) 144 B4
Saint-Marcel-Paulel (31) 169 G5
Saint-Marcel-sur-Aude (11) .. 188 A3
Saint-Marcelin-de-
  Cray (71) 115 H2
Saint-Marcellin (38) 144 D3
Saint-Marcellin-en-
  Forez (42) 129 E5
Saint-Marcellin-lès-
  Vaison (84) 158 D5
Saint-Marcet (31) 184 B3
Saint-Marcory (24) 151 H1
Saint-Marcouf (14) 13 F5
Saint-Marcouf (50) 13 E3
Saint-Mard (02) 22 C5
Saint-Mard (17) 107 F5
Saint-Mard (54) 69 G1
Saint-Mard (77) 43 F2
Saint-Mard (80) 21 E2
Saint-Mard-de-Réno (61) 60 D1
Saint-Mard-de-Vaux (71) 101 F5
Saint-Mard-lès-Rouffy (51) ... 45 F3
Saint-Mard-sur-Auve (51) 46 B2
Saint-Mard-sur-le-
  Mont (51) 46 C3

Saint-Mards (76) 17 G3
Saint-Mards-de-
  Blacarville (27) 15 H3
Saint-Mards-de-
  Fresne (27) 39 H2
Saint-Mards-en-Othe (10) 65 H4
Saint-Marien (23) 112 A3
Saint-Mariens (33) 135 F3
Saint-Mars-de-Coutais (44) .. 74 B6
Saint-Mars-de-
  Locquenay (72) 60 C6
Saint-Mars-d'Égrenne (61) .. 38 A6
Saint-Mars-d'Outillé (72) 78 B1
Saint-Mars-du-Désert (44) 75 E4
Saint-Mars-du-Désert (53) 59 G3
Saint-Mars-la-Brière (72) 60 C5
Saint-Mars-la-Jaille (44) 75 F2
Saint-Mars-la-Réorthe (85) .. 92 B4
Saint-Mars-sur-
  Colmont (53) 58 D2
Saint-Mars-sur-la-
  Futaie (53) 58 B1
Saint-Mars-Vieux-
  Maisons (77) 44 B5
Saint-Marsal (66) 200 D4
Saint-Martial (07) 143 E5
Saint-Martial (15) 141 E5
Saint-Martial (16) 122 B6
Saint-Martial (17) 107 H6
Saint-Martial (30) 173 E1
Saint-Martial (33) 150 A1
Saint-Martial-
  d'Albarède (24) 137 H1
Saint-Martial-
  d'Artenset (24) 136 C4
Saint-Martial-de-Gimel (19) .. 139 F2
Saint-Martial-de-
  Mirambeau (17) 121 C6
Saint-Martial-de-
  Nabirat (24) 152 B1
Saint-Martial-de-
  Valette (24) 123 F5
Saint-Martial-de-
  Vitaterne (17) 121 F5
Saint-Martial-
  Entraygues (19) 139 F3
Saint-Martial-le-Mont (23) .. 111 H6
Saint-Martial-le-Vieux (23) .. 126 A4
Saint-Martial-sur-Isop (87) .. 109 H5
Saint-Martial-sur-Né (17) .. 121 G4
Saint-Martial-Viveyrol (24) .. 136 D1
Saint-Martin (32) 167 F6
Saint-Martin (54) 49 C6
Saint-Martin (65) 183 E3
Saint-Martin (67) 71 F2
Saint-Martin-au-Bosc (76) 6 C6
Saint-Martin-aux-
  Arbres (76) 17 F4
Saint-Martin-aux-Bois (60) .. 20 D3
Saint-Martin-aux-
  Buneaux (76) 16 D2
Saint-Martin-aux-
  Champs (51) 46 A4
Saint-Martin-aux-
  Chartrains (14) 15 F3
Saint-Martin-Belle-
  Roche (71) 116 B3
Saint-Martin-
  Boulogne (62) 1 F4
Saint-Martin-Cantalès (15) .. 139 H3
Saint-Martin-Château (23) .. 125 E2
Saint-Martin-Choquel (62) 1 G4
Saint-Martin-Curton (47) 150 B4
Saint-Martin-d'Abbat (45) 81 F1
Saint-Martin-d'Ablois (51) 45 E2
Saint-Martin-d'Août (26) 144 B2
Saint-Martin-
  d'Arberoue (64) 181 E1
Saint-Martin-d'Arc (73) 146 D2
Saint-Martin-
  d'Ardèche (07) 157 H5
Saint-Martin-
  d'Armagnac (32) 166 D4
Saint-Martin-
  d'Arrossa (64) 180 D2
Saint-Martin-d'Ary (17) 135 H2
Saint-Martin-
  d'Aubigny (50) 12 D6
Saint-Martin-
  d'Audouville (50) 12 D3
Saint-Martin-
  d'Auxigny (18) 97 H1
Saint-Martin-d'Auxy (71) .. 101 E6
Saint-Martin-de-Bavel (01) .. 131 F2
Saint-Martin-de-
  Beauville (47) 151 G5
Saint-Martin-de-
  Bernegoue (79) 107 H4
Saint-Martin-de-Bienfaite-
  la-Cressonnière (14) 39 G2
Saint-Martin-de-
  Blagny (14) 13 G5
Saint-Martin-de-
  Bonfossé (50) 37 F1
Saint-Martin-de-
  Boscherville (76) 18 C4
Saint-Martin-de-
  Bossenay (10) 65 G2
Saint-Martin-de-
  Boubaux (48) 156 D6
Saint-Martin-de-
  Bréthencourt (78) 62 D1
Saint-Martin-de-
  Brômes (04) 176 D3
Saint-Martin-de-
  Caralp (09) 185 G5
Saint-Martin-de-
  Castillon (84) 176 A3

Saint-Martin-de-
  Cenilly (50) 37 E2
Saint-Martin-de-
  Clelles (38) 145 F5
Saint-Martin-de-
  Commune (71) 101 E4
Saint-Martin-de-
  Connée (53) 59 G3
Saint-Martin-de-Coux (17) .. 136 A3
Saint-Martin-de-Crau (13) .. 175 E5
Saint-Martin-de-
  Fenouillet (66) 200 C1
Saint-Martin-de-
  Fontenay (14) 14 B5
Saint-Martin-de-
  Fraigneau (85) 107 F2
Saint-Martin-de-
  Fressengeas (24) 123 G6
Saint-Martin-de-
  Fugères (43) 142 C5
Saint-Martin-de-
  Goyne (32) 167 H2
Saint-Martin-de-
  Gurson (24) 136 B4
Saint-Martin-de-Hinx (40) .. 164 C5
Saint-Martin-de-
  Juillers (17) 121 G1
Saint-Martin-de-
  Jussac (87) 123 G2
Saint-Martin-de-la-
  Brasque (84) 176 B4
Saint-Martin-de-la-
  Cluze (38) 145 G4
Saint-Martin-de-la-
  Lieue (14) 15 F5
Saint-Martin-de-la-
  Mer (21) 100 C1
Saint-Martin-de-la-
  Place (49) 77 G6
Saint-Martin-de-la-
  Porte (73) 146 D2
Saint-Martin-de-
  Lansuscle (48) 156 C6
Saint-Martin-de-
  l'Arçon (34) 171 H6
Saint-Martin-de-Laye (33) .. 135 H3
Saint-Martin-de-Lenne (12) .. 155 E4
Saint-Martin-de-Lerm (33) .. 150 B1
Saint Martin de l'If (76) 18 B3
Saint-Martin-de-Lixy (71).... 115 F5
Saint-Martin-de-
  Londres (34) 173 E4
Saint-Martin-de-
  Mâcon (79) 93 G3
Saint-Martin-de-
  Mailloc (14) 15 F5
Saint-Martin-de-Mieux (14) .. 38 D3
Saint-Martin-de-
  Nigelles (28) 41 G6
Saint-Martin-de-
  Pallières (83) 176 D5
Saint-Martin-de-
  Queyrières (05) 147 E5
Saint-Martin-de-Ré (17) 106 B4
Saint-Martin-de-
  Ribérac (24) 136 D2
Saint-Martin-de-Saint-
  Maixent (79) 108 B3
Saint-Martin-de-
  Salencey (71) 115 H2
Saint-Martin-de-
  Sanzay (79) 93 G2
Saint-Martin-de-
  Seignanx (40) 164 C5
Saint-Martin-de-
  Sescas (33) 150 A2
Saint-Martin-de-
  Valamas (07) 143 F5
Saint-Martin-de-
  Valgalgues (30) 157 E6
Saint-Martin-de-
  Varreville (50) 13 E4
Saint-Martin-de-
  Vaulserre (38) 131 G5
Saint-Martin-de-
  Villeréal (47) 151 G2
Saint-Martin-de-
  Villereglan (11) 186 D4
Saint-Martin-
  d'Écublei (61) 40 A4
Saint-Martin-
  d'Entraunes (06) 161 G6
Saint-Martin-des-Bois (41) 79 E2
Saint-Martin-des-
  Champs (18) 98 C2
Saint-Martin-des-
  Champs (29) 32 A3
Saint-Martin-des-
  Champs (50) 35 H3
Saint-Martin-des-
  Champs (77) 44 B4
Saint-Martin-des-
  Champs (78) 41 H3
Saint-Martin-des-
  Champs (89) 82 C3
Saint-Martin-des-
  Combes (24) 137 E4
Saint-Martin-des-
  Entrées (14) 14 A4
Saint-Martin-des-
  Fontaines (85) 107 E1
Saint-Martin-des-Lais (03) 99 G6
Saint-Martin-des-
  Landes (61) 38 D6
Saint-Martin-des-
  Monts (72) 60 D4
Saint-Martin-des-
  Noyers (85) 91 H4

Saint-Martin-des-
  Olmes (63) 128 B5
Saint-Martin-des-
  Pézerits (61) 39 H6
Saint-Martin-des-
  Plains (63) 127 G5
Saint-Martin-des-Prés (22) .. 33 F6
Saint-Martin-des-Puits (11) .. 187 F5
Saint-Martin-des-
  Tilleuls (85) 92 B3
Saint-Martin-
  d'Estréaux (42) 114 C5
Saint-Martin-
  d'Hardinghem (62) 2 A5
Saint-Martin-d'Hères (38) .. 145 G2
Saint-Martin-d'Heuille (58) .. 99 E3
Saint-Martin-d'Ollières (63) .. 127 H6
Saint-Martin-d'Oney (40) .. 165 H2
Saint-Martin-d'Ordon (89) .. 64 D6
Saint-Martin-d'Oydes (09) .. 185 G3
Saint-Martin-du-Bec (76) 16 B4
Saint-Martin-du-Bois (33) .. 135 G4
Saint-Martin-du-
  Boschet (77) 44 B5
Saint-Martin-du-
  Clocher (16) 108 D6
Saint-Martin-du-
  Fouilloux (49) 76 D5
Saint-Martin-du-
  Fouilloux (79) 108 B1
Saint-Martin-du-Frêne (01) .. 117 G5
Saint-Martin-du-Lac (71) .. 115 E4
Saint-Martin-du-Limet (53) .. 76 B1
Saint-Martin-du-
  Manoir (76) 15 F1
Saint-Martin-du-Mont (01) .. 117 C5
Saint-Martin-du-Mont (21) .. 85 F5
Saint-Martin-du-Mont (71) .. 117 E1
Saint-Martin-du-
  Tartre (71) 116 A1
Saint-Martin-du-Tertre (89) .. 65 E4
Saint-Martin-du-Tertre (95) .. 42 D1
Saint-Martin-du-Tilleul (27) .. 15 H5
Saint-Martin-du-Var (06) .. 179 E3
Saint-Martin-du-Vieux-
  Bellême (61) 60 D2
Saint-Martin-du-Vieux (76) .. 18 D4
Saint-Martin-d'Uriage (38) .. 145 H3
Saint-Martin-en-Bière (77) .. 63 H2
Saint-Martin-en-
  Bresse (71) 101 H5
Saint-Martin-en-
  Gâtinois (71) 101 H4
Saint-Martin-en-Haut (69) .. 129 G4
Saint-Martin-en-
  Vercors (26) 145 E4
Saint-Martin-Gimois (32) .. 168 B6
Saint-Martin-la-
  Campagne (27) 40 D2
Saint-Martin-la-
  Garenne (78) 41 H2
Saint-Martin-la-
  Méanne (19) 139 F3
Saint Martin la Pallu (86) 94 B5
Saint-Martin-la-
  Patrouille (71) 115 H1
Saint-Martin-la-Plaine (42) .. 129 G5
Saint-Martin-la-
  Sauveté (42) 128 C2
Saint-Martin-
  Labouval (46) 153 E3
Saint-Martin-
  Lacaussade (33) 135 E2
Saint-Martin-Laguépie (81) .. 153 G6
Saint-Martin-
  l'Aiguillon (61) 38 D6
Saint-Martin-Lalande (11) .. 186 C2
Saint-Martin-l'Ars (86) 109 F4
Saint-Martin-Lars-en-
  Sainte-Hermine (85) 107 E1
Saint-Martin-l'Astier (24) .. 136 C3
Saint-Martin-le-Beau (37) 79 F6
Saint-Martin-le-
  Bouillant (50) 37 F4
Saint-Martin-le-Châtel (01) .. 116 D4
Saint-Martin-le-
  Colonel (26) 144 D4
Saint-Martin-le-
  Gaillard (76) 6 A5
Saint-Martin-le-Gréard (50) .. 12 C2
Saint-Martin-le-Mault (87) .. 110 C3
Saint-Martin-le-Nœud (60) .. 20 A5
Saint-Martin-le-Pin (24) 123 E5
Saint-Martin-le-Redon (46) .. 152 A3
Saint-Martin-le-Vieil (11) .. 186 C2
Saint-Martin-
  le-Vieux (87) 124 A1
Saint-Martin-le-Vinoux (38) .. 145 G2
Saint-Martin-les-Eaux (04) .. 176 C3
Saint-Martin-lès-
  Langres (52) 86 A1
Saint-Martin-lès-Melle (79) .. 108 B4
Saint-Martin-lès-
  Seyne (04) 160 D4
Saint-Martin-Lestra (42) 129 F3
Saint-Martin-lez-
  Tatinghem (62) 2 B4
Saint-Martin-
  l'Heureux (51) 23 G6
Saint-Martin-l'Hortier (76) .. 19 E1
Saint-Martin-
  Longueau (60) 21 E5
Saint-Martin-Lys (11) 200 A1
Saint-Martin-
  Osmonville (76) 19 E2
Saint-Martin-Petit (47) 150 B2
Saint-Martin-Rivière (02) 9 F4

Saint-Martin-Saint-
  Firmin (27) 15 H4
Saint-Martin-Sainte-
  Catherine (23) 124 D1
Saint-Martin-Sepert (19) .. 124 C6
Saint-Martin-sous-
  Montaigu (71) 101 F5
Saint-Martin-sous-
  Vigouroux (15) 140 D5
Saint-Martin-sur-
  Armançon (89) 84 B1
Saint-Martin-sur-
  Cojeul (62) 8 B3
Saint-Martin-sur-
  Écaillon (59) 9 F3
Saint-Martin-sur-la-
  Chambre (73) 132 C6
Saint-Martin-sur-
  Lavezon (07) 158 A2
Saint-Martin-sur-le-Pré (51) .. 45 H3
Saint-Martin-sur-
  Nohain (58) 82 C6
Saint-Martin-sur-Ocre (45) .. 82 A3
Saint-Martin-sur-Oust (56) .. 56 B6
Saint-Martin-Terressus (87) .. 124 C2
Saint-Martin-
  Valmeroux (15) 140 A3
Saint-Martin-Vésubie (06) .. 162 D6
Saint-Martinien (03) 112 C4
Saint-Martory (31) 184 C4
Saint-Mary (16) 122 D2
Saint-Mary-le-Plain (15) 141 F3
Saint-Masmes (51) 23 G5
Saint-Mathieu (87) 123 F3
Saint-Mathieu-de-
  Tréviers (34) 173 F4
Saint-Mathurin (85) 91 E5
Saint-Matré (46) 152 A4
Saint-Maudan (22) 55 G2
Saint-Maugan (35) 56 C2
Saint-Maulvis (80) 6 D6
Saint-Maur (18) 112 B1
Saint-Maur (32) 167 F4
Saint-Maur (36) 96 C5
Saint-Maur (39) 117 G1
Saint-Maur (60) 19 H3
Saint-Maur-des-Bois (50) 37 F3
Saint-Maur-des-
  Fossés (94) 43 E4
Saint-Maur-sur-le-Loir (28) .. 62 A4
Saint-Maurice (52) 86 B1
Saint-Maurice (58) 99 G2
Saint-Maurice (63) 127 F4
Saint-Maurice (67) 71 F2
Saint-Maurice (94) 42 D4
Saint-Maurice-aux-
  Forges (54) 49 G6
Saint-Maurice-aux-Riches-
  Hommes (89) 65 F3
Saint-Maurice-
  Colombier (25) 88 B5
Saint-Maurice-Crillat (39) .. 117 H1
Saint-Maurice-
  d'Ardèche (07) 157 G3
Saint-Maurice-de-
  Beynost (01) 130 B2
Saint-Maurice-de-
  Cazevieille (30) 174 A1
Saint-Maurice-de-
  Gourdans (01) 130 C2
Saint-Maurice-de-
  Lestapel (47) 151 E2
Saint-Maurice-de-
  Lignon (43) 143 E2
Saint-Maurice-de-
  Rémens (01) 130 D1
Saint-Maurice-de-
  Rotherens (73) 131 G4
Saint-Maurice-de-
  Satonnay (71) 116 B3
Saint-Maurice-des-
  Champs (71) 116 A1
Saint-Maurice-des-
  Lions (16) 123 F1
Saint-Maurice-des-
  Noues (85) 107 F1
Saint-Maurice-
  d'Ételan (76) 15 H2
Saint-Maurice-d'Ibie (07) .. 157 G3
Saint-Maurice-en-
  Chalencon (07) 143 G5
Saint-Maurice-en-
  Cotentin (50) 12 B4
Saint-Maurice-en-
  Gourgois (42) 129 E6
Saint-Maurice-en-
  Quercy (46) 153 G1
Saint-Maurice-en-
  Rivière (71) 101 H5
Saint-Maurice-en-
  Trièves (38) 145 G6
Saint-Maurice-en-
  Valgodemard (05) 146 B6
Saint Maurice Étusson (79) .. 93 E3
Saint-Maurice-la-
  Clouère (86) 109 E3
Saint-Maurice-la-
  Souterraine (23) 110 D5
Saint-Maurice-le-
  Girard (85) 92 C6
Saint-Maurice-le-Vieil (89) .. 83 E2
Saint-Maurice-lès-
  Brousses (87) 124 B3
Saint-Maurice-lès-
  Charencey (61) 40 B5
Saint-Maurice-lès-
  Châteauneuf (71) 115 F5

Saint-Maurice-lès-
  Couches (71) 101 F4
Saint-Maurice-l'Exil (38) .. 130 A6
Saint-Maurice-
  Montcouronne (91) 42 B6
Saint-Maurice-
  Navacelles (34) 172 D3
Saint-Maurice-près-
  Crocq (23) 126 A2
Saint-Maurice-près-
  Pionsat (63) 112 D6
Saint-Maurice-Saint-
  Germain (28) 61 G1
Saint-Maurice-sous-les-
  Côtes (55) 47 H2
Saint-Maurice-sur-
  Adour (40) 166 A3
Saint-Maurice-sur-
  Aveyron (45) 82 C1
Saint-Maurice-sur-
  Eygues (26) 158 C5
Saint-Maurice-sur-
  Fessard (45) 64 A6
Saint-Maurice-sur-
  Mortagne (88) 70 A2
Saint-Maurice-sur-
  Moselle (88) 88 C2
Saint-Maurice-sur-
  Vingeanne (21) 86 B4
Saint-Maurice-sur-
  Thizouaille (89) 83 E2
Saint-Maurin (47) 151 G5
Saint-Max (54) 48 C5
Saint-Maxent (80) 6 C5
Saint-Maximin (30) 174 B2
Saint-Maximin (38) 132 A6
Saint-Maximin (60) 20 D6
Saint-Maximin-la-Sainte-
  Baume (83) 193 E2
Saint-Maxire (79) 107 H3
Saint-May (26) 159 E3
Saint-Mayeux (22) 55 E1
Saint-Méard-de-Drône (24) .. 136 D2
Saint-Méard-de-
  Gurçon (24) 136 B5
Saint-Médard (16) 121 H5
Saint-Médard (17) 121 G6
Saint-Médard (31) 184 B4
Saint-Médard (32) 167 G6
Saint-Médard (36) 95 H3
Saint-Médard (46) 152 B3
Saint-Médard (57) 49 F4
Saint-Médard (64) 165 H5
Saint-Médard (79) 108 A4
Saint-Médard-d'Aunis (17) .. 106 D5
Saint-Médard-de-
  Guizières (33) 136 A4
Saint-Médard-de-
  Mussidan (24) 136 C4
Saint-Médard-de-
  Presque (46) 139 E5
Saint-Médard-
  d'Excideuil (24) 137 H1
Saint-Médard-
  d'Eyrans (33) 135 F6
Saint-Médard-en-
  Forez (42) 129 F4
Saint-Médard-en-
  Jalles (33) 134 D5
Saint-Médard-la-
  Rochette (23) 112 A6
Saint-Médard-
  Nicourby (46) 139 F6
Saint-Médard-sur-Ille (35) .. 57 F1
Saint-Méen (29) 31 F3
Saint-Méen-le-Grand (35) .. 56 C2
Saint-Melaine-sur-
  Aubance (35) 77 E5
Saint-Mélany (07) 157 E3
Saint-Melon-des-Bois (22) .. 34 B5
Saint-Méloir-des-
  Ondes (35) 35 G4
Saint-Même-les-
  Carrières (16) 121 H4
Saint-Memmie (51) 45 H3
Saint-Menge (88) 69 E3
Saint-Menges (08) 24 C1
Saint-Menoux (03) 113 G1
Saint-Merd-de-
  Lapleau (19) 139 G2
Saint-Merd-
  la-Breuille (23) 126 A3
Saint-Merd-les-
  Oussines (19) 125 G4
Saint-Méry (77) 43 G5
Saint-Meslin-du-Bosc (27) .. 18 B6
Saint-Mesmes (77) 43 F3
Saint-Mesmin (10) 66 A2
Saint-Mesmin (21) 85 E6
Saint-Mesmin (24) 138 A1
Saint-Mesmin (85) 92 C5
Saint-Mexant (19) 138 D2
Saint-Mézard (32) 167 H1
Saint-M'Hervé (35) 58 A4
Saint-M'Hervon (35) 56 C1
Saint-Micaud (71) 101 E6
Saint-Michel (02) 10 B6
Saint-Michel (09) 185 G4
Saint-Michel (16) 122 B4
Saint-Michel (31) 184 D3
Saint-Michel (32) 183 H1
Saint-Michel (34) 172 C3
Saint-Michel (45) 63 G5
Saint-Michel (64) 180 D3
Saint-Michel (82) 168 C1
Saint-Michel-Chef-
  Chef (44) 73 H5

Saint-Michel-d'Aurance (07) 143 G5
Saint-Michel-de-Bannières (46) 138 D4
Saint-Michel-de-Boulogne (07) 157 G1
Saint-Michel-de-Castelnau (33) 150 A5
Saint-Michel-de-Chabrillanoux (07) ... 143 H6
Saint-Michel-de-Chaillol (05) 160 C1
Saint-Michel-de-Chavaignes (72) 60 D5
Saint-Michel-de-Dèze (48) 156 D5
Saint-Michel-de-Double (24) 136 C3
Saint-Michel-de-Feins (53) 76 D2
Saint-Michel-de-Fronsac (33) 135 G4
Saint-Michel-de-la-Pierre (50) 12 D6
Saint-Michel-de-la-Roë (53) 58 A6
Saint-Michel-de-Lanès (11) 186 A2
Saint-Michel-de-Lapujade (33) 150 B2
Saint-Michel-de-Llotes (66) .. 200 D3
Saint-Michel-de-Maurienne (73) 146 D2
Saint-Michel-de-Montaigne (24) 136 A5
Saint-Michel-de-Montjoie (50) 37 G4
Saint-Michel-de-Plélan (22) 34 C5
Saint-Michel-de-Rieufret (33) 149 G1
Saint-Michel-de-Saint-Geoirs (38) 145 E1
Saint-Michel-de-Vax (81) .. 169 H1
Saint-Michel-de-Veisse (23) 125 G1
Saint-Michel-de-Villadeix (24) 137 F4
Saint-Michel-de-Volangis (18) 97 H2
Saint-Michel-d'Euzet (30) .. 157 H6
Saint-Michel-d'Halescourt (76) 19 G3
Saint-Michel-en-Beaumont (38) 145 H5
Saint-Michel-en-Brenne (36) 95 G5
Saint-Michel-en-Grève (22) 32 B2
Saint-Michel-en-l'Herm (85) 106 C3
Saint-Michel-Escalus (40) 164 D2
Saint-Michel-Labadié (81) ... 171 E2
Saint-Michel-le-Cloucq (85).. 107 F2
Saint-Michel-les-Portes (38) 145 F5
Saint-Michel-l'Observatoire (04) ... 176 C2
Saint-Michel-Loubéjou (46).. 139 E5
Saint-Michel-sous-Bois (62) 1 G6
Saint-Michel-sur-Meurthe (88) 70 C2
Saint-Michel-sur-Orge (91) 42 C6
Saint-Michel-sur-Rhône (42) 129 H6
Saint-Michel-sur-Savasse (26) 144 C3
Saint-Michel-sur-Ternoise (62) 7 G1
Saint-Mihiel-Tubœuf (61)...... 40 B4
Saint-Mihiel (55) 47 G3
Saint-Mitre-les-Remparts (13) 191 G4
Saint-Molf (44) 73 F3
Saint-Momelin (59) 2 B3
Saint-Mont (32) 166 C4
Saint-Montan (07) 158 A3
Saint-Moré (89) 83 H4
Saint-Moreil (23) 124 D2
Saint-Morel (08) 24 A5
Saint-Morillon (33) 149 F1
Saint-Mury-Monteymond (38) 145 H2
Saint-Myon (63) 127 F1
Saint-Nabor (67) 71 F1
Saint-Nabord (88) 70 A5
Saint-Nabord-sur-Aube (10) 66 C1
Saint-Nauphary (82) 169 F2
Saint-Nazaire (30) 158 A6
Saint-Nazaire (44) 73 G4
Saint-Nazaire (66) 201 G2
Saint-Nazaire-d'Aude (11).. 187 H3
Saint-Nazaire-de-Ladarez (34) 172 A6
Saint-Nazaire-de-Pézan (34) 173 H5
Saint-Nazaire-de-Valentane (82) 151 H5
Saint-Nazaire-des-Gardies (30) 173 G2
Saint-Nazaire-en-Royans (26) 144 D3
Saint-Nazaire-le-Désert (26) 159 E2
Saint-Nazaire-les-Eymes (38) 145 H2
Saint-Nazaire-sur-Charente (17) 120 C1
Saint-Nectaire (63) 127 E5
Saint-Nexans (24) 137 E6
Saint-Nic (29) 31 F6

Saint-Nicodème (22) 32 D6
Saint-Nicolas (62) 8 B2
Saint-Nicolas-aux-Bois (02) ... 22 B3
Saint-Nicolas-d'Aliermont (76) 17 H2
Saint-Nicolas-de-Bourgueil (37) 78 A6
Saint-Nicolas-de-la-Balerme (47) 151 G6
Saint-Nicolas-de-la-Grave (82) 168 C1
Saint-Nicolas-de-la-Haie (76) 15 H1
Saint-Nicolas-de-la-Taille (76) 15 G2
Saint-Nicolas-de-Macherin (38) 131 F6
Saint-Nicolas-de-Pierrepont (50) 12 C4
Saint-Nicolas-de-Redon (44) 74 A1
Saint-Nicolas-de-Sommaire (61) 40 A4
Saint-Nicolas-des-Biefs (03) 114 C6
Saint-Nicolas-des-Bois (50) 37 F4
Saint-Nicolas-des-Bois (61) 59 H1
Saint-Nicolas-des-Motets (37) 79 F4
Saint-Nicolas-du-Pélem (22) 33 E6
Saint-Nicolas-du-Tertre (56) 56 B5
Saint-Nicolas-la-Chapelle (10) 65 F1
Saint-Nicolas-la-Chapelle (73) 132 D2
Saint-Nicolas-lès-Cîteaux (21) 102 A2
Saint-Nizier-d'Azergues (69) 115 H6
Saint-Nizier-de-Fornas (42) ... 128 D6
Saint-Nizier-du-Moucherotte (38) 145 F2
Saint-Nizier-le-Bouchoux (01) 116 D2
Saint-Nizier-le-Désert (01).. 116 D6
Saint-Nizier-sous-Charlieu (42) 115 E5
Saint-Nizier-sur-Arroux (71) 100 C5
Saint-Nolff (56) 55 G6
Saint-Nom-la-Bretèche (78) 42 B4
Saint-Offenge (73) 132 A3
Saint-Omer (14) 38 C3
Saint-Omer (62) 2 B4
Saint-Omer-Capelle (62) 2 A2
Saint-Omer-en-Chaussée (60) 20 A3
Saint-Ondras (38) 131 F5
Saint-Onen-la-Chapelle (35) 56 C2
Saint-Oradoux-de-Chirouze (23) 126 A3
Saint-Oradoux-près-Crocq (23) 126 A2
Saint-Orens (32) 168 B4
Saint-Orens-de-Gameville (31) 169 F6
Saint-Orens-Pouy-Petit (32).. 167 G2
Saint-Ost (32) 183 H1
Saint-Ouen (41) 79 G2
Saint-Ouen (80) 7 F5
Saint-Ouen (93) 42 D3
Saint-Ouen-d'Aunis (17).. 106 D4
Saint-Ouen-de-Mimbré (72) 60 A3
Saint-Ouen-de-Pontcheuil (27) 18 C6
Saint-Ouen-de-Sécherouvre (61) 39 H6
Saint-Ouen-de-Thouberville (27) 18 B5
Saint-Ouen-des-Alleux (35)... 57 G1
Saint-Ouen-des-Champs (27) 15 H3
Saint-Ouën-des-Toits (53)..... 58 C4
Saint-Ouën-des-Vallons (53) 58 D4
Saint-Ouen-Domprot (51)..... 45 H6
Saint-Ouen-du-Breuil (76) 17 G4
Saint-Ouen-du-Mesnil-Oger (14) 14 D5
Saint-Ouen-du-Tilleul (27)... 18 B5
Saint-Ouen-en-Belin (72)..... 78 B1
Saint-Ouen-en-Brie (77) 64 C1
Saint-Ouen-en-Champagne (72) 59 G6
Saint-Ouen-la-Rouërie (35).... 35 G5
Saint-Ouen-la-Thène (17)..... 121 H2
Saint-Ouen-l'Aumône (95) 42 B2
Saint-Ouen-le-Brisoult (61) ... 59 H1
Saint-Ouen-le-Mauger (76)... 17 F3
Saint-Ouen-le-Pin (14) 15 E5
Saint-Ouen-lès-Parey (88) 68 D4
Saint-Ouen-les-Vignes (37) ... 79 F5
Saint-Ouen-sous-Bailly (76) 6 A6
Saint-Ouen-sur-Gartempe (87) 110 B5
Saint-Ouen-sur-Iton (61) 40 B5
Saint-Ouen-sur-Loire (58) 99 E4
Saint-Ouen-sur-Morin (77) ... 44 A3
Saint-Oulph (10) 65 H1

Saint-Ours (63) 126 D2
Saint-Ours (73) 132 A3
Saint-Outrille (18) 96 D2
Saint-Ovin (50) 37 E5
Saint-Oyen (73) 132 D5
Saint-Pabu (29) 30 D3
Saint-Paër (76) 18 B3
Saint-Pair (14) 14 C5
Saint-Pair-sur-Mer (50) 36 D3
Saint-Pal-de-Chalencon (43) 142 C1
Saint-Pal-de-Mons (43) 143 E2
Saint-Pal-de-Senouire (43).. 142 A2
Saint-Palais (03) 112 B3
Saint-Palais (18) 97 H1
Saint-Palais (33) 135 E1
Saint-Palais (64) 181 F1
Saint-Palais-de-Négrignac (17) 135 H1
Saint-Palais-de-Phiolin (17).. 121 E5
Saint-Palais-du-Né (16) 121 G5
Saint-Palais-sur-Mer (17) 120 B3
Saint-Pancrace (24) 123 F6
Saint-Pancrace (73) 146 C1
Saint-Pancrasse (38) 145 H1
Saint-Pancré (54) 25 G3
Saint-Pandelon (40) 165 E4
Saint-Pantaléon (46) 152 B6
Saint-Pantaléon (84) 175 G3
Saint-Pantaléon-de-Lapleau (19) 139 H1
Saint-Pantaléon-de-Larche (19) 138 C3
Saint-Pantaléon-les-Vignes (26) 158 C4
Saint-Pantaly-d'Excideuil (24) 137 H1
Saint-Papoul (11) 186 C2
Saint-Pardon-de-Conques (33) 149 H2
Saint-Pardoult (17) 107 H6
Saint-Pardoux (63) 113 F6
Saint-Pardoux (79) 108 A1
Saint-Pardoux (87) 110 C6
Saint-Pardoux-Corbier (19).. 124 C6
Saint-Pardoux-d'Arnet (23).. 126 A2
Saint-Pardoux-de-Drône (24) 136 D2
Saint-Pardoux-du-Breuil (47) 150 C3
Saint-Pardoux-et-Vielvic (24) 137 H6
Saint-Pardoux-Isaac (47)..... 150 D2
Saint-Pardoux-la-Croisille (19) 139 F2
Saint-Pardoux-la-Rivière (24) 123 F5
Saint-Pardoux-le-Neuf (19)... 126 A4
Saint-Pardoux-le-Neuf (23)... 125 H2
Saint-Pardoux-le-Vieux (19) 125 H4
Saint-Pardoux-les-Cards (23) 111 H6
Saint-Pardoux-l'Ortigier (19) 138 D1
Saint-Pardoux-Morterolles (23) 125 E2
Saint-Pargoire (34) 172 D6
Saint-Parize-en-Viry (58) 99 F6
Saint-Parize-le-Châtel (58) ... 99 E5
Saint-Parres-aux-Tertres (10) 66 B3
Saint-Parres-lès-Vaudes (10) 66 C4
Saint-Parthem (12) 154 A2
Saint-Pastour (47) 151 F3
Saint-Pastous (65) 182 D5
Saint-Paterne - Le Chevain (72) 60 A2
Saint-Paterne-Racan (37) 78 C3
Saint-Pathus (77) 43 F2
Saint-Patrice-de-Claids (50).. 12 D5
Saint-Patrice-du-Désert (61) 38 C6
Saint-Paul (19) 139 F2
Saint-Paul (33) 135 G2
Saint-Paul (60) 20 A4
Saint-Paul (61) 38 A4
Saint-Paul (65) 183 H4
Saint-Paul (73) 131 G4
Saint-Paul (87) 124 C3
Saint-Paul (88) 69 E2
Saint-Paul-aux-Bois (02) 21 H3
Saint-Paul-Cap-de-Joux (81) 170 B5
Saint-Paul-de-Baïse (32) 167 G4
Saint-Paul-de-Salers (15) 140 B3
Saint-Paul-de-Serre (24) 137 E3
Saint-Paul-de-Tartas (43) 142 C4
Saint-Paul-de-Varax (01) 116 D6
Saint-Paul-de-Varces (38) ... 145 F3
Saint-Paul-de-Vence (06) 178 D2
Saint-Paul-de-Vern (46) 139 F6
Saint-Paul-de-Vézelin (42) .. 128 D2
Saint-Paul-des-Landes (15) .. 139 H5
Saint-Paul-d'Espis (82) 151 H6
Saint-Paul-d'Izeaux (38) 145 E1
Saint-Paul-d'Oueil (31) 197 F1
Saint-Paul-du-Bois (49) 93 E2
Saint-Paul-du-Vernay (14).... 13 H6
Saint-Paul-d'Uzore (42) 128 D4
Saint-Paul-en-Born (40) 148 B5
Saint-Paul-en-Chablais (74).. 119 F3

Saint-Paul-en-Cornillon (42) 129 E6
Saint-Paul-en-Forêt (83) 178 B5
Saint-Paul-en-Gâtine (79) 92 D6
Saint-Paul-en-Jarez (42) 129 G5
Saint-Paul-en-Pareds (85) 92 B4
Saint-Paul-et-Valmalle (34).. 173 E5
Saint-Paul-Flaugnac (46) ... 152 C5
Saint-Paul-la-Coste (30) 156 D6
Saint-Paul-la-Roche (24) 123 H5
Saint-Paul-le-Froid (48) 142 A6
Saint-Paul-le-Gaultier (72)... 59 G3
Saint-Paul-le-Jeune (07) 157 E4
Saint-Paul-lès-Dax (40) 165 E4
Saint-Paul-lès-Durance (13) 176 C4
Saint-Paul-les-Fonts (30) ... 174 C1
Saint-Paul-lès-Monestier (38) 145 F5
Saint-Paul-lès-Romans (26).. 144 C3
Saint-Paul-Lizonne (24) 136 C1
Saint-Paul-Mont-Penit (85) .. 91 E3
Saint-Paul-sur-Isère (73) 132 D4
Saint-Paul-sur-Save (31) 168 D4
Saint-Paul-sur-Ubaye (04)... 161 G2
Saint-Paul-Trois-Châteaux (26) 158 B4
Saint-Paulet (11) 186 B1
Saint-Paulet-de-Caisson (30) 157 H5
Saint-Paulien (43) 142 B3
Saint-Pavace (72) 60 A5
Saint-Pé-d'Ardet (31) 184 A5
Saint-Pé-de-Bigorre (65) ... 182 D4
Saint-Pé-de-Léren (64) 165 E6
Saint-Pé-Delbosc (31) 184 B2
Saint-Pé-Saint-Simon (47)... 167 E1
Saint-Pée-sur-Nivelle (64) .. 180 B1
Saint-Péran (35) 56 C3
Saint-Péravy-la-Colombe (45) 62 C6
Saint-Péray (07) 144 A5
Saint-Perdon (40) 165 H2
Saint-Perdoux (24) 137 E6
Saint-Perdoux (46) 153 G1
Saint-Père (58) 82 C5
Saint-Père (89) 83 H5
Saint-Père-en-Retz (44) 73 H5
Saint-Père-sur-Loire (45)..... 81 G2
Saint-Péreuse (58) 99 H3
Saint-Pern (35) 56 D1
Saint-Perreux (56) 73 H1
Saint-Péver (22) 33 E4
Saint-Pey-d'Armens (33) 135 H5
Saint-Pey-de-Castets (33)... 136 A6
Saint-Phal (10) 66 A5
Saint-Philbert-de-Bouaine (85) 91 F1
Saint-Philbert-de-Grand-Lieu (44) 91 F1
Saint-Philbert-des-Champs (14) 15 F4
Saint-Philbert-du-Peuple (49) 77 H5
Saint-Philbert-sur-Boissey (27) 18 B6
Saint-Philbert-sur-Orne (61) 38 C3
Saint-Philbert-sur-Risle (27) 18 A5
Saint-Philibert (21) 101 H1
Saint-Philibert (56) 72 C1
Saint-Philippe-d'Aiguille (33) 136 A5
Saint-Philippe-du-Seignal (33) 136 C5
Saint-Piat (28) 62 B1
Saint-Pierre (04) 178 C2
Saint-Pierre (15) 140 A1
Saint-Pierre (31) 169 G5
Saint-Pierre (39) 118 A1
Saint-Pierre (51) 45 G3
Saint-Pierre (67) 71 G2
Saint-Pierre-à-Arnes (08) 23 H5
Saint-Pierre-Aigle (02) 21 H5
Saint-Pierre-Avez (05) 159 H5
Saint-Pierre-Azif (14) 15 E3
Saint-Pierre-Bellevue (23)... 125 F2
Saint-Pierre-Bénouville (76) 17 F3
Saint-Pierre-Bois (67) 71 F2
Saint-Pierre-Brouck (59) 2 A2
Saint-Pierre-Canivet (14) 38 D3
Saint-Pierre-Chérignat (23) 124 D1
Saint-Pierre-Colamine (63).. 127 E5
Saint-Pierre-d'Albigny (73).. 132 B4
Saint-Pierre-d'Alvey (73) ... 131 G4
Saint-Pierre-d'Amilly (17) .. 107 F5
Saint-Pierre-d'Argençon (05) 159 H3
Saint-Pierre-d'Arthéglise (50) 12 B4
Saint-Pierre-d'Aubézies (32) 167 E5
Saint-Pierre-d'Aurillac (33).. 149 H2
Saint-Pierre-de-Bailleul (27) 41 F1
Saint-Pierre-de-Bat (33) 149 H1
Saint-Pierre-de-Belleville (73) 132 C5
Saint-Pierre-de-Bœuf (42)... 130 A6
Saint-Pierre-de-Bressieux (38) 144 D1
Saint-Pierre-de-Buzet (47) .. 150 C5
Saint-Pierre-de-Cernières (27) 40 A3

Saint-Pierre-de-Chandieu (69) 130 B4
Saint-Pierre-de-Chartreuse (38) 145 G1
Saint-Pierre-de-Chérennes (38) 145 E3
Saint-Pierre-de-Chevillé (72) 78 C3
Saint-Pierre-de-Chignac (24) 137 G3
Saint-Pierre-de-Clairac (47)... 151 G6
Saint-Pierre-de-Côle (24) ... 137 F1
Saint-Pierre-de-Colombier (07) 157 F1
Saint-Pierre-de-Cormeilles (27) 15 G4
Saint-Pierre-de-Coutances (50) 36 D1
Saint-Pierre-de-Curtille (73) 131 G3
Saint-Pierre-de-Frugie (24).. 123 H5
Saint-Pierre-de-Genebroz (73) 131 G6
Saint-Pierre-de-Jards (36) 97 E2
Saint-Pierre-de-la-Fage (34) 172 C4
Saint-Pierre-de-Lages (31).. 169 G6
Saint-Pierre-de-Lamps (36) .. 96 B4
Saint-Pierre-de-l'Isle (17) .. 107 H6
Saint-Pierre-de-Maillé (86) .. 95 E6
Saint-Pierre-de-Manneville (76) 18 B4
Saint-Pierre-de-Méaroz (38) 145 H5
Saint-Pierre-de-Mésage (38) 145 G3
Saint-Pierre-de-Mézoargues (13) 174 D3
Saint-Pierre-de-Mons (33) .. 149 H2
Saint-Pierre-de-Nogaret (48) 155 G3
Saint-Pierre-de-Plesguen (35) 34 D5
Saint-Pierre-de-Rivière (09).. 185 G5
Saint-Pierre-de-Salerne (27) 18 A6
Saint-Pierre-de-Semilly (50) 37 G1
Saint-Pierre-de-Soucy (73).. 132 B5
Saint-Pierre-de-Trivisy (81).. 171 E4
Saint-Pierre-de-Varengeville (76) 18 B3
Saint-Pierre-de-Varennes (71) 101 E5
Saint-Pierre-de-Vassols (84) 175 G1
Saint-Pierre-dels-Forcats (66) 200 A4
Saint-Pierre-d'Entremont (38) 131 H6
Saint-Pierre-d'Entremont (61) 38 A4
Saint-Pierre-d'Entremont (73) 131 H6
Saint-Pierre-des-Bois (72) 59 G6
Saint-Pierre-des-Champs (11) 187 F5
Saint-Pierre-des-Corps (37) .. 79 E5
Saint-Pierre-des-Échaubrognes (79)..... 92 D3
Saint-Pierre-des-Fleurs (27) 18 C6
Saint-Pierre-des-Ifs (14) 15 E5
Saint-Pierre-des-Ifs (27) 15 H4
Saint-Pierre-des-Jonquières (76) 6 B6
Saint-Pierre-des-Landes (53) 58 B3
Saint-Pierre-des-Loges (61).. 39 H4
Saint-Pierre-des-Nids (53) 59 H2
Saint-Pierre-des-Ormes (72) 60 C3
Saint-Pierre-des-Tripiers (48) 155 G6
Saint-Pierre-d'Exideuil (86)... 108 D5
Saint-Pierre-d'Eyraud (24) .. 136 C5
Saint-Pierre-d'Irube (64) 164 B6
Saint-Pierre-d'Oléron (17) .. 120 A1
Saint-Pierre-du-Bosguérand (27) 18 B6
Saint-Pierre-du-Bû (14) 38 D3
Saint-Pierre-du-Champ (43) 142 C2
Saint-Pierre-du-Chemin (85) 92 D6
Saint-Pierre-du-Fresne (14) .. 38 A2
Saint-Pierre-du-Jonquet (14) 14 D5
Saint-Pierre-du-Lorouër (72) 78 C2
Saint-Pierre-du-Mont (14) ... 13 G4
Saint-Pierre-du-Mont (40) .. 166 A2
Saint-Pierre-du-Mont (58) ... 83 F6
Saint-Pierre-du-Palais (17).. 135 H2
Saint-Pierre-du-Perray (91).. 43 E6
Saint-Pierre-du-Regard (61) 38 B3
Saint-Pierre-du-Val (27) 15 G3
Saint-Pierre-du-Vauvray (27) 18 D6
Saint-Pierre-Église (50) 12 D1
Saint-Pierre-en-Auge (14) 39 E2
Saint-Pierre-en-Faucigny (74) 118 D6
Saint-Pierre-en-Port (76) 16 D3
Saint-Pierre-en-Val (76) 6 B5

Saint-Pierre-en-Vaux (21) 101 E3
Saint-Pierre-es-Champs (60) 19 G4
Saint-Pierre-Eynac (43) 142 D4
Saint-Pierre-la-Bourlhonne (63) 128 B4
Saint-Pierre-la-Bruyère (61) 61 E2
Saint-Pierre-la-Cour (53) 58 B4
Saint-Pierre-la-Garenne (27) 41 F1
Saint-Pierre-la-Noaille (42).. 115 E5
Saint-Pierre-la-Palud (69) .. 129 G3
Saint-Pierre-la-Roche (07).. 157 H2
Saint-Pierre-Lafeuille (46).. 152 C3
Saint-Pierre-Langers (50) 36 D3
Saint-Pierre-Laval (03) 114 C5
Saint-Pierre-le-Bost (23) 112 A3
Saint-Pierre-le-Chastel (63) .. 126 D3
Saint-Pierre-le-Moûtier (58) 98 D5
Saint-Pierre-le-Vieux (48) .. 141 G6
Saint-Pierre-le-Vieux (71).. 115 H4
Saint-Pierre-le-Vieux (76) 17 F2
Saint-Pierre-le-Vieux (85) .. 107 F3
Saint-Pierre-le-Viger (76) 17 F3
Saint-Pierre-lès-Bitry (60) 21 G4
Saint-Pierre-lès-Bois (18) ... 97 G6
Saint-Pierre-lès-Elbeuf (76).. 18 C5
Saint-Pierre-lès-Étieux (18).. 98 A6
Saint-Pierre-lès-Franqueville (02) 22 D1
Saint-Pierre-lès-Nemours (77) 64 A3
Saint-Pierre-Quiberon (56) .. 72 B2
Saint-Pierre-Roche (63) 126 D3
Saint-Pierre-Saint-Jean (07) 157 E3
Saint-Pierre-sur-Doux (07) .. 143 G3
Saint-Pierre-sur-Dropt (47).. 150 C1
Saint-Pierre-sur-Erve (53) 59 F5
Saint-Pierre-sur-Orthe (53) .. 59 G3
Saint-Pierre-sur-Vence (08)... 24 A2
Saint-Pierre-Toirac (46) 153 G3
Saint-Pierremont (02) 22 D2
Saint-Pierremont (08) 24 C4
Saint-Pierremont (88) 70 A1
Saint-Pierreville (07) 143 G6
Saint-Pierrevillers (55) 25 G5
Saint-Plaisir (03) 113 F1
Saint-Plancard (31) 184 A3
Saint-Planchers (50) 36 D3
Saint-Plantaire (36) 111 F2
Saint-Point (71) 116 A3
Saint-Point-Lac (25) 103 H5
Saint-Pois (50) 37 G4
Saint-Poix (53) 58 B5
Saint-Pol-de-Léon (29) 31 H2
Saint-Pol-sur-Ternoise (62) 7 G1
Saint-Polgues (42) 128 C2
Saint-Polycarpe (11) 186 D5
Saint-Pompain (79) 107 G2
Saint-Pompont (24) 152 A1
Saint-Poncy (15) 141 F3
Saint-Pons (04) 161 F3
Saint-Pons (07) 157 H2
Saint-Pons-de-Mauchiens (34) 172 D6
Saint-Pons-de-Thomières (34) 187 G1
Saint-Pons-la-Calm (30) 174 C1
Saint-Pont (03) 113 H5
Saint-Porchaire (17) 120 D2
Saint-Porquier (82) 168 D2
Saint-Pôtan (22) 34 B4
Saint-Pouange (10) 66 B3
Saint-Pourçain-sur-Besbre (03) 114 B2
Saint-Pourçain-sur-Sioule (03) 113 H4
Saint-Prancher (88) 69 E2
Saint-Préjet-Armandon (43) 142 A2
Saint-Préjet-d'Allier (43) ... 142 A5
Saint-Prest (28) 62 B1
Saint-Preuil (16) 121 H4
Saint-Priest (07) 157 H1
Saint-Priest (23) 112 B6
Saint-Priest (69) 130 B3
Saint-Priest-Bramefant (63) 127 H1
Saint-Priest-d'Andelot (03).. 113 G6
Saint-Priest-de-Gimel (19) .. 139 F1
Saint-Priest-des-Champs (63) 126 D1
Saint-Priest-en-Jarez (42) .. 129 F6
Saint-Priest-en-Murat (03) .. 113 F3
Saint-Priest-la-Feuille (23) .. 111 E5
Saint-Priest-la-Marche (18).. 112 A3
Saint-Priest-la-Plaine (23) .. 111 E5
Saint-Priest-la-Prugne (42).. 128 B1
Saint-Priest-la-Roche (42) .. 128 D2
Saint-Priest-la-Vêtre (42) .. 128 B3
Saint-Priest-les-Fougères (24) 123 H5
Saint-Priest-Ligoure (87) ... 124 B4
Saint-Priest-Palus (23) 124 D2
Saint-Priest-sous-Aixe (87).. 124 A2
Saint-Priest-Taurion (87) ... 124 C2
Saint-Prim (38) 130 A6
Saint-Privat (07) 157 G2
Saint-Privat (19) 139 G3
Saint-Privat (34) 172 C4
Saint-Privat-d'Allier (43) ... 142 B4
Saint-Privat-de-Champclos (30) 157 G5
Saint-Privat-de-Vallongue (48) 156 C5

Saint-Privat-des-Vieux (30)... 157 E6
Saint-Privat-du-
  Dragon (43) 141 H2
Saint-Privat-du-Fau (48) 141 G5
Saint Privat en
  Périgord (24) 136 C2
Saint-Privat-la-
  Montagne (57) 26 B5
Saint-Privé (71) 101 E6
Saint-Privé (89) 82 C3
Saint-Prix (03) 114 B5
Saint-Prix (07) 143 G5
Saint-Prix (71) 100 B4
Saint-Prix (95) 42 C2
Saint-Prix-lès-Arnay (21).......101 L2
Saint-Projet (46) 152 D1
Saint-Projet (82) 153 F5
Saint-Projet-de-Salers (15) ... 140 B3
Saint-Projet-Saint-
  Constant (16) 122 D3
Saint-Prouant (85) 92 B5
Saint-Pryvé-Saint-
  Mesmin (45) 80 D1
Saint-Puy (32) 167 G3
Saint-Python (59) 9 F3
Saint-Quantin-de-
  Rançanne (17) 121 E5
Saint-Quay-Perros (22) 32 C1
Saint-Quay-Portrieux (22)....... 33 G3
Saint-Quentin (02) 9 E6
Saint-Quentin-de-
  Baron (33) 135 G5
Saint-Quentin-de-
  Blavou (61) 60 C1
Saint-Quentin-de-
  Caplong (33) 136 B6
Saint-Quentin-de-
  Chalais (16) 136 B2
Saint-Quentin-des-
  Isles (27) 40 A2
Saint-Quentin-des-
  Prés (60) 19 G3
Saint-Quentin-du-
  Dropt (47) 151 F1
Saint-Quentin-en-
  Tourmont (80) 6 C2
Saint-Quentin-
  Fallavier (38) 130 C4
Saint-Quentin-la-
  Chabanne (23) 125 G2
Saint-Quentin-la-Motte-
  Croix-au-Bailly (80) 6 B4
Saint-Quentin-la-
  Poterie (30) 174 B1
Saint-Quentin-la-Tour (09) .. 186 B5
Saint-Quentin-le-Petit (08) 23 E3
Saint-Quentin-le-
  Verger (51) 44 D6
Saint-Quentin-les-
  Anges (53) 76 C2
Saint-Quentin-les-
  Chardonnets (61) 38 A4
Saint-Quentin-les-
  Marais (51) 46 B4
Saint-Quentin-sur-
  Charente (16) 123 F2
Saint-Quentin-sur-
  Coole (51) 45 H4
Saint-Quentin-sur-
  Indrois (37) 95 G1
Saint-Quentin-sur-
  Isère (38) 145 F1
Saint-Quentin-sur-le-
  Homme (50) 35 H4
Saint-Quentin-sur-
  Nohain (58) 82 C6
Saint-Quentin-sur-
  Sauxillanges (63) 127 G5
Saint-Quentin-sur-
  Sioule (63) 113 G6
Saint-Quirc (09) 185 G2
Saint-Quirin (57) 50 A5
Saint-Rabier (24) 138 A3
Saint-Racho (71) 115 G4
Saint-Rambert-
  d'Albon (26) 144 A1
Saint-Rambert-en-
  Bugey (01) 131 E1
Saint-Raphaël (24) 137 H1
Saint-Raphaël (83) 194 C2
Saint-Régis-du-Coin (42) 143 F2
Saint-Règle (37) 79 G5
Saint-Remèze (07) 157 H4
Saint-Remimont (54) 69 G1
Saint-Remimont (88) 69 E3
Saint-Rémy (01) 116 D5
Saint-Rémy (12) 153 G4
Saint-Rémy (14) 38 B3
Saint-Rémy (19) 125 H4
Saint-Rémy (21) 84 C3
Saint-Rémy (24) 136 B4
Saint-Rémy (70) 87 F1
Saint-Rémy (71) 101 G5
Saint-Rémy (79) 107 G3
Saint-Remy (88) 70 C2
Saint-Rémy-au-Bois (62).......... 6 D2
Saint-Rémy-aux-Bois (54)....... 69 H2
Saint-Rémy-Blanzy (02) 22 A6
Saint-Rémy-
  Boscrocourt (76) 6 B5
Saint-Remy-Chaussée (59) 9 H3
Saint-Rémy-de-Blot (63) 113 F6
Saint-Rémy-de-
  Chargnat (63) 127 G5
Saint-Rémy-de-Chaudes-
  Aigues (15) 141 E6
Saint-Rémy-de-
  Maurienne (73) 132 C6

Saint-Rémy-de-
  Provence (13) 175 E4
Saint-Rémy-de-Sillé (72) 59 H4
Saint-Rémy-des-
  Monts (72) 60 C3
Saint-Rémy-du-Nord (59) 10 A3
Saint-Rémy-du-Plain (35) 35 F6
Saint-Rémy-du-Val (72) 60 B2
Saint-Remy-en-
  Bouzemont-Saint-
  Genest-et-Isson (51) 46 B6
Saint-Rémy-en-l'Eau (60) 20 D4
Saint-Rémy-en-Rollat (03) 114 A5
Saint-Remy-la-
  Calonne (55) 47 H2
Saint-Rémy-la-Vanne (77)....... 44 A4
Saint-Rémy-le-Petit (08) 23 F4
Saint-Rémy-lès-
  Chevreuse (78) 42 B5
Saint-Rémy-l'Honoré (78) 42 A5
Saint-Remy-sous-
  Barbuise (10) 66 B1
Saint-Remy-sous-
  Broyes (51) 44 D5
Saint-Remy-sur-Avre (28) 41 E4
Saint-Rémy-sur-Bussy (51) 46 B2
Saint-Rémy-sur-
  Creuse (86) 95 E4
Saint-Rémy-sur-
  Durolle (63) 128 A2
Saint-Renan (29) 30 D4
Saint-Restitut (26) 158 B4
Saint-Révérend (85) 90 D4
Saint-Révérien (58) 99 F1
Saint-Rieul (22) 34 A5
Saint-Rimay (41) 79 F2
Saint-Riquier (80) 7 E4
Saint-Riquier-en-
  Rivière (76) 6 B6
Saint-Riquier-ès-Plains (76) ... 17 E2
Saint-Rirand (42) 114 D6
Saint-Rivoal (29) 31 G5
Saint-Robert (19) 138 B2
Saint-Robert (47) 151 G5
Saint-Roch (37) 78 D5
Saint-Roch-sur-
  Égrenne (61) 38 A6
Saint-Rogatien (17) 106 D5
Saint-Romain (16) 136 B1
Saint-Romain (21) 101 F3
Saint-Romain (63) 128 C5
Saint-Romain (86) 109 E4
Saint-Romain-au-Mont-
  d'Or (69) 130 A2
Saint-Romain-d'Ay (07) 143 H3
Saint-Romain-de-
  Benet (17) 120 D3
Saint-Romain-de-
  Colbosc (76) 15 G1
Saint-Romain-de-
  Jalionas (38) 130 D3
Saint-Romain-de-
  Lerps (07) 144 A4
Saint-Romain-de-
  Monpazier (24) 151 G1
Saint-Romain-de-
  Popey (69) 129 G2
Saint-Romain-de-
  Surieu (38) 130 B6
Saint-Romain-d'Urfé (42) 128 B2
Saint-Romain-en-Gal (69)..... 130 A5
Saint-Romain-en-Gier (69) ... 129 H5
Saint-Romain-en-
  Jarez (42) 129 G5
Saint-Romain-en-
  Viennois (84) 158 D5
Saint-Romain-et-Saint-
  Clément (24) 123 G6
Saint-Romain-
  la-Motte (42) 115 E6
Saint-Romain-la-
  Virvée (33) 135 F4
Saint-Romain-
  Lachalm (43) 143 F2
Saint-Romain-le-
  Noble (47) 151 G6
Saint-Romain-le-Puy (42) 128 D5
Saint-Romain-les-
  Atheux (42) 143 F1
Saint-Romain-sous-
  Gourdon (71) 115 G1
Saint-Romain-sous-
  Versigny (71) 115 F1
Saint-Romain-sur-
  Cher (41) 80 A6
Saint-Romain-sur-
  Gironde (33) 120 D5
Saint-Roman (26) 159 F1
Saint-Roman-de-
  Codières (30) 173 F2
Saint-Roman-de-
  Malegarde (84) 158 C5
Saint-Romans (38) 144 D3
Saint-Romans-des-
  Champs (79) 107 H4
Saint-Romans-lès-
  Melle (79) 108 B4
Saint-Rome (31) 185 H1
Saint-Rome-de-
  Cernon (12) 171 H2
Saint-Rome-de-Tarn (12) 171 H1
Saint-Rustice (31) 169 E3
Saint-Saëns (76) 19 E2
Saint-Saire (76) 19 F2
Saint-Salvadour (19) 125 E6
Saint-Salvi-de-
  Carcavès (81) 171 F4
Saint-Salvy (47) 151 E5

Saint-Salvy-de-la-
  Balme (81) 170 D5
Saint-Samson (14) 14 D4
Saint-Samson-de-la-
  Roque (27) 15 G2
Saint-Samson-la-
  Poterie (60) 19 G3
Saint-Samson-sur-
  Rance (22) 34 D5
Saint-Sandoux (63) 127 F4
Saint-Santin (12) 153 H2
Saint-Santin-Cantalès (15)... 139 H4
Saint-Santin-de-Maurs (15)... 153 H2
Saint-Sardos (47) 151 E4
Saint-Sardos (82) 168 D3
Saint-Satur (18) 82 B6
Saint-Saturnin (15) 140 D2
Saint-Saturnin (16) 122 B4
Saint-Saturnin (18) 112 A2
Saint-Saturnin (48) 155 G4
Saint-Saturnin (51) 45 E6
Saint-Saturnin (63) 127 F4
Saint-Saturnin (72) 60 A5
Saint-Saturnin-de-
  Lenne (12) 155 F4
Saint-Saturnin-de-
  Lucian (34) 172 D5
Saint-Saturnin-du-
  Bois (17) 107 F5
Saint-Saturnin-du-
  Limet (53) 76 A1
Saint-Saturnin-lès-Apt (84)... 175 H2
Saint-Saturnin-lès-
  Avignon (84) 175 E2
Saint-Saud-
  Lacoussière (24) 123 G5
Saint-Sauflieu (80) 20 C1
Saint-Saulge (58) 99 G2
Saint-Saulve (59) 9 F2
Saint-Saury (15) 139 G5
Saint-Sauvant (17) 121 F3
Saint-Sauvant (86) 108 C3
Saint-Sauves-
  d'Auvergne (63) 126 C4
Saint-Sauveur (05) 161 G2
Saint-Sauveur (21) 86 B4
Saint-Sauveur (24) 137 E5
Saint-Sauveur (29) 31 G4
Saint-Sauveur (33) 169 F4
Saint-Sauveur (38) 144 D3
Saint-Sauveur (54) 49 H6
Saint-Sauveur (60) 21 F5
Saint-Sauveur (70) 87 H1
Saint-Sauveur (80) 7 F5
Saint-Sauveur-
  Camprieu (30) 172 D1
Saint-Sauveur-d'Aunis (17) .. 107 E4
Saint-Sauveur-de-
  Carrouges (61) 38 D6
Saint-Sauveur-de-
  Cruzières (07) 157 F5
Saint-Sauveur-de-
  Ginestoux (48) 156 B1
Saint-Sauveur-de-
  Meilhan (47) 150 B3
Saint-Sauveur-de-
  Montagut (07) 143 G6
Saint-Sauveur-de-
  Pierrepont (50) 12 C4
Saint-Sauveur-de-
  Puynormand (33) 136 A4
Saint-Sauveur-
  d'Émalleville (76) 16 B4
Saint-Sauveur-des-
  Landes (35) 35 H6
Saint-Sauveur-en-
  Diois (26) 158 D1
Saint-Sauveur-en-
  Puisaye (89) 82 D3
Saint-Sauveur-en-Rue (42) ... 143 G2
Saint-Sauveur-
  Gouvernet (26) 159 E4
Saint-Sauveur-la-
  Pommeraye (50) 36 D3
Saint-Sauveur-la-
  Sagne (63) 128 B6
Saint-Sauveur-Lalande (24).. 136 C4
Saint-Sauveur-le-
  Vicomte (50) 12 C4
Saint-Sauveur-
  Lendelin (50) 12 D6
Saint-Sauveur-lès-
  Bray (77) 64 D2
Saint-Sauveur-
  Marville (28) 41 E6
Saint-Sauveur-sur-
  École (77) 63 H1
Saint-Sauveur-sur-
  Tinée (06) 162 C6
Saint-Sauvier (03) 112 B3
Saint-Sauvy (32) 168 B4
Saint-Savin (33) 135 F2
Saint-Savin (38) 130 D2
Saint-Savin (65) 182 D5
Saint-Savin (86) 109 H1
Saint-Savinien (17) 121 E1
Saint-Saviol (86) 108 D5
Saint-Savournin (13) 192 B3
Saint-Sébastien (23) 111 E3
Saint-Sébastien-
  d'Aigrefeuille (30) 173 G1
Saint-Sébastien-de-
  Morsent (27) 40 D2
Saint-Sébastien-de-
  Raids (50) 12 D6
Saint-Sébastien-sur-
  Loire (44) 74 D1

Saint-Secondin (86) 109 F3
Saint-Ségal (29) 31 G6
Saint-Séglin (35) 56 D5
Saint-Seine (58) 100 A6
Saint-Seine-en-Bâche (21) ... 102 C2
Saint-Seine-l'Abbaye (21) 85 F5
Saint-Seine-sur-
  Vingeanne (21) 86 B4
Saint-Selve (33) 149 F1
Saint-Senier-de-
  Beuvron (50) 35 H4
Saint-Senier-sous-
  Avranches (50) 35 H3
Saint-Senoch (37) 95 F3
Saint-Senoux (35) 57 E4
Saint-Sériès (34) 173 H4
Saint-Sernin (07) 157 G2
Saint-Sernin (11) 186 A3
Saint-Sernin (47) 150 C1
Saint-Sernin-du-Bois (71)......101 E5
Saint-Sernin-du-Plain (71) 101 F4
Saint-Sernin-lès-
  Lavaur (81) 170 B6
Saint-Sernin-sur-
  Rance (12) 171 F3
Saint-Sérotin (89) 64 D4
Saint-Servais (22) 32 C5
Saint-Servais (29) 31 G4
Saint-Servant (56) 55 H4
Saint-Setiers (19) 125 G4
Saint-Seurin-de-Bourg (33) .. 135 E3
Saint-Seurin-de-
  Cadourne (33) 134 D1
Saint-Seurin-de-
  Cursac (33) 135 E2
Saint-Seurin-de-
  Palenne (17) 121 F4
Saint-Seurin-de-Prats (24) ... 136 B5
Saint-Seurin-sur-l'Isle (33) ... 136 A4
Saint-Sève (33) 150 B2
Saint-Sever (40) 165 H3
Saint-Sever-de-Rustan (65) .. 183 F2
Saint-Sever-de-
  Saintonge (17) 121 F3
Saint-Sever-du-
  Moustier (12) 171 F4
Saint-Séverin (16) 136 C1
Saint-Séverin-
  d'Estissac (24) 136 D3
Saint-Séverin-sur-
  Boutonne (17) 107 H5
Saint-Siffret (30) 174 B2
Saint-Sigismond (45) 62 C6
Saint-Sigismond (49) 76 B4
Saint-Sigismond (74) 119 F5
Saint-Sigismond (85) 107 F3
Saint-Sigismond-de-
  Clermont (17) 121 F5
Saint-Silvain-Bas-le-
  Roc (23) 112 A4
Saint-Silvain-
  Bellegarde (23) 125 H1
Saint-Silvain-
  Montaigut (23) 111 F5
Saint-Silvain-sous-
  Toulx (23) 112 A4
Saint-Siméon (27) 15 H4
Saint-Siméon (77) 44 A4
Saint-Siméon-de-
  Bressieux (38) 144 D1
Saint-Simeux (16) 122 A4
Saint-Simon (02) 21 H1
Saint-Simon (15) 140 B5
Saint-Simon (16) 122 A4
Saint-Simon (46) 153 F1
Saint-Simon-de-
  Bordes (17) 121 F6
Saint-Simon-de-
  Pellouaille (17) 121 E4
Saint-Sixt (74) 118 D6
Saint-Sixte (42) 128 C3
Saint-Sixte (47) 151 G6
Saint-Solve (19) 138 C1
Saint-Sorlin-d'Arves (73) 146 B2
Saint-Sorlin-de-Conac (17) .. 121 E6
Saint-Sorlin-de-
  Morestel (38) 131 E4
Saint-Sorlin-
  de-Vienne (38) 130 B6
Saint-Sorlin-en-Bugey (01).. 130 D2
Saint-Sorlin-en-
  Valloire (26) 144 B1
Saint-Sornin (03) 113 F3
Saint-Sornin (16) 122 D3
Saint-Sornin (17) 120 C2
Saint-Sornin-la-
  Marche (87) 110 A5
Saint-Sornin-Lavolps (19) 138 B1
Saint-Sornin-Leulac (87)...... 110 B6
Saint-Soulan (32) 168 B6
Saint-Souplet (59) 9 F4
Saint-Souplet-sur-Py (51) 23 H6
Saint-Soupplets (77) 43 F2
Saint-Sozy (46) 138 D5
Saint-Stail (88) 70 D2
Saint-Suliac (35) 34 D4
Saint-Sulpice (46) 153 F2
Saint-Sulpice (53) 58 D6
Saint-Sulpice (58) 99 F3
Saint-Sulpice (60) 20 B5
Saint-Sulpice (63) 126 C4
Saint-Sulpice (70) 88 A3
Saint-Sulpice (73) 131 H4
Saint-Sulpice-
  d'Arnoult (17) 120 D2
Saint-Sulpice-de-
  Cognac (16) 121 G3

Saint-Sulpice-de-
  Faleyrens (33) 135 H5
Saint-Sulpice-de-
  Favières (91) 63 F1
Saint-Sulpice-de-
  Grimbouville (27) 15 G3
Saint-Sulpice-de-
  Guilleragues (33) 150 B1
Saint-Sulpice-de-
  Pommeray (41) 79 H3
Saint-Sulpice-de-
  Pommiers (33) 150 A1
Saint-Sulpice-de-
  Roumagnac (24) 136 D2
Saint-Sulpice-de-
  Royan (17) 120 C3
Saint-Sulpice-de-
  Ruffec (16) 122 D1
Saint-Sulpice-des-
  Landes (35) 57 F6
Saint-Sulpice-des-
  Landes (44) 75 F2
Saint-Sulpice-des-
  Rivoires (38) 131 F5
Saint-Sulpice-
  d'Excideuil (24) 123 H6
Saint-Sulpice-en-
  Pareds (85) 92 C6
Saint-Sulpice-et-
  Cameyrac (33) 135 F5
Saint-Sulpice-la-Forêt (35) 57 F2
Saint-Sulpice-la-
  Pointe (81) 169 G4
Saint-Sulpice-Laurière (87) ...110 D6
Saint-Sulpice-le-
  Dunois (23) 111 F4
Saint-Sulpice-le-
  Guérétois (23) 111 F5
Saint-Sulpice-les-Bois (19) .. 125 G4
Saint-Sulpice-les-
  Champs (23) 125 G1
Saint-Sulpice-les-
  Feuilles (87) 110 D4
Saint-Sulpice-sur-Lèze (31).. 185 F2
Saint-Sulpice-sur-Risle (61) .. 40 A4
Saint-Supplet (54) 25 H4
Saint-Sylvain (14) 38 D2
Saint-Sylvain (19) 139 F3
Saint-Sylvain (76) 17 E2
Saint-Sylvestre (07) 144 A4
Saint-Sylvestre (74) 132 A2
Saint-Sylvestre (87) 124 C1
Saint-Sylvestre-Cappel (59).....2 C6
Saint-Sylvestre-de-
  Cormeilles (27) 15 G4
Saint-Sylvestre-
  Pragoulin (63) 114 A6
Saint-Sylvestre-sur-
  Lot (47) 151 G4
Saint-Symphorien (18) 97 G5
Saint-Symphorien (27) 15 G3
Saint-Symphorien (33) 149 F3
Saint-Symphorien (35) 57 E1
Saint-Symphorien (48) 142 A6
Saint-Symphorien (72) 59 G5
Saint-Symphorien (79) 107 G4
Saint-Symphorien-
  d'Ancelles (71) 116 B5
Saint-Symphorien-de-
  Lay (42) 129 E1
Saint-Symphorien-de-
  Mahun (07) 143 G3
Saint-Symphorien-de-
  Marmagne (71) 100 D5
Saint-Symphorien-de-
  Thénières (12) 154 D1
Saint-Symphorien-des-
  Bois (71) 115 F4
Saint-Symphorien-des-
  Bruyères (61) 40 A4
Saint-Symphorien-
  d'Ozon (69) 130 A4
Saint-Symphorien-sous-
  Chomérac (07) 158 A1
Saint-Symphorien-sur-
  Coise (69) 129 F4
Saint-Symphorien-sur-
  Couze (87) 110 C6
Saint-Symphorien-sur-
  Saône (21) 102 B2
Saint-Thégonnec Loc-
  Eguiner (29) 31 H4
Saint-Thélo (22) 55 F1
Saint-Théodorit (30) 173 H2
Saint-Théoffrey (38) 145 G4
Saint-Thibaud-de-
  Couz (73) 131 H5
Saint-Thibault (10) 66 B4
Saint-Thibault (21) 84 D6
Saint-Thibault (60) 19 H2
Saint-Thibault-des-
  Vignes (77) 43 F4
Saint-Thibaut (02) 22 C5
Saint-Thiébaud (39) 103 F3
Saint-Thiébault (52) 68 C4
Saint-Thierry (51) 23 E5
Saint-Thois (29) 53 H1
Saint-Thomas (31) 168 C6
Saint-Thomas-de-
  Conac (17) 121 E6
Saint-Thomas-de-
  Courceriers (53) 59 G2
Saint-Thomas-en-
  Argonne (51) 46 C1
Saint-Thomas-en-
  Royans (26) 144 D4

Saint-Thomas-la-
  Garde (42) 128 D5
Saint-Thomé (07) 158 A3
Saint-Thonan (29) 31 E4
Saint-Thual (35) 34 D6
Saint-Thurial (35) 56 D3
Saint-Thuriau (56) 55 F3
Saint-Thurien (27) 15 H3
Saint-Thurien (29) 54 B3
Saint-Thurin (42) 128 C3
Saint-Tricat (62) 1 G2
Saint-Trimoël (22) 34 A5
Saint-Trinit (84) 159 F6
Saint-Trivier-de-
  Courtes (01) 116 D2
Saint-Trivier-sur-
  Moignans (01) 116 C6
Saint-Trojan (33) 135 E3
Saint-Trojan-les-Bains (17) .. 120 B2
Saint-Tropez (83) 194 B4
Saint-Tugdual (56) 54 C2
Saint-Ulphace (72) 61 E4
Saint-Ulrich (68) 89 E3
Saint-Uniac (35) 56 D2
Saint-Urbain (29) 31 F5
Saint-Urbain (85) 90 C2
Saint-Urbain-
  Maconcourt (52) 68 A2
Saint-Urcisse (47) 151 G6
Saint-Urcisse (81) 169 G2
Saint-Urcize (15) 155 F1
Saint-Usage (10) 67 E5
Saint-Usage (21) 102 B2
Saint-Usuge (71) 102 B6
Saint-Utin (51) 66 D1
Saint-Uze (26) 144 A2
Saint-Vaast-de-
  Longmont (60) 21 E5
Saint-Vaast-
  d'Équiqueville (76) 17 H3
Saint-Vaast-
  Dieppedalle (76) 17 E3
Saint-Vaast-du-Val (76) 17 G4
Saint-Vaast-en-Auge (14)....... 15 E4
Saint-Vaast-en-
  Cambrésis (59) 9 F3
Saint-Vaast-en-
  Chaussée (80) 7 F5
Saint-Vaast-la-Hougue (50) ... 13 E2
Saint-Vaast-lès-Mello (60) 20 C6
Saint-Vaast-sur-Seulles (14) .. 14 A5
Saint-Vaize (17) 121 F3
Saint-Valbert (70) 87 H1
Saint-Valentin (36) 96 D4
Saint-Valérien (85) 107 E1
Saint-Valérien (89) 64 D4
Saint-Valery (60) 19 G2
Saint-Valery-en-Caux (76)...... 17 E2
Saint-Valery-sur-
  Somme (80) 6 C3
Saint-Vallerin (71) 101 F6
Saint-Vallier (16) 136 A1
Saint-Vallier (26) 144 A2
Saint-Vallier (71) 115 G1
Saint-Vallier (88) 69 G3
Saint-Vallier-de-Thiey (06) ... 178 C4
Saint-Vallier-sur-
  Marne (52) 86 B1
Saint-Varent (79) 93 G4
Saint-Vaury (23) 111 F5
Saint-Venant (62) 2 C5
Saint-Vénérand (43) 142 B5
Saint-Vérain (58) 82 C5
Saint-Véran (05) 147 G6
Saint-Vérand (38) 144 D2
Saint-Vérand (69) 129 G2
Saint-Vérand (71) 116 A4
Saint-Vert (43) 142 A1
Saint-Viance (19) 138 C2
Saint-Viâtre (41) 80 D4
Saint-Viaud (44) 74 A4
Saint-Victeur (72) 60 A3
Saint-Victor (03) 112 D3
Saint-Victor (07) 143 H3
Saint-Victor (15) 139 H4
Saint-Victor (24) 136 D2
Saint-Victor-de-
  Buthon (28) 61 F2
Saint-Victor-de-
  Cessieu (38) 131 E5
Saint-Victor-de-
  Chrétienville (27) 39 H2
Saint-Victor-de-
  Malcap (30) 157 F5
Saint-Victor-de-
  Morestel (38) 131 E3
Saint-Victor-d'Épine (27)........ 15 H4
Saint-Victor-des-Oules (30)... 174 B1
Saint-Victor-en-
  Marche (23) 111 F5
Saint-Victor-et-
  Melvieu (12) 171 G1
Saint-Victor-la-Coste (30) 174 C1
Saint-Victor-la-Rivière (63) .. 127 E5
Saint-Victor-l'Abbaye (76) 17 G4
Saint-Victor-
  Malescours (43) 143 F2
Saint-Victor-
  Montvianeix (63) 128 A1
Saint-Victor-Rouzaud (09) ... 185 G4
Saint-Victor-sur-Arlanc (43) .. 142 B1
Saint-Victor-sur-Avre (27) 40 C5
Saint-Victor-sur-Ouche (21) ...101 F1
Saint-Victor-sur-Rhins (42)... 129 E1
Saint-Victoret (13) 191 H4
Saint-Victour (19) 126 A6
Saint-Victurnien (87) 123 H2
Saint-Vidal (43) 142 B4

Saint-Vigor (27) 41 E2
Saint-Vigor-des-Monts (50) 37 F3
Saint-Vigor-d'Ymonville (76) 15 G2
Saint-Vigor-le-Grand (14) 13 H5
Saint-Vincent (31) 186 A1
Saint-Vincent (43) 142 C3
Saint-Vincent (63) 127 F5
Saint-Vincent (64) 182 D3
Saint-Vincent-Bragny (71) 115 E2
Saint-Vincent-Cramesnil (76) 15 G2
Saint-Vincent-d'Autéjac (82) 152 C6
Saint-Vincent-de-Barbeyrargues (34)......... 173 F4
Saint-Vincent-de-Barrès (07) 158 A1
Saint-Vincent-de-Boisset (42) 128 D1
Saint-Vincent-de-Connezac (24) 136 D2
Saint-Vincent-de-Cosse (24) 138 A5
Saint-Vincent-de-Durfort (07) 143 H6
Saint-Vincent-de-Lamontjoie (47) 167 H1
Saint-Vincent-de-Mercuze (38)............. 131 H6
Saint-Vincent-de-Paul (33).. 135 F4
Saint-Vincent-de-Paul (40).. 165 E3
Saint-Vincent-de-Pertignas (33) 135 H6
Saint-Vincent-de-Reins (69).................115 G6
Saint-Vincent-de-Salers (15) 140 B2
Saint-Vincent-de-Tyrosse (40) 164 C4
Saint-Vincent-des-Bois (27).... 41 H2
Saint-Vincent-des-Landes (44) 74 D1
Saint-Vincent-des-Prés (71)..115 H2
Saint-Vincent-des-Prés (72).. 60 C3
Saint-Vincent-d'Olargues (34) 171 G6
Saint-Vincent-du-Boulay (27) 15 G3
Saint-Vincent-du-Lorouër (72) 78 C1
Saint-Vincent-du-Pendit (46) 139 F6
Saint-Vincent-en-Bresse (71) 102 A6
Saint-Vincent-Jalmoutiers (24) .. 136 C2
Saint-Vincent-la-Châtre (79) 108 C4
Saint-Vincent-la-Commanderie (26) 144 C5
Saint-Vincent-le-Paluel (24).. 138 B5
Saint-Vincent-Lespinasse (82) 151 H6
Saint-Vincent-Rive-d'Olt (46) 152 B3
Saint-Vincent-Sterlanges (85) 92 A5
Saint-Vincent-sur-Graon (85) 91 G6
Saint-Vincent-sur-Jabron (04) 159 H6
Saint-Vincent-sur-Jard (85)... 91 F6
Saint-Vincent-sur-l'Isle (24) .. 137 G2
Saint-Vincent-sur-Oust (56) .. 56 C6
Saint-Vit (25) 103 E1
Saint-Vital (73) 132 C4
Saint-Vite (47) 151 H3
Saint-Vitte (18) 112 C2
Saint-Vitte-sur-Briance (87) .. 124 D4
Saint-Vivien (17) 106 D5
Saint-Vivien (24) 136 B5
Saint-Vivien-de-Blaye (33)... 135 F3
Saint-Vivien-de-Médoc (33) 120 C5
Saint-Vivien-de-Monségur (33) 150 B2
Saint-Voir (03)............... 114 B3
Saint-Vougay (29) 31 G3
Saint-Vrain (51) 46 C5
Saint-Vrain (91) 63 G1
Saint-Vran (22) 56 A1
Saint-Vulbas (01) 130 D2
Saint-Waast (59) 9 G2
Saint-Witz (95) 43 E2
Saint-Xandre (17) 106 D4
Saint-Yaguen (40) 165 G2
Saint-Yan (71) 115 E3
Saint-Ybard (19) 124 C6
Saint-Ybars (09) 185 F3
Saint-Yon (91) 63 F1
Saint-Yorre (03) 114 A6
Saint-Yrieix-la-Montagne (23) 125 G2
Saint-Yrieix-la-Perche (87) .. 124 A5
Saint-Yrieix-le-Déjalat (19).. 125 F6
Saint-Yrieix-les-Bois (23).... 111 G6
Saint-Yrieix-sous-Aixe (87).. 123 H2
Saint-Yrieix-sur-Charente (16) 122 B4
Saint-Ythaire (71) 116 A1
Saint-Yvi (29) 53 G3
Saint-Yvoine (63) 127 G5
Saint-Yzan-de-Soudiac (33) 135 F2
Saint-Yzans-de-Médoc (33).. 134 D1
Saint-Zacharie (83) 192 D3
Sainte-Adresse (76) 15 E2

Sainte-Agathe (63) 128 A3
Sainte-Agathe-d'Aliermont (76) 6 A6
Sainte-Agathe-en-Donzy (42) 129 E2
Sainte-Agathe-la-Bouteresse (42) 128 D3
Sainte-Agnès (06) 179 I3
Sainte-Agnès (38) 145 H2
Sainte-Agnès (39) 117 F1
Sainte-Anastasie (30) 174 A2
Sainte-Anastasie-sur-Issole (83) 193 E3
Sainte-Anne (25) 103 F3
Sainte-Anne (32) 168 C4
Sainte-Anne (41) 79 G2
Sainte-Anne-d'Auray (56) 55 E6
Sainte-Anne-Saint-Priest (87) 124 D3
Sainte-Anne-sur-Brivet (44) 74 A3
Sainte-Anne-sur-Gervonde (38) 130 D5
Sainte-Anne-sur-Vilaine (35) 57 E6
Sainte-Aulde (77) 44 A3
Sainte-Aurence-Cazaux (32) 183 H1
Sainte-Austreberthe (62) 7 E2
Sainte-Austreberthe (76) 18 C3
Sainte-Barbe (57) 26 C5
Sainte-Barbe (88) 70 B2
Sainte-Bazeille (47) 150 B2
Sainte-Beuve-en-Rivière (76) 19 F1
Sainte-Blandine (38) 131 E5
Sainte-Blandine (79) 108 A4
Sainte-Brigitte (56) 55 E2
Sainte-Camelle (11) 186 A3
Sainte-Catherine (62) 8 B2
Sainte-Catherine (63) 127 H6
Sainte-Catherine (69) 129 G4
Sainte-Catherine-de-Fierbois (37) 94 D2
Sainte-Cécile (50) 37 F3
Sainte-Cécile (71) 116 A3
Sainte-Cécile (85) 92 A5
Sainte-Cécile-d'Andorge (30) 156 D5
Sainte-Cécile-du-Cayrou (81) 169 H2
Sainte-Cécile-les-Vignes (84) 158 B5
Sainte-Céronne-lès-Mortagne (61) 40 A6
Sainte-Cérotte (72) 78 D1
Sainte-Christie (32) 167 H4
Sainte-Christie-d'Armagnac (32) 166 D3
Sainte-Christine (63) 113 E6
Sainte-Colombe (05) 159 G5
Sainte-Colombe (16) 122 D2
Sainte-Colombe (17) 135 G1
Sainte-Colombe (25) 103 H4
Sainte-Colombe (33) 136 A5
Sainte-Colombe (35) 57 G5
Sainte-Colombe (40) 165 H4
Sainte-Colombe (46) 153 G1
Sainte-Colombe (50) 12 C4
Sainte-Colombe (69) 130 A5
Sainte-Colombe (76) 17 E3
Sainte-Colombe (89) 84 A4
Sainte-Colombe-de-Duras (47) 150 C1
Sainte-Colombe-de-la-Commanderie (66) 201 E3
Sainte-Colombe-de-Villeneuve (47) 151 F4
Sainte-Colombe-des-Bois (58) 82 D6
Sainte-Colombe-en-Auxois (21) 84 D5
Sainte-Colombe-en-Bruilhois (47) 151 E6
Sainte-Colombe-la-Commanderie (27) 40 C1
Sainte-Colombe-près-Vernon (27) 41 E1
Sainte-Colombe-sur-Gand (42) 129 E2
Sainte-Colombe-sur-Guette (11) 200 B2
Sainte-Colombe-sur-l'Hers (11) 186 B5
Sainte-Colombe-sur-Loing (89) 82 D4
Sainte-Colombe-sur-Seine (21) 85 E1
Sainte-Colome (64) 182 B4
Sainte-Consorce (69) 129 H3
Sainte-Croix (01) 130 D2
Sainte-Croix (02) 22 D4
Sainte-Croix (12) 153 G4
Sainte-Croix (24) 137 G6
Sainte-Croix (26) 144 D6
Sainte-Croix (71) 117 E1
Sainte-Croix (81) 170 B2
Sainte-Croix-à-Lauze (04) ... 176 B2
Sainte-Croix-aux-Mines (68) 71 E3
Sainte-Croix-de-Caderle (30) 173 F1
Sainte-Croix-de-Mareuil (24) 122 D5
Sainte-Croix-de-Quintillargues (34) 173 H4
Sainte-Croix-du-Mont (33).. 149 H2

Sainte-Croix-du-Verdon (04) 177 H1
Sainte-Croix-en-Jarez (42).. 129 H5
Sainte-Croix-en-Plaine (68) 71 F4
Sainte-Croix-sur-Buchy (76).. 19 E3
Sainte-Croix-sur-Mer (14) .. 14 B3
Sainte-Croix-Vallée-Française (48) 156 C6
Sainte-Croix-Volvestre (09).. 185 E4
Sainte-Dode (32) 183 G1
Sainte-Eanne (79) 108 B3
Sainte-Engrâce (64) 181 G4
Sainte-Eugénie-de-Villeneuve (43) 142 A3
Sainte-Eulalie (07) 143 E6
Sainte-Eulalie (11) 186 D3
Sainte-Eulalie (15) 140 A3
Sainte-Eulalie (33) 135 F5
Sainte-Eulalie (48) 141 H6
Sainte-Eulalie-d'Ans (24)... 137 H2
Sainte-Eulalie-de-Cernon (12) 172 A2
Sainte-Eulalie-d'Eymet (24) 150 D1
Sainte-Eulalie-d'Olt (12).... 155 E3
Sainte-Eulalie-en-Born (40).. 148 B4
Sainte-Eulalie-en-Royans (26) 144 D4
Sainte-Euphémie (01) 130 A1
Sainte-Euphémie-sur-Ouvèze (26) 159 F5
Sainte-Eusoye (60) 20 B3
Sainte-Fauste (36) 96 D5
Sainte-Féréole (19) 138 D2
Sainte-Feyre (23) 111 G5
Sainte-Feyre-la-Montagne (23) 125 H2
Sainte-Flaive-des-Loups (85) 91 F5
Sainte-Florence (33) 135 H5
Sainte-Florine (43) 127 G6
Sainte-Foi (09) 186 B4
Sainte-Fortunade (19) 139 E2
Sainte-Foy (40) 166 B2
Sainte-Foy (71) 115 E4
Sainte-Foy (76) 17 G3
Sainte-Foy (85) 91 E5
Sainte-Foy-d'Aigrefeuille (31) 169 G6
Sainte-Foy-de-Belvès (24) .. 152 A1
Sainte-Foy-de-Longas (24) .. 137 F5
Sainte-Foy-de-Peyrolières (31) 168 D6
Sainte-Foy-la-Grande (33) .. 136 C5
Sainte-Foy-la-Longue (33) .. 150 A2
Sainte-Foy-l'Argentière (69) 129 G3
Sainte-Foy-lès-Lyon (69)... 130 A3
Sainte-Foy-Saint-Sulpice (42) 128 D3
Sainte-Foy-Tarentaise (73).. 133 F4
Sainte-Gauburge-Sainte-Colombe (61) 39 H5
Sainte-Gemme (17) 120 D2
Sainte-Gemme (32) 168 B4
Sainte-Gemme (33) 150 B2
Sainte-Gemme (36) 96 A5
Sainte-Gemme (51) 44 D1
Sainte-Gemme (79) 93 F4
Sainte-Gemme (81) 170 C1
Sainte-Gemme-en-Sancerrois (18) 82 B5
Sainte-Gemme-la-Plaine (85) 106 D2
Sainte-Gemme-Martaillac (47) 150 C4
Sainte-Gemme-Moronval (28) 41 F5
Sainte-Gemmes-le-Robert (53) 59 F4
Sainte-Gemmes-sur-Loire (49) 76 D5
Sainte-Geneviève (02) 23 E2
Sainte-Geneviève (50) 13 E2
Sainte-Geneviève (54) 48 C3
Sainte-Geneviève (60) 20 B6
Sainte-Geneviève (76) 19 E2
Sainte-Geneviève-des-Bois (45) 82 B2
Sainte-Geneviève-des-Bois (91) 42 D6
Sainte-Geneviève-lès-Gasny (27) 41 G2
Sainte-Hélène (33) 134 C4
Sainte-Hélène (48) 156 B3
Sainte-Hélène (56) 54 D5
Sainte-Hélène (71) 101 F5
Sainte-Hélène (88) 70 B3
Sainte-Hélène-Bondeville (76) 16 C3
Sainte-Hélène-du-Lac (73).. 132 A5
Sainte-Hélène-sur-Isère (73) 132 C4
Sainte-Hermine (85) 106 D1
Sainte-Honorine-de-Ducy (14) 13 H6
Sainte-Honorine-du-Fay (14) 14 B5
Sainte-Honorine-la-Chardonne (61) 38 B4
Sainte-Honorine-la-Guillaume (61) 38 C4
Sainte-Innocence (24) 150 D1
Sainte-Jalle (26) 159 E4
Sainte-Jamme-sur-Sarthe (72) 60 A4
Sainte-Julie (01) 130 D2
Sainte-Juliette (82) 152 B5

Sainte-Juliette-sur-Viaur (12) 154 C6
Sainte-Léocadie (66) 199 H4
Sainte-Lheurine (17) 121 G5
Sainte-Livrade (31) 168 D5
Sainte-Livrade-sur-Lot (47).. 151 F4
Sainte-Lizaigne (36) 97 E3
Sainte-Luce (38) 145 H5
Sainte-Luce-sur-Loire (44) ... 74 D5
Sainte-Lucie-de-Tallano (2A) 207 E2
Sainte-Lunaise (18) 97 G4
Sainte-Magnance (89) 84 B5
Sainte-Marguerite (43) 142 A2
Sainte-Marguerite (88) 70 D3
Sainte-Marguerite-de-Carrouges (61) 38 D6
Sainte-Marguerite-d'Elle (14) 13 F6
Sainte-Marguerite-Lafigère (07) 156 D3
Sainte-Marguerite-sur-Duclair (76) 18 B3
Sainte-Marguerite-sur-Mer (76) 17 F2
Sainte-Marie (05) 159 F3
Sainte-Marie (08) 24 A5
Sainte-Marie (15) 140 D5
Sainte-Marie (25) 88 B4
Sainte-Marie (32) 168 B5
Sainte-Marie (35) 56 C6
Sainte-Marie (58) 99 F2
Sainte-Marie (65) 184 A5
Sainte-Marie-à-Py (51) 23 H6
Sainte-Marie-au-Bosc (76)... 16 B4
Sainte-Marie-aux-Chênes (57) 26 A5
Sainte-Marie-aux-Mines (68) 71 E3
Sainte-Marie-Cappel (59) 2 C3
Sainte-Marie-d'Alloix (38).. 132 A6
Sainte-Marie-d'Alvey (73).. 131 G4
Sainte-Marie-d'Attez (27).... 40 C4
Sainte-Marie-de-Cuines (73) 146 C1
Sainte-Marie-de-Gosse (40) 164 D5
Sainte-Marie-de-Ré (17)... 106 B5
Sainte-Marie-de-Vatimesnil (27) 19 F6
Sainte-Marie-de-Vaux (87).. 123 H2
Sainte-Marie-des-Champs (76) 17 E4
Sainte-Marie-du-Bois (53) ... 59 E1
Sainte-Marie-du-Lac-Nuisement (51) 46 C6
Sainte-Marie-du-Mont (38).. 131 H6
Sainte-Marie-du-Mont (50).. 13 E4
Sainte-Marie-en-Chanois (70) 88 A1
Sainte-Marie-en-Chaux (70) 87 H2
Sainte-Marie-Kerque (62) 2 A2
Sainte-Marie-la-Blanche (21) 101 G3
Sainte-Marie-la-Mer (66) ... 201 G2
Sainte-Marie-la-Robert (61).. 38 D5
Sainte-Marie-Lapanouze (19) 126 A6
Sainte-Marie-Outre-l'Eau (14) 37 G2
Sainte-Marie-sur-Ouche (21) 85 F6
Sainte-Marthe (27) 40 C3
Sainte-Marthe (47) 150 C3
Sainte-Maure (10) 66 B3
Sainte-Maure-de-Peyriac (47) 167 E1
Sainte-Maure-de-Touraine (37) 94 D2
Sainte-Maxime (83) 194 B3
Sainte-Même (17) 121 F2
Sainte-Menehould (51) 46 C2
Sainte-Mère (32) 167 H2
Sainte-Mère-Église (50) 13 E4
Sainte-Mesme (78) 62 D1
Sainte-Mondane (24) 138 B5
Sainte-Montaine (18) 81 G5
Sainte-Nathalène (24) 138 B5
Sainte-Néomaye (79) 108 A3
Sainte-Olive (01) 116 C6
Sainte-Opportune (61) 38 C4
Sainte-Opportune-du-Bosc (27) 40 C1
Sainte-Opportune-la-Mare (27) 15 H2
Sainte-Orse (24) 137 H2
Sainte-Osmane (72) 78 D1
Sainte-Ouenne (79) 107 H2
Sainte-Pallaye (89) 83 G3
Sainte-Paule (69) 129 G1
Sainte-Pazanne (44) 74 B6
Sainte-Pexine (85) 106 D1
Sainte-Pôle (54) 49 G6
Sainte-Preuve (02) 22 D3
Sainte-Radegonde (12) 154 C4
Sainte-Radegonde (17) 120 D2
Sainte-Radegonde (24) 151 F1
Sainte-Radegonde (32) 167 H3
Sainte-Radegonde (33) 136 A6
Sainte-Radegonde (71) 100 B6
Sainte-Radegonde (79) 93 G3
Sainte-Radegonde (86) 109 G1
Sainte-Radégonde-des-Noyers (85) 106 D3
Sainte-Ramée (17) 121 E6
Sainte-Reine (70) 87 E4
Sainte-Reine (73) 132 B4

Sainte-Reine-de-Bretagne (44) 73 H3
Sainte-Ruffine (57) 26 B5
Sainte-Sabine (21) 101 F2
Sainte-Sabine-sur-Longève (72) 60 A4
Sainte-Savine (10) 66 B3
Sainte-Scolasse-sur-Sarthe (61) 39 G6
Sainte-Segrée (80) 19 H1
Sainte-Sève (29) 31 H3
Sainte-Sévère (16) 121 H3
Sainte-Sévère-sur-Indre (36) 111 H2
Sainte-Sigolène (43) 143 E2
Sainte-Solange (18) 98 A2
Sainte-Soline (79) 108 C4
Sainte-Souline (16) 122 A6
Sainte-Soulle (17) 106 D4
Sainte-Suzanne (09) 185 F3
Sainte-Suzanne (25) 88 C3
Sainte-Suzanne-et-Chammes (53) 59 F4
Sainte-Suzanne-sur-Vire (50) 37 G1
Sainte-Terre (33) 135 H5
Sainte-Thérence (03) 112 C4
Sainte-Thorette (18) 97 F3
Sainte-Tréphine (22) 33 E6
Sainte-Trie (24) 138 A1
Sainte-Tulle (04) 176 C3
Sainte-Valière (11) 187 H3
Sainte-Vaubourg (08) 24 A4
Sainte-Verge (79) 93 G3
Sainte-Vertu (89) 84 B3
Saintes (17) 121 E3
Saintes-Maries-de-la-Mer (13) 190 C4
Saintines (60) 21 E5
Saintry-sur-Seine (91) 43 E6
Saints (77) 43 H5
Saints-en-Puisaye (89) 83 E3
Saints-Geosmes (52) 86 B1
Sainville (28) 62 D2
Saires (86) 94 B4
Saires-la-Verrerie (61) 38 B5
Saissac (11) 186 D2
Saisseval (80) 7 F6
Saisy (71) 101 E4
Saivres (79) 108 A2
le Saix (05) 160 A3
Saïx (81) 170 C6
Saix (86) 93 H2
Saizenay (39) 103 F3
Saizerais (54) 48 C4
Saizy (58) 83 G6
Sajas (31) 184 D2
Salagnac (24) 138 A1
Salagnon (38) 130 D4
Salaise-sur-Sanne (38) 144 A1
Salans (39) 103 E2
Salasc (34) 172 C5
Salaunes (33) 134 D4
Salavas (07) 157 G4
Salavre (01) 117 E3
Salazac (30) 157 H5
Salbris (41) 81 E5
les Salces (48) 155 G3
Saléchan (65) 184 A5
Saleich (31) 184 C5
Saleignes (17) 108 B6
Saleilles (66) 201 F2
les Salelles (07) 157 E4
les Salelles (48) 155 G3
Salency (60) 21 G3
Saléon (05) 159 H4
Salérans (05) 159 H5
Salerm (31) 184 B2
Salernes (83) 177 F5
Salers (15) 140 B3
Sales (74) 131 H2
Salesches (59) 9 G3
la Salette-Fallavaux (38) ... 146 A5
Salettes (26) 158 C2
Salettes (43) 142 C5
Saleux (80) 7 F6
Salice (2A) 204 D4
Saliceto (2B) 205 F1
Saliès (81) 170 C3
Salies-de-Béarn (64) 165 F6
Salies-du-Salat (31) 184 C4
Salignac (04) 160 B6
Salignac-de-Mirambeau (17) 121 F6
Salignac-Eyvigues (24) 138 B4
Salignac-sur-Charente (17).. 121 G3
Saligney (39) 102 D1
Saligny (89) 65 E4
Saligny-le-Vif (18) 98 B3
Saligny-sur-Roudon (03) ... 114 C2
Saligos (65) 182 D6
Salindres (30) 157 E6
Saline (14) 14 C4
Salinelles (30) 173 G3
Salins (15) 140 A2
Salins (77) 64 C2
Salins-Fontaine (73) 132 C5
Salins-les-Bains (39) 103 F4
Salives (21) 85 G3
Sallagriffon (06) 178 C2
Sallanches (74) 133 E1
Sallaumines (62) 8 B1
la Salle (71) 116 B3
la Salle (88) 70 C2
la Salle-en-Beaumont (38).. 145 H5
la Salle-les-Alpes (05) 147 E4
Sallebœuf (33) 135 F5
Sallèdes (63) 127 G4

Sallèles-Cabardès (11) 187 E2
Sallèles-d'Aude (11) 188 A3
Sallen (14) 37 H1
Sallenelles (14) 14 C4
Sallenôves (74) 118 B6
Sallertaine (85) 90 D2
Salles (33) 148 D2
les Salles (42) 128 B2
Salles (47) 151 G2
Salles (65) 182 D6
Salles (79) 108 B3
Salles (81) 170 B1
Salles-Adour (65) 183 E3
Salles-Arbuissonnas-en-Beaujolais (69) 116 A6
Salles-Courbatiès (12) 153 G3
Salles-Curan (12) 154 D6
Salles-d'Angles (16) 121 G4
Salles-d'Armagnac (32) 166 D3
Salles-d'Aude (11) 188 B3
Salles-de-Barbezieux (16).. 121 H5
Salles-de-Belvès (24) 151 H1
les Salles-de-Castillon (33).. 136 A5
Salles-de-Villefagnan (16).. 122 C1
Salles-du-Gardon (30) 157 E6
Salles-et-Pratviel (31) 197 F1
Salles-la-Source (12) 154 C4
Salles-Lavalette (16) 122 C6
les Salles-Lavauguyon (87).. 123 F3
Salles-Mongiscard (64) 165 F6
Salles-sous-Bois (26) 158 C3
Salles-sur-Garonne (31) 185 E2
Salles-sur-l'Hers (11) 186 A2
Salles-sur-Mer (17) 106 D5
les Salles-sur-Verdon (83).. 177 F3
Sallespisse (64) 165 G5
Salmagne (55) 47 F4
Salmaise (21) 85 E5
Salmbach (67) 51 G2
Salmiech (12) 154 C6
Salomé (59) 3 E6
Salon (10) 45 F6
Salon (24) 137 F4
Salon-de-Provence (13) 175 G5
Salon-la-Tour (19) 124 C5
Salornay-sur-Guye (71) 116 A2
Salouël (80) 7 F6
Salperwick (62) 2 A4
Salsein (09) 184 D6
Salses-le-Château (66) 201 F1
Salsigne (11) 187 E2
Salt-en-Donzy (42) 129 E3
Salvagnac (81) 169 G3
Salvagnac-Cajarc (12) 153 F3
la Salvetat-Belmontet (82).. 169 F2
la Salvetat-Lauragais (31)... 169 H6
la Salvetat-Peyralès (12) ... 153 H5
la Salvetat-Saint-Gilles (31) 169 E5
la Salvetat-sur-Agout (34).. 171 F5
Salvezines (11) 200 B1
Salviac (46) 152 B1
Salvizinet (42) 129 E3
Salza (11) 187 F5
Salzuit (43) 141 H2
Samadet (40) 166 A5
Saman (31) 184 B3
Samaran (32) 183 H1
Samatan (32) 168 B6
Samazan (47) 150 B3
Sambin (41) 79 H5
Sambourg (89) 84 A2
Saméon (59) 3 H6
Samer (62) 1 F5
Samerey (21) 102 B2
Sames (64) 164 D5
Sammarçolles (86) 94 A3
Sammeron (77) 43 H3
Samoëns (74) 119 F5
Samognat (01) 117 G4
Samogneux (55) 25 E6
Samois-sur-Seine (77) 64 B2
Samonac (33) 135 E3
Samoreau (77) 64 B2
Samouillan (31) 184 C3
Samoussy (02) 22 C3
Sampans (39) 102 C2
Sampigny (55) 47 G3
Sampigny-lès-Maranges (71) 101 F4
Sampolo (2A) 205 E6
Sampzon (07) 157 G4
Samson (25) 103 F3
Samsons-Lion (64) 182 D1
Samuran (31) 184 A5
San-Damiano (2B) 205 G1
San-Gavino-d'Ampugnani (2B) 205 G1
San-Gavino-di-Carbini (2A).. 207 F2
San-Gavino-di-Fiumorbo (2B) 205 F6
San-Gavino-di-Tenda (2B).. 203 F5
San-Giovanni-di-Moriani (2B) 205 G1
San-Giuliano (2B) 205 G2
San-Lorenzo (2B) 205 F1
San-Martino-di-Lota (2B).. 203 G3
San-Nicolao (2B) 205 H1
Sana (31) 184 D3
Sanary-sur-Mer (83) 192 D5
Sancé (71) 116 B3
Sancergues (18) 98 C2
Sancerre (18) 82 B5
Sancey (25) 88 B6
Sancheville (28) 62 B4
Sanchey (88) 69 H4
Sancoins (18) 98 C5

Sancourt (27) 19 G5
Sancourt (59) 8 D3
Sancourt (80) 21 G1
Sancy (54) 26 A3
Sancy (77) 43 G3
Sancy-les-Cheminots (02) 22 B4
Sancy-lès-Provins (77) 44 B5
Sand (67) 71 G2
Sandarville (28) 62 A3
Sandaucourt (88) 69 E3
Sandillon (45) 81 E1
Sandouville (76) 15 G2
Sandrans (01) 116 C6
Sangatte (62) 1 G2
Sanghen (62) 1 G4
Sanguinet (40) 148 C2
Sanilhac (07) 157 F3
Sanilhac (24) 137 F2
Sanilhac-Sagriès (30) 174 B2
Sannat (23) 112 B6
Sannes (84) 176 A4
Sannois (95) 42 C3
Sanous (65) 183 E1
Sanry-lès-Vigy (57) 26 C5
Sanry-sur-Nied (57) 48 D2
Sans-Vallois (88) 69 F4
Sansa (66) 200 A3
Sansac-de-Marmiesse (15) 140 A5
Sansac-Veinazès (15) 154 B1
Sansais (79) 107 G4
Sansan (32) 167 H6
Sanssac-l'Église (43) 142 B4
Sanssat (03) 114 A4
Santa-Lucia-di-
  Mercurio (2B) 205 F2
Santa-Lucia-di-
  Moriani (2B) 205 H1
Santa-Maria-di-Lota (2B) 203 G3
Santa-Maria-
  Figaniella (2A) 207 E2
Santa-Maria-Poggio (2B) 205 H2
Santa-Maria-Siché (2A) 204 D6
Santa-Reparata-di-
  Balagna (2B) 202 D5
Santa-Reparata-di-
  Moriani (2B) 205 G2
Sant'Andréa-di-Bozio (2B) 205 F2
Sant'Andréa-di-
  Cotone (2B) 205 G2
Sant'Andréa-d'Orcino (2A) 204 C5
Santans (39) 102 D3
Sant'Antonino (2B) 202 C5
Santeau (45) 63 F5
Santec (29) 31 G2
Santenay (21) 101 F4
Santenay (41) 79 G4
Santeny (94) 43 E5
Santes (59) 3 F5
Santeuil (28) 62 C2
Santeuil (95) 42 A1
Santigny (89) 84 B4
Santilly (28) 62 D4
Santilly (71) 116 A1
Santo-Pietro-di-Tenda (2B) 203 F5
Santo-Pietro-di-
  Venaco (2B) 205 E3
Santosse (21) 101 F3
Santranges (18) 82 B5
Sanvensa (12) 153 G5
Sanvignes-les-Mines (71) 100 D6
Sanxay (86) 108 C2
Sanzey (54) 48 A4
Saon (14) 13 G5
Saône (25) 103 G1
Saonnet (14) 13 G5
Saorge (06) 179 G1
Saosnes (72) 60 B3
Saou (26) 158 C2
le Sap-André (61) 39 G4
Sap-en-Auge (61) 39 G3
Sapignicourt (51) 46 C5
Sapignies (62) 8 B3
Sapogne-et-Feuchères (08) 24 B2
Sapogne-sur-Marche (08) 25 E3
Sapois (39) 103 F5
Sapois (88) 70 B5
Saponay (02) 22 B6
Saponcourt (70) 87 F1
le Sappey (74) 118 C5
le Sappey-en-
  Chartreuse (38) 145 G2
Saramon (32) 168 A6
Saran (45) 62 D6
Saraz (25) 103 F3
Sarbazan (40) 166 B1
Sarcé (72) 78 B2
Sarceaux (61) 39 E5
Sarcelles (95) 42 D3
Sarcenas (38) 145 G1
Sarcey (52) 68 A5
Sarcey (69) 129 G2
Sarcos (32) 184 B1
Sarcus (60) 19 H2
Sarcy (51) 22 D6
Sardan (30) 173 G3
Sardent (23) 111 G6
Sardieu (38) 144 D1
Sardon (63) 127 F1
Sardy-lès-Épiry (58) 99 H2
Sare (64) 180 B1
Sargé-lès-le-Mans (72) 60 B5
Sargé-sur-Braye (41) 61 E6
Sari-d'Orcino (2A) 204 C5
Sari-Solenzara (2A) 205 G6
Sariac-Magnoac (65) 183 H2
Sarlabous (65) 183 F4
Sarlande (24) 124 A6
Sarlat-la-Canéda (24) 138 A5

Sarliac-sur-l'Isle (24) 137 G2
Sarniguet (65) 183 E2
Sarnois (60) 19 H2
Saron-sur-Aube (51) 44 D6
Sarp (65) 184 A5
Sarpourenx (64) 165 G6
Sarragachies (32) 166 D4
Sarrageois (25) 103 H5
Sarraguzan (32) 183 G2
Sarralbe (57) 49 H2
Sarraltroff (57) 50 A4
Sarran (19) 125 F6
Sarrance (64) 182 A4
Sarrancolin (65) 183 G5
Sarrant (32) 168 B4
Sarras (07) 144 A2
Sarrazac (24) 123 H6
Sarrazac (46) 138 D4
Sarraziet (40) 166 A4
Sarre-Union (67) 50 A2
Sarrebourg (57) 50 A4
Sarrecave (31) 184 A3
Sarreguemines (57) 27 H5
Sarreinsming (57) 27 H5
Sarremezan (31) 184 A3
Sarrewerden (67) 50 A3
Sarrey (52) 68 B5
Sarriac-Bigorre (65) 183 F1
Sarrians (84) 175 F1
Sarrigné (49) 77 E4
Sarrogna (39) 117 G2
Sarrola-Carcopino (2A) 204 C5
Sarron (40) 166 B5
Sarrouilles (65) 183 F3
Sarroux - St Julien (19) 126 A6
Sarry (51) 45 H3
Sarry (71) 115 E4
Sarry (89) 84 B3
le Sars (62) 8 B4
Sars-et-Rosières (59) 9 E1
Sars-le-Bois (62) 7 H2
Sars-Poteries (59) 10 A3
Sartène (2A) 206 D3
Sartes (88) 68 D3
Sartilly-Baie-Bocage (50) 36 D4
Sarton (62) 7 H4
Sartrouville (78) 42 C3
Sarzay (36) 111 G1
Sarzeau (56) 72 D2
Sasnières (41) 79 F2
Sassangy (71) 101 F6
Sassay (41) 80 A5
Sassegnies (59) 9 H3
Sassenage (38) 145 G2
Sassenay (71) 101 H5
Sassetot-le-Malgardé (76) 17 F3
Sassetot-le-
  Mauconduit (76) 16 D3
Sasseville (76) 17 E3
Sassey (27) 41 E2
Sassey-sur-Meuse (55) 24 D4
Sassierges-Saint-
  Germain (36) 96 D5
Sassis (65) 182 D6
Sassy (14) 38 D2
Sathonay-Camp (69) 130 A2
Sathonay-Village (69) 130 A2
Satillieu (07) 143 H3
Satolas-et-Bonce (38) 130 C3
Saturargues (34) 173 H4
Saubens (31) 169 E6
Saubion (40) 164 C4
Saubole (64) 182 D2
Saubrigues (40) 164 C5
Saubusse (40) 164 C4
Saucats (33) 149 F1
Sauchay (76) 17 H2
Sauchy-Cauchy (62) 8 C3
Sauchy-Lestrée (62) 8 D3
Sauclières (12) 172 C2
Saudemont (62) 8 C3
Saudoy (51) 44 D5
Saudron (52) 68 B1
Saudrupt (55) 46 D5
Saugeot (39) 117 H1
Saugnac-et-Cambran (40) 165 E4
Saugnacq-et-Muret (40) 148 D3
Saugon (33) 135 F2
Saugues (43) 142 A5
Sauguis-Saint-Étienne (64) 181 G3
Saugy (18) 97 F4
Saujac (12) 153 F3
Saujon (17) 120 C3
la Saulce (05) 160 B3
Saulce-sur-Rhône (26) 158 B1
Saulces-
  Champenoises (08) 23 H4
Saulces-Monclin (08) 23 H3
Saulcet (03) 113 H4
Saulchery (02) 44 B3
le Saulchoy (60) 20 B2
Saulchoy (62) 6 D2
Saulchoy-sous-Poix (80) 20 A1
Saulcy (10) 67 F3
Saulcy-sur-Meurthe (88) 70 D3
Saules (25) 103 H2
Saules (71) 101 F6
Saulgé (86) 109 H3
Saulges (53) 59 F5
Saulgond (16) 123 G1
Sauliac-sur-Célé (46) 153 E3
Saulieu (21) 100 C1
Saulles (52) 86 C2
Saulmory-et-
  Villefranche (55) 24 D4

Saulnay (36) 95 H4
Saulnes (54) 25 H3
Saulnières (28) 41 E5
Saulnières (35) 57 F4
Saulnot (70) 88 B3
Saulny (57) 26 B5
Saulon-la-Chapelle (21) 102 A1
Saulon-la-Rue (21) 101 H1
la Saulsotte (10) 65 F1
Sault (84) 176 A1
Sault-Brénaz (01) 131 E2
Sault-de-Navailles (64) 165 G5
Sault-lès-Rethel (08) 23 G4
Sault-Saint-Remy (08) 23 F4
Saultain (59) 9 F2
Saulty (62) 7 H3
Saulvaux (55) 47 G5
Saulx (70) 87 G2
Saulx-le-Duc (21) 85 H4
Saulx-lès-Champlon (55) 47 H2
Saulx-les-Chartreux (91) 42 C5
Saulx-Marchais (78) 42 A4
Saulxerotte (54) 69 E1
Saulxures (52) 68 C6
Saulxures (67) 71 E2
Saulxures-lès-
  Bulgnéville (88) 68 D4
Saulxures-lès-Nancy (54) 48 D5
Saulxures-lès-Vannes (54) 68 D1
Saulxures-sur-
  Moselotte (88) 70 C6
Saulzais-le-Potier (18) 112 C1
Saulzet (03) 113 G5
Saulzet-le-Froid (63) 126 D4
Saulzoir (59) 9 F3
Saumane (04) 176 C1
Saumane (30) 173 E1
Saumane-de-Vaucluse (84) 175 F2
Sauméjan (47) 150 B5
Saumeray (28) 61 H3
Saumont (47) 151 E6
Saumont-la-Poterie (76) 19 F3
Saumos (33) 134 C4
Saumur (49) 77 G6
Saunay (37) 79 F3
la Saunière (23) 111 G5
Saunières (71) 102 A4
Sauqueville (76) 17 G2
Saurais (79) 108 B1
Saurat (09) 185 G6
Sauret-Besserve (63) 126 D1
Saurier (63) 127 E5
Sausheim (68) 89 F1
Saussan (34) 173 F6
Saussay (28) 41 F4
Saussay (76) 17 F4
Saussay-la-Campagne (27) 19 F5
la Saussaye (27) 18 C6
Saussemesnil (50) 12 D3
Saussenac (81) 170 D2
Saussens (31) 169 H5
Sausses (04) 178 B1
Sausset-les-Pins (13) 191 H5
Sausseuzemare-en-
  Caux (76) 16 C4
Saussey (21) 101 F3
Saussey (50) 36 D2
Saussignac (24) 136 C6
Saussines (34) 173 G4
Saussy (21) 85 G5
Sautel (09) 186 A5
Sauternes (33) 149 G2
Sauteyrargues (34) 173 G3
Sauto (66) 200 A4
Sautron (44) 74 C4
les Sauvages (69) 129 F2
Sauvagnac (16) 123 F3
Sauvagnas (47) 151 F5
Sauvagnat (63) 126 C3
Sauvagnat-Sainte-
  Marthe (63) 127 F5
Sauvagney (25) 87 E6
Sauvagnon (64) 182 B1
Sauvagny (03) 113 E3
Sauvain (42) 128 C4
Sauve (30) 173 G2
la Sauve (33) 135 G6
Sauvelade (64) 181 H1
Sauverny (01) 118 B3
Sauvessanges (63) 128 C6
la Sauvetat (32) 167 H3
la Sauvetat (63) 127 F4
la Sauvetat-de-
  Savères (47) 151 G3
la Sauvetat-du-Dropt (47) 150 D1
la Sauvetat-sur-Lède (47) 151 F3
Sauveterre (30) 174 D1
Sauveterre (32) 184 C1
Sauveterre (65) 167 E6
Sauveterre (81) 187 F1
Sauveterre (82) 152 B5
Sauveterre-de-Béarn (64) 181 F1
Sauveterre-de-
  Comminges (31) 184 A5
Sauveterre-de-
  Guyenne (33) 150 A1
Sauveterre-de-
  Rouergue (12) 154 A5
Sauveterre-la-
  Lémance (47) 151 H2
Sauveterre-Saint-
  Denis (47) 151 F5
Sauviac (32) 183 H1
Sauviac (33) 149 H3
Sauvian (34) 188 C2
Sauviat (63) 128 A3
Sauviat-sur-Vige (87) 124 D2

Sauvignac (16) 136 A2
Sauvigney-lès-Gray (70) 86 D5
Sauvigney-lès-Pesmes (70) 86 C6
Sauvigny (55) 68 D1
Sauvigny-le-Beuréal (89) 84 B5
Sauvigny-le-Bois (89) 84 A4
Sauvigny-les-Bois (58) 99 E4
Sauville (08) 24 B3
Sauville (88) 68 D4
Sauvillers-Mongival (80) 20 D2
Sauvimont (32) 184 C1
Sauvoy (55) 47 H5
Saux (12) 152 A4
Saux-et-Pomarède (31) 184 B3
Sauxillanges (63) 127 G5
Sauze (06) 161 G6
le Sauze-du-Lac (05) 160 D3
Sauzé-Vaussais (79) 108 C5
Sauzelles (36) 95 F6
Sauzet (26) 158 B2
Sauzet (30) 174 A2
Sauzet (46) 152 B4
la Sauzière-Saint-Jean (81) 169 G2
Sauzon (56) 72 A3
Savarthès (31) 184 B4
Savas (07) 143 H1
Savas-Mépin (38) 130 C5
Savasse (26) 158 B2
Savenay (44) 74 A4
Savenès (82) 168 D3
Savennes (23) 111 G6
Savennes (63) 126 B5
Savennières (49) 76 D5
Saverdun (09) 185 G3
Savères (31) 184 D2
Saverne (67) 50 C4
Saveuse (80) 7 F6
Savianges (71) 101 F6
Savières (10) 66 A2
Savignac (12) 153 G4
Savignac (33) 150 A2
Savignac-de-Duras (47) 150 C1
Savignac-de-l'Isle (33) 135 G4
Savignac-de-
  Miremont (24) 137 G4
Savignac-de-Nontron (24) 123 F5
Savignac-Lédrier (24) 124 A6
Savignac-les-Églises (24) 137 G2
Savignac-les-
  Ormeaux (09) 199 F2
Savignac-Mona (32) 168 C6
Savignac-sur-Leyze (47) 151 G3
Savignargues (30) 173 H2
Savigné (86) 109 E5
Savigné-l'Évêque (72) 60 B5
Savigné-sous-le-Lude (72) 77 H3
Savigné-sur-Lathan (37) 78 B5
Savigneux (01) 130 A1
Savigneux (42) 128 D4
Savignies (60) 20 A4
Savigny (50) 37 E1
Savigny (52) 86 D2
Savigny (69) 129 G2
Savigny (74) 118 A6
Savigny (88) 69 G2
Savigny-en-
  Revermont (71) 117 F2
Savigny-en-Sancerre (18) 82 B5
Savigny-en-Septaine (18) 98 A3
Savigny-en-Terre-
  Plaine (89) 84 B5
Savigny-en-Véron (37) 94 A1
Savigny-le-Sec (21) 85 H5
Savigny-le-Temple (77) 43 E6
Savigny-le-Vieux (50) 37 G6
Savigny-lès-Beaune (21) 101 G3
Savigny-Lévescault (86) 109 F2
Savigny-Poil-Fol (58) 100 A5
Savigny-sous-Faye (86) 94 B4
Savigny-sous-Mâlain (21) 85 F6
Savigny-sur-Aisne (08) 24 B5
Savigny-sur-Ardres (51) 22 D6
Savigny-sur-Braye (41) 79 E1
Savigny-sur-Clairis (89) 64 D5
Savigny-sur-Grosne (71) 116 A1
Savigny-sur-Orge (91) 42 D5
Savigny-sur-Seille (71) 116 D1
Savilly (21) 100 D2
Savines-le-Lac (05) 160 D2
Savins (77) 64 D1
Savoillan (84) 159 F6
Savoisy (21) 84 D2
Savolles (21) 86 A5
Savonnières (37) 78 C6
Savonnières-devant-
  Bar (55) 47 E4
Savonnières-en-
  Perthois (55) 47 E6
Savouges (21) 101 H2
Savournon (05) 159 H3
Savoyeux (70) 86 D4
Savy (02) 21 H1
Savy-Berlette (62) 7 H2
Saxel (74) 118 D4
Saxi-Bourdon (58) 99 F3
Saxon-Sion (54) 69 F2
Sayat (63) 127 E2
Saze (30) 174 D2
Sazeray (36) 111 H3
Sazeret (03) 113 F4
Sazilly (37) 94 C2
Sazos (65) 182 D6
Scaër (29) 54 A2
Scata (2B) 205 G1
Sceau-Saint-Angel (24) 123 F5
Sceautres (07) 157 H2
Sceaux (89) 84 B4
Sceaux (92) 42 C4

Sceaux-d'Anjou (49) 76 D3
Sceaux-du-Gâtinais (45) 63 H5
Sceaux-sur-Huisne (72) 60 D5
Scey-Maisières (25) 103 G2
Scey-sur-Saône-et-Saint-
  Albin (70) 87 F3
Schaeffersheim (67) 71 H1
Schalbach (57) 50 B3
Schalkendorf (67) 50 D3
Scharrachbergheim-
  Irmstett (67) 50 D5
Scheibenhard (67) 51 G2
Scherlenheim (67) 50 D4
Scherwiller (67) 71 F2
Schillersdorf (67) 50 D3
Schiltigheim (67) 51 E5
Schirmeck (67) 71 E1
Schirrhein (67) 51 F3
Schirrhoffen (67) 51 F3
Schleithal (67) 51 G2
Schlierbach (68) 89 G2
Schmittviller (57) 50 B2
Schneckenbusch (57) 50 A5
Schnersheim (67) 50 D5
Schœnau (67) 71 H3
Schœnbourg (67) 50 B3
Schœneck (57) 27 G4
Schœnenbourg (67) 51 F2
Schopperten (67) 50 A2
Schorbach (57) 28 B5
Schweighouse-sur-
  Moder (67) 51 E3
Schweighouse-Thann (68) 89 E2
Schwenheim (67) 50 C4
Schwerdorff (57) 27 E3
Schweyen (57) 28 B5
Schwindratzheim (67) 50 D4
Schwoben (68) 89 F3
Schwobsheim (67) 71 G3
Sciecq (79) 107 H3
Scientrier (74) 118 D5
Scieurac-et-Flourès (32) 167 E5
Sciez (74) 118 D3
Scillé (79) 107 G1
Scionzier (74) 119 E6
Scolca (2B) 203 F5
Scorbé-Clairvaux (86) 94 C5
Scrignac (29) 32 B5
Scrupt (51) 46 C5
Scy-Chazelles (57) 26 B5
Scye (70) 87 F3
Séailles (32) 167 E4
la Séauve-sur-Semène (43) 143 E1
Sébazac-Concourès (12) 154 C4
Sébécourt (27) 40 D3
Sébeville (50) 13 E4
Seboncourt (02) 9 F5
Sebourg (59) 9 G2
Sébrazac (12) 154 C3
Séby (64) 166 A6
Secenans (70) 88 B4
Séchault (08) 24 B6
Sécheras (07) 144 A3
Sécheval (08) 11 E6
Séchilienne (38) 145 H3
Séchin (25) 87 H6
Seclin (59) 3 H6
Secondigné-sur-Belle (79) 108 A5
Secondigny (79) 107 H1
Secourt (57) 48 D3
Sedan (08) 24 C2
Sédeilhac (31) 184 A3
Séderon (26) 159 G5
Sedze-Maubecq (64) 182 D1
Sedzère (64) 182 D2
Seebach (67) 51 F2
Sées (61) 39 F6
Séez (73) 133 F4
Ségalas (47) 151 E2
Ségalas (65) 183 F1
la Ségalassière (15) 139 H5
Séglien (56) 54 D2
Ségny (01) 118 B4
Segonzac (16) 121 H4
Segonzac (19) 138 B2
Segonzac (24) 136 D2
Ségos (32) 166 B5
Ségoufielle (32) 168 D5
Segré-en-Anjou Bleu (49) 76 C2
Ségreville (31) 169 H6
Ségrie (72) 59 H4
Segrois (21) 101 G2
Ségry (36) 97 E4
Séguret (84) 159 E6
Ségur (12) 155 E5
le Ségur (81) 170 B1
Ségur-le-Château (19) 124 B6
Ségur-les-Villas (15) 140 D2
Ségura (09) 185 H5
Ségus (65) 182 D4
Seich (65) 183 H5
Seichamps (54) 48 D5
Seichebrières (45) 63 F6
Seicheprey (54) 48 A3
Seiches-sur-le-Loir (49) 77 E3
Seignalens (11) 186 B4
Seigné (17) 121 H1
Seignelay (89) 83 G1
Seigneulles (55) 47 E4
Seignosse (40) 164 C4
Seigny (21) 84 D4
Seigy (41) 96 A1
Seilh (31) 169 E4
Seilhac (19) 139 E1
Seilhan (31) 184 A4

Seillans (83) 178 A4
Seillonnaz (01) 131 E2
Seillons-Source-
  d'Argens (83) 193 E2
Seine-Port (77) 63 H1
Seingbouse (57) 27 F5
Seissan (32) 167 H6
Seix (09) 185 E6
le Sel-de-Bretagne (35) 57 F5
Selaincourt (54) 69 E1
Selens (02) 21 H4
Sélestat (67) 71 G3
Séligné (79) 108 A5
Séligney (39) 102 D4
la Selle-Craonnaise (53) 76 B1
la Selle-en-Hermoy (45) 64 B6
la Selle-en-Luitré (35) 58 A2
la Selle-Guerchaise (35) 58 A6
la Selle-la-Forge (61) 38 B4
la Selle-sur-le-Bied (45) 64 B5
Selles (27) 15 H4
Selles (51) 23 G5
Selles (62) 1 G4
Selles (70) 69 F6
Selles-Saint-Denis (41) 80 D6
Selles-sur-Cher (41) 96 B1
Selles-sur-Nahon (36) 96 B3
Sellières (39) 102 D5
Selommes (41) 79 G2
Seloncourt (25) 88 C4
Selongey (21) 86 A4
Selonnet (04) 160 D4
Seltz (67) 51 G2
la Selve (02) 23 E3
la Selve (12) 171 E1
Sem (09) 198 D1
Sémalens (81) 170 B5
Semallé (61) 60 A1
Semarey (21) 101 F1
Sembadel (43) 142 B2
Sembas (47) 151 F4
Semblançay (37) 78 C4
Sembleçay (36) 96 C1
Semboués (32) 167 E6
Séméac (65) 183 E3
Séméacq-Blachon (64) 166 C6
Semécourt (57) 26 B5
Sémelay (58) 100 A5
Semens (33) 149 H2
Sementron (89) 83 E3
Séméries (59) 10 A4
Semezanges (21) 101 G1
Sémézies-Cachan (32) 168 A6
Semide (08) 24 A5
Semillac (17) 121 E6
Semilly (52) 68 B3
Semmadon (70) 87 E2
Semoine (10) 45 F5
Semond (21) 85 E2
Semondans (25) 88 B4
Semons (38) 130 C6
Semousies (59) 10 A3
Semoussac (17) 121 E6
Semoutiers-Montsaon (52) 67 H5
Semoy (45) 62 D6
Sempesserre (32) 168 A1
Sempigny (60) 21 G3
Sempy (62) 1 G6
Semur-en-Auxois (21) 84 C5
Semur-en-Brionnais (71) 115 E4
Semur-en-Vallon (72) 60 D5
Semussac (17) 120 C4
Semuy (08) 24 A4
le Sen (40) 149 F6
Sénac (65) 183 F2
Senaide (88) 69 E6
Sénaillac-Latronquière (46) 139 G6
Sénaillac-Lauzès (46) 153 E2
Senailly (21) 84 C4
Senan (89) 83 E1
Senantes (28) 41 G6
Senantes (60) 19 H4
Sénarens (31) 184 C2
Senargent-Mignafans (70) 88 A3
Senarpont (80) 6 C6
Sénas (13) 175 F4
Senaux (81) 171 F4
Sencenac-Puy-de-
  Fourches (24) 137 F1
Senconac (09) 199 F1
Sendets (33) 150 A3
Sendets (64) 182 C2
Séné (56) 72 D1
Sénéchas (30) 157 E5
Sénergues (12) 154 B2
Sénestis (47) 150 C3
Séneujols (43) 142 B5
Senez (04) 177 G2
Sénezergues (15) 154 B1
Sengouagnet (31) 184 B5
Séniergues (46) 152 D1
Senillé-Saint-Sauveur (86) 94 D5
Seninghem (62) 1 H4
Senlecques (62) 1 G5
Senlis (60) 20 D6
Senlis (62) 2 A6
Senlis-le-Sec (80) 8 A5
Senlisse (78) 42 B5
Sennecey-le-Grand (71) 116 B1
Sennecey-lès-Dijon (21) 85 H6
Sennely (45) 81 F3
Sennevières (37) 95 G2
Senneville-sur-
  Fécamp (76) 16 C3
Sennevoy-le-Bas (89) 84 C2
Sennevoy-le-Haut (89) 84 C2
Senon (55) 25 G4

Senonches (28)...................... 40 D6
Senoncourt (70)...................... 87 F1
Senoncourt-les-
　Maujouy (55)...................... 47 F2
Senones (88)...................... 70 D2
Senonges (88)...................... 69 F4
Senonnes (53)...................... 76 A1
Senots (60)...................... 20 A6
Senouillac (81)...................... 170 A2
Sénoville (50)...................... 12 B3
Senozan (71)...................... 116 B3
Sens (89)...................... 65 E4
Sens-Beaujeu (18)...................... 82 A6
Sens-de-Bretagne (35)...................... 35 G6
Sens-sur-Seille (71)...................... 102 B5
Sentein (09)...................... 184 C6
Sentelie (80)...................... 20 A2
Sentenac-de-Sérou (09)...................... 185 F5
Sentenac-d'Oust (09)...................... 185 E6
Sentheim (68)...................... 88 D2
Sentilly (61)...................... 38 D4
la Sentinelle (59)...................... 9 F2
Sentous (65)...................... 183 G2
Senuc (08)...................... 24 B5
Senven-Léhart (22)...................... 33 E5
Sépeaux-St Romain (89)...................... 64 D6
Sepmeries (59)...................... 9 F2
Sepmes (37)...................... 95 E3
Seppois-le-Bas (68)...................... 89 E4
Seppois-le-Haut (68)...................... 89 E4
Sept-Meules (76)...................... 6 B5
Sept-Saulx (51)...................... 45 G1
Sept-Sorts (77)...................... 43 H3
Septème (38)...................... 130 E5
Septèmes-les-Vallons (13)...................... 192 A3
Septeuil (78)...................... 41 G3
Septfonds (82)...................... 152 D6
Septfontaines (25)...................... 103 H3
Septmoncel les
　Molunes (39)...................... 118 A3
Septmonts (02)...................... 22 A5
Septsarges (55)...................... 24 D5
les Septvallons (02)...................... 22 C5
Septvaux (02)...................... 22 A3
Sepvigny (55)...................... 47 H6
Sepvret (79)...................... 108 B4
Sepx (31)...................... 184 C3
Sequedin (59)...................... 3 F5
Sequehart (02)...................... 9 E6
le Sequestre (81)...................... 170 B3
Serain (02)...................... 9 E5
Seraincourt (08)...................... 23 F3
Seraincourt (95)...................... 42 A2
Sérandon (19)...................... 140 A1
Séranon (06)...................... 178 B3
Serans (60)...................... 42 A1
Seranville (54)...................... 70 A1
Séranvillers-Forenville (59)...................... 9 E4
Seraucourt-le-Grand (02)...................... 21 H1
Seraumont (88)...................... 68 C2
Serazereux (28)...................... 41 F6
Serbannes (03)...................... 114 A6
Serbonnes (89)...................... 64 D3
Serches (02)...................... 22 B5
Sercœur (88)...................... 70 A3
Sercus (59)...................... 2 C4
Sercy (71)...................... 116 A1
Serdinya (66)...................... 200 B3
Sère (32)...................... 184 A1
Sère-en-Lavedan (65)...................... 182 D4
Sère-Lanso (65)...................... 183 E4
Sère-Rustaing (65)...................... 183 G2
Serécourt (88)...................... 69 E5
Séreilhac (87)...................... 124 A3
Serémange-Erzange (57)...................... 26 D3
Sérempuy (32)...................... 168 B4
Sérénac (81)...................... 170 D2
Sérent (56)...................... 55 H5
Sérévillers (60)...................... 20 D2
Serez (27)...................... 41 F3
Sérézin-de-la-Tour (38)...................... 130 D5
Sérézin-du-Rhône (69)...................... 130 A4
Sergeac (24)...................... 137 H4
Sergenaux (39)...................... 102 C4
Sergenon (39)...................... 102 C4
Sergines (89)...................... 65 E3
Sergy (01)...................... 118 B4
Sergy (02)...................... 44 C1
Séricourt (62)...................... 7 G2
Sérifontaine (60)...................... 19 G5
Sérignac (46)...................... 152 A3
Sérignac (82)...................... 168 C2
Sérignac-Péboudou (47)...................... 151 E2
Sérignac-sur-Garonne (47)...................... 151 E6
Sérignan (34)...................... 188 C3
Sérignan-du-Comtat (84)...................... 158 B6
Sérigné (85)...................... 107 E2
Sérigny (86)...................... 94 B4
Sérilhac (19)...................... 139 E3
Seringes-et-Nesles (02)...................... 22 B6
Séris (41)...................... 80 B2
Serley (71)...................... 102 B5
Sermages (58)...................... 100 A3
Sermaise (49)...................... 77 G4
Sermaise (91)...................... 63 E1
Sermaises (45)...................... 63 F3
Sermaize (60)...................... 21 G3
Sermaize-les-Bains (51)...................... 46 D4
Sermamagny (90)...................... 88 C2
Sermange (39)...................... 102 D1
Sermano (2B)...................... 205 F2
Sermentizon (63)...................... 127 H3
Sermérieu (38)...................... 131 E4
Sermersheim (67)...................... 71 G2
Sermesse (71)...................... 102 A4
Sermiers (51)...................... 45 F1
Sermizelles (89)...................... 83 H4
Sermoise (02)...................... 22 B5

Sermoise-sur-Loire (58)...................... 99 E4
Sermoyer (01)...................... 116 C2
Sermur (23)...................... 126 A1
Sernhac (30)...................... 174 C2
Serocourt (88)...................... 69 E5
Séron (65)...................... 182 D2
Serpaize (38)...................... 130 B5
la Serpent (11)...................... 186 D5
Serques (62)...................... 2 A3
Serqueux (52)...................... 68 D6
Serqueux (76)...................... 19 F2
Serquigny (27)...................... 40 B1
Serra-di-Ferro (2A)...................... 206 C2
Serra-di-Fiumorbo (2B)...................... 205 G5
Serra-di-Scopamène (2A)...................... 207 E2
Serralongue (66)...................... 200 D5
Serraval (74)...................... 132 C2
la Serre (12)...................... 171 F3
la Serre-Bussière-
　Vieille (23)...................... 112 B6
Serre-les-Moulières (39)...................... 102 D1
Serre-les-Sapins (25)...................... 103 F1
Serre-Nerpol (38)...................... 145 E2
Serres (05)...................... 159 H3
Serres (11)...................... 187 E6
Serres (54)...................... 49 E5
Serres-Castet (64)...................... 182 B1
Serres-et-Montguyard (24)...................... 151 E1
Serres-Gaston (40)...................... 166 A4
Serres-Morlaàs (64)...................... 182 C2
Serres-Sainte-Marie (64)...................... 182 A1
Serres-sur-Arget (09)...................... 185 G5
Serreslous-et-Arribans (40)...................... 166 A4
Serriera (2A)...................... 204 B2
Serrières (07)...................... 144 A1
Serrières (71)...................... 116 A4
Serrières-de-Briord (01)...................... 131 E2
Serrières-en-
　Chautagne (73)...................... 131 G2
Serrières-sur-Ain (01)...................... 117 F5
Serrigny (89)...................... 84 A2
Serrigny-en-Bresse (71)...................... 102 A5
Serris (77)...................... 43 F4
Serrouville (54)...................... 26 A3
Serruelles (18)...................... 97 G4
Sers (16)...................... 122 D4
Sers (65)...................... 183 E6
Servais (02)...................... 22 A3
Serval (02)...................... 22 C5
Servance-Miellin (70)...................... 88 B1
Servanches (24)...................... 136 B3
Servant (63)...................... 113 F5
Servas (01)...................... 116 D5
Servas (30)...................... 157 F6
Servaville-Salmonville (76)...................... 18 D4
Serverette (48)...................... 155 H1
Serves-sur-Rhône (26)...................... 144 A3
Servian (34)...................... 188 C1
Servières (48)...................... 155 H2
Servières-le-Château (19)...................... 139 F3
Serviers-et-Labaume (30)...................... 174 B1
Serviès (81)...................... 170 B5
Serviès-en-Val (11)...................... 187 F4
Servignat (01)...................... 116 D3
Servigney (70)...................... 87 H2
Servigny (50)...................... 36 D1
Servigny-lès-Raville (57)...................... 26 D6
Servigny-lès-Sainte-
　Barbe (57)...................... 26 C5
Serville (28)...................... 41 F4
Servilly (03)...................... 114 B4
Servin (25)...................... 88 A6
Servins (62)...................... 8 A1
Servon (50)...................... 35 G4
Servon (77)...................... 43 E5
Servon-Melzicourt (51)...................... 24 B6
Servon-sur-Vilaine (35)...................... 57 G3
Servoz (74)...................... 133 E2
Sery (08)...................... 23 G3
Sery (89)...................... 83 G3
Séry-lès-Mézières (02)...................... 22 B1
Séry-Magneval (60)...................... 21 F6
Serzy-et-Prin (51)...................... 22 D6
Sessenheim (67)...................... 51 F3
Sète (34)...................... 189 F1
Setques (62)...................... 2 A4
Seugy (95)...................... 42 D1
Seuil (08)...................... 23 H4
Seuil-d'Argonne (55)...................... 46 D3
Seuillet (03)...................... 114 A5
Seuilly (37)...................... 94 A2
Seulline (14)...................... 38 A2
Seur (41)...................... 79 H4
le Seure (17)...................... 121 G2
Seurre (21)...................... 102 A3
Seux (80)...................... 7 F6
Seuzey (55)...................... 47 G2
Sevelinges (42)...................... 115 F6
Sevenans (90)...................... 88 C3
Sévérac (44)...................... 73 H2
Sévérac d'Aveyron (12)...................... 155 F5
Seveux (70)...................... 86 D4
Sévignac (22)...................... 34 B6
Sévignacq (64)...................... 182 C1
Sévignacq-Meyracq (64)...................... 182 B4
Sévigny (61)...................... 39 E4
Sévigny-la-Forêt (08)...................... 10 D6
Sévigny-Waleppe (08)...................... 23 E3
Sévis (76)...................... 17 H4
Sevrai (61)...................... 38 D5
Sevran (93)...................... 43 E3
Sèvremoine (49)...................... 75 G6
Sèvremont (85)...................... 92 C4
Sèvres (92)...................... 42 C4
Sèvres-Anxaumont (86)...................... 109 F1
Sevrey (71)...................... 101 G2
Sévrier (74)...................... 132 B2
Sévry (18)...................... 98 B2

Sewen (68)...................... 88 D1
Sexcles (19)...................... 139 F4
Sexey-aux-Forges (54)...................... 48 C6
Sexey-les-Bois (54)...................... 48 B5
Sexfontaines (52)...................... 67 H4
Seychalles (63)...................... 127 G3
Seyches (47)...................... 150 D2
Seyne (04)...................... 160 D4
La Seyne-sur-Mer (83)...................... 193 E5
Seynes (30)...................... 174 A1
Seyre (31)...................... 185 H2
Seyresse (40)...................... 165 E4
Seyssel (01)...................... 131 G1
Seyssel (74)...................... 131 G1
Seysses (31)...................... 169 E6
Seysses-Savès (32)...................... 168 C6
Seyssinet-Pariset (38)...................... 145 G2
Seyssins (38)...................... 145 G3
Seyssuel (38)...................... 130 A5
Seytroux (74)...................... 119 F4
Sézanne (51)...................... 44 D5
Siarrouy (65)...................... 183 E2
Siaugues-Sainte-Marie (43)...142 A3
Sibiril (29)...................... 31 G2
Sibiville (62)...................... 7 G2
Siccieu-Saint-Julien-et-
　Carisieu (38)...................... 130 D3
Sichamps (58)...................... 99 E2
Sickert (68)...................... 88 D1
Sideville (50)...................... 12 C2
Sidiailles (18)...................... 112 B2
Siecq (17)...................... 121 H2
Siegen (67)...................... 51 G2
les Sièges (89)...................... 65 F4
Sierck-les-Bains (57)...................... 26 C2
Sierentz (68)...................... 89 G2
Soindres (78)...................... 41 G3
Siersthal (57)...................... 28 B6
Sierville (76)...................... 18 C3
Siest (40)...................... 164 D4
Sieurac (81)...................... 170 B3
Sieuras (09)...................... 185 F3
Siévoz (38)...................... 145 H5
Siewiller (67)...................... 50 B3
Sigale (06)...................... 178 C2
Sigalens (33)...................... 150 A3
Sigean (11)...................... 188 A5
Sigloy (45)...................... 81 F2
Signac (31)...................... 184 A6
Signes (83)...................... 193 E4
Signéville (52)...................... 68 A3
Signy-l'Abbaye (08)...................... 23 G2
Signy-le-Petit (08)...................... 10 C6
Signy-Montlibert (08)...................... 25 E3
Signy-Signets (77)...................... 43 H3
Sigogne (16)...................... 121 H3
Sigonce (04)...................... 176 D1
Sigottier (05)...................... 159 H3
Sigoulès (24)...................... 136 D6
Sigournais (85)...................... 92 B5
Sigoyer (04)...................... 160 B4
Sigoyer (05)...................... 160 B3
Siguer (09)...................... 199 E1
Sigy (77)...................... 64 D1
Sigy-en-Bray (76)...................... 19 F3
Sigy-le-Châtel (71)...................... 115 H2
Silfiac (56)...................... 55 E2
Silhac (07)...................... 143 H5
Sillans (38)...................... 145 E1
Sillans-la-Cascade (83)...................... 177 F5
Sillars (86)...................... 109 H3
Sillas (33)...................... 150 A4
Sillé-le-Guillaume (72)...................... 59 G4
Sillé-le-Philippe (72)...................... 60 B5
Sillegny (57)...................... 48 C2
Sillery (51)...................... 23 F6
Silley-Amancey (25)...................... 103 G3
Silley-Bléfond (25)...................... 87 H6
Sillingy (74)...................... 132 A1
Silly-en-Saulnois (57)...................... 48 D2
Silly-la-Poterie (02)...................... 21 H6
Silly-le-Long (60)...................... 43 F2
Silly-sur-Nied (57)...................... 26 D5
Silly-Tillard (60)...................... 20 B5
Silmont (55)...................... 47 F5
Siltzheim (67)...................... 27 H5
Silvareccio (2B)...................... 203 G6
Silvarouvres (52)...................... 67 F5
Simacourbe (64)...................... 182 D1
Simandre (71)...................... 116 C1
Simandre-sur-Suran (01)...................... 117 F4
Simandres (69)...................... 130 A4
Simard (71)...................... 102 A6
Simencourt (62)...................... 8 A3
Simeyrols (24)...................... 138 B5
Simiane-Collongue (13)...................... 192 B2
Simiane-la-Rotonde (04)...................... 176 B2
Simorre (32)...................... 184 B1
Simplé (53)...................... 58 C6
Sin-le-Noble (59)...................... 8 D2
Sinard (38)...................... 145 G4
Sinceny (02)...................... 21 H3
Sincey-lès-Rouvray (21)...................... 84 B5
Sindères (40)...................... 165 F1
Singles (63)...................... 126 B3
Singleyrac (24)...................... 136 D6
Singly (08)...................... 24 A2
Sinsat (09)...................... 199 E1
Sinzos (65)...................... 183 F3
Sion (32)...................... 166 D4
Sion-les-Mines (44)...................... 57 F6
Sioniac (19)...................... 139 E4
Sionne (88)...................... 68 C2
Sionviller (54)...................... 49 F5
Siorac-de-Ribérac (24)...................... 136 D2
Siorac-en-Périgord (24)...................... 137 H6
Siouville-Hague (50)...................... 12 B3
Sirac (32)...................... 168 C4
Siracourt (62)...................... 7 G1

Siradan (65)...................... 184 A5
Siran (15)...................... 139 G5
Siran (34)...................... 187 G2
Sireix (65)...................... 182 D5
Sireuil (16)...................... 122 B4
Sirod (39)...................... 103 F5
Siros (64)...................... 182 B1
Sisco (2B)...................... 203 G3
Sissonne (02)...................... 22 D3
Sissy (02)...................... 22 B1
Sistels (82)...................... 168 B1
Sisteron (04)...................... 160 B5
Sivergues (84)...................... 176 A3
Sivignon (71)...................... 115 H3
Sivry (51)...................... 48 C4
Sivry-Ante (51)...................... 46 C2
Sivry-Courtry (77)...................... 64 B1
Sivry-la-Perche (55)...................... 47 E1
Sivry-sur-Meuse (55)...................... 25 E5
Six-Fours-les-Plages (83)...................... 193 E5
Sixt-Fer-à-Cheval (74)...................... 119 G6
Sixt-sur-Aff (35)...................... 56 C5
Sizun (29)...................... 31 G5
Smarves (86)...................... 109 E2
Smermesnil (76)...................... 6 B6
Soccia (2A)...................... 204 D3
Sochaux (25)...................... 88 C4
Socourt (88)...................... 69 G2
Socx (59)...................... 2 C2
Sode (31)...................... 197 F1
Sognolles-en-Montois (77)...................... 64 D1
Sogny-aux-Moulins (51)...................... 45 H3
Sogny-en-l'Angle (51)...................... 46 C4
Soignolles (14)...................... 38 D2
Soignolles-en-Brie (77)...................... 43 F6
Soindres (28)...................... 41 G3
Soing-Cubry-
　Charentenay (70)...................... 87 E3
Soings-en-Sologne (41)...................... 80 B5
Soirans (21)...................... 102 B1
Soissons (02)...................... 22 A5
Soissons-sur-Nacey (21)...................... 102 C1
Soisy-sous-
　Montmorency (95)...................... 42 C3
Soisy-sur-École (91)...................... 63 H1
Soisy-sur-Seine (91)...................... 42 D6
Soize (02)...................... 23 E2
Soizé (28)...................... 61 F4
Soizy-aux-Bois (51)...................... 44 D4
Solaize (69)...................... 130 A4
Solaro (2B)...................... 205 G6
Solaure en Diois (26)...................... 159 F1
Solbach (67)...................... 71 E1
Soleilhas (04)...................... 178 A3
Solemont (25)...................... 88 B5
Solente (60)...................... 21 F2
le Soler (66)...................... 201 E2
Solérieux (26)...................... 158 B4
Solers (77)...................... 43 F6
Solesmes (59)...................... 9 E3
Solesmes (72)...................... 77 F1
Soleymieu (38)...................... 130 D3
Soleymieux (42)...................... 128 D5
Solférino (40)...................... 148 C6
Solgne (57)...................... 48 D2
Soliers (14)...................... 14 C5
Solignac (87)...................... 124 B3
Solignac-sous-Roche (43)...................... 142 D2
Solignac-sur-Loire (43)...................... 142 C4
Soligny-la-Trappe (61)...................... 39 H6
Soligny-les-Étangs (10)...................... 65 F2
Sollacaro (2A)...................... 206 D2
Solliès-Pont (83)...................... 193 F4
Solliès-Toucas (83)...................... 193 F4
Solliès-Ville (83)...................... 193 F4
Sologny (71)...................... 116 A3
Solomiac (32)...................... 168 B3
Solre-le-Château (59)...................... 10 B3
Solrinnes (59)...................... 10 B3
Solterre (45)...................... 82 A1
Solutré-Pouilly (71)...................... 116 A4
Somain (59)...................... 9 E2
Sombacour (25)...................... 103 H3
Sombernon (21)...................... 85 F6
Sombrin (62)...................... 7 H3
Sombrun (65)...................... 166 D6
Somloire (49)...................... 92 D3
Sommaing (59)...................... 9 F2
Sommancourt (52)...................... 67 G1
Sommand (71)...................... 100 C3
Sommauthe (08)...................... 24 C4
Somme-Bionne (51)...................... 46 B2
Somme-Suippe (51)...................... 46 B1
Somme-Tourbe (51)...................... 46 B1
Somme-Vesle (51)...................... 46 A3
Somme-Yèvre (51)...................... 46 C3
Sommecaise (89)...................... 82 D1
Sommedieue (55)...................... 47 G1
Sommeilles (55)...................... 46 D3
Sommelans (02)...................... 44 B1
Sommelonne (55)...................... 46 D5
Sommepy-Tahure (51)...................... 23 H6
Sommerance (08)...................... 24 C5
Sommercourt (52)...................... 68 D3
Sommereux (60)...................... 20 A2
Sommeron (02)...................... 10 A5
Sommervieu (14)...................... 14 A3
Sommerviller (54)...................... 49 E5
Sommery (76)...................... 19 E3
Sommesnil (76)...................... 17 E4
Sommesous (51)...................... 45 G5
la Sommette (25)...................... 88 A6
Sommette-Eaucourt (02)...................... 21 H2
Sommeval (10)...................... 66 A4
Sommevoire (52)...................... 67 F2

Sommières (30)...................... 173 H4
Sommières-du-Clain (86)...................... 109 E4
Sompt (79)...................... 108 B5
Sompuis (51)...................... 45 H5
Somsois (51)...................... 46 A6
Son (08)...................... 23 G3
Sonac (46)...................... 153 F1
Sonchamp (78)...................... 42 A6
Soncourt (88)...................... 69 E2
Soncourt-sur-Marne (52)...................... 67 H3
Sondernach (68)...................... 70 D5
Sondersdorf (68)...................... 89 E4
la Sône (38)...................... 144 D3
Songeons (60)...................... 19 H3
Songeson (39)...................... 103 E6
Songy (51)...................... 46 A4
Sonnac (12)...................... 153 H3
Sonnac (17)...................... 121 H2
Sonnac-sur-l'Hers (11)...................... 186 B5
Sonnay (38)...................... 144 B1
Sonnaz (73)...................... 131 H4
Sons-et-Ronchères (02)...................... 22 C1
Sonthonnax-la-
　Montagne (01)...................... 117 F3
Sonzay (37)...................... 78 C4
Soorts-Hossegor (40)...................... 164 B4
Soppe-le-Bas (68)...................... 89 E2
Sor (09)...................... 184 D6
Sorans-lès-Breurey (70)...................... 87 F5
Sorbais (02)...................... 9 H6
Sorbets (32)...................... 166 D4
Sorbets (40)...................... 166 B5
Sorbey (55)...................... 25 G4
Sorbey (57)...................... 48 D2
Sorbier (03)...................... 114 B3
Sorbiers (05)...................... 159 G4
Sorbiers (42)...................... 129 F5
Sorbo-Ocagnano (2B)...................... 203 G6
Sorbollano (2A)...................... 207 E2
Sorbon (08)...................... 23 G3
Sorbs (34)...................... 172 C3
Sorcy-Bauthémont (08)...................... 23 H3
Sorcy-Saint-Martin (55)...................... 47 H5
Sorde-l'Abbaye (40)...................... 165 E5
Sore (40)...................... 149 F4
Soréac (65)...................... 183 F2
Sorède (66)...................... 201 F4
Sorel (80)...................... 8 C5
Sorel-en-Vimeu (80)...................... 7 E5
Sorel-Moussel (28)...................... 41 F4
Sorèze (81)...................... 186 C1
Sorgeat (09)...................... 199 G2
Sorges et Ligueux en
　Périgord (24)...................... 137 G3
Sorgues (84)...................... 175 E2
Sorigny (37)...................... 95 E1
les Sorinières (44)...................... 74 D6
Sorio (2B)...................... 203 F5
Sormery (89)...................... 65 H5
Sormonne (08)...................... 23 H1
Sornac (19)...................... 125 H4
Sornay (39)...................... 103 E6
Sornay (71)...................... 116 C1
Sornéville (54)...................... 49 E4
Sorquainville (76)...................... 16 D4
Sorrus (62)...................... 6 D1
Sort-en-Chalosse (40)...................... 165 F4
Sortosville (50)...................... 12 D3
Sortosville-en-
　Beaumont (50)...................... 12 B4
Sos (47)...................... 167 E1
Sospel (06)...................... 179 F2
Sossais (86)...................... 94 C4
Sost (65)...................... 183 H5
Sotta (2A)...................... 207 F4
Sottevast (50)...................... 12 C3
Sotteville (50)...................... 12 B2
Sotteville-lès-Rouen (76)...................... 18 C4
Sotteville-sous-le-Val (76)...................... 18 D5
Sotteville-sur-Mer (76)...................... 17 F2
Soturac (46)...................... 151 H3
Sotzeling (57)...................... 49 F3
Souain-Perthes-lès-
　Hurlus (51)...................... 46 A1
Soual (81)...................... 170 B6
Souancé-au-Perche (28)...................... 61 F3
Souanyas (66)...................... 200 B3
Souastre (62)...................... 7 H3
Soubès (34)...................... 172 C4
Soubise (17)...................... 120 C1
Soublecause (65)...................... 166 D6
Soubran (17)...................... 121 F6
Soubrebost (23)...................... 125 E1
Soucé (53)...................... 58 D1
Soucelles (49)...................... 77 E3
la Souche (07)...................... 157 F2
Souchez (62)...................... 8 B1
Soucht (57)...................... 50 B2
Soucia (39)...................... 117 H1
Soucieu-en-Jarrest (69)...................... 129 H4
Soucirac (46)...................... 152 D1
Souclin (01)...................... 131 E2
Soucy (02)...................... 21 H5
Soucy (89)...................... 65 E4

Souesmes (41)...................... 81 F5
Souffelweyersheim (67)...................... 51 E5
Soufflenheim (67)...................... 51 F3
Souffrignac (16)...................... 123 E4
Sougé (36)...................... 96 B4
Sougé (41)...................... 79 E2
Sougé-le-Ganelon (72)...................... 59 H3
Sougéal (35)...................... 35 G5
Sougères-en-Puisaye (89)...................... 83 E4
Sougraigne (11)...................... 187 E6
Sougy (45)...................... 62 C5
Sougy-sur-Loire (58)...................... 99 F5
les Souhesmes-
　Rampont (55)...................... 47 E2
Souhey (21)...................... 84 D5
le Souich (62)...................... 7 G3
Souilhanels (11)...................... 186 B2
Souilhe (11)...................... 186 B2
Souillac (46)...................... 138 C5
Souillé (72)...................... 60 A4
Souilly (55)...................... 47 F2
Soula (09)...................... 185 H6
Soulac-sur-Mer (33)...................... 120 B5
Soulages (15)...................... 141 G3
Soulages-Bonneval (12)...................... 154 D1
Soulaines-Dhuys (10)...................... 67 C2
Soulaines-sur-
　Aubance (49)...................... 77 E5
Soulaire-et-Bourg (49)...................... 77 E3
Soulaires (28)...................... 62 B1
Soulan (09)...................... 185 E6
Soulanges (51)...................... 46 A4
Soulangis (18)...................... 97 H2
Soulangy (14)...................... 38 D3
Soulatgé (11)...................... 187 F6
Soulaucourt-sur-
　Mouzon (52)...................... 68 D4
Soulaures (24)...................... 151 H1
Soulce-Cernay (25)...................... 88 C4
Souleuvre en Bocage (14)...................... 37 H2
Soulgé-sur-Ouette (53)...................... 59 E5
le Soulié (34)...................... 171 F6
Soulières (51)...................... 45 E3
Soulignac (33)...................... 149 H1
Souligné-Flacé (72)...................... 59 H6
Souligné-sous-Ballon (72)...................... 60 B4
Soulignonne (17)...................... 120 D2
Souligny (10)...................... 66 A4
Soulitré (72)...................... 60 C5
Soullans (85)...................... 90 D3
Soulles (50)...................... 37 F2
Soulom (65)...................... 182 D5
Soulomès (46)...................... 152 D2
Soulosse-sous-Saint-
　Élophe (88)...................... 68 D2
Soultz-Haut-Rhin (68)...................... 71 E6
Soultz-les-Bains (67)...................... 50 D6
Soultz-sous-Forêts (67)...................... 51 F2
Soultzbach-les-Bains (68)...................... 71 E5
Soultzeren (68)...................... 71 E5
Soultzmatt (68)...................... 71 E6
Soulvache (44)...................... 57 G5
Soumaintrain (89)...................... 65 H6
Soumans (23)...................... 112 B4
Soumensac (47)...................... 150 D1
Souméras (17)...................... 135 F1
Soumont (34)...................... 172 C4
Soumont-Saint-
　Quentin (14)...................... 38 D2
Soumoulou (64)...................... 182 C2
Soupex (11)...................... 186 B2
Soupir (02)...................... 22 C5
Souppes-sur-Loing (77)...................... 64 A4
Souprosse (40)...................... 165 G3
Souraïde (64)...................... 180 C1
Sourans (25)...................... 88 B5
Source-Seine (21)...................... 85 F5
Sourcieux-les-Mines (69)...................... 129 G3
le Sourd (02)...................... 9 H6
Sourdeval (50)...................... 37 G4
Sourdeval-les-Bois (50)...................... 37 E3
Sourdon (80)...................... 20 C2
Sourdun (77)...................... 65 E1
le Sourn (56)...................... 55 E3
Sournia (66)...................... 200 C2
Sourniac (15)...................... 140 A2
Sourribes (04)...................... 160 B6
Sours (28)...................... 62 B2
Soursac (19)...................... 139 H2
Sourzac (24)...................... 136 D3
Sous-Parsat (23)...................... 111 G6
Sousceyrac-en-Quercy (46)...139 G5
Sousmoulins (17)...................... 135 G1
Souspierre (26)...................... 158 C2
Soussac (33)...................... 136 A6
Soussans (33)...................... 135 E3
Soussey-sur-Brionne (21)...................... 85 E6
Soustelle (30)...................... 156 D6
Soustons (40)...................... 164 C3
Sousville (38)...................... 145 H5
Souternon (42)...................... 128 C2
la Souterraine (23)...................... 110 D4
Soutiers (79)...................... 108 A1
Souvans (39)...................... 102 D3
Souvignargues (30)...................... 173 H3
Souvigné (16)...................... 122 B1
Souvigné (37)...................... 78 C4
Souvigné (79)...................... 108 B3
Souvigné-sur-Même (72)...................... 60 D4
Souvigné-sur-Sarthe (72)...................... 77 F1
Souvigny (03)...................... 113 G2
Souvigny-de-Touraine (37)...79 G5
Souvigny-en-Sologne (41)...... 81 F3
Souyeaux (65)...................... 183 F3
Souzay-Champigny (49)...................... 93 H1
Souzy (69)...................... 129 F3
Souzy-la-Briche (91)...................... 63 F1
Soveria (2B)...................... 205 E2

Soyans (26) 158 C2
Soyaux (16) 122 C4
Soye (25) 88 A5
Soye-en-Septaine (18) 97 H3
Soyécourt (80) 8 B6
Soyers (52) 86 D1
Soyons (07) 144 A5
Sparsbach (67) 50 C3
Spay (72) 60 A6
Spechbach (67) 89 E2
Speloncato (2B) 202 D5
Spéracèdes (06) 178 C4
Spézet (29) 54 A1
Spicheren (57) 27 G4
Spincourt (55) 25 G5
Sponville (54) 48 A2
Spoy (10) 67 E4
Spoy (21) 86 A5
Spycker (59) 2 B2
Squiffiec (22) 33 E3
Staffelfelden (68) 89 F1
Stains (93) 42 D3
Stainville (55) 47 E5
Staple (59) 2 C4
Stattmatten (67) 51 F3
Stazzona (2B) 205 G1
Steenbecque (59) 2 C4
Steene (59) 2 B2
Steenvoorde (59) 2 D3
Steenwerck (59) 3 E4
Steige (67) 71 E2
Steinbach (68) 89 E1
Steinbourg (67) 50 C4
Steinbrunn-le-Bas (68) 89 F2
Steinbrunn-le-Haut (68) ... 89 F2
Steinseltz (67) 51 F1
Steinsoultz (68) 89 F3
Stenay (55) 24 D4
Sternenberg (68) 89 E2
Stetten (68) 89 G3
Stigny (89) 84 C2
Still (67) 50 D4
Stiring-Wendel (57) 27 G4
Stonne (08) 24 C3
Storckensohn (68) 70 D6
Stosswihr (68) 71 E5
Stotzheim (67) 71 G2
Strasbourg (67) 51 E5
Strazeele (59) 2 D4
Strenquels (46) 138 D4
Strueth (68) 89 E3
Struth (67) 50 B3
Stuckange (57) 26 C3
Stundwiller (67) 51 F2
Sturzelbronn (57) 28 C5
Stutzheim-Offenheim (67) 50 D5
Suarce (90) 89 E3
Suaux (16) 123 E2
le Subdray (18) 97 G3
Sublaines (37) 95 G1
Subles (14) 13 H5
Subligny (18) 82 B5
Subligny (50) 37 E4
Subligny (89) 64 D4
Suc-et-Sentenac (09) 198 D1
Succieu (38) 130 D5
Sucé-sur-Erdre (44) 74 D4
Sucy-en-Brie (94) 43 E3
Suèvres (41) 80 A3
Sugères (63) 127 H4
Sugny (08) 24 A5
Suhescun (64) 181 E2
Suilly-la-Tour (58) 82 C6
Suin (71) 115 H3
Suippes (51) 46 A1
Suisse (57) 49 F2
Suizy-le-Franc (51) 44 D3
Sulignat (01) 116 C5
Sully (14) 13 H5
Sully (60) 19 G3
Sully (71) 101 E3
Sully-la-Chapelle (45) 63 F6
Sully-sur-Loire (45) 81 G2
Sulniac (56) 55 H6
Sumène (30) 173 G2
Sundhoffen (68) 71 F5
Sundhouse (67) 71 G3
Supt (39) 103 F4
Surat (63) 127 G1
Surba (09) 185 G6
Surbourg (67) 51 E2
Surcamps (80) 7 E4
Surdoux (87) 124 D4
Suré (61) 60 C2
La Sure en Chartreuse (38) .. 145 F1
Suresnes (92) 42 C4
Surfonds (72) 60 C6
Surfontaine (02) 22 B1
Surgères (17) 107 F5
Surgy (58) 83 F4
Suriauville (88) 69 E4
Surin (79) 107 H2
Surin (86) 109 E6
Suris (16) 123 F2
Surjoux (01) 117 H6
Surmont (25) 88 B6
Surques (62) 1 G4
Surrain (14) 13 G5
Surtainville (50) 12 B3
Surtauville (27) 18 C6
Surville (14) 15 F3
Surville (27) 18 C6
Survilliers (95) 43 E2
Sury (08) 24 A1
Sury-aux-Bois (45) 63 G6
Sury-en-Vaux (18) 82 B6
Sury-ès-Bois (18) 82 A5
Sury-le-Comtal (42) 129 E5

Sury-près-Léré (18) 82 B5
Surzur (56) 73 E1
Sus (64) 181 G2
Sus-Saint-Léger (62) 7 H3
Susmiou (64) 181 G2
Sussac (87) 124 D4
Sussargues (34) 173 G4
Sussat (03) 113 F5
Sussey (21) 100 D1
Susville (38) 145 G5
Sutrieu (01) 131 F1
Suzan (09) 185 F5
Suzanne (08) 24 A3
Suzanne (80) 8 B5
Suzannecourt (52) 68 A2
Suzay (27) 19 F6
Suze (26) 144 C6
Suze-la-Rousse (26) 158 B5
la Suze-sur-Sarthe (72) 77 H1
Suzette (84) 158 D6
Suzoy (60) 21 G3
Suzy (02) 22 B3
Sy (08) 24 B3
Syam (39) 103 F6
Sylvains-lès-Moulins (27) 40 D3
Sylvanès (12) 171 H3
le Syndicat (88) 70 B5

T

Tabaille-Usquain (64) 181 G1
Tabanac (33) 135 F6
la Table (73) 132 B5
le Tablier (85) 91 G5
Tabre (09) 186 B5
la Tâche (16) 122 D2
Tachoires (32) 167 H6
Tacoignières (78) 41 G4
Taconnay (58) 83 F6
Taden (22) 34 D5
Tadousse-Ussau (64) 166 C5
Taglio-Isolaccio (2B) 203 G6
la Tagnière (71) 100 C5
Tagnon (08) 23 G4
Tagolsheim (68) 89 F2
Tagsdorf (68) 89 F3
Tailhac (43) 141 H4
Taillades (84) 175 F3
le Taillan-Médoc (33) 135 E5
Taillancourt (55) 68 D1
Taillant (17) 121 E1
Taillebois (61) 38 A3
Taillebourg (17) 121 E2
Taillebourg (47) 150 C3
Taillecavat (33) 150 C1
Taillecourt (25) 88 C4
La Taillée (85) 107 E3
Taillefontaine (02) 21 G5
Taillepied (50) 12 C4
Taillet (66) 200 D4
Taillette (08) 10 D5
Taillis (35) 57 H2
Tailly (08) 24 D4
Tailly (21) 101 G3
Tailly (80) 7 E5
Tain-l'Hermitage (26) 144 A3
Taintrux (88) 70 C3
Taisnières-en-
  Thiérache (59) 9 H4
Taisnières-sur-Hon (59) 9 H2
Taissy (51) 23 F6
Taïx (81) 170 C2
Taizé (71) 116 A2
Taizé-Aizie (16) 108 D6
Taizé-Maulais (79) 93 G4
Taizy (08) 23 G3
Tajan (65) 183 H3
Talairan (11) 187 G5
Talais (33) 120 B5
Talange (57) 26 B4
Talant (21) 85 H6
Talasani (2B) 205 G1
la Talaudière (42) 129 F5
Talazac (65) 183 E2
Talcy (41) 80 A2
Talcy (89) 84 B4
Talence (33) 135 E5
Talencieux (07) 144 A2
Talensac (35) 56 D3
Talissieu (01) 131 G2
Talizat (15) 141 E3
Tallans (25) 87 H5
Tallard (05) 160 B3
Tallenay (25) 87 F6
Tallende (63) 127 F4
Taller (40) 165 E2
Talloires-Montmin (74) 132 B2
Tallone (2B) 205 G3
le Tallud (79) 93 F6
Tallud-Sainte-Gemme (85) 92 C6
Talmas (80) 7 G5
Talmay (21) 86 B6
Talmont-Saint-Hilaire (85) 91 F6
Talmont-sur-Gironde (17) 120 C4
Talmontiers (60) 19 G5
Talon (58) 83 F6
Talus-Saint-Prix (51) 44 D4
Taluyers (69) 129 H4
Tamerville (50) 12 D3
Tamnay-en-Bazois (58) 99 H3
Tamniès (24) 138 A4
Tanavelle (15) 141 E4
Tanay (21) 86 A5
Tancarville (76) 15 G2
Tancon (71) 115 F6
Tanconville (54) 49 H5
Tancrou (77) 43 H2
Tangry (62) 7 G1

Taninges (74) 119 E5
Tanis (50) 35 G4
Tanlay (89) 84 B1
Tannay (08) 24 B3
Tannay (58) 83 G6
Tanneron (83) 178 C5
Tannerre-en-Puisaye (89) 82 D2
Tannières (02) 22 B6
Tannois (55) 47 E5
Tanques (61) 39 E5
Tantonville (54) 69 F1
le Tanu (50) 37 E3
Tanus (81) 170 D1
Tanville (61) 39 E6
Tanzac (17) 121 E4
Taponas (69) 116 B5
Taponnat-Fleurignac (16) 122 D3
Taradeau (83) 194 A2
Tarare (69) 129 F2
Tarascon (13) 174 D3
Tarascon-sur-Ariège (09) 199 E1
Tarasteix (65) 183 E2
Tarbes (65) 183 E3
Tarcenay (25) 103 G2
Tardes (23) 112 B5
Tardets-Sorholus (64) 181 G3
la Tardière (85) 92 C6
Tarentaise (42) 143 G1
Tarerach (66) 200 C2
Targassonne (66) 199 H4
Target (03) 113 H4
Targon (33) 135 G6
Tarnac (19) 125 F4
Tarnès (33) 135 G4
Tarnos (40) 164 B5
Taron-Sadirac-
  Viellenave (64) 166 B6
Tarquimpol (57) 49 G4
Tarrano (2B) 205 G2
Tarsac (32) 166 C4
Tarsacq (64) 182 A1
Tarsul (21) 85 G4
Tart-l'Abbaye (21) 102 B1
Tart-le-Bas (21) 102 B1
Tart-le-Haut (21) 102 A1
Tartaras (42) 129 H5
Tartas (40) 165 G3
Tartécourt (70) 87 F1
Tartiers (02) 21 H4
Tartigny (60) 20 C2
Tartonne (04) 177 G1
le Tartre (71) 102 C5
le Tartre-Gaudran (78) 41 G5
Tarzy (08) 10 C6
Tasque (32) 166 D5
Tassé (72) 77 G1
Tassenières (39) 102 C4
Tassillé (72) 59 G5
Tassin-la-Demi-Lune (69) 130 A3
Tasso (2A) 205 E4
le Tâtre (16) 121 H6
Taulé (29) 31 H3
Taulignan (26) 158 C3
Taulis (66) 200 D4
Taupont (56) 56 A4
Tauriac (33) 135 F3
Tauriac (46) 139 E5
Tauriac (81) 169 G3
Tauriac-de-Camarès (12) 172 A4
Tauriac-de-Naucelle (12) 154 A6
Taurignan-Castet (09) 184 D5
Taurignan-Vieux (09) 184 D5
Taurinya (66) 200 C3
Taurize (11) 187 F4
Taussac (12) 140 C6
Taussac-la-Billière (34) 172 A5
Tautavel (66) 201 E1
Tauves (63) 126 C5
Tauxigny (37) 95 F1
Tavaco (2A) 204 D5
Tavant (37) 94 C2
Tavaux (39) 102 C3
Tavaux-et-
  Pontséricourt (02) 22 D2
Tavel (30) 174 D2
Tavera (2A) 204 D4
Tavernay (71) 100 C3
Tavernes (83) 177 E5
Taverny (95) 42 C2
Tavers (45) 80 B2
Tavey (70) 88 C3
Taxat-Senat (03) 113 G5
Taxenne (39) 102 D1
Tayac (33) 136 A4
Taybosc (32) 168 A4
Tayrac (12) 154 A6
Tayrac (47) 151 G2
Tazilly (58) 100 A5
le Tech (66) 200 D5
Têche (38) 145 E2
Técou (81) 170 A3
le Teich (33) 148 C1
Teigny (58) 83 G6
le Teil (07) 158 A2
Teilhède (63) 127 E1
Teilhet (09) 186 A4
Teilhet (63) 113 E6
Teillay (35) 57 F5
Teillé (44) 75 E3
Teillé (72) 60 B4
Teillet (81) 170 D3
Teillet-Argenty (03) 112 C4
Le Teilleul (50) 37 H6
Teillots (24) 138 A2

Teissières-de-Cornet (15) 140 A4
Teissières-lès-Bouliès (15) 140 B6
Telgruc-sur-Mer (29) 31 E5
Tellancourt (54) 25 G3
Tellecey (21) 86 B6
Teloché (72) 78 B1
le Temple (33) 134 C5
le Temple (41) 61 F6
le Temple-de-Bretagne (44) 74 B4
Temple-Laguyon (24) 137 H2
le Temple-sur-Lot (47) 151 E4
Templemars (59) 3 F5
Templeuve-en-Pévèle (59) 3 G6
Templeux-la-Fosse (80) 8 C5
Templeux-le-Guérard (80) 8 D5
Tenay (01) 131 F1
Tence (43) 143 F3
Tencin (38) 145 H1
Tende (06) 163 F6
Tendon (88) 70 B4
Tendron (18) 98 B4
Tendu (36) 111 E1
Teneur (62) 7 F1
Tennie (72) 59 H4
Tenteling (57) 27 G5
Tercé (86) 109 F2
Tercillat (23) 111 H3
Tercis-les-Bains (40) 165 E4
Terdeghem (59) 2 C3
Tergnier (02) 22 A2
Terjat (03) 112 D5
Termes (11) 187 F5
Termes (48) 141 F6
Termes-d'Armagnac (32) 166 D4
Terminiers (28) 62 C5
Ternand (69) 129 G1
Ternant (17) 121 F1
Ternant (21) 101 G1
Ternant (58) 100 A6
Ternant-les-Eaux (63) 127 F6
Ternas (62) 7 G2
Ternat (52) 67 H6
Ternay (41) 79 E2
Ternay (69) 130 A4
Ternay (86) 93 H3
les Ternes (15) 141 E4
Ternuay-Melay-et-Saint-
  Hilaire (70) 88 B1
Terny-Sorny (02) 22 A4
Terramesnil (80) 7 G4
Terranjou (49) 77 E6
la Terrasse (38) 145 H1
la Terrasse-sur-Dorlay (42) 129 G6
Terrasson-Lavilledieu (24) 138 B3
Terrats (66) 201 E3
Terraube (32) 167 H2
Terre-Clapier (81) 170 D3
Terre-et-Marais (50) 13 E5
Terrebasse (31) 184 C3
Terrefondrée (21) 85 G2
Terrehault (72) 60 C4
Terres de Bord (27) 18 C6
Terres-de-Caux (76) 16 D4
les Terres-de-Chaux (25) 88 C6
Terres de Druance (14) 38 A3
Terroles (11) 187 E5
Terrou (46) 139 F6
Tersanne (26) 144 B2
Tersannes (87) 110 B4
Terssac (81) 170 B2
le Tertre-Saint-Denis (78) 41 G3
Tertry (80) 8 D6
Terville (57) 26 B3
Tessancourt-sur-
  Aubette (78) 42 A2
Tessé-Froulay (61) 38 C3
Tessel (14) 14 A5
Tesson (17) 121 E4
Tessonnière (79) 93 G5
la Tessoualle (49) 92 C3
Tessy Bocage (50) 37 G2
la Teste-de-Buch (33) 148 B1
Tétaigne (08) 24 C2
Téteghem-Coudekerque-
  Village (59) 2 C1
Teting-sur-Nied (57) 49 F1
Teuillac (33) 135 F3
Teulat (81) 169 G5
Teurthéville-Bocage (50) 12 D2
Teurthéville-Hague (50) 12 B2
Teyjat (24) 123 E4
Teyran (34) 173 G5
Teyssières (26) 158 D3
Teyssieu (46) 139 F5
Teyssode (81) 170 A5
Thaas (51) 45 E6
Thaims (17) 120 D4
Thairé (17) 106 D5
Thaix (58) 99 H5
Thal-Drulingen (67) 50 A3
Thal-Marmoutier (67) 50 C4
Thalamy (19) 126 B5
Thann (68) 89 E1
Thannenkirch (68) 71 F3
Thanvillé (67) 71 F2
Thaon (14) 14 B4
Tharaux (30) 157 H5
Tharoiseau (89) 83 H5
Tharot (89) 83 H4
Thaumiers (18) 98 A5
Thauron (23) 125 E1
Thauvenay (18) 82 B6
Thèbe (65) 184 A5
Théding (57) 27 G5
Thédirac (46) 152 C2

Thégra (46) 139 E6
Théhillac (56) 73 H2
le Theil (03) 113 G3
le Theil-de-Bretagne (35) 57 G4
le Theil-en-Auge (14) 15 F3
le Theil-Nolent (27) 15 H5
Theil-Rabier (16) 108 C6
Theillay (41) 81 E6
le Theix-Noyalo (56) 73 E1
Theizé (69) 129 G1
Théligny (72) 61 E4
Thélis-la-Combe (42) 143 G1
Thélod (54) 48 C6
Thelonne (08) 24 C2
Thélus (62) 8 B2
Théméricourt (95) 42 A2
Thémines (46) 153 F1
Théminettes (46) 153 F1
Thénac (17) 121 E3
Thénac (24) 136 C6
Thenailles (02) 23 E1
Thenay (36) 110 D1
Thenay (41) 79 H5
Thenelles (02) 22 B1
Thénésol (73) 132 C3
Theneuil (37) 94 C2
Theneuille (03) 113 E1
Thénezay (79) 93 H5
Thénioux (18) 97 E1
Thenissey (21) 85 E4
Thénisy (77) 64 D1
Thennelières (10) 66 B3
Thennes (80) 20 D1
Thenon (24) 137 H3
Thénorgues (08) 24 C4
Thénouville (27) 18 A5
Théoule-sur-Mer (06) 178 C6
Therdonne (60) 20 B4
Thèreval (50) 37 F3
Thérines (70) 19 H3
Thermes-Magnoac (65) 184 A2
Thérondels (12) 140 C5
Thérouanne (62) 2 B5
Thérouldeville (76) 16 D3
Thervay (39) 102 D1
Thésée (41) 79 H6
Thésy (39) 103 F4
Theuley (70) 87 E3
Théus (05) 160 C3
Theuville (28) 62 B3
Theuville (95) 42 B1
Theuville-aux-Maillots (76) 16 D3
Thevet-Saint-Julien (36) 111 H1
Théville (50) 12 D2
They-sous-Montfort (88) 69 E3
They-sous-Vaudemont (54) 69 F2
Theys (38) 146 A1
Théza (66) 201 F3
Thézac (17) 120 D3
Thézac (47) 151 H3
Thézan-des-Corbières (11) 187 H4
Thézan-lès-Béziers (34) 188 B1
Thèze (04) 160 A4
Thèze (64) 166 B6
Thézey-Saint-Martin (54) 48 D3
Théziers (30) 174 C3
Thézillieu (01) 131 F2
Thézy-Glimont (80) 20 D1
Thiais (94) 42 D5
Thiancourt (90) 88 D4
Thianges (58) 99 F4
Thiant (59) 9 F2
Thiat (87) 110 A4
Thiaucourt-Regniéville (54) 48 A3
Thiaville-sur-Meurthe (54) 70 C2
Thiberville (27) 15 G5
Thibie (51) 45 G3
Thibivillers (60) 19 H5
Thibouville (27) 40 B1
Thicourt (57) 49 F2
Thiébauménil (54) 49 F6
Thiéblemont-
  Farémont (51) 46 B5
Thiébouhans (25) 88 C6
Thieffrain (10) 66 D4
Thieffrans (70) 87 H4
Thiéfosse (88) 70 B5
Thiel-sur-Acolin (03) 114 B2
Thiembronne (62) 1 H5
Thiénans (70) 87 H4
Thiennes (59) 2 C5
Thiepval (80) 8 A4
Thiergeville (76) 16 D3
Thiernu (02) 22 D1
Thiers (63) 128 A2
Thiers-sur-Thève (60) 43 E1
Thierville (27) 18 A6
Thierville-sur-Meuse (55) 47 F1
Thiéville (14) 14 D6
Thièvres (62) 7 H4
Thièvres (80) 7 H3
Thieulloy-la-Ville (80) 19 H1
Thieulloy-l'Abbaye (80) 7 E6
Thieuloy-Saint-
  Antoine (60) 20 A2
la Thieuloye (62) 7 H1
Thieux (60) 20 C3
Thieux (77) 43 F2
Thiézac (15) 140 C4
Thignonville (45) 63 F3
Thil (01) 130 B2
Thil (10) 67 E3
Thil (27) 19 F5
Thil (31) 168 D4
Thil (51) 23 E5

Thil (54) 26 A2
Thil-Manneville (76) 17 G2
le Thil-Riberpré (76) 19 F2
Thil-sur-Arroux (71) 100 B5
Thilay (08) 11 F6
le Thillay (95) 42 D2
Thilleux (52) 67 F2
les Thilliers-en-Vexin (27) 19 F6
Thillois (51) 23 E6
Thillombois (55) 47 F3
Thillot (55) 47 H2
le Thillot (88) 70 C6
Thilouze (37) 94 D1
Thimert-Gâtelles (28) 41 E6
Thimonville (57) 49 E2
Thimory (45) 81 H1
Thin-le-Moutier (08) 23 H2
Thiolières (63) 128 B5
Thionne (03) 114 A3
Thionville (57) 26 B3
Thiouville (76) 16 D4
Thiraucourt (88) 69 E3
Thiré (85) 106 D1
Thiron-Gardais (28) 61 F3
This (08) 24 A1
Thise (25) 87 F6
Thivars (28) 62 A2
Thivencelle (59) 9 G1
Thiverny (60) 20 D6
Thiverval-Grignon (78) 42 A4
Thivet (52) 68 A6
Thiviers (24) 123 G6
Thiville (28) 62 A5
Thizay (36) 96 D4
Thizay (37) 94 A2
Thizy (89) 84 B4
Thizy-les-Bourgs (69) 115 G6
Thoard (04) 160 C6
Thodure (38) 144 C1
Thoigné (72) 60 B3
Thoiras (30) 173 G1
Thoiré-sous-
  Contenson (72) 60 B3
Thoiré-sur-Dinan (72) 78 C2
Thoires (21) 67 E6
Thoirette-Coisia (39) 117 F4
Thoiria (39) 117 H2
Thoiry (01) 118 B4
Thoiry (73) 132 A4
Thoiry (78) 41 H4
Thoissey (01) 116 B5
Thoissia (39) 117 F3
Thoisy-la-Berchère (21) 100 D1
Thoisy-le-Désert (21) 101 E1
Thoix (80) 20 A2
Thol-lès-Millières (52) 68 C4
Thollet (86) 110 B3
Thollon-les-Mémises (74) 119 F3
le Tholonet (13) 192 B2
le Tholy (88) 70 B4
Thomery (77) 64 B2
Thomirey (21) 101 E3
Thonac (24) 138 A4
Thônes (74) 132 C2
Thonnance-lès-
  Joinville (52) 68 A1
Thonnance-les-
  Moulins (52) 68 A2
Thonne-la-Long (55) 25 F3
Thonne-le-Thil (55) 25 F3
Thonne-les-Près (55) 25 F3
Thonnelle (55) 25 F3
Thonon-les-Bains (74) 119 E3
les Thons (88) 69 E6
Thonville (57) 49 F2
le Thor (84) 175 F2
Thorailles (45) 64 B6
Thoraise (25) 103 F1
Thorame-Basse (04) 161 E6
Thorame-Haute (04) 161 F6
Thoras (43) 142 A5
Thoré-la-Rochette (41) 79 F2
Thorée-les-Pins (72) 77 H3
Thorey (89) 84 B1
Thorey-en-Plaine (21) 102 A1
Thorey-Lyautey (54) 69 F1
Thorey-sous-Charny (21) 84 D6
Thorey-sur-Ouche (21) 101 F2
Thorigné-d'Anjou (49) 76 D3
Thorigné-en-Charnie (53) 59 F5
Thorigné-Fouillard (35) 57 F2
Thorigné-sur-Dué (72) 60 D5
Thorigny (85) 91 H5
Thorigny-sur-le-
  Mignon (79) 107 G5
Thorigny-sur-Marne (77) 43 F4
Thorigny-sur-Oreuse (89) 65 E3
le Thoronet (83) 193 H2
Thorrenc (07) 144 A2
Thors (10) 67 E3
Thors (17) 121 G2
Thory (80) 20 D2
Thory (89) 84 A4
Thoste (21) 84 C5
le Thou (17) 107 E5
Thou (18) 82 A5
Thou (45) 82 B4
Thouaré-sur-Loire (44) 74 D5
Thouars (79) 93 G3
Thouars-sur-Arize (09) 185 E3
Thouars-sur-Garonne (47) 150 D5
Thouarsais-
  Bouildroux (85) 92 C6
le Thoult-Trosnay (51) 44 D4
le Thour (08) 23 F3
Thourie (35) 57 G5
Thouron (87) 124 B1
Thourotte (60) 21 F4

Thoury (41) 80 B3
Thoury-Férottes (77) 64 C3
Thoux (32) 168 A4
Thubœuf (53) 59 E1
Thue et Mue (14) 14 B4
le Thuel (02) 23 E2
Thuès-entre-Valls (66) 200 A4
Thueyts (07) 157 F1
Thugny-Trugny (08) 23 G4
la Thuile (73) 132 A5
les Thuiles (04) 161 F3
Thuilley-aux-
   Groseilles (54) 48 A6
Thuillières (88) 69 F4
Thuir (66) 201 E3
le Thuit (27) 19 E6
Le Thuit de l'Oison (27) 18 B6
Thulay (25) 88 C5
Thumeréville (54) 25 H6
Thumeries (59) 3 F6
Thun-l'Évêque (59) 9 E3
Thun-Saint-Amand (59) 4 A6
Thun-Saint-Martin (59) 9 E3
Thurageau (86) 94 B5
Thuré (86) 94 C5
Thuret (63) 127 G1
Thurey (71) 102 A5
Thurey-le-Mont (25) 87 G5
Thurins (69) 129 H4
Thury (21) 101 E3
Thury (89) 83 E4
Thury-en-Valois (60) 43 H1
Thury-sous-Clermont (60) 20 C5
Thusy (74) 131 H1
Thuy (65) 183 F2
Thyez (74) 119 E5
Tibiran-Jaunac (65) 183 H4
Ticheville (61) 39 G3
Tichey (21) 102 B3
Tieffenbach (67) 50 B3
Tiercé (49) 77 E3
Tiercelet (54) 26 A4
le Tiercent (35) 35 G6
Tieste-Uragnoux (32) 166 D5
la Tieule (48) 155 G4
Tiffauges (85) 92 A3
Tigeaux (77) 43 G4
Tigery (91) 43 E6
Tignac (09) 199 F2
Tignécourt (88) 69 E5
Tignes (73) 133 G5
le Tignet (06) 178 C4
Tignieu-Jameyzieu (38) 130 C3
Tigny-Noyelle (62) 6 C2
Tigy (45) 81 F2
Til-Châtel (21) 86 A4
Tilh (40) 165 F5
Tilhouse (65) 183 G4
Tillac (32) 167 F6
Tillay-le-Péneux (28) 62 C4
Tillé (60) 20 B5
Tillenay (21) 102 B2
le Tilleul (76) 16 B4
Tilleul-Dame-Agnès (27) 40 C2
le Tilleul-Lambert (27) 40 C2
le Tilleul-Othon (27) 40 B1
Tilleux (88) 68 D3
Tillières-sur-Avre (27) 40 D5
Tilloloy (80) 21 E2
Tillou (79) 108 B5
Tilloy-et-Bellay (51) 46 B2
Tilloy-Floriville (80) 6 C5
Tilloy-lès-Conty (80) 20 B1
Tilloy-lès-Hermaville (62) 7 H2
Tilloy-lès-Mofflaines (62) 8 B3
Tilloy-lez-Cambrai (59) 8 B3
Tilloy-lez-Marchiennes (59) 9 E1
Tilly (27) 41 G1
Tilly (36) 110 C3
Tilly (78) 41 G3
Tilly-Capelle (62) 7 F1
Tilly-la-Campagne (14) 14 C5
Tilly-sur-Meuse (55) 47 G2
Tilly-sur-Seulles (14) 14 A4
Tilques (62) 2 A4
Tincey-et-Pontrebeau (70) ... 87 E3
Tinchebray-Bocage (61) 38 A4
Tincourt-Boucly (80) 8 C5
Tincques (62) 7 H2
Tincry (57) 49 E3
Tingry (62) 1 F5
Tinqueux (51) 23 E6
Tinténiac (35) 35 E6
Tintry (71) 101 E4
Tintury (58) 99 G3
Tiranges (43) 142 D1
Tirent-Pontéjac (32) 168 B6
Tirepied (50) 37 E4
Tissey (89) 84 A1
le Titre (80) 6 D3
Tivernon (45) 62 C4
Tiviers (15) 141 F4
Tizac-de-Curton (33) 135 G5
Tizac-de-Lapouyade (33) ... 135 G3
Tocane-Saint-Apre (24) 137 E2
Tocqueville (27) 15 H3
Tocqueville (50) 13 E1
Tocqueville-en-Caux (76) 17 F3
Tocqueville-les-Murs (76) ... 16 D4
Tœufles (80) 6 C4
Toges (08) 24 B4
Togny-aux-Bœufs (51) 46 A4
Tolla (2A) 204 D5
Tollaincourt (88) 68 D3
Tollent (62) 7 E2
Tollevast (50) 12 C2
la Tombe (77) 64 D2
Tombebœuf (47) 151 E3

Tomblaine (54) 48 D5
Tomino (2B) 203 G1
les Tonils (26) 158 D2
Tonnac (81) 170 A1
Tonnay-Boutonne (17) 121 E1
Tonnay-Charente (17) 120 D1
Tonneins (47) 150 D4
Tonnerre (89) 84 A1
Tonnoy (54) 48 D6
Tonquédec (22) 32 C3
Torcé (35) 57 H3
Torcé-en-Vallée (72) 60 C4
Torcé-Viviers-en-
   Charnie (53) 59 F4
Torcenay (52) 86 C1
Torchamp (61) 38 A6
Torchefon (38) 131 E5
Torcheville (57) 49 G3
Torcieu (01) 131 E1
Torcy (62) 1 H6
Torcy (71) 101 E3
Torcy (77) 43 F4
Torcy-en-Valois (02) 44 B2
Torcy-et-Pouligny (21) 84 C5
Torcy-le-Grand (10) 66 B1
Torcy-le-Grand (76) 17 H3
Torcy-le-Petit (10) 66 B1
Torcy-le-Petit (76) 17 H3
Tordères (66) 201 E3
Torfou (91) 63 F1
Torigny-les-Villes (50) 37 G2
Tornac (30) 173 G2
Tornay (52) 86 C2
le Torp-Mesnil (76) 17 F3
Torpes (25) 103 F1
Torpes (71) 102 B5
le Torpt (27) 15 G3
le Torquesne (14) 15 F4
Torreilles (66) 201 G2
Torsac (16) 122 C5
Torsiac (43) 141 F1
Tortebesse (63) 126 C3
Tortefontaine (62) 7 E2
Tortequesne (62) 8 C2
Torteron (18) 98 C3
Tortezais (03) 113 E3
Torvilliers (10) 66 A3
Torxé (17) 121 E1
Tosse (40) 164 C4
Tossiat (01) 117 E5
Tostat (65) 183 E2
Totainville (88) 69 E2
Tôtes (76) 17 G4
Touchay (18) 97 F6
la Touche (26) 158 B3
les Touches (44) 74 C4
les Touches-de-Périgny (17) .. 121 H1
Toucy (89) 83 E2
Toudon (06) 178 D2
Touët-de-l'Escarène (06) ... 179 F2
Touët-sur-Var (06) 178 C2
Touffailles (82) 152 A5
Toufflers (59) 3 G5
Touffréville (14) 14 C4
Touffreville (27) 19 E5
Touffreville-la-
   Corbeline (76) 18 A3
Touffreville-sur-Eu (76) 6 A5
Touget (32) 168 B4
Touille (31) 184 C4
Touillon (21) 84 D3
Touillon-et-Loutelet (25) ... 104 A5
Toujouse (32) 166 C3
Toul (54) 48 B5
Toulaud (07) 144 A5
Toulenne (33) 149 H2
Touligny (08) 24 A2
Toulis-et-Attencourt (02) 22 C2
Toulon (83) 193 E5
Toulon-sur-Allier (03) 113 H2
Toulon-sur-Arroux (71) 100 C6
Toulonjac (12) 153 G4
Toulouges (66) 201 E3
Toulouse (31) 169 F5
Toulouse-le-Château (39) .. 102 D5
Toulouzette (40) 165 G4
Toulx-Sainte-Croix (23) 112 A4
Touques (14) 15 E3
le Touquet-Paris-Plage (62) ... 1 E6
Touquettes (61) 39 H4
Touquin (77) 43 H5
la Tour (06) 179 E2
la Tour (74) 118 D5
la Tour-Blanche-Cercles (24) .. 122 D6
la Tour-d'Aigues (84) 176 B4
la Tour-d'Auvergne (63) ... 126 C5
la Tour-de-Faure (46) 153 E3
la Tour-de-Salvagny (69) .. 129 H2
la Tour-de-Scay (25) 87 G5
la Tour-du-Crieu (09) 185 H4
la Tour-du-Meix (39) 117 G2
la Tour-du-Parc (56) 73 E2
la Tour-du-Pin (38) 131 E5
la Tour-en-Bessin (14) 13 H5
la Tour-en-Jarez (42) 129 F5
Tour-en-Sologne (41) 80 B4
la Tour-Saint-Gelin (37) 94 C3
la Tour-sur-Orb (34) 172 B5
Tourailles (41) 79 G3
Tourbes (34) 188 D1
Tourcelles-Chaumont (08) ... 24 A4
Tourcoing (59) 3 G4
Tourdun (32) 167 E5
la Tourette (42) 128 D6
la Tourette-Cabardès (11) .. 187 E2
Tourette-du-Château (06) .. 178 D2
Tourgéville (14) 15 E3

Tourliac (47) 151 G1
Tourly (60) 20 A6
Tourmignies (59) 3 F6
Tourmont (39) 103 E4
Tournai-sur-Dive (61) 39 E4
Tournan (32) 184 B1
Tournan-en-Brie (77) 43 F5
Tournans (25) 87 H5
Tournavaux (08) 11 F6
Tournay (65) 183 F3
le Tourne (33) 135 F6
Tournebu (14) 38 C2
Tournecoupe (32) 168 B3
Tournedos-Bois-
   Hubert (27) 40 C2
Tournedos-sur-Seine (27) ... 18 D6
Tournefeuille (31) 169 E5
Tournefort (06) 178 D2
Tournehem-sur-la-
   Hem (62) 1 H3
Tournemire (12) 171 H2
Tournemire (15) 140 B4
Tournes (08) 24 A1
Tourneville (27) 40 D1
Tournières (14) 13 G5
Tournissan (11) 187 G4
Tournon (73) 132 C4
Tournon-d'Agenais (47) 151 H4
Tournon-Saint-Martin (36) .. 95 H2
Tournon-Saint-Pierre (37) .. 95 F6
Tournon-sur-Rhône (07) ... 144 A3
Tournous-Darré (65) 183 G2
Tournous-Devant (65) 183 G3
Tournus (71) 116 C1
Tourouvre au Perche (61) ... 40 A6
Tourouzelle (11) 187 G3
Tourreilles (11) 186 D5
les Tourreilles (31) 183 H4
Tourrenquets (32) 168 A4
Tourrette-Levens (06) 179 E3
les Tourrettes (26) 158 B1
Tourrettes (83) 178 B5
Tourrettes-sur-Loup (06) ... 178 D4
Tourriers (16) 122 C2
Tours (37) 78 D5
Tours-en-Savoie (73) 132 C4
Tours-en-Vimeu (80) 6 C4
Tours-sur-Marne (51) 45 F2
Tours-sur-Meymont (63) ... 128 A4
Tourtenay (79) 93 G3
Tourteron (08) 24 A3
Tourtoirac (24) 137 H2
Tourtour (83) 177 G5
Tourtouse (09) 184 D4
Tourtrès (47) 151 E3
Tourtrol (09) 186 A4
Tourves (83) 193 E2
Tourville-
   la-Campagne (27) 18 B6
Tourville-la-Rivière (76) 18 C5
Tourville-les-Ifs (76) 16 C3
Tourville-sur-Arques (76) ... 17 G2
Tourville-sur-Odon (14) 14 B5
Tourville-sur-Pont-
   Audemer (27) 15 H3
Tourville-sur-Sienne (50) ... 36 D1
Toury (28) 62 D4
Toury-Lurcy (58) 99 F6
Toury-sur-Jour (58) 99 E6
Tourzel-Ronzières (63) 127 F5
Toussaint (76) 16 C3
Toussieu (69) 130 B4
Toussieux (01) 130 A1
Tousson (77) 63 G3
Toussus-le-Noble (78) 42 B5
Toutainville (27) 15 G3
Toutenant (71) 102 A4
Toutencourt (80) 7 H5
Toutens (31) 169 H6
Toutlemonde (49) 92 C2
Toutry (21) 84 B3
Touvérac (16) 121 H6
le Touvet (38) 131 H6
Touville (27) 18 A5
Touvois (44) 91 E2
Touvre (16) 122 C4
Touzac (46) 152 A3
Tox (2B) 205 G2
Toy-Viam (19) 125 F4
Tracy-Bocage (14) 38 A1
Tracy-le-Mont (60) 21 G4
Tracy-le-Val (60) 21 G4
Tracy-sur-Loire (58) 82 B6
Tracy-sur-Mer (14) 14 A3
Trades (69) 115 H4
Traenheim (67) 50 C5
Tragny (57) 48 D2
Traînou (45) 63 E6
le Trait (76) 18 B4
Traitiéfontaine (70) 87 F5
Traize (73) 131 G4
Tralaigues (63) 126 B2
Tralonca (2B) 205 F2
Tramain (22) 34 A5
Tramayes (71) 116 A4
Trambly (71) 115 H4
Tramecourt (62) 7 F1
Tramery (51) 22 D6
Tramezaïgues (65) 196 D1
Tramolé (38) 130 D5
Tramont-Émy (54) 69 E2
Tramont-Lassus (54) 69 E2
Tramont-Saint-André (54) ... 69 E2
Tramoyes (01) 130 B2
Trampot (88) 68 B2

Trancault (10) 65 F2
la Tranche-sur-Mer (85) 106 B3
la Tranclière (01) 117 E5
Trancrainville (28) 62 D4
Trangé (72) 60 A5
le Tranger (36) 95 H4
Trannes (10) 67 E3
Tranqueville-Graux (88) 69 E2
Trans (53) 59 F3
Trans-en-Provence (83) 194 A1
Trans-la-Forêt (35) 35 F5
Trans-sur-Erdre (44) 75 E3
le Transloy (62) 8 C4
le Translay (80) 6 C5
Tranzault (36) 111 G1
Trappes (78) 42 B4
Trassanel (11) 187 E2
Traubach-le-Bas (68) 89 E3
Traubach-le-Haut (68) 89 E2
Trausse (11) 187 F2
Travaillan (84) 158 C6
Travecy (02) 22 A2
Traversères (32) 167 H6
Traves (70) 87 F3
le Travet (81) 170 D3
Trayes (79) 93 E6
Tréal (56) 56 B5
Tréauville (50) 12 B3
Trébabu (29) 30 C5
Treban (03) 113 G3
Tréban (81) 170 D1
Trébas (81) 171 E2
Trébédan (22) 34 C6
Trèbes (11) 187 E3
Trébeurden (22) 32 C2
Trébons (65) 183 E3
Trébons-de-Luchon (31) 197 F1
Trébons-sur-la-Grasse (31) .. 186 A1
Trébrivan (22) 32 C6
Trébry (22) 33 H6
Tréclun (21) 102 B1
Trécon (51) 45 F4
Trédaniel (22) 33 H6
Trédarzec (22) 33 E2
Trédias (22) 34 B6
Trédion (56) 55 H5
Trédrez-Locquémeau (22) ... 32 B2
Tréduder (22) 32 B3
Trefcon (02) 8 D6
Treffendel (35) 56 D3
Treffiagat (29) 53 E4
Treffieux (44) 74 D1
Trefflean (56) 55 G6
Treffort (38) 145 G5
Treffrin (22) 32 B6
Tréflaouénan (29) 31 G3
Tréflévénez (29) 31 F4
Tréflez (29) 31 F3
Tréfols (51) 44 C4
Tréfumel (22) 34 D6
Trégarantec (29) 31 F3
Trégarvan (29) 31 F6
Trégastel (22) 32 C1
Tréglamus (22) 32 D4
Tréglonou (29) 30 D3
Trégomeur (22) 33 F3
Trégonneau (22) 33 E3
Trégourez (29) 53 H2
Tréguennec (29) 52 D3
Trégueux (22) 33 G4
Tréguidel (22) 33 F3
Tréguier (22) 33 E2
Tréhet (41) 78 D2
Tréhorenteuc (56) 56 B3
le Tréhou (29) 31 G5
Treignac (19) 125 E5
Treignat (03) 112 B3
Treigny (89) 82 D4
Treilles (11) 188 A6
Treilles-en-Gâtinais (45) 64 A5
Treillières (44) 74 C4
Treix (52) 68 A4
Treize-Septiers (85) 91 H1
Treize-Vents (85) 92 C3
Tréjouls (82) 152 B5
Trélans (48) 155 F3
Trélazé (49) 77 E5
Trélévern (22) 32 D1
Trelins (42) 128 D3
Trélissac (24) 137 F2
Trélivan (22) 34 C5
Trélon (59) 10 B4
Trélou-sur-Marne (02) 44 C2
Trémaouézan (29) 31 F4
Trémargat (22) 32 D6
Trémauville (76) 16 D4
la Tremblade (17) 120 B2
Tremblay (35) 35 G6
Tremblay-en-France (93) 43 E3
Tremblay-les-Villages (28) .. 41 F6
le Tremblay-
   Omonville (27) 40 C1
le Tremblay-sur-
   Mauldre (78) 42 A4
Tremblecourt (54) 48 B4
le Tremblois (70) 86 C5
Tremblois-lès-
   Carignan (08) 25 E2
Tremblois-lès-Rocroi (08) ... 10 D6
Trémeheuc (35) 35 F5
Trémel (22) 32 B3
Tréméloir (22) 33 F3
Trémentines (49) 92 C2
Tréméoc (29) 53 F3
Tréméreuc (22) 34 D4
Trémery (57) 26 C4

Trémeur (22) 34 B6
Tréméven (22) 33 F3
Tréméven (29) 54 B4
Trémilly (52) 67 F2
Tréminis (38) 145 G6
Trémoins (70) 88 B3
Trémolat (24) 137 G5
Trémons (47) 151 H4
Trémont (61) 39 G6
Trémont-sur-Saulx (55) 46 D5
Trémonzey (88) 69 G6
Trémouille (15) 140 C1
Trémouille-
   Saint-Loup (63) 126 B5
Trémouilles (12) 154 C5
Trémoulet (09) 185 H4
Trémuson (22) 33 G4
Trenal (39) 102 C6
Trensacq (40) 149 E5
Trentels (47) 151 H3
Tréogan (22) 54 B1
Tréogat (29) 53 E3
Tréon (28) 41 E5
Tréouergat (29) 30 D3
Trépail (51) 45 G1
le Tréport (76) 6 A4
Trépot (25) 103 G1
Tréprel (14) 38 C3
Trept (38) 130 D4
Trésauvaux (55) 47 H2
Tresboeuf (35) 57 F5
Trescault (62) 8 D4
Treschenu-Creyers (26) 145 F6
Trescléoux (05) 159 H4
Trésilley (70) 87 F5
Treslon (51) 22 D6
Tresnay (58) 99 E6
Trespoux-Rassiels (46) 152 C4
Tresques (30) 174 C1
Tressan (34) 172 D6
Tressandans (25) 87 H4
Tressange (57) 26 A3
Tressé (35) 35 E5
Tresserre (66) 201 E3
Tresserve (73) 131 H4
Tresses (33) 135 F5
Tressignaux (22) 33 F3
Tressin (59) 3 G5
Tresson (72) 78 D1
Treteau (03) 114 B3
la Trétoire (77) 44 A4
Trets (13) 192 D2
Treux (80) 8 A5
Treuzy-Levelay (77) 64 B3
Trévé (22) 55 G1
Trévenans (90) 88 C3
Tréveneuc (22) 33 G3
Tréveray (55) 47 F6
Trévérec (22) 33 E3
Trévérien (35) 34 D6
Trèves (30) 172 C1
Trèves (69) 129 H5
Trévien (81) 170 C1
Trévières (14) 13 G5
Trévignin (73) 131 H3
Trévillach (66) 200 D3
Tréville (11) 186 B5
Trévillers (25) 88 D6
Trévilly (89) 84 B4
Trévol (03) 113 H1
Trévou-Tréguignec (22) 32 D1
Trévoux (01) 130 A1
le Trévoux (29) 54 A4
Trévron (22) 34 D6
Trézelles (03) 114 B4
Trézény (22) 32 D2
Tréziers (11) 186 B5
Trézilidé (29) 31 H3
Trézioux (63) 127 H3
Triac-Lautrait (16) 122 A3
le Triadou (34) 173 F4
Triaize (85) 106 C2
Tribehou (50) 13 G6
Trichey (89) 66 B6
Tricot (60) 20 D3
Trie-Château (60) 19 H6
Trie-la-Ville (60) 19 H6
Trie-sur-Baïse (65) 183 G2
Triel-sur-Seine (78) 42 B3
Triembach-au-Val (67) 71 F2
Trieux (54) 26 A3
Trigance (83) 177 H3
Trignac (44) 73 G4
Trigny (51) 22 D5
Triguères (45) 64 C5
Trilbardou (77) 43 F3
Trilla (66) 200 D2
Trilport (77) 43 G3
Trimbach (67) 51 H3
Trimer (35) 34 D6
la Trimouille (86) 110 B2
Trinay (45) 62 D5
la Trinitat (15) 155 E1
la Trinité (06) 179 F3
la Trinité (27) 41 E2
la Trinité (50) 37 F4
la Trinité (73) 132 B5
la Trinité-de-Réville (27) 39 H3
la Trinité-de-
   Thouberville (27) 18 B5
la Trinité-des-Laitiers (61) .. 39 G4
la Trinité-du-Mont (76) 15 H1
la Trinité-Porhoët (56) 55 H1
la Trinité-Surzur (56) 73 E1
Triors (26) 144 C3
le Trioulou (15) 153 H1

Triqueville (27) 15 G3
Trith-Saint-Léger (59) 9 F2
Tritteling-Redlach (57) 27 E5
Trivy (71) 115 H3
Trizac (15) 140 B2
Trizay (17) 120 D1
Trizay-Coutretot-Saint-
   Serge (28) 61 F3
Trizay-lès-Bonneval (28) 62 A4
Troche (19) 124 C6
Trochères (21) 86 B6
Trocy-en-Multien (77) 43 G2
Troësnes (02) 44 A1
Troguéry (22) 33 E2
Trogues (37) 94 C2
Les Trois Châteaux (39) 117 E3
les Trois-Domaines (55) 47 F3
Trois-Fonds (23) 112 A4
Trois-Fontaines-
   l'Abbaye (51) 46 D5
Les Trois Lacs (27) 19 E6
Trois-Monts (14) 38 B2
les Trois-Moutiers (86) 93 H2
Trois-Palis (16) 122 B4
les Trois-Pierres (76) 15 G1
Trois-Puits (51) 23 E6
Trois-Vèvres (58) 99 F4
Trois-Villes (64) 181 G3
Troisfontaines (57) 50 A5
Troisfontaines-
   la-Ville (52) 67 G1
Troissereux (60) 20 A4
Troissy (51) 44 D2
Troisvaux (62) 7 G1
Troisvilles (59) 9 F4
Tromarey (70) 86 D6
Tromborn (57) 27 F4
Troncens (32) 167 E6
la Tronche (38) 145 G2
le Tronchet (35) 35 E5
le Tronchet (72) 60 A4
Tronchoy (89) 84 A1
Tronchy (71) 102 A6
le Troncq (27) 18 B6
Trondes (54) 48 A5
Tronget (03) 113 G3
Tronville-en-Barrois (55) 47 F5
Troo (41) 79 E2
Trosly-Breuil (60) 21 G5
Trosly-Loire (02) 21 H4
Trouans (10) 45 G6
Troubat (65) 184 A5
Trouhans (21) 102 B2
Trouhaut (21) 85 F5
Trouillas (66) 201 E3
Trouley-Labarthe (65) 183 F2
Troussencourt (60) 20 B3
Troussey (55) 47 H5
Trouvans (25) 87 H5
Trouville (76) 15 H1
Trouville-la-Haule (27) 15 H2
Trouville-sur-Mer (14) 15 E3
Trouy (18) 97 G3
Troye-d'Ariège (09) 186 B5
Troyes (10) 66 B3
Troyon (55) 47 G2
la Truchère (71) 116 C2
Truchtersheim (67) 50 D5
Trucy (02) 22 C4
Trucy-l'Orgueilleux (58) 83 F5
Trucy-sur-Yonne (89) 83 G3
le Truel (12) 171 G1
Trugny (21) 102 A3
Truinas (26) 158 D2
Trumilly (60) 21 F6
Trun (61) 39 E4
Trungy (14) 13 H6
Truyes (37) 95 F1
Tubersent (62) 1 F6
Tuchan (11) 187 G6
Tucquegnieux (54) 26 A4
Tudeils (19) 139 E4
Tudelle (32) 167 F4
Tuffalun (49) 77 F6
Tuffé Val de la
   Chéronne (72) 60 C5
Tugéras-Saint-
   Maurice (17) 121 G6
Tugny-et-Pont (02) 21 H1
la Tulière (42) 128 B1
Tulette (26) 158 C5
Tulle (19) 139 E2
Tullins (38) 145 E1
Tully (80) 6 B4
Tupigny (02) 9 G5
Tupin-et-Semons (69) 130 A5
la Turballe (44) 73 F3
la Turbie (06) 179 F3
Turcey (21) 85 F5
Turckheim (68) 71 F4
Turenne (19) 138 D4
Turgon (16) 122 D1
Turgy (10) 66 B5
Turny (89) 65 G3
Turquant (49) 93 H1
Turquestein-Blancrupt (57) .. 50 A6
Turqueville (50) 13 E4
Turretot (76) 16 B4
Turriers (04) 160 C3
Tursac (24) 137 H4
Tusson (16) 122 B1
Tuzaguet (65) 183 H4
le Tuzan (33) 149 G2
Tuzie (16) 122 C1

U

Ubaye-Serre-Ponçon (04) 160 D3
Ubexy (88) 69 G2
Ubraye (04) 178 A2
Ucciani (2A) 204 D5
Ucel (07) 157 G2
Uchacq-et-Parentis (40) 165 H2
Uchaud (30) 174 A4
Uchaux (84) 158 B5
Uchizy (71) 116 B2
Uchon (71) 100 C5
Uckange (57) 26 B4
Ueberstrass (68) 89 E3
Uffheim (68) 89 G2
Uffholtz (68) 89 E1
Ugine (73) 132 C3
Uglas (65) 183 H4
Ugnouas (65) 183 E2
Ugny (54) 25 G4
Ugny-le-Gay (02) 21 H2
Ugny-l'Équipée (80) 21 G1
Ugny-sur-Meuse (55) 48 A5
Uhart-Cize (64) 180 D3
Uhart-Mixe (64) 181 F2
Uhlwiller (67) 51 E1
Uhrwiller (67) 50 D3
Les Ulis (91) 42 C5
Ully-Saint-Georges (60) 20 C6
les Ulmes (49) 93 G1
Umpeau (28) 62 C1
Unac (09) 199 F1
Uncey-le-Franc (21) 85 E6
Unchair (51) 22 D6
Ungersheim (68) 71 F6
Unias (42) 129 E4
Unienville (10) 67 E3
Unieux (42) 129 E6
l'Union (31) 169 F5
Unverre (28) 61 G4
Unzent (09) 185 G3
Upaix (05) 160 A4
Upie (26) 144 B6
Ur (66) 199 G4
Urau (31) 184 C5
Urbalacque (2A) 206 D1
Urbanya (66) 200 B3
Urbeis (67) 71 E2
Urbès (68) 70 D6
Urbise (42) 114 C4
Urçay (03) 112 D1
Urcel (02) 22 B4
Urcerey (90) 88 C3
Urciers (36) 112 A2
Urcuit (64) 164 C6
Urcy (21) 101 G1
Urdens (32) 168 A3
Urdès (64) 165 H6
Urdos (64) 182 A6
Urepel (64) 180 C4
Urgons (40) 166 A4
Urgosse (32) 166 D4
Uriménil (88) 69 H4
Urmatt (67) 50 C6
Urost (64) 182 D1
Urrugne (64) 180 A1
Urs (09) 199 F1
Urschenheim (68) 71 G4
Urt (64) 164 C6
Urtaca (2B) 203 E5
Urtière (25) 88 D6
Uruffe (54) 48 A6
Urval (24) 137 G6
Urville (10) 67 E4
Urville (14) 38 C2
Urville (50) 12 D3
Urville (88) 68 D4
Urvillers (02) 22 A1
Ury (77) 63 H3
Urzy (58) 99 E3
Us (95) 42 A2
Usclades-et-Rieutord (07).... 143 E4
Usclas-d'Hérault (34) 172 D6
Usclas-du-Bosc (34) 172 C4
Usinens (74) 118 A6
Ussac (19) 138 C2
Ussat (09) 199 E1
Usseau (79) 107 G5
Usseau (86) 94 C4
Ussel (15) 141 E4
Ussel (19) 126 A5
Ussel (46) 152 D2
Ussel-d'Allier (03) 113 G5
Usson (63) 127 G5
Usson-du-Poitou (86) 109 F4
Usson-en-Forez (42) 142 C1
Ussy (14) 38 D3
Ussy-sur-Marne (77) 43 H3
Ustaritz (64) 180 C1
Ustou (09) 198 C1
Utelle (06) 179 E2
Uttenheim (67) 71 G1
Uttenhoffen (67) 50 D3
Uttwiller (67) 50 D3
Uvernet-Fours (04) 161 F4
Uxeau (71) 100 B6
Uxegney (88) 69 H4
Uxelles (39) 117 H1
Uxem (59) 2 C1
Uz (65) 182 D5
Uza (40) 164 D1
Uzan (64) 166 A4
Uzay-le-Venon (18) 97 H5
Uzech (46) 152 C2
Uzein (64) 182 B1
Uzel (22) 33 F6
Uzelle (25) 88 A4

Uzemain (88) 69 H5
Uzer (07) 157 F3
Uzer (65) 183 F4
Uzerche (19) 124 D6
Uzès (30) 174 B2
Uzeste (33) 149 G3
Uzos (64) 182 B2

V

Vaas (72) 78 B3
Vabre (81) 170 D5
Vabres (15) 141 F4
Vabres (30) 173 F1
Vabres-l'Abbaye (12) 171 G2
Vacherauville (55) 25 E6
Vachères (04) 176 B2
Vachères-en-Quint (26) 144 D6
Vacheresse (74) 119 F3
la Vacheresse-et-la-
    Rouillie (88) 68 D4
la Vacherie (27) 40 D1
Vacognes-Neuilly (14) 14 A5
la Vacquerie-et-Saint-
    Martin-de-Castries (34).... 172 D4
Vacquerie-le-Boucq (62) 7 F2
Vacqueriette-
    Erquières (62) 7 F2
Vacqueville (54) 70 C1
Vacqueyras (84) 158 C6
Vacquières (34) 173 G3
Vacquiers (31) 169 F4
Vadans (39) 103 E4
Vadans (70) 86 C6
Vadelaincourt (55) 47 F2
Vadenay (51) 45 H2
Vadencourt (02) 9 G5
Vadencourt (80) 7 H5
Vadonville (55) 47 G4
Vagnas (07) 157 G4
Vagney (88) 70 B5
Vahl-Ebersing (57) 49 G1
Vahl-lès-Bénestroff (57) 49 G3
Vahl-lès-Faulquemont (57) 49 F2
Vaiges (53) 59 E5
Vailhan (34) 172 C6
Vailhauquès (34) 173 E5
Vailhourles (12) 153 F5
Vaillac (46) 152 D3
Vaillant (52) 85 H2
Vailly (10) 66 B2
Vailly (74) 119 E3
Vailly-sur-Aisne (02) 22 B4
Vailly-sur-Sauldre (18) 82 A5
Vains (50) 35 H3
Vair-sur-Loire (44) 75 F3
Vaire (25) 87 G6
Vairé (85) 91 E5
Vaire-sous-Corbie (80) 7 F4
Vaires-sur-Marne (77) 43 E4
Vaison-la-Romaine (84) 158 D5
Vaïssac (82) 169 G1
Vaite (70) 86 D3
la Vaivre (70) 69 H6
Vaivre-et-Montoille (70) 87 F3
le Val (25) 103 F2
le Val (83) 193 F2
Val-au-Perche (61) 61 E3
Val Buëch-Méouge (05) 160 A5
Val-Cenis (73) 147 F1
le Val-d'Ajol (88) 70 A6
Val d'Anast (35) 56 D4
Val d'Arcomie (15) 141 F5
Val d'Arry (14) 14 A5
Val d'Auzon (10) 66 D2
le Val-David (27) 41 E2
Val-de-Bride (57) 49 F4
Val de Briey (54) 26 A4
Val de Chaise (74) 132 C3
Val-de-Chalvagne (04) 178 B2
Val de Drôme (14) 37 H1
Val-de-Fier (74) 131 H1
le Val-de-Gouhenans (70) 88 A3
le Val-de-Guéblange (57) 49 H2
Val-de-la-Haye (76) 18 C5
Val de Lambronne (11) 186 B4
Val de Livre (51) 45 F2
Val de Louyre et
    Caudeau (24) 137 F4
Val-de-Mercy (89) 83 G3
Val-de-Meuse (52) 68 C6
Val de Moder (67) 50 D3
Val-de-Reuil (27) 18 D6
Val-de-Roulans (25) 87 H5
Val-de-Saâne (76) 17 F4
Val-de-Vesle (51) 45 G1
Val-de-Vie (14) 39 F3
Val-de-Vière (51) 46 B4
Val de Virvée (33) 135 F4
Val d'Épy (39) 117 F3
Val d'Erdre-Auxence (49).... 76 B4
Val-des-Marais (51) 45 F4
Val-des-Prés (05) 147 E4
Val des Vignes (16) 122 A5
le Val d'Esnoms (52) 86 A3
Le Val d'Hazey (27) 41 E1
Val-d'Isère (73) 133 G5
Val d'Issoire (87) 110 A5
Val-d'Izé (35) 57 H2
Le Val d'Ocre (89) 83 E2
Val d'Oingt (69) 129 G2
Val d'Orger (27) 19 E5
Val d'Ornain (55) 46 D4
Val d'Oronaye (04) 161 G3
Val d'Oust (56) 56 A5
Val-du-Layon (49) 76 D6
Val-du-Maine (53) 59 E6
Val en Vignes (79) 93 F2

Val-et-Châtillon (54) 49 H6
Val-Fouzon (36) 96 C1
Val-Maravel (26) 159 G2
Val-Mont (21) 101 E3
Val-Revermont (01) 117 E4
le Val-Saint-Éloi (70) 87 G2
le Val-Saint-Germain (91) 42 B6
le Val-Saint-Père (50) 35 H3
Val-Sonnette (39) 117 F1
Val Suran (39) 117 F3
Val-Suzon (21) 85 G5
Valady (12) 154 B3
Valailles (27) 15 H5
Valaire (41) 79 H5
Valambray (14) 14 D5
Valaurie (26) 158 B4
Valavoire (04) 160 B5
Valay (70) 86 D6
Valbeleix (63) 127 E6
Valbelle (04) 160 A6
Valbois (55) 47 H3
Valbonnais (38) 145 H5
Valbonne (06) 178 D4
Valcabrère (31) 184 A5
Valcanville (50) 13 E2
Valcebollère (66) 199 H5
Valcivières (63) 128 B5
Valcourt (52) 46 D6
Valdahon (25) 104 A2
Valdallière (14) 38 A3
Valdampierre (60) 20 A5
Valdeblore (06) 162 C6
Valderiès (81) 170 C2
Valderoure (06) 178 B3
Valdieu-Lutran (68) 89 E3
Valdivienne (86) 109 G2
Valdoie (90) 88 C2
Valdrôme (26) 159 G3
Valdurenque (81) 170 D6
Valeille (42) 129 F3
Valeilles (82) 151 H4
Valeins (01) 116 B5
Valempoulières (39) 103 F5
Valençay (36) 96 B2
Valence (16) 122 D2
Valence (26) 144 B5
Valence (82) 151 G6
Valence-d'Albigeois (81).... 170 D2
Valence-en-Brie (77) 64 B2
Valence-sur-Baïse (32) 167 G3
Valenciennes (59) 9 F2
Valencin (38) 130 B4
Valencisse (41) 79 H4
Valencogne (38) 131 F5
Valennes (72) 61 E6
Valensole (04) 177 E3
Valentigney (25) 88 C4
Valentine (31) 184 B4
Valenton (94) 42 D5
Valergues (34) 173 G5
Valernes (04) 160 B5
Valescourt (60) 20 D4
Valette (15) 140 B2
la Valette (38) 145 H4
la Valette-du-Var (83) 193 F5
Valeuil (24) 137 E1
Valeyrac (33) 120 C6
Valff (67) 71 G1
Valfin-sur-Valouse (39) 117 F3
Valflaunès (34) 173 F4
Valfleury (42) 129 G5
Valframbert (61) 60 A1
Valfroicourt (88) 69 F4
Valgorge (07) 157 E2
Valhey (54) 49 E5
Valhuon (62) 7 G1
Valiergues (19) 125 H6
Valignat (03) 113 G5
Valigny (03) 98 B6
Valines (80) 6 C4
Valjouffrey (38) 146 A5
Valjouze (15) 141 E3
la Valla-en-Gier (42) 129 G6
la Valla-sur-Rochefort (42) 128 C3
Vallabrègues (30) 174 C3
Vallabrix (30) 174 B1
la Vallée (17) 120 D1
la Vallée-au-Blé (02) 9 H6
la Vallée-Mulâtre (02) 9 F5
Les Vallées de la
    Vanne (89) 65 F4
Vallées en
    Champagne (02) 44 D3
Vallègue (31) 186 A1
Valleiry (74) 118 B5
Vallenay (18) 97 G5
Vallentigny (10) 67 E2
Vallerange (57) 49 F2
Vallérargues (30) 157 G6
Valleraugue (30) 173 E1
Vallères (37) 78 C6
Valleret (52) 67 G1
Vallereuil (24) 137 E3
Vallerois-le-Bois (70) 87 H4
Vallerois-Lorioz (70) 87 G4
Valleroy (25) 87 G5
Valleroy (52) 86 D2

Valleroy (54) 26 A4
Valleroy-aux-Saules (88) 69 F3
Valleroy-le-Sec (88) 69 F4
Vallery (89) 64 C4
Vallesvilles (31) 169 G5
Vallet (44) 75 E6
Valletot (27) 15 H3
Vallica (2B) 202 D6
Vallière (23) 125 G2
Vallières (10) 66 B6
Vallières (74) 131 H1
Vallières-les-Grandes (41) 79 G5
Valliguières (30) 174 C2
Valliquerville (76) 17 E4
Valloire (73) 146 D2
Valloire-sur-Cisse (41) 79 H4
Vallois (54) 70 A1
les Vallois (88) 69 F4
Vallon-en-Sully (03) 112 D2
Vallon-Pont-d'Arc (07) 157 G4
Vallon-sur-Gée (72) 59 H6
Vallorcine (74) 119 H6
Vallouise-Pelvoux (05) 146 D5
Valmanya (66) 200 C4
Valmascle (34) 172 B5
Valmeinier (73) 146 D2
Valmestroff (57) 26 C3
Valmigère (11) 187 E5
Valmondois (95) 42 C2
Valmont (57) 27 F5
Valmont (76) 16 D3
Valmunster (57) 26 D4
Valmy (51) 46 C2
Valognes (50) 12 D3
Valojoulx (24) 138 A4
Valonne (25) 88 B5
Valorbiquet (14) 39 G2
Valoreille (25) 88 C6
Valouse (26) 158 D3
Valprivas (43) 142 D1
Valpuiseaux (91) 63 G2
Valras-Plage (34) 188 C3
Valravillon (89) 83 F1
Valréas (84) 158 C4
Valros (34) 188 D1
Vals (09) 186 A4
Vals-des-Tilles (52) 85 H3
Vals-le-Chastel (43) 142 A2
Vals-les-Bains (07) 157 G1
Vals-près-le-Puy (43) 142 C4
Valsemé (14) 15 E4
Valserres (05) 160 C3
Valsonne (69) 129 F1
le Valtin (88) 70 D4
Valuéjols (15) 141 E4
Valvignères (07) 157 H3
Valz-sous-
    Châteauneuf (63) 127 H6
Valzergues (12) 153 H3
Valzin en Petite
    Montagne (39) 117 G3
Vanault-le-Châtel (51) 46 B4
Vanault-les-Dames (51) 46 C4
Vançais (79) 108 C4
Vancé (72) 78 D1
la Vancelle (67) 71 F2
Vandeins (01) 116 D4
Vandelainville (54) 48 B2
Vandelans (70) 87 G5
Vandeléville (54) 69 E2
Vandélicourt (60) 21 F4
Vandenesse (58) 99 H4
Vandenesse-en-
    Auxois (21) 101 F1
Vandeuil (51) 22 D6
Vandières (51) 44 D1
Vandières (54) 48 B3
Vandœuvre-lès-Nancy (54).... 48 C5
Vandoncourt (25) 88 D4
Vandré (17) 107 F6
Vandrimare (27) 19 E5
Vandy (08) 24 A4
Vanlay (10) 66 A5
Vannaire (21) 85 E1
Vanne (70) 87 E3
le Vanneau-Irleau (79) 107 G3
Vannecourt (57) 49 F3
Vannecrocq (27) 15 G3
Vannes (56) 55 G6
Vannes-le-Châtel (54) 48 A6
Vannes-sur-Cosson (45) 81 F3
Vannoz (39) 103 F5
Vanosc (07) 143 G2
les Vans (07) 157 E4
Vantoux (57) 26 C5
Vantoux-et-Longevelle (70) 87 E5
Vanves (92) 42 C4
Vanvey (21) 85 F1
Vanville (77) 64 D1
Vanxains (24) 136 C2
Vany (57) 26 C5
Vanzac (17) 121 G6
Vanzay (79) 108 C4
Vanzy (74) 118 A6
Vaour (81) 169 H1
Varacieux (38) 144 D2
Varages (83) 176 D5
Varaignes (24) 123 E4
Varaire (46) 153 E4
Varaize (17) 121 G1
Varambon (01) 117 E6
Varanges (21) 102 A1
Varangéville (54) 48 D5
Varaville (14) 14 D4
Varces-Allières-et-
    Risset (38) 145 G3
Vareilles (23) 110 D4
Vareilles (71) 115 F4

Varen (82) 153 F6
Varengeville-sur-Mer (76) 17 G2
Varenguebec (50) 12 D4
Varenne-l'Arconce (71) 115 F4
Varenne-Saint-
    Germain (71) 115 E3
Varennes (24) 137 G5
Varennes (31) 185 H1
Varennes (37) 95 F3
Varennes (80) 7 H4
Varennes (82) 169 F3
Varennes (86) 94 B5
Varennes (89) 83 H1
Varennes-Changy (45) 82 A1
Varennes-en-Argonne (55) 24 C6
Varennes-Jarcy (91) 43 E5
Varennes-le-Grand (71) 101 G6
Varennes-lès-Mâcon (71).... 116 B4
Varennes-lès-Narcy (58) 98 D1
Varennes-Saint-
    Honorat (43) 142 A3
Varennes-Saint-
    Sauveur (71) 117 E2
Varennes-sous-Dun (71) 115 G4
Varennes-sur-Allier (03) 114 A4
Varennes-sur-Amance (52) 86 C1
Varennes-sur-Loire (49) 94 A1
Varennes-sur-Morge (63) 127 F1
Varennes-sur-Seine (77) 64 C2
Varennes-sur-Tèche (03) 114 B4
Varennes-sur-Usson (63) 127 G5
Varennes-Vauzelles (58) 98 D3
Varès (47) 150 D3
Varesnes (60) 21 G3
Varetz (19) 138 C2
Varilhes (09) 185 H5
Varinfroy (60) 43 H2
Variscourt (02) 23 E4
Varize (28) 62 B5
Varize-Vaudoncourt (57) 26 D5
Varmonzey (88) 69 G2
Varneville (55) 47 H3
Varneville-Bretteville (76) 17 G4
Varogne (70) 87 G2
Varois-et-Chaignot (21) 85 H6
Varouville (50) 12 D1
Varrains (49) 93 H1
Varreddes (77) 43 G2
Vars (05) 161 F2
Vars (16) 122 B3
Vars (70) 86 C4
Vars-sur-Roseix (19) 138 C2
Varsberg (57) 27 E5
Varzay (17) 121 E3
Varzy (58) 83 E6
Vascœuil (27) 19 E4
Vasles (79) 108 C1
Vasperviller (57) 50 A5
Vassel (63) 127 G3
Vasselay (18) 97 G2
Vasselin (38) 131 E4
Vassens (02) 21 H4
Vasseny (02) 22 B5
Vassieux-en-Vercors (26) 145 E5
Vassimont-et-
    Chapelaine (51) 45 G5
Vassincourt (55) 46 D4
Vassogne (02) 22 C4
Vassonville (76) 17 G4
Vassy-sous-Pisy (89) 84 B4
le Vast (50) 13 E2
les Vastres (43) 143 E4
Vatan (36) 96 D3
Vathiménil (54) 70 B1
Vatierville (76) 19 F1
Vatilieu (38) 145 E2
Vatimont (57) 49 E2
Vatry (51) 45 G4
Vattetot-sous-
    Beaumont (76) 16 C4
Vattetot-sur-Mer (76) 16 B3
Vatteville (27) 19 E6
Vatteville-la-Rue (76) 18 A4
Vauban (71) 115 F4
Vaubecourt (55) 47 E3
Vaubexy (88) 69 G3
Vaucelles (14) 13 H5
Vaucelles-et-
    Beffecourt (02) 22 B3
Vauchamps (25) 87 G6
Vauchamps (51) 44 D4
Vauchassis (10) 66 A4
Vauchelles (60) 21 G3
Vauchelles-lès-Authie (80) 7 H4
Vauchelles-lès-Domart (80) 7 E4
Vauchelles-les-
    Quesnoy (80) 6 D4
Vauchonvilliers (10) 66 D3
Vauchoux (70) 87 F3
Vauciennes (51) 45 E2
Vauciennes (60) 21 G6
Vauclaix (58) 100 A1
Vauclerc (51) 46 B5
Vaucluse (25) 88 B6
Vauclusotte (25) 88 C6
Vaucogne (10) 66 C1
Vauconcourt-
    Nervezain (70) 87 E3
Vaucouleurs (55) 47 H6
Vaucourt (54) 49 F5
Vaucourtois (77) 43 G3
Vaucresson (92) 42 C4
Vaudancourt (60) 19 G6
Vaudebarrier (71) 115 G3
Vaudelnay (49) 93 G2
Vaudemange (51) 45 G2
Vaudémont (54) 69 E2
Vaudes (10) 66 B4

Vaudesincourt (51) 23 G6
Vaudesson (02) 22 B4
Vaudeurs (89) 65 F5
Vaudevant (07) 143 H3
Vaudeville (54) 69 G1
Vaudéville (88) 70 A3
Vaudeville-le-Haut (55) 68 C1
Vaudherland (95) 43 E2
Vaudigny (54) 69 G1
le Vaudioux (39) 103 F6
Vaudoncourt (55) 25 G5
Vaudoncourt (88) 68 D3
le Vaudoué (77) 63 H3
Vaudoy-en-Brie (77) 43 H5
Vaudreching (57) 26 D4
Vaudrecourt (52) 68 D4
Vaudrémont (52) 67 G4
le Vaudreuil (27) 18 D6
Vaudreuille (31) 186 B1
Vaudreville (50) 12 D3
Vaudrey (39) 102 D3
Vaudricourt (62) 2 D6
Vaudricourt (80) 6 B4
Vaudrimesnil (50) 12 D6
Vaudringhem (62) 1 H5
Vaudrivillers (25) 88 A6
Vaufrey (25) 88 D5
Vaugines (84) 176 A4
Vaugneray (69) 129 H3
Vaugrigneuse (91) 42 B6
Vauhallan (91) 42 C5
Vaujany (38) 146 A2
Vaujours (93) 43 E3
le Vaulmier (15) 140 B2
Vaulnaveys-le-Bas (38) 145 G3
Vaulnaveys-le-Haut (38) 145 G3
Vaulry (87) 110 B6
Vault-de-Lugny (89) 83 H5
Vaulx (62) 7 F2
Vaulx (74) 132 A1
Vaulx-en-Velin (69) 130 B3
Vaulx-Milieu (38) 130 C4
Vaulx-Vraucourt (62) 8 C4
le Vaumain (60) 19 H5
Vaumas (03) 114 B3
Vaumeilh (04) 160 B5
Vaumoise (60) 21 G6
Vaumort (89) 65 F4
Vaunac (24) 137 G1
Vaunaveys-la-Rochette (26).... 144 C6
Vaunoise (61) 60 C2
la Vaupalière (76) 18 C4
Vaupillon (28) 61 F1
Vaupoisson (10) 66 C1
Vauquois (55) 24 D6
Vauréal (95) 42 B2
Vaureilles (12) 153 H3
le Vauroux (60) 19 H5
Vausseroux (79) 108 B1
Vautebis (79) 108 B1
Vauthiermont (90) 88 D2
Vautorte (53) 58 C3
Vauvenargues (13) 176 B5
Vauvert (30) 174 A4
Vauville (14) 15 E3
Vauvillers (70) 69 F6
Vauvillers (80) 8 A6
Vaux (03) 112 D3
Vaux (31) 186 A1
Vaux (57) 26 B5
Vaux (86) 108 D4
Vaux-Andigny (02) 9 F5
Vaux-Champagne (08) 23 H4
Vaux d'Amognes (58) 99 E3
Vaux-devant-Damloup (55) 25 F6
Vaux-en-Amiénois (80) 7 F5
Vaux-en-Beaujolais (69) 115 H6
Vaux-en-Bugey (01) 130 D1
Vaux-en-Dieulet (08) 24 C4
Vaux-en-Pré (71) 115 H1
Vaux-en-Vermandois (02) 21 H1
Vaux-et-Chantegrue (25).... 103 H5
Vaux-Lavalette (16) 122 C6
Vaux-le-Moncelot (70) 87 E4
Vaux-le-Pénil (77) 64 A1
Vaux-lès-Mouron (08) 24 B5
Vaux-lès-Mouzon (08) 24 D3
Vaux-lès-Palameix (55) 47 G2
Vaux-lès-Rubigny (08) 23 F2
Vaux-lès-Saint-Claude (39).... 117 H3
Vaux-Marquenneville (80) 6 D5
Vaux-Montreuil (08) 23 H3
Vaux-Rouillac (16) 122 A3
Vaux-Saules (21) 85 F5
Vaux-sur-Aure (14) 13 H5
Vaux-sur-Blaise (52) 67 G1
Vaux-sur-Eure (27) 41 E2
Vaux-sur-Lunain (77) 64 C3
Vaux-sur-Mer (17) 120 C3
Vaux-sur-Poligny (39) 103 E5
Vaux-sur-Saint-Urbain (52).... 68 A2
Vaux-sur-Seine (78) 42 A2
Vaux-sur-Seulles (14) 14 A4
Vaux-sur-Somme (80) 7 H6
Vaux-sur-Vienne (86) 94 D4
Vaux-Villaine (08) 23 H1
Vauxaillon (02) 22 B4
Vauxbons (52) 85 H1
Vauxbuin (02) 22 A5
Vauxrenard (69) 116 A5
Vauxrezis (02) 22 A4
Vauxtin (02) 22 C5
Vavincourt (55) 47 E4
Vavray-le-Grand (51) 46 B4
Vavray-le-Petit (51) 46 B4
Vaxainville (54) 49 G6
Vaxoncourt (88) 69 H3
Vaxy (57) 49 E3

Vay (44) 74 C2
Vaychis (09) 199 F2
Vaylats (46) 153 E4
Vayrac (46) 138 D5
Vayres (33) 135 G5
Vayres (87) 123 G3
Vayres-sur-Essonne (91) 63 G2
Vazeilles-Limandre (43) 142 B3
Vazerac (82) 152 B6
Veauce (03) 113 F5
Veauche (42) 129 E5
Veauchette (42) 129 E5
Veaugues (18) 98 B1
Veauville-lès-Baons (76) 17 E4
Veauville-lès-Quelles (76) 17 E3
Vèbre (09) 199 F1
Vebret (15) 140 B1
Vebron (48) 156 B5
Veckersviller (57) 50 B3
Veckring (57) 26 D3
Vecoux (88) 70 B5
Vecquemont (80) 7 H6
Vecqueville (52) 67 H1
Vedène (84) 175 E2
Védrines-Saint-Loup (15) 141 G4
Végennes (19) 139 E4
Vého (54) 49 G6
Veigné (37) 79 E6
Veigy-Foncenex (74) 118 C4
Veilhes (81) 169 H5
Veilleins (41) 80 C5
Veilly (21) 101 E2
Veix (19) 125 E5
Velaine-en-Haye (54) 48 B5
Velaine-sous-Amance (54) 48 D5
Velaines (55) 47 F5
Velanne (38) 131 F5
Velars-sur-Ouche (21) 85 G6
Velaux (13) 192 A2
Velennes (60) 20 B4
Velennes (80) 20 B1
Velesmes-Échevanne (70) 86 D5
Velesmes-Essarts (25) 103 F1
Velet (70) 86 C5
Vélieux (34) 187 G2
Vélines (33) 136 B5
Vélizy-Villacoublay (78) 42 C4
Velle-le-Châtel (70) 87 F3
Velle-sur-Moselle (54) 48 D6
Vellèches (86) 94 D4
Vellechevreux-et-Courbenans (70) 88 A4
Velleclaire (70) 87 E5
Vellefaux (70) 87 G4
Vellefrey-et-Vellefrange (70) 87 E5
Vellefrie (70) 87 G2
Velleguindry-et-Levrecey (70) 87 F4
Velleminfroy (70) 87 H3
Vellemoz (70) 87 E4
Velleron (84) 175 F2
Vellerot-lès-Belvoir (25) 88 B5
Vellerot-lès-Vercel (25) 104 A1
Velles (36) 96 C6
Velles (52) 86 D1
Vellescot (90) 88 D3
Vellevans (25) 88 A6
Vellexon-Queutrey-et-Vaudey (70) 87 E4
Velloreille-lès-Choye (70) 86 D5
Velluire (85) 107 E2
Velogny (21) 84 D5
Velone-Orneto (2B) 205 G1
Velorcey (70) 87 G2
Velosnes (55) 25 F3
Velotte-et-Tatignécourt (88) 69 G3
Vélu (62) 8 B3
Velving (57) 27 E4
Vélye (51) 45 G3
Vémars (95) 43 E2
Venaco (2B) 205 E3
Venansault (85) 91 F4
Venanson (06) 162 D6
Venarey-les-Laumes (21) 84 D4
Venas (03) 113 E2
Venasque (84) 175 G2
Vence (06) 178 D4
Vendargues (34) 173 G5
Vendat (03) 113 H5
Vendays-Montalivet (33) 120 B6
Vendegies-au-Bois (59) 9 G3
Vendegies-sur-Écaillon (59) 9 F3
Vendel (35) 57 H1
la Vendelée (50) 36 D1
Vendelles (02) 8 D6
Vendémian (34) 172 D6
Vendenesse-lès-Charolles (71) 115 G3
Vendenesse-sur-Arroux (71) 115 E1
Vendenheim (67) 51 E5
Vendes (14) 14 A5
Vendeuil (02) 22 A2
Vendeuil-Caply (60) 20 C3
Vendeuvre (14) 39 E2
Vendeuvre-sur-Barse (10) 66 D4
Vendeuvres (36) 96 A5
Vendoire (24) 122 C6
Vendôme (41) 79 G2
Vendranges (42) 128 D1

Vendrennes (85) 92 A4
Vendres (34) 188 C3
Vendresse-Beaulne (02) 24 B3
Vendrest (77) 43 H2
la Vendue-Mignot (10) 66 B4
Vénéjan (30) 158 A6
Venelles (13) 176 A5
Vénérand (17) 121 F2
Venère (70) 86 D6
Vénérieu (38) 130 D4
Vénérolles (02) 9 G5
Venerque (31) 185 G1
Vénès (81) 170 C4
Venesmes (18) 97 G5
Vénestanville (76) 17 F3
Venette (60) 21 F4
Veney (54) 70 C1
Venise (25) 87 G6
Venisey (70) 87 F1
Vénissieux (69) 130 A3
Venizel (02) 22 A5
Venizy (89) 65 G5
Vennans (25) 87 G6
Vennecy (45) 63 E6
Vennes (25) 104 B1
Vennezey (54) 69 H1
Venon (27) 40 D1
Venon (38) 145 G2
Venouse (89) 83 G1
Venoy (89) 83 G2
Vensac (33) 120 C6
Vensat (63) 113 G6
Ventabren (13) 192 A1
Ventalon en Cévennes (48) 156 C5
Ventavon (05) 160 A4
Ventelay (51) 22 D5
Venteuges (43) 141 H4
Venteuil (51) 45 E2
Venthon (73) 132 C3
Ventiseri (2B) 205 G6
Ventouse (16) 122 D2
Ventron (88) 70 C6
la Ventrouze (61) 40 B6
Venzolasca (2B) 203 G6
Ver (50) 37 E3
Ver-lès-Chartres (28) 62 B2
Ver-sur-Launette (60) 43 F2
Ver-sur-Mer (14) 14 B3
Vérac (33) 135 G4
Véranne (42) 143 H1
Vérargues (34) 173 H4
Véraza (11) 186 D5
Verberie (60) 21 E5
Verbiesles (52) 68 A5
Vercel-Villedieu-le-Camp (25) 104 A1
Verchain-Maugré (59) 9 F2
Verchaix (74) 119 F5
Vercheny (26) 159 E1
Verchin (62) 2 A6
Verchocq (62) 1 H5
Verclause (26) 159 F4
Vercoiran (26) 159 E5
Vercourt (80) 6 C2
Verdaches (04) 160 D5
Verdalle (81) 170 C6
Verdelais (33) 149 H2
Verdelot (77) 44 B4
Verdenal (54) 49 G6
Verderel-lès-Sauqueuse (60) 20 B4
Verderonne (60) 20 D5
Verdèse (2B) 205 G1
Verdets (64) 181 H2
le Verdier (81) 170 A2
la Verdière (83) 176 D5
Verdigny (18) 82 B6
Verdille (16) 122 A2
Verdilly (02) 44 B2
Verdon (24) 137 E6
Verdon (51) 44 D3
le Verdon-sur-Mer (33) 120 B4
Verdonnet (21) 84 C2
Verdun (09) 199 F1
Verdun (55) 47 F1
Verdun-en-Lauragais (11) 186 C2
Verdun-sur-Garonne (82) 168 D3
Verdun-sur-le-Doubs (71) 101 H4
Vereaux (18) 98 C4
Verel-de-Montbel (73) 131 G5
Verel-Pragondran (73) 131 H4
Véretz (37) 79 E6
Vereux (70) 86 D4
Verfeil (31) 169 G5
Verfeil (82) 153 F6
Verfeuil (30) 157 G6
Vergaville (57) 49 G3
Vergéal (35) 57 H3
la Vergenne (70) 88 A3
le Verger (35) 56 D3
Vergeroux (17) 106 D6
Verges (39) 103 E1
Vergetot (76) 16 B4
Vergezac (43) 142 B4
Vergheas (63) 126 C1
Vergies (80) 6 D5
Vergigny (89) 65 G5

Vergisson (71) 116 A4
Vergné (17) 107 G5
la Vergne (17) 121 F1
Vergoignan (32) 166 C4
Vergongheon (43) 141 G1
Vergons (04) 178 A2
Vergranne (25) 87 H5
Vergt (24) 137 F4
Vergt-de-Biron (24) 151 G2
le Verguier (02) 8 D6
Véria (39) 117 F2
Vérignon (83) 177 F4
Vérin (42) 130 A6
Vérines (17) 106 D4
Vérissey (71) 102 A6
Verjon (01) 117 E3
Verjux (71) 101 H4
Verlans (70) 88 C3
Verlhac-Tescou (82) 169 F2
Verlin (89) 64 D6
Verlincthun (62) 1 F5
Verlinghem (59) 3 F4
Verlus (32) 166 C5
Vermand (02) 8 D6
Vermandovillers (80) 8 B6
Vermelles (62) 2 D6
Vermenton (89) 83 G3
le Vermont (88) 70 D2
Vern-sur-Seiche (35) 57 F3
Vernais (18) 98 B5
Vernajoul (09) 185 H5
Vernancourt (51) 46 C4
Vernantes (49) 77 H5
Vernantois (39) 117 G1
la Vernarède (30) 156 D5
Vernas (38) 130 D3
Vernassal (43) 142 B3
Vernaux (09) 199 F1
Vernay (69) 115 H5
la Vernaz (74) 119 E3
Verne (25) 87 H5
Vernègues (13) 175 G4
Verneiges (23) 112 B4
le Verneil (73) 132 B5
Verneil-le-Chétif (72) 78 B2
Verneix (03) 112 D3
la Vernelle (36) 96 B1
le Vernet (03) 114 A6
le Vernet (04) 160 D5
le Vernet (09) 185 H3
le Vernet (31) 185 F1
le Vernet (43) 142 B4
Vernet-la-Varenne (63) 127 H6
Vernet-les-Bains (66) 200 C3
le Vernet-Sainte-Marguerite (63) 127 E4
Verneugheol (63) 126 B3
Verneuil (16) 123 F3
Verneuil (18) 98 A5
Verneuil (51) 44 D2
Verneuil (58) 99 G5
Verneuil d'Avre et d'Iton (27) 40 C5
Verneuil-en-Bourbonnais (03) 113 H4
Verneuil-en-Halatte (60) 20 D6
Verneuil-Grand (55) 25 F3
Verneuil-le-Château (37) 94 C3
Verneuil-l'Étang (77) 43 G6
Verneuil-Moustiers (87) 110 B3
Verneuil-Petit (55) 25 F3
Verneuil-sous-Coucy (02) 22 A3
Verneuil-sur-Igneraie (36) 111 H1
Verneuil-sur-Indre (37) 95 G3
Verneuil-sur-Seine (78) 42 B3
Verneuil-sur-Serre (02) 22 C2
Verneuil-sur-Vienne (87) 124 A2
Verneusses (27) 39 H3
Vernéville (57) 26 A5
Vernie (72) 59 H4
Vernierfontaine (25) 103 H2
Vernines (63) 126 D4
Verniolle (09) 185 H4
Vernioz (38) 130 B6
Vernix (50) 37 H4
Vernoil-le-Fourrier (49) 77 H5
le Vernois (39) 102 D5
Vernois-lès-Belvoir (25) 88 B6
Vernois-lès-Vesvres (21) 86 B1
Vernois-sur-Mance (70) 86 D1
Vernols (15) 140 D2
Vernon (07) 157 F3
Vernon (27) 41 F2
Vernon (86) 109 F2
Vernonvilliers (10) 67 E3
Vernosc-lès-Annonay (07) 143 H2
Vernot (21) 85 G4
la Vernotte (70) 87 E4
Vernou-en-Sologne (41) 80 C4
Vernou-la-Celle-sur-Seine (77) 64 B2
Vernou-sur-Brenne (37) 79 E5
Vernouillet (28) 41 F5
Vernouillet (78) 42 B3
Vernoux (01) 116 D2
Vernoux-en-Gâtine (79) 93 E6
Vernoux-en-Vivarais (07) 143 H5
Vernoux-sur-Boutonne (79) 108 A5
le Vernoy (25) 88 B3
Vernoy (89) 64 D5
Vernusse (03) 113 F4
Verny (57) 48 C1
Vero (2A) 204 D4
Véron (89) 65 E5
Véronne (26) 158 D1
Véronnes (21) 86 A4
Verosvres (71) 115 G3

Verpel (08) 24 C5
la Verpillière (38) 130 C4
Verpillières (80) 21 F2
Verpillières-sur-Ource (10) 67 E5
Verquières (13) 175 E3
Verquigneul (62) 2 D6
Verquin (62) 2 D6
Verrens-Arvey (73) 132 C4
Verreries-de-Moussans (34) 187 G1
Verrey-sous-Drée (21) 85 F6
Verrey-sous-Salmaise (21) 85 E5
Verricourt (10) 66 C2
Verrie (49) 77 G6
la Verrie (85) 92 B3
la Verrière (78) 42 A5
Verrières (08) 24 B4
Verrières (10) 66 B4
Verrières (12) 155 F6
Verrières (16) 121 H4
Verrières (51) 46 C2
Verrières (61) 61 E2
Verrières (63) 127 E5
Verrières (86) 109 G3
Verrières-de-Joux (25) 104 B4
Verrières-en-Anjou (49) 77 E4
Verrières-en-Forez (42) 128 D5
Verrières-le-Buisson (91) 42 C5
Verrue (86) 94 A4
Verruyes (79) 108 A2
Vers (71) 116 H1
Vers (74) 118 B5
Vers-en-Montagne (39) 103 F5
Vers-Pont-du-Gard (30) 174 C2
Vers-sous-Sellières (39) 102 D5
Vers-sur-Méouge (26) 159 G5
Vers-sur-Selle (80) 7 F6
Versailles (78) 42 B4
Versailleux (01) 130 C1
Versainville (14) 38 D3
la Versanne (42) 143 G1
Versaugues (71) 115 E3
Verseilles-le-Bas (52) 86 A2
Verseilles-le-Haut (52) 86 B2
Versigny (02) 22 B2
Versigny (60) 43 F1
Versols-et-Lapeyre (12) 171 H3
Verson (14) 14 B5
Versonnex (01) 118 B4
Versonnex (74) 131 H1
le Versoud (38) 145 H2
Vert (40) 149 F6
Vert (78) 41 H3
Vert-en-Drouais (28) 41 E5
Vert-le-Grand (91) 42 D6
Vert-le-Petit (91) 63 G1
Vert-Saint-Denis (77) 64 A1
Vert-Toulon (51) 45 E4
Vertain (59) 9 F3
Vertaizon (63) 127 G3
Vertamboz (39) 117 H1
Vertault (21) 84 C1
Verteillac (24) 136 D1
Verteuil-d'Agenais (47) 150 D3
Verteuil-sur-Charente (16) 122 C1
Verthemex (73) 131 G4
Vertheuil (33) 134 D1
Vertolaye (63) 128 B4
Verton (62) 6 C1
Vertou (44) 74 D5
Vertrieu (38) 130 D2
Vertus (51) 45 F3
Vervant (16) 122 B2
Vervant (17) 121 F1
Vervezelle (88) 70 B3
Vervins (02) 10 A6
Véry (55) 24 D6
Verzé (71) 116 A3
Verzeille (11) 187 E4
Verzenay (51) 45 G1
Verzy (51) 45 G1
Vesaignes-sous-Lafauche (52) 68 B3
Vesaignes-sur-Marne (52) 68 A6
Vesancy (01) 118 B3
Vesc (26) 158 D3
Vescemont (90) 88 C2
Vescheim (57) 50 B4
Vescles (39) 117 G3
Vescours (01) 116 C2
Vesdun (18) 112 C2
Vésigneul-sur-Marne (51) 46 A4
Vésines (01) 116 B3
le Vésinet (78) 42 B3
Vesles-et-Caumont (02) 22 D2
Veslud (02) 22 C3
Vesly (27) 19 G6
Vesly (50) 12 C5
Vesoul (70) 87 G3
La Vespière-Friardel (14) 39 H2
Vessaux (07) 157 G2
Vestric-et-Candiac (30) 174 A4
Vesvres (21) 85 E6
Vesvres-sous-Chalancey (52) 86 A3
Vétheuil (95) 41 H2
Vétraz-Monthoux (74) 118 C5
Vétrigne (90) 88 D2
Veuil (36) 96 B2
Veuilly-la-Poterie (02) 44 A2
Veules-les-Roses (76) 17 E2
Veulettes-sur-Mer (76) 16 D2
Veurey-Voroize (38) 145 F1
la Veuve (51) 45 H2
Veuvey-sur-Ouche (21) 101 F2

Veuxhaulles-sur-Aube (21) 67 F6
Veuzain-sur-Loire (41) 79 G4
Vevy (39) 102 D6
Vexaincourt (88) 70 D1
Vexin-sur-Epte (27) 41 G1
le Vey (14) 38 B3
Veynes (05) 160 A2
Veyrac (87) 124 A2
Veyras (07) 157 H1
Veyre-Monton (63) 127 F4
Veyreau (12) 155 H6
Veyrier-du-Lac (74) 132 B2
Veyrières (15) 140 A1
Veyrières (19) 126 A5
Veyrignac (24) 138 B6
Veyrines-de-Domme (24) 137 H6
Veyrines-de-Vergt (24) 137 F5
Veyssilieu (38) 130 D4
Vez (60) 21 G6
Vézac (15) 140 B5
Vézac (24) 138 A6
Vézannes (89) 83 H1
Vézaponin (02) 21 H4
Vèze (15) 141 E2
la Vèze (25) 103 G1
Vézelay (89) 83 H5
Vézelise (54) 69 F1
Vézelois (90) 88 D3
Vezels-Roussy (15) 140 B6
Vézénobres (30) 173 H1
Vézeronce-Curtin (38) 131 E4
Vézézoux (43) 127 G6
le Vézier (51) 44 C4
Vézières (86) 94 A2
Vézilly (02) 44 D1
Vezin-le-Coquet (35) 57 E2
Vézinnes (89) 84 A1
Vézins (49) 92 C2
Vézins-de-Lévézou (12) 155 E5
Vezot (72) 60 B2
Vezzani (2B) 205 F3
Viala-du-Pas-de-Jaux (12) 172 A2
Viala-du-Tarn (12) 171 G1
Vialas (48) 156 D4
Vialer (64) 166 C6
Viam (19) 125 F4
Viane (81) 171 F4
Vianges (21) 100 D2
Vianne (47) 150 D5
Viâpres-le-Petit (10) 66 B1
Viarmes (95) 42 D1
Vias (34) 188 D2
Viazac (46) 153 G2
le Vibal (12) 154 D5
Vibersviller (57) 49 H3
Vibeuf (76) 17 F4
Vibrac (16) 122 A4
Vibrac (17) 121 G6
Vibraye (72) 61 E5
Vic-de-Chassenay (21) 84 C5
Vic-des-Prés (21) 101 F2
Vic-en-Bigorre (65) 183 E1
Vic-Fezensac (32) 167 F4
Vic-la-Gardiole (34) 173 F6
Vic-le-Comte (63) 127 G4
Vic-le-Fesq (30) 173 H3
Vic-sous-Thil (21) 84 C6
Vic-sur-Aisne (02) 21 H5
Vic-sur-Cère (15) 140 C4
Vic-sur-Seille (57) 49 E4
Vicdessos (09) 198 D1
le Vicel (50) 13 E2
Vichel (63) 127 G6
Vichel-Nanteuil (02) 44 B1
Vichères (28) 61 F3
Vicherey (88) 69 E2
Vichy (03) 114 A5
Vico (2A) 204 C4
la Vicogne (80) 7 G4
la Vicomté-sur-Rance (22) 34 D5
Vicq (03) 113 G5
Vicq (52) 68 C6
Vicq (59) 9 G1
Vicq (78) 42 A4
Vicq-d'Auribat (40) 165 F3
Vicq-Exemplet (36) 112 A1
Vicq-sur-Breuilh (87) 124 C4
Vicq-sur-Gartempe (86) 95 F6
Vicq-sur-Mer (50) 12 D1
Vicq-sur-Nahon (36) 96 B2
Vicques (14) 39 E3
Victot-Pontfol (14) 14 D5
Vidai (61) 60 C1
Vidaillac (46) 153 F4
Vidaillat (23) 125 F1
Vidauban (83) 194 A2
Videcosville (50) 12 D2
Videix (87) 123 F3
Videlles (91) 63 G2
Vidou (65) 183 G2
Vidouze (65) 182 D1
Viefvillers (60) 20 B3
le Vieil-Dampierre (51) 46 C3
le Vieil-Évreux (27) 41 E2
Vieil-Hesdin (62) 7 F2
Vieil-Moutier (62) 1 G4
Vieille-Brioude (43) 141 H2
Vieille-Chapelle (62) 2 D5
Vieille-Église (62) 2 A2
Vieille-Église-en-Yvelines (78) 42 A5
la Vieille-Loye (39) 102 D3
la Vieille-Lyre (27) 40 B3
Vieille-Toulouse (31) 169 F6
Vieilles-Maisons-sur-Joudry (45) 81 G1
Vieillespesse (15) 141 F3

Vieillevie (15) 154 B2
Vieillevigne (31) 185 H1
Vieillevigne (44) 91 G1
Vieilley (25) 87 F6
Vieilmoulin (21) 85 F6
Viel-Arcy (02) 22 C5
Viel-Saint-Remy (08) 23 H2
Viella (32) 166 C5
Viella (65) 183 E6
Vielle-Adour (65) 183 E3
Vielle-Aure (65) 183 G6
Vielle-Louron (65) 183 G6
Vielle-Saint-Girons (40) 164 C1
Vielle-Soubiran (40) 166 C1
Vielle-Tursan (40) 166 A4
Viellenave-d'Arthez (64) 182 B1
Viellenave-de-Navarrenx (64) 181 G1
Vielleségure (64) 181 H1
Vielmanay (58) 98 D1
Vielmur-sur-Agout (81) 170 B5
Vielprat (43) 142 C5
Viels-Maisons (02) 44 B3
Vielverge (21) 102 C1
Viennay (79) 93 F6
Vienne (38) 130 A5
Vienne-en-Arthies (95) 41 H2
Vienne-en-Bessin (14) 14 A3
Vienne-en-Val (45) 81 E2
Vienne-la-Ville (51) 46 C1
Vienne-le-Château (51) 24 C6
Viens (84) 176 B2
Vienville (88) 70 C4
Vier-Bordes (65) 182 D5
Viersat (23) 112 C4
Vierville (28) 62 D2
Vierville (50) 13 E4
Vierville-sur-Mer (14) 13 G4
Vierzon (18) 97 E1
Vierzy (02) 22 A6
Viesly (59) 9 F3
Viéthorey (25) 88 A5
Vieu (01) 131 F2
Vieu-d'Izenave (01) 117 F6
Vieure (03) 113 E2
Vieussan (34) 171 H6
Vieuvicq (28) 61 H3
Vieuvy (53) 58 C1
Vieux (14) 14 B5
Vieux (81) 170 A2
Vieux-Berquin (59) 2 D4
Vieux-Boucau-les-Bains (40) 164 C3
Vieux-Bourg (14) 15 F3
le Vieux-Bourg (22) 33 F5
le Vieux-Cérier (16) 122 D1
Vieux-Champagne (77) 44 A6
Vieux-Charmont (25) 88 C4
Vieux-Château (21) 84 B5
Vieux-Condé (59) 9 F1
Vieux-Ferrette (68) 89 F4
Vieux-Lixheim (57) 50 A4
Vieux-Manoir (76) 19 E3
le Vieux-Marché (22) 32 C3
Vieux-Mesnil (59) 9 H3
Vieux-Moulin (60) 21 F5
Vieux-Moulin (88) 70 D2
Vieux-Pont (61) 38 D5
Vieux-Port (27) 15 H2
Vieux-Reng (59) 10 A2
Vieux-Rouen-sur-Bresle (76) 6 C6
la Vieux-Rue (76) 18 D4
Vieux-Ruffec (16) 109 E6
Vieux-Thann (68) 89 E1
Vieux-Viel (35) 35 G5
Vieux-Vy-sur-Couesnon (35) 35 G6
Vieuzos (65) 183 H2
Viévigne (21) 86 A5
Viéville (52) 67 H3
Viéville-en-Haye (54) 48 B3
Viévy (21) 101 E3
Vievy-le-Rayé (41) 79 H1
Viey (65) 183 E6
Vif (38) 145 G3
Viffort (02) 44 C3
le Vigan (30) 172 D2
le Vigan (46) 152 C1
le Vigeant (86) 109 G4
le Vigen (87) 124 B3
Vigeois (19) 138 C1
Viger (65) 182 D4
Vigeville (23) 111 H5
Viggianello (2A) 206 D3
Viglain (45) 81 F2
Vignacourt (80) 7 F5
Vignale (2B) 203 G5
Vignats (14) 39 E3
le Vignau (40) 166 B3
les Vigneaux (05) 147 E5
Vignec (65) 183 G6
Vignely (77) 43 F3
Vignemont (60) 21 F4
Vignes (64) 166 A6
Vignes (89) 84 B4
Vignes-la-Côte (52) 68 A3
Vigneul-sous-Montmédy (55) 25 E3
Vigneulles (54) 48 D6
Vigneulles-lès-Hattonchâtel (55) 47 H2
Vigneux-de-Bretagne (44) 74 C4
Vigneux-Hocquet (02) 23 E1
Vigneux-sur-Seine (91) 42 D5

Vignevieille (11) 187 F5
Vignieu (38) 131 E4
Vignoc (35) 57 E1
Vignol (58) 83 G6
Vignoles (21) 101 G3
Vignolles (16) 122 A5
Vignols (19) 138 B1
Vignonet (33) 135 H5
Vignory (52) 67 H3
Vignot (55) 47 H4
Vignoux-sous-les-Aix (18) 97 H2
Vignoux-sur-Barangeon (18) 97 F2
Vigny (57) 48 D2
Vigny (95) 42 A2
Vigoulant (36) 111 H3
Vigoulet-Auzil (31) 169 F6
Vigoux (36) 110 D2
Vigueron (82) 168 C3
Vigy (57) 26 C4
Vijon (36) 111 H3
Vilcey-sur-Trey (54) 48 B3
Vildé-Guingalan (22) 34 C5
le Vilhain (03) 113 E2
Vilhonneur (16) 122 D4
Villabé (91) 42 D6
Villabon (18) 98 A2
Villac (24) 138 B2
Villacerf (10) 66 A2
Villacourt (54) 69 H1
Villadin (10) 65 G3
Villafans (70) 88 A3
Village-Neuf (68) 89 H3
Villages du Lac de Paladru (38) 131 F5
les Villages Vovéens (28) 62 B3
Villaines-en-Duesmois (21) 85 E3
Villaines-la-Carelle (72) 60 B2
Villaines-la-Gonais (72) 60 D4
Villaines-la-Juhel (53) 59 F2
Villaines-les-Prévôtes (21) 84 C4
Villaines-les-Rochers (37) 94 C1
Villaines-sous-Bois (95) 42 D2
Villaines-sous-Lucé (72) 78 C1
Villaines-sous-Malicorne (72) 77 G2
Villainville (76) 16 B4
Villalier (11) 187 E3
Villamblain (45) 62 B6
Villamblard (24) 137 E4
Villamée (35) 58 A1
Villampuy (28) 62 B5
Villandraut (33) 149 G3
Villandry (37) 78 C6
Villanière (11) 187 E2
Villanova (2A) 204 B5
Villapourçon (58) 100 B4
Villar-d'Arêne (05) 146 C3
Villar-en-Val (11) 187 E4
Villar-Loubière (05) 146 B5
Villar-Saint-Anselme (11) 186 D5
Villar-Saint-Pancrace (05) 147 E5
Villard (23) 111 F4
Villard (74) 118 D4
Villard-Bonnot (38) 145 H2
Villard-de-Lans (38) 145 F3
Villard-d'Héry (73) 132 B5
Villard-Léger (73) 132 B5
Villard-Notre-Dame (38) 146 A4
Villard-Reculas (38) 146 A3
Villard-Reymond (38) 146 A4
Villard-Saint-Christophe (38) 145 G4
Villard-Saint-Sauveur (39) 118 A3
Villard-Sallet (73) 132 B5
Villard-sur-Bienne (39) 118 A2
Villard-sur-Doron (73) 132 D3
Villardebelle (11) 187 E5
Villardonnel (11) 187 E2
Villards-d'Héria (39) 117 H3
les Villards-sur-Thônes (74) 132 C1
Villarembert (73) 146 C2
Villargent (70) 88 A4
Villargoix (21) 84 C6
Villargondran (73) 146 C1
Villariès (31) 169 F4
Villarodin-Bourget (73) 147 G3
Villaroger (73) 133 F4
Villaroux (73) 132 A5
Villars (24) 123 F6
Villars (28) 62 B4
Villars (42) 129 F6
le Villars (71) 116 C2
Villars (84) 176 A2
Villars-Colmars (04) 161 F5
Villars-en-Azois (52) 67 F5
Villars-en-Pons (17) 121 E4
Villars-et-Villenotte (21) 84 D4
Villars-Fontaine (21) 101 G2
Villars-le-Pautel (70) 87 E1
Villars-le-Sec (90) 88 D4
Villars-lès-Blamont (25) 88 D5
Villars-les-Bois (17) 121 G2
Villars-les-Dombes (01) 130 B1
Villars-Saint-Georges (25) 103 E2
Villars-Santenoge (52) 85 G2
Villars-sous-Dampjoux (25) 88 C5
Villars-sous-Écot (25) 88 B5
Villars-sur-Var (06) 178 D2
Villarzel-Cabardès (11) 187 E3
Villarzel-du-Razès (11) 186 D4
Villasavary (11) 186 C3
Villate (31) 185 F1
Villaudric (31) 169 F4
Villautou (11) 186 A4
Villavard (41) 79 F2

Villaz (74) 132 B1
Ville (60) 21 G3
Villé (67) 71 F2
Ville-au-Montois (54) 25 H4
Ville-au-Val (54) 48 C3
la Ville-aux-Bois (10) 67 E2
la Ville-aux-Bois-lès-Dizy (02) 23 E2
la Ville-aux-Bois-lès-Pontavert (02) 22 D4
Ville-aux-Clercs (41) 61 G6
la Ville-aux-Dames (37) 79 E5
Ville-d'Avray (92) 42 C4
Ville-devant-Belrain (55) 47 F3
Ville-devant-Chaumont (55) 25 F5
Ville-di-Paraso (2B) 202 D5
Ville-di-Pietrabugno (2B) 203 G4
la Ville-Dieu-du-Temple (82) 168 D1
Ville-Dommange (51) 23 E6
Ville-du-Bois (91) 42 C5
Ville-du-Pont (25) 104 B3
Ville-en-Blaisois (52) 67 G2
Ville-en-Sallaz (74) 118 D5
Ville-en-Selve (51) 45 F1
Ville-en-Tardenois (51) 45 E1
Ville-en-Vermois (54) 48 D6
Ville-en-Woëvre (55) 47 H1
la Ville-ès-Nonais (35) 34 D4
Ville-Houdlémont (54) 25 G3
Ville-la-Grand (74) 118 C4
Ville-Langy (58) 99 F4
Ville-le-Marclet (80) 7 F5
Ville-Saint-Jacques (77) 64 B3
Ville-Savoye (02) 22 C6
Ville-sous-Anjou (38) 144 A1
Ville-sous-la-Ferté (10) 67 F5
la Ville-sous-Orbais (51) 44 D3
Ville-sur-Ancre (80) 8 A5
Ville-sur-Arce (10) 66 D5
Ville-sur-Cousances (55) 47 E2
Ville-sur-Illon (88) 69 G4
Ville-sur-Jarnioux (69) 129 C1
Ville-sur-Lumes (08) 24 B1
Ville-sur-Retourne (08) 23 H5
Ville-sur-Saulx (55) 46 D5
Ville-sur-Terre (10) 67 F3
Ville-sur-Tourbe (51) 46 B1
Ville-sur-Yron (54) 26 A5
Villeau (28) 62 B4
Villebarou (41) 79 H3
Villebaudon (50) 37 F2
Villebazy (11) 187 E4
Villebéon (77) 64 C4
Villeberny (21) 85 E5
Villebichot (21) 101 H2
Villeblevin (89) 64 C3
Villebois (01) 131 E2
Villebois-Lavalette (16) 122 C5
Villebois-les-Pins (26) 159 G4
Villebon (28) 61 H2
Villebon-sur-Yvette (91) 42 C5
Villebougis (89) 64 C3
Villebourg (37) 78 C3
Villebout (41) 61 G6
Villebramar (47) 151 E2
Villebret (03) 112 D4
Villebrumier (82) 169 F3
Villecelin (18) 97 F5
Villecerf (77) 64 B3
Villecey-sur-Mad (54) 48 B2
Villechauve (41) 79 F3
Villechenève (69) 129 F3
Villechétif (10) 66 B3
Villechétive (89) 65 E6
Villecien (89) 65 E6
Villécloye (55) 25 E3
Villecomtal (12) 154 C3
Villecomtal-sur-Arros (32) 183 F1
Villeconin (91) 63 E1
Villecourt (80) 21 G1
Villecresnes (94) 43 E5
Villecroze (83) 177 G5
Villedaigne (11) 187 H3
Villedieu (15) 141 E4
la Villedieu (17) 108 A6
Villedieu (21) 84 D1
la Villedieu (23) 125 F3
les Villedieu (25) 103 H5
la Villedieu (48) 156 A1
Villedieu (84) 158 C5
la Villedieu-du-Clain (86) 109 E2
la Villedieu-en-Fontenette (70) 87 G2
Villedieu-le-Château (41) 78 D2
Villedieu-lès-Bailleul (61) 39 E4
Villedieu-les-Poêles-Rouffigny (50) 37 F3
Villedieu-sur-Indre (36) 96 B5
Villedômain (37) 95 H3
Villedômer (37) 79 F4
Villedoux (17) 106 D4
Villedubert (11) 187 E3
Villefagnan (16) 108 C6
Villefargeau (89) 83 F2
Villefavard (87) 110 C5
Villeferry (21) 85 E5
Villefloure (11) 187 E4
Villefollet (79) 108 A5
Villefontaine (38) 130 C4
Villefort (11) 186 C5
Villefort (48) 156 D3
Villefranche (32) 184 B1
Villefranche-d'Albigeois (81) 170 D3

Villefranche-d'Allier (03) 113 E3
Villefranche-de-Conflent (66) 200 B3
Villefranche-de-Lauragais (31) 186 A1
Villefranche-de-Lonchat (24) 136 B4
Villefranche-de-Panat (12) 171 F1
Villefranche-de-Rouergue (12) 153 G4
Villefranche-du-Périgord (24) 152 A2
Villefranche-du-Queyran (47) 150 C4
Villefranche-le-Château (26) 159 G5
Villefranche-sur-Cher (41) 80 C6
Villefranche-sur-Mer (06) 179 F4
Villefranche-sur-Saône (69) 129 H1
Villefrancœur (41) 79 H3
Villefranon (70) 86 D5
Villefranque (64) 164 B6
Villefranque (65) 166 D6
Villegailhenc (11) 187 E3
Villegats (16) 122 C1
Villegats (27) 41 F2
Villegaudin (71) 102 A5
Villegenon (18) 82 A5
Villegly (11) 187 E2
Villegongis (36) 96 B4
Villegouge (33) 135 G4
Villegouin (36) 96 A4
Villegusien-le-Lac (52) 86 B2
Villeherviers (41) 80 C6
Villejésus (16) 122 B2
Villejoubert (16) 122 C2
Villejuif (94) 42 D4
Villejust (91) 42 C5
Villelaure (84) 176 A4
Villeloin-Coulangé (37) 95 H2
Villelongue (65) 182 D5
Villelongue-d'Aude (11) 186 C5
Villelongue-de-la-Salanque (66) 201 F2
Villelongue-dels-Monts (66) 201 F4
Villeloup (10) 65 H2
Villemade (82) 169 E1
Villemagne (11) 186 C2
Villemagne-l'Argentière (34) 172 A5
Villemain (79) 108 B6
Villemandeur (45) 64 A6
Villemanoche (89) 64 D3
Villemardy (41) 79 G2
Villemaréchal (77) 64 B3
Villemareuil (77) 43 G3
Villematier (31) 169 F3
Villemaury (28) 62 A5
Villembits (65) 183 G2
Villembray (60) 19 H4
Villemer (77) 64 B3
Villemereuil (10) 66 B4
Villemeux-sur-Eure (28) 41 F5
Villemoirieu (38) 130 D3
Villemoiron-en-Othe (10) 65 H4
Villemoisson-sur-Orge (91) 42 D5
Villemolaque (66) 201 F3
Villemomble (93) 43 E3
Villemontais (42) 128 C1
Villemontoire (02) 22 A5
Villemorien (10) 66 C5
Villemorin (17) 108 A6
Villemort (86) 110 A1
Villemotier (01) 117 E2
Villemoustaussou (11) 187 E3
Villemoutiers (45) 63 H6
Villemoyenne (10) 66 C4
Villemur (65) 183 H3
Villemur-sur-Tarn (31) 169 F3
Villemurlin (45) 81 G3
Villemus (04) 176 C3
Villenauxe-la-Grande (10) 44 C6
Villenauxe-la-Petite (77) 65 E2
Villenave (40) 165 G1
Villenave-de-Rions (33) 149 G1
Villenave-d'Ornon (33) 135 E6
Villenave-près-Béarn (65) 182 D1
Villenave-près-Marsac (65) 183 E2
Villenavotte (89) 64 D4
Villeneuve (01) 116 B6
Villeneuve (04) 176 D2
Villeneuve (09) 184 C5
Villeneuve (12) 153 G4
la Villeneuve (23) 126 A2
Villeneuve (33) 135 E4
Villeneuve (63) 127 F6
la Villeneuve-au-Châtelot (10) 65 G1
la Villeneuve-au-Chemin (10) 66 A4
la Villeneuve-au-Chêne (10) 66 D4
la Villeneuve-Bellenoye-et-la-Maize (70) 87 G2
Villeneuve-d'Allier (43) 141 G2
Villeneuve-d'Amont (25) 103 G4
Villeneuve-d'Ascq (59) 3 G5
Villeneuve-d'Aval (39) 103 E3
Villeneuve-de-Berg (07) 157 H2
Villeneuve-de-Duras (47) 136 C6
Villeneuve-de-la-Raho (66) 201 F3
Villeneuve-de-Marc (38) 130 C5
Villeneuve-de-Marsan (40) 166 B2
Villeneuve-de-Mézin (47) 151 E4
Villeneuve-d'Entraunes (06) 161 G6
Villeneuve-d'Olmes (09) 186 A6
Villeneuve-du-Latou (09) 185 F3
Villeneuve-du-Paréage (09) 185 H4

la Villeneuve-en-Chevrie (78) 41 G2
Villeneuve-en-Montagne (71) 101 F5
Villeneuve-en-Perseigne (72) 60 B1
Villeneuve-en-Retz (44) 90 D1
Villeneuve-Frouville (41) 79 H2
Villeneuve-la-Comptal (11) 186 B2
Villeneuve-la-Comtesse (17) 107 G5
Villeneuve-la-Dondagre (89) 64 D5
Villeneuve-la-Garenne (92) 42 D3
Villeneuve-la-Guyard (89) 64 C3
Villeneuve-la-Lionne (51) 44 C5
Villeneuve-la-Rivière (66) 201 E2
Villeneuve-l'Archevêque (89) 65 F4
Villeneuve-le-Comte (77) 43 G4
Villeneuve-le-Roi (94) 42 D5
Villeneuve-Lécussan (31) 183 H3
Villeneuve-lès-Avignon (30) 174 D2
Villeneuve-lès-Béziers (34) 188 C2
Villeneuve-lès-Bordes (77) 64 C1
Villeneuve-lès-Bouloc (31) 169 F4
Villeneuve-lès-Cerfs (63) 127 G1
la Villeneuve-lès-Charleville (51) 44 D4
la Villeneuve-les-Convers (21) 85 E4
Villeneuve-les-Corbières (11) 187 H5
Villeneuve-les-Genêts (89) 82 D2
Villeneuve-lès-Lavaur (81) 169 H5
Villeneuve-lès-Maguelone (34) 173 F6
Villeneuve-lès-Montréal (11) 186 C3
Villeneuve-lès-Sablons (60) 20 A6
Villeneuve-Loubet (06) 178 D4
Villeneuve-Minervois (11) 187 F2
Villeneuve-Renneville-Chevigny (51) 45 F3
Villeneuve-Saint-Denis (77) 43 F4
Villeneuve-Saint-Georges (94) 42 D5
Villeneuve-Saint-Germain (02) 22 A5
Villeneuve-Saint-Salves (89) 83 G1
Villeneuve-Saint-Vistre-et-Villevotte (51) 44 D6
Villeneuve-sous-Charigny (21) 84 D5
Villeneuve-sous-Dammartin (77) 43 E2
Villeneuve-sous-Pymont (39) 102 D6
la Villeneuve-sous-Thury (60) 43 H1
Villeneuve-sur-Allier (03) 113 H1
Villeneuve-sur-Auvers (91) 63 F1
Villeneuve-sur-Bellot (77) 44 B4
Villeneuve-sur-Cher (18) 97 F3
Villeneuve-sur-Conie (45) 62 C5
Villeneuve-sur-Fère (02) 44 C1
Villeneuve-sur-Lot (47) 151 F4
Villeneuve-sur-Verberie (60) 21 E6
Villeneuve-sur-Vère (81) 170 B2
Villeneuve-sur-Yonne (89) 65 E5
Villeneuve-Tolosane (31) 169 E6
Villeneuvette (34) 172 C5
Villennes-sur-Seine (78) 42 B3
Villenouvelle (31) 185 H1
Villenoy (77) 43 G3
Villentrois (36) 96 B2
Villeny (41) 80 C3
Villepail (53) 59 G2
Villeparisis (77) 43 E3
Villeparois (70) 87 G3
Villeperdrix (26) 159 E3
Villeperdue (37) 94 D1
Villeperrot (89) 64 D3
Villepinte (11) 186 C2
Villepinte (93) 43 E3
Villeporcher (41) 79 F3
Villepot (44) 57 H6
Villepreux (78) 42 B4
Villequier-Aumont (02) 21 H2
Villequiers (18) 98 B3
Viller (57) 49 F2
Villerable (41) 79 F2
Villerbon (41) 80 A3
Villeréal (47) 151 G2
Villereau (45) 63 E5
Villereau (59) 9 H3
Villerest (42) 128 C1
Villeret (02) 8 D5
Villeret (10) 67 E1
Villereversure (01) 117 F5
Villermain (41) 80 B1
Villeromain (41) 79 G2
Villeron (95) 43 E2
Villerouge-Termenès (11) 187 G5
Villeroy (77) 43 F3
Villeroy (80) 6 C5
Villeroy (89) 64 D4
Villeroy-sur-Méholle (55) 47 H6
Villers (42) 115 F5
Villers (88) 69 G3
Villers-Agron-Aiguizy (02) 44 D1
Villers-Allerand (51) 45 F1

Villers-au-Bois (62) 8 A2
Villers-au-Flos (62) 8 C4
Villers-au-Tertre (59) 8 D2
Villers-aux-Bois (51) 45 E3
Villers-aux-Érables (80) 20 D1
Villers-aux-Nœuds (51) 45 F1
Villers-aux-Vents (55) 46 D4
Villers-Bocage (14) 14 A5
Villers-Bocage (80) 7 G5
Villers-Bouton (70) 87 F5
Villers-Bretonneux (80) 7 H6
Villers-Brûlin (62) 7 H2
Villers-Buzon (25) 103 E1
Villers-Campsart (80) 6 D6
Villers-Canivet (14) 38 D3
Villers-Carbonnel (80) 8 C6
Villers-Châtel (62) 8 A1
Villers-Chemin-et-Mont-lès-Étrelles (70) 87 E5
Villers-Chief (25) 104 A1
Villers-Cotterêts (02) 21 G6
Villers-devant-Dun (55) 24 D4
Villers-devant-le-Thour (08) 23 H4
Villers-devant-Mouzon (08) 24 C2
Villers-Écalles (76) 18 B3
Villers-en-Argonne (51) 46 D2
Villers-en-Arthies (95) 41 H2
Villers-en-Cauchies (59) 9 E3
Villers-en-Haye (54) 48 B4
Villers-en-Vexin (27) 19 F6
Villers-Farlay (39) 103 E3
Villers-Faucon (80) 8 C5
Villers-Franqueux (51) 23 E5
Villers-Grélot (25) 87 G5
Villers-Guislain (59) 8 D5
Villers-Hélon (02) 22 A6
Villers-la-Chèvre (54) 25 G3
Villers-la-Combe (25) 104 A1
Villers-la-Faye (21) 101 G2
Villers-la-Montagne (54) 25 H4
Villers-la-Ville (70) 88 A4
Villers-le-Château (51) 45 G3
Villers-le-Lac (25) 104 C2
Villers-le-Rond (54) 25 F4
Villers-le-Sec (02) 22 B1
Villers-le-Sec (51) 46 C4
Villers-le-Sec (55) 47 F6
Villers-le-Sec (70) 87 G3
Villers-le-Tilleul (08) 24 B2
Villers-le-Tourneur (08) 23 H2
Villers-les-Bois (39) 102 D4
Villers-lès-Cagnicourt (62) 8 C3
Villers-lès-Guise (02) 9 G6
Villers-lès-Luxeuil (70) 87 G2
Villers-lès-Mangiennes (55) 25 F5
Villers-lès-Moivrons (54) 48 D4
Villers-lès-Nancy (54) 48 C5
Villers-les-Pots (21) 102 B1
Villers-lès-Roye (80) 21 E2
Villers-l'Hôpital (62) 7 F3
Villers-Marmery (51) 45 G1
Villers-Outréaux (59) 9 E5
Villers-Pater (70) 87 G4
Villers-Patras (21) 67 E6
Villers-Plouich (59) 8 D4
Villers-Pol (59) 9 G2
Villers-Robert (39) 102 C4
Villers-Rotin (21) 102 C2
Villers-Saint-Barthélemy (60) 19 H5
Villers-Saint-Christophe (02) 21 G1
Villers-Saint-Frambourg (60) 21 E6
Villers-Saint-Genest (60) 43 G1
Villers-Saint-Martin (25) 88 A6
Villers-Saint-Paul (60) 20 D6
Villers-Saint-Sépulcre (60) 20 B5
Villers-Semeuse (08) 24 B1
Villers-Sir-Simon (62) 7 H2
Villers-Sire-Nicole (59) 10 A2
Villers-sous-Ailly (80) 7 E4
Villers-sous-Chalamont (25) 103 G4
Villers-sous-Châtillon (51) 45 E2
Villers-sous-Foucarment (76) 6 B6
Villers-sous-Montrond (25) 103 G2
Villers-sous-Pareid (55) 48 A1
Villers-sous-Prény (54) 48 B3
Villers-sous-Saint-Leu (60) 20 C6
Villers-Stoncourt (57) 49 E2
Villers-sur-Auchy (60) 19 G4
Villers-sur-Authie (80) 6 C2
Villers-sur-Bar (08) 24 B2
Villers-sur-Bonnières (60) 20 A3
Villers-sur-Coudun (60) 21 F4
Villers-sur-le-Mont (08) 24 A2
Villers-sur-Mer (14) 15 E3
Villers-sur-Meuse (55) 47 F2
Villers-sur-Nied (57) 49 E3
Villers-sur-Port (70) 87 F3
Villers-sur-Saulnot (70) 88 B4
Villers-sur-Trie (60) 19 H5
Villers-Tournelle (80) 20 D2
Villers-Vaudey (70) 86 D3
Villers-Vermont (60) 19 G3
Villers-Vicomte (60) 20 B2
Villerserine (70) 102 D4
Villersexel (70) 88 A4
Villerupt (54) 26 A3
Villerville (14) 15 E3
Villery (10) 66 A4
Villes (01) 117 H6

Villes-sur-Auzon (84) 175 G1
Villeselve (60) 21 G2
Villesèque (11) 45 G4
Villesèque (46) 152 C4
Villesèque-des-Corbières (11) 187 H5
Villesèquelande (11) 186 D3
Villesiscle (11) 186 C3
Villespassans (34) 188 C2
Villespy (11) 186 C2
Villetaneuse (93) 42 D3
la Villetelle (23) 126 A2
Villételle (34) 173 H4
Villethierry (89) 64 C3
Villeton (47) 150 C4
Villetoureix (24) 136 D2
Villetritouls (11) 187 F4
Villetrun (41) 79 G2
la Villette (14) 38 B3
Villette (54) 25 F4
Villette (78) 41 H3
Villette-d'Anthon (38) 130 C3
Villette-de-Vienne (38) 130 B4
Villette-lès-Arbois (39) 103 E4
Villette-lès-Dole (39) 102 C3
Villette-sur-Ain (01) 130 D1
Villette-sur-Aube (10) 66 B1
Villettes (27) 40 D1
les Villettes (43) 143 E2
Villeurbanne (69) 130 A3
Villevallier (89) 65 E6
Villevaudé (77) 43 F3
Villevenard (51) 45 E4
Villevêque (49) 77 E4
Villeveyrac (34) 173 E6
Villevieille (30) 173 H4
Villevieux (39) 102 C5
Villevocance (07) 143 G2
Villevoques (45) 64 A5
Villexanton (41) 80 A2
Villexavier (17) 121 F6
le Villey (39) 102 C4
Villey-le-Sec (54) 48 B5
Villey-Saint-Étienne (54) 48 B5
Villey-sur-Tille (21) 85 H4
Villez-sous-Bailleul (27) 41 F1
Villez-sur-le-Neubourg (27) 40 C1
Villié-Morgon (69) 116 A5
Villiers (36) 95 H4
Villiers (86) 94 A6
Villiers-Adam (95) 42 C2
Villiers-au-Bouin (37) 78 B4
Villiers-aux-Corneilles (51) 44 D6
Villiers-Charlemagne (53) 58 D2
Villiers-Couture (17) 122 A1
Villiers-en-Bière (77) 63 H1
Villiers-en-Bois (79) 107 H5
Villiers-en-Désœuvre (27) 41 F3
Villiers-en-Lieu (52) 46 C5
Villiers-en-Morvan (21) 100 C2
Villiers-en-Plaine (79) 107 G2
Villiers-Fossard (50) 13 F6
Villiers-Herbisse (10) 45 G6
Villiers-le-Bâcle (91) 42 B5
Villiers-le-Bel (95) 42 D2
Villiers-le-Bois (10) 66 B6
Villiers-le-Duc (21) 85 E2
Villiers-le-Mahieu (78) 41 H4
Villiers-le-Morhier (28) 41 H5
Villiers-le-Roux (16) 108 C6
Villiers-le-Sec (52) 67 H5
Villiers-le-Sec (58) 83 F6
Villiers-le-Sec (95) 42 D2
Villiers-lès-Aprey (52) 86 A2
Villiers-les-Hauts (89) 84 B2
Villiers-Louis (89) 65 E4
Villiers-Saint-Benoît (89) 82 D2
Villiers-Saint-Denis (02) 44 A3
Villiers-Saint-Frédéric (78) 42 A4
Villiers-Saint-Georges (77) 44 B6
Villiers-Saint-Orien (28) 62 B4
Villiers-sous-Grez (77) 64 A3
Villiers-sous-Mortagne (61) 60 D1
Villiers-sous-Praslin (10) 66 C5
Villiers-sur-Chizé (79) 108 A5
Villiers-sur-Loir (41) 79 F2
Villiers-sur-Marne (94) 43 E4
Villiers-sur-Morin (77) 43 G4
Villiers-sur-Orge (91) 42 C6
Villiers-sur-Seine (77) 65 E2
Villiers-sur-Suize (52) 68 A6
Villiers-sur-Yonne (58) 83 G5
Villiers-Vineux (89) 65 H6
Villiersfaux (41) 79 F2
Villieu-Loyes-Mollon (01) 130 D1
Villing (57) 27 E4
Villognon (16) 122 B2
Villon (89) 84 B1
Villoncourt (88) 70 A3
Villons-les-Buissons (14) 14 B4
Villorceau (45) 80 B2
Villosanges (63) 126 C2
Villotran (60) 20 A5
Villotte (88) 68 D5
Villotte-devant-Louppy (55) 46 D3
Villotte-Saint-Seine (21) 85 F5
Villotte-sur-Aire (55) 47 F4
Villotte-sur-Ource (21) 85 E1
Villouxel (88) 68 C2
Villuis (77) 65 E2
Villy (08) 24 C3
Villy (89) 83 H1
Villy-Bocage (14) 14 A5
Villy-en-Auxois (21) 85 E5
Villy-en-Trodes (10) 66 D4
Villy-le-Bois (10) 66 B4

Villy-le-Bouveret (74) 118 C6
Villy-le-Maréchal (10) 66 B4
Villy-le-Moutier (21) 101 H3
Villy-le-Pelloux (74) 118 C6
Villy-lez-Falaise (14) 38 D3
Villy-sur-Yères (76) 6 B5
Vilory (70) 87 G2
Vilosnes-Haraumont (55) 25 E5
Vilsberg (57) 50 B4
Vimarcé (53) 59 G4
Vimenet (12) 155 E4
Viménil (88) 70 B3
Vimines (73) 131 H5
Vimont (14) 14 C5
Vimory (45) 64 A6
Vimoutiers (61) 39 F3
Vimpelles (77) 64 D2
Vimy (62) 8 B2
Vinantes (77) 43 F2
Vinassan (11) 188 B3
Vinax (17) 108 A6
Vinay (38) 145 E2
Vinay (51) 45 E2
Vinça (66) 200 D3
Vincelles (51) 44 D2
Vincelles (71) 102 B6
Vincelles (89) 83 G3
Vincelottes (89) 83 G3
Vincennes (94) 42 D4
Vincent-Froideville (39) 102 C5
Vincey (88) 69 H2
Vincly (62) 2 A6
Vincy-Manœuvre (77) 43 G2
Vincy-Reuil-et-Magny (02) 23 E2
Vindecy (71) 115 E3
Vindelle (16) 122 B3
Vindey (51) 44 D5
Vindrac-Alayrac (81) 170 A1
Vinets (10) 66 C1
Vineuil (36) 96 C4
Vineuil (41) 80 A4
Vineuil-Saint-Firmin (60) 43 E1
la Vineuse sur
  Fregande (71) 115 H2
Vinezac (07) 157 F3
Vingrau (66) 201 E1
Vinnemerville (76) 16 D3
Vinneuf (89) 64 D3
Vinon (18) 98 B1
Vinon-sur-Verdon (83) 176 C4
Vins-sur-Caramy (83) 193 G2
Vinsobres (26) 158 D4
le Vintrou (81) 171 E6
Vinzelles (63) 127 G2
Vinzelles (71) 116 B4
Vinzier (74) 119 E3
Vinzieux (07) 143 H1
Viocourt (88) 69 E3
Viodos-Abense-de-Bas (64) ...181 G2
Violaines (62) 3 E6
Violay (42) 129 F2
Violès (84) 158 C6
Violot (52) 86 B2
Viols-en-Laval (34) 173 E4
Viols-le-Fort (34) 173 E4
Vioménil (88) 69 G5
Vion (07) 144 A3
Vion (72) 77 G1
Vions (73) 131 G2
Vionville (57) 26 A6
Viozan (32) 183 H1
Viplaix (03) 112 B2
Vira (09) 186 A5
Vira (66) 200 C1
Virac (81) 170 B1
Virandeville (50) 12 B2
Virargues (15) 140 D3
Virazeil (47) 150 C3
Viré (71) 116 B2
Viré-en-Champagne (72) 59 F5
Vire Normandie (14) 37 H3
Vire-sur-Lot (46) 152 A3
Vireaux (89) 84 B2
Virecourt (54) 69 G1
Virelade (33) 149 G1
Vireux-Molhain (08) 11 E4
Vireux-Wallerand (08) 11 E4
Virey-le-Grand (71) 101 G3
Virey-sous-Bar (10) 66 C4
Virginy (51) 46 C1
Viriat (01) 116 D2
Viricelles (42) 129 F4
Virieu (38) 131 E5
Virieu-le-Grand (01) 131 F2
Virieu-le-Petit (01) 131 G1
Virignin (01) 131 G3
Viriville (38) 144 D1
Virlet (63) 112 D5
Virming (57) 49 G2
Viroflay (78) 42 C4
Virollet (17) 107 E4
Vironchaux (80) 6 D2
Vironvay (27) 18 D6
Virsac (33) 135 F3
Virson (17) 107 E5
Virville (76) 15 G1
Viry (39) 117 H4
Viry (71) 115 G2
Viry (74) 118 B5
Viry-Châtillon (91) 42 D5
Viry-Noureuil (02) 21 H2
Vis-en-Artois (62) 8 C3
Visan (84) 158 C4
Viscomtat (63) 128 B2
Viscos (65) 182 D5
Viserny (21) 84 C4
Visker (65) 183 E3

Vismes (80) 6 C5
Visoncourt (70) 87 H2
Vissac-Auteyrac (43) 142 A3
Vissec (30) 172 D3
Visseiche (35) 57 H4
Viterbe (81) 170 A5
Viterne (54) 48 C6
Vitot (27) 40 C1
Vitrac (15) 139 H6
Vitrac (24) 138 A6
Vitrac (63) 126 D1
Vitrac-Saint-Vincent (16) 123 E3
Vitrac-sur-Montane (19) 139 E2
Vitrai-sous-Laigle (61) 40 B5
Vitray-en-Beauce (28) 62 A3
Vitré (35) 58 A4
Vitreux (39) 102 D1
Vitrey (54) 69 F1
Vitrey-sur-Mance (70) 86 D1
Vitrimont (54) 49 E6
Vitrolles (05) 160 B3
Vitrolles (13) 192 A2
Vitrolles-en-Lubéron (84) 176 B3
Vitry-aux-Loges (45) 63 F6
Vitry-en-Artois (62) 8 C2
Vitry-en-Charollais (71) 115 E2
Vitry-en-Montagne (52) 85 H1
Vitry-en-Perthois (51) 46 B5
Vitry-la-Ville (51) 46 A4
Vitry-Laché (58) 99 G2
Vitry-le-Croisé (10) 67 E4
Vitry-le-François (51) 46 B5
Vitry-lès-Nogent (52) 68 B6
Vitry-sur-Loire (71) 99 H6
Vitry-sur-Orne (57) 26 B4
Vitry-sur-Seine (94) 42 D4
Vittarville (55) 25 F4
Vitteaux (21) 85 E5
Vittefleur (76) 17 E3
Vittel (88) 69 E4
Vittersbourg (57) 49 H2
Vittoncourt (57) 49 E2
Vittonville (54) 48 C2
Vitz-sur-Authie (80) 7 E3
Viuz-en-Sallaz (74) 118 D5
Viuz-la-Chiésaz (74) 132 A2
Vivaise (02) 22 B3
Vivans (42) 114 D1
Vivario (2B) 205 E3
Viven (64) 166 B6
Viverols (63) 128 C6
Vivès (66) 201 E4
Vivey (52) 85 H2
le Vivier (66) 200 C1
Vivier-au-Court (08) 24 B1
le Vivier-sur-Mer (35) 35 E4
Vivières (02) 21 G5
Viviers (07) 158 A3
Viviers (57) 49 E3
Viviers (89) 84 A2
Viviers-du-Lac (73) 131 H4
Viviers-le-Gras (88) 69 E4
Viviers-lès-Lavaur (81) 169 H5
Viviers-lès-Montagnes (81) ..170 C6
Viviers-lès-Offroicourt (88) ...69 F3
Viviers-sur-Artaut (10) 66 D5
Viviers-sur-Chiers (54) 25 G4
Viviès (09) 186 A4
Viviez (12) 153 H2
Vivoin (72) 60 A3
Vivonne (86) 109 E2
Vivy (49) 77 G6
Vix (21) 85 E1
Vix (85) 107 E3
Vizille (38) 145 G3
Vocance (07) 143 G2
Vodable (63) 127 F5
Vœgtlinshoffen (68) 71 F5
Vœlfling-lès-
  Bouzonville (57) 27 E4
Vœllerdingen (67) 50 A2
Vœuil-et-Giget (16) 122 B4
La Vôge-les-Bains (88) 69 G5
Vogelgrun (68) 71 G5
Voglans (73) 131 H4
Vogüé (07) 157 G2
Voharies (02) 22 D1
Void-Vacon (55) 47 H5
Voigny (10) 67 F3
Voilemont (51) 46 C2
Voillans (25) 88 A5
Voillecomte (52) 67 F1
Voimhaut (57) 49 E2
Voinémont (54) 69 F1
Voingt (63) 126 B3
Voinsles (77) 43 H5
Voipreux (51) 45 F3
Voires (25) 103 H2
Voiron (38) 145 F1
Voiscreville (27) 18 A5
Voise (28) 62 C2
Voisenon (77) 43 F6
Voisey (52) 86 D1
Voisines (52) 86 A1
Voisines (89) 65 E6
Voisins-le-Bretonneux (78) ...42 B5
Voissant (38) 131 G5
Voissay (17) 121 F1
Voiteur (39) 102 D5
la Voivre (70) 88 A1
la Voivre (88) 70 C2
les Voivres (88) 69 G5
Voivres-lès-le-Mans (72) 60 A6
Volckerinckhove (59) 2 B3
Volesvres (71) 115 F2
Volgelsheim (68) 71 G5
Volgré (89) 83 E2
Volksberg (67) 50 B2
Vollore-Montagne (63) 128 B3

Vollore-Ville (63) 128 A3
Volmerange-lès-
  Boulay (57) 26 D5
Volmerange-les-Mines (57) ...26 B2
Volmunster (57) 28 B5
Volnay (21) 101 G3
Volnay (72) 60 C6
Volon (70) 86 D3
Volonne (04) 160 B6
Volpajola (2B) 203 F5
Volstroff (57) 26 C3
Volvic (63) 127 E2
Volx (04) 176 D3
Vomécourt (88) 70 B2
Vomécourt-sur-Madon (88) ...69 G2
Voncourt (52) 86 D2
Voncq (08) 24 A4
Vonges (21) 86 B6
Vongnes (01) 131 G2
Vonnas (01) 116 C4
Voray-sur-l'Ognon (70) 87 F6
Voreppe (38) 145 F1
Vorey (43) 142 C2
Vorges (02) 22 C3
Vorges-les-Pins (25) 103 F2
Vorly (18) 97 H4
Vornay (18) 98 A4
Vosbles (39) 117 F3
Vosne-Romanée (21) 101 H2
Vosnon (10) 65 H5
Vou (37) 95 F2
Vouarces (51) 45 E6
Voudenay (21) 100 D2
Voué (10) 66 B2
Vougécourt (70) 69 F6
Vougeot (21) 101 H2
Vougrey (10) 66 C5
Vougy (42) 115 E6
Vougy (74) 119 E6
Vouharte (16) 122 B2
Vouhé (17) 107 E5
Vouhé (79) 108 A1
Vouhenans (70) 88 A3
Vouillé (79) 107 H3
Vouillé (86) 94 A6
Vouillé-les-Marais (85) 107 E3
Vouillers (51) 46 C5
Vouillon (36) 96 D5
Voujeaucourt (25) 88 C4
Voulaines-les-
  Templiers (21) 85 F2
Voulangis (77) 43 G4
Voulême (86) 108 D5
Voulgézac (16) 122 B5
Voulmentin (79) 93 E3
Voulon (86) 108 D3
Voulpaix (02) 22 D1
la Voulte-sur-Rhône (07) 144 A6
Voulton (77) 44 B6
Voulx (77) 64 C3
Vouneuil-sous-Biard (86) 109 E1
Vouneuil-sur-Vienne (86) 94 D6
Vourey (38) 145 F1
Vourles (69) 130 A4
Voussac (03) 113 F4
Voutenay-sur-Cure (89) 83 H4
Voutezac (19) 138 C1
Vouthon (16) 122 D4
Vouthon-Bas (55) 68 C1
Vouthon-Haut (55) 68 C1
Voutré (53) 59 F4
Vouvant (85) 107 F1
Vouvray (37) 79 E5
Vouvray-sur-Huisne (72) 60 D5
Vouxey (88) 69 E2
Vouzailles (86) 94 A6
Vouzan (16) 122 D4
Vouzeron (18) 97 F1
Vouziers (08) 24 A4
Vouzon (41) 81 E3
Vouzy (51) 45 F3
Vovray-en-Bornes (74) 118 C6
Voyenne (02) 22 C2
Voyennes (80) 21 G1
Voyer (57) 50 A5
la Vraie-Croix (56) 55 H6
Vraignes-en-
  Vermandois (80) 8 D6
Vraignes-lès-Hornoy (80) 19 H1
Vraincourt (52) 67 H3
Vraiville (27) 18 C6
Vraux (51) 45 G2
Vrécourt (88) 68 D4
Vred (59) 8 D1
Vregille (70) 87 E6
Vregny (02) 22 B4
Vrély (80) 21 E1
Vriange (39) 102 D1
Vrigne-Meuse (08) 24 B2
Vrigne aux Bois (08) 24 B1
Vrigny (45) 63 F5
Vrigny (51) 23 E6
Vritz (44) 75 G2
Vrocourt (60) 19 H3
Vroil (51) 46 D4
Vron (80) 6 D2
Vroncourt (54) 69 F1
Vroncourt-la-Côte (52) 68 C4
Vroville (88) 69 G3
Vry (57) 26 C5
Vue (44) 74 B5
Vuillafans (25) 103 H2
Vuillecin (25) 104 A3
Vuillery (02) 22 A4
Vulaines (10) 65 G4
Vulaines-lès-Provins (77) 44 A6

Vulaines-sur-Seine (77) 64 B2
Vulbens (74) 118 A5
Vulmont (57) 48 D3
Vulvoz (39) 117 H3
Vy-le-Ferroux (70) 87 F3
Vy-lès-Filain (70) 87 G4
Vy-lès-Lure (70) 88 A3
Vy-lès-Rupt (70) 87 E3
Vyans-le-Val (70) 88 C4
Vyt-lès-Belvoir (25) 88 B5

W

Waben (62) 6 C1
Wacquemoulin (60) 21 E4
Wacquinghen (62) 1 F3
Wadelincourt (08) 24 C2
Wadonville-lès-
  Marmoutier (67) 50 C5
Wagnon (08) 23 H2
Wahagnies (59) 3 F6
Wahlbach (68) 89 F3
Wahlenheim (67) 51 E4
Wail (62) 7 F2
Wailly (62) 8 B3
Wailly-Beaucamp (62) 6 D1
Walbach (68) 71 E5
Walbourg (67) 51 E3
Waldambach (67) 50 B3
Waldersbach (67) 71 E1
Waldhambach (67) 50 B2
Waldhouse (57) 28 B5
Waldighofen (68) 89 F3
Waldolwisheim (67) 50 C4
Waldweistroff (57) 26 D3
Waldwisse (57) 26 D2
Walheim (68) 89 F3
Walincourt-Selvigny (59) 9 E4
Wallers (59) 9 E1
Wallers-en-Fagne (59) 10 B4
Wallon-Cappel (59) 2 C4
Walschbronn (57) 28 B5
Walscheid (57) 50 A5
Waltembourg (57) 50 B4
Waltenheim (68) 89 G2
Waltenheim-sur-Zorn (67) 50 D4
Waly (55) 47 E2
Wambaix (59) 9 E4
Wambercourt (62) 7 E1
Wambez (60) 19 H3
Wambrechies (59) 3 F4
Wamin (62) 7 E1
Wanchy-Capval (76) 6 A6
Wancourt (62) 8 B3
Wandignies-Hamage (59) 9 E1
Wangen (67) 50 C5
Wangenbourg-
  Engenthal (67) 50 B5
Wannehain (59) 3 G5
Wanquetin (62) 8 A2
la Wantzenau (67) 51 F5
Warcq (08) 24 A1
Warcq (55) 25 G6
Wardrecques (62) 2 B4
Wargemoulin-Hurlus (51) 46 B1
Wargnies (80) 7 G6
Wargnies-le-Grand (59) 9 G2
Wargnies-le-Petit (59) 9 G2
Warhem (59) 2 C2
Warlaing (59) 9 E1
Warlencourt-Eaucourt (62) 8 B4
Warlincourt-lès-Pas (62) 7 H3
Warloy-Baillon (80) 7 H5
Warluis (60) 20 B5
Warlus (62) 8 A2
Warlus (80) 7 E6
Warluzel (62) 7 H3
Warmeriville (51) 23 F5
Warnécourt (08) 24 A1
Warneton (59) 3 F4
Warsy (80) 21 E2
Warvillers (80) 21 E1
Wasigny (08) 23 G2
Wasnes-au-Bac (59) 9 E2
Wasquehal (59) 3 G5
Wasselonne (67) 50 C5
Wasserbourg (68) 71 E5
Wassigny (02) 9 G5
Wassy (52) 67 G1
le Wast (62) 1 G4
Watigny (02) 10 B6
Watronville (55) 47 G1
Watten (59) 2 A3
Wattignies (59) 3 F5
Wattignies-la-Victoire (59) 10 A3
Wattrelos (59) 3 G4
Wattwiller (68) 89 E1
Wavignies (60) 20 C3
Waville (54) 48 B2
Wavrans-sur-l'Aa (62) 2 A4
Wavrans-sur-Ternoise (62) ...7 G1
Wavrechain-sous-
  Denain (59) 9 F2
Wavrechain-sous-
  Faulx (59) 9 E2
Wavrille (55) 25 E5
Wavrin (59) 3 F5
Waziers (59) 8 D1
Weckolsheim (68) 71 G5
Wegscheid (68) 88 D1
Weinbourg (67) 50 C3
Weislingen (67) 50 B3
Weitbruch (67) 51 E4
Weiterswiller (67) 50 C3
Welles-Pérennes (60) 20 D3
Wemaers-Cappel (59) 2 C3
Wentzwiller (68) 89 G3
Werentzhouse (68) 89 F4
Wervicq-Sud (59) 3 F4
West-Cappel (59) 2 C2

Westhalten (68) 71 F5
Westhoffen (67) 50 C5
Westhouse (67) 71 G1
Westhouse-
  Marmoutier (67) 50 C5
Westrehem (62) 2 B4
Wettolsheim (68) 71 F5
Weyer (67) 50 A3
Weyersheim (67) 51 E4
Wickerschwihr (68) 71 G4
Wickersheim-
  Wilshausen (67) 50 D4
Wicquinghem (62) 1 H5
Wicres (59) 3 E5
Widehem (62) 1 F5
Widensolen (68) 71 G4
Wiège-Faty (02) 9 G6
Wiencourt-l'Équipée (80) 8 A6
Wierre-au-Bois (62) 1 F5
Wierre-Effroy (62) 1 F4
Wiesviller (57) 27 H5
Wignehies (59) 10 A5
Wignicourt (08) 24 A3
Wihr-au-Val (68) 71 E5
Wildenstein (68) 70 D5
Wildersbach (67) 71 E1
Willeman (62) 7 F2
Willems (59) 3 G5
Willencourt (62) 7 F3
Willer (68) 89 F3
Willer-sur-Thur (68) 89 E1
Willeroncourt (55) 47 F5
Willerval (62) 8 B2
Willerwald (57) 49 H2
Willgottheim (67) 50 D5
Williers (08) 25 E2
Willies (59) 10 B4
Wilwisheim (67) 50 D4
Wimereux (62) 1 F4
Wimille (62) 1 F4
Wimmenau (67) 50 C3
Wimy (02) 10 A5
Windstein (67) 50 D2
Wingen (67) 29 E6
Wingen-sur-Moder (67) 50 C2
Wingersheim les Quatre
  Bans (67) 50 D4
Wingles (62) 3 E6
Winkel (68) 89 F4
Winnezeele (59) 2 C3
Wintersbourg (57) 50 B4
Wintershouse (67) 51 E4
Wintzenbach (67) 51 G2
Wintzenheim (68) 71 F4
Wintzenheim-
  Kochersberg (67) 50 D5
Wirwignes (62) 1 F4
Wiry-au-Mont (80) 6 D5
Wisches (67) 50 B6
Wisembach (88) 71 E3
Wiseppe (55) 24 D4
Wismes (62) 1 H5
Wisques (62) 2 A4
Wissant (62) 1 F3
Wissembourg (67) 29 E5
Wissignicourt (02) 22 B3
Wissous (91) 42 D5
Witry-lès-Reims (51) 23 F5
Wittelsheim (68) 89 F1
Wittenheim (68) 89 F1
Witternesse (62) 2 B5
Witternheim (67) 71 H2
Wittersdorf (68) 89 F3
Wittersheim (67) 50 D4
Wittes (62) 2 B5
Wittisheim (67) 71 G3
Wittring (57) 27 H6
Wiwersheim (67) 50 D5
Wizernes (62) 2 A4
Wœl (55) 47 H2
Wœlfling-lès-
  Sarreguemines (57) 28 A5
Wœrth (67) 51 E2
Woignarue (80) 6 B4
Woimbey (55) 47 G2
Woincourt (80) 6 B4
Woippy (57) 26 B5
Woirel (80) 6 D5
Wolfersdorf (68) 89 E3
Wolfgantzen (68) 71 G5
Wolfisheim (67) 51 E5
Wolfskirchen (67) 50 A3
Wolschheim (67) 50 C4
Wolschwiller (68) 89 G4
Wolxheim (67) 50 D6
Wormhout (59) 2 C3
Woustviller (57) 27 G5
Wuenheim (68) 71 E6
Wuisse (57) 49 F3
Wulverdinghe (59) 2 B3
Wy-dit-Joli-Village (95) 42 A1
Wylder (59) 2 C2

X

Xaffévillers (88) 70 A2
Xaintrailles (47) 150 C5
Xaintray (79) 107 H2
Xambes (16) 122 B2
Xammes (54) 48 A2
Xamontarupt (88) 70 B4
Xanrey (57) 49 G2
Xanton-Chassenon (85) 107 F2
Xaronval (88) 69 G2
Xermaménil (54) 49 E6
Xertigny (88) 69 H5
Xeuilley (54) 48 C6

Xirocourt (54) 69 G2
Xivray-et-Marvoisin (55) 48 A3
Xivry-Circourt (54) 25 H5
Xocourt (57) 48 D3
Xonrupt-Longemer (88) 70 D4
Xonville (57) 48 A2
Xouaxange (57) 49 H5
Xousse (54) 49 G5
Xures (54) 49 F5

Y

Y (80) 21 G1
Yainville (76) 18 B4
Yaucourt-Bussus (80) 7 G3
Ychoux (40) 148 C4
Ydes (15) 140 A1
Yébleron (76) 16 D4
Yèbles (77) 43 F6
Yenne (73) 131 G3
Yermenonville (28) 62 B1
Yerres (91) 43 E5
Yerville (76) 17 F4
Yèvre-la-Ville (45) 63 G4
Yèvres (28) 61 H4
Yèvres-le-Petit (10) 66 D1
Yffiniac (22) 33 H5
Ygos-Saint-Saturnin (40) 165 G1
Ygrande (03) 113 F2
Ymare (76) 18 D5
Ymeray (28) 62 C1
Ymonville (28) 62 C3
Yolet (15) 140 B5
Yoncq (08) 24 C3
Yonval (80) 6 D4
Youx (63) 113 E5
Yport (76) 16 C3
Ypreville-Biville (76) 16 D4
Yquebeuf (76) 18 D3
Yquelon (50) 36 D3
Yronde-et-Buron (63) 127 G4
Yrouerre (89) 84 A2
Yssac-la-Tourette (63) 127 F2
Yssandon (19) 138 B2
Yssingeaux (43) 142 D3
Ytrac (15) 140 A5
Ytres (62) 8 C4
Yutz (57) 26 B3
Yvecrique (76) 17 E4
Yvernaumont (08) 24 A2
Yversay (86) 94 B6
Yves (17) 106 D6
les Yveteaux (61) 38 D5
Yvetot (76) 17 E4
Yvetot-Bocage (50) 12 D3
Yvias (22) 33 F2
Yviers (16) 136 A1
Yvignac-la-Tour (22) 34 C6
Yville-sur-Seine (76) 18 B4
Yvoire (74) 118 D3
Yvoy-le-Marron (41) 80 D3
Yvrac (33) 135 F5
Yvrac-et-Malleyrand (16) 122 D3
Yvré-le-Pôlin (72) 78 A1
Yvré-l'Évêque (72) 60 B5
Yvrench (80) 7 E3
Yvrencheux (80) 7 E3
Yzengremer (80) 6 B4
Yzernay (49) 92 D3
Yzeron (69) 129 G3
Yzeure (03) 113 H2
Yzeures-sur-Creuse (37) 95 H3
Yzeux (80) 7 F5
Yzosse (40) 165 E4

Z

Zaessingue (68) 89 F3
Zalana (2B) 205 G2
Zarbeling (57) 49 F3
Zegerscappel (59) 2 B3
Zehnacker (67) 50 C5
Zeinheim (67) 50 D5
Zellenberg (68) 71 F4
Zellwiller (67) 71 G1
Zermezeele (59) 2 C3
Zérubia (2A) 207 E2
Zetting (57) 27 H5
Zévaco (2A) 205 E6
Zicavo (2A) 205 E6
Zigliara (2A) 206 D1
Zilia (2B) 202 C6
Zilling (57) 50 B4
Zillisheim (68) 89 F2
Zimmerbach (68) 71 E4
Zimmersheim (68) 89 F2
Zimming (57) 27 G5
Zinswiller (67) 50 D3
Zittersheim (67) 50 C3
Zœbersdorf (67) 50 D4
Zommange (57) 49 G4
Zonza (2A) 207 F2
Zoteux (62) 1 G5
Zœufdues (67) 1 H3
Zouafftgen (57) 26 B2
Zoza (2A) 207 E2
Zuani (2B) 205 G2
Zudausques (62) 2 A4
Zutkerque (62) 1 H3
Zuydcoote (59) 2 C1
Zuytpeene (59) 2 C3

Contents

The OFFICIAL Everton FC Annual 2005

0. ...s Zone
...Manager

08. ...adden
...le track

10. Joseph Yobo
A dream fulfilled

14. Quiz time
Come and have a go...

15. Marcus Bent
20 Questions for our striker

16. The Academy
A day in the life...

20. Fun time
Spot the difference

21. Lee Carsley
20 Questions

22. Everton Ladies
Girl power at Goodison

24. Richard Wright
Speedway dream of our goalkeeper

27. David Weir
A clever investment by Everton

28. Quiz time
Test your Everton knowledge

32. The Goodison Game
Can you score a big match hat-trick?

35. Steve Watson
20 questions for our defender

36. Goodison Park
A day in the life of our famous stadium

40. Power To The People's Club
We highlight your remarkable fan passion

46. Leon Osman Interview
What it takes to make the grade

48. And if you know your history...
The super heroes of Goodison

54. Training Ground
Taking you behind the scenes

56. How to play like the stars
Top tips from Alan Irvine

59. Who said that?
Famous blue quotes

61. Alessandro Pistone
20 questions for our defender

MoyesZone

The man who inspired the People's Club tag is still leading us with real passion

David Moyes is one of the finest young managers in the game. Bill Kenwright showed tremendous judgement when he swooped for the Preston North End boss on March 14, 2002. The former Celtic player followed the vastly experienced Walter Smith into the Goodison Park hot-seat after a four-year managerial apprenticeship at Deepdale. He had gained promotion to the First Division with Preston in May 2000. The club missed out on promotion to the Premiership the following season with a 3-0 defeat against Bolton Wanderers in the First Division play-off final.

However, David had set down a marker as to his potential and offers soon came in from Manchester City, Southampton and West Ham United. In the final reckoning, it was going to take something special to tempt the Scot away from his beloved North End, where he had also figured as a player. He felt the Everton challenge was simply too good to turn down, highlighting his immediate belief in the potential of the Mersey Blues.

It was no surprise that David made an instant impact with the Evertonians when he declared in his first press conference that he had come to "the People's Club." The smile on Bill Kenrwight's face when those words came out indicated straight away that he knew he had made exactly the right decision in overlooking some more famous names to go for the ambitious young boss. There had been a certain amount of press specualtion at that time that David might be asked to join Manchester United as assistant to Sir Alex Ferguson before the eventual appointment of Steve McClaren.

Moyes immediately set about his first Everton challenge - to avoid relegation. He was given a tremendous welcome by the fans and when David Unsworth lashed home a goal thirty seconds into the opening game against Fulham, David's bond of respect with the Goodison faithful was sealed. Duncan Ferguson bagged a second in a 2-1 victory and the new manager quickly instilled a level of consistency into a side that would see the Blues move into a position of safety.

The 2002/03 season began very brightly and the Blues were the surprise package in the first half of the season as a run of six consecutive wins - their best since the Championship winning season of 1986/87 - helped Everton to climb as high as third before Christmas. The club's form earned David Moyes the Barclaycard manager of the month award for November and by the end of the year the team had continued to respond to his inspirational leadership. Europe was still in Everton's sights. Unfortunately for David, a 2-1 final day home defeat to champions Manchester United enabled Blackburn to snatch the final UEFA Cup place from their grasp with the Blues seventh in the Premiership table.

It still marked a massive jump of eight places from the previous year and earned our boss the League Managers Association's Manager of the Year award.

The 2003/04 campaign would prove to be be much more testing, but David Moyes is amongst the most focused in the business and 2004/05 saw our famous club shock all of the pundits by surging into third spot early on, despite the fact that only limited summer signings had been added to the squad during the transfer window.

David's standing with the fans has gone from strength to strength. Former Celtic giant Bill

If you know your History... **1878**

● Club formed as St. Domingo's. We play our first game in Stanley Park and beat St. Peter's 6-0

McNeill says that he has not been surprised, declaring: "David has learned things at every club he has gone to and at every stage in his career. He has always had leadership qualities and he has put his ambition, determination and his attitude into his managerial career. Things have progressed very well for him.

"I was always hoping he would get a big club and so I was delighted when he went to Goodison. Everton have got someone who is capable of reproducing the stirring seasons of the past."

All Evertonians will agree with that. We have a great manager and one we are very proud of.

He's got red hair

And we don't care

Davie, Davie Moyes

1879 ● We decide to adopt the name EVERTON

1892 ● Goodison Park is opened in August

1893 ● We reach our first FA Cup Final, losing to Wolves

James
McFadden

1 Favourite pop artist/group:
DAVID GRAY

2 Favourite holiday destination:
MEXICO

3 Favourite Christmas present as a kid:
PLAYSTATION

4 Favourite board game:
SCRABBLE

5 Favourite computer game:
PRO-EVOLUTION SOCCER

6 First ever football shirt
CELTIC

7 First footballing hero:
PAUL MCSTAY

8 Best footballing advice you've been given:
WORK HARD AND ENJOY IT

9 One thing you have changed in your game:
NOT ARGUING WITH REFEREES

10 Your hobbies outside of football:
SNOOKER

11 The best concert you've been to:
DAVID GRAY

12 Favourite film:
SHAWSHANK REDEMPTION

13 Favourite actor/actress:
KEVIN SPACEY

14 Favourite other sport:
I LIKE THEM ALL

15 The first team you played for:
CELTIC NORTH

16 Favourite food:
CHICKEN

17 Favourite newspaper:
SCOTTISH DAILY RECORD

18 Favourite item of clothing:
T-SHIRT

19 First car you drove:
RENAULT MEGANE

20 Best player you've played against:
CRISTIAN CHIVU

If you know your History... **1906** ● We beat Newcastle to win our first FA Cup

JOSEPH YOBO

A dream fulfilled for our travelling defender

Everton star Joseph Yobo is still a relatively young man at 24, but he has already lived in five different countries - Nigeria, Belgium, France, Spain (Tenerife) and England.

The talented defender left his family in Nigeria when he was still a teenager to pursue his footballing dream. Six years later, he has captained his country and achieved his goal of playing in the Premiership.

Despite his success, it's been a difficult road for the Nigerian international, as he's had to adapt to different cultures and styles, both on and off the pitch.

He said: "I was playing for a team in

Nigeria when I was 17. Nigeria is a football country so a lot of scouts come to watch.

"I've got an older brother who plays football too. He left Nigeria a year before I did but he told his agent about me. I'd had an opportunity to leave before then but my parents said I was too young. The agent came over when I was 17 and because he'd worked with my brother it was easier for my family to let him work with me as well."

He added: "Going to Belgium and to Standard Liege was a big decision for me. It was a good opportunity, but life was pretty difficult.

"I was still quite young and everything was different. The language was difficult and it was very hard because my family wasn't there. For me the African culture is about family. Families are always together and you've always got people around you. Here people tend to have a good time but keep themselves to themselves.

"When I grew up I was always with my family but when I came to Europe it was very different, especially when I didn't speak the language."

TAKING CHARGE: Against Theirry Henry

HIGH JUMP: Yobo challenges against Burnley in pre-season

Yobo spent a season in Liege, before moving to French giants Marseille in the summer of 2001. He spent two years there, including a stint on loan with Tenerife, before moving to Everton, as David Moyes' first signing in 2002.

"As I grew up I started to watch the Premiership games and I thought that I'd give it a go when the time came," he said. "When the opportunity to play in England arrived I didn't hesitate.

"I think I've improved in every aspect since I've been here. When I arrived I was 21 and still on a learning curve. Since then I've worked with the coaches and they've helped me a lot. Now I can take control while I'm playing and that's all credit to Everton."

If you know your History...   1928   ● Dixie Dean hits his record-breaking 60th league goal against Arsenal

"When I arrived I was 21 and still on a learning curve. Since then I've worked with the coaches and they've helped me a lot. Now I can take control while I'm playing and that's all credit to Everton"

GET IN THERE: Yobo celebrates with Peter Clarke

1948 ● September 18 - more than 78,000 pack into Goodison to watch the Blues take on Liverpool to set our record attendance

1966 ● Everton complete one of the greatest comebacks of all-time to beat Sheffield Wednesday at Wembley and lift the FA Cup

COME AND HAVE A GO

IF YOU THINK YOU'RE CLEVER ENOUGH

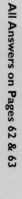

All Answers on Pages 62 & 63

1 Against which club did Nigel Martyn make his Everton debut, coming on as a substitute for Richard Wright?

2 Who scored the first goal of David Moyes' reign as manager?

3 Which Everton player finished as top scorer in the 2002/03 campaign?

4 From which club did Everton sign Kevin Campbell?

5 Former Everton midfielder Tony Grant is currently playing with which Coca-Cola Championship club?

6 Which former Everton player manages Swindon Town?

7 Who was Neville Southall's Australian deputy during the early 1990s?

8 At which club did Kevin Kilbane start his professional footballing career?

9 From which club did Everton sign David Ginola?

10 Against which club did Paul Gascoigne score the only goal of his Everton career?

5

11 What was midfielder Thomas Gravesen's nickname at his former club Hamburg?

12 At which Scottish club did David Moyes start his playing career?

13 Which Spanish club did Howard Kendall manage?

14 Who is the Golden Vision?

15 Legendary Goodison striker Graeme Sharp used to manage which club?

9

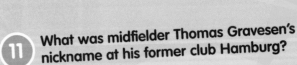

15

INSIDE TRACK

1 Favourite pop artist/group:
50 CENT

2 Favourite holiday destination:
CARIBBEAN

3 Favourite Christmas present as a kid:
A BIKE

4 Favourite board game:
MONOPOLY

5 Favourite computer game:
PRO-EVOLUTION SOCCER

6 First football shirt you got:
ENGLAND

7 First footballing hero:
JOHN BARNES – For England

8 Your hero outside of football:
MUHAMMAD ALI

9 Best footballing advice you've been given:
ALWAYS GIVE YOUR BEST

10 Your hobbies outside of football:
MUSIC AND OTHER SPORTS

20 QUESTIONS FOR...

Marcus Bent

11 The best concert you've been to:
ROBBIE WILLIAMS

12 Favourite film:
SHAWSHANK REDEMPTION

13 Favourite actor/actress:
SAMUEL L. JACKSON

14 Favourite other sport:
ANY

15 The first team you played for:
BRENTFORD

16 Favourite food:
PASTA

17 Favourite newspaper:
NOT REALLY GOT ONE

18 Favourite item of clothing:
JEANS

19 First car you drove:
DON'T WANT TO SAY!

20 Best player you've played against:
ANY OF OUR LADS IN TRAINING

If you know your History... **1966** ● Legends Pele (Brazil) and Eusebio (Portugal) grace Goodison in the World Cup

TheACADEMY

An Academy is not just a building.
It is not just a group of people.
It is not just a scheme.

Yes, it is all of those,
but more importantly it is
a philosophy, a culture,
a way of doing things.

A day in the life of Everton's Academy is certainly an interesting one.
The Academy day starts five miles away from the Netherton training
camp in the Academy Lodge, that houses about ten of the club's
youngsters, and is located in the Waterloo area of the City.

Everton

What goes on behind the scenes at the Academy

7.00am

John and Linda King, the house parents, wake the youngsters up and give them their breakfast. They leave the Lodge at 7.45am, and meet up at Netherton to join the rest of our full-time Academy professionals.

8.00am

They start an hour and 15 minutes worth of physical work, with our Fitness and Conditioning coach, Phil Hewitt. During that period, the rest of the coaching and support staff arrive, including Academy Manager, Ray Hall (right).

10.00am

They complete the session with a warm down by 10am - and then they have a light meal in the canteen. After that, they go back outside to work on technical elements of the programme, under the direction of Neil Dewsnip and Gary Ablett (below).

12.00pm

The players have lunch and then they can relax for an hour.

2.00pm

The lads make their way back to the field ready for work again at 2.00pm. That particular session finishes between 3.00pm and 4.00pm and then they go home.

Between office hours, there is a hard-working staff at the Academy, who make sure that all the administrative responsibilities - such as arranging fixtures, wages and player registrations - are organised properly.

The Academy's kit manager, Mick O'Brien, who won the FA Youth Cup with Everton as a player, has to deal with 140 sets of kit per day. The medical team is also vital, as they help all of the young players recover from injury.

Mick O'Brien

The Education, Social and Welfare needs of the players and the Academy's Child Protection Policy are taken care of by Mike Dickinson, while Kevin O'Brien looks after the goalkeepers on a day-to-day basis.

At 5pm, the evening coaching starts when all of the younger age groups come in to work at Netherton. The 9-11 year-olds work at Bellefield and the 13-16 age groups, including the keepers, work at Netherton. A number of part-time coaches, first-aiders and administrative people are on hand to ensure that the operation runs smoothly. At 8pm we finish - but it doesn't stop there, as for the next two hours the facilities are used by such groups as Everton Ladies and the club's disabled teams.

Then the following day...the whole process begins again!

TheACADEMY

Everton's Academy is rightfully regarded as one of the best in the country. It's record for producing players is second to none. Teams all over the world have been contacting the club to see how they produce their stars of the future.

So, do you think you have got what it takes to play for Everton? Do you dream of wearing the famous royal blue jersey and running out to the tune of Z-Cars at Goodison Park? Here our Academy Manager, Ray Hall offers some helpful tips for all those youngsters to one day see their dream come true...

"Anyone who wants to follow in the footsteps of Tony Hibbert, Leon Osman and Nick Chadwick has got to have talent," said Ray. "Then you've got to get yourself into a club and be seen.

"Once you have been recommended to us here at the

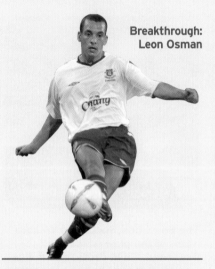

Breakthrough: Leon Osman

Academy - either by your manager, teacher or a scout - then we will do our best to see you in action. It's then that we identify players we believe are talented enough to join our Academy or one of our preparation groups. If we do sign you up then the development programme starts from the minute you arrive at the Academy. You may be here for 12 months or you may be here for 25 years!

"Obviously, we're not just about developing quality footballers, we want to develop quality people as well. We work very hard on developing young boys' footballing skills, but we also work hard to make sure that their education is the best it can be. Because of this,

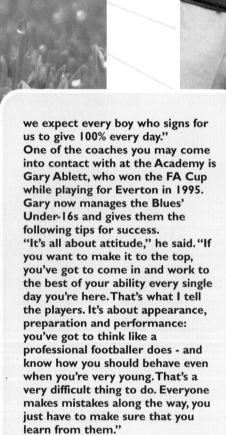

we expect every boy who signs for us to give 100% every day."

One of the coaches you may come into contact with at the Academy is Gary Ablett, who won the FA Cup while playing for Everton in 1995. Gary now manages the Blues' Under-16s and gives them the following tips for success.

"It's all about attitude," he said. "If you want to make it to the top, you've got to come in and work to the best of your ability every single day you're here. That's what I tell the players. It's about appearance, preparation and performance: you've got to think like a professional footballer does - and know how you should behave even when you're very young. That's a very difficult thing to do. Everyone makes mistakes along the way, you just have to make sure that you learn from them."

'...we're not just about dev
we want to develop qualit

Everton

New kids on the block :
The Everton Academy squad.
Back Row (L-R): Victor Anichebe,
James Vaughan, Mark Hughes,
Alan Kearney, Anthony Gerrard
Middle Row (L-R): Christian Seargeant,
Lawrence Wilson, Matthew Holt,
Craig Gallagher, Sean Lake, Daniel Fox,
James Potter, Patrick Boyle
Front Row (L-R): Andrew Fowler,
Sean Wright, Damon Martland,
James Harris, Paul Hopkins,
Scott Phelan, Stephen Wynne

oping quality footballers,
eople as well'

Can you spot the TEN differences in the action picture. Use a pencil or pen and circle the changes.

Answers on Pages 62 & 63

INSIDE TRACK

1 Favourite pop artist/group:
UB40

2 Favourite holiday destination:
PORTUGAL

3 Favourite Christmas present as a kid:
A BIKE

4 Favourite board game:
MONOPOLY

5 Favourite computer game:
PRO-EVOLUTION SOCCER

6 First football shirt you got:
THE CATHOLIC COMMUNITY CENTRE

7 First footballing hero:
BRYAN ROBSON

8 Your hero outside of football:
BILL ELLABY - The Players' Liason Officer

9 Best footballing advice you've been given:
TRAIN HARD

10 Your hobbies outside of football:
TRAVELLING HOME TO BIRMINGHAM!

20 QUESTIONS FOR... Lee Carsley

11 The best concert you've been to:
BLUE - The only one I've been to!

12 Favourite film:
RAMBO

13 Favourite actor/actress:
SYLVESTER STALLONE

14 Favourite other sport:
BOXING

15 The first team you played for:
THE CATHOLIC COMMUNITY CENTRE

16 Favourite food:
PASTA

17 Favourite newspaper:
DON'T READ THEM

18 Favourite item of clothing:
TRAINERS

19 First car you drove:
A MINI

20 Best player you've played against:
GABRIEL BATISTUTA

If you know your History... **1974**

● December: The chant of 'Bobby Latchford Walks On Water' is born as the striker scores at Derby County on a waterlogged pitch

Girl power is growing for the Everton Ladies

It's not just the boys who have the chance to play for Everton. The club has no fewer than EIGHT separate ladies teams - and they're inviting all girls with talent to join them for a trial!

"If you want to play for Everton Ladies, you should get in touch with the County FA," says manager Mo Marley, "and they will give you a list of clubs and their contact information. Our name will be included on that. Then we will probably invite you for a trial.

"If you're exceptionally good, we'll probably sign you up immediately, but if we don't feel that you should play for our teams then we would recommend another club for you to join. The standard of all our sides is very high indeed, but we are keen to see everyone enjoying their football. We have a lot of age groups: under 8s, under 10s, under 12s, under 14s, under 16s, an 'A' team, which is basically an under 19 youth team, a reserve team and a youth team - so we're massive! In total, we've got about 168 players, but that varies every year."

A player who has come through the ranks with the ladies is 20-year-old defender Kelly Vaughan. You may recognise her as the model of the club's current ladies' kit, but she's also a talented player in her own right.

"I had a trial for Everton's under-14s when I was 12," she said. "Before that I hadn't played for a team.

"I passed all my trials and was playing for the under 14s for two years before moving to the under 16s. I played there for a year and then moved up to the reserve team. At that time I was also playing at Tranmere's Centre of

BIG TALENT:
Kelly Vaughan

Excellence because Everton didn't have one at the time - but they do now!

"I spent about a season and a half in the reserves before I was involved in the first team. Obviously I didn't start regularly but it was great to train with the players and I learned a lot.

"Now I'm in my third full season playing for the first team and I think I've played in most of the games. I've learned a lot from Everton. We've had really tough seasons; we've had relegation battles but I've improved so much as a player. Now we've got a very strong side and it just goes to show that all the hard work that's gone on behind the scenes has paid off.

"I can't see myself playing for anyone else except Everton."

18 78
NIL SATIS NISI OPTIMUM
Everton

RICHARD WRIGHT

'I didn't want to be a goalkeeper when I was a kid, I wanted to be a speedway rider'

If you ask professional footballers what they wanted to be when they were growing up – for most the answer is usually the same. Almost all of them wanted to do what they are doing now - kicking a ball around on a Saturday afternoon.

But Richard Wright is a little bit different. He didn't have dreams of Premiership or England glory - which he has since achieved - he thought his future lay on the track - not as an athlete or a jockey, but on a motorbike!

"I didn't want to be a goalkeeper when I was a kid, I wanted to be a speedway rider," he said.

"But my dad got made redundant in his job and we couldn't afford to do it so my brother and I chose football. He was the goalkeeper then, but I really wanted to be between the sticks. Then, when he was 12-years-old, he suddenly wanted a change and he shoved me in goal and that fortunately worked out well for me!

"I was 11 when I got recognised by Ipswich and I went in to train at their Centre of Excellence. I was at the club from that point until the age of 24 when I left - so I spent 13 years there.

"Since I've been at Everton, it's been great to work with Nigel Martyn and Chris Woods. They can help me out and it can only be good for my career and I think I am improving all the time."

On May 6, 2005, it will be ten years since made his debut for Ipswich. Since then, he has won promotion with the Tractor Boys, a Championship medal with Arsenal and two England caps.

Now in his third full season with the Blues, the Suffolk-born stopper is hoping to keep improving over the course of the season. He agrees a lot of effort has to go in if you want to become a good 'keeper - and the hard work doesn't stop when you reach the top.

"You've got to have a good temperament and be unflappable because there will be times when you're under a lot of pressure and you've got to keep your concentration," he said.

"You've got to be switched on for 90 minutes. Sometimes you may not have anything to do for 89 minutes but in the last minute you may get called upon and if you do you have to do your job, so it's important that you concentrate all the time.

"My advice to anyone who wants to be a 'keeper is this: make sure that you enjoy your football and everything will move on from there. I think the main thing is to work hard. As a goalkeeper you're going to concede goals and if you make a mistake just forget about it and get on with the next game."

...AND STRETCH: Wrighty tipping over the bar

David
Weir

You don't have to put football before your education

Many Evertonians think David Weir is one of the club's best buys of all time. The dependable defender signed from Hearts in 1999 for a fee of just £250,000 and since then has made over 150 appearances for the Blues.

Not only that, he is one of a handful of players in the game who have successfully combined studies with his soccer. Before he made his name as a professional footballer, he obtained a University degree.

A lot of people still think that a youngster must make a choice between whether he is going to be a good player or a good pupil, but David insists that it's very easy to do both, providing that you work hard.

"Don't let anybody tell you that you can't combine studies with playing football," he said. "Don't listen to people who say you've got to take either one or the other, because that's not the case and I think I've shown that.

"I went to University in America when I was 18. I studied over there while playing football at the same time. I got my degree and four years of football as well. It was an ideal opportunity for me.

"Going to University was a fantastic experience - I would recommend it to anyone.

"When I came back, I wrote to a few clubs to see if I could maybe get a trial. Falkirk asked me to come down and I signed a contract with them within a couple of weeks.

"I want to play football for as long as I can and hopefully I'll never have to use my degree - it was in Advertising and PR, although I suppose it does give me something to fall back on when I eventually retire."

It's not only at club level where he has excelled; David has also won 37 caps for his native Scotland.

"Playing for your country is a fantastic experience," he said.

"It's one of the best experiences that you can ever have. When you're a kid it's the one thing you want to do. You want to represent your country and play in front of your own people. I've been fortunate enough to do that.

"I knew I wanted to play football at the highest standard that I could when I was at University, and the Premiership is one of the best leagues in the world. When the move came for me to join Everton, I didn't hesitate."

If you know your History... **1980** ● March 1, Dixie Dean passes away at his beloved Goodison as he watches a Merseyside derby

FUN TIME

ROUTE ONE?

Can you help?
David Moyes has got to get to the match on time. The only problem is which route should he take to make sure he makes it to Goodison to finalise his match-winning tactics?

GOODISON

CAR BREAKS DOWN

TRAFFI JAM

A B C

START

GOODISON RIDDLE

I share the same name as a Welsh lady. I always stand even when everybody else sits down.

What am I?

SPOT THE BALL

Can you find the missing ball in the game from Everton v Arsenal...

1878

Everton

NIL SATIS NISI OPTIMUM

Try your luck with our EFC Wordsearch...

```
S D F G W L A D Y S S T R E E T J O K M
H A B I F M R A T C L I F F E O C T A L
A S A L S S J M O J E N U R T F J W S A
R O P Q W A Z J C E E O J I C F W H K T
P J S E Y O M O F J J P A J I E J H S C
H O W A R D S D K E N D A L L S J E F H
R I T H I N G R J J C J J J H S J E K F
I R E M I T J O A J A W I A I J S D B O
L V L J B T J K Y J S D J J S B A L D L
D I N B A A Y L M I E J N J B T A A U D
R N J C J J L E J I M C A S E R S F E M
S E J A L S J I C J Y S M J R I K C S M
O J Y T J L N O S I J S G T P J M K E M
U S A T E S O J B I N G O O D I S O N M
T C J E J J T H A R V E Y J J J V J C M
H N S R J J R J R T J J G A T I I H K O
A J D I X I E D E A N S H J A S M A I C
L Y O C J S V I S J N A Y S M I T H E M
L R A K I Z E D S S J S W A G O J C E M
G O L D E N G S T U B B S A R N J A P M
```

Words to find:

ACADEMY
BALL
BLUES
CATTERICK
DIXIE DEAN
EVERTON
GOLDEN
GOODISON
GWLADYS STREET
HARVEY
HIBBERT
HOWARD KENDALL
IRVINE
JOE ROYLE
LATCHFORD
MCFADDEN
MOYES
NAYSMITH
OSMAN
RATCLIFFE
SHARP
SOUTHALL
STUBBS
TOFFEES
VISION

Can you identify our three current players in these anagrams...

① **LITMA LICH**

② **NASTY HAYGRIM**

③ **TOWES VETANS**

GUESS THE PLAYERS

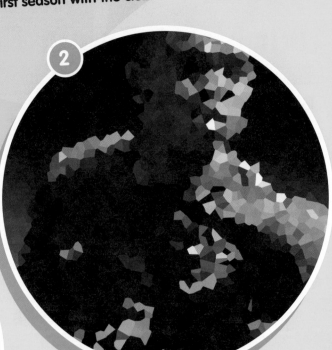

1
I was born in Preston.
I have played in the World Cup Finals for my country.
My goal against Fulham in the 2003/04 campaign was voted Goal of the Season.

2
I am a defender but I have played in midfield for my country.
I was playing in France before I moved to Everton.
I was sent off against Newcastle in my first season with the club.

3
I scored the first hat-trick of my Everton career against Leeds last season.
I have also played for a team wearing claret and blue.
I am probably best known as a defender but I am regularly used in midfield.

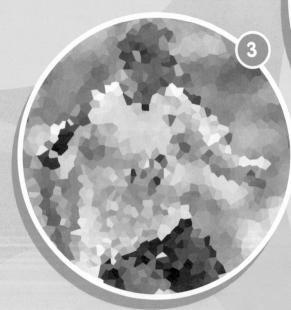

4
I'm a skilful and battling Dane who signed from a German club. I have a special relationship with the Evertonians.
I am a key member of my international side and work all over the pitch to inspire my team.

Answers on Pages 62 & 63

Alan **Stubbs**

Everton

Come and Play
GOODISON GLORY

Kick-off for the big game at Goodsion is just a few minutes away.
Your boots feel like lead and your legs feel like jelly. Understandable, considering you are about to **make your debut for Everton**. You are sat in the dressing room, looking at your name on the back of the famous royal blue jersey when Alan Stubbs comes over and pats you on the back. "Just relax and enjoy yourself!" he says. Big Dunc jumps up, fists clenched, shouting "Come on boys!". The boss gives you a wink as you head into the tunnel. The sound of Z Cars makes the hairs stand up on the back of your neck, and the Evertonians roar as you run out onto the pitch with your team-mates. Before you know it, the warm-up is over and the referee has blown his whistle to signal the start of the biggest day of your life. . .

Bad corner straight to the goalkeeper.
Move Back One Space

Ambitious 40-yard cross field pass lands at Marcus Bent's feet
Move Forward Two Spaces

You are tackled before passing to a team-mate
Move Back Two Spaces

GWLADYS STREET
PENALTY SHOOT-OUT
Throw an even
Move Forward Two Spaces
Throw an odd
Move Back Two Spaces
Throw a SIX **Advance to GOAL!!!**

Good Corner to the near post
Move Forward One Space

Clumsy tackle leads to a Yellow card
Move Back One Space

Solid Tackle leads to a break away
Move Forward One Space

MAI

A long throw by
the corner flag
**Move Forward
One Space**

Yellow
card for
high tackle
**Move Back
Two Spaces**

INJURY-TIME
You pick up a
knock and go
off for
treatment.
MISS A TURN.

BULLEN

The crowd are
on your back
after a mistake
**Move Back
Two Spaces**

PARK END

MARCHING ORDERS
Dangerous tackle
warrants a red card.
Roll a SIX or
Go Back to START

Are you ready for the challenge?

All you have to do now is put in a
good performance and score a
hat-trick to win the game . . .

How to play:

For two or more players. Just
make some counters for
each player to move around
the board, take turns to roll
the dice and follow the instructions
along the way. (Reaching the end is
the equivalent of scoring one goal.
You must do this three times to
win) Good luck!

GOAL!!!

The crowd go
wild. Carry on
until you score
THREE goals

...TAND

ALF-TIME CHANCE
O ADVANCE

hrow a SIX
o advance to
ullens Road.
you don't, wait
our turn

The crowd chant
your name after an
impressive start
**Move Forward
Two Spaces**

Bad First
Touch
**Move Back
One Space**

START

INSIDE TRACK

20 QUESTIONS FOR...
Steve Watson

1 Favourite pop artist/group:
U2 or OASIS

2 Favourite holiday destination:
MARBELLA

3 Favourite Christmas present as a kid:
A GRIFTER (BIKE)

4 Favourite board game:
TRIVIAL PURSUIT

5 Your hero outside of football:
NICK FALDO

6 First ever football shirt:
AN ENGLAND ONE

7 First footballing hero:
CHRIS WADDLE

8 Favourite computer game:
TIGER WOODS

9 Best footballing advice you've been given:
ALWAYS GIVE 100% IN EVERYTHING

10 Your hobbies outside of football:
GOLF

11 The best concert you've been to:
GUNS 'N ROSES

12 Favourite film:
GOODFELLAS

13 Favourite actors:
ROBERT DE NIRO AND AL PACINO

14 Favourite other sport:
GOLF

15 The first team you played for:
WALLSEND BOYS CLUB

16 Favourite food:
CHINESE

17 Favourite newspaper:
DAILY MIRROR

18 Favourite item of clothing:
JEANS

19 First car you drove:
SUZUKI VITARA

20 Best player you've played against:
THIERRY HENRY

GOODISON

Have you ever wondered what happens at Goodison Park on a matchday - from the moment the first gate is opened at 7.00am until the very last person leaves the stadium?
And who is the last one out, having that final responsibility to turn the final lock in the door?

GOODISON

Most of us just turn up to watch the 90 minutes of football. We might arrive a bit early to soak up the atmosphere and leave a bit late if we've taken all three points, but what we sometimes forget is that a tremendous amount of work goes on behind the scenes to make sure the game can go ahead.

The stadium is opened up at 7am, when most of us are still in bed, and in the hours that follow after that, thousands of faces - some familiar, some not - file through the gates.

One of the most familiar faces is that of Alan "the pieman" who arrives from his Preston base shortly after 9am on a matchday. His award-winning pies are dropped off around the ground over the next couple of hours, to stock up the 26 food bars around the stadium.

7.00am

Around the same time the television crew arrives to start setting up. There are six cameras positioned around the ground to capture the action. These are directed from a huge truck in the Park End car park.

10.00am

Kit man Jimmy Martin arrives soon after 10am to get the players' kit ready in the dressing room.

THE MANAGER ARRIVES...

12.00pm

Around midday the management start to arrive at the ground to prepare for that afternoon's match. At the same time, head groundsman Bob Lennon makes the final touches to the pitch, placing the four corner flags.

The players also start to arrive around this time and enter the ground at the corner of the Park End and Bullens Road stands. Upstairs in the Park End stand, the head stewards are meeting to discuss what lies ahead.

2.55pm

Special guests arrive at the Goodison Road reception right up until kick-off. Former manager Howard Kendall is a regular visitor to the ground while ex-players like Dave Hickson and Brian Labone help out behind the scenes.

At 2.55pm the two teams run out to Z-Cars and huge applause from the Goodison crowd, hoping for a victory. Come on you Blues!

A couple of hours before kick-off, the match referee and his assistants inspect the pitch, as the 300 stewards are briefed on their duties in the stands.

1.30pm

At 1.30 the turnstiles open and the fans start to file into the ground, as the players start drifting out onto the pitch to warm up. As they do that, the coach carrying the opposition team pulls up outside of the stadium.

4.45pm

Once the match is over there is a hive of activity still taking place. Once he is changed out of his tracksuit, the manager meets the press to give them his thoughts on what has just happened. The fans file back out of the stadium - happy or not - and the staff in the lounges serve the final drinks of the day to their guests.

7.15pm

The real final whistle as the caretaker, the man who opened the stadium at the beginning of the day, now locks the stadium up. The lights go out - until next time!

1984

● Andy Gray and Graeme Sharp are on the scoresheet as the Blues lift the FA Cup thanks to a 2-0 win over Watford

Power to the People's Club . . .

A picture tells a thousand words. This one not only shows the passion of strikers Gary Lineker and Graeme Sharp in 1986, but also the incredible support of our fans.

It is this love of the Blues that inspired David Moyes to say that he had come to the People's Club.

In this special section of your Official Everton Annual, we have researched some of the great images that demonstrate why Evertonians are in a class of their own when it comes to backing the Blues.

We hope you enjoy this fan-tastic journey. We know it will make you proud to be a Blue Nose. This section is dedicated to YOU.

1985
● Everton overcome Bayern Munich in the semi-final of the European Cup Winners' Cup and then beat Rapid Vienna to claim the trophy

● Graeme Sharp's goal against QPR clinches the League Championship - our first title success since that legendary success of 1970

The remarkable scenes at Goodison Park after the Blues drew with Coventry City on the final day of the 1997/98 season to ensure we would retain our proud Premiership status. No one will ever forget the sheer sense of relief.

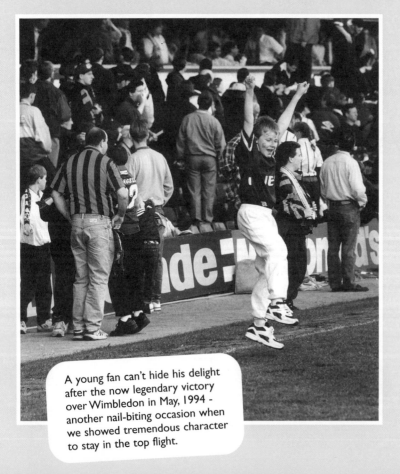

A young fan can't hide his delight after the now legendary victory over Wimbledon in May, 1994 - another nail-biting occasion when we showed tremendous character to stay in the top flight.

This Evertonian made sure the whole neighbourhood was in no doubts as to his allegiance. Harold Boswell of Birkenhead painted his house blue and white in 1977 and named it Goodison Park.

If you know your History...   **1985**   ● Everton legend Harry Catterick passes away at Goodison Park during the FA Cup quarter-final against Ipswich in March

It's December, 1975 and this young fan grabs an unusual vantage point to watch the game against Manchester Unirted.

We Shall Not Be Moved! Defiant scenes as we secure top flight status in 1998

Evertonians are in London in 1966 for the FA Cup Final clash with Sheffield Wednesday. They meet a world sporting legend in Hyde Park. Muhammad Ali asks the question: "Who Is The Greatest?" The answer, of course - EVERTON

1986 ● Gary Lineker is presented with the Golden Boot during his brief stay at Goodison after scoring 40 goals in the 1985-86 season

1987 ● Kevin Ratcliffe hoists the Championship trophy aloft following a win at Norwich

The Boys From The Bluestuff was a banner linked with Alan Bleasdale's famous TV documentary "Boys From The Blackstuff." This was Wenbley '84 - the League Cup Final against arch-rivals Liverpool.

The passion of Evertonians lasts a lifetime. This young boy is ready to look you in the face and declare: "I'm a true Blue!" These are the fans of tomorrow who will ensure the club is in safe hands.

Who said that football is not for girls? The ladies who support the Blues – young and old – are as passionate as any of the lads as this tremendous picture shows.

Baby Blue - you can't start them young enough when it comes to supporting the Blues. This young fan had a special vantage point and a helping hand as he begins to understand the Goodison sights.

Two-goal hero Graham Stuart claims the matchball after the famous 1994 Wimbledon relegation battle. He is swamped by elated fans as he heads for the players' tunnel.

1989 ● Stuart McCall hits a 90th minute equaliser in the FA Cup Final - but the Blues come away empty-handed

1990 ● Howard Kendall returns from Spain to start his second spell as Everton's proud manager

LEON OSMAN

Leon Osman tells us how he was made for the game

Leon Osman is the latest Academy youngster to break through into the Everton first team. In the 2003/04 season he made his full debut, against Wolverhampton Wanderers at Molineux, and scored within 90 seconds!

Leon has always been a football fanatic but he has had to travel a 13-year long road to get to where he is today, including stints at Skelmersdale Boys, Oldham - and in his living room!

"For as long as I can remember I've known that this game is the one for me," he said. "My parents tell me that I was well into football even when I was a baby. I'd drink my drink as quickly as I could, and then kick the plastic cup around the house!

"I joined Everton when I was ten. I'd been playing for Skelmersdale Boys for a season when Oldham picked me up. Everton had been to see me on a few occasions. They asked me to come to the club but I was enjoying my time at Oldham back then so I stayed there for another year before deciding that Everton was the place to be.

"In the 13 years I've been here, there have been plenty of ups and downs - both for me and the club. I had a bad knee injury and people were saying that I might never come back from it, but I

always believed that I could. I hadn't broken into the first team at that point but I was determined that I was going to, so I got my head down and worked hard."

'Ossie' thinks the most important thing a person needs to succeed is self-belief and is adamant that with hard work and determination you can reach your goals.

"If I was to give anyone advice on how to follow in my footsteps, I'd say that firstly you've got to work hard," said the 23 year-old. "You have to believe in your own ability - and don't let people knock you. People might say that you're not good enough, or you're too small, or you're not strong enough, but if you have belief in your own ability then you'll eventually come through.

"Any footballer needs determination - first of all determination to make it as a professional, but also determination to be on the teamsheet playing every week. Every footballer needs it."

20 QUESTIONS FOR... Leon

Osman

7 First footballing hero:
JOHN BARNES

8 Your hero outside of football:
MUHAMMAD ALI

9 Best footballing advice you've been given:
'GET AFTER IT' – Colin Harvey

10 Your hobbies outside of football:
READING

11 The best concert you've been to:
OASIS

12 Favourite film:
BACK TO THE FUTURE

13 Favourite actor/actress:
TOM HANKS

14 Favourite other sport:
AMERICAN FOOTBALL

15 The first team you played for:
ELMERS GREEN

16 Favourite food:
CHIPS

17 Favourite newspaper:
DAILY STAR

18 Favourite item of clothing:
MY D&G JEANS

19 First car you drove:
MEGANE COUPE

20 Who's the best player you played against:
THIERRY HENRY

1 Favourite pop artist/group:
BARRY WHITE

2 Favourite holiday destination:
CANCUN

3 Favourite Christmas present as a kid:
REMOTE-CONTROLLED CAR

4 Favourite board game:
CLUEDO

5 Favourite computer game:
JOHN MADDEN NFL

6 First football shirt you got:
ENGLAND

AND IF YOU

In 2000, as the nation celebrated the Millennium, Everton conducted an in-depth search to find the Giants who would stand proudly in the club's first official Hall of Fame.

Here we salute some of those heroes

Sam Chedgzoy

How often have you been to the match and heard the fans proudly singing 'If you Know Your History'?

Hundreds of times probably. That's because Everton Football Club has a history second to none.

Last season we celebrated our 125th anniversary. The year before we were singing it from the rooftops that we had completed 100 years of football in the top flight.

During that time, we have won the First Division championship nine times, and finished runner-up seven times. We have won the FA Cup five times, won the Charity Shield outright eight times, and lifted the European Cup Winners' Cup.

And a whole host of top players have helped us to achieve that.

No matter how old you are you will have your Everton heroes, but for those of us not quite old enough to remember all the great names, here's a quick rundown of the club's Millennium Giants, and a few other great men to have taken to the hallowed Goodison turf.

Jack Sharp was Everton's regular outside right for eleven seasons. He ended up playing 300 league games for the Blues before retiring in 1910. He scored his fair share of goals too, finding the back of the net 80 times during his Goodison career. He played in Everton's two FA Cup Finals of 1906 and 1907 and won two England caps. Sharp was also a fine cricketer, winning three test caps and scoring 105 against Australia at The Oval in 1909.

Jack Sharp

KNOW YOUR HISTORY.

1910-1926

Sam Chedgzoy was the man responsible for bringing about a major change to the rules of the game. He spotted a flaw in the rule concerning corner kicks and chose to test it out. Sammy took a corner against Spurs at White Hart Lane in 1924 and dribbled the ball in without crossing first time or passing to a team mate. It resulted in a goal and sparked tremendous controversy. As a result, twelve months on, the Football Association introduced a new rule saying that the taker of a corner could not dribble the ball in. Sam played in the outside-right position and won a League Championship medal in 1914-15.

**1951-56
1957-59**

Dave Hickson is one of few men to have played for all three Merseyside clubs, but it is his time at Everton that he is best remembered for.

Hickson was a talented and tough centre-forward who scored 111 goals for Everton in 243 appearances. Off the pitch, he was a quiet man but when he pulled on the blue shirt of Everton it was a different story. He became an aggressive, robust player who often found himself having a chat or two with the referees.

Dave Hickson

1924-38

Dixie Dean is Everton's most famous player. In season 1927-28 he scored a record 60 league goals, scoring a hat-trick against Arsenal on the final day of the season to take him to that record tally. Many say he was the greatest goalscorer football has ever seen. He scored 383 goals for Everton during his 14 seasons at the club and collected 16 England caps. In total, he scored an amazing 36 hat-tricks during his time at Everton, easily a club record. Dean left Everton for Notts County in 1938. He died at Goodison Park in March 1980, minutes after the final whistle had blown on a Merseyside derby match.

Dixie Dean

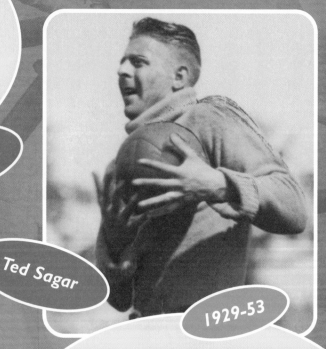

Ted Sagar

1929-53

Ted Sagar was one of the finest goalkeepers of all time. He made a massive 499 appearances for Everton and spent a record 24 years and one month with the club. He won his first England cap against Northern Ireland in October 1935 and was to be honoured by his country another three times after that. During his time at Everton he won two League Championship medals and an FA Cup winners' medal. Sagar was famous for throwing himself at the ball regardless of how many players were in his way.

1960-68

Alex Young was hero-worshipped at Goodison Park. He was nicknamed 'The Golden Vision', for he used to almost glide across the pitch - a nickname he retains to this day. People used to say he had magic boots. He was a graceful player who could change the game in the blink of an eye. In fact, people thought so much of him that they made him the subject of a television play called 'The Golden Vision'. He won Championship and FA Cup winners' medals with the Blues and scored 87 goals in 273 appearances for the club.

Alex Young

1936-49

TG Jones was known as 'The Prince of Wales'. The Welsh centre-half made more than 170 appearances for the Blues after being signed from Wrexham for £8,000 in 1936. He won a League Championship medal with the Blues in 1939, in only his second season at the club. War brought a halt to his career for five seasons, but Jones did return to Goodison in 1945 and was eventually made skipper in 1949. He also collected 17 caps for Wales before retiring in 1950.

TG jones

Neville Southall

1966-71

Grown men cried when it was announced that Alan Ball was leaving for Arsenal in December 1971. Ball, who was famous for the white boots he wore, was one of the greatest players ever to pull on an Everton shirt. The fiery character inspired England to success in the 1966 World Cup and was an important part of the Everton team that won the league in 1970. Alongside Howard Kendall and Colin Harvey, Ball was part of the midfield trio that formed a key part of that successful side. He had an amazing appetite for learning and a huge desire to win every time he set foot on the pitch.

Alan Ball

1964-69

Anyone who watched him play say Ray Wilson was the best left back ever to be seen at Everton. He was also one of the victorious World Cup winning side of 1966 and was widely regarded as the finest full-back in Europe at that time. He made 153 appearances for Everton and collected a massive 63 England caps during his career. Wilson's tackling was tough and he was tactically sharp. Sadly, his career was cut short by a knee injury.

Ray Wilson

1981-97

Neville Southall is one of the finest goalkeepers football has ever seen. In fact, his teammates will tell you he was one of the main reasons why Everton were so successful in the 1980's, when they won the League Championship twice, the FA Cup and the European Cup Winners Cup. Indeed, he was voted Footballer of the Year by the Football Writers' Association in 1985. Southall joined Everton from Bury in July 1981 as one of manager Howard Kendall's first signings. He was magnificent in the air and would amaze opposition strikers with the speed of his reflexes. He went on to make a record 750 appearances for the club and collected a massive 92 caps for his country, Wales.

1986-2001

Dave Watson won a League Championship winners medal at the very start of his Everton career - although there were some lows during his 15 years with the club, as the Blues struggled against relegation. He did get the chance to hold the FA Cup aloft in 1995, however, and when Joe Royle left the club in 1996 he took over as caretaker manager for a short time. Dave Watson is one of the most loyal, brave and committed players ever to have played for Everton. He wore the captain's armband for many years and no-one would argue that he didn't deserve to. He made 528 appearances for Everton, scoring 38 goals. He is quite simply a Goodison legend.

Dave Watson

1974-81

Bob Latchford was a bustling centre-forward who seemed to be able to score goals out of almost nothing. Although he was not particularly tall, Latchford was lethal in the air and finished as top League scorer in his first four full seasons with the club. In season 1977-78 he became the first Division One player in six years to score 30 goals in one season. He left Everton for Swansea City in July 1981 as the Blues' highest league goalscorer since the Second World War, netting 106 goals in 235 games.

Bob Latchford

TRAINING GROUND

What goes on behind the four walls of the training ground is largely kept secret. After all, it's where the manager and his coaching staff hatch plans to beat the rest of the teams in the Premiership.

But there are some things we can let you in on.

Everton's Bellefield training headquarters have been home to some of the game's finest talent over the years. It's where Howard Kendall, Colin Harvey and Alan Ball practiced their skills, and it's where the current squad train for a matchday.

Back in the days of Harry Catterick, who managed Everton in the 1960's, players had to sign in every morning. The book was taken away at 10.00am and if they hadn't turned up by then they were fined.

It's not quite that strict these days although the players are, as they were then, expected in by 10.00am.

● There are plenty of balls and shirts for the players to sign before - and after - training, with the club's charity department working hard to meet the demands of the local organisations, but when the players are changed into their training gear it's generally into the gym to warm up.

● Some players like to have a massage before training while others get treatment from one of the three physiotherapists - and everything is usually accompanied by a blast of loud music, picked by one of the squad.

● Training begins at 10.30am when the players are usually taken on a light jog around the training ground by one of the fitness coaches. They'll then do a bit of light stretching before the main part of the session begins.

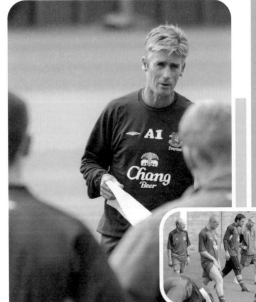

● Most of the players are changed into their training kit by 10.00am, with players like Nigel Martyn in as early as 8.00am some days.

● The manager and his assistants arrive not long after that to plan the day ahead.

Everton

By 12.00pm the training session is usually over - unless, of course, they are in for a double one, in which case they will have something to eat and a bit of a breather before starting all over again.

If it is only a morning session that has been lined up for them that day then when it's all over it's either up to the canteen for a spot of lunch, or off home.

Depending upon how many days are left until match day they may work on some of their techniques such as shooting, heading and long and short passing.

Once a week, the press are invited down to Bellefield and the manager will be interviewed by journalists from newspapers, television and radio. Sometimes a player or two will be interviewed as well, as people look forward to the upcoming game.

And then it's back in again the next day to start all over again!

They may also watch a video of the opposition to work on their tactics ahead of the big game or take a look back at their previous games to see what they could have done better. A sports scientist is based at the ground and he provides the manager with fascinating statistics from the matches - like how far each player has run during the game, how many passes were successful, or if the players really were offside when that decision was given. These days, statistics like that are available to the manager at the touch of a button.

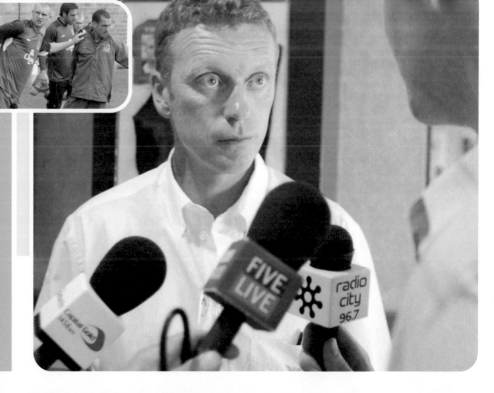

ALAN iRViNE....

David Moyes' assistant Alan Irvine was a talented Everton player in the early 1980s, and in recent years he has established himself as one of the country's top coaches at Premiership and Academy level.

At Blackburn, he nurtured the likes of Damien Duff and James Beattie, and at Newcastle he helped Kieron Dyer and Shola Ameobi achieve their full potential. He has worked with hundreds of youngsters over the years and here he passes on some handy hints on to those of you with aspirations of becoming the next young Everton hero.

"The biggest thing of all is to do everything you possibly can to make yourself better," said Alan. "If you're not particularly good at one aspect of the game, you must work really hard to try and make it better. Don't expect it to get better without any work. That doesn't mean you should forget about your strengths, because it's important that you also improve at the things you're already good at. Give things your best shot. Don't do anything in half measures. If you want to become better, it is your responsibility. Take advantage of anyone who can help you along the way to improve, but always remember that it is your career and you are responsible for how you develop.

"Most of all enjoy it! Hopefully, these hints will help you on your way. Play as much football as you can, because you learn by practice - and if you join a team, not only will it help you become a better footballer, but you might make some good friends too."

2. Heading

If you don't think you're a particularly good header of the ball, take a football into an open space and keep heading it. You will learn and improve your technique that way, without any coaching. You can try and play head tennis with a friend or against a wall to improve your accuracy and power, or you can simply try and head the ball long distances. Practice is also the key to becoming a good header of the ball. If you head the ball 100 times, you'll learn a lot more than if you only head it 10 times.

3. Developing your weaker foot

Again, practice is the key. Take a ball and kick it against the wall with the foot you think is your strongest. Do it slowly and notice how you strike. Look at the way you stand, the way you approach the ball, what part of the foot you kick it with, where on the ball you kick it, what your body shape is when you kick it and the strength you use. Then try and do exactly the same with the other foot. I firmly believe that any player can become two-footed. I see no reason why they shouldn't be. You'll get better by continual, proper practice.

4. Accurate Shooting

To become an accurate striker of the ball you have to be able to pick your spot. Rather than hitting and hoping, it's important that you can place the ball into the goal, especially if you're a striker. To help you do this, draw a goal on a wall and divide it into a number of areas, for example nine, or 12 if you're feeling confident. Number the squares and then try to shoot the ball (with either foot) into each of the areas. See how many times it takes you to hit the ball into each one. I am sure the more you do it, the less times it will take. When you are comfortable with that, try changing the distances. Try it from further away as well. That will help you get both power and accuracy into your shot.

1. Dribbling

It is important that you feel confident when you've got the ball at your feet. To begin with, I would run with the ball over long distances, practising turning with the ball and then you can move on to more complicated techniques. Use cones or markers and spread them out over a distance of about 30 metres. Run with the ball, snaking your way between the markers - without touching them, then try and get faster and faster. See if you can get someone to time you while you do it. Then, to improve your skill, shorten the space between each marker, so it gets even trickier.

If you know your History... **1994** ● Barry Horne's thunderbolt helps Everton remain in the Premiership as the Blues secure a crucial victory over Wimbledon on the final day of the season

TOFFEE TEASER

Fill in the blanks to reveal an Everton associated word in the yellow boxes...

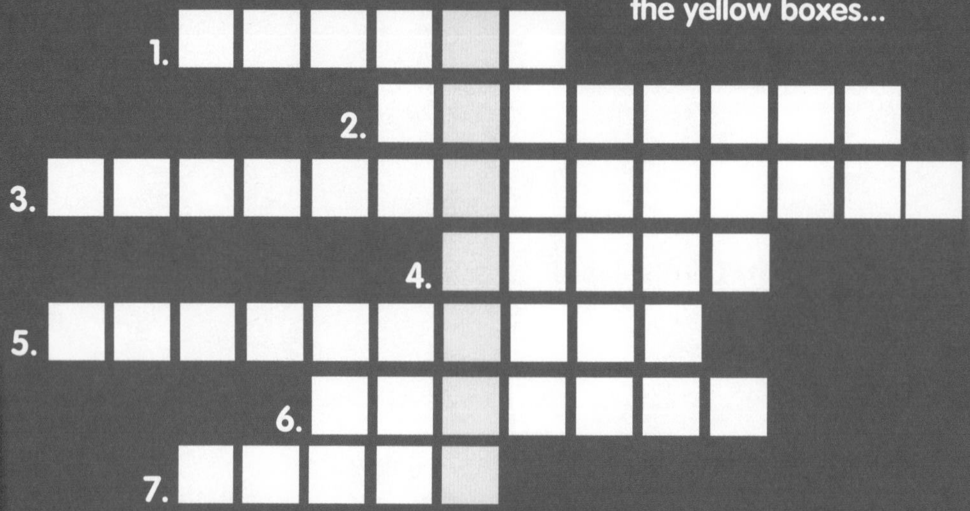

1. ☐☐☐☐☐☐
2. ☐☐☐☐☐☐☐☐☐
3. ☐☐☐☐☐☐☐☐☐☐☐☐
4. ☐☐☐☐☐
5. ☐☐☐☐☐☐☐☐☐☐
6. ☐☐☐☐☐
7. ☐☐☐☐☐

1. Former Player and U-16s manager
2. Home of Everton Football Club
3. Giant number 10
4. Trophy we won in 1995
5. Position played by Richard Wright and Nigel Martyn
6. Kevin Kilbane and Lee Carsley represent this country
7. Everton manager

NUMBERS QUIZ

- Marcus Bent wears the number ☐ Shirt
- Everton have won the First Division championship ☐ times
- Dixie Dean scored ☐ league goals in the 1927/28 season
- Howard Kendall managed the club on ☐ separate occasions
- Alex Nyarko used to wear the number ☐ on his back

Fill in the blanks and then add all the numbers up to find the answer to the question below...

- The number of years of top flight football celebrated in the 2002/03 season = ☐

Everton

WHO SAID THAT?

"Once Everton has touched you, nothing will be the same"
Alan Ball

"The reason Everton are a big club is because of their history but now we need to make history of our own"
David Moyes

"One Evertonian is worth 20 Liverpudlians"
Brian Labone

"I'll only ever manage a team that wears Blue"
Joe Royle

"I'd have broken bones for all the clubs I played for but I'd have died for Everton"
Dave Hickson

"The player I admire most is Peter Reid - he deserves a medal for running on those legs"
Neville Southall

"Everton supporters have always been fantastic. I always thought they had a great knowledge of the game and their loyalty was unquestioned"
Andy Gray

"I've been a Blue Nose all my life and I always will be. I'm a very proud and privileged man to be able to say that"
Derek Mountfield

"When you score against Liverpool it's the best feeling in the world and anything goes"
Kevin Ratcliffe

"Goodison Park just seems to be a magical place. There was something that made the back of my neck tingle when I ran onto the pitch even when the place was empty"
Alex Young

If you know your History... **1995** ● Daniel Amokachi scores a double in the 4-1 FA Cup semi-final win over Tottenham Hotspur and Paul Rideout heads a Cup Final winner against Man. Utd

20 QUESTIONS FOR...

Alessandro Pistone

1 Favourite pop artist/group:
THE BEATLES

2 Favourite holiday destination:
THE MALDIVES

3 Favourite Christmas present as a kid:
REMOTE-CONTROLLED CAR

4 Favourite board game:
WHO WANTS TO BE A MILLIONAIRE?

5 Favourite computer game:
ANY FOOTBALL ONE

6 First football shirt you got:
AC MILAN

7 First footballing hero:
GEORGE WEAH

8 Your hero outside of football:
MUHAMMAD ALI

9 Best footballing advice you've been given:
GIVE 100% - EVEN IN TRAINING

10 Your hobbies outside of football:
COMPUTERS & READING

11 The best concert you've been to:
DON'T REALLY GO

12 Favourite film:
FIGHT CLUB

13 Favourite actor/actress:
AL PACINO

14 Favourite other sport:
ATHLETICS

15 The first team you played for:
ALCIONE

16 Favourite food:
SEAFOOD

17 Favourite newspaper:
THE DAILY TELEGRAPH

18 Favourite items of clothing:
JEANS

19 First car you drove:
FIAT PUNTO

20 Best player you've played against:
THIERRY HENRY

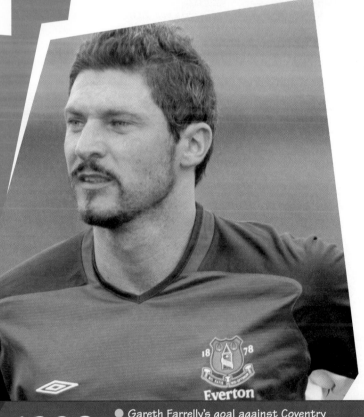

If you know your History...

1998

● Gareth Farrelly's goal against Coventry on the final day of the season keeps Everton in the Premiership

ANSWERS

We reveal all...

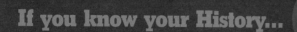